Shielding Humanity

Shielding Humanity

*Essays in International Law in Honour
of Judge Abdul G. Koroma*

Edited by

Charles Chernor Jalloh
Olufemi Elias

BRILL
NIJHOFF

LEIDEN | BOSTON

Library of Congress Cataloging-in-Publication Data

Shielding humanity : essays in international law in honour of Judge Abdul G. Koroma / edited by Charles C. Jalloh, Olufemi Elias.
   pages cm
 Includes bibliographical references and index.
 ISBN 978-90-04-23650-9 (hardback : alk. paper) -- ISBN 978-90-04-29313-7 (e-book : alk. paper) 1. International law. 2. International courts. 3. International law--Africa. 4. Koroma, Abdul G. I. Jalloh, Charles, editor. II. Elias, Olufemi, editor. III. Koroma, Abdul G., honouree.

KZ3410.S543 2015
341--dc23

2015009633

This publication has been typeset in the multilingual "Brill" typeface. With over 5,100 characters covering Latin, IPA, Greek, and Cyrillic, this typeface is especially suitable for use in the humanities. For more information, please see brill.com/brill-typeface.

ISBN 978-90-04-23650-9 (hardback)
ISBN 978-90-04-29313-7 (e-book)

Copyright 2015 by Koninklijke Brill NV, Leiden, The Netherlands.
Koninklijke Brill NV incorporates the imprints Brill, Brill Hes & De Graaf, Brill Nijhoff, Brill Rodopi and Hotei Publishing.
All rights reserved. No part of this publication may be reproduced, translated, stored in a retrieval system, or transmitted in any form or by any means, electronic, mechanical, photocopying, recording or otherwise, without prior written permission from the publisher.
Authorization to photocopy items for internal or personal use is granted by Koninklijke Brill NV provided that the appropriate fees are paid directly to The Copyright Clearance Center, 222 Rosewood Drive, Suite 910, Danvers, MA 01923, USA.
Fees are subject to change.

This book is printed on acid-free paper.

Contents

Preface and Acknowledgments   IX
Biographical Summary   XVI
Abbreviations   XX
Editors' Biographies   XXV
Contributors   XXVI

PART 1
Reflections on Abdul G. Koroma's Contributions to International Law

1. Judge Abdul Koroma in the Service of Universal International Law   3
   P.S. Rao
2. A Tribute to Abdul Koroma   14
   Tommy Koh
3. Abdul Koroma: Good Neighbour, Friend and Colleague   16
   Kenneth Keith

PART 2
Peaceful Dispute Settlement and the International Court of Justice

4. The Peaceful Settlement of International Disputes: The Rainbow Warrior Affair – Experiences of a Small State   21
   Kenneth Keith
5. The International Court of Justice and the Latin American Experience   35
   Bernardo Sepúlveda-Amor
6. Abdul Koroma, Territorial Integrity and the *Kosovo* Opinion   50
   John Dugard
7. Provisional Measures in Interpretation Proceedings – A New Way to Extend the Court's Jurisdiction? The Practice of the Court in the Avena and Temple of Preah Vihear Cases   61
   Karin Oellers-Frahm
8. Twailing the Bakassi Case: Colonialist Logic, Self-Determining Agents and the Concept of Legitimate Statehood in our Time   85
   Obiora Chinedu Okafor and Chikeziri Igwe

9   The International Court and the Legacy of the Barcelona Traction
    Case in the Field of Diplomatic Protection   104
      Phoebe Okowa

PART 3
International Law – General Subjects

10 The Competition between and among Intrinsic and Instrumental
    Values in Selected Competing Visions of the World   133
      Sienho Yee
11 Democratizing International Law-Making   144
      Babafemi Akinrinade
12 An Innovative Solution to an Ambitious Project: Dispute Resolution
    in the 1982 Convention on the Law of the Sea   163
      Surya P. Subedi
13 An Analysis of the Adequacy of the Dispute Settlement Mechanism
    Under UNCLOS: Maritime Boundary Delimitation Disputes   187
      Osman Keh Kamara
14 Constitutional Law and the Settlement of Investor-State Disputes:
    Some Interplays   230
      Laurence Boisson de Chazournes and Brian McGarry
15 Legal Aspects of Competition between International
    Organizations   242
      Konstantinos D Magliveras

PART 4
International Criminal Law And Humanitarian Law

16 The International Court of Justice and International Humanitarian
    Law   263
      Christopher Greenwood
17 The Prevention of Genocide as A *Jus Cogens* Norm? A Formula for
    Lawful Humanitarian Intervention   289
      Manuel J. Ventura
18 A Reflection on the Phrase "Widespread or Systematic" As Part of the
    Definition of Crimes Against Humanity   352
      Avitus A. Agbor

19	Justice And Gender: Prosecuting Gender-Based and Sexual Violence Crimes at the International Criminal Tribunal for Rwanda and the Special Court for Sierra Leone 379	
	Tamara Cummings-John	
20	International Crimes, Immunities and the Protocol on Amendments to the Protocol of the Merged African Court: Some Observations 406	
	Adejoké Babington-Ashaye	
21	Africa and the International Criminal Court: Legitimacy and Credibility Challenges 426	
	Abdul Tejan-Cole	
22	International Criminal Justice Processes in Rwanda and Sierra Leone: Lessons for Liberia 447	
	Charles Chernor Jalloh and Andrew Morgan	

PART 5
Africa and International Law

23	The Public Law of Africa and International Law: Broadening the Scope of Application of International Rules and Enriching Them for Intra-Africa Purposes 513	
	Abdulqawi A. Yusuf	
24	The Development and Enforcement of Community Law in the African Regional Economic Communities: Conceptual Issues, Architecture and Institutions 536	
	Tiyanjana Maluwa	
25	Africa's Contribution to the Advancement of the Right to Development in International Law 565	
	Olajumoke O. Oduwole	
26	Aspects of Africa's Contribution to the Development of International Law 591	
	Adetola Onayemi and Olufemi Elias	
27	The African Union and Questions Arising from Efforts to Resolve the Ivorian and Libyan Conflicts 614	
	Vincent O. Nmehielle	
28	Democratic Succession in Africa: Enhancing Orderly Transition through the African Charter on Democracy, Elections and Governance 639	
	Lydia A. Nkansah	
29	Secession: The African Experience 680	
	Gino J. Naldi	

30 Can Regional and Sub-Regional African Courts Strengthen the Rule of Law in Africa? Questions of Impact and Enforcement   705
     Mia Swart
31 Rethinking Anti-Corruption Strategies in Africa: Constitutional Entrenchment as Basis for Credible and Effective Anti-Corruption Clean-Ups   726
     Charles Manga Fombad and Madeleine Choe-Amusimo Fombad

Index   775

Preface and Acknowledgments

On the contemporary international and national law scene, there are not many jurists whose eminence and stature compare to those of Judge Abdul Gadire Koroma. His exemplary devotion to international law and his stellar career command a befitting tribute. We have attempted such a tribute in the publication of this book in his honor and in deserving recognition of his outstanding contribution to international law and justice.

In the course of an illustrious career, albeit one characterized throughout by great modesty and humility, Judge Koroma worked on and contributed to a truly wide range of significant issues of international law. Born and raised in Sierra Leone, West Africa, he obtained his legal education in different parts of the world and served in several legal and diplomatic roles across the globe. His commitment to the values of peace and law has benefited from his exposure to different cultures and has certainly contributed to his dynamic approach of promoting international justice in the various capacities he served. The numerous roles he held at the United Nations, ranging from being ambassador of his country to distinguished member of the International Law Commission (ILC) and to judge of the International Court of Justice (ICJ) for eighteen years, positioned him well to participate in several ground-breaking aspects of contemporary international law and international justice – as set out in the biographical summary in Part I of this volume.

Throughout his decades of unwavering commitment to the ideals of international law, Africa has been and remains an important focus of his work. To give but a few examples, he headed several United Nations missions on the observance of the exercise of the right of self-determination in various non-self-governing territories; served on the General Assembly's Sixth Committee from 1977 to 1994 and was Chairman of the United Nations Special Committee on the granting of independence to colonial countries and people (Committee of 24). Furthermore, he was the Chairman of the African Group and signatory at the Third United Nations Conference on the Law of the Sea (UNCLOS III) – where the African Group made major contributions to the development of concepts such as the exclusive economic zone.

But, like a true international lawyer, Judge Koroma's work and contributions did not focus only on Africa. For example, as a member of the ILC between 1982–1994 and Chair of its Forty-Third Session (1991), Judge Koroma was an active participant and contributor to the elaboration, codification and progressive development of numerous important international legal instruments. These include the Draft Code of Crimes against the Peace and Security of

Mankind; relations between States and international organizations; the jurisdictional immunities of states and their property; the law of state responsibility; the proposed Statute of an International Criminal Court; and the convention on non-navigational uses of international watercourses; the articles on most-favoured-nation clauses; the draft articles on the status of the diplomatic courier and the diplomatic bag not accompanied by diplomatic courier, to name but a few. The scope of his activities, interests and contributions to international law, when taken together between his fourteen years of service at the ILC through to his eighteen years on the bench of the ICJ (a total of thirty-two years), is no mean feat for any international lawyer regardless of their background or country of origin.

This volume seeks to reflect the breadth of the issues in which Judge Koroma was interested. The essays, written by his colleagues, admirers and friends, from all four corners of the world, discuss both classical and contemporary topics of significant relevance to the current and future of international law. These range from dispute settlement in international law and at the ICJ to general topics of public international law, international criminal law and international humanitarian law and Africa's contribution to the development of international law as well as issues at the intersection of international law and regional integration in Africa.

The first substantive part of this collection contains personal reflections fondly written by three of Judge Koroma's close friends and colleagues. P.S. Rao, who served with him at the ILC, reviews some key contributions of Judge Koroma to international law and his vision of the role of law in the international community. Tommy Koh, also from his New York days, reminisces about personal experiences of Judge Koroma based on their friendship which has lasted over several decades. Judge Kenneth Keith provides the third personal note, speaking of Judge Koroma as a neighbour, friend and colleague during the time that they worked together at the Peace Palace in The Hague.

Part II of the volume, which brings together contributions from a mix of ICJ judges and scholars, focuses on critical issues centred on international dispute settlement and the some of the jurisprudence of the ICJ. Judge Keith, in his second contribution to this work, opens with a chapter on the infamous 10 July 1985 sinking by French agents while moored in Auckland Harbor of a converted research trawler owned by Greenpeace and used to protest nuclear testing and commercial whaling and offshore oil and gas drilling in the South Pacific. What subsequently became etched in the minds of international lawyers as the *Rainbow Warrior* Affair resulted in the destruction of the ship, the death of a Dutch crewmember, and a major diplomatic row between New Zealand and France. The dispute lasted several years and only ended following a ruling by then UN Secretary-General Javier Pérez de Cuéllar, binding arbitration and a French apology and compensation. The paper, coming from someone who participated in the arbitration, demonstrates international law's relevance, flexibility and efficacy even in situations where disputes are resolved ad hoc and outside the formal adjudicatory mechanisms of the ICJ. This, of course, was consistent with the ideals of pacific dispute settlement between states found in the Charter of the United Nations.

Judge Bernardo Sepúlveda-Amor, another former ICJ colleague of Judge Koroma's, examines the role that judicial settlement of disputes plays in the maintenance of international peace and security in light of the experience of Latin American States before the World Court. John Dugard, who has also served as a judge ad hoc at the Court and on the ILC before that, analyses the ICJ's advisory opinion on the *Accordance with International Law of the Unilateral Declaration of Independence in Respect of Kosovo*,[1] in which Judge Koroma delivered a dissenting opinion, and its effect on the scope of the principle of territorial integrity. Examining the Court's decisions in *Avena*[2] and *Temple of Preah Vihear*,[3] Karin Oellers-Frahm, a scholar with a long running interest in the ICJ, asks a question that in essence proposes a solution to the Court's lack of compulsory enforcement jurisdiction. Obiora Chinedu Okafor and Chikeziri Igwe provide a TWAIL[4] critique of the ICJ's decision in *Cameroon v. Nigeria*,[5] while Phoebe Okowa assesses the legacy of the decision of the International Court of Justice in the classic *Barcelona Traction Case*[6] and its impact on the modern law of diplomatic protection.

Switching from ICJ decisions to substantive international law, in Part III of the volume, a group of scholars and practitioners take on several important general topics in the field. Sienho Yee writes on the "Competition between and among Intrinsic and Instrumental Values in Selected Competing Visions of the World", where he attempts to draw up a framework for rationalising the world and for analysing competing values. Babafemi Akinrinade writes on democratising international law-making to reflect and adapt to the challenges of an

---

[1] Accordance with International Law of the Unilateral Declaration of Independence in Respect of Kosovo, ICJ Reports 2010.
[2] Case concerning Avena and Other Mexican Nationals, (Mexico v. United States of America), Provisional Measures, ICJ Reports 2008.
[3] Request for Interpretation of the Judgment of 15 June 1962 in the Case Concerning the Temple of Preah Vihear (Cambodia v. Thailand), Provisional Measures, ICJ Reports 2011.
[4] TWAIL is the acronym for "Third World Approaches to International Law".
[5] Case Concerning the Land and Maritime Boundary between Cameroon and Nigeria (Cameroon v. Nigeria: Equatorial Guinea intervening), Judgment, ICJ Reports 2002.
[6] Barcelona Traction Case (Belgium v. Spain) ICJ Reports 1970.

ever-evolving international legal order. While extolling the 1982 Convention of the Law of the Sea as perhaps the most comprehensive of all international treaties, Surya Subedi scrutinises the mechanism established under UNCLOS III for the settlement of disputes and analyses how effective it has been in resolving disputes and maintaining order in the seas and oceans around the world. Osman Keh Kamara writes on the adequacy of the dispute settlement mechanisms contained in Part XV of UNLOS to disputes arising from boundary delimitations in the territorial sea, the exclusive economic zone and the continental shelf between coastal states. The interaction and inter-relation between constitutional law and the settlement of investor-state disputes is examined by Laurence Boisson de Chazournes and Brian McGarry, while Konstantinos Magliveras examines the application of competition rules and principles and their implications for the law of international organizations.

Moving from general international law to the conjoined twin sub-fields of international criminal law and international humanitarian law, both of which have been of special attraction to Judge Koroma as evidenced by his contributions to the Draft Code of Crimes Against the Peace and Security of Mankind and the International Committee of the Red Cross, Judge Sir Christopher Greenwood of the ICJ traces the important jurisprudence of the Court relating to the latter beginning from the *Corfu Channel,* through to the recent *Jurisdictional Immunities*[7] *and Obligation to Prosecute or Extradite*[8] cases. Manuel Ventura analyses a core international instrument through his analysis of the Genocide Convention. He examines its role in the prevention of genocide especially in the light of the emerging doctrines of humanitarian intervention, the responsibility to protect and the prohibition of the use of force. Avitus Agbor scrutinises the chapeau requirement of "widespread or systematic attack" as part of the definition of crimes against humanity, as an offense under international criminal law, while the jurisprudence of the Special Court for Sierra Leone on gender-based and sexual violence crimes is examined by Tamara Cummings-John. The provision of the 2014 Protocol on Amendments to the Protocol on the Statute of the African Court of Justice and Human and Peoples Rights – which temporarily exempts from prosecution any serving African head of state or government or his deputy or any other senior state official during their tenure in office – is analysed by Adejoké Babington-Ashaye for its consistency with existing law, including the infamous ICJ decision in the *Arrest Warrant* case. Abdul Tejan-Cole takes up and largely debunks the recent myths and criticisms of the International Criminal Court (ICC) from a small but vocal group of African States that allege that the world penal court unduly targets

---

[7] Jurisdictional Immunities of the State (Germany v. Italy, Greece intervening), ICJ Reports 2012.
[8] Obligation to Prosecute or Extradite (Belgium v. Senegal), ICJ Reports 2012.

PREFACE AND ACKNOWLEDGMENTS   XIII

Africa in a manner that reflects "legal imperialism". Charles Chernor Jalloh and Andrew Morgan round off this part of the volume with an evaluation of the role and contribution of the UN International Criminal Tribunal for Rwanda and the Special Court for Sierra Leone to the administration of international criminal justice following the horrific Rwandan genocide and the brutal Sierra Leonean conflict in the 1990s. They extrapolate lessons for Liberia where, for various reasons relating more to pragmatics than principle, no prosecutions of atrocity crimes have taken place. This despite substantial evidence of the widespread commission of heinous international crimes by all the parties to the conflict during that country's notorious civil war.

Part V of the volume, which highlights another of Judge Koroma's areas of long standing interest including in his writings and speeches, focuses on the theme Africa and International law. Judge Abdulqawi Yusuf, also currently on the ICJ bench and its current vice-president, discusses the "public law of Africa", comprising rules, principles and practices applicable to intra-African relations and reflecting the African conceptualisation of international law, while Tiyanjana Maluwa examines the development of "community law" in Africa. Jumoke Oduwole examines the conceptualisation, application and development of the Right to Development and highlights the contributions of the African Charter on Human and People's Right and the pragmatic interpretation of it by African regional and sub-regional bodies. Lydia Apori Nkansah discusses the question of democratic succession in Africa and the challenges that bedevil smooth transition of governments, including weak national institutions and the responsibility in this context of credible leadership committed to the advancement of democracy and the welfare of citizens. Adetola Onayemi and Olufemi Elias consider the contribution of African regional and sub-regional institutions and international instruments to the development of international law norms and standards. Vincent Nmehielle, currently the Legal Counsel to the African Union (AU) Commission, analyses the complex dynamics of resolving conflicts in Africa and the role of the AU using the Ivorian and Libyan conflicts as case studies. Gino Naldi examines the controversial topic of secession from an African perspective, drawing on the experiences of Eritrea, Somaliland and South Sudan. Mia Swart explores the effect of the decisions of African regional and sub-regional judicial institutions on domestic judicial institutions in African states, with the view to answering the question whether there is a positive trickle-down effect of these regional and sub-regional decisions.

Last but not least, in a joint paper, Charles Manga Fombad and Madeline Choe-Amusimo Fombad contend that endemic corruption in Africa and the failure to seriously control it poses one of the greatest threats to peace and security on the continent. This undermines Africa's development prospects. In arguing that the fight against corruption is not simply about occasional campaigns designed to catch a few bad apples, the duo makes the case for the establishment of a robust and sustainable legal framework that will improve overall governance, accountability and transparency. The crux of their claim is that only a robust constitutionally entrenched framework of measures and institutions, protected by certain fundamental principles, can provide a solid and effective basis to bring rampant corruption on the continent under control.

∙ ∙ ∙

Judge Koroma's many judicial pronouncements reflect his vision for international society and the role of law within it. Of these pronouncements, despite the many possible candidates, we have selected the following statement made in his Dissenting Opinion in the ICJ's advisory opinion on the *Legality of the Threat of Use of Nuclear Weapons*. He stated as follows:

> In my view, the prevention of war, by the use of nuclear weapons, is a matter for international law and, if the Court is requested to determine such an issue, it falls within its competence to do so. Its decision can contribute to the prevention of war by ensuring respect for the law. The Court in the Corfu Channel case described as its function the need to "ensure respect for international law, of which it is the organ" (I.C.J. Reports 1949, p. 35). The late Judge Nagendra Singh, a former Member and President of this Court, commenting on that statement, observed that it was made by the Court without reference to the United Nations Charter or to its own Statute. He observed that "the Court has thus to be conscious of this fact, as something inherent to its existence in relation to the law which it administers" (The Role and Record of the International Court of Justice, p. 173). Today a system of war prevention exists in international law, and comprises the prohibition of the use of force, the collective security provisions of the United Nations Charter for the maintenance of international peace, the obligation to resort to peaceful means for the settlement of international disputes and the regulations on weapons prohibition, arms limitation and disarmament. The Court's Advisory Opinion in this case could have strengthened this régime *by serving as a shield of humanity*.[9]

---

9   ICJ Reports (1995), p. 557.

This conception of the place of law in international affairs reflects Judge Koroma's view of the function of international law in the international community. International law can contribute to the prevention of war by ensuring respect for the law. Thus, beyond hiding behind technicalities in the fear of confronting the obviously political when confronted with questions about the legality of using the ultimate weapon with a frightening capacity to wipe out humankind, international law should first and foremost be invoked by the Court in the service of humanity's perennial search for peace and security. In choosing the last sentence of this passage as the title of this volume, we firmly believe that it perfectly encapsulates the essence of Judge Koroma's views and is a true reflection of his ideological standpoint: that law should never be shy to stare power in the face, and if necessary, to bring power to its knees. It is our hope that the chapters and other contributions in this volume will enrich the perspectives of those who have dedicated themselves, as Judge Koroma has done, to the pursuit of international law and international justice.

⋯

Finally, as editors, we have benefitted from the generosity, kindness and collegiality of each and every contributor to this book all of whom heartily endorsed the project when we first approached them. We therefore wish to acknowledge and thank them all for their tremendous patience as we gathered and edited contributions. In this regard, although we appreciate all their support through some unplanned delays, we are particularly indebted to Judge Keith for his invaluable role and always sound advice throughout the process as we worked hard to see this book through. We are also grateful to the Registrar of the ICJ, H. E. Philippe Couvreur, for permission to reproduce the photograph of Judge Koroma. Adetola Onayemi assisted with the preparation of the index. Jonathan Davis assisted with reviews and collation of the proofs. We are also grateful to Lindy Melman, Ingeborg van der Laan, Wilma de Weert and all their fine colleagues at Brill for their helpful support and professionalism throughout the process of producing and publishing this book.

Charles Chernor Jalloh and Olufemi Elias

Abdul G. Koroma – Biographical Summary

Abdul Gadire Koroma was born in Freetown, Sierra Leone, West Africa. He earned an LL.M. (Honours), from Kiev State University; a Master of Philosophy (International Law), Kings College, University of London; and was awarded an Honorary Doctorate from the University of Sierra Leone. He has been a Barrister-at-Law and Honorary Bencher, Honourable Society of Lincoln's Inn, London and a Honorary Professor at the Gujarat National Law University, Gujarat, India.

He joined the Government service of Sierra Leone in 1964 and the Ministry of Foreign Affairs in 1969. As a Barrister and Legal Practitioner of the High Court of Sierra Leone, he was appointed State Counsel and Special Adviser to the Attorney-General and Minister of Justice. He subsequently served as Legal Adviser to the Permanent Mission of Sierra Leone to the United Nations and as Ambassador Extraordinary and Plenipotentiary of Sierra Leone to the United Nations, New York, while concurrently accredited as High Commissioner of Sierra Leone to Jamaica and Trinidad and Tobago, and Ambassador to the Republic of Korea (Seoul) and Cuba (1981–1985). He was also Ambassador Extraordinary and Plenipotentiary to Belgium, France, Luxembourg and The Netherlands while concurrently accredited to the European Communities and to the United Nations Educational, Scientific and Cultural Organization (UNESCO) (1985–1988). He later became Ambassador Extraordinary and Plenipotentiary of Sierra Leone to the Organization of African Unity (OAU), with concurrent accreditation to Ethiopia, Kenya, the United Republic of Tanzania and Zambia (1988–1992); and was also accredited to Republic of Korea (Seoul) and High Commissioner to Barbados, Jamaica, Trinidad and Tobago (1988).

As delegate to the General Assembly, he served on the Sixth Committee (Legal) from 1977 to 1994 and was elected Chairman and as delegate of Sierra Leone to the following United Nations bodies: the Special Committee on the Review of the Charter and on the Strengthening of the Role of the Organization; the United Nations Commission on International Trade Law (UNCITRAL); the United Nations Committee on the Peaceful Uses of Outer Space; the United Nations Programme of Assistance in the Teaching, Study, Dissemination and Wider Appreciation of International Law; served as Chairman of the United Nations Special Committee on the granting of independence to colonial countries and people (Committee of 24); headed various United Nations missions on the observance of the exercise of the right of self-determination in various non-self-governing territories.

He has represented Sierra Leone at many plenipotentiary conferences, including the United Nations Conference on the Succession of States in respect of Property, Debts and Archives, and was a signatory of the Convention; the Third United Nations Conference on the Law of the Sea (UNCLOS III) and Chairman of the African Group at the Conference. In that capacity, he was closely associated with the elaboration of some of the key provisions of the resulting Convention. Was a signatory of the Convention.

He has also played an active role in and contributed to the elaboration of various contemporary legal instruments as a member of the International Law Commission (January 1982–1994) and Chairman of the Commission during its forty-third session (1991). He formerly was Chairman of the Committee mandated to elaborate a Draft Statute for an International Criminal Court and was an active participant and contributor to the codification and progressive development of such important international legal instruments as the Draft Code of Crimes against the Peace and Security of Mankind; Relations between States and International Organizations; the Jurisdictional Immunities of States and their Property; the Law of State Responsibility; the proposed Statute of an International Criminal Court; and the Law of the Non-Navigational Uses of International Water Courses; the articles on most-favoured-nation clauses; the draft articles on the status of the diplomatic courier and the diplomatic bag not accompanied by diplomatic courier, and of the optional protocols thereto.

He has made contributions to other major areas of international law, including the law of self-determination, human rights law, international humanitarian law, and the peaceful settlement of disputes, and has written and lectured on these subjects. Further, he was an expert consultant with the International Committee of the Red Cross (ICRC) at Geneva on the implementation of and respect for international humanitarian law. Has delivered lectures on all of these topics in many countries, including Cameroon, Canada, China, Ethiopia, Germany, Greece, India, Italy, Japan, Republic of Korea, Malta, Norway, Peru, Sweden, the United Republic of Tanzania and the United States of America.

Over the course of his career, Judge Koroma participated in conferences, symposiums and seminars on international law, including those held by the International Ocean Institute (Malta and Halifax, Nova Scotia); the International Law Institute (Hawaii); the International Criminal Jurisdiction (Talloires); the International Institute of Higher Studies in Criminal Sciences; Centre for International Studies, New York University School of Law; the Asian-African Legal Consultative Committee. And, in service to the academy, he was an external examiner in international law for Ph.D. candidates of the University of Dalhousie, Halifax, Nova Scotia, Canada.

He has been a member of the American Society of International Law and of the Planning Council of the International Ocean Institute (Halifax and Malta); Member and Vice-President of the African Association of International Law and Comparative Law; President of the African Society of International and Comparative Law; President, Henry Dunant Centre for Humanitarian Dialogue (Geneva) (1999–2006); Member of the International Institute of Humanitarian Law, San Remo; Member of the Institute of International Law; Member of the Committee of Experts on the Application of Conventions and Recommendations, International Labour Office (Geneva); Member of the Advisory Board of the *Manchester Journal of International Economic Law*; Member of the Scientific Advisory Board of the Cologne Commentary on Space Law, Institute of Air and Space Law, University of Cologne; May 2009 Member of the Advisory Board of the *Journal of International Humanitarian Legal Studies (JIHLS)*.

Judge Koroma has received many honors. He was awarded the Order of Commander of Rokel by the Government of Sierra Leone for outstanding professional service (1991); the International Institute of Humanitarian Law Prize for the Promotion, Dissemination and Teaching of International Humanitarian Law (2005); and the Order of Grand Officer of the Republic of Sierra Leone (the highest national award) in recognition of his service to the nation in the field of international law and international justice as a judge at the International Court of Justice (2007).

He has written widely on international law issues. He was an author of a thesis on the *Settlement of Territorial and Boundary Disputes in Africa* (University of London). Among articles published are the following: "Humanitarian Intervention and Contemporary International Law", *Swiss Review of International and European Law*, No. 4, 1995; "The Peaceful Settlement of International Disputes", *Netherlands International Review*, Vol. XLIII, 1996/7; "50th Anniversary of the Universal Declaration of Human Rights: Human Rights and International Humanitarian Law", *International Review of the Red Cross*, 1998; "The Influence of the Universal Declaration of Human Rights in Africa – Fifty Years After Its Adoption – A Legal Perspective", *Africa Legal Aid Quarterly*, 1998; "International Justice in Relation to the International Court of Justice", *Thesaurus Acroasium*, Vol. XXVI, Thessaloniki; "Implementation of the Law of the Sea Convention Through Its Institutions: An Overview", in D. Vidas and W. Østreng (eds.) *Order for the Oceans at the Turn of the Century*; "The Humanitarian Consequences of Small Arms Proliferation", Paper delivered under the auspices of the Henry Dunant Centre for Humanitarian Dialogue; "The Future of the Common Heritage of Mankind", *1982 Convention on the Law of the Sea*, published by the Law of the Sea Institute, University of Hawaii, Honolulu; "Provisional Measures in Disputes between African States before the International Court of

Justice", in Laurence Boisson de Chazournes and Vera Gowlland-Debbas (eds.) *The International Legal System in Quest of Equity and Universality*, Liber Amicorum Georges Abi-Saab, 2001; "Social Justice and the Role of an International Judge", Paper delivered at the Colloquium on Social Justice and International Law in Honour of Professor Georges Abi-Saab, 2001; Book review on *Human Rights in Africa Series*, in Professor Christof Heyns (ed.) *Leiden Journal of International Law*, 2001; "Africa's Place in the International Justice System", Paper delivered at the 643rd Wilton Park Conference: Justice in Africa, 2001; "Refugees: A Continuing Challenge", Paper delivered at the 25th Round Table on Current Problems of International Humanitarian Law, International Institute of Humanitarian Law, San Remo, 2001; "The Protection of Civilian Populations in Non-International Armed Conflicts", Paper delivered at the Third Meeting of Experts, International Institute of Humanitarian Law, Stockholm, 2001; "Rules of Court and Practice Directions", *Max Planck Encyclopedia of Public International Law*, 2005.

Abbreviations

ACHPR	African Charter of Human and People's Rights
AFRC	Armed Forces Revolutionary Council
AMISOM	African Union Mission in Somalia
AMU	Arab Maghreb Union
APC	All People's Congress
ASEAN	Association of South East Asian Nations
ASP	Assembly of States Parties of the International Criminal Court
AU	African Union
APSA	African Union Peace and Security Architecture
AUPSC	Peace and Security Council of the African Union
AZAPO	Azanian Peoples Organization
CAR	Central African Republic
CAT	Convention Against Torture
CCJEU	Court of Justice of the Europen Union
CDF	Civil Defense Forces
CEDAW	Convention on the Elimination of All Forms of Discrimination Against Women
CEN-SAD	Community of Sahel-Saharan States
CIS	Commonwealth of Independent States
CODESRIA	Council for Development and Social Research in Africa
COE	Council of Europe
COMECON	Council of Mutual Economic Assistance
COMESA	Common Market of Eastern and Southern Africa
CPI	Corruption Perception Index
CRC	Convention on the Rights of the Child
CSOS	Civil Society Organizations
CSTO	Collective Security Treaty Organization
DRC	Democratic Republic of the Congo
EAC	East African Community
EBRD	European Bank of Reconstruction and Development
ECCAS	Economic Community of Central African States
ECCC	Extraordinary Chambers in the Courts of Cambodia
ECGLC	Economic Community of Great Lakes Countries
ECHR	European Convention on Human Rights
ECJ	European Court of Justice
ECtHR	European Court of Human Rights

ECOMOG	Economic Community of West African States Monitoring Group
ECOWAS	Economic Community of West African States
ECOSOC	Economic and Social Council – an organ of the United Nations
EEC	European Economic Community
EFTA	European Free Trade Association
EIDHR	European Instrument for Democracy and Human Rights
ELN	National Liberation Army (Colombia)
EMA	Electoral Management Agencies
EMB	Election Management Bodies
EU	European Union
FARC	Revolutionary Armed Forces of Colombia
FAO	Food and Agriculture Organization
FRY	Federal Republic of Yugoslavia
GATT	General Agreement on Tarriffs and Trade
GNU	Government of National Unity
HRW	Human Rights Watch
IAEA	International Atomic Energy Agency
ICC	International Criminal Court
ICC&Ts	International Criminal Courts and Tribunals
ICG	International Crisis Group
ICL	International Criminal Law
ICLS	International Criminal Law Section
ICJ	International Court of Justice
ICPR	International Covenant on Civil and Political Rights
ICESCR	Interntional Covenant on Economic, Social and Cultural Rights
ICRC	International Committee of the Red Cross
ICSID	International Center for Settlement of Investment Disputes
ICTR	International Criminal Tribunal for Rwanda
ICTY	International Criminal Tribunal for the former Yugoslavia
IDP	Internally Displaced Persons
IGAD	Intergovernmental Authority on Development
IHL	International Humanitarian Law
ILC	International Law Commission
IMF	International Monetary Fund
IMT	International Military Tribunal at Nuremberg
IMTFEE	International Military Tribunal for the Far East
IPI	Ivorian Popular Front
IOS	International Organizations

ITLOS	International Tribunal for the Law of the Sea
JCE	Joint Criminal Enterprise
LAIA	Latin American Integration Association
LRA	Lord's Resistance Army
MICT	Mechanism for International Criminal Tribunals
M & A	Merger and Acquisition
NAFTA	North American Free Trade Agreement
NAM	Non-Aligned Movement
NATO	North Atlantic Treaty Organization
NDPP	Natioanl Directorate of Public Prosecutions (South Africa)
NEPAD	New Partnership for Africa's Development
NIEO	New International Economic Order
NPFL	National Patriotic Front of Liberia
NPRC	National Provisional Ruling Council
NPWJ	No Peace Without Justice
OAS	Organization of American States
OAU	Organization of African Unity (later transformed into the African Union)
OECD	Organization of Economic Cooperation and Development
OEECC	Organization for European Economic Cooperation
OIC	Organization of Islamic Conference
OHADA	Organisation for the Harmonisation of Business Law in Africa
OHCHR	Office of the High Commissioner for Human Rights
OPEC	Organization of Petroleum Exporting Countries
OPCW	Organization for Prohibition of Chemical Weapons
OAPEC	Organization of Arab Petroleum Exporting Countries
OSIWA	Open Society Initiative for West Africa
OTP	Office of the Prosecutor
PTC	Pre-Trial Chamber of the International Criminal Court
PTRD	People's Right to Development
RECS	Regional Economic Communities
RPE	Rules of Procedure and Evidence
RPF	Rwandan Patriotic Front
RSCSL	Residual Special Court for Sierra Leone
R2P	Responsibility to Protect
RTD	Right to Development
RUF	Revolutionary United Front
RUF/SL	Revolutionary United Front of Sierra Leone
RUFP	Revolutionary United Front Party
Rules	Rules of Procedure and Evidence

SACU	Southern African Customs Union
SADC	Southern African Development Community
SCO	Shanghai Cooperation Organization
SCSL	Special Court for Sierra Leone
SEATO	Southeast Asia Treaty Organization
SERAC	Social and Economic Rights Action Centre
SL	Sierra Leone
SLA	Sierra Leone Army
SLPP	Sierra Leone People's Party
SPLM	Sudan People's Liberation Army/Movement (SPLA/M)
STL	Special Tribunal for Lebanon
TRC	Truth and Reconciliation Commission
TWAIL	Third World Approaches to International Law
UEAMO	Economic and Monetary Union of West Africa
UIA	Union of International Associations
UK	United Kingdom
UN	United Nations
UNGA	United Nations General Assembly
UNDP	United Nations Development Programme
UNEP	United Nations Environmental Programme
UNESCO	United Nations Education, Scientific and Cultural Organization
UNIDO	United Nations International Development Organization
UNSC	United Nations Security Council
UDHR	Universal Declaration of Human Rights
UNAMID	United Nations Assistance Mission in Darfur
UNAMSIL	United Nations Assistance Mission in Sierra Leone
UNAMIR	United Nations Assistance Mission for Rwanda
UNCLOS	United Nations Convention on the Law of the Sea
UNCTAD	United Nations Conference on Trade and Development
UNHRC	United Nations Human Rights Council
UNICEF	United Nations Children's Fund
UNMIK	United Nations Mission in Kosovo
UNMIL	United Nations Mission in Liberia
UNOMSIL	United Nations Observer Mission in Sierra Leone
UNSG	United Nations Secretary-General
UNTAET	UN Transitional Administration in East Timor
UNWCC	United Nations War Crimes Commission
UPDF	Uganda Peoples Defence Force
US or USA	United States of America
WEU	Western European Union

WHO	World Health Organization
WVS	Witness and Victims Section
WVSS	Witness and Victims Support Section

Editors' Biographies

Charles Chernor Jalloh
B.A. (Guelph) LLB/BCL (McGill) M St (Oxon), is an Associate Professor at Florida International University (FIU) College of Law, USA. Before joining FIU, he taught international and criminal law at the University of Pittsburgh School of Law where he was selected as the Buchanan Ingersoll & Rooney Faculty Scholar for 2013–2014. He has been a legal adviser in the Canadian Department of Justice, the Special Court for Sierra Leone, the International Criminal Tribunal for Rwanda as well as a Visiting Professional in the International Criminal Court. He has published widely on aspects of international criminal justice in leading journals and is author or editor of several books with leading academic presses. The Founding Editor-in-Chief of the *African Journal of Legal Studies* and *African Journal of International Criminal Justice*, he is a member of the International Law Association's Committee on Complementarity in International Criminal Law; the Advisory Board to the President of the International Criminal Tribunal for the former Yugoslavia; the Advisory Board to the War Crimes Committee, International Bar Association, and between 2012–2014, was a Co-Chair of the American Society of International Law's International Criminal Law Interest Group.

Olufemi Elias
M.A. (Oxon) LLM (Cambridge) Ph.D. (London), is the Legal Adviser and Director of the Office of Legal Affairs at the Organization for the Prohibition of Chemical Weapons based in The Hague. Prior to that, he was the Executive Secretary of the World Bank Administrative Tribunal, in Washington, D.C., after having served as a legal adviser at the United Nations Compensation Commission in Geneva. He is a Visiting Professor in international law at Queen Mary University of London. He has taught international law at King's College, London, and has held teaching positions in a number of other universities. He is a member of the Nigerian Bar. He has written widely on various aspects of international law. He is the Secretary-General of the African Association of International Law, and a member of the Executive Council of the American Society of International Law.

Contributors

Avitus A. Agbor
LLB (Buea) LLM (Notre Dame) PhD (Witwatersrand), is currently a Senior Lecturer at the Faculty of Law, North-West University, Mafikeng Campus, Mafikeng, South Africa. He is an NRF-rated researcher with interests in International Criminal Law, Criminal Law and International Human Rights Law.

Babafemi Akinrinade
LLB, LLM (Ife) LLM JSD (Notre Dame) is currently Associate Professor of Human Rights, Fairhaven College of Interdisciplinary Studies, Western Washington University. He is a Barrister and Solicitor of the Supreme Court of Nigeria

Adejoké Babington-Ashaye
LLM (London School of Economics and Political Science), is currently counsel at the World Bank Administrative Tribunal. A member of the New York Bar, she was formerly an Associate Legal Officer at the International Court of Justice and an Investigator in the Office of the Prosecutor, International Criminal Court.

Laurence Boisson de Chazournes
is Professor of international law and international organization at the Faculty of Law of the University of Geneva since 1999 and has published widely in international economic law, international environmental law and in the area of dispute settlement. She is a Member of the Court, Permanent Court of Arbitration. She has served as chairperson of WTO arbitration panels on pre-shipment inspections, has pleaded before the International Court of Justice (ICJ) and has been an arbitrator in international and investment arbitrations.

Tamara Cummings-John
is currently a Legal Officer in the Office of Legal Affairs at the United Nations in New York. She previously worked in the Office of the Prosecutor at both the Special Court for Sierra Leone and at the International Criminal Tribunal for Rwanda. She studied at the University of Manchester, Université de Bourgogne, and the College of Law, Store Street and holds a Masters in International and Comparative Legal Studies from the School of Oriental and African Studies, University of London.

John Dugard

SC, Professor Emeritus, Leiden University, Honorary Professor, University of Pretoria, and judge ad hoc of the International Court of Justice, was a member of the International Law Commission (1997–2011) and Special Rapporteur to the Human Rights Council and Commission on Human Rights on the Human Rights Situation in the Occupied Palestinian Territory (2001–2008).

Olufemi Elias

MA (Oxon) LLM (Cambridge) PhD (London), Legal Adviser and Director of the Office of Legal Affairs, Organisation for the Prohibition of Chemical Weapons and Visiting Professor in international law, Queen Mary, University of London. He is former Executive Secretary, World Bank Administrative Tribunal, and former legal adviser, United Nations Compensation Commission; and currently a Visiting Professor in international law, Queen Mary, University of London.

Christopher Greenwood

QC is a Judge of the International Court of Justice. He was formerly Professor of International Law at the London School of Economics and Political Science and a barrister practising before the English and international courts. He taught at the University of Cambridge for nearly twenty years and is a Queen's Counsel. He has published widely in the field of international law. He was made a Companion of the Order of St Michael and St George (CMG) for services to public international law in 2002 and knighted in 2009.

Chikeziri Igwe

PhD (Osgoode Hall Law School, York) LLM (Manitoba) and LLB (Hons) (Calabar, Nigeria), Crown Prosecutor, Government of Ontario, Toronto, Canada. He has published several works in international law.

Osman Keh Kamara

LL.B. Hons. (Fourah Bay College, University of Sierra Leone) BL (Sierra Leone Law School), MPA (Columbia, New York, USA), Post-Graduate Diploma (Rhodes Academy of Ocean Law and Policy, Greece), is currently Sierra Leone's Ambassador to the African Union with concurrent accreditation to the Federal Republic of Ethiopia and the United Nations Economic Commission for Africa. He was formerly Ambassador and Deputy Permanent Representative of Sierra Leone at its Permanent Mission to the United Nations in New York. He has been a Nippon Foundation Fellow at the International Tribunal of the Law of the Sea in Hamburg, where he spent time at the Max Planck Institute for Comparative Public Law and International Law in Heidelberg, Germany. He has also been a co-counsel at the United Nations-backed Special Court for Sierra Leone.

Charles Manga Fombad
Lic-en-Droit (Yaounde) LLM PhD (London), is Professor of Law, Institute for International and Comparative Law in Africa, Faculty of Law, University of Pretoria, South Africa.

Madeline Choe-Amusimo Fombad
Lic-en-Droit (Yaounde) MLIS (Botswana), PhD (Pretoria), is Senior Lecturer, Department of Information Science, Faculty of Humanities, University of Pretoria, South Africa.

Charles Chernor Jalloh
BA (Guelph) LLB and BCL (McGill) M St (Oxon), is Associate Professor at Florida International University College of Law, USA. He has been counsel in the Canadian Department of Justice, the Special Court for Sierra Leone and the International Criminal Tribunal for Rwanda. He has published widely on issues of international criminal justice.

Kenneth Keith
was a Judge of the International Court of Justice from 2006 to 2015. He is a Queen's Counsel, a former judge at the Supreme Court of New Zealand and former Dean of the Victoria University of Wellington. Judge Keith is a knight and a member of the Order of New Zealand, that country's highest honour, as well as a member of the Institut de Droit International.

Tommy Koh
is currently Ambassador-at-Large at the Ministry of Foreign Affairs, Special Adviser of the Institute of Policy Studies and Chairman of the Centre for International Law, National University of Singapore. He is former Dean of the Faculty of Law of the University of Singapore from 1971 to 1974, and subsequently, Singapore's Permanent Representative to the United Nations and its ambassador to Canada, Mexico and the United States. He holds a First Class Honours degree in Law from the National University of Singapore, a Masters in Law from Harvard University and an honorary degree of Doctor of Laws from Yale University.

Tiyanjana Maluwa
LLB (Malawi) LLM (Sheffield) PhD (Cantab), holds the H. Laddie Montague Chair in Law at the Dickinson School of Law of Pennsylvania State University,

where he is concurrently Associate Dean for International Affairs and Director of the School of International Affairs. He previously worked as the Legal Counsel of the OAU (now African Union) and, subsequently, as the legal adviser to the Office of the UN High Commissioner for Human Rights. He has been a Professor of Law at the University of Cape Town, and Extraordinary Professor of Law at the University of Pretoria, South Africa.

Konstantinos D. Magliveras

LLM (Exon) DPhil (Oxon), Professor, Department of Mediterranean Studies, University of the Aegean; Attorney at Law, Greece. He has published widely on aspects of international law and international institutions.

Brian McGarry

BA (Rutgers) JD (Tulane) LLM (The Graduate Institute), Member of the Bar of New York, is a PhD Researcher in the Faculty of Law, University of Geneva.

Andrew Morgan

Esq., BA (NYU) JD *cum laude* (Pittsburgh), Executive Director, JURIST Legal News and Research Services, Inc., Member of the Bar of the Commonwealth of Pennsylvania; formerly an intern at the International Criminal Tribunal for Rwanda.

Gino J. Naldi

LLB LLM PhD (Birmingham), after many years in academia, is currently an independent scholar. He has published extensively on issues of international law with a focus on African affairs especially on the Organization of African Unity/African Union.

Lydia A. Nkansah

LLB, LLM, PhD is a Senior Lecturer in Law, Kwame Nkrumah University of Science and Technology, Ghana. She was a Senior Legal Officer at the Ghana Human Rights Commission, Head of the Research Unit of the Truth and Reconciliation Commission for Sierra Leone, and International Expert Advisor to the Liberian Transitional Legislative Assembly on Truth and Reconciliation Bill.

Vincent O. Nmehielle

LLB BL LLM SJD, is General Counsel of the African Union. He is also a Professor of Law and the Head of the Wits Programme in Law, Justice and Development in Africa at the University of the Witwatersrand School of Law, Johannesburg, South Africa (currently on leave). Nmehielle held the Bram Fischer Chair in

Human Rights Law at Wits Law School from 2002–2004. From 2005–2008, he served as the Principal Defender of the United Nations-Backed Special Court for Sierra Leone in Freetown, Sierra Leone.

Karin Oellers-Frahm
is a Senior Research fellow at the Max Planck Institute for Comparative Public Law and International Law in Heidelberg, Germany. She has written widely on issues of international law, focusing in particular, on aspects of public international law and the International Court of Justice.

Olajumoke O. Oduwole
LLB (Unilag) LLM (Cantab) JSM JSD (Stanford), is Professor to the Prince Claus Chair in Development and Equity 2013/2015 at the International Institute of Social Studies, The Hague, The Netherlands; Lecturer, Department of Jurisprudence and International Law, Faculty of Law, University of Lagos, Nigeria.

Obiora Chinedu Okafor
University Research Chair in International and Transnational Legal Studies at the Osgoode Hall Law School, York University, Toronto, Canada; and the Vice-Chair/Rapporteur, UN Human Rights Council Advisory Committee. He has visited at several universities, including Harvard, and most recently was the Gani Fawehinmi Distinguished Professor of Human Rights Law at the Nigerian Institute of Advanced Legal Studies, Abuja. He has published extensively in the fields of international human rights law, immigration and refugee law, and general public international law.

Phoebe Okowa
is Professor of Public International Law at Queen Mary, University of London. She previously taught at the University of Bristol and in 2011, she was a Global Visiting Professor at New York University, School of Law. Okowa is the joint editor of Foundations of Public International Law (Oxford University Press) and the Queen Mary Studies in International Law (Brill). She has published extensively on a wide range of topics in public international law.

Adetola Onayemi
LLB (Lagos) LLM (Cambridge), serves as legal counsel to Form+ (Winner, Google API award 2012) and Blendology (UK), and currently works at the Office of the Legal Adviser, Organisation for the Prohibition of Chemical Weapons. He previously worked at the legal office of Ikeyi & Arifayan Barristers and Solicitors, Lagos and Citibank Nigeria, and has written in international intel-

lectual property law, investment and trade law, technology law and international law.

Pemmaraju Sreenivasa Rao
BL and ML (Andhra University, India), LLM and JSD (Yale), is a (1999-2004) Associate member, Member (2005-) and the First Vice-President (2013-2015) of the Institut de Droit International, Special Adviser, Office of the Attorney-General, State of Qatar (2006-), Member, Advisory Council, the Asian Society of International Law (2014-, Judge Ad Hoc, ICJ, Sovereignty over Pedra Branca/Pulau Batu Puteh (2004-2008), Middle Rocks and South Ledge (Malaysia/Singapore), Arbitrator, Bay of Bengal Maritime Boundary Arbitration between Bangladesh and India (2010-2014), the Legal Adviser to the Ministry of External Affairs of India (1985-2002), a former Member (1987-2006), Chairman (1995) and Special Rapporteur (1997-2006) of the International Law Commission, President of the Asian-African Legal Consultative Organization (1998, 2001). Author of Public Order of the Ocean Resources (MIT, 1975), contributed chapters to various edited volumes and published articles on different subjects of international law.

Bernardo Sepúlveda-Amor
was a Judge of the International Court of Justice and was its Vice-President between 2012 and 2015. Before joining the Court, he was a distinguished professor of international law, a diplomat representing Mexico, and subsequently, its foreign minister as well as a member of the International Law Commission between 1996 and 2005. His education includes law degrees from National University of Mexico, a Master of Laws and Diploma in International Law from Cambridge, and an honorary doctorate from the University of San Diego.

Surya P. Subedi
OBE DPhil (Oxon); LLM with Distinction (Hull); LLB and MA (Tribhuvan University), is Professor of International Law at the University of Leeds and a practising barrister in England and Wales. He has published extensively in international law and has advised a number of countries on international legal matters. He has been designated to serve on the Panels of Arbitrators and of Conciliators of the intergovernmental International Centre for Settlement of Investment Disputes and on the Panels of the Dispute Settlement Body of the World Trade Organization. He is the UN Special Rapporteur for Human Rights in Cambodia and an Associate Member of the Institut de Droit International.

Mia Swart
BA (UNISA) LLB (UCT) LLM (Humboldt) PhD (Leiden) is Professor of International Law at the University of Johannesburg where she coordinates and teaches the LLM programme in international law at the University of Johannesburg. Mia previously worked as Associate Professor at the University of the Witwatersrand, Research Fellow at the Bingham Centre for the Rule of Law in London and as Assistant Professor of Public International Law and Global Justice at Leiden University, The Netherlands.

Abdul Tejan-Cole
is the executive director of the Open Society Initiative for West Africa. Prior to that, he served as commissioner of the Anti-Corruption Commission in Sierra Leone from December 2007 through April 2010. His previous positions include: senior trial attorney in the Office of the Prosecutor, Special Court for Sierra Leone; deputy director for the International Center for Transitional Justice's Cape Town Office; and president of the Sierra Leone Bar Association. He has published several articles and book chapters on various topics in international law.

Manuel J. Ventura
BA/LLB (University of Western Sydney), BEcSocSc (Hons) (University of Sydney), LLM (Hons) (Geneva Academy of International Humanitarian Law and Human Rights), is a Director of The Peace and Justice Initiative, a non-governmental organization that assists states in the domestic implementation of the Rome Statute of the International Criminal Court; an Adjunct Fellow at the School of Law, University of Western Sydney; and a member of the Council of Advisers of the Global Institute for the Prevention of Aggression. He publishes regularly on topics related to international criminal law and justice.

Sienho Yee
is Changjiang Xuezhe Professor and Chief Expert, China Institute for Boundary and Ocean Studies and Institute of International Law at Wuhan University, China; member of the Institut de Droit International; Editor-in-Chief of the *Chinese Journal of International Law*; Special Rapporteur of the Informal Expert Group on Customary International Law of the Asian-African Legal Consultative Organization; formerly Sub-reporter on ICJ Matters for the ILA Study Group on UN Reform and Chair of the ILA American Branch Committee on Inter-State Dispute Settlement; and the author of many articles and essays on diverse issues in international law.

Abdulqawi A. Yusuf
is a Judge of the International Court of Justice, The Hague, The Netherlands and Vice-President of the Court since February 2015. He is a member of the Institut de Droit International, Geneva, Switzerland, a former Legal Adviser to various intergovernmental organizations, including UNESCO and UNIDO, the founder and General Editor of the African Yearbook of International Law, a former lecturer in international law at the Somali National University in Mogadishu and other universities, and author of numerous publications on international legal matters. He holds a Ph.D. in international law, IUHEI, Geneva.

PART 1

Reflections on Abdul G. Koroma's Contributions to International Law

∴

CHAPTER 1

Judge Abdul Koroma in the Service of Universal International Law

Pemmaraju Sreenivasa Rao

Judge Abdul Koroma, for long truly a citizen of the international community, has been a major player in the development, practice and application of international law. His contribution as a negotiator, diplomat and permanent representative of Sierra Leone to the United Nations, and as a member of the International Law Commission and as a judge of the International Court of Justice has many sides to it. But chiefly it added value and strength to the work of the Third World international law scholars and practitioners, in particular from Africa. This is all the more noteworthy as it came at a time when it was needed most in the formative years of the Law of the Sea Convention, during the fashioning of the various declarations of the UN General Assembly and in the context of the early efforts of the UN to codify and progressively develop international law. His work is a towering example of how scholars and practitioners from the Third World have been working constantly and consistently to enlarge the foundations of international law to make it more universal.

The Third World's contribution to international law and its impact on the development and codification of international law in the post-UN period, despite many scholarly assessments, still is little appreciated and understood in the global context and much less in the Third World itself. This is partly due to lack of seriousness with which international law ought to be taken as a discipline in its own right distinct from the national law. One of course should not take this to mean that there are two water-tight legal systems in the classical sense of monist and dualist schools of international law. The contemporary reality of globalization apart, the two disciplines do closely interact and are even to some extent integrated, particularly in the fields of foreign investment, environmental protection and especially in promoting fundamental human rights. Nevertheless, the nature of international law as a discipline is fundamentally different from national law because its primary focus and purpose is to establish and regulate the rule of law at the global level. It is easy to see the difference between the system and values that govern a national community and the system and values that govern the international community.[1] More fundamentally, while the Austinian system prevails to govern national legal order, consent and consensus and consistent and uniform practice followed by perceived sense of obligation weaves the system of international law and world order. This is in turn maintained not by a centralized command and control mechanism that sustains national legal order but by a more nuanced system of 'common interests',[2] reciprocity[3] and retaliation.[4]

The second reason is that Third World countries are still so preoccupied with nation-building and even survival – some are engulfed in ethnic and religious conflicts – that they have little time to fully grasp the role and function of international law in the world order much less to focus on building national international law expertise. Just to illustrate this point, whereas the economic and foreign policy of western European and other States is well served by large groups of highly trained international law specialists, supported by influential schools of thought and doctrines of international law articulated by fellow scholars and practitioners, such expertise scarcely exists in the Third World countries, and there is much less appreciation and utilization of such expertise that exists. Even a small country like Belgium or the Netherlands can boast of more international law specialists than most other Third World countries. Teaching and research in the field of international law as a distinct discipline commenced in Europe when the University of Salamanca in Spain first developed it in the early sixteenth century, whereas it is being developed only now and that too in a few countries in the Third World.

In this context as noted above, it is necessary to highlight the remarkable achievements and contributions of Judge Abdul Koroma. Following his education in Freetown, Kiev and London, he entered the diplomatic service of Sierra

---

1   On the nature and significance of the "international community", see P.S. Rao, "The Concept of International Community in International Law and the Developing Countries", in Ulrich Fastenrath et al. (eds.), *From Bilateralism to Community Interest: Essays in Honour of Bruno Simma* (2011), p. 326; and "The Concept of International Community in International Law in Theory and Reality", in *International Law between Universalism and Fragmentation: Festschrift in Honour of Gerhard Hafner* (2008), p. 85.

2   On the concept of 'common interests', see the work and contributions of the New Haven School of Law, pioneered by Professors Myres S. McDougal and Harold D. Lasswell of the Yale Law School. See McDougal, Lasswell and Vlasic, Law and Public Order in Space (Yale Uni.Press, 1963), pp. 150–151.

3   See Bruno Simma, 'Reciprocity', in the Max Planck Encyclopedia of Public International Law.

4   Retaliation is a milder form of unilateral action as opposed to reprisals. On the lawfulness of unilateral actions not amounting to the use of force, see the work of the International Law Commission on state responsibility; James Crawford, *The International Law Commission's Articles on State Responsibility* (2002).

Leone but remained essentially a student and practitioner of international law. Even when he was the Permanent Representative of Sierra Leone to the UN, he paid particular attention to the work of the Sixth (Legal) Committee and contributed to the work of the UN Charter Committee and to the finalization of Declarations on the non-use of force and the peaceful settlements of disputes.

Later, as member of the International Law Commission for 10 years (1982–1993), Koroma took deep interest in its work. He took a firm stand in favor of the establishment of the International Criminal Court at a time when there were still pending issues and political hurdles. In 1990 intervening in the debate on the jurisdiction of an international criminal court, which at that time was being discussed in response to a request from the General Assembly[5] but as part of the broader item on the draft code of crimes against the peace and security of mankind, he observed thus:

> The International Criminal Court would assist the United Nations in maintaining international peace and security and in encouraging respect for human rights and fundamental freedoms for all, without distinction as to race, colour or creed. It would ensure the implementation of the future code of crimes against the peace and security of mankind and its establishment, together with the adoption of the code, would obviate the criticism of lack of legal force in criminal law which had been levelled in the past against tribunals set up to try crimes on an ex post facto basis. The code would thus strengthen the rule of law in international relations, and the International Criminal Court, if it ever came to be established, would act both as a deterrent and as a safeguard for States whose institutions were currently being threatened.[6]

In this connection he was in favor of allowing "international organizations, non-governmental organizations or even private individuals" to bring cases "where States were not prepared to prosecute their own nationals", noting that some nongovernmental organizations had proved their worth in the field of international humanitarian law and could be regarded as impartial institu-

---

5   See the General Assembly's request, at the behest of Trinidad and Tobago, in resolution 44/39 of 4 December 1989 for a legal opinion on the question of establishing an international criminal court or other international criminal trial mechanism with jurisdiction over illicit trafficking in narcotic drugs and other transnational criminal activities. See A/RES/44/39.,
6   Yearbook of the International Law Commission, vol 1, A/CN.4/Series A/1990, 2157th meeting, 15 May 1990, para. 81, p. 58

tions.[7] He also declared himself against death penalty.[8] Koroma was certainly ahead of the times when he took these positions, but he drew inspiration from the need to establish rule of law at the global level, broaden the participation of inter-governmental and non-governmental entities in the international legal order and was responding to the growing demand to end impunity for perpetrators of egregious breaches of human rights and international crimes.

Another of the important subjects considered by the Commission during Koroma's membership was the non-navigational uses of international watercourses. Noting the applicable principles of the duty to co-operate and prevent serious harm, promote equitable utilization of resources and the duty to exchange information or to consult,[9] Koroma was in favour of the regulation of international watercourses and the need for joint institutional arrangements. In so doing he was again motivated by a desire to promote a more integrated and international management of vital resources that transcend national and political boundaries. But he was not an idealist and was aware of the need to balance any such management against the legitimate demands of States and the sovereignty they enjoy over their natural resources. Accordingly, he recommended that proposals on regulation and joint management of international watercourses "should not be couched in mandatory terms" and "be made more flexible so as to command general acceptance".[10] He pointed out that it was necessary "first, because watercourse States might have different priorities with regard to the regulation of a watercourse, and secondly, because some States still considered that projects being carried out within their boundaries were a matter exclusively for them and not for other States".[11]

In the same vein, Koroma's focus, when it came to the subject of international liability for injurious consequences arising out acts not prohibited by international law, was on protection of the environment. On this topic he submitted that

> the Commission would have to determine the obligations of States with regard to the environment, as damage to the environment and environmental degradation, whose consequences affected the whole world, were the subject of universal disapproval. The Commission must decide whether the standard to be adopted in that connection should be strict

---

7   Ibid., para. 85, p. 58
8   Ibid., para. 89, p. 59.
9   Ibid., 2164th meeting – 29 May 1990, para. 51, p. 115
10 Ibid.
11 Ibid.

liability or liability based on due diligence, as in the 1982 United Nations Convention on the Law of the Sea. He agreed that, in determining the obligations of States regarding the environment, account must be taken of the need to ensure a balance of interests, as, for instance, in the 1988 Convention on the Regulation of Antarctic Mineral Resource Activities (see A/CN.4/428 and Add.l, footnote 37). The Commission must also decide whether, in the matter of liability, the same standards should apply to activities conducted in the territory of States and to activities that caused harm to the global commons or to the environment.[12]

Judge Koroma's concern for the environment and human rights became a leitmotif as he came to deal with cases as judge of the International Court of Justice (ICJ). For reasons of space and brevity, it is apt to focus on his views in the matter of the advisory opinion on the question of the legality of the use and legal effects of the use of nuclear weapons in an armed conflict under international law. While the General Assembly of the UN sought the advisory opinion of the ICJ on the matter of legality of the use of nuclear weapons, the World Health Organization (WHO) sought the advisory opinion on the breach of legal obligations of State under international law and the Constitution of the WHO in terms of its duty to protect health and environment because of the use of the nuclear weapons. The Court declined the WHO's request, concluding that the request did not conform to the 'rule of specialty', as it did not relate to a question "arising within the scope of [the] activities" of the Organization in accordance with Article 96, paragraph 2, of the Charter, a precondition for a Specialized Agency like the WHO to seek an advisory opinion.

In his lengthy dissenting opinion, Koroma vigorously contested this decision and argued that the Court erred in equating the question raised by the WHO with the question submitted by the UN General Assembly.[13] He took the view that the latter request related to the legality of the use of nuclear weapons under international law and the former question raised by the WHO was more on the legal obligations of a State under international law and in particular under international humanitarian law to protect health of peoples and envi-

---

12   Ibid., 2185th meeting, 3 July 1990, para. 64, p 267.
13   He noted that to reach such a conclusion, the Court "interpreted" the question posed as relating not to the obligations which might arise in view of the health and environmental effects of the use of nuclear weapons, but as to the *"legality of the use of such weapons",* a function according to the Court not assigned to the WHO. See *Legality of the Use by State of Nuclear Weapons in Armed Conflict,* ICJ Rep (1996), p. 189.

ronment on which it depends, given the colossal loss of human life and immediate and long-term devastating effects on environment. He observed that

> Civilized and organized community life would come to an end not only in the countries involved in the conflict but even in those not involved; millions would die from the effects of intense and widespread radioactive fallout. Such a catastrophe, it was argued, would be in violation of the health and environmental obligations undertaken by States under international law, particularly international humanitarian law, as well as under the Constitution of the WHO. Whether or not such obligations exist for States and whether they would be violated in the course of war or other armed conflict involving the use of nuclear weapons is, in my view, an eminently suitable matter for the Court to determine in accordance with its Statute.[14]

Further, referring to the report of the WHO presented to the Court on the impact of a devastated environment on health and health services and the socio-economic effects of the use of nuclear weapons, he established that the essential function of the WHO lay in "taking of measures to prevent health problems on a catastrophic scale, such as those which may result from the use of nuclear weapons".[15] He went on to detail the various health and environmental obligations of States.[16] He also examined the *jurisprudence constante* that governed the function of the Court in rendering advisory opinions in general and as applicable in the present case and concluded:

> In my view, since the responsibility of the WHO includes the promotion and protection of international public health, including the taking of preventive measures, a question that seeks the opinion of the Court as to whether in view of their health and environmental effects, a State using nuclear weapons would be in breach of its obligations under international law, including the WHO Constitution, relates to a matter eminently within the competence and scope of activities of the Organization.

> The legal question in the request is directed to the factual effects of the use of nuclear weapons and not to the legality or illegality of such weapons *per* se. ... The request cannot be considered as incompatible with the

---

14   Ibid. p. 173
15   Ibid, p. 180.
16   Ibid, pp. 182–187.

purpose and objective of WHO nor can it be considered as detrimental to the interests of member States in excess of what they had accepted as a basis of their membership.[17]

Despite its own finding that the question raised by the WHO was eminently a legal question that was within its competence to ask, the Court declined to take it on board, according to Koroma, because it chose to refrain from pronouncing upon a controversial matter. He noted, citing the *Namibia* case,[18] that "the Court has never declined a request for the reason that it is controversial or might prove to be an embarrassment",[19] and as such provided no valid ground. Similarly, he rejected the argument that it was prudent on the part of the Court to decline rendering an advisory opinion in this case because matters relating to nuclear weapons were being discussed in other fora.[20] Accordingly, he stated that

> on the basis of the material before the Court, applying the law to that material, I am of the firm conviction that a State would be in breach of its obligations under international law, including the WHO Constitution, were it to use nuclear weapons in war or other armed conflict in view of the health and environmental consequences. To put a question of this kind to the Court is indeed within the competence and scope of the activities of the WHO.[21]

Koroma also dissented from the advisory opinion the Court agreed to render in respect of the question of legality of the use of nuclear weapons requested by the UN General Assembly.[22] The Court first found no specific authorization[23] or prohibition[24] of the threat or use of nuclear weapons as such in either customary or conventional international law. The Court unanimously held

---

17 Ibid, pp. 221–222.
18 See ibid, p. 222, citing the *Legal Consequences for States of the Continued Presence of South Africa in Namibia (South West Africa) notwithstanding Security Council Resolution 276 (1970)*, ICJ Rep (1971), p. 23.
19 Ibid.
20 Ibid, p. 223, using the authority of the Court in the *Fisheries Jurisdiction* cases, ICJ Reports 1974, p. 192.
21 Ibid, pp. 223–224.
22 The vote on this decision was 13 to 1 with Judge Oda dissenting.
23 By unanimous vote.
24 On this decision the vote was 11 to 3, Judges Koroma, Shahbuddeen and Weeramantry dissenting.

that any threat or use of force that is not in conformity with Articles 2(4) and requirements of 51 of the UN Charter was unlawful. In addition, the Court noted that the threat or use of force should also be compatible with the requirements of international law applicable in armed conflicts particularly those of the principles and rules of international humanitarian law, as well as with specific obligations under treaties and other undertakings which expressly deal with nuclear weapons. It follows from this, the Court held, by seven votes for and seven against, and by the casting vote of the President, that the threat or use of nuclear weapons would "generally" be contrary to the rules of international law applicable in armed conflict, and in particular the principles and rules of humanitarian law. However, "in view of the current state of international law, and of the elements of fact at its disposal, the Court cannot conclude definitively whether the threat or use of nuclear weapons would be lawful or unlawful in an extreme circumstance of self-defence, in which the very survival of a State would be at stake" (paragraph 2E, second sentence, of the *dispositif*).

Koroma fundamentally disagreed with this part of the opinion, secured by the President's casting vote. He deplored the failure of the Court to utilize its authority to defend and promote a system of law that exists in the form of the UN Charter prohibiting the use of force and regulating the inherent right of self-defence.[25] Noting that a "finding of *non liquet* is wholly unfounded in the present case",[26] but would

> appear tantamount to judicial legislation which undermines the régime of the non-use of force as enshrined in Article 2, paragraph 4, of the Charter, and that of self defence as embodied in Article 51, but the doctrine of the survival of the State represents a throwback to the law before the adoption of the United Nations Charter and is even redolent of a period long before that. Grotius, writing in the seventeenth century, stated that: "[the right of self-defence ... has its origin directly, and chiefly, in the fact that nature commits to each his own protection" (De Jure Belli Ac Pacis,

---

[25] He noted that "Today a system of war prevention exists in international law, and comprises the prohibition of the use of force, the collective security provisions of the United Nations Charter for the maintenance of international peace, the obligation to resort to peaceful means for the settlement of international disputes and the regulations on weapons prohibition, arms limitation and disarmament. The Court's Advisory Opinion in this case could have strengthened this régime by serving as a shield of humanity". See Legality of the Threat or Use of Nuclear Weapons, Advisory Opinion, ICJ Reports 1996, p. 226, p. 557.

[26] p. 558.

Book II, Chap. 1, Part III, at p. 172 (Carnegie Endowment trans. 1925) (1646)).[27]

He reminded us that "in its historical garb 'of the fundamental right of self-preservation', such a right was used in the past as a pretext for the violation of the sovereignty of other States. Such acts are now considered unlawful under contemporary international law".[28] "The question therefore", he continued, "is not whether a State is entitled to exercise its right of self-defence in an extreme circumstance in which the very survival of that State would be at stake, but rather whether the use of nuclear weapons would be lawful or unlawful under any circumstance including an extreme circumstance in which its very survival was at stake – or, in other words, whether it is possible to conceive of consequences of the use of such weapons which do not entail an infringement of international law applicable in armed conflict, particularly international humanitarian law".[29] The answer to this question was clear for Judge Koroma:

> In my considered opinion, the unlawfulness of the use of nuclear weapons is not predicated on the circumstances in which the use takes place, but rather on the unique and established characteristics of those weapons which under any circumstance would violate international law by their use. It is therefore most inappropriate for the Court's finding to have turned on the question of State survival when what is in issue is the lawfulness of nuclear weapons. Such a misconception of the question deprives the Court's finding of any legal basis.[30]

These dissenting opinions highlight several qualities of Judge Koroma. He departs from his usual reticence, and his usual characteristic of stating his reasons as economically as possible. In this case he not only dissented but did so at length, sometimes betraying emotions for the plight of victims who suffered or might suffer the horrors and untold miseries caused by the use nuclear weapons in an armed conflict. His concern here is not only the well-being of human beings but also of the environment. The advocate in him also led him to write a comprehensive defense in favor of the right of the WHO to seek the advisory opinion it did, drawing studiously from the *jurisprudence constante*. In the process the opinion bears out his intense involvement in the work of the

---

27 p. 560.
28 p. 561.
29 p. 562.
30 p. 571.

UN and his firm commitment as citizen of the international community to promote its objectives and purposes aimed at securing peace and justice associated with sovereign equality and fair and equitable economic development of all "the peoples of the United Nations". Once again, the opinion could not have come out the way it did were he not schooled in world affairs and trained to appreciate the value of international law as an instrument for the promotion of those objectives and purposes. The effect of his tenure as a member of the ILC was equally evident in so far as he alluded to the obligations entailed on account of the duty to prevent and issues of State responsibility to protect environment.

∙ ∙ ∙

His dissent regarding the request of the UN General Assembly on the legality of the threat or use of nuclear weapons, on the other hand, registered his opposition to and disapproval of the unilateral use of force invoking self-defense or self-preservation, and the methods and means employed to sustain colonialism and domination over sections of the world population. His dissent also embraced the function of law in the international community and value of advisory opinions of the Court. Above all, he faulted the majority opinion because it was "all too reluctant to take a position of principle on a question involving what the late Judge Nagendra Singh has described as the most important aspect of international law facing humanity today (*Nuclear Weapons and International Law*, p. 17)". He went on to observe that the Court also failed to recognize the *jus cogens* character of rules of humanitarian law which, in the opinion of the International Law Commission as far back as 1980, had acquired that status.[31] As he put it, the Court missed the opportunity to allow its advisory opinion to serve as a "shield of humanity".[32]

Judge Koroma's dissent brings out vividly the essence of the function of a judge of the ICJ. As the principal judicial organ of the UN, the Court's advisory opinions are to be developed or rendered keeping in mind the objectives and purposes of the UN, the legal framework that is developed over the years through relevant treaties and uniform and consistent State practice, the work of the International Law Commission and full appreciation of the forces at work and dynamics governing the contemporary international society, including the lessons of two world wars and the age of colonialism, and the scourge of apartheid, and denial of human rights and dignity to a great majority of the

---

31 Ibid., p. 574.
32 Ibid., p. 557.

peoples struggling to liberate themselves from the miseries of poverty. In this sense, the way the personality and intellectual orientation of a judge is shaped or takes shape is crucial when it comes to issues of fundamental importance to "the peoples of the United Nations" as opposed to the 'peoples' of a nation. There is a fundamental difference the way the 'United Nations' is structured on the basis of sovereign equality, with no central authority of the kind that exist within a State, to enforce decisions taken in pursuance of the 'rule of law' at the global level, which is yet to be fully formed or framed. Breakdown of order is common at the national level also and there is no doubt that a culture of compliance is the ultimate guarantor of any system of rule of law. But while such breakdowns of law and order within a State are rarely left unattended for too long, the issue at the global level is not one of correcting the breakdown of law and order but building one on a durable and equitable basis. Here, personalities which evolved essentially in the international environment, and which have been exposed consistently to the "power"[33] politics that still permeates the policies that guide the "rule of law" at the universal level, make a difference as Judge Koroma's personality amply demonstrates not only in terms of the dissenting opinions noted above but many other opinions he so eloquently and with great conviction crafted.

For international law to serve truly the needs and values of an international community as diverse and divided as ours presently, its foundations must continue to be broadened to encompass civilizations, the social, economic and cultural ethos and values of peoples of the world going beyond the European and western civilizations. Equally those chosen to represent our different legal systems as judges of the ICJ and other international judicial and legal fora must strive hard to acquire necessary orientation, training, and experience to rise up to the occasion and demands of the office. Judge Koroma's life and times as a representative of Sierra Leone in international fora and as member of the International Law Commission and as a judge for 18 long years and his continued service as a decision-maker and scholar of international law should be inspiration to all of us, particularly those from the Third World.

---

33 'Power' should be understood not merely as a value by itself, in the sense of military power, but as a compendium of different values like wealth and enlightenment.

CHAPTER 2

A Tribute to Abdul Koroma

Tommy Koh

I have been a friend and admirer of Judge Abdul Koroma since the 1970s. We first met during the Third UN Conference on the Law of the Sea (1973 to 1982). He represented Sierra Leone and I represented Singapore. He became Chairman of the African Group at the Conference. In the two final years of the Conference, I served as its President, succeeding Shirley Hamilton Amerasinghe of Sri Lanka, who passed away in 1980. In December 1982, in Montego Bay, in Jamaica, Judge Koroma signed the UN Convention on the Law of the Sea (UNCLOS) on behalf of his country.

Judge Koroma served as the Permanent Representative of Sierra Leone to the United Nations, in New York, from 1981 to 1985. I served as Singapore's Permanent Representative to the UN from 1968 to 1971 and from 1974 to 1984. We were therefore colleagues in New York for three years. Because delegations were seated in an alphabetical order, Sierra Leone and Singapore were neighbours. There were other affinities which drew us together and made us good friends. We were two relatively young Ambassadors, representing two small countries. We were legally educated and shared a common vision of promoting the rule of law in the relations between and among states.

In 1984, I left New York for Washington. In the following year, Judge Koroma also left New York for his postings in Europe. We kept in touch and I followed his career with interest. He had served as Chairman of the Sixth (Legal) Committee of the UN General Assembly. He was a Member of the International Law Commission from 1982 to 1994, serving as its Chairman in 1991.

I knew it was a matter of time before the Government of Sierra Leone would put him up as a candidate for election to the International Court of Justice. In 1993, I was happy to support his candidacy and was delighted when he was successfully elected to the court. Nine years later, I also supported his campaign for re-election. Judge Abdul Koroma was a distinguished member of the International Court of Justice for 18 years, from 1994 to 2012. He gained a good reputation as a learned, conscientious and fair-minded judge.

In 1995, the Singapore Government appointed me as its Agent in a legal dispute between Malaysia and Singapore. Both countries claimed to have sovereignty over three maritime features: Pedra Branca/Pulau Batu Puteh, Middle

Rocks and South Ledge. By a special agreement concluded between the two governments, the dispute was referred to the International Court of Justice.

The oral proceedings began on Tuesday, 6 November 2007. I had unfortunately fallen ill during the previous weekend. When I woke up that morning, my voice had become a hoarse whisper. After taking a double dose of the medication which had been prescribed by a Dutch doctor, I was able to speak in a weak but audible voice. Judge Koroma had noticed that I was ill and had difficulty speaking and kindly sent some throat lozenges for me to my hotel. I was very touched by his kind gesture. It was a token of our friendship. I recovered from my illness. On 20 November 2007, when I had to make the final submission on behalf of Singapore, my voice had completely recovered and I was able to speak clearly.

The judgement of the court was delivered on Friday, 28 May 2008. The Singapore delegation had turned up in full force and listened attentively as the Acting President of the Court read the 2-hour long judgement. The Court had ruled, by a majority of 12 to 4, that Singapore had sovereignty over Pedra Branca/Pulau Batu Puteh. The court ruled, by 15 to 1, to award sovereignty over Middle Rocks to Malaysia. The court also ruled, by 15 to 1, that sovereignty over South Ledge belongs to the state in the territorial waters of which it is located. In all three instances, Judge Koroma voted with the majority.

In 2013, the Singapore Government appointed Professor S Jayakumar and me to co-chair an International Advisory Panel on Transboundary Pollution. The Government asked the Co-chairs to recommend the names of some of the world's most distinguished international lawyers for appointment to the panel. We recommended six such experts, including Judge Koroma. We were delighted when he accepted our request to be a member of the panel. The panel met in Singapore from 21–24 May in Singapore. The panel adopted an unanimous report advising the Singapore on the trends and developments in international law relating to transboundary pollution, the issues arising under international law from the impact of transboundary pollution as well as on the related solutions and practical steps which Singapore can adopt in the light of the foregoing. Judge Koroma made many important contributions to the deliberations of the panel and the writing of its report.

I am very pleased to be able to join many of Judge Koroma's friends, colleagues and admirers in paying a tribute through this collection of essays. I wish him continued good health and peace of mind. May he continue to work for peace, the rule of law and a better world.

CHAPTER 3

Abdul Koroma: Good Neighbour, Friend and Colleague

Kenneth Keith

Ridderlaan 81, The Hague, Sunday 5 February 2006, 8.30 am

It is our second day in our apartment. The doorbell rings. Abdul appears with his large lovely smile, croissants and marmalade, with apologies for not also bringing the newspaper: the English language newspapers had not yet arrived at the Kaashuis Jan de Bruijn, a splendid cheese shop in Hoytemastraat, which Jocelyn and I, following Abdul's precedent, must have visited on 200 or more Sunday mornings since.

Opposite Ridderlaan 81, our car parked on the street, January 2012, freezing cold weather

On the front window of the car, a flattened cardboard box, held in place by the windscreen wipers, the box in recent use to assist the Judge, following his 18 years of excellent service to the cause of international justice at the Peace Palace, to empty his room, but in use now to prevent his neighbour's car window from icing up.

United Nations, New York, 28 October 1997

To my great surprise I was invited to deliver a paper to, and participate in, a seminar held at the UN to mark the 50th anniversary of the adoption of the Statute of the International Law Commission. A major contributor was Abdul Koroma, at the time an ILC member, and among other participants were future colleagues Peter Tomka, then Chair of the Sixth Committee, Hisashi Owada and Bruno Simma, as well as Alain Pellet, Georges Abi-Saab, Maurice Kamto, Brigitte Stern, Frank Berman and James Crawford, all of whom have appeared as counsel in my time on the Court (*Making Better International Law – The International Law Commission at 50* (United Nations, 1998)).

Waitangi, the Bay of Islands, New Zealand, 6 February 1840 and The Hague, 6 February 2006

The first date is the day of the signing of the Treaty of Waitangi by Maori Chiefs in the northern area of New Zealand and by Captain William Hobson as a British Consul which led to the British colonisation of New Zealand, the second the day on which I became a member of the International Court of Justice, joining Abdul and our thirteen colleagues. I take the opportunity of this coincidence of dates to call attention to striking parallels between the wording of the Treaty of Waitangi and that of a Treaty signed 15 years earlier between the King of Sherbro, in Sierra Leone, and the British Governor in that area. In both the local chiefs cede sovereignty to the British Crown, the local people are accorded the rights and privileges of British subjects, and the local peoples are guaranteed the full, free and undisturbed possession of their properties.[1]

And over the years much good friendship, for instance in The Hague and at the two yearly sessions of the Institut de Droit International in Bruges, Cracow, Santiago de Chile, Naples and Rhodes.

---

1 Convention between Great Britain and the Chiefs of the Barra and Sancong families for the cession of Bacca Loco to Great Britain (12 December 1825) 75 Consolidated Treaty Series (*CTS*) 379, and Treaty of Waitangi, between the United Kingdom of Great Britain and Ireland and the Native Chiefs and Tribes of New Zealand (6 February 1840) 89 CTS 473.

PART 2

*Peaceful Dispute Settlement
and the International Court of Justice*

CHAPTER 4

The Peaceful Settlement of International Disputes: The Rainbow Warrior Affair – Experiences of a Small State

Kenneth Keith

I begin with a listing of the various means available to States and other international actors to settle their disputes by peaceful means. Lawyers tend to begin with, and sometimes not to get past, adjudication as the means, but that is far too narrow a focus. Further means of settling disputes appear as long ago as 1899 and 1907 in the Hague Conventions of those years for the Pacific Settlement of International Disputes, the Covenant of the League of Nations (1919), the Constitution of the International Labour Organisation (1919), the General Act for the Pacific Settlement of International Disputes which provides for conciliation, arbitration and judicial settlement (1928) and the Revised Act (1948), the Charter of the United Nations, particularly Article 33, and the Statute of the International Court of Justice (1945), the 1949 Geneva Conventions for the Protection of War Victims and their 1977 Protocols, the various mechanisms in human rights treaties, the International Center for the Settlement of Investment Disputes, the Statutes of the International Criminal Court, and ad hoc tribunals and resolutions adopted by the General Assembly on Friendly Relations and Co-operation among States (1970),[1] the World Summit (2005),[2] Mediation (2011),[3] and the Rule of Law (2012).[4]

The means include negotiation, good offices, mediation, conciliation, arbitration and adjudication. They may be public or private. They may lead to

---

* I was one of the arbitrators in the 1989–1990 arbitration discussed in this paper. Thanks to Amelia Keene for excellent research assistance.
1 UN General Assembly [UNGA], *Declaration on Principles of International Law concerning Friendly Relations and Co-operation among States in accordance with the Charter of the United Nations*, UN Doc A/Res/25/2625, (October 24, 1970).
2 UN General Assembly [UNGA],*2005 World Summit Outcome*, UN Doc A/Res/60/1, (September 10, 2005).
3 UN General Assembly [UNGA], *Strengthening the role of mediation in the peaceful settlement of disputes, conflict prevention and resolution*, UN Doc A/Res/65/283, (July 28, 2011).
4 UN General Assembly [UNGA, *The Rule of Law at the National and International Levels*, UN Doc A/Res/67/93, (December 14, 2012).

recommendations or to binding decisions. If the latter the decisions might be final and binding or subject to interpretation, revision, review or appeal. The decision might be reached according to law or on a broader basis such as equity and good conscience. The relevant institutions might be permanent ones or be established for the particular purpose. The processes might be confined to particular subject matters – law of the sea, trade, investment, human rights, for instance, or be available more generally. That is to say the parties to an international dispute are increasingly likely to have a wide choice of means available to them if they wish to settle their disputes by peaceful means. None of this is to minimize the important role of formal adjudication, especially in establishing an equal playing field on which international law disputes can be resolved, but it is to recognise that international adjudication is not always the best, first, or only option.

I have omitted at least two other ways of approaching international disputes. The first is to put the dispute to one side, as spectacularly demonstrated by the agreement in the Antarctic Treaty 1959 in respect of territorial claims to that vast continent.[5] Another, bilateral, example involving New Zealand relates to the dispute with the United States which arose in 1985 from the ban on the access of nuclear armed and powered ships to New Zealand waters and ports.[6] Or consider the many unresolved territorial and maritime disputes, some going back over centuries.

The second means that is often neglected is the resolution of international disputes through national processes, especially national courts. Consider the great number of disputes about State immunity and jurisdiction involving foreign elements decided by national courts. Many, including one New Zealand case,[7] were cited by the ICJ in the recent case, *Germany v. Italy*.[8] In respect of jurisdiction I mention one New Zealand case which predated the *Lotus*[9] in the Permanent Court of International Justice by 50 years and presented a related

---

5 Our honorand is one of those who played in the legendary cricket match at Scott Base between the MCC (captained by Arthur Watts, legal adviser at the Foreign and Commonwealth Office) and the rest of the world (captained by Christopher Beeby, a redoubtable New Zealand diplomat). As a proud New Zealander it would be wrong of me to mention which side won!
6 For an account, see: Geoffrey Palmer, 'Perspectives on International Dispute Settlement from a Participant', 43 *Victoria University of Wellington Law Review* (*VUWLR*) (2012) 39.
7 *Fang v. Jiang* [2007] *New Zealand Administrative Reports* (*NZAR*) 420 (New Zealand High Court).
8 *Jurisdictional Immunities of the State (Germany v. Italy: Greece Intervening)*, Judgment, International Court of Justice, (3 February 2012), at paras 74–76 and 85–87.
9 *The Case of the S.S. Lotus (France v. Turkey)* (1927) Permanent Court of International Justice (*PCIJ*) Series A No 10 (PCIJ).

issue: *The Case of the Barque Oneco, (R v. Dodd)*.[10] The New Zealand Court of Appeal on the basis of an argument presented by a newly qualified lawyer and the first law teacher in New Zealand, Robert Stout, who was later to be Attorney-General, Premier and Chief Justice, was persuaded that New Zealand courts did not have jurisdiction over an alleged murder committed on the high seas on a foreign ship.[11] Only the flag State did. Stout relied on major texts on international law written by Vattel,[12] Westlake,[13] Phillimore,[14] Wheaton,[15] Story,[16] and Kent,[17] a testament to the splendid law libraries in Dunedin, the Edinburgh of the South, the City of the first university in New Zealand and with what is still claimed to be the southernmost law school in the world.[18] The PCIJ by contrast, referring to court decisions given in Great Britain, Germany, France, Italy and Belgium, but not to *Dodd*, held that the jurisdiction of the flag State was not exclusive – a view of the law which was to be rejected by treaty.[19] In the New Zealand case, the holding by the Court of Appeal meant that there was no potential dispute with the United States, by contrast to the case of the *Lotus* where the Turkish authorities were taking steps to prosecute the French naval officer of the watch, a course which France opposed.

Another quite different set of decisions of national courts on international law matters illustrates yet another area in which international disputes may arise – the classification of imported goods for tariff purposes. In recent years New Zealand courts have decided on the valuation of cars being imported

---

10 The trial is reported as: *The Oneco Affair (R v. Dodd) Tuapeku Times*, Rorahi VII, Putanga 401, 21 Whiringa-a-nuku, 1874, p. 5 (Supreme Court of New Zealand).
11 *R v. Dodd* (1876) 2 *The New Zealand Jurist (NZJ)* 52 (New Zealand Court of Appeal) (8 December 1874).
12 Emer de Vattel, *Law of Nations*, (Ed. Charles G. Fenwick (Translator), London, 1760, Original, 1758).
13 John Westlake, *A Treatise on Private International Law* (W. Maxwell, London, 1858).
14 Sir Robert Phillimore, *Commentaries upon international law* (W.G. Benning, London, 1854–61).
15 Henry Wheaton, *Elements of International Law*, William B. Lawrence (ed) (2nd ed, S. Low, London, 1863).
16 Joseph Story, *Commentaries on the Conflict of Laws, Foreign and Domestic* (Little, Brown, Boston, 1872).
17 James Kent, *Commentaries on American Law* (Little, Brown and Co, Boston, 1858).
18 See, Jeremy Finn, "New Zealand Lawyers and 'Overseas' Precedent 1874–1973 – Lessons from the Otago District Law Society Library" (2007) 11 *Otago Law Review* [OLR] 469.
19 See now United Nations Convention on the Law of the Sea, art. 94(1). See *Sellars v. Maritime Safety Inspector* [1999] 2 NZLR 44 (NZCA).

from Japan,[20] shoes from the Philippines,[21] and agricultural equipment from Canada and the United States.[22] If the decisions went against the importer (and accordingly against the exporter and the country of origin) a dispute with the country of origin could arise and became the subject of the processes under the Dispute Settlement Undertaking of the World Trade Organisation – a possibility that is one reason for the national courts to be alert to the relevant rules of international law, including those relating to the interpretation of treaties, and to relevant rulings of the World Customs Union and of the WTO panels and Appellate Body.

I now focus on the Rainbow Warrior case to consider how, in practice, dispute resolution might take place both inside and outside formal adjudicatory bodies.[23] The case involved a very wide range of procedures, national and international, and it highlights various issues to be addressed by those considering how best to settle a particular international dispute. Following the explosions which sank the Greenpeace vessel, the Rainbow Warrior, which carried the British flag, in Auckland Harbour, and killed a Greenpeace photographer Fernando Pereira, a Dutch national, two of the French agents, Major Alain Mafart and Captain Dominique Prieur, who had been involved in the lead up to the explosion were arrested on passport offences. (They were travelling on false Swiss passports.) At that early stage, the French undertook an internal inquiry, which led it to the conclusion that there was no French involvement in the explosion. The two agents were soon charged in New Zealand with the murder of the Dutch photographer, and wilful damage to a ship by means of an explosion. The murder charges were reduced to manslaughter, the two agents pleaded guilty and the Chief Justice of New Zealand sentenced them to ten years imprisonment.[24] By that time, the Prime Minister of France had acknowledged that France was responsible for the action and the Foreign Minister pointed out that France was willing to make reparation for the consequences of its action. Attempts to resolve the dispute by negotiation began in September 1985. Those attempts did not lead to a settlement. On the initiative of the

---

20   *Integrity Cars (Wholesale) Ltd v. Chief Executive of New Zealand Customs Service (Autos case)* (2001) NZCA 86.

21   *Elitunnel Merchanting Ltd v. Regional Collector of Customs* CA305/98, 12 April 2000 (NZCA).

22   *Chief Executive of the New Zealand Customs Service v. Rakaia Engineering & Contracting Ltd* [2002] 3 NZLR 24 (NZCA).

23   For a background to the Rainbow Warrior affair, see Christina Hoss and Jason Morgan-Foster, 'The Rainbow Warrior', *Max Plank Encyclopedia of Public International Law* (*MPEPIL*) 198 (2010).

24   Chief Justice Sir Ronald Davison, "Sentencing for manslaughter – pleas of guilty – mitigation of sentence for terrorist activities" (1986) 74 International Law Reports (*ILR*) 241.

good offices of the Netherlands Prime Minister, the Dutch occupying the Chair of the European Union at the time and having the specific interest arising from the death of one of its nationals, the New Zealand and French Governments agreed on 19 June 1986 to refer all the problems arising from the affair for a binding ruling by the UN Secretary-General. The ruling was to be "principled and equitable".

The two states filed memoranda with the Secretary-General who made diplomatic contact with the two Governments to ensure he had a full understanding of their positions. France contended that it followed from its acknowledgement that it was responsible, from its willingness to apologize and to pay compensation to New Zealand for the damage caused and from the fact that the agents acted under military orders, that they should be released. For New Zealand that was not possible. The sinking of the Rainbow Warrior was both a serious breach of international law and the commission of a serious crime in New Zealand. The release of the agents to freedom would undermine the integrity of the New Zealand judicial system. The Secretary-General noted that New Zealand had indicated in bilateral negotiations with France that it was ready to explore possibilities for the prisoners serving their sentences outside New Zealand. And just 17 days after receiving the task, the Secretary-General gave his Ruling,[25] the substance of which was, within three days, incorporated into three agreements signed by the two States.

In terms of the first agreement the two military officers were to be transferred to the French military facility on the island of Hao in French Polynesia for a period of not less than three years. They were prohibited from leaving the island for any reason, except with the mutual consent of the two governments. Provision was also made for reporting by the French authorities to New Zealand on the condition of the agents on the island and for visits by an agreed observer. In making that Ruling the Secretary-General rejected the French contention that because it was willing to assume *all* responsibility in place of the persons who had acted on its behalf they should be released. In other words individual responsibility and state responsibility could and did exist in parallel. One did not exclude the other. The ICJ applied the same proposition in

---

[25] *Case concerning the differences between New Zealand and France arising from the Rainbow Warrior affair* (*New Zealand v. France*) Ruling of 6 July 1986 by the Secretary-General of the United Nations, Vol. XIX, Reports of International Arbitral Awards (*RIAA*) Vol. XIX, p. 199 (1986); also reported as: *Rainbow Warrior Case* (*New Zealand v. France*) (1987) 26 International Law Materials (*ILM*) 1346, (1987) 74 ILR 546 [*Rainbow Warrior I*].

Bosnia v. Serbia in 2007 in rejecting the Serbian contention that individual criminal responsibility for genocide excluded state responsibility.[26]

The proposed removal of the two agents from New Zealand led to further proceedings in a New Zealand court, with the filing of a private prosecution against them. That was however brought to an end by the Solicitor-General filing a stay of proceedings, which was in turn the subject of an unsuccessful application for judicial review.[27]

The Ruling and the Agreements also dealt with:

- the formal and unqualified apology to be made by the French Prime Minister,
- monetary compensation to be paid to New Zealand,
- trade matters, and
- an arbitral process for the resolution of any disputes about the interpretation or application of the agreements, the process which was invoked by New Zealand after the two agents left the island within the three year period fixed by the agreement and the subject of the second ruling which I discuss.

I recall two other aspects of the ruling of the Secretary-General. New Zealand in its submission to him said that, in its negotiations with France, it had indicated that a settlement would be possible only if adequate compensation, in respect of the damage to Greenpeace and the family of the dead man, had been paid or there were reasonable and binding arrangements in place that assured that this would be done. Because the vessel was British and the dead man was Dutch, New Zealand accepted that it was unable to assert formal standing to claim on behalf of either. By the time of the ruling, the payment had been made to the family and a binding procedure for private arbitration, to fix the sum payable to Greenpeace, was under way.

Within 16 months, in one case, and 18 months, in the other, the two agents left the island for Paris and never returned. In 1989 New Zealand initiated the arbitration process provided for in one of the 1986 Agreements. Following two rounds of written pleadings and two rounds of hearings, the Tribunal handed down its award.[28] It was required to reach its award on the basis of the 1986

---

26   *Application of the Convention on the Prevention and Punishment of the Crime of Genocide (Bosnia and Herzegovina v. Serbia and Montenegro)* Judgment, ICJ Reports 2007, p. 43.
27   *Amery v. Solicitor-General* [1987] 2 New Zealand Law Reports (NZLR) 292 (NZCA).
28   *Case concerning the difference between New Zealand and France concerning the interpretation or application of two agreements, concluded on 9 July 1986 between the two States and*

Agreements, the Agreement establishing it and applicable rules and principles of international law, a contrast to "equitable and principled basis" for the Secretary-General's ruling. It held that France had acted (1) lawfully in removing Major Mafart (by majority), (2) unlawfully in removing Captain Prieur, and (3) unlawfully in not returning them, and that the three year period had continued to run while the agents were in Paris (again by majority) with the consequence that there was no question of their being returned to the island. Further, the condemnation of the French Republic ((2) and (3) above) for its breaches of its obligations, made public by the decision of the Tribunal, constituted appropriate satisfaction for the legal and moral damage to New Zealand, which had not sought a monetary remedy. The Tribunal did, however, recommend that the two governments set up a fund to promote close and friendly relations between the citizens of the two countries and that France make the first contribution of US$2 million. That recommendation was accepted by both governments and a year later was put in treaty form by the two Prime Ministers at an official lunch in Wellington with the New Zealand Prime Minister declaring that this unhappy affair was now at an end.[29] Well, not quite, since in 1991, the following year, another of the French agents who was still the subject of an Interpol arrest warrant issued by New Zealand entered Switzerland without appropriate papers. Did New Zealand wish to have him extradited, the Swiss authorities inquired? (The two agents arrested in New Zealand in 1985, it will be recalled, were using false Swiss passports.) No, said the responsible New Zealand Minister, referring to his Prime Minister's statement about the end of "the unhappy affair" and recalling the ICJ's ruling about the binding force of certain unilateral acts, made in the Nuclear Tests cases in 1974.[30] In addition, all the outstanding arrest warrants were withdrawn.

I have set out the foregoing account of steps taken in this case for number of reasons. One is that the account mentions about ten international processes and a similar number of national processes. How are choices to be made between the different means? I take two instances: the agreement to have the UN Secretary-General make a binding ruling in a process called mediation (which is generally thought not to lead to a binding outcome). The ruling was to be principled and equitable. It followed a very summary process, which was completed in a little over two weeks. The ruling was barely reasoned. The

---

which related to the problems arising from the Rainbow Warrior Affair (New Zealand v. France) Vol. XX, RIAA, p. 215 (1990), 82 ILR 500 (1990) [Rainbow Warrior II].

29 Prime Minister James Bolger, Ministerial Statement on the signing of the Agreement with France (April 1991).
30 Doug Graham, Minister of Justice, 18 December 1991.

indications are that the two governments were very close to agreement on all aspects of the dispute when they submitted the matter to the Secretary-General. One may speculate that they required a neutral, authoritative third party to make the ruling, one which each government would have had difficulty selling to their public were they to agree to it without more.

By contrast, to move to a second choice, the arbitration process initiated by New Zealand, after the removal of the two agents from the island, was facilitated by the existence of substantive obligations relating to the agents set out in the 1986 Agreement and of the related agreement for arbitration. Although the latter provided for arbitration at the option of one party, much remained to be agreed, namely:

1. the composition of the Tribunal (especially the appointment of its President);
2. the place of hearing;
3. the choice of registrar and registry;
4. the law or standard to be applied, in this case, as noted above, the 1986 Agreements, the 1989 Agreement establishing the Tribunal and the applicable rules and principles of international law;
5. the need for reasons;
6. the procedural steps – numbers of pleadings, time limits; and
7. costs and expenses.

The ICJ Statute, Rules and practice provide ready made answers to these questions – and present no issue of the costs of the tribunal since they are borne by the budget of the Court, as part of the general UN budget. But States may nevertheless decide that ad hoc arbitration has advantages in a particular context, for instance in respect of the composition of the Tribunal.[31]

A second issue, or really the first, arising from the processes summarised above arises from the word "the dispute", which is to be "settled". Much writing about the peaceful settlement of disputes turns too quickly to the means – the matters just discussed – and assumes that no real issues arise about the definition of "the dispute" or about "settlement", both sounding like tidy legal terms.

Also, too often, judicial settlement is put at the centre, ignoring the wise reflections of a great American scholar, Lon Fuller, who said this in 1960:[32]

---

[31] Arthur Watts, "Preparation for international litigation", in Tafsir Malick Ndiaye and Rüdiger Wolfrum (eds.) *Law of the Sea, Environmental Law and Settlement of Disputes: Liber Amicorum Judge Thomas A. Mensah*, (Martinus Nijhoff Publishers, 2007).

[32] Lon Fuller, "Adjudication and the Rule of Law" (1960) 54 Proceedings of the American Society of International Law 1, 1.

We cannot solve all our problems and disputes by referring them to judges or arbitrators. Anyone who discharges a judicial function works within a particular institutional framework. That framework is like a specialised tool; the very qualities which make it apt for one purpose make it useless for another. A sledge-hammer is a fine thing for driving stakes. It is cumbersome device for cracking nuts, though it can be used for that purpose at a pinch. It is hopeless as a substitute for a can-opener. So it is with adjudication. Some social tasks confront it with an opportunity to display its fullest powers. For others it can be at best a *pis aller*. For still others it is completely useless.

As already indicated, New Zealand, while recognizing that it could not formally exercise its power of diplomatic protection in respect of the death of a Dutch citizen and the sinking of a British flagged vessel, nevertheless included those matters within the scope of the overall dispute as it saw it by insisting that a settlement would be possible only if those matters were resolved, as they had been by the time of the Secretary-General's ruling.

New Zealand also claimed in its memorandum to the Secretary-General that the French government by its own action and statements had introduced trade matters into the dispute which New Zealand had taken to the Organisation for Economic Cooperation and Development and to the General Agreement on Tariffs and Trade (to add to the list of international methods noted earlier). According to it, a French Minister had said that a total ban of New Zealand butter imports was in contemplation by France. But said France, the checks on certain New Zealand exports had no connection with the dispute submitted to the Secretary-General. Further, they had been terminated, and France did not intend to oppose the continuation of butter imports or to take any steps in breach of an agreement between New Zealand and the EEC. On that matter, the Secretary-General gave a ruling in terms of "undertakings ... as sought by ... New Zealand".

The foregoing discussion of "the dispute" is limited to the sinking of the Rainbow Warrior and the related matters arising between the two governments. One wider context was of course the continuation of French nuclear testing in the South Pacific, which had been the subject of New Zealand diplomatic, judicial, and other action from 1963. France in its memorandum to the Secretary-General in fact stated that "the attack against the Rainbow Warrior" could not be understood without recalling the interventions of certain New Zealand authorities in French internal affairs, especially with respect to nuclear tests conducted on Mururoa. These interventions all the more aroused French public opinion as they proceeded from a country, which as the New Zealand Memorandum properly stresses, "was traditionally a close friend and ally." In the 1970s France had emphasised the development of its *force de frappe* as essential to protect its national security.

The New Zealand concern is, and has been for some time, wider than testing in the South Pacific. It is the opposition to the development of nuclear weapons, their testing, their proliferation, their installation and their use. In the words of a major New Zealand historian of foreign affairs "New Zealand's antipathy to all things nuclear has become deeply embedded in their collective psyche".[33] That much wider set of issues shows the inadequacy of the words "dispute" and "settlement" or, more accurately, their inapplicability in such matters. The Charter of the UN makes the point by using the words "questions",[34] "matters",[35] "the principles governing disarmament and the regulation of armaments",[36] and "situations",[37] as well as "disputes".[38]

My final comment about the processes for the settlement of the dispute concerns "the parties". Consider, first, the position of the two agents who were convicted and sentenced, the third who was detained in Switzerland, and the others who were the subject of the Interpol arrest warrants. In not taking action in respect of the agent detained in Switzerland, and in withdrawing the outstanding warrants, New Zealand appears to have accepted that the 1990 award and the 1991 agreement had indeed brought the "unhappy affair" to an end and that no individual responsibility had remained. But what if the two agents had, while on Hao, resigned their commissions and claimed freedom of movement under the European Convention of Human Rights? Or consider, next, the rights and interests of the Pereira family and of Greenpeace. In the former case at least, there was no continuing issue between them and France once their claims had been dealt with by the payment of compensation.

By contrast consider the ongoing relations between New Zealand and France, a matter that was the subject of the recommendation, which the Tribunal made and the agreement implementing that recommendation. That recommendation recognized that the relationship between the two countries would continue into the future. The relevant part of the award began with this passage:[39]

---

33   Malcolm Templeton, *Standing Upright Here: New Zealand in the Nuclear Age 1945–1990* (Wellington: Victoria University Press [VUP], 2007), 511.
34   Art. 10, UN Charter.
35   Ibid, art. 22.
36   Ibid, art. 12.
37   Ibid, art. 14.
38   Ibid, art. 34 – 36.
39   *Rainbow Warrior II*, at [124].

> New Zealand and France have had close and continuing relations since the early days of European exploration of the South Pacific. The relationship has grown more intense and friendly since the beginning of constitutional government in New Zealand exactly 150 years ago. It includes the friendship of many of the citizens of the two countries forged in peace and war, particularly in the two world wars; and, notwithstanding difficulties of great distance, it extends to the full range of cultural, social, economic and political matters.

The Tribunal recalled that:[40]

> In the hearing before the Tribunal, the Agents of the two Governments emphasized the warming of the relationship, referring for instance to a relevant statement made by Mr. Rocard, the French Prime Minister, during his visit in August 1989 to the South Pacific. Moreover, Mr. Lange, now Attorney-General of New Zealand and from July 1984 to August 1989 Prime Minister, spoke before the Tribunal of the dynamic of reconciliation now operating between the two countries.

It concluded that:[41]

> The recommendation, addressed to the two Governments, is intended to assist them in putting an end to the present unhappy affair.

Such a recommendation – which has led to many young citizens of the two countries visiting the other – can perhaps be made more easily by such a three member tribunal than a larger permanent Court over the composition of which the Parties have no or only limited influence.

The process of adjudication, in addition to settling the dispute in question, may, of course, also contribute to the clarification and development of the law. That aspect of the judicial process may assist the settlement of disputes in the future, by removing uncertainties and facilitating settlement by negotiation. I mention features of the Award, which may be seen as making that contribution.

In argument before the Tribunal, New Zealand emphasised the 1986 Agreements, the relevant treaty obligations. The agents were not to leave the island without the mutual consent of the two governments. France, by contrast, contended that the treaty obligations had to be read along with, indeed subject to,

---

40   Ibid, at [125].
41   Ibid, at [126].

the customary international law of State responsibility and in particular the rules which may exclude wrongfulness and the rules about remedies. The Tribunal ruled as follows on that matter:[42]

> The legal consequences of a breach of a treaty, including the determination of the circumstances that may exclude wrongfulness (and render the breach only apparent) and the appropriate remedies for breach, are subjects that belong to the customary Law of State Responsibility.
>
> [Further,] without prejudice to the terms of the agreement which the Parties signed and the applicability of certain important provisions of the Vienna Convention on the Law of Treaties, the existence in this case of circumstances excluding wrongfulness as well as the questions of appropriate remedies, should be answered in the context and in the light of the customary Law of State Responsibility.

Where were those rules about the exclusion of wrongfulness and remedies to be found? The Tribunal, guided by the written and oral arguments presented to it, consulted the draft articles on State Responsibility being prepared at that stage by the International Law Commission. Although that was more than 10 years before the text was completed by the Commission, the text was already seen as having real authority.

France contended that the removal of the two agents from the island was justified on any one of three grounds, grounds then being elaborated by the ILC.[43] They were *force majeure*, a state of necessity and distress. The Tribunal rejected the argument of *force majeure*: "the test of its applicability is of absolute and material impossibility; a circumstance rendering performance more difficult or burdensome does not constitute a case of *force majeure*."[44] It emphasised the controversial character of the proposal on the State of necessity. It was more positive about the excuse of distress. It set out the requirements in the following way:[45]

> The question … is to determine whether the circumstances of distress in a case of extreme urgency involving elementary humanitarian considerations affecting the acting organs of the State may exclude wrongfulness in this case.

---

42   Ibid, at [75].
43   International Law Commission (*ILC*), Draft Articles on State Responsibility (First Reading, provisionally adopted, 32nd session of the ILC, Yearbook of the International Law Commission, 1980, vol. II(1)), "Circumstances Precluding Wrongfulness", arts 19–35.
44   *Rainbow Warrior II*, at [77].
45   Ibid, at [78]–[79].

In accordance with the previous legal considerations, three conditions would be required to justify the conduct followed by France in respect of Major Mafart and Captain Prieur:

(1) The existence of very exceptional circumstances of extreme urgency involving medical or other considerations of an elementary nature provided always that a prompt recognition of the existence of those exceptional circumstances is subsequently obtained from the other interested party or is clearly demonstrated.
(2) The reestablishment of the original situation of compliance with the assignment in Hao as soon as the reasons of emergency invoked to justify the repatriation had disappeared.
(3) The existence of a good faith effort to try to obtain the consent of New Zealand in terms of the 1986 Agreement.

In my separate opinion, I said this:[46]

I would agree with counsel for France on the lawfulness of the urgent removal of an agent to Papeete for necessary life-saving surgery there following a shark attack at Hao and allowing no time to get New Zealand's prior consent. All legal systems recognize such exceptions to the strict letter for the law.

This aspect for the case gives us a good reminder of seeing particular legal rules in their broader context. The conditions, which the Tribunal sets out, required as well that very close attention be given to the particular circumstances of the two agents. The Tribunal divided in its assessment of those circumstances in one of the two cases.

The ICJ had also made use of some of those early draft provisions on State responsibility and when the ILC came to complete the text of the articles in its second reading it was able to draw on those decisions. This is an instance of the ongoing international legal process, which continues to this day with courts and tribunals, as well as the executive branches of government in their practice, making use of the texts and their commentaries. The process is one which may involve the same individuals wearing different hats at different times – as scholars, law reformers, advocates, arbitrators or judges. The Tribunal also drew on provisions of the draft articles relating to the duration of obligations and remedies, a usage, which in turn helped inform the Commission in completing its work.

• • •

---

46   Ibid, Separate opinion of Sir Kenneth Keith, at [4].

I conclude with five possible lessons from this affair, in part by way of repetition. Much more could be and has been said about it.

The first is to recall again that States have many means of resolving and handling disputes available to them. It is a mistake to think only of courts.[47]

A second lesson is that the varying elements of an affair might be assembled in various ways, reflecting the different interests and the different parties involved – here consider the family of the photographer, the French agents (not just the two who were arrested), Greenpeace, New Zealand exporters and European and other importers and the two States – and the different character of the relationships between them, some fleeting, some very long lasting. Those variations bring to mind the last words of Gertrude Stein, the American writer and supporter of the arts. She asked "what is the answer?" She apparently received none. She then asked "what is the question?" And then she died.[48]

Third, it is important to see the particular legal issue in context. As John Donne said, "no man is an island entire of itself".[49]

Fourth, Leo Cullum, the great New Yorker cartoonist, reminds us of the central importance of facts in litigation. One of his cartoons has a lawyer urging the Judge, no doubt without success, with these words: "Can we, just for a moment, Your Honor, ignore the facts?"

Finally, the case alerts us to some of the different and interacting ways by which international law gets clarified and developed. We should not have our vision unnecessarily channelled by formal lists such as those sometimes constructed out of Article 38 of the Statute of the ICJ. Significant in this context are the not infrequent references to principles, often undefined, in the reasons of judges and arbitrators – considerations of an elementary nature, exceptional circumstances, humanity, dignity, fairness, reasonableness, good faith and the like. Recall from 190 years ago Shelley's declaration that poets are "the unacknowledged legislators of the world".[50]

---

47 Consider the role, as at the moment (October 2013), of our honorand as Chair of an African Union body established to give an advisory opinion relating to the border between Sudan and South Sudan, following the earlier peace agreement and arbitration; in respect of the Malawi v. Tanzania dispute; as a judge of the World Bank Administrative Tribunal; and as a member of the International Labour Organisation Committee of Experts on the Application of Conventions and Recommendations.

48 For an excellent account of the life of Gertrude Stein, see Janet Malcolm, *Two Lives: Gertrude and Alice* (Yale University Press, New Haven, 2007).

49 John Donne, 'Meditation XVII', *Devotions upon Emergent Occasions* (1624, London).

50 Percy Bysshe Shelley, 'A Defence of Poetry', (1821), in Mary Shelley (ed.), *Essays, Letters from Abroad, Translations and Fragments* (Edward Moxon, London, 1840).

CHAPTER 5

The International Court of Justice and the Latin American Experience

Bernado Sepúlveda-Amor

It is a pleasure to participate in a collection of essays devoted to recognize and honour the achievements of Abdul Koroma, my distinguished colleague for six years in the International Court of Justice. Judge Koroma's contributions to the development of international law are embedded in each of the Judgments, Advisory Opinions and Orders delivered by the Court in the long period – eighteen years – in which Judge Koroma performed his judicial functions. Additionally, his declarations, separate or dissenting opinions, provide a source of inspiration for those wishing to learn the nuances in the decisions of the World Court.

I   Judicial Decisions, Peace and Security

In recognition of Judge Koroma's interest in the role of regionalism in international law, I have decided in this essay to examine the role of judicial settlement in the maintenance of international peace and security through the lens of the Latin American experience before the International Court of Justice (ICJ).

To associate the work of the ICJ with the maintenance of international peace and security might not strike as self-evident. Although the development of international law by the Court is no small matter – and, indeed, is closely related to the maintenance of peaceful relations in a broad sense – it seems accurate to say that it has been a side-benefit of, rather than a rationale for, the Court's establishment.

Paraphrasing the great Hersch Lauterpacht, I would say the Court's primary function is to contribute to the maintenance of international peace in so far as this aim can be achieved through law.

---

* Dr. Cristina Villarino-Villa's contribution to the preparation of this article is much appreciated.

The consensual nature of the Court's contentious jurisdiction places a structural limit on the Court's ability to engage in the settlement of international disputes. Although, under the United Nations Charter States are obliged to settle their disputes peacefully, there is no obligation to do so through judicial means.

A glance at the Court's docket, however, shows that the Court's inherent jurisdictional limits have been no obstacle to the Court becoming an active participant, as well as a useful instrument, in the settlement of acute international conflicts, becoming a legitimate force and a relevant voice in matters of general interest to the international community as a whole.

For instance, the Court's Advisory Opinions in the *South West Africa* cases and the *Western Sahara* played a pivotal role in the articulation of the right of the self-determination of peoples and supported the work of the General Assembly on this matter.

More recent examples of decisions touching upon crucial questions of international policy (and politics) include the Court's Advisory Opinions on the *Legality of the Use or Threat of Use of Nuclear Weapons, the Legal Consequences of a Wall in the Occupied Palestinian Territory* or the *Accordance with International Law of the unilateral declaration of independence in respect of Kosovo*.

With regard to inter-state disputes, the Court's decisions in *Nicaragua*, the *Genocide* case, or in *Democratic Republic of Congo* v. *Uganda* are good examples of the Court's engagement with major conflicts, thus directly touching upon the maintenance of international peace and security.

Depending on the subject-matter of the dispute and the scope of States' consent to the Court's contentious jurisdiction, judicial settlement may be just one aspect of the solution to a particular conflict. It is well-known that reaching a peaceful solution often requires employing political and judicial means. For instance, the Court's decisions in *El Salvador* v. *Honduras* and *Nigeria* v. *Cameroon* – both involving extremely delicate territorial questions and a highly volatile security environment – were preceded and succeeded by intense multilateral negotiations, within the OAS and the UN, respectively.

I may add that, whereas the Court has often worked in tandem with the UN political organs, namely the General Assembly and the Security Council, it has not hesitated to vindicate its own independent role in the maintenance of international peace and security. One such example is the Court's decision in *Nicaragua*, where it declared the United States – a permanent member of the Security Council – responsible for violations of the prohibition on the use of force in international relations.

Inseparable from the Court's role in the maintenance of international peace and security through the resolution of specific, individual disputes, is its contribution to the development and clarification of international law, a function I evoked earlier in this note.

Let me emphasize the importance of this role: specific judgments of the Court, although issued in relation to specific disputes, have provided stepping stones in the identification and formulation of principles of general application. This has been a slow but steady process that has afforded the Court the opportunity of knitting an increasingly dense web of legal principles with regard to the most important areas of international relations.

Latin American countries have become relevant actors in this enterprise by entrusting to the Court the settlement of complex regional disputes, particularly in the last decade. The successes, failures and idiosyncrasies surrounding the Latin American practice speak volumes about the role, potential and limits of the Court and, more generally, of judicial settlement in the maintenance of peaceful relations between States. What follows is an impressionistic overview of the most salient elements of that practice.

II   The Trilogy Haya de la Torre

It is useful to begin with a brief reference to the trilogy Haya de la Torre. I speak of a "trilogy", because it took no less than two judgments on the merits and a frustrated request for interpretation to settle the controversy that so sharply opposed Colombia and Peru on the rules governing diplomatic asylum under the Havana Convention of 1928.

This episode lies too far in the past to fully appreciate the extent to which Colombia's decision to accord diplomatic asylum to the Peruvian opposition leader Raúl Haya de la Torre in its Embassy in Lima strained its bilateral relations with Peru back in 1949.

Ultimately, the Court ruled that Colombia had acted in contravention of the Havana Convention of 1928 by affording diplomatic asylum in circumstances not justified by reason of "urgency". At the same time, however, the Court found that Colombia was not obliged to deliver Haya de la Torre to the Peruvian authorities, ruling that the 1928 Convention allowed such decisions to be based upon a political assessment on the part of the State wishing to grant the requested asylum. In short, on the basis of the applicable law, it was for the parties to find a negotiated solution to the granting (or not) of the asylum.

The parties only managed to settle their differences by an agreement concluded on 22 March 1954, that is, after Haya de la Torre had spent more than five years confined in the Colombian Embassy in Lima. Under the terms of that agreement, Haya de la Torre was delivered to Peru from where he was expelled to Mexico on 6 April 1954.

It is interesting to note that the Court's decisions in *Haya de la Torre* ultimately led to the adoption of a new regional Convention on Diplomatic Asylum in Caracas in 1954. The Court's interpretation of the Havana Convention of 1928 was instrumental in identifying gaps and ambiguities in the conventional regime on diplomatic asylum then in force amongst a number of Latin American States, and the need to bring it into line with contemporary norms. The new regulation expressly recognized *inter alia* a right of unilateral qualification on the part of the State according asylum and the corresponding obligation on the territorial State to accord safe-conduct to the refugee at the request of the State of asylum, both of which were rejected by the Court on the basis of the Havana Convention of 1928.

III   Nicaragua

In terms of complexity, scope and symbolic value, the Court's Judgment in *Nicaragua* remains to date the single most important decision involving a Latin American country. It was also a milestone in the history of the Court's jurisprudence at large.

In few contentious cases before the Court have the political and legal stakes been as high as in *Nicaragua*, set against the backdrop of one of the most turbulent chapters in the recent history of Latin America, namely the rise of revolutionary and counter-revolutionary armed movements in Central America in the late 70's and the 80's, and the concurrent intervention of the United States in the region, both direct and covert.

The dispute has several defining features. First of all, the asymmetry of its protagonists: a small developing country, on the one hand, and the world's superpower, on the other. Second, the political and legal scope of the matters submitted for the Court's consideration, which included the scrutiny of controversial aspects of the United States' foreign policy in Latin America. Finally, the specific circumstances that preceded the Court's seisin, namely Nicaragua's failed attempts to involve the Security Council as a result of the United States' exercise of its veto.

An entire treatise is required just to examine the Court's Judgment on preliminary objections. For the purposes of this note, it will suffice to evoke the extraordinary opportunity that *Nicaragua* afforded to the Court to develop and clarify, in the merits phase of the case, the rules of international law on a number of sensitive areas, including the law on the use of force and self-defence;

the relationship between the Security Council and the Court under the United Nations Charter; the content and scope of the principle of non-intervention; the separate existence of conventional and customary law as sources of international law; or the rules governing the attribution of internationally wrongful acts to States at a time when the International Law Commission was light-years away from finalizing its project on the responsibility of States for wrongful acts under international law.

From the standpoint of the role, potential and limits of the ICJ as an international judicial organ, the extra-legal factors that surrounded this case are as instructive as the Court's own substantive findings on the applicable law.

I refer, in particular, to the United States' decision to withdraw its unilateral declaration recognizing the Court's compulsory jurisdiction in reaction to Nicaragua's Application as well as the United States' refusal to participate in the proceedings on the merits.

More importantly, the Judgment that came out of the *Nicaragua* case was to gain notoriety for being one of few (and most unfortunate) instances of non-compliance by a State with a judgment of the Court, in light of the issues involved in the case: the mining of the Nicaraguan ports, the covert operations against Nicaragua, the organization, financing, training and arming of the Contras aiming to overthrow the Nicaraguan government, the breach of the rule of non-intervention, as well as other violations of international law. Claiming that the Court had acted *ultra vires* and erred in its appraisal of both the facts and applicable law, the United States refused to pay compensation for the damages caused to Nicaragua as a result of the violations of international law of which it was found responsible. Nicaragua's recourse to the Security Council under Article 94(2) of the UN Charter was to no avail, for the United States' veto excluded any prospect of executive action in support of the enforcement of the Judgment.

Ultimately, it was neither the Council nor the Court, but a change in the political wind that prompted a change in US policy towards Nicaragua, most notably the outbreak of the Iran-contra scandal and the defeat of the Sandinistas in the presidential elections of 1990. After the United States Government announced an aid package of 500 million dollars and assistance to Nicaragua through international financial institutions, in 1991 Nicaragua notified the Court of its intention to discontinue the proceedings on damages.

Notwithstanding the difficulties raised by the United States' attitude, the Nicaragua Judgment remains by and large a success story in the jurisprudence of the Court. Paramount in this assessment is the Court's vindication of the role of judicial settlement in the maintenance of peace and security, including in a context of on-going armed conflict.

It is no exaggeration to say that *Nicaragua* marked a before and after in the Court's own history, particularly in the public's perception of this organ which, as a result of this landmark decision, gained wide recognition as an impartial forum capable of successfully solving the most complex and politically sensitive disputes.

One important consequence in the settlement of disputes and the *Nicaragua* Judgment is that it re-established the Court's legitimacy as the principal judicial organ of the UN, after a period of questioning that followed the Court's decision in the *South West Africa* case. From 1986 onwards, the flow of cases submitted to the Court from the developing world, became a constant and welcome feature. This can only be interpreted as a show of trust.

IV   Avena

Although perhaps lacking the evocative force of the *Nicaragua* Judgment, subsequent disputes involving Latin American countries have invariably touched upon important national interests of the States concerned.

Life and death issues were at stake in *Avena*, involving the diplomatic protection of 51 Mexican citizens sentenced to death as a result of the commission of serious felonies on United States' soil. Like the cases *Breard* and *LaGrand* before it, *Avena* brought to the forefront the crucial importance of the obligations in Article 36 of the Vienna Convention on Consular Relations to protect the rights of arrested individuals in a foreign country.

Prior to this case, in *LaGrand*, the Court had already defined the nature and scope of the rights under the Vienna Convention, including the notion that Article 36(1) recognized true individual rights in the field of consular protection.

With regard to the right to be informed "without delay" of the rights of notification and access to consular authorities under Article 36(1)(b) of the Convention, in *Avena* the Court specified that the corresponding obligation on the arresting authorities to provide that information arose as "soon as it is realized that the person is a foreign national, or once there are grounds to think that the person is probably a foreign national".

As in *LaGrand*, the Court confirmed in *Avena* the conformity with international law of the procedural default rule; the US federal rule that prescribes that, before a state criminal defendant can obtain relief in federal court, the claim must be presented in the first instance to a State court.

This rule proved an insurmountable obstacle to federal appeal in those cases where violation of consular rights was not alleged at state level due to ignorance of the existence of these rights by the affected individual.

In substantive terms, one of the most important contributions of this decision relates to the Court's unravelling of the content of the obligation to provide review and reconsideration of the sentences entered in violation of the Vienna Convention. Whereas in principle the United States had the choice of means as to how this should be achieved, the Court specified that review and reconsideration should be effective as well as take into account the violation of the right violated. Both the violation and any potential resulting prejudice had to be fully examined and considered in relation to both the sentence and the conviction.

The Court further noted that the review and reconsideration process should occur as part of the judicial proceedings within the overall judicial proceedings relating to the individual defendant concerned. On the facts, it concluded that, as practiced within the United States' criminal justice system, the clemency process did not meet the requirements set forth by the Court and thus was not an appropriate means of review and reconsideration.

The Court's Judgment in *Avena* prompted immediate action on the part of the United States' administration, leading to two decisions that at first glance may strike as contradictory. On the one hand, then President George W. Bush issued a memorandum to the Attorney General expressing the determination of the United States' government to discharge its international obligations by having state courts give effect to the Court's Judgment.

On the other hand, the United States withdrew from the Optional Protocol to the Vienna Convention on Consular Relations concerning the Compulsory Settlement of Disputes, thus barring any future proceedings against the United States before the Court on matters relating to the interpretation and/or application of this Convention.

The troubled journey of the presidential memorandum within the United States judiciary, however, showed the true scope of the United States Government's decision: In *Medellín v. Texas* (2008), the United States Supreme Court found that the President had no constitutional authority to order state courts to enforce ICJ decisions. Moreover, that neither the Vienna Convention on Consular Relations nor ICJ Judgments were self-executing within the United States legal order.[1]

The bottom line is that an act of Congress is required to ensure respect for the rights to consular protection enshrined in the Convention as well as to pro-

---

1 For a more detailed analysis of these matters, see B. Sepúlveda-Amor, "Diplomatic and Consular Protection: The rights of the State and the Rights of the Individual in the *LaGrand* and *Avena* cases". In Fastenrath, V. (et al.), *From Bilateralism to Community Interest* (*Essays in Honour of Judge Bruno Simma*, Oxford University Press, 2011.).

vide effective review and consideration in the event of violation of those rights. To date, the requisite federal legislation has not yet been enacted.

In its Judgment of 19 January 2009 dismissing Mexico's request for interpretation of the *Avena* Judgment, the Court emphasized that the obligation to provide means for review and reconsideration "is indeed an obligation of result which clearly must be performed unconditionally; non-performance of it constitutes internationally wrongful conduct".

The above was of no solace to the family of José Ernesto Medellín, executed five months earlier in Texas in violation of both the Court's Judgment in *Avena* and its Order indicating provisional measures pending the resolution of Mexico's request for interpretation. Three other Mexican nationals listed in the *Avena* Judgment have been executed without the benefit of the "review and reconsideration" obligation.

v   Territorial and Maritime Boundary Disputes

Territorial and maritime boundary disputes are a category of cases that, over the years, have come to be viewed as the Court's classic field of expertise. Together with the use and exploitation of shared natural resources, the delimitation of land and maritime frontiers has been the main rationale for resort to the Court by Latin American countries in the past decade. To this we may add disputes involving allegations of trans-boundary environmental damage, such as those underlying the cases *Construction of a Road in Costa Rica along the San Juan River* (*Nicaragua* v. *Costa Rica*) still pending before the Court and *Aerial Herbicide Spraying* (*Ecuador* v. *Colombia*), a case withdrawn days before the beginning of the oral proceedings before the Court as a result of an agreement reached by the parties.

Whereas the specific application of the principle *uti possidetis juris* has been at the core of territorial conflicts, maritime boundary disputes have mainly concerned the delimitation of maritime areas in accordance with modern concepts of the international customary law of the sea.

Be it on land or at sea, the delimitation of international boundaries counts as one of the most sensitive matters that States can entrust to judicial determination. Frontiers are not just logical corollaries of abstract notions of sovereignty and jurisdiction, they are also inextricably linked to economic development and access to natural resources by the relevant States (think, for instance, of the economic dimension of States' rights over the exclusive economic zone and the continental shelf). Most importantly, they are inseparable from deep-seated feelings of national pride and identity. This explains the highly volatile nature of frontier disputes, and their deeply destabilizing effects on the international plane whenever they occur.

A good example of the thin line that all too often separates contested international borders and armed conflict is the scenario submitted for resolution in the *Land, Island and Maritime Frontier Dispute between El Salvador and Honduras*, decided by a Chamber of the Court in 1992. The Court's Judgment put an end to a three-pronged dispute that poisoned the relations between the two neighboring countries for more than a century and which eventually culminated in a short-lived armed struggle in the summer of 1969. The intervention of the OAS was instrumental in the adoption of a cease-fire and the subsequent withdrawal of the troops, but the state of war was to persist between El Salvador and Honduras for more than ten years.

Together with the *Frontier Dispute* between Burkina Faso and Mali, the Judgment in the *Land, Island and Maritime Frontier Dispute* constitutes a landmark in the Court's jurisprudence with regard to the *uti possidetis juris* principle and other principles applicable to contested territorial title; principles that the Court has had occasion to implement time and again since, most recently in the cases *Nicaragua* v. *Honduras* and *Nicaragua* v. *Colombia*.

On a more general note, the dispute that opposed El Salvador and Honduras, in particular the role played by the OAS before and after the Judgment, offers unique insights into how political and judicial means of settlement may complement each other and even require the other to bring about the final resolution of a complex inter-state dispute.

With regard to *Nicaragua* v. *Honduras* and *Nicaragua* v. *Colombia*, the Court's rulings on the maritime claims are perhaps the most noteworthy aspects of the Judgments.

In the first case, the Court rejected Honduras' thesis as to the existence of a traditional maritime boundary between Nicaragua and Honduras along the 15th parallel on the basis of the *uti possidetis juris* and the practice of the parties.

One of the most interesting aspects of this decision concerns the delimitation method chosen by the Court and the geographic circumstances that led it to discard the application of the equidistance method to delimit the parties' maritime areas under customary international law. By geographic circumstances, I mean the morpho-dynamic nature of the mouth of the River Coco, where the eastward terminus of the land boundary between both States was located. As a result of the changes in the morphology of the mouth of the river over the years, the coordinates once agreed upon as describing the location of the terminus of the land boundary no longer corresponded to that point.

Given that it was impossible to identify stable base points on both banks of the River, and aware that any variation or error in their identification would have disproportionate effects in the course of the equidistance line, the Court opted for the bisector method, based on the macro-geography of the coastline as represented by a line drawn between two points on the coast.

Furthermore, on account of the instability of the mouth of the River Coco, with the agreement of the parties, the Court fixed the starting point of the maritime boundary 3 nautical miles seaward. Accordingly, the course of the delimitation line between the terminus of the land boundary and the starting point of the maritime boundary was left unsettled, subject to the subsequent agreement of the Parties.

As with *Nicaragua* v. *Honduras*, disagreement as to the actual existence of a maritime boundary was at the center of the *Territorial and Maritime Dispute* between Nicaragua and Colombia, settled by a judgment of the Court of 19 November 2012.

In this instance, the Court found that neither the 1928 Bárcenas-Esguerra Treaty nor the 1930 Protocol of Exchange of Ratifications concluded by Nicaragua and Colombia effected a maritime delimitation along the 82nd meridian, as claimed by Colombia. On that basis, the Court proceeded to plot a single maritime boundary between Nicaragua's mainland coast and a number of islands located in the Caribbean Sea found to belong to Colombia, in accordance with applicable customary principles of the law of the sea.

The location of the Colombian islands (at a considerable distance from one another) was such that an equidistance line between them and Nicaragua's mainland coast would have cut Nicaragua off from some three quarters of the area into which its coast projected. In addition, there was considerable disparity in the lengths of the relevant coasts.

The Court concluded that these were relevant circumstances calling for the adjustment of the original equidistance line, which the Court shifted eastwards.

In particular, the Court found that, for delimitation purposes, those islands should not be treated as though they were a continuous mainland coast stretching for over 100 nautical miles and cutting off Nicaraguan access to the sea-bed and waters to their east.

In order to understand the Court's démarche in this case, it is important to bear in mind the principles governing single maritime boundaries under customary international law, most notably the overarching principle that delimitation of the economic exclusive zone and the continental shelf is to rest upon equitable principles.

The Court's decision met with sharp criticism in Colombian official circles. President Santos denounced the Pact of Bogota almost immediately, on 27 November 2012. He also declared that the Court had mistakenly delimited the maritime boundary and thus the Judgment was "inapplicable" to Colombia.

A recent decision of the ICJ, delivered on 27 January 2014, settled a dispute between Peru and Chile as to whether there was a maritime boundary dividing the waters of the two neighbouring States. Peru argued that no agreed maritime boundary existed between the two countries and asked the Court to plot a boundary line using the equidistance method in order to achieve an equitable result. Chile argued that the 1952 Santiago Declaration, signed by Peru, Chile and Ecuador, established an international maritime boundary along the parallel of latitude, having as a starting point the Peru-Chile land boundary and extending to a minimum of 200 nautical miles.

In its decision, the Court invoked the terms of the 1954 Special Maritime Frontier Zone Agreement, conducted by Peru, Chile and Ecuador, which acknowledges that a maritime boundary already exists. However, it was recognized by the Court that the Agreement does not indicate when and by what means that boundary was agreed upon. The Court concluded that by acknowledging the existence of a maritime boundary, the Parties were reflecting a tacit agreement which they had reached earlier. It was said that the 1947 Proclamations of Peru and Chile, claiming a 200 nautical miles territorial sea, and the 1952 Declaration of Santiago with a similar claim, suggested an evolving understanding between the Parties concerning their maritime boundary.

The 1954 Agreement gives no indication of the nature of the maritime boundary nor does it indicate its extent. Resorting to the 1947 Proclamations and the 1952 Declaration of Santiago, the Court noted that these instruments expressed claims to the sea-bed and to waters above the sea-bed and their resources. Thus the Court concluded that the boundary is an all-purpose one.

To determine the extent of the maritime boundary, the Court examined the practice of the Parties in the early 1950s, since the 1954 Agreement referred to a maritime boundary serving a specific purpose: to establish a zone of tolerance for fishing activity operated by small vessels. The available information before the Court indicated that the species that were being taken by the Parties at that time were generally to be found within a range of 60 nautical miles from the coast. In the view of the Court, the Parties were unlikely to have considered that the acknowledged maritime boundary extended to a 200-nautical-mile limit. The Court thus concluded that the agreed maritime boundary did not extend beyond 80 nautical miles from its starting-point.

Unusual for a maritime delimitation undertaken by the Court, in the *Peru* v. *Chile* case it decided that the delimitation of the maritime area must begin at the established endpoint of the parallel line, namely 80 nautical miles. From there on, the Court proceeded to apply its usual methodology and constructed a provisional equidistance line, selecting the appropriate base points. The line runs in a general south-west direction, until it reaches the 200 nm limit measured from the Chilean baselines. In line with its "three-step methodology" the Court found no basis for adjusting the provisional equidistance line and found no significant disproportion that would affect the equitable nature of the result.

As previously indicated, in its Judgment the Court determined that there was a tacit agreement between Peru and Chile establishing a maritime boundary, one that had been acknowledged by the three signatories of the Santiago Declaration in its 1954 Agreement. However, the existence of a tacit agreement was questioned by several Judges, who did not find a compelling reason to retreat from the stringent standard of proof formulated in the *Nicaragua v. Honduras* case.

Be that as it may, the fact is that the decision of the Court and its implementation by the two Parties is a significant step towards resolving a dispute that for years affected the friendly relations between Peru and Chile. The Court's resolution puts an end to a difficult controversy regarding a bilateral maritime delimitation. The two Parties now enjoy the legal certainty afforded by a judgment of the Court, dispelling doubts that were a constant source of friction.

Of special relevance is the positive reaction of Peru and Chile after the delivery of the Court's decision, proceeding immediately to implement the Judgment. In a short span of time – exactly two months after the delivery of the Judgment – the two governments reached an agreement on the coordinates of their maritime boundary.

This achievement sets an example to be followed by other countries, an example that shows political will to comply with the Court's decisions and sends a clear message about the strengthening of the rule of law in Latin American international relations.

VI   Shared Natural Resources

The cases referred to above show how frontier disputes can be an important source of tension between neighbouring countries and even become a threat to regional stability. Although international borders are crucial in an international community made up of independent, sovereign States, it would be a mistake to reduce the richness of border relations to the notions of separation and exclusion. Borders are, above all, points of encounter between political communities linked by an invisible thread of common – albeit not necessarily convergent - interests. By interests, I mean questions as important as security, economic development or the preservation and exploitation of shared natural resources.

In the Latin American context, the case relating to the *Pulp Mills on the River Uruguay (Argentina v. Uruguay)* and the *Dispute regarding Navigational and Related Rights (Costa Rica v. Nicaragua)* are good examples of the complex nature of transborder relations in connection with the shared used of the quintessential natural resource: water.

The case relating to the *Pulp Mills on the River Uruguay* originated from the decision of the Uruguayan government to authorize the construction of two pulp mills on the bank of the River Uruguay, the natural frontier between Argentina and Uruguay, under the terms of the Treaty of Montevideo of 1961.

The dispute turned on the interpretation of the Treaty of Salto of 1975, which lays down a number of procedural and substantive obligations within a cooperative framework for the common use of the River, the preservation of animal life and the prevention of pollution.

According to Argentina, in addition to important procedural obligations, Uruguay violated conventional obligations concerning the protection of the environment. The location of the pulp mills was one of Argentina's main concerns, based on the fear that, in addition to inflicting damage to the quality of the waters and the environment, the pulp mills would adversely affect tourism and other economic interest in the area.

Ultimately, the Court ruled that, whereas Uruguay had violated a number of important procedural obligations aimed at ensuring bilateral cooperation in respect of projects and activities likely to cause harm to the other party, Argentina had failed to prove that, by its actions and decisions, Uruguay had caused any damage to the quality of the waters or the environment.

Significantly, in this decision the Court suggested for the first time that "it may now be considered a requirement under general international law to undertake an environmental impact assessment where the risk that the proposed industrial activity may have a significant adverse impact in a transboundary context, in particular, on a shared resource".[2]

In the case of the *Dispute regarding Navigational and Related Rights (Costa Rica v. Nicaragua)*, the controversy turned on the interpretation of the scope of Costa Rica's navigational rights in the San Juan River under the terms of the Treaty Jerez-Cañas of 1858. An important difference between the rivers Uruguay and San Juan is that, whereas the waters of the former are subject to the

---

2   At para. 204.

sovereignty of both Argentina and Uruguay, Nicaragua enjoys full sovereignty over the waters of the San Juan. That is, the land boundary between Costa Rica and Nicaragua runs along the Costa Rican bank of the San Juan.

In its Judgment, the Court clarified that Costa Rica's navigational rights are not limited to the transport of goods – as claimed by Nicaragua – but also extend to the transport of persons for commercial purposes (i.e., tourists). They also include navigational rights of private and non-commercial character in favour of the riparian Costa Rican population with a view to satisfying basic needs of daily life, such as commuting to school or going to the doctor.

The Court also recognized that, in its capacity as a sovereign State, Nicaragua was entitled to regulate navigation on the San Juan, within certain limits, namely regulation:

1. could only subject navigation to certain rules without rendering impossible or substantially impeding the exercise of the right of free navigation;
2. had to be consistent with the terms of the 1858 Treaty;
3. had to have a legitimate purpose, such as safety of navigation, crime prevention and public safety and border control;
4. could not be discriminatory; and, finally
5. could not be unreasonable, that is, its negative impact on the exercise of the right of navigation could not be manifestly excessive.

On this basis, the Court concluded that certain restrictions imposed by Nicaragua upon Costa Rica's navigational rights were contrary to the Treaty of 1858.

VII The ICJ: A Positive Role in Latin America

It seems accurate to say that, overall, the Court has played a meaningful role in the settlement of important disputes in the Latin American context. In so doing, it has formulated rules of international law that apply beyond the specifics of each individual conflict.

The role played by the Court, including its contribution to international stability and the development of international law in each particular instance, depends on a number of factors, including the nature of the dispute, the content of the applicable law, and the prevailing political climate, most notably, States' attitudes towards the Court's decisions.

The Court's function, potential and limits reflect the degree of political maturity of the society whose laws it administers. In this regard, States' attitudes hold the key to greater involvement and influence on the part of the Court in international relations.

Inevitably, adverse judicial decisions exact a political toll on the losing party. This price, however, is minimal compared to the cost of not having access to an impartial judicial organ whenever the need arises to settle disputes dispassionately in accordance with international law. Recent history has shown Latin American States that this need is indeed frequent.

Of course, the Court does not stand alone in its endeavour to bring about the peaceful settlement of disputes and, more often than not, judicial and political means are complementary. The Court, however, stands out for the unique means that it applies in the discharge of its functions: international law as agreed by States, be it bilaterally or within a multilateral framework. States should therefore be wary of hasty decisions tending to insulate themselves from the reach of the Court's jurisdiction for, in so doing, they are in reality insulating themselves from the reach and protection of the rule of law.

CHAPTER 6

Abdul Koroma, Territorial Integrity and the *Kosovo* Opinion

John Dugard

I am pleased to have been invited to contribute to this collection of essays to honor Abdul Koroma. Abdul and I have been friends for many years. We first met in the 1970s at a seminar on sanctions against the apartheid regime of South Africa held at MIT in Boston. Thereafter we met regularly at meetings of the now defunct African Society of International and Comparative Law, whose dynamic Secretary-General, the late Emile Yakyo, succeeded in holding in many countries on the continent. Abdul and I served together on the Society's Governing Body and participated in the unfortunate winding-up of the Society – unfortunate because the Society had done much to promote the cause of international law in Africa. Later Abdul and I worked together on the International Court of Justice, he as a judge and I as a judge *ad hoc*.

In 2002, our friendship was put to the test when we competed for the African seat on the International Court of Justice. Any bitterness that I harbored on this election was directed at the South African government for its failure to support my candidacy[1] and not at Abdul. Abdul and his agent in the election,

---

[1] My experience in that election may have been unique in the history of elections to the International Court of Justice and for his reason warrants telling, even if only in a footnote. In 2002, I was nominated by South Africa's national group that was presided over by Chief Justice Arthur Chaskalson and included his successor, Pius Langa. The national group meticulously followed the procedure laid down in Article 6 of the ICJ Statute and consulted South Africa's highest court of justice, law faculties and organized legal profession before making the nomination. My nomination was duly forwarded to the UN Secretary-General by the South African government and placed on the list of nominees prepared by the Secretary-General in terms of Article 7 of the Statute. But there the support of the South African government ended. At no stage did the government inform me that it would not support my candidacy. It simply refused to publicly endorse my candidacy or to lobby on my behalf. Repeated appeals to President Mbeki and Foreign Minister Nxosazana Dlamini – Zuma for support or clarification of the government's position were met with silence, which left me with little choice but to lobby on my own behalf by fax, phone and meetings at the United Nations in New York in the hope that the South African government would at some stage decide to publicly endorse my candidacy and campaign for me. The South African ambassador in New York, Dumisani Kumalo, recieived no instructions from Pretoria on this matter despite repeated requests.

the ambassador of Sierra Leone to the United Nations, not only behaved honorably throughout the election but in addition ensured that our friendship remained intact. Indeed this experience seemed to strengthen our friendship and respect for each other.

I have chosen to write about Abdul and territorial integrity because it is a subject of special interest to him and one on which he holds strong views. This interest was demonstrated early in Abdul's career when he submitted a thesis on the "Settlement of Territorial and Boundary Disputes" for his Master's degree at Kings College, London.

Abdul's views on territorial integrity were first revealed to me at a meeting of the African Society of International and Comparative law held near Rustenburg, South Africa, in 1995. One of the panels at this meeting was addressed by an African-American scholar who mistakenly thought that he would endear himself to an African audience by assailing colonial boundaries in Africa. African boundaries, he proclaimed, were the products of European imperialist colonialism and should be redrawn to accord with principle of self-determination. Koroma was the first to comment. Politely, but *very* firmly, he told the speaker that he was completely out of touch with African aspirations and the opinions of its people on existing boundaries. *Uti possidetis* was part of customary international law in general and African customary international law in particular. Without respect for the territorial integrity of states, premised on respect for colonial boundaries, Africa would fall into conflict and chaos. The speaker was advised to more fully inform himself about African opinion before he sought to advise Africa on how to manage its affairs.

My next exposure to Koroma's views on African boundaries occurred during the ICJ elections of 2002. The South African ambassador in New York took me into the Security Council during a break in its proceedings and introduced me to a number of ambassadors as South Africa's candidate for the ICJ. With one exception they replied that they would consider supporting me when they received official endorsement of my candidacy from Pretoria – which in the event was not forthcoming.[2] The one exception was the ambassador of Camer-

---

Many governments promised to vote for me provided that they received official confirmation from Pretoria that I enjoyed the support of the government. This confirmation was not forthcoming and Amabassador Kumalo was obliged to cast his vote without instructions from Pretoria. Surprisingly, I received a respectable number of votes in both the Security Council and the General Assembly, but Abdul Koroma won handsomely. No candidate can succeed in an election in the United Nations without the support of his or her own government. As far as I know, this is the only occasion on which a candidate has contested an election without any support whatever from his own government!

2 See above, footnote 1.

oon. He put his arm around my shoulder and warmly informed me that I could rely on the unconditional support of Cameroon. (I was later informed that this promise had been kept.) I was amazed and surprised by this extravagant show of support at a time when my campaign was going nowhere. Only afterwards did I understand the reason for Cameroon's open display of support. This was Koroma's dissenting opinion attached to the International Court's judgment in *Land and Maritime Boundary between Cameroon and Nigeria*,[3] handed down in October 2002, in which he supported Nigeria's territorial claim based largely on a cautious reading of the law governing territorial title.

In the light of these experiences it was no surprise for me to read Abdul's dissenting opinion in the *Kosovo* Advisory Opinion.

1   **The Kosovo Advisory Opinion and Territorial Integrity**

On 8 October 2008 the General Assembly asked the International Court of Justice to render an advisory opinion on the question "Is the unilateral declaration of independence by the provisional Institutions of Self-Government of Kosovo in accordance with international law?"[4] On 22 July 2010 the International Court handed down its advisory opinion on *Accordance with International Law of the Unilateral Declaration of Independence in Respect of Kosovo*.[5] In this opinion the Court found by 10 votes to 4 that the unilateral declaration of independence issued by the representatives of the people of Kosovo did not violate any general rule of international law or the *lex specialis* created by Security Council resolution 1244 (1999), establishing a civil and military presence in Kosovo, known as UNMIK,[6] which governed the territory for ten years. Undoubtedly the narrowness of the question asked, and its failure to ask the Court to address the consequences of the unilateral declaration of independence,[7] allowed the Court to avoid pronouncing on broader issues relating to the se-

---

[3] *Cameroon v. Nigeria, Equatorial Guinea Intervening*, 2002 ICJ Reports p. 303, at p. 474.

[4] Resolution 63/3.

[5] 2010 ICJ Reports 403. Much has been written about this Opinion. See, for example, J.Dugard, "The Secession of States and their Recognition in the Wake of Kosovo" (2011) 357 *Recueil des Cours* p. 9 (at p. 178, footnote 630, there is a comprehensive bibliography of writings on this Opinion); P. Hilpold(ed.) *Kosovo and International Law. The ICJ Advisory Opinion of 22 July 2010*, Leiden, Martinus Nijhoff, 2012; J.Summers (ed.), *Kosovo: A Precedent? The Declaration of Independence, the Advisory Opinion, and Implications for Statehood, Self-Determination and Monrity Rights*, Leiden, Martinus Nijhoff, 2011.

[6] United Nations Interim Administration in Kosovo.

[7] See the comments of the Court in para. 51, *supra* footnote 5, pp. 423–424.

cession of states, such as the scope of self-determination in a post-colonial world, the relationship between self-determination and territorial integrity and remedial secession, despite the fact that the arguments presented by 43 states before the Court had fully examined such matters.

The Court's advisory opinion did not, with one exception, pronounce on any matter of substance relating to the secession of states. This exception concerned the limits of territorial integrity. In paragraph 80 of its opinion, the Court declared that "the scope of the principle of territorial integrity is confined to the sphere of relations between states".[8] In support of its finding the Court invoked Article 2(4) of the UN Charter, the Declaration on the Principles of International Law Concerning Friendly Relations Among States[9] contained in General Assembly resolution 2625 (XXV), and the Helsinki Accords,[10] which require *states* (and not by implication non-state actors) to respect the territorial integrity of other states, but made no mention of several important Security Council resolutions that require non-state actors – liberation movements acting in pursuance of the right of self-determination – to respect the territorial of the state against which their action is directed.

It was this finding of the Court that provoked a powerful dissent from Abdul Koroma.

Koroma began by stating that the effect of Kosovo's unilateral declaration of independence was to create the new state of Kosovo which violated both Security Council resolution 1244 (1999) and general international law.[11] In the first place, he stressed that both the text and the spirit of Security Council resolution 1244(1999) recognized the territorial integrity of Serbia (the Federal Republic of Yugoslavia) as the basis for any future settlement.[12] Then he turned to general international law. Citing Article 2(4) of the UN Charter, which requires states to "refrain in their international relations from the threat or use of force against the territorial integrity or political independence of any State", and General Assembly resolution 2625 (XXV), which provides that "any attempt aimed at the partial or total disruption of the national unity and territo-

---

8   Ibid, p. 437.
9   The full title of this Declaration is Declaration on Principles of International Law Concerning Friendly Relations and Co-operation among States in Accordance with the Charter of the United Nations.
10 Article IV of the Final Act of the Helsinki Conference on Security and Co-operation in Europe of 1 August 1975.
11 2010 ICJ Reports, pp. 467, 469–474, paras 2, 9–19.
12 Ibid. pp. 471–473, paras 13–16.

rial integrity of a State or country ... is incompatible with the purposes and principles of the Charter",[13] he declared that:

> One of the fundamental principles of contemporary international law is that of respect for the sovereignty and territorial integrity of States. This principle entails an obligation to respect the definition, delineation and territorial integrity of an existing State.[14]

The principle of self-determination did not allow for the dismemberment of an existing state without its consent. Resolution 2625 (XXV) left "no doubt that the principles of the sovereignty and territorial integrity of States prevail over the principle of self-determination".[15]

Koroma was concerned that the Court's opinion would create a precedent that would give support to secessionist movements. He declared:

> International law does not confer a right on ethnic, linguistic or religious groups to break away from the territory of a State of which they form part, without that State's consent, merely by expressing their wish to do so. To accept otherwise, to allow any ethnic, linguistic or religious group to declare independence and break away from the territory of which it forms part, outside the context of decolonization, creates a very dangerous precedent. Indeed, it amounts to nothing less than announcing to any and all dissident groups around the world that they are free to circumvent international law simply by acting in a certain way and crafting a unilateral declaration of independence, using certain terms. The Court's Opinion will serve as a guide and instruction manual for secessionist groups the world over, and the stability of international law will be severely undermined.[16]

2 The Scope of the Principle of Territorial Integrity in Today's World

Koroma was correct that the Court's Opinion in *Kosovo* does substantially change the understanding of states on the subject of territorial integrity.

---

13 The Declaration on the Granting of Independence to Colonial Countries and Peoples, General Assembly resolution 1514 (XV) contains a similar prohibition.
14 Ibid. p. 475, para. 21.
15 Ibid. p. 476, para. 22.
16 Ibid. p. 468, para. 4.

Although Article 2(4) of the UN Charter, the Declaration on the Principles of International Law Concerning Friendly Relations Among States and the Helsinki Accords do provide that only states are required to respect the territorial integrity of other states and make no mention whether this obligation extends to non-state actors, the practice of the United Nations and of states strongly suggests – indeed, *indicates* – that non-state actors are bound, outside the context of decolonization, to respect the territorial integrity of states to which they belong and not to take action that might impair the national unity or territorial integrity of existing states.

The most recent general pronouncement of the General Assembly – the World Summit Outcome Resolution of 2005[17] – does not follow the formulation of the principle of territorial integrity of Article 2(4) of the UN Charter, Resolution 2625 (XXV) or the Helsinki Accords. Instead heads of state and government simply "rededicate" themselves to respect for territorial integrity[18] without any suggestion that this principle applies only to relations between states. Moreover the 2007 Declaration on the Rights of Indigenous Peoples makes it clear that the principle of respect for territorial integrity extends to non-state actors. Article 46 of this Declaration provides

> Nothing in this Declaration may be interpreted as implying for any State, *people, group or person* any right to engage in any activity or to perform any act contrary to the Charter of the United Nations or construed as authorizing or encouraging any action which would dismember or impair, totally or in part, the territorial integrity or political unity of sovereign and independent States (emphasis added).

Security Council resolutions provide no support for the interpretation of the principle of territorial integrity placed upon it by the International Court in the *Kosovo* Opinion. In resolution 787 (1992) on the subject of the territorial integrity of Bosnia-Herzegovina – invoked by the Court in *Kosovo* in another connection[19] – the Security Council declared that "any entities unilaterally declared" (clearly a reference to the Republic of Srpska, a non-state actor) would "not be accepted" and called for strict respect for the territorial integrity of Bosnia-Herzegovina. In a number of subsequent resolutions the Security

---

17   Resolution 60/L.1.
18   Para. I(5).
19   2010 ICJ Reports pp. 437–438, para. 81.

Council condemned "Bosnian Serbs" – *non-state actors* – within Bosnia-Herzegovina for their refusal to respect the territorial integrity of that state.[20]

Serbs (again non-state actors) within Croatia that set up the Serb enclave of Krajina were likewise condemned for their refusal to respect the territorial integrity of Croatia.[21] In Darfur the Security Council has made it clear that it does not support the secession of any group by reaffirming the territorial integrity of Sudan.[22] The Security Council has rejected the secessionist aspirations of the people of Somaliland and Puntland (non-state actors) by its reaffirmations of the territorial integrity of Somalia.[23] Before the intervention of the Russian Federation in Georgia in August 2008, the Security Council reaffirmed the territorial integrity of Georgia at the expense of a secessionist movement in Abkhazia.[24] Resolutions of this kind were invoked by several states in the proceedings before the International Court in order to support the argument that that the principle of territorial integrity applied to non-state actors. For instance, Argentina argued on the basis of these resolutions that

> Respect for the principle of territorial integrity is an obligation that applies not only to states and international organizations, but also to other international actors, particularly those involved in internal conflicts threatening international peace and security.[25]

The argument advanced by the United States that the Security Council in these resolutions had simply "included language designed to promote the maintenance of the unity of a particular state where it had concluded that so doing will advance international peace and security"[26] is not convincing. The resolutions make it clear that non-state actors are bound to respect the territorial integrity of states.

The practice of states accords with the practice of the Security Council in the pre-Kosovo era. Western states repeatedly reaffirmed respect for the terri-

---

20 Resolutions 859 (1993), 942 (1994).
21 Resolution 981 (1995).
22 Resolutions 1566 (2004), 1769 (2007).
23 Resolutions 1766 (2007), 1772 (2007).
24 Resolutions 896 (1994), 1065 (1996).
25 See the proceedings before the ICJ in *Kosovo*, Written statement of Argentina, 17 April 2009, p. 30, para. 75. See, too, the written statements of Cyprus (July 2009, pp. 6–8, paras 15–18), Spain (July 2009, p. 3, para. 4), Iran (17 April 2009, p. 4, para. 3.1) and Serbia (15 April 2009, p. 152, para. 423).
26 Ibid. Written statement, July 2009, p. 18, Chap. IV, Section 1, B

torial integrity of the Russian Federation in respect of Chechnya.[27] France declared that Chechnya was part of the Russian Federation, whose territorial integrity was to be respected[28] and the United States proclaimed

> We support the sovereignty and territorial integrity of the Russian Federation ... We oppose attempts to alter international boundaries by force, whether in the form of aggression by one state against another or in the form of armed secessionist movements ...[29]

The West similarly demanded respect for the territorial integrity of Georgia on the part of those who had declared the Republic of Abkhazia in the 1990s.[30]

3   The Court's Opinion: Some Criticisms

It seems clear that the United Nations and states have interpreted the principle of respect for territorial integrity to extend to both states and non-state actors, despite the language of Article 2(4) of the UN Charter, Resolution 2625 (XXV) and the Helsinki Accords that expressly confine the principle to relations between states. Does this mean that the letter of these instruments has been changed by subsequent practice on the part of states and the United Nations in terms of Article 31(3) of the Vienna Convention on the Law of Treaties? Is this a case similar to the practice of abstention in the Security Council which has varied the strict letter of Article 27(3) of the Charter on the veto?[31] Or is it similar to the practice of the United Nations on colonialism which has seen the language of Chapter XI of the Charter, which impliedly recognized the lawfulness of colonialism, ignored to allow colonialism to be declared unlawful?[32]

---

27   See A. Buchanan, *Justice, Legitimacy and Self-Determination. Moral Foundations for International Law*, Oxford, Oxford University Press, 2004, pp. 340–341.
28   (1995) 41 *Annuaire francais de droit international* 911.
29   Deputy Secretary of State Talbott, (1995) 6 US Department of State Dispatch, pp. 119–120.
30   See J. Dugard and D. Raic, "The Role of Recognition in the Law and Practice of Secession" in M.G. Kohen, *Secession. International Law Perspectives,* Cambridge, Cambridge University Press, 2006, p. 117,
31   This interpretation of Article 27(3) was upheld by the International Court in *Legal Consequences for States of the Continued Presence of South Africa in Namibia(South West Africa) notwithstanding Security Council Resolution 276 (1970),* 1971 ICJ Reports p. 16 at p. 22.
32   See J.Dugard, *International Law. A South African Perspective*, 4th ed, Cape Town, Juta, 2011, pp. 93–94.

This is not an easy question to answer. However, it is surely a question that should have been carefully and thoroughly examined by the Court in *Kosovo*. The Court's terse finding that "the scope of the principle of territorial integrity is confined to the sphere of relations between States"[33] makes no attempt whatsoever to consider the practice of states or the United Nations let alone the question whether the interpretation of Article 2(4) of the Charter and other instruments it cites has been influenced by such practice. On other occasions the Court has used the advisory opinion to fully examine the law, and indeed to develop it,[34] but in this Opinion the Court chose to be thoroughly economical in its reasoning.

Another criticism of the Court's Opinion on the subject of territorial integrity concerns the failure of the Court to examine the meaning of the controversial paragraph in the Declaration on Principles of International Law Concerning Friendly Relations Among States – Resolution 2625 (XXV) – which declares that

> Nothing in the foregoing paragraphs (asserting the right of self-determination) shall be construed as authorizing or encouraging any action which would dismember or impair, totally or in part, the territorial integrity or political unity of sovereign independent States conducting themselves in compliance with the principles of equal rights and self-determination of peoples ... and thus possessed of a government representing the whole people belonging to the territory without distinction as to race, creed or colour.[35]

This paragraph clearly means that states are prohibited from engaging in action that would impair the territorial integrity of a state unless that state denies the right of self-determination to its people.[36] But does it also mean that a non-state actor is prohibited from engaging in action that would dismember or impair the territorial integrity of a state *unless* the state failed to act

---

[33] 2010 ICJ Reports, p. 437, para. 80.

[34] As, for example, in the *Namibia* Opinion (*supra* footnote 31) and *Legal Consequences of the Construction of a Wall in the Occupied Palestinian Territory* 2004 ICJ Reports p. 136.

[35] This paragraph is substantially reaffirmed by paragraph 2 of the Vienna Declaration and Programme of Action adopted by the UN World Conference on Human Rights of 1993 (1993) 32 *International Legal Materials* 1661.

[36] It seems clear that this paragraph was directed at states. See Dugard, *supra*, footnote 5 at p. 109; A. Cassese, *Self-Determination of Peoples,* Cambridge, Cambridge University Press, 1995, pp. 333–334. However, it is not clear that this paragraph of Resolution 2625 (XXV) was directed at states alone.

in compliance with the principle of self-determination and was thus possessed of a government that did not represent the whole people belonging to the territory? If this is so, it follows that where the state does comply with the principle of self-determination and has a government representing the people of the territory as a whole that both non-state actors and third states are obliged to respect the territorial integrity of a state. If this latter interpretation is accepted it would lend support to the notion of remedial secession, which allows secession when a people occupying a distinct part of the territory of a state are denied the right of internal self-determination, subjected to an abuse of their human rights and have exhausted all avenues to secure their right of internal self-determination.[37] However, the Court in *Kosovo* refused to pronounce on the question whether international law recognizes such a right.[38] The Court would have contributed substantially to our understanding of the role of self-determination in a post-colonial world and of the limits of secession had it examined the scope of this controversial paragraph and whether it recognized a right of remedial secession. Unfortunately it elected not to do so.

4   The Present Status of Territorial Integrity

Respect for territorial integrity remains a fundamental principle of international law. There is, however, no doubt that it has been weakened by the International Court's finding in *Kosovo* that the scope of the principle "is confined to the sphere of relations between States" as this indicates that non-state actors who in today's world undoubtedly pose the greatest threat to the territorial integrity of states, are not bound by the principle. There is therefore substance in the warning of Abdul Koroma that the Opinion "will serve as a guide and instruction manual for secessionist groups the world over",[39] a warning that was repeated by Judge Yusuf in a separate opinion,[40] and has been echoed by academic commentators on the Opinion.[41]

---

37   See Dugard, *supra*, footnote 5, pp. 112–121; A. Cassese, *supra*, footnote 35, pp. 118–119.
38   *Supra*, footnote 5, p. 438, paras 82–83.
39   See above at footnote 16.
40   Judge Yusuf declared that the Court's Opinion "may be misinterpreted as legitimizing" unilateral declarations of independence "by all kinds of separatist groups or entities": *supra* footnote 5 at p. 620, para. 6.
41   According to Ralph Wilde, "All sub-groups in the world are now on notice that … there would not appear to be a general international rule barring them from declaring independence", "Self-Determination, Secession, and Dispute Settlement after the Kosovo Advisory Opinion" (2011) 24 *Leiden Journal of International Law*, p. 149 at p. 152. See, too,

The history of the post – Westphalian era demonstrates that the boundaries of states do not and will not remain static. Change is inevitable. Empires have come and gone; states have emerged, disappeared, enlarged and reduced in size. Yet international peace and stability demand that every effort be made to retain states within their existing boundaries. Only in extreme situations should change be allowed. The principles of respect for territorial integrity and *uti possidetis* have ensured a measure of certainty and stability in today's world. Where, however, the government of a state denies the right of internal self-determination to a part of its people inhabiting a distinct territory, suppresses their human rights and closes the door to negotiation, the secession of the people of that territory should not be resisted. Nor should the principle of territorial integrity be permitted to obstruct this secession. This is the meaning of resolution 2625(XXV). The principle of remedial secession that permits secession where the right of self-determination has been denied and human rights suppressed provides an instrument for change that balances self-determination and territorial integrity. The wholesale removal of the principle of respect for territorial integrity from this process does, however, remove a necessary legal restraint on territorial change. This, in effect, is what the International Court has done in its *Kosovo* Opinion. Arguably, we have already seen the consequences of this weakening of respect for territorial integrity in the Crimea, where a secessionist group of Russian-speakers was able to secede from Ukraine and join the Russian Federation in an exercise of self-determination where there was no suggestion that their right to internal self-determination in Ukraine had been denied or their human rights suppressed. It seems, sadly, that Koroma's warning has already been fulfilled.

T. Christakis, "The ICJ Advisory Opinion: Has International Law Something to say about Secession?" ibid, p. 73 at p. 5; R.Falk, "The Kosovo Advisory Opinion: Conflict Resolution and Precedent" (2011) 105 *American Journal of International Law*, p. 58.

CHAPTER 7

Provisional Measures in Interpretation Proceedings – A New Way to Extend the Court's Jurisdiction? The Practice of the Court in the Avena and Temple of Preah Vihear Cases

Karin Oellers-Frahm

I Introduction

Judge Abdul G. Koroma served for two terms at the ICJ, from 6 February 1994 to 5 February 2012. This was one of the most interesting periods of the Court which was characterized by a significant development not only with regard to the increasing number of cases reaching the Court, but also with regard to the acceptance the Court gained all over the world with cases being brought no longer only or foremost from Western European states, but also from Eastern Europe, Africa, Asia and the Americas. New developments of the international community created new legal problems which the judges of the Court had to resolve on the basis of the existing law but not without paving the way for new developments in international law. Judge Abdul G. Koroma made an important contribution to the work of the Court by putting the accent in his well-pondered and concise separate opinions in particular on humanitarian aspects and cultural diversity in international law. It is a great honor to contribute to a collection of essays dedicated to Judge Koroma and I decided to tackle a topic that had emerged right at the end of his term of office and which seems to relate simply to procedural questions but does, in fact, reflect a new facet of the central problem of international dispute settlement, namely the lack of obligatory jurisdiction of the Court and means to overcome it by a flexible use of the available instruments.

II Interpretation Proceedings: The Legal Requirements

According to Art. 60 of the ICJ Statute "The judgment is final and without appeal"; it is, however, open to interpretation (Art. 60 Statute) and revision (Art. 61 Statute). While revision may lead to a partially or totally different/new judgment, interpretation does not affect the *res iudicata*, it adds nothing to the decision, but only allows for guidance to be given by the Court with regard to the meaning or scope of the judgment. Both means of "review" of judgments are extremely rarely used[1] and in no interpretation case any of the "incidental proceedings"[2] such as interim protection, preliminary objections, counter-claims or intervention was used. This situation changed when on 5 June 2008 Mexico filed a request for interpretation of the Court's judgment of 31 March 2004 in the case *Avena and other Mexican Nationals (Mexico v. United States of America)*[3] submitting the same day also a request for the indication of provisional measures. This example was followed on 28 April 2011 by Cambodia when it applied for the interpretation of the Judgment of 15 June 1962 requesting at the same time the indication of provisional measures.[4]

Due to the fact that interim measures aim at protecting the rights to be adjudged in the merits of the case and that in interpretation proceedings the underlying judgment remains as it stands, i.e. the rights adjudicated as such are no longer in dispute, it may appear doubtful whether there is at all any room for provisional protection.[5] It is thus necessary to succinctly characterize the two kinds of proceedings in order to assess the relationship between them.

Interpretation proceedings[6] are rather limited in scope because the Court may only construe, not touch upon the *res iudicata* of the underlying judgment. The exercise of the Court's jurisdiction is unproblematic as the competence to construe the judgment follows from the competence to decide the underlying case. Even if one or both parties to the original case have meanwhile

---

1 *Request for Interpretation of the Judgment of 20 November 1950 in the Asylum case (Colombia v. Peru), Judgment,* ICJ Reports 1950, p. 401; *Application for Revision and Interpretation of the Judgment of 24 February 1982 in the Case concerning the Continental Shelf (Tunisia/Libyan Arab Jamahiriya), (Tunisia v. Libyan Arab Jamahiriya), Judgment,* ICJ Reports 1985, p. 223, para. 56; *Request for Interpretation of the Judgment of 11 June 1998 in the Case concerning the Land and Maritime Boundary between Cameroon and Nigeria (Cameroon v. Nigeria), Preliminary Objections, (Nigeria v. Cameroon),* ICJ Reports 1999, pp. 31 et seq., *Case concerning Avena and Other Mexican Nationals, (Mexico v. United States of America),* ICJ Reports 2009, p. 3 et seq.; *Case Concerning the Temple of Preah Vihear (Cambodia v. Thailand)* which is still pending.
2 Section D of the Rules of Court, Art. 73 et seq.
3 ICJ Reports 2004, p. 12.
4 *Request for Interpretation of the Judgment of 15 June 1962 in the case concerning the* Temple of Preah Vihear *(Cambodia v. Thailand),* Order of 18 July 2011, available on the website of the ICJ.
5 Ibid. Diss. Op. Judge Donoghue.
6 For a comprehensive analysis cf. A. Zimmermann, Art. 60, in A. Zimmermann/C. Tomuschat/ K. Oellers-Frahm/C. Tams (eds.), The Statute of the International Court of Justice – A Commentary, 2nd ed., 2012, 1469 et seq.

withdrawn their consent to the Court's jurisdiction, the competence to decide an interpretation request is not affected, a fact that may explain a request for interpretation if the jurisdiction of the Court is otherwise lacking even where the meaning of the underlying judgment is uncontroversial, but where the follow-up to the judgment is critical. Furthermore and in difference to a request for revision, there is no time-limit for requesting the interpretation of a former judgment so that a request for interpretation reaching the Court in 2011 with regard to a judgment delivered in 1962 is no bar to admissibility. All that is required is that there is a dispute ("contestation" in the French version of the Statute) as to the meaning or scope of the judgment.

The preconditions for interim protection[7] on the other hand include the existence of at least *prima facie* jurisdiction – which in interpretation proceedings is unproblematic –, urgency, imminent irreparable harm, plausibility of the asserted rights and a link between those rights and the measures requested. In the context of the limited jurisdiction under Art. 60 of the Statute, the rights to be protected must plausibly be derivable from the original judgment and thus may only be rights said to have been established with the force of *res judicata* in the original judgment but the meaning or scope of which are unclear and need interpretation in the view of the Applicant.[8] It was, in fact, in both cases the link between the measures requested and the rights to be protected in the interpretation request which gave rise to concern what will be explained more in detail in the following considerations.

III   The *Avena* Case

1   *The Decision of the Court*

The underlying case concerned the death sentences against several Mexican nationals in the United States who had been convicted in disregard of the obligations of the United States flowing from Art. 36 of the Vienna Convention on Consular Relations, namely the lack of information of the consular representative concerning detention and sentencing of one of its nationals. In its original judgment the Court found *inter alia,* that "the appropriate reparation in this case consists in the obligation of the United States of America to provide, by means of its own choosing, review and reconsideration of the convictions and sentences of the Mexican nationals" (para. 153 (9) of the Judgment). With a

---

7   For a comprehensive analysis cf. K. Oellers-Frahm, Art. 41, in A. Zimmermann et al., (fn. 6), 1029 et seq.

8   *Avena* case, ICJ Reports 2008, pp. 311, 326, para. 58; *Temple of Preah Vihear* case, para. 34.

view to the follow-up given to the judgment by the United States, and in particular due to decisions of the Texas courts disregarding the ICJ judgment, Mexico was of the opinion that a dispute existed between the two parties with regard to the meaning of the relevant passage of the judgment. While Mexico was of the opinion that the obligation to provide review and reconsideration of the sentences and convictions constituted an "obligation of result", the United States considered it, so the argument of Mexico, rather as "an obligation of means". It was thus for the Court to construe this part of the judgment. The request for provisional measures resulted from the fear of Mexico that Mexican nationals faced execution in the nearest future without having received the required review or reconsideration of their case.

The central question in this case was whether there was in fact a "dispute" in the sense of Art. 60 of the Statute between the parties since the United States explicitly agreed that also in their view the obligation concerning review and reconsideration of the cases of the Mexican nationals concerned was an obligation of result. If the Court would have shared this statement there would neither have been any room for the indication of provisional measures nor for upholding the case which would have to be dismissed as inadmissible. The Court found, however, that there was a "dispute" between the parties. In this context the Court referred to the French version of Art. 60 Statute which does not use the term "différend" in translating the English term "dispute", as is the case in Art. 36 (2) of the Statute, but the term "contestation". In the view of the Court the term "contestation" is wider in scope and more flexible than the term "différend" in that it need not satisfy the same criteria as a "dispute" under Art. 36 (2) of the Statute but only requires the presence of "opposing views" as to the scope of the underlying judgment. On this basis the Court concluded that the Parties "apparently hold different views as to the meaning and scope of that obligation of result, namely whether that understanding is shared by all United States federal and state authorities and whether that obligation falls upon those authorities".[9] On the basis of this finding the Court decided that the circumstances of the case required the indication of provisional measures since the Mexican nationals concerned were at risk of being executed before having received review and reconsideration of their case which would cause irreparable harm. The Court consequently ordered that the Mexican nationals concerned shall not be executed pending the judgment on the request for interpretation unless they had received review and reconsideration of their case and that the United States shall keep the Court informed on the measures taken to implement the order.

---

9   Para. 55 of the Order of 2008 (fn. 8).

This decision was accompanied by the dissent of five judges of the Court[10] which related in particular to the statement that there was a "dispute/contestation" in the sense of Art. 60 of the Statute, but which expressed also concern with regard to the measures ordered. As to the first concern, the existence of a dispute/contestation, the arguments of the dissenters are far more convincing than the argument of the Court because it cannot be contested that at the international level it is the United States Executive, not its component organs at all levels, that represent the State. Therefore the position taken by the authorities of a state of the United States is of no relevance with regard to the obligations of the parties to the case, namely the United States and Mexico who, in fact, were in complete agreement with regard to the obligation flowing from the judgment of the Court. The attitude of component organs or state authorities of the United States could only become relevant under the aspect of state responsibility if the judgment of 2004 were not complied with, irrespective of whether this would be imputable to acts of federal or state authorities. As the Court itself noted that this kind of responsibility would become relevant if the United States – by acts or omissions of any of its political subdivisions – were unable to fulfill its international obligations under the *Avena* judgment its decision as to the existence of a "dispute/contestation" seems rather artificial.

The same is true for the measures ordered which simply repeat what was decided with binding force in the Judgment of 2004, namely that no Mexican national shall be executed unless review and reconsideration of the sentence has been granted. This obligation is binding upon the United States without any time limit, while the measures ordered in the context of the request for interpretation are only binding until the judgment on the merits is delivered and in fact expired when by judgment of 19 January 2009 the Court found that the request for interpretation had to be dismissed. The reason for this finding was, however, not that there was no "dispute/contestation" between the parties in the sense of Art. 60 of the Statute, but that the request for interpretation concerned a matter which had not been decided by the Court in its judgment of 31 March 2004, namely whether the understanding that the judgment established an obligation of result was shared by all United States federal and state authorities and whether that obligation falls upon those authorities. This finding is, in fact, astonishing because a decision concerning the concrete obligations of federal or state authorities would not have been within the competence of the Court; such decision would interfere with the internal system of the United States administration and relate to issues which are irrelevant in the

---

10 Order of 2008 (fn. 8), diss. op. Judge Buergenthal, joint diss. op. Judges Owada, Tomka and Keith; diss. op. Judge Skotnikov.

relations between Mexico and the United States in proceedings and judgments before the ICJ. With a view to this state of affairs the decision of the Court looks rather like a lesson in international law given to Mexico because Mexico's alleged understanding of the judgment would be *ultra vires,* a fact that manifestly and *a limine litis* excluded the indication of provisional measures.

2   Analysis of the Decision

Although the concern of Mexico that one of the Mexican nationals would be executed without having received review and reconsideration of his sentence is understandable and in fact unfortunately proved well founded as one of the nationals was executed on 5 August 2008, it was rather obvious that Mexico's request for interpretation aimed more at a confirmation of what had been decided with binding force in 2004. By admitting the request on a *prima facie* basis in order to indicate provisional measures the Court opened the way for (ab)using the interpretation procedure in cases where not the interpretation of the judgment, but its implementation, is at stake. In distinction to the *Temple* case, there were not even any new developments in the *Avena* case; the situation leading to the seizing of the Court resulted clearly from the imminent non-implementation of the final judgment and was thus the expression of a desperate attempt to save the life of a Mexican national. As in international law the execution of judgments lies with the parties, the "request for interpretation" was a cover-up to have the Court remind the United States of their obligations following from the judgment because no other means are available for the enforcement of the judgment. In contrast to other international courts, as for example the European Court of Human Rights, where the Committee of Ministers "shall supervise the execution" (Art. 46 ECHR), the involvement of the Security Council in the execution of the judgments of the ICJ under Art. 94 (2) of the UN Charter is far from efficiently guaranteeing implementation,[11] and the possibilities of the Court are extremely limited if at all existent; in proceedings concerning the indication of provisional measures, however, the Court has developed a standard according to which it has to be informed of the measures taken by the party(ies) in compliance of the order and moreover declares itself to remain seised of the matters which form the subject of the order. This is in conformity with the possibility to revise the measures or indicate

---

11   For the "enforcement mechanism" seemingly resulting from Art. 94 (2) UN Charter cf. K. Oellers-Frahm, Souveräne Gleichheit der Staaten in der internationalen gerichtlichen Streitbeilegung? Überlegungen zu Art. 94 Abs. 2 und Art. 27 UN Charta, in J.A. Frowein/ K. Scharioth/I. Winkelmann/R. Wolfrum (eds.), Verhandeln für den Frieden, Liber Amicorum *Tono Eitel,* 2003, 69–91.

other ones whenever circumstances so require and gives the Court at least some power to supervise compliance with provisional measures. Once the judgment is delivered, neither the Court nor any other organ – the Security Council's powers being also of only limited effect – is empowered to supervise or take measures to enforce the judgment. As provisional measures have binding force until the judgment is delivered, implementation of provisional measures enjoys thus a better, although still limited guarantee than the implementation of a judgment which in particular cases may even be identical to the order of provisional measures. This situation seems rather odd and may explain that not only parties but also the Court use any possibility to urge the State concerned to comply with the judgment. To this end a request for the interpretation of a judgment is in fact a promising means because the most delicate problem in provisional measures proceedings, the question of jurisdiction, does not even arise; the only relevant aspect being the imminent and irreparable damage to the rights at stake. Of course, in interpretation proceedings the "rights at stake" are linked to the terms to be construed, but it cannot be expected that the Court as an organ of the United Nations charged with the peaceful settlement of disputes could pass in silence the disregard of a former judgment including the risk of execution of human beings who did not enjoy all possible procedural guarantees in their proceedings. Therefore, there are good reasons to justify the indication of provisional measures in interpretation proceedings which finally aim at compliance with the underlying judgment. The "activism" of the Court granting provisional measures in such cases somehow remedies the lack of any supervisory powers concerning compliance with the judgment. Nevertheless and under a strict legal appreciation, the indication of provisional measures in cases like the *Avena* case is not unproblematic, but ethically understandable. In order to keep within the legal framework it would, however, be preferable that the Court would dismiss a request for interpretation if there is manifestly no "dispute" concerning the meaning of the underlying judgment as in the *Avena* case, while including in the reasons, not the operative part of the order dismissing the case, a reminder to the parties of their obligations resulting from the judgment. Such attitude would be in line with the Court's powers even in cases where the interpretation request merely aims at such reminder. If the Court admits the request for provisional measures as in the *Avena* case and includes such reminder in the operative part of its order, there is no problem as long as the sovereign rights of the parties are not affected because any interference with sovereign rights of the parties must strictly relate to the case at hand, i.e. the rights to be construed in the interpretation proceedings, an aspect which became crucial in the *Temple* case. As it would require an amendment of the Statute, which is an integral part of the UN

Charter and thus dependent on the same amendment requirements, to give the Court or some other organ the power to supervise compliance with a judgment by means of an interpretation request may be justified as long as the Court keeps within the legal framework and does not indicate provisional measures affecting the sovereign powers of the parties – unless there is a link to the interpretation problem, a situation that will probably be rather the exception.

IV The *Temple of Preah Vihear* Case

1 *The Decision of the Court*

The dispute concerning the question under whose sovereignty, Cambodia or Thailand, the Temple of Preah Vihear is situated, was decided in 1962. With regard to this date it seems in fact rather strange that questions concerning the interpretation of that judgment arose only nearly 50 years later, in 2011, and more so as this happened when serious armed incidents occurred in the area of the Temple. In 2008 the Temple was classified as a world cultural heritage and included in the UNESCO list; since then, several armed incidents occurred, in particular in February and April of 2011, for which, in the view of Cambodia, Thailand was responsible.

In its judgment of 1962 the Court had decided in the first paragraph of the operative clause that "the Temple of Preah Vihear is situated in territory under the sovereignty of Cambodia"; and in the second paragraph of the operative clause the Court declared that "Thailand is under an obligation to withdraw any military or police forces or other guards or keepers, stationed by her at the Temple, or in its vicinity on Cambodian territory". According to Cambodia this finding implies the conclusion that a legally established frontier existed between the two Parties in the area in question, while according to Cambodia, Thailand believes that Cambodia's sovereignty is confined to the Temple only and does not extend to the area surrounding it. Therefore a dispute existed – in the view of Cambodia – as to the meaning and scope of the 1962 Judgment, in particular with regard to the extent of Cambodia's sovereignty and the meaning of the words "vicinity on Cambodian territory" and furthermore with regard to the continuing duration of Thailand's obligation to withdraw any forces from the Temple and its vicinity. Cambodia's request for interpretation thus asked the Court to declare that Thailand is under a continuing obligation to respect "the integrity of the territory of Cambodia, that territory having been delimited in the area of the Temple and its vicinity by the line on the Annex I map, on which the Judgment of the Court is based".[12] The request for the indication of provisional measures of the same date aimed at an order to "cause the incursions into its territory (by Thailand) to cease", and moreover "to avoid aggravation of the dispute".[13]

Thailand maintained that there was no dispute as to the meaning and scope of the 1962 judgment because it recognized that the Temple is situated on Cambodian territory and that it is under an obligation to withdraw its military forces from the Temple and its vicinity in so far as those forces were situated on Cambodian territory. This obligation has fully been met by Thailand and cannot give rise to an interpretative judgment so that the Court manifestly lacks jurisdiction to rule on the request and to indicate provisional measures. Thailand claims, moreover, that the aim of Cambodia's request for interpretation is to have the Court decide that the frontier between the two countries derives from the Annex I map on which the Court did in fact "base" its judgment of 1962, but which it did not consider as delimiting the entire frontier in this area refusing clearly to rule in the operative clause of the judgment on the legal status of the Annex I map and the frontier line in the disputed area.

On the basis of the positions of the Parties, the Court found that there was a dispute as to the scope and meaning of the 1962 Judgment relating in the first place to the meaning of the phrase "vicinity on Cambodian territory" and second to the nature of the obligation to withdraw any military or police forces, in particular whether this obligation was of a continuing character; finally the difference of opinion concerned the question whether the Judgment did or did not recognize with binding force the line shown on the Annex I map as representing the frontier between the two Parties.[14]

In the *Temple* case the most relevant question was not, as in the *Avena* case, whether there was a dispute/contestation concerning the meaning and scope of the underlying judgment, but whether the rights to be adjudged on the merits are plausible and whether a link existed between the rights at stake, i.e. the interpretation, and the measures requested. Both questions were answered positively by the Court. As to the question of urgency and irreparable harm required for the indication of provisional measures, the Court came to the conclusion that armed clashes had taken place and continued to take place in the area, in particular between 4 and 7 February 2011, leading to fatalities, injuries

---

12 *Request for Interpretation of the Judgment of 15 June 1962 in the Case Concerning the* Temple of Preah Vihear (Cambodia v. Thailand), ICJ website, para. 5 of the Order on the Request for the Indication of Provisional Measures, 18 July 2011.
13 Ibid. para. 10.
14 Ibid. para. 31.

and the displacement of local inhabitants. The Court also determined that, because of these clashes, there was a real and imminent risk of irreparable prejudice being caused to the rights claimed by Cambodia thereby justifying the indication of provisional measures. With a view to ensure that no irreparable damage is caused to persons or property in the area of the Temple, the Court decided to indicate measures other than those requested by Cambodia – as it is empowered to do under Art. 75 (2) of the Rules of Court. It decided to address the order indicating provisional measures to both Parties, namely that all armed forces should, pending the Judgment on the merits, be excluded from a zone around the area of the Temple. To this end, the Court defined a provisional demilitarized zone from which both Parties had to withdraw their military personnel and where they had to refrain from any military armed activity; furthermore, it decided *inter alia* that "both Parties shall refrain from any action which might aggravate or extend the dispute before the Court or make it more difficult to resolve".[15] The decision of the Court in particular with regard to the two points of the operative clause mentioned above met with the dissent of Judges Al-Khasawneh, Xue, Donoghe and Cot who addressed in particular the legal limits of interpretation proceedings and the room they leave for provisional measures.

2   Analysis of the decision
a   The creation of a demilitarized zone

This is not the place to go into the well-founded criticism of the dissenters regarding the establishment of a provisional demilitarized zone, which they all consider as going too far because it includes undisputed territory of both parties and orders the parties to withdraw troops or personnel from their own territory, in particular as the Court does not give detailed reasons for this decision. This is, in fact, an unprecedented decision of the Court which in former cases of territorial disputes has always confined measures ordering the withdrawal of military personnel to the "disputed territories" and never gone beyond such areas.[16] In the present context the question is, however, rather whether the creation of a provisional demilitarized zone maintains the

---

15   Ibid. para. 69, paragraph B (4) of the operative clause.
16   *Certain Activities carried out by Nicaragua in the Border Area (Costa Rica v. Nicaragua), Provisional Measures, Order of 8 March 2011*, para. 86; *Land and Maritime Boundary between Cameroon and Nigeria (Cameroon v. Nigeria), Provisional Measures, Order of 15 March 1996*, ICJ Reports 1996 (I), pp. 24–25, para. 49; *Frontier Dispute (Burkina Faso/Republic of Mali), Provisional Measures, Order of 10 January 1986*, ICJ Reports 1986, pp. 11–12, para. 31; cf. Order of 2011, *Temple of Preah Vihear case* (fn. 12), D.O Judge Xue; M. Barnett, Cambodia v. Thailand: A Case Study on the Use of Provisional Measures to Protect Human Rights in International Border Disputes, Brooklyn Journal of International Law 38 (2012); 269–303.

necessary link to the rights at stake in the merits, here the interpretation of the 1962 judgment, a question that has to be answered in the negative. The measures imposed go far beyond the preservation of rights to be adjudged in the interpretation proceeding, since there is no dispute/contestation concerning the interpretation of the sovereignty over the Temple itself, and consequently no "rights" needed to be preserved pending a decision on the interpretation request. The same is true for the areas within the territory of each Party that fall within the provisional demilitarized zone; they are not in dispute in the Art. 60 proceeding. Therefore, the Court should have limited its order to the obligation addressed to both parties to restrain from military activity in the "disputed area",[17] because the creation of a provisional demilitarized zone is not linked in any way to the interpretation to be given to the 1962 Judgment. Even if the order of the Court would have been delivered in an Art. 36 proceeding and not in an Art. 60 proceeding, the interference into the exercise of sovereignty over undisputed territory would raise at least concern. But in such situation it could be argued that this far reaching measure would be necessary to prevent further clashes in the area and that therefore the temporal restriction of sovereign rights was justifiable when weighed against loss of life or injuries to persons or cultural heritage. As, however, in this case the dispute is not a dispute in the sense of Art. 36 of the Statute, but a "contestation" relating to the interpretation of a judgment that had already more than 50 years ago settled the original dispute regarding the sovereignty over the Temple, the measure adopted seems excessive from a legal point of view:[18] it does neither relate to the question of the duration of the obligations resulting from the 1962 judgment, nor to the question of the status of the frontier line and also not the definition of the meaning of the words "vicinity on Cambodian territory".

A.C. Traviss, Temple of Preah Vihear: Lessons on Provisional Measures, Chicago Journal of International Law 13 (2012), 317–344, 336.

17 The reference to the "disputed area" is the usual approach of the Court in indicating provisional measures in border disputes, cf. *Certain Activities carried out by Nicaragua in the Border Area (Costa Rica v. Nicaragua), Provisional Measures, Order of 8 March 2011*, para. 86; *Land and Maritime Boundary between Cameroon and Nigeria (Cameroon v. Nigeria), Provisional Measures, Order of 15 March 1996*, ICJ Reports 1996 (I), pp. 24–25, para. 49; *Frontier Dispute (Burkina Faso/Republic of Mali), Provisional Measures, Order of 10 January 1986*, ICJ Reports 1986, pp. 11–12, para. 31.

18 Traviss, (fn. 16) 334.

b   The non-aggravation measures

The same is true with regard to the other controversial measure indicated, which is closely linked to the previous one, ordering the Parties to refrain from any action which might aggravate or extend the dispute. In fact, the Court refers in this context to its previous cases indicating non-aggravation measures which, however, all related to a dispute under Art. 36 of the Statute, not a dispute/contestation in Art. 60 proceedings. This situation does therefore support the impression that in the present case the provisional measures were rather linked to the aggravation or revival of the old conflict decided definitely by the underlying judgment or a new conflict between the parties which, however, the Court cannot decide for lack of jurisdiction than to the dispute/contestation concerning the scope of the judgment of 1962. Judge Donoghue brought this concern to the point in stating that "the conduct of the Parties in the border region would not "aggravate" the narrow and limited dispute about the meaning or scope of the words in a judgment".[19] This raises the question whether a non-aggravation provisional order may at all be in place in interpretation proceedings; in any case, if at all imaginable, it would be limited to very special cases. In the case at hand, the interpretation of the 1962 judgment does not justify these measures which instead relate to a new dispute or the revival of the original dispute between the parties. The Court cannot decide the latter because of the lack of a jurisdictional basis. As in the *Avena* case, the Court was confronted with a situation involving military force and endangering human lives. Therefore it could not be expected to pass this fact in silence; it has thus to be asked whether there are arguments justifying the decision of the Court in legal, not only ethical terms.

v   Tentative Justification of the Court's Decisions

1   *The Extent of the Power of the Court to Issue Provisional Measures*

The orders of the Court in the *Avena* and the *Temple* case have been supported by the majority of the Court which undoubtedly was aware of the sweeping legal basis on which the orders relied. This has explicitly been praised as a reassuring step because the Court used its competence in an anticipatory way to *prevent* violent acts and not only in a conservatory manner to *preserve* the rights of the parties, and to protect cultural diversity and thus international

---

19   Order of 2011 (fn. 12), para. 26 of the dissenting opinion Judge Donoghue.

law.[20] It has also been understood as a re-enforcement of human rights by the ICJ, an aspect gaining increasing relevance also before the Court.[21] And, in fact, in the *Temple* case, this strategy was successful; both parties stated their will to comply with the measures and withdrew their troops so that the provisional measures did in fact prevent further violence thereby supporting regional stability and human rights.[22] In the *Avena* case, however, the provisional measures were not complied with. But it may be regarded as comforting that the Court did at least make an attempt to prevent the execution of the death sentence and to remind the party concerned once more of its obligations. This may be deemed to be justified simply because it may be successful.

In legal terms this state of affairs raises the question whether there is in fact "future potential for the ICJ in weighing competing international principles with an international bias that can be respected and not feared",[23] e.g. that the end justifies the means and whether, if it does, this kind of activism of the Court may not only interfere with the sovereign rights of the states concerned, but also with the powers and function of the Security Council.

This question is all the more relevant as the cases commented upon are not isolated, but only particularly relevant and recent examples. They have to be seen in context with those cases where the Court indicated provisional measures in Art. 36 proceedings, although it was rather clear that it lacked jurisdiction to decide the case on the merits[24] or where it found that it lacked *prima*

---

[20] Order of 2011 (fn. 12), S.O. Trindade, paras 64/65 and para. 117; cf. P. D'Argent, Juge ou policier? Les mesures conservatoires dans l'Affaire du *Temple de Préah Vihéar*, AFDI 2011, 147–163, 162.

[21] Barnett, (fn. 16).; A. Zimmermann, Human Rights Treaty Bodies and the Jurisdiction of the International Court of Justice, The Law and Practice of International Courts and Tribunals 12 (2013), 5–29.

[22] K. Shulman, *The case Concerning the Temple of Preah Vihear (Cambodia v. Thailand):* The ICJ Orders Sweeping Provisional Measures To Prevent Armed Conflict at the Expense of Sovereignty, Tulane Journal of International and Comparative Law, 20 (2012), 555–570, p. 569/70.

[23] Shulman, (fn. 22) p. 570.

[24] *Armed Activities on the Territory of the Congo (New Application: 2002) (Democratic Republic of the Congo v. Rwanda)*, Provisional Measures, ICJ Reports 2002, 219; *Application of the International Convention on the Elimination of All Forms of Racial Discrimination (Georgia v. Russia)*, Provisional Measures, ICJ Reports 2008, 353. Similar developments may be observed in other courts, too: cf. ITLOS, *M/V "Louisa" Case (St. Vincent and the Grenadine v. Kingdom of Spain)*, Order on provisional measures of 23 December 2010 and judgment dismissing the case for lack of jurisdiction of 28 May 2013. In this case provisional measures were not granted, however, the problem under consideration was approached in the separate and dissenting votes.

facie jurisdiction, but nevertheless inserted in its order a statement calling on the parties to respect their obligations under international law and not to aggravate the dispute,[25] or where it did indicate provisional measures, and additionally explicitly reminded the parties of their obligations under international law.[26] These precedents have to be weighed against those cases where the Court declined to adopt general provisional measures concerning the non-aggravation of the dispute because there was no reason to adopt concrete interim measures for the preservation of the rights at stake[27] or where it dismissed a new request for provisional measures because those already indicated were still in force since the merits of the case were not yet decided.[28]

All these cases reflect the attempt of states to involve the Court in situations where the requesting state needs some support in order to have the defendant state comply with the Court's decision, judgment or previous provisional measures, or where the Court is used as a forum to publicly advance the state's po-

---

25 *Legality of the Use of Force (Yugoslavia v. Belgium)* (*and other NATO States*), Provisional Measures, ICJ Reports 1999, 124 et seq., 140, para. 49.
26 *Nuclear Tests case*, ICJ Reports 1973, 99, 106; *Frontier Dispute case (Burkina Faso /Mali)*, ICJ Reports 1986, 3, 9, 11; *Bosnian Genocide case*, ICJ Reports 1993, 3, 23/24; and 349/350; *Land and Maritime Boundary case (Cameroon v. Nigeria)*, ICJ Reports 1996, 13, 22–24; *Armed Activities case (DRC v. Uganda)*, ICJ Reports 2000, 11, 129; *Bosnian Genocide case*, Provisional Measures, ICJ Reports 1993, 24; *Application of the Convention on the Eliminations of all Forms of Racial Discrimination*, Provisional Measures, ICJ Reports 2008, 353.
27 *Pulp Mills case (Argentina v. Uruguay)*, ICJ Reports 2007, 3, 16.
28 *Bosnian Genocide case*, ICJ Reports 1993, 325, 349. In this context reference has to be made to the most recent case where "a modification" of the formerly indicated provisional measures was requested by both parties (*Certain Activities Carried Out by Nicaragua in the Border Area (Cost Rica v. Nicaragua)* and *Construction of a Road in Costa Rica along the San Juan River (Nicaragua v. Costa Rica)*, both cases were joined by an Order of 17 April 2013). In this case the Court found with regard to the request of Costa Rica and the one of Nicaragua that in fact there was a change in the situation underlying the provisional measures of 8 March 2011, but it could not find that this change caused a risk of irreparable harm to the rights at stake. Nevertheless, the Court noted that "the presence of organized groups of Nicaraguan nationals in the disputed area carries the risk of incidents which might aggravate the present dispute (para. 37) and thus reaffirmed the measures indicated in its Order of 8 March 2011 concerning the requirement that the Parties "shall refrain from any action which might aggravate or extend the dispute before the Court or make it more difficult to resolve" (para. 38). In this case the Court did not indicate new provisional measures, but explicitly reaffirmed in the operative part of the Order the non-aggravation measures which were, however, of an exhortative character constituting thus no problem with regard to sovereign rights of the parties.

sition in a disputed situation, mostly involving the use of force.[29] There are good reasons – from a humanitarian point of view – to support action of the Court in such cases which benefit on the prestige of the Court and which are based on legal reasoning and thus not dependent on political tensions which govern the actions of the Security Council. As, however, the competence of the Court still today requires the consent of the states parties to a case it has to be examined whether the Court is at all – in Art. 36 and more so in Art. 60 proceedings – justified to indicate *any* provisional measures. The core question, which was more evident in the *Temple* case than in the *Avena* case, concerns the issue whether the Court may order measures aimed at preventing the aggravation of the dispute. And whether such measures may only be indicated in addition to other concrete measures relating to the rights at stake or also independently from such other measures, i.e. measures aimed merely at the non-aggravation of the dispute in order to prevent or terminate use of force between the parties not manifestly linked to the case at hand.

2 Additional Provisional Measures Concerning the Non-aggravation of the Dispute

Until the *Pulp Mills* case the practice of the Court clearly supports the view that the Court felt justified to indicate provisional measures with a view to preventing the aggravation or extension of the dispute.[30] In its early case law,[31] the Court besides granting specific provisional measures often included an indication that the parties should ensure that no action of any kind is taken which might aggravate or extend the dispute submitted to the Court.[32] Such indication appeared to be a standard clause additional to specific provisional measures relating strictly to the preservation of the rights to be adjudged on the merits. In the *Aegean Sea Continental Shelf case*,[33] the question was raised whether the Court was empowered to indicate provisional measures for the sole purpose of preventing the aggravation of the dispute. As the Court held

---

29 Cf. K. Oellers-Frahm, Article 41, in The Statute of the International Court of Justice – A Commentary (fn. 7), 1056, MN 69.
30 *Land and Maritime Boundary case, (Cameroon v. Nigeria)*, ICJ Reports 1996, 22/23.
31 Cf. e.g. *Anglo-Iranian Oil Co. Case (United Kingdom v. Iran)* Provisional Measures, ICJ Reports 1951, 89, 93; *Fisheries Jurisdiction (United Kingdom v. Ireland)*, Interim Protection, ICJ Reports 1972, 12, 17; *Nuclear Tests (Australia v. France)*, Interim Protection, ICJ Reports 1973, 99, 106.
32 Cf. P. Palchetti, The Power of the International Court of Justice to Indicate Provisional Measures to Prevent the Aggravation of a Dispute, Leiden Journal of International Law 21 (2008), 623–642.
33 *Aegean Sea Continental Shelf (Greece v. Turkey)*, Interim Protection, ICJ Reports 1976, 3, 13.

that there was no risk of aggravation, this question was not answered. Ten years later, however, in the *Frontier Dispute case (Burkina Faso/Mali)* which related to the delimitation of the boundary between the two states a Chamber of the Court held that "independently of the requests submitted by the Parties for the indication of provisional measures, the Court or, accordingly, the chamber possesses by virtue of Art. 41 of the Statute the power to indicate provisional measures with a view to preventing the aggravation or extension of the dispute whenever it considers that circumstances so require".[34] This approach was followed by the full Court in the *Land and Maritime Boundary between Cameroon and Nigeria case*[35] and in the *Armed Activities case*.[36] In these cases the non-aggravation measures were additional to specific measures although there were already voices supporting that the indication of provisional measures "in general terms of an exhortation to all parties not to aggravate or extend the dispute ... does not in any way depend upon the indication of other, more specific provisional measures."[37] The measures concerning non-aggravation or recalling the prohibition of the use of force may thus be interpreted as a mere reminder of obligations binding upon the parties under general international law and existing independently of any case before the Court. Such general "exhortation" does thus not imply any interference with the sovereignty of the states concerned and does therefore not raise concern with a view to the consent based jurisdiction of the Court. As, moreover, at this time it was not even generally recognized that interim measures had binding force,[38] the general reminder to refrain from any measures that might aggravate or extent the dispute together with or independent from particular measures preserving the rights at stake may be supported with good reasons. Although the concern remains that it construes Art. 41 Statute in the sense of giving the Court a general prevention power which in the system of the United Nations is rather attributed to the Security Council.[39]

---

34   ICJ Reports 1986, 3, 9.

35   *Land and Maritime Boundary case (Cameroon v. Nigeria)*, Provisional Measures, ICJ Reports 1996, 13, 22.

36   *Armed Activities in the Congo (DRC v. Uganda)*, Provisional Measures, ICJ Reports 2000, 111, 128.

37   Diss. Op. of Judge Bedjaoui, *Aerial Incident at Lockerbie (Libyan Arab Jamahiriya v. United States of America)*, Provisional Measures, ICJ Reports 1992, 143, 158.

38   This question was decided by the Court in the judgment on the merits in the *LaGrand case (Germany v. United States of America)*, ICJ Reports 2001, 466, 505, para. 107.

39   J. Sztucki, Case Concerning Land and Maritime Boundary (Cameroon v. Nicaragua), Provisional Measures, Order of 15 March 1996, Leiden Journal of International Law Law 10 (1997), 341–358, 357–358.

3   Independent Non-aggravation Measures

The question of indicating non-aggravation measures independently from particular preservation measures which had been argued in theoretical terms because in practice such measures had always been accompanied by concrete preservation measures became decisive in 2007, when the scene had changed in so far as the binding character of provisional measures was no longer controversial. In the *Pulp Mills* case[40] the Court declined to indicate provisional measures aiming merely at the non-aggravation of the dispute. As the Court dismissed the request for specific measures requested by Uruguay because it found that there was no risk of irreparable prejudice to the rights at stake, the Court refrained from granting the requested measures concerning non-aggravation of the dispute arguing that in all cases where non-aggravation measures had been indicated also other measures were ordered which aimed at preventing irreparable harm. The Court did not discuss this matter in depth but seems to suggest that non-aggravation measures can be granted only where the circumstances of the case require the indication of measures aimed at preventing irreparable harm to the disputed rights of the parties, thus only in addition to specific measures.[41] The Court thus gave – voluntarily? – raise to a vivid discussion which it easily could have avoided by indicating specific provisional measures what would have been in that case and would in general be possible without causing particular problems. In particular Judge Buergenthal criticized this decision of the Court as too restrictive an interpretation of Art. 41. He referred to situations "in which one party to the case resorts to extrajudicial coercive measures, unrelated to the subject matter in dispute, that aggravate the dispute by seeking to undermine or interfere with the rights of the other party ...",[42] and which under the findings of the Court in the *Pulp Mills case* could not adequately be addressed. According to Judge Buergenthal interim protection has to be granted also where "the challenged actions are having a serious adverse effect on the ability of the party seeking the provisional measures to fully protect its rights in the judicial proceedings".[43]

---

40   *Pulp Mills on the River Uruguay (Argentina v. Uruguay)*, Provisional Measures, ICJ Reports 2001, 3.
41   Palchetti, (fn. 32), 636.
42   *Pulp Mills case*, (fn. 40), Declaration Judge Buergenthal, p. 24, para. 11.
43   Ibid.

4   Legal Basis for Independent Non-aggravation Measures

In fact it would be difficult to require the Court to close its eyes – and its mouth – in situations involving use or threat of use of armed force between the parties to a case pending before it. It is thus not surprising that several explanations have been offered to justify the power of the Court to issue independent non-aggravation measures.

a) A first explanation starts directly from the terms of Art. 41 of the Statute.[44] According to its English version this provision empowers the Court "to indicate ... *any* (emphasis added) provisional measure" and the Rules of Procedure explicitly provide that the Court may indicate measures that are in whole or in part other than those requested (Art. 75, para. 2 of the Rules) and moreover empower the Court to indicate provisional measures even *proprio motu* (Art. 75, para. 1 of the Rules). This would support the view that also independent non-aggravation measures are covered by these provisions. This argument suffers, however, from the fact that it regards the provisions of the Rules of Procedure independently from Art. 41 of the Statute, and Art. 41 of the Statute independently from its context. Art. 41 of the Statute refers to the preservation of "the respective rights of either party"[45] and these rights are not *any* rights of the parties including those existing under general international law, but only the rights in dispute in the concrete case which, according to Art. 40 of the Statute have to be indicated in the application. Interim protection is one of the "incidental proceedings" regulated in more detail in Section D of the Rules of Court and accordingly the discretion left to the Court in indicating provisional measures has always to be assessed under this premise. Accordingly, the power of the Court under Art. 41 of the Statute and Art. 75, para. 1 and 2 of the Rules is limited to the preservation of the rights of either party in the case at stake. This is consistent with the jurisprudence of the Court which always refers to an aggravation of the "dispute" which has to be distinguished from an aggravation of the "relations between the parties" or the "aggravation of the overall situation". This would not prevent the Court from including a mere reminder of the general obligations under international law in the reasoning, not the operative clause, of a decision. Particular measures, however, concerning the non-aggravation of a dispute, such as withdrawal of troops or the creation of a demilitarized zone depend upon the particular circumstances of the case and must relate to the rights in dispute, because the Rules of Procedure cannot be understood as going further than the rights conferred upon the Court in Art. 41 of the

---

44   P. D'Argent, (fn. 20), 161.
45   P. D'Argent, (fn. 20), 161 et seq.

Statute; and Art. 41 of the Statute only addresses an incidental proceeding related to a particular case. The limitation of the Court's power results from the fact that consent to the Court's jurisdiction is still the indispensible requirement for any action of the Court. Understanding Art. 75, para. 1 and 2 of the Rules as empowering the Court to issue any measures including independent non-aggravation measures would lead to the result that the powers of the Court in the stage of a procedure for the indication of provisional measures are broader than in the stage of deciding on the merits of the case since here the Court can only decide on the concrete rights in dispute. This consequence is hardly compatible with the principles of international jurisdiction and the provisions of the Statute of the ICJ. Moreover, raises concern with regard to the admissibility of non-aggravation measures issued in addition to, not independent of, particular measures preserving the rights at stake. Strict legal reasoning therefore leads to the result that general non-aggravation measures, not strictly linked to the rights at stake, are not justified at all, because they exceed the Court's powers.

b) Another justification starting also from the terms of Art. 41 of the Statute argues that, if *prima facie* jurisdiction is found to exist, the action of the Court depends essentially from a principle of necessity resulting from the Court's perception of the imminent irreparable damage to the rights at stake.[46] According to this opinion the fact that there is a risk or even already use of armed violence is evidence in the sense that there are nearly no rights not at risk of being prejudiced; the rights at stake in the case are thus preserved by measures aiming primarily at reducing the tension between the parties and preventing the deterioration of their relations what means that independent non-aggravation measures are within the Art. 41 power of the Court. But also this approach suffers, as the first one considered above, from the fact that interim protection is an incidental procedure that is aimed at guaranteeing the efficiency of the final judgment with the consequence that the Court's powers are defined and limited by its jurisdiction to decide the case. Any act interfering with the sovereign rights of the parties not in dispute in the merits would be *ultra vires* and would support the view that non-aggravation measures must be linked to the subject-matter of the case.

c) Finally, there is third approach to justify independent non-aggravation measures which does not, however, explicitly refer to Art. 41 of the Statute but rather recalls the origins of the institute of interim protection which found a first expression in Art. XVIII of the Convention for the Establishment of a Cen-

---

46   Ibid.

tral American Court of Justice[47] which provided: "From the moment in which any suit is instituted against any one or more governments up to that in which a final decision has been pronounced, the court may at the solicitation of any one of the Parties fix the situation in which the contending Parties must remain, to the end that the difficulty shall not be aggravated and that things shall be conserved in *statu quo* pending a final decision". This provision clearly focuses on the non-aggravation aspect which may be considered as one of the reasons, or even a general principle, of interim protection: as judicial settlement of disputes serves the maintenance of peace, the aggravation of the situation pending the procedure may become a threat to peace and has to be prevented. This line of argument may also be applied to the ICJ although Art. 41 of the Statute seems to be more restrictive than Art. XVIII of the 1907 Washington Convention in that it aims explicitly at the preservation of the rights at stake on the merits. But as it is widely accepted that the power to indicate provisional measures of protection exists irrespective of an explicit provision as an implied power of international courts and tribunals,[48] the indication of non-aggravation measures may be based on this general power which serves not only the preservation of the rights at stake, but also the good and orderly administration of justice,[49] and which is not set aside by Art. 41 of the Statute. Thus, the power of the Court to grant interim protection does not only result from Art. 41 of the Statute but is a "principle universally accepted by international tribunals ... to the effect that the parties to a case must abstain from any measure capable of exercising a prejudicial effect in regard to the execution of the decision to be given and, in general, not allow any step of any kind to be taken which might aggravate or extend the dispute".[50]

This approach seems in fact to support the power of the Court to issue independent non-aggravation measures. This does not, however, answer the question as to the kind of non-aggravation measures which may be issued by the Court, a question that is relevant in particular with a view to the fact that provisional measures are binding upon the parties and thus admissible only in so far as the parties consented to the Court's jurisdiction. If i.e. the Court indicates particular non-aggravation measures such as in the *Temple* case the creation of a demilitarized zone (even without comprising uncontroversial

---

47 Convention of 20 December 1907, AJIL 2 (Suppl. 1908), 238; cf. also Oellers-Frahm, Art. 41 ICJ Statute (fn. 7), 1029.
48 Oellers-Frahm, Art: 41, (fn. 7), 1034, MN 17 with bibliographical indications.
49 Cf. *Pulp Mills* case (fn. 40), Decl. Judge Buergenthal, 22/23, para. 6.
50 *Electricity Company of Sofia and Bulgaria*, Order of 5 December 1939, P.C.I.J. Series A/B, No. 79, 199.

sovereign territory of one or both parties) its powers would be overstepped if such measure would not be linked to a right in dispute in the merits. If the Court restricts such non-aggravation measures however to a general exhortation not to aggravate the dispute and to refrain from use of force it would not act *ultra vires* because such measures would not interfere with the sovereign rights of the parties which in any case and independently from any proceedings before any court are obliged to refrain from the use of force. Such measures would therefore seem to be justifiable as a measure for guaranteeing the orderly exercise of the judicial function; nevertheless there remains some concern because such action of the Court would clearly be in collision with the function of the Security Council because it would empower the Court to act, unrelated to the dispute at stake, as an organ for the maintenance of peace and security.

This concern increases when considering the power of the Court in interpretation proceedings. Although the Court's jurisdiction is limited in Art. 60 proceedings to the mere interpretation of the underlying judgment without any power to touch upon the judgment as such, the necessity of maintaining the orderly exercise of the judicial function is the same as in Art. 36 cases so that non-aggravation measures would be as justified as in Art. 36 proceedings. The fact, however, that in Art. 60 proceedings the jurisdiction of the Court is uncontroversial would open a way to request the Court to issue non-aggravation measures of a general kind, i.e. to act as an organ of maintenance of peace, not as a judicial organ. This situation is in fact problematic because the Court could be used under the cover of an interpretation request to issue provisional non-aggravation measures not at all linked to the case as such, the interpretation request, but solely to a peace-threatening situation existing between the parties. This concern gives much support to the Court's reasoning in the *Pulp Mills* case as an attempt to draw a balance between the Court's competence to decide a case and its powers to issue provisional measures: where the dispute submitted to the Court, i.e. the rights or obligations to be adjudged by the Court are not exposed to an imminent and irreparable damage there is no room for any provisional measures what so ever, because interim protection relates to the dispute at stake only. With a view to interim protection as a tool to secure the orderly function of the administration of justice the Court would, however, be empowered to urge the parties – in an Order dismissing concrete provisional measures for lack of imminent and irreparable damage – to respect their general international obligations, in particular the prohibition of use of force, however rather in the reasons to its decision than in the operative part of the Order. In any case such non-aggravation "measures" cannot order the parties to take or refrain from any steps interfering with their sovereign rights unless such measures are linked to the merits of the case.

VI   Concluding Remarks

The above considerations lead to the result that the Court does have the power to issue non-aggravation measures orders, albeit only if the aggravation of the situation has an impact on the case at stake because interim protection is merely an incidental phase in a dispute which defines the jurisdiction of the Court. Therefore, the decision of the Court in the provisional measures stage cannot affect rights or obligations of the parties which are not at stake in the merits. This does not mean that the Court could not issue non-aggravation measures, together with or independent from particular measures as long as such measures do not interfere with sovereign rights of the parties not in dispute in the case. Consequently, the Court would only be empowered to remind the parties of their general obligations under international law if the extrajudicial measures of one or both parties have an adverse effect on the full protection of the rights in the case. In Art. 36 cases the fact that the Court has to find at least *prima facie* in favor of its jurisdiction on the merits can be considered as constituting a bar to non-aggravation measures unrelated to the pending proceedings, a hurdle that is not present in interpretation cases. Therefore, and with a view to the fact that the dispute in Art. 60 proceedings is not related to disputed rights and obligations of the parties, but to the meaning and scope of a judgment which has already settled the dispute, the necessity of non-aggravation measures has to be submitted to an even stricter scrutiny and in principle would justify no more than a standard exhortation to the parties to respect their international law obligations.

The decision of the Court in the *Pulp Mills* case denying the power to issue independent non-aggravation measures has thus the advantage of requiring a clear relationship between non-aggravation measures and the pending dispute. This may be regarded as a confidence building measure to states in the sense that the Court will not exceed its powers. There is, on the other side, no question that the Court will always be able to issue particular provisional measures if it considers that non-aggravation measures should be issued so that a requirement of this kind serves rather as a fig leaf to demonstrate the link between non-aggravation measures and the dispute.

Under the aspect of the orderly administration of justice, which the Court has to protect, independent non-aggravation measures can be indicated. Such measures have however to keep within the framework of the Court's jurisdiction on the merits which means that in general only a general exhortation in the reasoning of the order rather than the operative part would be acceptable. Only where the subject-matter of the dispute is affected by the measures of the parties, provisional non-aggravation measures ordering concrete action of the parties and thus affecting their sovereign rights are admissible. In view of these parameters, the Court exceeded its jurisdiction in the *Temple* case where only a general exhortation would have been within the limits of the Court's jurisdiction.

As already mentioned, such general exhortation touches upon the function of the Security Council, however, as long as there is no interference with sovereign rights of the parties, the standing and authority that the Court enjoys meanwhile allows it to issue such admonition. The Court as an organ of the UN serving the peaceful settlement of disputes cannot be expected to remain silent when the peaceful relations between the parties in the pending case are endangered. Such "activism" of the Court may be seen, referring to the words of Judge Koroma in his declaration appended to the Order in the *Temple of Preah Vihear case*, "as an effort to prevent further armed conflict between the two Parties while preserving the sovereign rights of each of them".[51] The request for provisional measures in interpretation proceedings thus opens a way for the Court to use its prestige and authority at least to *remind* the parties of their respective obligations. Measures going beyond such general reminder are justified only when linked to the rights in dispute, a situation that seems rather unrealistic in interpretation proceedings. Nevertheless, the use of interpretation proceedings combined with a request for provisional measures extends the power of the Court to react to measures threatening the peace between the parties and to at least urge them to refrain from any aggravating measures. It is the Court which has to find the balance between such extensive, but not abusive recourse, to provisional protection in order not to overstretch the flexibility of an instrument that was clearly not aimed at the use increasingly made thereof. This could lead undermine the authority of the Court as well as the acceptability of its decisions.

As to the overlap of such action with the functions of the Security Council, it may be stated that although the Security Council has a monopoly with regard to the use of force, all organs of the United Nations are involved in the maintenance of international peace and security, especially the ICJ as the principal judicial organ of the Organization. Consequently, any appeal of the ICJ to states parties in a proceeding to refrain from aggravating a dispute and any use of the ICJ enabling it to issue such appeal – since the Court cannot act on its

---

51   Order of 2011, (fn. 12), Decl. Judge Koroma, para. 4.

own initiative, but only if seized by a state – are admissible as long as the Court remains within the limits of the jurisdiction transferred upon it. The fact that institutions such as provisional measures and interpretation proceedings are used in a broader way than originally expected and intended, reflects the standing that the Court has gained in the international community and the confidence in its action. It is up to the Court to benefit from this situation in a balanced way while contributing to upholding and implementing the most basic values of mankind, namely peace and security, while keeping in mind that it is is still and will remain without significant power with regard to compliance with its decisions, which lies with the States, as was demonstrated, unfortunately again in a negative sense, in the *Avena* Case.

CHAPTER 8

TWAILing the Bakassi Case: Colonialist Logic, Self-Determining Agents and the Concept of Legitimate Statehood in Our Time

Obiora Chinedu Okafor and Chikeziri Igwe

> ... to contend that an international personality has disappeared by consent is *verging on fraud*.[1]

I   Introduction

On the 10th of October 2002, the International Court of Justice (ICJ) issued its now famous (and certainly controversial) decision in the so-called *Bakassi case*.[2] Focusing on the aspects of the case that concern sovereignty over the oil-rich Bakassi Peninsula (the aspect of the case that is most germane to this chapter), the facts of the Bakassi case in summary form, are that following a series of long-standing, low-intensity and localized conflicts in some spots along its border with Nigeria (mostly in the Lake Chad and Bakassi Peninsula regions), Cameroon brought the matter before the ICJ.

Cameroon's prayer to the court was, inter alia, to hold that it had sovereignty over the oil rich Bakassi Peninsula. Cameroon's main argument in this regard was that it possessed sovereignty over this Peninsula because, inter alia, that:

a. through the Anglo-German Demarcation Agreement of 12 April 1913, that peninsula had been ceded by Britain to the Germans (its then colonial power)
b. the Thomson/Marchand Declaration confirmed by the Exchange of Letters of 9 January 1931 further evidenced this transfer of sovereignty

---

1   See *Case Concerning the Land and Maritime Boundary between Cameroon and Nigeria* (Cameroon v. Nigeria: Equatorial Guinea intervening), *Judgment*, (2002) ICJ Reports 303 (hereinafter "the Bakassi case), Separate Opinion of Judge Ranjeva, at paragraph 3 (emphasis supplied).
2   See the Bakassi case, ibid.

c. since the 1960s, Nigeria had acknowledged Cameroon's title to the Bakassi Peninsula
d. the city states of Old Calabar (in present-day Nigeria) which had exercised control over the Bakassi Peninsula long before the advent of the British in the area and whose Kings and Chiefs had concluded the Treaty of Protection of 10 September 1884 with Britain were not really states properly so-called, and that as such the agreement they had signed with Britain could not really be treated as a treaty, and especially since Britain did not regard that agreement as such.

For its own part, Nigeria disputed the soundness of each of these grounds, especially the contention that the city states of Old Calabar lacked international legal personality before they were colonized by Britain, and argued that, in any case, the Kings and Chiefs of Old Calabar had exercised control over this territory since precolonial times, and that Nigeria's historical consolidation of sovereignty over the area over a very long time grounded its claim to sovereignty over the area.

With regard to the specific question of sovereignty over the Bakassi Peninsula, the aspect on which this chapter mainly focuses, a majority of the ICJ found for Cameroon and ordered Nigeria to hand over the territory to Cameroon forthwith. The court applied the Anglo-German Demarcation Agreement of 12 April 1913 (in which Britain had purported to cede the Bakassi Peninsula), while refusing to apply the plain words of the Treaty of Protection of 10 September 1884 between the Kings and Chiefs of Old Calabar and Britain (which did not authorize Britain to cede the territory to another power). The court also held that over the years, Nigeria had consistently acknowledged Cameroon's sovereignty over the area. More importantly for the purposes of this chapter, though, the majority decision embraced Cameroon's arguments regarding the non-applicability of this Treaty of Protection between Old Calabar and Britain, on the basis that the Kingdoms of Old Calabar could not properly be regarded as states in international law that were capable of entering into treaties. The majority of the court also held that, in any case, and contrary to its plain words, that treaty was in reality and at best a treaty of cession of all of Old Calabar's territories to Britain, and was not in fact a treaty of protection.[3]

However, this last aspect of the overall rationale for the court's decision (i.e. the aspect concerned with the twin issues of the statehood of Old Calabar and the status of its treaty with Britain) was challenged by the strong objections on that specific point that was raised by five of the sixteen judges who sat on the case. The five who raised this kind of objection were Judges Ranjeva, Al-Kha-

---

3 See the Bakassi case, paragraphs 209–216.

sawneh, Rezek, Ajibola (ad hoc), and Koroma (in whose honor this book was written). Instructively, nestled among these five objectors were two judges who voted with the majority of the court on the overall question of the entitlement of Cameroon to sovereignty over the Bakassi Peninsula (namely Justices Ranjeva and Al-Khasawneh). All of the judges who dissented on the present point argued forcefully that, as Judge Al-Khasawneh put it in his separate opinion:

> ... the Court chose, quite unnecessarily, to revert to the question of the validity of the 1913 Agreement between Great Britain and Germany under which the former ceded the entire territory of the Kings and Chiefs of Calabar ... to Germany without the consent of those Kings and Chiefs, notwithstanding that Great Britain had entered earlier into a Treaty of Protection with them in 1884 under which ... Her Majesty would extend Her 'favour and protection' to them.[4]

In effect, these dissenters accused the majority of the court of gratuitously engaging in a form of colonialist logic that effectively denied the international legal personality and human agency of the leadership and peoples of the Kingdoms of Old Calabar. It is in part for this reason that three of these judges effectively saw the reasoning of the majority of the court in this case as "fundamentally flawed."[5]

Against this contentious background, the chief objective of this chapter is to "TWAIL" the judgment of the majority of the court in the Bakassi case. By this is meant that the goal here is to subject that judicial decision to a critical third world approaches to international law (i.e. TWAIL) interrogation and analysis.[6] As the broad intent and character of TWAIL analysis has been exhaustively explained elsewhere,[7] that task will not detain us here. Suffice it to emphasize that, as internally diverse as their approaches and conclusions can often be:

---

4   See paragraph 2, Separate Opinion of Judge Al-Khasawneh.
5   See paragraph 3, Separate Opinion of Judge Koroma.
6   See M. Mutua, "What is TWAIL?" (2000) 94 ASIL Proceedings 31.
7   See for example, A. Anghie, *Imperialism, Sovereignty and the Making of International Law* (Cambridge: Cambridge University Press, 2004); M. Mutua, "What is TWAIL?," ibid.; J. Gathii, "Alternative and Critical: The Contribution of Research and Scholarship on Developing Countries to International Legal Theory" (2000) 41 Harvard International Law Journal 263; K. Mickelson, "Rhetoric and Rage: Third World Voices in International Legal Discourse" (1998) 16 Wisconsin International Law Journal 353; O.C. Okafor, "Critical Third World Approaches to International Law (TWAIL): Theory, Methodology, or Both?" (2008) 10 International Community Law Review 37; O.C. Okafor, "Newness, Imperialism, and International Legal Reform in Our Time: A TWAIL Perspective" (2005) 43 Osgoode Hall

TWAIL scholars (or "TWAILers") are solidly united by a shared ethical commitment to the intellectual and practical struggle to expose, reform, or even retrench those features of the international legal system that help create or maintain the generally unequal, unfair, or unjust global order ... a commitment to centre the *rest* rather then merely the *west*, thereby taking the lives and experiences of those who have self-identified as Third World much more seriously than has generally been the case.[8]

More specifically, the chapter's stated goal of TWAILing the Bakassi case will be achieved largely by applying to that decision aspects of a conceptual framework that was worked out in the book *Re-Defining Legitimate Statehood*.[9] It was argued in that book that international law's historical conception of state legitimacy in the third world (and in particular in Africa) has been shaped by four tendencies and attitudes, namely: deference to European peer review; deference to the effectiveness principle; the glorification of empire; and homogenization.[10] Here, we deploy the first three of these ideas in an effort to illuminate the deep structure of, and dominant sensibilities within, the judgment under study. The main questions which preoccupy us are: to what extent was the decision shaped by a colonialist logic that assaults the agency of the people of the Bakassi peninsula? To what extent does the legal reasoning in the decision support or impede the realization of the right to self-determination of the relevant people? What concept of legitimate statehood frames, orients and shapes the decision? And what are its implications?

In order to answer these questions, the analysis conducted in the rest of the chapter is organized into four sections. In section II, the decision is analyzed from the perspective of the tendency in the traditional international law of state legitimacy to excessively privilege and defer to European peer review. Section III is devoted to an analysis of the extent to which the judgment conformed to the traditional international law tendency to treat effectiveness as conferring legitimacy. In section IV, the extent to which the decision at issue succumbs to the tendency within traditional international law to glorify empire is considered. Section V concludes the chapter by considering briefly the

---

Law Journal 171; J. Gathii, O.C. Okafor, and A. Anghie, "Africa and TWAIL" (2012) African Yearbook of International Law (forthcoming); and B. Rajagopal, *International Law from Below* (Cambridge: Cambridge University Press, 2003).

8   See O.C. Okafor, "Newness" ibid, at 176–177.
9   See O.C. Okafor, *Re-Defining Legitimate Statehood: International Law and State Fragmentation in Africa* (The Hague: Martinus Nijhoff, 2000).
10 Ibid.

nature of the concept of legitimate statehood that is revealed by the analysis in the preceding chapters and what it reveals about the tensions and contradictions that too often trouble the "post-colonial mind."

11 Deference to European Peer Review

At least since the onset of dominant international legal positivism in the 19th century,[11] the dominant tendency in traditional international law was for other states, the so-called peers of a would-be or established state, to decide whether or not to admit that state to membership in the family of nations.[12] This determination was not necessarily based on the nature or qualities of the candidate state or of any of its sub-state groups. This is what is meant by the deference of international law to peer review.[13] While this tendency was and remains theoretically capable of accommodating all existing states, the historical reality was that – at least until relatively recently – it was the *ipse dixit* or "say-so" of mostly European States that really counted in this peer-review process.[14] These states assumed this self-appointed role largely due to the sheer fact of their vastly disproportionate power in world affairs at that time. Thus, in reality, over the relevant period of world history, international law's deference to peer review has more or less translated into its deference to European peer review. Thus, the garb of state legitimacy (i.e. legitimate statehood) tended therefore to be adorned on "candidate" states only to the degree of their recognition as such by European states and not necessary because of their objective qualifications as such. It was how these polities were regarded or "viewed" in the European gaze that more or less defined the legitimacy or otherwise of their statehood.

It appears that the legal reasoning adopted by the majority of the ICJ in the Bakassi case was in conformity with this traditionally dominant (though waning)[15] attitude of international law to legitimate statehood. To the majority of the court, it is what may be styled "the European super gaze" that must

---

11   See J. Crawford, *The Creation of States in International Law* (Oxford: Clarendon Press, 1979) at 7–12. See also, N.L. Wallace-Bruce, *Claims to Statehood in International Law* (New York: Carlton Press, 1994)
12   See O.C. Okafor, "After Martyrdom: International Law, Sub-State Groups, and the Construction of Legitimate Statehood in Africa" (2000) 41 Harvard International Law Journal 504, at 515.
13   Ibid.
14   Ibid.
15   O.C. Okafor, "After Martyrdom," *supra* note 12, at 517.

orient and direct any analysis of state legitimacy. It is what the European mind thinks and what the European eye sees that must define the European encounter with the natives of the Third World. The converse was hardly ever true. For example, to the majority of the court, the "internal" British perspective on how it had itself treated with the polities/peoples that it encountered in the Third World was to the court the controlling consideration. The "internal" perspective of the relevant Third World polity/peoples – "the other" – did not figure significantly or matter at all in the majority's analysis. This much can be easily gleaned, inter alia, from the majority's contention that "the choice of a protectorate treaty by Britain [in its dealings with the Kingdom of Old Calabar] was a question of *the preferred manner of rule*,"[16] as well as from the majority's heavy reliance on the fact that "Britain *regarded itself* as administering the territories comprised in the 1884 Treaty, and not just protecting them."[17] Importantly, nowhere in the majority decision are we told by what alchemy that which Britain "regarded itself" as doing when it entered into the relevant treaty should be the determining factor, as opposed to what the parties had explicitly agreed to in writing. Yet, if all that really mattered in the determination of the reality and the construction of the normative position was what the European state (Britain) thought and/or did, or regarded itself as doing, then the "native" polity (Old Calabar) is virtually displaced from view, and is all but erased from normative significance; a result that Judge Ranjeva characterizes as "the disappearance from the international scene of this ancient entity, the Chiefs of Old Calabar."[18] Thus, British behavior is, a la Homi Bhabha, elevated to "a sign taken for wonder."[19]

That this kind of attitude has deeply permeated, colored and refracted the prism through which international law is deciphered is evident from the fact that even while strongly disagreeing with the attempt of the majority of the court to erase the statehood and international legal personality of Old Calabar, Judge Ajibola still felt constrained to hinge the legitimacy of the statehood of Old Calabar on the "say-so" and agency of the British. In his own words, Old Calabar was a state because "the political and legal personality of the Kings and Chiefs of Old Calabar were recognized in the treaty making of the British Crown."[20]

---

16   Paragraph 206. Emphasis supplied.
17   Ibid, at paragraph 207. Emphasis supplied
18   Ibid, at paragraph 2, Separate Opinion.
19   See H. Bhabha, "Signs Taken for Wonders: Questions of Ambivalence and Authority under a Tree Outside Delhi, May 1817" (1985) 12 Critical Inquiry 144.
20   Paragraph 87, Separate Opinion.

More importantly, the majority decision's deployment of the basically colonialist mentality and methodology of viewing state legitimacy exclusively through European eyes, i.e. via the European super-gaze, and therefore of bowing enthusiastically to the traditional international legal tendency to privilege European peer review, was a legal maneuver that was directed at conceptually erasing (and in any case did have the effect of erasing) the statehood of Old Calabar and the agency of its leaders and people. This, the majority judgment did, notwithstanding the obvious and undeniable fact of Old Calabar's real life existence at the time as a state and as a people. This point is easy to illustrate, because the majority judgment is littered with explicit or implied evidence of this kind of colonialist logic. For example, that judgment states rather curiously that "in Sub-Saharan Africa treaties termed 'treaties of protection' were entered into *not with States*, but rather with important indigenous rulers exercising local rule over identifiable areas of territory."[21] Ad hoc Judge Keba Mbaye's intervention on this specific issue is even more telling. In his own words, "when historians speak of African kingdoms or empires what is very often actually meant is groupings of settlements whose inhabitants acknowledged the suzerainty of a particular king or chief."[22] In sum, the point that was made by the majority in this respect was that despite the obvious reality of its existence at the time as an independent kingdom, Old Calabar was not really a state properly so-called largely because Britain and other Europeans did not view and treat with it in that way.[23]

Much to the discredit of the majority decision, no established historians of African statehood testified in this matter or were even cited in the majority decision![24] The closest that the majority came to doing so was in Judge Mbaye's separate opinion in which, while making no reference at all to the work of a single African scholar, let alone historian, he rather preferred to liberally and extensively cite an European lawyer as "one of the greatest experts in African law"![25] It is no wonder then that, at least on this specific point, the majority decision displayed a troubling level of ignorance of the historical record, and

---

21 Paragraph 205.
22 Paragraph 73.
23 Paragraphs 89–93.
24 The rank of experts in this area includes a host of Africans and non-Africans. For example, see A. Boahen, *Topics in West African History* (Essex: Longman, 1986); K.O. Dike, *Trade and Politics in the Niger Delta 1830–1885* (London: Oxford University Press, 1956); C.A. Diop, *Pre-Colonial Black Africa* (Westport, Conn: Lawrence Hill, 1987); and C.M. Warner, "The Political Economy of "Quasi-Statehood" and the Demise of 19th Century African Polities" (1999) 25 Review of International Studies 233.
25 See Paragraphs 74–75, Separate Opinion of Judge Mbaye.

revealed how heavily it's reasoning was shaped by widespread and heavily racialized misconceptions about pre-colonial Black African statehood. Had the majority bothered to study and refer to the actual historical evidence, it would have realized that the very same states that it derided as unworthy of international legal personality held undisputed sway for nearly four centuries over the Coastlines and near hinterland; were paid obeisance and steep taxes by British traders and officials; and that many had exchanged envoys with Portugal, Spain and even Britain, well before the onset of colonialism.[26]

Much to their credit, Judges Rezek, Ranjeva, Al-Khasawneh, Ajibola and Koroma (some of whom – on other grounds – still voted with the majority as to the final outcome) explicitly resisted the majority's colonialist logic. For example, Ad Hoc Judge Ajibola's convincing dissenting argument on this question was that:

> In deciding whether the City States of Old Calabar is an international legal entity, one should look to the nature of the Treaty entered into between Great Britain and the Kings and Chiefs of Old Calabar in 1884. In the first place, this is not the first treaty of this kind signed by the Kings and Chiefs. As I have already mentioned, Great Britain signed altogether 17 treaties of this kind with the Kings and Chiefs of Old Calabar. Secondly, Great Britain referred to it not as a mere agreement, a declaration or exchange of Notes, but as a treaty – 'Treaty with the Kings and Chiefs of Old Calabar, September 10, 1884' (Counter-Memorial of Nigeria, Vol. IV, Ann. NC-M 23, p. 109). How then could Great Britain sign a document, and call it a treaty if it were not so? It would have been described as an 'ordinance' had it been a document involving a colony of Great Britain. There is therefore no doubt that the City States of Old Calabar have international legal personality.[27]

Reinforcing his rejection of the conceptual erasure of the statehood of Old Calabar in the majority decision, he noted further that it should be instructive that Britain actually "dealt with the City States of Old Calabar as such [i.e. as international legal persons] *de facto* and *de jure* from 1884 till the time of independence of Nigeria in 1960."[28] Reminding the court of the *Western Sahara* case,[29] where the notion that a European power could unilaterally appropriate

---

26   See K.O. Dike, *supra* note 24.
27   Paragraph 95, Dissenting Opinion of Judge Ajibola.
28   Paragraph 88.
29   [(1975) ICJ Reports p. 39, paragraph 80

a territory inhabited by indigenous communities was rejected, Judge Rezek registered as strong an objection to the majority's reasoning in the current respect.[30]

Having established that the intended effect of the near-complete deference in the majority decision to the say-so and self-appointed state legitimating authority of European states was the normative erasure and disappearance from the realm of international legal personality of an ancient African state that nevertheless existed in reality (i.e. the state of Old Calabar), as well as the denial of the legitimacy of both its statehood and the agency of its leaders and peoples, it is important at this point to consider the principal use to which this legal maneuver was ultimately put in the majority decision. What was the intended effect of the attempt in the majority decision to erase the statehood of Old Calabar? What result did this achieve in the end? An analysis of the majority decision easily reveals the fact that the intended effect of the normative erasure in the majority decision of Old Calabar's statehood was, in effect, the denial of its capacity to enter into the very kind of international treaties it had in reality entered into. Here was a solution searching for a problem! In the majority's view, not being recognized by European eyes as a state in international law, Old Calabar could not enter into a treaty on an equal basis with Britain, and as such – so the majority implied – the treaty of protection it had signed with Britain should be read as much more like a document outlining the internal organization of a colonial territory, than as an international treaty properly so-called.[31] Ad Hoc Judge Mbaye's argument in this connection captured the essence of the majority decision's logic here. This was that the treaties signed by Britain with Old Calabar were not really treaties because Britain did not intend them to be viewed and treated as treaties, and that such treaties were signed by the dozen and were rarely signed by duly authorized reps of the colonizing state, and were instead signed by merchants and junior military officers.[32] In the course of making this argument, he even went as far as developing a non-established and rather strange distinction between colonial treaties and international treaties.[33]

And this denial of the international legal capacity of Old Calabar to make treaties properly so-called then functioned to justify the puzzling refusal of the court to apply the plain words of the British treaty of protection with Old Calabar, which did not authorize the alienation of the latter's territory by Britain.

---

30 Paragraph 2, Separate Opinion of Judge Rezek.
31 Majority Decision, Paragraphs 203–209.
32 Paragraphs 67–74, Separate Opinion of Judge Mbaye.
33 Ibid.

To paraphrase Judge Ranjeva (who dissented on this point), no satisfactory explanation was provided by the majority as to how it came to be in this case that the operative doctrine of international law became *pacta non servanda sunt*, rather than *pacta sunt servanda*?![34]

However, as the judges who dissented from the majority decision on the set of issues discussed in this section of the chapter noted, the notion that a state that existed in fact, and which treated with Britain and other Europeans in matters of trade and so on, ought not to be recognized as a state in international law because a European power like Britain did not really think it was a state (even though it had in fact treated with it on that basis); and should not be thought of as capable of entering into treaties with other states because Britain and other European states did not think that of the treaties that they signed with it as capable of international legal significance, is supremely illogical and unjust. So is the curious notion that runs through the majority decision that the provisions of such treaties ought *not* be given their plain meaning; that since the British did not say what they meant and mean what they said, the unstated intention of only one party to the agreement, one that was masked in subterfuge, should over-determine and control the meaning to be ascribed to the treaty. As was powerfully articulated by Judge Rezek:

> It is rare to find in classic international law propositions as flimsy – and as inadmissibly so in moral terms – as those which would have it that agreements entered into [in] the past between colonial powers and indigenous communities – organized communities which had been masters of their own territories for centuries and were subject to a recognized authority – are not treaties, because 'native chiefs and tribes are neither states nor International Organizations; and thus possess no treaty-making capacity.'[35]

He went further to note that:

> if the Kings and Chiefs of Old Calabar did not have capacity to enter into an international agreement, if the 1884 Treaty was not a treaty and had no legal force whatsoever, it must be asked what was the basis for Great Britain to assert its authority over those territories, by what mysterious divine right did it set itself up as the protecting State of these areas of Africa.[36]

---

34 See Paragraph 3, Separate Opinion of Judge Ranjeva.
35 Paragraph 1, Separate Opinion of Judge Rezek.
36 Paragraph 3, ibid.

For his own part, Judge Koroma was of view that the Old Calabar was fully capable of entering into treaties properly so-called, and that as such its treaty of protection with Britain ought to have been applied by the court. Thus, in his view, as a consequence of the majority's failure to do so, its:

> ... findings are in clear violation of the express provisions of the 1884 treaty and contrary to the intention of one of the parties to the 1884 treaty – that of the Kings and Chiefs of Old Calabar – and hence to the rule of *pacta sunt servanda*, i.e., the sanctity of treaties. This finding, in violation of the applicable treaty and clearly in breach of the principle of *pacta sunt servanda*, is not only illegal but unjust.[37]

The question of inter-temporal law, which the court also relied on, is also relevant to a full understanding of the set of rationales through which the majority of the court "kow-towed" to European peer-review, attempted the normative erasure of the statehood of Old Calabar, denied the capacity of that ancient state to enter into treaties, and refused to apply the plain words of the treaty of protection that it had entered into with Britain. According to the majority, the rules of international law with which one must asses the behavior of the relevant actors in the nineteenth century and the legality of their actions are not the rules of contemporary international law but those established by the international law that was in force during the relevant period.[38] But as Judge Al-Khasawneh has noted, the obvious fact that "no African State had participated in the formation of the alleged [state] practices," should mean that the said practices ought not to be invoked to justify any European rules that disadvantage these African states.[39] And in Judge Ranjeva's language, "the problem is whether, in this case, the rules of intertemporal law are sufficient to explain and justify the disappearance from the international scene of this ancient entity, the Chiefs of Old Calabar."[40] By what alchemy, it must be asked, did the fact of European states deciding among themselves that the law that governed their own regional inter-relations will apply outside Europe to non-Europeans automatically transform that inter-European law into the law that governed the relations of one (European) party to the colonial encounter with the other (non-European) party? Here again, the European super-gaze trumps rather predictably and tendentiously over the African perspective. And European

---

37   Paragraph 7.
38   See Paragraph 205, Majority Decision.
39   Paragraph 9, Separate Opinion of Judge Al-Khasawneh.
40   Paragraph 2, Separate Opinion of Judge Koroma.

agency is privileged and celebrated while African agency is ignored and even erased in conceptual terms. We are not told why the so-called "applicable law at the time" was not the inter-African rules that governed commerce, diplomatic relations, and external contact with other African and Europeans alike? Why must inter-temporality take on an exclusively European orientation and wear a decidedly European garb? No satisfactory explanation is provided on this point in the majority decision. We are also not told what exactly happened to African agency as this colonialist rendering of a part of the story of British/Old Calabar contact was crafted.

The argument that was developed in this section was that the near-complete deference in the majority decision to the self-appointed role played by many European states as the legitimizers of third world statehood, and the resulting normative erasure and disappearance from the realm of international legal personality of ancient African states that nevertheless existed in reality, led to the incoherent denial in the majority decision of the capacity of that state to enter into treaties, and justified the refusal of the majority of the court to apply the plain words of the British treaty of protection with Old Calabar to the dispute at hand. Thus, the structure and sensibility of the court's logic was curiously colonialist, and was therefore highly problematic in its marked contribution to the motley variety of the performances of international discourse and action that have functioned too often over the last few centuries to, inter alia, deny the agency of most third world peoples and the legitimacy of most of their states.

III   Deference to the Effectiveness Principle

It is a fairly non-controversial proposition that, at least since the 19th century, at traditional international law, effectiveness tended to confer legitimacy.[41] The idea was that when once an act had been effectively done, it was *ipso facto* legitimate and lawful.[42] Thus, traditional international law tended to be viewed and discussed by mainstream commentators as consisting of a series of responses to social events, and as a reflection of social power.[43]

---

41   See O.C. Okafor, "Re-Defining Legitimate Statehood," *supra* note 9, at 65–70.

42   See T. Christian, "Introduction" in L.C. Green and O. Dickason, eds., *The Law of Nations and the New World* (Edmonton: The University of Alberta Press, 1989), at x.

43   See M. Koskenniemi, "The Wonderful Artificiality of States" (1994) ASIL Proceedings 22, at 24.

The way in which the doctrine has been applied to the specific question of state legitimacy has been ably re-stated by James Crawford. According to him, with regard to state legitimacy, that doctrine asserts that where a state actually exists, the legality or legitimacy of its creation or existence must be purely an abstract question since the law must take account of the reality despite its legality.[44] This understanding of the doctrine as it applies to the question of state legitimacy has enjoyed and still enjoys widespread support in the literature; even though – like the core doctrine itself – it has now begun to slowly wane.[45]

It was against this normative and discursive background that the majority decision in the Bakassi case dismissed Nigeria's claim of title to the Bakassi Peninsula via a form of historical consolidation which largely occurred through its effective occupation and administration of that territory.[46] According to the court, Nigeria's invocation of the effectiveness of its historical consolidation of its occupation and administration of the territory "cannot in any event vest [lawful or legitimate] title to Bakassi in Nigeria, where its 'occupation' of the peninsula is adverse to Cameroon's prior treaty title and where, moreover, the possession has been for a limited period."[47] Yet the same majority decision held that the effectiveness of British subversion of the plain words of the treaty of protection it had entered into with Old Calabar conferred legitimacy on the British claim to title over the Bakassi Peninsula and this in spite of the clear contrary words of that treaty (title that it therefore lawfully transferred at a later date to Germany – Cameroon's then colonial power).

This is a rather curious contradiction. For, was the effectiveness of British occupation of Bakassi, post the treaty of protection it had entered into with Old Calabar, not clearly adverse to the latter's treaty-recognized title to Bakassi? And was Britain's effective (albeit illegal) possession of Bakassi not also similarly adverse for a limited time (before it handed over the territory to Germany)? Why then did the effectiveness of British colonial occupation count and the effectiveness of Nigerian post-colonial possession did not? It appears that according to the deeper logic of the court's reasoning on this issue, effectiveness does indeed confer legitimacy, but only if the occupying power is European.

---

44   See J. Crawford, *The Creation of States in International Law* (Oxford: Clarendon Press, 1979) at 3–4.
45   Ibid. See also T.M. Franck, *Fairness in International Law and Institutions* (Oxford: Clarendon Press, 1995, at 7; H. Kelsen, *Principles of International Law* (New York: Holt, Rinehart and Winston, 1966) at 424; R.H. Jackson and C. Rosberg, "Sovereignty and Underdevelopment: Juridical Statehood in the African Crisis" (1986) 24 The Journal of Modern African Studies 1; and O.C. Okafor, "Re-Defining Legitimate Statehood," *supra* note 9, at 65–70.
46   Paragraphs 220–225.
47   Paragraph 220.

Connecting the dots in the majority's reasoning, it becomes clear that the presence of this apparent contradiction in its reasoning needed to be cured in some way if the decision is to have some measure of coherence. This appears to be why the court resorted to the colonialist logic discussed in the last section that sought to deny and de-legitimize Old Calabar's statehood. For, it was only by erasing Old Calabar's international legal personality, and thereby constructing the treaty it signed with Britain as not really a treaty properly so-called, that the majority decision could plausibly reach the conclusion that Britain was in a position to transfer a part of Old Calabar's territory to Germany in spite of the clearly contrary provisions of the relevant treaty.

Much to their credit, the three judges who dissented from the court's overall finding that Cameroon held lawful title to Bakassi strongly questioned the majority's treatment of this issue of effectiveness conferring legitimacy. Accusing the majority of going as far as even refusing to as much as assess the evidence that supported Nigeria's claim to title via historical consolidation,[48] Judge Koroma argued that:

> In my opinion, founded on the jurisprudence of the Court ... historical consolidation, if supported by the requisite evidence, can be a sound and valid means of establishing territorial title in international law. When, therefore, such evidence is presented to the Court, as in this case, it does not seem legally justified to reject such evidence because it is characterized under a particular rubric.[49]

For his own part, Judge Ajibola noted that the net effect of the majority decision was that:

> ... the Court fails to take into consideration the situation on the ground in the Bakassi peninsula, despite the fact that no one is left in doubt that at the moment this territory, and indeed since independence, is occupied by and firmly in the possession of Nigeria and inhabited by Nigerian people ... This is an artificial decision that fails blatantly to take into consideration, contrary to all the accepted principles of international law and practice, that *effectivités* must invariably be given consideration in a matter of this nature.[50]

---

48   See paragraph 20, Dissenting Opinion.
49   Paragraph 8.
50   Paragraph 64.

In any case, as Judge Koroma argued, the bottom line is that – aside from through the possible operation of this very effectiveness principle – Britain simply did not have any color of international legal right to alienate Old Calabar's territory to Germany. For, the treaty of protection on which it relied clearly forbade this possibility.[51] As such, the majority's contradictory application of the effectiveness principle to benefit the British colonial claim to title over Bakassi while at the same time refusing to apply the same principle to benefit the Nigerian post-colonial claim to that territory is, at best, incoherent and unconvincing.

However, it may well be plausibly argued on behalf of the majority that this contradiction is resolved by the invocation of the doctrine of inter-temporal law; that while the traditional international law in force at the time of the British colonial takeover of control over Bakassi may have legitimized the acquisition of title through effective possession, that the modern international law norms that have been in force between the 1960s or so and the date of the judgment no longer allow this. While it may be true that contemporary international law frowns more on the forcible acquisition of title to territory than traditional international law, the same cannot necessarily be said of its attitude to the acquisition of territory by the kind of more peaceful means of historical consolidation that Nigeria also relied on.[52] Even the majority of the ICJ did not rule out the possibility that this could found title to territory in appropriate cases.[53] More importantly, the difficulty with the invocation of inter-temporal law in a bid to resolve the apparent contradiction in the majority decision's treatment of the separate British and Nigerian reliance on the effectiveness doctrine lies in the fact that, as has already been argued, the so-called law in force at that time was merely the law brought to the table by one side of the dispute. By what alchemy it must be emphasized, did inter-European law apply to govern relations between the African Kingdom of Old Calabar and the European Kingdom of Britain? As Judge Ranjeva warned (even while ultimately voting with the majority):

> In the present case, application of the rules of intertemporal law raises the problem of the judgment's acceptance of the conduct of the protecting Power, which proceeded to liquidate the entity of Old Calabar" and

---

[51] Paragraph 15.
[52] See the Court's cursory reference to the *Fisheries (United Kingdom v. Norway) case* (1951) ICJ Reports 130.
[53] Paragraph 65, Majority Decision.

that the ICJ ought not be "seeking to legitimize colonial law by reliance on the rules of intertemporal law."[54]

IV   The Glorification of Empire

As was demonstrated in the book *Re-Defining Legitimate Statehood*, there is little doubt that traditional international law praxis tended to glorify and/or facilitate empire, at least from about the 19th century.[55] By the "glorification of empire" is meant the fact that despite not formally outlawing or requiring the non-recognition of de-centralized states, and in spite of the fact that it has never really imposed a lower limit on the size of a state, traditional international law praxis tended to glorify scale, centralization, and the power to conquer other states/peoples, as important attributes of states properly so-called, as measures of legitimate statehood.[56] The larger, more centralized, and more militarily/politically/economically strong a political entity was, the more it seemed to merit recognition and legitimization by other states (especially the more powerful ones) as one of them.[57]

In keeping with the traditional international legal tendency at issue here, the majority decision in the Bakassi case explicitly deployed its rough standard in assessing and rejecting the legitimacy of the statehood of Old Calabar. In a telling passage, the majority held that Old Calabar:

> ... was one of a multitude in a region where local Rulers were not regarded as States [read European states]. Indeed apart from parallel declarations of various lesser Chiefs agreeing to be bound by the 1884 Treaty, *there is not even convincing evidence of a central federal power*. There appears in Old Calabar rather to have been individual townships, headed by Chiefs, who regarded themselves as owing a general allegiance to more important Kings and Chiefs.[58]

---

54   Paragraph 4.
55   See O.C. Okafor, "Re-Defining Legitimate Statehood," *supra* note9, at 70–72. See also J. Anaya, "The Capacity of International Law to Advance Ethnic or Minority Rights Claims (1991) 13 Human Rights Quarterly 403, at 405; and C.H. Alexandrowicz, "The Role of Treaties in the European-African Confrontation in the Nineteenth Century," in A.K. Mensah-Brown, ed., *African International Legal History* (New York: UNITAR, 1975) at 32.
56   Ibid.
57   Ibid.
58   Paragraph 207.

Thus, in the majority's view, aside from the fact of its supposed non-acceptance as a state properly so-called by Britain, Old Calabar was not a state, in part at least, because it did not in reality look like the typical European states that they knew, was not sufficiently centralized, and as such did not have sufficient empire-like characteristics.

Almost needless to say, the five judges who dissented from the court's majority decision on the issue of Old Calabar's statehood and capacity to make treaties did not share this adherence by the court to the tendency of traditional international law to glorify empire. These five judges recognized Old Calabar's statehood and international legal personality in spite of the fact that that Kingdom was not as large, centralized and strong, as the majority would have wanted.

V   The Concept of Legitimate Statehood in the Bakassi Decision and the "In-between-ness of the Post-colonial Mind"

Colonialism is dead, long live colonialism! This appears to be one important lesson that can be learned from the majority decision in the Bakkassi case. For, as the foregoing analysis demonstrates, the majority decision is to a large degree structured, framed and driven by a form of colonialist logic that would today seem rather quaint to most discerning minds, but which is no less troubling in its reflection of the mindsets of all-too-many contemporary international lawyers. What is more, this colonialist logic unfolded in a way that unabashedly denied the agency of at least one third world people, subjected and subjugated them to the indignity of European review and legitimization, privileged the European gaze, and sought to erase the actuality of their statehoods. These are all tendencies that characterized European colonialism in the third world. Thus, the concept of legitimate statehood in the Bakkassi judgment is much more colonialist than post-colonialist, much more regressive than progressive, and far more harmful than helpful. It has in fact significantly pushed back the hitherto swelling progressive tide that has been ramming against the rocky cliffs of traditional international law, seeking to denude them of some of their potency. It has helped set back the seemingly progressive redefinition in international law of the concept of legitimate statehood from one founded much more on raw power and European superiority and privilege to one founded to a significantly greater extent on the self-determination and equality of peoples.

Given this reality, it may at first glance surprise some that Cameroon (itself a formerly colonized African country) appeared to embrace and purvey this kind of harmful colonialist logic; perhaps because it served its end-goal of winning control of the oil-rich Bakkassi peninsula. For, one of Cameroon's main contentions in the case was that it would be inappropriate to talk of Old Calabar as if it possessed international legal personality or as if it was recognized by Europeans as a state during the relevant period.[59] And as we have seen, the Senegalese (African) ad-hoc judge whom Cameroon had appointed to the ICJ for the purposes of hearing this particular case, i.e. Judge Mbaye, expressed very similar views.[60]

Without absolving Cameroon and Judge Mbaye of their responsibility for choosing to lend credence to the much-discredited colonialist logic that framed, shaped and drove the majority decision, it is also fair to say that with their preferred end-goals in mind, these two African actors selected a number of arguments from the range that was available and in play; from among the types that they thought would meet with favor among the majority of the court. This is a common strategy among trial lawyers. And so, these two actors clearly possess and exhibit agency. However, in seeking to win the case in the particular way they did, in deploying the specific strategy they adopted, they appeared to have been caught between and betwixt the super-powerful structure and effect of European ideas and practice in our time and their own assertion of agency in choosing a winning legal strategy. Unfortunately, it is in this somewhat complicated way that the postcolonial mind too often participates in the kind of tragic drama in which Cameroon and Judge Mbaye found themselves. The nature of the tragedy here is that colonial logic is reproduced even by the very post-colonial minds whose lives have been so negatively affected by it on the whole. This is, in part, because of the kind of cards that the post-colonial subject has been dealt, the type of ground it has been allowed to stand on.

Such a phenomenon could be described as the "in-between-ness of the postcolonial mind": the post-colonial subject's tendency to argue all-too-often from within the very "prison house" of European colonial logic that it has been forced to inhabit. This felt necessity to adhere to otherwise rejected colonialist logic in pursuit of current self-interest, is in part driven by the performance of European agency over the last couple of centuries or so as a form of "super-agency." By this is meant the fact that, in the dominant international legal praxis, European gaze, desire, ideas and actions almost always trump their third world equivalent. As Judge Rezek incisively recognized:

---

59 This Cameroonian argument was recounted in Judge Koroma's dissenting opinion. See paragraph 12 thereof.
60 Paragraph 73.

In the present case, the Bakassi Peninsula was part of the territory of Old Calabar, subject to the original rule of its Kings and Chiefs. The Applicant itself [Cameroon], [was] *paradoxically required by the circumstances* to espouse some particularly unacceptable propositions of colonialist discourse ...[61]

In conclusion, it is only fair to state that because it rests so heavily (if unnecessarily) on the praxis of "European super-agency," since it has helped legitimize the silencing/displacing of the voices of the Bakassi people, and because it has pushed in favor of the erasure of the statehood of the ancient polity of the African city states of Old Calabar, the ICJ's majority decision in the Bakkassi case and Cameroon's victory in that matter, sits upon a very shaky foundational structure, one that was erected through the instrumentality of colonialist logic. Yet, it is gratifying from a TWAIL perspective that the distinguished international lawyer, scholar, diplomat, and jurist in whose honor this book has been published was among a handful of ICJ judges who, as best they could, boldly resisted the majority's troubling and incoherent lapse into a colonialist logic that at best belongs to a time past (if at all). It is in part for this intelligent and courageous stand that we celebrate him.

---

61   Paragraph 3, Separate Opinion of Judge Rezek. Emphasis supplied.

CHAPTER 9

The International Court and the Legacy of the Barcelona Traction Case

Phoebe Okowa

1   Introduction

The decision of the International Court of Justice, in the *Barcelona Traction Case*[1] on diplomatic protection generated a considerable amount of interest in the academic literature.[2] In that case, the Court confirmed the centrality of diplomatic protection by States as the principal means for safeguarding the interests of foreign nationals harmed by a violation of international law. Specifically, it noted that States who admitted foreign investments or foreign nationals on their territory had direct obligations towards them. However, in a significant dictum, it also recognized obligations that were not owed to individual states, but the international community as a whole.[3] In one of the most cited passages, the Court drew a distinction between obligations arising by way of diplomatic protection and those owed to the international community as a whole. It observed that:

> When a State admits into its territory foreign investments or foreign nationals, whether natural or juristic persons, it is bound to extend to them the protection of the law and assume obligations concerning the treatment to be afforded them. These obligations, however, are neither

---

1   *Barcelona Traction Case* (Belgium V. Spain) 1970 ICJ Reports, 4.
2   Christian Tams *Erga Omnes Obligations*, (Cambridge 2002) and the references cited. M. Ragazzi, 'The Concept of International Obligations Erga omnes (Oxford 1997); C. Tomuschat, 'Obligations Arising for States With or Without Their Will' 241 *Recueil des Cours* (1993) 185. See J. Crawford, *Responsibility for Breaches of Communitarian Norms: An Appraisal of Article 48 of the ILC Articles of Responsibility of States for Internationally Wrongful Acts'* in U. Fastenrath, R. Geiger, D.E. Khan et al., eds. *From Bilateralism to Community Interest: Essays in Honour of Judge Bruno Simma* (Oxford, 2011).
3   M. Ragazzi, 'The Concept of International Obligations Erga omnes (Oxford 1997); C. Tomuschat, 'Obligations Arising for States With or Without Their Will' 241 *Recueil des Cours* (1993) 185.

absolute nor unqualified. In particular, an essential distinction should be drawn between obligations of a state towards the international community as a whole and those arising *vis-a-vis* another state in the field of diplomatic protection. By their very nature the former are the concern of all states in view of the importance of the rights involved, all States can be held to have a legal interest in their protection, they are obligations *erga omnes*. Such obligations derive for example in contemporary international law, from the outlawing of aggression, and of genocide, as also from the principles and rules concerning the basic rights of the human person, including protection from slavery and racial discrimination. Some of the corresponding rights of protection have entered into the body of general international law while others are conferred by international instruments of a universal or quasi-universal character. Obligations the performance of which is the subject of diplomatic protection are not of the same category. It cannot be held, when one such obligation in particular is in question, in a specific case, that all States have a legal interest in its observance.

The pronouncements on *erga omnes* obligations were clearly provisional since the exact consequences were not spelt out. Was the Court anticipating bilateral enforcement on a private rights model or was this the beginning of the recognition of a system of public order subject to international oversight? It is doubtful that the Court was proposing a set of obligations for which there would be no accountability. Furthermore, if international law was moving towards a law of consensus, this was certainly a new development. The dominant positivist tradition was clear, that states, were only bound by obligations they had expressly consented to. Moreover, in the prevailing system of international law, dispute settlement mechanisms were limited to inter-state claims on the basis of diplomatic protection. In the literature, the decision created an expectation that as far as community interests were concerned, international law would in time embrace a liberal approach to questions of standing, quite possibly resulting in the recognition of an *actio popularis*.[4] Enough time has passed now to allow for a critical evaluation of the decision and its impact on

---

4   See J. Crawford, *Responsibility for Breaches of Communitarian Norms: An Appraisal of Article 48 of the ILC Articles of Responsibility of States for Internationally Wrongful Acts'* in U. Fastenrath, R. Geiger, D.E. Khan et al., eds. *From Bilateralism to Community Interest: Essays in Honour of Judge Bruno Simma* (Oxford, 2011); Institute of International Law, *'Obligations Erga Omnes in International Law*, Fifth Commission, Krakow Session – 2005, www.idi-iil.org/idiE/resolutionsE/2005_kra_01_en.pdf.

the international court's subsequent jurisprudence. The article also attempts to assess the impact of the judgment on national decisions dealing with issues of diplomatic protection in circumstances politically different from those prevailing in the period leading to the Barcelona decision. The first part of this essay is an attempt to understand the reasons for the general decline in diplomatic protection as an institution of international law after the *Barcelona Traction Case,* but it also seeks to offer some insights into the decisions of the International Court on the subject during Judge Koroma's tenure on the Court. The cases considered involved a reconsideration of the Court's landmark judgment in the case on the specific subject of diplomatic protection of nationals but also in relation to the legal consequences of designating certain obligations as owed to the international community as a whole. The increased public sensitivity to the importance of human rights and environmental values raised the expectation that the Court would play a pivotal role in their enforcement even if the exact modalities were yet to be worked out.

The right of states to protect their nationals, by bringing international claims on their behalf, when they had suffered a wrong was of long standing and its *lex lata* character was never in doubt. Indeed as far back as 1758 Emer de Vattel wrote that

> whoever offends the State injures its rights, disturbs its tranquility or does it a prejudice in any manner whatsoever, declares himself its enemy and exposes himself to be justly punished for it. Whoever uses a citizen ill indirectly offends the State which is bound to protect this citizen and the sovereign of the latter should avenge his wrongs, punish the aggressor and if possible oblige him to make full reparation; since otherwise the citizen would not obtain the great end of the civil association which is safety.[5]

However, the idea that international law also recognized obligations of solidarity, based not on individual but on shared community values, was both untested and underdeveloped. It is for this reason that the Court's pronouncement on this matter generated much interest in the academic literature both immediately before the decision and afterwards. On the facts, the pronouncement on the *erga omnes* character of certain international obligations was unnecessary; the *Barcelona Traction Case* itself concerned the question of Belgium's entitlement to exercise diplomatic protection on behalf of its shareholders.

---

[5] Principles of the Law of Nations Applied to the Conduct and Affairs of Nations and Sovereigns (F ed. 1797) Book 2 Chapter VI at 71; H. Lauterpacht, *'Allegiance, Diplomatic Protection and Criminal Jurisdiction over Aliens'* (1945–47), Cambridge Law Journal, 330.

This *obiter dictum* nevertheless had a profound effect in the literature, and it was readily accepted as authority for the existence of two distinct categories of obligations in international law; those in the nature of a civil law right and which were owed to individual states; and those which created a regulatory framework for dealing with public order concerns and therefore owed to the international community as a whole. Referring to its judgment in the *Barcelona Traction*, the International Court in the *Bosnia Genocide Case*,[6] noted that the erga omnes character of the duty to prevent genocide was not territorially circumscribed and all states had a duty to prevent it. Moreover, the Barcelona judgment generated the expectation that the implications of these obligations would be worked out either by International Court itself or in state practice in future cases. If the obligations were owed to the international community as a whole, to what extent did they incorporate a general right of states to bring an action in vindication of the public interest? The evidence so far indicates that the strong affirmative support for a category of obligations owed to the international community, as a whole, has not been matched by the development of parallel institutions for the enforcement of law.[7] In its earlier Judgment in the *South West Africa Cases*, the Court denied the existence of an *actio popularis* in international law.[8]

The judgment in the *Barcelona Traction Case* coincided with profound changes in the composition and membership of the international community following the processes of decolonization. There was therefore an implicit expectation that like much of the law that had been developed to protect imperial interests, the law in this area too would undergo some revision to reflect the changed composition of the international community, an overwhelmingly non-European majority. Much of the law on diplomatic protection had been concerned with the protection of the interests of colonial powers, principally as capital exporting countries.[9] International law had recognized that these nationals of imperial nations were entitled to a higher standard of treatment than that which prevailed in their host countries; the failure to comply with international standards was buttressed by institution of diplomatic protection, entitling states to bring an action on the international plane in those situations where the international minimum standard was not complied with.

---

6   *Application of the Convention on the Prevention and Punishment of the Crime of Genocide*, (Bosnia and Herzegovina V. Serbia and Montenegro) ICJ Reports 1996, 595 at 616 (para. 31).
7   On the proposition *lex ferenda* that international law should recognize such an institution, see part three of the ILC's Articles on the Responsibility of States for Internationally Wrongful Acts (Specifically Articles 42, 48 and 54) (Yearbook of the ILC, 2001, Vol. II, at p. 33.
8   *South West Africa Case (Ethiopia/South Africa, Liberia/ South Africa* (merits) ICJ Reports 1966, 6.
9   See K. Bourne, *The Foreign Policy of Victorian England* (Oxford: Clarendon press, 1970).

Diplomatic protection, it is suggested encouraged a two tier system of international protection, where those from powerful states could always lay claim to preferential treatment backed by governmental support where domestic remedies were either not forthcoming, or were simply inadequate on the protection of their governments as a last resort in those situations where domestic remedies were either not forthcoming or were simply inadequate;[10] whilst those from weak marginalized communities would remain outside it. This inequity at its core was not lost on Latin American scholars and was frequently subjected to trenchant criticism.[11] A look at the international law reports reveals that the majority of diplomatic protection cases related to American or European interests in South America.[12] Intuitively, there was an expectation that this avowedly imperial institution was unlikely to survive in light of the changed composition of the international community following the processes of decolonization. The judgment also came at a time of increased public awareness on the importance of human rights as universal values, at once inalienable and fundamental to the dignity of every human being on state territory. This renewed emphasis on the equal protection of the law was at odds with diplomatic protection, predicated as it was, on the exceptionalism of European or American interests. If diplomatic protection was to survive as an institution of international law, how could it be reconciled with the increased emphasis on universality of human rights? Moreover, at its core was an implicit assumption that third world legal systems were inferior, at once and falling short of standards expected of civilized nations. This did not augur well with the newly independent states.

It is suggested that diplomatic protection was not just at odds with an international system committed to the sovereign equality of states, but there are arguments too that the new institutions of international law may have rendered it redundant. Specifically, the consensus around the universality of human rights made any special regimes of protection based on ties of nationality unnecessary. The right of diplomatic protection is dependent on nationality, since it is only the State of which a person is a national who can exercise it. Yet those most at risk from violations of fundamental human rights are the displaced, refugees and stateless persons. Inherently, diplomatic protection emerged as an institution that lacked a democratic spirit at its core and only

---

10 See F.S Dunn, *The Protection of Nationals* (Baltimore: John Hopkins press, 1932).
11 See D.R. Shea, *The Calvo Clause* (Minneapolis: University of Minnesota Press) at 10.
12 Marjorie Whiteman, Digest of International Law; Flutie *Case* (USA v. Venezuela) 9 RIAA 148 (1904); *Kunhardt Case* (USA v. Venezuela) (1903) 9 RIAA 171; *North American Dredging Co* (USA v. Mexico) 4 RIAA 26 (1926); *Sapphire International Petroleum Ltd V. National Iranian oil co. 35 ILR* 136 (1963); *Kuwait v. Amin oil* 66 ILR 518, 21 ILM 976 (1982).

served to perpetuate existing inequalities in the system of human rights protections. In other ways, it could be argued that the consensus around the universality of human rights rendered any special regimes of protection redundant.

Both national and international courts have grappled in different ways with the Barcelona legacy and it therefore seems an appropriate moment to reflect on the Court's contribution to the law on diplomatic protection. What is most striking is that while remaining faithful to the spirit of its judgment in *Barcelona Traction case*, the Court's decisions have not advanced the substantive law of diplomatic protection or extended the law (in relation to legal standing) to new frontiers of protection. It has remained in form, and substance, essentially a tool for the protection of the bilateral interests of states. The promise of extending it to community interests much heralded in Barcelona has in fact not been realized. It is therefore appropriate to consider why a judgment that promised so much achieved so little.

2   Obligations *Erga Omnes*

In the years after the *Barcelona Traction Case,* there was much speculation as to the legal consequences of designating certain obligations as binding *erga omnes.* Substantively there was the difficult question of which of the many obligations in the field of international law could be designated as having an *erga omnes* character and the criteria for their inclusion.[13] Elsewhere in the judgment, it is apparent that the Court in *Barcelona Traction* did not regard the existence of *erga omnes* obligations as necessarily entailing the recognition of *actio popularis*. Standing to enforce a claim in the Court's view only existed in those instances where the obligation was strictly speaking binding *erga omnes partes*. It observed that:

> With regard more particularly to human rights, to which reference has already been made in paragraph 34 of this judgment, it should be noted that these include protection against denial of justice. However, on the universal level, the instruments, which embody human rights, do not confer on states the capacity to protect the victims of infringements of such rights irrespective of their nationality. It is therefore still on the regional level that a solution to this problem has had to be sought; thus within the Council of Europe, of which Spain is not a member, the

---

13   C. Tams, Enforcing *Obligations Erga Omnes in International Law,* Cambridge 2005; Institute of International Law, Articles 1 and 2.

problem of admissibility encountered by the claim in the present case has been resolved by the European Convention on Human Rights, which entitles each State which is a party to the Convention to lodge a complaint against any other contracting state for the violation of the convention, irrespective of the nationality of the victim.

In the period after the decision, there was much speculation at least in the literature, that the international community would in due course recognize litigation in the public interest. However, because States are naturally reticent to involve themselves in cases that do not affect their direct interests, the International Court of Justice had very few opportunities to examine the legal implications of designating certain obligations as binding *erga omnes* and its failure to develop the law is in part a direct consequence of the largely bilateral character of the cases referred to it. The first clear opportunity arose in the *East Timor* Case. The context may be restated briefly. In that case, Portugal brought an action against Australia arguing that by entering into a treaty with Indonesia regarding the delimitation of the East Timorese continental shelf, Australia had interfered with the right of the East Timorese people to self-determination, a right whose *erga omnes* character was impeccable. Yet a judgment on the merits required the Court to rule first on the incidental question concerning the legality of Indonesia's invasion of East Timor, and the subsequent jurisdictional authority enjoyed by Indonesia over the East Timorese. Indonesia was not a party to the dispute, nor had it accepted the Court's jurisdiction. It was therefore immediately apparent that the Court was being asked to rule on the rights and obligations of a third party to the dispute contrary to its previous jurisprudence as laid down in the *Monetary Gold* case, that it could only entertain a claim with the parties' consent. Portugal argued that limitations on the Court's jurisdiction under the *Monetary Gold*[14] principle had no application in view of the *erga omnes* character of the right of self-determination at the centre of the dispute.. The Court rejected the claim and observed that:

> ... Portugal's assertion that right of people's to self-determination as it evolved from the Charter and the UN practice has an *erga omnes* character is irreproachable. The principle of self-determination of peoples has been recognized in the United Nations Charter and in the jurisprudence of the Court. It is one of the essential principles of contemporary international law. However, the Court considers that the *erga omnes* character of a norm and the rule of consent are two different things. Whatever the nature of obligations invoked, the Court could not rule on the lawfulness

---

14   *Monetary Gold Case* (Italy v. United Kingdom, France, United States) ICJ Reports 1954, 19.

of the conduct of a State when its judgment would imply an evaluation of the lawfulness of the conduct of another State which is not a party to the Case. Where this is so, the Court cannot act even if the right in question is a right *erga omnes*[15]

The consensual basis of the Court's jurisdiction remains in almost all cases an effective bar to the Court's jurisdiction over *erga omnes* claims. Moreover, even in those cases where states have accepted the Court's jurisdiction, there is a real possibility that States would simply immunize themselves from *erga omnes* suits by staying away from the International Court's jurisdictional system or making reservations to *erga omnes* cases. In principle there are no limits to the Court's *proprio motu* powers and there is nothing to stop the court in the exercise of its inherent jurisdiction to give effect *to erga omnes* obligations which arise in cases before it and even in circumstances where these have not formed the basis of the parties' formal submissions.[16] The Court, it could be argued, has a judicial duty as the principal guardian of the rule of law to enforce the core values of the international system in which it operates. But this too presupposes that the Court is already seised of a matter through the normal consensual basis of its jurisdiction. In practical terms, it is unlikely that the Court could do much beyond a declaratory order. It is unlikely to compel states to take specific measures by way of upholding *erga omnes* duties.

In its Advisory Opinion on the *Legal Consequences for the Construction of a Wall in Palestinian Territory*,[17] the International Court observed that Israel's obligations in the field of self-determination and humanitarian law were binding *erga omnes*; that the construction of the wall violated these obligations and all states were under a duty not to recognize the illegal situation resulting from the construction of the wall in the occupied Palestinian territory. It said:

> ... the obligations violated by Israel include certain obligations *erga onmes*. As the Court indicated in the *Barcelona Traction* Case, such obligations are by their nature "the concern of all states" and in view of the importance of the rights involved, all states can be held to have a legal interest in their protection ... the obligations *erga omnes* violated by Israel are the obligation to respect the right of the Palestinian people to

---

15 *East Timor Case (Portugal v. Australia), Judgment,* ICJ Reports 1995, p. 90, para. 29.
16 A. Orakhelashvili, *Peremptory Norms in International Law* (Oxford 2006) p. 496.
17 *Legal Consequences of the Construction of the Construction of a Wall in the Occupied Palestinian Territory,* ICJ Reports, 2004, 136 at para. 155–159; Separate opinion of Judge Koroma, p. 204.

self-determination, and certain of its obligations under international humanitarian law.

Strictly speaking characterization of the obligations as *erga omnes* was not necessary for the decision, since the duties of non-recognition as Christian Tams has pointed out, attach to all illegal acts of state, and not just those characterized as binding *erga omnes*.[18] Judge Koroma emphasized the 'the international community as a whole bears an obligation towards the Palestinian people as a former mandate, on whose behalf the international community holds a 'sacred trust' not to recognize any unilateral change in the status of the territory brought about by the construction of the wall'.[19] The pronouncement was nevertheless significant as an attempt to concretize community obligations. For Koroma, the onus was on the General Assembly who had requested the opinion to act on it by taking concrete steps towards the resolution of the Palestinian conflict.

In the DRC v. *Rwanda Case*, the Court was again faced with argument that the *erga omnes or jus cogens character* of a norm conferred jurisdiction on it even in the absence of express jurisdictional consent from the parties. Rwanda had made a reservation to Article IX of the Genocide Convention, the provision conferring the Court with jurisdiction in relation to the interpretation of the Convention. The DRC argued that the reservation was invalid in so far as it purported to deprive the Court of the means of giving effect to *erga omnes* obligations and therefore fulfilling 'its noble mission of safeguarding peremptory norms'. Recalling its judgment in the *East Timor Case*, and in the cases brought by Yugoslavia against some of the NATO states concerning alleged aggression on the territory of Yugoslavia, the Court again reiterated 'that the fact that a dispute relates to compliance with a norm having such a character, which is assuredly the case with regard to the prohibition of genocide, cannot of itself provide a basis for the jurisdiction of the Court to entertain the dispute'.[20] The Court also rejected the argument put forward in DRC's Counter-Memorial, that since article 66 of the Vienna Convention gave the Court jurisdiction to rule on the validity of a treaty that is contrary to *jus cogens*, the court therefore had jurisdiction irrespective of the parties consent on all *jus*

---

18 C. Tams and Alessandra Asterriti, 'Erga Omnes "Jus Cogens and their Impact on the Law of Responsibility" in Evans and Koutrakis, The International Responsibility of the European Union' (Hart 2013). Separate Opinion of Judge Higgins, paras 38–39.
19 Separate Opinion of Judge Koroma, para. 7.
20 DRC v. Rwanda (New Application (Provisional measures) ICJ Reports 2002 para. 64 and *Case Concerning Armed Activities on the Territory of the Congo (New Application: 2002) Democratic Republic of Congo v. Rwanda*) Jurisdiction of the Court and admissibility of the application, Judgment of 3rd February 2006.

cogens norms and not just those concerning questions of interpretation under the Vienna Convention.

Judge Koroma dissented from the majority judgment, arguing that article IX envisaged dispute settlement by the Court in all disputes concerning the interpretation of the Genocide Convention and to exclude the Court's jurisdiction was in principle contrary to the object and purpose of the Convention.[21] But strictly speaking, his conclusions were based on the interpretation of the Convention *qua* treaty and not because obligations having *erga omnes* or *jus cogens* status were in a special category for jurisdictional purposes. The treaty in question he noted, specifically provided for prevention and punishment, with the International Court forming an essential part of the accountability mechanisms envisaged. He noted that it was:

> ... Not to claim that the seriousness of an obligation, the *jus cogens* status of a norm or the *erga omnes* nature of an obligation per se confers jurisdiction on the Court, as was recognized in the Judgment, it is nevertheless my opinion that it is incumbent on Rwanda in this case, as a State party to the Genocide Convention-and which itself was a victim of genocide and rightly referred the matter to the competent organ of the United Nations-to allow scrutiny of the allegation that it had breached its obligations under the Genocide Convention'[22]

He further observed that the court has a special responsibility to safeguard the interests of the international community, and the views of an individual state on whether the Court had jurisdiction or not could not be regarded as determinative.[23]

Other judges were equally critical of the Court's conclusion that the *erga omnes* character of a norm did not automatically confer on the Court jurisdiction, but accepted that the conclusion was incontrovertible, in the *lex lata* content of international law. In their joint Separate opinion, Judges Kooijmans, Elaraby, Owada, Simma and Higgins observed that it was a:

> ... A matter for serious concern that at the beginning of the twenty-first century, it is still for States to choose whether they consent to Court adjudicating claims that they have committed genocide. It must be regarded as a very grave matter that a State should be in a position to shield from

---

21 Dissenting opinion of Judge Koroma, *Armed Activities on the Territory of the Congo* (New Application 2002) Democratic Republic of Congo v. Rwanda, para. 4.
22 Dissenting Opinion of Judge Koroma, para. 22.
23 Dissenting opinion of Judge Koroma, para. 14.

international scrutiny any claim that might be made against it concerning genocide A state so doing shows the world scant confidence that it would never, ever, commit genocide, one of the greatest crimes known.[24]

In regarding itself as effectively powerless, to interpret a convention incorporating rules for the maintenance of international public order /community values in the absence of specific state consent to its jurisdiction, the court appears to have ignored its central role as custodian of the rule of law. The idea that the international system recognized a category of super-norms projecting the values of that system but on the whole unenforceable seems problematic.

The right of all states to enforce community norms was eloquently advanced by Judge Simma in *Armed activities in the Territory of the Congo (DRC v. Uganda)*. The Court had refused to entertain Uganda's counter-claim concerning the alleged mistreatment by Congolese soldiers of persons whose nationality had not been established. Judge Simma argued that the Court should have entertained the claim since the obligation in question was binding *erga omnes*. He said that:

> ... the question of standing of a claimant state for violations of human rights committed against persons which might or might not possess the nationality of that state, the jurisdiction of the court not being at issue the contemporary law of state responsibility provides a positive answer as well ... The obligations deriving from the human rights cited above and breached by the DRC are instances par excellence of obligations that are owed to a group of states including Uganda, and are established for the protection of a collective interest of the States parties to the covenant.[25]

The issue of standing to enforce *erga omnes* obligations formed a central element of the Bosnian pleadings in the *Bosnia Genocide Case*. In addition to claims on its own behalf, Bosnia also argued that the obligations imposed on Serbia were not bilateral but were owed to the International community as a whole. In addition to claims on its own behalf, Bosnia also argued that the obligations imposed on Serbia were not bilateral but were owed to the International Community as a whole. It submitted that as a result, the right to seize the Court for such disputes, even when the claimant state or its nationals are not direct victims of the genocidal acts, is nothing but the logical consequence of the fact that the' rights and obligations enshrined by the Convention are

---

24   Joint Separate opinion, paras 2–5.
25   *Armed Activities in the Territory of the Congo* (DRC V. Uganda), Judgment of 19th December 2005, para 35 ICJ-CIJ.org

rights and obligations *erga omnes*.[26] It supplied evidence that Serbia had committed acts of Genocide not only on the territory of Bosnia but elsewhere on the territory of the former Yugoslavia. In particular, those atrocities were committed not only on citizens of Bosnia and Herzegovina but also on Albanians, Sandak Muslims, Croats, Hungarians and other minorities. It is true that some of these minorities were nationals of Bosnia, but Bosnia also made it clear that it was bringing claims for acts of genocide against persons who were nationals of Yugoslavia itself and that the nature of obligations involved, entitled it to bring claims on behalf of third state nationals.[27]

The Court found it unnecessary to give a definitive judgment on this point. It noted that genocide was a crime that required a specific intent to eliminate a targeted group, and that as a result the group had to be identified positively, a burden which the applicant had failed to discharge.[28] Moreover, as the Court had reached the conclusion that Serbia had not been involved in the direct commission of acts of genocide, it was not necessary for it to speculate as to which groups would fall within the ambit of protection. It is possible to read from this passage that the Court was not contesting the applicant's right to bring a claim in respect of atrocities committed against persons who are not its nationals. The Court was merely concerned that, on the specific facts before it, the applicant had been unable to prove that these nationals of a third state had been the victims of genocide. The opportunity to clarify whether international law recognized an *actio popularis* in a clear and decisive manner was nevertheless missed. It is in the area of international crimes that the possibility of litigation *actio popularis* holds the greatest promise. Many of the atrocities are committed by governments against their own populations and unless third states can bring claims, there is little possibility that these states would be held to account. There are of course a number of justifiable concerns in connection with the recognition about permitting an *actio popularis* in this context as in others. There is nothing to stop states from bringing politically motivated cases on the international plane for the sole purpose of causing difficulty for the respondent state. It is also possible to see the Court's decision on this point as part of its general reticence on the issue of standing, in relation to claims brought by states when their direct interests are not affected.

The Court's subsequent consideration of *erga omnes* obligations has not advanced the argument much beyond *erga omnes partes* (that a state party to a convention may be able to rely on its provisions even where it has not been

---

26   *Case Concerning Application of the Convention on the Prevention and Punishment of the Crime of Genocide*, Judgement of 26th February 2007. Para. 185.
27   Reply of the Government of Bosnia and Herzegovina (23rd April 1998) at 972.
28   Judgment of 26th February 2007, paras 368, 369 and 373.

specifically affected by the breach of the obligations in the Convention). In the *Questions Relating to the Obligation to Prosecute or Extradite (Belgium v. Senegal)*[29] under the UN Convention against Torture, Belgium had argued that Senegal, by failing to prosecute or extradite persons accused of having committed acts of torture, was in breach of his obligations under the convention. None of the alleged victims of the torture had Belgian nationality and Belgium's standing to bring the claim was contested by Senegal. In support of its right to bring the claim, Belgium argued that the obligations in question were opposable to all parties to the convention.

Furthermore, that the obligations in question were also binding on states as a matter of customary law.[30] Referring specifically to obligations under the torture convention, the Court noted that:

> The common interest in compliance with the relevant obligations under the Convention against torture implies entitlement of each State Party to the Convention to make a claim concerning the cessation of an alleged breach by another State party. If the Special interest were required for that purpose, in many cases no State would be in a position to make such a claim. It follows that any State Party to the Convention may invoke the responsibility of another State Party with a view to ascertaining the alleged failure to comply with obligations *erga omnes* partes such as under article 6 Para. 2 and article 7, Para. 1 of the Convention and to bring the failure to an end.[31]

The court's finding did not exclude the possibility that what was initially an obligation binding only on state parties to the convention had through state practice acquired customary law status. It rejected Belgium's argument based on customary law because on the specific facts of the case, the contention that customary law had been violated had not formed part of the parties' diplomatic exchanges before the dispute was filed.

The possibility of a duty to prevent torture, binding *erga omnes* on all states was conceded by counsel for Senegal in reply to a question by Judge Cancado Trindade[32] and was also in part the basis of the Belgian application. In his separate opinion Judge Trindade was unequivocal that the obligation to

---

29 2012 ICJ Reports 448. The case was referred to the Court and considered during Judge Koroma's tenure but the final judgment was given after he left the Court.

30 Memorial of Belgium of 1st July 2010, p. 83, submission 1 (b); Final submission of Belgium, of 19th March 2012, submission 1 (b).

31 Judgment, para. 69.

32 Separate opinion of Judge Cancado Trindade, 2012 ICJ Reports 529, para. 107.

prevent torture had a parallel existence under customary international law. In his view:

> ... what the Court really wished to say, in my perception, is that there was no material object for the exercise of its jurisdiction in respect of obligations under customary international law rather than a lack of its own jurisdiction *per se*. The finding that, in the circumstances of the present case, a dispute did not exist between the contending parties as to the matter at issue does not necessarily mean that, as a matter of law, the Court would automatically lack jurisdiction, to be exercised in relation in relation to the determination of the existence of a dispute concerning breaches of alleged obligations under customary law[33]

Further obstacles in the path of litigation *actio popularis* as a way of enforcing *erga omnes* have been noted. Schachter for instance, has suggested that States are reluctant to set precedents which could be used in future litigation against them and so are unlikely to lodge claims even in respect of *erga omnes* obligations unless their direct interests were involved. Moreover, he warns that there is a real risk that an expansive concept of *actio popularis* is likely to deter even further state acceptance of the International Court's compulsory jurisdiction, and those who accept the compulsory jurisdiction will invariably protect themselves from its consequences by making reservations against *actio popularis* suits.[34] In any case, it is abundantly clear from the few occasions that the Court has considered the matter, that it has been particularly reticent to acknowledge public interest litigation as a means of enforcing *erga omnes* obligations.

The articles finally adopted by the ILC in 2001, explicitly recognize the right of states other than those directly injured to bring an action in the public interest. The special rapporteur, in the commentary to article 48, acknowledged that the article involved elements of progressive development of the law in so far as it entitled States to bring claims for restitution and reparation on behalf of the beneficiaries of the obligation even when they were not directly affected. The Articles were commended to States by the UN GA in GA Resolution 56/83 (12 December 2001) but it remains an open question whether this positive endorsement will be reflected in actual state behavior.[35]

---

33   Separate opinion of Judge Cancado Trindade, para. 144.
34   Oscar Schachter, International Law in Theory and in Practice (Dordrecht Nijhoff, 1991, p. 212).
35   International Law Commission's Articles on Responsibility of States for Internationally Wrongful Acts (2001).

3 Diplomatic Protection of Corporations after Barcelona Case

Much of the law on diplomatic protection had been largely developed to protect the interests of capital exporting countries, usually foreign investments of their nationals, in jurisdictions whose legal systems were widely regarded as falling short of a'mythical' international standard of treatment.[36] In the period following decolonization, diplomatic protection was increasingly subjected to trenchant criticism as perpetuating the relations of inequality and subordination in international relations by newly independent states. The leading arbitral decisions in this field had been mainly concerned with the protection extended to American or British nationals in Mexico or Venezuela. Moreover, the uncertainties of outcome in litigation led many capital-exporting countries to the conclusion that their interests were better served through guarantees contained in bilateral investment treaties. The *Barcelona Traction Case* itself, had resulted in a rather negative outcome for Belgium, the applicant state. After litigation lasting close to three decades, the International Court concluded that Belgium had no right to protect the interests of its shareholders in a Canadian registered company. The Court argued, that, the rights at issue belonged to the company not its shareholders. It is not surprising that in the intervening period states chose to protect their interests through bilateral investment treaties rather than litigation through the institution of diplomatic protection.[37]

However, in the *Ahmadou Sadio Diallo Case*, brought by the Democratic Republic of Congo (DRC) against Guinea,[38] Guinea sought to protect the shareholding interest in a Congolese registered company, owned by a Guinean national but a long time resident of the DRC. The International Court was therefore for the first time called upon to revisit its judgment in the *Barcelona Traction Case*, in relation to diplomatic protection of companies as well as the shareholding interest in those corporations. In the *Barcelona Traction Case*, it will be recalled that the International Court had concluded that the nationality of a company had to be determined by reference to the laws of a state in which it was incorporated or had its registered office. The majority was of the view that the simple fact of incorporation under the law of a State was conclusive. Moreover, the majority thought that it was not necessary to lift the corporate veil in order to determine the economic reality of a company, even if this

---

36   C. Amerasinghe, *State Responsibility for Injury to Aliens* (Oxford, Clarendon Press; 1967).
37   See generally Z. Douglas, *International Law of Investment Claims* (Cambridge 2009).
38   *Ahmadou Sadio Diallo* (Guinea v. Congo), *Preliminary Objections*, Judgment of 24th May 2007, p. 66.

indicated that the corporation had links with a state other than that of incorporation. The Court thus denied Belgium the right to bring an action in respect of wrongs done to a Canadian company, in circumstances where the majority of the shareholders were Belgian. In rejecting Belgium's claim, the Court noted that a company, as an institution of municipal law was an entity distinct from its shareholders. As such, where wrong was done to the company, while the interests of the shareholders might be affected it was the company alone that had the right to maintain an action in international law.

A significant majority of the Court in the Barcelona Traction case nevertheless thought that there were a number of instances in which the State of which the shareholders were nationals might be entitled to bring a claim on the international plane. This included those situations where the direct rights of shareholders were affected. Examples given by the Court included: (a) their rights to dividends; (b) the right to attend and vote at general meetings; (c) the right to share in the assets of the company after liquidation. Some judges thought that shareholders may be entitled to diplomatic protection in cases where the company had the nationality of the respondent state. The Court refrained from expressing an opinion on the correctness of this proposition, noting that the issue did not arise on the facts of the case since it was Canada, not Spain which was the country of nationality of the company. The correctness of this proposition, which, the Court had the opportunity to reconsider in the *Ahmadou Diallo Case,* was in any case open to challenge. First, it ignored the traditional rule that a state is not guilty of violating international law when it harms one of its nationals. Second, it is difficult to reconcile with the argument advanced by the majority that, when a wrong is done to a company, the interests of the shareholders may be affected but only the company has rights, which are capable of legal protection. If shareholders are entitled to protection in the situation where the wrong is done to the company by the state of incorporation and therefore to its own national, what is the precise legal basis of the protection? The minority did not articulate how mere interests could be transformed into rights capable of legal protection.

The Court also thought that shareholders may be entitled to protection where the company had ceased to exist. On the facts, the Court took the view that although the Barcelona Traction Company was in receivership, it was formally still in existence, and for this reason Belgium could not exercise protection on behalf of the shareholders. Other judges were prepared to extend diplomatic protection in those instances where, although a company was still formally in existence, it had become practically paralyzed.

The Court advanced some policy-based justifications to support its conclusions. It denied that shareholders as a category had any general right of protection under international law. It noted that the extension of protection to shareholders, by exposing the allegedly wrongdoing State to a wide range of claimants could introduce an element of uncertainty and insecurity in international economic relations. The court was also concerned with the practical difficulty of ascertaining shareholding interests since such shares frequently change hands, and in many instances it could be difficult to determine which state was entitled to exercise protection, especially where the nominee and the beneficiaries were from different states. In the *Barcelona Traction Case* itself, there was some doubt whether the Belgian interest in the shares had been continuous and in particular whether Belgium could have satisfied the test at the time of injury. The decision is therefore an unequivocal authority in support of the view that, when a company is injured, it is the national state of the company alone that may bring an action and shareholders as a category are not entitled to diplomatic protection.

However, it is clear that some judges were prepared to extend protection to shareholders. Moreover, a number of them favoured a different test for corporations and would have applied the genuine link test as formulated in the *Nottebohm* case with the result that the State of incorporation would not have an automatic right protection in the absence of some tangible connection. Such a genuine link could be demonstrated by proving that the majority of shareholders were from the state asserting the right of diplomatic protection. Furthermore, there is evidence that in practice, states have been prepared to extend diplomatic protection to shareholding interests in foreign corporations and such a right has been unequivocally advocated by the International Law Commission in its 2000 report on the law of diplomatic protection. There is also evidence that States have been reluctant to extend protection to companies incorporated in their territory in the absence of substantial link with the national economy. However, the law in this area cannot be stated with certainty. In the *Oil Platforms Case*, Iran denied that the USA had the right as a matter of international law to extend diplomatic protection to US flagged but foreign owned merchant ships, on the basis that there was an absence of a genuine link between the ships and the US government as required by international law. The Court's judgment, however, does not suggest that it was particularly troubled by the absence of a genuine link with the USA.

The protection of corporations and shareholding interests received extended consideration by the ICJ in the *Case Concerning Ahmadou Diallo*,[39] its first significant decision on this point since *Barcelona Traction Case*. Mr. Diallo had settled in Zaire for 32 years. During this time, he established two companies

---

39   Ibid.

that were at the centre of the dispute. Africom-Zaire and Africontainers Zaire. These companies, it was contended, had lost substantial sums in the course of their dealings with the Government authorities in the DRC. The attempts by Mr. Diallo and his companies to recover the monies owed were unfavourably reviewed by the Congolese authorities and his attempts to access judicial remedies in the Congolese courts were equally fruitless. Guinea argued that the decision of the Congolese authorities to expel Mr. Diallo in November 1995 was taken in order to frustrate his efforts to enforce a judgment obtained by him against Zaire Shell for the sum of 60 billion dollars.

The Congolese arguments in the pleadings had a particular resonance with those put forward by Spain in the *Barcelona Traction Case*. The DRC raised a number of preliminary objections.[40] It argued that Guinea lacked standing to bring the application, in so far as it related to wrongs allegedly done to Africom-Zaire and Africacontainers –Zaire, these being Congolese companies. The DRC relied directly on the *Barcelona Traction* case in support of its arguments that the two companies were corporations under Congolese law, with rights distinct and separate from those of Mr. Diallo, a shareholder. DRC argued that positive international law did not entitle a State to bring an action in respect of a wrong done to a shareholder in a company registered in another State. It further denied that international law recognized a process of 'substitution,' whereby the rights of a company could be assigned to a shareholder for purposes of litigation when the state whose responsibility is at issue is also the national state of the company.

The Court accepted that Mr. Diallo's rights as a shareholder in the two companies were affected, and as a result Guinea had *locus standi* to bring the claims. It drew a distinction between Mr. Diallo's rights and those of the company, and concluded that Guinea as the national State was entitled to exercise diplomatic protection in relation to its shareholding interests. The right to protect shareholders' direct interests was explicitly recognized by the majority in the *Barcelona Traction Case*. The judgment of the Court in the Barcelona Traction Case left unresolved the question whether shareholders were entitled to diplomatic protection if the company had the nationality of the wrongdoing state. In the *Diallo Case*, Guinea's third claim rested squarely on the alleged existence of this exception, claiming a right of diplomatic protection by way of substitution on the ground that the wrongdoing state was also the state of nationality of Africom – Zaire and Africontainers – Zaire, the companies concerned.

The Court categorically denied the existence of this exception as a matter of customary international law. In support of its claim for a right of diplomatic

---

40   DRC written pleadings.

protection by way of substitution, Guinea had relied on arbitral awards, decisions of the European Commission on Human Rights, ICSID jurisprudence, and bilateral treaties for the promotion and protection of investment disputes, which had recognized protection of shareholding interests where the respondent state was also the national state of the company. The Court regarded these arbitral awards and treaty provisions as *lex specialis*, which did not support the existence of any general right of diplomatic protection by way of substitution. It distinguished its earlier decision in the *Electtronica Sicula* case,[41] where a Chamber of the Court had allowed the USA to bring a claim in respect of a wrong done to an Italian company, the shares of which were held by two American corporations. It argued that the decision in *Electronnica Sicula* was not based on general international but on treaty provisions allowing the protection of shareholding interests.

In its draft articles on diplomatic protection, the ILC had considered a more limited exception, allowing protection of shareholding interests only where a company's incorporation in a respondent state was a mandatory condition for doing business in that country.[42] The Court noted that, on the facts before it, there was no evidence that Africom-Zaire and Africontainers-Zaire had been incorporated in Zaire (DRC) as a mandatory pre-condition for doing business there. It therefore expressed no opinion on the validity of the ILC's proposed exception as a matter of customary law.

Thus more than 40 years after its landmark decision in the *Barcelona Traction* case, the Court has reaffirmed that judgment in almost all respects. The significance of the Court's judgment should not however be exaggerated. The court itself noted that the role of diplomatic protection has largely fallen into disuse since most issues relating to diplomatic protection of corporations and shareholding interests are now dealt with comprehensively in international treaties. The significant delays that accompany claims arising by way of diplomatic protection also account for lack of interest in the process. The litigation in the *Barcelona Traction* case lasted almost two decades, while in *Diallo*, it took more than 10 years to reach the final judgment.

---

41 *Case Concerning Elettronica Sicula S.P.A.* (ELSI) United States of America v. Italy, Judgment of 20 July 1989.
42 Article 11 of the 'Draft Articles on Diplomatic Protection' 2006, Official Records of the General Assembly, Sixty – First Session, Supplement No. 10(A/61/10).

4 Nationality of Claims: Diplomatic Protection of Natural Persons

In its judgment in *Nottebohm*,[43] the International Court observed that for nationality to form the basis of diplomatic protection in international claims it must be based on a genuine link between the claimant state and the national on whose behalf it was claiming. It was the bond of nationality that established a claimant state's interest in the claim. In its subsequent judgments though, the Court has been far from unequivocal in insisting on the genuine link requirement. In *Barcelona Traction*, it qualified this proposition and observed that no general requirement of genuine link applied to nationality of corporations – that the fact of incorporation under the law of a state was in any case conclusive. Moreover, the majority thought that it was not necessary to lift the corporate veil in order to determine the economic reality of a company, even if this indicated that it had links with a state other than that of incorporation. The Court thus denied Belgium the right to bring an action in respect of wrongs done to a Canadian company, in circumstances where the majority of the shareholders were Belgian. In rejecting Belgium's claim, the Court noted that a company, as an institution of municipal law was an entity distinct from its shareholders. As such, where a wrong was done to the company, while the interests of shareholders might be affected, it was the company alone that had the right to maintain an action in international law. It noted that: 'Whenever shareholder's interests are harmed by an act done to the company, it is to the latter that he must look to institute appropriate action; for although two separate entities may have suffered from the same wrong, it is only one entity whose rights have been infringed.'

In any case the Court's formal conclusion that nationality must be supported by a 'genuine link' in order to be opposable in the field of diplomatic protection has also been criticized for two reasons. First, it has been argued that as a matter of policy, it is desirable that the test for nationality be capable of objective determination. The requirement of a genuine link introduces into this area of law a vague and uncertain test and is therefore open to abuse. Second, that by denying the validity of certain forms of nationality, it has the practical effect of severely restricting the scope of diplomatic protection. It has been argued that it is undesirable as a matter of policy that a wrong should go without redress simply because the links between the State and the national on whose behalf he is claiming are weak. In its decision in the *Ahmadou Sadio Diallo* case, the International Court was not particularly troubled by the genuine link

---

[43] (Liechtenstein v. Guatemala, Second Phase) 1955 ICJ Reports, p. 3.

requirement when treating as admissible Guinea's claims against the Democratic Republic of Congo (DRC).

Guinea had instituted proceedings by way of diplomatic protection on behalf of Ahmadou Sadio Diallo, a businessman of Guinean nationality who had been resident in the DRC for 32 years. His connections with Guinea were at best tenuous, yet the Court's approach to the nationality question was in marked contrast to that taken in *Nottebohm*. That Guinea was able to bring this action without any challenge by the respondent State or adverse comment by the Court is a further indication of the prevailing uncertainty as to the exact reach of the 'genuine link' requirement. Until his expulsion from the DRC, it appears that all of Mr. Diallo's links for a period of 32 years were with that state-a period not dissimilar to the 34-year link between Nottebohm and Guatemala in the *Nottebohm Case*. The *Diallo* decision lends some support to the view that the *Nottebohm* decision should be confined to its own facts and not treated as laying rules of general application.

In *La Grand*,[44] Germany made an application to the International Court for alleged violations by the United States of obligations owed to Germany as a state party to the Vienna Convention on Consular Relations. Specifically, Germany complained that the US authorities had failed to notify the German consular officials of the arrest and detention of the two German nationals; Furthermore, that they had failed to inform the La Grand brothers of their right to consular assistance under the consular relations convention. As a result, Germany argued that she had been deprived of her right to render more effective and timely assistance to the two brothers, in particular by helping them to obtain adequate legal representation during the decisive phases of their trial.[45]

The application was made by Germany on its own behalf but also by way of diplomatic protection on behalf of Walter and Karl La Grand, two nationals who had been executed in the United States and in circumstances where their right to consular assistance had not been complied with. Germany argued that the obligations in the Vienna Convention were not just state obligations owed to it by the United States but that crucially they were also individual human rights owed to the nationals in question. Throughout the proceedings, the United States emphasized the tenuous links between the La Grand brothers and Germany. Both had emigrated to the United States as young children and for all practical purposes severed links with the country of their birth. The counter-memorial of the United States noted that at the time of the murder in

---

44   *La Grand Case* (Germany v. United States), Judgment of 27th June 2001,icj-cij.org.
45   Memorial of the Federal Republic of Germany, 16 September, 1999, icj-cij.org.

1982: ... 'the brothers appeared in all respects to be native citizens of the United States ... by their appearance, mannerisms and characteristics ... and were fully American in outlook'.[46]

In the proceedings before the Court, Germany's case proceeded principally on the basis that the United States had violated obligations owed directly to her and the alternative case on the basis of diplomatic protection was not explored at length. It is nevertheless apparent that at all stages of the proceedings, the ICJ was not particularly troubled by the absence of recent ties between the La Grand brothers and Germany. Germany did not deny that for nationality to be the basis of diplomatic protection it had to be based on a genuine link but maintained that on the facts the relevant links were provided by the fact that the two brothers had been born in Germany.[47]

These decisions indicate that the Court has by and large remained committed to the ties of nationality as the basic premise of diplomatic protection. It has been less troubled by absence of a genuine link between the state and the national on whose behalf the claim is brought. It could nevertheless be argued that in appropriate cases, the absence of genuine link between a litigant and a national on whose behalf a claim is brought could play a crucial role in eliminating claims that are frivolous or *mala fides*. The Court has not had the occasion to pronounce on claims by refugees or stateless persons and therefore revisit, in a more fundamental way, the compatibility of the genuine link requirement as the basis of diplomatic protection and the increasing recognition that human rights apply to all individuals and the duties of protection as state obligations are not dependent on formal ties of nationality. In *La Grand,* a significant majority of the court treated the rights under the Vienna Convention as individual rights and not just state rights, putatively opening the door for future claims without the constraints of nationality.

5   Diplomatic Protection in National Decisions

The decision in the *Barcelona Traction Case* has also had a profound impact on the decisions of national courts implementing the right of diplomatic protection. First, there has been a consistent body of jurisprudence confirming the right of diplomatic protection as essentially discretionary and exercisable at the behest of national governments. This has proved a particularly useful

---

46   *La Grand Case* (Germany v. United States) Written Pleadings.
47   International Court of Justice, CR2000/26, public sitting held on 13 November 2000, at 10 am, arguments of Mr. Simma 21–22.

weapon in the hands of national governments resisting claims made by their citizens that right of diplomatic protection was a mandatory justiciable right of citizenship. In the *Barcelona Traction* case the International Court emphasized the discretionary character of diplomatic protection. It said that:

> ... Within the limits prescribed by international law, a State may exercise diplomatic protection by whatever means and to whatever extent it thinks fit, for it is its own right that the State is asserting. Should the natural or legal person on whose behalf it is acting consider that their rights are not adequately protected, they have no remedy in international law. All they can do is resort to municipal law, if means are available, with a view to furthering their cause or obtaining redress. The municipal legislator may lay upon the state an obligation to protect its citizens abroad, and may also confer upon the national a right to demand the performance of the obligation, and clothe the right with corresponding sanctions. However, all these questions remain within the province of municipal law and do not affect the position internationally. The State must be viewed as the sole judge to decide whether its protection will be granted, to what extent it is granted, and when it will cease. It retains in this respect a discretionary power the exercise of which may be determined by considerations of a political or other nature, unrelated to the particular case. Since the claim of the state is not identical with that of the individual or corporate person whose cause is espoused, the State enjoys complete freedom of action.[48]

But to what extent could this essentially discretionary obligation be regarded as consistent with human rights, as well as national constitutions that place obligations on governments to secure fundamental rights to all individuals under their jurisdiction? The matter has now come to fore in face of the war against terror and the arbitrary deprivation of liberty involved in some of the measures employed by foreign governments, especially in connection with those detained by the United States authorities in Guantanamo Bay.[49] Many of the individuals affected have turned to national governments for assistance, invoking an enforceable right of diplomatic protection. Not surprisingly, an institution that was widely viewed as obsolete has again become of central

---

[48] *Barcelona Traction, Light and Power Company, Limited,* Second Phase, Judgment, ICJ Reports 1970, p. 3, paras 78–9.

[49] For an extended discussion of the cases involved; see C.R.G Murray, '*In the Shadow of Haw Haw:* Guantanamo Bay,' Diplomatic Protection and Allegiance [2011] Public Law, p. 115.

importance. Notwithstanding these profound developments in humans rights law, the bulk of national decisions have consistently affirmed the discretionary character of diplomatic protection as outlined in the *Barcelona* case. In *Al Rawi*,[50] the English Court of Appeal accepted that international law on nationality decides who is entitled to diplomatic protection and that as a result, a person who is not a British national is not entitled to the protection of the state. It was argued on behalf of the applicant that a state has a duty to secure fundamental rights for all those on its territory but the argument failed because the alleged violations occurred extra-territorially, in circumstances where the state was not complicit in the wrongdoing. The suggestion, *lex ferenda*,[51] by the ILC that a state should be able to extend diplomatic protection to resident refugees was considered and rejected by the Court of Appeal. This insistence on ties of nationality is a significant shortcoming since those most at risk from violations of fundamental human rights are the displaced, refugees and stateless persons. It is suggested that limiting diplomatic protection to nationals lacks a democratic spirit at its core and only serves to perpetuate existing inequalities in the system of human rights protection. A number of constitutions now provide either directly or implicitly for a constitutional right of diplomatic protection.[52] It remains an open question whether constitutional entrenchment extends the ambit of protection. It is easy to see the dangers inherent in a constitutional right of diplomatic protection. Ensuring that the guarantees of a national constitution are respected abroad could potentially be seen as a jurisdictional overreach and a violation of the sovereign of equality of states, especially when states insist that due process rights guaranteed to their nationals at home should be respected when they act abroad.

It is nevertheless significant that national courts have consistently confirmed that despite its discretionary character the right is justiciable and subject to judicial oversight.

In *Abbasi v. Secretary for Foreign and Common wealth Affairs*,[53] the applicant who was detained by the US authorities at Guantanamo Bay, sought judicial

---

50   R. (*On the Application of Al Rawi*) v. *Secretary of State for Foreign and Commonwealth Affairs* [2006] EWCA Civ 1279 [2008] QB 289.

51   Article 8 of the articles on diplomatic protection, *Report of the International Law Commission, Fifty-Eigth Session*, UN DOC./A/61/10 (2006).

52   See for instance the Constitution of the Republic of South Africa, as discussed in *Kaunda and Others V. President of the Republic of South Africa* (2004) 4S.A.L.R 235; For the position under the Canadian Constitution see, Canada (Prime Minister v. Khadr) (2009) F.C.A246; [2010] 1 FCR 73 at [2010] 1 SCR 44.

53   *Abbasi v. Secretary of Foreign and Commonwealth Affairs and Secretary of Home Office*, EWCA Civ 1598, 6 November 2002.

review to compel the UK foreign office to take up his case and make appropriate representations on his behalf to the US government. In the alternative, he asked that the UK government be compelled to give an explanation as to why representations on his behalf had not been undertaken. The English Court of Appeal, after an extended review of authorities confirmed the orthodox position that diplomatic protection was a right of States and did not as such give right to an enforceable duty under English law. However, it noted that this discretion was subject to judicial review, especially if it could be shown that decision was irrational, or contrary to the rules of natural justice.

In *Kaunda and others v. President of the Republic of South Africa and others*,[54] the South African Constitutional Court recognized that the right to request diplomatic protection was a constitutional entitlement under the South African constitution but it went on to hold that its actual exercise was a matter of foreign policy and therefore within the discretion of the executive branch. The decision in Kaunda has been confirmed in two subsequent decisions of the Supreme Court of South Africa. In *Rootman v. President of the Republic of South Africa*,[55] the Supreme Court refused a request by the applicant that the South African Government be compelled to take steps to assist him in securing the execution of a money judgment in his favour, granted by the Pretoria High Court, against the government of the Democratic Republic of Congo (DRC). The applicant had argued that the rule of law created an expectation that the State would assist a citizen enforce his or her rights. The Court however noted that, although the State may engage in diplomatic negotiations with a foreign state to secure the rights of its citizens, it could not be compelled to do so.

In *Omar Khadr v. The Prime Minister of Canada*,[56] the applicant argued that, the failure of the Canadian Government, to make representations to the US government for his release from Guantanamo Bay, was a violation of his rights under the Canadian Charter of Rights and freedoms. This was contested by the Canadian Government, which argued that it had an 'unfettered discretion to decide whether to request the return of a citizen detained in a foreign country, this being a matter within its exclusive authority to conduct foreign affairs'. The Court was therefore called upon to examine whether Canada had a legal duty to protect Mr. Khadr and what the ambit of that duty might be. The Canadian Supreme Court concluded that, in general, the right of protection was not enforceable as it fell within the executives' conduct of foreign policy. However, the Court would intervene if the government's position was irrational or

---

54 Case CCT 23/04, 2005 (4) SA 235 (CC).
55 Case 016/06 [2006] SCA 80 (RSA).
56 2009 FCA 246.

contrary to a legitimate expectation. The Court concluded that in the specific circumstances of the case, the failure to exercise diplomatic protection was a violation of the applicant's rights to life, liberty and security of the person. The Supreme Court explained that in Canada, the rule of law entailed an expectation that all government action was potentially subject to the Charter of Rights and Freedoms and the individual rights which it guaranteed. The crown prerogative in the conduct of foreign affairs was also subject to the Charter.

The decisions of national courts on these constitutional provisions support the thesis that general international law as it stands does not contain an enforceable legal duty of diplomatic protection. In this sense the discretionary character of diplomatic protection remains the primary legal position despite the developments as outlined in the human rights field. Human rights obligations and treaties protecting the economic interests of individuals have nevertheless substantially eroded the centrality of diplomatic protection as a mechanism for the protection of aggrieved individuals by creating directly enforceable rights even as against the state of which the individual is a national.[57] When contrasted with its traditional role, it is probably accurate to say that diplomatic protection is today more of a default mechanism for the enforcement of claims where there are no direct avenues provided for by international law. A better view, it is suggested, is to see diplomatic protection and enforcement mechanisms in human rights instruments as operating in parallel, serving related-but at times discrete objectives. For example, vindication of the rule of law may require that an action be brought on the international plane by a State even in the face of opposition by the wronged individual. It must also be accepted that States may have wider concerns going beyond the immediate interests of the wronged individual; these interests will at times be better served by exercising the discretion not to bring an action on the international plane. Where the exercise of its discretion results in the denial of a fundamental human right, it is suggested that the right of the state should be subordinated to the rights of the aggrieved individual. The existence of a human rights obligation, it is suggested, creates a strong expectation that the state will exercise its discretion in support of the aggrieved individual.

---

57   *Report of the International Law Commission, Fifty-Second Session*, UN Doc. A/55/10 (2000); See also J.R. Dugard, 'Diplomatic Protection and Human Rights: The Draft Articles of the International Law Commission' (2005) Aust. Yearbook of International Law, 75 at 80.

5 Conclusions

The cases surveyed confirm in their own different ways the recognition of a distinct set of communitarian obligations as part of international law. Not a single case has retracted from the *erga omnes* character of fundamental obligations first recognized in the *Barcelona Traction Case*. The international justiciability of these obligations as the cases illustrate remain problematic and none of the cases considered during Judge Koroma's tenure on the court has advanced the jurisprudence much. The conservative jurisprudence can in part be attributed to the fact that very few cases brought before the court directly raised the issue of *erga omnes* obligations. A court whose jurisdiction is directly derived from the consent of states has understandably been reticent to pronounce on issues not directly before it. The court's confirmation of the *erga omnes* character of obligations has nevertheless been real enough in all the cases that raised the issue – if only as a promise, a high aim of what the international system, collectively regards as important. The classical cases of diplomatic protection have largely disappeared from the international court's caseload. It was widely anticipated that the institution would gradually fall into desuetude as a result of developments confirming the universality of human rights law and the institutions for their enforcement. In the area of foreign investment it is also increasingly apparent that the protection of economic interests was better assured through bilateral investment treaties and not through the uncertainties that attend to diplomatic protection. The *Diallo, La Grand* and *Avena* cases nevertheless confirm that the institution has residual value, providing a remedy of last resort when other options have either been exhausted or are unavailable. The increasing number of cases in national jurisdictions invoking the right of diplomatic protection to compel governments to intervene when nationals have been deprived of their rights, indicates that it is probably premature to consign diplomatic protection to legal history. The increased public sensitivity to the importance of human rights values, and the development of a legitimate expectation that protection in the area of human rights is a right of citizenship in democracies, is likely to lead to more claims for governmental intervention on the basis of diplomatic protection. The increased awareness of the importance of human rights values comes at a time when disregard for due process requirements is on the rise even in democracies otherwise committed to the rule of law. It is for instance no surprise that the largest number of cases challenging detention orders have been from detainees held at Guantanamo Bay.

PART 3

International Law – General Subjects

∴

CHAPTER 10

The Competition Between and Among Intrinsic and Instrumental Values in Selected Competing Visions of the World

Sienho Yee

It is with great pleasure that I contribute at this time this paper on value and diversity to the festschrift for Judge Koroma. First of all, I am privileged to have had pleasant conversations with him from time to time on international law and some larger issues at The Hague and during the meetings of the *Institut de droit international*. Secondly, recently there has been a great deal of talk about visions and alternative visions of the world and the values involved in each vision.[1]

Obviously it is important for us to see clearly the various visions of the world. But the picture is quite murky and there is really no end to history, and there will be no conquering of one vision over another anytime soon. In the meantime, it is more important for us to be good decision-makers in any vision of the world that we find ourselves in, or choose to live in. To illustrate, if we are capitalists, we'd better be good capitalist decision-makers; if we are socialists, we'd better be good socialist decision-makers. How can we become good decision-makers? One way is to identify the competing values involved in any decision, do a value calculation and properly resolve the competition before a decision is made, as any decision ultimately embodies the resolution of such a competition. As there is an infinite variety of values involved in any decision, depending on the perspective of each person involved, it will be impossible for me to deal with each and every value in a raw fashion. Fortunately, philosophers have organized the world into two basic values – intrinsic and instrumental values. I will follow this approach here to try to bring out into the open some

---

* The preparation of this paper benefited from the support from Research Project No. 08&ZD055 of the China Social Sciences Foundation and the Fundamental Research Funds for the Central Universities in China. A slightly different version of this paper first appeared in 13 Chinese Journal of International Law (2014), 241–250. The websites were current as of 14 August 2014.

1   As my participation in this debate, this paper, in part, draws heavily upon, but also represents an effort to generalize, the discussions in Sienho Yee, The Intrinsic and Instrumental Values of Diversity: Some Philosophical and Legal Considerations, in: Sienho Yee & Jacques-Yvan Morin (eds), Multiculturalism and International Law: Essays in Honour of Edward McWhinney (Martinus Nijhoff 2009), 207–226.

implicit ways of, or a framework for, seeing and rationalizing the world, and to generalize the issues to a certain level so as to order our examination, analysis and rationalization in a better way. Probably at this "basic level" we will already have enough food for thought and, if we are conscientious, we will be moved in however small a way in our decision-making, for the better.

1   Intrinsic and Instrumental Values as Two Basic Values

The idea is basically this: For almost everything or every phenomenon in the world, one can find in it or assign to it two values: intrinsic value and instrumental value. This is also true with human beings. As we will see, each value is virtuous in a different way. Often "inherent" is used as synonymous with "intrinsic".[2]

An instrumental value is that which is good only as an instrument for something else. I want one US Dollar not to keep it for good, but to use it to buy a cup of coffee. The dollar bill is an instrument for me to obtain my coffee. On the other hand, an intrinsic value is an end value in itself. For example, my experience is an intrinsic value to me: it is unique and it forms part of me, my personhood, and that's it. Period.

Generally speaking, the two values may exist in the same thing at once: a value, independently evaluated, can be an intrinsic value; yet it may be an instrument for another intrinsic value. To this extent, these two values signify ways of seeing values and the world. One may see one value or another, depending on one's world view and orientation.

As is obvious, what follows from being treated as an instrumental value may be vastly different from what follows from being treated as an intrinsic value. For example, if indeed we are so special as an end in itself, as philosophers taught us long ago, we (or humanity) would reign supreme as end units, and not as instrumental units for the glory of the community, nation, society, or even God. If we were only instrumental members in a community, nation, society, or fellowship in Christ, we would have to sacrifice ourselves for the benefit of the community, nation, society, or God. Of course, closer to the truth is the position that both values may co-exist in us, and one may inform or promote the other. When they do come into conflict, which one should prevail is a perennial question.

An instrumental value will expire when the end for which the instrumental value is an instrument has been achieved. That is to say, the *raison d'être* of the

---

2   At the most difficult level, there may be a question of degree or vantage point here.

instrumental value no longer exists and the instrumental value should not exist any further. In contrast, an intrinsic value, or an end in itself, may not expire as a value, although I am not sure whether it is wise to say never. Therefore, if we can find an intrinsic value in a thing or a phenomenon, there can be better and longer life for that thing or phenomenon.

Perhaps for these and for other reasons, it has been observed that, "Intrinsic value [...] has a certain priority over extrinsic value. The latter is derivative from or reflective of the former and is to be explained in terms of the former. It is for this reason that philosophers have tended to focus on intrinsic value in particular."[3]

11 Intrinsic and Instrumental Values in Practical Decision-making

It is not just philosophers who have applied such a value analysis to the world. Practical decision-makers such as political leaders as well as legal decision-makers also have been doing this, although not yet in an ideal way.

First, we have legal instruments expressly recognizing the various values. The Universal Declaration of Human Rights declares in its preamble that "recognition of the inherent dignity and of the equal and inalienable rights of all members of the human family is the foundation of freedom, justice and peace in the world". This is repeated in both the International Covenant on Civil and Political Rights (ICCPR) and the International Covenant on Economic, Social and Cultural Rights (ICESCR). The latter two further recognize, in the preamble to each, that "these rights derive from the inherent dignity of the human person".

Second, even when decision-makers do not use the philosophers' parlance, we know for sure that they are doing the same analysis in a fuzzy way. Good examples are the US Supreme Court's decisions on affirmative action in education, to which we will come shortly.

Or even when decision-makers do not do any such analysis, their decisions can be rationalized as such. And there is a cottage industry in academia to do such rationalizing. For example, there has been a lot of literature on the rationale for the property law principle, *numerus clausus*, that under legislation there is a mandatory limit to the types of property interests available and judges cannot expand that list. An influential view seems to be that the principle reflects the instrumental value of efficiency: it is easier for the transfer

---

[3] See Intrinsic vs. Extrinsic Value, in: Stanford Encyclopedia of Philosophy (http://plato.stanford.edu/entries/value-intrinsic-extrinsic/#WhaIntVal).

of property if we have a fixed typology so that we can easily tell what we are giving and what we are getting. But the *numerus clausus* principle was adopted a long time ago, before the economic analysis of law came about. So such reasoning at best is a latter-day *post-facto* rationalization. Personally, I believe that this principle embodies the intrinsic value of self-determination and sovereignty: typology of property is an important matter on which only the representative of the people – Parliament – decides, and that's where sovereignty is located. Judges steer clear of that type of decision. This version jibes better with the history of the emergence of the principle.

III Resolution of the Competition between and among Intrinsic and Instrumental Values

If the world can be seen through such a lens so that intrinsic and instrumental values can be observed in every thing and every phenomenon, many disputes in society can be cast as conflicts or clashes of these values. The resolution of such disputes is then a choice between such values within the same category (an intrinsic value vs. another intrinsic value, or an instrumental value vs. another instrumental value) or between two values from different categories (an intrinsic value vs. an instrumental value). Roughly speaking, a reasonable person under normal circumstances would probably choose the more efficient one between two instrumental values and the more important one between two intrinsic values or between an intrinsic value and an instrumental value. Furthermore, one would give priority to an intrinsic value in the last scenario, if the intrinsic value is as important as or perhaps slightly less so than the instrumental value. A society as a whole, however, most likely would opt for the value perceived to be more important and achievable, often in a most un-nuanced fashion and without the benefit of an explicit intrinsic vs. instrumental value analysis. Such a choice may exhibit itself in law. In the following observations, I shall attempt to bring into the open such an analysis, by some concrete and interesting examples.

III.A ICCPR

A clear example of decision-makers consciously resolving the competition or conflict between and among intrinsic and instrumental values is the "general exception" under Article 4 of the ICCPR. Under paragraph 1 of that article, either the "life of the nation" is considered a value more important than the intrinsic value of many of the human rights protected under the ICCPR; or the instrumental value of the forfeiture of many of these rights is more important than the intrinsic value of these rights. That provision states:

> In time of public emergency which threatens the life of the nation and the existence of which is officially proclaimed, the States Parties to the present Covenant may take measures derogating from their obligations under the present Covenant to the extent strictly required by the exigencies of the situation, provided that such measures are not inconsistent with their other obligations under international law and do not involve discrimination solely on the ground of race, colour, sex, language, religion or social origin.

That calculation does not work with respect to some rights. Under paragraph 2 of Article 4, "No derogation from articles 6, 7, 8 (paragraphs 1 and 2), 11, 15, 16 and 18 may be made under this provision". The rights delineated under these enumerated articles, and the intrinsic value thereof, are considered more important than the instrumental value of the forfeiture of them. Probably one cannot say that a conscious decision has been made to prioritize the intrinsic value of these rights over that of the "life of the nation". Rather, the decision is probably that the enjoyment of the rights under the enumerated articles would not threaten the "life of the nation"; or that the forfeiture of these rights would not lessen or eliminate such a threat if it exists.

III.B   *Affirmative Action Cases in Education in the USA*

Similarly, many disputes relating to diversity can also be seen as conflicts between intrinsic and instrumental values. The resulting choices may be rationalized as one value being given priority over another. However, decision-makers may not have seen things through such a lens. Or, if they have, the pictures they have seen are incomplete or even garbled.

In national law, an obvious example is the *Grutter* case[4] in the US Supreme Court. In that case, the University of Michigan Law School applied a nuanced affirmative action policy in order to attain a critical mass of disadvantaged minority students in its student body. The Supreme Court upheld that policy. The Court clearly recognized the instrumental value of diversity – the resulting educational benefits – and its ultimate decision could be rationalized as one championing one value – the instrumental value according to the Court – over another, the intrinsic value of Grutter's right not to be discriminated against. In whatever manner the Court would like to explain its decision, by necessary implication, it must have decided this way.

However, the *modus operandi* in the Court's decision-making in this and similar cases appears not to pit these two values against each other expressly,

---

4   Grutter v. Bollinger, 539 U.S. 306 (2003).

but to ask: "Whether diversity is a compelling interest that can justify the narrowly tailored use of race in selecting applicants for admission to public universities."[5] This question was analyzed and answered in a way so that the challenger – Grutter – seemed to have disappeared from the picture, as if the compelling interest, which was an instrument to obtain the assorted educational benefits, were some sort of *force majeure* making it futile to address other rights and interests. Still, by necessary implication, the Court gave priority to an instrumental value – diversity as a means of securing the educational benefits – over an intrinsic value in not being discriminated against.

Such a governmental interest and/or educational benefits as an overriding "trump" over equal protection rights seem not to be based on some textual home in the Constitution but on the Court's own constitutional doctrine-making. Neither can one find such a home for "diversity" as such. As has been noted by Rehnquist, the received wisdom is that constitutional rights, not intrinsic worth, prevail in constitutional decision-making.[6] One thus is left only with the option of locating diversity in an established constitutional right in order to endow it with the fair power to override equal protection rights. It seems to be such a reasoning that was at work in Justice Powell's opinion in *Bakke*, where he did notice in his analysis a conflict of values or, as he may call it, a conflict of interests, as can be inferred from his choice of word "interest". But he did not pursue such a line of reasoning till the end. He said,

> in arguing that its universities must be accorded the right to select those students who will contribute the most to the "robust exchange of ideas," petitioner [the Regents of the University of California] invokes a countervailing constitutional interest, that of the First Amendment. In this light, petitioner must be viewed as seeking to achieve a goal that is of paramount importance in the fulfillment of its mission.[7]

Pitting a First Amendment interest against an equal protection right, an eminently intrinsic value, would seem to be presenting a better fight than pitting the assorted educational benefits against an equal protection right. Letting a First Amendment interest prevail over an equal protection right would seem to be more reasonable than letting the assorted educational benefits prevail over an equal protection right. It would seem that the triumph of one intrinsic value

---

5 Ibid., 321.
6 William H. Rehnquist, The Notion of a Living Constitution, 29 Harvard J. of Law and Public Policy (2006) (reprinting an earlier article), 401, 412.
7 Regents of the University of California v. Bakke, 438 U.S. 265 (1978), 313 (opinion of Powell, J.).

over another intrinsic value would make one feel better than the triumph of an instrumental value over an intrinsic value. If the First Amendment interest can be considered to have intrinsic value (probably not the version that Justice Powell had in mind), the conflict will then be between two intrinsic values. One wonders whether, under US law, there could ever be a plausible analysis that would treat diversity as an intrinsic value without going through the avenue of the First Amendment and would tackle the conflict between diversity and equal protection rights or other rights directly as a conflict between two intrinsic values.

III.C *Mr. Diallo's Case*

Mr. Diallo's case[8] in the Bronx, New York, is heartbreaking. Mr. Diallo was a young African immigrant who had returned to his building on the night of 4 February 1999. About 12:40 a.m. on that night, four New York police officers, all in street clothes, approached Mr. Diallo on the stoop of his building and fired 41 shots, striking him 19 times, as he retreated inside. The officers, who are white, said they had thought he had a gun. It turned out to be a wallet. The police perpetrators were acquitted in a subsequent prosecution by a jury consisting of four blacks and eight whites, because in its view what the officers were doing was considered not unreasonable so as to persuade it to convict them. So, the police perpetrators were reasonably conducting self-defence. In the jury's mind, then, although what the perpetrators did was *in fact* wrong, it was considered to be legitimate *in belief* and *in law,* for the good of society.

We do not see any express explanation of its action by the jury, but what it did can be rationalized this way: while the mistaken self-defence cost the life of Mr. Diallo, it was believed to be necessary for society (at least the particular version of it in the Bronx) to survive, and legitimately so. That is to say, it was all right for Mr. Diallo to die for the good of society. Two versions of the conflict of values are apparent: one between Mr. Diallo's life as an intrinsic value to him and his death as an instrumental value to society, and one between his life as an intrinsic value and the survival of society (ultimately) as an intrinsic value. The intrinsic value of Mr. Diallo's life was apparently considered not as important as his death's instrumental value to society *or* as the intrinsic value of the survival of society. This shows that at a critical moment even a capitalistic or

---

8   Jane Fritsch, The Overview: 4 Officers in Diallo Shooting Are Acquitted of All Charges, NY Times, 26 Feb. 2000 (http://partners.nytimes.com/library/ national/regional/022600ny-diallo.html). On subsequent similar tragedies, see Reuters stories relating to Mr. Trayvon Martin (http://www.reuters.com/search?blob=trayvon+martin) and Mr. Michael Brown (http://www.reuters.com/search?blob=ferguson).

liberal society (New York), which champions human rights, freedom or liberalism, ultimately sacrifices individuals for its own good, although one might not like to see the events in this light.

Well, the jury's logic, writ large, may hang over a conscientious analysis of the responsibility for the Iraq war in search of weapons of mass destruction. This version of the narrative apparently is yet to be done conscientiously.

III.D   Two Tales of the Lunar Embassy

At present there is an entity called the Lunar Embassy, with its headquarters in Nevada, USA, and with branches all over the world, which is selling land on the moon to willing takers.

In China, a branch incorporating as a company was also doing the same. The local business administration considered that to be unlawful conduct of business and imposed penalties on the company. The company sought judicial review. An intermediate people's court in Beijing ruled that the sales of land on the moon indeed constituted unlawful conduct of business and upheld the administrative decision, because the Outer Space Treaty prohibits the appropriation of outer space objects.[9]

In the Lunar Embassy's home state of Nevada, selling land to which one cannot walk, drive or fly is perfectly legal. Once Tom Sargent, spokesman for Nevada's Attorney General, was asked about this particular piece of business. Apparently, as long as the company pays its yearly $100 fee and no one complains, the Lunar Embassy is licensed in good standing. So far, no complaints have been received. People in Sargent's office – and his own family – have bought parcels. Do they believe they have purchased a real acre? "Well, my son certainly thinks he owns one," Sargent replied, "He's 10. It's on his wall in his bedroom."[10] Thus, a humorous remark takes care of a problem that has gone all the way to a higher, appellate court in China.

The two different approaches epitomize two different ways to resolve the competition between intrinsic and instrumental values. The Chinese administrative and judicial decisions perhaps can be characterized as giving priority to the instrumental value of a stable and quality business order over the intrinsic value of free enterprise or freedom of conducting business. This apparently results from a belief that the general populace is in need of protection. The Nevada approach can be characterized as giving priority to the intrinsic value of the autonomous decision-making of the buyers over the instrumental value

---

[9]   Beijing First Immediate People's Court, Beijing Yueqiucun Hangtiankeji Youxiangongsi, (2007) yizhong xingzhongzi No. 128.

[10] AP News, Man Sells Lunar Plots for $19.99 an Acre, Mar. 28, 2004.

of a stable business order. Obviously, this occurs against the background of a trust in the mature mentality of the populace.

One might perhaps say that the two approaches also epitomize two different ways to view business regulation in the larger sense. It seems that the Chinese approach emphasizes the quality of business products, an instrumental value consideration, while the Nevada approach privileges autonomy in decision-making – an intrinsic value consideration – by the purchasers, which usually also emphasizes disclosure of relevant information. This contrast perhaps epitomizes that between the entire social arrangements of China and those of the USA, or, writ large, between socialism and capitalism.

The clear disadvantages of the Chinese approach are in the difficulty in ensuring quality of business products and the inefficiency in attempting to do so. The felt need to liberate creative energy from suffocating bureaucracy, aggravated by perhaps unsavory self-interest or even irrationality in many aspects of decision-making and life in general, is real and seems to be getting stronger. This liberation is no doubt a herculean task, if ever achievable. The not-so-clear disadvantage to this approach is the fact that someone else may be making a decision on the quality of a product for the purchaser.

The disadvantages of the Nevada approach are in the difficulty in providing perfect disclosure or in reaching a rational decision even with perfect disclosure of information. The liberal capitalism loop seems to consist of these presumptions: information can be perfectly disclosed; once disclosed, information can be perfectly digested; once information is digested, rational decisions can be perfectly made. This finds no better reflection than in securities regulation in the USA in the modern era. But the liberal capitalism loop is full of bumpers at any juncture: information may not be perfectly disclosed; once disclosed, information may not be perfectly digested; or once information is digested, rational decisions may not be perfectly made. The animal spirit in humans may predominate. And we know that any one of these bumpers would be sufficient to break the loop and wreak havoc in a particular sector or even the whole system.

Perhaps one can see images of the two approaches in the unfolding and the aftermath of the 2008 world financial crisis in which both imperfect disclosure and irrational decision-making played an important part. Different approaches to economic activity management thus led to different damage in the world. This is common knowledge now and need not be described here.

Our analysis here may call for a reconsideration of which values are more important and achievable, and perhaps a resultant change in the fundamental rules of the game so that they would ultimately reflect a nuanced combination of the two approaches discussed. These changes in the rules of the game should have the capacity of removing the bumpers or, if necessary, changing the loop itself as we are talking about. The current regulations in the USA and elsewhere to strengthen consumer protection will only fix small potholes, leaving systemic and structural ills in place, probably to wreak greater havoc still in the next worldwide financial crisis.

Perhaps the *numerus clausus* principle, as a principle if not in its detailed content, should be applied to financial products with some proactive rigor, so that the bumpers in the liberal capitalism loop will not come about to begin with. Perhaps certain financial products should simply be banned. This of course would necessitate an adjustment in the value calculation, as we talked about. Policy-makers will no doubt have an interesting task in making this adjustment.

III.E *Democratic Intervention*

Democratic intervention has been a topic that has consumed a substantial amount of collective time at various forums and figured prominently in the literature. An analysis of this topic under the framework sketched out here could reveal important considerations for the decision-makers.

Often the choice presented for consideration is between a democratic government and the existing regime under attack. Even in this scenario, it would be interesting to conduct an analysis of the competition between intrinsic and instrumental values involved, which is rarely presented openly.

Another choice for analysis would be between democracy as a form of social arrangement and the existing form of that arrangement in the State where democratic intervention is being conducted. The analysis may not be too easy, as one might find it difficult to assign an intrinsic value to democracy as such, even if one were to subscribe to the famous view that "Democracy is the worst form of government, except for all those other forms that have been tried from time to time."

Another choice may be between democracy and the lives of those people who would be killed inevitably during the intervention. Here the analysis of the values involved can get very difficult. If one were to ask the mothers of those who were killed, the analysis might not be so difficult.

Still another choice may be between (1) the sudden and dramatic suffering including the deaths of the finite number of victims during the democratic intervention, even if successful, and (2) the slower and less dramatic suffering of a much larger number of victims who would be mistreated under the regime being attacked during the democratic intervention.

The intrinsic and instrumental values involved in each of these choices may appear different from different angles. The competition between and among them can be fierce. The choice of one value over another may be unappetizing or even nauseating. One hopes that decision-makers carefully resolve such competition in their decision-making.

IV   Conclusions

Society has taken cognition of the competition between intrinsic and instrumental values. Yet it is not always conscious of whether it is intrinsic value or instrumental value that it is championing in its decision-making. I am not championing a particular vision of the world, not here in this comment anyway. I leave the decisions to the decision-makers. What I am asking for is clearer and better analyses that tackle such conflicts of values in a more direct way. Indeed, it would be desirable that before any important decision is made, the relevant decision-maker(s) should conduct a calculation of the intrinsic and instrumental values involved and resolve the competition between them in a formal way. Such clearer and more direct analyses would help to concentrate the mind so as to allow conscious and perhaps tough decision-making. Such further work will inform society's efforts to prioritize the more important value over others. This will improve the quality of the exercise of decision-making power and, of course, the ultimate result of that exercise.

One may wonder whether the calculation between intrinsic and instrumental values can be of such use or significance. Knowing that computer scientists can do so many beautiful things with 0 and 1, we perhaps should be confident that important decision-makers in society can do a lot with intrinsic and instrumental values.

CHAPTER 11

Democratizing International Law-Making

Babafemi Akinrinade

Recent developments in the international system have led to calls for international law to adapt and meet extant and future challenges to the international legal order. There are perennial questions about the interface of many aspects of international law with questions of national security and the protection of human rights. Other old and new challenges include environmental concerns, climate change, cybersecurity, global regulation of international finance with its linkages to money laundering, terrorism and narco-trafficking.[1] There are also emerging or recurrent tensions between diverse fields of international law, including human rights and the environment, international trade, and the World Trade Organization's intellectual property regime and its impact on public health. Within international law, there is the concern about the proliferation of judicial tribunals and the "danger" of fragmentation of international law.[2]

The challenge posed to international law by these developments is magnified because of the State-centric nature of international law and the supposed inflexibility of this regime in adapting to change. States are not perceived to be in a hurry to deal with some of these challenges to the international order despite their seeming urgency, and their potential impact on human and other lives. The classic understanding of international law as law between nations means that, despite the progress of recent years, actors and participants[3] in the international system other than States are still relatively marginalized.

---

1   See e.g. Joel P. Trachtman, The Future of International Law: Global Government (2012)
2   On fragmentation of international law, implicit in the Report of the Study Group of the International Law Commission on the subject is the lack of consensus on fragmentation within international law. According to the report, "[w]hile the reality and importance of fragmentation cannot be doubted, assessments of the phenomenon have varied. *Some commentators have been highly critical of what they have seen as the erosion of general international law, emergence of conflicting jurisprudence, forum-shopping and loss of legal security.*" (Emphasis supplied). Fragmentation of International Law: Difficulties Arising from the Diversification and Expansion of International Law, *Report of the Study Group of the International Law Commission*, UN Doc. A/CN.4/L.702, 18 July 2006, p. 4.
3   On the utility of "participants" rather than "subjects" or "objects" of international law, See Rosalyn Higgins, Problems and Process: International Law and How We Use It, 50 (1994).

States are thus the only and "proper" subjects of international law. Only States and other State-sanctioned entities ratify international treaties and as long as State consent is material to the architecture of the international system, international law-making will always be held "hostage" to State consent. The materiality of State consent makes it more difficult for a nimbler response to these current challenges and others that may arise in the future.

The conflicted nature of the international legal order is reflected in calls for accepting the reality of the "democratization" of international law-making, and a recognition of the role of actors other than States in the law-making process.[4] Factors contributing to the democratization of international law include the end of the Cold War and the subsequent removal of the "constraints ... [confining] the activities of smaller actors,"[5] the technological revolution providing access to non-State actors, as well as the "privatization" of international law-making,[6] "involving the voluntary withdrawal in some states of the state apparatus from activities ... previously deemed to be inherently "public"."[7]

Yet, moving beyond the State-centric process by recognizing other participants on equal footing with States is *eo ipso* a challenge to the international legal system as conceived presently.[8] Those other actors have interests that are not necessarily congruent with those of States and, sometimes, these interests are totally opposed to State interests. International law, going forward, is thus expected to recognize these multiple interests and embrace a multiplicity of actors in the law-making process to ensure its continued relevance and enhance the legitimacy of the law. That these actors have influenced State conduct and international legislation in recent years is undeniable. The question

---

4   See e.g. W. Michael Reisman, *The Democratization of Contemporary International Law-Making Processes and the Differentiation of Their Application*, in Developments Of International Law In Treaty Making, pp. 15–30 (Rüdiger Wolfrum & Volker Röben, eds., 2005)

5   Reisman, id., at 24.

6   Id.

7   Id.

8   *Compare* the following: "Now, the greater clout they [non-State actors] have come to enjoy has led some observers to believe that they have shaken the existing international legal order and they are likely to be a force in the future. This has led some commentators, very powerful and influential commentators like Jessica Matthews to the conclusion that they deserve to be treated on par and as equal to states." Rabmatullah Khan, *Comment* on Eibe Riedel, *The Development of International Law: Alternatives to Treaty-Making? International Organizations and Non-State Actors*, in Developments Of International Law In Treaty Making, *supra* note 4, at 332.

is the extent to which these voices become as dominant as States and the basis of the claims that they be vested with such influence.

Moving forward and accepting the claims for democratization of international law-making still calls for a recognition and affirmation of the past of international law, one devoted largely to State interests and State consent. Arguably, international law today exists only because States exist, States – and the international system – provide the *raison d'être* for the existence of international law. As presently constituted, the implementation of that law depends very much on States, whether willingly or coerced. If willingly, it is the will of the State concerned. If unwilling or coerced, other States have to do the coercion.[9] Thus, willingly or coerced, international law still depends on States for its existence and survival. The absence of a central legislative body for international law means that each State, and States generally, has/have a very important role in the realization of the aims of international law.

As noted, other actors have interests not aligned with those of States. There is constant friction developing between multiple areas of international law[10] and there are struggles in the efforts to mediate those tensions. Apart from conflicts related to substantive and procedural aspects of international law, one emerging tension relates to the varying regional expressions of international law.[11] The existence of judicial tribunals within regional organizations for the purposes of interpreting the laws of those organizations has the potential of creating diverse body of laws that theoretically can lead to conflicts with other regional or global bodies in their interpretation of international law. As commentators have noted, these "different fora have taken different approaches to analyzing the relationship among the international, regional, and nation-

---

9   Other actors may of course be involved in getting other States to demand or force compliance by the targeted State.

10 See for example the tensions between the implementation of international human rights law in the context of international crimes and the related issue of State and personal immunities conferred by international law.

11 On regional expressions of international law, three meanings of "regionalism" in international law are offered in the Analytical Study of the Study Group of the International Law Commission. First, "regionalism" may refer to "a set of approaches and methods for examining international law." The second is "regionalism" as a "technique for international law-making," while the third sees "regionalism" as "the pursuit of a geographical exceptions to universal international law rules." It is with the second and third meanings that this essay is concerned. See Fragmentation of International Law: Difficulties Arising from the Diversification and Expansion of International Law, Report of the Study Group of the International Law Commission (Finalized by Martti Koskenniemi), UN Doc. A/CN.4/L.682, 13 April 2006, pp. 102–112.

al legal orders."[12] An example is the direct challenge to the authority of the UN Security Council by the decisions of the European Court of Justice, the European Court of Human Rights and national courts. The challenge arises in the context of the interpretation of the constitutive instruments of those bodies which are implicated by the decisions of the UN Security Council.[13] One of those challenges arose in *Kadi and Al Barakaat* where the European Court of Justice (ECJ) decided it could review the lawfulness of a European Community measure aimed at implementing a resolution of the UN Security Council. The primacy of the UN Security Council in maintaining international peace and security is uncontested, given the provisions of the UN Charter. But the question remains whether this primacy of the UN Security Council means that the body is above the law and its decisions are beyond judicial review.[14]

The contemplation of the drafters of the UN Charter[15] in Chapter VIII is of "regional arrangements" complementing the work of the UN,[16] and not necessarily challenging the UN's authority. It is arguable though that the *Kadi and Al Barakaat* decision is a welcome development as it raises the notion of accountability of the UN Security Council,[17] although at the same time it could be argued that the European Court of Justice is not a supranational authority over the UN Security Council. As the international legal system evolves, there will be further expressions of regional dimensions of international law which may be opposed to what is currently accepted as the norm. Increasingly, these challenges may be to the substantive aspects of international law, rather than being mere "methodologies" for understanding or interpreting international law.[18] The consequences for international law can only be imagined when such as-

---

12 Jeffrey L. Dunoff, Steven R. Ratner & David Wippman, International Law: Norms, Actors, Process: A Problem-Oriented Approach 916 (2010).
13 Id.
14 See *Yassin Abdullah Kadi and Al Barakaat International Foundation v. Council of the European Union and Commission of the European Communities*, 3 C.M.L.R. 41 (2008) For a sample of the debate on this issue, see Jeffrey L. Dunoff et al, id., at 924–926.
15 See Charter of the United Nations (As Amended), concluded at San Francisco, 26 June 1945. Entered into force, 24 October 1945. 1 U.N.T.S. XVI, 1976 Y.B.U.N. 1043; 1945 Can. T.S. 7; 1945 S.A.T.S. 6; 1946 U.K.T.S. 67. Cmd. 7015, 145 B.F.S.P. 805; U.S.T.S. 993, 59 Stat. 1031; reprinted in Supplement of Basic Documents To International Law And World Order, 11 (Burns H. Weston, Richard A. Falk & Hilary Charlesworth, eds., 1997).
16 See Articles 52–54, UN Charter, *supra* note 3 (Chapter VIII – Regional Arrangements).
17 See e.g. Nikolaos Lavranos, *Judicial Review of UN Sanctions by the European Court of Justice*, 78 Nordic J. Int'l L. 343, 357–358. See Dunoff et al., *supra* note 12, 925.
18 This would be the third meaning of "regionalism" as opposed to the first meaning offered in the Analytical Study. See *supra* note 11.

sertions of regional autonomy are made by judicial bodies protecting constitutional arrangements that birthed them, which then places them in direct conflict with the global order.

Now as Then: Marching to the Future

In a strict sense, the future of international law belongs to its past. That future cannot be totally divorced from States as custodians and guardians of the law. The present international order constituted by States is accepted as following the Treaty of Westphalia, 1648.[19] The rise of the nation-State in Europe is thus tied to the rise of international law. As presently enacted and implemented, many consider international law to be largely a European venture,[20] to which other States have been invited or coopted, by design or by accident.[21] The flexibility and expansiveness of international law rules means that other States are welcome to become parties to this venture which has served the interest of non-European States, especially the new States that were created after World War II. Given the rise of the United States and its imprint on international law, that body of laws is arguably now more reflective of Euro-American interests,[22] while accommodating the interests of other States. Norms that reflect or pro-

---

19 Peace Treaty between the Holy Roman Emperor and the King of France and their Respective Allies, concluded at Munster in Westphalia, October 24, 1648. For the text see Treaty of Westphalia at http://avalon.law.yale.edu/17th_century/westphal.asp.
20 See e.g. Antony Anghie, *Imperialism, Sovereignty And the Making of International Law* (2004)
21 See e.g. Martti Koskenniemi, *International Law in Europe: Between Tradition and Renewal*, 16 Eur. J. Int'l. L. 113 (2005). Koskenniemi offers a critique of the supposed universality of international law. However, Dupuy offers a vigorous rebuttal of Koskenniemi's (and similar) arguments. See Pierre-Marie Dupuy, *Some Reflections on Contemporary International Law and the Appeal to Universal Values: A Response to Martti Koskenniemi*, 16 Eur. J. Int'l. L. 131–137 (2005).
22 This essay follows Dianne Otto's position:
    In using the term "Europe," I do not mean the geographical entity. The term refers to the West in the broad sense of those interests or regimes of power which benefit from the reproduction of European knowledges and, in so doing, affirm European or Western dominance. This term includes postcolonial elites who have embraced European knowledges and institutions, albeit with indigenous variations, as well as the elites of the West.
    Dianne Otto, *Rethinking the "Universality" of Human Rights Law*, 29 Colum. Hum. Rts. L. Rev. 1 (1997–1998)

tect the interests of the new States have since been adopted[23] but those States still find themselves marginalized on issues that materially affect them, issues which may be opposed by Euro-American States.[24] Despite this situation,

---

[23] According to Dupuy, "it is to the aforementioned 'Third World' countries that we owe, from the 1960s onwards, the proposal that any treaties contrary to 'peremptory norms' should be null and void in their entirety." Thus, the "concept of *jus cogens* and its initial inclusion in Article 53 of the Vienna Convention on the Law of Treaties were above all a victory of the South over the West." Dupuy, *supra* note 20, 134. Dupuy also notes that "'obligations *erga omnes*', set forth in the famous paragraph 33 of the [ICJ's] ruling in the *Barcelona Traction* case," was meant to appease not Western but Third World States to "once again go down the ICJ route, which they had abandoned following its ultra-conservative decision in the *South-West African* case." Id. Further, Dupuy cites the adoption of Resolution 1803 of the General Assembly, where Third World countries obtained an affirmation of the principle of permanent sovereignty over natural resources, as well as the adoption of the Charter of Economic Rights and Duties of States. Id., at 135. See also Resolution on Permanent Sovereignty Over Natural Resources, adopted by the UN General Assembly, Dec. 14, 1962. G.A. Res. 1803, UN GAOR, 17th Sess., Supp. No. 17, at 15, UN Doc. A/5217 (1963); reprinted in 2 I.L.M. 223 (1963); Charter of Economic Rights and Duties of States, adopted by the UN General Assembly, Dec. 12, 1974. G.A. Res. 3281, UN GAOR, 29th Sess., Supp. No. 31, at 50, UN Doc. A/9631 (1975); *reprinted in* 14 I.L.M. 251 (1975).

[24] An example is the process that led to the adoption of the Bamako Convention in 1991. Following a series of incidents on the unlawful dumping of hazardous wastes produced in industrialized countries in developing countries, a conference convened under the auspices of the United Nations Environmental Programme (UNEP) adopted the Basel Convention on the Control of Transboundary Movement of Hazardous Wastes and the Disposal in 1989. The Basel Convention for the most part reflected the position of the industrialized countries in the tensions between that set of countries and developing countries. Developed countries wanted to keep their options open, while developing countries, especially African countries, wanted a ban on international trade in hazardous wastes. See Phillipe Sands, Principles Of International Environmental Law 690 (2ed, 2003). The Basel Convention was criticized for legitimating the trade in hazardous and other wastes and leaving "developing states in the third world vulnerable to unsafe disposal practices." See Patricia W. Birnie & Alan E. Boyle, International Law And The Environment 341 (1992). Consequently, African countries that had favored a total ban on the export of these wastes to African countries adopted the Bamako Convention to reflect their interests. The Convention on the Ban of Imports into Africa and the Control of Transboundary Movement and Management of Hazardous Wastes within Africa, 1991 (Bamako Convention), gives effect to the positions African countries had adopted in the negotiations leading to the adoption of the Basel Convention. See David Hunter, James Salzman, & Durwood Zaelke, International Environmental Law And Policy 878 (1998). See also Sands, id., at 696. Had their interests been reflected in the Basel Convention, there would have been no need for the Bamako Convention. For the Conventions, see Basel Convention on the Control of Transboundary Movement of Hazardous Wastes,

countries of the Global South still invoke international law and do not challenge its applicability.[25]

In moving forward, there are calls for international law to be more nimble, easily adapted to changing circumstances. To achieve this, rules have to be rewritten since some of these were developed in the pre-1945 world and events have dramatically changed since then. Such rules include the prohibition on the use of force in Article 2(4) of the UN Charter and those on permissible use of force in Article 51. These changes, for example, will allow the use of force for the purposes of realizing the emergent "responsibility to protect" (R2P) doctrine,[26] in the place of the doctrine of humanitarian intervention which is of doubtful legality under international law.[27] Some view current international law-making processes as old-fashioned, "essentially oligarchical,"[28] slow and not particularly responsive to ever-changing circumstances.[29] This leads to calls for expanding the recognition of soft-law in moving international law forward. While there is considerable skepticism on the utility of soft-law, it is considered nimble enough to recognize it as a form of law, "soft" or not.[30] Relatedly, given the "creaky time-consuming"[31] nature of treaty-making, other ways of making international law should be considered. Treaty-making and other traditional modes of making international law, or "state-made law"[32] should be paired with a more democratic form of international law-making.[33]

---

concluded at Basel, March 22, 1989, entered into force May 24, 1992. UN Doc. UNEP/WG.190/4; reprinted in 28 I.L.M. 657 (1989). See also Bamako Convention on the Ban of Import into Africa and the Control of Transboundary Movement and Management of Hazardous Wastes within Africa, concluded at Bamako, January 29, 1991, entered into force April 22, 1998; 30 I.L.M. 775 (1991).

25 See Dupuy, *supra* note 21, 135.
26 See James Crawford, Brownlie's Principles of Public International Law 755–756 (8th ed., 2012).
27 Id., 752–753
28 Reisman, *supra* note 4, at 23.
29 See Hanspeter Neuhold, *The Inadequacy of Law-Making by International Treaties: "Soft-Law" as an Alternative?*, in Developments of International Law in Treaty Making, pp. 39–52, esp. 46–47 (Rüdiger Wolfrum & Volker Röben, eds., 2005). According to Reisman, the treaty-making (and ratification) process is "creaky" and "time-consuming." See Reisman, *supra* note 4, p. 29. According to Neuhold, treaties "often fail to meet four requirements for an effective legal regime" which he identifies as speed, clarity and uniformity, universality of participation, and flexibility and adaptability. See p. 40.
30 See Neuhold, id., pp. 47–52. See also Reisman, *supra* note 4, pp. 17, 28–29.
31 Reisman, *supra* note 4, at 29.
32 See Reisman, id., at 24
33 See Reisman, id., at 22 *et seq.*

This other form, the "media-made law"[34] is "a much larger and more open law-making process, which is transmitted through multiple electronic and media channels and operates directly on the politically relevant strata of the great democratic states and the governments dependent on them."[35] It is one which "continuously shapes expectations and demands of what is right and wrong and, more urgently, which wrongs require some legal remedy."[36]

The "expectations shaped" by this media-made law is not necessarily "congruent" with that of "state-made law."[37] Media-made law may characterize events significantly differently from state-made law and is not necessarily bound by the restrictions suffered by state-made law. Given the fluidity of those involved in shaping this new legal realization, "characterization of legal violation[s] and demand for remedy" may not be consistent across countries.[38] However, as Reisman notes, this media-made law also has a "problematic feature."[39] According to Reisman, "the remedial component of state-made law is cautious (perhaps to a fault) and acutely aware of the difficulties and costs of enforcement."[40] On the other hand, "the remedial component of media-made law is based on the demand for immediate satisfaction and has a sense of political possibility that is not tempered by experience."[41] As Reisman concedes, media-made law "[i]ndeed ... is sometimes romantic and unreal."[42]

Nonetheless, to Reisman, media-made law is a "more democratic," if not "necessarily egalitarian"[43] way of making international law. But state-made law, to the extent that it comprises the traditional sources of international law,[44] mirrors the problems inherent in that mode of law-making. It does have

---

[34] Media-made law "takes its name from the channels through which the communications are delivered rather than the extraordinary range of groups and individuals who act through it, shaping expectations and having their own expectations shaped." Id., at 25.

[35] Id., at 24.

[36] Id.

[37] Id., at 25.

[38] Id.

[39] Id., at 26.

[40] Id.

[41] Id.

[42] Id.

[43] Reisman, id., at 23.

[44] These include Article 38(1) provisions of the Statute of the International Court of Justice. See *infra* note 46.

its advantages as well, in terms of the near – certainty and the expectations of the law and its symbols.[45]

Calls for moving international law forward and adapting to the challenges of the 21st and subsequent centuries go in tandem with calls for democratization of international law-making. These ideas are not necessarily the same, as international law can still be adapted to the new century, essentially employing the same mode of lawmaking to which it has been attuned in the past. But, given the multitude of challenges, a more favorable perception of international law certainly helps, in view of the general views of impotency or irrelevancy of international law to the realities of many peoples around the world. International law cannot afford to be marginalized by the same States that should be upholding the prescriptions of the law.

Sources of International Law and International Law-Making Fora

Another important element of the democratization of international law-making process is the question of recognition of other sources of international law beyond those listed in Article 38 of the Statute of the International Court of Justice (ICJ) which provides:

1. The Court, whose functions is to decide in accordance with international law such disputes as are submitted to it, shall apply
   a. international conventions, whether general or particular, establishing rules expressly recognized by the contesting states;
   b. international custom, as evidence of a general practice accepted as law;
   c. the general principles of law recognized by civilized nations;
   d. subject to the provisions of Article 59, judicial decisions and the teachings of the most highly qualified publicists of the various nations, as subsidiary means for the determination of rules of law.
2. This provision shall not prejudice the power of the Court to decide a case *ex aequo et bono*, if the parties agree thereto.[46]

---

45   See Georges Abi-Saab, *Comment, in* Developments Of International Law In Treaty Making, pp. 30–37, at 33 (Rüdiger Wolfrum & Volker Röben, eds., 2005).

46   Article 38, Statute of the International Court of Justice, concluded at San Francisco, 26 June 1945. Entered into force, 24 October 1945. 1978 Y.B.U.N. 1052; 1945 Can. T.S. 7; 1945 S.A.T.S. 6; 1946 U.K.T.S. 67. Cmd. 7015, 145 B.F.S.P. 832; U.S.T.S. 993, 59 Stat. 1031; *reprinted in*

Strictly, Article 38 enumerates the sources of law which the ICJ shall apply in deciding disputes submitted to it[47] and does not claim to be the final authority on the sources of international law. But there has been deference over the years to the provisions of Article 38. At the same time, law is being made and expressed through judicial decisions, including interpretations of the law, by international bodies other than the ICJ and by regional judicial institutions.[48] It is arguable that the continued relevance of Article 38 is dependent on litigation before the ICJ. Absent contentious cases and requests for advisory opinion before the Court, the judges cannot pronounce on what the law is. Anything offered by the judges beyond the confines of the particular cases before them would be mere opinion of the members of the judicial tribunals and would probably qualify or rank as "the teachings of the most highly qualified publicists." These would "not actually qualify as sources of law but rather as means to establish the existence of sources of law."[49]

The ICJ plays a dominant role in making international law through the fulfilment of its assigned role under the UN Charter and the ICJ Statute annexed to the Charter. Another relevant institution is the International Law Commission (ILC), a body tasked with the "promotion of the progressive development and codification of international law."[50] According to the Statute of the ILC, "progressive development of international law" is a term of convenience "meaning the preparation of draft conventions on subjects which have not yet been regulated by international law or in regard to which the law has not yet been sufficiently developed in the practice of States."[51] The ILC Statute distinguishes this term from "codification of international law" which is a term of convenience "meaning the more precise formulation and systematization of

---

Supplement Of Basic Documents To International Law And World Order, *supra* note 15, at 32.

[47] Higgins, *supra* note 3, 18. As Judge Koroma notes, the list in Article 38 "is not *de facto* law that the Court has to apply, it is merely descriptive." Abdul G. Koroma, Comment, *International Court and Tribunals: Alternative to Treaty Making*, in Developments Of International Law In Treaty Making, pp. 621–625, at 622, (Rüdiger Wolfrum & Volker Röben, eds., 2005).

[48] See Koroma, id., at 621.

[49] Rüdiger Wolfrum, *Sources of International Law*, in The Max Planck Encyclopedia Of Public International Law, Vol. IX, 301 (2012)

[50] Article 1, Statute of the International Law Commission, adopted by the General Assembly in Resolution 174 (II) of 21 November 1947, as amended by Resolutions 485 (V) of 12 December 1950, 984 (X) of 3 December 1955, 985 (X) of 3 December 1955 and 36/39 of 18 November 1981.

[51] Article 15, id.

rules of international law in fields where there already has been extensive State practice, precedent and doctrine."[52] The work of the ILC has been primarily around these two concepts and it has laid the groundwork for many treaties adopted in the international system.

Of course, these two institutions, coupled with other intergovernmental organizations that engage in international law-making, are predominantly State organized institutions. As they are creatures of States they do primarily represent and project State interests. Thus, they suffer from the same problems Reisman attributes to "state-made law." International law is also made through conferences convened by the UN General Assembly[53] and States generally, through regional organizations, and the majority of treaties are made by States, either as bilateral or plurilateral treaties. Treaties, as one of the primary sources of international law, are made by States or State-created entities. The other significant source of international law is customary international law. This also is structured around State practice that is accepted as law. Other sources of law in Article 38 are related to States and State interests, except the "teachings of the most highly qualified publicists of the various nations," which are "subsidiary means for the determination of rules of law."[54]

Any refinement of these various sources and fora as a way of meeting the challenges of this century would be unacceptable for those seeking democratization of the law-making process, as it "border[s] on fantasy to imagine that [they] could be spiffed up and made into the principal law-making modality of contemporary international law."[55] Further, neither "can the portmanteau process of customary-law making, deriving from state practice accompanied by subjective perceptions of law itself fill the need, for in a context of rapid technological change the need to craft normative arrangements is a eufunction of the change itself and must often precede rather than follow from state practice."[56] Obviously, to its proponents, there is something about "contemporary" international law that warrants bypassing current modes of law-making to make that law acceptable and capable of meeting modern challenges.

---

52   Id.
53   Generally, the UN has been an important source and forum for the initiation and creation of international law, through its principal organs and the specialized agencies. See also Mary Ellen O'Connell, Richard F. Scott & Naomi Roht-Arriaza, The International Legal System 1187–1188 (2010).
54   Article 38, ICJ Statute, *supra* note 46.
55   Reisman, *supra* note 4, at 29.
56   Reisman, id., at 29–30.

Expanding the Space and Participants in International Law-Making

In the context of democratization of international law-making, given the problems associated with State-made law, media-made law is an attractive proposition. According to its proponents, it is a "dynamic form of international law-making … a process of norm generation that does not conform to many of the policies we demand of conventional law-making."[57] It is a form of law that "political decision makers cannot afford to ignore," but which critics would "err in dismissing it."[58] According to Reisman, this is "the imperative version of what is presented as right that appears in editorials of leading newspapers, is repeated relentlessly in the visual and audial media and that comes to be reflected in popular expectation."[59] It is these expectations that are in turn "recorded in incessant opinion polls which are then regularly checked by nervous decision-makers and their "spin-meisters.""[60]

But as Abi-Saab rightly notes, the idea of "media-made law" is "antithetical to the very concept of law." There is no evidence that that form of law would follow procedures that "ensure their social perceptibility and recognition as law." While law can, and does "change in response to social demands," it "cannot change according to opinion polls every fortnight, every week or every day; or for that matter every night following the leaders of the morning press."[61] For such social demands to become law, they need "to go through certain processes and procedures." Thereafter, subjects can

> perceive it and react to it as a general rule of international law, representing the general will of the international community as a whole; and not the will of the decision-maker in one country, who decides that this is the rule the world needs or should have, who acts upon it, even in violation of well (and pre-)established rules, and who then claims that this is "practice" that established" the new rule, because it has "surrounded it by the symbols of authority" of law, by demonstrating a "willingness to act to make it effective."[62]

---

57   Id., at 23.
58   Id.
59   Id.
60   Id.
61   Abi-Saab, *supra* note 45, at 33.
62   Id., 33–34.

Rather than depending on *vox populi*[63] as a way of expanding participation in international law-making,[64] we may wish to focus rather on making the current system more egalitarian and truly representative of all countries within the international system, not only in the creation but also in the application of international law. There is still a feeling that international law represents mostly Western (Euro-American) interests. Customary international law only has meaning in the context of State practice from that region. Assertions of progressive development of international law and the creation of new norms are mostly in the context of the will of the powerful States.[65] International law sometimes appears to serve as the law of (made by) the strong for the weak.[66]

Given the marginality of small States, especially States in the Third World or the Global South in shaping international law, efforts could be directed at focusing on the concerns of those States, critically examining their claims and seeing how to accommodate those interests within the framework of current international law. The tensions within the law of immunity and its relationship with international human rights and international criminal law is one area of contestation.[67] While the current trend is to deny immunity to State officials alleged to have committed human rights atrocities, this is particularized to those branches of the law. There is still a law of immunity granting serving heads of States immunity from criminal processes. To the extent that it is denied, it is in relation to the heads of States of the weaker countries. The ongoing prosecutorial efforts in the International Criminal Court (ICC) of the

---

63 Daniel Thürer, *Comment, The Democratization of Contemporary Law-Making Processes and the Differentiation of Their Application*, in Developments Of International Law In Treaty Making, pp. 53–59, at 55 (Rüdiger Wolfrum & Volker Röben, eds., 2005).

64 As Jessica Matthews notes, an expansion in "international decision-making" will "exacerbate the so-called democratic deficit, as decisions that elected representatives once made shift to unelected international bodies." Jessica T. Matthews, *Power Shift*, 76 (1) Foreign. Aff. 50–66, 65 (1997). This can be analogized to the current calls for democratization of international law-making. It definitely shifts power from States to unelected and unaccountable networks of actors.

65 For example, only the very powerful States are quick to assert the emergence of a norm of humanitarian intervention simply because the target States for intervention are usually the weaker States.

66 As Julius Nyerere, the former Tanzanian President characterizes it in relation to the place of the "Third World" in the international legal and economic order, "In international rule-making, we are recipients not participants." Julius K. Nyerere, *South-South Option*, in The Third World Strategy: Economic And Political Cohesion In The South, 9, 10 (Altaf Gauhar, ed., 1983). See Makau Mutua, *What is TWAIL?* 94 Am. Soc'y Int'l L. Proc. 31, 35 (2000).

67 Crawford, *supra* note 26, 505, 688. See also Dapo Akande, *International Law Immunities and the International Criminal Court*, 98 Am. J. Int'l L. 407–433 (2004).

Kenyan President and Vice-President is illustrative of this situation.[68] The African Union (AU) requested a one year deferral of the prosecutions. The response of the UN Security Council was essentially to deny the request by adopting the resolution.[69] The request was in accordance with Article 16 of the ICC Statute,[70] which was grounded in the AU's reaffirmation of the "principles deriving from national laws and customary international law by which sitting Heads of State and other senior state officials are granted immunities during their tenure of office."[71]

The rationale for denial of the request, veiled as abstention from voting for or against the resolution is partly grounded on the lack of nexus between the request and "threat to international peace and security"[72] which is implied in Article 16 of the ICC Statute. Others ground their abstention in the Assembly of States Parties to the ICC Statute being the proper forum for resolving the issue.[73] As far as the latter excuse is concerned, no reading of Article 16 supports

---

[68] See *The Prosecutor v. Uhuru Muigai Kenyatta*, ICC-01/09-02/11; and *The Prosecutor v. William Samoei Ruto and Joshua Arap Sang*, ICC-01/09-01/11.

[69] Press Release, Security Council, Security Council Resolution Seeking Deferral of Kenyan Leaders' Trial Fails to Win Adoption, with 7 Voting in Favour, 8 Abstaining, UN Doc. SC/11176 (Nov. 15, 2013).

[70] Statute of the International Criminal Court, July 17, 1998, UN Doc. A/CONF.183/9 (ICC Statute). Article 16 provides: "No investigation or prosecution may be commenced or proceeded with under this Statute for a period of 12 months after the Security Council, in a resolution adopted under Chapter VII of the Charter of the United Nations, has requested the Court to that effect; that request may be renewed by the Council under the same conditions."

[71] Decision on Africa's Relationship with the International Criminal Court (ICC), A.U. Res. Ext/Assembly/AU/Dec.1 (Oct. 2013), adopted at the Extraordinary Session of the Assembly of the African Union, Addis Ababa, Ethiopia, October 12, 2013, at http://www.au.int/en/sites/default/files/Ext%20Assembly%20AU%20Dec%20&%20Decl%20_E.pdf. However, it can be argued that States Parties to the ICC Statute have consented to a limitation on the customary law of immunities by ratifying the Statute which limits the assertion of personal immunity in cases before the ICC. See Akande, *supra* note 67, 432. For an argument that the customary law of immunities is unaffected by human rights and international criminal law, see Ingrid Wuerth, *Pinochet's Legacy Reassessed*, 106 Am. J. Int'l L. 731–768 (2012). According to Wuerth, "under customary international law as it stands today, there is no human rights or international criminal law exception (human rights exception) to the customary international law of functional immunity." Id., 732.

[72] According to María Cristina Perceval, Argentina's Permanent Representative to the United Nations, her delegation abstained from voting "because it was the Council's duty to interpret strictly whether the trial posed a threat to international peace and security, and Argentina did not think it did." See Press Release, *supra* note 69.

[73] Id.

the claim and is thus an excuse to deny the request. Supporters of the resolution rightly maintained that nothing in the resolution undermined the integrity of the ICC Statute,[74] and it could also be argued that the request was not inconsistent with extant international law. Of course, it is not incongruous to note that some of the States voting on the resolution are not parties to the Rome Statute.[75] The AU request is not an argument for the immunity of these officials from prosecution or an assertion of the innocence of said officials.[76] Neither can it be construed as an argument for impunity, as the Argentine ambassador seemed to have implied in her statement that "the rights of victims could not be forgotten or the subject of indifference; they deserved truth, justice and reconciliation."[77] It is only a request for the honoring of international

---

74 Id.
75 The United States, not a party to the Rome Statute, abstained from voting, claiming through Samantha Power, its Permanent Representative, that she had abstained because Kenya's concerns were best addressed in the Court and in the Assembly of States Parties. All seven countries that voted in favor of the resolution (Azerbaijan, China, Morocco, Pakistan, Russia, Rwanda and Togo) are not State parties to the Rome Statute. See id.
76 See Article 27, ICC Statute:
   1. This Statute shall apply equally to all persons without any distinction based on official capacity. In particular, official capacity as a Head of State or Government, a member of a Government or parliament, an elected representative or a government official shall in no case exempt a person from criminal responsibility under this Statute, nor shall it, in and of itself, constitute a ground for reduction of sentence.
   2. Immunities or special procedural rules which may attach to the official capacity of a person, whether under national or international law, shall not bar the Court from exercising its jurisdiction over such a person.

   Given the cautious framing of the AU request, while Kenya could be argued to have signed away its right to head of State immunity by ratifying the Rome Statute, the provision of Article 27 is irrelevant to the request, which is for a deferral of prosecution, and not a claim for absolute immunity from prosecution.

   It should be noted that the AU was also publicly opposed to the denial of immunity to the serving President of The Sudan, Omar al-Bashir, in the cases related to the Darfur Genocide before the International Criminal Court. See AU Assembly Decision 245 (XIII), July 3, 2009; AU Assembly Decision 296 (XV), July 27, 2010; AU Assembly Decision 334 (XVI), January 31, 2011; AU Assembly Decision 366 (XVII), July 1, 2011. See also Crawford, *supra* note 26, 501.
77 See Press Release, *supra* note 69.

law of immunity that precludes the trial[78] of serving heads of States and other senior officials.[79]

The above is arguably one instance of the marginality of weaker States within the current structure of international law, especially in terms of the application of international law. To the extent that the prosecutorial efforts succeeds, it then creates a precedent that can be applied to similarly placed officials of Third World countries that are unable to negotiate their exit from such prosecutions. Any expansion of participation in law-making would be welcome to the extent that the exercise is cognizant of this imbalance in the application of the law, which itself can be an exercise in law-making. Such expansion is welcome if it does not replicate the current imbalance within international law, of the power differential between small/weak States and States mostly in the Global North that wield disproportionate influence in shaping and making international law. The *vox populi* to be admitted to the law-making table, that form that appears "in the editorials of leading newspapers, [and] repeated relentlessly in the visual and audial media"[80] are essentially those of the Global North,[81] even if there are occasional disagreements within that group on what should be done as a matter of international public policy.[82] The role of particu-

---

78 In the Kenya case involving President Kenyatta, the acts were committed before assumption of office as President of the Republic. There can be no immunity, functional or otherwise, for the said acts. Honoring the law of immunity would have the consequence of deferring the trial until he vacates office. If he was not prosecuted before his election, there is certainly no demonstrated urgency for conducting the prosecutions while in office. It is arguable that the prosecution would even be more difficult, giving the accused person's status, with the possibility of tampering with witnesses and witnesses may simply be unwilling to assume the risk of testifying against their President for fear of possible repercussions. The case of Omar al-Bashir is quite different since the alleged acts were performed while serving as head of State of The Sudan.

79 In the Arrest Warrant Case, Belgium had issued a warrant of arrest for a serving Minister of Foreign Affairs of the Democratic Republic of Congo. The issuance of the warrant, and its circulation was held to be a violation of the immunity of the person entitled to that immunity under international law. See Arrest Warrant of 11 April 2000 (Dem. Rep. Congo v. Belg.) (Feb. 14, 2002), 41 I.L.M. 536 (2002). But see Certain Questions of Mutual Assistance in Criminal Matters (Djibouti v. France), 2008 ICJ 177, 243–244, where the ICJ was not prepared to extend personal immunity to certain officials of Djibouti. Crawford notes that "the lack of clarity in Djibouti's submission ... may have affected the Court's position." Crawford, *supra* note 26, 500.

80 Reisman, *supra* note 4, at 23.

81 These are the same "global networks of power, of exploitation and domination." See Otto, *supra* note 22, at 33

82 See Thürer, *supra* note 63, at 55.

lar non-State actors in the making and shaping of international law has been noted. Non-governmental organizations, corporations, and networks of individuals have been impactful on the making of international law, for example in the adoption of the Rome Statute of the ICC, as well as in the adoption of the Landmines Convention of 1997.[83] They have also influenced the adoption of treaties on international environmental law.[84] But, disproportionately, these tend to reflect the influence of Northern actors and the agenda they seek to accomplish. They do have collaborators in the Global South, who adopt these same agenda, thus giving it a veneer of universality.

This new, "inclusive," universal law-making efforts cannot be considered inclusive or universal. The fora is limited to those controlled by the powerful States, and those they cannot control are marginalized.[85] The whole exercise lends credence and affirmation to claims that the "regime of international law is illegitimate [and] is a predatory system that legitimizes, reproduces and sustains the plunder and subordination of Third World States by the West."[86] For the exercise to be meaningful, there must be "full representativity of all voices,"[87] not only of those small and weak States that are marginalized through the international legal system but also "those non-State, nongovernmental, rural and urban poor who constitute the majority in the Third World."[88]

Recognition of these voices and the concerns articulated by Third World voices, States and government should not be mere tokenism. As Vaughan Lowe noted, Africa has been quite marginalized in international law.[89] As with other

---

83   Convention on the Prohibition of the Use, Stockpiling, Production, and Transfer of Anti-Personnel Mines and on Their Destruction, concluded Sept. 18, 1997, entered into force Mar. 1, 1999, 226 U.N.T.S. 211.

84   See Sands, *supra* note 24, 114. One prominent organization is the International Union for Conservation of Nature (IUCN), founded in 1948, which claims its "ever-growing influence" as one of the benefits of membership. Among the achievements of its Environmental Law Programme is its "[m]ajor contribution to the development of international treaty law through *the preparation of draft instruments*" (emphasis supplied). It also claims "[m]ajor contribution to international "soft law" as well as "[s]ignificant contributions to the negotiation process of international treaties." Major international and regional treaties on environmental law are highlighted in its work. See IUCN: Achievements, at http://www.iucn.org/about/work/programmes/environmental_law/elp_about/elp_about_achieve

85   See Mutua, *supra* note 66, at 37.

86   Mutua, id., at 31. See also O'Connell, *et al.*, *supra* note 53, at 1174: "[International law] cannot arguably be viewed today as legitimate, as worthy to be law for all people."

87   Mutua, id., at 37.

88   Id.

89   Vaughan Lowe, *The Marginalization of Africa*, 94 Am. Soc'y Int'l L. Proc. 231–232 (2000).

developing regions, it is "underrepresented" in the study of international law, in the processes of the creation of international law and in the development of the doctrine.[90] And without the voices of the marginalized in deciding the priorities of the international legal system, their concerns are usually ignored.[91] The attempts at democratizing international law-making through "media-made law" risks furthering that marginalization.

On the other hand, one can argue that recognition and acceptance of Third World voices and contributions to the law is not a matter of democratization *per se*; it is just righting the imbalance that always existed. For the most part, the central doctrines of international law including the sovereign equality of States, the centrality of sovereignty and that of territorial integrity of States have existed as notions. These are accepted only relative to powerful States. Today, it is common to assert that sovereignty is no longer absolute, which can be translated to mean the sovereignty of small and weak States is no longer absolute. The role of the State itself is contested as an organizing principle of society. But this again relates only to the weaker States, especially because of the authoritarian tendencies of some of the governments in those States. This has in turn led to calls for creation of "liberal zones," which is "constituted by liberal states practicing a higher degree of civilization, to which other states will be admitted only when they meet the requisite standards."[92] Related calls include a process of "reform" of the law of treaties, "to allow only representatives of democratic governments to obligate their populations through treaties."[93] The Vienna Convention on the Law of Treaties would then be amended to "require that the credentials of the signatories be *properly democratic*" (emphasis supplied) as "judged by other states" under human rights treaties and UN General Assembly resolutions on democracy.[94]

---

90 Id.
91 Id.
92 Benedict Kingsbury, *Sovereignty and Inequality,* in Inequality, Globalization, And World Politics 66, 90 (Andrew Hurrell & Ngaire Woods, eds, 1999). See David P. Fidler, *The Return of the Standard of Civilization* 2 Chi. J. Int'l L. 137, 147 (2001)
93 Fernando Tesón, Remarks, *The Project of Reconfiguration: How Can International Law Be Reconstituted?* 94 Am. Soc'y Int'l L. Proc. 73, 78–79 (2000).
94 Id. Other ideas include changing "the law of recognition of states and governments" to ensure the non-recognition of "undemocratic" States and governments. Diplomatic law should also be changed to "require rejecting diplomats who purport to represent a state but who are simply henchmen of its current dictators." Id. While States have generally chosen to recognize other States and governments as they deemed fit, as well as engaging

Thus, the argument here is that questions of "inclusion, exclusion, and marginality"[95] in international law-making are not totally resolved by the calls for democratization of the law-making process to include actors who generate "media-made law" as opposed to "state-made law." It is one thing to argue for recognition of actors and participants other than States to have better representation and status in the law-making process. It is quite another argument to recognize the output of the *vox populi* process as legitimate law or source of law. While some argue for accepting the legitimacy of that process and these differing participants, it remains a contestable notion that what essentially privileges them is the notion of self-determination or self-interests of those actors, coupled with the irresponsibility of certain governments.[96] It is certainly not the case that non-State actors, especially non-governmental organizations, are the sole repository of knowledge of how to solve the world's problems. And to the extent that the agenda is controlled by the same powerful interests that marginalize others, it cannot be called an inclusive regime, it is not egalitarian by any means. If as Reisman concedes, the process is not necessarily egalitarian, why simply replicate the same agenda all over again? It would amount to no more than a modern and thus more acceptable form of the same process of marginalization and exclusivity, the promulgation of a new "standard of civilization"[97] in international law and a means of controlling the agenda for the weaker countries.

---

        in diplomatic relations with other States, to change these into a *requirement* of international law would perpetuate the divide that currently pervades the law. It stands to reason that this would be applied only to the weaker States in the international legal order.

95   Dianne Otto, Remarks, *The Third World and International Law: Voices from the Margins*, 94 Am. Soc'y Int'l L. Proc. 50 (2000).

96   Volker Röben, *Proliferation of Actors*, *in* Developments Of International Law In Treaty Making, pp. 511–536, esp. 522–530, (Rüdiger Wolfrum & Volker Röben, eds., 2005). See also Steve Charnovitz, Comment, *The Relevance of Non-State Actors to International Law*, *in* Developments Of International Law In Treaty Making, pp. 542–556, esp. 548–552, (Rüdiger Wolfrum & Volker Röben, eds., 2005).

97   Fidler, *supra* note 92.

CHAPTER 12

An Innovative Solution to an Ambitious Project: Dispute Resolution in the 1982 Convention on the Law of the Sea

Surya P. Subedi

Introduction

The mechanism for the settlement of disputes arising out of the implementation and interpretation of the provisions of a treaty is an important part of any international treaty. This is especially true of the 1982 Convention on the Law of the Sea,[1] which deals with so many complex issues concerning the governance of the seas and oceans that cover more than two-thirds of the globe. The Convention known as the 'Charter of the seas and oceans' is perhaps the most comprehensive of all international treaties resulting from intensive negotiations lasting for nine years. It deals with more or less every aspect of human activity in the seas and oceans of the world – these covering two-thirds of the area of planet earth. Equally elaborate, innovative and sophisticated is its dispute settlement mechanism designed to resolve different kinds of maritime disputes between States. As stated by Rothwell and Stephens, this complex mechanism "is unusual in public international law because it is comprehensive and compulsory, subject to limited exceptions."[2]

The development of the law of the sea has gone through three phases: articulation and acceptance of its major principles, such as the freedom of the high seas; codification of the rules and principles through international legal instruments, such as the four 1958 Geneva Conventions on the Law of the Sea; and the elaboration of the rules and principles through a comprehensive treaty with a provision for mechanisms for the resolution of disputes relating to the interpretation and application or implementation of the treaty. Accordingly, this Chapter is designed to examine the background to the mechanism

---

1 United Nations, *The Law of the Sea: Official Texts of the United Nations Convention on the Law of the Sea and of the Agreement Relating to the Implementation of Part XI with Excerpts from the Final Act of the Third Conference* (New York: United Nations, 1997).
2 D.R. Rothwell and T. Stephens, *The International Law of the Sea* (Hart Publishing, Oxford, 2010), p. 439.

established by the Convention for the settlement of disputes concerning the matters covered by it, asses the nature and scope of the mechanism, comparing and contrasting it with other international dispute settlement mechanisms, and analyse how effective it has been in resolving disputes between States in order to maintain law and order in the seas and oceans around the globe.

History of Maritime Disputes

Much of the history of the law of the sea is the history of international law itself and there have been disputes between states since time immemorial with regard to the use and control of the seas and oceans. The desire to control the seas in order to control navigation and exploit maritime resources probably dates back to the days when the Egyptians first plied the Mediterranean in papyrus rafts. Over the centuries, countries possessing vast ocean-going fleets or small fishing flotillas, husbanding rich fishing grounds close to shore or eyeing distant harvests, have all vied for the control of the seas. When various missions of exploration or 'discoveries' were taking place, Spain and Portugal, two great maritime powers of the day, were competing for the control of the seas and oceans of the globe. In 1494, two years after Christopher Columbus's first expedition to America, Pope Alexander VI met with representatives of these two nations and divided the Atlantic Ocean between them. Everything west of the line the Pope drew down the Atlantic belonged to Spain and everything east of it to Portugal. On the basis of this Papal decree, the Pacific and the Gulf of Mexico were claimed by Spain, and Portugal claimed the South Atlantic and the Indian Ocean, effectively dividing the world into two halves.

As other European countries such as the Netherlands, France and Great Britain expanded their maritime power, they began to challenge the division of the world's seas and oceans between Spain and Portugal. It was around this time that Hugo Grotius published his monograph *Mare Liberum*, advocating the freedom of the seas rather than control by a few states.[3] When Britain became more powerful, British authors such as John Selden sought to revive the idea of the closed sea, *mare clausum*. This idea was challenged by other maritime powers and legal scholars of the day. Consequently, the freedom of the high seas was accepted as a cardinal principle of the law of the sea.

However, when the balance of political power shifted and England emerged as a more powerful European state, an English legal antiquarian and politician,

---

3   Hugo Grotius, *De Jure Belli Ac Pacis* (The Hague, Martinus Nijhoff, 1625, 1948 trans), book 2.

John Selden, argued in favour of the *mare clausum* (closed sea) in 1635, a justification of a single nation's rule over the high seas. This was in contrast to Grotius's argument in favour of the free sea (*mare liberum*). However, the idea advanced by Selden was short lived. Most of the scholars and major maritime powers of the day supported the idea of the freedom of the seas. Nevertheless, the idea of the closed sea found its expression in a limited manner in the principle of a territorial sea, under which coastal states would have rights over a narrow belt of water around the coast lines. Thus, the traditional law of the sea accepted that states could claim some part of the seas beyond their shores as part of their territory, as a zone of protection to be patrolled against smugglers, pirates, warships and other intruders. This came to be known as the territorial sea, and its boundary evolved from the eighteenth century 'cannon-shot' rule to a three-mile rule and eventually to a 12-mile rule.

Another Dutch jurist, Cornelius van Bynkershoek, formulated the principle of a territorial sea according to which the waters adjoining the shores of a country within the range of artillery on land were not included in the juridical meaning of the term 'high seas' and would come under the territorial sovereignty of that country.[4] This principle received wide support throughout the world, and many coastal states began to claim an area of the sea up to three nautical miles from the baselines as their territorial waters. Gradually, certain states began to claim six or even 12 nautical miles as their territorial waters. (It should be noted here that traditionally 'nautical' rather than imperial miles have been used in relation to marine matters.) At the same time, the right of 'innocent passage', a term that is generally recognised to mean passage 'not prejudicial to the peace, good order or security of the coastal state', has been accepted so that foreign ships can traverse the waters of the territorial sea of a coastal state. This means that the law of the sea has protected and preserved one of its original purposes, and one of the five principles of the freedoms of the sea – the freedom of navigation – even in the territorial sea. In this sense, the navigational aspect of the centuries-old principle of *mare liberum* is still valid in almost all areas of the seas.[5]

---

4   Cornelius van Bynkershoek, *De Dominio Maris Dissertatio* (New York, Ocean, 1744, 1923 trans, 1964 (rep)).
5   See generally, P.B. Potter, *The Freedom of the Seas in History, Law and Politics* (London, 1924); R.P. Anand, *Origin and Development of the Law of the Sea: History of International Law Revisited* (The Hague: Martinus Nijhoff, 1983); R. Bernhardt, 'Custom and Treaty in the Law of the Sea', 205 *Recueil des cours* (1989.vi), pp. 167–412.

Attempts to Codify the Law

We know that as early as the fourth millennium BC there were maritime trade routes connecting Mesopotamia with the Indus valley. It is also known that commercial contacts between the Mediterranean basin and lands to the east existed as early as the Old Kingdom epoch in Egypt (third millennium BC). Ancient commercial contacts between the nations of the Mediterranean basin and the Red Sea-Indian Ocean regions were documented from the Ptolemaic-Roman period (third century BC until the late second/early third centuries AD). In Hellenistic-Roman times, there were several maritime trade routes connecting the Mediterranean world with those lands to the East. When trading relations through sea routes began to grow in the Mediterranean region, trading nations began to develop rules for the conduct of maritime trade in the form of various codes for maritime commerce. One prominent example is the 'Rhodian Sea Law'.

While the peaceful maritime trade continued to be governed by some rudimentary rules of international law for some time, it was during the twentieth century that most significant developments took place within the law of the sea. It was also during this century that the law of the sea acquired a truly global character. Until the establishment of the United Nations, the maritime powers of Europe and the United States dominated the law and practice in the law of the sea. Furthermore, traditionally maritime questions were handled on an ad hoc basis, via bilateral international agreements on particular issues within the law of the sea. There was no international institution dealing comprehensively with maritime questions prior to 1945. Until the establishment of the UN, only a small number of agencies existed dealing with some specialised matters relating to the law of the sea. An example would be the International Council for the Exploration of the Sea, set up in 1902 to encourage and co-ordinate scientific investigation of the eastern North Atlantic, including the waters off Greenland and Iceland.

The use of the seas by submarines and aircraft in an unregulated manner during the First World War demonstrated the inadequacy of international law with respect to freedom of the seas. Many traditional principles of the law of the sea were disregarded by the warring parties, including both Germany and Great Britain, in the pursuit of the war, especially during the British blockade of the European continent and Germany's attempt to isolate the British Isles from the rest of the world. Indeed, interference by Germany in American trade through the sea route with Britain was one of the causes of the entry of the United States into the war in 1917, resulting in the victory for the allied powers.[6]

Hague Codification Conference

Following the establishment of the League of Nations after the First World War, the League convened a conference in 1930 in The Hague with a view to developing and codifying the rules of the law of the sea, among other subjects. It was attended by 47 states from different parts of the world. It was perhaps the first global conference of this nature to deal with the law of the sea. The Conference demonstrated a gradual decline in the ability of the European imperial states to dictate the law, an emergence of the influence of middle-ranking states and a shift in the development of the law of the sea from a Eurocentric to a more international perspective.

One of the main purposes of the Conference was to reach agreement on the standard limits to territorial waters, as the traditional cannon-shot rule – which said that waters adjoining the shores of a country within the range of artillery on land were not included in the term 'high seas' – was considered too vague a measure and different states were making different claims to the waters around their coast. For instance, the UK and US had settled on a three-mile limit, whereas the Scandinavian countries had a four-mile limit, France had claimed six and Russia a 12-mile territorial sea. In addition, there were the issues of mineral resources and offshore drilling for oil. States were concerned that the codification of customary international law into a binding legal instrument might hinder the exploration and exploitation of the sea as well as the development of the law of the sea itself.

Only a few countries supported a three-mile limit for territorial waters for all purposes. It was not possible to agree on a compromise proposal for a 'contiguous zone' beyond the territorial sea either, since the breadth of the latter was not agreed; the breadth of the contiguous zone depended on the breadth of the territorial sea. Consequently, the Hague Codification Conference ended without the adoption of any final agreement. Nevertheless, the Conference did recognise the following principles as widely accepted principles of the law of the sea:

---

6   D.P. O'Connell, *The International Law of the Sea*, vol.1 (Oxford, Clarendon press, 1982); D.R. Rothwell and T. Stephens, *The International Law of the Sea* (Hart Publishing, Oxford, 2010), chapt 1.

- the territorial sea as subject to the sovereignty of the relevant coastal state
- the general right of innocent passage in territorial waters
- the general right of hot pursuit by vessels of a coastal state beyond its territorial waters.

The conference was significant in the sense that it demonstrated that the three-mile limit preferred by the major maritime powers of the day was not acceptable to other states and international conferences such as this were important in developing international law. It also heralded the beginning of a wider debate on various uses of the seas and oceans. Consequently, the law of the sea became a matter high on the international agenda after the establishment of the UN.

The Aftermath of the Second World War

The conduct of the belligerent powers during the Second World War demonstrated the need for a more orderly system of using the seas and oceans for various purposes. During the war, the rights of neutrals were largely disregarded by the belligerent powers and many other rules of the law of the sea as well as the rules of international humanitarian law were violated because of the desperate urgency on both sides to utilise every means of achieving victory. Because the war was of a global character, violations of the rules of the law of the sea also took place in different parts of the world, affecting many more states than had been the case in previous wars.

When the UN was established many nations began to express a need to conclude comprehensive international instruments designed, *inter alia*, to safeguard their legitimate interests and to extend national claims seaward to include mineral resources off their coasts, to protect fish stocks around their coastlines and to have the means to enforce pollution controls around their coastal area. Furthermore, certain states had begun to apply wartime technological advances to peacetime uses of the sea, enabling amongst other things, the exploitation of the resources of the seabed. With post-war shortages in oil, amongst other things, there was a trend towards coastal states claiming more and more maritime areas contiguous to their coasts. The Truman Declaration of 1945, which asserted US claims over the continental shelf around the US land mass, is one such example. This American declaration led to many other coastal States making similar claims of their own. Such unilateral claims heralded an era of seaward expansion by coastal States.

The First UN Conference on the Law of the Sea

The scope of issues before the First UN Conference on the Law of the Sea (UNCLOS I) in 1958 was much wider than those covered at the Hague Conference in 1930. There was now an International Law Commission (ILC) whose purpose was to promote 'the progressive development of international law and its codification', and one of the tasks it had undertaken in the early years of its establishment as a subsidiary body of the UN General Assembly was to prepare 73 draft articles on the law of the sea for discussion in four separate committees. Composed of members of recognised competence in international law, the ILC had spent seven years preparing the draft articles, circulating them to states and reviewing them in light of comments received. Therefore, by the time UNCLOS I got underway, the legal texts were already available, albeit in a skeleton form, and could be debated and voted on with relative ease at the conference.[7]

The number of states participating in UNCLOS I was bigger than that at the Hague Codification Conference of 1930, and the representation was global. Many of the newly independent and developing states, such as Mexico, India and Sri Lanka, exerted a substantial influence. The Conference ended by adopting four historic Conventions on the Law of the Sea.[8] They were adopted by a solid majority of the 86 states involved. The four Geneva Conventions on the Law of the Sea of 1958 were not part of a single comprehensive framework – they established four different regimes.[9] Although they served to clarify and codify the law in many respects, they were not widely ratified. They represented a huge milestone in the development of the law of the sea, but their impact was limited due to a number of deficiencies within them.[10]

Although UNCLOS I left some difficult issues such as the actual breadth of the territorial sea undecided, it was considered a success in codifying much of the law of the sea. What was missing in the Conventions was a distinct dispute

---

7   International Law Commission, 'Articles concerning the Law of the Sea with Commentaries' (1956), *Yearbook of the International Law Commission*, vol 2, 265–301.
8   The four Conventions adopted by the First UN Conference on the Law of the Sea are as follows: (i) Convention on the Territorial Sea and the Contiguous Zone, 1958 (ii) Convention on the High Seas 1958 (iii) Convention on Fishing and Conservation of Living Resources in the High Seas 1958 and (iv) Convention on the Continental Shelf 1958.
9   Philip C. Jessup, 'The Geneva Conferences on the Law of the Sea: A Study of International Law-Making' (1958) 52 *American Journal of International Law* 730, 732.
10 For travaux préparatoires and the proceedings of the First UN Conference on the Law of the Sea, see *United Nations Official Records of the United Nations Conference on the Law of the Sea*, Volumes I to VII, Sales No.: 58.V.4.

settlement mechanism to resolve maritime disputes between States. Of course, the ICJ and all other means of general international dispute settlements such as arbitration would be available to States to resolve any maritime disputes, but the Conventions themselves did not contain any separate dedicated dispute settlement mechanism as has the 1982 Convention done. The international community was still focused on codifying the law rather than devising mechanisms for their implementation.[11] Only one of the four Geneva Conventions, i.e. the Convention on Fishing and Conservation of the Living Resources of the High Seas had a provision for a limited number of fisheries disputes to be submitted for settlement by a 'special commission' of five members. Instead, the Geneva Conference adopted a separate Optional Protocol of Signature Concerning the Compulsory Settlement of Disputes Arising from the Law of the Sea Conventions. Although the under the Protocol disputes lie within the compulsory jurisdiction of the ICJ, the very nature of the opt-in mechanism, as summed up by Rothwell and Stephens, "added little to the ICJ's optional clause system".[12] Indeed, in reality, only a small number of states ratified the Protocol and it has never been invoked to resolve a dispute.

Second UN Conference on the Law of the Sea

Since the four Geneva Conventions had not resolved some important issues within the law of the sea, the UN decided to convene a second conference, UNCLOS II, in 1960, soon after the conclusion of UNCLOS I. UNCLOS II sought to reach agreement on the limits of coastal states' exclusive control of fisheries exploitation and conservation. The formula proposed for this allowed for a territorial sea of six miles plus an additional six-mile fisheries zone.

However, the efforts did not result in any international agreements; the issues of fishing zones and the limits of the territorial sea remained unresolved. Those states which had habitually and historically fished in the 3–12 mile zone, those which had wanted a 12-mile territorial sea and those which were advancing the claim of a 200-mile territorial sea, especially from the Latin American region, were not prepared to compromise. Since there was no agreement on one of the most crucial issues in the law of the sea – the breadth of the territorial sea – UNCLOS II ended without any international agreement. The prospect

---

11   Arthur H Dean, 'The Geneva Conference on the Law of the Sea: What was Accomplished' (1958) 52 *American Journal of International Law*, 607, 627.

12   D.R. Rothwell and T. Stephens, *The International Law of the Sea* (Hart Publishing, Oxford, 2010), p. 444.

of a dedicated separate mechanism for the settlement of maritime disputes was thus rather dim during UNCLOS II.[13]

Third UN Conference on the Law of the Sea

Since neither UNCLOS I nor UNCLOS II had been able to resolve some crucial issues within the law of the sea, especially the limits of the territorial sea, different states began to assert different claims over the maritime areas off their coasts in the 1960s. Following the first major challenge to the centuries-old principle of the freedom of the seas through the Truman Proclamation of 1945, by which the U.S. tried to claim for itself the resources of the continental shelf off its coasts, many states began to assert their own unilateral claims to various maritime zones around their coasts in order to safeguard the natural resources therein. In sum, the free-for-all situation in the seas and oceans generated both dangers and promises, risks and hopes. There was a multitude of claims, counterclaims and sovereignty disputes, warranting a further major international conference on the law of the sea to address comprehensively the issues relating to the numerous uses of the seas and oceans.[14] By the end of the 1960s, there was a huge drive to undertake a full-scale review of the extant rules of the law of the sea and adopt a comprehensive set of new rules for the management of the seas and oceans and the resources therein. Accordingly, the UN decided to hold the Third UN Conference on the Law of the Sea (UNCLOS III) in 1973.

The objective was for a more stable order, promoting greater use and better management of sea and ocean resources and generating harmony and goodwill among states. It was recognised that, in the absence of a comprehensive international framework, legal uncertainties would remain and chaos might accelerate if states went on unilaterally asserting their own rules and offering their own interpretations of the basic principles of the law of the sea, including the freedom of the seas. Therefore, the need to negotiate and draft a comprehensive framework convention on the law of the sea had become imperative and the core of that endeavour was a dedicated and distinct mechanism to resolve maritime disputes rather than rely on the ICJ or other traditional

---

13   D.W. Bowett, 'The Second United Nations Conference on the Law of the Sea (1960), 9 *International and Comparative Law Quarterly* 415.
14   See generally, P. Allott, 'Power Sharing in the Law of the Sea', 77 *American Journal of International Law* (1983), pp. 1ff.

means of pacific settlement of disputes.[15] Consequently, one of the key features of the 1982 Convention is that disputes can be submitted to a dedicated and standing tribunal – the International Tribunal for the Law of the Sea established under the Convention – or to the International Court of Justice, or to arbitration.

The adoption of the 1982 Convention[16] was a huge triumph of diplomacy and has been described as the result of a 'silent revolution' in the history of the law of the sea and in international diplomatic history. It represented an unprecedented attempt by the international community to regulate all major aspects of the resources of the seas and oceans and their uses. It deals with a huge range of areas, including navigational rights, territorial sea limits, economic jurisdiction, the legal status of resources on the seabed beyond the limits of national jurisdiction, the passage of ships through narrow straits, the conservation and management of living marine resources, the protection of the marine environment, a marine research regime, the rights of land-locked states and, a more unique feature, a binding procedure for the settlement of disputes between states. This 'world constitution for the seas' was adopted as a 'package deal' and had to be accepted as a whole in all its parts without reservation on any aspect.

The Nature and Scope of the Dispute Settlement Mechanism

Traditionally, provisions for the settlement of disputes arising out of an international treaty are contained in a separate optional protocol, giving parties to the treaty the opportunity to choose to be bound by those provisions by accepting it or not to be bound by not accepting it. This choice does not often affect their participation in the main treaty. But the 1982 Convention on the Law of the Sea is different in that the mechanism for the settlement of disputes is incorporated into the main Convention, making it obligatory for parties to the Convention to go through the settlement procedure in case of a dispute with another party. In other words, if a state wishes to participate in the Convention it must *ipso facto* accept the dispute settlement mechanism provided

---

15 See D. Freestone, R. Barnes and D. Ong (eds) *The Law of the Sea: Progress and Prospects* (Oxford: Oxford University Press, 2006).

16 As of January 2013, 165 States had ratified the 1982 Convention on the Law of the Sea.

for in the Convention, albeit that the Convention itself offers a number of options for the settlement of such disputes.[17]

During the negotiation of the Convention at UNCLOS III, many countries were opposed in principle to binding settlement to be decided by third-party judges or arbitrators, insisting that issues could best be resolved by direct negotiations between states without requiring them to bring in outsiders. However, other states pointed to a history of failed negotiations and long-standing disputes and argued that the only sure chance for peaceful settlement lay in the willingness of states to bind themselves in advance to accept the decisions of judicial bodies. Consequently, what emerged from the negotiations was a novel mechanism which combined both of these approaches. This novelty in creating a compulsory dispute settlement mechanism has been regarded by many as a landmark in international law.

The Compromise

In the face of the differing views of States, the Convention gives disputing states a choice of four procedures if direct talks between them fail or if they fail to resort to other means of dispute settlement:

- submission of the dispute to the International Tribunal for the Law of the Sea;
- adjudication by the International Court of Justice;
- submission to binding international arbitration procedures;
- submission to special arbitration tribunals with expertise in specific types of disputes.

All these procedures involve binding third-party settlement in which a party other than the disputing parties hands down a decision that the parties are committed in advance to respect. The Convention makes an exception to these provisions for sensitive cases involving national sovereignty. In such cases, the

---

[17] See generally, O. Adede, *The System for Settlement of Disputes under the United Nations Convention on the Law of the Sea* (Dordrecht: Nijhoff, 1987); A.E. Boyle, 'Dispute Settlement and the Law of the Sea Convention: Problems of Fragmentation and Jurisdiction', 46 *International and Comparative Law Quarterly* (1997), pp. 37–54; N. Klein, *Dispute Settlement in the UN Convention on the Law of the Sea* (Cambridge: Cambridge University Press, 2005); D. Freestone, R. Barnes and D. Ong (eds) *Law of the Sea: Progress and Prospects* (Oxford: Oxford University Press, 2006) Chapters 20–22.

parties are obliged to submit their dispute to a conciliation commission rather than to any of the four methods outlined above. What is more, the disputing parties will not be bound by any decision or finding of the commission. The Convention also allows for the so-called 'optional exceptions' under which a state can specify at the time of signing, ratifying or acceding to the Convention, or at any later time, that it chooses not to be bound by one or more of the mandatory procedures if they involve existing maritime boundary disputes, military activities or issues under discussion in the United Nations Security Council.

There is also a general exception contained in Article 280 of the Convention according to which nothing in the Convention impairs the right of any states parties to agree at any time to settle a dispute between them concerning the interpretation or application of this Convention by any peaceful means of their own choice. This provision has proved highly significant in at least two cases, *Southern Bluefin Tuna*[18] and *MOX Plant*,[19] where parties have insisted on a regional dispute settlement mechanism superseding that established by the Convention.[20] Similarly, if states parties to the Convention are parties to a dispute concerning the interpretation or application of the Convention and agree to seek settlement of the dispute by a peaceful means of their own choice, the procedures provided for in the Convention apply only where no settlement has been reached by recourse to such means and the agreement between the parties does not exclude any further procedure.

---

18   Southern Bluefin Tuna (New Zealand v. Japan; Australia v. Japan) (provisional measures) 1999 117 ILR 148 (jurisdiction and admissibility) (2000) 119 ILR 508.

19   Mox Plant (Ireland v. United Kingdom) (provisional measures) (2002) 41 ILM 405.

20   For instance, in the Mox Plant case, the dispute initiated by Ireland related to the operation of the plant located in the UK on the coast off the Irish Sea, and to international movements of radioactive materials and the protection of the marine environment of the Irish Sea. The plant was designed to recycle plutonium from spent nuclear fuel by mixing plutonium dioxide with depleted uranium dioxide, and Ireland was concerned about the possible environmental harm of such activities. Ireland had claimed before the Tribunal that the UK had failed to take the necessary steps to prevent, reduce and control pollution of the marine environment when granting a licence to operate the MOX Plant. However, the Tribunal suspended hearings on the case in November 2004. The European Commission decided to bring the case before the European Court of Justice (ECJ), and the ECJ in turn found that Ireland had violated the Treaty Establishing the European Community by instituting proceedings against the United Kingdom before an arbitral tribunal under the 1982 Convention on the Law of the Sea, rather than seeking to resolve the dispute using EC mechanisms. The Tribunal therefore suspended hearings in order to have the issue of jurisdiction and the Community law competence resolved.

Another provision concerns the existence of other mechanisms applicable to the dispute. If the states parties to the Convention which are parties to a dispute concerning the interpretation or application of the Convention have agreed, through a general, regional or bilateral agreement or otherwise, that such dispute shall, at the request of any party to the dispute, be submitted to a procedure that entails a binding decision, that procedure shall apply in lieu of the procedures provided for in the Convention, unless the parties to the dispute agree otherwise. The choice of states to resort to conciliation has also been preserved in the Convention for certain cases. A state party to the Convention which is a party to a dispute concerning the interpretation or application of this Convention may invite the other party or parties to submit the dispute to conciliation. If the invitation is accepted and the parties agree upon the conciliation procedure to be applied, any party may submit the dispute to that procedure. If the invitation is accepted and the parties agree upon the conciliation procedure to be applied, any party may submit the dispute to that procedure. If the invitation is not accepted or the parties do not agree upon the procedure, the conciliation proceedings will be deemed to be terminated.

The Mechanism

The provisions for the settlement of disputes are contained in Part XV of the Convention. Article 279 stipulates the obligation of States to settle disputes by peaceful means and Article 280 allows the Sates the flexibility of settling disputes by any peaceful means chosen by the parties themselves. Only when States fail to resolve their disputes through other means, the specific dispute settlement mechanisms outlined in the Convention come into play. According to Article 286 of the 1982 Convention, where no settlement has been reached by recourse to other mechanisms, any dispute concerning the interpretation or application of the Convention will be submitted at the request of any party to the dispute to the court or tribunal having jurisdiction under this section. Article 287 outlines the options available to states party to the Convention:

> *Article 287*
> Choice of procedure
> 1. When signing, ratifying or acceding to this Convention or at any time thereafter, a State shall be free to choose, by means of a written declaration, one or more of the following means for the settlement of disputes concerning the interpretation or application of this Convention:

(a) the International Tribunal for the Law of the Sea established in accordance with Annex VI;

(b) the International Court of Justice;

(c) an arbitral tribunal constituted in accordance with Annex VII;

(d) a special arbitral tribunal constituted in accordance with Annex VIII for one or more of the categories of disputes specified therein.

2. A declaration made under paragraph 1 shall not affect or be affected by the obligation of a State Party to accept the jurisdiction of the Seabed Disputes Chamber of the International Tribunal for the Law of the Sea to the extent and in the manner provided for in Part XI, section 5.

3. A State Party, which is a party to a dispute not covered by a declaration in force, shall be deemed to have accepted arbitration in accordance with Annex VII.

4. If the parties to a dispute have accepted the same procedure for the settlement of the dispute, it may be submitted only to that procedure, unless the parties otherwise agree.

5. If the parties to a dispute have not accepted the same procedure for the settlement of the dispute, it may be submitted only to arbitration in accordance with Annex VII, unless the parties otherwise agree.

6. A declaration made under paragraph 1 shall remain in force until three months after notice of revocation has been deposited with the Secretary-General of the United Nations.

7. A new declaration, a notice of revocation or the expiry of a declaration does not in any way affect proceedings pending before a court or tribunal having jurisdiction under this article, unless the parties otherwise agree.

8. Declarations and notices referred to in this article shall be deposited with the Secretary-General of the United Nations, who shall transmit copies thereof to the States Parties.

As can be seen from the above provision, the 1982 Convention was one of the first international treaties providing for a dispute settlement mechanism with compulsory jurisdiction. Neither the ICJ nor its predecessor, the Permanent Court of International Justice, had such powers. Under the Law of the Sea Convention, a State party to the Convention can unilaterally refer a dispute with another State to the dispute settlement mechanism stipulated in the Convention.

Broad Jurisdiction

Article 288 goes on to outline jurisdiction of the above-listed courts or tribunals which are accorded a very broad jurisdiction. They can exercise jurisdiction over any dispute concerning the interpretation or application of the 1982 Convention which is submitted to them in accordance with the provisions outlines in the Convention. Article 288 reads as follows:

> *Article 288*
> Jurisdiction
> 1. A court or tribunal referred to in article 287 shall have jurisdiction over any dispute concerning the interpretation or application of this Convention which is submitted to it in accordance with this Part.
> 2. A court or tribunal referred to in article 287 shall also have jurisdiction over any dispute concerning the interpretation or application of an international agreement related to the purposes of this Convention, which is submitted to it in accordance with the agreement.
> 3. The Seabed Disputes Chamber of the International Tribunal for the Law of the Sea established in accordance with Annex VI, and any other chamber or arbitral tribunal referred to in Part XI, section 5, shall have jurisdiction in any matter which is submitted to it in accordance therewith.
> 4. In the event of a dispute as to whether a court or tribunal has jurisdiction, the matter shall be settled by decision of that court or tribunal.

It can be seen from the above provision that a court or tribunal referred to in Article 287 of the Convention has broad jurisdiction over any dispute concerning the interpretation or application of the Convention. Combined with the mandatory nature of jurisdiction, these broad powers make the dispute settlement mechanism under the 1982 Convention unusually strong in international law.

Applicability of a Wider Body of Law

The law that a court or tribunal having jurisdiction under the Convention should apply is the provisions of the Convention itself and other rules of international law not incompatible with the Convention. The phrase 'other rules of international law' should be understood to refer to the sources of international law listed in Article 38 of the Statute of the International Court of Justice, namely, customary rules of international law, treaty law, general principles of law and the law flowing from the decisions of international courts and tribunals and the writings of publicists.[21]

Exhaustion of Local Remedies

According to Article 295 of the 1982 Convention, any dispute between states parties concerning the interpretation or application of the Convention may be submitted to the procedures provided for in this section only after local remedies have been exhausted, where this is required by international law.

Provisional Measures

Article 290 of the 1982 Convention empowers a court or tribunal which considers that *prima facie* it has jurisdiction on the matter referred to it by states party to the Convention, including the International Tribunal for the Law of the Sea, to prescribe any provisional measures which it considers appropriate under the circumstances to preserve the respective rights of the parties to the dispute or to prevent serious harm to the marine environment, pending the final decision. Such measures may be modified or revoked as soon as the circumstances justifying them have changed or ceased to exist.

This article also allows the International Tribunal for the Law of the Sea to prescribe provisional measures in other situations. Pending the constitution of an arbitral tribunal to which a dispute is being submitted under the 1982 Convention, any court or tribunal agreed upon by the parties, including the Tribunal, may prescribe, modify or revoke provisional measures in accordance with this article, if it considers (a) that *prima facie* the tribunal which is to be constituted would have jurisdiction and (b) that the urgency of the situation so requires. The Tribunal may also prescribe, modify or revoke such provisional measures if, within two weeks of the date of the request for provisional measures, the parties have failed to agree on a court or tribunal. Several of the cases

---

21   Article 38 of the Statute of the International Court of Justice reads as follows: (1) The Court, whose function is to decide in accordance with international law such disputes as are submitted to it, shall apply: (a) international conventions, whether general or particular, establishing rules expressly recognized by the contesting states; (b) international custom, as evidence of a general practice accepted as law; (c) the general principles of law recognized by civilized nations; (d) subject to the provisions of Article 59, judicial decisions and the teachings of the most highly qualified publicists of the various nations, as subsidiary means for the determination of rules of law.

that the Tribunal has dealt with to date have concerned applications for provisional measures, notably the *Blue Fin Tuna* cases and the *Land Reclamation* case between Malaysia.

Finality and Binding Force of Decisions

Any decision rendered by a court or tribunal having jurisdiction under the Convention will be final and shall be complied with by all the parties to the dispute. Any such decision will have no binding force except between the parties and in respect of that particular dispute.

International Tribunal for the Law of the Sea (ITLOS)

One of the significant achievements of UNCLOS III was the creation of an International Tribunal for the Law of the Sea (ITLOS), whose seat is in Hamburg in Germany. The Tribunal is permanent and is composed of 21 independent members, elected from among persons enjoying the highest reputation for fairness and integrity and of recognised competence in the field of the law of the sea. The members of the Tribunal are elected for nine years and may be re-elected. The Statute of the Tribunal establishes a Seabed Disputes Chamber to consider cases concerning the deep seabed provisions of Part XI of the Convention. The Tribunal may form such chambers, composed of three or more of its elected members, as it considers necessary for dealing with particular categories of disputes.

Although ITLOS is one of the four mechanisms available to States for settling their disputes relating to the law of the sea, it came into existence with high expectations. Commentators often put it in the ranks of the WTOs Dispute Settlement Body or the International Criminal Court. The Tribunal is open to all states parties to the Convention. It has jurisdiction in all disputes and all applications submitted to it in accordance with the Convention and all matters specifically provided for in any other agreement which confers jurisdiction on the Tribunal. Disputes are submitted to the Tribunal, as the case may be, either by notification of a special agreement or by written application addressed to the Registrar, who should in turn forthwith notify the special agreement or the application to all concerned. The Registrar should also notify all states parties. All questions are to be decided by a majority of the members of the Tribunal who are present.

The Tribunal can also be called upon to give its advisory opinion on matters relating to the law of the sea. It is not only the States party to the Convention, but also regional and international organisations can request for an advisory opinion.[22] As of July 2013, a total of 21 cases, including both contentious and advisory, had been referred to the Tribunal.[23] The number of cases referred to it and the number and quality of judgements and orders delivered by the Tribunal indicate that it is gaining the trust and confidence of the States party to the Convention. It also has demonstrated its flexibility and an interest in delivering speedy justice by forming chambers in different areas of the law of the sea. Pursuant to the provisions of its Statute, the Tribunal has the Chamber of Summary Procedure, the Chamber for Fisheries Disputes, the Chamber for Marine Environment Disputes and the Chamber for Maritime Delimitation Disputes. So much so that at the request of Chile and the European Community, the Tribunal also formed a special chamber to deal with the *Case con-*

---

[22] An example is the request of 28 March 2013 by the Sub-Regional Fisheries Commission (SRFC) to render an Advisory Opinion. The SRFC is based in Dakar, Senegal, and comprises seven member States, all of which are States Parties to the Convention: Cape Verde, the Gambia, Guinea, Guinea-Bissau, Mauritania, Senegal and Sierra Leone.

[23] They are as follows: Case No. 1: The M/V "SAIGA" Case (Saint Vincent and the Grenadines v. Guinea), Prompt Release; Case No. 2: The M/V "SAIGA" (No. 2) Case (Saint Vincent and the Grenadines v. Guinea); Cases Nos 3 & 4: Southern Bluefin Tuna Cases (New Zealand v. Japan; Australia v. Japan), Provisional Measures; Case No. 5: The "Camouco" Case (Panama v. France), Prompt Release; Case No. 6: The "Monte Confurco" Case (Seychelles v. France), Prompt Release; Case No. 7: Case concerning the Conservation and Sustainable Exploitation of Swordfish Stocks in the South-Eastern Pacific Ocean (Chile / European Union); Case No. 8: The "Grand Prince" Case (Belize v. France), Prompt Release; Case No. 9: The "Chaisiri Reefer 2" Case (Panama v. Yemen), Prompt Release; Case No. 10: The MOX Plant Case (Ireland v. United Kingdom), Provisional Measures; Case No. 11: The "Volga" Case (Russian Federation v. Australia), Prompt Release; Case No. 12: Case concerning Land Reclamation by Singapore in and around the Straits of Johor; (Malaysia v. Singapore), Provisional Measures; Case No. 13: The "Juno Trader" Case (Saint Vincent and the Grenadines v. Guinea-Bissau), Prompt Release; Case No. 14: The "Hoshinmaru" Case (Japan v. Russian Federation), Prompt Release; Case No. 15: The "Tomimaru" Case (Japan v. Russian Federation), Prompt Release; Case No. 16: Dispute concerning delimitation of the maritime boundary between Bangladesh and Myanmar in the Bay of Bengal (Bangladesh/Myanmar); Case No. 17: Responsibilities and obligations of States sponsoring persons and entities with respect to activities in the Area (Request for Advisory Opinion submitted to the Seabed Disputes Chamber); Case No. 18: The M/V "Louisa" Case (Saint Vincent and the Grenadines v. Kingdom of Spain); Case No. 19: The M/V "Virginia G" Case (Panama/Guinea-Bissau); Case No. 20: The "ARA Libertad" Case (Argentina v. Ghana), Provisional Measures; Case No. 21: Request for an advisory opinion submitted by the Sub-Regional Fisheries Commission (SRFC).

cerning the Conservation and Sustainable Exploitation of Swordfish Stocks in the South-Eastern Pacific Ocean (Chile/European Community). With regard to the disputes relating to activities in the International Seabed Area, they are submitted to the Seabed Disputes Chamber of the Tribunal, consisting of 11 judges. What is more, any party to a dispute over which the Seabed Disputes Chamber has jurisdiction may request the Seabed Disputes Chamber to form an *ad hoc* chamber composed of three members of the Seabed Disputes Chamber.

Seabed Disputes Chamber

Disputes over seabed activities are to be arbitrated by an 11-member Seabed Disputes Chamber within the Tribunal. The Chamber has compulsory jurisdiction over all conflicts concerning the deep seabed provisions of Part XI of the Convention. Article 187 of the 1982 Convention contains the following provision with regard to the jurisdiction of the Chamber:

> *Article 187*
> Jurisdiction of the Seabed Disputes Chamber
> The Seabed Disputes Chamber shall have jurisdiction under this Part and the Annexes relating thereto in disputes with respect to activities in the Area falling within the following categories:
> (a) disputes between States Parties concerning the interpretation or application of this Part and the Annexes relating thereto;
> (b) disputes between a State Party and the Authority concerning:
> (i) acts or omissions of the Authority or of a State Party alleged to be in violation of this Part or the Annexes relating thereto or of rules, regulations and procedures of the Authority adopted in accordance therewith; or
> (ii) acts of the Authority alleged to be in excess of jurisdiction or a misuse of power;
> (c) disputes between parties to a contract, being States Parties, the Authority or the Enterprise, state enterprises and natural or juridical persons referred to in article 153, paragraph 2(b), concerning:
> (i) the interpretation or application of a relevant contract or a plan of work; or
> (ii) acts or omissions of a party to the contract relating to activities in the Area and directed to the other party or directly affecting its legitimate interests;
> (d) disputes between the Authority and a prospective contractor who has been sponsored by a State as provided in article 153, paragraph 2(b), and has

duly fulfilled the conditions referred to in Annex III, article 4, paragraph 6, and article 13, paragraph 2, concerning the refusal of a contract or a legal issue arising in the negotiation of the contract;

(e) disputes between the Authority and a State Party, a state enterprise or a natural or juridical person sponsored by a State Party as provided for in article 153, paragraph 2(b), where it is alleged that the Authority has incurred liability as provided in Annex III, article 22;

(f) any other disputes for which the jurisdiction of the Chamber is specifically provided in this Convention.

It is particularly interesting to note that the Chamber can entertain cases involving not only states and the International Seabed Authority (an intergovernmental organisation), but also companies or individuals with seabed mining contracts. In this respect the jurisdiction of the Tribunal is different from that of the International Court of Justice, before which only sovereign states can appear as disputing parties. The Seabed Disputes Chamber is entitled to give advisory opinions at the request of the Assembly or the Council of the International Seabed Authority on legal questions arising within the scope of their activities.

The Commission on the Limits of the Continental Shelf

In accordance with the provisions of Article 76, the 1982 Convention establishes a Commission on the Limits of the Continental Shelf.[24] Although the

---

24   See generally on the work of the Commission and the outer limits of the continental shelf, L.D.M. Nelson, "The Continental Shelf: Interplay of Law and Science", in: N. Ando, E. McWhinney and R. Wolfrum (eds.) *Liber Amicorum Judge Shigeru Oda* (The Hague: Kluwer Law International, 2002) 1235–1253; Suzette v. Suarez, *The Outer Limits of the Continental Shelf – Legal Aspects of their Establishment* (Berlin: Springer, 2008) and especially Chapter 5: "Establishment of the Outer Limits of the Continental Shelf Beyond 200 Nautical Miles – the Legal, Scientific and Technical Interface"; Betsy Baker, "States Parties and the Commission on the Limits of the Continental Shelf ", in: R. Wolfrum and T. Malik Ndiaye (eds.) *Liber Amicorum Judge Thomas A. Mensah: Law of the Sea, Protection of the Marine Environment and Settlement of Disputes* (Leiden: Martinus Nijhoff, 2007) 669–686; Peter J. Cook and Chris M. Carleton (eds.), *Continental Shelf Limits: The Scientific and Legal Interface* (Oxford: Oxford University Press, 2000); Myron H. Nordquist, John Norton Moore, and Tomas H. Heidar (eds.) *Legal and Scientific Aspects of Continental Shelf Limits* (Centre for Oceans Law and Policy, University of Virginia (Leiden: Martinus Nijhoff, 2004); R.R. Churchill and A.V. Lowe, *The Law of the Sea* (3rd edition, Manchester:

Commission is not necessarily a dispute settlement mechanism, it is perceived to be one in many quarters since it receives submissions from States with regard to the determination of the outer limits of their continental shelf. As all States have a right to a continental shelf up to the 200-nm point, the Commission is concerned only with an area beyond the 200-nm point and the maximum outer limit that a coastal State can establish as its continental shelf. The Commission consists of 21 members who are experts in the fields of geology, geophysics or hydrography, and who are elected by States Parties to the Convention from among their nationals, having due regard for the need to ensure equitable geographical representation. The members serve in a personal capacity. They are elected for a term of five years and are eligible for re-election.

The functions of the Commission are: (a) to consider data and other material submitted by coastal States concerning the outer limits of the continental shelf in areas where those limits extend beyond 200 nm, and to make recommendations in accordance with Article 76 and the Statement of Understanding adopted on 29 August 1980 by the Third United Nations Conference on the Law of the Sea (UNCLOS III) and contained in Annex II to the Final Act of UNCLOS III; and (b) if requested by a coastal state, to provide scientific and technical advice during the preparation of data to be submitted to the Commission. Where a coastal state intends to establish the outer limits of its continental shelf beyond 200 nm in accordance with Article 76, that state is required to submit to the Commission particulars of such limits, along with supporting scientific and technical data, as soon as possible, and in any case within ten years of the entry into force of the 1982 Convention for that state.

The Commission's recommendations are to be submitted in writing to the coastal state that made the submission and to the UN Secretary-General. This process is already under way and many States have now made their submissions. In addition to the submissions by individual States, groups of

---

Manchester University Press, 1999) at Ch. 8; Constance Johnson and Alex G. Oude Elferink, "Submission to the Commission on the Limits of the Continental Shelf in Cases of Unresolved Land and Maritime Disputes: The Significance of Article 76 (10) of the Convention on the Law of the Sea", in: Freestone et al., op. cit. *supra* note 6 at 161–179; Clive Schofield and I Made Andi Arsana, "Beyond the Limits?: Outer Continental Shelf Opportunities and Challenges in East and Southeast Asia" (2008) 31(1) *Contemporary Southeast Asia* 28–63; Huw Llewellyn, "The Commission on the Limits of the Continental Shelf: Joint Submission by France, Ireland, Spain and the United Kingdom" (2007) 56 *International and Comparative Law Quarterly* 677–694; Surya P. Subedi, "Problems and Prospects for the Commission on the Limits of the Continental Shelf in Dealing with Submissions by Coastal States in Relation to the Ocean Territory Beyond 200 Nautical Miles', *The International Journal of Marine and Coastal Law* 26 (2011) 413–431.

States have also made joint submissions, of which one example is the joint application made by the UK, France, Ireland, and Spain over a particular sector of the Atlantic Ocean, off the Bay of Biscay, and in the Celtic Sea.

In accordance with Rule 50 of the Commission's Rules of Procedure, a coastal State is required to make public the proposed outer limits of the extended continental shelf. Upon completion of its task, the Commission is required to make recommendations to the submitting State in accordance with Article 76 of the 1982 Convention. The limits of the continental shelf established by the State concerned on the basis of these recommendations are final and binding and the UN Secretary-General is required to give due publicity to the limits thus established.

The Commission makes a recommendation based on the scientific data and other materials submitted by a coastal state about the outer limit of its continental shelf. Upon receipt of submissions from coastal States, the Commission assigns the matter to a sub-commission, which makes recommendations to the Commission. Altogether about 80 States are expected to make an overlapping submission for the outer limit of their continental shelf under this mechanism. With an estimated two-thirds of the 460 or so maritime boundaries between coastal States being either disputed or unresolved, the work of the Commission will remain a focus of attention for many decades. What is more, because the Commission may not examine claims for sovereignty over territories under dispute, many submissions for the establishment of the outer limit of the continental shelves made to it may have to wait until issues of territorial sovereignty in disputed areas have been resolved.

The Commission can do no more than to make a recommendation to the State concerned after considering its submission; it has no powers to enforce its recommendations. States with divergent views may make submissions or send communications in the form of *notes verbales* to the Commission. Article 8 of Annex II to the 1982 Convention provides that: "In the case of disagreement by the coastal State with the recommendations of the Commission, the coastal State shall, within a reasonable time, make a revised or new submission to the Commission." If the State concerned is dissatisfied with the Commission's recommendation, the latter may reconsider. However, once the Commission has completed its work, it would be up to the disputing parties to accept its recommendations. In the absence of such an acceptance, they will have to resort either to bilateral negotiations or to referring the matter either to the International Court of Justice, to the International Tribunal for the Law of the Sea, or to an international arbitration.

It should also be noted that, one way or the other, the Commission, which consists of non-lawyers, is likely to find itself in a position of interpreting some provisions of the LOS Convention or the Statement of Understanding, or the Guidelines, and it remains to be seen what the ramifications of this would be for the application or implementation of the Commission's recommendations. The Commission is neither a judicial body nor a purely administrative body. It bears little resemblance to a quasi-judicial body, as none of the members of this body are individuals with a background in law, even though some of its functions are akin to those of a judicial body. Its status seems to fall somewhere between a quasi-judicial and an administrative body; it could perhaps best be described as a technical-*cum* scientific body consisting of members with technical and scientific expertise. However, it is a very important intergovernmental body exercising powers under an international legal instrument. Its decisions, formally known as recommendations, will have far-reaching implications for the States concerned, for the 1982 Convention, and for international governance of the global commons.

Conclusions

As seen in the preceding paragraphs, the dispute settlement mechanism of the 1982 Convention is both flexible and comprehensive, allowing states several choices of method to settle their disputes. The mechanism on the whole is the result of an innovative diplomatic exercise not witnessed prior to the adoption of the Convention. It covers more or less every situation concerning the law of the sea, including disputes not only between states but also between states and intergovernmental entities and even private entities involved in the exploration and exploitation of the natural resources of the seabed. The dispute settlement mechanism represents a landmark institution in the history of the international dispute settlement mechanisms offered by international law.

As can be seen from the foregoing analysis, this innovative, flexible and sophisticated mechanism of settling maritime disputes outlined in the 1982 Convention is working well. Although the number of disputes referred to the International Tribunal on the Law of the Sea is relatively small and there was some pessimism in the early years of its inception, the Tribunal has already delivered some land mark judgements on some of the complex issues within the law of the sea such as the Dispute concerning delimitation of the maritime boundary between Bangladesh and Myanmar in the Bay of Bengal (Bangladesh/Myanmar) and established itself as a body that works well, and works to deliver the vision envisaged in the Convention. Not many other international treaties contain such a detailed and flexible dispute settlement mechanism as does the 1982 Convention which itself is a mammoth comprehensive treaty.

The beauty is that in spite of being such an ambitious project in the annals of international law, both the 1982 Convention and its innovative dispute settlement mechanism, are likely to support the vision of keeping peace in the seas and oceans and their use for peaceful purposes for the betterment of humanity for a long time to come.

CHAPTER 13

An Analysis of the Adequacy of the Dispute Settlement Mechanism Under UNCLOS: Maritime Boundary Delimitation Disputes

Osman Keh Kamara

1 Introduction

The Law of the Sea is an accretion of numerous treaties and customary rules dating back since time immemorial. The United Nations Convention on the Law of the Sea ('UNCLOS' or 'The Convention') epitomizes efforts to codify and reform the law of the sea in line with the modern era.[1] It is widely acclaimed as the most significant development of international law in recent decades. UNCLOS establishes the normative framework under which coastal States should delimit their maritime boundaries. In the course of this process, disputes are inevitable.[2] It has been reasonably asserted that maritime boundary delimitation disputes are among the most complicated international disputes with inordinate propensity to evolve into tensions and eventual conflicts if the appropriate international dispute settlement mechanisms are not initiated to resolve these disputes.[3]

Undoubtedly, oceans are among the most important resources on the planet. They consist of approximately seventy percent of the earth surface and play a pivotal role in the existence and survival of mankind. Among other things, a wide array of biological species such as fish are caught from the ocean; it also serves as useful terrain for both passenger and cargo transportation; a source of raw materials like crude oil, gas, and other important mineral resources; and finally, diverse military activities are carried on, above, upon, and below it.

---

1 The United Nations Convention on the Law of the Sea was adopted on 30 April 1982 at Montego Bay Jamaica following nine years of negotiation at various sessions of the Third United Nations Conference on the Law of the Sea. It came into force on 16 November 1994. (Source: http://www.un.org/depts/los/reference_files/status2005.pdf).
2 J.G Merrills, *International Dispute Settlement,* Third edition, (1998), at p. 1.
3 Catley and Makmur Keliat, *Spratlys: The Dispute in the South China Sea,* (1997), at 2. Between 1919 and 1975 there were 86 international conflicts, 39 of which originated from territorial dispute. Currently there is an ongoing dispute initiated by the Philippine against China at the International Tribunal on Law of the Sea (ITLOS).

Since the very inception of the Westphalian state system in 1648, governments have been concerned with what goes on at sea; and because they differ so much in their geography, economy, politics, and capacities, their interests invariably lead to competition.[4] The panoply of interests inevitably result in disputes. Some of the disputes may relate solely to maritime boundary delimitation while others may constitute mixed-disputes encompassing complex issues of sea boundary delimitation and sovereignty over insular land territory.

The consequences of these disputes are enormous. Apart from affecting the bilateral relationship between the opposite or adjacent coastal states concerned, it would jeopardize their economic activities especially were naval forces are involved with the attendant effect of disrupting international peace and security. The inviolability of the territorial issue to the States in question has the effect of making these disputes extremely difficult to resolve. Nevertheless, States are required, under international law, to refrain from actions that are tantamount to threat or use of force to resolve their international disputes. Instead, they must resolve disputes by peaceful means and in conformity with the principles of justice and international law so that international peace, security, and justice will not be breached.[5]

Dubbed as the constitution for the oceans,[6] UNCLOS was successfully negotiated and eventually adopted as the normative framework for the effective and sustainable exploitation of the sea and its wide biological diversity. The Convention sets out an international legal order containing provisions on the basis of which the plethora of activities in the oceans and seas must be carried out. As a comprehensive legal framework, the Convention has elucidated the rights and obligations of all States, including but not limited to: coastal, landlocked, and geographical disadvantaged States, international organizations and entities in various functional maritime areas; the protection of marine environment; marine scientific research; activities in the seabed (the Area) as well as mechanisms for the settlement of disputes that may arise during the implementation and interpretation of the Convention. The dispute settlement mechanism enshrined in Part XV of UNCLOS, which is characterized by 'compulsory procedures entailing binding decisions', has made UNCLOS unique among major lawmaking treaties and as one commentator puts it: "one of an

---

[4] M.H. Mendelson, Oxford Journal of Legal Studies, *The Flux and Reflux of the Law of the Sea* 5(2) 285.

[5] Article 1 and 2 of the Charter of the United Nations.

[6] Remarks by Tommy T.B. Koh, President of the Third United Nations Conference on the Law of the Sea at the final session of the Conference.

extremely small number of global treaties that prescribe mandatory jurisdiction for disputes arising from interpretation and application of its terms."[7]

This chapter, which will hopefully serve as a fitting tribute to the work, interests and contributions of His Excellency Judge Abdul G. Koroma in the area of the law of the sea, examines the adequacy of the dispute settlement mechanisms contained in Part XV of UNCLOS for disputes arising from boundary delimitations in the Territorial Sea, the Exclusive Economic Zone and the Continental Shelf between coastal states. My core argument is that UNCLOS provides principled guidance in the resolution of all facets of disputes pertaining to the law of the sea.

Basically, Articles[8] 15, 74 and 83 of UNCLOS contain provisions that deal with delimitation of the territorial sea, exclusive economic zone and the continental shelf between States with opposite or adjacent coasts, respectively. Accordingly, any dispute concerning the interpretation and application of those provisions would invite the dispute settlement procedures set out in Part XV of the Convention. Paragraph 2 of articles 74 and 83 further provides that, if no agreement is reached within a reasonable period of time, the "States concerned shall resort to the procedures provided for in Part XV" of the convention.[9] To what extent are delimitation disputes covered by the procedures provided for in Part XV?[10] Are these provisions adequate enough to settle sea boundary delimitation disputes? The pith and marrow of this chapter essentially aim to reflect answers to these questions.

The first part of this chapter situates the dispute settlement provisions of UNCLOS in a wider perspective. Section 2 addresses delimitation of maritime boundaries. Section 3 considers the regime regarding disputes pertaining to

---

7   Natalie Klein, *Dispute Settlement in the UN Convention on the Law of the Sea* (2005), at 2.
8   Unless otherwise specified, references to articles are to be taken as references to the articles of the United Nations Convention on the Law of the Sea (UNCLOS).
9   See the Award dated 11 April 2006 of the Arbitral Tribunal constituted pursuant to article 287, and in accordance with Annex VII, of UNCLOS in the matter of an arbitration between: Barbados and The Republic of Trinidad and Tobago (the "Arbitral Award of 2006").
10 See United Nation Convention on the Law of the Sea 1982: A Commentary, Vol. V, pp. 107–141 (Shabtai Rosenne and Louis B. Sohn eds., 1989) ("Virginia Commentary"); Tullio Treves, "What have the United Nations Convention and the International Tribunal for the Law of the Sea to offer as regards Maritime Delimitation Disputes?", in Rainer Lagoni and Daniel Vignes (eds.), *Maritime Delimitation*, 2006, pp. 63–78; Alan E. Boyle, "Dispute Settlement and the Law of the Sea Convention: Problems of Fragmentation and Jurisdiction", 46 *International and Comparative Law Quarterly* (1997), pp. 37–54; Natalie Klein, *Dispute settlement in the UN Convention on the Law of the Sea* (2005), pp. 253–263.

sea boundary delimitation. The conclusion restates the key arguments of the chapter.

1 Part XV of UNCLOS in Perspective

Heralding a new era in international law, the third United Nations Conference on the law of the sea, which adopted UNCLOS, introduced what was considered to be innovative and far-reaching compulsory dispute settlement mechanisms.[11] Drafters were cognizant of two important issues. First, the fact that the interpretation and application of the provisions of UNCLOS might give rise to differences in opinion among States and other entities involved in the application of its provisions, in particular, application and interpretation relating to the powers, rights and obligations of the coastal States *vis-a-vis* other states and entities in the maritime zones declared to be within national jurisdiction. Second, the conference decided to adopt a dispute settlement mechanism through which all differences connected with the interpretation and application of UNCLOS should be resolved. This was to ensure that those dealing with powers and responsibilities of the International Sea Bed Authority in its relations with State parties, entities or persons engaged in activities in the International Area were covered.

1.1 The Regime of Part XV

The dispute settlement regime encapsulated in Part XV of UNCLOS is viewed by many scholars and commentators as a necessary balancing device designed to streamline the interests of all States against the increased jurisdictional competence enjoyed by coastal States under UNCLOS.[12] As remarked by the First President of the Conference, "effective dispute settlement would ... guarantee that the substance and intention within the legislative language of the Convention will be interpreted consistently and equitably."[13] Against this backdrop, the conference agreed to establish procedures for dispute settlement which would be acceptable to States.

---

11 Tommy T.B. Koh, "A Constitution for the Oceans" Remark made by the President of the Third United Nations Conference on the Law of the Sea, in Official Text of the United Nations Convention on the Law of the Sea with Annexes and Index(1983) E 83V5, xxxiii.

12 See Rosemary Rayfuse, *The Future of Compulsory Dispute Settlement Under the Law of the Sea Convention*, (Victoria University of Wellington Law Review), p. 2.

13 See Article by Thomas A. Mensah, *"Dispute Settlement Regime of UNCLOS"*, Max Planck Yearbook of United Nations Law (1998) p. 307. The entire Statement is reproduced in Doc. A/CONF.62/WP.9/Add.1, para. 6. Third United Nations Conference on the Law of the Sea, Official Records, Vol. 5, 122;

But the Conference was aware that States are not always willing to submit their disputes for binding settlement to the existing international bodies. The reasons for the reluctance of States to accept compulsory and binding settlement of their disputes by international courts are many.[14] Suffice it to say that many States have been unwilling to agree unconditionally to submit all disputes with other States to international courts for binding decision; and many of those who accept the jurisdiction of such courts generally seek to limit the scope of their acceptance. For this reason it was not considered realistic to require all States parties to agree, without reservation, to submit all disputes under the UNCLOS to a particular international judicial body. Consequently the Conference did not attempt to endow a single judicial body with exclusive jurisdiction to deal with disputes arising in connection with its application and interpretation.[15]

On the other hand, there was general recognition of the need to ensure that all disputes concerning the interpretation and application of the Convention would be settled by peaceful means. In line with the relevant provisions of the United Nations Charter and the general principles of international Law, it was accepted that peaceful settlement should involve, as a first step, recourse to procedures mutually acceptable to the parties to the disputes, i.e. through "peaceful means of their own choice."[16] For this reasons the Convention specifically states that nothing in the regime established under it would "impair the right of any State Parties to agree at any time to settle a dispute between them concerning the interpretation or application of this Convention by any peaceful means of their own choice."[17]

However, there was consensus in the conference that, where States are not able to settle their disputes through such means of their choice, they should be obliged to submit the disputes for settlement by mechanisms established internationally.[18] The dispute settlement procedures are contained in all three

---

[14] E.D. Brown, "Dispute settlement and the Law of the Sea: the UN Convention regime", Mar. Pol'y. 21 (1997), 17 et seq. (18).

[15] See Article by Thomas A. Mensah, *"Dispute Settlement Regime of UNCLOS"*, Max Planck Yearbook of United Nations Law (1998), p. 308.

[16] Charter of the United Nations, Article 33 para. 1.

[17] Article 280.

[18] The world community's interest in the peaceful settlement of disputes ... has been advanced by the Mandatory System of Disputes Settlement of the Convention": T.T.B. Koh, "A Constitution for the Oceans", Statement of the President of the Conference, 6 and 11 December 1982. Reproduced in: *The Law of the Sea: The United Nations Convention on the Law of the Sea,* United Nations Publication, xxxiii, see also A.O. Adede, *The System for*

sections of Part XV. Section 1 lays down voluntary procedures;[19] section 2 contains compulsory procedures entailing binding decisions;[20] and section 3 addresses "limitations and exceptions" to the applicability of section 2 and (non-binding) compulsory conciliation.[21] Each of these are considered in turn below.

1.2 Section 1: Voluntary Procedures

The voluntary procedures contained in Section 1 of Part XV reiterate the general obligation of States to resolve their disputes by an agreement and to do so peacefully in accordance with the established procedures provided for under general international law pursuant to Article 33 paragraph 1 of the United Nations Charter.[22] This mechanism preserves the right of States to agree at any time to settle their disputes by means of their own choice, in which case, the dispute is exempted from Part XV procedures except where no settlement has been reached and the agreement does not exclude any further procedure.[23]

The Convention also provides that a dispute concerning the interpretation and application of the convention may be submitted to a particular procedure for binding decision if the parties to the dispute have agreed, pursuant to a general regional or bilateral international agreement, that such a dispute shall be settled through that procedure. In such a case, that procedure applies in lieu of the procedures enshrined in Part XV, unless the parties to the dispute otherwise agree.[24] Such procedure establishes compulsory jurisdiction invokable at the instance of any party to the dispute. It is thus open to states parties to submit their disputes, by agreement, to any binding dispute settlement procedure, including any procedure provided for in section 2.

Primarily, whenever a dispute arises, the States parties thereto are required to expeditiously exchange views regarding its settlement by peaceful means either through negotiation, inquiries, mediation, arbitration, exchange of views between the parties, or alternately, elect to proceed to voluntary concili-

---

Settlement of Dispute Under the United Nations Convention on the Law of the Sea, 1987, 240 et seq.

19   Articles 279 to 285 of the Convention.
20   Articles 286 to 296.
21   Articles 297 to 299.
22   Article 279 of the Convention, i.e. through negotiation, inquiries, mediation, conciliation, arbitration, exchange of views between the parties or judicial settlement; see American Treaty on Pacific settlement of Dispute (Pact of Bogota)
23   Articles 280 to 281.
24   Article 282.

ation.[25] A similar exchange is also required: (i) where a procedure for the settlement of such a dispute has been terminated without settlement; or (ii) where a settlement has been reached and the circumstances require consultation regarding the manner of implementing the settlement.[26] Where the parties agree to settle the dispute by conciliation, they can take advantage of the procedures set out in section 1 of Annex V to the Convention.[27] This involves the use of a Conciliation Commission whose members are selected by the parties to the dispute. The conclusions of and recommendations of the Commission are to assist the parties if they wish, but are not binding upon them.[28] It is important to note that a State Party to a dispute is at liberty to accept or refuse an invitation from the other disputant to submit the dispute to conciliation and, if the invitation is not accepted or the parties do not agree upon the procedure, the conciliation proceedings are deemed to be terminated.[29]

It follows therefore, that Section 1 enunciates several procedures and the application of any of the procedures depends on the facts and circumstances of each case. If, for instance, the parties are bound by a previous agreement to settle the dispute by a procedure of their choice (article 281) or to submit their dispute to a procedure entailing a binding decision (article 282), then that procedure applies to the exclusion of the other procedures. If the parties start with a clean slate, then the provision requiring the parties to exchange views regarding settlement by negotiation or other peaceful means applies. In certain cases, more than one procedure may apply. It seems notable that each of the peaceful ways of addressing disagreements mentioned in the two preceding paragraphs originate from and comport with the express provisions of the general dispute resolution regime contemplated by the Charter of the United Nations.

1.3 Section 2: Compulsory Procedures

Where the states concerned have been unable to resolve their disputes concerning the interpretation or application of any provision of the Convention pursuant to any of the procedures enshrined in Section 1 of Part XV of the Convention, they are obliged to submit the dispute to an appropriate standing judicial procedures for binding decision in accordance with the provisions for

---

25 Article 283. paragraph 1
26 Article 283, paragraph 2
27 Article 284.
28 Annex V, article 7 para. 2.
29 Article 284.

"compulsory procedures entailing binding decisions" enumerated in Section 2 of Part XV of the Convention.

However, section 2 lays down certain pre-conditions which need to be satisfied before any compulsory procedure entailing binding decision is invoked. Either party may invoke a compulsory procedure only if its application is not negated by the limitations and exceptions referred to in section 3 and no settlement has been reached by recourse to section 1. If these pre-conditions are satisfied, any dispute concerning the interpretation or application of the convention may be submitted at the instance of any party to it to the court or tribunal having jurisdiction under section 2.

In this regard, state parties are empowered to choose from a list of the under-mentioned alternative standing judicial bodies endowed with compulsory procedures for the settlement of their disputes concerning the interpretation and application of the Convention. These bodies include: (a) the International Tribunal for the Law of the Sea established in accordance with Annex VI; (b) the International Court of Justice; (c) an Arbitral Tribunal constituted in accordance with Annex VII to the Convention; and (d) a special Arbitral Tribunal constituted pursuant to Annex VIII to the Convention for disputes falling within the categories specified therein.[30]

In most cases, the choice of a forum will depend on prior declarations made by parties in favor of one of the standing judicial bodies of the Convention. Where no declaration is made at all, or where declarations are made for two distinct standing judicial bodies such that no common choice is agreed, the parties are deemed to have chosen Annex VII arbitration which is the default procedure regarding the choice of forum. It follows, therefore, that Annex VII arbitral tribunal is the inherent choice of compulsory dispute settlement procedures entailing binding decisions for State parties to the Convention unless there is a declaration to the contrary.[31]

A court or tribunal referred to in article 287 exercises jurisdiction over any dispute concerning:

> (i) "The interpretation or application of the Convention which is submitted to it in accordance with this Part; and, (ii) The Interpretation or application of an international agreement related to the purposes of Convention, which is submitted to it in accordance with the agreement. (iii) In the event of a dispute over the jurisdiction of a court or tribunal, under article 287, that court or tribunal, exercising its Compétence de la Compétence, settles the matter by its decision."[32]

---

30   Article 287 paragraph 1, (a), (b), (c) and (d).
31   Articles 286 to 287 of the Convention.
32   Article 288, paragraphs 1, 2 and 4 of the Convention.

That being said, it is now pertinent to briefly adumbrate the rationale behind the establishment of several judicial fora under the Convention. Primarily, the International Court of Justice ("ICJ") is established under the Charter of the United Nations as the principal judicial organ of the United Nations. The Statute of the Court is annexed to the Charter of the United Nations of which it is an integral part. Although it is a principal organ of the United Nations, the ICJ does not have automatic jurisdiction to deal with disputes involving all member states of the United Nations. In effect, it can only adjudicate on cases if the parties involved have specifically accepted its jurisdiction pursuant to articles 34, 35 and 36 of its statutes. Obviously, some states have been wary, unwilling or at least reluctant to accept the jurisdiction of the Court, although some others have been quite happy and willing to submit to the Court without hesitation. In the light of such differences in the attitudes of States to the Court, the framers of UNCLOS did not consider it realistic to make the Court the sole forum for the settlement of disputes in connection with the Convention. What they did was to make recourse to the Court as one of the possible procedures available to States Parties who wish to rely on the Court. For such states, the ICJ will have the competence to give binding decisions on disputes in which they are involved.[33] This seems to make practical sense, at least from the perspective of many countries.

The other standing judicial body which States may choose is the International Tribunal for the Law of the Sea ("ITLOS" or "The Tribunal"). This is a new court established by UNCLOS. The Statute of the Tribunal is contained in Annex VI to the Convention, which is an integral part of UNCLOS.[34] The Tribunal was created because, as stated above, some states are not willing to accept the jurisdiction of the ICJ without reservation. There was general agreement in the Third United Nations Convention on the need for a standing court, with an established membership and well-known rules and procedure, to which disputes concerning the interpretation or application of the provisions of the new Convention could be submitted for final and binding decisions. The Conference therefore, decided to established another tribunal or court which would be available to the States which might wish to have recourse to a standing court but which might, for one reason or another, not be comfortable with the ICJ. In other words, it was felt that even if an international court of general

---

[33] Article 296 of the Convention provides that a decision of a court or tribunal having jurisdiction under the Convention "shall be final and shall be complied with by all the parties to the disputes."

[34] Article 318 of the Convention.

compulsory jurisdiction did not exist, a special court addressing specific subject matter may be politically acceptable to States.

Conversely, the Conference also recognized that some states might consider the Tribunal equally unacceptable as a compulsory forum for the settlement of all their disputes. This is particularly so in the case of those states which object in principle to a mandatory obligation to submit their disputes to an international judicial body. To cater for such states it was decided to provide other alternative procedure which will give to States parties a greater measure of choice in the composition of the bodies to which their disputes might be submitted.[35]

Consequently, the conference adopted two methods of arbitration as contained in annexes VII and VIII of the Convention respectively; the composition of which to a large extent, will be determined by States parties to the dispute in question. The former is a comprehensive procedure designed to adjudicate on all facets of disputes arising from the interpretation and application of the provisions of the Convention as a whole,[36] whereas the latter is specifically designed and restricted to deal with special disputes relating to fisheries, the protection and conservation of the marine environment, marine scientific research and navigation, including pollution from vessels and by dumping.[37] In this connection, States who do not wish to submit their disputes to the ICJ and ITLOS can agree to submit their disputes for settlement by any of the two arbitral tribunals whose members will be selected pursuant to the dictates of the Convention.[38]

Each arbitral tribunal will normally consist of five members duly appointed in accordance with the relevant but different procedures laid down in the respective annexes to the Convention.[39] The members of an arbitral tribunal constituted under the provisions contained in Annex VII are selected from a general list of arbitrators drawn up and maintained by the Secretary-General of the United Nations. This list contains the names of persons nominated by the State parties, with each State Party entitled to nominate not more than four persons.[40]

The members of the arbitral tribunal for any particular dispute are selected by the parties to the dispute from among the list in the following manner: one

---

35	See Thomas A. Mensah, Max-Planck Year Book of United Nations Law (1998), p. 312.
36	Annex VII, article 1.
37	Annex VIII, article 1.
38	Article 287 para. 1, (c) & (d).
39	Annex VII, article 3; and Annex VIII, article 3.
40	Annex VII, article 2.

member each is selected by the party initiating the proceedings and the respondent party. The remaining three members are selected by agreement between the members, and the president of the arbitral tribunal is selected by an agreement between the parties to the dispute. If no agreement is reached on the selection of the three members or the president of the arbitral tribunal, the choice will be made by a person or a third state agreed by the parties to the dispute. If no agreement is reached by the parties, the choice will be made by the President of the ITLOS.[41]

With respect to the special arbitral tribunal constituted under annex VIII to the Convention, members are selected from "special lists of experts" maintained by specified international organizations to which responsibility has been assigned by the Convention. These organizations include: (a)"The Food and Agricultural organization (FAO) for fisheries related disputes; (b)The Intergovernmental Oceanographic Commission (IOC) for disputes relating to marine scientific research; (c)The UNEP disputes relating to the protection and preservation of the marine environment; and (d)The International Maritime Organization (IMO) for navigation, including the prevention of marine pollution from vessels and dumping."[42]

This list contains the names of experts nominated by the State Parties, with each being entitled to nominate not more than two experts. The five members of the special arbitral tribunal for any particular dispute are selected by the parties to the dispute from among the appropriate list in the following manner: two members each are selected by the party initiating the proceedings and a further two by the respondent party. The fifth member, who acts as the president of the special arbitral tribunal for any particular dispute is selected from the same list of experts by agreement between the parties to the dispute. In event of disagreement on the selection of the president, the choice will be made by a person or a third state agreed upon between the parties to the dispute. If the parties cannot agree on such a person or third state, the selection will be made by the Secretary-General of the United Nations.[43]

1.4 Section 3: Limitations and Exceptions to the Applicability of Section 2

While every State Party to UNCLOS is obliged to accept a "compulsory procedure entailing binding decisions" regarding disputes in which it may be involved, section 3 carves out a plethora of limitations and exceptions to the

---

41 Annex VII, article 3 lit. (d), (e) and sequence.
42 Annex VIII, article 2.
43 Annex VIII, article 3.

applicability of section 2. Primarily, the respective courts and tribunals listed in paragraph 1 of article 287 of UNCLOS accepted by a particular State Party will have automatic jurisdictional competence to adjudicate on disputes in which it is alleged that the State Party has acted contrary to the provisions relating to the freedom, rights or obligations in regard to specified "international lawful uses of the sea"[44] or in contravention to the laws and regulations of the coastal State enacted pursuant to UNCLOS or other rules of international law generally,[45] or other relevant international rules and standards for the protection and preservation of the marine environment.[46] However, this jurisdictional competence is subject to a number of limitations and exceptions enunciated in articles 297 and 298 respectively of UNCLOS.

The "limitations" set out in article 297 are automatic in the sense that their applicability is not dependent on any action of the States Parties to UNCLOS. They do not, however, extend to delimitation disputes. Thus a coastal State Party is not obliged to submit or accept the submission to a court or tribunal of certain disputes arising out of the exercise by that State of a right or discretion in respect of marine scientific research.[47] Moreover, the Convention excludes from the jurisdiction of the respective courts and tribunals listed in article 287 disputes concerning the sovereign rights of the coastal States with regard to the exploitation of the living resources in the exclusive economic zone or the exercise of such rights.[48]

In contrast, the "optional exceptions" specified in article 298 to the applicability of section 2 prevail only when declarations are made by States. Article 298 makes provision for a State to declare (when signing, ratifying or acceding to the convention or at any time thereafter) that it does not accept any one or more of the compulsory procedures provided for in section 2 with respect to one or more of the following categories of disputes: (a) Disputes relating to the interpretation or application of the provisions of the Convention in respect of sea boundary delimitations or those involving historic bays or titles provided for in articles 15, 74 and 83 of the Convention;[49] (b) Disputes relating to military activities involving the use of government vessels and aircraft engaged in non-commercial service; and disputes concerning law enforcement activities by a coastal State with respect to fisheries and marine scientific research in areas

---

44 Article 297 para. 1 (a).
45 Ibid., (b).
46 Ibid., (c).
47 Article 297 para. 2.
48 Ibid., para. 3
49 Article 298 para. 1 (a)

subject to its jurisdiction but excluded from the jurisdiction of the tribunal in accordance with paragraphs 2 and 3 of article 297 of the Convention; and, (c) Disputes in respect of which the United Nations Security Council is exercising its functions under the Charter of the United Nations, unless the Security Council decides to remove the matter from its agenda or calls upon the parties to settle it by the means provided for in UNCLOS.

Article 298, paragraph 1 (a)(i), further provides that when a State makes a declaration that it does not accept any of the compulsory procedures in regard to the disputes specified in (a) above, "It shall, when such a dispute arises subsequent to the entry into force of this Convention and where no agreement within a reasonable period of time is reached in negotiations between the parties, at the request of any party to the dispute, accept submission of the matter to conciliation under Annex V, section 2;" and "provided further that any dispute that necessarily involves the concurrent consideration of any unsettled dispute concerning sovereignty or other rights over continental or insular land territory shall be excluded from such submission."[50] In any event, article 7 paragraph 2 of Annex V provides that the conclusions and recommendations of a conciliation commission appointed under that Annex are not binding on the parties. Therefore even such disputes cannot be considered as covered by the compulsory procedures entailing binding decisions under section 2 of Part XV of UNCLOS.

A State therefore has many options to exercise under article 298. It may not accept any one or more of the compulsory procedures with respect to disputes specified in article 298, paragraphs 1(a) (i), 1(b) and 1(c). Or, it may accept only any one or more of the compulsory procedures with respect to certain categories of disputes and not the other. Paragraphs 1(a) (i) and 1(b) of article 298 contain more than one category of disputes. For instance, disputes relating to sea boundary delimitations specified in article 15 appertain to a category of disputes which is separate from the category of disputes relating to delimitations specified in article 74 or article 83. Since declarations under article 298 constitute exceptions to the application of compulsory procedures, and since it is reasonable to expect that UNCLOS would want to keep the exceptions to the minimum and within narrow limits, article 298 may be construed as permitting exceptions even narrower than those stated expressly therein[51]

The declarations made under article 298 do not in any way affect the obligations arising under section 1 of Part XV.[52] A State may at any time withdraw its

---

50   Article 298 para. 1 (a) (i).
51   *Virginia commentary; supra* note 10. p. 115.
52   See article 298, paragraph 1.

declaration.[53] However, a new declaration, or the withdrawal of a declaration, has no retroactive effect on the proceedings pending before a court or tribunal.[54] A State may agree to submit a dispute excluded by its declaration to "any procedure specified in this convention".[55] The "procedure" mentioned here obviously refers to a compulsory procedure provided for in section 2, since article 298 declarations are without prejudice to the obligations arising under section 1. The agreement with the other party in this regard will be an ad hoc one, for the declaration as such is not withdrawn.

When a State Party has made a declaration, it cannot submit any dispute falling within the excepted category of disputes to "any compulsory procedure provided for in section 2 of UNCLOS" against another State Party.[56] Article 298, paragraph 4, provides that, if any of the State Parties has made a declaration under paragraph 1 (a), any other State Party may submit any dispute falling within the excepted category against the declarant party to "the procedure Specified in such declaration." It cannot be that the expression "the procedure specified in such declaration" refers to a compulsory procedure specified in section 2; it has been suggested that the expression should be understood as referring to the compulsory conciliation procedure specified in article 298, paragraph 1(a).[57] Even so, there is the need for the declaration in question to specify a procedure, since paragraph 1 (a) expressly states that conciliation procedure becomes obligatory "at the request of any party to the dispute."

Declarations and notices of withdrawal of declarations under article 298 are required to be deposited with the Secretary-General of the United Nations, who in turn, is required to transmit copies thereof to the States Parties.[58] It appears that such declarations and notices take effect from the moment they are received by the Secretary-General.[59] Unless excluded by a declaration made under article 298, paragraph 1 (a) (i), compulsory procedures provided for in section 2 are available in respect of delimitation disputes or those involving historic bays or titles, whether they have arisen before the entry into force of UNCLOS or arise subsequent to its entry into force. Any State making a declaration excluding any or all delimitation disputes is, nevertheless, bound by different settlement procedures with respect to post-Convention disputes. The

---

53 See article 298, paragraph 1.
54 See article 298, paragraph 5.
55 See article 298, paragraph 2.
56 See article 298, paragraph 3.
57 See *Virginia Commentary, supra* note 10, p. 116.
58 See article 298, paragraph 6.
59 See *Virginia Commentary, supra* note 10, pp. 140–141.

Convention calls upon the parties to enter into negotiations with a view to reaching agreement in regard to such disputes.[60] If no agreement is reached "within a reasonable period of time", conciliation under Annex V, section 2, at the request of any party to the dispute, becomes compulsory.[61] Article 298 thus uses compulsory conciliation as a subsidiary procedure of dispute settlement.

Even in regard to post-Convention disputes, there are further exclusions from any submission to conciliation. These are as follows: (a) mixed disputes referred to in the second proviso in article 298, paragraph 1(a) (i); (b) disputes finally settled by an arrangement between the parties;[62] and, (c) disputes that are to be settled in accordance with a bilateral or multilateral agreement binding on the parties.[63]

The procedure for conciliation may be stated in accordance with Annex V, section 2. The commission is empowered to decide disagreements as to its competence.[64] Articles 2 to 10 of section 1 of Annex V govern different aspects of the constitution and functioning of the conciliation commission. Generally speaking, the conciliation procedure is less adversarial and less legalistic than any compulsory and binding procedure. It involves assisted negotiation.[65] This aspect is particularly underlined in Annex V, which invites the commission to draw the attention of the parties to any measures which might facilitate an amicable settlement of the disputes[66] and to make proposals to the parties with a view to reaching such settlement.[67]

The conciliation commission is given a specific time limit: twelve months from the time the commission is constituted to submit its report.[68] The report must record any agreements reached and, failing agreement, the commission's conclusion on all questions of fact or law relevant to the matter in dispute and such recommendations as the commission may deem appropriate for an amicable settlement.[69] It is required to be deposited with the Secretary-General of the United Nations for transmission to the parties to the dispute.[70]

---

60   See article 298, paragraph 1(a) (i).
61   Ibid.
62   See article 298, paragraph 1 (a) (iii).
63   Ibid.
64   See article 13 of Annex V.
65   See Paul C. Irwin, *supra* note 10, p. 129.
66   See article 5 of Annex V.
67   See article 6 of Annex V.
68   See article 7 of Annex V.
69   Ibid.
70   Ibid.

The report of the commission, including its conclusions and recommendations, is not binding upon the parties.[71] However, it cannot be dismissed as being of no value. Any party to the dispute ignoring the report may invite adverse international opinion. Further, the conclusions and recommendations of the commission may be used in any eventual settlement of the dispute. The Convention itself calls upon the parties to negotiate an agreement on the basis of the report.[72] It is a legal requirement that the parties should negotiate in good faith[73] and with a view to arriving at an agreement, and not merely go through a formal process of negotiation.[74] Article 298, paragraph 1 (a)(ii), states that, if the negotiations do not result in an agreement, the parties "shall, by mutual consent, submit the question to one of the procedures provided for in section 2, unless the parties otherwise agree". If no such agreement can be reached, the obligations under article 283 in section 1 of Part XV come fully in to play.[75]

A dispute excepted by a declaration made under article 298 may be submitted to a procedure provided for in section 2 only by agreement of the parties to the dispute.[76] Notwithstanding requirement of section 3 of Part XV, the parties to the dispute may agree to some other procedure for the settlement of such dispute or reach an amicable settlement.[77]

It bears emphasis that the Convention does not restrict the freedom of the parties to go their own way for the settlement of the dispute provided the means chosen by them for the settlement are peaceful. Subject to the provisions of article 309, it does not impose any public policy consideration on their freedom to devise their own procedures different from those enshrined in the Convention.

1.5   Jurisdiction of the Sea-bed Dispute Chamber

Within the ITLOS, the Convention also establishes the Sea bed Dispute Chamber and entrusts it with compulsory, independent and exclusive jurisdictional competence to adjudicate on various categories of disputes arising with respect to activities in the Area.[78] Article 187 of UNCLOS provides that: "The Sea

---

71   Ibid.
72   See article 298, paragraph 1 (a) (ii).
73   See article 300.
74   See North Sea Continental Shelf, ICJ Reports 1969, p. 4, paragraph 85.
75   See the Virginia Commentary, *supra* note 10, p. 134.
76   Article 299, paragraph 1.
77   Article 299, paragraph 2.
78   Part XI, Section 5, articles 186 to 191 of the Convention; and Statute of the International Tribunal for the Law of the Sea (Annex VI to the Convention).

Bed Disputes Chamber shall have jurisdiction under this Part and the Annexes relating thereto in disputes with respect to activities in the Area falling within the following categories." These categories are provided for in paragraphs (a) to (f) of this Article and are specified as follows: (a) Disputes between States Parties concerning the interpretation or application of this Part and its relevant Annexes;[79] (b) Disputes between States Parties and the International Sea-bed Authority as to whether or not the acts or decisions of the Authority are in accordance with the applicable provisions of the Convention;[80] (c) Dispute between parties to a contract, being either State parties, the Sea-Bed Authority or the Enterprise, State enterprises and natural and juridical persons as provided in article 153, paragraph 2(b) of the Convention; concerning the interpretation or application of a specific contract or plan of work or an act of omission of a part to the contract;[81] (d) Disputes between the Authority and a prospective contractor who has been sponsored by a State, or the failure to conclude a contract or a legal issue arising in the negotiation of the contract;[82] (e) Disputes between the authority and a State Party, a state enterprise or a natural or juridical person within the spirit and framework of article 187 of the Convention; concerning a claim of liability made against the authority for a wrongful act or omission pursuant to a relevant provisions of the Convention or as provided in article 22 of Annex III to the Convention;[83] and (f) Any other disputes for which the Jurisdiction of the Chamber is specifically provided for in the Convention.[84]

It is clear from the above that the Jurisdiction of the Sea-Bed Dispute Chamber in respect of these categories is distinct, enormous and does not depend on the choice of procedure or declarations made under paragraph 1 of article 187 of the Convention. In fact paragraph 2 of article 187 is imperative as it provides as follows: "A declaration made under paragraph 1 shall not affect or be affected by the obligation of the State Party to accept the jurisdiction of the Sea-Bed Disputes Chamber of the International Tribunal for the Law of the Sea to the extent and in the manner provided for in Part XI, Section 5."

In spite of the wide scope jurisdiction wielded in the Sea-bed Dispute Chamber, one cannot conclude with certainty that the competence of the Chamber is without limitations. Thus, there are certain nuances on the competence of

---

79   Article 187, paragraph (a).
80   Article 187, paragraph (b).
81   Article 187, paragraph (c).
82   Article 187, paragraph (d).
83   Article 187, paragraph (e).
84   Article 187, paragraph (f).

the Sea-Bed Disputes Chamber in connection with disputes arising from decisions of the International Sea-Bed Authority. Article 189 of the Convention expressly provides that the Sea-Bed Disputes Chamber has "no jurisdiction with regard to the exercise by the Authority of its discretionary powers" under Part XI of the Convention. In particular, the Chamber shall not "substitute its discretion for that of the Authority" and shall not "pronounce itself" on the question of whether any rules, regulations and procedures of the Authority are in conformity with the Convention. The Chamber may also not declare invalid any such rules, regulations and procedures of the Authority. The jurisdiction of the Chamber in this regard is "confined to" deciding "claims that the application of any rules, regulations and procedures of the authority in individual cases would be in conflict with the contractual obligations of the parties to the dispute or their obligations under the Convention;" to claims concerning excess of jurisdiction or misuse of powers; or to claims for damages for failure to comply with contractual obligations or obligations under the Convention.

These are significant limitations to the jurisdiction of the Chamber and were included in the Convention to ensure that, to the extent compatible with the requirement of fairness and accountability in the exercise of its powers and prerogatives, the International Sea-Bed Authority would be afforded the freedom, powers and discretion it needs to discharge its important and innovative responsibilities on behalf of "mankind as a whole."[85] However, they give to the Sea-Bed Dispute Chamber considerable power of oversight on the decisions and actions of the Authority where they impact on the rights and interests of States and other entities operating in the International Area. And they also endow the Chamber with the necessary competence to pronounce on the rights and responsibilities of the various parties to the contracts, and on their entitlement to compensation and other appropriate remedies when their rights have been unjustifiably infringed upon.

Further, the Sea-Bed Dispute Chamber is also empowered to give advisory opinions, at the request of the Assembly or Council of the Authority, on legal questions arising within the scope of the activities of these organs of the Authority.[86]

---

85   Article 137 paragraph 2.
86   Article 191 of the Convention. The Seabed dispute Chamber of the International Tribunal on Law of the Sea had issued the following advisory opinions: *1. Responsibilities and obligations of States sponsoring persons and entities with respect to activities in the Area (Request for Advisory Opinion submitted to the Seabed Disputes Chamber) 2. Request for an advisory opinion submitted by the Sub-Regional Fisheries Commission (SRFC) in the West African Region* – http://www.itlos.org/ for reports.

1.6 Provisional Measures

Part XV also contain substantive provisions relating to the prescription of provisional measures in appropriate situations when it becomes absolutely necessary to protect and preserve the respective rights of the parties to the dispute pending the hearing and final determination of the dispute. The Tribunal is the judicial organ mandated by the Convention to perform this responsibility. Apart from its competence to prescribe provisional measures in disputes specifically submitted to it, the ITLOS also has jurisdiction to prescribe, modify or revoke provisional measures in a dispute over which the tribunal has no jurisdiction to determine the substantive issue. For instance the Tribunal can prescribe provisional measures in a dispute to protect the rights of the parties where the parties involved have agreed to submit the dispute to arbitration in accordance with the provisions of Article 297 paragraph 1(c) of UNCLOS. Other courts and tribunals under article 287 of the Convention can equally grant provisional measures for the preservation of the respective rights of either party to a dispute or to prevent violence, the use of force, and to safeguard the peace pending the court's decision.[87] The Convention provides that "If a dispute has been duly submitted to a court or tribunal which considers that *prima facie* it has jurisdiction under ... Part XV or Part XI Section 5, the court or tribunal may prescribe any provisional measures which it considers appropriate under the circumstances to preserve the respective rights of the parties to the dispute or to prevent serious harm to the marine environment, pending the final decision."[88]

However, the jurisdiction of the ITLOS to prescribe provisional measures is subject to specific pre-condition. These are that: (a) the parties have agreed to submit the case to an arbitral tribunal; (b) the constitution of the arbitral tribunal has not yet been completed; (c) one of the parties to the dispute has requested provisional measures; and (d) the parties have failed to agree, within two weeks from the date of the request for provisional measures, on a court or tribunal to which the request should be submitted.

---

[87] In the dispute between Yugoslavia and USA, the International Court of Justice granted provisional measures to prevent violence, irreparable harm and further actions that might aggravate or extend the dispute pending the Court's decision (Yugoslavia vs. USA, ICJ Reports, Declaration, order, 2-6-99) – see separate declaration of Judge Koroma, p. 99.

[88] Article 290 paragraphs 1 to 5 of the Convention. Cases relating to provisional measures dealt with by the International Tribunal on Law of the Sea are as follows: *1. Southern Bluefin Tuna Cases (New Zealand v. Japan; Australia v. Japan), 2. The MOX Plant Case (Ireland v. United Kingdom), 3. Case concerning Land Reclamation by Singapore in and around the Straits of Johor (Malaysia v. Singapore, 4. The "ARA Libertad" Case (Argentina v. Ghana).* See http://www.itlos.org/ for reports.

Where these conditions are fulfilled, the Tribunal will have the jurisdiction, at the request of the party concerned, to prescribe, modify or revoke appropriate provisional measures. Paragraph 5 of article 290 stipulates that in prescribing provisional measures, ITLOS must be satisfied firstly, that *prima facie* the Tribunal which is to be constituted would have jurisdiction to deal with the dispute, and secondly, the urgency of the situation requires the prescription of the measures requested. Such measures may be modified, revoked or affirmed by the appropriate tribunal when it is constituted. Until so modified or revoked, provisional measures prescribed by the Tribunal are binding on the parties.[89] A court or tribunal under article 287 of the Convention can decline to grant provisional measures on account of lack of jurisdiction.[90]

The Sea-Bed Disputes Chamber has similar jurisdictional competence to prescribe, revoke or modify provisional measures in respect of disputes relating to activities in the international sea-bed area. That competence is subject to the same conditions and limitations.

1.7   Prompt Release of Vessels and Crew

Another innovative and distinct feature of Part XV is the compulsory jurisdiction of the ITLOS designed to ensure the prompt release of vessels and crews. This jurisdiction is exercised pursuant to Article 292 of the Convention. Paragraph 1 of this articles provides that where the authorities of a State Party have detained a vessel flying the flag of another State Party and it is alleged that the detaining state has not complied with the provisions of the conventions for the prompt release of the vessel or its crews upon the posting of a reasonable bond or other financial security, the question of the release from detention may be submitted to any court or tribunal agreed upon by the parties. This article mandates the Tribunal to address applications submitted to it on the question of the prompt release of vessels and its crews. It has no competence to look into the merits of substantive case pending before the national or domestic courts of the detaining State Party. Even after the ITLOS is properly seized of the matter, the authorities of the detaining state are at liberty to release the vessel at any time and has no obligation to wait for the decision of the Tribunal.

Thus, the jurisdiction of the Tribunal in this respect is dependent upon the occurrence of certain factors, i.e.; the parties to the application must have

---

89   Article 290 paragraph 6.
90   In the dispute between New Zealand and France – (Nuclear Tests (New Zealand v. France), ICJ Reports 1974), the International Court of Justice declined to New Zealand's request for an Indication of Provisional Measures on account of lack of Jurisdiction. See separate dissenting opinion of Judge Koroma, p. 364,

failed to reach an agreement regarding the choice of a court or tribunal; the application must be submitted to the Court within ten days commencing from the time of the detention; and the application must be submitted by or on behalf of the flag State as non-state entities do not have *'locus standi'* before the Tribunal under article 292 of the convention.

Where these requirements are fulfilled, the jurisdiction of the ITLOS becomes compulsory irrespective of the choices or declarations which the flag State or detaining State may have made under article 287 paragraph 1 of UNCLOS. Thus, the authorities of the detaining State are obliged to respect the competence of the tribunal and to abide by its decision in accordance with article 292 paragraph 4 of the Convention.[91]

2 Delimitation of Maritime Boundaries

2.1 Applicable Law

Articles 15, 74 and 83 respectively of UNCLOS are the relevant provisions enunciated for the delimitation of the territorial sea, the exclusive economic zone and the continental shelf between opposites or adjacent coastal States. These articles and their practical application have been influenced by judgments of international courts and tribunals.[92]

The maritime rights of a coastal State are derived from its sovereignty over a particular land territory.[93] The land is the legal source of the power which a coastal State may exercise over territorial extensions to seaward.[94] Thus, the terrestrial territorial situation constitutes the starting point for the determination of the maritime rights of a coastal State.[95] Islands too enjoy the same status and therefore generate the same maritime rights as other land territory.[96]

---

[91] Since the inception of its judicial mandate, the International Tribunal on Law of the Sea had adjudicated the undermentioned cases of prompt release of vessels and crews: *1. The M/V "SAIGA" Case (Saint Vincent and the Grenadines v. Guinea), 2. The "Camouco" Case (Panama v. France),3. The "Monte Confurco" Case (Seychelles v. France), 4. The "Grand Prince" Case (Belize v. France), 5. The "Chaisiri Reefer 2" Case (Panama v. Yemen), 6. The "Volga" Case (Russian Federation v. Australia),7. The "Juno Trader" Case (Saint Vincent and the Grenadines v. Guinea-Bissau), 8. The "Hoshinmaru" Case (Japan v. Russian Federation), 9.The "Tomimaru" Case (Japan v. Russian Federation)* – http://www.itlos.org – for Reports.

[92] D.C. Kapoor and Adam J. Kerr, *A Guide to Maritime Boundary Delimitation*(1986) p. 71

[93] *North Sea Continental Shelf*, ICJ Reports 1969, p. 51. Paragraph 96; Aegean Sea Continental Shelf, I.C.J Reports 1978, p. 36, paragraph 86; see also Churchill & Geir Ulfsyein (1992: 38).

[94] *North Sea Continental Shelf*, ICJ Reports 1969, p. 51.

[95] *Maritime Delimitation and Territorial Questions between Qatar and Bahrain, Merits, Judgment*, ICJ Reports 2001, p. 40, paragraph 185.

[96] Ibid.

There may be a number of situations in which the determination of entitlements over land is a prerequisite before disputes concerning sea boundary delimitations are resolved. For example, in the *Case concerning Maritime Delimitation and Territorial Questions between Qatar and Bahrain*, the ICJ found that "[i]n order to determine what constitutes Bahrain's relevant coasts and what are the relevant baselines on the Bahraini side, the Court must first establish which islands come under Bahraini sovereignty."[97] A similar approach was adopted by the ICJ in the case of *Romania v. Ukraine* where the Court first of all established the relevant islands which fall under both Romania and Ukraine.[98]

2.2 Delimitation of the Territorial Sea between States with Opposite or Adjacent Coasts

Article 15 of UNCLOS specifies the mechanism for the delimitation of the Territorial Sea. This article provides that: "Where the coasts of two States are opposite or adjacent to each other, neither of the two States is entitled, failing agreement between them to the contrary, to extend its territorial sea beyond the median line every point of which is equidistant from the nearest points on the baselines from which the breadth of territorial seas of each of the two States is measured. The above provision does not apply, however, where it is necessary by reason of historic title or other special circumstances to delimit the territorial seas of two States in a way which is at variance therewith". The general rule as can be discerned from this article is that, the relevant method for the delimitation of the territorial sea has to be conducted by the construction of an equidistant line between the opposite or adjacent coasts, although it does not rule out the possibility of negotiating the boundary line between the respective coastal states in question.

2.3 Delimitation of the Exclusive Economic Zones and Continental Shelf

Article 74 of UNCLOS sets out the procedures for the delimitation of the Exclusive Economic Zone which are similar to those sets out in article 83 relating to the delimitation of the continental shelf. These articles provide that: "(i) The

---

[97] *Maritime Delimitation and Territorial Questions between Qatar and Bahrain, Merits, Judgment*, ICJ Reports 16 March 2001 at para. 186.

[98] David J. Bederman, International Decisions, Maritime Delimitation in the Black Sea (Romania v. Ukraine), p. 543 to 549 at 547. See also htt://www.icj-cij.org. for the Judgment of the International Court of Justice, February 3, 2009.

delimitation of the exclusive economic zones (continental shelf) between States with opposite or adjacent coasts shall be effected by agreement on the basis of international law, as referred to in Article 38[99] of the Statute of the International Court of Justice, in order to achieve an equitable solution. (ii) If no agreement can be reached within a reasonable period of time, the States concerned shall resort to the procedures provided for in Part xv. (iii) Pending Agreement, as provided for in paragraph 1, the States concerned, in a spirit of understanding and cooperation, shall make every effort to enter into provisional arrangements of a practical nature and, during this transitional period, not to jeopardize the reaching of the final agreement. Such arrangements shall be without prejudice to the final delimitation. (iv)Where there is an agreement in force between the States concerned, questions relating to the delimitation of exclusive economic zone (or continental shelf) shall be determined in accordance with the provisions of that agreement".

For all intent and purposes, articles 74 and 83 of UNCLOS stress the necessity for negotiation in maritime boundary delimitation in order to achieve an equitable solution. The basic requirement is that maritime boundary delimitation shall be effected by an agreement between the parties concerned in order to achieve an "equitable solution" taking into account all relevant circumstances.[100] Each boundary negotiation whether, bilateral or multilateral, presents a set of unique problems stemming from differences in coastline configuration, the presence of small or large islands, seabed morphology, distribution of living and non-living resources etc. Hence, delimitation on an equitable basis entails numerous political, strategic, historical and economic considerations

---

99 Article 38 of the ICJ Statutes provides that, 1. the Court, whose function is to decide in accordance with international law such disputes as are submitted to it, shall apply: (a) international conventions, whether general or particular, establishing rules expressly recognized by the contesting States; (b) international custom, as evidence of a general practice accepted as law; (c) the general principles of law recognized by civilized nations; (d) subject to the provisions of Article 59, judicial decisions and the teachings of the most highly qualified publicists of the various nations, as subsidiary means for the determination of rules of law; 2. this provision shall not prejudice the power of the Court to decide a case *ex aequo et bono*, if the parties agree thereto.

100 North Sea cases, ICJ Reports (1969), paragraph 85; The concept of relevant or special circumstances did not appear in the UNCLOS, but its implications have certainly found expression in Articles 74 and 83 of the UNCLOS, which provide for boundary delimitation on the basis of international law in order to achieve an equitable solution, (Mahmoudi, 1990: 162).

which govern the actual laying down of a boundary.[101] Every coastal State Party to UNCLOS is empowered to establish a 200 nautical miles Exclusive Economic Zone and Continental Shelf respectively with the possibility of extending the Continental Shelf beyond 200 nautical miles if the geophysical configuration allows. It must be noted that the exclusive economic zone regime applies to the water column and its resources whereas the continental shelf applies to the seabed, its subsoil and resources therein.

2.4 Principles Governing Maritime Boundary Delimitation

There are several legal precedents and numerous definitions of geometrical principles governing sea boundary delimitation between opposite or adjacent coastal States. The North Sea Continental Shelf Case[102] is the classic example of legal precedent which articulates the basic principles governing sea boundary delimitation.

The median line is another principle commonly used in maritime boundary delimitation. It is synonymous with the equidistance line as far as both results from the geometrical application of the same method. The principles of the median line originate from the recommendation of the International Law Commission's (ILC) preparatory work for UNCLOS 1. It was presented by the experts in response to question relating to how a lateral boundary line should be drawn through the adjoining territorial sea of two adjacent states. The substance of the recommendation was to the effect that the lateral boundary through the territorial sea if not already fixed otherwise – should be drawn according to the principles of equidistance from the respective coastlines (that is, it should be a median line). In some cases, where this may not lead to an equitable solution, such a solution should be achieved by negotiation.

As a geometric principle, an equidistance line between any two points in the same plane is the perpendicular bisector of the line joining them. This principle is embodied in the median line concept. This concept can be applied in a variety of geographical situations where States are situated opposite or adjacent to each other or where islands or other features may be present in the vicinity of the baselines. The application of the equidistance concept to boundary delimitation between opposite or adjacent States can be carried out on the

---

101 D.C. Kapoor and Adam J. Kerr, *A Guide to Maritime Boundary Delimitation* (1986) p. 72; Prescott & Clive Schofield (2005: 210).

102 ICJ Reports (1969) 1; 41 ILR. In this case, the Court recognized the use of equidistant line but also made it clear that in special circumstances other methods may be more suitable for maritime boundary delimitation.

surface of a geodetic ellipsoid in most cases using the appropriate computer programs or other software technologies in order to overcome the inaccuracies introduced by map projections.[103]

2.5 Boundary Agreement

It is an accepted rule of international law that maritime boundaries are established by an agreement between the states concerned. This principle can be applied in several ways using variety of methods relevant to a particular situation taking into account the relevant factors.[104] Another element to be considered was a reasonable degree of proportionality. States practice shows that numerous methods have been used for boundary delimitation. In some situations, modifications have been made to equidistance line in order to accommodate special circumstances, such as the presence of small islands that may be situated in such a way as to distort the boundary line.[105] In other circumstances, the presence of Small Island in the vicinity of a median line, or a marked protrusion along the coastline, may produce a disproportionate effect on a median line. The States parties may, therefore, agree to give full or partial effect to these features. Some boundary Agreements choose to totally ignore the presence of islands, or to award them only a limited area of specified distance.[106] In some situations where early agreement on boundary settlement cannot be reached, and the countries involved desire to proceed expeditiously with exploration of resources, they may decide to establish joint development agreements.[107]

2.6 The Delimitation Method

In the delimitation of the territorial sea, exclusive economic zone and continental shelf, the general principle of equity should be applied in boundary

---

[103] D.C. Kapoor and Adam J. Kerr, *A Guide to Maritime Boundary Delimitation* (1986) p. 77.
[104] Ibid. In the North Sea Continental Shelf Case, the Court ruled that the use of the equidistance method of delimitation was not obligatory and factors to be taken into consideration should inter alia include the general configuration of the coasts, as well as the physical and geological structures and natural resources of the Shelf. Another element to be considered was a reasonable degree of proportionality
[105] Ibid: For instance in the case of the delimitation of the continental shelf between United Kingdom and France, it was decided to give 'half effect' to the Scilly Isles.
[106] Ibid. This is true of the Italy-Yugoslavia and Italy Tunisia agreements.
[107] Ibid. This course was followed in the 1975 Japan-South Korea Joint development Zone agreement and the Malaysia-Thailand Memorandum of understanding pertaining to an area in the Gulf of Thailand

agreements. The requirement in establishing a sea boundary between opposite or adjacent states is that the States parties must basically endeavor to negotiate a mutually acceptable agreement. If they fail in this attempt, the next step is to seek solution through some form of third party arbitration. Alternatively, the States parties concerned may seek solution pursuant to the provisions of Part XV of UNCLOS in which case they will be guided by the relevant provisions of articles 15, 74 and 83.

Although articles 15 advocates application of an equidistance line, it also notes that other methods may be more suitable in order to produce a result that is appropriate, fair and acceptable to all parties in accordance with the principles of equity.[108] In applying the equitable concepts, the negotiated single boundary agreements are not based on a particular legal theory, but may best be characterized as "developed on the basis of principles deemed by the parties to be equitable in view of the relevant circumstances."[109] For instance, in the delimitation of the exclusive economic zone, circumstances regarding geographical features of the maritime area, historic use and economic dependency on the resources of the exclusive economic zone may be relevant in order to achieve an equitable solution.[110]

Although equitable principles are commonly utilized in maritime boundary delimitation, it has however, been found useful to reduce them to geometric principles when it actually comes to defining the location of the final delimitation line. The most favored geometric method is termed "half-effect." The equidistant itself as defined in the 1958 and 1982 Conventions is a precise geometrical method[111] but it has been discovered that in some cases it does not produce an equitable solution. In other cases, "half-effect," or "partial-effect" has been used to achieve a more equitable solution.

---

108   Shortly after the Geneva Convention of 1958, the use of the equidistance line had been disputed by some States, and in the North Sea Continental Shelf Case (1969), the Court discounted this method of delimitation in customary law.
109   Moore, John Norton & Samuel Pyeatt, *Cases and Materials on Oceans Law and Policy*, Volume III, pp. 21–4, 21–5.
110   The importance of geographical features in relation to the delimitation method and outcome has also been emphasized in the following cases: Saint Pierre and Miquelon, (International Law Reports, Vol. 95, p. 660, para. 24); Continental Shelf (Libyan Arab Jamahiriya/Malta), Judgment (ICJ Reports 1985, pp. 42 et seq.); Maritime Delimitation in the Area between Greenland and Jan Mayen, Judgment (ICJ Reports 1993, pp. 74–75); Land and Maritime Boundary between Cameroon and Nigeria (Cameroon v. Nigeria: Equatorial Guinea intervening), Judgment (ICJ Reports 2002, p. 339, para. 49).
111   Beazley, P. B. (1994: 7), *Technical aspects of Maritime Boundary Delimitation*, Volume 1 No. 2, International Research Unit Durham University, UK.

In the recent case of Maritime Delimitation between *Romania vs. Ukraine*, the Serpent Island off the Coast of Ukraine was given half-effect.[112] In most cases, account has been taken of special circumstances leading to a great diversity of solutions in order to accommodate the relevant factors of each case. Sometimes equidistance is used for the delimitation of part of the boundary line, but other principles are applied for the delimitation of other parts of the same boundary. Thus, for example, equidistance may be utilized for the delimitation of the first part of the boundary, but abandoned in favor of proportionality when coastline configuration begins to produce an inequitable equidistance line with particular reference being paid to those protuberant coastal points situated nearest to the area to be delimited.[113] In some situations, an equitable division may best be effected through the application of the equidistance method.[114] The reason for this relates to its mathematical precision, lack of ambiguity and its accordance with equity where the parties' coastlines are broadly comparable. Thus, an equidistance line would be drawn between adjacent coasts "unless there are compelling reasons that make this unfeasible."[115]

In situations where the maritime boundary areas of three or more coastal states converge or overlap, it is always prudent for the three coastal states to agree on tri-points or interception points before completing the delimitation of the area as the ICJ held in the case of Romania and Ukraine where the delimitation terminus is yet to be concluded having regard to the interest of adjacent and opposite States.[116]

---

[112] See Maritime delimitation in the Black Sea case Romania vs Ukraine Judgment, 2009 paragraph 166; See Article by David H. Anderson, Maritime Delimitation in the Black Sea (Romania vs. Ukraine), Law and Practice of the International Courts and Tribunals 8 (2009) 305–327 at 315; See also *Nicaragua v. Honduras* case ICJ Reports 2007, paragraph 281 where the method of the bisector between coastal fronts was followed

[113] Moore, John Norton & Samuel Pyeatt, *Cases and Materials on Oceans Law and Policy*, Volume III, pp. 21–5.

[114] Ibid.

[115] Nicaragua v. Honduras case ICJ Reports 2007, paragraph 281 where the method of the bisector between coastal fronts was followed – Separate Opinion of Judge Koroma, Nicaragua v. Honduras Judgment, 8–10–07; See also Maritime delimitation in the Black Sea case Romania vs. Ukraine Judgment, 2009 paragraph 166; See Article by David H. Anderson, Maritime Delimitation in the Black Sea (Romania vs. Ukraine), Law and Practice of the International Courts and Tribunals 8 (2009) 305–327 at 315.

[116] In the Maritime Delimitation in the Black Sea (Romania vs. Ukraine), Law and Practice of the International Courts and Tribunals 8 (2009) 305–327, the court left the equidistance line opened for future negotiations and eventual agreement on a tri-point by Romania, Ukraine and either Turkey or Bulgaria.

2.7 Delimitation of the Extended Continental Shelf

The general provisions on the continental shelf are laid down in Articles 76 to 85 of Part VI of UNCLOS, Annex II concerning the Commission on the Limits of the Continental Shelf, and Annex II of the Final Act which contains a statement of understanding with respect to the specific methods to be used in establishing the outer limits of the continental margin for the distinct situation of the Bay of Bengal.

Prior to the 20th Century, the seabed was generally regarded as international area but this notion changed completely in the first half of the 20th Century as coastal States made declarations of sovereign rights over the seabed and its array of resources. The "Truman Proclamation" of 1945 is commonly regarded as the first clear assertion of the notion that the resources of the continental shelf belongs to the coastal State. The proclamation asserted that "the Government of the United States regards the natural resources of the subsoil and seabed of the continental shelf beneath the high seas but contiguous to the coasts of the USA as appertaining to the USA, subject to its jurisdiction and control."[117] It was a simple but clear assertion of jurisdiction and control over the resources of the continental shelf based on the physical proximity, or contiguity of the continental shelf to the land mass of the coastal State. This declaration was followed by several claims of other states. Within a decade, a consistent states practice had evolved recognized by other States. This practice is widely regarded as a classic example of the formation of customary international law.

In 1958, the practice was legalized and embodied in the Geneva Convention on the Continental Shelf. This Convention provides that the coastal States have sovereignty for the purpose of exploring and exploiting the natural resources of the continental shelf. It also made it clear that the rights of the coastal State over the continental shelf did not affect the legal status of the superjacent waters as high seas or that of the air space above.[118] In the North Sea Continental shelf cases in 1969, the ICJ confirmed that these provisions of the Geneva Convention represented customary international law and further emphasized that "more fundamental than the notion of proximity appears to be the principle ... of the natural prolongation or continuation of the land territory ..."[119] This dic-

---

117 See *Legal and Scientific Aspects of the Continental Shelf*, edited by Myron H. Nordquist et al, p. 21; *The Truman Proclamation No. 2667*, 10 Fed. Reg. 12303; (University of Cambridge, 1992: 3); Public Papers of the Presidents of the United States: Harry S, Truman (1945), p. 353 (1961).
118 Articles 2(1) and (2) of the 1958 Convention on the Continental Shelf.
119 North Sea Continental Shelf cases (1969) International Court of Justice Report at p. 31.

tum of the Court had significant impact on the development of this issue at the Third United Nations Conference on the Law of the Sea in 1973 to 1982.

The exploitative criterion used in the 1958 Geneva Convention to define the limits of the Continental Shelf was considered to be imprecise and unclear. It observed that if it was to be maintained, new technology would push the limits farther and farther from the shore and that eventually, coastal State's continental shelf would cover the entire ocean floor. In 1970 the UN adopted a resolution were the deep seabed beyond national jurisdiction was declared the common heritage of mankind.[120] At the Third Conference on the Law of the Sea, although there was agreement to build on the provision of the 1958 Geneva Convention on the legal status and inner limits of the Continental Shelf, there were disagreements with respect to its outer limits. The majority of the States favored the 200 miles limit. After protracted negotiations, a compromise was reached and the provisions of Article 76 were drafted containing detailed modalities to be employed in determining the extension of the continental shelf beyond 200 nautical miles by coastal states.[121]

2.8   Determination of the Outer Limits of the Continental Shelf
The practical use of the continental shelf is provided for in article 76 consisting of 10 paragraphs, which deal with a number of distinct but interrelated issues. Paragraph 1 of article 76 sets out the general legal definition of the continental shelf:

> The continental shelf of a coastal State comprises the seabed and subsoil of the submarine areas that extend beyond its territorial sea through the natural prolongation of its land territory to the outer edge of the continental margin, or to a distance of 200 nautical miles from the baselines from which the breadth of the territorial sea is measured where the outer edge of the continental margin does not extend up to that distance.

This paragraph establishes the legal rights of coastal States to determine the outer limits of the continental shelf albeit using two alternative criteria based on either natural prolongation or distance i.e. at 200 nautical miles from the baselines, or to the outer edge of the continental margin where it extends

---

120   General Assembly Resolution 2749 (XXV) of 17 December 1970.
121   United Nations Convention on the Law of the Sea 1982 – A Commentary, ed. Myron H. Nordquist et al., Center for Ocean Law and Policy, University of Virginia School of Law, vol. II, 1993. pp. 841–890 and p. 932.

beyond that distance. The continental margin is in turn described in paragraph 3 of article 76 as comprising "the submerged prolongation of the land mass of the coastal State," and as consisting "of the seabed and subsoil of the shelf, the slope and the rise." In short, it consists of the geophysical shelf, the slope and the rise. Paragraph 2 of article 76 qualifies this definition. It indicates that the continental shelf shall not extend beyond the outer limit lines specified in paragraphs 4 to 6 of Article 76.

2.9   The Foot of the Slope

Article 76, 4(a) suggests the formulation of a test of appurtenance in order to entitle a coastal State to extend the outer limits of the continental shelf beyond the limit set by the 200 nautical miles criterion. This is designed to demonstrate that the natural prolongation of its land territory to the outer edge of the continental margin extends beyond 200 nautical miles. Paragraphs 4 to 6 of Article 76 provide specific formula to establish the outer edge of the continental margin where it extends beyond 200 nautical miles.[122] Paragraph 4 further contains dual regime or formulas for the determination of the outer edge of the continental margin. Both formulas take as their starting point the foot of the continental slope which is a primary and distinct feature in the delineation of the continental shelf beyond the 200 nautical miles limit. Pursuant to paragraph 4(a) of the article in question, the slope is the reference baseline from which the breadth of the limits specified by the Irish and Hedberg formulas is measured. The basic objective of these formulae is to ensure that coastal States' sovereign rights would extend to a major portion of the continental rise where significant hydrocarbon resources were expected to exist as succinctly provided for in the Scientific and Technical Guidelines of the Commission on the Limits of the Continental Shelf. Both formulae may be applied by a coastal State alternatively; it may apply the Irish formula in certain portions of its continental shelf and the Hedberg formula in the other portions, in a manner to maximize its entitlement.

From the foot of the slope, outer limit points can be determined by sediment thickness (also referred to as the Irish or Gardiner formula) or a distance of sixty nautical miles (the distance criterion is also known as the Hedberg formula). Pursuant to the Scientific and Technical Guidelines of the Commission on the Limits of the Continental Shelf, the rule is that the foot of the slope shall be determined as the point of maximum change in the gradient at its base. This implies that morphological and bathymetric evidence shall be

---

[122]   Scientific and Technical Guidelines of the Commission on the Limits of the Continental Shelf, United Nations Doc. CLCS/11, adopted on 13 May 1999, pp. 12–13.

applied whenever possible.[123] If the evidence identified by the maximum change in the gradient cannot precisely establish the foot of the slope at its base, coastal states are allowed to use evidence to the contrary to the general rule, i.e. the best geological and geophysical evidence available to them to locate the foot of the slope.[124]

2.10   Maximum Limits of the Continental Shelf

Paragraphs 5 and 6 describe two restraint formulae i.e. the maximum limits. If the fixed points defined under paragraph 4 fall seaward of both restraint lines they cannot be employed. The two restraints are defined by distance from the baseline of the territorial sea (350 nautical miles) and distance from the 2,500-metre isobath (100 nautical miles from that isobath). In the case of submarine ridges the latter restraint cannot be applied.[125] The maximum limit on such ridges is fixed at 350 M. This exception does not apply to submarine elevations that are natural components of the continental margin, such as its plateau, rises, caps, banks and spurs. The first constraint is specifically based on a distance criterion, whereas the second is based on a combination of depth and distance criteria. It important to point out that, the two constraints may, as a general rule, be utilized alternatively and only one of them has to be respected in each portion of the continental shelf. Moreover, the constraints do not provide yardstick for entitlement to an extended continental shelf. Instead, they are solely constraints to the lines produced in accordance with the two formulae identified in paragraph 4(a) of the article under discussion in order to delineate the outer limits of the continental shelf.

Paragraph 7 lays down criteria for the coastal state to delineate the outer limit of its continental shelf. Paragraph 7 provides that fixed points defined by "coordinates of latitude and longitude" selected by application of paragraphs 4 to 6 cannot be more than 60 nautical miles apart, and at each of the connecting points the thickness of sediments is at least one percent of the shortest distance from such point to the foot of the slope. Therefore, if the formula is to apply at a distance of 100 M from the foot of the slope, one-metre thickness of sediment must be present. Such connecting points are to be defined by coordinates of latitude and longitude.

---

123   Scientific and Technical Guidelines of the Commission on the Limits of the Continental Shelf, United Nations Doc. CLCS/11, adopted on 13 May 1999, pp. 37–42.
124   Scientific and Technical Guidelines of the Commission on the Limits of the Continental Shelf, United Nations Doc. CLCS/11, adopted on 13 May 1999, pp. 43–49.
125   Article 7(6) of the 1982 United Nations Convention of the Law of the Sea (UNCLOS).

2.11   Commission on the Limits of the Continental Shelf (CLCS)

Paragraph 8 of Article 76 defines the role of the Commission on the Limits of Continental Shelf in the process of establishing the outer limits by the coastal state as contained in Annex II to the Convention. As paragraph 8 indicates, after reviewing the submitted information, the Commission shall then proceed to issue recommendations to the coastal State on matters related to the establishment of the outer limits of the continental shelf. The significance of the Commission's recommendations is indicated by the provision that outer limits established by the coastal State on the basis of the recommendations of the Commission shall be "final and binding." No such provision is included in any of the other provisions of UNCLOS on outer limits of maritime zones.

A further indication of the significance of the Commission's recommendations is provided by Article 8 of Annex II to UNCLOS, which Annex sets out the terms of reference of the Commission. Article 8 provides that in case of disagreement with the recommendations of the Commission the coastal State shall make a new or revised submission. Thus, Article 8 imposes a legal obligation on the coastal State to follow a specific course of action if it does not agree with the recommendations.

With respect to submissions relating to areas of unresolved land or maritime disputes, or submissions for which the Commission has received objections from opposite or adjacent States, Article 9 of Annex II to the Convention provides that the actions of the Commission shall not prejudice matters relating to sea boundary delimitation disputes between States with opposite or adjacent coasts.[126] The rules of procedure of the Commission make it clear that resolution of those disputes rests with the competence of the particular States concerned.[127] Nevertheless, partial submissions can be made in respect of an undisputed portion without prejudice to make submission for the disputed portion at a later date after the resolution of the dispute.[128] In certain cases with the consent of the disputing States Parties, the Commission shall examine submissions made in respect of portions under disputes.[129] The Rules of Procedure also provides for joint or separate submissions pursuant to an agree-

---

126   See Rules of Procedures of the Commission on the Limits of The Continental Shelf, United Nations Doc. CLCS/3/Rev.2, adopted on 4th September 1998. A third revised version of the Rules, United Nations Doc. CLCS/3/Rev.3, adopted on 6th February 2001.
127   Ibid., Annex I, paragraph 1.
128   Ibid., Annex I, paragraph 3.
129   Ibid., Annex I, paragraph 5(a).

ment between the respective States Parties concerned.[130] The provisions of the rules of procedure are flexible and vital as they are geared toward ensuring the competence of the Commission to make recommendation since the outer limits of the Continental shelf will not be finally established without recommendation by the Commission.[131] In order to resolve the issues over a disputed extended Continental shelf, it is submitted that, the respective States Parties must first of all take steps to delineate the outer limits of the disputed area from the area under the regime of the International Seabed Authority. After securing the recommendation of the Commission, the disputed parties will then proceed to either divide the disputed area pursuant to an agreement, or alternatively agree to a joint exploration and exploitation of the area.

Upon completion of the process of delineation of the outer limits of the continental shelf and the relevant delimitation boundaries are established, it is imperative pursuant to paragraph 9 of article 76 of the Convention to submit to the Secretary General of the United Nations charts and ancillary information including geodetic data, permanently describing the outer limits of its continental shelf for ultimate publication. The publicity is designed to ensure that States and institutions are duly informed of the extent of a coastal State's continental shelf.

It is important to note that pursuant to paragraph (2) of article 121 of UNCLOS, the continental shelf of an island is determined in accordance with the provisions of the Convention applicable to other land territory. There is no distinction, as far as UNCLOS is concerned, between the determinations of the outer limits of the continental shelf of an island on the one hand and that of a mainland on the other hand.[132]

---

[130] Ibid., Annex I, paragraph 4.
[131] See Article 76(8) of the 1982 Law of the Sea Convention
[132] See Article 121 of the 1982 Convention on the Law of the Sea; see also Myron H. Nordquist et al, *Legal and Scientific Aspect of the Continental Shelf Limits*, Center for Oceans Law and Policy, pp. 1–34.

3   Settlement of Sea Boundary Delimitation Disputes

3.1   Preliminary issues

Part XV of UNCLOS was part of a delicate "package deal"[133] painstakingly negotiated in a spirit of what one author refers to as "give a little – get a little."[134] The rationale behind the deal was predicated on the assumption that the competing rights and interests of the parties to UNCLOS so evenly balanced in the substantive provisions of the Convention would easily disintegrate through unilateral interpretations of the treaty itself in the case of a dispute. It was felt absolutely expedient as part of the compromise to establish a viable third-party dispute settlement procedures, including judicial procedures for the settlement of disputes that may arise under the Convention.[135] Through such procedures, it was recognized, there would be a possibility of achieving objective interpretation and application of the treaty so as to ensure the maintenance of the delicate balance of rights and interests embodied in it. It was the desire of the framers of UNCLOS to establish a unified system of peaceful settlement of all sea related disputes where every State party to UNCLOS will have equal treatment before the law in accordance with the principle of sovereign equality of States. Thus, a flexible dispute settlement regime was billed as one of the strong pillars of the new order in the oceans which the comprehensive law of the sea Convention was intended to create.[136]

While that principle was widely accepted, its application to the question of maritime boundary delimitation disputes and other aspects of State sovereignty was both sensitive and controversial. The compromise that emerged has the effect of ousting the jurisdiction of the dispute settlement procedures enshrined in section 2 of Part XV of UNCLOS from adjudicating on a plethora of maritime disputes which are likely to arise in the course of the exercise of coastal States rights within the territorial sea, the exclusive economic zone and the continental shelf on account of declarations made under article 298(1) (a) of UNCLOS. Pursuant to this provision, a State may declare that a court or tribunal established within the context of section 2 of Part XV is barred from adjudicating on disputes relating to scientific research and fisheries; military activities; sea boundary delimitation disputes; and disputes in respect of which

---

133   See H. Caminos and M. Molito, *Progressive Development of International Law and the Package Deal* 79 AJIL, P. 871 to 890 (1985) (providing a thorough explanation of the concept of "package deal" in relation to the negotiations that led to the adoption of UNCLOS).

134   A.O. Adede, *The System For Settlement of Disputes Under the United Nations Convention on the Law of the Sea*, p. 24.

135   Ibid.

136   Ibid., A.O. Adede, *Settlement of disputes Arising Under the Law of the Sea Convention* G9 AJIL, p. 798, at 816–818 (1975).

the United Nations Security Council is exercising its functions under the Charter.

However, the second proviso of this article contains an express exclusion of unsettled disputes concerning the concurrent consideration of sovereignty or other rights over continental or insular land territory from conciliation process required by that article. It therefore implies that a court or tribunal established under section 2 of Part XV of the Conventions might take up such disputes if a State does not exercise its rights under article 298(1)(a)(i).

Where a sea boundary delimitation dispute arises and the matter is eventually submitted[137] to a court or tribunal established under section 2 of Part XV of UNCLOS for adjudication, the judicial forum to which the matter is submitted will primarily determine certain procedural issues before proceeding with the substantive matter on the merits. These include a preliminary determination of: (a) the *locus standi* of the parties to initiate proceedings under the Convention and to further establish whether declarations were made by the disputants pursuant to article 287 (1) of UNCLOS; (b) whether sea boundary delimitation disputes fall within the ambit of disputes concerning the interpretation or application of the Convention; (c) whether the dispute in question exclusively relates to sea boundary delimitation or a combination of both sea and land boundary disputes (mixed delimitation dispute) and to establish whether this type of disputes concern the interpretation or application of the Convention; and (d) whether declarations were made under article 298(1)(a) ousting the jurisdiction of the intended court or tribunal and whether the parties have failed to settle their dispute in accordance with section I of Part XV of UNCLOS.

3.2 Scope of the Dispute

In accordance with the consistent ICJ jurisprudence and the Permanent Court of International Justice,[138] its predecessor, a dispute arises at a time when the

---

137 In the case of the International Tribunal for the Law of the Sea(ITLOS), disputes are submitted either by notification of a special agreement or by written application, addressed to the Registrar, see article 24 of its Statute; see also Corfu Channel Case(Preliminary Objection), ICJ Reports, 1947, Judgment of 25 March 1948, p. 15.

138 In paragraph 24 of its Judgment of 10 February 2005 in the Case Concerning Certain Property (Liechtenstein v. Germany), the Court stated: "... a dispute is a disagreement on a point of law or fact, a conflict of legal views or interests between parties" (see *Northern Cameroons, Judgment,* ICJ Reports 1963, p. 27; *Applicability of obligation to Arbitrate under Section 21 of the United Nations Headquarters Agreement of 26 June 1947; Advisory Opinion,* ICJ Reports 1988, p. 27, paragraph 35; *East Timor Judgment,* ICJ Reports 1995, pp. 99–100, paragraph 22). Moreover, for the purposes of verifying the existence of a legal dispute it falls to the Court to determine whether 'the claim of one party is positively opposed by

opposing views of the parties on a point of law or fact take definite shape.[139] The existence of the dispute does not depend on the articulation of its precise scope, so long as the record indicates with reasonable clarity the scope of the legal differences between the parties.[140] The negotiations between the parties towards reconciling the divergent views should reach a deadlock and the dispute warrants solution by other means. The dispute settlement mechanisms of UNCLOS are designed to foster the resolution of disputes relating to the interpretation of the Convention or an international agreement related to the purposes of the Convention.[141] This applies both to a court or tribunal referred to in article 287.[142] When there are clear provisions in the Convention or the international agreement referred to above on any matter, disputes relating to them obviously fall within the jurisdiction of the dispute settlement mechanisms of Part XV.

Where the parties differ as to the scope of the matters which constitute the dispute referred to a court or tribunal, it is arguable that that body may hold that the dispute also includes matters which are "sufficiently closely related" to the dispute submitted to it.[143] In other words, the ambit of the dispute mentioned in the submission may become wider because of the close connection between what is expressly submitted to a court or tribunal and what has to be decided as part of that submission.[144] This may be so especially where all the

---

the other' (*South West Africa, Preliminary Objections, Judgment*, ICJ Reports 1962, p. 328) see Judgment, ICJ 2005, paragraph 24, at http://www.icj-cij.org/icjwww/idocket/ila/index.htm.

139   See the *Mavromatis Palestine Concessions Case (jurisdiction)*, 1924, P.C.I.J., Series A, No. 2, p. 11.

140   See the Arbitral Award of 2006, between Barbados and the Republic of Trinidad and Tobago, paragraph 198.

141   See Part XV of the Convention and, in particular, article 288, paragraphs 1 and 2.

142   In the case of the Tribunal, see also article 21 of its Statute.

143   In the *Corfu Channel Case*, following Albania's failure to attend 'in the third stage of the *Corfu Channel Case* in which the International Court of Justice was to determine the amount of the compensation to be paid to the United Kingdom, Albania maintaining that the special agreement of 25th March 1948 did not confer jurisdiction on the Court to fix the amount of the compensation, the Court had to throw out the argument, recalling its judgment of 25th March 1948, by means of which competence was conferred on the Court and stating "in accordance with the Statute (Article 60), which, for the settlement of the present dispute is binding on the Albania Government", ICJ Reports 1949, p. 248.

144   In the matter of arbitration between Barbados and the Republic of Trinidad and Tobago, the parties differed on the question as to whether the dispute submitted to the Annex VIII Tribunal included the delimitation of the maritime boundary in relation to that part of the continental shelf extending beyond 200 nautical miles. The Tribunal, while answering

matters said to fall within the scope of the dispute are dealt with expressly in the Convention. This brings the discussion to a rather complex issue involving a mixed delimitation dispute denoting a dispute concerning sea boundary delimitation and insular land territory part of which is governed by the provisions of the Convention. UNCLOS does not claim to deal with this question in direct terms. It may be fruitful to discuss this question with respect to a maritime boundary delimitation dispute. It is far from being disputed that a dispute directly involving sovereignty or other rights over land territory may not be a dispute governed by the provisions of UNCLOS. Does it become part of a dispute under UNCLOS when its consideration is indispensable for the disposal of a maritime boundary delimitation dispute?

The optional exceptions to the applicability of Section 2 contained in Article 298 of UNCLOS are silent on this issue. Pursuant to paragraph 1(a) (i) of this article, States are required to accept submission of "only" sea boundary delimitation disputes to a conciliation commission established under section 2 of Annex V to the Convention. The second proviso of this article is imperative and unambiguous. It makes it abundantly clear that any dispute that concerns the concurrent determination of unsettled dispute concerning sovereignty or other rights over continental or insular land territory must 'not' be submitted to conciliation. Although the second proviso excludes upon declaration delimitation disputes from the jurisdiction of compulsory procedures and any other substituted dispute settlement mechanism, there is no specific provision that expressly excludes mixed disputes involving land and sea delimitations from the purview of Part XV. Plainly, the second proviso categorically excludes the submission of maritime boundary delimitation disputes to a Conciliation Commission where the thrust of that dispute concerns the concurrent consideration of any unsettled dispute concerning sovereignty or other rights over continental or insular land territory.[145]

---

the question in the affirmative, relied upon more than one ground in the regard. The Tribunal observed: "The Tribunal considers that the dispute to be dealt with by the Tribunal includes the outer continental shelf, since (i) it either forms part of, or is sufficiently closely related to, the dispute submitted by Barbados, (ii) the record of the negotiations shows that it was part of the subject-matter on the table during those negotiations, and (iii) in any event there is in law only a single continental shelf rather than an inner continental shelf and a separate extended or outer continental shelf." See the Arbitral Award of 2006, *supra* note 136, Paragraph 213.

145 The present text of article 298, paragraph 1 (a)(i), is based on the provision contained in the ICNT/Rev, 2, For text see Virginia Commentary, *supra* note 13, p. 114.

Taking its ordinary meaning, the exclusionary clause suggests that but for its inclusion in the second proviso in article 298, paragraph (a)(i), the question of a mixed dispute would have remained within the competence of a conciliation commission. As a logical corollary to this, it follows that, since the exclusionary clause does not apply to a compulsory procedure provided for in section 2 of Part XV, a mixed dispute, whether it arose before or after the entry into force of UNCLOS, falls within the jurisdiction of a compulsory procedure. If the intention of the framers of UNCLOS is to provide that the exclusionary clause in the second proviso made applicable to conciliation should apply with equal force to the compulsory procedures in section 2 of article 298, then it ought to have been expressly specified in article 298 or in a similar provision of Part XV.[146]

In the absence of specific provisions in the Convention mandating a court or tribunal established there-under to deal with mixed disputes, paragraph 1 of article 293 should be construed as the applicable law which provides that "... court or tribunal having jurisdiction under this section shall apply this Convention and other rules of international law not incompatible with the Convention." The last paragraph of the preamble of the Convention also affirms the competence of a court or tribunal established in accordance with articles 287 and 288 to deal with mixed disputes. This paragraph reads as follows: "Affirming that matters not regulated by this Convention continue to be governed by the rules and principles of international law." Therefore, where no declaration is made with respect to delimitation disputes under article 298(1)(a), a court or tribunal within the meaning of articles 287 and 288 would have jurisdiction to deal with a mixed dispute. It may not deal with disputed land territory issues alone if there is no necessary nexus between them and the dispute concerning sea boundary delimitation, unless with the mutual consent of the parties.

3.3 Application of the Choice of Procedures in Sea Boundary Delimitation Dispute Settlement

If the competent court or tribunal is not barred by an article 298 declaration from proceeding with the dispute, then it will have to inquire into whether the

---

[146] See *Territorial Disputes (Libyan Arab Jamahiriya/Chad), Judgment*, ICJ Reports 1994, pp. 21–22. Paragraph 41. The ICJ held: In accordance with customary international law, reflected in Article 31 of the 1969 Vienna Convention on the Law of Treaties, a treaty must be interpreted in good faith in accordance with the ordinary meaning to be given to its terms in their context and in the light of its object and purpose. Interpretation must be based above all upon the text of the treaty.

parties to the delimitation dispute made efforts to reach settlement by recourse to section 1 of Part XV, more particularly, under articles 74 and 83. Where there is an agreement in force between the States concerned, questions relating to the delimitation of the exclusive economic zone and of the continental shelf are to be determined in accordance with the provisions of that agreement.[147] Where there is no agreement, the States concerned are given a reasonable period of time to reach agreement on the basis of international law, as referred to in article 38 of the Statute of the ICJ, in order to achieve an equitable solution.[148] If no such agreement can be reached, the States concerned shall resort to the procedures provided for in Part XV.[149]

Article 283, paragraph 2, also requires an expeditious exchange of views where a procedure for the settlement of such a dispute has been terminated without a settlement. This further exchange is obviously intended to enable the parties to agree on other peaceful means for settlement such as good offices or conciliation or identification of appropriate compulsory procedure among the several procedures provided for in article 287.[150] As held by the Tribunal, it should be kept in view that a State Party is not obliged to continue with an exchange of views when it concludes that the possibilities of reaching agreement have been exhausted.[151] The requirement of article 283 regarding an exchange of views is not, however, an empty formality to be dispensed with at the whims of a disputant. The obligation in this regard, like any other international obligation must be discharged in good faith, and it is the inherent duty of a competent court or tribunal to examine the facts and circumstances of the case whether this obligation has been complied with.[152] The intended Court or Tribunal can only proceed to determine the merits of the dispute submitted to it after it has determined that the requirements of article 283 have been fully complied with.

---

147 See articles 74 and 83, paragraphs 4 of UNCLOS respectively.
148 See article 74, paragraph 2, and article 83, paragraph 2.
149 See article 74, paragraph 2, and article 83, paragraph 2
150 See also A.O Adede, *Settlement of Disputes arising under the law of the Sea Convention* 69 American Journal of International Law (1975), p. 798 at p. 803.
151 (*Ireland v. United Kingdom*) *Provisional Measures, Order of 3 December 2001*, ITLOS Reports 2001, p. 95, paragraph 60.
152 *Land Reclamation in and around the straits of Johor (Malaysia v. Singapore), Provisional Measures, order of 8 October 2003,* Separate Opinion of Judge Chandrasekhara Rao, p. 3, paragraph 11

3.4 Proceedings on the Merits

The parties to the dispute are normally represented by their respective Agents and Counsel who assist them in the preparation and presentation of their cases before the Tribunal. The names of the agents who do not necessarily need to be a national of either of the disputed States parties are required to be indicated in the special agreement transmitting the dispute to the Registrar. This method of transmitting the dispute to the court or tribunal is designed to obviate the possibility of making preliminary objections regarding the jurisdiction of the court. The reason is that the special agreement concluded by the parties prior to the submission of the dispute did not only replace[153] the traditional procedure based on unilateral application, but also confers jurisdiction on the court so that it could be seized of the case.[154] In any event, it is the responsibility of the court or tribunal to determine its jurisdiction when a matter is submitted to it for adjudication.[155] Thus, the latter's competence depends on the prior consent of the parties as no sovereign State can be a party to a case before an international tribunal if it had not consented thereto.[156]

The same scenario is followed in the context of cases relating to requests for provisional measures and prompt release of vessels pursuant to articles 290(5) and 292 respectively of UNCLOS. An application may also be filled in the con-

---

153   Corfu Channel Case, special agreement concluded on 25th March 1948; see Judgment of 9th April 1949 (Merits), ICJ Reports, 1949, p. 6.
154   In analyzing the number of signatories to the special agreement in the North Sea Continental Shelf case, M. Bedjaoui stated that "It will be noted in passing that introducing a case by way of a special agreement has henceforth become the most common method of submitting cases to the Court. This is a welcome development which has largely made up for the disappointment felt at the "optional clause" system instigated to encourage States to accept the jurisdiction of the Court in advance in all disputes in which they had to appear before the latter, or in all those cases falling into specific categories. As we know, that system was not as successful as had been expected and has frequently been the source of controversy as regards the competence of the Court, whilst that competence cannot be placed in doubt when a case is submitted by means of a special agreement". M. Bedjaoui, La "fabrication" des arrêts de la Cour international de Justice", in Mélanges Michel Virally, Paris, Pedone, 1991, p. 88.
155   See Article 288, paragraph 4, of the United Nations Convention on the Law of the Sea.
156   Article 288, paragraph 1, provides that the Tribunal "shall have jurisdiction over any dispute concerning the interpretation or application of this Convention which is submitted to it in accordance with this part". Similarly, article 21 of the Statute states: "The jurisdiction of the Tribunal comprises all disputes and all applications submitted to it in accordance with this Convention and all matters specifically provided for in any other agreement which confers jurisdiction on the Tribunal".

text of preliminary proceedings pursuant to article 294 of UNCLOS, a request to intervene under articles 31 and 32 of the Statute of the International Tribunal on Law of the Sea; a request for discontinuance under article 106(1) of the Rules, or for the purpose of interpretation or revision of a judgment of the Tribunal pursuant to article 24(1) of the Statute and article 54(1) of the Rules and procedures of the aforesaid tribunal.

In the conduct of the matter, the Tribunal, as the case may be, makes orders concerning matters of procedures including the admissibility of evidence.[157] In most cases, it does so in consultation with the agents[158] of the parties to the dispute until final judgment is delivered.

11   Conclusion

The dispute settlement mechanism of UNCLOS plays a pivotal role in enhancing cooperation among coastal states. Over three decades after the adoption of UNCLOS, Part XV has justified its adequacy to resolve maritime boundary delimitation disputes. The courts and tribunals established under Articles 287 of UNCLOS normally collaborate with the global scientific community to address delimitation disputes that may otherwise threaten international peace and security. These institutions may not handle delimitation dispute on direct terms but with the express consent of the parties coupled with the judicial acumen of judges drawn from all corners of the globe. Part XV has stood the test of time and exhibited its pliability to address maritime boundary delimitation disputes. In most cases, disputes occur over the ownership of a common pool resource in the ocean; the delimitation of maritime zones to states; and conflicts over the jurisdiction and management of resources of the territorial seas, exclusive economic zone, continental shelf, high seas and seabed. Absent a resolution of these claims, costly international conflicts can arise.

The recent judgment of the maritime boundary delimitation dispute between Bangladesh and Myanmar in the Bay of Bengal is an excellent case in point where the Judges of the International Tribunal on Law of the Sea used judicial craftsmanship to adjudicate and resolved all facets of this dispute (including the delineation of the extended continental shelves of the two na-

---

157   Article 27 of the Statute.
158   Article 45 of the Statute, See also article 59 of Rules of the Tribunal.

tions) to the satisfaction of the parties and the international community.[159] As expected in academic and judicial spheres, some pundits argued that the Tribunal at some point in this case actually performed the functions of another organ of the Convention. Jurisprudentially, the decision of the Tribunal was designed to meet the intention of the framers of Part XV and the spirit of the Convention i.e. to encourage the respective parties in dispute to find peaceful solution to their dispute on the basis of law, to promote international cooperation and contribute to the maintenance of international peace and security. I take the view that the tribunal's judgment essentially met these criteria. It properly took consideration of its prima facie jurisdiction in light of the parties' overall submissions, made an assessment of the necessity to preserve the parties' respective rights, and did not foreclose the parties from making further requests of the Court for it to delineate their continental shelves should these rights be threatened in the future. Therefore the omnibus decision reached by the Tribunal was and still is consistent with the judicial role of courts and tribunals established under the Convention.[160]

It has been submitted that UNCLOS has been the only multilateral treaty in which compulsory judicial mechanisms are part and parcel of the Convention rather than being made an optional protocol annexed to the main body of the Convention. This appears to be a major step forward in the evolution of international dispute settlement processes. Every State Party to the Convention is deemed to have consented to be bound by the compulsory dispute settlement procedures set out in Part XV thereof.[161]

Finally, it has also been submitted that the residual and or mandatory jurisdiction of the seabed dispute chamber and the ITLOS help to promote the paramount interest of the international community in the settlement of international dispute for the maintenance of international peace, security and justice.[162] The parties are at liberty to submit disputes to these standing judicial

---

159 *Dispute concerning delimitation of the maritime boundary between Bangladesh and Myanmar in the Bay of Bengal (Bangladesh/Myanmar)*, Judgment of the International Tribunal on Law of the Sea delivered in 2012 – http://www.itlos.org/.

160 For the importance of courts to encourage parties to settle their disputes peacefully, see Decision of the International court of Justice and separate declaration of Judge Koroma in Argentina V. Uruguay (Pulp Mill case), ICJ Reports, Declaration, order, 23-1-2007.

161 Since the 1969 Vienna Convention on the Law of Treaties and its annex on compulsory conciliation as the primary third-party procedure under the Treaty, no diplomatic conference producing a multilateral convention has included compulsory disputes settlement procedures as an integral part of the convention.

162 United Nations Charter, Article 2 paragraph 3.

bodies at any time once they are unable to agree on mutually acceptable procedures for the settlement of their disputes. In this regard, the Convention provides a reasonable degree of certainty that there will always be an identifiable avenue for peaceful settlement of disputes without in each case requiring the agreement of each of the parties which may be cumbersome if not almost impossible to obtain in some cases.[163]

---

163   See article by Thomas A. Mensah, Max-Planck Year Book of United Nations Law (1998) p. 322.

CHAPTER 14

Constitutional Law and the Settlement of Investor-State Disputes: Some Interplays

Laurence Boisson de Chazournes and Brian McGarry

1 Introduction

The State's role in the international legal order is a thread that can be traced throughout Judge Koroma's scholarship. In particular, his contributions to dialogues on the international judicial law-making function as well as emerging themes in international law, such as solidarity and multiculturalism, demonstrate a reflective approach to questions of normative harmony and conflict. It is in this spirit that the authors present the following brief observation on the synergies between domestic and international legal regimes which may appear in the context of investor-State claims and defenses. While issues of constitutional law may arise directly in the ratification process of investment treaties and the execution of arbitral awards, well-established hurdles to the application of domestic law in transnational fora substantially limit the degree to which such issues factor into the merits of investor-State disputes. Nevertheless, they may gain prominence through informal paths. Rather than directly applying constitutional law per se, tribunals may utilize other paths such as deferring to domestic interpretations of constitutional principles, or to constitutional procedures that appear, for example, to protect fair and equitable treatment.

From the outset, we may note that links between international and domestic spheres can play a role in rooting arbitral awards in what the WTO Appellate Body in the *EC – Hormones* case described in memorably stark terms: "the real world where people live, work and die."[1] The following year, an *ad hoc* tribunal in the *Himpurna California Energy* case echoed this sentiment in an investment context.[2] As to the applicable norms in a case involving corruption, that tribunal declared that it "do[es] not live in an ivory tower [...] [n]or does [it]

---

1 *EC Measures Affecting Meat and Meat Products (Hormones)*, Report of the Appellate Body, WT/DS26&48/AB/R (13 Feb. 1998), para. 187.
2 *Himpurna California Energy v. Indonesia*, Final Award (4 May 1999). Reprinted in Mealey's International Arbitration Report, vol. 14, no. 14 (Dec. 1999); Yearbook of Commercial Arbitration, vol. 25 (2000), p. 186.

view the arbitral process as one which operates in a vacuum, divorced from reality."[3] The year thereafter, the *S.D. Myers* tribunal introduced this view into dispute settlement under the North American Free Trade Agreement (NAFTA).[4] Moreover, it stressed its approach as deferential to democratic processes. In its evaluation of minimum standards of treatment, the tribunal stated that it "does not have an open-ended mandate to second-guess government decision-making,"[5] finding instead that "[t]he ordinary remedy [...] for errors in modern governments is through internal political and legal processes."[6]

In terms of tribunals' analysis and consideration of domestic constitutions during the course of arbitrations, we can draw attention to two broad paths. The first concerns informal comity toward constitutional principles and idiosyncrasies that may lie at the heart of an investment dispute. The second is the extent to which a host-State may formally rely upon constitutional guarantees to its people as a defense to a claim, particularly in the context of a domestic crisis.

2   Informal Deference to Constitutional Expertise

A general theme that emerges with respect to the former is tribunals' willingness or reluctance to 'second-guess' domestic courts' interpretations of their own constitutional safeguards and domestic legal complexities.[7] The extent to which tribunals have regarded host-State constitutions should not be viewed as a measure of the legal force of constitutional provisions against international law. Rather, we may see deference to national interpretations of principles enshrined in both domestic law and international law. Foremost among these principles is that of fair and equitable treatment. This is a fundamental principle of most domestic laws and the basis for a pervasive claim in investment dispute settlement.

---

3   Ibid., paras 219–220.
4   *S.D. Myers v. Canada*, First Partial Award on Liability (13 Nov. 2000), ICSID Reports, vol. 8 (2005), p. 18.
5   Ibid., para. 261.
6   Ibid.
7   Review of domestic judiciaries in this manner may raise internal issues concerning separation of powers. See, e.g., the discussion of *Chevron Corporation (USA) and Texaco Petroleum Company (USA) v. Republic of Ecuador*, PCA Case No. 2009-23, First Interim Award on Interim Measures, 25 January 2012, in T. Tucker, 'Investment Agreements versus the Rule of Law?', Investment Policy Hub, 9 October 2013, available at: http://investmentpolicyhub.unctad.org/Views/Public/FeaturedDiscussionDetails.aspx?fdid=25.

It is possible for a treaty to refer directly to constitutional State norms, as is the case in the CARICOM-Cuba investment treaty.[8] This treaty incorporates by reference the fair and equitable treatment standards found in the domestic legislation of the host-State.[9] However, such direct formulations are unique for straightforward reasons. If the meaning of fair and equitable is defined exclusively by the legal framework of the host-State, tribunals may arguably lack interpretative norms for gauging State compliance.[10]

Yet the difference between purely domestic versus international conceptions of fair and equitable treatment is not as distinct as it may seem.[11] An examination of the element of 'proportionality' illuminates this point. In a purely domestic sense, this concept primarily serves to limit the involvement of public authorities within the private sphere.[12] From these State-based origins, proportionality tests have increasingly penetrated transnational legal systems. Most notably, the adoption of such a test in the jurisprudence of the Court of Justice of the European Union (CJEU) has diffused this concept into

---

8   Agreement on Reciprocal Promotion and Protection of Investments [between the Caribbean Community (CARICOM) and the Republic of Cuba] (1990).

9   Ibid., Art. 4 ("Each Party shall ensure fair and equitable treatment of Investments of Investors of the other Party under and subject to national laws and regulations").

10 See R. Kläger, 'Fair and Equitable Treatment' in International Investment Law (Cambridge: Cambridge University Press, 2011), p. 21. On the general interpretation of fair and equitable treatment standards in the absence of such direct formulations, see R. Dolzer & M. Stevens, Bilateral Investment Treaties (The Hague: Martinus Nijhoff, 1995), p. 58; S. Vasciannie, 'The Fair and Equitable Treatment Standard in International Investment Law and Practice', British Yearbook of International Law, vol. 70, no. 1 (1999), p. 99. See also S. Montt, State Liability in Investment Treaty Arbitration – Global Constitutional and Administrative Law in the BIT Generation (Oxford: Hart Publishing, 2009), Ch. VI ('Controlling Arbitrariness through the Fair and Equitable Standard'), p. 293 et seq.

11 Similarly, other guarantees against investor discrimination such as the national treatment standard are common to federal constitutions (such as the U.S.), supranational entities (such as the EU), and, in particular, the WTO. In an investment context, most treaties take a minimalist approach to national treatment guarantees that results in a comparatively amorphous and complex study of trends. For an excellent analysis of the state of jurisprudence on this particular issue, see J. Kurtz, 'The Merits and Limits of Comparativism: National Treatment in International Investment Law and the WTO', in S.W. Schill (ed.), International Investment Law and Comparative Public Law (Oxford: Oxford University Press, 2010), pp. 243–278.

12 R. Kläger, op. cit., pp. 236–237. This function of proportionality may have originated in the administrative law of Germany. The concept has since developed into a doctrinal element of constitutional law in that State.

the legal systems of States across Europe.¹³ This has paved two-way streets between domestic and international interpretations of fair and equitable treatment. A similar influence may be ascribed to the jurisprudence of the European Court of Human Rights (ECtHR). With respect to the latter, proportionality is firmly established as an important tool to restrict the discretion left to State authorities, and to scrutinize the legitimacy of their measures.¹⁴ The concept is also well-known in WTO law. In this area, analysis under Article XX of the General Agreement on Tariffs and Trade (GATT) has utilized a sort of proportionality test.¹⁵

For the purposes of our review, however, it may suffice to narrow the focus toward those claims that specifically allege a denial of justice. Foreign investor claims that question the legal effectiveness of host-State administrative procedures may informally trigger issues of comity. This is due to a true distinction between the aforementioned institutions and investment tribunals. Such tribunals are not constituted to serve as appellate courts reviewing domestic judicial decisions, much less very fine points of national law. To that extent, Jan Paulsson has submitted that even "gross or notorious injustice [...] is not a denial of justice merely because the conclusion appears to be demonstrably wrong in substance; it must impel the adjudicator to conclude that it could not have been reached by an impartial judicial body worthy of that name."¹⁶

Denial of justice allegations do not direct arbitrators to gauge the substantive accuracy of a State's application of its own laws. We must therefore consider fair and equitable treatment in this regard as a principle related to procedural fairness.¹⁷ With this in mind, we may turn to some recent NAFTA

---

13   See J. Schwarze, *European Administrative Law* (Office for Official Publications of the European Communities, 2006), pp. 680 et seq. For a non-regional perspective on the diffusion of proportionality analysis, see A. Stone Sweet & J. Mathews, 'Proportionality Balancing and Global Constitutionalism,' *Columbia Journal of Transnational Law*, vol. 47 (2008), pp. 111 et seq.

14   See A. Stone Sweet & J. Mathews, op. cit., pp. 145 et seq.

15   See M. Hilf & S. Puth, 'The Principle of Proportionality on its Way into WTO/GATT Law', in A. von Bogdandy, et al. (eds.), *European Integration and International Co-ordination* (The Hague: Kluwer Law International, 2002), p. 199. For a case example of the WTO Dispute Settlement Body [DSB] developing its dynamic approach to Article XX of the GATT, see *U.S. – Import Prohibition of Certain Shrimp and Shrimp Products*, Report of the Appellate Body, WT/DS58/AB/R (12 Oct. 1998).

16   J. Paulsson, *Denial of Justice in International Law* (Cambridge: Cambridge University Press, 2005), p. 65. See, similarly, I. Brownlie, *Principles of Public International Law*, 7th ed. (Oxford: Oxford University Press, 2008), p. 530.

17   It is in this light that some commentators have posited that the unifying theory behind the fair and equitable treatment standard is the concept of legality. Such a view concludes

arbitrations that have raised related and complex constitutional issues. We can now more concretely appreciate how a tribunal – by emphasizing the procedural character of its FET analysis – may therefore draw inspiration from domestic interpretations of this principle.

For example, the tribunal in the *Glamis Gold* case dealt with a U.S. agency's "lengthy, reasoned legal opinion" of constitutional law.[18] The namesake Canadian corporation in this case was engaged in the exploration and extraction of precious metals throughout the continent. In 1994, Glamis Gold acquired mining rights for a proposed open-pit gold mine on U.S. federal lands, in the California desert lands known as Imperial Valley. Given the potential ecological damages associated with the firm's proposed mining practices, permission to commence exploration hinged on a thorough environmental review. This review considered, *inter alia*, the rights of indigenous populations in the area. In 2001, after years of study, the relevant federal agency formally denied the Glamis Gold project.

This rejection was based in large part on an apparent conflict between the longstanding U.S. mining statute liberalizing mining rights in the American west, and the religious freedoms guaranteed under the State's federal constitution.[19] Noting that a local tribe's religion required it to worship in a pathway traversing the proposed mining area – and analogizing U.S. Supreme Court precedents addressing other natural resource agencies – the executive order found that the federal government was bound to "preserv[e] the physical integrity of the sites unless such a choice [was] impracticable, forbidden by law, or clearly inconsistent with essential agency functions."[20]

However, following a change in presidential administrations the same year, this opinion was reversed and the Imperial Valley Project was approved. In response to this federal turnaround, California adopted an emergency regulation implementing onerous remediation requirements designed to preserve lands near tribal sacred sites. This example of dual regulatory sovereignty results from a constitutionally enshrined federalism that surfaces somewhat fre-

---

that investment tribunals implicitly interpret this standard as requiring treatment in accordance with the concept of the rule of law. See, e.g., B. Kingsbury & S. Schill, 'Investor-State Arbitration as Governance: Fair and Equitable Treatment, Proportionality and the Emerging Global Administrative Law', New York University School of Law, Public Law & Legal Theory Research Working Paper No. 09–46 (2009), p. 10.

18   *Glamis Gold v. United States of America*, Award, NAFTA/UNCITRAL (16 May 2009), para. 761.
19   Constitution of the United States of America, amend. I.
20   *Glamis Gold*, op. cit., para. 142.

quently in NAFTA Chapter 11 claims,[21] which are what Glamis Gold brought next. The firm filed NAFTA claims alleging regulatory expropriation under Article 1110 and a violation of fair and equitable treatment under Article 1105, stemming from both the initial federal ruling and the eventual state measures.

The latter claim serves as our focal point, as it required the tribunal to review what it called "[the U.S. agency's] complicated legal opinion on an issue of first impression that changed a [...] century-old regime upon which Claimant had based reasonable expectations."[22] The question, therefore, was whether this administrative interpretation of constitutional law violated NAFTA's incorporation of customary international standards of fair and equitable treatment by altering the investor's legitimate expectations. The tribunal's response cast NAFTA Article 1105 as deferential to the due process interpretations of domestic constitutional courts. The tribunal stated that it would not 'second-guess' the original federal opinion or California measures relying upon it unless such decisions had appeared "blatantly unfair or evidently discriminatory" or "evidence[d] a complete lack of process."[23] In so doing, the tribunal left the claimant's only potential recourse at the courthouse steps.

In this manner, the tribunal implied a notable give-and-take in Chapter 11 disputes. Foreign investors may be inclined to select arbitration over domestic U.S. litigation, as NAFTA tribunals may construe expropriation more broadly

---

21   NAFTA Chapter 11 is a notable prism through which we can view international and domestic legal interplay. One reason for this is that the basic constitutional tensions at play in federalist States are particularly visible in investment dispute settlement. NAFTA's States Parties vest substantial constitutional authority in sub-federal sovereigns, governing economic and environmental matters alike. In Canada, for example, the federal government in 2010 settled a Chapter 11 claim brought by U.S. investor AbitibiBowater, arising from an expropriation by the province of Newfoundland and Labrador. Canada's constitution, however, does not include any mechanism whereby Ottawa can recoup its C$130 million settlement – the largest in NAFTA history at the time – from its province through legal action. See L.L. Herman, 'Federalism and international investment disputes', IISD Investment Treaty News (12 July 2011), available at: http://www.iisd.org/itn/2011/07/12/federalism-and-international-investment-disputes/. Similar issues abound in the U.S. constitutional model, and are easily capable of yielding the opposite imbalance. For example, following the *Methanex* arbitration, Washington was able to recoup its arbitral costs from the unsuccessful Canadian claimant. However, California has no direct avenue in U.S. constitutional law to claim from this sum its considerable expenses in preparing to defend the water health regulation at issue. See M. Bottari & L. Wallach, 'Federalism and Global Governance', Public Citizen Global Trade Watch (2008), available at: http://www.citizen.org/documents/federalism.pdf.

22   *Glamis Gold*, op. cit., para. 761.

23   Ibid., para. 24.

under Article 1110 than federal courts would construe the term under the U.S. constitution.[24] Yet when it comes to Article 1105 claims concerning fair and equitable treatment, investor-State tribunals – such as in the *Glamis Gold* case – may demonstrate more reluctance than their domestic judicial counterparts to review administrative decisions and constitutional interpretations.

The *Grand River* case was a subsequent NAFTA dispute with facts even more intertwined with domestic federalism issues and informal issues of 'second-guessing' domestic institutions.[25] In this case, the investor, a Canadian cigarette distributor, arranged a business strategy that would mitigate its financial obligations under the contemporary tobacco laws in many U.S. states. Such obligations required tobacco distributors to place large sums into escrow accounts in order to settle claims related to the damaging health effects of cigarettes.

However, Grand River attempted to circumvent these state requirements by distributing its product primarily through the quasi-sovereign 'Indian territories' occupied by federally recognized tribes. The major question for the tribunal in the eventual NAFTA case, therefore, was whether U.S. constitutional law and federalism granted U.S. states the regulatory authority to impose their escrow laws on commerce in tribal reservations within a state's territory.[26]

Striking a deferential note similar to *Glamis Gold*, the tribunal stated that "U.S. federal Indian law is a complex and not altogether consistent mixture of constitutional provisions, federal statutes, and judicial decisions by the U.S. Supreme Court [...]."[27] Finding that "U.S. domestic law is currently far from conclusive about the question raised here of the extent of permissible state regulation," the *Grand River* tribunal cautiously noted that "[d]etermining the contents of that law ... often calls for necessarily uncertain predictions of how future courts will apply past decisions involving different [state regulations]."[28]

From this context, the tribunal forcefully returned to the themes of the *Glamis Gold* tribunal's treatment of claims based on NAFTA Article 1105 fair and equitable treatment, stating that it "is loath to purport to address ... delicate

---

24 U.S. Constitution, amend. v.
25 *Grand River Enterprises Six Nations v. United States of America*, Award, NAFTA/UNCITRAL (12 Jan. 2011).
26 Ibid., para. 132.
27 Ibid., para. 137.
28 Ibid., para. 138. The tribunal in a more recent NAFTA arbitration was similarly reluctant to make determinations regarding the division of federal and provincial competences under Canada's constitution. *Bilcon of Delaware et al v. Government of Canada*, Award, NAFTA/UNCITRAL, PCA Case No. 2009-04 (17 Mar. 2015), para. 526 ("The Tribunal recognizes that constitutional doctrine can be complex, controversial and shifting [...]").

and complex questions of U.S. constitutional [law]."[29] Dismissing Grand River's claims in full, the tribunal asserted its reluctance to address delicate matters of federal law, finding instead that such "issues of national law belong in national courts, not in an international tribunal."[30] In other words, because U.S. authorities' determination on the matter had not presented a *prima facie* case of denial of justice cognizable at the high threshold of customary international law under NAFTA Article 1105, the tribunal in *Grand River* refused to 'second-guess' domestic constitutional interpretations.

This comity toward executive opinions on 'complex' questions of constitutional law is particularly noteworthy because claimant Grand River argued that U.S. authorities had violated one of the State's international human rights obligations: the duty to consult with indigenous peoples prior to making important regulatory decisions affecting their interests.[31] As this legal duty arguably formed part of the claimant's reasonable expectations at the time of contracting, the *Grand River* tribunal essentially deferred to domestic treatment of federalism questions in lieu of its own competence to counterbalance legitimate investor expectations.[32]

On this point, we may return to our earlier discussion of the role of constitutional law in instances where an international treaty does not address relevant fundamental rights. Under NAFTA, a tribunal "shall decide the issues in dispute in accordance with this Agreement and applicable rules of international law."[33] This mandate does not refer expressly to constitutional or any State law, and yet we have seen NAFTA tribunals in *Glamis Gold* and *Grand River* find cause to show informal deference to domestic law. Concerning the legal interests of local populations that are intertwined in these cases, one may begin to discern a certain tendency in investor-State arbitration to recognize a

---

29   Ibid., para. 234.
30   Ibid.
31   Ibid., paras 180–181.
32   Another NAFTA Chapter 11 arbitration recently initiated by a Canadian investor against the U.S. followed on the heels of a separate, ongoing arbitration between the parties concerning the relative authority of investment tribunals to affirm or refute domestic judiciaries' treatment of their own constitutions. Canadian pharmaceutical company Apotex argued unsuccessfully that U.S. courts misapplied statutory and constitutional law in multiple decisions, in what amounts to a violation of NAFTA commitments concerning national treatment, fair and equitable treatment, and expropriation. Apotex Holdings Inc. and Apotex Inc. v. United States of America, Award, ICSID Case No. ARB(AF)/12/1 (25 Aug. 2015).
33   NAFTA, Art. 1131.

rather broad margin for governments to make their own choices in ensuring the respect of constitutional norms within their jurisdictions.[34]

3 Formal Application of Constitutional Obligations

The right of compensation in case of expropriation, like the guarantee of fair and equitable treatment, is a fundamental principle common to a majority of domestic legal systems, and many of these States codify this right at the constitutional level (including Croatia, Denmark, Germany and Italy).[35] U.S. jurisprudence has explained that State's constitutional permission of compensated takings on the basis of States' implicit police powers: exercises of a government's sovereign right to protect its people's lives, health, morals, comfort and general welfare, at a level paramount to any rights under contracts between individuals.[36] In more recent decades, the U.S. Supreme Court extended this reasoning to contracts between individuals and the entities of the states.[37]

Like the constitutional courts of these domestic legal systems, those of transnational jurisdiction broadly support the principle that States may terminate or otherwise modify contracts with private parties in the event of superseding public interests. This authority is indeed so uncontroversial that it is generally read as an implied exception to investment treaty umbrella clauses.[38]

However, despite overlaps between domestic and international legal principles in this context, direct reference to constitutional law as a host-State defense against foreign investors' claims has proven problematic in practice. This is because it is a *formal* path to applying domestic law. As such, it may be examined in contrast with the *informal* paths we have just seen in the context of fair and equitable treatment claims.

For example, if proof of a taking is established in an investment arbitration, constitutional law may inform the fact of whether sufficient justification exists

---

34 L. Boisson de Chazournes, 'Fundamental Rights and International Arbitration: Arbitral Awards and Constitutional Law', in A. J. van den Berg (ed.), *Arbitration Advocacy in Changing Times*, ICCA Congress Series No. 15 (Alphen aan de Rijn: Wolters Kluwer, 2011), p. 321.

35 F. Lenzerini, 'Property Protection and Protection of Cultural Heritage', in S.W. Schill (ed.), op. cit., p. 566.

36 See B. Meyler, 'Economic Emergency and the Rule of Law', *DePaul Law Review*, vol. 56 (2007), p. 558 et seq.

37 *City of El Paso v. Simmons*, 379 US 497, 506 et seq. (1965); *U.S. Trust Co. v. New Jersey*, 431 US 1, 14 et seq. (1977).

38 S.W. Schill, 'Umbrella Clauses as Public Law Concepts in Comparative Perspective', in S.W. Schill (ed.), op. cit., p. 340.

to excuse the host-State from any required and outstanding compensation. However, domestic constitutions vary widely on this point and may not provide substantive clarity to the tribunal concerning a government's conformity or non-conformity with its own laws defining states of emergency. For example, France's 1958 constitution vests broad discretion and powers in the President when "the proper functioning of the constitutional public authorities is interrupted."[39] The U.S. not only similarly lacks any clear constitutional discussion of economic emergencies, but also lacks any constitutional provision on emergency authorities beyond the rudimentary suspension of *habeas corpus* "when in cases of rebellion or invasion the public safety may require it."[40]

In contrast, investment tribunals have incrementally contributed to a more static norm of emergency powers, notably involving defenses based on the human rights elements of State constitutions. For example, in several disputes arising from its financial crisis, Argentina has explicitly referred to resulting threats to its 'constitutional order', in both the societal and legal senses of the term.[41] The intriguing point here is the manner in which conflicts with human rights obligations appear to arise.

In some instances, Argentina has argued that it took measures in response to its financial crisis that were necessary to uphold the basic rights and liberties of the Argentine public, and has at times cited the supremacy of human rights treaty obligations within its Constitution.[42] The first investment tribunal to render an award in such a dispute was the *CMS* case, which not only rejected Argentina's human rights defense, but deemed that the human rights and investor obligations in question were not in conflict, and therefore led to no issues of constitutional supremacy.[43] Meanwhile, the tribunal in the *Sempra* case simply concluded on the same facts that no danger of societal collapse existed to have even necessitated the suspension of liberties.[44] In contrast, an ICSID tribunal's award in the *Continental Casualty* case reached opposite con-

---

39 Constitution of the Fifth Republic of France, Art. XVI. See C. Binder & A. Reinisch, 'Economic Emergency Powers: a Comparative Law Perspective', in S.W. Schill (ed.), op. cit., pp. 520–521.

40 U.S. Constitution, Art. I, sec. 9. See B. Ackerman, 'The Emergency Constitution', *Yale Law Journal*, vol. 113 (2004), p. 1041.

41 See 'Selected Recent Developments in IIA Arbitration and Human Rights', UN Conference on Trade and Development [UNCTAD] International Investment Agreement Monitor, no. 2 (2009), p. 4. Electronic version available at: http://unctad.org/en/Docs/webdiaeia20097_en.pdf.

42 Ibid., pp. 8–12.

43 *CMS Gas Transmission v. Argentina*, Award, ICSID Case No. ARB/01/08 (12 May 2005).

44 *Sempra Energy v. Argentina*, Award, ICSID Case No. ARB/02/16 (28 Sep. 2007).

clusions on both the effectiveness of Argentina's emergency defense and the preeminence of its human rights obligations.[45] Of particular note to our discussion of constitutional interplay is the tribunal's remark that Argentina's protection of fundamental liberties was a proactive step that removed the necessity of later suspending such liberties to enforce social order.[46]

The resulting deference that the *Continental Casualty* tribunal granted to Argentina's crisis management decisions stands in stark contrast to the limited margin of appreciation that had been granted to Argentina under the same circumstances by the tribunal in the *Siemens* case.[47] Indeed, that tribunal had rejected as unformed Argentina's argument that the property rights claimed by Siemens would have forced Argentina to violate its constitutionally preeminent international human rights treaty obligations.[48]

In a more recent case arising from the Argentine financial crisis, the tribunal in *SAUR International* acknowledged fundamental human rights, and in particular the right to water, as safeguarded by both the Argentine constitution and general principles of international law.[49] However, the tribunal held that this regulatory concern must be combined with investors' treaty rights to compensation for property.[50]

4 Concluding Remarks

As the application of domestic law in international dispute settlement is an exercise in overcoming well-established hurdles – and as investment arbitration today offers an evolving but inherently fragmented body of precedents – it

---

45   *Continental Casualty v. Argentina*, Award, ICSID Case No. ARB/03/9 (5 Sept. 2008).
46   Ibid., paras 180–181, 270. See also *LG&E Energy v. Argentina*, Decision on Liability, ICSID Case No. ARB/01/1 (3 Oct. 2006), para. 234. Argentina's necessity defense was successful in the *LG&E Energy* case, although that tribunal relied upon a different rationale than in the subsequent *Continental Casualty* case. The *LG&E Energy* decision did not expressly refer to Argentina's human rights obligations, but rather emphasized the social and health-related effects of the financial crisis.
47   *Siemens v. Argentina*, Award, ICSID Case No. ARB/02/08 (6 Feb. 2007).
48   Ibid., para. 79.
49   *SAUR International v. Argentine Republic* (Case No ARB/04/4), *Decision on Jurisdiction and Liability* (6 June 2012). For a detailed review of the dispute in English, see 'Newly-Released Saur v. Argentina Decision Touches on Illegality, Test for Expropriation, and Financial "Strangulation" of a Concessionaire', *IA Reporter* (14 June 2012). Electronic version available at: <http://www.iareporter.com/articles/20120615_1 (accessed 18 December 2012).
50   Ibid.

should not surprise that different tribunals have thus exhibited varying degrees of comity toward States' administrative and judicial procedures. The informal paths that we have traced between constitutional law and investment arbitration rely upon such comity. It entails tribunals' reluctance to probe alleged denials of justice when host-State procedures do not appear to contradict principles of due process and the rule of law. Moreover, it may compel those tribunals' deference to domestic interpretations of constitutional complexities. In practice, these paths have more effectively assimilated constitutional law than have more formal approaches, such as we have seen in host-State defenses based on emergency powers.

Yet these faint but clearing paths between the two legal spheres do not tell the end of the story. There may be marked trails as well, such as our earlier mention of investment treaties incorporating host-State norms by reference. Still another portal may be found in the premise of comparative constitutional analysis. This is not a merely theoretical model or a one-sided push to 'domesticate' investor-State dispute settlement through traditional constitutional constraints. It acknowledges that the standards and tests embraced by tribunals are likely to influence both the future conduct of States and the decisions of other tribunals. Moreover, the trend toward viewing investor-State arbitration as part of a global governance structure naturally encourages resort to principles of comparative constitutional law, particularly when assessing the concept of fair and equitable treatment.

In this sense, the content of such treatment standards is poised to evolve further in the coming years of investment arbitration. Despite the general supremacy of international law, tribunals called upon to decide matters of transnational law may well serve the institutional interests of investment arbitration by integrating a mutually supportive understanding of constitutional and international norms. The doorways between these constructs may remain works in progress for the time being, but as tribunals have increasingly implied, no such edifice is an "ivory tower" of limited view or reach.[51]

---

51   *Himpurna California Energy*, op. cit., para. 219.

CHAPTER 15

Legal Aspects of Competition between International Organizations

Konstantinos D. Magliveras

1   Introduction

We are surrounded by competition. Wherever and whenever there is more than one thing of the same kind there is bound to be competition between them. Even when there are two principles of law regulating the same subject matter, invariably they are competing with each other. And not only are they competing but at same stage the one will take precedence over the other. In his Dissenting Opinion in *Threat or Use of Nuclear Weapons*, Judge Koroma submitted that "[w]hen the [International] Court [of Justice] is faced with two competing principles or rights,[1] it should jurisprudentially assign a priority to one of them and cause it to prevail".[2] The present contribution attempts to examine the application of competition rules and principles as they pertain to international organizations, an area that arguably has not attracted much attention in the bibliography. It examines how the most important rules of competition law apply to international organizations and offers pertinent examples from practice.

---

1   In casu, the obligation of states to comply with the principles and rules of international law applicable in armed conflict *versus* the right of states to self-defence, especially when their survival is at stake.
2   International Court of Justice, *Legality of the Threat or Use of Nuclear Weapons*, Advisory Opinion of 8 July 1996, [1996] ICJ Reports 226, Dissenting Opinion of Judge Koroma 556, 559, at www.icj-cij.org/docket/files/95/7523.pdf (accessed 1 October 2014). In support of his submission, Judge Koroma cited Sir Hersch Lauterpacht, *The Development of International Law by the International Court* (Cambridge University Press 1958) 146.

11 Applying the Concept of Competition to International Organizations. The Advantages of Competition

Competition has always been a healthy process.[3] It has the power to distinguish the good from the bad, the successful from the disasters and it offers to entities being in competition the opportunity to acquire a new dynamic. Traditionally, competition has been viewed from an economic point of view. Its foundations, processes and players have been defined accordingly: the relevant markets and their interchangeability, undertakings and enterprises, consumers and recipients of services, market shares, the dominant position and its abuse, the monopoly, the monopsony, concerted practices, cartels, access to market and barriers to it, they are all primarily economic notions and principles. Even though not immediately identifiable, competition exists and takes place in many non-economic spheres. To offer illustrations of this diversity, reference could be made to competition among political parties in a democratic society,[4] among public bodies including universities and research centers,[5] among churches,[6] and so on. Generally speaking, competition exists between all those entities (whether private, public or semi public), which aim at gaining power at the expense of others and endeavour to consolidate their power and their control in a given area (in competition jargon the 'the market') where they pursue specific activities ('the product').

Even though Schumpeter's 'gales of creative destruction' might not apply to international organizations (IOs), at least to the extent that it applies to

---

3   For those questioning whether competition is advantageous at all times, see M.E. Stucke, "Is Competition Always Good?" (2013) 1 *Journal of Antitrust Enforcement* 162.
4   M. Morlok, "Parteienrecht als Wettbewerbsrecht" in P. Häberle, M. Morlok and V. Skouris (eds.), *Festschrift für Dimitris Th. Tsatsos zum 70. Geburtstag am 5. Mai 2003* (Nomos Verlag 2003) 408; C. DeMuth, "Competition and the Constitution", *National Affairs*, Fall 2011, No. 9, 38. The principle of free competition among political parties has been expressly enshrined in a number of national Constitutions: see e.g. Article 5 of the Constitution of the Czech Republic (1992), available in English translation in http://legislationline.org/documents/section/constitutions (accessed on 10 October 2014).
5   G. De Fraja and E. Lossa, "Competition Among Universities and the Emergence of the Élite Institution" (2002) 54 *Bulletin of Economic Research* 275.
6   The first to talk about competition in religious markets was Adam Smith, see A. Smith, *An Inquiry into the Nature and Causes of the Wealth of Nations*, 1776, published as R.H. Campbell and A.S. Skinner (eds), *Vol. II of the Glasgow Edition of the Works and Correspondence of Adam Smith* (Liberty Fund 1981) V.i.g: 788–814. And in June 2010 The Guardian newspaper put the question "Should religions compete?"; for the replies see: www.theguardian.com/commentisfree/belief/2010/jun/28/conversion-religion-christianity (accessed 1 October 2014).

companies,[7] the fact is that competition does exist between IOs as well. For open IOs, i.e. institutions where the accession of new Members is permitted usually upon the satisfaction of specific criteria, the purpose of competition would be twofold: on the one hand, to attract as many new Members as possible and, on the other hand, to persuade Members of competing IOs to withdraw and join them. But why would existing Members decide to join another international organization (IO)? In other words, which are the competitive advantages of an IO that would induce the Members of a third IO either to secede from it and accede to the other IO or to join the other IO as well? It is submitted that, all things being equal, these advantages are not different from those that a consumer might see in a new product and decides to replace the old product with the new one and/or to additionally buy the new product.

The following four advantages, which have been drawn by making broad analogies with competition between undertakings, shall be mentioned. The first is that, on account of the leading status that an IO has achieved (i.e. the IO has a 'dominant position') in a specific area of activities (the 'relevant market'), states might seek to reinforce their power by joining a particularly strong and powerful IO. The second is that an IO might have shown effectiveness and a stellar performance in specific areas of activities (e.g. economic cooperation and free trade) where competing IOs have failed; consequently, states, which are eager to promote their goals in economic integration, will be drawn by this IO. The third is that an IO might offer more benefits and advantages to its membership than other comparable IOs do. Equally, it might have superior infrastructure, offer more advanced services and employ better qualified personnel, elements which would be regarded as added value to the membership. The fourth is that an IO might have gained the reputation that those states that have joined it acquire a specific status, e.g. are regarded as democratic countries (with reservations, the example of the Council of Europe) or as economically advanced countries (the example of the Organization of Economic Cooperation and Development (OECD)).

III   Applying the Notion of 'Relevant Market' to IOs

Before examining the parameters of competition between IOs, two factors ought to be addressed. The first is to determine the existence of actual competitors, which are capable of constraining the behaviour of those entities that are active in a specific market. The second is to assess the degree of real competition in that market. If all IOs are put together, they constitute a single

---

7   J. Schumpeter, *Capitalism, Socialism, and Democracy* (Harper & Row 1942).

market, namely 'the market of international organizations'. However, as this market is extremely large and exhibits considerable variations, it is necessary to break it into smaller and more concrete (and consequently comparable) segments, which will become the 'relevant markets'. According to the definition of the term 'relevant market, as given in European Union law, it is made up of two elements: a 'relevant geographic market' and a 'relevant product market'. The former comprises the area in which the entities concerned supply their products and services in sufficiently homogeneous conditions of competition. The latter comprises all those products and services which consumers regard as interchangeable or substitutable by reason of their characteristics, prices and intended use.[8]

A   *The Relevant Geographic Market*

Applying this distinction to the IOs market, in the 'relevant geographic market' one could distinguish four different markets. In descending order, they are: the relevant geographic market of global IOs; the relevant geographic market of intra-regional IOs; the relevant geographic market of regional IOs; and the relevant geographic market of sub-regional IOs. This categorization is consistent with the classification adopted by the Union of International Associations (UIA), a research institute and documentation centre established in Brussels more than one hundred years ago and the publisher of the *Yearbook of International Organizations*.[9] The UIA has developed a 'hierarchical typology' of IOs which is extremely broadly defined and currently consists of 15 different types of organizations. Three of these types are of direct relevance to the 'relevant geographic market' suggested here: universal membership organizations (it corresponds to the relevant geographic market of global IOs); intercontinental membership organizations (it corresponds to the intra-regional IOs market); and regionally defined membership organizations (it corresponds to the regional and sub-regional IOs markets).[10]

---

[8]   European Commission, *Commission notice on the definition of relevant market for the purposes of Community competition law*, Official Journal of the European Community, C 372 of 9 December 1997, p. 5. See further Articles 101–109 of the Treaty for the Functioning of the European Union (2009). For another definition of the relevant market, see United Nations Conference on Trade and Development, UNCTAD *Model Law on Competition*, Chapter II(1)(D), UN Doc. TD/RBP/CONF.7/8, August 2010, at: http://unctad.org/en/Docs/tdrbpconf7d8_en.pdf (accessed 1 October 2014).

[9]   For the current edition, see Union of International Associations (ed.), *Yearbook of International Organizations 2014–2015*, Guide to Global Civil Society Networks, Edition 51 (Brill 2014).

[10]   See www.uia.be/node/325608#typeb (accessed 1 October 2014).

As regards the relevant geographic market of global IOs, the United Nations has undoubtedly a monopoly or a very strong dominant position, if, as will later be explained, the Group of 77 or the Non-Aligned Movement (NAM) were considered as its direct competitors. Moreover, the United Nations has the monopoly of adopting and/or authorizing legally binding measures of a punitive nature (sanctions), which specifically involve the use of force. Effectively, these measures can be applied against each and every country of the world considering that almost all sovereign independent states have opted to join the United Nations.[11] However, the infliction of these measures does not have to do with the relevant geographic market but with the relevant product market, which will be discussed later. Moreover, all of the current 15 Specialized Agencies participating in the UN family (defined by the United Nations as 'autonomous organizations linked to the UN through special agreements')[12] would also fall into the relevant geographic market of global IOs. And this because the vast majority of states have chosen to join them, presumably drawn by the services and the benefits offered to Members. By the same token, the World Trade Organization (WTO), the Organization for the Prohibition of Chemical Weapons (OPCW) and the International Atomic Energy Agency (IAEA), three IOs closely connected to the United Nations but not forming part of the UN family, should also be considered as part of the relevant geographic market of global IOs.

The relevant geographic market of intra-regional IOs covers those IOs, whose membership comes from more than one specific region. For practical reasons, each region could be equated to a continent. Examples include: (a) the Organization of Islamic Cooperation (OIC) (membership from all continents bar Oceana); (b) the Organization of Petroleum Exporting Countries (OPEC), the European Bank for Reconstruction and Development (EBRD) as well as the OECD (membership from three continents); and (c) the League of Arab States and the Council of Europe (membership from two continents).

The relevant geographic market of regional IOs covers those IOs that satisfy two conditions. The first is that the membership comes exclusively from a single region. The second is that the majority of the states belonging to the region in question have joined an IO belonging to this market. Examples include the Organization of American States (OAS), the European Union (EU), and the Af-

---

11   See Article 25 in conjunction with Articles 41 et seq. of the UN Charter and Chapter VIII thereof.
12   For the list, see www.un.org/en/aboutun/structure/index.shtml (accessed 1 October 2014).

rican Union (AU).[13] Finally, the relevant geographic market of sub-regional IOs comprises those IOs whose membership covers only some of the states belonging to a specific region/continent. Examples can be found in America (the Andean Community of Nations (CAN), the Latin American Integration Association (LAIA), and the Southern Common Market (Mercosur)); in Africa (the Southern African Development Community (SADC), the Common Market of Eastern and Southern Africa (COMESA), the Economic Community of Western African States (ECOWAS), the East African Community (EAC), and the Intergovernmental Authority on Development (IGAD)); in Europe (the European Free Trade Association (EFTA)); and in Asia (the Association of South East Asian Nations (ASEAN), the Commonwealth of Independent States (CIS), the Collective Security Treaty Organization (CSTO), and the Shanghai Cooperation Organization (SCO)). A particular characteristic of the relevant market in sub-regional IOs is the overlapping membership, namely that the same states participate in two or more IOs with similar or comparable aims and objectives. For all intents and purposes, they could be regarded as rival IOs, especially if the product market is not deep enough to accommodate all of them or if the available resources are scarce and the IOs in question 'fight' each other to get hold of them.

B The Relevant Product Market

As far as the 'relevant product market' is concerned, one could categorize IOs (irrespective of whether they are global/intra-regional/regional/sub-regional, i.e. irrespective of the 'relevant geographic market') according to their principal area of activity, where an activity is deemed to correspond to a product. Thus, one could envisage the relevant product market in political IOs, the relevant product market in military and defense IOs, the relevant product market in peace and security IOs, the relevant product market in technical IOs, the relevant product market in economic, financial and monetary IOs, the relevant product market in human rights IOs, and so on. If the scope of these relevant markets appears too broad, it should be explained that similar 'products' have been combined, in other words activities with considerably more similarities than dissimilarities have been grouped together. It is rather difficult to

---

13   The League of Arab States poses a problem: it has been placed in the relevant market of intra-regional IOs because its membership comes from both Africa and Asia. But if the Arab world is considered as a specific region, on account of the very strong common characteristics that it exhibits (language, religion, history), it could also be placed among the regional IOs. However, since it does not meet the two characteristics of the relevant market of regional IOs suggested here, it will be treated as an intra-regional IO.

categorize IOs in single product relevant markets, since their constitutive instruments may envisage different areas of activities and, through their evolutionary development, they could have acquired additional mandates.

Therefore, this grouping together will also be applied in the case of regional IOs which commenced with specific aims but, in the course of their life, have been endowed with other objectives belonging to different spheres of activities. A good case in point is the aforementioned African sub-regional IOs. As their name suggests, they started off with specific objectives placing them in the relevant product market of free trade / customs union / economic integration IOs. However, over the years, Member States decided to grant them powers and functions falling into the ambit of the relevant product market of peace and security and into the relevant product market of human rights. Arguably, their Member States could have established new and separate single product IOs, e.g. IOs for the protection and the promotion of human rights. In the event, they opted for significantly augmenting the role of existing IOs.[14] The same could be argued for the European Union, which, following the entry into force of the Lisbon Reform Treaty in 2009, has augmented its structures by firmly embedding a Common Foreign and Security Policy, including a Common Security and Defense Policy.[15] In these instances, it is clear that the relevant IOs will belong to more than one relevant product markets, a fact which should lead to increased competition.

Finally, in order to distinguish among the relevant product markets, the notion of 'global public goods' could be employed: one such global public good would correspond to a specific product market. This notion is a much augmented application of the concept of 'public goods', another concept emanating from the economics literature, projected to cover a global audience.[16] Examples of global public goods include human rights and fundamental freedoms, peace and security, and environmental protection. States may or may not be capable to offer them on an individual basis but (on account of the synergies achieved) IOs are definitely in a much better position to provide them.

---

14 Note that the ECOWAS and the SADC have courts of justice with jurisdiction to rule on alleged human rights violations, while the EAC is expected to adopt a protocol to that effect in the near future.

15 See Articles 23–46 of the Treaty on European Union (2009).

16 Generally, see I. Kaul, I. Grunberg and M.A. Stern (eds), *Global Public Goods: International Cooperation in the 21st Century* (United Nations Development Programme/Oxford University Press 1999); I. Kaul, P. Conceicao, K. Le Goulven and R.U. Mendoza (eds), *Providing Global Public Goods: Managing Globalization* (United Nations Development Programme/Oxford University Press 2003); and S. Barrett, *Why Cooperate? The Incentive to Supply Global Public Goods* (Oxford University Press 2007).

However, as the notion of global public goods is still rather underdeveloped,[17] it might be better to use the above categorization of IOs in order to distinguish among the various relevant product markets.

IV   Actual and Potential Competition between International Institutions

Having defined the 'relevant geographical market' and the 'relevant product market' as they apply to IOs, the next issue to be explored is 'actual competition' and 'potential competition', the two different forms through which competition is manifested. According to the former, two or more IOs are in a state of competition on account of having similar goals or because their activities are comparable and/or because they operate in the same relevant geographical market. Indeed, two or more IOs might be in direct competition because they were actually established as rivals (admittedly an infrequent phaenomenon). According to the latter, on account of their aims, functions, powers, membership, etc., two or more IOs might be considered as competitors but, for whatever reason, they have not entered into competition with each other (although this could happen in the future). Suffice to mention two explanations for this: the IOs in question have deliberately not engaged in competition or the opportunity has not yet arisen. In both instances there exists the possibility for competition and if the causes preventing them from being in competition lapse, the IOs in question could become actual competitors.

Actual competition does not necessarily mean that the IOs, which belong to a specific relevant market, take decisions and adopt policies solely behaving as rivals. To exemplify these arguments, the following four instances of actual competition will be cited. The first and second instances concern IOs, which were created during the Cold War by each of the then two ideological adversaries with the specific aim of acting as direct competitors. Thus, the creation of the North Atlantic Treaty Organization (NATO) by the Western group in 1949[18] was answered by the Eastern group with the establishment of the Warsaw Treaty Organization in the mid 1950s.[19] Moreover, the advances by the Eastern

---

17   Cf. D. Long and F. Woolley, "Global Public Goods: Critique of a UN Discourse" (2009) 15 *Global Governance* 107.
18   Established under the North Atlantic Treaty, concluded in Washington, D.C., 4 April 1949, 34 *UNTS* 243.
19   Established under the Treaty of Friendship, Cooperation and Mutual Assistance, concluded in Warsaw, Poland (the 'Warsaw Pact'), 1 May 1955, 219 *UNTS* 3.

group in Southeast Asia, prompted the creation of the Southeast Asia Treaty Organization (SEATO) also in the mid 1950s.[20] However, even before that, the creation of the Organization for European Economic Cooperation (OEEC) by the Western group in 1948 was answered, only the following year, with the creation of the Council of Mutual Economic Assistance (better known as COMECON).[21] Later on, COMECON would be called the 'European Economic Community of Eastern Europe',[22] a reference to the fact that it attempted to bring about (unsuccessfully as it turned out) the economic integration of its ten Member States.

The collapse of the Eastern group in the late 1980s–early 1990s rendered the Cold War objectless (no war can be fought by only one party and without rivals!). Even though the 'winners' of the Cold War chose to maintain NATO[23] and have since attempted to change its purposes and enlarge the geographical area of activities, the 'losers' did not have any further use for their own institutions and promptly disbanded them. Notwithstanding this development, in the period 1991–1992 the Russian Federation, taking advantage of being the most powerful state to emerge from the dissolution of the USSR, exerted considerable pressure on the other former Soviet republics, which were now referred to as the 'new democracies'. In the end, the pressure paid off. A new political/military/security IO, the CIS, was created.[24] It has attracted to membership states such as Georgia (it joined in December 1993) which would have

---

20   Established under the Southeast Asia Collective Defense Treaty, concluded in Manila, Philippines (the 'Manila Pact'), 8 September 1954, 209 *UNTS* 28. See A. Hall, "Anglo-US Relations in the Formation of SEATO" (2005) 5 *Stanford Journal of East Asian Affairs* 113.

21   Established under a Communiqué signed by the Soviet Union, Bulgaria, Czechoslovakia, Hungary, Poland, and Romania in Moscow on 25 January 1949. On 14 December 1959, a Charter was adopted, 368 *UNTS* 264, as well as a Convention on its legal personality, 368 *UNTS* 242. See R. Bideleux and I. Jeffries, *A History of Eastern Europe: Crisis and Change* (Routledge 1998) 534 et seq.

22   M.K. Goodrich, The Library of Congress Federal Research Division, *Country Studies: Germany, East (Former), Appendix B. The Council of Mutual Economic Assistance*, no date, at http://memory.loc.gov/frd/cs/germany_east/gx_appnb.html (accessed 1 October 2014).

23   As regards the OEEC, in 1961 it was transformed into the OECD, a completely different institution both in scope and in activities; it has since become a forum of loose economic cooperation among developed countries.

24   Established under the Agreement Establishing the Commonwealth of Independent States of 8 December 1991, (1992) 31 *ILM* 138, and the Alma-Ata Declaration and Protocol of 21 December 1991, (1992) 31 *ILM* 147. The CIS performs its activities on the basis of its Charter adopted on 22 January 1993, 1819 *UNTS* 37; (1995) 34 *ILM* 1279. See Z. Kembayev, *Legal Aspects of the Regional Integration Processes in the Post-Soviet Area* (Springer 2009) 25–94.

ideally preferred to stay away due to animosity with the Russian Federation.[25] The CIS, together with other IOs of the sub-regional type (e.g. the Collective Security Treaty Organization (CSTO))[26] could be regarded as NATO's competitors.

The third instance concerns (in chronological order of creation) the Western European Union (WEU)[27] and NATO, two regional IOs belonging to the same relevant product market (that of mutual defense IOs). They both belonged to the Western group and were basically established to address the threat of the Eastern group at a time when Europe was divided along ideological lines. Quite predictably, they had overlapping membership.[28] In the event, the WEU never managed to operate as an ardent competitor to NATO (perhaps there was no room for more than one IO in that specific market) and, despite the occasional bloodline administered in the 1980s and some security activities carried out in the 1990s, it fell into disuse. It was finally absorbed by a (remotely) potential competitor, the European Union, in a move that could be described as mergers and acquisitions (M&A). As a treaty-based IO, the WEU ceased functioning on 30 June 2011.[29]

The fourth instance concerns the European Economic Community (EEC) and its successor the European Union (EU), on the one hand, and the European Free Trade Association (EFTA), on the other hand. Both IOs belong in the same relevant geographic market and relevant product market, namely that of European regional economic integration. They have co-existed since the early 1960s when the United Kingdom, having been left outside the EEC due to French opposition, was instrumental in forming EFTA as a rival IO under its leadership.[30] However, EFTA proved unable to match the services and benefits

---

25   Note that Georgia withdrew from the CIS in August 2009 citing the occupation of part of its territory by the Russian Federation in August 2008.

26   Established in May 1992 and currently operating under its Charter concluded in Kishinev, Moldova, 7 October 2002, 2235 *UNTS* 79.

27   Established under the Treaty of Economic, Social, and Cultural Collaboration and Collective Self-Defense, concluded in Brussels, Belgium ('Treaty of Brussels'), 17 March 1948, 19 *UNTS* 51.

28   The Treaty of Brussels has been regarded as a stepping stone for the conclusion of the North Atlantic Treaty, see NATO Public Diplomacy Division, *NATO Handbook* (NATO Publications 2006) 17.

29   See European Union, *Council Decision 2011/297/CFSP of 23 May 2011 amending Joint Action 2001/555/CFSP on the establishment of a European Union Satellite Centre*, Official Journal of the European Union, L 136 of 24 May 2011, p. 62.

30   Established under the Treaty on European Free Trade Association, concluded in Stockholm, Sweden, 4 January 1960, 370 *UNTS* 3.

that its competitor was offering to its own Member States. EFTA lacked the vision and the audacity that has turned the EEC/ EU into the most successful IO ever. The United Kingdom withdrew from EFTA in 1972 in order to join the EEC in January 1973, since membership in the latter was incompatible with continued participation in the former. Five other EFTA Members followed suit for the same reason (in alphabetical order): Austria, Denmark, Finland, Sweden, and Portugal. Until today, EFTA has survived the competition in the relevant product market presumably because the current membership (Island, Liechtenstein, Norway, and Switzerland) prefers this kind of multilateral institution as being more appropriate to its needs.[31] On the other hand, due to its small membership, there exists no real competition with the EU in the relevant geographic market.

Examples of potential competition include, on the one hand, the OPEC[32] and the Organization of Arab Petroleum Exporting Countries (OAPEC),[33] and, on the other hand, the United Nations, the Group of 77 and the Non-Aligned Movement (examined in more detail later). In the former case there is a considerable overlap in membership (eight out of the ten OAPEC Members are among the 12 OPEC Member States) as well as in purpose (both operate as oil cartels aiming at ensuring the best prices for participating states). For these reasons it would be difficult to be direct competitors and, had it not been for the apparent desire to maintain the 'Arab' character of the OAPEC, there would be no adequate reasons to keep it alive.

V Competition between International Institutions in Specific Relevant Product Markets

Over and above the existence of competition between IOs as a whole (i.e. one IO competing with another IO or with a number of IOs in all spheres of endeavour), one could also envisage IOs acting as competitors in specific relevant product markets. Three such illustrations will be given.

---

31 K. Magliveras, "Membership in International Organizations" in J. Klabbers and Åsa Wallendahl (eds), *Research Handbook on the Law of International Organizations* (Edward Elgar Publishing 2011) 84, 99.

32 Established by the Baghdad Conference in September 1960, which adopted its Statute, 443 *UNTS* 247; (1965) 4 *ILM* 1175.

33 Established under the Agreement the establishment of the Arab Organization for the Petroleum Exporting States, concluded in Beirut, Lebanon, 9 January 1968, 681 *UNTS* 235; (1968) 7 ILM 759.

The first illustration concerns the 'relevant product market in the international protection and promotion of human rights and humanitarian law'. Currently, there is an impressive number of organs and entities active in this market. They could be categorized as follows: the entities operating on a global scale under United Nations' auspices;[34] the human rights courts operating at a regional level[35] as well as the regional human rights commissions;[36] and the International Criminal Court (ICC). Arguably, all of them compete with each other in the relevant product market of safeguarding fundamental freedoms, sheltering individuals from human rights abuses, and preventing breaches of humanitarian law (broadly defined). Most of them have the power, subject to a number of conditions, to receive and to adjudicate inter-state complaints as well as (subject to stricter prerequisites) individual complaints alleging that human rights violations have taken place within the territory of a contracting state.[37]

To demonstrate competition in this relevant product market,[38] suppose that a number of victims of human rights' abuse meet the criteria for bringing complaints before any of these bodies and entities. With the obvious limitation that a complaint may not be filed before a regional human rights court or

---

34   This group comprises (a) the Human Rights Council, which was set up in March 2006 by the UN General Assembly under Resolution 60/251 and replaced the Commission on Human Rights, and (b) the so-called 'treaty bodies', namely the ten entities established under human rights treaties adopted under UN auspices, see www.ohchr.org/EN/HRBOdies/Pages/HumanRightsBodies.aspx (accessed 1 October 2014).

35   This group comprises principally the European Court of Human Rights, the Inter-American Court of Human Rights and the African Court on Human and Peoples' Rights. However other regional courts exist whose judgments, depending on the circumstances, could have a human rights dimension, e.g. the Court of Justice of the European Union and the entities mentioned in note 14.

36   E.g. the Inter-American Commission of Human Rights, the African Commission on Human and Peoples' Rights, the Arab Human Rights Committee, Independent Permanent Human Rights Commission of the Organization of Islamic Cooperation and the ASEAN Intergovernmental Commission on Human Rights. Note that their functions and powers vary considerably.

37   Note that the UN Human Rights Council may only receive individual complaints, while the ICC cannot receive actionable complaints by individuals and states cannot be defendants before it.

38   Cf. N. Rodley, "The United Nations Human Rights Council, Its Special Procedure, and its Relationship with the Treaty Bodies: Complementarity or Competition?" in K. Boyle (ed.), *New Institutions for Human Rights Protection* (Oxford University Press 2009) 49. Note that the UN General Assembly initiated intergovernmental process for strengthening the effective functioning of the human rights treaty body culminated to Resolution 68/268 of 9 April 2014.

before a treaty body in which the state where the alleged abuse took place does not participate, the victims may choose among different options. For example, if they were victims of slavery in an African state, they should be able to lodge complaints (a) before the African Court on Human and Peoples' Rights, (b) before two UN treaty bodies (the Human Rights Committee and the Committee against Torture), and (c) before the judicial organ of certain African sub-regional organizations. Thus, competition offers choice to victims. If there was only one relevant entity (i.e. monopoly), the choice would be curtailed and, if there was only one entity with dominant position, which it abused, the choice could be negated.

Theoretically speaking, the victims, being faced with a number of choices, will look into the qualities and benefits that each of the relevant bodies and entities (viewed as competitors) has to offer before lodging a complaint.[39] The qualities that would make a competitor stand out include: its overall effectiveness; the easiness of the application process and the speedy completion of proceedings; the proximity of the entity to the applicants-victims; the opportunities it offers as regards restitution, compensation and other forms of satisfaction; and the impact of its decisions. An evaluation based on these criteria should lead the victims opting for different entities.

The second illustration concerns the competition in the 'relevant product market of international fact-finding and inquiry'. It is made up of smaller markets, one of them being the relevant product market of international fact-finding and inquiry for violations of human rights and humanitarian law. Of the diverse services, which could be offered by permanent or by ad-hoc institutions and entities,[40] suffice to mention the following: the (permanent) International Humanitarian Fact-Finding Commission, which has been recognized by more than 70 states;[41] the (ad hoc) bodies set up by the UN Human Rights Council (e.g. the United Nations Fact Finding Mission on the Gaza Conflict in

---

[39] Note that competition is invariably curtailed by the rule that the same complaint cannot be adjudicated at the same time by different entities; a rule of exclusivity is applied.

[40] For a list of missions instituted to investigate violations of humanitarian law and human rights during international and domestic armed conflicts since the end of World War II, see Harvard University, Program on Humanitarian Policy and Conflict Research, Monitoring, Reporting, and Fact-Finding Digital Library, at www.hpcrresearch.org/mrf-database (accessed 1 October 2014).

[41] Established pursuant to Article 90 of the Protocol Additional to the Geneva Conventions of 12 August 1949, and relating to the Protection of Victims of International Armed Conflicts (Protocol I), 8 June 1977, 1125 *UNTS* 3.

2009,[42] the Independent International Commission of Inquiry on the Syrian Arab Republic in 2011[43] or the International Fact-Finding Mission on Israeli Settlements in the Occupied Palestinian Territory in 2012)[44]; the (ad hoc) fact finding commissions established by the European Union (e.g. the Independent International Fact-Finding Mission on the Conflict in Georgia in 2008/9)[45]; and the (ad hoc) commissions set up by the African Commission on Human and Peoples' Rights (e.g. the Fact-Finding Mission to the Republic of Sudan in the Darfur Region in 2004/5).[46]

The competition in this relevant product market lies in that states, in order to investigate particular situations and events and instead of undertaking this task themselves, have the option to choose, depending on the circumstances, between different mechanisms and show their preference for a specific mechanism over the others. For the sake of argument, if the signatory parties to the African Charter on Human and Peoples' Rights, the instrument that has created the namesake Commission, wish to investigate post-election violence that led to human rights abuses in an African country and had spill-over effects in other states as well, they might opt to approach the UN Human Rights Council and not the African Commission because they believe that the former offers more competitive advantages than the latter.

The third illustration concerns the 'relevant product market in the judicial settlement of international disputes'. Again, this is a very broad market and, for present purposes, reference will be made to the 'relevant product market in the judicial settlement of international disputes relating to the law of the sea'. Assuming that the states to the dispute fulfil the required substantive and procedural requirements and depending on the nature of the dispute, they could submit their dispute to one of the following institutions and entities: (a) the International Court of Justice; (b) the International Court of the Law of the

---

[42] Established under Resolution S-9/1 of 12 January 2009, at http://www.ohchr.org/EN/HRBodies/HRC/SpecialSessions/Session9/Pages/FactFindingMission.aspx (accessed 20 March 2015).

[43] Established under Resolution S-17/1 of 22 August 2011, at www.ohchr.org/EN/HRBodies/HRC/IICISyria/Pages/IndependentInternationalCommission.aspx (accessed 1 October 2014).

[44] Established under Resolution 19/17 of 22 March 2012, at www.ohchr.org/EN/HRBodies/HRC/RegularSessions/Session19/Pages/IsraeliSettlementsInTheOPT.aspx (accessed 1 October 2014).

[45] Established under Council Decision 2008/901/CFSP of 2 December 2008 concerning an independent international fact-finding mission on the conflict in Georgia, Official Journal of the European Union, L 323, 3 December 2008, p. 66.

[46] Established under Resolution ACHPR/Res. 68 (XXXV) 04, adopted by the 35th Ordinary Session on 4 June 2004.

Sea;[47] (c) the (general) arbitral tribunals envisaged in Annex VII of the Convention on the Law of the Sea; (d) the (special) arbitral tribunals envisaged in Annex VIII of the Convention on the Law of the Sea; or (e) to an (ad hoc) arbitral tribunal of the own liking.

The ability of litigant parties to choose the jurisdiction or the venue of the judicial mechanism to settle their disputes is usually referred to as 'forum shopping'. Traditionally, forum shopping has not been viewed favourably (especially in domestic judicial proceedings), because it allows a litigant to exploit the rules so as to affect (or at least to attempt to affect) the outcome of the proceedings.[48] Notwithstanding the advantages or disadvantages of forum shopping,[49] what it shows is that there exists competition between judicial methods of dispute resolution and that customers (in casu, the states to a dispute) have the ability to opt for one institution over another. Thus, states could choose a specific institution because they believe that, on the basis of its earlier jurisprudence, it will render a decision closer to their argumentation or because its decisions ordering interim measures are treated as mandatory[50] or because they will have the benefit of an ad hoc judge of their own choosing[51] or because (in the case of ad hoc arbitral tribunals) they wish the dispute and its settlement to remain undisclosed, etc.

Arguably, there is nothing wrong when states try to preserve their rights by choosing the mechanism that they feel would serve best their interests. It is up to the judicial mechanisms themselves, on the one hand, to win over litigant parties by persuading them that they are the only appropriate venue and, on

---

[47] See Articles 279 and 287 of the Convention on the Law of the Sea (1982), 1833 UNTS 3.

[48] F.K. Juenger, "The Internationalization of Law and Legal Practice: Forum Shopping, Domestic and International" (1989) 63 *Tulane Law Review* 553.

[49] Note that, according to Article 344 of the Treaty for the Functioning of the European Union (2009), Member States have undertaken not to submit disputes concerning its interpretation or application to methods of settlement other than those provided for therein; see European Court of Justice, Case C-459/03, *Commission v. Ireland*, Judgment of 20 May 2006, [2006] ECR I-4635, concerning this obligation *vis-à-vis* the dispute settlement method envisaged in the Convention on the Law of the Sea.

[50] For the International Court of the Law of the Sea, see Article 290(6) Convention on the Law of the Sea. Even though Article 41 of the Statute of the International Court of Justice does not stipulate expressly the binding nature of interim measures' orders, the ICJ has held that they enjoy mandatory character: *LaGrand (Germany v. United States of America)*, Judgment of 27 June 2001, [2001] *International Court of Justice Reports* 466, paras 99–103; *Application of the Convention on the Prevention and Punishment of the Crime of Genocide (Bosnia and Herzegovina v. Serbia and Montenegro)*, Judgment of 26 February 2007, [2007] *International Court of Justice Reports* 43, paras 452, 468.

[51] Cf. Article 31 of the Statute of the International Court of Justice.

the other hand, to minimize the negative effects of forum shopping. If states, which have the ability to choose among the available mechanisms, regarded them as competing institutions and showed their clear preference for a specific mechanism, the latter would acquire a dominant position in the relevant product market. In such circumstances, the other institutions would have to make the services they offer more competitive, if they wanted to remain players in the relevant market.

VI The Question of Market Entry

A further important issue in competition law and policy is the existence of adequate 'market entry', namely the ability of new players to gain entry and compete in an existing market and the obligation of those entities already in the market in question not to take measures (the so called 'concerted practices') to prevent it. As will be later explained, if the market in question is a monopoly, the price that a new player will have to pay could be prohibitive. This will discourage the entry of new players and, consequently, will perpetuate the existence of the monopoly.[52] Put into context, entry in the market of IOs has two manifestations. The first concerns the possibilities existing for new IOs to enter into a relevant geographic and product market or for existing IOs to enter into a market different from the one in which they are already active. The second concerns the difficulties that such IOs might face as a result of actions, which are orchestrated by those IOs already operating in that particular relevant market and attempting to maintain their power.[53]

As an illustration of market entry in the relevant geographic market of global IOs and in the relevant product market of political IOs, currently dominated by the United Nations, one could mention the Group of 77 and the Non-Aligned Movement. The former was created in June 1964 when 77 developing countries signed a Joint Declaration at the end of the first session of the United Nations Conference on Trade and Development (UNCTAD).[54] Three years later, a ministerial level meeting in Algiers adopted the namesake Charter.[55] Over time, a

---

52   Monopolies per se are neither prohibited nor are they a bad thing. However, abusing their position in the relevant market is.
53   B.S. Frey, "Outside and Inside Competition for International Organizations – From Analysis to Innovations" (2008) 3 *The Review of International Organizations* 335. The author refers to the 'costs to enter' for an IO on a particular market (pp. 338 et seq.) but does not explain what these costs consist of.
54   Text at http://www.g77.org/doc/Joint%20Declaration.html (accessed 1 October 2014).
55   Text at www.g77.org/doc/algier~1.htm (accessed 1 October 2014).

permanent institutional structure has emerged, which is characterized by the existence of Chapters in various capital cities, which happen to be the headquarters of UN Specialized Agencies or UN subsidiary organs: Rome (seat of the Food and Agriculture Organization (FAO)), Vienna (seat of the UN Industrial Development Organization (UNIDO)), Paris (seat of UNESCO), Nairobi (seat of the UN Environment Programme (UNEP)), and Washington, D.C. (seat of both the International Monetary Fund (IMF) and the World Bank). The Group of 77, with a current membership of 134 states, operates as a 'soft IO' and assists the developing world, on the one hand, to articulate and promote its collective economic interests and, on the other hand, to enhance its joint negotiating capacity on all major international issues within the UN system. The Group of 77 not only operates as a pressure group with unrivalled force due to its vast membership in the UN Assembly and its six Committees but also in other UN organs. It also produces action programmes and agreements on development issues. To that extent, it could act as a competitor to the United Nations, provided that it is endowed with formal structures and mechanisms.

The Non-Aligned Movement (NAM) is older than the Group of 77. It was established in September 1961 as the brainchild of India's Nehru, Indonesia's Sukarno, Egypt's Nasser, Ghana's Nkrumah, and Yugoslavia's Tito.[56] The NAM, with a current membership of 118 states, was originally concerned, as its name reveals, with the consequences of the race between the Soviet Union and the USA in acquiring spheres of influence. The subsequent augmentation of its membership with countries of the developing world gave to the NAM a specific political agenda, which centered on the denunciation of Western colonialism and foreign military installations. When the East-West antagonism receded in the early 1990s, the NAM moved its focus on economic and social problems and the relation between North and South. The NAM could also act as a competitor to the United Nations. Given that there is considerable overlap with the Group of 77 (both in terms of membership and mandate) these two institutions could not be considered as competitors but as two interchangeable institutions operating in the similar relevant geographic and products markets.

The fact that in the 1960s the Group of 77 and the NAM entered into the relevant geographic market of global IOs could indicate that there was adequate competition at the time. On the contrary, the fact that since then there has been no 'market penetration' by other IOs in the same relevant market might be an indication that the United Nations is abusing its dominant

---

56   See the Declaration of Belgrade of 6 September 1961 at http://namiran.org/wp-content/uploads/2013/04/Declarations-of-All-Previous-NAM-Summits.pdf (accessed 20 March 2015).

position and has been raising obstacles to market entry and unhindered competition. Or it could be an indication that the United Nations has become such an effective IO that no group of states would seriously undertake to set up a new IO to act as competitor. In these circumstances, the cost of establishing a new IO is deemed to exceed significantly the benefits that could be expected from competing with the United Nations. As a result, to create a new IO does not appear to be a viable proposition. At the same time, it has long been recognized that the United Nations is in need of fundamental reform which, however, has not been materialized. As has been argued, the 'sclerosis of reform' inside the United Nations could be met by resorting to outside competition,[57] which arguably could mean, due to the current lack of other international institutions with near-universal participation, the Group of 77 and the NAM.

VII Conclusions

The present contribution has discussed the existence of competition between international organizations and institutions and has demonstrated how the principles of competition law are applied. Unlike companies competing in a given relevant market, IOs do not necessarily aim at engaging in competition with each other. However, at the end of the day, open IOs strive to enlarge their membership basis. On the other hand, the very large number of IOs which characterizes the contemporary international community offers states a plethora of choices. In many areas of activities, states have the ability to choose which IO to join. Leaving aside considerations that have to do with foreign policy, it is only logical that states will opt to participate in those IOs, which have shown a very strong performance and have acquired a dominant position or even a monopoly. At the same time, the existing Members of an IO may withdraw from it in order to join another IO lured by its stellar performance and the significant benefits afforded to its membership. There has always been undisputed dynamism in the relations among IOs, which could be examined from the point of view of the law of competition.

---

57   R. Wedgwood, "Give the United Nations a Little Competition", *The New York Times*, 5 December 2005, at www.nytimes.com (accessed on 17 October 2013).

PART 4

International Criminal Law and Humanitarian Law

CHAPTER 16

The International Court of Justice and International Humanitarian Law

Christopher Greenwood

Introduction

It is a personal pleasure, as well as an honour, to have been invited to contribute to this collection of essays in honour of my friend and former colleague, Abdul Koroma. I had the privilege of serving on the International Court of Justice during the last three years of Abdul's eighteen years as a Judge but our friendship stems from a much earlier date. Not long after Abdul was elected to the Court, he and I attended a conference on humanitarian law held at the Kurhaus in Scheveningen. It was there that we met and that I first experienced the warmth and generosity which Abdul showed to younger colleagues. My most abiding memory of the conference is of the conversation which I had with him – as we both held on to the passenger straps on a crowded tram going from the Kurhaus to the Peace Palace – during which he shared with me some of his experiences in working on the implementation of international humanitarian law and gave me what proved to be some excellent career advice. When I was elected to the Court, many years later, I mentioned this conversation to him and was touched to find that he also remembered it.

In view of Abdul Koroma's longstanding commitment to international humanitarian law and his many years of service to the International Court of Justice, it seemed fitting that one of the essays in the present volume should focus on the impact which the jurisprudence of the Court has had on that particular body of international law. It is the more appropriate because, although the Court had touched on various issues of international humanitarian law before Abdul Koroma became a Judge in February 1994, its most important contributions to the subject to date are to be found in a series of judgments and advisory opinions given between 1994 and 2012. It is on those that this essay will concentrate. It is not my intention to attempt a comprehensive survey. That has already been most successfully carried out by Professor Kreß in his chapter in a recent work on the Court.[1] Rather, after a brief survey of the case law, this

---

[1] C. Kreß, "The International Court of Justice and the Law of Armed Conflicts" in C. Tams and J. Sloan (eds.), *The Development of International Law by the International Court of Justice* (Oxford, 2013), p. 263.

essay will concentrate upon three themes which run through the work of the Court on international humanitarian law and which seem to me to be of particular importance.

1 The Jurisprudence of the Court on International Humanitarian Law

A *The Early Cases*
Corfu Channel

The International Court of Justice addressed questions of humanitarian law came on two occasions before 1994. In the *Corfu Channel* case,[2] the United Kingdom brought proceedings against Albania concerning the loss of two British warships which struck mines in Albanian territorial waters while the ships were passing through the Corfu Channel. The United Kingdom alleged that the mines were laid "by or with the connivance or knowledge of the Albanian Government" or that "the Albanian Government knew that the said minefield was lying in a part of its territorial waters" and that, in either event, "the Albanian Government did not notify the existence of these mines as required by the Hague Convention VIII of 1907 in accordance with the general principles of international law and humanity".[3] The Court did not base its judgment on the Convention, which it considered applicable only in time of war, but on "certain well-recognized principles", amongst which it included "elementary considerations of humanity, even more exacting in peace than in war".[4] That approach is hardly surprising. The terms of the Convention make clear that it was intended to apply in time of war and, even then, only when all the belligerents were parties to the Convention.[5] There was no suggestion that the United Kingdom was at war with Albania[6] and Albania was not party to the

---

2   *Corfu Channel Case (United Kingdom v. Albania) (Merits), Judgment of 9th April 1949*, ICJ Reports 1949, p. 4.
3   ICJ Reports 1949, p. 10.
4   ICJ Reports 1949, p. 22.
5   Hague Convention VIII, Article 7.
6   Today, the prevailing view is that the 1907 Conventions on the laws of war, or, at least, the customary international law principles which they codify, are applicable to an international armed conflict irrespective of whether there is a formal state of war; see C. Greenwood, "The Concept of War in Modern International Law", 36 *International and Comparative Law Quarterly* (1987), p. 283. Since the British warships were asserting a right of passage through the Corfu Channel following an earlier incident in which British warships had been fired on by Albanian artillery, an interesting question might have arisen as

Convention. Reference to the Convention was, nevertheless, a clear indication that the United Kingdom considered that the Convention was still in force and that its provisions reflected rules of customary international law. It was also an affirmation by the United Kingdom that the laws of war (as international humanitarian law was then more commonly known) remained valid and effective in the era of the United Nations Charter, notwithstanding suggestions that the Charter had superseded that body of law.[7] The passing reference to the Convention in the Judgment appears to endorse the view that it continued to be valid and effective.

Military and Paramilitary Activities in and against Nicaragua

That reference to general humanitarian principles was taken up by the Court forty years later in *Military and Paramilitary Activities in and against Nicaragua*.[8] While the main focus of that case was on the compatibility of United States action with the customary international law regarding recourse to force,[9] Nicaragua also made allegations about the mining of Nicaraguan ports and the commission of atrocities by the US-sponsored "*contra*" rebels. Nicaragua did not, however, allege that it was engaged in an armed conflict and did not accuse the United States of violations of international humanitarian law as such.[10] The Court nevertheless held that:

> The conflict between the *contras'* forces and those of the Government of Nicaragua is an armed conflict which is "not of an international character". The acts of the *contras* towards the Nicaraguan Government are therefore governed by the law applicable to conflicts of that character; whereas the actions of the United States in and against Nicaragua fall under the legal rules relating to international conflicts.[11]

---

to whether there was an armed conflict between the two States, especially in view of the very broad definition of armed conflict favoured by the International Committee of the Red Cross: "any difference between two States and leading to the intervention of members of the armed forces is an armed conflict" (J. Pictet (ed), *Commentary to Geneva Convention III Relative to the Treatment of Prisoners of War* (ICRC, 1960, p. 23).

7   For consideration of that question, see H. Lauterpacht, "The Problem of the Revision of the Law of War", 30 *British Yearbook of International Law* (1952), p. 206.
8   *Military and Paramilitary Activities in and against Nicaragua (Nicaragua v. United States of America) (Merits), Judgment of 27 June 1986,* ICJ Reports 1986, p. 3.
9   The Court was unable to apply the relevant provisions of the Charter for jurisdictional reasons; see ICJ Reports 1986, pp. 92–97.
10 ICJ Reports 1986, p. 112, para. 216.
11 ICJ Reports 1986, p. 114, para. 219.

By implication, the Court thus found that there were two separate armed conflicts – one of an international and the other an internal character – existing in parallel. Nevertheless, it avoided the need to explore the resulting differences between the substantive humanitarian law applicable to the international conflict and that applicable to the internal conflict by characterising the provisions of common Article 3 of the 1949 Geneva Conventions (which apply to conflicts "not of an international character occurring in the territory of one of the High Contracting Parties") as "a minimum yardstick" applicable to any armed conflict, whether international or non-international in character.[12] Referring back to the *Corfu Channel* case, the Court also found that those provisions "reflect what the Court in 1949 called 'elementary considerations of humanity'".[13] That finding, which amounted to a decision that the provisions of Article 3 had acquired the status of rules of customary international law, rendered it unnecessary for the Court to consider whether the United States' multilateral treaty reservation meant that it lacked jurisdiction to apply the provisions of the Geneva Conventions. On the mining of harbours, the Court followed the same approach taken in the *Corfu Channel* case. Rather than applying the provisions of Hague Convention VIII as such,[14] the Court found the United States to have committed "a breach of the principles of humanitarian law underlying the specific provisions of Convention No. VIII of 1907".[15]

Neither *Corfu Channel* nor *Nicaragua* can be regarded as making a major contribution to the development of international humanitarian law. In *Corfu Channel* a treaty on the laws of war at sea was invoked by the Applicant but in circumstances where its provisions were not directly applicable and the Court (like the United Kingdom) considered those provisions important more by way of analogy, or as an example in the context of war of more general principles applicable at all times. In *Nicaragua,* the Court invoked the principles of international humanitarian law even though the Applicant State had not invited it to do so. Its finding that the provisions of Article 3 – undoubtedly an innovation when they were adopted in 1949 – had become declaratory of customary international law was significant, though hardly surprising. The reference to those provisions as "a minimum yardstick" and the Court's subsequent reliance upon that yardstick meant that the judgment did not develop the law applicable to international armed conflicts.

---

12 ICJ Reports 1986, p. 114, para. 218. Neither Nicaragua nor the United States was at that time party to the Additional Protocols to the 1949 Geneva Conventions.
13 Loc. cit.
14 Both Nicaragua and the United States were parties to Hague Convention VIII.
15 ICJ Reports 1986, p. 112, para. 215.

B Cases in the Period 1994–2012

By contrast, the period in which Abdul Koroma served as a judge of the Court saw the Court squarely confronted with some of the most difficult questions of international humanitarian law in three major cases. That challenge began almost as soon as Judge Koroma took office.

Nuclear Weapons

In December 1994 the General Assembly asked the International Court of Justice to give an advisory opinion on the question –

> Is the threat or use of nuclear weapons in any circumstances permitted under international law?[16]

For the first time, therefore, the Court was confronted with a case in which international humanitarian law occupied the central position.[17] The question posed by the General Assembly also, of course, involved other areas of international law. The Court naturally emphasised that the threat or use of nuclear weapons would be unlawful if it was contrary to the principles of the *jus ad bellum* enshrined in the United Nations Charter, although it rejected an argument that any use of nuclear weapons would inevitably amount to a disproportionate use of force and thus be incapable of constituting an exercise of the right of self-defence preserved by Article 51 of the Charter.[18] The Court also considered the relevance of international human rights law and international environmental law (a matter to which we shall return in the next part of this chapter). But the Court was clear that the principal focus had to be on international humanitarian law.[19]

Most of the Opinion was, therefore, devoted to a consideration of international humanitarian law. Three points stand out in the Court's analysis. First, the Court rejected the argument that there had emerged a specific rule of in-

---

16 *Legality of the Threat or Use of Nuclear Weapons (Request by the United Nations General Assembly for an Advisory Opinion)*, ICJ Reports 1996, p. 226.

17 For a collection of different views on the Court's advisory opinion, see Boisson de Chazournes and Sands, *International Law, the International Court of Justice and Nuclear Weapons* (1999). The present author contributed a chapter to that volume, op. cit., pp. 247–266.

18 *Legality of the Threat or Use of Nuclear Weapons (Request by the United Nations General Assembly for an Advisory Opinion)*, ICJ Reports 1996, p. 245, para. 43.

19 *Legality of the Threat or Use of Nuclear Weapons (Request by the United Nations General Assembly for an Advisory Opinion)*, ICJ Reports 1996, p. 243, para. 34.

ternational humanitarian law prohibiting all use of nuclear weapons.[20] No such prohibition could be deduced from treaties which restricted particular activities concerned with nuclear weapons, such as the ban on atmospheric nuclear tests or the creation of zones in which States agreed not to deploy nuclear weapons.[21] The Court also rejected the theory that nuclear weapons were somehow included within the prohibitions of poisons and chemical weapons. Although this theory had been popular in some quarters for many years,[22] the Court dismissed it as incompatible with the understanding of the terms used at the times the relevant treaties were concluded, as well as with the subsequent practice of the parties to those treaties.[23] Finally, the Court held that no customary humanitarian law rule had emerged specifically banning nuclear weapons. In this context, the Court acknowledged the importance of the series of General Assembly resolutions on the subject, which the Court held "reveals the desire of a very large section of the international community to take, by a specific and express prohibition of the use of nuclear weapons, a significant step forward along the road to complete nuclear disarmament".[24] Nevertheless, the Court noted that none of the resolutions concerned suggested that there was a specific prohibition of nuclear weapons in customary international law and that the support which they had received had to be balanced against the substantial opposition they had attracted and the other instances of State practice which contradicted the existence of such a rule. The Court concluded –

> The emergence, as *lex lata,* of a customary rule specifically prohibiting the use of nuclear weapons as such is hampered by the continuing tensions between the nascent *opinio juris* on the one hand, and the still strong adherence to the practice of deterrence on the other.[25]

---

20   *Legality of the Threat or Use of Nuclear Weapons (Request by the United Nations General Assembly for an Advisory Opinion)*, ICJ Reports 1996, p. 266, para. 105(E); this paragraph of the *dispositive* was adopted by eleven votes to three, Judge Koroma being one of the dissenters.

21   *Legality of the Threat or Use of Nuclear Weapons (Request by the United Nations General Assembly for an Advisory Opinion)*, ICJ Reports 1996, pp. 248–253, paras 59–63.

22   See, e.g., Nagendra Singh, *Nuclear Weapons and International Law* (1959).

23   *Legality of the Threat or Use of Nuclear Weapons (Request by the United Nations General Assembly for an Advisory Opinion)*, ICJ Reports 1996, p. 248, paras 53–57.

24   *Legality of the Threat or Use of Nuclear Weapons (Request by the United Nations General Assembly for an Advisory Opinion)*, ICJ Reports 1996, p. 255, para. 73.

25   *Legality of the Threat or Use of Nuclear Weapons (Request by the United Nations General Assembly for an Advisory Opinion)*, ICJ Reports 1996, p. 255, para. 73.

Secondly, the Court held that the general principles of international humanitarian law were applicable to the use of nuclear weapons, even though those principles had become part of customary international law before nuclear weapons technology came into existence.[26] In doing so, the Court rejected an argument once vigorously advanced by a number of States and writers, that the use of nuclear weapons would be something that lay outside the scope of international humanitarian law unless and until States concluded a treaty to prohibit or regulate that use.[27] The Court thus found that the use of nuclear weapons, like the use of any other weapon, in armed conflict was subject to the principle of distinction and the prohibition of unnecessary suffering.[28] In doing so, it made reference to the famous Martens clause.[29] The Court did not, however, base any findings upon this provision and its failure to do so suggests it did not accept the suggestion that the Martens Clause is the basis for freestanding obligations which find no other expression in international humanitarian law. The Court also found that the use of nuclear weapons was subject to the principle of neutrality, in respect of which the Court said –

> ... international law leaves no doubt that the principle of neutrality, whatever its content, which is of a fundamental character similar to that of the humanitarian principles and rules, is applicable (subject to the relevant provisions of the United Nations Charter) to all international armed conflict, whatever type of weapons might be used.[30]

This brief passage may prove to have been a little too concise. The Court was concerned with that part of the law of neutrality which prohibits the use of force by a belligerent on the territory of a neutral. That principle is undoubt-

---

26 *Legality of the Threat or Use of Nuclear Weapons (Request by the United Nations General Assembly for an Advisory Opinion)*, ICJ Reports 1996, p. 259, paras 85–6.
27 It is noticeable, however, that none of the 33 States which participated in the proceedings chose to advance this argument.
28 *Legality of the Threat or Use of Nuclear Weapons (Request by the United Nations General Assembly for an Advisory Opinion)*, ICJ Reports 1996, pp. 257–9, paras 78–84.
29 This clause, which first appeared in the Hague Convention II with respect to the Laws and Customs of War on Land, 1899, takes modern form in Article 1(2) of 1977 Additional Protocol I to the 1949 Geneva Conventions: "In cases not covered by this Protocol or by other international agreements, civilians and combatants remain under the protection and authority of the principles of international law derived from established custom, from the principles of humanity and from the dictates of the public conscience".
30 *Legality of the Threat or Use of Nuclear Weapons (Request by the United Nations General Assembly for an Advisory Opinion)*, ICJ Reports 1996, p. 261, para. 89.

edly applicable to any international armed conflict. However, whether it extends to belligerent acts outside neutral territory which cause harm within neutral territory is more questionable and the Court's refusal to indicate the content of the principle may lead to difficulties in the future. Moreover, examination of State practice since 1945 (during which time very few armed conflicts have had the formal status of war) suggests that most States do not consider themselves bound to apply other principles of the law of neutrality[31] in the absence of a state of war.

Thirdly, when the Court came to apply these principles to a possible use of nuclear weapons, its conclusion was equivocal. After examining the arguments advanced on each side of the debate, the Court explained that it lacked a sufficient basis for a determination of the validity of the view that the use of tactical nuclear weapons might be lawful. The Court went on to state –

> Nor can the Court make a determination of the validity of the view that the recourse to nuclear weapons would be illegal in any circumstance owing to their inherent and total incompatibility with the law applicable in armed conflict. Certainly, as the Court has already indicated, the principles and rules of law applicable in armed conflict – at the heart of which is the overriding consideration of humanity – make the conduct of armed hostilities subject to a number of strict requirements. Thus, methods and means of warfare, which would preclude any distinction between civilian and military targets, or which would result in unnecessary suffering to combatants, are prohibited. In view of the unique characteristics of nuclear weapons ... the use of such weapons in fact seems scarcely reconcilable with respect for such requirements. Nevertheless, the Court considers that it does not have sufficient elements to enable it to conclude with certainty that the use of nuclear weapons would necessarily be at variance with the principles and rules of law applicable in armed conflict in any circumstance.[32]

The Court concluded that –

> Accordingly, in view of the present state of international law viewed as a whole, as examined above by the Court, and of the elements of fact at its disposal, the Court is led to observe that it cannot reach a definitive

---

[31] For example, those limiting the use of neutral harbours by belligerent warships or imposing a duty of impartiality upon neutrals.

[32] *Legality of the Threat or Use of Nuclear Weapons (Request by the United Nations General Assembly for an Advisory Opinion)*, ICJ Reports 1996, pp. 262–3, para. 95.

conclusion as to the legality or illegality of the use of nuclear weapons by a State in an extreme circumstance of self-defence, in which its very survival would be at stake.[33]

That conclusion was then reflected, albeit in slightly different language, in paragraph (E) of the *dispositif*, in which the Court, by seven votes to seven on the casting vote of the President, found that –

> ... the threat or use of nuclear weapons would generally be contrary to the rules of international law applicable in armed conflict, and in particular the principles and rules of humanitarian law;
> However, in view of the current state of international law, and of the elements of fact at its disposal, the Court cannot conclude definitively whether the threat or use of nuclear weapons would be lawful or unlawful in an extreme circumstance of self-defence in which the very survival of a State would be at stake.[34]

Of the seven Judges who voted against this paragraph of the *dispositif*, four considered that the paragraph went too far in finding limits on the legality of using nuclear weapons, while three thought that the Court should have found that any use of nuclear weapons was unlawful. Judge Koroma was one of the latter group. His dissenting opinion was based on the firm conclusion that the Court's findings on humanitarian law and the effects of using nuclear weapons "should have led it inexorably to conclude that any use of nuclear weapons is unlawful under international law, in particular the law applicable in armed conflict including humanitarian law".[35] Judge Koroma considered that any use of nuclear weapons was prohibited not only by the application of the general principles of international humanitarian law but also by a specific prohibition of their use. His analysis of the law on this subject and of the effects which he held would be produced by any use of nuclear weapons also led him to dissent from the advisory opinion, given on the same day, in which the Court held that it could not give the advisory opinion requested by the World Health Organization on a question similar to that posed by the General Assembly.[36]

---

33 *Legality of the Threat or Use of Nuclear Weapons (Request by the United Nations General Assembly for an Advisory Opinion)*, ICJ Reports 1996, p. 263, para. 97.
34 *Legality of the Threat or Use of Nuclear Weapons (Request by the United Nations General Assembly for an Advisory Opinion)*, ICJ Reports 1996, p. 266, para. 105(2)(E).
35 *Legality of the Threat or Use of Nuclear Weapons (Request by the United Nations General Assembly for an Advisory Opinion)*, ICJ Reports 1996, p. 570.
36 *Legality of the Use by a State of Nuclear Weapons in Armed Conflict (Request by the World Health Organization for an Advisory Opinion)*, ICJ Reports 1996, p. 66. Judge Koroma's dissenting opinion begins at p. 172.

Construction of a Wall in the Occupied Palestinian Territory

The Court was again confronted with difficult questions of international humanitarian law in *Legal Consequences of the Construction of a Wall in the Occupied Palestinian Territory* in 2004.[37] In that case, the General Assembly sought an advisory opinion on the question –

> What are the legal consequences arising from the construction of the wall being built by Israel, the occupying Power, in the Occupied Palestinian Territory, including in and around East Jerusalem, as described in the report of the Secretary-General, considering the rules and principles of international law, including the Fourth Geneva Convention of 1949 and relevant Security Council and General Assembly resolutions?

Although the question concerned the legal consequences of the construction of the wall, the Court held that it had to begin by determining for itself whether the construction of the wall was contrary to international law[38] and to that end it began by determining whether Israel was indeed the occupying Power of the territory in question and what law was applicable to its conduct there.

The Court had no doubt that Israel was the occupying Power in the territories situated between the "Green Line" (the armistice delimitation line fixed in 1949) and the former eastern boundary of the Palestine Mandate, including East Jerusalem.[39] All of these territories had been controlled by Jordan between 1949 and 1967 and came under the control of the Israeli armed forces during the armed conflict between Israel and Jordan in 1967. They thus became occupied territories under customary international law. The Court held that none of the events since 1967 – including Israel's declaration that East Jerusalem was part of Israel, the 1994 peace treaty between Israel and Jordan and the agreements between Israel and the Palestinian authorities – had altered their status as occupied territory or Israel's status as the occupying Power. The Court therefore held that Israel was bound by the customary international law of belligerent occupation, including those rules contained in Section III of the 1907 Hague Regulations respecting the Laws and Customs of War on Land, the provisions of which have long been regarded as an authoritative statement of the

---

[37] *Legal Consequences of the Construction of a Wall in the Occupied Palestinian Territory*, ICJ Reports 2004, p. 136.

[38] *Legal Consequences of the Construction of a Wall in the Occupied Palestinian Territory*, ICJ Reports 2004, p. 164, para. 68.

[39] *Legal Consequences of the Construction of a Wall in the Occupied Palestinian Territory*, ICJ Reports 2004, p. 167, para. 78.

customary law.[40] The 1907 Regulations had been supplemented in 1949 by the Fourth Geneva Convention Relative to the Protection of Civilian Persons in Time of War, most of the provisions of which are concerned with occupied territory.

Israel had, however, long maintained the position that the Fourth Convention was not applicable to the West Bank and East Jerusalem, although it undertook to apply the "humanitarian provisions" of the Convention.[41] This argument was grounded in Israel's reading of Article 2 of the Convention, the relevant parts of which provide –

> ... the present Convention shall apply to all cases of declared war or of any other armed conflict which may arise between two or more of the High Contracting Parties, even if the state of war is not recognized by one of them.
> The Convention shall also apply to all cases of partial or total occupation of the territory of a High Contracting Party, even if the said occupation meets with no armed resistance.

According to Israel, the West Bank and East Jerusalem, though controlled by Jordan between 1949 and 1967, had never lawfully been part of the territory of Jordan so that when Israel occupied them in 1967 it was not, in the words of Article 2(2), an "occupation of the territory of a High Contracting Party".[42] This argument attracted almost no support outside Israel[43] and, indeed, was widely criticised by leading Israeli international lawyers,[44] on the ground that the applicability of the Fourth Convention was determined by Article 2(1), the conditions of which were manifestly satisfied by the armed conflict between Israel and Jordan. The Court had no hesitation in holding that the Fourth Convention was applicable. The text of Article 2, taken as a whole, the *travaux préparatoires* and the subsequent practice of the parties all pointed to such a conclusion.[45]

---

40 The International Military Tribunal at Nuremberg had come to that conclusion in its 1946 Judgment.
41 See Shamgar (ed.), *Military Government in the Territories Administered by Israel* (1982), p. 31 et seq.
42 Both Israel and Jordan were parties to the 1949 Geneva Conventions long before 1967.
43 For further discussion of this issue, see Greenwood, 'The Administration of Occupied Territory in International Law' in Playfair (ed.), *International law and the Administration of Occupied Territories* (1992), p. 241 et seq.
44 See, e.g., Dinstein, *The International Law of Belligerent Occupation* (2009), pp. 20–21.
45 *Legal Consequences of the Construction of a Wall in the Occupied Palestinian Territory*, ICJ Reports 2004, pp. 173–7, paras 90–101.

More unexpected is what the Court said about Article 6(3) of the Convention, which provides that –

> In the case of occupied territory, the application of the present Convention shall cease one year after the general close of military operations; however, the Occupying Power shall be bound, for the duration of the occupation, to the extent that such Power exercises the functions of government in such territory, by the provisions of the following Articles of the present Convention: 1 to 12, 27, 29 to 34, 47, 49, 51, 52, 53, 59, 61 to 77, 143.

The potential application of this provision had generally been ignored or discounted in the literature about the occupation, with most governments and commentators tending to assume that the Convention applied in its entirety.[46] The Court, however, held that "the military operations leading to the occupation of the West Bank in 1967 ended a long time ago" and that, consequently, only those provisions of the Convention listed in Article 6(3) were applicable.[47] This is the first judicial application of Article 6(3) and it is interesting that the Court considered that it was triggered by the close of military operations by contending regular armed forces, notwithstanding the high level of violence which the occupied territories continued to experience after the ceasefire between Israeli and Jordanian regular forces. The result is perhaps unfortunate in that the list of provisions which continue to apply is somewhat arbitrary (although the Court cannot be blamed for that). It is difficult, for example, to understand why the duties in relation to education and the provision of food and essential supplies imposed upon the occupying Power by Articles 50 and 55 respectively, or its obligations regarding hospitals and health services under Articles 56 and 57, should cease one year after the close of military operations even though the occupation remains. To a large extent, however, the Court's decision (considered below) that the occupying Power continues to be bound by the provisions of the International Covenants on Civil and Political Rights and Economic and Social Rights, as well as the Convention on the Rights of the Child,[48] filled the void left by the inapplicability of those provisions of the

---

46 See, e.g., Roberts 'Prolonged Military Occupation' in Playfair, op. cit. n. 44, above, at pp. 36–39.
47 *Legal Consequences of the Construction of a Wall in the Occupied Palestinian Territory*, ICJ Reports 2004, p. 185, para. 125.
48 *Legal Consequences of the Construction of a Wall in the Occupied Palestinian Territory*, ICJ Reports 2004, pp. 177–181, paras 102–113.

Fourth Convention excluded by Article 6(3). On the nature of the legal regime thus applicable, the Court was careful to point out that –

> Whilst the drafters of the Hague Regulations of 1907 were as much concerned with protecting the rights of a State whose territory is occupied, as with protecting the inhabitants of that territory, the drafters of the Fourth Geneva Convention sought to guarantee the protection of civilians in time of war regardless of the status of the occupied territories, as is shown by Article 47 of the Convention.[49]

Applying the provisions of the humanitarian law on belligerent occupation which it had found to be applicable and the relevant provisions of human rights law, the Court concluded that Israel's construction of the wall in the occupied territory[50] was a breach of its obligations. In this context, the Court relied, *inter alia*, upon the prohibition on an occupying Power to transfer parts of its own population into the occupied territory (Article 49 of the Fourth Convention), which it held was violated by the establishment of Israeli settlements in the occupied territory.[51] It also found that the deprivation of private property involved either in the construction of the wall or as a consequence thereof was a breach of the rules stated in Articles 46 and 52 of the Hague Regulations and the provisions of Article 53 of the Fourth Convention.[52] Perhaps most importantly, the Court found that the conditions of life which the wall imposed upon Palestinian residents in the area which it enclosed and the overall deprivation of liberty of movement violated both humanitarian law and human rights principles, including the right of self-determination.[53]

As for the consequences of these violations of the law, the Court held that they engaged the responsibility of Israel, which was under an obligation to cease the violations and to ensure *restitutio in integrum* or, if that was not pos-

---

[49] *Legal Consequences of the Construction of a Wall in the Occupied Palestinian Territory*, ICJ Reports 2004, p. 175, para. 95.

[50] To the extent that the wall was to be constructed in Israel itself, the Court found that it was not called upon to examine the legal consequences of the construction of that part of the wall; *Legal Consequences of the Construction of a Wall in the Occupied Palestinian Territory*, ICJ Reports 2004, p. 164, para. 67.

[51] *Legal Consequences of the Construction of a Wall in the Occupied Palestinian Territory*, ICJ Reports 2004, pp. 183–4, para. 120, and pp. 191–2, para. 134.

[52] *Legal Consequences of the Construction of a Wall in the Occupied Palestinian Territory*, ICJ Reports 2004, p. 189, para. 132.

[53] *Legal Consequences of the Construction of a Wall in the Occupied Palestinian Territory*, ICJ Reports 2004, pp. 189–192, paras 133–134.

sible, to make compensation.[54] It could not rely upon either self-defence or necessity to preclude the wrongfulness of its actions. The issue of self-defence will be considered below. With regard to necessity, the Court considered that, to the extent that humanitarian law permitted reliance upon a concept of necessity, that concept was built in to the specific provisions of the relevant treaty. Hence, it noted that, while there was a limited necessity qualification upon the general obligation in Article 49(1) regarding deportation and transfer of population, no such qualification applied to the obligation in Article 49(6).[55] On the consequences for States other than Israel, the Court concluded that Article 1 of the Fourth Geneva Convention – by which "the High Contracting Parties undertake to respect and ensure respect for the present Convention in all circumstances" – placed them "under an obligation, while respecting the United Nations Charter and international law, to ensure compliance by Israel with international humanitarian law as embodied in that Convention".[56]

The Court's opinion was supported by a very large majority of the judges.[57] Judge Koroma was part of that majority. He added a brief separate opinion in which he stated his view that Israel's conduct had gone so far as to amount to an annexation of parts of the West Bank and East Jerusalem, thus contravening the "fundamental international law principle of the non-acquisition of territory by force" and adding that "under the regime of occupation, the division or partition of an occupied territory by the occupying Power is illegal".[58]

Armed Activities on the Territory of the Congo

The third major case involving international humanitarian law was *Armed Activities on the Territory of the Congo*, in which the Court gave judgment only

---

54 *Legal Consequences of the Construction of a Wall in the Occupied Palestinian Territory*, ICJ Reports 2004, p. 197, para. 147 et seq.
55 *Legal Consequences of the Construction of a Wall in the Occupied Palestinian Territory*, ICJ Reports 2004, p. 192, para. 135.
56 *Legal Consequences of the Construction of a Wall in the Occupied Palestinian Territory*, ICJ Reports 2004, p. 200, para. 159.
57 Judge Buergenthal, who voted against all five paragraphs of that portion of the *dispositif* which contained the answer to the question posed by the General Assembly, did so because he considered the Court should have declined to answer the question and because he considered that the Court lacked the necessary evidential basis for its findings. He concurred in most of the reasoning about the applicability and content of international humanitarian law; *Legal Consequences of the Construction of a Wall in the Occupied Palestinian Territory*, ICJ Reports 2004, p. 240, paras 1–2. Judge Kooijmans' disagreement with the Court's reasoning regarding Article 1 of the Fourth Convention is considered below.
58 *Legal Consequences of the Construction of a Wall in the Occupied Palestinian Territory*, ICJ Reports 2004, p. 204, para. 2 and p. 205, para. 4.

eighteen months after its opinion in the *Wall* case.[59] Unlike the *Nuclear Weapons* and *Wall* cases, *Armed Activities* was a contentious case, so that there was a far more substantial body of evidence before the Court.[60] Moreover, the basis for the jurisdiction of the Court in *Armed Activities* was the declarations made by the Parties under the Optional Clause; since these contained no sweeping reservations, the Court was able to consider the full range of allegations about violation of both customary and treaty-based international humanitarian law.[61] By contrast, in the other contentious case from this period in which the Court was confronted with allegations of illegal conduct in armed conflict, *Application of the Convention on the Prevention and Punishment of the Crime of Genocide*,[62] the Court's jurisdiction was confined to determining whether or not there had been a breach of the provisions of the Genocide Convention.

Three points in relation to international humanitarian law particularly stand out from a comparatively long judgment. First, in relation to the applicable law, the Court reaffirmed the approach it had earlier taken in the *Nuclear Weapons* and *Wall* cases that international humanitarian law and international human rights law applied in tandem.[63] In this case, however, it was able to apply a more extensive list of humanitarian law instruments since, for the first time, it was confronted with a case in which both parties to the armed conflict were party to 1977 Additional Protocol I to the Geneva Conventions. The Court also considered the application of the international law on natural resources alongside the specific principles of humanitarian law and human rights law relating to the exploitation of natural resources in occupied territory.

Secondly, the Court applied the law on belligerent occupation in a context very different from that with which it was faced in the *Wall* case. Whereas the *Wall* had concerned a small, densely populated region with a substantial Israeli military presence and undoubted exercise by Israel of governmental authority,

---

59 *Armed Activities on the Territory of the Congo (Democratic Republic of the Congo v. Uganda)*, ICJ Reports 2005, p. 168.

60 In addition, the principles concerning burden and standard of proof and their implications for the Court's findings of fact were applicable. These principles cannot apply in the same way when the Court exercises its advisory jurisdiction; see Greenwood, 'Judicial Integrity and the Advisory Jurisdiction of the International Court of Justice' in Gaja and Grote Stoutenberg (eds.), *Enhancing the Rule of Law through the International Court of Justice* (2014), p. 61.

61 The Court was also able to rule on allegations of violation of the prohibition of the use of force in the United Nations Charter but that falls outside the scope of the present Chapter.

62 *Application of the Convention on the Prevention and Punishment of the Crime of Genocide (Bosnia and Herzegovina v. Serbia and Montenegro)*, ICJ Reports 2007, p. 43.

63 *Armed Activities on the Territory of the Congo (Democratic Republic of the Congo v. Uganda)*, ICJ Reports 2005, pp. 242–4, paras 216–7.

Armed Activities concerned a vast area of the Congo in which the numbers of Ugandan troops present at any given time was comparatively small and the exercise by them of governmental authority far more difficult to establish. Moreover, in marked contrast to the Wall, the occupation here was said to exist at a time when hostilities were still ongoing. The Court applied the test laid down in Article 42 of the Hague Regulations on the Laws and Customs of War on Land that territory was considered occupied only when actually placed under the authority of the hostile army and extended only to those areas where such authority had actually been established and could be exercised.[64] On that basis, it considered that it had to –

> ... satisfy itself that the Ugandan armed forces were not merely stationed in particular locations but also that they had substituted their own authority for that of the Congolese Government. In that event, any justification given by Uganda for its occupation would be of no relevance; nor would it be relevant whether or not Uganda had established a structured military administration.[65]

On that basis, the Court held that –

> ... the territorial limits of any zone of occupation by Uganda in the DRC cannot be determined by simply drawing a line connecting the geographic locations where Ugandan troops were present, as has been done on the sketch map presented by the DRC ... [66]

Only in Ituri, where the Ugandan commander had appointed a governor to administer the territory, did the Court find that Uganda had become the occupying Power. The fact that the commander may have acted without authority did not alter that conclusion.[67]

Thirdly, the Court examined allegations that Uganda had engaged in a practice of looting the natural resources of the occupied territory and other parts of the DRC in which its forces were operating. The Court found insufficient evidence to warrant a finding that such looting was the product of a policy

---

64 *Armed Activities on the Territory of the Congo (Democratic Republic of the Congo v. Uganda)*, ICJ Reports 2005, p. 230, paras 173–4.
65 *Armed Activities on the Territory of the Congo (Democratic Republic of the Congo v. Uganda)*, ICJ Reports 2005, p. 230, para. 173.
66 *Armed Activities on the Territory of the Congo (Democratic Republic of the Congo v. Uganda)*, ICJ Reports 2005, p. 230, para. 174.
67 *Armed Activities on the Territory of the Congo (Democratic Republic of the Congo v. Uganda)*, ICJ Reports 2005, p. 230, para. 176.

adopted by the Ugandan Government but held that there had been widespread looting, including of natural resources, in which Ugandan officers and soldiers had engaged.[68] Since Uganda was responsible for all acts of members of its armed forces, irrespective of whether they had acted pursuant to, or in contravention of, their orders,[69] this looting engaged the responsibility of Uganda and was a violation of the prohibition of pillage in Article 47 of the Hague Regulations and Article 33 of the Fourth Geneva Convention.[70] In the occupied area of Ituri, there was also a failure, attributable to Uganda, by the military authorities to take the steps required in exercise of the duty to govern under Article 43 of the Hague Regulations because those authorities had failed to take steps to prevent looting by private persons, particularly members of Congolese rebel groups.

The Court concluded, by a large majority, that Uganda was responsible for serious violations of international humanitarian law and international human rights law, most noticeably in causing – or, in some instances, failing to prevent – the deaths of large numbers of civilians[71] and in pillaging the natural resources of the DRC. Judge Koroma joined in that majority and appended a declaration in which he emphasized the gravity of the violations and the importance of the rules of humanitarian law in issue.[72]

Other Cases

While the three cases discussed above were the most important instances of the Court pronouncing on issues of humanitarian law during Judge Koroma's time on the Court, questions of humanitarian law also arose in a number of other cases. In its mammoth judgment in *Application of the Convention on the Prevention and Punishment of the Crime of Genocide*, delivered in 2007, the Court dealt at length with the requirements of the Genocide Convention and the nature of State responsibility under that Convention.[73] In *Jurisdictional*

---

68 *Armed Activities on the Territory of the Congo (Democratic Republic of the Congo v. Uganda)*, ICJ Reports 2005, pp. 249–253, paras 237–250.
69 See Article 3, Hague Convention IV, 1907, and Article 92, Additional Protocol I, 1977; *Armed Activities on the Territory of the Congo (Democratic Republic of the Congo v. Uganda)*, ICJ Reports 2005, p. 242, paras 213–4.
70 *Armed Activities on the Territory of the Congo (Democratic Republic of the Congo v. Uganda)*, ICJ Reports 2005, p. 252, para. 245.
71 *Armed Activities on the Territory of the Congo (Democratic Republic of the Congo v. Uganda)*, ICJ Reports 2005, pp. 239–241, paras 2017–211.
72 *Armed Activities on the Territory of the Congo (Democratic Republic of the Congo v. Uganda)*, ICJ Reports 2005, p. 284.
73 *Application of the Convention on the Prevention and Punishment of the Crime of Genocide (Bosnia and Herzegovina v. Serbia and Montenegro)*, ICJ Reports 2007, p. 43.

Immunities,[74] the Court held that the fact that a State was accused of (and indeed accepted that it had committed) war crimes did not remove entitlement to sovereign immunity before the courts of another State, even if the laws violated had the status of *jus cogens*.[75] Finally, in *Arrest Warrant*[76] and *Obligation to Prosecute or Extradite*[77] the Court gave important judgments about aspects of international criminal law which have repercussions for the future prosecution of war crimes. With the exception of the last case (in which he did not sit), Judge Koroma played an active part in all of these cases, appending an opinion or declaration to the judgment.

2 An Evaluation of the Court's Contribution

Little of what the Court has said regarding international humanitarian law will have come as a surprise to anyone who has taken an interest in that area of international law. That is only to be expected, since the role of a court is very different from that of a legislature and most of humanitarian law was already well established before the Court first had occasion to consider it. Nevertheless, the jurisprudence examined in the previous section has made a significant contribution to the development of international humanitarian law in a number of ways on which space permits comment upon only a few.

A Reaffirmation of the Law

It is appropriate to begin by observing that one important contribution which the Court has made has been to reaffirm the continuing validity and effect of international humanitarian law. Ever since the Second World War doubt has been cast upon the continued significance of the rules of international humanitarian law. Those doubts have been voiced by those who maintained that the existence of a body of law governing hostilities which applied equally both to an aggressor and to a victim of aggression, as well as by those who (often from very different perspectives) have questioned whether rules which evolved in an earlier age are suitable for application in the conditions of modern warfare.

---

74   *Jurisdictional Immunities of the State (Germany v. Italy, Greece intervening)*, ICJ Reports 2012, p. 99.

75   As in the *Nuclear Weapons* case, the Court did not consider it necessary to decide whether the relevant rules of international humanitarian law had the status of *jus cogens*.

76   *Arrest Warrant of 11 April 2000 (Democratic Republic of the Congo v. Belgium)*, ICJ Reports 2002, p. 3.

77   *Obligation to Prosecute or Extradite (Belgium v. Senegal)*, ICJ Reports 2012, p. 422.

The Court, however, has consistently upheld the force and effect of international humanitarian law and has applied it to modern conflicts in a way that convincingly refutes the suggestion that this branch of international law has become even partially obsolescent. That approach by the Court can be discerned in its assumption, in *Corfu Channel* and then in *Military and Paramilitary Activities*, that the humanitarian requirements of Hague Convention VIII continued to have effect. Even more striking is the insistence, in *Nuclear Weapons*, that general principles of international humanitarian law such as the requirement to distinguish between civilians and combatants and the prohibition of methods of warfare likely to cause unnecessary suffering, which had their origins at the end of the nineteenth century, had to be applied to the use of nuclear weapons.

The approach of the Court in this respect reflects the preponderance of State practice and scholarly opinion but it is nonetheless a significant and welcome rejection of the competing approach which would have left the conduct of warfare largely unregulated. Moreover, while the Court's early jurisprudence (in particular its judgment in *Military and Paramilitary Activities*) suggested a temptation to disregard the often difficult detail of humanitarian law in favour of broad "considerations of humanity, even more exacting in peace than in war",[78] in its more recent cases the Court has not succumbed to that temptation. It did not hesitate in *Wall* and *Armed Activities*, for example, to deal with the detail of the law of belligerent occupation, including difficult questions of precisely when that law would be applicable.

B   The Relationship between International Humanitarian Law and International Law as a Whole

Another important feature of the Court's jurisprudence has been the way in which it has dealt with the relationship between international humanitarian law and other bodies of international law and, thus, with the former's position in the overall structure of international law. In *Nuclear Weapons*, and then in *Wall* and *Armed Activities*, the Court considered the complex relationship between international humanitarian law and international human rights law, as well as the even more vexed question of the relationship between humanitarian law and the law regulating recourse to force.

With regard to the former, the Court has rejected both the notion that human rights law has no application in the context of international armed

---

[78]   Judge Higgins was critical of the *Nuclear Weapons* Opinion for its failure to be sufficiently rigorous in examining the detail of the law; *Legality of the Threat or Use of Nuclear Weapons (Request by the United Nations General Assembly for an Advisory Opinion)*, ICJ Reports 1996, p. 584, paras 9–10.

conflict and the suggestion that its principles on such matters as the right to life have somehow superseded the rules of international humanitarian law. Thus, in the *Nuclear Weapons* case, the Court observed that –

> ... the protection of the International Covenant on Civil and Political Rights does not cease in times of war, except by operation of Article 4 of the Covenant whereby certain provisions mat be derogated from in a time of national emergency. Respect for the right to life is not, however, such a provision. In principle, the right not arbitrarily to be deprived of one's life applies also in hostilities.[79]

The Court then went on to say –

> The test of what is an arbitrary deprivation of life, however, then falls to be determined by the applicable *lex specialis*, namely the law applicable in armed conflict which is deigned to regulate the conduct of hostilities. Thus whether a particular loss of life, through the use of a certain weapon in warfare, is to be considered an arbitrary deprivation of life contrary to Article 6 of the Covenant, can only be decided by reference to the law applicable in armed conflict and not deduced from the terms of the Covenant itself.[80]

This approach, by which the term "arbitrary" in Article 6 operates to ensure a *renvoi* to humanitarian law where the Article is applied in the context of an international armed conflict, ensures that human rights law can continue to apply without undermining the *lex specialis*. The same approach would logically apply to other provisions of the Covenant in which similar language is used. Thus, Article 9 provides that "no-one shall be subjected to arbitrary arrest or detention". The reasoning employed by the Court would suggest that the detention of a member of enemy armed forces as a prisoner of war would not violate this provision, as long as he or she was treated in accordance with the Third Geneva Convention.

Nevertheless, this approach is not free from difficulty. A State is required to ensure the protection of the rights contained in the Covenant "to all individuals within its territory and subject to its jurisdiction".[81] If one party to an inter-

---

[79] *Legality of the Threat or Use of Nuclear Weapons (Request by the United Nations General Assembly for an Advisory Opinion)*, ICJ Reports 1996, p. 240, para. 25.

[80] *Legality of the Threat or Use of Nuclear Weapons (Request by the United Nations General Assembly for an Advisory Opinion)*, ICJ Reports 1996, p. 240, para. 25.

[81] Article 2(1). This phrase is generally interpreted disjunctively, so that it applies to persons

national armed conflict bombards the territory of the rival belligerent, does that action bring the population of the latter within its jurisdiction? In *Banković v. Belgium and Others* in 2001, a Grand Chamber of the European Court of Human Rights unanimously held that it does not.[82] The position may be different in occupied territory, where it is easier to see the population of the occupied territory as falling within the jurisdiction of the occupying Power.[83] There, the approach taken by the International Court of Justice has the particular advantage that the provisions of the Covenants offer a protection to the population which goes beyond that afforded by humanitarian law, particularly in the case of a prolonged occupation such as that in the *Wall* case.

The approach taken by the Court in *Nuclear Weapons* and then briefly recalled in the *Wall* towards the relationship between humanitarian law and the *jus ad bellum* is more problematic. The Court's conclusion that "it cannot reach a definitive conclusion as to the legality or illegality of the use of nuclear weapons by a State in an extreme circumstance of self-defence, in which its very survival would be at stake"[84] could be taken as suggesting that the right of self-defence might justify conduct which was contrary to the requirements of hu-

---

within the jurisdiction of a State but outside its territory; see UN Human Rights Committee General Comment 31, para. 10; CCPR/C/21/Rev. 1/Add 13 (2004).

[82] *Banković v. Belgium and Others*, 123 *International Law Reports* 94 (2001). The Grand Chamber was applying Article 1 of the European Convention on Human Rights, which requires each State Party to secure the rights laid down in the Convention to "everyone within their jurisdiction". However, while Article 1 of the European Convention is, in this respect, very similar to Article 2(1) of the International Covenant on Civil and Political Rights, the substantive provisions of the two treaties are couched in rather different terms. In particular, the provisions on the right to life (Article 2) and the right to liberty of the person (Article 5) of the European Convention do not use the term "arbitrary" and are therefore more difficult to interpret in the way that the International Court of Justice has interpreted the corresponding provisions of the Covenant. Nevertheless, the Grand Chamber of the European Court of Human Rights, in a judgment clearly influenced by the jurisprudence of the International Court of Justice, has held that the detention of a prisoner of war in compliance with the Third Geneva Convention does not violate Article 5 of the European Convention on Human Rights. See Hassan v. United Kingdom (App. No. 29750/09), Judgment of 16 September 2014, to be reported in volume 161 of the International Law Reports.

[83] The European Court of Human Rights has held that the United Kingdom was required to apply the European Convention in two cases concerning persons in a part of Iraq occupied by the United Kingdom in 2003–04; see *Al-Jedda v. United Kingdom*, 147 *International Law Reports* 107 (2011) and *Al-Skeini v. United Kingdom*, 147 *International Law Reports* 181 (2011).

[84] *Legality of the Threat or Use of Nuclear Weapons (Request by the United Nations General Assembly for an Advisory Opinion)*, ICJ Reports 1996, p. 263, para. 97.

manitarian law.[85] Such a conclusion – which, it may be noted, was not supported by any of the States taking part in the proceedings – would run counter to the long established principle that humanitarian law and the *jus ad bellum* operate independently of one another and that compliance with one cannot justify or excuse the violation of the other.[86] It is not, however, at all clear that the Court meant to suggest that a State acting in self-defence – even in an extreme case – might be justified in departing from the requirements of humanitarian law.[87] Paragraphs 2(C) and 2(D) of the *dispositif* and the earlier reasoning of the Court uphold the traditional approach that for a use of force to be lawful it must comply with the requirements of both bodies of law. That approach was also applied by the International Court in its Judgment in *Armed Activities*.

C   *The Law of Belligerent Occupation*

Perhaps the area of humanitarian law to which the Court has made the biggest contribution is the law of belligerent occupation. Although this body of law was substantially updated by the Fourth Geneva Convention in 1949, many of the most important principles, including the basic legal regime for the governance of occupied territory and the powers of the occupant to take property, are still governed primarily by the rules of customary international law stated in the 1907 Hague Regulations. As such, it has frequently been suggested that the law of belligerent occupation is not adequate to cope with contemporary demands. Certainly, there have been very few cases since 1945 in which a State that acquired control of territory by the use of force has acknowledged its status as an occupying Power and been willing to apply the law of belligerent occupation.[88] The Court's Opinion in the *Wall* case and its Judgment in *Armed Activities* are therefore of the utmost importance in reaffirming that the law laid down in 1907 and 1949 remains applicable today and in clarifying the circumstances in which that legal regime becomes applicable. In particular, its

---

85   That appears to have been the view of Judge Fleischhauer, *Legality of the Threat or Use of Nuclear Weapons (Request by the United Nations General Assembly for an Advisory Opinion)*, ICJ Reports 1996, p. 255; it was heavily criticized by Judge Koroma.

86   See, e.g., Greenwood, 'The Relationship between *Ius ad Bellum* and *Ius in Bello*', 9 *Review of International Studies* (1983), p. 133.

87   Contrast Greenwood, '*Jus ad bellum* and *jus in bello* in the Nuclear Weapons Advisory Opinion', Boisson de Chazournes and Sands, *International Law, the International Court of Justice and Nuclear Weapons* (1999), p. 264, with Kreß, "The International Court of Justice and the Law of Armed Conflicts" in C. Tams and J. Sloan (eds.), *The Development of International Law by the International Court of Justice* (Oxford, 2013), p. 294.

88   See, e.g., Roberts, 'What is a Military Occupation', 55 *British Year Book of International Law* (1984), p. 249.

rejection, in the *Wall*,[89] of the theory that application of the Fourth Geneva Convention is in some way contingent upon the title of the State controlling the territory immediately prior to the occupation, and, in *Armed Activities*,[90] of the suggestion that a State which acquires control of territory as the result of a lawful use of force in self-defence is not subject to the law of belligerent occupation provide an important element of clarity.

The Court has also provided useful clarification of the conditions which must be met if an area of territory is to be treated as occupied and thus as subject to the law of belligerent occupation. As explained above, in the *Armed Activities* case, the Court insisted that it was not enough that a State's troops were stationed in the area; they must have substituted their own authority for that of the displaced government, although it was not necessary that a structured administration be established.[91] Nevertheless, once the substitution had occurred, the occupying Power had positive duties of government. Thus, the Court made clear that Uganda was not merely required not to engage in the despoliation of the occupied territory; it also had a positive obligation to prevent its despoliation by others. Even more important was the positive obligation to protect the population from murderous activities by rebel groups, notwithstanding that the Court had found that there was insufficient evidence to conclude that those groups were controlled by Uganda.[92]

In this context, the Court's melding of the law of belligerent occupation with the law of human rights is of particular significance. The decision that an occupying Power is obliged to apply the provisions of the 1966 Covenants goes a long way to giving substance in a contemporary context to the general duty of governance laid down by Article 43 of the Hague Regulations. In its *Armed Activities* Judgment, the Court, after finding that Uganda was an occupying Power in the Ituri area, added that –

---

[89] *Legal Consequences of the Construction of a Wall in the Occupied Palestinian Territory*, ICJ Reports 2004, pp. 173–7, paras 90–101.

[90] *Armed Activities on the Territory of the Congo (Democratic Republic of the Congo v. Uganda)*, ICJ Reports 2005, p. 230, para. 173. The Court rejected Uganda's argument that its resort to force was lawful but its comment that "any justification given by Uganda for its occupation would be of no relevance" shows that it considered that, even if Uganda had acted lawfully, the territory which it thereby acquired would still have been occupied territory and the law of belligerent occupation would have been applicable.

[91] *Armed Activities on the Territory of the Congo (Democratic Republic of the Congo v. Uganda)*, ICJ Reports 2005, p. 230, para. 173.

[92] *Armed Activities on the Territory of the Congo (Democratic Republic of the Congo v. Uganda)*, ICJ Reports 2005, p. 253, para. 248. In this respect, the Court distinguished between Uganda's duties as occupying Power in Ituri and the absence of an obligation with regard to the acts of rebel groups elsewhere; see para. 247.

As such it was under an obligation to take all the measures in its power to restore, and ensure, as far as possible, public order and safety in the occupied area, while respecting, unless absolutely prevented, the laws in force in the DRC. This obligation comprised the duty to secure respect for the applicable rules of international human rights law and international humanitarian law, to protect the inhabitants of the occupied territory against acts of violence, and not to tolerate such violence by any third party.[93]

While a requirement to apply the provisions of a regional human rights treaty to occupied territory outside that region might well create serious difficulties, since it could easily involve the imposition of the standards of the occupying power's region on a population with a different culture and thus conflict with the duty in Article 43 to respect the law already in force in the occupied territory, such problems should not arise with the global human rights instruments, particularly where those were already applicable prior to the occupation.

D   *Enforcement and Implementation*

Finally, a word about the Court's contribution to the enforcement and implementation of humanitarian law is called for. In recent years, the focus of any discussion of this subject has been the enforcement of the law through the prosecution of individuals. In that respect, huge advances have been made by the International Criminal Tribunals for the Former Yugoslavia and Rwanda, the International Criminal Court, the Special Court for Sierra Leone and the Extraordinary Chambers in the Courts of Cambodia. The International Court of Justice has, of course, no jurisdiction over individuals and its contribution to these developments has thus been indirect.[94] Its jurisprudence has, however, made a more direct contribution to the enforcement of humanitarian law through the medium of State responsibility. While much of what the Court has said on this subject is no more than an application in the field of humanitarian law of general principles regarding State responsibility as codified by the

---

93 *Armed Activities on the Territory of the Congo (Democratic Republic of the Congo v. Uganda)*, ICJ Reports 2005, p. 231, para. 178.

94 That is not to say that it has not been significant. The Judgments in *Arrest Warrant of 11 April 2000 (Democratic Republic of the Congo v. Belgium)*, ICJ Reports 2002, p. 3 and *Obligation to Prosecute or Extradite (Belgium v. Senegal)*, ICJ Reports 2012, p. 422 have dealt with important issues regarding the exercise of criminal jurisdiction. The Judgment in *Application of the Convention on the Prevention and Punishment of the Crime of Genocide (Bosnia and Herzegovina v. Serbia and Montenegro)*, ICJ Reports 2007, p. 43 addressed issues of aiding and abetting and the responsibility of a State to ensure that persons responsible for genocide are brought to justice.

International Law Commission in the Articles on State Responsibility adopted in 2001,[95] the Court has gone beyond those principles in one respect. In *Armed Activities*, it treated the principle laid down in Article 3 of Hague Convention IV, 1907, and Article 91 of Additional Protocol I, 1977, that a belligerent "shall be responsible for all acts committed by members of its armed forces" as going beyond the principle in Article 7 of the ILC Articles on State Responsibility. The latter provision makes *ultra vires* acts of an organ of the State (which, of course, includes members of that State's armed forces) attributable to the State "if the organ ... acts in that capacity". That leaves open the possibility that the act of such an organ will not be attributable to the State on the ground that the organ did not act in its capacity as an organ of the State. Article 3 of the Hague Convention, however, was intended to make the belligerent State responsible for *all* acts of members of its armed forces, without the need to inquire into the capacity in which they acted.[96] Since the Court did not inquire into the capacity in which members of the Ugandan armed forces had acted, it seems to have adopted this interpretation.

The Court's finding in that regard confirmed what was already a widely held belief. Its interpretation of Article 1 of the Fourth Convention (a provision common to all four Geneva Conventions) in the *Wall* Opinion (which is set out above) is more controversial. The Court found that Article 1 places on all States an obligation to ensure compliance by Israel with its obligations under the Convention. It is very doubtful that the provision was intended to have any such effect. The most comprehensive study of the subject suggests that Article 1 was inserted into the 1949 Conventions to make clear that a belligerent was required to ensure that those subject to its control complied with the Convention, rather than to require each State to take action to ensure compliance with the Convention by other States.[97] Nor is there much sign in the subsequent practice of States to suggest that States have considered themselves under any such obligation. As Judge Kooijmans pointed out in his separate opinion in the *wall*, it is to be regretted that the Court did not explain its reasoning on this point more fully and explore precisely what other States might be required to do to comply with this broader understanding of Article 1.[98] The approach

---

95   See, e.g., *Legal Consequences of the Construction of a Wall in the Occupied Palestinian Territory*, ICJ Reports 2004, pp. 197–8, paras 147–153 and *Armed Activities on the Territory of the Congo (Democratic Republic of the Congo v. Uganda)*, ICJ Reports 2005, p. 257, para. 259.

96   See, e.g., Kalshoven, 'State Responsibility for Warlike Acts of the Armed Forces', 40 *International and Comparative Law Quarterly* (1990), p. 827.

97   Kalshoven, 'The Undertaking to Respect and Ensure respect in all Circumstances', 2 *Year Book of International Humanitarian Law* (1999), p. 3.

98   *Legal Consequences of the Construction of a Wall in the Occupied Palestinian Territory*, ICJ Reports 2004, p. 233, para. 47.

taken by the Court does, however, indicate a further way in which the machinery for ensuring compliance with international humanitarian law can be strengthened.

Much else could be said about the jurisprudence of the International Court of Justice on international humanitarian law but it is hoped that this chapter has sufficed to consider the principal features and also to acknowledge how much that jurisprudence developed during the eighteen years of Judge Koroma's service to the Court.

CHAPTER 17

The Prevention of Genocide as a *Jus Cogens* Norm? A Formula for Lawful Humanitarian Intervention

Manuel J. Ventura

1   Introduction

At the heart of this chapter lies the desire to seek a greater understanding of, and to develop, the meaning of the following words of the Convention on the Prevention and Punishment of the Crime of Genocide (1948) ('Genocide Convention'):

> The Contracting Parties confirm that genocide, whether committed in time of peace or in time of war, is a crime under international law which they undertake *to prevent* and punish.
> [...]
> Any Contracting Party may call upon the competent organs of the United Nations to take such action under the Charter of the United Nations as they consider appropriate *for the prevention and suppression* of acts of genocide or any of the other acts enumerated in Article III.[1]

While many trees have been felled in the efforts to explore the prohibition on the commission of genocide, less academic time and energy has been invested into the prevention of genocide as such. Indeed, it was only in February 2007 with the International Court of Justice ('ICJ')'s judgment in *Case Concerning Application of the Convention on the Prevention and Punishment of the Crime of Genocide (Bosnia and Herzegovina v. Serbia and Montenegro)*[2] (*'Genocide Case'*) that we were first offered a detailed judicial glimpse of its substantive legal content when it held, *inter alia*, that 'the obligation of States parties is

---

*   The author would like to thank Dr. Guido Acquaviva and Judge Sir David Baragwanath of the Special Tribunal for Lebanon for their thoughtful comments and suggestions on a prior version of this chapter.
1   Articles I, VIII, Convention on the Prevention and Punishment of the Crime of Genocide (1948) ('Genocide Convention') (emphasis added).
2   ICJ, *Case Concerning Application of the Convention on the Prevention and Punishment of the Crime of Genocide (Bosnia and Herzegovina v. Serbia and Montenegro)*, Judgment of 26 February 2007, ICJ Reports 2007, p. 43 (*'Genocide Case'*).

[...] to employ all means reasonably available to them, so as to prevent genocide so far as possible.'[3] Since then, scholarly legal writing on the subject, as such, has been sparse.[4]

However, in June 2007 – a mere four months after the ICJ's judgment – a novel claim was brought before the Dutch courts. In *Mothers of Srebrenica and Others v. The Netherlands and the United Nations* the applicants sought to hold the United Nations ('UN') (and The Netherlands) responsible for failing in their (supposed) duty to prevent genocide by their stepping aside as the Srebrenica enclave was overrun during the civil war in Bosnia and Herzegovina in July 1995, resulting in the deaths of between 7,000–8,000 people.[5] This was the first time, outside of the aforementioned ICJ litigation, that a court had considered such a claim. In particular, the claimants argued that the UN's immunity before Dutch courts should be set aside on the basis of genocide's *jus cogens* status. While the claim was ultimately dismissed by the Dutch Supreme Court[6] and held to be inadmissible before the European Court of Human Rights ('ECtHR'),[7] it brought to light an interesting question that remained unexplored through-

---

3   ICJ, *Genocide Case*, p. 221, para. 430. See also ICJ, *Case Concerning Application of the Convention on the Prevention and Punishment of the Crime of Genocide (Bosnia and Herzegovina v. Serbia and Montenegro)*, Judgment of 26 February 2007 – Joint Declaration of Judges Shi and Koroma, ICJ Reports 2007, p. 282, para. 5: [W]e believe in the intrinsic humanitarian value of the conclusion reached by the Court and recognize the overriding legal imperative established by Article I of the Convention, namely: the duty of a State to do what it properly can, within its means and the law, to try and prevent genocide when there is a serious danger to its occurrence of which the State is or should be aware.

4   While there are certainly some explorations of the subject in the literature (see for example, W.A. Schabas, *Genocide in International Law: The Crime of Crimes*, 2nd Edition (Cambridge, Cambridge University Press: 2009), pp. 520–592; P. Akhavan, 'Preventing Genocide: Measuring Success by What Does Not Happen', (2011) 22(1–2) *Criminal Law Forum* 1; C.J. Tams, 'Article 1', in C.J. Tams, L. Berster, and B. Schiffbauer, *Convention on the Prevention and Punishment of the Crime of Genocide: A Commentary* (C.H. Beck/Hart Publishing/Nomos, Munich/Oxford/Baden-Baden: 2014), pp. 45–54), these are dwarfed by the discussions of the prevention of genocide alongside the prevention of war crimes, crimes against humanity and ethnic cleansing in the context of the responsibility to protect. Academic discussion of the prevention of genocide as a stand-alone principle has thus been much less prevalent.

5   See ICTY, *Prosecutor v. Krstić*, Trial Judgment, Case No IT-98-33-T, 2 August 2001, para. 84 (this finding was not overturned on appeal); ICTY, *Prosecutor v. Popović* et al., Trial Judgment, Case No. IT-05-88-T, 10 June 2010, para. 664 (appeal pending).

6   Supreme Court of the Netherlands, *Stichting Mothers of Srebrenica and Others v. The Netherlands and the United Nations*, LJN: BW1999, ILDC 1760 (NL 2012), 13 April 2012.

7   European Court of Human Rights ('ECtHR') – Third Section, *Stichting Mothers of Srebrenica and Others v. The Netherlands*, Admissibility, Application No. 65542/12, 11 June 2013.

out the entire litigation: is the prevention of genocide actually *jus cogens*? While the answer to this question, as the present author and Akande have previously pointed out, would not have affected the final outcome of these cases,[8] it nonetheless opens very interesting and relatively unexplored legal terrain on account of its potential *jus cogens* status vis-à-vis humanitarian intervention and the use of force.[9]

Having considered the legal terrain, this chapter aims to present and explore the following argument: if the prevention of genocide actually attains *jus cogens* status then it can override and/or modify other substantive norms of international law – for our purposes, and under certain conditions, the prohibition on the use of force. This would remain unchanged even if this prohibition were also of a *jus cogens* character; it would simply be a situation where a subsequent *jus cogens* norm modifies an existing *jus cogens* norm.[10] In other words, this is potentially a key to unlocking the door for humanitarian intervention to prevent genocide. However, unlike the predominant view on humanitarian intervention, this formula sits perfectly well within established principles of international law – no international law is harmed in the process. In short, what will be proposed is nothing less than *legal* humanitarian intervention, albeit in a relatively narrow set of circumstances.

To explain this theory, the present chapter consists of four parts, aside from the present introduction. First, historical research will be presented that provides a window into the original intent of the drafters of the Genocide Convention (1948) from 1946–1948 with respect to the prevention of genocide.

---

[8] This is because of the difference between procedural versus substantive clashes, a distinction recently drawn by the ICJ: ICJ, *Jurisdictional Immunities of the State (Germany v. Italy: Greece intervening)*, Judgment of 3 February 2012, ICJ Reports 2012, p. 140, para. 92. See generally M.J. Ventura and D. Akande, '*Mothers of Srebrenica*: The Obligation to Prevent Genocide and *Jus Cogens* – Implications for Humanitarian Intervention', *EJIL: Talk!* Blog, 6 September 2013, available at: http://www.ejiltalk.org/ignoring-the-elephant-in-the-room-in-mothers-of-srebrenica-is-the-obligation-to-prevent-genocide-jus-cogens (accessed 30 June 2014).

[9] This argument was previously invoked without too much sophistication during the NATO intervention in Kosovo in 1999. See W.A. Schabas, *Genocide in International Law: The Crime of Crimes*, 2nd Edition (Cambridge, Cambridge University Press: 2009), p. 530: 'It was argued that the duty to prevent genocide was a peremptory or *jus cogens* norm, and that consequently it trumped any incompatible obligation, even one dictated by the Charter of the United Nations.' For an example, see R. Tomes, 'Operation Allied Force and the Legal Basis for Humanitarian Interventions', (2000) 30(1) *Parameters* 38, at 49–50.

[10] As per Article 53 of the Vienna Convention on the Law of Treaties (1969) ('Vienna Convention'), *jus cogens* norms 'can be modified only by a subsequent norm of general international law having the same character.'

Second, the content and characteristics of *jus cogens* norms are discussed together with an overview of judicial practice on the prevention of genocide as well as State practice during the Rwandan genocide in 1994. It aims to demonstrate not that the prevention of genocide is currently a *jus cogens* norm, but that it could perhaps in the future become a peremptory norm of international law, depending on how subsequent events unfold. Third, the implications of such a status being accorded to the prevention of genocide are explored, in particular with respect to humanitarian intervention, the responsibility to protect, and the prohibition on the use of force. This structure seeks to roughly trace the prevention of genocide from the past, to the present, and into the future. Concluding remarks then follow.

2   The Prevention of Genocide in the *Travaux Préparatoires* of the Genocide Convention (1948)

Article 31 of the Vienna Convention on the Law of Treaties (1969) ('Vienna Convention'), reflective of customary international law,[11] directs that treaties 'shall be interpreted in good faith in accordance with the ordinary meaning to be given to the terms of the treaty in their context and in the light of its object and purpose.' Unfortunately, the term 'prevent' in Article 1 of the Genocide Convention (1948) is so broad and difficult to delineate that its meaning should be complemented by going outside the basic traditional approach to interpretation outlined above, since a plain reading on its face 'leaves the meaning ambiguous [and] obscure'.[12] Further, as one commentator in a detailed study of the *travaux préparatoires* of the Vienna Convention (1969) has recently pointed out, the drafters of that treaty intended that 'interpreters should rely on drafting history in every plausible contestable case to shed light on the meaning of th[e] text – and in some cases even to override what had initially seemed like its clear import.'[13] It is therefore relevant, probative and useful to probe into the *travaux préparatoires* of Article 1 of the Genocide Convention

---

[11]   ICJ, *Dispute Regarding Navigational and Related Rights (Costa Rica v. Nicaragua)*, Judgment of 13 July 2009, ICJ Reports 2009, p. 237, para. 47 (and other sources cited therein). The same source recognizes that Article 32 of the Vienna Convention (1969) is also reflective of customary international law.

[12]   Article 32(a), Vienna Convention (1969).

[13]   J.D. Mortenson, 'The *Travaux* of *Travaux*: Is the Vienna Convention Hostile to Drafting History?', (2013) 107(4) *The American Journal of International Law* 780, at 821.

(1948), as directed by Article 32 of the Vienna Convention (1969) in addition to today's contemporary legal milieu.

A   UN *General Assembly Resolution 96(1)*

From the beginning of the process that eventually led to UN General Assembly ('GA') Resolution 96(1), the notion that States should prevent genocide was clear and unambiguous. Thus, the very first draft resolution relating to genocide proposed jointly by Cuba, India and Panama resolved that genocide be brought to the UN Economic and Social Council ('ECOSOC')'s attention for it to study and 'prepare a report on the possibilities of declaring genocide an international crime and assuring international cooperation *for its prevention* and punishment.'[14] Similarly, the very first draft proposal for a genocide convention, an initiative presented by Saudi Arabia, not only refers to the prevention of genocide in its preamble,[15] but also in Article II (entitled 'International Action'):

> The parties to this protocol agree to make effective use of every means at their disposal, acting separately or in cooperation *to prevent* and penalize genocide.[16]

The Saudi Arabian delegate Riad Bey repeated his country's position at the UN General Assembly Sixth Committee (Legal) ('Sixth Committee') by asserting that any convention on genocide should include 'provisions for assuring the prevention and repression of [the crime of] genocide.'[17]

---

14   UN Doc. A/BUR/50, Annex 15, 2 November 1946, in H. Abtahi and P. Webb, *The Genocide Convention: The* Travaux Préparatoires, Volume 1 (Leiden/Boston, Martinus Nijhoff Publishers: 2008), at p. 3 (emphasis added).

15   *Whereas* the atrocities committed against humanity which violated the rules of international law and shocked public conscience make it imperative for the nations of the world to take concerted action *to prevent* and penalize the commission of such acts in the future;

   [...]

   Therefore the nations signatories to this protocol declare that genocide is an international crime against humanity, and agree to co-operate *to prevent* and suppress it as herein provided[.]

   UN Doc. A/C.6/86, Annex 15b, 26 November 1946, in *supra* fn. 14, at p. 6 (emphasis added on prevention language).

16   UN Doc. A/C.6/86, Annex 15b, 26 November 1946, in *supra* fn. 14, at p. 7 (emphasis added).

17   UN Doc. A/C.6/91, 30 November 1946, Mr. Riad Bey (Saudi Arabia), in *supra* fn. 14, at p. 15.

Other States were also on board with genocide prevention language. Thus, a proposed amendment by Chile to the preamble of the Cuban, Indian and Panamanian draft resolution included the following text:

> *Recommends* that international co-operation be organized between States with a view to facilitating *the speedy prevention* and punishment of the crime of genocide.[18]

Another preambular paragraph invited States to prevent and punish genocide within the scope of their domestic legislation.[19] During the debates at the Sixth Committee on the draft resolution, the Dutch representative also asserted that 'action taken by the United Nations should aim at prevention of the crime rather than its repression.'[20] The Polish representative – who later became an ICJ judge and its President (1973–1976) – likewise posited that the crime of genocide 'necessitated preventive rules which should be drawn up with the greatest of care', making reference to hate propaganda and domestic Polish legislative measures on the subject.[21] China spoke in support of the draft resolution and the amendment proposed by Chile and further suggested that the UN GA 'should also draw up a declaration enjoining upon Governments the duty of introducing effective measures to prevent and punish the crime of genocide.'[22]

The Sixth Committee debates led to the appointment of a sub-committee to draft what eventually became GA Resolution 96(I). The report of this committee agreed 'that it was desirable for Member States to enact legislation for the prevention and punishment of the crime of genocide'[23] and thus their draft resolution, passed without amendment by the GA, included the following text:

> *Invites* the Member States to enact the necessary legislation for the prevention and punishment of this crime [of genocide];
> [...]

---

18   UN Doc. A/C.6/94, Annex 15d, 1946, para. 3, in *supra* fn. 14, at p. 17 (emphasis added on prevention language).
19   UN Doc. A/C.6/94, Annex 15d, 1946, para. 2, in *supra* fn. 14, at p. 17.
20   UN Doc. A/C.6/96, 2 December 1946, Mr. Beucker Andrae (The Netherlands), in *supra* fn. 14, at p. 20.
21   UN Doc. A/C.6/96, 2 December 1946, Mr. Manfred Lachs (incorrectly spelled in the original document as 'Laks') (Poland), in *supra* fn. 14, at p. 22.
22   UN Doc. A/C.6/96, 2 December 1946, Mr. Liu (China), in *supra* fn. 14, at p. 22.
23   UN Doc. A/231, Annex 63, 1946, para. 5, in *supra* fn. 14, at p. 32.

Recommends that international co-operation be organized between States with a view to facilitating the speedy prevention and punishment of the crime of genocide[.][24]

A subsequent note by the UN Secretary-General on the resolution noted that the first of these two paragraphs was a 'question of internal measures to be taken by each State' and that the ECOSOC had 'no immediate step in view in this connection.'[25] With respect to the second paragraph, the note merely asserted that it was up to the ECOSOC to fulfill this task in view of drawing up a draft treaty.[26]

B First Draft Genocide Convention Prepared by the UN Secretary-General

In addition to the inclusion of prevention language reproduced above, GA Resolution 96(I) requested the ECOSOC to draw up a draft convention on genocide. After some debate, this was entrusted to the UN Secretary-General.[27] This draft convention included a number of interesting provisions related to the prevention of genocide.

First, in the preamble, the UN Secretary-General suggested that the High Contracting Parties proclaim 'that the fundamental exigencies of civilization, international order and peace require the[] prevention and punishment [of genocide]' and that '[t]hey pledge themselves to prevent and to repress such acts *wherever they may occur*.'[28] Second, the operative articles further emphasized the issue of prevention. Thus, Article 1 stated that the purpose of the convention was to 'prevent the destruction of racial, national, linguistic, religious or political groups of human beings.'[29] But perhaps more interesting was Article XII of the draft which was entitled 'Action by the United Nations to Prevent or to Stop Genocide'. It read:

---

24 UN GA Resolution 96(I), 11 December 1946, in *supra* fn. 14, at p. 34.
25 UN Doc. E/330, 12 March 1947, in *supra* fn. 14, at p. 36.
26 UN Doc. E/330, 12 March 1947, in *supra* fn. 14, at pp. 36–37.
27 UN Doc. E/325, ECOSOC Resolution 47(IV), 28 March 1947, in *supra* fn. 14, at p. 60.
28 UN Doc. E/447, Draft Convention on the Crime of Genocide, 26 June 1947, Preamble, paras 2–3, in *supra* fn. 14, at p. 214 (emphasis added). This draft was also contained in UN Doc. A/AC.10/42/Rev.1, 12 June 1947, in *supra* fn. 14, at p. 124. Both documents are English translations of the original French: UN Doc. A/AC.10/41, 6 June 1947, in *supra* fn. 14, at p. 61.
29 UN Doc. E/447, Draft Convention on the Crime of Genocide, 26 June 1947, Article I, in *supra* fn. 14, at p. 214 (also at UN Doc. A/AC.10/42/Rev.1, 12 June 1947, Article 1, in *supra* fn. 14, at p. 124).

> Notwithstanding any provisions in the foregoing articles, should the crimes as defined in this Convention be committed in any part of the world, or should there be serious reasons to suspect that such crimes have been committed, the High Contracting Parties may call upon the competent organs of the United Nations to take measures for the suppression or prevention of such crimes.
>
> In such case the said Parties shall do everything in their power to give full effect to the intervention of the United Nations.[30]

The accompanying note of the UN Secretariat/Secretary-General elaborated that the draft had been couched in the widest possible terms in order to form the basis for debate and that it was up to UN Member States and the various organs of the UN to resolve among themselves 'those problems of a political nature which may arise in connection with the prevention and punishment of the crime of genocide.'[31] For us, the commentary accompanying Article XII, which was to later be adopted in the final treaty in an amended form as Article VIII, is most interesting. After noting the general deterrent effect of domestic law criminal law, it then continued:

> In the international field even more than in the national, it is essential to exercise constant vigilance, and preventive action must be taken, either before the harm is done or before it has assumed wide proportions, for then it takes on the nature of a catastrophe, the effects of which are to a great extent irreparable.
>
> There is no need to expatiate on the preventive action which would be taken by the United Nations, for this is a question of the general competence of the United Nations being applied in a particular case.
>
> It must nevertheless be pointed out that, if preventive action is to have the maximum chances of success, the Members of the United Nations must not remain passive or indifferent. The Convention for the punishment of crimes of genocide should, therefore, bind the States to do everything in their power to support any action by the United Nations intended to prevent or stop these crimes.[32]

---

30   UN Doc. E/447, Draft Convention on the Crime of Genocide, 26 June 1947, Article XII, in *supra* fn. 14, at p. 218 (also at UN Doc. A/AC.10/42/Rev.1, 12 June 1947, Article 12, in *supra* fn. 14, at p. 128).

31   UN Doc. A/AC.10/42/Add.1, 10 June 1947, in *supra* fn. 14, at p. 133. See also UN Doc. E/447, in *supra* fn. 14, at p. 223.

32   UN Doc. E/447, 26 June 1947, in *supra* fn. 14, at p. 248.

This draft was submitted to the Committee on the Progressive Development of International Law and its Codification and elicited debate among States, initially mostly along the lines that they had not been accorded enough time to properly consider the draft. Nevertheless, in amongst these discussions, the Egyptian representative expressed the hope that 'future plans for preventing the crime of genocide would be farsighted enough not only to eliminate this crime in one direction, but also to prevent it from developing in another direction',[33] whilst the Union of Soviet Socialist Republics ('USSR') insisted that governments 'surely had a right to insist that effective measures be taken to prevent and punish this crime.'[34]

Nevertheless, comments received from UN Member States on the whole supported Article XII. Haiti for example, proposed also allowing human groups affected by genocide to call upon the UN to take measures in response,[35] while the United States of America ('US') suggested an amendment to Article XII so that UN Member States 'agree[d] to concert their action as [UN] Members to assure that the United Nations takes such action as may be appropriate under the Charter for the prevention and suppression of genocide.'[36] France stated that it could not 'but support a measure designed to prevent the recurrence of the racial persecutions' carried out by the Nazis,[37] but Venezuela however expressed concerns that the draft went beyond GA Resolution 96(I), but nevertheless stated that 'the spirit of [GA Resolution 96(I)] was to ensure that Members should prevent and punish the hateful acts that constitute genocide and establish a principle of international co-operation with this object'.[38]

Further discussions in the Sixth Committee then ensued. France would express the view that the draft did not go far enough, asserting that 'the present draft did not propose any effective machinery for the prevention of the crime of genocide'.[39] Nonetheless some, like Egypt and Australia, questioned the very utility of a convention, positing that it could not work as a preventive measure[40] and that the Nuremberg and Tokyo judgments 'would have a far greater effect towards preventing genocide than a convention'.[41] Pakistan on the other hand, 'favoured a convention on genocide, believing that it would prove effective in

---

[33] UN Doc. A/AC.10/SR.29, 24 June 1947, Mr. Ebeid (Egypt), in *supra* fn. 14, at p. 173.
[34] UN Doc. A/AC.10/SR.29, 24 June 1947, Professor Koretsky (USSR), in *supra* fn. 14, at p. 176.
[35] UN Doc. A/401, Annex 3a, 27 September 1947, in *supra* fn. 14, at p. 368.
[36] UN Doc. A/401, Annex 3a, 27 September 1947, in *supra* fn. 14, at p. 380.
[37] UN Doc. A/401, Annex 3a, 27 September 1947, in *supra* fn. 14, at p. 383.
[38] UN Doc. A/401, Annex 3a, 27 September 1947, in *supra* fn. 14, at p. 370.
[39] UN Doc. A/C.6/SR.39, 29 September 1947, Mr. Chaumont (France), in *supra* fn. 14, at p. 388.
[40] UN Doc. A/C.6/SR.40, 2 October 1947, Mr. Raafat (Egypt), in *supra* fn. 14, at p. 392.
[41] UN Doc. A/C.6/SR.42, 6 October 1947, Mr. Oldham (Australia), in *supra* fn. 14, at p. 404.

preventing the crime, and that the General Assembly resolution [96(I)] demanded it.'[42]

The United Kingdom representative – and the former lead British Prosecutor at Nuremberg – called to attention Article XII's reference to UN Member States calling upon the UN's competent organs to take suppressive measures against genocide anywhere in the world and that Article IX defined as the competent organ for trials a proposed international court. He questioned whether any State would likely surrender their nationals to such an institution, stating that '[t]he only real sanction against genocide was war' and that the draft was unrealistic.[43]

A Sub-Committee then decided that the appropriate organ to proceed with the matter was the ECOSOC,[44] and the Sixth Committee then urged the GA to adopt what became GA Resolution 180(II), which formally asked the ECOSOC to be seized of the issue.[45] During the GA debate concerning GA Resolution 180(II), the Norwegian delegate emphasized that part of GA Resolution 96(I) was 'an invitation to Member States to enact the necessary legislation for the prevention and punishment of this crime' and urged the GA to 'now work out the convention on genocide in order to do what little we can to prevent it from happening again; and let us do it now while our memories [from World War II] are still fresh.'[46] Importantly for us, the Mexican delegate emphasized that:

> [T]he mere fact of the occurrence of genocide, in whatever part of the world, suffices to make my Government consider that, both individually and collectively through our international organization, every one of the States ought to feel it their bounden duty and a matter of the greatest importance to eliminate and above all to prevent this crime against whole groups of human beings, which criminally destroys great potentialities of culture, energy and vital activities, and constitute a direct and serious threat to the welfare of the human race.[47]

---

[42] UN Doc. A/C.6/SR.41, 3 October 1947, Mr. Pirzada (Pakistan), in *supra* fn. 14, at p. 397.
[43] UN Doc. A/C.6/SR.42, 6 October 1947, Sir Hartley Shawcross (United Kingdom), in *supra* fn. 14, at pp. 403–404.
[44] UN Doc. A/C.6/190, 11 November 1947, in *supra* fn. 14, at p. 412.
[45] UN GA Resolution 180(II), 21 November 1947, in *supra* fn. 14, at p. 467.
[46] UN Doc. A/PV.123, 21 November 1947, Mr. Seyersted (Norway), in *supra* fn. 14, at pp. 451–452.
[47] UN Doc. A/PV.123, 21 November 1947, Mr. Villa Michel (Mexico), in *supra* fn. 14, at p. 454 (translated from original Spanish).

THE PREVENTION OF GENOCIDE AS A *JUS COGENS* NORM?   299

He went on to express the view that 'the prevention of genocide deserves special attention over and above that given to it in the draft convention drawn up by the Secretariat' and that the prevention of genocide could not rest on the punishment of attempts or preparatory acts, or on the effectiveness of exemplary punishment, but instead, 'more emphasis [should be placed] on the elimination, through the operation of the convention, of certain reprehensible acts which may also be regarded as giving rise to conditions causing, or at least predisposing to, genocide.'[48] These remarks elicited no objections. In response to some skepticism as to the utility of a convention on genocide, the Dominican Republic representative opined that 'the convention would at least carry great moral weight and might, by that moral weight alone, prevent many errors and excesses, because the convention[] [...] would be the most forceful denunciation of that heinous crime, and would therefore mean the final condemnation of its instigators before the moral tribunal of the world.'[49]

C   The Economic and Social Council and the Ad Hoc Committee on Genocide

Despite being given terms of reference outlining specific issues the ECOSOC needed to resolve, a perusal of that document reveals that the prevention of genocide, as such, was not chief among them.[50] Notwithstanding, during initial debates at the ECOSOC the Brazilian representative insisted that '[w]hile it could not be expected that such a convention would prevent genocide, any more than the criminal laws of various countries prevented crime, such considerations should not discourage the United Nations from taking action in the matter.'[51] Likewise, the USSR representative expressed the view that preventing genocide meant also fighting against discrimination and the stirring up of hatred against certain groups by not only developing friendly relations between States, but also between groups living within the State.[52] In the end, an *ad hoc* committee (consisting of representatives from the US, USSR, Lebanon, China, France, Poland and Venezuela) was established in order to further prepare the draft convention taking into account the views of UN Member States

---

48   UN Doc. A/PV.123, 21 November 1947, Mr. Villa Michel (Mexico), in *supra* fn. 14, at p. 455 (translated from original Spanish).
49   UN Doc. A/PV.123, 21 November 1947, Mr. Henriquez Ureña (Dominican Republic), in *supra* fn. 14, at p. 459 (translated from original Spanish).
50   See UN Doc. E/622, 3 February 1948, in *supra* fn. 14, at pp. 572–576 (translated from the original French).
51   UN Doc. E/SR.139, 12 February 1948, Mr. Muniz (Brazil), in *supra* fn. 14, at p. 591.
52   UN Doc. E/SR.140, 13 February 1948, Mr. Arutiunian (USSR), in *supra* fn. 14, at p. 596.

and other UN bodies.[53] The committee's terms of reference did not include specific reference to the prevention of genocide as such.[54]

During the *ad hoc* committee's debates, expressions on the prevention on genocide revolved around the protected groups[55] and whether governmental complicity should be an element.[56] However, the USSR delegation produced a set of basic principles wherein it stated that '[t]he campaign against genocide requires all civilized peoples to take decisive measures to prevent such crimes and also to suppress and prohibit the stimulation of racial, national (and religious) hatred' and as such was of the position that the convention should oblige States to enactment domestic legislation on genocide.[57] The USSR representative would repeat these views during the *ad hoc* committee's debates[58] which were also echoed by Poland.[59] This elicited debates surrounding free speech, propaganda for genocide, and incitement to commit genocide.[60] Initially, the *ad hoc* committee rejected the USSR proposal for the inclusion of language that obliged States to criminalize genocide in their municipal law, despite in principle support from countries like China and France.[61] Later in the negotiations it was revived by the USSR and after further discussions, and

---

53   ECOSOC Resolution 117(VI) (UN Doc. E/734), 3 March 1948, in *supra* fn. 14, at p. 619.
54   See UN Doc E/AC.25/2, 1 April 1948, in *supra* fn. 14, at p. 643 (translated from the original French).
55   See UN Doc. E/AC.25/SR.1, 7 April 1948, Mr. Perez-Perozo (Venezuela), in *supra* fn. 14, at p. 686 (translated from the original French); UN Doc. E/AC.25/SR.2, 6 April 1948, Mr. Azkoul (Lebanon), in *supra* fn. 14, at p. 692 (translated from the original French).
56   UN Doc E/AC.25/SR.4, 15 April 1948, Mr. Rudzinski (Poland), Mr. Ordonneau (France), Mr. Maktos (US), Mr. Perez-Perozo (Venezuela), in *supra* fn. 14, at pp. 714–715 (translated from the original French).
57   UN Doc. E/AC.25/7, 7 April 1948, Principles I, VIII(b), in *supra* fn. 14, at pp. 696, 697–698 (translated from the original Russian).
58   UN Doc. E/AC.25/SR.3, 13 April 1948, Mr. Morozov (USSR), in *supra* fn. 14, at p. 701 (translated from the original French).
59   UN Doc. E/AC.25/SR.3, 13 April 1948, Mr. Rudzinski (Poland), in *supra* fn. 14, at p. 702 (translated from the original French).
60   UN Doc. E/AC.25/SR.5, 16 April 1948, Mr. Maktos (US), Mr. Rudzinski (Poland), Mr. Morozov (USSR), in *supra* fn. 14, at pp. 731–733 (translated from the original French).
61   UN Doc. E/AC.25/SR.6, 18 April 1948, Mr. Lin Mousheng (China), Mr. Ordonneau (France), Mr. Rudzinski (Poland), in *supra* fn. 14, at pp. 746, 749–756 (translated from the original French).

despite reservations from Venezuela,[62] its inclusion was approved as a measure to prevent the occurrence of genocide.[63]

However, Venezuela also pointed to the danger of resort to the UN Security Council in a genocide context, rather than each State formally pledging to suppress and endeavouring to prevent genocide themselves:

> [A]n armed expeditionary force in the territory of a State guilty of genocide would inevitably lead to war; yet the United Nations had been set up for the purpose of avoiding war.[64]

Others, such as Lebanon, supported the idea that some form of international 'control' be set up, either entrusted to the UN Security Council, an international penal court, or an *ad hoc* international court, for '[t]he aim[] [...] was not only to put a stop to criminal acts; they should also be prevented. The fear of legal reprisals would be the most effective means of preventing them.'[65] Poland, on the other hand thought that the UN Security Council and States taking domestic legislative measures to prevent genocide was sufficient and opposed any international tribunal.[66] The proposal to establish an international court was eventually put to a vote and was approved,[67] however, it would later be watered down so that States would only pledge to submit persons guilty of genocide to competent national courts or a future international court, and then subsequently removed it from the draft altogether but was nonetheless included in the final report.[68]

The committee would return to the basic principles proposed by the USSR, particularly Principle X, which stated:

---

62   UN Doc. E/AC.25/SR.19, 5 May 1948, Mr. Perez-Perozo (Venezuela), in *supra* fn. 14, at p. 937.

63   UN Doc. E/AC.25/SR.18, 26 April 1948, in *supra* fn. 14, at pp. 927–930; UN Doc. E/AC.25/SR.19, 5 May 1948, in *supra* fn. 14, at pp. 934–939. The approved text read:
The High Contracting Parties undertake to enact the necessary legislation, in accordance with their constitutional procedures, to give effect to the provisions of the present convention.

64   UN Doc. E/AC.25/SR.7, 20 April 1948, Mr. Perez-Perozo (Venezuela), in *supra* fn. 14, at p. 782 (translated from the original French).

65   UN Doc. E/AC.25/SR.7, 20 April 1948, Mr. Azkoul (Lebanon), in *supra* fn. 14, at p. 785 (translated from the original French).

66   UN Doc. E/AC.25/SR.7, 20 April 1948, Mr. Rudzinski (Poland), in *supra* fn. 14, at p. 786 (translated from the original French).

67   UN Doc. E/AC.25/SR.8, 17 April 1948, in *supra* fn. 14, at pp. 805 (translated from the original French).

68   UN Doc. E/AC.25/SR.20, 4 May 1948, in *supra* fn. 14, at pp. 943–944.

The convention should provide that the signatories to the convention must report to the Security Council all cases of genocide and all cases of a breach of the obligations imposed by the convention, so that the necessary measures may be taken in accordance with Chapter VI of the United Nations Charter.[69]

The USSR representative explained that 'an act of genocide might necessitate the taking of measures outside the scope of an international court of justice or national courts. It would thus belong to the Security Council to decide whether measures should be taken in accordance with Chapter VI of the Charter'.[70] Furthermore, he emphasized that if humanity were again to witness genocide, the adoption of Principle X 'would enable the United Nations to take the measures necessary for the restoration of order and the prevention of further crimes. The signatories to the convention should not only have the right to report all cases of genocide to the Security Council; but it should be their obligation to do so.'[71] Poland expressed support for the USSR's principle, opining that '[t]o make the convention fully effective, provision had to be made for the intervention of the only organ of the United Nations invested with authority to take decisions, that is, the Security Council.'[72] Lebanon and France were also on board, so long as the principle was intended to merely specify an obligation to bring genocide to the Security Council's attention.[73] France added that 'the Security Council did not necessarily have to be seized of all violations of the convention' as it was a matter for the Security Council to decide.[74]

China's representative spoke against, arguing that it raised difficulties, particularly with respect to the correct UN organ to deal with matters like cultural genocide and asked why Chapter VII was not included in Principle X. Nevertheless, he expressed a preference for a provision similar to Article XII of the

---

69 UN Doc. E/AC.25/7, 7 April 1948, Principle X, in *supra* fn. 14, at p. 698 (translated from the original Russian).

70 UN Doc. E/AC.25/SR.8, 17 April 1948, Mr. Morozov (USSR), in *supra* fn. 14, at p. 807 (translated from the original French).

71 UN Doc. E/AC.25/SR.8, 17 April 1948, Mr. Morozov (USSR), in *supra* fn. 14, at p. 807 (translated from the original French).

72 UN Doc. E/AC.25/SR.8, 17 April 1948, Mr. Rudzinski (Poland), in *supra* fn. 14, at p. 808 (translated from the original French); UN Doc. E/AC.25/SR.9, 21 April 1948, Mr. Rudzinski (Poland), in *supra* fn. 14, at p. 821 (translated from the original French).

73 UN Doc. E/AC.25/SR.8, 17 April 1948, Mr. Rudzinski (Poland), Mr. Ordonneau (France), in *supra* fn. 14, at pp. 808, 809 (translated from the original French).

74 UN Doc. E/AC.25/SR.8, 17 April 1948, Mr. Ordonneau (France), in *supra* fn. 14, at p. 809 (translated from the original French).

UN Secretary-General's draft,[75] and proposed that 'that states should be given the option, rather than placed under the obligation, of having recourse to the appropriate organ of the United Nations.'[76] Similarly, the US believed that Principle X was somewhat superfluous given that UN Member States could already bring such matters to the attention to the UN Security Council and also showed support for Article XII as it had a wider field of application.[77] In the end, the principle of obligatory notification of genocide was defeated in a vote[78] and instead the *ad hoc* committee adopted a proposal by the US for UN Member States to instead take concerted action to assure that the UN took action to prevent and suppress genocide as may be appropriate under the UN Charter (1945).[79]

During this time a note by the Secretariat was drafted on the relationship between the Genocide Convention and the formulation of the Nuremberg Principles and the Draft Code of Offences Against Peace and Security of Mankind, which spoke to the issue of the prevention of genocide and what it would mean for the Genocide Convention. Aside from penal measures for acts that do not themselves constitute genocide (e.g. inciting hatred), the document stated that:

> There may be international prevention of a political nature. That would be the case if it was provided that the States parties to the convention should inform the organs of the United Nations in order that they might prevent the Commission of genocide.[80]

In the meantime, States continued to submit further views. The Netherlands' comments on what was then Article XII ('Action by the United Nations to Prevent or to Stop Genocide') stated that the provision required closer scrutiny. In

---

75   UN Doc. E/AC.25/SR.8, 17 April 1948, Mr. Lin Mousheng (China), in *supra* fn. 14, at pp. 809, 815–816 (translated from the original French).

76   UN Doc. E/AC.25/SR.9, 21 April 1948, Mr. Lin Mousheng (China), in *supra* fn. 14, at p. 821 (translated from the original French).

77   UN Doc. E/AC.25/SR.8, 17 April 1948, Mr. Maktos (US), in *supra* fn. 14, at pp. 809–810 (translated from the original French); UN Doc. E/AC.25/SR.9, 21 April 1948, Mr. Maktos (US), in *supra* fn. 14, at pp. 820–821 (translated from the original French).

78   UN Doc. E/AC.25/SR.9, 21 April 1948, Mr. Maktos (US), in *supra* fn. 14, at p. 822 (translated from the original French).

79   UN Doc. E/AC.25/SR.9, 21 April 1948, Mr. Maktos (US), in *supra* fn. 14, at pp. 821, 822 (translated from the original French).

80   UN Doc E/AC.25/3/Rev.1, 12 April 1948, in *supra* fn. 14, at p. 675 (translated from the original French).

particular, it opined that Article XII contained elements that were self-evident, such as the stipulation that States were to do everything in their power to give full effect to UN intervention and that it felt the same about the US proposal articulated above.[81] The Netherlands suggested 'either to consider as self-evident that the new treaty does not infringe upon the rights and duties under the Charter, or to insert a general article to this effect, so that all action of the United Nations which is now desirable and permissible shall remain so in future.'[82]

Back at the *ad hoc* committee, China presented its own draft articles for inclusion into the Genocide Convention. This draft included language whereby States parties agreed to prevent and punish genocide, however it was included in the preamble.[83] This proposed preamble did not elicit debate in the committee. However, the rest of the articles were discussed line by line. Article IV of the Chinese draft is of interest to us. It stated that '[a]ny Signatory to this Convention may call upon any competent organ of the United Nations to take such action as may be appropriate under the Charter for the prevention and suppression of genocide.'[84] This proposed article elicited some debate in the *ad hoc* committee, with the USSR proposing to amend its wording so as to also include an obligation (not just the right) to report any violation of the convention as well as acts of genocide to the UN Security Council. This amendment was promptly rejected in a vote.[85] Notwithstanding, support for the Chinese proposal was evident and was approved (originally as Article 7 of the draft convention, but which later became Article VIII), although with amendments, to read:

> Any signatory of this Convention may call upon any competent organ of the United Nations to take such action as may be appropriate under the Charter for the prevention and suppression of genocide. Any signatory to this Convention may bring to the attention of any competent organ of the United Nations any case of violation of this Convention.[86]

---

81 UN Doc. E/623/Add.2, 22 April 1948, in *supra* fn. 14, at p. 638. For the US proposal, see *supra* fn. 36.

82 UN Doc. E/623/Add.2, 22 April 1948, in *supra* fn. 14, at p. 638.

83 UN Doc. E/AC.25/9, 16 April 1948, Preamble, in *supra* fn. 14, at p. 833.

84 UN Doc. E/AC.25/9, 16 April 1948, Article IV, in *supra* fn. 14, at p. 833.

85 UN Doc. E/AC.25/SR.20, 4 May 1948, Mr. Morozov (USSR), in *supra* fn. 14, at p. 944–945. See also the final report of the *ad hoc* committee: UN Doc. E/794, 24 May 1948, in *supra* fn. 14, at pp. 1142–1143.

86 UN Doc. E/AC.25/SR.20, 4 May 1948, in *supra* fn. 14, at pp. 944–945 (corrected at UN Doc. E/AC.25/SR.20/Corr.1, 14 May 1948, in *supra* fn. 14, at p. 950). See also the final report of the *ad hoc* committee: UN Doc. E/794, 24 May 1948, in *supra* fn. 14, at p. 1143.

Prolonged discussions also surrounded what became the Preamble of the draft Genocide Convention (whose prevention language would later find its way into Article I of the final convention) however, they did not focus too much on the prevention of genocide as such.[87] Nevertheless, a US proposal to include language in the Preamble that 'the parties to the [...] Convention agree to prevent and punish [genocide] as herein provided' was defeated,[88] but a similar proposal by the USSR, focusing more on the repression of preparatory acts was approved instead.[89] Further discussions saw this whittled down and reference being made to the then recent judgment of the International Military Tribunal at Nuremberg. The approved preamble read:

> The High Contracting Parties declare that genocide is a grave crime against mankind which violates the spirit and aims of the United Nations and which the civilized world condemns;
>
> The High Contracting Parties, having been profoundly shocked by many recent instances of genocide, and having taken note of the fact that the International Military Tribunal at Nuremberg, in its judgment of September 30 and October 1, 1946 has punished certain persons who have committed analogous acts, and being convinced that the prevention and punishment of genocide requires international co-operation, hereby agrees to prevent and punish the crime as provided in this Convention.[90]

Finally, last minute amendments were passed during the final readings of the approved convention text. This included language about putting to trial before domestic courts or before a competent international tribunal persons alleged

---

87   See UN Doc. E/AC.25/SR.20, 4 May 1948, in *supra* fn. 14, at pp. 948–949; UN Doc. E/AC.25/SR.21, 5 May 1948, in *supra* fn. 14, at pp. 953–959; UN Doc. E/AC.25/SR.22, 5 May 1948, in *supra* fn. 14, at pp. 961–968; UN Doc. E/AC.25/SR.23, 4 May 1948, in *supra* fn. 14, at pp. 970–973.
88   UN Doc. E/AC.25/SR.22, 5 May 1948, in *supra* fn. 14, at pp. 962–963;
89   UN Doc. E/AC.25/SR.22, 5 May 1948, in *supra* fn. 14, at pp. 967–968. The approved USSR proposal read:
   That the struggle against genocide requires all civilized peoples to take decisive measures aimed at the prevention of such crimes and also at the suppression and prohibition of the instigation of racial, national (and religious) hatred and at the severe punishment of the persons guilty of inciting, committing or preparing the commission of the crimes mentioned above.
90   UN Doc. E/AC.25/SR.23, 4 May 1948, in *supra* fn. 14, at p. 973 (translated from the original French).

to have committed genocide in Article 6 of the draft[91] and minor changes to Article 7 of the draft.[92] However, the USSR insisted that States should instead undertake in the treaty to report occurrences of genocide and violations of the convention to the UN Security Council for it to deal with under Chapter VI, expressing its preference for a differently worded article to that effect.[93] Similarly, small changes were made to the Preamble,[94] but the prevention language outlined above was kept intact,[95] despite insistence from the USSR that the preamble also include language with respect to measures aiming to suppress and prohibit instigation of hatred and preparatory acts of genocide.[96] However, a new Article I was introduced which declared genocide to be an international crime during peace and war, thus shifting the rest of the articles down one number.[97] The final vote for the convention as a whole by the *ad hoc* committee on genocide was five for (China, France, Lebanon, US, Venezuela), one against (USSR) with one abstention (Poland),[98] and was promptly delivered to the ECOSOC, which in turn, after some discussions[99] transmitted the draft convention and the committee's report to the UN GA for its consideration.[100]

D   *The UN General Assembly and the Final Genocide Convention*

The Sixth Committee then proceeded to discuss the *ad hoc* committee's draft. During the initial debates, the representative from Yugoslavia criticized the draft as it had 'no provision designed to prevent genocide; the whole text dealt only with punishment of the crime' and suggested that a fresh draft be prepared providing for the prevention as well as punishment of genocide.[101] The

---

91   UN Doc. E/AC.25/SR.24, 12 May 1948, in *supra* fn. 14, at p. 1020–1021.
92   See *supra* fn. 86; UN Doc. E/AC.25/SR.24, 12 May 1948, in *supra* fn. 14, at p. 1021–1022.
93   UN Doc. E/AC.25/SR.24, 12 May 1948, Mr. Morozov (USSR), in *supra* fn. 14, at p. 1022.
94   UN Doc. E/AC.25/SR.24, 12 May 1948, in *supra* fn. 14, at pp. 1023–1025.
95   See *supra* fn. 90.
96   UN Doc. E/AC.25/SR.24, 12 May 1948, Mr. Morozov (USSR), in *supra* fn. 14, at p. 1025.
97   UN Doc. E/AC.25/W.1/Add.3, in *supra* fn. 14, at pp. 1003–1004.
98   UN Doc. E/AC.25/SR.26, 12 May 1948, in *supra* fn. 14, at p. 1040 (translated from the original French). See also the final report of the *ad hoc* committee: UN Doc. E/794, 24 May 1948, in *supra* fn. 14, at p. 1154. The final draft convention was attached as an annex: UN Doc. E/794, 24 May 1948, in *supra* fn. 14, at pp. 1155–1159 (also in UN Doc. E/AC.25/12, 19 May 1948, in *supra* fn. 14, at pp. 1161–1166).
99   See UN Doc. E/SR.218, 26 August 1948, in *supra* fn. 14, at pp. 1219–1239; UN Doc. E/SR.219, 26 August 1948, in *supra* fn. 14, at pp. 1240–1251.
100   ECOSOC Resolution 153(VII) (UN Doc. E/1049), 26 August 1948, in *supra* fn. 14, at p. 619.
101   UN Doc. A/C.6/SR.63, 30 September 1948, Mr. Bartos (Yugoslavia), in H. Abtahi and P. Webb, *The Genocide Convention: The* Travaux Préparatoires, Volume 2 (Leiden/Boston, Martinus Nijhoff Publishers: 2008), at p. 1297.

United Kingdom again expressed doubt as to the utility of a convention on genocide, noting that 'individual genocide was already punishable by the laws of all countries, whereas genocide committed by States was punishable only by war.'[102] Others like Poland praised the draft, particularly its provisions on incitement to commit genocide, stating that '[t]he instigators of hatred were numerous at the present time and should be prevented from carrying out their dangerous work'.[103] Egypt likewise supported such clauses as a means to prevent genocide.[104] A number of States including Belgium[105] and Czechoslovakia[106] also stated the importance of passing domestic legislation to suppress and prevent genocide, while Iran highlighted the ability of States parties to bring to the attention of the competent bodies of the UN instances of genocide so that measures could be taken to prevent and suppress it.[107]

Each of the articles of the draft were then examined by the Sixth Committee. With respect to Article I, The Netherlands proposed adding language to ensure that not only was genocide recognized as an international crime during war and peace, but that it was also a crime that States undertook to prevent and punish,[108] a move that was supported by Iran, Syria, Denmark, the United Kingdom.[109] On the other hand, the USSR was skeptical and argued that it should be moved to the preamble,[110] a position supported by the Dominican Republic.[111] Against this proposal were Mexico and The Netherlands.[112] In the

---

[102] UN Doc. A/C.6/SR.63, 30 September 1948, Sir Hartley Shawcross (United Kingdom), in *supra* fn. 101, at p. 1307.
[103] UN Doc. A/C.6/SR.63, 30 September 1948, Mr. Manfred Lachs (Poland), in *supra* fn. 101, at p. 1309.
[104] UN Doc. A/C.6/SR.63, 30 September 1948, Mr. Raafat (Egypt), in *supra* fn. 101, at p. 1317.
[105] UN Doc. A/C.6/SR.63, 30 September 1948, Mr. Kaeckenbeeck (Belgium), in *supra* fn. 101, at p. 1313.
[106] UN Doc. A/C.6/SR.66, 4 October 1948, Mr. Prochazka (Czechoslovakia), in *supra* fn. 101, at p. 1323.
[107] UN Doc. A/C.6/SR.66, 4 October 1948, Mr. Abdoh (Iran), in *supra* fn. 101, at p. 1325.
[108] UN Doc. A/C.6/SR.68, 6 October 1948, Mr. de Beus (The Netherlands), in *supra* fn. 101, at p. 1342.
[109] UN Doc. A/C.6/SR.68, 6 October 1948, Mr. Abdoh (Iran), Mr. Tarazi (Syria), Mr. Federspiel (Denmark), Sir Hartley Shawcross (United Kingdom), in *supra* fn. 101, at p. 1344–1346.
[110] UN Doc. A/C.6/SR.68, 6 October 1948, Mr. Morozov (USSR), in *supra* fn. 101, at p. 1347.
[111] UN Doc. A/C.6/SR.68, 6 October 1948, Mr. Mezina (Dominican Republic), in *supra* fn. 101, at p. 1347.
[112] UN Doc. A/C.6/SR.68, 6 October 1948, Mr. Noriega (Mexico), Mr. de Beus (The Netherlands), in *supra* fn. 101, at p. 1348.

end the USSR's move was defeated decisively in a vote,[113] and after some wrangling as to the exact wording, the following was approved:

> The High Contracting Parties confirm that genocide is a crime under international law, whether committed in time of peace or of war, which they *undertake to prevent and to punish*.[114]

Despite this, some delegations including Brazil, Czechoslovakia, Chile and Venezuela expressed the view that Article I should instead appear in the preamble.[115] It should be noted that the words 'to prevent' did not elicit significant debate.

In amongst discussions of other provisions – such as the definition of genocide, the protected groups and preparatory acts of genocide (incitement, instigation, etc.) – there were some discussions about the prevention genocide. For example, in response to a French proposal for the introduction of a State involvement element into Article II,[116] the US brought up the issue of State responsibility for genocide, stating that it would be against the notion that a State that had fulfilled its obligation under the Genocide Convention but had not succeeded in preventing genocide could nonetheless incur international responsibility. However, 'if a State had not done all it could to prevent or punish the crime, international responsibility would come under consideration.'[117] This view was repeated by Sweden, Uruguay[118] and France.[119] However, these discussions centered around the issue of responsibility for genocide within the borders of the relevant State, not outside those borders. In any event, the French proposal was rejected.[120]

Additionally, when moves were made by the US to remove direct incitement to commit genocide from the convention,[121] various States objected, arguing that this would undermine the convention's efforts to prevent genocide before

---

113 UN Doc. A/C.6/SR.68, 6 October 1948, in *supra* fn. 101, at p. 1350.
114 UN Doc. A/C.6/SR.68, 6 October 1948, in *supra* fn. 101, at p. 1352 (emphasis added).
115 UN Doc. A/C.6/SR.68, 6 October 1948, Mr. Amado (Brazil), Mr. Zourek (Czechoslovakia), Mr. Arancibia Lazo (Chile), Mr. Pérez Perozo (Venezuela), in *supra* fn. 101, at p. 1353.
116 UN Doc. A/C/224/Corr.1, 8 October 1948, in in *supra* fn. 101, at p. 1978.
117 UN Doc. A/C.6/SR.79, 20 October 1948, Mr. Maktos (US), in *supra* fn. 101, at p. 1461.
118 UN Doc. A/C.6/SR.79, 20 October 1948, Mr. Petren (Sweden), Mr. Manini y Ríos (Uruguay), in *supra* fn. 101, at pp. 1463, 1464.
119 UN Doc. A/C.6/SR.80, 21 October 1948, Mr. Spanien (France), in *supra* fn. 101, at pp. 1469–1470.
120 UN Doc. A/C.6/SR.80, 21 October 1948, in *supra* fn. 101, at p. 1471.
121 UN Doc. A/C.6/214, 4 October 1948, in *supra* fn. 101, at p. 1968.

it occurred. Such views were expressed by Poland, Yugoslavia, Denmark, Czechoslovakia, Uruguay, Egypt, and the USSR.[122] The US proposal was eventually defeated.[123] Similarly, in debates surrounding a proposal by the USSR to add further preparatory acts to the list of punishable acts,[124] States such as the USSR, The Netherlands, Yugoslavia, Denmark, Poland, Czechoslovakia and Haiti[125] all emphasized the need to prevent genocide before it materialized, and Yugoslavia went as far as to say that the 'rejection of the Soviet Union amendment would be equivalent to depriving the convention of all preventive force.'[126] However, the USSR amendment was defeated.[127] Likewise, when the issue of competent courts for genocide arose (in the documents this was Article VII, but it would eventually become Article VI in the final Genocide Convention (1948)), States such as Pakistan, Iran, Ecuador and Belgium were of the view that some form of provision for control at the international level was necessary to prevent the crime in the future.[128]

Attention would eventually turn to Article VIII. The USSR tried to replace the existing draft with an article that again introduced language that States would 'undertake to report to the Security Council all cases of genocide and all cases of a breach of the obligations imposed by the Convention' so that necessary Chapter VI action would be taken.[129] In the debates, the USSR expressed the view that it 'was not pessimistic in regard to the United Nations' ability to prevent and repress genocide. Chapters VI and VII of the Charter provided means for the prevention and punishment of genocide, means far more concrete and effective than anything possible in the sphere of international

---

122   UN Doc. A/C.6/SR.84, Mr. Manfred Lachs (Poland), Mr. Bartos (Yugoslavia), 26 October 1948, in *supra* fn. 101, at pp. 1529, 1530–1531; UN Doc. A/C.6/SR.85, Mr. Federspiel (Denmark), Mr. Zourek (Czechoslovakia), Mr. Manini y Ríos (Uruguay), Mr. Raafat (Egypt), Mr. Manfred Lachs (Poland), Mr. Morozov (USSR), 27 October 1948, in *supra* fn. 101, at pp. 1536, 1538, 1539–1540, 1543–1544, 1545.

123   UN Doc. A/C.6/SR.85, 27 October 1948, in *supra* fn. 101, at p. 1547.

124   UN Doc. A/C.6/215/Rev.1, proposed Article IV, 4 October 1948, in *supra* fn. 101, at p. 1970.

125   UN Doc. A/C.6/SR.86, Mr. Morozov (USSR), Mr. de Beus (The Netherlands), Mr. Bartos (Yugoslavia), Mr. Federspiel (Denmark), Mr. Manfred Lachs (Poland), Mr. Zourek (Czechoslovakia), Mr. Demesmin (Haiti), 28 October 1948, in *supra* fn. 101, at pp. 1553–1554, 1554–1555, 1555–1556, 1558–1559, 1560–1561, 1562–1563, 1571.

126   UN Doc. A/C.6/SR.86, Mr. Bartos (Yugoslavia), 28 October 1948, in *supra* fn. 101, at p. 1563.

127   UN Doc. A/C.6/SR.86, 28 October 1948, in *supra* fn. 101, at pp. 1567, 1579.

128   UN Doc. A/C.6/SR.97, Mr. Sadar Bahadur Khan (Pakistan), Mr. Abdoh (Iran), Mr. Correa (Ecuador), Mr. Kaeckenbeeck (Belgium), 9 November 1948, in *supra* fn. 101, at pp. 1678–1679, 1679–1680, 1687–1688, 1688–1689.

129   UN Doc. A/C.6/215/Rev.1, proposed Article VIII, 4 October 1948, in *supra* fn. 101, at p. 1971.

jurisdiction.'[130] This was supported by France, who proposed their own amendment to the USSR model which removed 'all', so that States 'may call the attention of the Security Council to the cases of genocide and of violations of the present Convention likely to constitute a threat to international peace and security' so that the UN Security could take action it deemed necessary.[131] Others such as the United Kingdom, Greece, France, Belgium, the US and Siam spoke for the elimination of Article VIII on the grounds that it was superfluous.[132] Nevertheless, Belgium and Greece expressed support for the French proposal.[133] Peru on the other hand, thought it unwise to give the UN Security Council 'jurisdiction' over the prevention and repression of genocide as it 'would, in fact, be to give penal jurisdiction to that body. [...] [M]easures to be taken against genocide should be juridical and not political.'[134] The US expressed a similar view as Peru, as 'the whole question of the veto would be involved.'[135] Egypt, Syria, Poland, Iran, and Czechoslovakia all expressed support for Article VIII in its USSR/French form and were against its deletion.[136] In particular, Czechoslovakia pointed out that entrusting the UN Security Council would be the most effective way given that it 'was in permanent session and was therefore capable of swift and effective action. It was also the organ entrusted with the primary responsibility for the maintenance of international peace and security [...] and it was the only organ of the United Nations which had the power to impose effective sanctions.'[137] Poland also stated that '[t]he prevention of genocide was extremely important and if the commission of genocide were linked with threats to international peace and security, it would be a useful deterrent.'[138]

---

130   UN Doc. A/C.6/SR.101, Mr. Morozov (USSR), 11 November 1948, in *supra* fn. 101, at p. 1734.
131   UN Doc. A/C.6/SR.101, Mr. Mr. Chaumont (France), 11 November 1948, in *supra* fn. 101, at p. 1735.
132   UN Doc. A/C.6/SR.101, Mr. Fitzmaurice (United Kingdom), Mr. Spiropoulos (Greece), Mr. Chaumont (France), Mr. Kaeckenbeeck (Belgium), Mr. Maktos (US), Prince Wan Waithayakon (Siam), 11 November 1948, in *supra* fn. 101, at pp. 1734, 1735, 1739.
133   UN Doc. A/C.6/SR.101, Mr. Kaeckenbeeck (Belgium), Mr. Spiropoulos (Greece), 11 November 1948, in *supra* fn. 101, at pp. 1735, 1740.
134   UN Doc. A/C.6/SR.101, Mr. Maûrtua (Peru), 11 November 1948, in *supra* fn. 101, at p. 1736.
135   UN Doc. A/C.6/SR.101, Mr. Maktos (US), 11 November 1948, in *supra* fn. 101, at p. 1739.
136   UN Doc. A/C.6/SR.101, Mr. Raafat (Egypt), Mr. Tarazi (Syria), Mr. Manfred Lachs (Poland), Mr. Abdoh, Mr. Zourek (Czechoslovakia), 11 November 1948, in *supra* fn. 101, at pp. 1736–1737, 1738–1739, 1740–1741.
137   UN Doc. A/C.6/SR.101, Mr. Zourek (Czechoslovakia), 11 November 1948, in *supra* fn. 101, at p. 1741.
138   UN Doc. A/C.6/SR.101, Mr. Manfred Lachs (Poland), 11 November 1948, in *supra* fn. 101, at p. 1741.

Although Article VIII was initially voted out of existence,[139] the USSR/French proposal remained on the table, albeit in an amended form that also included the possibility of seizing the UN General Assembly as well as the UN Security Council of genocide and violations of the convention.[140] However this too was rejected in a vote,[141] but shortly after, upon the initiative of the USSR – which had vowed to fight for Article VIII – there was an attempt to reopen debate surrounding Article VIII on procedural grounds, however this too was defeated.[142]

Thus, it appeared that Article VIII was doomed to the dustbin of history. However, in discussions on Article X – concerning dispute procedures that included an ICJ compromissory clause (which later became Article IX of the final Genocide Convention (1948)), the Australian representative attempted to re-introduce Article VIII via the backdoor as an amendment to Article X,[143] and although the Chairman ruled that it was out of order given the prior rejection of Article VIII, he was overruled by a two-thirds majority vote.[144] This amendment received support from China, and after short consideration was approved in Article X.[145] The United Kingdom and The Netherlands explained that they had voted in favour because they wanted it to be clear that the ICJ was not the only recourse in instances of genocide.[146]

---

139 UN Doc. A/C.6/SR.101, 11 November 1948, in *supra* fn. 101, at p. 1744–1745.
140 UN Doc. A/C.6/SR.102, 12 November 1948, in *supra* fn. 101, at p. 1750. The joint USSR/French/Iranian proposal read:
     The High Contracting Parties may call the attention of the Security Council or, if necessary, of the General Assembly to the cases of genocide and of violations of the present Convention likely to constitute a threat to international peace and security, in order that the Security Council may take such measures as it may deem necessary to stop that threat.
141 UN Doc. A/C.6/SR.102, 12 November 1948, in *supra* fn. 101, at p. 1753.
142 UN Doc. A/C.6/SR.102, Mr. Morozov (USSR), 12 November 1948, in *supra* fn. 101, at p. 1776–1757.
143 UN Doc. A/C.6/SR.105, 13 November 1948, in *supra* fn. 101, at p. 1793 (also at UN Doc. A/C.6/265). This amendment to Article X added a second paragraph to Article X:
     With respect to the prevention and suppression of acts of genocide, a Party to this Convention may call upon any competent organ of the United Nations to take such action as may be appropriate under the Charter of the United Nations.
144 UN Doc. A/C.6/SR.105, 13 November 1948, in *supra* fn. 101, at pp. 1794–1795.
145 UN Doc. A/C.6/SR.105, 13 November 1948, in *supra* fn. 101, at pp. 1796–1797, 1799.
146 UN Doc. A/C.6/SR.105, Mr. Fitzmaurice (United Kingdom), Mr. de Beus (The Netherlands), 13 November 1948, in *supra* fn. 101, at pp. 1796–1797, 1798.

Notwithstanding the approval of Article X with a paragraph inspired by the former Article VIII,[147] it appears that it was eventually moved and renumbered to become the final Article VIII. A search of the historical record is not entirely clear on exactly how this process came to be or the discussions surrounding it. The final Sixth Committee's report merely noted the approval of Article X (including the former Article VIII language) and in a footnote explained that:

> By the rearrangement and renumbering of the articles decided upon by the Drafting Committee, the second paragraph of article X became article VIII of the final text.[148]

The final Convention, annexed to the report, contains the language of what is now Article VIII:

> Any Contracting Party may call upon the competent organs of the United Nations to take such action under the Charter of the United Nations as they consider appropriate for the prevention and suppression of acts of genocide or any of the other acts enumerated in article III.[149]

The draft as a whole was then approved by the Sixth Committee,[150] passed on to the UN General Assembly, and was then approved despite some last minute amendments by the USSR and Venezuela on 9 December 1948.[151]

E Observations from the travaux préparatoires of the Genocide Convention (1948)

What observations or conclusions can we draw from the above historical record as it pertains to the original intention and foresight of the drafters of the

---

147   See UN Doc. A/C.6/269, 15 November 1948, in *supra* fn. 101, at pp. 2006–2007. The approved Article X read:

> Any dispute between the High Contracting Parties relating to the interpretation, application or fulfilment of the present Convention, including disputes relating to the responsibility of a State for any of the acts enumerated in articles II and IV, shall be submitted to the International Court of Justice at the request of any of the parties to the dispute.
>
> With respect to the prevention and suppression of acts of genocide, a party to the present Convention may call upon any competent organ of the United Nations to take such action as may be appropriate under the Charter of the United Nations.

148   UN Doc. A/760, 3 December 1948, in *supra* fn. 101, at p. 2027.
149   UN Doc. A/760, 3 December 1948, Annex, Article VIII, in *supra* fn. 101, at p. 2034.
150   UN Doc. A/C.6/SR.132, 1 December 1948, in *supra* fn. 101, at pp. 1919–1922.
151   UN Doc. A/PV.179, 9 December 1948, in *supra* fn. 101, at pp. 2083–2085.

Genocide Convention (1948) with respect to the prevention of genocide? It is submitted that the *travaux préparatoires* demonstrate that the preventive aspect of genocide encompasses two separate notions. The first was the notion of prevention through the criminalization of genocide at international law. This is evident from the debates surrounding incitement and other preparatory acts of genocide. The drafters hoped that in mandating the force of an international treaty against genocide, it would act as a general deterrent in preventing its future occurrence. This method of prevention is akin to the reasons for the criminalisation of any domestic offence – it was assumed that individuals would think twice before committing genocide in the face of a treaty declaring it a crime under international law. Related to this, was the notion of the domestic implementation of genocide into municipal law and the mandating of penal sanction for such acts as per Article v. This was reinforced by what became Article vi, which mandated that persons accused of genocide would be tried by domestic courts or some future international court with jurisdiction over the crime. This in turn was linked to the obligation to punish genocide also included in Article i. In short, the convention and its various articles, as such, were seen as a tool for preventing genocide in the future.

The second, of most relevance to us, is the notion encompassed in Article viii: that States parties could decide to inform competent organs of the UN of genocide so that the UN could take preventive action as they saw fit.[152] In this context, it is pertinent to consider the comments made by Judge *Ad Hoc* Lauterpacht in his separate opinion in the icj's ruling on provisional measures in the *Genocide Case*:

> [D]oes the duty of prevention that rests upon a party [to the Genocide Convention (1948)] in respect of its *own* conduct, or that of persons subject to its authority or control, outside its territory also mean that every party is under an obligation individually and actively to intervene to prevent genocide outside its territory when committed by or under the

---

152 However, as the icj's interpretation of Article viii confirms, this was not intended to be an exhaustive provision:

[The prevention of genocide] extends beyond the particular case envisaged in Article viii, namely reference to the competent organs of the United Nations, for them to take such action as they deem appropriate. Even if and when these organs have been called upon, this does not mean that the States parties to the Convention are relieved of the obligation to take such action as they can to prevent genocide from occurring, while respecting the United Nations Charter and any decisions that may have been taken by its competent organs.

icj, *Genocide Case*, p. 220, para. 427.

authority of some other party? [...] I do not feel able, in the absence of a full treatment of this subject by both sides to express a view on it at this stage[.][153]

Article VIII reveals an important and relevant matter in this respect. It is clear from the debates that States did not consider the extraterritorial occurrence of genocide to be none of their concern.[154] Far from it. Indeed, the idea that States should have some sort of role to play in such circumstances was one of the primary concerns that lay behind Article VIII's drafting and subsequent approval. This was undoubtedly a reflection of the times. We must recall that during the drafting of the Genocide Convention (1948), the horrors of the holocaust perpetrated by the Nazis in Europe were only a few years old. It was a vivid memory fresh in the minds of the drafters and was raised many times in various contexts by numerous State representatives during the debates, and rightly so. We must also recall that these crimes were perpetrated in territories under the control or occupation of the Nazis and therefore beyond the borders of the allied States fighting against them.

Thus, the primary impetus behind the drafting and finalization of the convention was *exactly* genocide committed extra-territorially, that is, beyond the territory over which States exercised their jurisdiction. As the ICJ would later confirm, 'the obligation each State thus has to prevent and punish the crime of genocide is not territorially limited by the Convention.'[155] One cannot therefore ignore the treaty's particular historical context. In other words, there was a general recognition that States parties to the Genocide Convention (1948) should not be indifferent to genocide of the kind described by Judge

---

153　ICJ, *Case Concerning Application of the Convention on the Prevention and Punishment of the Crime of Genocide (Bosnia and Herzegovina v. Yugoslavia (Serbia and Montenegro))*, Provisional Measures, Order of 13 September 1993 – Separate Opinion of Judge Lauterpacht, ICJ Reports 1993, pp. 444–445, para. 115.

154　Indeed, Raphael Lemkin – the architect of the genocide concept – wrote in 1947 that '[b]y declaring genocide a crime under international law and by making it a problem of international concern [via UN GA Resolution 96(1) (1946)], the right of intervention on behalf of minorities slated for destruction has been established.' R. Lemkin, 'Genocide as a Crime under International Law', (1947) 41(1) *The American Journal of International Law* 145, at 150.

155　For further discussion of the territorial application of the Genocide Convention (1948), see M. Milanović, 'Territorial Application of the Genocide Convention and State Succession', in P. Gaeta (ed.), *The Genocide Convention: A Commentary* (Oxford, Oxford University Press: 2009), pp. 474–483.

Ad Hoc Lauterpacht above.[156] To say otherwise would be to negate the defining event – the holocaust – that resulted in the treaty coming into existence in the first place.

While it is true that there was a sense during the discussions that the UN was the most appropriate body at the international level to be seized of genocide[157] – as reflected in the final Article VIII – it is also true that States did not give serious thought to State obligations for the prevention of genocide in the absence of UN or other UN-related/based action. There is nothing in the historical record that suggests States explicitly considered, discussed and rejected the cutting of the Gordian knot of our times: humanitarian intervention as a last resort in the event of a stalemate at or inaction by the UN Security Council. This lack of foresight is also apparent in discussions relating to Article 1, since what exactly preventing genocide encompassed was not broached or elaborated upon in any significant detail as such.[158] In other words, in the absence of serious consideration of the matter, the *travaux préparatoires* do not themselves reveal that States categorically ruled out action to prevent genocide in the territory of another State, at least in such a manner that it conformed to the accepted principles of international law regarding the use of force.

It is submitted that the historical record and the intent of the drafters are therefore not an impediment *per se* to the theory advanced in this chapter. What can be said instead is that the drafters, unfortunately, were not properly attuned to future potential eventualities. Whilst silence should not always be interpreted as permitting that on which a treaty (or its drafter) expresses no

---

156   However, one should note that the USSR's proposal for a mandatory system of notification, particularly to the UN Security Council, was rejected during the negotiations. See *supra* fns 78, 85.

157   See B. Schiffbauer, 'Article VIII', in C.J. Tams, L. Berster, and B. Schiffbauer, *Convention on the Prevention and Punishment of the Crime of Genocide: A Commentary* (C.H. Beck/Hart Publishing/Nomos, Munich/Oxford/Baden-Baden: 2014), pp. 272–274. See also N. Ruhashyankiko, *Study of the Question of the Prevention and Punishment of the Crime of Genocide*, UN Doc. E/CN.4/Sub.2/416, 4 July 1978, para. 304.

158   See also W.A. Schabas, *Genocide in International Law: The Crime of Crimes*, 2nd Edition (Cambridge, Cambridge University Press: 2009), p. 81:

    [W]hile the final Convention has much to say about [the] punishment of genocide, there is little to suggest what prevention of genocide really means. Certainly, nothing in the debates about Article 1 provides the slightest clue as to the scope of the obligation to prevent.

view,[159] we should nevertheless properly take into account this fact, in addition to other relevant material, when considering the prevention of genocide.

3   Future *Jus Cogens* Status for the Prevention of Genocide

Notwithstanding the exploration of the *travaux préparatoires* elucidated above, Article 31 of the Vienna Convention (1969) still offers a place at the table for contemporary context in considering the prevention of genocide. Thus, Article 31(3)(b) permits consideration of 'subsequent practice in the application of the treaty which establishes the agreement of the parties regarding its interpretation' together with 'relevant rules of international law applicable in the relations between the parties' as directed in Article 31(3)(c). It is to this that this chapter now turns. However, it should be first made clear as to what this chapter will not attempt to do. It will not be argued that the prevention of genocide is a *jus cogens* norm at present. There is an insufficient amount of practice and judicial consideration of the issue to safely arrive at that conclusion at this time.[160] Rather, by looking at State reactions during the Rwandan genocide as a case study and State attitudes to genocide generally, together with judicial consideration of the matter, we can see hints as to how States

---

159   But see *contra*, United States Supreme Court, *United States v. Alvarez-Machain*, 650 U.S. 655 (1992). This case held (by majority) that since the applicable US/Mexico extradition treaty did not explicitly forbid forcible abduction, resorting to such means to bring a Mexican national from Mexico to the US to face a criminal trial before her courts was permitted. This holding has been bluntly described by a prominent academic as a 'preposterous position': M.C. Bassiouni, *International Extradition: United States Law and Practice*, 6th Edition, (Oxford, Oxford University Press: 2014), p. 281. See also *contra* by analogy, Permanent Court of International Justice ('PCIJ'), *The Case of the S. S. "Lotus"* (France v. Turkey), Series A – No. 10, 7 September 1927, pp. 18–19 (often cited for the maxim that international law permits that which is not prohibited by international law (that is, when international law is silent)).

160   See S. Forlati, 'The Legal Obligation to Prevent Genocide: *Bosnia v. Serbia* and Beyond', in *Polish Yearbook of International Law – Volume 31 (2011)* (Warsaw, Wydawnictwo Tekst Sp. z o.o.: 2012), p. 196: '[it] would seem […] that the obligation [to prevent genocide], albeit legally binding, is not (yet) part of the peremptory core of the prohibition of genocide.' But see *contra*, O. Ben-Naftali, 'The Obligation to Prevent and to Punish Genocide', in P. Gaeta (ed.), *The Genocide Convention: A Commentary* (Oxford, Oxford University Press: 2009), p. 36:

> The prohibition on genocide is a *jus cogens* obligation. The peremptory nature of the norm attached to the obligation to prevent, for otherwise the normative status of the prohibition – and its legal implications – would be rendered meaningless.

consider, and the level of importance placed upon, the prevention of genocide as a legal norm. It will be argued that in the future, depending on further practice, the prevention of genocide could perhaps move into the realm of *jus cogens*.

A   **The Content and Substance of Jus Cogens *Norms and Subsequent* Erga Omnes *Obligations***

Jus cogens norms are notoriously difficult to pin down. They are norms to which one can easily invoke (US) Justice Potter Stewart's (in)famous dictum of 'I know it when I see it'.[161] Although some scholars (stubbornly) dispute the very premise and legitimacy of *jus cogens*,[162] it is beyond doubt that today it forms an important and integral part of the international legal order. Indeed, from its humble beginnings, *jus cogens* has blossomed to touch and concern a seemingly endless number of diverse areas of international law and international affairs. As the Inter-American Court of Human Rights ('IACtHR') rightly put it:

> In its development and by its definition, *jus cogens* is not limited to treaty law. The sphere of *jus cogens* has expanded to encompass general international law, including all legal acts. *Jus cogens* has also emerged in the law of the international responsibility of States and, finally, has had an influence on the basic principles of the international legal order.[163]

Similarly, in a separate opinion, (now ICJ) Judge Cançado Trindade further explained that *jus cogens* 'is an open category, which expands itself to the extent that the universal juridical conscience [...] awakens for the necessity to protect the rights inherent to each human being in every and any situation.'[164]

---

161 United States Supreme Court, *Jacobellis v. Ohio*, 378 U.S. 184 (1964), at 197 (per Stewart J., concurring) (concerning possible obscenity in the 1958 French film '*Les Amants*').

162 See for example, R.P. Barnidge, Jr., 'Questioning the Legitimacy of *Jus Cogens* in the Global Legal Order', (2008) 38 *Israel Yearbook on Human Rights* 199; U. Linderfalk, 'The Effect of *Jus Cogens* Norms: Whoever Opened Pandora's Box, Did You Ever Think About the Consequences?', (2007) 18(5) *European Journal of International Law* 853; A. D'Amato, 'It's a Bird, It's a Plane, It's *Jus Cogens*!', (1990–1991) 6(1) *Connecticut Journal of International Law* 1. For a critique prior to its finalization in the Vienna Convention (1969), see G. Schwarzenberger, 'International *Jus Cogens*?', (1965) 43(4) *Texas Law Review* 455.

163 IACtHR, *Juridical Conditions and Rights of Undocumented Migrants*, Advisory Opinion OC-18/03, 17 September 2003, para. 99.

164 IACtHR, *Juridical Conditions and Rights of Undocumented Migrants*, Advisory Opinion OC-18/03, Concurring Opinion of Judge A.A. Cançado Trindade, 17 September 2003, para.

At its most basic, we can say that *jus cogens* consists of 'norm[s] that enjoy[] a higher rank in the international hierarchy than treaty law and even "ordinary" customary rules.'[165] As the late Professor Antonio Cassese explained, they have 'achieved such prominence in the international community that States and other international legal subjects[166] may not derogate from it either in their international dealings or in their own national legislation'[167] unless overtaken by another rule of international law endowed with the same normative force. This is of course reflected in the positivist origin of *jus cogens*, which can be found in Article 53 of the Vienna Convention (1969):[168]

---

68. See also A.A. Cançado Trindade, *International Law for Humankind: Towards a New* Jus Gentium, 2nd Edition, (Leiden/Boston, Martinus Nijhoff Publishers: 2013), pp. 295–309.

165   ICTY, *Prosecutor v. Furundžija*, Trial Judgement, Case No. IT-95-17/1-T, 10 December 1998, para. 153.

166   The Second Chamber of the European Court of Justice held, for example, that *jus cogens* binds the UN Security Council, a non-State entity: ECJ – Second Chamber, *Kadi v. Council of the European Union and Commission of the European Communities*, Case T-135/01, 21 September 2005, paras 226, 230; ECJ – Second Chamber, *Yusuf and Al Barakaat International Foundation v. Council of the European Union and Commission of the European Communities*, Case T-306/01, 21 September 2005, paras 277, 281. Although both these decisions were ultimately overturned on appeal, this was so because it was held that the ECJ did not have the competence to declare itself on the acts and conduct of the UN Security Council, not because *jus cogens* were not binding upon it: ECJ – Grand Chamber, *Kadi and Al Barakaat International Foundation v. Council of the European Union*, Cases C-402/05 P and C-415/05 p, 3 September 2008, para. 287. Judge *Ad Hoc* Lauterpacht has also expressed the view that *jus cogens* binds the UN Security Council: ICJ, *Case Concerning Application of the Convention on the Prevention and Punishment of the Crime of Genocide (Bosnia and Herzegovina v. Yugoslavia (Serbia and Montenegro))*, Provisional Measures, Order of 13 September 1993 – Separate Opinion of Judge Lauterpacht, p. 440, para. 100.

167   STL, *In re El Sayed*, Order Assigning Matter to Pre-Trial Judge, Case No. CH/PRES/2010/01, 15 April 2010, para. 29.

168   Pointing to the Vienna Convention (1969) as the positivist origin of *jus cogens* does not mean that, as a concept, it was a 20th century innovation. *Jus cogens*' pedigree can be traced back to the pens of eminent historical jurists such as Hugo Grotius (writing in 1625) and Emer de Vattel (writing in 1758):

[T]he Law of Nature is so unalterable, that God himself cannot change it. For tho' the Power of God be infinite, yet we may say, that there some Things to which this infinite Power does not extend, because they cannot be expressed by Propositions that contain any Sense, but manifestly imply a Contradiction.

H. Grotius (R. Tuck (ed.)), *The Rights of War and Peace – Book I*, (Indianapolis, Liberty Fund, Inc.: 2005), p. 155 (providing as an example, that not even God could alter the fact that 2 + 2 = 4). This concept was subsequently extended, by implication, to State behaviour by Vattel:

THE PREVENTION OF GENOCIDE AS A *JUS COGENS* NORM?

[A] peremptory [*jus cogens*] norm of general international law is a norm accepted and recognized by the international community of States as a whole as a norm from which no derogation is permitted and which can be modified only by a subsequent norm of general international law having the same character.[169]

Unfortunately, this does not tell us that much about *jus cogens*' foundations, formative process or even an indication of which norms have attained such status. This situation can be traced back to the drafting process that eventually led to Article 53 (and Article 64).[170] During the negotiations, States simply could not agree on the contours and legal flesh of this newly christened concept, and so instead they included only that on which there was a common understanding and agreement – or to put it another way, only the lowest common denominator was included in the Vienna Convention (1969).[171] The rest was left for the future to be developed by courts, practitioners and academics.

Over the decades, many have taken up the cause of further clarifying the almost mythical properties and composition of *jus cogens*, but ambiguity and disagreement continue to permeate, particularly with respect to its conceptual framework.[172] Nevertheless, because of the work of various authors we are in a

---

Since therefore the necessary law of nations consists in the application of the law of nature to states, – which law is immutable, as being founded on the nature of things, and particularly on the nature of man, – it follows, that the necessary law of nations is immutable. Whence, as this law is immutable, and the obligations that arise from it necessary and indispensable, nations can neither make any changes in it by their conventions, dispense with it in their own conduct, nor reciprocally release each other from the observance of it.

E. de Vattel (B. Kapossy and R. Whatmore (eds)), *The Law of Nations, or, Principles of the Law of Nature, Applied to the Conduct and Affairs of Nations and Sovereigns* (Indianapolis, Liberty Fund, Inc.: 2008), p. 70.

169 Article 53, Vienna Convention (1969). This language was subsequently replicated verbatim in Article 53, Vienna Convention on the Law of Treaties between States and International Organizations or between International Organizations (1986).

170 Article 64, Vienna Convention (1969) reads: 'If a new peremptory norm of international law emerges, any treaty which is in conflict with that norm becomes void and terminates.'

171 Report of the International Law Commission Covering the Work of its Fifteenth Session, 6 May – 12 July 1963, UN Doc. A/5509, Commentary to Article 37 of the Draft Articles on the Law of Treaties (1962), in *Yearbook of the International Law Commission 1963 – Volume II* (New York, United Nations: 1964), UN Doc. A/CN.4/SER.A/1963/Add.1, pp. 198–199.

172 E.J. Criddle and E. Fox-Decent, 'A Fiduciary Theory of *Jus Cogens*', (2009) 34(2) *The Yale Journal of International Law* 331, at 345–346: 'In sum, *jus cogens* remains a popular concept in search of a viable theory. The prevailing accounts of peremptory norms' legal status are

far better position today in attempting to peer into the eyes of *jus cogens* than we were in 1969. Thus for Orakhelashvili for example, the key defining characteristics of peremptory norms are:

> [T]he link to community interest as distinct from individual interests of States[.] [...] It must be asked whether a norm is intended to benefit a given actor in the interest of the community. It must also be asked whether a valid derogation would be possible from a given norm[.][173]

Similarly, Yarwood has explained that:

> [*J*]*us cogens* exists if these norms are understood as one component[] [...] in a wider movement to protect the fundamental interests of more than simply states. [...] [*J*]*us cogens* norms seek to protect the interests of the international community as a whole and can be distinguished because they have the additional characteristic of being non-derogable.[174]

On the other hand, De Hoogh posed the issue of non-derogation a little differently in stating that 'the essence of *jus cogens* lies not in the impossibility of derogation, but in the impossibility of eluding the application of norms of *jus cogens*.'[175] Kadelbach purported to sum up the literature in the following words:

> [T]he concept of *jus cogens* is founded on community interests and characterized by the prohibition against disposing over certain rights, be it to one's own disadvantage or to the detriment of others who are not in a position to provide effectively for their protection themselves, such as peoples, groups or individuals.[176]

---

premised upon, and shaped by, normative political theories of consent, natural law, and international order – none of which has proven adequate to the task.'

173 A. Orakhelashvili, *Peremptory Norms in International Law* (Oxford, Oxford University Press: 2006), p. 47.

174 L. Yarwood, *State Accountability under International Law: Holding States Accountable for a Breach of Jus Cogens Norms* (Abingdon/New York, Routledge: 2011), p. 72.

175 A. de Hoogh, 'The Relationship between *Jus Cogens*, Obligations *Erga Omnes* and International Crimes: *Jus Cogens* Norms in Perspectives', (1991) 42 *Austrian Journal of Public and International Law* 183, at 186.

176 S. Kadelbach, '*Jus Cogens*, Obligations *Erga Omnes* and other Rules – The Identification of Fundamental Norms', in C. Tomuschat and J-M. Thouvenin (eds), *The Fundamental Rules*

For its part, the International Law Commission ('ILC') in its commentary to its Draft Articles on the Responsibility of States for Internationally Wrongful Acts (2001) concluded that *jus cogens* 'arise from those substantive rules of conduct that prohibit what has come to be seen as intolerable because of the threat it presents to the survival of States and their peoples and the most basic human values.'[177]

But *jus cogens* has another important characteristic: its relationship to obligations *erga omnes* (owed to the international community as a whole) and in particular, the relevance of the former to the latter. Here, it is often said that *jus cogens* necessarily create or bring about obligations *erga omnes*.[178] Thus the ICJ, in its foray into the subject in the *Barcelona Traction* case, gave as examples of *erga omnes* obligations those that arose from the prohibitions on aggression, genocide, slavery, and racial discrimination[179] all of which are readily accepted as *jus cogens* norms.[180] Notwithstanding, this is (yet) another area where the literature is mixed and murky, with a spectrum of academic opinion ranging from *erga omnes* and *jus cogens*' 'mere overlap, to partial identity (all peremptory norms imposing obligations *erga omnes*), or complete identity.'[181] Whilst there is some ambiguity, space does not permit a thorough exploration of this

---

    of the International Legal Order: Jus Cogens *and Obligations* Erga Omnes (Leiden/Boston, Martinus Nijhoff Publishers: 2006), p. 35.

[177] Report of the International Law Commission on the Work of its Fifty-Third Session, 23 April – 1 June and 2 July – 10 August 2001, UN Doc. A/56/10, Commentary to Article 40 of the Draft Articles on the Responsibility of States for Internationally Wrongful Acts (2001), in *Yearbook of the International Law Commission 2001 – Volume II, Part Two* (New York, United Nations: 2007), UN Doc. A/CN.4/SER.A/2001/Add.1 (Part 2), p. 112, para. 3.

[178] M.C. Bassiouni, 'International Crimes: *Jus Cogens* and *Obligatio Erga Omnes*', (1996) 59(4) *Law and Contemporary Problems* 63, at 72; A.A. Cançado Trindade, *International Law for Humankind: Towards a New* Jus Gentium, 2nd Edition, (Leiden/Boston, Martinus Nijhoff Publishers: 2013), p. 312.

[179] ICJ, *Case Concerning the Barcelona Traction, Light and Power Company, Limited (New Application: 1962 – Second Phase) (Belgium v. Spain)*, Judgment of 5 February 1970, ICJ Reports 1970, p. 32, paras 33–34.

[180] See *Fragmentation of International Law: Difficulties Arising from the Diversification and Expansion of International Law – Report of the Study Group of the International Law Commission*, UN Doc. A/CN.4/L.702, 18 July 2006, para. 14(33), adopted and reproduced in Report of the International Law Commission on the Work of its Fifty-Eight Session, 1 May – 9 June and 3 July – 11 August 2006, UN Doc. A/61/10, in *Yearbook of International Law Commission 2006 – Volume II, Part Two* (New York, United Nations: 2007), UN Doc. A/CN.4/SER.A/2006/Add.1 (Part 2), para. 251(33).

[181] C J. Tams, *Enforcing Obligations* Erga Omnes *in International Law* (Cambridge, Cambridge University Press: 2005), p. 146 (see in particular, the authors cited therein).

issue, nor is it this chapter's aim. What can be said with certainty however is that *jus cogens* and *erga omnes* are undeniably linked. Although academics disagree on the exact nature of the link – whether it is a cause and effect-type link – it is sufficient for our purposes to point to and recognize this relationship, as no discussion of *jus cogens* can be completely bereft of *erga omnes*.

It is thus evident from the discussion above, that *jus cogens* acts, to a certain degree, as a sort of Martens Clause for general international law (extending beyond international humanitarian law), in that it can be said that it is the legal manifestation of a desire to ensure that action in the international arena does not contradict humanity's common conscience. Of course, this looks good on paper, but pinpointing exactly what 'humanity's common conscience' contains is far from an exact science. Despite all the ink that has been spilled in trying to address this question, we can nevertheless identify at the very least four important *jus cogens* ingredients from Article 53 of the Vienna Convention (1969): (i) it must be a norm of general international law; (ii) it must be accepted and recognized as a whole by States; (iii) it must be a norm from which one cannot depart, and (iv) it can only be altered by another subsequent *jus cogens* norm. The question that presently concerns us is whether the prevention of genocide could move into this realm. To this we now turn.

B *Rwanda in 1994 and State and Judicial Practice on the Prevention of Genocide: Potential for Future* Jus Cogens *Status?*

Although international criminal law does not formally recognize a hierarchy among different international crimes,[182] there can be little doubt that genocide holds a high and exalted place in the pantheon of criminality. This perhaps helps to explain the attitudes of defendants before international criminal tribunals: they appear far more comfortable with being convicted of war

---

182 See ICTY, *Prosecutor v. Tadić*, Judgement in Sentencing Appeals, Case No. IT-94–1-A *bis*, 26 January 2000, para. 69; ICTR, *Prosecutor v. Kayishema and Ruzindana*, Appeal Judgement, Case No. ICTR-95–1-A, 1 June 2001, para. 367; ICTY, *Prosecutor v. Mrkšić and Šljivančanin*, Appeal Judgement, Case No. IT-95–13/1-A, 5 May 2009, para. 375; ICTR, *Bikindi v. The Prosecutor*, Appeal Judgement, Case No. ICTR-01–72-A, 18 March 2010, para. 145. It is often forgotten however, that this was not the initial position taken by international criminal law. See ICTY, *Prosecutor v. Erdemović*, Appeal Judgement – Joint Separate Opinion of Judge McDonald and Judge Vohrah, Case No. IT-96-22-A, 7 October 1997, paras 20–27 (Judges Cassese and Stephen concurring: ICTY, *Prosecutor v. Erdemović*, Appeal Judgement, Case No. IT-96–22-A, 7 October 1997, para. 20). For a discussion of the reversal of this position, see P. Akhavan, *Reducing Genocide to Law: Definition, Meaning, and the Ultimate Crime* (Cambridge, Cambridge University Press: 2012), pp. 67–81.

crimes or crimes against humanity than being labeled a *genocidaire*.[183] This, it is submitted, also helps to explain the attitudes and reactions of States in the midst of genocide.

For the purposes of this chapter, there have not been, thankfully, large numbers of genocides (as defined in the Genocide Convention (1948)) by which to properly assess the attitudes of States on its prevention during their occurrence, particularly when they are sustained and systematic. Any analysis will not have the benefit of a large swathe of State practice. On the other hand, it could be said that in the absence of widespread genocides, the relatively few instances of their occurrence take on a larger significance in that greater weight should be attached to the little State practice arising from such events.[184] In this light, what we can do is hone our efforts on events surrounding the one clear-cut instance where the entire world unanimously agreed that genocide ran rampart for a significant amount of time: Rwanda in 1994. A perusal of political reactions and statements of the time made by States help us to not only identify their behaviour, but also gives us an important insight as to the underlying *reasons* that lay behind such behaviour. Our specific concern here are the obligations that States felt they had (or did not have) in the face of genocide and whether this had any role to play in how events unfolded in the way they did. Our attention will also turn to judicial pronouncements on the prevention of genocide, all of which touch and concern the events that occurred in Srebrenica, Bosnia and Herzegovina during July 1995, with a view to similarly explore State obligations in the face of genocide.

When the genocide began in Rwanda in 1994, we began to witness a most interesting phenomenon among States. Time after time, statement after statement, the word 'genocide' (or the dreaded 'g' word) was avoided at all costs. Only years after the events at issue was this readily acknowledged by persons who were on the frontlines of the formulation and execution of their respective governments' positions. Conrad K. Harper (Legal Adviser of the US Department of State during the Clinton Administration) for example, when asked to comment on the matter responded that 'there were a lot of policy concerns about being that blunt [calling it 'genocide'], including what obligation we had

---

183 W.A. Schabas, *Genocide in International Law: The Crime of Crimes*, 2nd Edition (Cambridge, Cambridge University Press: 2009), p. 11, fn. 32: 'Plea agreements systematically involve withdrawing charges of genocide in favour of convictions for crimes against humanity, which is not what would be expected if there was no hierarchy.'

184 This was most evident, for example, in the early days of space exploration and the development of customary international space law. See generally V.S. Vereshchetin and G.M. Danilenko, 'Custom as a Source of International Law of Outer Space, (1985) 13(1) *Journal of Outer Space* 22.

under the Genocide Convention to act – so there was a tap dance.' He went to say that 'I never had any doubt in my own mind, and I made it clear that was my own view [that it was genocide]. But the Legal Adviser doesn't make the ultimate decisions, even about characterizing something as an international crime.'[185] Michael J. Matheson (Acting Legal Adviser of the US Department of State during the (George H. W.) Bush and Clinton Administrations) added that even when a decision was made to use the term 'for some reason the policy-makers were more comfortable with the euphemism that it was "acts of genocide", which was, somehow, better from their point of view that just saying it was genocide.'[186]

This attitude to the 'g' word was exemplified in a memorable 10 June 1994 press briefing by US Department of State spokesperson Christine Shelley:

> Q: How would you describe the events taking place in Rwanda?
> MS. SHELLY: Based on the evidence we have seen from observations on the ground, we have every reason to believe that acts of genocide have occurred in Rwanda.
> Q: What's the difference between "acts of genocide" and "genocide"?
> MS. SHELLY: As you know, there is a legal definition of this. There has been a lot of discussion about how the definition applies under the definition of "genocide" contained in the 1948 convention. If you're looking at that for your determination about genocide, clearly, not all of the killings that have taken place in Rwanda are killings to which you might apply that label.
> [...]
> Q: How many acts of genocide does it take to make genocide?
> MS. SHELLY: Alan, that's just not a question that I'm in a position to answer.
> Q: Well, is it true that you have specific guidance not to use the word "genocide" in isolation but always to preface it with these words "acts of"?
> MS. SHELLY: I have guidance which I try to use as best as I can. There are formulations that we are using that we are trying to be consistent of our use of. I don't have an absolute categorical prescription against

---

185   Discussion with C.K. Harper, in M.P. Scharf and P.R. Williams, *Shaping Foreign Policy in Times of Crisis: The Role of International Law and the State Department Legal Adviser* (Cambridge, Cambridge University Press: 2010), p. 110.

186   Discussion with M.J. Matheson, in M.P. Scharf and P.R. Williams, *Shaping Foreign Policy in Times of Crisis: The Role of International Law and the State Department Legal Adviser* (Cambridge, Cambridge University Press: 2010), p. 110.

something, but I have the definitions. I have phraseology which has been carefully examined and arrived at as best as we can apply to exactly the situation and the actions which have taken place.[187]

This last response was at best misleading or at worst a plain lie. As Michael J. Matheson noted, and confirmed by declassified records from the period, there was indeed a concerted effort within the US government to ensure that the word 'genocide' was not used and to avoid making any public declaration that genocide was in fact occurring in Rwanda.

Thus, a declassified 1 May 1994 Rwanda discussion paper from the US Department of Defense states the following: 'Be Careful. Legal at [US Department of] State was worried about [Rwandan events] yesterday – Genocide finding could commit USG [US Government] to actually "do something".'[188] Another declassified 21 May 1994 action memorandum entitled 'Has Genocide Occurred in Rwanda?' (and signed by then US Secretary of State Warren Christopher), specifically instructed US Department of State personnel to only use the words 'acts of genocide' when referring to the Rwandan situation. The reason? Because it was believed that '[a] USG [US Government] statement that acts of genocide have occurred would not have any particular legal consequences.'[189] An unnamed senior Clinton Administration official speaking to the New York Times in June 1994 confirmed this sentiment, stating that '[g]enocide is a word that carries an enormous amount of responsibility' and that it would be natural for the population to expect the response to include dispatching US troops.[190] The US Ambassador to Rwanda was on the same page, asserting that '[a]s a responsible Government, you don't just go around hollering "genocide". You say that acts of genocide may have occurred and they need to be investigated.'[191]

---

187 US State Department Daily Press Briefing, 10 June 1994, available at: http://dosfan.lib.uic.edu/ERC/briefing/daily_briefings/1994/9406/940610db.html (accessed 30 June 2014).

188 Discussion Paper – Rwanda, Office of the Deputy Assistant Secretary of Defense for Middle East/Africa Region, Department of Defense, 1 May 1994, p. 1 (declassified), available at: http://www2.gwu.edu/~nsarchiv/NSAEBB/NSAEBB53/rw050194.pdf (accessed 30 June 2014).

189 Action Memorandum to US Secretary of State Warren Christopher, 'Has Genocide Occurred in Rwanda?', 21 May 1994, p. 2 (declassified), available at http://www2.gwu.edu/~nsarchiv/NSAEBB/NSAEBB53/rw052194.pdf (accessed 30 June 2014).

190 D. Jehl, 'Officials Told to Avoid Calling Rwanda Killings "Genocide"', *The New York Times*, 10 June 1994, available at http://www.nytimes.com/1994/06/10/world/officials-told-to-avoid-calling-rwanda-killings-genocide.html (accessed 30 June 2014).

191 D. Rawson, in D. Jehl, 'Officials Told to Avoid Calling Rwanda Killings "Genocide"', *The New York Times*, 10 June 1994, available at http://www.nytimes.com/1994/06/10/world/officials-

The US was not alone in holding such views. The United Kingdom ('UK') also reacted in the same way. Thus, interviews with former UK Foreign and Commonwealth Office staff and members of the 1994 British Cabinet revealed that:

> It was [UK Foreign Secretary] Douglas Hurd who said 'We are not to call this genocide'. The reason is because that then brings up obligations under, you know, the Genocide Convention. [...] [Also] the American [...] Madeleine Albright, she was totally against calling it genocide.
>
> [W]e [the UK Foreign and Commonwealth Office] kept referring the issue [use of the word 'genocide' to describe events in Rwanda] to some committee of experts until they decided what actually happened and dictated we weren't going to use this word ['genocide']. It was Douglas Hurd who was responsible for this, by the way – it[] [was not] people at the bottom, it definitely came from the top.[192]

The categorical refusal by the UK to recognize or use the word 'genocide' to describe what was going on in Rwanda was:

> Because the lawyers claimed that in international law, that as soon as you use the word genocide, then you are bound to take certain actions and they [the United Kingdom] didn't have the resource[s] to take those actions [...] that is basically the reason, because of international law and the obligations and such like so it wasn't the fact that they just didn't think that it was genocide.[193]

The French also refused to use the term 'genocide' in discussing ongoing events Rwanda. Thus, at the very height of the massacres, French Foreign Minister Alain Juppé downplayed the entire situation telling the National Assembly in Paris 'that the large-scale massacres were part of a vicious 'tribal war', with abuses on both sides.'[194]

This mentality also found its way into the UN Security Council. And so, when the then President of the UN Security Council Colin Keating (New Zea-

---

told-to-avoid-calling-rwanda-killings-genocide.html (accessed 30 June 2014).

192   Interview with Hazel Cameron, London, 2006, in H. Cameron, *Britain's Hidden Role in the Rwandan Genocide: The Cat's Paw* (Abingdon/New York, Routledge: 2013), p. 105.

193   Interview with Hazel Cameron, London, 2006, in H. Cameron, *Britain's Hidden Role in the Rwandan Genocide: The Cat's Paw* (Abingdon/New York, Routledge: 2013), p. 105.

194   A. Juppé, National Assembly, Paris, 28 April 1994, in A. Wallis, *Silent Accomplice: The Untold Story of France's Role in Rwandan Genocide* (London, I.B. Tauris: 2006), p. 106.

THE PREVENTION OF GENOCIDE AS A *JUS COGENS* NORM? 327

land) tabled a draft Presidential Statement that included the 'g' word (in the hope that its invocation would trigger an obligation to act), objections were raised by China (together with the US, the UK and France) to have the language removed. The British complained that if the word 'genocide' was used the UN Security Council would become a 'laughing stock' due to its inaction, while Djibouti's representative was against the statement because it was 'sensationalist'.[195] The result was that a statement that originally read:

> [T]he horrors of Rwanda's killing fields have few precedents in the recent history of the world. The Security Council reaffirms that the systematic killing of any ethnic group, with the intent to destroy it in whole or in part constitutes an act of genocide [...] The council further points out that an important body of international law exists that deals with perpetrators of genocide.[196]

Ended up a little differently – devoid of the word 'genocide':

> The Security Council condemns all these breaches of international humanitarian law in Rwanda, particularly those perpetrated against the civilian population, and recalls that persons who instigate or participate in such acts are individually responsible. In this context, the Security Council recalls that the killing of members of an ethnic group with the intention of destroying such a group in whole or in part constitutes a crime punishable by international law.[197]

But even this language, as LeBor notes, emerged out of a compromise only after Keating threatened a vote on his draft which 'would have revealed which countries were opposed to calling the Rwandan slaughter genocide.'[198] In fact,

---

195   L. Melvern, *A People Betrayed: The Role of the West in Rwanda's Genocide* (London, Zed Books: 2009), p. 203; K.C. Moghalu, *Rwanda's Genocide: The Politics of Global Justice* (New York/Basingstoke, Palgrave Macmillan: 2005), p. 20.

196   K.C. Moghalu, *Rwanda's Genocide: The Politics of Global Justice* (New York/Basingstoke, Palgrave Macmillan: 2005), p. 20; L. Melvern, *A People Betrayed: The Role of the West in Rwanda's Genocide* (London, Zed Books: 2009), pp. 202–203; M. Barnett, *Eyewitness to a Genocide: The United Nations and Rwanda* (Ithaca/London, Cornell University Press, 2002), p. 134.

197   *Statement by the President of the Security Council*, UN Doc. S/PRST/1994/21, 30 April 1994.

198   A. LeBor, *"Complicity with Evil": The United Nations in the Age of Modern Genocide* (New Haven/London, Yale University Press: 2006), p. 178. See also L. Melvern, *A People Betrayed: The Role of the West in Rwanda's Genocide* (London, Zed Books: 2009), p. 203; L.R. Melvern,

'for hours the [UN Security] Council had discussed the use of the word genocide – from 11 a.m. until the final vote the following day at 1.15 a.m. on Saturday, 30 April [1994].'[199]

This short narrative is of course not a complete picture of State practice in the face of Rwanda, but there is little to suggest that many other countries thought otherwise. The invocation of the 'g' word undoubtedly invokes a knee-jerk reaction amongst States for action to be taken – even when being committed in a faraway land where they have absolutely no direct or indirect control. It is also particularly interesting, since we are concerned with the potential for humanitarian intervention, to see the reactions of States that had the most capacity and ability to intervene to stop events on the ground – it appears that they were the most ardent in avoiding the 'g' word at all costs. This is not to suggest that the practice of say Tuvalu and/or Barbados does not concern us at all, but simply that their practice, at least in terms of the potential for the use of force, is not as illuminating as the practice of States with such means at their disposal. The ICJ itself has recognized this view in elaborating on the requirement of State practice in the formation of customary international law:

> [A]n indispensible requirement would be that within the period in question, short though it might be, State practice, *including that of States whose interests are specially affected*, should have been both extensive and virtually uniform[.][200]

As a consequence, as Klabbers has explained:

> [L]andlocked states such as Austria and Switzerland will not have much practice when it comes to maritime affairs; consequently, a focus on their practice will not be very revealing. By the same token, the development of customary space law will owe more to the practices of the USA, Russia and France than those of Sierra Leone or Norway.[201]

'The Security Council: Behind the Scenes in the Rwanda Genocide', in A. Jones (ed.), *Genocide, War Crimes and the West: History and Complicity* (London/New York, Zed Books: 2004), pp. 262–263.

[199] L. Melvern, *A People Betrayed: The Role of the West in Rwanda's Genocide* (London, Zed Books: 2000), p. 203.

[200] ICJ, *North Sea Continental Shelf Cases (Germany/Denmark; Germany/The Netherlands)*, Judgment of 20 February 1969, ICJ Reports 1969, p. 43, para. 74 (emphasis added).

[201] J. Klabbers, *International Law*, (Cambridge, Cambridge University Press: 2013), p. 27. See also M. Shaw, *International Law*, 6th Edition, (Cambridge, Cambridge University Press:

Similar logic should apply here. While a *jus cogens* norm requires, *inter alia*, recognition from 'States as a whole',[202] this does not necessarily mean that States without the capacity to act would in fact act differently if they did have such capacity. It is simply that they have not been faced with the same dilemma of seeing genocide unfold before them in the knowledge that they are actually able to stop it using military force should they so choose.[203]

Nevertheless, it clear from the reactions of States, particularly those who had the most capacity to act in 1994, that the word 'genocide' invoked a heightened sense of not only moral obligation, but of *legal* obligation. It is as though States believed that the word 'genocide' had some sort of mythical property, a word whose mere invocation would set a genie free. In subsequent years many of these same States would come to regret standing still and a number formally apologized for their inaction in the face of genocide in Rwanda, including the US, France, and Belgium. Interestingly, even clubs of States such as the European Union and the African Union have also expressed similar regret at their inaction.[204]

So what are we to make of this avoidance of the 'g' word and the above historical record? The point to be emphasized is that States do not react like this when war crimes or crimes against humanity are taking place. Whether we like

---

2008), pp. 79–80; G. Boas, *Public International Law: Contemporary Principles and Perspectives*, (Cheltenham/Northampton, Edward Elgar Publishing: 2012), p. 76.

[202] It must be made clear that the wording choice of 'States as a whole' in (what eventually became) Article 53, Vienna Convention (1969) was never intended to produce a result whereby one or a few number of States could 'veto' the emergence of a *jus cogens* norm. As the *travaux préparatoires* reveal, for a *jus cogens* norm to emerge:

[I]t would be enough if a very large majority [of States accepted and recognized it]; that would mean that, if one State in isolation refused to accept the peremptory character of a rule, or if that State was supported by a very small number of States, the acceptance and recognition of the peremptory character of the rule by the international community as a whole would not be affected.

United Nations Conference on the Law of Treaties, First Session: 26 March – 24 May 1968, Summary Records of the Plenary Meetings and of the Meetings of the Committee of the Whole, (New York, United Nations: 1969), UN Doc. A/CONF.39/11, p. 472 (Mr. Mustafa Kamil Yasseen (Iraq) – Chairman of the Drafting Committee).

[203] Nevertheless, as will be articulated later, the use of force is only one of a number of means by which a potential *jus cogens* obligation to prevent of genocide could be satisfied. Thus, this would not absolve smaller States from positive action within their capabilities – that do not involve the use of force – in the face of genocide should a *jus cogens* obligation to prevent it crystallize in the future.

[204] See F. Grünfeld and A. Huijboom, *The Failure to Prevent Genocide in Rwanda: The Role of Bystanders* (Leiden/Boston, Martinus Nijhoff Publishers: 2007), pp. 231–238.

it or not, States view genocide as *special and uniquely abhorrent*; this is clear from the brief outline to reactions to Rwanda. What is the consequence of States behaving in such a fashion? The view advanced here is that States believe that 'genocide' triggers an obligation to act – to undertake positive action – in order to try and stop it so as to satisfy an extraterritorial obligation to prevent genocide *even to situations where they exercise no level of (direct or indirect) control*. In order to avoid such an obligation, States simply refused to call events by their rightful name. One can draw parallels here to an argument raised during the *Nicaragua* case with respect to the customary rule of non-intervention in the domestic affairs of a State (given the fact many States *do* in fact intervene in the affairs of others), where the ICJ stated:

> If a State acts in a way *prima facie* incompatible with a recognized rule, but defends its conduct by appealing to exceptions or justifications contained within the rule itself, then whether or not the State's conduct is in fact justifiable on that basis, the significance of that attitude is to confirm rather than to weaken the rule.[205]

It is submitted that the same should apply here. Thus the inaction in Rwanda by the consistent avoidance of invoking the word 'genocide', in the fear of being obliged to act, further reinforces an obligation to prevent rather than undermining it.

But this proposition is not new in of itself. Article I (and VIII) of the Genocide Convention (1948) has explicit prevention language that was held as early as 1993 by the ICJ as indeed providing for a binding obligation to prevent genocide (but without providing much detail on what this obligation entailed in practice).[206] More substantive detail was only forthcoming in the ICJ's *Genocide Case* in February 2007, where it did not state that the prevention obligation under the Genocide Convention (1948) was territorially or jurisdictionally

---

[205] ICJ, *Case Concerning Military and Paramilitary Activities in and Against Nicaragua (Nicaragua v. United States of America)*, Merits, Judgment of 27 June 1986, ICJ Reports 1986, p. 98, para. 186 (emphasis added).

[206] See ICJ, *Case Concerning Application of the Convention on the Prevention and Punishment of the Crime of Genocide (Bosnia and Herzegovina v. Yugoslavia (Serbia and Montenegro))*, Provisional Measures, Order of 8 April 1993, ICJ Reports 1993, p. 22, para. 45; ICJ, *Case Concerning Application of the Convention on the Prevention and Punishment of the Crime of Genocide (Bosnia and Herzegovina v. Yugoslavia (Serbia and Montenegro))*, Provisional Measures, Order of 13 September 1993, ICJ Reports 1993, pp. 346–347, para. 46.

THE PREVENTION OF GENOCIDE AS A *JUS COGENS* NORM? 331

limited, but articulated an obligation that could potentially apply to genocide anywhere in the world.²⁰⁷

However, this holding came with one important caveat: the ICJ stated that it was specifically interpreting treaty law only, refusing to step outside the Genocide Convention's (1948) boundaries:

> The Court will therefore confine itself to determining the specific scope of the duty to prevent in the Genocide Convention, and to the extent that such a determination is necessary to the decision to be given on the dispute before it.²⁰⁸

The view being offered here is that, regardless of this statement, there is likely already in existence at least a customary obligation to prevent genocide.²⁰⁹ After all, the ICJ stated as early as 1951 'that the principles underlying the Convention are principles which are recognized by civilized nations as binding on States even without any conventional obligation',²¹⁰ and at that time the treaty

---

207 See ICJ, *Genocide Case*, pp. 221–222, paras 430–431. See also ICJ, *Case Concerning Application of the Convention on the Prevention and Punishment of the Crime of Genocide (Bosnia and Herzegovina v. Yugoslavia)*, Preliminary Objections, Judgment of 11 July 1996, ICJ Reports 1996, p. 616, para. 31: 'the obligation each State thus has to prevent and to punish the crime of genocide is not territorially limited by the Convention'; C.J. Tams, 'Article 1', in C.J. Tams, L. Berster, and B. Schiffbauer, *Convention on the Prevention and Punishment of the Crime of Genocide: A Commentary* (C.H. Beck/Hart Publishing/Nomos, Munich/Oxford/Baden-Baden: 2014), pp. 47–48; A. Gattini, 'Breach of the Obligation to Prevent and Reparation Thereof in the ICJ's Genocide Judgment', (2007) 18(4) *European Journal of International Law* 695, at 699–700. But see *contra*: ICJ, *Genocide Case*, Separate Opinion of Judge Tomka, pp. 345–348, paras 66–67 (favouring a prevention obligation when a State exercises jurisdiction outside its territory or exercises control over persons outside its territory); Declaration of Judge Skotnikov, pp. 377–379 (favouring a prevention obligation where territory is under a State's jurisdiction or control). However, neither Judge Tomka nor Skotnikov provide any explanation as to why, during Rwanda for example, a number of States that had no control (either directly or indirectly) over the relevant territory or actors on the ground still nonetheless felt they had an obligation to act, and hence the need to avoid triggering this obligation by avoiding the 'g' word).

208 ICJ, *Genocide Case*, pp. 220–221, para. 429.

209 See also S. Forlati, 'The Legal Obligation to Prevent Genocide: *Bosnia v. Serbia* and Beyond', in *Polish Yearbook of International Law – Volume 31 (2011)* (Warsaw, Wydawnictwo Tekst Sp. z o.o.: 2012), p. 193: 'It may safely be postulated that, in addition to being incorporated in the 1948 UN Convention, the obligation to prevent genocide is a customary rule of international law.'

210 ICJ, *Reservations to the Convention on the Prevention and Punishment of the Crime of Genocide*, Advisory Opinion of 28 May 1951, ICJ Reports 1951, p. 23. This view was reaffirmed by

had a meagre 25 States parties. Today, that number has ballooned to over 144 States, a significantly larger and more diverse part of the international community (about 75% of UN member States). In addition, the ICJ has also recognized that treaty law and customary law can exist in parallel, simultaneously and separate from each other. Thus in *Nicaragua*, the prohibition on the use of force originally contained in Article 2(4) of the UN Charter (1945) (as treaty law) was found to have an entirely separate – but parallel – customary basis.[211] There is nothing that prevents Article 1 of the Genocide Convention (1948) from having the same existence.

Further evidence can be found in light of other sources, such as the emerging responsibility to protect ('R2P') doctrine. As is well known, this was adopted by the UN General Assembly in the 2005 World Summit Outcome document and provided that:

> Each individual State has the responsibility to protect its populations from genocide, war crimes, ethnic cleansing and crimes against humanity. This responsibility entails the prevention of such crimes[.] [...] The international community, through the United Nations, also has the responsibility to use appropriate diplomatic, humanitarian and other peaceful means, in accordance with Chapters VI and VIII of the Charter, to help to protect populations from genocide, war crimes, ethnic cleansing and crimes against humanity. In this context, we are prepared to take collective action, in a timely and decisive manner, through the Security Council, in accordance with the Charter, including Chapter VII, on a case-by-case basis and in cooperation with relevant regional organizations as appropriate, should peaceful means be inadequate and national authorities are manifestly failing to protect their populations from genocide, war crimes, ethnic cleansing and crimes against humanity.[212]

---

the ICJ in 2006: ICJ, *Case Concerning Armed Activities on the Territory of the Congo (New Application: 2002) (Democratic Republic of the Congo v. Rwanda)*, Jurisdiction of the Court and Admissibility of the Application, Judgment of 3 February 2006, ICJ Reports 2006, p. 31, para. 64.

211 The result was that although the United States had entered a reservation to the ICJ's compulsory jurisdiction (under Article 36, ICJ Statute) in cases concerning multilateral treaties (such as the UN Charter (1945)), this did not deprive the ICJ of jurisdiction over alleged breaches of the prohibition on the use of force (Article 2(4)) as customary international law: ICJ, *Case Concerning Military and Paramilitary Activities in and Against Nicaragua (Nicaragua v. United States of America)*, Jurisdiction and Admissibility, Judgment of 26 November 1984, ICJ Reports 1984, p. 424, para. 73.

212 UN Doc. A/Res/60/1, 24 October 2005, at paras 138–140.

A similar notion can be found on the African continent as well, where the Constitutive Act of the African Union ('AU') (2000) provides that the AU shall function in accordance to, *inter alia*, 'the right of the Union to intervene in a Member State pursuant to a decision of the Assembly in respect of grave circumstances, namely: war crimes, genocide and crimes against humanity.'[213] But one might well ask why the author does not make an equivalent argument with respect to other international crimes such as crimes against humanity and war crimes. After all, these are also mentioned alongside genocide with respect to R2P and in the Constitutive Act of the AU (2000). The reason, it is submitted, is twofold.

First, from a positivist perspective, there is no clear obligation directed at States to prevent any of these crimes at international law (other than in R2P of course, which standing alone, is non-binding in character). For example, the Constitutive Act of the AU (2000) is directed at the AU (as opposed to individual States) and neither the Geneva Conventions (1949) nor any of the two Additional Protocols (1977) include any provision mandating the *prevention* of war crimes. The closest one comes is in Common Article 1, Geneva Conventions (1949) which merely provides that States parties should respect and ensure respect for the Geneva Conventions.[214] Neither is there any such a positivist obligation with respect to crimes against humanity or ethnic cleansing, since there is no treaty on the former[215] and the latter is not recognized as

---

[213] Article 4(h), Constitutive Act of the African Union ('AU') (2000). For more on this particular article, see D. Kuwali, *The Responsibility to Protect: Implementation of Article 4(h) Intervention* (Leiden/Boston, Martinus Nijhoff Publishers: 2011); D. Kuwali and F. Viljoen (eds), *Africa and the Responsibility to Protect: Article 4(h) of the African Union Constitutive Act* (Abingdon/New York, Routledge: 2014).

[214] But see J. Heieck, 'Illegal Vetoes in the Security Council – How Russia and China Breached their Duty under *Jus Cogens* to Prevent War Crimes in Syria', *Opinio Juris* Blog, 14 August 2013, available at: http://opiniojuris.org/2013/08/14/emerging-voices-illegal-vetoes-in-the-security-council-how-russia-and-china-breached-their-duty-under-jus-cogens-to-prevent-war-crimes-in-syria (last accessed 30 June 2014) (where the author takes Common Article 1, Geneva Conventions (1949) too far by stretching its meaning to argue that a *jus cogens* obligation to prevent war crimes exists).

[215] It is worth noting that there currently exists a draft convention concerning crimes against humanity that was drafted by a group of internationally renowned experts led by a seven-member Steering Committee headed by Professor Leila Nadya Sadat. This was the result of the Crimes Against Humanity Initiative of the Whitney R. Harris World Law Institute of the Washington University in St. Louis School of Law. See L.N. Sadat (ed.), *Forging a Convention for Crimes Against Humanity* (Cambridge, Cambridge University Press: 2011). On 30 July 2013, the ILC voted to add the drafting of a convention on crimes against humanity to its long-term work programme. See generally, Report of the International Law Commission – Sixty-fifth Session, 6 May – 7 June and 8 July – 9 August 2013, UN Doc.

an autonomous international crime as such.[216] One cannot point to the ICC Statute (1998) either as it only serves to criminalize and impose individual responsibility for the commission of international crimes and includes no operative article concerning a duty among States to prevent any of them.[217]

This is to be contrasted with Articles I and VIII of the Genocide Convention (1948) which *explicitly* include such a duty and were recognized as doing so by the ICJ in the *Genocide Case*. But what about torture? Unlike the aforementioned treaties, the Torture Convention (1984) actually has explicit language to the effect that States parties undertake to prevent torture:

> Each State Party shall take effective legislative, administrative, judicial or other measures to prevent acts of torture *in any territory under its jurisdiction*.[218]

Nevertheless, as is apparent, that obligation is limited to territory under the State's jurisdiction, and while this does not prohibit its extraterritorial application, it does entail an element of control over such territory or persons as recognized by the Committee Against Torture.[219] In other words, the duty to

---

A/68/10, Annex B, in *Yearbook of the International Law Commission 2013 – Volume II, Part Two* (New York, United Nations) (forthcoming).

[216] The closest one comes is deportation/forcible transfers as a war crime and/or crimes against humanity.

[217] But note ICC Statute (1998), Preamble, para. 5: 'Determined to put an end to impunity for the perpetrators or these [international] crimes and thus contribute to the prevention of such crimes[.]'

[218] Article 2(1), Convention Against Torture and Other Cruel, Inhuman or Degrading Treatment of Punishment (1984) (emphasis added).

[219] *General Comment No. 2 – Implementation of Article 2 by States Parties*, UN Doc. CAT/C/GC/2, 24 January 2008, para. 16. This would generally entail some sort of extra-territorial physical presence by the relevant State. See for example, *Al-Skeini*: ECtHR – Grand Chamber, *Al-Skeini and Others v. The United Kingdom*, Judgment, Application No. 55721/07, 7 July 2011. Without such presence one could be entering *Banković* territory, where jurisdiction would be much more difficult to establish: ECtHR – Grand Chamber, *Banković and Others v. Belgium and Others*, Admissibility, Application No. 52207/99, 12 December 2001. Nevertheless, it is important to remember that the Grand Chamber of the ECtHR has held that the provision of substantial military, economic, and political support for an insurgent movement, where such support ensures its survival, is enough to bring their human rights violations within the extraterritorial jurisdiction of the relevant supporting State: ECtHR – Grand Chamber, *Ilaşcu and Others v. Moldova and Russia*, Judgment, Application No. 48787/99, 8 July 2004, at paras 379–94. See also ECtHR – Former Fourth Section, *Ivanţoc and Others v. Moldova and Russia*, Judgment, Application No. 23687/05, 15

prevent torture cannot be in the same league as the seemingly wide-ranging obligation to prevent of genocide contained in Article 1 of the Genocide Convention (1948) as articulated by the ICJ.

The second reason has already been touched upon: State reactions when genocide is taking place. We do not and – more importantly – States do not have the looming tower of a 'w' word, 'c' word, or 't' word in the face of war crimes, crimes against humanity or torture. Take the current Syrian civil war as an example. In the face of widespread and well-documented war crimes and crimes against humanity by the Independent International Commission of Inquiry on the Syrian Arab Republic,[220] we do not see State representatives trying to avoid calling the crimes by their proper name at all costs. It would seem that the conscience of humanity is not quite as rattled or the imperative to act quite as forceful as it would be in the face of genocide.[221] Genocide is special and unique; it is inherently linked with a special heightened sense of revulsion together with an impetus to act. This is not to say that States welcome the commission of war crimes, crimes against humanity or torture with open arms, but simply that the same reactions are not accorded them. We may not like to hear it, but it remains a fact that States treat genocide differently to other international crimes – as heinous and repulsive as they also are. As a corollary, we may conclude that States do not appear to consider that the legal obligations that might stem from calling acts 'crimes against humanity', 'war crimes' or 'torture' to be in the same league as genocide; they do not appear as concerned about an obligation 'do something'. The consciences of States appear far more visibly disturbed in the face of genocide. It is not a stretch to further suggest that States (and others) attempt to tap into this sentiment by referring to domestic situations as 'genocide' where it is not warranted, perhaps in the hope that this will invoke a reaction – an obligation to act – that might otherwise not be forthcoming without its invocation.[222]

November 2011; ECtHR – Grand Chamber, *Catan and Others v. Moldova and Russia*, Judgment, Application Nos. 43370/04, 8252/05, 18454/06, 19 October 2012.

[220] See for example UN Doc. A/HRC/21/50, 16 August 2012; UN Doc. A/HRC/22/59, 5 February 2013; UN Doc. A/HRC/23/58, 4 June 2013.

[221] One possible exception to this was the reactions of States when it was revealed that chemical weapons were used in the conflict. On this, see C. Stahn, 'Syria and the Semantics of Intervention, Aggression and Punishment: On "Red Lines" and "Blurred Lines"', (2013) 11(5) *Journal of International Criminal Justice* 955.

[222] 'Genocide' was invoked during the Libyan civil war by the rebels: BBC, 'Libya's deputy envoy to the UN: "What's happening is genocide"', 21 February 2011, available at http://www.bbc.co.uk/news/world-middle-east-12527601 (accessed 30 June 2014). It was similarly invoked by Serbia in the context of the Serbian minority in Kosovo: The Guardian,

Nevertheless, the question of what status to accord the prevention of genocide outside of the Genocide Convention (1948) arose squarely in the *Mothers of Srebrenica and Others v. The Netherlands and the United Nations* litigation that was initiated in June 2007 originally before the Dutch courts[223] and eventually made its way to the ECtHR.[224] As mentioned in the introduction,[225] this case sought to hold the UN (and The Netherlands) responsible for failing to prevent the genocide at Srebrenica in July 1995.[226] With respect to The Netherlands, this was not problematic – as a State party to the treaty, Article I applied to them as treaty law. But with respect to the UN, two problems arose. First, the UN was not a party to the Genocide Convention (1948). It could not be, as Article XI makes it plain that it is only open to States to join. Therefore there had

---

'Serbian President Nikolic warns of Kosovo genocide', 29 July 2012, available at http://www.theguardian.com/world/2012/jul/29/serbian-president-nikolic-kosovo-genocide (accessed 30 June 2014). One could say the same about the Darfur, Sudan example where the US was virtually alone among States in invoking 'genocide' to describe events on the ground; even established NGOs, like Amnesty International and Human Rights Watch avoided using the term: The Guardian, 'Sudan massacres are not genocide, says EU', 10 August 2004, available at http://www.theguardian.com/world/2004/aug/10/eu.sudan (accessed 30 June 2014).

223   See The Hague District Court of The Netherlands, *Stichting Mothers of Srebrenica and Others v. The Netherlands and the United Nations*, LJN: BD6795, 10 July 2008; The Hague Court of Appeal of The Netherlands, *Stichting Mothers of Srebrenica and Others v. The Netherlands and the United Nations*, LJN: BL8979, 30 March 2010; Supreme Court of the Netherlands, *Stichting Mothers of Srebrenica and Others v. The Netherlands and the United Nations*, LJN: BW1999, ILDC 1760 (NL 2012), 13 April 2012.

224   ECtHR – Third Section, *Stichting Mothers of Srebrenica and Others v. The Netherlands*, Admissibility, Application No. 65542/12, 11 June 2013.

225   A number of the thoughts concerning this case outlined below have been first expressed elsewhere. See M.J. Ventura and D. Akande, '*Mothers of Srebrenica*: The Obligation to Prevent Genocide and *Jus Cogens* – Implications for Humanitarian Intervention', *EJIL: Talk!* Blog, 6 September 2013, available at: http://www.ejiltalk.org/ignoring-the-elephant-in-the-room-in-mothers-of-srebrenica-is-the-obligation-to-prevent-genocide-jus-cogens (accessed 30 June 2014).

226   It is worth noting that the avoidance of the 'g' word, like in Rwanda, was also present with respect to events in Bosnia and Herzegovina:

The [George H. W.] Bush administration assiduously avoided the word. "Genocide" was shunned because a genocide finding would create a moral imperative. [...] Policymakers preferred the phrase "ethnic cleansing". [US National Security Advisor] Scowcroft believes genocide would have demanded a U.S. response, but ethnic cleansing, which is the label he uses for what occurred in Bosnia did not[.]

S. Power, *"A Problem From Hell": America and the Age of Genocide* (New York, Basic Books: 2013), p. 288.

to be another non-treaty basis for attaching an obligation to prevent genocide upon the UN. Second, even assuming that a non-treaty basis for the obligation existed, there was still the problem that the UN was entitled to immunity before Dutch courts pursuant to Article 105 of the UN Charter (1945) and the Convention on the Privileges and Immunities of the United Nations (1946), to both of which The Netherlands was a State party.

Faced with these problems, the plaintiffs argued that the UN's immunity should be set aside on the basis of genocide's *jus cogens* status. This was a smart move: it killed the proverbial two birds with one stone. On the one hand, this satisfied the need for a non-treaty basis for the prevention of genocide, and on the other it potentially nullified the UN's immunity, as it would presumably be trumped by the legal prowess of a *jus cogens* norm.[227] In other words, the framing of the case by the plaintiffs put the issue squarely on the judicial table: is the prevention of genocide *jus cogens* or not? The answer to that question should have been dispositive. If it was not, then the plaintiff's legal theory fell apart; another non-treaty basis upon which to attach the prevention of genocide to the UN would have been required, and then they still would have faced the UN's immunity.[228] Only if the prevention of genocide was *jus cogens* would it have been worthwhile moving into the subsequent question of clashes of legal norms. Unfortunately, neither the Dutch courts not the ECtHR ever addressed the question head on. Instead, they simply assumed that the prevention of genocide was *jus cogens* on account of the prohibition on the commission of genocide also being *jus cogens*. Thus, when the case reached Strasbourg after being dismissed by the Dutch Supreme Court, it was enough for it to be stated that '[t]he Court [ECtHR] [has] recognized the prohibition of genocide as a rule of *jus cogens*'.[229] But as the ICJ has made clear in the *Genocide Case*, the prohibition on the commission of genocide and the prevention

---

227 The latter was a legal technique that had then been recently adopted by Italy's highest court in the *Ferrini* case: Italian Court of Cassation, *Ferrini v. Federal Republic of Germany*, Decision No. 5044/2004, 11 March 2004 (where Germany's sovereign immunity before Italian courts was set aside on account of World War II crimes being violations of *jus cogens*).

228 Perhaps the plaintiffs could have pointed to a customary basis for the prevention of genocide (as advocated previously in this chapter) that was binding upon the UN. But even if this were true, a customary norm can be displaced by treaty (as indeed Article 105 of the UN Charter (1945) and the Convention on the Privileges and Immunities of the United Nations (1946) appeared to do).

229 ECtHR – Third Section, *Stichting Mothers of Srebrenica and Others v. The Netherlands*, Admissibility, Application No. 65542/12, 11 June 2013, para. 157.

of genocide are two distinct and separate legal obligations.²³⁰ Just because the former is (undoubtedly) a *jus cogens* norm it does not follow, without a further careful analysis of international law, that the latter is also a *jus cogens* norm, otherwise we would have a case of *jus cogens* 'by association'(!)

This is not to say that the case would have turned out differently had the requisite analysis been undertaken to properly conclude that the prevention of genocide was indeed a *jus cogens* norm. The dismissal of the claims seemed all but the inevitable result of the recent ICJ holding in *Jurisdictional Immunities of the State* that substantive *jus cogens* norms (i.e. the prohibition of the commission of genocide) are different from procedural norms (i.e. immunity before domestic courts) so that the two are incapable of conflict.²³¹ Indeed, this was the very basis upon which the case was dismissed by the Dutch Supreme Court²³² and the ECtHR.²³³ However, the reasoning employed by the ECtHR

---

230   ICJ, *Genocide Case*, pp. 219–220, para. 427.
231   ICJ, *Jurisdictional Immunities of the State (Germany v. Italy: Greece intervening)*, Judgment of 3 February 2012, ICJ Reports 2012, p. 140, para. 92. Nevertheless, the *Mothers of Srebrenica* case differed in one important respect. Unlike the ICJ case where the claimants had the opportunity to appear before German courts to have their claims for compensation heard, in the *Mothers of Srebrenica* case, the claimants have *no* court in which they can make their claims for compensation against the UN because of the UN's absolute immunity before domestic courts and because the UN has not set up courts to hear and adjudicate such claims, notwithstanding Article VIII, Section 29(a) of the Convention on the Privileges and Immunities of the United Nations (1946): 'The United Nations shall make provisions for appropriate modes of settlement of[] [...] disputes arising out of contracts or other disputes of a private law charter to which the United Nations is a party[.]'
232   Supreme Court of the Netherlands, *Stichting Mothers of Srebrenica and Others v. The Netherlands and the United Nations*, LJN: BW1999, ILDC 1760 (NL 2012), 13 April 2012, paras 4.3.12, 4.3.14 :

> [T]he ICJ [in *Jurisdictional Immunities of the State (Germany v. Italy: Greece intervening)* did not] accept the argument that, since the rules that were breached by the German forces had the character of *ius cogens*, they should prevail over Germany's immunity.
> [...]
> Although UN immunity should be distinguished from State immunity, the difference is not such as to justify ruling on the relationship between the former and the right of access to the courts in a way that differs from the ICJ's decision on the relationship between State immunity and the right of access to the courts. The UN is entitled to immunity regardless of the extreme seriousness of the accusations on which the Association [Mothers of Srebrenica] et al. base their claim.

233   ECtHR – Third Section, *Stichting Mothers of Srebrenica and Others v. The Netherlands*, Admissibility, Application No. 65542/12, 11 June 2013, para. 158:

> International law does not support the position that a civil claim should override immunity from suit for the sole reason that it is based on an allegation of a particularly

and the Dutch courts can be seen as artificial, particularly when one appreciates the fact that they stand on a supposed *jus cogens* norm whose existence was neither confirmed nor denied.[234] The point was argued by the parties and properly before the courts; it should have received a judicial response.

The corollary of this state of affairs is that it also unfortunately robs this chapter of a definite legal opinion of the current state of the prevention of genocide outside of the Genocide Convention (1948). Notwithstanding, the ICJ, in the *Genocide Case*, in elaborating upon what the obligation to prevent genocide entailed made it plain that in acting to prevent genocide 'every State may only act within the limits permitted by international law'.[235] The ICJ's view that the prevention of genocide is subservient to other norms significantly undermines an argument that it is presently *jus cogens* since if it cannot prevail over other rules of international law then this would effectively rob a *jus cogens* norm of one of its central defining characteristics; a *jus cogens* norm that cannot trump all other norms of international law (including prior *jus cogens* norms) hardly sounds like *jus cogens*. On the other hand, the ICJ, unlike the ECtHR and the Dutch courts, were never briefed on and called upon to consider the proposition that the prevention of genocide is a rule of *jus cogens* (or even a customary rule). Therefore, from another perspective one could say that the ICJ's ruling may not have intended to say anything on the question. In any event, it certainly does not prohibit its future development and growth.

> grave violation of a norm of international law, even a norm of *ius cogens*. In respect of the sovereign immunity of foreign States this been clearly stated by the ICJ in *Jurisdictional Immunities of the State (Germany v. Italy: Greece intervening)*[] [...]. In the Court's opinion this also holds true as regards the immunity enjoyed by the United Nations.

234 One could also point out that the ICJ in *Jurisdictional Immunities of the State* similarly did not actually address Italy's argument that the rules violated by Germany during World War II were in fact *jus cogens*:

> *Assuming for this purpose* that the rules of the law of armed conflict which prohibit the murder of civilians in occupied territory, the deportation of civilian inhabitants to slave labour and the deportation of prisoners of war to slave labour are rules of *jus cogens*[] [...] [.]

> ICJ, *Jurisdictional Immunities of the State (Germany v. Italy: Greece intervening)*, Judgment of 3 February 2012, ICJ Reports 2012, p. 140, para. 93 (emphasis added). But see ICJ, *Jurisdictional Immunities of the State (Germany v. Italy: Greece intervening)*, Judgment of 3 February 2012 – Separate Opinion of Judge Koroma, ICJ Reports 2012, p. 157, para. 3:

> The question in this case is limited to whether Germany is legally entitled to immunity before the Italian domestic courts with respect to the conduct of its armed forces in the course of the armed conflict. The Court did not need to address the substantive matter of the legality of Germany's conduct to resolve the issue of sovereign immunity.

235 ICJ, *Genocide Case*, p. 221, para. 430.

So then this still leaves us with the lingering question: could the prevention of genocide become a *jus cogens* norm in the future? As we know, *jus cogens* are in some ways tied to moral or natural law principles. It acts, in a way, as the world's conscience – norms that no self-respecting country would deviate from. Could one not describe the prevention of genocide, considering both the positivist considerations outlined above together with State practice, in the same way? It is not radical to suggest that in this day and age that States will not sit idly by and unflinching while watching another Rwanda unfold on their television screens. Indeed, States react all the time to war crimes and crimes against humanity. The question that concerns us, however, is whether there is the potential to overcome the prohibition on the use of force pursuant to Article 2(4) of the UN Charter (1945). Clearly, States do not consider that the prevention of crimes against humanity and/or war crimes merits this kind of action. Nevertheless, it is apparent that States believe that their obligation to prevent genocide is somehow of a different nature; there is an undeniable fear among States in even using the 'g' word and what their obligations to prevent genocide would entail. It is suggested here that the potential for military force is one such fear. Of course, one might consider it far fetched to suggest that States would feel obliged to use military force in order to prevent genocide. But consider this: the US was prepared only very recently to use force – without any prior UN Security Council authorization and clearly not in self defence – on the basis of the Syrian people being subjected to chemical weapons attack by their own government.

All of this is of course is pure speculation. We have no sure way of truly knowing how States will in fact react to another Rwanda. But it will only be through the practice of States that we will be able to identify the rise of new *jus cogens* norms– it will inevitably depend on future reactions of States in the face of genocide. Thus, to be able to gauge this more definitively, we will have to closely watch the future reactions and stances of States in the face of genocide. In particular, we will have to see how States react to inaction by the UN Security Council. Arguably, this exact situation was avoided in Rwanda by a simple recourse of avoiding the 'g' word. However, if in the future we see similar inaction and States step up to act, perhaps militarily, and such action is defended in order to prevent genocide and is accepted as such by the community of States, then one could say that such action begins to support the emergence of a new *jus cogens* norm. In other words, under those conditions, it could be said that States are inclined to believe that the obligation to prevent genocide could – under the right circumstances – be enough to override Article 2(4) of the UN Charter (1945). And if the prohibition on the use of force is indeed a *jus cogens* norm as some suggest, then this could be evidence of a subsequent *jus cogens* norm overriding a prior *jus cogens* norm as provided for in Article 53 of the Vienna Convention (1969).

4 The Prevention of Genocide as *Jus Cogens* and Lawful Humanitarian Intervention: Overcoming the Prohibition on the Use of Force

Having traced historical and contemporary attitudes with respect to the prevention of genocide, we now take a legal leap to consider the implications should it actually attain full *jus cogens* status. The author will attempt to explore some of the substantive content that such a concept would entail and what an obligation to prevent genocide might actually look like in practice.

A The Prohibition of the Use of Force in the Face of a Jus Cogens Obligation to Prevent Genocide: Possible Implications for the UN Charter

In this context, it is trite to say that *jus cogens* trumps other norms of international law – both treaty and customary law. It is beyond question that the prohibition on the use of force is part of treaty law as well as customary international law. However, as aforementioned, some scholars also assert that it has attained *jus cogens* status, although arguments can be made to the contrary.[236] Nevertheless, even if the prohibition on the use of force were *jus cogens*, this does not prevent a subsequent norm of the same character overriding or modifying its application; the Vienna Convention (1969) expressly recognizes this.[237] Therefore if we accept the argument that a *jus cogens* norm can have 'built in' exceptions,[238] and should the prevention of genocide attain *jus cogens* status,

---

[236] See generally J.A. Green, 'Questioning the Peremptory Status of the Prohibition of the Use of Force', (2011) 32(2) *Michigan Journal of International Law* 215 (noting at fns 4–7 various authors who support this view).

[237] Article 53, Vienna Convention (1969).

[238] Accepting the view that the use of force is *jus cogens* entails accepting the notion that *jus cogens* can have exceptions 'built in'. Otherwise, we would have a situation whereby the UN Security Council can validly authorize the violation of a *jus cogens* norm (pursuant to Article 42, Chapter VII of the UN Charter (1945)). And when one accepts that, then it must follow that it can also validly authorize the commission of genocide or torture. This simply cannot be. While this is not the place to argue whether *jus cogens* can indeed have 'built in exceptions', it is interesting to note that the ILC, in listing norms it believed to have attained *jus cogens* status, did not include the prohibition on the use of force but rather the prohibition of aggression, which unlike the former does not contain any

then the prohibition on the use of force also having this same status would not stand in the way of the argument being proposed here – it sits perfectly well within the established orthodox principles of international law. It is also entirely consistent with the original drafters' vision for a dynamic *jus cogens* that is subject to the law of judicial evolution.[239] As the commentary to Article 50 of the ILC's then Draft Vienna Convention (1966) (which eventually became Article 53 of the final treaty) makes plain, 'it would clearly be wrong to regard even rules of *jus cogens* as immutable and incapable of modification in light of future developments.'[240]

However, from a policy perspective, one could argue that the prevention of genocide as *jus cogens* would present unreasonable and problematic consequences for the international legal order. Here, we must recall the effects of *jus cogens* on treaty law and note that the prohibition on the use of force is found in Article 2(4) of the UN Charter (1945) (but also and independently under customary law, as held by the ICJ).[241] While it is true that a *jus cogens* norm can be modified or terminated only by a subsequent peremptory norm, it is also true that it invalidates any treaty that is in conflict with *jus cogens*.[242] So if Article 2(4) were to conflict with a future *jus cogens* norm on the prevention of genocide, two consequences are possible. It could be argued that the whole UN

---

exceptions: Report of the International Law Commission on the Work of its Fifty-Third Session, 23 April – 1 June and 2 July – 10 August 2001, UN Doc. A/56/10, Commentary to Article 26 of the Draft Articles on the Responsibility of States for Internationally Wrongful Acts (2001), in *Yearbook of the International Law Commission 2001 – Volume II, Part Two* (New York, United Nations: 2007), UN Doc. A/CN.4/SER.A/2001/Add.1 (Part 2), p. 85, para. 5. This reflects the ICJ's pronouncement in 1970 that *erga omnes* obligations derived from, *inter* alia, aggression (remaining silent on the prohibition on the use of force): ICJ, *Case Concerning the Barcelona Traction, Light and Power Company, Limited (New Application: 1962 – Second Phase) (Belgium v. Spain)*, Judgment of 5 February 1970, ICJ Reports 1970, p. 32, para. 34. See also S. T. Helmersen, 'The Prohibition of the Use of Force as *Jus Cogens*: Explaining Apparent Derogations', (2014) 61(2) Netherlands International Law Review 167.

239　M.E. Villiger, *Commentary on the 1969 Vienna Convention on the Law of Treaties* (Leiden/Boston, Martinus Nijhoff Publishers: 2009), pp. 672–673.

240　Part II – Report of the International Law Commission on the Work of its Eighteenth Session, 4 May – 19 July 1966, UN Doc. A/6309/Rev.1, Commentary to Article 50 of the Draft Articles on the Law of Treaties (1966), in *Yearbook of the International Law Commission 1966 – Volume II* (New York, United Nations: 1967), UN Doc. A/CN.4/SER.A/1966/Add.1, p. 248.

241　ICJ, *Case Concerning Military and Paramilitary Activities in and Against Nicaragua (Nicaragua v. United States of America)*, Jurisdiction and Admissibility, Judgment of 26 November 1984, ICJ Reports 1984, pp. 424–425, para. 73.

242　Articles 53, 64, Vienna Convention (1969).

Charter (1945) becomes null and void, as this is not a circumstance where only one treaty provision may be modified or invalidated. As Article 44(5) of the Vienna Convention (1969) on the separability of treaty provisions provides, the possibility to isolate and nullify one single article is specifically rejected when it conflicts with *jus cogens* norms pursuant to Article 53.[243] On the other hand, it could also be argued that separability is in fact available:

> According to Art[icle] 44 para. 5, no separation is permitted in cases falling under Art[icle] 53. By way of not referring to Art[icle] 64,[244] Art[icle] 44 [as a whole] is applicable to treaties that have been valid at the time of their conclusion but subsequently conflict with newly emerging peremptory rules. Consequently, the ground of invalidity, *ie* the subsequent *ius cogens* conflict, affects only conflicting treaty provision[s] whereas the remaining treaty provisions are legally valid, provided they are separable from the affected provision (Art[icle] 44 para. 3).[245]

The point is that either view leaves us with most undesirable outcomes: either the UN Charter (1945) dies as a whole or Article 2(4) becomes null and void. Avoiding either one of these situations is a good policy argument against recognizing the prevention of genocide as *jus cogens*.

Yet, there is an important *caveat* to this: the Vienna Convention (1969) was not intended to apply to treaties concluded before its entry into force, as spelled out in Article 4.[246] This includes, for our purposes, the provisions regarding the invalidity of treaties vis-à-vis violations of *jus cogens*. It means this:

---

243 Article 44(5), Vienna Convention (1969) reads;
> In cases falling under articles 51, 52 and 53, no separation of the provisions of the treaty is permitted.

244 Article 64, Vienna Convention (1969) reads:
> If a new peremptory norm of international law emerges, any existing treaty which is conflict with that norm become void and terminates.

245 K. Schmalenbach, 'Article 64: Emergence of a New Peremptory Norm of General International Law (*"Jus Cogens"*)', in O. Dörr and K. Schmalenbach (eds), *Vienna Convention on the Law of Treaties: A Commentary* (Berlin/Heidelberg, Springer: 2012), p. 1124. See also M.E. Villiger, *Commentary on the 1969 Vienna Convention on the Law of Treaties* (Leiden/Boston, Martinus Nijhoff Publishers: 2009), p. 794:
> Article 53 [...] differs from Article 64 in that the latter envisages the separability of treaty provisions [...]. It is, therefore, possible that only individual treaty provisions will come into conflict with the *jus cogens* rule, and only these provisions will become void and terminate. All other provisions of the treaty remain in force.

246 Article 4, Vienna Convention (1969) reads:
> Without prejudice to the application of any rules set forth in the present Convention to which treaties would be subject under international law independently of the Conven-

jus cogens cannot invalidate treaties concluded before 1980 (when the Vienna Convention (1969) entered into force), unless perhaps *jus cogens* crystallized prior to this date (since Article 4 does not displace pre-existing treaty rules).[247] *Jus cogens*, as positive law, was born with advent of Articles 53 and 64 the Vienna Convention (1969). Of course, the reality is that the ICJ has applied provisions of the convention to treaties concluded many years before 1980, but it has only really done so with respect to the interpretation of such treaties – usually Article 31 as reflecting customary international law.[248] There are also very good policy and practical arguments against the retroactive application of *jus cogens* to nullify historical treaties. For example, consider the world-wide uncertainty that could ensue were we to nullify historical treaties that validated historical conquests and territorial acquisitions through what we would today qualify as the crime of aggression.[249] The moment we accept that *jus cogens* can apply retroactively, then the map of Europe could become unstable, a

---

tion, the Convention applies only to treaties which are concluded by States after the entry into force of the present Convention with regard to such States.

See also M.E. Villiger, *Commentary on the 1969 Vienna Convention on the Law of Treaties* (Leiden/Boston, Martinus Nijhoff Publishers: 2009), p. 112; K. Schmalenbach, 'Article 4: Non-retroactivity of the Present Convention', in O. Dörr and K. Schmalenbach (eds), *Vienna Convention on the Law of Treaties: A Commentary* (Berlin/Heidelberg, Springer: 2012), pp. 86–87.

247 See also J. Crawford, *Brownlie's Principles of Public International Law*, 8th Edition (Oxford, Oxford University Press: 2012), p. 389.

248 See for example, ICJ, *Dispute Regarding Navigational and Related Rights (Costa Rica v. Nicaragua)*, Judgment of 13 July 2009, ICJ Reports 2009, p. 236, para. 47 (where the court applied Article 31, Vienna Convention (1969) to a treaty that was concluded in 1857). For a discussion of this case, see M. Dawidowicz, 'The Effect of Passage of Time on the Interpretation of Treaties: Some Reflections on *Costa Rica v. Nicaragua*' (2011) 24(1) *Leiden Journal of International Law* 201. See also ICJ, *Case Concerning Kasikili/Sedudu Island (Botswana/Namibia)*, Judgment of 13 December 1999, ICJ Reports 1999, p. 1059, para. 18 (where the court applied Article 31, Vienna Convention (1969) to a treaty that was concluded in 1890); ICJ, *Case Concerning Sovereignty Over Pulau Ligitan and Pulau Sipadan (Indonesia/Malaysia)*, Judgment of 17 December 2002, ICJ Reports 2002, pp. 645–646, para. 38 (where the court applied Article 31, Vienna Convention (1969) to a treaty that was concluded in 1891).

249 See also the recently initiated *Case Concerning the Obligation to Negotiate Access to the Pacific Ocean (Bolivia v. Chile)* at the ICJ, concerning negotiations to resolve the 19th century conquest by Chile of former Bolivian territory which, had it occurred today, would have violated *jus cogens* norms. For a discussion of this case and its *jus cogens* angle, see E. Santalla Vargas, 'Bolivia's Centenarian Maritime Claim before the International Court of Justice', *Peace Palace Library* Blog, 14 May 2013, available at: http://www.peacepalacelibrary.nl/2013/05/bolivias-centenarian-maritime-claim-before-the-international-court-of-justice/ (accessed 30 June 2014).

most undesirable outcome.[250] It also raises the question as to exactly how far back in time such a norm would reach.

For this reason, the recognition of the prevention of genocide as *jus cogens* should not mark the end of the UN Charter (1945) or Article 2(4) and international relations as we know it. It would very much remain alive and well. However, what would occur is that a new exception to the prohibition on the use of force would emerge as the *jus cogens* prohibition on the use of force would be modified by another subsequent *jus cogens* norm, albeit one that applies in specific circumstances.

B *A Jus Cogens Obligation to Prevent Genocide in Practice*

The crystallization of a *jus cogens* norm to prevent genocide would mark an important step in the development of international law. Whereas the great majority of established *jus cogens* norms involve negative obligations (i.e prohibition on genocide, slavery, apartheid, aggression, etc.), the prevention of genocide would entail a *positive* obligation – an obligation to act, to 'do something'.[251] This might sound problematic, but this is not all that dissimilar from the concept that 'all basic rights involve some positive obligations [upon the State].'[252] The difference is that in this instance such an obligation is extended to events beyond the standard jurisdictional limits of the State, as indeed it

---

250 It should be noted, however, that boundary treaties are considered to be a special category of treaties. They create obligations *erga omnes* and the boundaries they create are generally considered to continue to apply even if the treaty itself does not. See Arbitration Tribunal, *Eritrea/Yemen Arbitration (Phase One: Territorial Sovereignty and Scope of the Dispute)*, 9 October 1998, 114 ILR 1, p. 48, para. 153; ICJ, *Territorial Dispute (Libyan Arab Jamahiriya/Chad)*, Judgment of 3 February 1994, ICJ Reports 1994, p. 37, paras 72–73. Their unique character is reflected in the fact that, for example, boundary treaties remain unaffected in cases of State succession (G. Hafner and G. Novak, 'State Succession in Respect of Treaties' in D.B. Hollis, *The Oxford Guide to Treaties* (Oxford, Oxford University Press: 2012), pp. 399, 419; Article 11, Vienna Convention on Succession of States in Respect of Treaties (1978)) and that fundamental changes of circumstances do not terminate such treaties nor provide grounds for withdrawing from them (Article 62(2)(a), Vienna Convention (1969)). Whether boundary treaties and the boundaries they create could continue to exist even in the face of the retroactive application of *jus cogens* is less certain.

251 See generally, K. Schmalenbach, 'Article 53: Treaties Conflicting with a Peremptory Norm of General International Law (*"Jus Cogens"*)', in O. Dörr and K. Schmalenbach (eds), *Vienna Convention on the Law of Treaties: A Commentary* (Berlin/Heidelberg, Springer: 2012), p. 917.

252 A. Mowbray, *The Development of Positive Obligations under the European Convention on Human Rights by the European Court of Human Rights* (Oxford/Portland, Hart Publishing: 2004), p. 224.

already appears to be with respect to States parties to the Genocide Convention (1948).

We are thus left with the inquiry of what a *jus cogens* obligation to prevent genocide could look like in practice. It surely cannot automatically mean the use of force in all instances of genocide. Of course, the present work is not the first to explore this sort of issue. The ICJ did so in its *Genocide Case* when it recognized an obligation to prevent genocide, holding that:

> [I]t is clear that the obligation in question is one of conduct and not one of result, in the sense that a State cannot be under an obligation to succeed, whatever the circumstances, in preventing the commission of genocide: the obligation of States parties is rather to employ all means reasonably available to them, so as to prevent genocide so far as possible. A State does not incur responsibility simply because the desired result is not achieved; responsibility is however incurred if the State manifestly failed to take all measures to prevent genocide which were within its power, and which might have contributed to preventing the genocide.[253]

It went on to state that:

> Various parameters operate when assessing whether a State has duly discharged the obligation concerned. The first, which varies greatly from one State to another, is clearly the capacity to influence effectively the action of persons likely to commit, or already committing, genocide. This capacity itself depends, among other things, on the geographical distance of the State concerned from the scene of the events, and on the strength of the political links, as well as links of all other kinds, between the authorities of that State and the main actors in the events. The State's capacity to influence must also be assessed by legal criteria, since it is clear that every State may only act within the limits permitted by international law; seen thus, a State's capacity to influence may vary depending

---

253 ICJ, *Case Concerning Application of the Convention on the Prevention and Punishment of the Crime of Genocide (Bosnia and Herzegovina v. Serbia and Montenegro)*, Judgment of 26 February 2007, ICJ Reports 2007, p. 221, para. 430. See also See also ICJ, *Case Concerning Application of the Convention on the Prevention and Punishment of the Crime of Genocide (Bosnia and Herzegovina v. Serbia and Montenegro)*, Judgment of 26 February 2007 – Joint Declaration of Judges Shi and Koroma, ICJ Reports 2007, p. 282, para. 5.

on its particular legal position vis-à-vis the situations and persons facing the danger, or the reality, of genocide.[254]

While the ICJ was careful in limiting its holding to obligations under the Genocide Convention (1948) only,[255] there is no apparent or pressing reason why it should be different when considering the same principle as *jus cogens*. Therefore, it is submitted that a *jus cogens* obligation to prevent genocide would look much the same as that under the Genocide Convention (1948) as elaborated above by the ICJ. However, there is one important difference: no derogations are permitted in the face of *jus cogens* obligations. States that are not parties to the Genocide Convention (1948) cannot escape this prevention obligation by simply asserting that they had not subscribed to the treaty. Nevertheless, 'the principles underlying the Convention are principles which are recognized by civilized nations as binding on States, even without any conventional obligation.'[256] On the assumption that the prevention of genocide is also a part of customary international law, States can point to various circumstances that preclude the wrongfulness of violating this obligation including consent, self defence, countermeasures, necessity, etc. One cannot point to any of these in the face of a violation of *jus cogens*. So what does this mean for a *jus cogens* obligation to prevent genocide?

It is submitted that the prevention of genocide is broad enough to encompass a wide range of actions depending on the capacities, capabilities and abilities of the relevant State to prevent genocide. In other words, there is a wide and ever increasing spectrum of State action that would satisfy this *jus cogens* obligation depending on the State at issue and the circumstances of any given case. Imagine a sliding scale for the prevention of genocide as *jus cogens*. On one end of this scale would be measures that all States – including small and less prominent ones – have the capacity to undertake when they are made aware of genocide taking place or that genocide is imminent. This would

---

254   ICJ, *Case Concerning Application of the Convention on the Prevention and Punishment of the Crime of Genocide (Bosnia and Herzegovina v. Serbia and Montenegro)*, Judgment of 26 February 2007, ICJ Reports 2007, p. 221, para. 430.

255   ICJ, *Case Concerning Application of the Convention on the Prevention and Punishment of the Crime of Genocide (Bosnia and Herzegovina v. Serbia and Montenegro)*, Judgment of 26 February 2007, ICJ Reports 2007, p. 220, para. 429.

256   ICJ, *Reservations to the Convention on the Prevention and Punishment of the Crime of Genocide*, Advisory Opinion of 28 May 1951, ICJ Reports 1951, p. 23; ICJ, *Case Concerning Armed Activities on the Territory of the Congo (New Application: 2002) (Democratic Republic of the Congo v. Rwanda)*, Jurisdiction of the Court and Admissibility of the Application, Judgment of 3 February 2006, ICJ Reports 2006, p. 31, para. 64.

include, for example, bringing this knowledge to the attention of the international community and regional agencies, engaging with the relevant State authorities where appropriate, diplomatic protests, the recalling of diplomats, or other peaceful means of action such as international litigation.[257] For developing countries that do not have the capacity to intervene in any significant way this could be enough to satisfy their *jus cogens* obligation; it is the best that they can practically do – and that they can be expected to do – given their particular circumstances. This would be in line with the ICJ's pronouncement on the prevention of genocide as outlined above (albeit with respect to conventional obligations under the Genocide Convention (1948)).

It is to be noted at this instance that such a minimum obligation for States does not really introduce anything new to their conduct (nor is it inconsistent with international law) – they do this already in the face of genocide. No State even today sits completely motionless in such circumstances. Of course as we have seen during the Rwandan genocide, States may try to deny the very existence of genocide or appeal to technicalities in its definition as a means to justify inaction. But as explained earlier, this could merely serve to reinforce the general norm rather than undermine it.

On the other end of the spectrum, we have the use of force. However, it must be ensured that reliance on such a measure be exercised in a cautious and responsible manner. This raises the question of what this could look like. In this respect, much of the potentially applicable principles and framework can be found in the R2P context; much of the work has been done already, at least in theory. Hence, any use of force in order to prevent genocide would ideally abide by the various precautionary principles that are outlined in R2P. That is, right intention (the primary purpose being to halt or avert genocide), last resort (the exhausting of peaceful options for the prevention of genocide,

---

257 With respect to litigation before the ICJ, it is worth noting that a number of States have included reservations to the compromissory clause contained in Article IX of the Genocide Convention (1948), thus limiting the ICJ's ability to resolve disputes arising from the treaty between States parties. Despite Judge Koroma's strong protestations to the contrary, the ICJ has held that such reservations are not inconsistent with the object and purpose of the Genocide Convention (1948). See ICJ, *Case Concerning Armed Activities on the Territory of the Congo (New Application: 2002) (Democratic Republic of the Congo v. Rwanda)*, Jurisdiction of the Court and Admissibility of the Application, Judgment of 3 February 2006, ICJ Reports 2006, pp. 32–33, paras 66–68. But see *contra*, ICJ, *Case Concerning Armed Activities on the Territory of the Congo (New Application: 2002) (Democratic Republic of the Congo v. Rwanda)*, Jurisdiction of the Court and Admissibility of the Application, Judgment of 3 February 2006 – Dissenting Opinion of Judge Koroma, ICJ Reports 2006, pp. 55–64, paras 1–29.

or reasonable grounds for the belief that lesser action would not prevent genocide), proportional means (the scale, duration and intensity of the intervention being the minimum necessary to prevent genocide), and reasonable prospects (reasonable prospects of success in preventing genocide through intervention, with its consequences not likely being worse than those brought on by inaction).[258]

Utilising these principles, the use of force pursuant to a *jus cogens* norm to prevent genocide could well be articulated in such a way as to avert or minimize excesses. Borrowing from the R2P model, the use of force to prevent genocide would be the last port of call after the entire spectrum of other State action has been exhausted. This would generally come after seizing the UN Security Council of the matter so as to be dealt with under Chapter VII of the UN Charter (1945), after State protests, and after every other non-forceful measure wields no success. In other words, the use of force pursuant to a *jus cogens* obligation to prevent genocide would be a last, not first, resort. Only when it would be unfeasible to go through the entire spectrum of action in order to satisfy this obligation, and depending on the particular factual matrix, could a State perhaps depart from such principles.

Therefore, in the face of large scale massacres where global inaction is resulting in the deaths of tens of thousands – another Rwanda – States could be justified in using limited force for the sole purpose of bringing to a halt senseless killing. It should be exercised with particular care, foresight and in good faith. But, as explained by the ICJ, such action would not be for every State. Not every State has the capacity to undertake such operations, nor should they be expected to. A State may be geographically distant, such action may be economically untenable, or the State may simply lack the capability to undertake such an endeavour. This would not mean that such a State is in violation of a *jus cogens* norm, so long as that State did everything else within its capabilities to prevent genocide. But should a State be in a clear position to 'do something', it could, in the most unique of circumstances and as a last resort, intervene unilaterally in order to prevent genocide; the use of force under this model would be limited and narrow in scope. Further, it must be appreciated that there would be an inherent and unusual amount of flexibility in a *jus cogens* norm that bends and curves depending on the circumstances surrounding the genocidal events and the circumstances of the particular State at issue.

---

258 See International Commission on Intervention and State Sovereignty, *The Responsibility to Protect: Report of the International Commission on Intervention and State Sovereignty* (Ottawa, International Development Research Centre: 2001), paras 4.33–4.43.

Of course, such a concept could be open to abuse. This has always been the inherent problem with humanitarian intervention. But this concern is hardly news to international lawyers, nor is it confined to the law on the use of force. It touches most, if not all, areas of international law. This is an unavoidable situation when operating within a legal system where States primarily determine for themselves whether they are abiding by their international obligations or not. Having said that, should States act contrary to the applicable principles for humanitarian intervention to prevent genocide, they of course then open themselves up to at best, accusations of an unlawful use of force, and/or at worst their leaders could face charges of aggression before the International Criminal Court,[259] as well as the political and economic fallout that comes with it.

5   Conclusion

The theory espoused in this chapter is controversial. This is because it upsets one of the cornerstones of international affairs since the end of World War II: the legal notion that no State has the right to intervene militarily into the affairs of another. Nevertheless, there comes a time in any legal system – whether domestic or international – when the needs and hopes of the community which it is supposed to serve is no longer matched by the outcomes that it decrees. It is then that the law is most ripe for change. It is submitted that the prohibition on the use of force under international law is rapidly approaching this pivotal point. It cannot be denied that the international legal system is moving ever more rapidly away from the traditional State-centric Westphalian model of international relations and into a new era where the individual is far more in focus than ever before. Yet, despite this shift, the prohibition on the use of force as it stands today still decrees that individuals should perish in the most brutal and shocking of circumstances for the sake of Westphalian sovereignty. As one jurist has put it, States pay 'unreasonable homage [...] to the doctrine of non-interference in each other's affairs.'[260] Consequently, Article

---

259   On the assumption that the ICC's jurisdiction over aggression as per Article 8 *bis* of the Rome Statute (1998) has been activated and that the factual situation satisfies the ICC's jurisdictional parameters.

260   D.D.N. Nsereko, 'Genocide: A Crime Against Mankind', in G. K. McDonald and O. Swaak-Goldman (eds), *Substantive and Procedural Aspects of International Criminal Law: The Experience of International and National Courts – Volume 1: Commentary* (The Hague, Kluwer Law International: 2000), p. 139.

2(4) of the UN Charter (1945) is becoming more and more detached from the increasing attention that the international system pays to individuals and human rights. Left unchecked, the current prohibition on the use of force will likely be left behind in the face of global inaction to tomorrow's Rwanda.

In light of this, all that this paper has attempted to do is to provide a legal theory by which to express these desires for change but within the existing legal system. However, it is undoubtedly an idea whose time has not yet arrived. It is an idea for tomorrow, not for today; this chapter has dealt with *lex ferenda* not *lex lata*. There are still a number of areas that would need to be expanded and addressed.[261] Indeed, as Judge Bennouna of the ICJ points out, in the present climate the theory presented herein 'would be tantamount to recognising a right of trusteeship for powerful States over weaker ones.'[262] Plainly, in today's legal milieu the ideas expressed above do not sit comfortably with orthodox views of sovereignty (and the use of force). Then again, the orthodoxy of today could very well become the relic of tomorrow. Only time will tell. But the seeds of change are certainly in the ground.[263] However, if history teaches us anything, it is that humanity are generally a reactive, rather than a proactive, species. Very rarely do we act in advance of the foreseeable ills of tomorrow. Generally, we tend to live through their effects before the impetus to change is fortified. Perhaps it will only take something of the magnitude of Rwanda for the idea advocated in this chapter to be raised, recognized and accepted. But one can hope – perhaps naïvely – that it need not come to that.

---

261 For example, it ought to be explored how a violation of a *jus cogens* obligation to prevent genocide would work in light of Article 41(2) of the ILC's Draft Articles on the Responsibility of States for Internationally Wrongful Acts (2001) whereby '[n]o State shall recognize as lawful a situation created by a serious breach [of a *jus cogens* norm], nor render aid or assistance in maintaining that situation.' See generally Report of the International Law Commission on the Work of its Fifty-Third Session, 23 April – 1 June and 2 July – 10 August 2001, UN Doc. A/56/10, Commentary to Article 41 of the Draft Articles on the Responsibility of States for Internationally Wrongful Acts (2001), in *Yearbook of the International Law Commission 2001 – Volume II, Part Two* (New York, United Nations: 2007), UN Doc. A/CN.4/SER.A/2001/Add.1 (Part 2), pp. 113–116, paras 1–14. Another area worth exploring is how such a norm would apply beyond States and to, for example, the UN as an organization endowed with international legal personality.

262 M. Bennouna, 'Prevention in International Law', in *Collected Courses of the Xiamen Academy of International Law – Volume 4: 2011* (Leiden/Boston, Martinus Nijhoff Publishers: 2013), p. 166.

263 See for example E. Benvenisti, 'Sovereigns as Trustees of Humanity: On the Accountability of States to Foreign Stakeholders', (2013) 107(2) *The American Journal of International Law* 295 (where the author posits a theory of sovereignty as a trusteeship not only towards a State's own citizens, but also towards humanity as a whole).

CHAPTER 18

A Reflection on the Phrase "Widespread or Systematic" as Part of the Definition of Crimes Against Humanity

Avitus A. Agbor

1 Introduction

The definition of what constitutes serious crimes in international law has been subjected to numerous variations ever since the birth of international criminal justice in 1945. While little variance has been made with regard to the content of serious crimes in international law, the definition of these crimes have undergone sufficient vacillations. However, in the last decade of the last century, events that unfolded in the former Yugoslavia, Rwanda, and Sierra Leone gave the international community the opportunity to develop and adopt definitions of these crimes, which, since, then, have suffered minor changes.[1] Three crimes are recurrent: war crimes, genocide and crimes against humanity.[2] International instruments in the last decades have not failed in constituting these as serious crimes in international law. As acknowledged by the Trial

---

1   See generally the following international instruments: Statute of the Special Court for Sierra Leone (hereinafter referred to as the SCSL), annexed to the Agreement between the United Nations and the Government of Sierra Leone on the Establishment of a Special Court for Sierra Leone pursuant to United Nations Security Council Resolution 1315, UN SCOR, 4186th meeting, UN Doc. S/RES/1315 (2000); Statute of the International Criminal Tribunal for Rwanda (hereinafter referred to as the ICTR), annexed to United Nations Security Council Resolution 955, UN SCOR, 3453rd meeting, UN Doc. S/RES/955 (1994); Statute of the International Criminal Tribunal for the former Yugoslavia (hereinafter referred to as the ICTY), annexed to United Nations Security Council Resolution 827, UN SCOR, 3217th meeting, UN Doc. S/RES/827 (1993). In addition to these events, the establishment of the International Criminal Court was a colossal breakthrough in international criminal justice, and more importantly, the adoption of what constitute serious crimes in international law. See Rome Statute of the International Criminal Court, UN Doc. A/CONF.183/9 (1998), reprinted in 37 I.L.M. 999 (1998) (hereinafter referred to as the Rome Statute of the ICC).

2   Rome Statute of the ICC, Articles 6–8 respectively; Statute of the SCSL, Articles 2–4; Statute of the ICTR, Articles 2–4; Statute of the ICTY, Articles 2–5.

Chambers in the *ad hoc* tribunals, these three crimes are very distinct from each other and do protect different interests.[3]

One of these crimes, the crime of crimes against humanity, has not been immune to these definitional variations. In fact, it became very worrying to notice that two different definitions were given by the same institution within a two-year period in response to the nature of atrocities perpetrated: the definitions of crimes against humanity as contained in the Statute of the ICTY and the Statute of the ICTR are completely different.[4] However, international instruments subsequent to the Statute of the ICTR have retained most of the definitional elements.[5] These definitional elements as well as the jurisprudence of the *ad hoc* Tribunals have contributed to the development of what David Luban calls 'the common law of crimes against humanity'.[6]

An examination of these definitional elements reveals that two specific but alternate phrases are used: 'systematic or widespread'. The inclusion of these two alternating words highlight a distinguishing feature of crimes against humanity from other serious crimes in international law: they are group crimes because they require group participation for their planning, preparation or execution. This makes it very different from the crime of genocide where the key distinguishing feature is the requirement of a genocidal intent: to destroy a people, in part or in whole;[7] and war crimes, which requires the presence of an armed conflict for any such crime(s) to be committed.[8]

This paper argues that the inclusion of a caveat – 'widespread or systematic' – descriptive of the attack, implicitly speaks of crimes against humanity

---

3 *The Prosecutor v. Jean-Paul Akayesu*, Judgment, Case No. ICTR-96-4-T 2, T. Ch. I, September 1998, para. 469.
4 See generally the Statute of the ICTY, Article 5 (which defined crimes against humanity by requiring that any of the enlisted crimes be committed within an armed conflict, international or internal in character, and directed against any civilian population) as different from the Statute of the ICTR, Article 3 (which defined crimes against humanity by requiring that any of the enlisted crimes be committed as a part of a widespread or systematic attack and directed against any civilian population based on any of the stipulated discriminatory grounds).
5 See for example, the Rome Statute of the ICC, Article 7(1); the Statute of the SCSL, Article 2.
6 David Luban, 'A Theory of Crimes against Humanity' (2004) 29 *Yale J. Int'l L.* 85, 93–109.
7 See the Rome Statute of the ICC, Article 6; Statute of the ICTR, Article 2(2); Statute of the ICTY, Article 4(2). See also the *Convention on the Prevention and Punishment of the Crime of Genocide*, United Nations General Assembly Resolution 260(III), UN GAOR, 3rd Session, 179th meeting, UN Doc. A/RES/260A (1948), Article 2.
8 See the Rome Statute of the ICC, Article 8; Statute of the ICTR, Article 4; Statute of the ICTY, Articles 2–3.

as group crimes which require the existence of a joint criminal enterprise for their planning, preparation or commission.

In making this argument, first, I give a synoptic account of the evolution of crimes against humanity. Secondly, I take a look at the definitional elements of crimes against humanity, with specific focus on the 'widespread or systematic' nature of the attack as prescribed by international instruments. Thirdly, I construe these definitional elements to expose the implicit existence or requirement of a group of persons which, logically, is a joint criminal enterprise, for the planning, preparation or commission of the crime of crimes against humanity.

2   The Evolution of Crimes against humanity

Despite the protracted slowness in prescribing an acceptable definition of what constitutes crimes against humanity, the various formulations between 1945 and 1992 helped in identifying what would be considered the common law of crimes against humanity. However, with the definition advanced by the UNSC second ad hoc international criminal tribunal (ICTR) which, for the most part, incorporated into the Rome Statute of the ICC, I argue that the crime of crimes against humanity carries a key distinguishing characteristic which makes it sui generis: they are group crimes (can be committed only by a group, or in more precise legal jargon, a joint criminal enterprise).

2.1   *The Charters of the International Military Tribunals, Nuremberg and Tokyo, and Allied Control Council Law No. 10*

Though considered as old as humanity itself,[9] prior to 1945, crimes against humanity resided in the realm of international discourse as a 'term of art',[10] a concept that was dismissed by Americans as 'not the object of punishment by a court of justice', but rather one of 'moral law' that lacked any 'fixed and universal standard'.[11] Following the London Agreement that established the IMT,

---

9   Jean Graven, 'Les Crimes Contre l'Humanité' (1950–1) 76 *Receuil des Cours* 427, 433.
10 Roger S. Clark, 'Crimes against Humanity' in George Ginsburgs & V N Kudriavtsev (eds), *The Nuremberg Trial and International Law* (Martinus Nijhoff Publishers 1990) 177–212, 177.
11 Commission on the Responsibility of the Authors of the War and on Enforcement of Penalties, *Report Presented to the Preliminary Peace Conference,* 29 March 1919, reprinted in (1920) 14 *AJIL* 95, 144. See also Lord Wright 'War Crimes Under International Law' (1946) 62 *Law Q. Rev.* 40, 48–49; Graven (n. 9) 446–51.

Nuremberg,[12] it became a positive crime in international law, with Nuremberg residing as its baptismal locus. Established to try and punish the major war criminals,[13] it had jurisdiction over three crimes, amongst which were crimes against humanity. The Charter of the IMT defined crimes against humanity as follows:

> murder, extermination, enslavement, deportations, and other inhumane acts committed against any civilian population, before or during the war; or persecutions on political, racial or religious grounds in execution of or in connection with any crime within the jurisdiction of the Tribunal, whether or not in violation of the domestic law of the country where perpetrated.[14]

The wording of Article 6(c) required that the acts must be committed against a civilian population before or during the war. It statutorily established a nexus between the crimes and the war in order for them to qualify as crimes against humanity.[15]

The Nuremberg Charter was succeeded by two historic international instruments. The first was the Allied Control Council Law No. 10, enacted in 1945 by the Allied Powers.[16] Allied Control Council Law No. 10 defined crimes against humanity as

---

12   Nineteen states subsequently acceded to the Agreement. Annexed to this Agreement was the Charter of the IMT. See Agreement for the Prosecution and Punishment of the Major War Criminals of the European Axis, 8 August 1945, 59 Stat. 1544, 82 UNTS 279; M. Cherif Bassiouni, *Crimes against Humanity in International Criminal Law* (Kluwer Law International 1999) 1.

13   Charter of IMT, Nuremberg, Article 1. Under the 1943 Moscow Declaration by the Allies, the trial and judgment of minor war criminals would take place in the countries where they committed their crimes.

14   Charter of IMT, Nuremberg, Article 6(c).

15   However, vagueness, ambiguities and uncertainties in the wording of Article 6(c) resulted in intense debates by international law scholars. Conflicting interpretations of the various versions of the text defining crimes against humanity arose, which led to the Berlin Protocol of 6 October 1945. It eliminated the semicolon and replaced it with a comma. This new phrasing of the Berlin Protocol buried every doubt and made clear that 'in execution of or in connection with any crime within the jurisdiction of the Tribunal' would be construed to apply to the entire context of the paragraph. It would also constitute an important restriction on the scope of the concept of crimes against humanity. See Bassiouni (n. 12) 227–32; Clark (n. 10) 177–92.

16   This was a piece of municipal legislation enacted by the Allied Powers following the unconditional surrender of Germany on 8 May 1945. Having supreme legislative authority

> [A]trocities and offences, including but not limited to murder, extermination, enslavement, deportation, imprisonment, torture, rape, or other inhumane acts committed against any civilian population, or persecutions on political, racial or religious grounds, whether or not in violation of the domestic laws of the country where perpetrated.[17]

The definition contained in Article 11(c) of Allied Control Council Law No. 10 had some similarities and differences that pertained to the definition in Article 6(c) of the Charter of the Nuremberg Tribunal.[18] The second instrument after Nuremberg was the Charter of the International Military Tribunal for the Far East (hereinafter referred to as the IMTFE), Tokyo. It established the Tokyo Tribunal 'for the just and prompt trial and punishment of major war criminals in the Far East',[19] and simply repeated *mutatis mutandis* the wording of Article 6(c) of the Nuremberg Charter. Entitled 'Jurisdiction over Persons and Offenses', the Tokyo Charter created and defined crimes against humanity to mean

> murder, extermination, enslavement, deportation, and other inhumane acts against any civilian population, before or during the war, or perse-

---

over Germany, the Control Council Law No. 10 was not intended to be an international instrument, but a piece of national legislation providing the Allied Powers the legal basis for subsequent criminal prosecutions in Germany. Its applicability was to the various zones of occupation by the Allied Powers. Bassiouni (n. 12) 3–6.

17 Allied Control Council Law No. 10, Article 11 (c).

18 First, in its wording, the Allied Powers stated that Control Council Law No. 10 was enacted for the 'prosecution of war criminals and other similar offenders other than those dealt with by the International Military Tribunal' In the wording of crimes against humanity, an enlistment of the crimes was preceded by the words 'Atrocities and offences' (Article 11(1)(c)), whereas the Charter of the IMT, Nuremberg, defined crimes against humanity without such annotation. The Allied Control Council Law No. 10 also made use of broad phraseology in the definition of crimes against humanity, injecting the words 'included but not limited to' (Article 11(1)(c)). New crimes like rape and imprisonment were added despite the possibility of sub-classifying them under the umbrella of 'other inhumane acts' like the Charter of the IMT, Nuremberg, did (see Article 6(c)). Article 6(c) of the Charter of the IMT, Nuremberg, required that the acts amounting to crimes against humanity be committed 'in execution of, or in connection with any crime [crimes against peace, war crimes and crimes against humanity] within the jurisdiction of the Tribunal, whether or not in violation of the domestic law of the country where perpetrated.' By inserting the clause 'whether or not in violation of the domestic laws of the country where perpetrated' (Article 11(1)(c)), the nexus requirement was made redundant in the formulation articulated by Allied Control Council Law No. 10 (Article 11(1)(c)).

19 Charter of the IMTFE, Tokyo, Article 1.

cutions on political or racial grounds in execution of or in connection with any crime within the jurisdiction of the Tribunal, whether or not in violation of the domestic law of the country where perpetrated.[20]

Like the Charter of the Nuremberg Tribunal, it stated that the category of persons who would be subject to the jurisdiction of the IMTFE, Tokyo, included 'leaders, organizers, instigators and accomplices participating in the formulation or execution of a common plan or conspiracy to commit any of the foregoing crimes ....'[21] It also mentioned that the commission of these crimes would be 'before or during the war,' and 'in execution of or in connection with any crime within the jurisdiction of the Tribunal'.[22] However, a noticeable variation existed in the definitions stipulated in these two Charters. Article 5(c) of the Charter of the IMTFE, Tokyo, did not make 'persecution' subject to 'religious' grounds. It confined it to 'political or racial grounds'.[23] This variation, though slight, seemed to be triggered by a significant difference in the events leading to them: Nazi atrocities in Europe, especially the extermination of millions of Jews and treatment of citizens in occupied countries, had no exact equivalent in the Asian region or conflict.[24]

---

20   Ibid Article 5(c). Though crimes against humanity were subject to the jurisdiction of the IMTFE, Tokyo, no individual was indicted and charged for crimes against humanity. The Tokyo Tribunal indicted individuals for murder; making it a distinct novelty. At Nuremberg, the crime of murder was not considered a specific crime, except where it was committed as a means of perpetrating war crimes or crimes against humanity. The prosecution's argument was based on the theory that killings in an unlawful war would constitute murder by virtue of the illegal nature of the war. With no legal precedents, the murder charges became the subject of much controversy, and have since then, never been repeated in international law. Neil Boister & Robert Cryer, *The Tokyo International Military Tribunal: A Reappraisal* (Oxford University Press 2008) 154.
21   Charter of the IMT, Nuremberg, Article 6(c); and Charter of the IMTFE, Tokyo, Article 5(c).
22   Charter of the IMTFE, Tokyo, Article 5(c).
23   Ibid.
24   None of the indicted individuals was charged for crimes against humanity. However, they were tried for the offence of murder, which appeared unprecedented and controversial, and has never been repeated in any international criminal tribunal. See Boister & Cryer (n. 20).

2.2 The Works of the United Nations War Crimes Commission[25]

Beyond these three different formulations by the Allied Powers, the United Nations War Crimes Commission (UNWCC) worked on developing a definition of crimes against humanity.

The UNWCC was able to extrapolate and postulate some basic guidelines in understanding the meaning of crimes against humanity. First, it propounded that there were two categories of crimes against humanity: the 'murder' type, which covered crimes such as murder, extermination, enslavement, deportation; and the 'persecution' type, which covered crimes committed based on racial, religious or political grounds. Second, it established that crimes against humanity of the 'murder' and 'persecution' type needed to be perpetrated against a civilian population. This meant they would obviously fall out of its scope if they were inflicted upon military personnel. It added a caveat related to the pattern in which the crimes are committed: they needed to be systematic or widespread in pattern. By this requirement, isolated incidents of crimes would not qualify as crimes against humanity. This requirement that the crimes be committed as part of a widespread or systematic attack was aimed at altering the nature of the crimes and elevate them from ordinary crimes prohibited and punishable by municipal penal laws to serious crimes under international law.

Another conclusion reached at by the UNWCC was that it was irrelevant if the crimes were committed before, during, or after a war. So too were the nationalities of the victims. It was immaterial whether the crimes committed were in violation of the laws of the place (*lex loci*) where they were committed. Lastly, it held that the classification of responsible persons would be widened to cover not just the ringleaders, but also the actual perpetrators of the crimes. It posited that crimes against humanity may be committed by simply enacting

---

25 The United Nations War Crimes Commission was set up by a decision of a diplomatic conference on 20 October 1943 The UNWCC was created on 20 October 1943 by representatives of the seventeen Allied nations. It was the only international framework that dealt with the issue of war crimes and war criminals during the Second World War, and it continued to operate until 31 March 1948. In the course of its existence, it had created a total of 8,178 files (representing 36,810 individuals and groups). Most important notions elaborated by the UNWCC found their way into the Nuremberg Charter. See generally Michael S. Blayney, 'Herbert C. Pell, War Crimes and the Jews' (1976) 65 *American Jewish Historical Quarterly* 335–52; Donald Bloxham, *Genocide on Trial: War Crimes Trials and the Formation of Holocaust History and Memory* (Oxford University Press 2001); Arieh J. Kochavi, *Prelude to Nuremberg: Allied War Crimes Policy and the Question of Punishment* (University of North Carolina Press 1998); Bradley F. Smith, *The Road to Nuremberg* (Basic Books 1981); Clark (n. 10).

a piece of legislation that encourages, orders or permits the commission of any of the crimes, such as unjustified killings, racial discrimination, mass deportations, torture and rape.[26]

2.3 The Travails of the International Law Commission (ILC)[27]

In post-Nuremberg, the international community directed its efforts towards the drafting of a Code of Offences Against the Peace and Security of Mankind.[28] The ILC, barely over a year after its creation, had its first session in 1949. This session was characterised by deliberations, and in 1950, the ILC presented a report in which crimes against humanity were defined as

> Murder, extermination, enslavement, deportation and other inhuman acts done against any civilian population, or persecutions on political, racial or religious grounds, when such acts are done or such persecutions are carried on in execution of or in connexion with any crime against peace or any war crime.[29]

After 1950, four decades elapsed without any formal adoption of a definition of what constituted crimes against humanity. In 1991, the International Law Commission made another formulation.[30] The International Law Commission, at

---

26   Ibid.
27   The International Law Commission was created for the purpose of promoting 'the progressive development of international law and its codification'. See the United Nations General Assembly Resolution 174(II), UN GAOR, 2nd Session, 123rd meeting, UN Doc. A/RES/174(II) of 21 November 1947. The United Nations General Assembly Resolution 177(II) mandated the International Law Commission to formulate 'the principles of international law recognised' in the Charter of the IMT, Nuremberg, and 'in the judgment of the Tribunal.' See the United Nations General Assembly Resolution 177(II), UN GAOR, 2nd Session, 123rd meeting, UN Doc. A/RES/177(II) of 21 November 1947; Bassiouni (n. 12) 179.
28   It was an effort that was begun on 21 November 1947, which resulted in the Draft Code of Crimes against Peace and Security of Mankind. It has not been adopted by the United Nations General Assembly. By 1987, it had become the Code of Crimes against the Peace and Security of Mankind. See Bassiouni (n. 12) 179.
29   Principle VI(c) of *Principles of International Law Recognized by the Charter of the Nuremberg Tribunal and the Judgment of the Tribunal*. See also Bassiouni (n. 12) 180.
30   'An individual who commits or orders the combination of any of the following violations of human rights:
   – Murder
   – Torture
   – Establishing or maintaining over persons a status of slavery, servitude or forced labour

its 43rd session, considered, amongst other things,[31] a Draft Code of Crimes against the Peace and Security of Mankind.[32] At the 2236th meeting, the Commission continued deliberations on the Draft Code of Crimes against the Peace and Security of Mankind.[33] The deliberations of this meeting would be limited to general principles. At its 2237th and 2239th meetings, the Commission deliberated on the core content of what constitute crimes against the peace and security of mankind. These crimes included aggression (Article 15); the threat of aggression (article 16); intervention (Article 17); colonial domination and

- Persecution on social, political, racial, religious or cultural grounds in a systematic manner or on a mass scale; or
- Deportation or forcible transfer of population ….' (Article 21 of the 1991 Draft Code of Crimes).

[31] Different items on the ILC's agenda included state responsibility, jurisdictional immunities of States and their property, the law of the non-navigational uses of international watercourses, international liability for injurious consequences arising out of acts not prohibited by international law, relationsn between States and international organisations.

[32] The Officers of the ILC included Mr Abdul G. Koroma (Sierra Leone), Chairman; Mr John Alan Beesley (Canada), First Vice-Chairman; Second Vice – Chairman: Mr. César Sepúlveda Gutiérrez (Mexico), Second Vice-Chairman; Mr. Husain Al – Baharna (Bahrain), Rapporteur; and Mr. Stanislaw Pawlak (Poland), Chairman of the Drafting Committee. The members of the Commission were Prince Bola Adesumbo Ajibola (Nigeria); Mr. Husain Al – Baharna (Bahrain); Mr. Awn Al-Khasawneh (Jordan); Mr. Riyadh Mahmoud Sami Al-Qaysi (Iraq); Mr. Gaetano Arangio-Ruiz (Italy); Mr. Julio Barboza (Argentina); Mr. Juri G. Barsegov (Union of Soviet Socialist Republics); Mr. John Alan Beesley (Canada); Mr. Mohamed Bennouna (Morocco); Mr. Boutros Boutros-Ghali (Egypt); Mr. Carlos Calero Rodrigues (Brazil); Mr. Leonardo Díaz González (Venezuela); Mr. Gudmundur Eiriksson (Iceland); Mr. Laurel B. Francis (Jamaica); Mr. Bernhard Graefrath (German Democratic Republic); Mr. Francis Mahon Hayes (Ireland);Mr. Jorge E. Illueca (Panama); Mr. Andreas J. Jacovides (Cyprus); Mr. Abdul G. Koroma (Sierra Leone); Mr. Ahmed Mahiou (Algeria); Mr. Stephen C. McCaffrey (United States of America); Mr. Frank X.J.C. Njenga (Kenya); Mr. Motoo Ogiso (Japan); Mr. Stanislaw Pawlak (Poland); Mr. Alain Pellet (France); Mr. Pemmaraju Sreenivasa Rao (India); Mr. Edilbert Razafindralambo (Madagascar); Mr. Emmanuel J. Roucounas (Greece); Mr. César Sepúlveda Gutiérrez (Mexico); Mr. Jiuyong Shi (China); Mr. Luis Solari Tudela (Peru); Mr. Doudou Thiam (Senegal); Mr. Christian Tomuschat (Germany); and Mr. Alexander Yankov (Bulgaria). <<http://legal.un.org/ilc/sessions/43/43sess.htm>> accessed on 18 June, 2014.

[33] It resumed from the 2214th meeting. (A/CN.4/435 and Add.1 (reproduced in Yearbook of the ILC 1991, vol. II (Part One)), A/CN.4/L.456, sect. B, A/CN.4/L.459 and Corr. 1 and Add. 1, ILC (XLIII)/Conf.Room Dc.3).

other forms of alien domination (article 18); genocide (article 19); apartheid (article 20); and systematic or mass violations of human rights (article 21).[34]

Article 21 defined what constituted systematic or mass violations of human rights as follows:

> An individual who commits or orders the commission by another individual of any of the following shall, on conviction thereof, be sentenced [to ...]:
> – violation of human rights in a systematic manner or on a mass scale consisting of any of the following acts:
> (a) murder;
> (b) torture;
> (c) establishing or maintaining over persons a status of slavery, servitude or forced labour;
> (d) deportation or forcible transfer of population;
> (e) persecution on social, political, racial, religious or cultural grounds.[35]

Even though not characterised as 'crimes against humanity', the records of the Drafting Committee give clues that this was the crime the drafters had in mind.[36] The grouping of these crimes under a common rubric was attributable to the fact that they were all violations of human rights. In the opinion of the Commission, '[a]ll violations of human rights, whatever their degree, were abhorrent and intolerable ... '.[37] However, in order to escalate them to crimes against the peace and security of mankind, they had to be 'sufficiently serious'.[38]

Article 21 of the Draft Code introduces some definitional elements. Obviously, focus is not made on the enlisted crimes such as murder, torture, etc., but

---

34 These deliberations, however, spawned to the 2240th meeting where attention was given to the sequencing of the definition of the crime of systematic or mass violations of human rights'.
35 One of the challenges the Commission faced was choosing the crimes to be covered. Even though this list has expanded over the years, the basic concept (definitional element) has not changed that much. As noted below, the seriousness of these crimes is indicated by the systematic or massive nature, the main criterion for them to be qualified as crimes against the peace and security of mankind. Summary of Records of the meetings of the forty-third session, para. 79.
36 Ibid., para. 61.
37 Ibid.
38 Ibid.

on the general principle and criteria by which these crimes would be committed. These definitional elements of a 'systematic manner or on a mass scale' excludes single and isolated cases of human rights violations from the scope of Article 21. The sub-paragraphs (a) to (e) simply enlist the different crimes which the definitional requirement applies to.[39]

However, three years later (in 1994), the ILC would depart significantly from its own earlier definition when it produced a Draft Statute for an ICC.[40] Two years after this extensive formulation, the ILC reconsidered its definition of crimes against humanity and propounded a more abridged version. It defined crimes against humanity to mean

---

[39] Ibid., para. 62.
[40] 'A person commits crimes against humanity, whether in time or peace or war, when:
(a) he is in a position of authority and orders, commands, or fails to prevent the systematic commission of the acts described below, against a given segment of the civilian population;
(b) he is in a position of authority and participates in the making of a policy or program designed to systematically carry out the acts described below against a given segment of the civilian population;
(c) he is in a senior military or political position and knowingly carries out or orders others to carry out systematically the acts described below against a segment of the civilian population;
(d) he knowingly commits the acts described below with the intent to further a policy of systematic persecution against a segment of the civilian population without having a moral choice to do otherwise.
1. The acts constituting 'crimes against humanity' when committed systematically against a segment of the civilian population are:
a. extermination;
b. murder, including killings done by creating conditions likely to cause death;
c. enslavement, including slave-related practices;
d. discriminatory and arbitrary deportation;
e. imprisonment, in violation of international norms on the prohibition of arbitrary arrest and detention;
f. torture;
g. rape and other serious assaults of a sexual nature;
h. persecution, whether based on laws or practices targeting select groups or their members in ways that seriously and adversely affect their ethnic, cultural or religious life, their collective well-being, and welfare, or their ability to group identity;
i. other inhumane acts, including but not limited to serious attacks upon physical integrity, personal safety, and individual dignity, such as physical mutilation, forced impregnation or forced carrying to term foetuses that are the product of forced impregnation, and unlawful human experimentation.'

... any of the following acts, when committed in a systematic manner or on a large scale and instigated or directed by a Government or by any organization or group:
(a) murder;
(b) extermination;
(c) torture;
(d) enslavement;
(e) persecution on political, racial, religious or ethnic grounds;
(f) institutionalized discrimination on racial, ethnic or religious grounds involving the violation of fundamental human rights and freedoms and resulting in seriously disadvantaging a part of the population;
(g) arbitrary deportation of forcible transfer of population;
(h) arbitrary imprisonment;
(i) forced disappearance of persons;
(j) rape, enforced prostitution and other forms of sexual abuse;
(k) other inhumane acts which severely damage physical or mental integrity, health or human dignity, such as mutilation and severe bodily harm.[41]

Approximately four decades after the Charter of the IMT, Nuremberg, events in the territory of the former Yugoslavia created a fecund ground upon which another formulation of crimes against humanity would be made. Evidence of war crimes and other gruesome human rights violations that occurred in the territory of the former Yugoslavia attracted the attention of the international community. The United Nations Security Council expressed concern over violations of international law in the territory, and affirmed the concept of individual criminal responsibility for such violations.[42]

2.4 The Statutes of the United Nations' ad hoc Tribunals

On 6 October 1992, the United Nations Security Council created a Commission of Experts to examine the violations of international law that had taken place in the region.[43] In its interim report, the Commission concluded that serious

---

41 The Draft Code of Crimes Against the Peace and Security of Mankind, 1996, Article 18.
42 For example, United Nations Security Council Resolution 713, UN SCOR, 3009th meeting, UN Doc. S/RES/713 (1991), 25 September 1991.
43 United Nations Security Council Resolution 780, UN SCOR, 3119th meeting, UN Doc. S/RES/713 (1992). The Commission of Experts' mandate was not just to reach legal conclusions, but also to obtain evidence that would be used for prosecution; and also establish a

violations of international law were taking place. It recommended the creation of an *ad hoc* international criminal tribunal.[44] Following the Commission's report, on 11 February 1993, the United Nations Security Council declared that the violations of international humanitarian law in the former Yugoslavia amounted to, and constituted a grave threat to international peace and security. The United Nations Security Council created an international tribunal to address them; and requested the Secretary-General of the United Nations to prepare a report implementing this decision.[45] The Secretary-General's Report contained a draft statute for an *ad hoc* international criminal tribunal. It also took the view that such an *ad hoc* international criminal tribunal be established by resolution rather than treaty.[46]

The United Nations Security Council, pursuant to Chapter VII of the United Nations' Charter, unanimously passed Resolution 827 on 25 May 1993. This created the ICTY. It was the first time an *ad hoc* international criminal tribunal was created in international law. Resolution 827 adopted the draft Statute of the ICTY as expressed in the Secretary-General's report.

---

database of information. See Letter of 9 February 1993, from the Secretary-General, addressed to the President of the Security Council, 10 February 1993, UN Doc. S/25274, at 7–11 (hereinafter referred to as Yugoslavia Commission First Interim Report).

44   Yugoslavia Commission First Interim Report (n. 34). A second interim report was produced by the Commission in October 1993, and then a final report in May 1994. See Letter dated 5 October 1993, from the Secretary-General to the President of the Security Council, 6 October 1993, UN Doc. 2/26545; Letter dated 24 May 1994, from the Secretary-General to the President of the Security Council, 27 May 1994, UN Doc. S/1994/674. The Commission on Human Rights also appointed a Special Rapporteur whose activities were coordinated with those of the Commission of Experts. See The Situation of Human Rights in the Territory of the Former Yugoslavia, 3 September 1992, UN Doc. A/47/418-S/24516; The Situation of Human Rights in the Territory of the Former Yugoslavia, 6 November 1992, UN Doc. A/47/635-S/24766.

45   United Nations Security Council Resolution 808, UN SCOR, 3175th meeting, UN Doc. S/RES/808 (1993), 22 February 1993.

46   Report of the Secretary-General pursuant to paragraph 2 of the United Nations Security Council Resolution 808, 3 May 1993, UN Doc. S/25704 (hereinafter referred to as the Secretary-General's Yugoslavia Report). The consideration to have the Statute adopted by a United Nations Security Council Resolution under pursuant to Chapter VII of the United Nations' Charter was influenced by a number of factors: first, a treaty would be a laborious exercise, whereas a Security Council Resolution would be much quicker and easier. Second, such a Security Council Resolution would bind all states, whereas a treaty would bind only those states that are parties to it. Third, it would be more difficult to secure active participation and cooperation of some member states.

The Statute of the ICTY gave the ICTY jurisdiction over crimes against humanity which it defined as

> ... the following crimes when committed in armed conflict, whether international or internal in character, and directed against any civilian population:
> (a) murder;
> (b) extermination;
> (c) enslavement;
> (d) deportation;
> (e) imprisonment;
> (f) torture;
> (g) rape;
> (h) persecutions on political, racial and religious grounds;
> (i) other inhumane acts.[47]

Except for the addition of rape and imprisonment and some other slight differences,[48] the wording was akin to that of Article 6(c) of the Nuremberg Charter. Article 5 of the Statute took a major departure from the UNWCC's conclusions on crimes against humanity, which required that the crimes committed be systematic or widespread. In departing from this requirement, it articulates that the crimes be 'committed in armed conflict'.[49] However, it specifically defines the crime of persecution as based on political, racial and religious grounds. Like some other formulations,[50] it adds the words 'other inhumane acts',[51] with no specificity as to what may amount to an inhumane act.

On 8 November 1994, the United Nations Security Council established the second *ad hoc* tribunal, the ICTR.[52] Like the first, the United Nations Security

---

47 Statute of the ICTY, Article 5.
48 The Statute made redundant the Nuremberg requirement that the commission of crimes against humanity be connected to the other crimes (crimes against peace and war crimes). See generally the Charter of the IMT, Nuremberg, Article 6(c).
49 Ibid.
50 See the Charter of the IMT, Nuremberg, Article 6(c); Charter of the IMTFE, Tokyo, Article 5(c); the Statute of the ICTY, Article 5(i). See also, other (recent) international developments leading to the definition of crimes against humanity. For example, the Rome Statute of the ICC, Article 7(k); the Statute of the SCSL, Article 2(i).
51 Statute of the ICTY, Article 5(i).
52 United Nations Security Council Resolution 955, UN SCOR, 3453rd meeting, UN Doc. S/RES/955 (1994) to which was annexed the Statute of the International Criminal

Council acted pursuant to Chapter VII of the United Nations' Charter.[53] The Statute of the ICTR articulated the crimes over which it has jurisdiction.[54] It has jurisdiction over crimes against humanity, and defines it to mean

> ... the following crimes when committed as part of a widespread or systematic attack against any civilian population on national, political, ethnic, racial or religious grounds:
> (a) murder;
> (b) extermination;
> (c) enslavement;
> (d) deportation;
> (e) imprisonment;
> (f) torture;
> (g) rape;
> (h) persecutions on political, racial and religious grounds;
> (i) other inhumane acts.[55]

In defining crimes against humanity, the Statute of the ICTR reiterates one of the conclusions of the UNWCC: that the attack on civilian population constituting these enumerated crimes be 'systematic or widespread'.[56] It deviates from the definition offered by the preceding Statute of the ICTY, which articulates that crimes against humanity be 'committed in armed conflict',[57] while

---

Tribunal for Rwanda. See also Report of the Secretary-General Pursuant to Paragraph 5 of Security Council Resolution 955 (1994), 13 February 1995, UN Doc. S/1995/134, at 2 (reasons for establishing the ICTR under Chapter VII).

53 The organisation and functioning of the ICTR were similar to those of the ICTY in numerous aspects. First, they were all created pursuant to Chapter VII of the United Nations' Charter. Second, they are all subsidiary, though independent, organs of the Security Council. Third, their organisational structures are identical, with separate prosecutorial, adjudicative and administrative organs. The adjudicative organs comprise of three Trial Chambers and an Appeals Chamber, having similar rules of organisation and procedures. Furthermore, they share a common Appellate Chamber, a common prosecutor and some common prosecutorial staff. See the Statute of the ICTR, Articles 10, 11, 12 (2), 15(3), and 16(3). However, unlike the ICTY, the ICTR carries its operations in different locations. The Office of the Prosecutor and Appeals Chambers are located in The Hague; the investigatory and prosecutorial units operate in Rwanda, and the Trial Chambers sit in Arusha, United Republic of Tanzania.

54 Statute of the ICTR, Articles 2, 3, and 4.
55 Statute of the ICTR, Article 3.
56 Ibid.
57 Statute of the ICTY, Article 5.

the Statute of the ICTR defined them to be 'crimes committed as part of a widespread or systematic attack against any civilian population ....'[58] As will be seen later, this requirement and its accompanying characteristics of an attack now make up the core elements of the definition of crimes against humanity. In other words, an accused would be convicted of crimes against humanity only when it is proved that he did not only commit any of the enlisted crimes, but that such enlisted crime was committed within the framework of an attack, which was widespread or systematic in pattern, directed against a civilian population, and such an attack was based on 'national, political, ethnic, racial or religious grounds.'[59]

2.5 The Rome Statute of the International Criminal Court

Despite the differences in these two *ad hoc* Statutes, the Statute of the ICTR served as a blueprint used in formulating a definition of crimes against humanity in the Rome Statute of the ICC. It provided the conceptual framework from which the definitional elements of crimes against humanity would be borrowed.[60] Established to 'exercise its jurisdiction over persons for the most serious crimes of international concern',[61] its definition of crimes against humanity was akin to the formulation of the Statute of the ICTR.[62] It defines crimes against humanity as

> ... any of the following acts when committed as part of a widespread or systematic attack directed against any civilian population, with knowledge of the attack:
> a) Murder;
> b) Extermination;
> c) Enslavement;
> d) Deportation or forcible transfer of population;
> e) Imprisonment or other severe deprivation of physical liberty in violation of fundamental rules of international law;
> f) Torture;

---

[58] Statute of the ICTR, Article 3.
[59] Ibid. See the discussion below for a thorough analysis of the meaning of these words which jointly constitute the definitional requirements of crimes against humanity.
[60] The formulation stipulated in Article 3 of the Statute of the ICTR provided much of the framework upon which subsequent formulations were made, except for the slight deviations. See the Rome Statute of the ICC, Article 7(1); the Statute of the SCSL, Article 2.
[61] Rome Statute of the ICC, Article 1.
[62] Statute of the ICTR, Article 3. See also the Statute of the ICTY, Article 5.

g) Rape, sexual slavery, enforced prostitution, forced pregnancy, enforced sterilization, or any other form of sexual violence of comparable gravity;
h) Persecution against any identifiable group or collectivity on political, racial, national, ethnic, cultural, religious, gender as defined in paragraph 3, or other grounds that are universally recognized as impermissible under international law, in connection with any act referred to in this paragraph or any crime within the jurisdiction of the Court;
i) Enforced disappearance of persons;
j) The crime of apartheid;
k) Other inhumane acts of a similar character intentionally causing great suffering, or serious injury to body or to mental or physical health.[63]

Fifty three years after the Charter of the Nuremberg Tribunal, the definition of crimes against humanity had undergone a tremendous evolution,[64] resulting in the formal adoption of the distinct definitional requirements of crimes against humanity. It departed significantly from previous definitions of crimes against humanity preceding the Statute of the ICTR, and incorporated, with slight changes, the definition contained in the Statute of the ICTR. It discarded the stipulation of the Statute of the ICTY that the crimes be committed when 'in armed conflict'.[65] The stipulated discriminatory grounds ('national, political, ethnic, racial or religious')[66] were deleted by the Rome Statute of the ICC.[67] To a greater extent, the definition of crimes against humanity under the Rome Statute of the ICC is similar to that of the Statute of the ICTR. Like the Statute of the ICTR, the Rome Statute of the ICC articulates definitional elements: these crimes must be committed as part of an attack that is widespread or systematic in pattern, and, directed against any civilian population.[68] Furthermore, it imports and expands the constituent crimes, with definitions as to their meanings.[69]

---

63 Rome Statute of the ICC, Article 7(1).
64 Bassiouni (n. 12).
65 Statute of the ICTY, Article 5.
66 Statute of the ICTR, Article 3.
67 See generally the wording of Rome Statute of the ICC, Article 7(1).
68 The Rome Statute of the ICC, Article 7(1), which makes express mention that these crimes be committed as part of an attack, and ' ... with knowledge of the attack'.
69 Rome Statute of the ICC, Article 7(1).

The Rome Statute of the ICC is a significant development in international criminal law. Unlike most of the preceding formulations, it is not an *ex post facto* treaty with a retroactive effect.[70] It offers a working definition with the consensus of the global community, not just on its definition and constituent crimes, but even its classification as a serious crime under international law.[71] An issue that comes up is whether this formulation of crimes against humanity per the Rome Statute of the ICC closes every hitherto existing gap, and serves as an acceptable paradigm to other developments in international law. Events that have unfolded beyond the Rome Statute leading to the formulation of crimes against humanity help answer this question.[72]

From the above discussion, it is settled in international law that the definition of crimes against humanity requires that the act of the accused be committed as part of a widespread or systematic attack that is directed against a civilian population, with knowledge of the attack.[73] The requirement of 'knowledge of the attack' was introduced by the Rome Statute of the ICC.[74] Under the Statute of the ICTR, that requirement is absent. Rather, it requires that such an attack be discriminatory: that is, it must be perpetrated on racial, ethnic, religious, national or political grounds.[75]

3   The Definitional Elements of Crimes against Humanity under the Statute of the ICTR

The Statute of the ICTR defines crimes against humanity as ' ... the following crimes when committed as part of a widespread or systematic attack against any civilian population on national, political, ethnic, racial or religious grounds ... ' Per this definition under the Statute of the ICTR, for there to be crimes against humanity, it must be proved that any of the enlisted crimes was committed as part of a 'widespread or systematic attack against a civilian population'.[76] Such an attack must be perpetrated on discriminatory grounds

---

[70] Rome Statute of the ICC, Article 11(1).
[71] Rome Statute of the ICC, Article 7(1).
[72] Statute of the SCSL.
[73] Rome Statute of the ICC, Article 7(1); Statute of the SCSL, Article 2.
[74] Rome Statute of the ICC, Article 7(1).
[75] Statute of the ICTR, Article 3.
[76] *The Prosecutor v. Laurent Semanza*, Judgment, Case No. ICTR-97-20, T. Ch. II, 15 May 2003, para. 326; *Akayesu*, (n. 3) paras 460–69; *The Prosecutor v. Alfred Musema*, Judgment, Case No. ICTR-96-13, T. Ch. I, 27 January 2000, Paras 199–211; *The Prosecutor v. George Rutaganda*, Judgment, Case No. ICTR-96-3-T, T. Ch. I, 6 December 1999, Paras 65–71; *The*

(racial, ethnic, national, religious or political). The accused must commit any of the enlisted crimes with knowledge that there is a widespread or systematic attack.[77] These definitional elements can be summarised as follows:

(i) there must be an attack;
(ii) the attack is widespread or systematic;
(iii) the crime committed by the accused must be within, part or in furtherance of, the widespread or systematic attack;
(iv) the widespread or systematic attack is directed against a civilian population;
(v) the widespread or systematic attack is discriminatory in nature: that is, it is perpetrated on racial, ethnic, religious, national or political grounds;
(vi) and the perpetrator acted with knowledge of the attack (the *mens rea* or mental element).

These elements are five in number. However, I will focus on the prescriptive description of the qualifiers of the nature of the attack that must be directed against any civilian population. These qualifiers are that such an attack must be either 'widespread or systematic'.[78] These two adjectives are disjunctive in nature: in other words, the attack must be either widespread or systematic. As would be discussed later, the dissection of both of these words reveals that there is an implicit element of the involvement of a plurality of persons for the attack to meet the requirement of widespread or systematic.

Given the fact that the Trial and Appeal Chambers of the ICTR have used the jurisprudence of the ICTY, I will make intermittent references to cases from the ICTY.

3.1 An Attack

The requirement of an attack as part of the definitional elements of crimes against humanity denotes 'a course of conduct involving the commission of acts of violence.'[79] The requirement of an attack is not limited to the conduct

---

Prosecutor v. *Clément Kayishema and Obed Ruzindana*, Judgment, Case No. ICTR-95-1-T, T. Ch. I, 21 May 1999, Paras 119–34.

77 Rome Statute of the ICC, Article 7(1).
78 See Statute of the ICTR, Article 3. See also Rome Statute of the ICC, Article 7(1); Statute of the Special Court for Sierra Leone, Article 2.
79 Guénaël Mettraux, *International Crimes and the ad hoc Tribunals* (Oxford University Press 2005) 156. See the following cases: *Kayishema and Ruzindanda* (n. 76) (TC) para. 122 where the Trial Chamber described the *attack* as 'the event in which the enumerated crimes must form part'. In *Akayesu* (n. 3), the Trial Chamber gave a slightly different definition of

of hostilities. An attack may occur without the presence of hostilities. The requirement of an attack covers the maltreatment of persons who take no active part in hostilities.[80] Furthermore, there is no requirement that the attack be directed against the enemy.[81] The attack may be directed against any civilian population, including any part of the state's population.

An attack in itself does not constitute a crime against humanity. It merely serves as the 'vehicle for the commission of crimes against humanity.'[82] It is the framework or foundation, within and upon which the enlisted crimes are perpetrated.[83]

The definitional requirement of an attack connotes an enterprise that is being executed as part of a policy or plan. It is the framework within which a common purpose is established and materialised; and the acts of the accused persons are in furtherance of that common purpose. It uncovers the existence of a joint criminal enterprise. Within this joint criminal enterprise, there are different actors who may be at different places and times, play different roles, but acting individually or collectively to perpetrate the acts within the framework of the attack. The perpetration of these acts constitutes the materialisa-

---

the meaning of 'attack': 'The concept of "attack" may be defined as an unlawful act of the kind enumerated in Article 3(a) to (i) under the Statute, like murder, extermination, enslavement, etc.' (para. 581); *The Prosecutor v. Juvénal Kajelijeli*, Judgment, Case No. ICTR-96–44-T, T. Ch. II, 1 December 2003, para. 867; *Musema* (n. 76) para. 205; *Rutaganda* (n. 76) para. 70; and the Rome Statute of the ICC, 17 July 1998, Article 7, para. 2, UN Doc. A/CONF.183/9 (1998), which defined an attack in the following words: '"Attack directed against any civilian population" means a course of conduct involving the multiple commission of acts referred to in paragraph 1 against any civilian population, pursuant to or in furtherance of a state of organisational policy to commit such attack.' For an analysis of the challenges that the ICC has faced in interpreting the latter part of that phrase, and a proposal for an amendment to the ICC Statute, see Charles C. Jalloh, "What Makes a Crime Against Humanity a Crime Against Humanity", 28 *American University International Law Review* 2 (2013) 381–441.

80 The Appeal Chamber held that 'the attack in the context of a crime against humanity is not limited to the use of armed force; it encompasses any mistreatment of the civilian population ....' See *Dargoljub Kunarac, Radomir Kovač & Zoran Vuković v. The Prosecutor*, Judgment, Case No. IT-96–23 & 23/1-T, Appeal Chamber, 12 June 2002, para. 86; *The Prosecutor v. Dargoljub Kunarac, Radomir Kovač & Zoran Vuković*, Judgment, Case No. IT-96-23 & 23/1-T, T. Ch., 22 February 2001, para. 416.

81 Pursuant to the definition of crimes against humanity, 'civilian population' is the phraseology used, which can be construed to be opposite to 'armed population'. See the subsection on 'civilian population' below.

82 Mettraux (n. 79) 157.

83 Ibid.

tion and consummation of the attack contained in the policy of the joint criminal enterprise. As Mettraux puts it,

> ... the attack requirement appears to be a descriptive device that captures in one word a pattern of criminal activity, in the context of which the acts of the accused must have taken place to be regarded as crimes against humanity. To the extent that the acts of the accused can be sufficiently linked to that attack, they acquire a greater criminal dimension which sets them apart from purely domestic crimes and differentiates them from ordinary war crimes.[84]

3.2 The Attack Must be Either Widespread or Systematic

The words 'widespread or systematic' as part of the qualifier of the attack disclose the scale (widespread) or the organised nature (systematic) of the attack.[85] Either or both of these two definitional requirements will suffice to translate a crime to crimes against humanity. The adjectives alternate, and have a disjunctive rather than conjunctive effect: proof that the attacks were

---

84   Ibid. 161.
85   In *The Prosecutor v. Fatmir Limaj, Haradin Baa and Isak Muslui*, Judgment, Case No. IT-03-66-T, T. Ch. II, 30 November 2005, it was held that the requirements of widespread or systematic are 'disjunctive rather than cumulative', holding that the word 'widespread' refers to 'the large scale nature of the attack and the number of victims,' while 'systematic' means 'the organized nature of the acts of violence and the improbability of their random occurrence.' The inclusion of the words 'widespread or systematic' distinguishes 'non-accidental repetition of similar conduct on a regular basis,' which reveals the systematic nature of the attacks. See also *Tihomir Blaškić v. The Prosecutor*, Judgment, Case No. IT-95-14, Appeal Chamber, 29 July 2004, para. 101 (citing *Kunarac* et al. (n. 80) (AC) para. 94). In *Kunarac* et al. (n. 80), the Appeal Chamber stated its view that 'the assessment of what constitutes a "widespread" or "systematic" attack is essentially a relative exercise in that it depends upon the civilian population which, allegedly, was being attacked. A Trial Chamber must therefore "first identify the population which is the object of the attack and, in light of the means, methods, resources and result of the attack upon the population, ascertain whether the attack was indeed widespread or systematic". The consequences of the attack upon the targeted population, the number of victims, the nature of the acts, the possible participation of officials or authorities or any identifiable patterns of crimes, could be taken into account to determine whether the attack satisfies either or both requirements of a "widespread" or "systematic" attack vis-à-vis this civilian population.' Para. 95.

either widespread or systematic is sufficient to amount to crimes against humanity.[86]

The word 'widespread' has been used to mean the large-scale nature of the attack, measured by the number of victims involved.[87] An attack may be widespread as a result of the cumulative effect of a series of acts. It may also be widespread based on the effect of a single act of extraordinary magnitude.[88] 'Systematic' refers to the organised nature of the attack, including the improbability of their random occurrence. The systematic pattern of an attack is revealed by the non-accidental repetition of similar acts or conduct on a regular basis.[89]

In practice, these two adjectives describing the nature of the attacks do overlap. An attack that is widespread may also be systematic.[90] A widespread attack targeting a civilian population requires some level of planning or organisation. So too is an attack that is systematic in pattern, as it has the purpose, potential, frequency and effect of reaching and affecting many people, thereby satisfying the widespread requirement. The history of the situation may be examined in its entirety to determine whether there was a widespread or systematic attack. Mettraux has outlined some factors to be considered by a Trial Chamber in determining whether there was a widespread or systematic

---

[86] *Kunarac* et al. (n. 80) (AC) para. 93 (and the references cited therein); *Blaškić* (n. 85) para. 101. In the Report of the Secretary-General (ICTY), the Statute of the ICC and the work of the ILC, the conditions of scale and 'systematicity' are not necessarily cumulative. In other words, any of the acts, even inhumane acts, can be characterised as crimes against humanity if any of the two conditions is met. See *The Prosecutor v. Tihomir Blaškić*, Judgment, Case No. IT-95-14. T. Ch., 3 March 2000, para. 207; *Kunarac* et al. (n. 80) (TC) para. 427; *The Prosecutor v. Jean de Dieu Kamuhanda*, Judgment, Case No. ICTR-95-54A-T, T. Ch. II, 22 January 2004, para. 664; *Kajelijeli* (n. 79) paras 869–70; *Rutaganda* (n. 76) paras 67–68; *Akayesu* (n. 3) para. 579. See also the ILC, 1991 ILC Report and 1996 ILC Report.

[87] See *Akayesu* (n. 3) para. 580; Mettraux (n. 79) 170–72; William A. Schabas, *The UN International Criminal Tribunals: The Former Yugoslavia, Rwanda and Sierra Leone* (Cambridge University Press 2006) 191–96.

[88] The Trial Chamber in *Rutaganda* defined widespread to mean 'massive, frequent, large-scale action, carried out collectively with considerable seriousness and directed against a multiplicity of victims'. See *Rutaganda* (n. 76) para. 68.

[89] *Rutaganda* (n. 76) para. 68. See also the Trial Chamber's definition of systematic which it held to be a 'thoroughly organized action, following a regular pattern on the basis of a common policy and involving substantial public or private resources.'

[90] Numerous Chambers (Trial) in the *ad hoc* tribunals have found that the attacks waged against the population were both widespread and systematic. See *The Prosecutor v. Duško Tadić*, Judgment, Case No. IT-94-1, T. Ch., 7 May 1997, para. 660; *Rutaganda* (n. 76), para. 67; *Kayishema and Ruzindanda* (n. 76) para. 576; *Akayesu* (n. 3) para. 652.

attack: the number of criminal acts, the number of victims, the existence of criminal patterns, the existence of a policy or plan targeting specific group(s) of individuals, the inescapability of the attack, the involvement of military or political authorities, the logistics and financial resources involved, the existence of public statements or political views underpinning the events, the means and methods used in the attacks and the adoption of discriminatory measures.[91]

In determining whether an attack was widespread or systematic in pattern, the Trial Chamber examines the totality of the circumstances pertaining to the situation or events. The Trial Chamber must identify the population which has been targeted and determine whether there was an attack against this population. As to the pattern of the attack, the Trial Chamber considers the means, methods and resources used, and the outcome(s) of the attack to determine if the attack in question was widespread or systematic.[92]

Under the definitional requirements of crimes against humanity, only the attack must be widespread or systematic in pattern.[93] It is not necessary that the accused's specific act is 'widespread' or 'systematic'. Unless it was isolated, a single act would qualify as a crime against humanity if it was perpetrated within the framework of an attack.[94] In the Rwandan experience, a good example would be the single killing of a Tutsi. If such a killing was perpetrated against a Tutsi as part of a widespread or systematic attack directed against the Tutsis (a civilian population), then, that single act qualifies as murder as a crime against humanity. As long as the crime committed by the accused is part of an attack and this attack is widespread or systematic, then, the numerical value (in terms of impact) of the accused's crime becomes irrelevant.

---

91 Mettraux (n. 79) 171.
92 *Kunarac* et al. (n. 71) (TC) para. 430. On appeal, it was held that in determining whether an attack satisfies either or both requirements of 'widespread' or 'systematic' attack against a civilian population, it would take into account factors such as the nature of the acts, the consequences of such acts upon the targeted population, the number of victims, the participation of officials and other authorities, civilian or military, and any identifiable pattern in the commission of crimes. *Kunarac* et al. (n. 80) (AC) para. 95.
93 *Kunarac* et al. (n. 80) (AC) para. 96; *Kunarac* et al. (n. 80) (TC) para. 430; *Blaškić* (n. 85) para. 101.
94 *Kunarac* et al. (n. 80) (AC) para. 96; *The Prosecutor v. Zoran Kupreškić, Drago Josipović, Vladimir Šantić, Mirjan Kupreškić, Vlatko Kupreškić, Dragan Papić*, Judgment, Case No. IT-95–16-T, T. Ch., 14 January 2000, para. 550, where the Trial Chamber held: 'For example, the act of denouncing a Jewish neighbour to the Nazi authorities – if committed against a background of widespread persecution – has been regarded as amounting to a crime against humanity. An isolated act, however – i.e. an atrocity which did not occur within such a context – cannot.'

3.3 Meeting the 'Widespread or Systematic' Threshold: The Implicit Existence or Requirement of a Joint Criminal Enterprise

As discussed above, the definition of crimes against humanity requires that the act of the perpetrators forms part of an attack that is either widespread or systematic. The use of the disjunctive word 'or' instead of a conjunctive 'and' suggests that such an attack needs to fulfil only any of the caveats: it could be widespread or systematic.

The qualification 'widespread' refers to the scale of atrocities. It therefore distinguishes these crimes from random acts of criminality, especially group crimes. On the other hand, 'systematic' is used to mean the organised nature of the crimes.

The logical interpretation of these two caveats leads one to make the inference that there is an implicit involvement of a group of persons for crimes against humanity. If an attack has to be widespread or systematic in scale, it is therefore common-sensical to establish that it requires a group of persons to be involved either in its planning, preparation or execution. In other words, a single individual cannot engage in the planning, preparation or execution of a crime that would satisfy the widespread or systematic qualification.

In jurisprudential parlance, when a group of persons concert to a criminal activity, that is called a joint criminal enterprise. It describes situations wherein a multiplicity of persons act with a common purpose: the commission of (a) crime(s). In such cases, the imposition of criminal responsibility on such individuals requires that they are treated as principal offenders.[95] Furthermore,

---

[95] This is the case in most common law countries. Australia is an example. See *Osland v. R* (1998) 73 ALJR 173, HC of A. Joint criminal enterprise or joint unlawful enterprise has been a debatable doctrine as to whether it carries a distinct form of liability. However, it is used to describe cases where two or more persons embark on a joint enterprise to commit a crime or crimes. They would obviously have planned and agreed beforehand to commit such crimes. While this remains the clearest case, it is however possible to have such an agreement made immediately before or even during the commission of the crimes(s). The key and distinguishing ingredient of cases of joint criminal enterprise is the presence of a shared common purpose, or 'a shared common intention': in other words, each individual participating in the commission of the crime has the same intention as the others, and each individual knows that the others do intend the same thing (usually the result). As a consequence, each individual is criminally responsible for any (or whatever) crimes that the others commit which come within the scope of the common purpose or design. The doctrine of joint criminal enterprise has been the subject of numerous academic papers by many experts in the field of international criminal law. Their discussions, however, focus on where to draw a precise line as to which persons to hold responsible for the crimes committed by a joint criminal enterprise. This has been a recurrent issue ever since the Nuremberg Tribunals, but gathered much momentum after some landmark decisions rendered by both the Trial and Appeal Chambers of the *ad hoc* Tribunals (the

the capacity in which one of the persons acted in a joint criminal enterprise is immaterial. In cases where it is necessary to make a distinction, the test is this: did the accused by his or her own act (as distinct from anything done by the other accused persons) contribute to the *actus reus*? If in the affirmative, then, the accused is a principal offender. If the accused did not, then, some difficulties arise. If the accused is innocent, then, there is no crime the accused could have aided or abetted because of the accused's lack of *mens rea* and also knowledge that the accused aided and abetted the crime. The accused ought to be seen as an innocent agent in such cases.

With an understanding of the nature of joint criminal enterprise, it is logical to argue that a distinguishing element of crimes against humanity is the

---

ICTY and the ICTR). The points raised and approaches advanced by these scholars are very significant and eloquent, yet, remain different from the way I approach joint criminal enterprise in this thesis. Whereas their issue is on where to draw a line in holding persons responsible, my focus is the bigger picture of a joint criminal enterprise as it reflects the different roles played by different individuals at different times. In other words, it asks and answers the 'how' question: the role played towards the planning, preparation or execution of the crimes. Putting this into play, instigators should have been perceived as having played a role towards any of the stages of any of the crimes over which the ICTR has jurisdiction. Inasmuch as there is a cornucopia of literature on the issue of joint criminal enterprise, it is important that the approaches and focus are distinguished from what I do in this Chapter particularly and in the entire thesis generally. For an understanding of the approaches raised by some leading academic experts, see generally Allison Marston Danner and Jenny S. Martinez, 'Guilty Associations: Joint Criminal Enterprise, Command Responsibility, and the Development of International Criminal Law' (2005) Vol. 93, 1 *California Law Review*, 75–169; Antonio Cassese, 'The Proper Limits of Individual Responsibility under the Doctrine of Joint Criminal Enterprise' (2007) Vol. 5, 1 *J Int Criminal Justice* 109–133; Elies van Slierdregt, 'Joint Criminal Enterprise as a Pathway to Convicting Individuals for Genocide' (2007) Vol. 5, 1 *J Int Criminal Justice* 184–207; Harmen van der Wilt, 'Joint Criminal Enterprise Possibilities and Limitations', (2007) Vol. 5, 1 *J Int Criminal Justice* 91–108; Jens David Ohlin, 'Three Conceptual Problems with the Doctrine of Joint Criminal Enterprise' (2007) Vol. 5, 1 *J Int Criminal Justice* 69–90; Kai Ambos, 'Joint Criminal Enterprise and Command Responsibility', (2007) Vol. 5, 1 *J Int Criminal Justice* 159–183; Kai Hamdorf, 'The Concept of a Joint Enterprise and Domestic Modes of Liability for Parties to a Crime: A Comparison of German and English Law' (2007) Vol. 5, 1 *J Int Criminal Justice* 208–226; Rebecca L. Haffajee, 'Prosecuting Crimes of Rape and Sexual Violence at the ICTR: The Application of Joint Criminal Enterprise Theory' (2006) 29 *Harv. J. L. & Gender* 201–221; Steven Powles, Joint Criminal Enterprise – Criminal Liability by Prosecutorial Ingenuity and Judicial Creativity' (2004) 2 *J. Int'l Crim. Just.* 606–619; Verena Han, 'The Development of the Concept of Joint Criminal Enterprise at the International Criminal Tribunal for the Former Yugoslavia' (2005) 5 *Int'l Crim. L. Rev.* 167–201.

implicit existence or requirement that a group or multiplicity of persons concert to wage an attack against any civilian population. Unlike any other attack, international instruments have required that the attack meets any of the following criteria: widespread or systematic. The widespread nature is revealed by the scale of victimisation while the systematic nature is dictated by the organised nature of such attacks. While these two caveats are disjunctive in nature, an attack could still be widespread and systematic.

These alternating adjectives highlight the key difference between crimes against humanity and other serious crimes in international law. More importantly, they distinguish random acts of criminality from organised, large-scale atrocities perpetrated against a civilian population. In summation, it can be said that crimes against humanity are group crimes, a logical conclusion from the inclusion of the caveats of an attack that must be either widespread or systematic.

3.4 Conclusion

The above illustrates first, the legislative evolution of crimes against humanity, from when it resided in international discourse as a 'term of art',[96] to when it finally got crystallised as a positive and serious crime in international law;[97] and second, the definitional elements of crimes against humanity under the Statute of the ICTR.

The above discussion does not merely highlight the evolution of crimes against humanity as a serious crime in international law. Neither does it only consider the definitional requirements of crimes against humanity. The discussion portrays the uniqueness of crimes against humanity, and in stipulating these chapeau elements, I bring out the necessity of group involvement for the planning, preparation and execution of crimes against humanity as implied by the definitional elements of crimes against humanity under the Statute of the ICTR. As Mettraux outlined what factors can be looked at in determining whether an attack was widespread or systematic,[98] it is impossible to have an

---

96 Clark (n. 10).
97 See the Charter of the IMT, Nuremberg, Article 6(c), the Charter of the IMTFE, Article 5(c), the Statute of the ICTY, Article 5, the Statute of the ICTR, Article 3, the Rome Statute of the ICC, Article 7(1), the Statute of the SCSL, Article 2 (at least, these are formulations which highlight not just the recognition of crimes against humanity as a serious crime, but (with the exclusion of the ICC) had individuals tried and convicted of crimes against humanity).
98 Mettraux (n. 79).

attack that meets this threshold without the involvement of different individuals who play different roles at different times. The involvement of numerous individuals who partook in different ways in the atrocities in Rwanda helped in the formulation of both the definition of crimes against humanity (containing numerous and fundamental differences from the Statute of the ICTY) and the imposition of criminal responsibility. By stipulating the various modes of participation, which must lead to any of the stages of any of the crimes (planning, preparation or execution), the drafters clearly knew that a joint criminal enterprise must have been in place for atrocities of such a scale and magnitude to be executed. It is within this conceptual framework of the existence of a joint criminal enterprise that I propound this theory of crimes against humanity: that they are group crimes because they require an organizational element since they focus more on the scale of victimisation.

CHAPTER 19

Justice and Gender: Prosecuting Gender-Based and Sexual Violence Crimes at the International Criminal Tribunal for Rwanda and the Special Court for Sierra Leone

Tamara Cummings-John

Introduction

The jurisprudence of the two African-based International Tribunals that were established in the wake of unprecedented atrocities has made a significant contribution to international criminal justice. In particular the case law from the International Criminal Tribunal for Rwanda (ICTR) and the Special Court for Sierra Leone (Special Court or SCSL) on gender-based and sexual violence crimes is ground-breaking in many respects. This chapter will explore the ICTR's and the Special Court's case law as they relate to gender-based and sexual violence crimes. It will attempt to examine what role, if any, a gender-sensitive approach played in the pleadings of the Prosecutors of both tribunals, the treatment of witnesses and evidence and, ultimately, the decisions of the judges.

Both the ICTR and the SCSL make for interesting case study not least of all because they were the first of international tribunals on the continent, created in response to two conflicts that witnessed unprecedented levels of mass murder, mass rape and other human rights violations. While these conflicts – one involving a Genocide – and the other a non-international armed conflict differ, the International Criminal Tribunal for Rwanda set the stage for the Special Court for Sierra Leone to some extent – the SCSL Statute provided for the Court to apply the ICTR's Rules of Procedure and Evidence *mutatis mutandis*.[1] As far as the SCSL's jurisprudence is concerned, there were many examples of Special Court judges relying on precedents set by the ICTR, for example when it came to determining the elements of rape, the SCSL relied on the ICTR, in particular

---

1   Statute of the Special Court For Sierra Leone, Article 14 http://www.rscsl.org/Documents/scsl-statute.pdf.

the latter court's findings in its landmark Akayesu case.[2] Rather than take a broad view of the contributions made by these two African-based international criminal tribunals, the paper will consider their jurisprudence in relation to gender-based and sexual violence crimes.

The first part of this chapter will examine the approach of the ICTR to gender-based and sexual violence crimes and discuss what emerged from its jurisprudence. The assessment will consider how the judges dealt with the inclusion or absence of gender-based and sexual violence crimes in the indictments of the accused and will touch briefly on how witness testimonies relating to these crimes were dealt with in the courtroom.

The second part will consider the SCSL's treatment of three key gender-based and sexual violence crimes – forced marriage, sexual slavery and rape. In reviewing the SCSL's approach, an attempt will be made to critique this through a gender-sensitive lens. The reference to gender applies, of course, to a social construct and by extension will take on board certain cultural considerations. It will consider the existence of women as well as men in the context of these conflicts and the judicial mechanisms that have sought to address them.

As this paper focuses, however, on the jurisprudence of the ICTR and SCSL, the role of women perpetrators will not figure prominently. The ICTR only indicted one woman, Pauline Nyiramasuhuko, a former social worker, and the Minister of Family Affairs and Women's Development. All of the 14 persons[3] indicted by the Prosecutor of the SCSL were men. The absence of female indictees at the International Criminal Tribunal for Rwanda and the Special Court for Sierra Leone may be explained by the fact that the both court's mandates were limited to prosecuting those bearing the greatest responsibility for the genocide in the case of the ICTR and the crimes perpetrated during the conflict in the case of the SCSL. One could therefore argue that the lack of prosecution of women implied that they were not considered – at least by the prosecution – as falling among the category of those most responsible. However, a more complex picture emerges when one considers the factual account of these two conflicts as well as some of the evidence elicited from witnesses.

Agnes Ntamabyariro, who was Minister of Justice in the *genocidaire* government, was tried in Rwanda where witnesses testified to her ordering the killing of a Tutsi local leader and distributing weapons to killers. Valerie Bemeriki was

---

2   Prosecutor v. Akayesu, Case No. ICTR-96-4-T, Judgment (Int'l Crim. Trib. For Rwanda Trial Chamber, Sept. 2, 1998).
3   Sam Bockarie, Alex Brima, Moinina Fofana, Augustine Gbao, Morris Kallon, Brima Kamara, Santigie Kanu, Alieu Kondewa, Johnny Paul Koroma, Sam Hinga Norman, Foday Sankoh, Issa Sesay, and Charles Taylor.

an extremist journalist who was tried and sentenced by the traditional Gacaca Court for her role in the Genocide.[4] There were many other female perpetrators from the Rwandan Genocide that seemed to have been overlooked by the ICTR, some of them were tried in Rwanda. Witnesses also provided evidence of a number of women actors in the war who were senior commanders or otherwise established their notoriety for the brutality of their conduct. These witnesses from both the SCSL and the Sierra Leone Truth and Reconciliation Commission (TRC) implicated ruthless female perpetrators like Adama 'Cut Hand'[5] and Monica Pearson who was described in the TRC Report as "perhaps the RUF's most notorious female combatant".[6] Some have argued that the mere fact of holding a senior position within these armed groups should not have been regarded in and of itself as equating to "bearing the greatest responsibility" and that the notoriety of a perpetrator should also speak to the question of responsibility.[7] While there may be some merit to not taking a strictly scientific approach to the question of responsibility, it must be said in a conflict and a genocide as brutal as those that took place in Sierra Leone and Rwanda, focus on actors by virtue of their barbarity may have produced far more indictees than either tribunal could have handled. The SCSL was grappling with meagre resources and expectations that it would able to complete its work far quicker than the ad hoc tribunals (as the ICTR and its sister tribunal the International Tribunal for the former Yugoslavia or ICTY are often called). The scale of the Rwandan Genocide was such that the ICTR could only hope to scratch the surface, accountability for these heinous crimes required both international and national efforts.[8]

Despite their shortcomings, a key purported advantage of hybrid tribunals like the SCSL, over international courts like the ICTR, was said to be the higher likelihood that they will produce jurisprudence or other positive transformative effects on the domestic legal system. For this reason, I will also briefly consider the effect of the SCSL on Sierra Leone's treatment of gender-based and sexual violence crimes, especially in light of the Sexual Offences Act of 2012.

---

4   Donna J Baier, Women Leaders in the Rwandan Genocide: When Women Choose To Kill, Universitas, Volume 8 (2012–2013).
5   Prosecutor vs. Brima, Kamara and Kanu, Case no SCSL-2004–16-T, Transcript, 25 July 2005, page 20.
6   Sierra Leone TRC Report, Vol. 3 A, Chapter 4, Nature of the Conflict, para. 73 (2004).
7   Charles Chernor Jalloh, Special Court for Sierra Leone: Achieving Justice?, Legal Studies Research Paper Series Working Paper No. 2010–31, 421 (2011).
8   Over 120,000 people were suspected of having played a part in the Rwandan Genocide and detained – The Justice and Reconciliation Process in Rwanda, Background Note on Outreach Programme of the Rwanda Genocide and the United Nations, (March 2014).

The question is whether the treatment of gender-based and sexual violence crimes in the country's national courts has evolved, since the Special Court's establishment, and if so, whether we can identify evidence that could establish causal links to the jurisprudence and practice of the SCSL.

Throughout the chapter, reference will be made to gender-based and sexual violence crimes – this is in an attempt to capture all gender-related crimes including those that may not be sexual in nature but are perpetrated against a person because of their socially-constructed gender role.

Finally, this paper will conclude by discussing the lessons learned by both the ICTR and the SCSL in their treatment of gender-based and sexual violence crimes. It will attempt to distil those that may be most valuable from a gender-sensitive perspective.

1   ICTR Jurisprudence on Sexual Violence

In the context of jurisprudence relating to gender-based and sexual violence crimes, the role of the International Criminal Tribunal for Rwanda is worth analysing. The ICTR was the first international tribunal to define rape in international criminal law and to recognise rape as a means of perpetrating genocide.[9] The ICTR also defined sexual violence crimes as primary violations under the crimes of genocide, war crimes, and crimes against humanity. The judgments that emerged from the ICTR included various forms of sexual violence such as rape as crimes against humanity, rape as a war crime, rape as genocide and finally rape and/or other sexual violence amounting to torture in one case (the Semanza case).[10] Although these achievements are noteworthy, given the context of the Rwandan Genocide – where sexual violence crimes were endemic and many Tutsi women were portrayed as *femmes fatales* and seductive agents of the enemy and therefore justified targets for 'extermination',[11] – they still fell short of adequately addressing a conflict where sexual violence crimes were so systemic.

---

9   The Akayesu Judgment represented the first time an international Tribunal had to interpret the definition of genocide as defined in the Genocide Convention, *Prosecutor v. Akayesu*, Trial Chamber Judgment, 2 (September 1998).

10 Review of the Sexual Violence Elements of the Judgments of the International Criminal Tribunal for the Former Yugoslavia, the International Criminal Tribunal for Rwanda, and the Special Court for Sierra Leone in the light of Security Council Resolution 1820, Department of Peacekeeping Operations, March 2009, p. 47.

11 *Prosecutor v. Nahimana*, Case No. ICTR-99–52-T, Judgment and Sentence, ¶ 1079, (Dec. 3, 2003).

According to the United Nations Special Rapporteur, there were between 250,000 and 500,000 rapes during the Rwandan Genocide.[12] The ICTR brought charges of rape against 52 of its 95 indictees, many of these cases resulted in plea bargains and some were transferred to national jurisdictions. To date there have been only thirteen convictions at the trial stage, on rape charges, seven of which were later confirmed at the Appeals stage with the remaining six pending appeal.[13] When the totality of the conflict is viewed and sheer number of sexual-violence crimes, one can conclude that the ICTR could have or at least should have done more.

1 *Combined Efforts – Civil Society Advocacy and Gender-sensitive Adjudicators* – **Prosecutor v. Jean Paul Akayesu**

Although the case of the *Prosecutor v. Jean-Paul Akayesu* has been lauded for setting a precedent in terms of its treatment of sexual violence – representing the first time an International Criminal Tribunal recognized the link between sexual violence and genocide –it was not the prosecutor, but rather a female judge who recognized elements of sexual violence during the testimonies of several witnesses.

Although the first Prosecutor of the ICTR, Richard Goldstone appointed a Legal Advisor for gender-related crimes – Ms Patricia Viseur-Sellers – very few of his indictments included charges of sexual violence crimes during the tribunal's early years. It was rather through the testimonies of witnesses, recognised by the Court's only female judge (at the time), Judge Navanathem Pillay, who also had experience working in gender issues, that a gap was identified. Judge Pillay encouraged the Prosecutor to go back and investigate sexual violence crimes in view of the related evidence that she had heard from several witnesses in the case of the Akayesu case.[14] At the same time an amicus curiae

---

12 Special Rapporteur of the Commission on Human Rights, Report of the Situation of Human Rights in Rwanda, UN Doc E/CN.4/1996/68 (Jan. 29 1996).

13 The Prosecutor won convictions at the trial stage, for charges of sexual violence crimes in relation to the following persons: Ngirabatware, Ntahobali, Ndayambaje, Nizeyimana, Nyiramasuhuko; nine sexual violence convictions were upheld at the appeals stage: Akayesu, Bagosora, Bizimungu, Gacumbitsi, Hategekimana, Karemera, Muhimana, Ngirumpatse and Semanza. Best Practices Manual for the Investigation and Prosecution of Sexual Violence Crimes in Post-Conflict Regions: Lessons Learned from the Office of the Prosecutor for the International Criminal Tribunal for Rwanda, http://www.unictr.org/sites/unictr.org/files/publications/ICTR-Prosecution-of-Sexual-Violence.pdf.

14 Richard Goldstone and Estelle Dehon, Engendering Accountability: Gender Crimes Under International Law, *New England Journal of Public Policy*, Volume 19. Issue 1, Article 8.

brief filed by the Coalition for Women's Human Rights urged the Tribunal to allow for the inclusion of sexual violence crimes in the Akayesu indictment. The Coalition argued that the failure to include charges of rape in the first case before the Tribunal in Arusha, despite evidence of rape, set an "unwelcome precedent for the prosecutions to come and discourage[d] women witnesses from participating in the further investigations and prosecutions of the Tribunal."[15] The amicus brief also emphasized the effect of a lack of prosecution of sexual violence crimes by the ICTR on women in Rwanda who, it argued, would conclude that these crimes, which had had a devastating effect on their lives, were not considered important enough to warrant inclusion in cases before the tribunal. While the Coalition's arguments rested on a matter of principle, Judge Pillay's position resulted from the evidence that was before her. This combined effort led to an adjournment which allowed the Prosecutor to investigate these allegations and uncover evidence of widespread rape and forced nudity implicating Akayesu.

As a result of this major turn of events, the Trial Chamber was able to connect sexual violence with genocide, and found Akayesu guilty of genocide for crimes including rape and sexual assault despite the lack of evidence that he had physically committed these acts himself. The Chamber found that rapes of Tutsi women and girls had been widespread and systematic, and that the accused had been present at many of the rapes. The Judges found that Akayesu's presence, attitude, and words could be considered as encouragement of sexual violence. Perhaps the most significant aspect of the Judgment was the finding that crimes of sexual violence could be committed with the intent of killing members of a group.[16] The Trial Chamber identified rape and sexual assaults as independent crimes and noted that sexual violence could also constitute "serious bodily and mental harm" and "outrages upon personal dignity" under the ICTR Statute.

It is worth noting that the Trial Chamber in the Akayesu case was also the first to make a distinction between rape and sexual violence. It defined rape as "a physical invasion of a sexual nature committed on a person under circumstances which are coercive," while sexual violence was broadly defined as "any act of a sexual nature which is committed on a person under circumstances

---

15 Amicus Curiae Brief Respecting Amendment of the Indictment and Supplementation of the Evidence to Ensure the Prosecutor of Rape and Other Sexual Violence within the competence of the Tribunal, http://www.iccwomen.org/publications/briefs/docs/Prosecutor_v_Akayesu_ICTR.pdf.

16 Paras. 503, 509, 731 and 733, Judgment, *Prosecutor v. Jean-Paul Akayesu*, ICTR-96–4-T, 2 (September 1998).

which are coercive." In view of the fact that physical invasion was not considered necessary in constituting sexual violence, the instance of a student being forced to publicly undress and do gymnastics in front of a crowd[17] in the nude was also found to constitute sexual violence in the judgment.[18]

2   After Akayesu – *How the Treatment of Gender-based and Sexual Violence Crimes Evolved in the* ICTR

The Akayesu case established numerous precedents in its treatment of gender-based and sexual violence crimes. The issue of evidence of a victim being coerced was examined by the Trial Chamber and the judges ruled that coercive circumstances did not need to be evidenced by a show of physical force. They noted that "threats, intimidation, extortion and other forms of duress which prey on fear or desperation may constitute coercion, and coercion may be inherent in certain circumstances, such as armed conflict or the military presence of *Interahamwe,* the militia that was used by the *genocidaire* government, among refugee Tutsi women at the bureau communal."[19] In the same vein, the Chamber ruled that the discussion of consent was not necessary as a victim could not consent to sexually violent conduct.[20]

In the case of the *Prosecutor v. Gacumbitsi,* the Chamber was of the opinion that any penetration of the victim's vagina by the rapist with his genitals or with any object constituted rape.[21] This definition of the crime of rape as including the penetration by objects was particularly relevant to the conflict in Sierra Leone where sticks, guns, and other objects were regularly and systematically used to rape.

In *Musema,* the Trial Chamber found that Musema raped a Tutsi woman himself, and that he had the knowledge of a widespread or systematic attack, as such the Chamber concluded that he was individually criminally responsible for the crime against humanity of rape. However the Chamber ruled that

---

17   Para. 688, Judgment, *Prosecutor v. Jean-Paul Akayesu,* ICTR-96-4-T, 2 (September 1998).
18   See Siobhan Kehoe Dubin, A Comparative Study of Sexual Violence Trials in the ICTY and ICTR Comparing Six Particular Issues, 2003, pp. 9–10, available at http://law.case.edu/Academics/AcademicCenters/Cox/WarCrimesResearchPortal/memoranda/SexualViolence.pdf. Also see K. Alexa Koenig, Ryan Lincoln and Lauren Groth, The Jurisprudence of Sexual Violence, Sexual Violence & Accountability Project Working Paper Series, May 2011, pp. 9–10.
19   Para. 688, Judgment, *Prosecutor v. Jean-Paul Akayesu,* ICTR-96-4-T, 2 (September 1998).
20   Patricia Viseur Sellers, *The Prosecution of Sexual Violence in conflict: The Importance of Human Rights as Means of Interpretation,* p. 20.
21   Para. 321, Judgment, *Prosecutor v. Gacumbitsi,* Case No. ICTR-2001-64-T, 17 June 2004. Also see Akayesu Judgment (TC), paras 597 to 598 and ICTY, Kunarac and Others, (AC), paras 127 to 133.

the Prosecutor had failed to prove command responsibility beyond a reasonable doubt. The standard for this mode of liability required evidence that acts of rape had been committed by Musema's subordinates and that Musema knew or had reason to know of them, and by extension, either failed to take reasonable measures to prevent or failed to punish the perpetrators.[22]

The ICTR's jurisprudence reflected the standard that individual responsibility for rape as a crime against humanity would require that the accused actually perpetrated the rape himself, whereas command responsibility for the same act as a crime against humanity, requires evidence of the accused's direct orders, physical presence at the crime scene, and evidence of the rape occurring. Article 6(3) of the ICTR Statute addresses the question of command responsibility by introducing the need for knowledge – the superior is required to know or have reason to know "that the subordinate was about to commit such acts or had done so and the superior failed to take the necessary and reasonable measures to prevent such acts or to punish the perpetrators hereof".[23] This relatively high standard may account for the difficulties in establishing superior responsibility for sexual violence. In particular there are many instances where there is no allegation of physical contact between the accused and the victim and no evidence of the accused explicitly ordering or inciting the rape; it may also be that the accused's presence at the crime scene cannot be established – in such instances the nexus between the accused and the crime would be extremely difficult to establish.[24]

Given the widespread nature of gender-based and sexual violence crimes, one would expect international criminal tribunals to exercise some flexibility and creativity in their assessment of evidence. That gender-based and sexual violence crimes form part of the arsenal of perpetrators of serious crimes of international concern cannot be in dispute. As such, "knowledge" must be viewed in broader terms and must take into consideration the nature of a particular conflict. Indeed Judge Chile Eboe Osuji, formerly a trial attorney at the ICTR and SCSL, has argued that a duty to take "all reasonable measures to prevent rapes" should be imposed upon superiors in light of the frequency of rape and other sexual violence crimes in armed conflicts.[25]

---

[22] Paras. 966–968, Judgment, Prosecutor v. Musema, Case No. ICTR-93–13-I, 27 January 2000.

[23] Statute of the International Tribunal for Rwanda, Article 6 (3).

[24] Anne-Marie de Brouwer, Supranational Criminal Prosecution of Sexual Violence, para. 3.1.1.1, pp. 64–65, The ICC and the Practice of the ICTY and the ICTR, Intersentia nv, 2005.

[25] Chile Eboe-Osuji, Rape and Superior Responsibility in International Criminal Law in need of adjustment, Protecting humanity : essays in international law and policy in honour of Navanethem Pillay, p. 163 (2010).

3   Adjudicating Gender-based and Sexual Violence Crimes in the ICTR – Lessons Learned

Although the *Akayesu* judgment can be described as ground-breaking in advancing gender jurisprudence worldwide,[26] the ICTR should have done considerably more to address the prevalence of gender-based and sexual violence crimes in the context of the Rwandan Genocide. An additional lesson learned, at least from the early part of the ICTR's lifetime, is the importance of adequate female representation in the entire process and in every sphere. That said, female representation in and of itself must not be regarded as enough to guarantee a gender-sensitive approach to international criminal justice. The ICTR serves in this regard as a case in point; although the Court's second Prosecutor was a woman and by this time, it had welcomed many female judges including Judge Andresia Vaz and Judge Khalida Khan, both of whom had experience in gender-related issues,[27] the ICTR continued to fall short where prosecutions and convictions for crimes of sexual violence were concerned. The ICTR and other international criminal tribunals should take cognisance of the need to address impunity for gender-based and sexual violence crimes in a multi-faceted way. Such a strategy should cover both the investigation stages, including how witnesses are approached and by whom and the way in which those witnesses, particular those who are also victims of sexual violence crimes, are prepared before giving testimony. Equally important is the Prosecutor's decision to bring specific charges that relate to gender-based and sexual violence crimes and the way in which those charges are pleaded in Court.

The number of successful prosecutions at the ICTR of gender-based and sexual violence crimes do not adequately reflect the nature of the Genocide, and within that context, the widespread and systematic use of sexual violence as a means to target in whole or part the Tutsi population. That said, the Prosecutor's strategy evolved over the years, reflecting a more concerted effort to prosecute gender-based and sexual violence crimes. The present Prosecutor, Hassan Bubacar Jallow has himself acknowledged falling short on some of the challenges in relation to the effective prosecution of sexual violence crimes. On 30 January 2014, he published a best practices manual[28] that took stock of

---

26   Rebecca L. Haffajee, Prosecuting Crimes of Rape and Sexual Violence at the ICTR: The Application of Joint Criminal Enterprise Theory, 2006, p. 206.

27   Rebecca L. Haffajee, Prosecuting Crimes of Rape and Sexual Violence at the ICTR: The Application of Joint Criminal Enterprise Theory, 2006, p. 206.

28   Best Practices Manual for the Investigation and Prosecution of Sexual Violence Crimes in Post-Conflict Regions: Lessons Learned from the Office of the Prosecutor for the International Criminal Tribunal for Rwanda, http://www.unictr.org/sites/unictr.org/files/publications/ICTR-Prosecution-of-Sexual-Violence.pdf.

the lessons learned over the past 19 years since the ICTR opened its doors. The manual includes recommendations aimed at guiding future prosecutions. This will hopefully serve not only the successor body of the ICTR (the Mechanism for International Criminal Tribunals – MICT) but also other tribunals whose work continues especially the only permanent example of such bodies, the International Criminal Court.

11 Addressing Gender-based and Sexual Violence in the Jurisprudence of the Special Court for Sierra Leone

The approach of the Special Court for Sierra Leone (SCSL) towards gender-based and sexual violence crimes has been more comprehensive than that of the International Criminal Tribunal for Rwanda. Like the Rwandan Genocide, the decade long war in Sierra Leone was characterized by the systematic use of sexual violence crimes as a tool – some would say an effective tool of war. Far from being incidental to the brutal acts of murder and maiming, crimes of sexual violence were employed as a means to achieving the objectives of the actors.

According to Human Rights Watch, thousands of women were subjected to widespread and systematic sexual violence, which included individual and gang rape, and rape with objects such as weapons, firewood, umbrellas, and pestles.[29] In some instances women and girls were viewed as the spoils of war, combatants rewarded themselves after military operations by raping the women of the town or village they had attacked and in many instances taking them as slaves or what became known as "bush wives". Physicians for Human Rights concluded that 13% of household members surveyed reported war-related sexual violence – perpetrated primarily by the Revolutionary United Front (RUF).[30] The Special Rapporteur on violence against women, its causes and consequences, Radhika Coomaraswamy, took note of the failure to investigate, prosecute and punish those responsible for rape and other forms of gender-based violence thus contributing to an environment of impunity that perpetuates violence against women in Sierra Leone, including rape and domestic violence.[31]

---

29 "We'll Kill You If You Cry", 16 January 2003, ISBN: A1501.
30 War-Related Sexual Violence in Sierra Leone – A Population Based Assessment, June 2002, http://physiciansforhumanrights.org/library/reports/war-related-sexual-violence-sierra-leone-2002.html.
31 Report of the Special Rapporteur on violence against women, its causes and consequences, Ms. Radhika Coomaraswamy, submitted in accordance with Commission on Human

It came as no surprise therefore that the Prosecutor would charge ten out of the thirteen accused with the crimes against humanity of rape and sexual slavery, and the war crime of outrages upon personal dignity. Rather, it was surprising that the Prosecutor at the time did not charge sexual violence crimes in the case of *Prosecutor v. Norman, Fofana & Kondewa* (the CDF case). When the Prosecutor attempted to amend the indictment in order to add gender-based and sexual-violence crimes, his request was rejected by the judges.[32] The Chamber considered that the rights of the Accused to be tried without undue delay and to have adequate time to prepare their case was of primary importance. In the Prosecution Reply to Defence's Response regarding the issue of the decision to not allow the amendment, the Prosecutor contended that the high profile nature of gender-based crimes under international law constitutes "[an] exceptional circumstance".[33] While jurisprudence from international tribunals including the International Criminal Court would tend to suggest that gender-based and sexual violence crimes have yet to obtain the "high profile" status alluded to by the SCSL Prosecutor, there is certainly increasing recognition that including such crimes in prosecutorial strategy of international criminal tribunals is imperative.

The Trial Chamber's majority decision in the CDF case rejected the Prosecutor's request to bring evidence of crimes of sexual violence committed by the accused. However, Judge Pierre Boutet in his Dissenting Opinion argued that "victims of sexual violence have the right to have crimes that are committed against them prosecuted with all due respect to the Rule of Law. I consider these factors to constitute, in themselves, exceptional circumstances within the meaning of Rule 73(B) of the Rules in that not to do so in these circumstances would not be in the interests of justice".[34] In her partially dissenting opinion in the Appeals Judgment, Justice Renate Winter, an expert in women's rights echoed Judge Boutet's view by highlighting the importance of pro-

---

Rights resolution 2001/49*, Addendum, Mission to Sierra Leone, 21–29 August 2001, http://www.refworld.org/pdfid/3c84a38a4.pdf.

32   *Prosecutor v. Norman, Fofana & Kondewa*, Case No. SCSL-04-14-PT, Decision on Prosecution Request for Leave to Amend the Indictment, ¶ 6 (May 20, 2004).

33   *Prosecutor v. Norman, Fofana & Kondewa*, Case No. SCSL-04-14-T, Prosecution Reply to Defence Joint Response to Prosecution's Application for Leave to File an Interlocutory Appeal against the Decision on Request for Leave to Amend the Indictment, ¶ 12 July 2005.

34   *Prosecutor v. Sam Hinga Norman, Moinina Fofana & Alieu Kondewa*, Case No. SCSL-04-14-T, Partially Dissenting Opinion of Judge Pierre Boutet to Majority Decision on Request for Leave to Appeal Decision on Prosecution Motion for Ruling on Admissibility of Evidence, para. 10, (9 December 2005).

secuting sexual violence crimes. Justice Winter argued that the rights of the accused should have been balanced with the need for victims of gender-based violence to see their case adjudicated before the Special Court. She added that this was particularly relevant in light of the fact that such victims had no remedy in the national courts as a result of amnesties granted under the Lomé Peace Accord. The female judge concluded that "denying the Prosecution [the possibility of prosecuting] acts of gender-based violence committed against women and girls during the armed conflict in Sierra Leone impeded the Special Court's fulfilment of its mandate".[35]

Despite this omission, the Special Court nonetheless had the largest percentage of indictments containing charges of gender-based and sexual violence crimes than any other tribunal to date. The SCSL established noteworthy international legal precedents in relation to gender-based and sexual violence crimes. In the case of *Prosecutor vs. Alex Tamba Brima, Ibrahim Bazzy Kamara and Santigie Borbor Kanu* (the AFRC case), the court was able to provide important details about the prohibited acts of sexual slavery and forced marriage. Both the trial judgment and the appeals judgment in the case of *Prosecutor vs. Issa Sesay, Morris Kallon and Augustin Gbao* contributed significantly to the development of jurisprudence of sexual violence.[36]

Likewise the case of the *Prosecutor v. Charles Taylor* (the Taylor case) reinforced the jurisprudence that had emerged from the RUF and AFRC cases, particularly in relation to rape. By acknowledging the inevitable need to rely on circumstantial evidence in relation to act of rape, the Trial Chamber was cognizant of the cultural and social context of the conflict where many victims of sexual violence suffered social stigma and therefore it found that the restrictive test set out in the elements of the crime would be difficult to satisfy.[37]

1 *The Treatment of Forced Marriage*

Perhaps the most noteworthy jurisprudence to emerge from the Special Court for Sierra Leone relates to its treatment of the phenomenon of "bush wives". Ms. Zainab Hawa Bangura, the Special Representative of the United Nations Secretary-General on Sexual Violence in Conflict who was at the time a civil society activist and campaigner for women's rights in Sierra Leone, testified as

---

35 *Prosecutor v. Sam Hinga Norman, Moinina Fofana & Alieu Kondewa*, Case No. SCSL-04–14-A, Judgment, Partially Dissenting Opinion of Honourable Justice Renate Winter, (28 May 2008).

36 Valerie Oosterveld, *The Gender Jurisprudence of the Special Court for Sierra Leone: Progress in the Revolutionary United Front Judgments*, p. 51 (2011).

37 *Prosecutor v. Charles Taylor*, Case No. SCSL-03–01-T, Trial Chamber II, Judgment, ¶ 416 (May 18, 2012).

an expert witness for the Prosecutor in the AFRC case. Her report focused on the question of forced "marriage" within the context of the conflict in Sierra Leone.[38] The Defence sought to block the entry into evidence of Ms. Bangura's report by arguing that she could not be considered independent as she had been "agitating for women's rights".[39] The Chamber rejected this bizarre argument which seemed to suggest that advocating for women's rights was incompatible with a witness' independence on gender-based and sexual violence crimes. Ms. Bangura's report was accepted into evidence by the Chamber after her cross-examination.

In her report, Ms. Bangura described forced marriage within the Sierra Leone context as the physical abduction of a girl or woman by a combatant during the war. She noted that when an attack was carried out, the perpetrator would restrain the girl or woman and proclaim her to be his "wife" thus implying control and permanence of the relationship that did not necessarily exist within the context of sexual slavery. Ms. Bangura testified that she met many of these girls and women known as "bush wives" or "junta wives" and that even after the war many of them remained with their "husbands" and some even legitimised their "marriages". The fear of being stigmatised if they were to return to their communities was, according to this expert, a crucial factor.[40] The expert witness provided both in her report and testimony, a cultural and gender context vis-à-vis the use of bush wives and the notion of forced marriage.

When it came to pleading forced marriage, the Prosecutor needed to satisfy a set of criteria in order to justify its inclusion within the category of crimes against humanity by proving that it constituted "other inhumane acts" as specified in the SCSL Statute. This meant in accordance with Article 2(i), that four requirements had to be fulfilled:

i. great suffering inflicted by means of the inhumane act;
ii. similarities in character to other crimes against humanity;

---

38 *Prosecutor v. Alex Tamba Brima, Ibrahim Bazzy Kamara and Santigie Borbor Kanu*, Case No. SCSL-04-15-PT, Prosecution Request for Leave to call an additional witness pursuant to Rule 73bis(E), (4 May 2005), Annex B, Expert Report on the phenomenon of forced "marriage" in the context of the conflict in Sierra Leone, and more specifically in the context of the trials against the RUF and the AFRC Accused only, (May 2005.

39 Ibrahim Jalloh, Examining The Role of Expert Witnesses in the AFRC Trials at the Special Court for Sierra Leone, 18 December 2005 (http://www.carl-sl.org/home/articles/44-examining-the-role-of-expert-witnesses-in-the-afrc-trials-at-the-special-court-for-sierra-leone).

40 *Prosecutor vs. Brima, Kamara and Kanu*, Case no SCSL-2004–16-T, Transcript, 3 October 2005, page 16.

iii. a nexus between the enumerated act and broader widespread and systematic violence; and
iv. the need to create a new, distinct category of crime.[41]

The only obstacle the Prosecutor faced was demonstrating that forced marriage contained elements that were distinct enough to justify a new category of crime based on the "exact same factual context".[42] In this regard, the Prosecutor argued at the time that the new count of forced marriage better reflected the full culpability of the Accused. This argument was rejected by the judges of the Trial Chamber who concluded that the treatment being characterized as forced marriage was already included in the crime of sexual slavery.[43]

The AFRC Trial Chamber held that the use of the term "wife" by the perpetrator was indicative of the intent of the perpetrator to exercise ownership over the victim, and not an intent to assume a marital or quasi-marital status with the victim in the sense of establishing mutual obligations inherent in a husband wife relationship. In fact all a rebel needed do was to declare a captive, his "wife" and this pronouncement in and of itself seemed sufficient to change her status.[44] At the same time, the Chamber acknowledged that the relationship of the rebels to their "wives" was generally one of exclusive ownership, even though the victim could be passed on or given to another rebel at the discretion of the perpetrator.[45]

Justice Doherty disagreed with the majority opinion that dismissed sexual slavery as duplicitous with forced marriage.[46] In her detailed partially dissenting opinion which makes numerous reasoned arguments, she captures the particularity of the phenomenon of forced marriage in the context of the Sierra Leone conflict. She referred to the Ms. Bangura's Expert Report in presenting her arguments regarding the distinct and separate nature of the two crimes – sexual slavery and forced marriage. In particular, she contended that

---

41 Statute of the Special Court For Sierra Leone, Article 2(i) http://www.rscsl.org/Documents/scsl-statute.pdf.
42 Para. 38, Decision on Prosecution Request for Leave to Amend the Indictment, RUF case, Case No. SCSL-04–15-PT, 6 May 2004.
43 Rachel Slater, Gender Violence or Violence against Women? The Treatment of Forced marriage in the Special Court for Sierra Leone, *Melbourne Journal of International Law*, pp. 738–739.
44 Michael P. Scharf, Forced marriage as a Separate Crime against Humanity, The Sierra Leone Special Court and its Legacy, (2014) p. 197.
45 Para. 711, *Prosecutor vs. Brima, Kamara and Kanu*, Trial Judgment, Special Court for Sierra Leone, 20 June 2007.
46 *Prosecutor vs. Brima, Kamara and Kanu*, Trial Judgment, 20 June 2007, para. 108.

forced marriage focused on the harm stemming from the label 'wife' and the resulting stigmatisation. She reiterated what had been said by the Prosecution expert that many girls were unable to return to their schools or communities as they were ostracized for becoming "tainted and acquiring rebel behaviour".[47]

The Appeals Chamber disagreed with the Trial Chamber and decided that forced marriage was indeed an inhumane act by virtue of the fact that it caused severe suffering and injury. They agreed with Justice Doherty's dissenting opinion, that the act of forced marriage is of similar gravity and nature to others that fall under crimes against humanity and that the act causes serious bodily or mental harm, which can be qualified to constitute a crime against humanity.[48] The Appeals Chamber defined the crime as "a situation in which the perpetrator through his words or conduct or those of someone of whose actions he is responsible, compels a person by force, threat or force or coercion to serve as a conjugal partner resulting in severe suffering, or physical, mental or psychological injury to the victim."[49]

The RUF judgment was able to benefit from the AFRC Appeals Chamber's ruling on the question of forced marriage being treated under the rubric of 'other inhumane acts', as such the Trial Chamber's focus was on whether the elements of forced marriage could be said to fulfil the definition of an inhumane act. It was interesting to note that the Chamber, while recognising that certain aspects of forced marriage did fall under the definition of slavery, acknowledged that the real distinction was reflected in the fact that the term "wife" was used.[50]

The reference in the indictment in the Taylor case to the phenomenon of "bush wives" was subsumed within sexual slavery. As a result the Trial Chamber felt compelled to consider forced marriage in light of evidence relating to "bush wives". In doing so the Chamber disagreed with the Prosecutor and concluded that forced marriage should not have been charged under crime against

---

47 Rachel Slater, *Gender Violence or Violence against Women? The Treatment of Forced marriage in the Special Court for Sierra Leone*, Melbourne Journal of International Law, pp. 739–740.
48 *Prosecutor vs. Brima, Kamara and Kanu*, SCSL-04–16-T, Trial Judgment, Partly Dissenting Opinion of Justice Doherty on Count 7(Sexual slavery) and Count 8(' Forced marriage'), pp. 584–595 (20 June 2007).
49 *Prosecutor vs. Brima, Kamara and Kanu*, SCSL-04–16-A, Appeals Judgment, p. 195 (2008).
50 Rachel Slater, *Gender Violence or Violence against Women? The Treatment of Forced marriage in the Special Court for Sierra Leone*, Melbourne Journal of International Law, pp. 740–741.

humanity of other inhumane acts.[51] The Chamber seemed to take exception to the use of the term "marriage" which it considered inappropriate because there was no "marriage".[52] Instead the Chamber preferred the term conjugal slavery which, it contended considered both the sexual and non-sexual aspects of the act.

The lack of recognition of the "marriage" as it was labelled by the Prosecutor in international or Sierra Leonean law should not in and of itself negate the existence of the phenomenon, however perverse the practice. Patricia Viseur Sellers has argued that the reference to "marriage" is in fact a "linguistic camouflage" and that the crime against humanity of enslavement is adequate.[53] Jennifer Gong-Gerhowitz echoes Sellers' view of the use of term "marriage" and argues that this "implies mutual benefits and obligations".[54] These arguments appear to set aside the reality of the Sierra Leonean conflict generally, and the phenomenon of "bush wives" in particular. The focus on consensual marriage or even arranged marriages which are sometimes referred to as forced marriages may account for this reluctance to accept the term "marriage". However the reality was and in some instances may continue to be far more complex that the crime of sexual slavery allows.

The reference to bush wives was by no means accidental – the intention was indeed to inflict psychological suffering on these women and girls. According to the Sierra Leone Truth and Reconciliation Commission Report, rape was not merely used as a weapon against women, it concluded "it was a devastating tool of terror wielded intentionally to strike a sense of vulnerability into the wider society."[55] In order to fully appreciate why forced "marriage" is justifiable and should not be subsumed within sexual enslavement, it is necessary to look critically at the perpetrator's intention. By focusing on the union of marriage as we know it during times of peace, we ignore the fact that society itself accepted the term of "bush wives" and in so doing went on to punish these victims again by virtue of their so-called protected status. They were viewed as accomplices in a way that those who were abducted as used as sexual slaves

---

51 *Prosecutor vs. Charles Taylor*, Judgment, Case No. SCSL-03–01-T, Trial Chamber II, Paras. 424–430, (18 May 2012).

52 Valerie Oosterveld, Gender and the Charles Taylor Case at the Special Court for Sierra Leone, p. 20 (2012).

53 Patricia Viseur Sellers, Wartime Female Slavery: Enslavement?, 44 Cornell Int'l L.J. 115, page 137 (2011).

54 Jennifer Gong-Gerhowitz, Forced marriage: A "New" Crime Against Humanity?, 8 NW INT'L HUM. RTS, para. 65 (2009).

55 Sierra Leone TRC Report, Vol. 3 A, Chapter 4, Nature of the Conflict, para. 74 (2004).

were not.[56] In some instances some of these "bush wives" remained with their captors although it is unclear whether this was due to their fear of rejection by their communities or fear of their captors. In this regard, the Secretary-General reported in May 2000 that many of these wives who were abductees of rebels, "would most likely not feel free to express their wish to return to their original families" if they were not interviewed separately from their so-called husbands.[57] Even in the absence of evidence of the fear experienced by victims of forced marriage, it would be impossible to assign any responsibility to these women due to the fact that they were taken against their will and put through both physical and psychological torture by their captors thus depriving them of any real sense of agency.

Indeed the RUF Trial Chamber believed that the use of the term 'wife' by the rebels was deliberate and strategic, with the aim of enslaving and psychologically manipulating the women and with the purpose of treating them like possessions. It found that the perpetrators intended to exercise control and ownership over their victims who were unable to leave or escape for fear that they would be killed or sent to the front lines as combatants.[58] Witnesses in the AFRC trial testified about the justice system among rebel groups, known as "jungle justice". Within this system, one of the more serious crimes that could result in death was the raping of a soldier's "wife"[59] thus reinforcing the idea of a "protected status" of the "bush wife" and highlighting the complex nature of this gender-based crime.

2 *Sexual Slavery*

The crime of Sexual slavery was examined in the AFRC, RUF and Taylor cases. Prior to the SCSL's establishment however, the TRC had looked at the question of sexual slavery and the TRC Commissioners noted that sexual slavery became a gendered form of persecution, in that the individual was enslaved because of his or her function in society. Women were used for cooking and cleaning or for sex and reproduction.[60]

---

56 Stephen Rapp, Press Conference by Prosecutor for special Court for Sierra Leone, (17 July 2009).
57 Fourth report of the Secretary-General on UNAMSIL, S/2000/455, Section v. Human Rights, para. 45 (19 May 2000).
58 *Prosecutor v. Sesay, Kallon & Gbao*, Case No. SCSL-04–15-T, Judgment, Paras. 1466 and 1467(2 Mar 2009).
59 *Prosecutor vs. Brima, Kamara and Kanu*, Trial Judgment, para. 1139 (20 June 2007).
60 Sierra Leone TRC Report, Vol. 3 B, Chapter 3, Women and Armed Conflict in Sierra Leone, para. 194 (2004).

In the AFRC Trial Judgment, the Chamber adopted the elements of sexual slavery as contained in the Rome statute of the International Criminal Court, namely:

1. The perpetrator exercised any or all of the powers attaching to the right of ownership over one or more persons, such as by purchasing, selling, lending or bartering such a person or persons, or by imposing on them a similar deprivation of liberty.
2. The perpetrator caused such person or persons to engage in one or more acts of a sexual nature.
3. The perpetrator committed such conduct intending to engage in the act of sexual slavery or in the reasonable knowledge that it was likely to occur.[61]

Although the first element lists various powers of ownership, the list was not intended to be exhaustive. Furthermore payment or any form of exchange in order to establish the exercise of ownership is not required. With regard to the removal of liberty, this may include extracting forced labour or otherwise reducing a person to servile status. Another qualification in relation to ownership, as indicated by possession, is that it does not require confinement to a particular place. The consent of the free will of the victim is absent under conditions of enslavement.[62]

The treatment of sexual slavery in the RUF case is perhaps most noteworthy as it was the first time that an international tribunal had entered a conviction for sexual slavery as a crime against humanity.[63] In the RUF case, the Chamber recognized that the codification of sexual slavery in the Rome Statute and the SCSL's Statute was intended to draw attention to serious crimes that have been historically overlooked and to recognize the particular nature of sexual violence that has been used [...][64] The Chamber deemed that the *actus reus* of the offence of sexual slavery was made up of two elements:

i. the Accused exercised any or all of the powers attaching to the right of ownership over a person or persons (the slavery element); and

---

61 *Prosecutor vs. Brima, Kamara and Kanu*, Trial Judgment, para. 708 (20 June 2007).
62 *Prosecutor vs. Brima, Kamara and Kanu*, Trial Judgment, para. 709 (20 June 2007).
63 Valerie Oosterveld, *The Gender Jurisprudence of the Special Court for Sierra Leone*, p. 61 (2011).
64 *Prosecutor v. Sesay, Kallon & Gbao*, Case No. SCSL-04-15-T, Judgment, Special Court for Sierra Leone, Trial Chamber I, para. 156, (2 March 2009).

ii. the enslavement involved sexual acts (the sexual element).[65]

The RUF Trial Chamber concluded that "similar deprivation of liberty", one of the elements of the crime listed in the AFRC Judgment, could encompass situations in which the victims may not have been physically confined, but were otherwise unable to leave as they would have nowhere else to go and feared for their lives.[66]

When considering the issue of consent, the RUF Trial Chamber ruled that the sexual relations with the rebels could not be consensual because of the state of uncertainty and subjugation in which the victims lived. The Chamber's position was unambiguous – in such hostile and coercive circumstances, there should be a presumption of absence of genuine consent to having sexual relations or contracting marriages with the said RUF fighters.[67] The Appeals Chamber cited the ICTY Appeals Chamber which confirmed that "circumstances which render it impossible to express consent may be sufficient to presume the absence of consent. As such, the Chamber stressed that the lack of consent of the victim to the enslavement or to the sexual acts did not need to be proved by the Prosecution.[68]

The Trial Chamber concluded that the pattern of sexual enslavement employed by the RUF was a deliberate system intended to spread terror by the mass abductions of women, regardless of their age or existing marital status, from legitimate husbands and families.[69]

The Chamber was satisfied that the manner in which the rebels ravaged through villages targeting the female population effectively disempowered the civilian population and had a direct effect of instilling fear on entire communities. It found that these acts were not intended merely for personal satisfaction or a means of sexual gratification for the fighter. The savage nature of such conduct against the most vulnerable members of the society demonstrated that they were committed with the specific intent of spreading fear amongst

---

[65] Prosecutor v. Sesay, Kallon & Gbao, Case No. SCSL-04-15-T, Judgment, Special Court for Sierra Leone, Trial Chamber I, para. 159 (2 Mar 2009).

[66] Prosecutor v. Sesay, Kallon & Gbao, Case No. SCSL-04-15-T, Judgment, Trial Chamber I, Paras. 160–161, (Mar. 2, 2009).

[67] Prosecutor v. Sesay, Kallon & Gbao, Case No. SCSL-04-15-T, Judgment, Trial Chamber I, Paras. 1470–1471 (2 Mar 2009).

[68] Prosecutor v. Sesay, Kallon & Gbao, Case No. SCSL-04-15-T, Judgment, Trial Chamber I, para. 163 (Mar. 2, 2009).

[69] Prosecutor v. Sesay, Kallon & Gbao, Case No. SCSL-04-15-T, Judgment, Special Court for Sierra Leone, Trial Chamber I, para. 1351, (Mar. 2, 2009).

the civilian population as a whole, in order to break the will of the population and ensure their submission to AFRC/RUF control.[70]

The Taylor case produced some significant precedents vis-à-vis the treatment of sexual slavery – it defined sexual slavery as:

i. The perpetrator exercised any or all of the powers attaching to the right of ownership over one or more persons, such as by purchasing, selling, or bartering such a person or persons, or by imposing on them a similar deprivation of liberty.
ii. The perpetrator caused such a person or persons to engage in one or more acts of sexual nature.
iii. The perpetrator intended to engage in the act of sexual slavery or acted with the reasonable knowledge that this was likely to occur.[71]

The Trial Chamber in Taylor took a two-pronged approach when considering sexual slavery; in the first instance it focused on the enslavement aspect and then it considered the sexual aspect.[72] At the same time the judges recognised a hierarchical system with regard to ownership which reflected the changing context of ownership. The Chamber also considered the question of "control" as it related to victims – their movement, their environment, and their psychological state. In the Trial Judgment, the Chamber confirmed its view that physical confinement is not necessary for a victim to be considered "enslaved". This was particularly relevant to the Sierra Leonean conflict, given that armed groups moved around considerably so slaves were not necessarily confined in one place. It also took into consideration the psychological state of a victim, in particular the fear of punishment, which sometimes prevented victims from pursuing freedom even if or when the situation presented itself.

3   Rape as a Crime against Humanity in the RUF Case

At the onset of the trials before the Special Court for Sierra Leone, experts and witnesses testified to the systematic and widespread nature of sexual violence crimes, in particular rape among the RUF. In the Trial Judgment, the judges concluded that the RUF's plan was to adopt "a calculated and concerted pat-

---

[70]   Prosecutor v. Sesay, Kallon & Gbao, Case No. SCSL-04-15-T, Judgment, Special Court for Sierra Leone, Trial Chamber I, para. 1348 (Mar. 2, 2009).
[71]   Prosecutor v. Taylor, Case No. SCSL-03-01-T, Judgment, para. 418 (May 18, 2012).
[72]   Prosecutor v. Taylor, Case No. SCSL-03-01-T, Judgment, para. 2175 (May 18, 2012).

tern" of gender-based and sexual violence including many forms of rape, sexual slavery and forced marriage.[73]

In that case, the Trial Chamber provided the constitutive elements of rape as:

i. The Accused invaded the body of a person by conduct resulting in penetration, however slight, of any part of the body of the victim or of the Accused with a sexual organ, or of the anal or genital opening of the victim with any object or any other part of the body;
ii. The invasion was committed by force, or by threat of force or coercion, such as that caused by fear of violence, duress, detention, psychological oppression or abuse of power against such person or another person or by taking advantage of a coercive environment, or the invasion was committed against a person incapable of giving genuine consent;
iii. The Accused intended to effect the sexual penetration or acted in the reasonable knowledge that this was likely to occur; and
iv. The Accused knew or had reason to know that the victim did not consent.[74]

When considering the evidence, the Trial Chamber found that the widespread and systematic rape of women instilled fear and a sense of insecurity among the civilian population. The Chamber further ruled that the deliberate and concerted campaign to rape women constituted an extension of the battlefield to the women's bodies, a degrading treatment that inflicted physical, mental and sexual suffering to the victims and to their community. It also found that widespread and systematic sexual violence, including rape, constitutes an act of terrorism as charged under Count 1 of the Indictment.[75]

Rebels and other fighters employed perverse methods of sexual violence against women and men of all ages ranging from brutal gang rapes, the insertion of various objects into victims' genitalia, the raping of pregnant women and forced sexual intercourse between male and female civilian abductees.[76] The level of depravity was unprecedented in Sierra Leone and seemed to strike

---

73 *Prosecutor v. Sesay, Kallon & Gbao*, Case No. SCSL-04-15-T, Judgment Paras 1347, 1351, (Mar. 2, 2009).
74 Prosecutor v. Sesay, Kallon & Gbao, Case No. SCSL-04-15-T, Judgment, Trial Chamber I, para. 145 (Mar. 2, 2009).
75 Prosecutor v. Sesay, Kallon & Gbao, Case No. SCSL-04-15-T, Judgment, Trial Chamber I, para. 1602, (Mar. 2, 2009).
76 Prosecutor v. Sesay, Kallon & Gbao, Case No. SCSL-04-15-T, Judgment, Special Court for Sierra Leone, Trial Chamber I, para. 1347, (Mar. 2, 2009).

the very core of family and community values. Previously taboo practices such as the raping of pregnant women and old women became part and parcel of warfare, thus scarring not only the female or male victims but also the society as a whole, in particular its men who were powerless to prevent these heinous acts.

The AFRC Trial Chamber concluded that all rape, sexual slavery, forced "marriage" and outrages on personal dignity, when committed against a civilian population with the specific intent to terrorise, amount to an act of terror.[77]

In keeping with the AFRC trial judgment and with the approach of the ICTY in *Prosecutor v. Kunarac,* the *Taylor* Trial Chamber adopted three elements of crime for rape which were non-consensual penetration, the intent to effect such penetration and intention to engage in the act or the reasonable knowledge that it was likely to occur.[78] It confirmed the approach of the RUF case and reiterated the Court's jurisprudence that rape, sexual slavery, forced marriages, and outrages on personal dignity, when committed against a civilian population with the specific intent to terrorise, amount to an act of terror. The expert, Beth Vann, who interviewed refugees from Kono and Kailahun District reported that victims suffered from sexually transmitted diseases, exhibited signs of post-traumatic stress disorder, and were often socially isolated, stigmatized and rejected by their families.[79]

The Trial Chamber found further that committing crimes of sexual violence in public was a deliberate tactic on the part of the perpetrators to spread terror. Such crimes were part of a campaign of rape and sexual slavery committed by members of the AFRC/RUF against the women of Kono District not merely as a means of sexual indulgence, but as a means to spread terror among the civilian population.[80]

Rape was considered in the AFRC, RUF and Taylor cases in different terms. The AFRC case mainly focused on the use of gang rape as a tactic within the conflict, whereas the RUF case referred to the employment of gang rape, multiple rapes, rape with weapons and other objects, rape in public, rape in which family members were forced to watch and forced rape between family members or among captured civilians by the rebel group all of which was intended

---

77 Prosecutor v. Sesay, Kallon & Gbao, Case No. SCSL-04–15-T, Judgment, Special Court for Sierra Leone, Trial Chamber I, para. 1352, (Mar. 2, 2009).
78 Prosecutor vs. Charles Taylor, Judgment, Case No. SCSL-03–01-T, Trial Chamber II, para. 418, (18 May 2012).
79 Prosecutor vs. Charles Taylor, Judgment, Case No. SCSL-03–01-T, Trial Chamber II, para. 2035, (18 May 2012).
80 Prosecutor vs. Charles Taylor, Judgment, Case No. SCSL-03–01-T, Trial Chamber II, para. 2037, (18 May 2012).

to accomplish its strategic goals.[81] Evidence in the Taylor case revealed the practice of deliberately targeting breast-feeding mothers.[82] The three cases confirmed the Prosecutor's argument that incidents of rape or other gender-based or sexual violence crimes did not take place in isolation. On the contrary, they were committed with a number of other violations such as murder, abduction, mutilation, forced nudity, sexual slavery, forced labour, forced marriage and physical assault – all of which were perpetrated in order to achieve the same goal – to terrorise the population.[83]

The Taylor case referred to "women and girls" as the victims of the sexual violence crimes thus ignoring the plight of men and boys. The RUF trial judgment recognized the Prosecutor's effort of providing clear, timely and consistent attention to sexual violence crimes directed against men and boy and further confirmed the effects of the rape directed against women and girls on men and boys.[84]

The International Criminal Court's elements of crimes of outrages upon personal dignity were widely applied in AFRC, RUF and Taylor case. This category of crime was not merely limited to rape and sexual slavery but rather included other acts, such as forced nudity and threats of sexual mutilation, were also included within this scope.[85]

Interestingly the SCSL considered the war crime of committing acts of terror as a gender-based crime, it was alleged by the Prosecutor that the acts of terror were perpetrated in various forms including gender-based and sexual violence crimes. In the RUF case, the Chamber found that through acts of sexual violence the accused had demonstrated the specific intent to terrorize the civilian population. So did the Taylor case. Since the outcome of this violence turned out to effectively disempower the civilian population and to instil fear in entire communities, the court believed that the war crime of committing acts of terror was committed.[86]

---

81 Valerie Oosterveld, Gender and the Charles Taylor Case at the Special Court for Sierra Leone, 2012, p. 10.
82 Ibid, p. 11.
83 Ibid, p. 11.
84 Ibid, p. 14.
85 Ibid, p. 25.
86 Ibid, pp. 25–26. Also see Paras. 2035 and 2037, Prosecutor vs. Charles Taylor, Judgment, Case No. SCSL-03–01-T, Trial Chamber II, 18 May 2012.

The RUF Trial Chamber found that the crimes of rape, sexual slavery and 'forced marriage' constitute in each case a severe humiliation, degradation and violation of the dignity of the victims and the perpetrators knew that their acts would have this effect.[87]

4   National Efforts in Sierra Leone to Address Gender-base and Sexual Violence Crimes

As a hybrid Court, the Special Court for Sierra Leone incorporated domestic Sierra Leonean Law in its statute as well as international law. One of the two domestic acts included related to the abuse of girls pursuant to the Prevention of Cruelty to Children Act of 1926.[88] This demonstrated that the law of Sierra Leone dating back to the early 1900s had already addressed certain aspects of gender-based violence. That said, at the time that the Special Court was established, the Sierra Leone judiciary had crumbled following over a decade of war. In a report on the country's judiciary, it was said that "restoration of the rule of law [was] still being threatened by a pattern of criminal impunity, won by the perpetrators of human rights abuses and crimes."[89] The authors went as far as arguing that Sierra Leoneans had accepted the amnesties provided for by the Lomé Peace Accord because of their sense that retributive justice through the domestic courts was beyond their reach.[90]

The conflict in Sierra Leone decimated an already inefficient court system and police force creating a persistent climate of impunity in the country. Many perpetrators of sexual enslavement were never brought to justice and the number of women and girls who remain with their rebel "husbands" as a result of the practice of forced "marriage" is not known. As a result of the 1999 Lomé Peace Accord's "blanket amnesty under Sierra Leonean law," many perpetrators have remained outside of the reach of Sierra Leone's justice system – many of whom would have committed gender-based and sexual violence crimes during the conflict.[91] In a stark example of the pervasiveness of impunity, a British newspaper reported in 2000 that one of the most notorious female per-

---

87   Prosecutor v. Sesay, Kallon & Gbao, Case No. SCSL-04–15-T, Judgment, Special Court for Sierra Leone, Trial Chamber I, para. 1583, (Mar. 2, 2009).
88   Statute of the Special Court For Sierra Leone, Article 5, http://www.rscsl.org/Documents/scsl-statute.pdf.
89   Niobe Thompson and Mohammed Pa Momo Fofanah, In Pursuit of Justice: a report on the Judiciary in Sierra Leone, para. 5.4 (2002).
90   Id.
91   Deanna Simpson, Women under Siege, Sierra Leone. (February 7 2013).

petrators of the war known as Adama "Cut Hand" was being trained by the British Army as part of their efforts to reintegrate ex-rebels into the Sierra Leonean army.[92]

While the SCSL went some way to filling the justice lacuna that had existed for years, it is clear that a sense of impunity for serious crimes including gender-based and sexual violence crimes still exists. In particular, given the widespread use of sexual violence during the war, it would be naïve to assume that a cessation of hostilities or the closure of the cases against a small number of perpetrators, could equate to an end or significant reduction in such crimes.

The Special Court was somewhat limited with regard to its ability to build capacity in the domestic system, due in a large part to it being a treaty body. In fact the Court's Appeals Chamber had ruled that the treaty-based nature of the court removed it from the national legal system and rendered it an international tribunal.[93] The United Nations' expectation was that SCSL would be able be to build the capacity of the country's judiciary,[94] this proved impossible due to the fact that the Court only dealt with international crimes. However the Security Council in its resolution 1688 of 16 June 2006 recognised the Special Court's "vital contribution" to establishing the Rule of Law in the country.[95]

Recognising the need to address gender-based and sexual violence crimes, the Sierra Leone Government introduced in 2007, the Domestic Violence Act. The Act granted authorities the power to respond to gender-based and sexual crimes through measures such as issuing protection orders or barring perpetrators from their homes.[96] Five years later, the Government introduced the Sexual Offences Act, which made violence or sexual abuse against women, including within marriage, a criminal act.[97] The Sexual Offences Act defines rape as "an act of sexual penetration with another person without the consent of that other person" and the crime carries a sentence of 5–15 years.

While neither the Domestic Violence Act nor the Social Offences Act fully responds to the scope of gender-based and sexual violence crimes in post-conflict Sierra Leone, they do go some way to addressing the culture of impunity

---

[92] Phillip Sherwell, How Britain hones the skill of killers, The Daily Telegraph, (10 September 2000).

[93] *Prosecutor v. Morris Kallon, Sam Hinga Norman, Brima Bazzy Kamara*, Decision on Constitutionality and Lack of Jurisdiction, para. 2, (13 March 2004).

[94] OHCHR, Rule of Law Tools for Post-Conflict States, Maximizing the Legacy of Hybrid Courts, HR/PUB/08/2, pp. 28–5, (New York and Geneva, 2008).

[95] Security Council Resolution 1688, S/RES/1688 (2006).

[96] Karen Barnes, Addressing Gender-based violence in Sierra Leone, p. 16 (August 2007).

[97] Supplement to the Sierra Leone Gazette Vol. CXLIII, No. 60, (1 November 2012).

for such crimes. In February 2011, the Government established Saturday Courts with support of the United Nations in an attempt to tackle gender-based and sexual violence crimes by providing access to women and girls. According to UNDP reports, the Saturday Courts have helped clear a backlog of 700 such cases within a few months of the courts being established.[98]

In 2012, after the Sexual Offences Act was introduced, the Chief Justice, a woman, apparently took a tough stance on sexual offences *inter alia* by revoking bail for all persons accused of sexual offences at the beginning of the first High Court session of 2012.[99] Regrettably neither address forced marriage nor sexual slavery despite there being victims who continue to live through untold suffering because the y have either remained with their captors or they have been unable to return to their communities.[100] There is a sense among Sierra Leonean women that the SCSL did not fully address gender-based and sexual violence and that justice should be more localised, with many viewing the Special Court as far removed from their lives.[101] However it would be disingenuous to lay the responsibility for the absence of accountability for gender-based and sexual violence crimes at the feet of the SCSL alone. Prior to its establishment of the SCSL, as early as 2001, the Sierra Leone Government had already set up Family Support Units made up of members of the police force who had been trained to work with victims of sexual and domestic violence[102] and yet according to report issued by a non-governmental organization, sexual violence and gender-based crimes were on the rise in 2013[103] despite numerous efforts by the government. Such reports highlight the need for a multi-faceted approach to gender-based and sexual violence crimes – an approach where justice can play a central role but it cannot be seen as the panacea for such deplorable crimes.

---

98 Saturday Courts help tackle Sexual and Gender-Based Violence in Sierra Leone, http://www.sl.undp.org/content/sierraleone/en/home/ourwork/democraticgovernance/successstories/Saturday_Courts_Help_Tackle_SGBV/
99 Lisa Denney and Aisha Fofana Ibrahim, Violence against women in Sierra Leone: How women seek redress, p. 6 (December 2012).
100 Barbara Bangura, Returning the girls home: Reintegration and Resocialisation of Abducted and Ex-Soldier girls, p. 7.
101 Lotta Teale, Addressing gender-based violence in the Sierra Leone conflict: Notes from the field,
102 UN Women, End Violence Against Women and Girls, http://www.endvawnow.org/en/articles/1092-overview.html.
103 Don Bosco Girls Shelter, "Brutal Violence Against Girls in Sierra Leone" (2013).

III Conclusion

The judicial approach to gender-based and sexual violence crimes has evolved since the establishment of the first modern ad hoc tribunal, the International Criminal Tribunal for the former Yugoslavia. Since then, both the International Criminal Tribunal for Rwanda and the Special Court for Sierra Leone have made significant contributions, in particular towards a more systematic approach to dealing with such gender-based and sexual violence crimes. From the ICTR's treatment of rape as genocide to the SCSL's reference to forced marriage as a crime against humanity, the guidelines, in the form of the jurisprudence that have emerged, offer a more robust approach for dealing with such crimes. While these precedents are by no means binding on the world's permanent criminal court, they serve as solid building blocks, providing reasoned arguments upon which the ICC would, if it chooses, be able to build.

Gender-based and sexual violence crimes seem to characterise modern day conflicts with chilling brutality. They also seem to occur with a frequency that we were unaccustomed to and one that calls for robust action. While justice forms a part of the solution for dealing with such crimes, it cannot be seen as the only solution – there is a need to engage that the national and international level in order to address impunity for gender-based and sexual violence crimes.

What is clear from the two African-based international criminal tribunals is that there are numerous stakeholders in the push for accountability for gender-based and sexual violence crimes; where Prosecutors fail to see the importance of charging such crimes where they have taken place, gender-sensitive judges are able to step in. Likewise civil society have a role to play in demanding that truths that paint a full picture of a conflict are told in courtrooms. The role of victims and witnesses is likewise indispensable; successful prosecutions for gender-based and sexual violence crimes will no doubt strengthen their resolve in always seeking justice for such irreprehensible crimes.

Both the Rwandan Genocide and the Sierra Leonean conflict act as proof of the fundamental need to address impunity for gender-based and sexual violence crimes particularly in light of the prominent role they played in these conflicts. With the comprehensive body of jurisprudence at our disposal today, hopefully ensuring accountability for gender-based and sexual violence crimes will become the norm, both at the national and international level.

CHAPTER 20

International Crimes, Immunities and the Protocol on Amendments to the Protocol of the Merged African Court: Some Observations

Adejoké Babington-Ashaye

Introduction

In June 2014 the Assembly of the African Union[1] adopted the Protocol on Amendments to the Protocol on the Statute of the African Court of Justice and Human and Peoples Rights (Protocol) at its 23rd Ordinary Session in Malabo, Equatorial Guinea.[2] The Protocol contains noteworthy amendments including the creation of an International Criminal Law Section (ICLS) with jurisdiction over a wide-range of internationally recognized crimes. Yet what has drawn the greatest attention and criticism is the inclusion of Article 46A*bis* which provides that:

> No charges shall be commenced or continued before the Court against any serving AU Head of State or Government, or anybody acting or entitled to act in such capacity, or other senior state officials based on their functions, during their tenure of office.

Some have argued that inclusion of Article 46A*bis* in the Protocol severely undermines the barely existing Court and disregards the trend in international criminal law of non-recognition of immunity for state agents before international criminal courts and tribunals.[3] Others have challenged the extension of

---

1 The African Union Assembly comprises of Heads of State and Government of the African Union. See www.au.int.
2 Decision on the Draft Legal Instruments, Assembly/AU/Dec.529 (XXIII).The Protocol revises the Protocol on the Statute of the African Court of Justice and Human Rights which was adopted in 2008 and is not yet in force. This protocol merged the African Court on Human and Peoples Rights and the African Court of Justice. The text of the draft protocol is available here: http://www.au.int/en/content/protocol-amendments-protocol-statute-african-court-justice-and-human-rights.
3 See Amnesty International, *Open Letter to Heads of State and Government of the African Union: Article 46Abis of the Draft Protocol on Amendments to the Protocol on the Statute of the African*

immunity to "senior state officials based on their functions," arguing that there is no basis for such a provision in international law.[4]

This paper will address Article 46A*bis* in four parts. It will assess the extent to which Article 46A*bis* detracts from the law governing the interplay between immunities for state agents and prosecution for international crimes before international courts or tribunals. It will not address the question of immunities before national courts, or immunities of former Heads of State or Government, since Article 46A*bis* expressly limits immunity to their term in office. The first part of the paper places Article 46A*bis* in the context of the international law rules governing the immunities of state agents charged with international crimes before international courts and tribunals. The second part considers the first clause in Article 46A*bis* which provides that "no charges shall be commenced or continued before the Court against any serving AU Head of State or Government." The third addresses the second clause of the article namely "... or anybody acting or entitled to act in such capacity", while the fourth part addresses the final clause of the article namely "or other senior state officials based on their functions, during their tenure of office."

I   Immunities of State Agents Charged with International Crimes before International Courts and Tribunals.

It is appropriate to commence this section with an overview of the immunities recognized in international law as attaching to certain state agents.[5] Immunity is generally defined as "the exception or exclusion of the entity, individual, or property enjoying it from the jurisdiction of"[6] a foreign State. International law recognizes two broad types of immunities which are applicable to an agent of

---

  Court of Justice and Human Rights, AFR 01/012/2014, 20 June 2014. *Available at*: http://www.amnesty.org/en/library/info/AFR01/012/2014/en.
4 See Dan Kuwali, *Article 46Abis: A Step Backward in Ending Impunity in Africa*, kujenga amani, (22 Sept. 2014), http://forums.ssrc.org/kujenga-amani/2014/09/22/article-46a-bis-a-step-backward-in-ending-impunity-in-africa/#.VSQqEdLETLI.
5 For a detailed review of this body of law see Hazel Fox, *The Law of State Immunity*, (2002). See also Arthur Watts, *The Legal Position in International Law of Heads of States, Heads of Governments and Foreign Ministers*, 247 Recuil Des Cours 13 (1994 III).
6 ILC, Preliminary Report of the Special Rapporteur on Immunity of State Officials from Foreign Criminal Jurisdiction, UN Doc. A/CN.4/601, at para.56 [Hereinafter ILC Preliminary Report].

the State but are derived as a "corollary of the immunity of the state itself."[7] The first is immunity *ratione personae* or personal immunity which "extends to acts performed by a State official in both an official and a private capacity, both before and while occupying his post."[8] This type of immunity is limited to certain officials and is recognized as attaching, under customary international law, to the Head of State, the Head of Government, or the foreign minister.[9] Diplomats and other officials on special mission in foreign states are also accorded personal immunity under the Vienna Convention on Diplomatic Relations (1961)[10] and the United Nations Convention on Special Missions (1969).[11] Personal immunity is described as "full", "absolute", "complete", or "integral"[12] since it covers acts performed in both an official and personal capacity,[13] and precludes the exercise of criminal jurisdiction over these acts.[14] Such immunity is conferred on those with primary responsibility for the smooth conduct of international relations.[15]

---

7   The Netherlands Ministry of Foreign Affairs, Advisory Committee on Issues of Public International Law, *Advisory Report on the Immunity of Foreign State Officials (Translation)*, Advisory Report No. 20, (The Hague, 2011), at 11. *Available at*: http://cms.webbeat.net/Con tentSuite/upload/cav/doc/cavv-report-nr-20-immunity_foreign_officials.pdf.

8   ILC Preliminary Report, para. 79.

9   Arthur Watts, *supra* note 5. See also Arrest Warrant of 11 April 2000 (Democratic Republic of the Congo v. Belgium) Judgment, ICJ Reports 2002, p. 3 [hereinafter the Arrest Warrant case].

10 Vienna Convention on Diplomatic Relations, 18 April 1961, 500 UNTS, 95.

11 United Nations Convention on Special Missions, 8 December 1969, 1400 UNTS, 231.

12 ILC, Memorandum prepared by the Secretariat, UN Doc. A/CN.4/596, para. 137.

13 Id.

14 See for example Article 1 of the Resolution of the Institut de Droit International of 26 August 2001 on Immunities from Jurisdiction and Execution of Heads of State and of Government in International Law: "when in the territory of a foreign State, the person of the Head of State is inviolable. While there, he or she may not be placed under any form of arrest or detention. The Head of State shall be treated by authorities with due respect and all reasonable steps shall be taken to prevent any infringement of his or her person, liberty, or dignity." *Available at*: http://www.idi-iil.org/idiE/resolutionsE/2001_van_02_en.PDF.

15 Chanaka Wickremasinghe, *Immunities Enjoyed by Officials of States and International Organizations*, in International Law (Malcom D. Evans ed., 2003) at 389. Regarding personal immunity attaching to the Head of State, the ICC Pre-Trial Chamber I in *The Prosecutor v. Omar Al Bashir*, stated that such immunity is "ensured under international law for the purpose of the effective performance of the functions of sitting Heads of State." para. 25. Prosecutor v. Omar Al Bashir, Decision on the Cooperation of the Democratic Republic of Congo Regarding Omar Al Bashir's Arrest and Surrender to the Court, ICC-02/05-01/09-195 (9 April 2014). *Available at*: http://www.icc-cpi.int/iccdocs/doc/doc1759849.pdf.

The second type of immunity is immunity *ratione materiae*. Also referred to as functional immunity or 'official acts immunity',[16] immunity *ratione materiae* applies to all "representatives of the State acting in that capacity."[17] Unlike immunity *ratione personae* 'representatives of the State' refers to a much broader category of individuals and may be relied upon by current or former state officials who, regardless of their status, have acted on behalf of the State.[18] The application of functional immunity is derived from the belief that the acts in question are attributable to the State rather than the individual, and the need to prevent indirect adjudication by one state over the acts of another.[19] In its commentary to the draft articles on consular relations the International Law Commission (ILC), noted that "[t]his exemption represents an immunity which the sending State is recognized as possessing in respect of acts which are those of a sovereign State. By their very nature such acts are outside the jurisdiction of the receiving State, whether civil, criminal or administrative. Since official acts are outside the jurisdiction of the receiving State, no criminal proceedings may be instituted in respect of them."[20]

Unlike personal immunity which is temporary in nature and offers the holder only a procedural defence while in office, functional immunity is a substantive defence and outlives the cessation of office.[21] These two types of immunity coexist for instance with a Head of State who would enjoy both

---

16   Pierre D'Argent, *Immunity of State Officials and the Obligation to Prosecute*, CeDIE Working Paper No. 2013/04, http://www.uclouvain.be/cps/ucl/doc/ssh-cdie/documents/2013-04-PdArgent.pdf, retrieved 5 October 2014.

17   Article 2(1)(b)(iv), United Nations Convention on Jurisdictional Immunities of States and Their Property, UN Doc. A/RES/59/38 (not in force). Article 2(1)(b)(iv) provides that "[f]or the purposes of the present Convention "State" means ... representatives of the State acting in that capacity."

18   H.F. Van Panhuys, *In the Borderland Between the Act of State Doctrine and Questions of Jurisdictional Immunities*, 13 Int'l & Comp. L.Q. (1964), 1193–1218 at 1206. See also Kuwait Airways Corp. v. Iraq Airways Co. [1995] 3 All E.R. 694 (H.L.); Kaitlin R. O'Donnell, *Certain Criminal Proceedings in France (Republic of Congo v. France) and Head of State Immunity: How Impenetrable Should the Immunity Veil Remain?*, 26 Boston Univ. Int'l Law Journ. (2008), 384–385; and Michael A. Tunks, *Diplomats or Defendants? Defining the Future of Head-of-State Immunity*, 52 Duke L.J. (2002), 651–682.

19   Dapo Akande, *International Law Immunities and the International Criminal Court*, 98(3) Am. J. Int'l L, (2004) 407–433 at 413.

20   Report of the International Law Commission on the work of its thirteenth session, (1961) vol. II, *Yearbook of the International Law Commission*, A/CN.4/SER.A/1961/Add.1, at 117.

21   Anthony Cassese, *When May Senior State Officials Be Tried for International Crimes? Some Comments on the Congo v. Belgium Case*, 13(4) Eur. J. Int'l L. (2002), 853–875 at 862. Micaela Frulli, *The Question of Charles Taylor's Immunity: Still in Search of a Balanced Application of Personal Immunities?*, 2 J.Int'l Crim. Just. (2004), 1118–1129, at 1125.

functional and personal immunities while in office. Once the Head of State leaves office he or she would benefit only from functional immunity in relation to 'official acts'.

The central question explored in this paper is whether Article 46A*bis* detracts from any recognizable rules in international law concerning immunities before international criminal courts or tribunals. The 2002 *Arrest Warrant* case provides a useful starting point. The case concerned the issuance of an international arrest warrant by Belgium against Mr. Abdoulaye Yerodia Ndombasi, then the incumbent Minister for Foreign Affairs of the Democratic Republic of Congo (DRC). Belgium argued that Mr. Yerodia Ndombasi committed offences constituting grave breaches of the Geneva Conventions of 1949 and of the Additional Protocols thereto. Mr. Yerodia Ndombasi was also charged with committing crimes against humanity. Belgium asserted that international law recognized an exception to the inviolability of state immunity for the prosecution of international crimes.

Though the case concerned the exercise of jurisdiction by foreign courts, the ICJ made notable *obiter dicta* which are relevant to the question of immunities before international criminal courts and tribunals. First the ICJ observed that, having carefully examined State practice, including national legislation and decisions of national higher courts, it was "unable to deduce from this practice that there exists under customary international law any form of exception to the rule according immunity from criminal jurisdiction and inviolability to incumbent Ministers for Foreign Affairs, where they are suspected of having committed war crimes or crimes against humanity."[22] The Court nevertheless recognized that "an incumbent or former Minister for Foreign Affairs may be subject to criminal proceedings before certain international criminal courts, where they have jurisdiction,"[23] noting examples such as the International Criminal Tribunal for the former Yugoslavia (ICTY), the International Criminal Tribunal for Rwanda (ICTR) and the International Criminal Court (ICC).

Through this observation it seems clear that the jurisdiction of an international court or tribunal over such senior officials is not automatic, but rather is dependent on the statutory provisions of the court in question, and whether these provisions give the court jurisdiction over those who would otherwise be accorded immunity under international law.[24] The 1998 Rome Statute estab-

---

22   *Arrest Warrant case, supra* note 9, para. 58.
23   Id., para. 61.
24   See Akande, *supra* note 19 at 418.

lishing the ICC expressly removes immunities which attach to the officials of States Parties to the Rome Statute.[25] Article 27(2) provides that:

> Immunities or special procedural rules which may attach to the official capacity of a person, whether under national or international law, shall not bar the Court from exercising its jurisdiction over such a person.

The statutes of the ICTY, ICTR and the Special Court for Sierra Leone (SCSL) have also noted the irrelevance of official capacity in the execution of the tribunals' mandates.[26] In 2003 the prosecutor of the SCSL issued an indictment against former Liberian President Charles Taylor for war crimes and crimes against humanity committed in Sierra Leone. Taylor filed a motion contending that at the time the indictment was issued he was the incumbent Head of State and enjoyed absolute immunity from criminal process, including the issuance of an international arrest warrant.[27] Relying on the *Arrest Warrant* case, Taylor

---

[25] Though not relevant here, it is worth noting that a tension exists between Article 27 and Article 98 of the Rome Statute which addresses cooperation with respect to waiver of immunity and consent to surrender. Article 98(1) provides that "[t]he Court may not proceed with a request for surrender or assistance which would require the requested State to act inconsistently with its obligations under international law with respect to the State or diplomatic immunity of a person or property of a third State, unless the Court can first obtain the cooperation of that third State for the waiver of the immunity." Since the ICC does not have police powers, it relies upon States to execute arrest warrants. This is particularly important in cases, such as that of Al-Bashir of Sudan, where the accused is the subject of a non-State party to the Rome Statute. Article 98(1) provides that the Court must first secure the agreement of that State before requesting the surrender or assistance of member States in relation to that accused. This tension has been addressed here: Dapo Akande, *The Legal Nature of Security Council Referrals to the ICC and its Impact on Al Bashir's Immunities*, 7(2) J. Int. Criminal Justice (2009), 333–352, and The Prosecutor v. Omar Al Bashir, Decision Pursuant to Article 87(7) of the Rome Statute on the Failure by the Republic of Malawi to Comply with the Cooperation Requests Issued by the Court with Respect to the Arrest and Surrender of Omar Hassan Ahmad Al Bashir, ICC-02/05-01/09 (12 December 2009). *Available at*: http://www.icc-cpi.int/iccdocs/doc/doc1287184.pdf.

[26] Article 7(2) Statute of the International Criminal Tribunal for the former Yugoslavia, Article 6(2) Statute of the International Criminal Tribunal for Rwanda (1994), and Article 6(2) Statute of the Special Court for Sierra Leone provide that "[t]he official position of any accused person, whether as Head of State or Government or as a responsible Government official, shall not relieve such person of criminal responsibility nor mitigate punishment."

[27] Applicant's Motion made under Protest and without Waiving of Immunity accorded to a Head of State President, SCSL-2003-01-I-015 (23 July 2003).

argued that there was nothing in the instruments establishing the SCSL to suggest that it was an international criminal court.[28]

The SCSL Appeals Chamber centered its ruling against Taylor's motion on the legal character of the special court as an international court.[29] The Appeals Chamber first noted that the special court was established by the Agreement between the United Nations (UN) and Sierra Leone pursuant to Security Council Resolution 1315 (2000) for the sole purpose of prosecuting those who bore the greatest responsibility for "serious violations of humanitarian law and Sierra Leonean law committed in the territory of Sierra Leone".[30] Article 1 of the SCSL Statute specifically refers to this mandate. The Appeals Chamber further observed that in performing its duty to maintain international peace and security, the UN Security Council acts on behalf of all UN member states.[31] It noted that the "Agreement between the United Nations and Sierra Leone is thus an agreement between all members of the United Nations and Sierra Leone",[32] making it "an expression of the will of the international community".[33] According to the Appeals Chambers the Special Court was established to "fulfil an international mandate and is part of the machinery of international justice."[34]

With respect to immunity before the SCSL, the Appeals Chamber observed that Article 6(2) of its statute expressly provides that the official position of such a person shall not relieve them of criminal responsibility nor mitigate punishment. The Appeals Chamber noted the substantial similarity between Article 6(2) and Article 7(2) of the Statute of the ICTY, Article 6(2) of the Statute of the ICTR and Article 27(2) of the ICC Statute. Taking into account the statement by the ICJ in the *Arrest Warrant* case[35] and the view expressed by

---

28 Id.
29 Prosecutor v. Taylor (Charles Ghankay), Decision on immunity from jurisdiction, Case No SCSL-2003-01-I, SCSL-03-01-I-059, (2004) 128 ILR 239, ICL 25 (SCSL 2004), 31st May 2004, Appeals Chamber (SCSL). [Hereinafter SCSL Immunities Decision].
30 SCSL Immunities Decision, paras 34–42. See also Security Council Resolution 1315 (2000) of 14 August 2000, UN Doc S/RES/1315.
31 Article 24(1) of the UN Charter.
32 SCSL Immunities Decision, para. 38.
33 Id.
34 Id., para. 39.
35 "... an incumbent or former Minister for Foreign Affairs may be subject to criminal proceedings before *certain international criminal courts*, where they have jurisdiction. Examples include the International Criminal tribunal for the former Yugoslavia, and the International Criminal tribunal for Rwanda, established pursuant to Security Council resolutions under *Chapter VII of the United Nations Charter*, and the future International Criminal Court created by the *1998 Rome Convention*. The latter's statute expressly provides, in *Article 27, paragraph 2*, that '[i]mmunities or special procedural rules which may

Lord Slynn of Hadley in the *Pinochet case*,[36] the SCSL Appeals Chamber concluded that "the principle seems now established that the sovereign equality of states does not prevent a Head of State from being prosecuted before an international criminal tribunal or court."[37]

It is necessary to note that while the Appeals Chamber is correct to deny immunity to Taylor on the basis of the legal instruments governing the SCSL, the waiver of immunities before an international criminal court or tribunal cannot be considered automatic. The international character of a criminal court or tribunal does not inherently indicate the inapplicability of internationally recognized immunities. In his dissenting opinion in *Krstic* Judge Shahabudeen observed that "there is no substance in the suggested automacity of disappearance of the immunity just because of the establishment of international criminal courts. ... A presumption of continuance of their immunities as these exist under international law is only offset where some element in the decision to establish such a court shows that they agreed otherwise."[38] International criminal tribunals and courts derive their mandate and jurisdiction from their constitutive instruments. That these governing statutes have included express provisions removing immunities accorded to state officials does not indicate the emergence of a rule of customary international law that such immunity is automatically waived before international courts and tribunals. Rather, it only illustrates a trend in the establishment of international criminal courts and tribunals to expressly remove immunities which are otherwise recognized in international law. The relevance or irrelevance of immunities of state officials as a bar to jurisdiction thereby depends on the statutes of these judicial bodies.[39]

---

attach to the official capacity of a person, whether under national or international law, shall not bar the Court from exercising its jurisdiction over such person", *supra* note 9, para. 61 (emphasis added).

36 Regina v. Bartle and the Commissioner of Police for the Metropolis and others, Ex parte Pinochet, 37 I.L.M. 1302 1313–1314 (H.L. 1998). He stated "there is ... no doubt that states have been moving towards the recognition of some crimes as those which should not be covered by claims of state or Head of State or other official or diplomatic immunity when charges are brought before international tribunals."

37 SCSL Immunities Decision, para. 52.

38 *Prosecutor v. Krstić*, Case IT-98-33-A, Decision on Application for Subpoenas, 1 July 2003, paras 11–12. *Available at*: http://www.icty.org/x/cases/krstic/acdec/en/030701do.htm.

39 Dapo Akande reaches the same conclusion noting that "In sum, the statement that international immunities may not be pleaded before certain international tribunals must be read subject to the condition (1) that the instruments creating those tribunals expressly or implicitly remove the relevant immunity, and (2) that the state of the official concerned

Assuming, *arguendo*, that a waiver of immunity automatically applies to prosecution before international criminal courts and tribunals, could the ICLS of the African Court be characterized as an international criminal court? It may appear to be one since its jurisdiction is similar to that of the ICC and the *ad hoc* tribunals, and international criminal law is the applicable law. Yet, adopting the criteria set out by the SCSL, it may also be possible to argue that the ICLS falls short of the definition of an international criminal court. First, unlike the ICC which derives its mandate from a treaty open to the international community, the ICLS derives its mandate from the Protocol whose provisions bind only those of the 54 AU member states that opt to sign and ratify it. Secondly, unlike the ICTY, ICTR, and the Special Tribunal for Lebanon (STL) the mandate of the ICLS is not derived from UN Security Council resolutions. Thirdly, unlike the SCSL, the Extraordinary Chambers in the Courts of Cambodia (ECCC), the ICLS was not created pursuant to an agreement between the African Union and the United Nations which could suggest an agreement with the international community. Regardless of the position adopted, it is clear that the ICLS is bound by the provisions of the Protocol in determining the relevance or irrelevance of immunities of state officials.

II   "No Charges Shall be Commenced or Continued before the Court against Any Serving AU Head of State or Government"

In light of the foregoing, it is apparent that the first clause in Article 46A*bis* does not deviate from current international law. In other words, there is nothing in international law which prohibits inclusion of provisions such as Article 46A*bis* in the Protocol, and doing so does not derogate from a peremptory norm.

Even so, however, the rationale behind the inclusion of this clause in Article 46A*bis* raises a number of concerns. During a press conference on 11 July 2014, Vincent Nmehielle, the Legal Counsel and Director for Legal Affairs of the African Union Commission revealed that the rationale behind the inclusion of Article 46A*bis* was to extend, to the regional court, immunities recognized in international law which prevent prosecution of sitting Heads of State or Government in domestic courts. He stated that member states expressed the

---

is bound by the instrument removing the immunity. Therefore, a senior serving state official entitled to immunity ratione personae (for example, a head of state is entitled to such immunity before an international tribunal that the state concerned has not consented to." Akande, *supra* note 19 at 418–419.

sentiment that "we want that principle that applies in domestic courts [for] other sovereigns ... we want to preserve that for the regional mechanism".[40] He also noted that Article 46A*bis* was a compromise as the initial proposition was to accord 'blanket immunity' to Heads of State or Government which would continue after their term in office.

The introduction of a principle which applies in domestic courts to the statute of the African Court has, as one of its effects, the restriction of access to the region's court of last resort for victims where the accused is an incumbent Head of State or Government. Many African states have included immunity for incumbent Heads of State or Government in domestic legislation. When such Heads of State or Government are accused of committing crimes such as genocide, crimes against humanity and corruption of a "serious nature affecting the stability of a state, region or the Union,"[41] they are immune from prosecution within their legal systems for the duration of their term in office. Since international law has not yet recognized an exception to immunity from foreign courts for international crimes, victims would not have recourse to the long arm of the law by petitioning the courts of AU member states. With the inclusion of Article 46A*bis* in the Protocol, the option remaining for victims is to wait for the Head of State or Government in question to step down, be deposed, or submit a request to the ICC Prosecutor where that State is a state party to the Rome Statute. It is observed that the jurisdiction of the African Court was extended to international crimes to address the alleged "targeting" of African leaders by the ICC. It seems ironic that, after the introduction of Article 46A*bis*, the option left for victims in the case of incumbent Heads of State or Government remains the ICC.

III "... Or Anybody Acting or Entitled to Act in Such Capacity"

In 2013, Kenya proposed an amendment to Article 27 of the Rome Statute which would introduce immunity for Heads of State or Government, "their deputies and anybody acting or is entitled to act as such" during their term in

---

[40] Press Conference on the AU Summit Decision on the Protocol on African Court of Human and Peoples Rights, 11 July 2014 at 11:30 a.m. (GMT +3). *Available at*: http://new.livestream.com/accounts/2466140/events/3177260.

[41] Article 28I of the Protocol.

office.⁴² This proposal was supported by the AU which decided at its 11–12 October 2013 Extraordinary Summit on ICC that:⁴³

> To safeguard the constitutional order, stability and, integrity of Member States, no charges shall be commenced or continued before any International Court or Tribunal against any serving AU Head of State or Government or anybody acting or entitled to act in such capacity during their term in office.

The second clause in Article 46A*bis* is a reflection of this 2013 decision and proposal by the Kenyan Government. This clause appears to extend personal immunity to deputies, assignees and conceivably any person who has been authorized to act in the capacity of a Head of State or Government. Such a provision could apply for instance to heads of transitional governments, or a vice-president acting in the place of an incapacitated president. While the text does not include qualifications on who "is acting or entitled to act" one could logically interpret this clause as requiring any assignment of authority to be predicated upon constitutional provisions or domestic legislation of the State. Such an interpretation would preclude those who succeed Heads of State or Government in violation of constitutional provisions from claiming immunity on the basis that they are 'acting' in such capacity. Examples include the installation of military officials as Heads of Government following a coup d'état, or the succession of a relative following the death of the Head of State. An illustration of the latter is Joseph Kabila's succession to the presidency of the DRC after his father's assassination in January 2001. It was reported that this succession was the realization of Laurent Kabila's wishes expressed prior to his death.⁴⁴ The requirement that the individual who 'acts' in the capacity of a

---

42 Submission by the Republic of Kenya on Amendments to Rome Statute of the International Criminal Court for Consideration by the Working Group on Amendments, UN Doc. C.N.1026.2013.TREATIES-XVIII.10 (Depositary Notification), 14 March 2014. *Available at*: https://treaties.un.org/doc/Publication/CN/2013/CN.1026.2013-Eng.pdf.

43 Extraordinary Session of the Assembly of the African Union, Decision on Africa's Relationship with The International Criminal Court (ICC), Ext/Assembly/AU/Dec.1 (Oct.2013). *Available at*: http://www.iccnow.org/documents/Ext_Assembly_AU_Dec_Decl_12Oct2013.pdf.

44 Joseph Kabila's presidency was affirmed by the 2002 Global and Inclusive Agreement of Sun City, South Africa which ended the Second Congo War. The Agreement provided that "[t]o ensure the stability of the transitional institutions, the President, the Vice-Presidents and the Presidents of the National Assembly and the Senate shall remain in office during the whole transitional period, unless they resign, die, are impeached, or convicted

Head of State must represent the expression of the people following free and fair elections, or a legal appointment process should be read into this provision.

The word "entitled" also raises some confusion since the concept of entitlement could extend to a broad range of individuals.[45] It is proposed that the African Court should be the final arbiter in this matter, requiring the claimant to identify a legal basis for his or her claim to entitlement. The Court could consider whether, independent of the individual's assertions, based on domestic legislation and international law, the individual seeking immunity was entitled to represent the state. In doing so, the Court could consider whether an entitlement can be recognized under special circumstances (for example a president who was deposed by a military coup and is still recognized as such by the international community).

IV   "Or Other Senior State Officials Based on Their Functions, During Their Tenure of Office"

The third clause in Article 46A*bis* is open to at least two interpretations. The first possible interpretation is that it is the function of the state official which qualifies him or her for the "class" of senior state officials granted personal immunity under the Protocol. Such an interpretation would be consistent with the findings of the ICJ in the *Arrest Warrant* case. The ICJ observed that in order to determine the extent of the immunities accorded to a minister for foreign affairs, it was necessary to consider the nature of his or her functions. It noted that:[46]

> He or she is in charge of his or her Government's diplomatic activities and generally acts as its representative in international negotiations and intergovernmental meetings. Ambassadors and other diplomatic agents carry out their duties under his or her authority. His or her acts may bind the State represented, and there is a presumption that a Minister for Foreign Affairs, simply by virtue of that office, has full powers to act on behalf of the State (see, for example, Article 7, paragraph 2 (a), of the 1969

---

for high treason, misappropriation of public funds, extortion or corruption." Presidential elections were eventually held in 2006.

45   An argument, certainly on the outer limits of potential claims, could be made by paramount chiefs and kings who, based on the customary law origins of their title prior to colonization, may be perceived as 'entitled' to act in the capacity of a Head of State.

46   Arrest Warrant case, *supra* note 9, paras 53–54.

Vienna Convention on the Law of Treaties). In the performance of these functions, he or she is frequently required to travel internationally, and thus must be in a position freely to do so whenever the need should arise. He or she must also be in constant communication with the Government, and with its diplomatic missions around the world, and be capable at any time of communicating with representatives of other States. The Court further observes that a Minister for Foreign Affairs, responsible for the conduct of his or her State's relations with all other States, occupies a position such that, like the Head of State or the Head of Government, he or she is recognized under international law as representative of the State solely by virtue of his or her office. He or she does not have to present letters of credence: to the contrary, it is generally the Minister who determines the authority to be conferred upon diplomatic agents and countersigns their letters of credence. Finally, it is to the Minister for Foreign Affairs that chargés d'affaires are accredited.

The Court accordingly concludes that the functions of a Minister for Foreign Affairs are such that, throughout the duration of his or her office, he or she when abroad enjoys full immunity from criminal jurisdiction and inviolability.

The second possible interpretation is that immunity is granted on the basis of *what is done*, rather than *who* performs the act. If this interpretation is correct then the individual would be granted functional immunity.

The apparent absence of a basis in international law for the extension of immunities to "senior state officials" was discussed during the meetings of the African Union Specialized Technical Committee (STC) on Justice and Legal Affairs[47] which debated the Protocol. The delegates "raised concerns regarding extension of immunities to senior state officials and its conformity with international law, domestic laws of Member States and jurisprudence, underlining the challenges inherent in widening immunities and especially considering the lack of a precise definition of 'senior state official,' as well as the difficulty in providing an exhaustive list of persons who should be included in the category of senior state officials".[48] The ensuing report notes that:[49]

---

[47] The Report, The Draft Legal Instruments and Recommendations of the Specialized Technical Committee on Justice and Legal Affairs, EX.CL/846(XXV). *Available at*: http://justsecurity.org/wp-content/uploads/2014/07/Legal-Instruments-Adopted-in-Malabo-July-2014.pdf.
[48] Id., para. 25.
[49] Id., para. 26.

> After exhaustive deliberations, taking into consideration the relevant Decisions of the Assembly of the Union, and appreciating that some senior state officials are entitled to *functional immunities* by virtue of their functions, the meeting resolved that Article 46A*Bis* should include the provision "senior state officials based on their functions." The meeting further resolved that interpretation of "senior state official" would be determined by the Court, on a case-by-case basis taking their functions into account in accordance with international law. (Emphasis added).

During the press conference of 11 July 2014, Mr. Nmehielle confirmed the interpretation that this clause grants some senior state officials functional immunity.[50]

This second interpretation is markedly different from the first. Functional immunities, or as Cassese termed them "organic immunities",[51] apply only to official acts and would not shield the holder from prosecution for acts performed in his or her private capacity. If "senior state officials" are awarded functional immunity under Article 46A*bis* it would be incorrect to state that such immunity is only available "during their tenure of office". Furthermore, the question at the heart of functional immunity is whether the acts in question are official acts; the seniority of the individual is inconsequential.

Discussion on the effect of functional immunity on international criminal jurisdiction has often included an assessment of whether the acts in question could be considered "official acts." Could the acts, over which the African Court has jurisdiction, be considered official acts for the purposes of recognizing functional immunity? Article 28A enumerates the Court's international criminal jurisdiction, noting that:

> Subject to the right of appeal, the International Criminal Law Section of the Court shall have power to try persons for the crimes provided hereunder:

---

50 *Supra* note 40. Nmehielle noted that "if you look at that provision it says based on their functions. Now that accords with international law principle that ... accords functional immunity to a person who performs a particular function." He stated "... functional immunity does not apply to every Tom, Dick and Harry. It applies to those whose specific functions, by virtue of those functions under international law enables them to enjoy some immunity. It is not every general who would be entitled to immunity. It is not every soldier who says 'well I've risen to a high rank,' or not even every minister. ... It is an issue of fact and law to be determined by a constituted court and there is a plethora of precedents on functional immunity."

51 Cassese, *supra* note 21, at 862.

1) Genocide
2) Crimes Against Humanity
3) The Crime of Unconstitutional Change of Government
4) Piracy
5) Terrorism
6) Mercenarism
7) Corruption
8) Money Laundering
9) Trafficking in Persons
10) Trafficking in Drugs
11) Trafficking in Hazardous Wastes
12) Illicit Exploitation of Natural Resources
13) The Crime of Aggression

The idea that international crimes could be considered official acts protected by functional immunity has been rejected in some national courts[52] and by some scholars.[53] In 2000, the Amsterdam Court of Appeal held in *Bouterse* that "[t]he commission of very serious offences as are concerned here – cannot be considered to be one of the official duties of a head of state."[54] Speaking with respect to the crime of torture and its prohibition under the Torture Convention, Lord Browne-Wilkinson stated in *Re Pinochet*:[55]

> How can it be for international law purposes an official function to do something which international law itself prohibits and criminalises? ...

---

52   See for example *Attorney General v. Adolf Eichmann*, Judgment of the Supreme Court of Israel of 29 May 1962, in 36 ILR, 277–342 and *Fédération National des Déportées et Internés Résistants et Patriotes and Others v. Barbie*, 78 ILR 125 (Court of Cassation (Criminal Chamber), 1983 and 1984). Cassese for instance observes that many of these cases "where military officials were brought to trial before foreign courts demonstrate that state agents accused of war crimes, crimes against humanity or genocide may not invoke before national courts, as a valid defence, their official capacity." *Supra* note 21 at 870.

53   See for example Cassese, *supra* note 21 at 870–874.

54   Wijngaarde et al. v. Bouterse, Court of Appeal, Amsterdam, 20 November 2000, LJN: AA8395, available at http://ljn.rechtspraak.nl. English translation provided by the International Commission of Jurists. *Available at*: https://www.icrc.org. Desi Bouterse, Surinamese Head of State, was charged with ordering his military to execute fifteen people in Suriname in December 1982. For more information see Elies Van Sliedregt, *International Crimes before Dutch Courts: Recent Developments*, Leiden J. Int'l L., 20 (2007), pp. 895–908.

55   Judgment – Regina v. Bartle and the Commissioner of Police for the Metropolis and Others Ex Parte Pinochet, 38 I.L.M. 581 (H.L. 1999).

> [A]n essential feature of the international crime of torture is that it must be committed "by or with the acquiescence of a public official or other person acting in an official capacity." As a result all defendants in torture cases will be state officials. Yet, if the former head of state has immunity, the man most responsible will escape liability while his inferiors (the chiefs of police, junior army officers) who carried out his orders will be liable. I find it impossible to accept that this was the intention.
>
> ... if the implementation of a torture regime is a public function giving rise to immunity ratione materiae, this produces bizarre results. Immunity ratione materiae applies not only to ex-heads of state and ex-ambassadors but to all state officials who have been involved in carrying out the functions of the state.

In their joint separate opinion in the *Arrest Warrant* case Judges Higgins, Koijmans and Beurgenthal also noted that:[56]

> It is now increasingly claimed in the literature [...] that serious international crimes cannot be regarded as official acts because they are neither normal State functions nor functions that a State alone (in contrast to an individual) can perform [...]. This view is underscored by the increasing realization that State-related motives are not the proper test for determining what constitutes public state acts. The same view is gradually also finding expression in State practice, as evidenced in judicial decisions and opinions.

Not everyone agrees with the position that international crimes cannot be considered official acts. Article 7 of the International Law Commission's Articles on State Responsibility provides that "[t]he conduct of an organ of a state or of a person or entity empowered to exercise elements of the governmental authority shall be considered an act of the state under international law if the organ, person or entity acts in that capacity, even if it exceeds its authority or contravenes instructions."[57] According to Akande and Shah:[58]

---

[56] Arrest Warrant case, *supra* note 9, Joint Separate Opinion of Judges Higgins, Kooijmans and Buergenthal, para. 85.

[57] Article 7, Responsibility of States for Internationally Wrongful Acts (2001), Yearbook of the International Law Commission, 2001, vol. II (Part Two).

[58] Dapo Akande and Sangeeta Shah, *Immunities of State Officials, International Crimes, and Foreign Domestic Courts*, 21 Eur.J.Int'l L. (2011) 815–852 at 832.

whether or not acts of state officials are regarded as official acts does not depend on the legality, in international or domestic law, of those acts. Rather, whether or not the acts of individuals are to be deemed official depends on the purposes for which the acts were done and the means through which the official carried them out.

They argue that if those acts were performed in furtherance of the policies of the State, and carried out using the state apparatus, then they are considered official acts.[59] Judge van den Wyngaert expressed the same view in her dissenting opinion in the *Arrest Warrant* case, noting that "[s]ome crimes under international law (e.g. certain acts of genocide and of aggression) can, for practical purposes, only be committed with the means and mechanisms of a State and as part of a State policy. They cannot, from that perspective, be anything other than 'official' acts."[60]

Perhaps what matters the most is not so much the characterization of the acts as "official acts", but rather whether the individual can be held criminally responsible. It submitted that state officials, regardless of whether they commit international crimes in furtherance of state policies or in their personal capacities, are individually responsible for these crimes. The fact that these crimes were committed at the behest of the Government and are also attributable to the State does not relieve the individual of responsibility. This view is consistent with the position that the evolution of international law has led to the recognition of individuals as subjects of international law.[61] They too, just as States, can violate international norms, and can be held responsible.

---

59 Id.
60 Arrest Warrant case, *supra* note 9, Dissenting Opinion of Judge van den Wyngaert, para.36. She notes that "[i]mmunity should never apply to crimes under international law, neither before international courts nor national courts. I am in full agreement with the statement of Lord Steyn in the first *Pinochet* case, where he observed that: '[i]t follows that when Hitler ordered the 'final solution' his act must be regarded as an official act deriving from the exercise of his functions as Head of State. That is where the reasoning of the Divisional Court inexorably leads."
61 See P.K Menon, *Individuals as Subjects of International Law*, in Revue de Droit International, de Sciences Diplomatiques et Politiques, Vol. 70, Issue 4, 295–327; and Andrew Clapham, *The Role of the Individual in International Law*, 21 Eur. J. Int'l L 25–30. Clapham states "So we find the individual as the bearer of individual obligations under international criminal law in the context of international armed conflicts. Almost 50 years later, in the Tadic decision of the Appeals Chamber of the International Criminal Tribunal for the former Yugoslavia, the idea is applied to individual criminal responsibility for certain violations of humanitarian law committed in non-international armed conflicts. By 2002 we have a Statute in force for a permanent International Criminal Court with jurisdiction

In the context of the Protocol, this view does not do violence to the object and purpose of the instrument. Instead it brings Article 46A*bis* in conformity with Article 46B. Article 46(B)(1) provides that "[a] person who commits an offence under this Statute shall be held individually responsible for the crime". Furthermore, Article 46B(2) notes that "[s]ubject to the provisions of Article 46A*bis* of this Statute, the official position of any accused person shall not relieve such person of criminal responsibility nor mitigate punishment." Finally, Article 46B(4) provides that "[t]he fact that an accused person acted pursuant to the order of a Government or of a superior shall not relieve him or her of criminal responsibility, but may be considered in mitigation of punishment if the Court determines that justice so requires." Article 46B(4) refers to the defence of superior orders. It also, by extension, recognizes that functional immunity cannot apply to relieve an individual of criminal responsibility for the acts.

In light of the Report which notes that the intent of the drafters was to afford functional immunity to senior state officials, Article 46A*bis* should be understood as affording a modified form of functional immunity to certain "senior state officials," or rather, extending the regime of personal immunity to certain "senior state officials". Unlike *true* functional immunity, "senior state officials" are not afforded a substantive defense under the Protocol. Pursuant to Article 46(B)(2) and (4) they will be held individually responsible for the crimes regardless of whether these acts are considered official acts. As provided in Article 46A*bis*, the immunity afforded to them exists only during their tenure in office.

The final question of which "senior state official" is entitled to immunity under the Protocol should be carefully addressed by the African Court with the goal of construing the term narrowly. More than before ministers, senators, and other government officials engage in international activities on behalf of their governments. Seniority among government officials can be a nebulous concept, and there are insufficient precedents to support the conclusion that all holders of ministerial appointments, or members of parliament, for example, are entitled to personal immunity.[62] Such a view is consistent with the

---

over individuals covering not only war crimes but also genocide and crimes against humanity," p. 27. According to Ian Brownlie "[t]here is no general rule that the individual cannot be a "subject of international law", and in particular contexts he appears as a legal person on the international plane." Principles of International Law, 7th edition, 2008, at 65.

62 The Netherlands Ministry of Foreign Affairs, Advisory Committee on Issues of Public International Law observed that "[i]n view of the growing acceptance described in chapter 3 that punishment for international crimes should, in principle, take precedence over

judgment of the ICJ in *Djibouti v. France*.[63] In that case Djibouti challenged the issuance of witness summons by France to the Procureur de la République and the Head of National Security of Djibouti, asserting that these summons violated the immunities held by these state agents.[64] The ICJ noted that "there are no grounds in international law upon which it could be said that the officials concerned were entitled to personal immunities, not being diplomats within the meaning of the Vienna Convention on Diplomatic Relations of 1961, and the Convention on Special Missions of 1969 not being applicable in this case."[65]

In determining criteria to define which senior state officials are entitled to claim immunity under the Protocol, the African Court may wish to obtain guidance from paragraphs 53–54 of the ICJ judgment in the *Arrest Warrant* case noted above. An in-exhaustive list of criteria could include:

a. whether the "senior state official" acts as a representative of his or her Government in international negotiations and intergovernmental meetings;
b. whether the performance of his or her functions requires frequent international travel; and
c. whether his or her acts bind the State represented.

Conclusion

The inclusion of Article 46A*bis* in the Protocol comes in the wake of several AU decisions emphasizing respect for the immunity of Heads of State or Govern-

---

immunity, the CAVV advocates that extreme caution should be observed when considering whether to expand the categories of persons entitled to claim personal immunity. The CAVV is therefore not in favor of granting the personal immunities presently enjoyed by incumbent heads of state, heads of government and ministers of foreign affairs to other government ministers, ministers of parliament, heads of national administrative authorities and (high-ranking) officials." *Supra* note 7 at 31, para. 4.3.1.

63 *Certain Questions of Mutual Assistance in Criminal Matters (Djibouti v. France)*, Judgment, ICJ Reports 2008, p. 177.

64 Djibouti initially contended that the Procureur de la République and the Head of National Security benefited from personal immunities from criminal jurisdiction. It then argued on the basis of functional immunity stating that "it is a principle of international law that a person cannot be held individually criminally liable for acts performed as an organ of State, and while there may be certain exceptions to that rule, there is no doubt as to its applicability in the present case." Id., para. 185.

65 Id., para. 194.

ment before the International Criminal Court. This paper has examined the extent to which Article 46A*bis* detracts from international law and finds that international law does not preclude the recognition of the inviolability of Heads of State or Government before international courts and tribunals. However, Article 46A*bis* goes a step further and possibly extends personal immunity to individuals hitherto unprotected by such immunity under international law. Whatever the motivation of the African Union, it is noted that the desire to accord immunity to certain state agents is not uniformly shared by African States. In July 2014 the Government of the Republic of Botswana issued a statement on the amendments to the Protocol on the Statute of the African Court of Justice and Human Rights. Clarifying that it is not a state party to the Statute establishing the African Court, Botswana noted that "the Summit decision in question runs contrary to Botswana's position on human rights as well as the principles of human rights as enshrined in the African Union's own instruments, and other international legal instruments towards the promotion of human rights".[66]

While immunity does not necessarily equate to impunity, the African Court has jurisdiction over crimes the majority of which are likely to require, at the very least, the acquiescence of state agents. The introduction of Article 46A*bis* thus raises legitimate questions on the extent to which the African Court is a viable option for the protection of victims of international crimes in Africa.

---

66   Republic of Botswana, Ministry of Foreign Affairs & International Cooperation, Gaborone: 03 July 2014. *Available at*: http://www.mofaic.gov.bw/index.php?option=com_content&view=category&id=13&Itemid=248.

CHAPTER 21

Africa and the International Criminal Court: Legitimacy and Credibility Challenges

Abdul Tejan-Cole

Introduction

The International Criminal Court (ICC) continues to face increasing criticism about its' singularly African case docket with all 9 active investigations (situations) and 21 prosecutions (cases) against Africans.[1] The overall prosecutorial strategy and the Court's expanding global reach in selecting situations has raised concerns about the legitimacy of the ICC and its ability to dispense impartial justice for crimes under its jurisdiction. The ICC's focus on Africa has prompted many within and beyond Africa to ask why it is only Africans facing justice in The Hague yet international crimes are prevalent in other parts of the world.

Some have gone so far as to accuse the ICC of being a neo-colonialist institution. In this narrative, the Court is accused of advancing a Western agenda that seeks to influence and control African politics through its ICC investigations and prosecutions. This perception of the ICC, held by some Africans and non-Africans alike and particularly by some individuals in countries where the ICC operates, should not be ignored. Supporters of the Court, which includes most victims, see it as the only avenue to hold certain military and political leaders accountable. They know all too well that without the ICC, impunity will prevail for state-sponsored and other mass crimes. In many African countries, it is impossible to prosecute the 'big men' in authority because of the enormous powers of the executive over the other state organs such as the judiciary and police and the intimidation of witnesses. However, there is need for a stronger complementarity agenda and more substantive engagement with African leaders, civil society and victims if the Court is to be successful and effective in administering justice in Africa.

---

[1] http://www.icc-cpi.int/en_menus/icc/situations%20and%20cases/Pages/situations%20 and%20cases.aspx (last visited on 15 November 2014).

Assessing the legitimacy[2] and fairness of ICC's pursuit of cases in Africa requires a more detailed analysis that goes beyond the geographical make-up of its case docket. This paper seeks to contribute to the debate by focusing on whether the Situations and Cases before the Court, despite being African in character, are justified from a legal standpoint. It also focuses on the jurisdictional limitations, including referrals and complementarity matters that have made it more likely that cases in Africa are more often pursued than elsewhere. This author takes the view that the ICC's focus on Africa is both necessary and appropriate. This approach, however, does not detract from legitimate calls for the Office of the Prosecutor (OTP), as the triggering force of ICC jurisdiction, to similarly pursue justice in other regions under its authority where international crimes have been committed. Victims everywhere deserve some form of national or international justice.

Ideally, victims should have recourse to justice and accountability in domestic courts that are more easily accessible to them and closer to the evidence, perpetrators, context and other necessary information. Countries in Africa would do well to pursue this option as this may indeed be the best means to curtail the ICC's intervention wherever crimes within its jurisdiction may be found. It is in recognition of this fact that the AU has encouraged states to strengthen their local justice systems by initiating programs of cooperation and capacity building, and training of members of their police and judiciary in order to enhance their legal capacity. In addition, the African Union recently adopted a model law on Universal Jurisdiction which gives national courts extended jurisdiction over the offences of genocide, crimes against humanity, war crimes, piracy, trafficking in narcotics and terrorism committed abroad provided that the accused person "shall be within the territory of the State at the time of the commencement of the trial."

While there are many reasons in favour of the ICC's involvement in Africa, we must not forget that such intervention signals foremost a failure of States, which have the primary responsibility to fairly and impartially investigate and prosecute crimes within their jurisdiction. Other reasons include widespread systematic conflicts on the continent, the nature of the crimes, lack of capacity due to partial or complete collapse of institutions in post-conflict societies or unwillingness to hold perpetrators accountable, thereby failing to provide redress to victims. The Court's delicate relationship with Africa highlights its role in on-going conflicts and the present geopolitics between Africa and the West

---

[2] Legitimacy is assessed by examining inter alia the function, output, fairness and prosecutorial discretion of the Court.

through referrals and deferrals by the United Nations Security Council ("UNSC").

This paper begins with a background on the ICC's jurisdictional issues and then proceeds to review the OTP's preliminary examinations and discusses whether intervention in those non-African countries is appropriate. The paper then concludes with an examination of African States Parties positive actions in bringing Situations currently before the Court, to illustrate the misperception of alleged African bias. Notwithstanding its broader geographical scope of open preliminary examinations, given the nascent character of this international institution, it is argued that it is too early to substantively judge its trajectory and ability to deliver justice beyond Africa.

The ICC's Involvement in Africa

Jurisdiction

Founded on the principle of complementarity, the Rome Statute recognizes the primary responsibility of national systems and the complementary role of ICC only where the relevant state is either unwilling or unable to investigate or prosecute international crimes.[3] Having been hailed as the first permanent international criminal court, there are many misconceptions about the scope of ICC's powers and consequently expectations of its ability to take action in any part of the world. In reality, the Court has inherent jurisdictional limitations and capacity constraints that prevent it from acting against all individuals and in all situations where ICC intervention is desirable; not to mention enforcement challenges which are central to ICC's effectiveness in those areas where it decides to operate. Ensuring enforcement of ICC decisions is the collective responsibility of the international community.

Personal or Territorial Jurisdiction

Principally, the ICC lacks universal jurisdiction to make it a truly global institution. While that remains an achievable goal, with a membership of 122 State Parties,[4] the Court cannot choose to automatically assert territorial or personal jurisdiction to open investigations and therefore prosecutions in the 71 other countries within the United Nations ("UN") system or against their nationals. Those non-State Parties beyond the ICC's reach include Syria, Israel and Iraq,

---

3 Preamble of the Rome Statute.
4 http://www.icc-cpi.int/en_menus/asp/states%20parties/Pages/the%20states%20parties%20to%20the%20rome%20statute.aspx (last visited on 14 November 2014).

as well as powerful nations like Russia, China and the United States of America. The only way the ICC can assert jurisdiction over non-State Parties is where it is invited by that State through a formal declaration or by the UNSC using its chapter VII powers under the UN Charter.[5] In other words, beyond serious crimes conducted on the territory of a State Party or involving a State Party's nationals,[6] the ICC's ability to intervene is seriously hampered. Considering its present predicament, Syria provides a good illustration – the ICC's possible intervention is solely dependent on a referral by the UNSC since it is improbable that the Assad regime will declare an acceptance of the Court's jurisdiction. It is unlikely that this will happen soon as Russia, and possibly China, would likely use their veto to prevent ICC intervention. Thus illustrating that part of the problem affecting the perception of the ICC as an impartial judicial entity, is more political than legal.

Subject Matter and Temporal Jurisdiction

The ICC's jurisdiction is further limited to war crimes, crimes against humanity and genocide[7] occurring from July 2002.[8] Therefore the Court does not have subject-matter jurisdiction over other serious crimes such as terrorism or piracy; whilst for non-State Parties, the referring authority[9] can further limit the ICC's temporal jurisdiction to a period after July 2002. The reality is that the ICC and other international tribunals cannot prosecute everyone involved in the various conflicts, many of which find their bases in historical injustices or infighting that are well beyond the temporal jurisdiction of the ICC. Even then, from July 2002, there have been several major incidents within the 122 ICC states parties that may meet the threshold to warrant the Court's intervention. The majority of these have been conflicts in Africa.

To a large extent, in practical terms, the method of referral determines the level of state cooperation that the OTP can expect to receive for its investigations and prosecutions from the affected government. State cooperation includes access to crime scenes, victims, official records, witness protection, enforcement of arrest warrants and securing witness attendance in court. This reality favours self-referrals and voluntary acceptance of jurisdiction by non-

---

5 Articles 12 and 13 of the Rome Statute.
6 Articles 12 and 13 of the Rome Statute.
7 The Court will only have jurisdiction over the crime of aggression in 2017 after the State Parties activate this provision.
8 Articles 5 and 11 of the Rome Statute.
9 Either of the UN Security Council or non-State Party declaration.

State Parties over and above UNSC referrals and the Prosecutor's unprompted powers to open investigations and initiate proceedings (*proprio motu*).

Complementarity

In its interventions, the ICC must respect the principle of complementarity, which the OTP defines as:

> an examination of the existence of relevant national proceedings in relation to the potential cases being considered for investigation by the Office, taking into consideration the Office's policy to focus on those who appear to bear the greatest responsibility for the most serious crimes. Where relevant domestic investigations or prosecutions exist, the Prosecution will assess their genuineness.[10]

This means that inaction by state law enforcement authorities mandates the Court to act. Any State action is subject to an assessment of its ability to administer justice and whether or not it is intended to shield an individual from accountability. The ICC's Appeals Chamber has adopted a same person /same conduct test, which requires the national investigation or prosecution of the same individual for the same crimes, in order to determine whether a case currently before the Court should be inadmissible.[11] In the Libya case, the Appeals Chambers stated that "(T)o be successful, this challenge must be able to show what is being investigated by the State (the contours or parameters of the case) such that the Court is able to compare this against what is being investigated by the Prosecutor. It may be that those contours will develop as time goes on, but again, any investigation, irrespective of its stage, will have defining parameters. If a State is imable to present such parameters to the Court, no assessment of whether the same case is being investigated can be meaningfully made. In such circumstances, it would be unreasonable to suggest that the Court should accept that an investigation, capable of rendering a case inadmissible before the Court, is underway."[12]

---

10   OTP Report on Preliminary Examinations, November 2012, pages 3–4: http://www.icc-cpi.int/NR/rdonlyres/C433C462-7C4E-4358-8A72-8D99FD00E8CD/285209/OTP2012ReportonPreliminaryExaminations22Nov2012.pdf (last visited on 14 November 2014).

11   Judgment on the appeal of the Republic of Kenya against the decision of Pre-Trial Chamber II of 30 May 2011 entitled "Decision on the Application by the Government of Kenya Challenging the Admissibility of the Case Pursuant to Article 19(2)(b) of the Statute" Para. 1 at page 3.

12   In the Case of the Prosecutor V. Saif Al-Islam Gaddafi and Abdullah Al-Senussi No. ICC-01/11–01/11 OA 4, http://www.icc-cpi.int/iccdocs/doc/doc1779877.pdf.

The conventional wisdom is that the ICC can only prosecute the very senior persons among alleged perpetrators while national courts can focus on other alleged perpetrators. The OTP's policy of charging the person(s) most responsible, based on the complementarity principle and guided by some measure of realism, inevitably means that even in spite of the Court's intervention, its capacity constraints will result in some victims being denied access to justice unless states shoulder their primary responsibility to hold perpetrators accountable. The OTP's new investigation strategy signals a possible shift towards first investigating and prosecuting mid and high-level or even possibly low-level perpetrators where their conduct has been particularly grave, before gradually building upwards to those bearing the greatest responsibility.[13] However, regardless of the Court's involvement, domestic action is indispensable for an effective international justice system. In addition, the Court will consider the sufficient gravity of the crimes by assessing the scale, nature, manner and impact of the alleged crimes; as well as the vague provision of 'interests of justice' to determine whether an investigation would not be desirable.[14]

ICC Situations and Cases – justified legal intervention

> With due respect, what offends me most when I hear criticisms about the so-called African bias is how quick we are to focus on the words and propaganda of a few powerful, influential individuals and to forget about the millions of anonymous people that suffer from these crimes ... because all the victims are African victims.
> FATOU BENSOUDA, *ICC Prosecutor*[15]

Even though any State Party can refer the situation of another state party to the Court, so far no state has done so outside of the UNSC framework. This is unlikely to change soon. Two Situations, Darfur (Sudan) and Libya, were referred by the UN Security Council, a global system subscribed to by 193 nations that

---

13   OTP strategic plan June | 2012–2015 issued on 11 October 2013, http://www.icc-cpi.int/en_menus/icc/structure%20of%20the%20court/office%20of%20the%20prosecutor/policies%20and%20strategies/Documents/OTP-Strategic-Plan-2012–2015.pdf, page 6.
14   OTP Report on Preliminary Examinations, November 2012, page 4: http://www.icc-cpi.int/NR/rdonlyres/C433C462–7C4E-4358–8A72–8D99FD00E8CD/285209/OTP2012Reporton-PreliminaryExaminations22Nov2012.pdf (last visited on 5 November 2013).
15   http://www.guardian.co.uk/law/2012/may/23/chief-prosecutor-international-criminal-court (last visited on 27 February 2013); and http://www.osisa.org/law/blog/law-tool-world-peace-and-security (last visited on 27 February 2013).

include 53 African States. Notably, 6 African States directly voted in favour of one or the other referral. Gabon, Nigeria and South Africa supported the Libyan referral,[16] while Algeria, Tanzania and Benin backed the Darfur referral.[17] African Countries which constitute the largest block of any continent with 34 State Parties, have referred 4 of the 8 Situations presently before the Court. These referrals regarding cases in Uganda, Democratic Republic of Congo, Central African Republic and Mali were made by their respective governments. Another African State, Cote d'Ivoire, accepted the Court's jurisdiction despite not being a state party to the Rome Statute at that time,[18] thereby inviting the Prosecutor to open investigations using *proprio motu* powers. In only one Situation, Kenya, has the OTP made a decision to intervene without direct prompting by the affected State Party or by the Security Council. This was only after sufficient time had been given to the Kenyan authorities by Kofi Annan and the panel of eminent African personalities[19] to take appropriate action to ensure accountability for the post-election violence of 2007. Even though to date all the ICC's 18 cases and all 29 persons publicly indicted are, so far, Africans, it is insincere to completely blame the ICC when African Governments have played a very active role in referring matters to the Court.

The core mandate of the ICC is "to put an end to impunity for the perpetrators of these crimes and thus to contribute to the prevention of such crimes."[20] As noted by the Court's Chief Prosecutor, Fatou Bensouda, in a recent meeting with NGOs in The Hague, rather than accusing the ICC of focusing on Africa, it is African states that are coming to the ICC for good reason.[21] African States Parties to the ICC presently contribute less than 1 per cent of the Court's budget yet African citizens are making significant use of the Court. The first ratification of the Rome Statute by any country was from Senegal, and this growing commitment by countries in Africa continued with subsequent self-referrals and strong State Cooperation. It is necessary to look at these situations separately in order to put the ICC's involvement in these countries into proper perspective.

---

16 http://www.un.org/News/Press/docs/2011/sc10187.doc.htm (last visited on 5 November 2013).
17 http://www.un.org/News/Press/docs/2005/sc8351.doc.htm (last visited on 5 November 2013).
18 Cote d'Ivoire subsequently became a State Party on 15 February 2013: http://www.icc-cpi.int/en_menus/icc/press%20and%20media/press%20releases/Pages/pr873.aspx (last visited on 5 November 2013).
19 http://kofiannanfoundation.org/kenya-national-dialogue-and-reconciliation.
20 Preamble of the Rome Statute.
21 ICC-NGO roundtable meeting that was held in The Hague, 29 May 2012.

Uganda

Uganda became the first country to make use of this new institution when, in December 2003, the government referred the situation involving atrocities committed by the Lord's Resistance Army (LRA) to the ICC.[22] This referral by the Ugandan government happened after a blanket amnesty in 2000, aimed at bringing the conflict to an end, had been granted to the LRA. The amnesty did not end the atrocities, thus leading the Ugandan President, Yoweri Museveni, to refer the Situation to the ICC. Of course, Museveni had other considerations in mind. He used it to build credibility with the West and he dangled the carrot of amnesty/local tribunal and stick of ICC throughout the subsequent 2006–7 peace negotiations, resulting in no peace for Northern Ugandans in the end.

In 2004, the ICC Prosecutor sought arrest warrants for the LRA leadership. The position of the OTP regarding the Ugandan Army, Uganda People's Defence Force ("UPDF"), remains uncertain. The official ICC position is that it has "investigated both sides but that the crimes committed by the UPDF do not meet the stringent 'gravity' test devised to ensure that the ICC only pursues the most egregious of criminals. The ICC maintains that according to their investigations, the crimes committed by the UPDF were neither systematic nor part of a military strategy with a command chain. It is also claimed that the UPDF committed fewer breaches than the LRA and that the soldiers responsible faced some measure of censure or punishment." It is unclear whether the investigation of the UPDF is still ongoing, so far the nature and gravity of the crimes committed by the LRA have led to arrest warrants only being issued against LRA commanders. The uncertainty regarding the UPDF and the decision by the former Prosecutor of the ICC to announce his investigation in the Uganda Situation with President Museveni by his side raised many questions about the objectivity and impartiality of the ICC.

In 2008, as part of a peace agreement with the LRA,[23] the Ugandan authorities took steps towards domestic accountability by establishing a War Crimes Division within the Uganda High Court. While the War Crimes Division has faced its fair share of challenges,[24] it presents a unique opportunity for complementarity between the ICC and a domestic justice system. With the level of

---

22 See http://www.icc-cpi.int/en_menus/icc/situations%20and%20cases/situations/situation%20icc%200204/Pages/situation%20index.aspx (last visited 15 November 2014).

23 Agreement on Accountability and Reconciliation signed in 2007 by the Ugandan government and LRA/M representatives at the Peace negotiations. http://www.amicc.org/docs/Agreement_on_Accountability_and_Reconciliation.pdf.

24 For example, the Division cannot try UPDF soldiers or officers implicated in any crime because of the parallel and primary role of the Court Martial system.

atrocities committed during the conflict in Uganda, the ICC could indeed maintain its arrest warrants for the LRA leadership – a couple of whom are already dead. To date, the ICC has had a positive relationship with the War Crimes Division as the OTP, engaged in positive complementarity, has assisted in capacity building efforts for its personnel judges in an effort to advance domestic action.[25] It remains to be seen, however, whether it will fulfil its promise to deliver domestic justice or remain hampered by decisions around amnesties.

Democratic Republic of Congo

The Democratic Republic of Congo ("DRC") has been ravaged by a protracted and complicated conflict for over a decade. By the Government's own admission, the Congolese judicial system is completely incapable of conducting any meaningful trials for alleged perpetrators of serious crimes. As a result, the government referred the Situation to the ICC in April 2004.[26] While the ICC's investigations have focused mainly on crimes committed in the Ituri and Kivu region of eastern Congo, there is a need for broader efforts to ensure accountability at the local level especially for serious crimes committed in the same region by persons other than those currently in ICC custody and in other parts of the country. Recent efforts to establish a hybrid tribunal in DRC have yet to yield success as law makers in the country cannot agree on a statute for this purpose.

Central African Republic

The situation in the Central African Republic ("CAR") is closely linked with the DRC as the subject of proceedings is the former Vice President of the DRC, Jean Pierre Bemba.[27] Bemba is being tried for crimes committed by his fighting forces who intervened in the CAR to help the former government of then President Ange Félix Patasse ("Patasse") fight against rebel forces. The then government in CAR referred the situation to the ICC in December 2004, stating clearly that CAR is unable to conduct credible investigations and prosecutions for serious crimes committed in the country's territory. Whereas Bemba was

---

25 OTP personnel presentation and ICC-NGO roundtable meeting in The Hague, 29 May 2012.

26 See http://www.icc-cpi.int/en_menus/icc/press%20and%20media/press%20releases/2004/Pages/prosecutor%20receives%20referral%20of%20the%20situation%20in%20the%20democratic%20republic%20of%20congo.aspx.

27 See http://www.icc-cpi.int/EN_Menus/ICC/Situations%20and%20Cases/Situations/Situation%20ICC%200105/Pages/situation%20icc-0105.aspx (last visited on 15 November 2014).

arrested, there was no significant attempt to indict his co-perpetrator, former CAR President, Patassé who passed away in April 2011.[28] After his arrest, Bemba challenged the ICC's jurisdiction to try him on the basis that local investigations had commenced in CAR prior to his arrest. In response, the CAR Government made oral and written submissions to ICC judges, stating that there had been no proceedings against Bemba in the CAR. The Government explained that although it had commenced proceedings against Mr Bemba, these were quickly abandoned due to his immunity as the vice-president of the DRC and thus the inability to prosecute him. The Appeals Chamber of the ICC eventually issued a decision stating that the case against Bemba could proceed to trial at the ICC.[29]

Kenya

Kenya presents the only situation where the ICC's Prosecutor, using his *proprio moto* powers, initiated investigations without the State's or UNSC's urging.[30] This followed the bitterly contested 2007 elections and the violence and commission of serious crimes that ensued. In this instance it can be argued that Kofi Annan in his role as peace mediator gave the Kenyan authorities significant time to institute domestic proceedings for the crimes within the ICC's purview. However, law makers could not agree on a bill to establish a hybrid tribunal within the domestic justice system and there were calls for "Don't be vague, let's go to The Hague".[31] Thus, the ICC prosecutor eventually brought charges against key political figures. The Kenyan government later filed admissibility challenges before the ICC explaining that it was in a position to conduct credible proceedings at the national level. The Pre-Trial Chamber ruled, and the Appeals Chamber confirmed, that the state had to prove that it was investigating the "same persons" and for the "same conduct" if it wanted remove the cases from the ICC jurisdiction. Subsequently, civil society and victims groups filed petitions against the government in Kenyan courts seeking compensation from the government for police shootings and sexual and gender based violence crimes committed by persons other than those who are now subjects of ICC proceedings.[32]

---

28 See http://www.theguardian.com/world/2011/jun/14/ange-felix-patasse-obituary.
29 Judgment on the appeal of Mr Jean-Pierre Bemba Gombo against the decision of Trial Chamber III of 24 June 2010 entitled "Decision on the Admissibility and Abuse of Process Challenges".
30 See http://www.icc-cpi.int/EN_Menus/ICC/Situations%20and%20Cases/Situations/Situation%20ICC%200109/Pages/situation%20index.aspx (last visited on 15 November 2014).
31 http://www.newsafrica.net/en/news/1489/kid-gloves-are-off.html.
32 http://www.capitalfm.co.ke/news/2013/02/pev-victims-file-case-for-compensation/.

As part of its judicial reform efforts, Kenya has also taken steps to establish a Serious Crimes Division within its justice system. Though with challenges, a witness protection agency has also been established and the Truth, Justice and Reconciliation Commission has a mandate to order reparations for victims of the post-election violence. These efforts, if properly and effectively managed, could have achieved significant complementarity objectives in Kenya. However, there has been little domestic action whilst proceedings at the ICC have been affected by allegations of unprecedented witness interference, which has so far culminated into the issuance of an arrest warrant for offences against the administration of justice.[33]

Côte d'Ivoire

In 2003 the Côte d'Ivoire government of Laurent Gbagbo submitted a declaration accepting the jurisdiction of the ICC for crimes committed from the start of the conflict in 2002, even though it was not a State Party to the ICC's Rome Statute at the time.[34] When violence escalated following disputed elections in 2010, the new government of Alassane Ouattara reaffirmed the 2003 declaration.[35] So far, the Court has issued arrest warrants for three persons in the country – former President Laurent Gbagbo, his wife Simone Gbagbo, and a member of his inner circle Charles Blé Goudé.[36] Laurent Gbagbo was taken into the custody of the ICC in November 2011. The Ivorian government has since brought charges in the national court against Simone Gbagbo and other alleged perpetrators of crimes.[37] Recently, judges at the ICC declined to confirm charges against the former president of Ivory Coast, Laurent Gbagbo, after the OTP failed to present compelling evidence linking him to crimes on the ground. Gbagbo remains in custody while the prosecution appeals against this decision. There have also been discussions on how the ICC and the national courts could complement each other as they conduct proceedings for different individuals.

---

33   http://www.icc-cpi.int/iccdocs/doc/doc1650592.pdf (last visited on 15 November 2014).
34   http://www.icc-cpi.int/EN_Menus/ICC/Situations%20and%20Cases/Situations/ICC0211/Pages/situation%20index.aspx (last visited on 14 November 2014).
35   http://www.icc-cpi.int/NR/rdonlyres/498E8FEB-7A72-4005-A209-C14BA374804F/0/ReconCPI.pdf (last visited on 14 November 2014).
36   http://www.icc-cpi.int/en_menus/icc/situations%20and%20cases/situations/icc0211/Pages/situation%20index.aspx (last visited on 14 November 2014).
37   In a recent report, Amnesty International accused the Ivorian Government of pursuing victor's justice. http://www.amnesty.org/en/library/asset/AFR31/001/2013/en/028f70d7-8f37-4a40-ad71-71c9e8369a41/afr310012013fr.pdf (last visited on 4 March 2013).

The previous prosecutor of the Court told NGOs at a meeting in May 2012 that his office was willing to collaborate with the Ivorian authorities in furtherance of their domestic accountability efforts.[38] This approach holds immense promise for complementarity as it is an example of how the ICC can better prosecute the senior commanders while national justice systems can focus on middle level or other perpetrators. It is a concern however, that investigations and prosecutions have only targeted one faction of the conflict – Gbagbo and his supporters, and this is the case for both the ICC and national proceedings. If accountability mechanisms, both at the ICC and national levels are to be credible, then they have to investigate all parties to the conflict, not just one faction.

Mali

Following calls for ICC intervention by the Economic Community of West African States ("ECOWAS"),[39] the Mali government became the latest country to refer a situation to the Prosecutor of the ICC.[40] Mali is still the site of an ongoing conflict and an uncontroverted fact is that the Malian justice system lacks the ability to investigate and prosecute crimes committed since the military coup of March 21, 2012.[41] In a statement, the Prosecutor urged 'the Malian authorities to put an immediate stop to the alleged abuses and on the basis of the principle of complementarity, to investigate and prosecute those responsible for the alleged crimes. "I remind all parties to the on-going conflict in Mali that my Office has jurisdiction over all serious crimes committed within the territory of Mali, from January 2012 onwards. All those alleged to be responsible for serious crimes in Mali must be held accountable."[42] Considering that there are on-going negotiations based on the June 18 Ouagadougou agreement (Preliminary Agreement to the Presidential Election and Inclusive Peace Talks in Mali) under which the transitional government of Dioncounda Traoré agreed with the MNLA to set a 60-day deadline after the establishment of the

---

38   Comments made by former Prosecutor of the ICC, Luis Moreno Ocampo, at the bi-annual ICC-NGO meeting in The Hague, May 29 2012.
39   http://www.icc-cpi.int/en_menus/icc/situations%20and%20cases/situations/icc0112/Documents/SASMaliArticle53_1PublicReportENG16Jan2013.pdf (last visited on 6 November 2014).
40   http://www.icc-cpi.int/NR/rdonlyres/A245A47F-BFD1-45B6-891C-3BCB5B173F57/0/ReferralLetterMali130712.pdf (last visited on 6 November 2014).
41   http://www.icc-cpi.int/en_menus/icc/situations%20and%20cases/situations/icc0112/Pages/situation%20index.aspx (last visited on 4 November 2014).
42   http://www.icc-cpi.int/en_menus/icc/press%20and%20media/press%20releases/news%20and%20highlights/Pages/otpstatement280113.aspx.

new government for the reopening of negotiations, it is very unlikely that the Malian justice system will be able to prosecute any of the negotiating parties. It may well be the case that without the ICC, prosecution may be unlikely. In the long run, as the ICC can only prosecute a few people, a strengthened Malian justice system will be in a position to ensure accountability for other alleged perpetrators outside the ICC. As the conflict ensues in the north, it will be important to assess the impact of the ICC on the peace negotiations.

UNSC Referrals: Sudan and Libya

Two complex situations are Darfur, Sudan[43] and Libya,[44] both countries that became the subject of ICC's jurisdiction based on referrals by the UNSC.

Sudan

In the case of Sudan, two suspects – Abdallah Banda Abakaer Nourain and Saleh Mohammed Jerbo Jamus, both of whom are commanders of a rebel faction in the Dafur region have already voluntarily subjected themselves to the ICC. A third rebel commander – Bahar Idriss Abu Garda also voluntarily submitted himself to the Court but no charges were confirmed against him. The Court's biggest challenge in the Sudan situation is how to execute the arrest warrants against persons who are affiliated with the Sudanese government, including the country's President, Omar al-Bashir.[45] A major controversy in the Sudan situation was the timing of the Prosecutor's announcement of an arrest warrant against President Al-Bashir. This decision led to discussions as to how the ICC could contribute to or undermine peace. Concerns have been expressed that the Court's action in this regard had a negative impact on peace efforts and humanitarian services in the Dafur region. The AU High-Level Panel on Darfur, headed by former South African President Thabo Mbeki ("Mbeki panel") set up to explore ways to secure peace, justice, and reconciliation in Darfur concluded that the "people of Darfur have suffered extreme violence and gross violations of human rights." The Mbeki panel recommended the establishment of a hybrid court comprising of Sudanese judges and judges appointed by the AU to prosecute the most serious crimes committed in Darfur. It also led to tensions between the ICC and the African Union as the latter in-

---

43   http://www.icc-cpi.int/EN_Menus/ICC/Situations%20and%20Cases/Situations/Situation%20ICC%200205/Pages/situation%20icc-0205.aspx (last visited on 4 March 2013).

44   http://www.icc-cpi.int/EN_Menus/ICC/Situations%20and%20Cases/Situations/ICC0111/Pages/situation%20index.aspx (last visited on 4 March 2013).

45   http://www.icc-cpi.int/en_menus/icc/situations%20and%20cases/situations/situation%20icc%200205/Pages/situation%20icc-0205.aspx (last visited 6 November 2013).

structed its member states not to cooperate with the ICC in the arrest of President Omar al-Bashir. According to the African Union, the Security Council refused to respond to its request for investigations to be deferred in the interest of peace in Dafur as provided for in Article 16 of the Rome Statute.[46] In spite of this, some African countries continue to express their support for the Court and co-operate with the OTP. While the issue of deferral remains a source of debate between the African Union, Security Council and the ICC, no guidelines have been tabled on what issues should be considered as being in the interest of peace and justice to warrant a deferral of an investigation by the Prosecutor of the Court.

Libya

The situation in Libya has also become very controversial after the UNSC referred the situation to the ICC. This followed efforts by revolutionary fighters to topple the regime of the late Muammar Gaddafi. The Prosecutor of the Court announced arrest warrants for Gaddafi, his son Saif Al Islam and his intelligence chief, Abdullah al-Sanusi. While Muammar Gaddafi was killed in the fighting, the new Libyan regime has insisted on prosecuting Saif Gaddafi and al-Sanusi in Libya instead of sending them to the ICC. In a decision advancing complementarity by allowing domestic measures where possible, the ICC judges recently allowed Libyan authorities to try al-Sanusi in Libya.[47] Conversely, the ICC judges denied Libya's attempt to try Saif Gaddafi in Libya, ruling that he should be surrendered to the Court.[48] Although both decisions are currently under appeal, the distinction made by the judges appears to be based on circumstances surrounding Saif's custody by rebels in Zintan versus Al-Sanusi's custody by Libyan authorities. Many have argued that al-Sanusi and Saif Gaddafi will not get fair trials in Libyan courts, with their respective defence teams arguing that they should be taken to The Hague. These arguments present new perspectives to the complementarity debate, including whether it is for the ICC to monitor defence rights or concerns in domestic proceedings. Reading the Rome Statute's complementarity provision, it establishes that domestic proceedings will be rated as credible if they are not meant to shield the accused person, with no mention of whether the proceedings are fair to the

---

46   See Africa and the International Criminal Court: Collision Course or Cooperation? Charles Chernor Jalloh North Carolina Central Law Review, Vol. 34, p. 203, 2012.
47   http://www.icc-cpi.int/iccdocs/doc/doc1663102.pdf (last visited on 6 November 2013).
48   http://www.icc-cpi.int/iccdocs/doc/doc1599307.pdf (last visited on 6 November 2013).

accused.[49] This has been a key argument advanced by lawyers working on behalf of the Libyan government.

The Libyan situation has also led to a debate on whether foreign forces intervening in a country's conflict must be held to account. Many have argued, and the previous prosecutor of the Court suggested, that it would be possible to investigate possible crimes committed by NATO forces in Libya in their efforts to assist revolutionary forces trying to topple the Gadaffi regime. We can only wait and see whether the Prosecutor of the Court will ever investigate NATO forces.

There have been suggestions that the Sudan and Libyan situations have been the most controversial because of the subjects of the Court's arrest warrants and the manner of their referrals – African heads of states referred by the UN Security Council. For some, especially a few African heads of states, the ICC has evolved into a political and a neo-colonial tool that is meant to target only Africans heads of state for regime change. Many have pointed to the crisis in Syria as an example of how selective the ICC's involvement in situations could be. It can be argued that accusations of ICC bias are misdirected. Prosecution of non-State Parties are less about the ICC and more to do with the UNSC – which has five veto wielding and ten non-veto states with the responsibility to refer situations for states that are not parties to the Rome Statute. As such, any accusation of bias in this regard is better directed towards the UNSC rather than the ICC.

ICC (Non-African) Preliminary Examinations

Beyond Africa, the OTP is conducting preliminary examinations in other continents that may result in Situations and Cases at the Court. A fundamental objective for the OTP is to "... consider, as a matter of policy, the extent to which its preliminary examination activities can stimulate genuine national proceedings against those who appear to bear the greatest responsibility for the most serious crimes."[50] This puts states on notice that the ICC will intervene once jurisdiction is established if national measures are not forthcoming. Outside the African continent, this current analysis affects Afghanistan, Honduras, Republic of Korea, Colombia, Georgia and Comoros as potential Situation coun-

---

49   See Article 17 (2) (a) of the Rome Statute.
50   http://www.icc-cpi.int/NR/rdonlyres/C433C462-7C4E-4358-8A72-8D99FD00E8CD/285209/OTP2012ReportonPreliminaryExaminations22Nov2012.pdf, page 5 (last visited on 5 November 2013).

tries.[51] The most advanced analysis, and therefore likely involvement of the Court outside Africa, relate to Colombia and Georgia where the OTP has already established that it has subject-matter jurisdiction.[52] For these two countries, the main reason for non-intervention by the ICC so far is due to ongoing domestic investigations and/or proceedings being undertaken by state authorities.

Colombia

The Situation in Colombia has been under preliminary examination since June 2004.[53] Following Colombia's ratification of the Rome Statute, the Court may exercise its jurisdiction over ICC crimes committed on the territory or by the nationals of Colombia since 1 November 2002 but its jurisdiction over war crimes is from 1 November 2009.[54] However, Colombia has enacted legislation and carried out investigations and prosecutions that have led to various convictions and sentences of different factions and this process is on-going.[55] For example, the OTP's last report on preliminary examinations notes, that "[a]ccording to the information available, a large number of FARC and ELN members, including senior leaders, have been the subject of national proceedings under the ordinary criminal justice system in Colombia."[56] The OTP continues to liaise with the Colombian authorities to monitor domestic efforts to ensure that those most responsible are brought to justice.

---

51 http://www.icc-cpi.int/NR/rdonlyres/C433C462-7C4E-4358-8A72-8D99FD00E8CD/285209/OTP2012ReportonPreliminaryExaminations22Nov2012.pdf (last visited on 5 November 2013).

52 http://www.icc-cpi.int/NR/rdonlyres/C433C462-7C4E-4358-8A72-8D99FD00E8CD/285209/OTP2012ReportonPreliminaryExaminations22Nov2012.pdf, page 6 (last visited on 5 November 2013).

53 http://www.icc-cpi.int/NR/rdonlyres/C433C462-7C4E-4358-8A72-8D99FD00E8CD/285209/OTP2012ReportonPreliminaryExaminations22Nov2012.pdf, page 23 (last visited on 5 November 2013).

54 See, Article 124 which allows a State to delay jurisdiction for war crimes for a period of 7 years after entry into force of the Rome Statute for that State; See, http://www.icc-cpi.int/NR/rdonlyres/C433C462-7C4E-4358-8A72-8D99FD00E8CD/285209/OTP2012ReportonPreliminaryExaminations22Nov2012.pdf, page 23 (last visited on 5 November 2013).

55 http://www.icc-cpi.int/NR/rdonlyres/C433C462-7C4E-4358-8A72-8D99FD00E8CD/285209/OTP2012ReportonPreliminaryExaminations22Nov2012.pdf, pages 25 to 28 (last visited on 5 November 2013).

56 http://www.icc-cpi.int/NR/rdonlyres/C433C462-7C4E-4358-8A72-8D99FD00E8CD/285209/OTP2012ReportonPreliminaryExaminations22Nov2012.pdf, page 26 (last visited on 5 November 2013).

Supporter of the ICC have tried to distinguish the current African situations by stating that in the African cases there were no domestic action taken or the actions taken fell short of addressing the most responsible for the specific crimes investigated by the OTP. Critics on the other hand accused the OTP for failing to work with African governments in the same way as it worked with the government of Columbia in the spirit of complementarity. As regards the 5 persons in the DRC Situation, Lubanga and Katanga were in pre-trial detention before and were under investigation by Congolese courts at the time of their transfer to the ICC. Ngudjolo had an arrest warrant issued against him by a Congolese military prosecutor but Congolese authorities opted to surrender him to the ICC instead of handing him to the Congolese judge. With Bosco Ntaganda, the ICC arrest warrant was issued before Congolese courts could act against him. Congolese civil society brought an action against him before a military prosecutor but the Congolese government sent a letter to all military and civilian prosecutors asking them not to act against any of the CNDP commanders after the 23 March 2009 agreement. Only Mbarushimana was either not formally prosecuted or beyond the reach of Congolese courts, leaving abroad. These cases clearly showed that the OTP never showed the same level of deference to Congolese authorities as it showed to Colombian authorities.

Georgia

The OTP began the preliminary examination of the situation in Georgia on 14 August 2008 following its ratification of the Rome Statute, thereby giving the Court jurisdiction as of 1 December 2003. At issue are the crimes committed during the August 2008 conflict between South Ossetian forces and the Georgian army, which led to the armed involvement of Russia. Both Georgia and Russia have since pursued seemingly relevant investigations into alleged crimes committed. However, there have been no prosecutions as both countries claim either the lack of cooperation by the other side, lack of access to the crime scene or immunity, as a barrier. As both countries continue their interactions with the OTP, the Prosecutor's decision to open a Situation is dependent on

> ... seeking clarification as to whether the respective investigations have halted; whether any additional information remains to be provided to the Office; and whether the lack of cooperation identified as an obstacle both by the Russian and Georgian authorities may be overcome through enhanced mutual legal assistance between the two States.

Once the OTP has established that investigations and/or prosecutions are not continuing especially in relation to the most responsible, the Court would have to intervene, unless it deemed that it would not be in the interests of justice to proceed. This illustrates that verifiable national measures serve the dual function of administering justice to victims by holding perpetrators accountable and keeping the ICC at bay. However, any such situation is subject to review by the ICC as events unfold in the domestic arena. Citing Central Africa Republic as an example, critics have pointed out that the OTP never sought clarification as to whether the investigations commenced by the government of Ange Félix Patesse had been halted but rushed to act as soon as Francoise Bozize installed himself as president and referred the matter to the ICC.

Conclusion

The existential legitimacy of the Court and its expanding jurisdiction should be a foregone conclusion. Through progressive ratification of the Rome Statute, the ICC has gained increasing acceptance that has solidified its guardianship of the international criminal justice regime. In fact, the adoption of a definition for the controversial crime of aggression in June 2010 that is pending implementation should be seen as a vote of confidence by the State Parties. Additionally, various non-State Parties have demonstrated faith in the Court by supporting Security Council referrals or declaring an acceptance of its jurisdiction. Although many criticize the Court's financial expenditure, there is growing recognition that accountability for the most serious international crimes is linked to their future prevention and sustainable peace.

The ICC's statutory complementarity role in international justice demonstrates its utility. The Court's focus on Africa in its first decade does not appear to have been deliberate but rather as a result of a combination of factors including State failure and self-referrals for which the ICC should not now be blamed, and whose intervention is justifiable and required. Through complementarity, the Court's intervention has been instrumental towards the garguntum task of ending impunity as States have been either unable or unwilling to take credible or verifiable national measures. Failures within the affected African States have occasioned the ICC's involvement. However, these States should be commended for noting their obligations and thus taking remedial measures through self-referrals. Yet States cannot merely delegate their responsibilities to the ICC without taking additional steps to combat impunity, such as implementing adequate legislation, investigating and prosecuting low and mid-level perpetrators, and exercising universal jurisdiction. At the thirteenth ordinary session of the Assembly of the African Union held in Libya on 1–3 July 2009, member states took a decision to encourage:

> Member States to initiate programmes of cooperation and capacity building to enhance the capacity of legal personnel in their respective countries regarding the drafting and safety of model legislation dealing with serious crimes of international concern, training of members of the police and the judiciary, and the strengthening of cooperation amongst judicial and investigative agencies.[57]

ICC is also having an impact on continental standard setting and also on peace processes. One of the reasons the Mali-MNLA peace deal did not have amnesty provisions was because of the existing ICC referral. Another very positive move has been steps recently taken by the African Union and Senegal in respect of the upcoming prosecution of the former Chadian President, Hissène Habré and the adoption by the AU of a model law on Universal Jurisdiction for incorporation by member states into their national jurisdictions to allow for the prosecution of international crimes in domestic courts.

Many who criticize the ICC for targeting Africans simultaneously denounce it for not prosecuting more cases or pursuing broader charges in the relevant African Situations. Indeed, the Court's intervention is absolutely essential in other parts of the globe. The OTP should address crimes under its jurisdiction where those States have failed to hold perpetrators accountable, thereby activating complementarity. Nevertheless, regardless of whether the ICC opens a Situation outside of Africa, the need to address the perception of alleged African bias is vital to its success in Africa. The OTP cannot afford to isolate the very people it seeks to help and who will assist in its mandate. The Court needs more substantive engagement with all levels of African society, from leaders to civil society to the general populace, in order to effectively investigate and prosecute crimes as well as contribute to their prevention. For example, the OTP should push for, rather than simply not oppose or generally support, conducting entire trials or key parts of the trials in locations proximate to affected victims. A more victim centred approach would bring greater legitimacy to the work of the Court and quell allegations of a Western agenda.

---

57   Decision on the Meeting of African States Parties to the Rome Statute of the International Criminal Court (ICC) Doc. Assembly/AU/13(XIII) http://www.au.int/en/sites/default/files/ASSEMBLY_EN_1_3_JULY_2009_AUC_THIRTEENTH_ORDINARY_SESSION_DECISIONS_DECLARATIONS_%20MESSAGE_CONGRATULATIONS_MOTION_0.pdf.

Considering also that the Court's location is distant from crime scenes, it must ensure a more constructive engagement with local civil society in order to reach and impact affected communities. Such engagement includes greater use of civil society as intermediaries in reaching out to victims' communities. For example, a major success of the Special Court for Sierra Leone, a hybrid tribunal established to investigate and prosecute crimes committed during Sierra Leone's bloody civil conflict, was the establishment and implementation of an effective outreach program. The Court's use of and engagement with local civil society to reach various communities around the country facilitated the successful conduct of trials, and winning the confidence of the public. It is only through such greater access by victims and potential perpetrators alike, that ICC trials can have a more meaningful impact.

International criminal justice system continues to be misunderstood by many in Africa. African politicians have succeeded in politicising it and linking international criminal justice to the politics around the ICC. At the inauguration of Uhuru Kenyatta as President of the Republic of Kenya, Uganda's President Yoweri Museveni declared,

> I want to salute the Kenyan voters on one issue – the rejection of the blackmail by the International Criminal Court (ICC) and those who seek to abuse this institution for their own agenda ... I was one of those that supported the ICC because I abhor impunity. However, the usual opinionated and arrogant actors using their careless analysis have distorted the purpose of that institution. They are now using it to install leaders of their choice in Africa and eliminate the ones they do not like.

Ironically, Museveni made the first self-referral to the ICC. His turnaround clearly shows that leaders will use the Court when it suits their political interest but dump it when it does not. It can also be argued that the courts own challenges – lack of outreach, limited resources, biased case selection, politicization and bias surrounding UN Security Council referrals has gradually eroded support for the Court across the Continent. It is important to note that many of the referrals by African States to the ICC were not done in the genuine pursuit of justice but as a means of settling internal political scores. In many instances, the ICC allowed itself to be used in this process. It may have avoided this in most cases by investigating and prosecuting those who referred the cases to it but it did not. The UN Security Council can help the court immensely by setting out and widely publicising objective criteria for its referrals. It is already bizarre that three out of the five permanent members of the UN Security Council do not see it fit to ratify the Rome Statute but can make referrals to the

Court. It gets worse when some of them wield their vetoes to protect their allies and defeat the ends of justice.

The ICC must combat this crisis of credibility, perceived or real, by administering objective and impartial justice in all cases and for all sides under its jurisdiction. For the ICC to regain ground it cannot simply rely on outreach through the Western media – and making a moral argument – or purist legal arguments after all the perpetrators have shown themselves to have a propensity for immorality and lawlessness. This is why there is an urgent need to promote a greater and broader acceptance of international criminal justice in Africa. There is no doubt in my mind that there is still immense passion amongst Africans to see justice done. The legitimate concern remains ICC's independence and neutrality as a vehicle to ensure that that justice is delivered impartially.

CHAPTER 22

International Criminal Justice Processes in Rwanda and Sierra Leone: Lessons for Liberia

Charles Chernor Jalloh and Andrew Morgan

1   Introduction

Although by no means unique, the late 20th century and early 21st century saw a spate of violent conflicts across Africa. These include the horrific genocide in Rwanda in 1994, the brutal civil wars in Liberia and Sierra Leone, and the ongoing conflicts in the Central African Republic (CAR), the Democratic Republic of Congo (DRC) and Uganda. In Rwanda and Sierra Leone, at the request of the national authorities, the "international community,"[1] as represented by the United Nations, sought to establish ad hoc mechanisms through which to prosecute the leading perpetrators of atrocities. Similarly, following in the footsteps of Rwanda and Sierra Leone, the CAR, DRC and Uganda have invited international intervention in their own territories, but not to set up special ad hoc courts. Rather, they referred their own situations to the Prosecutor of the Hague-based permanent International Criminal Court (ICC) in the hope that she will undertake further investigations and prosecutions.

This paper seeks to assess the role of the two ad hoc courts, the International Criminal Tribunal for Rwanda (ICTR) and the Special Court for Sierra Leone (SCSL or "the Special Court"), and their normative impact on the national communities in whose name they were created to render credible justice. It contrasts these two situations to that of Liberia, where a truth commission was established in lieu of criminal accountability. A key lesson we derive from the Rwanda and Sierra Leone accountability experiments is that a strong governmental commitment in the affected state is a necessary, if not sufficient, condition in the ongoing fight against impunity.

We proceed as follows. In Part II, in order to manage expectations, we set out the outer parameters of this study. Our argument is that the ad hoc

---

[1] For a deeper discussion on the loaded meaning of the term "international community," see, Edward Kwakwa, The International Community, International Law and the United States: Three in One, Two against One, or One and the Same? in United States Hegemony and the Foundations of International Law 25 (Michael Byers and George Nolte eds., Oxford Univ. Press 2008).

criminal courts for Rwanda and Sierra Leone should be assessed principally on whether they have fulfilled their statutory mandates to hold fair trials. Any other benefits that accrue from their investigations and prosecutions are to be welcomed, but should not be treated as a benchmark against which they are evaluated. Having made the case for more realistic grounds for the assessment of the legacy of these courts, we identify eight factors that affected the choice of and consequently the operations of each of the two mechanisms in Part III. In Part IV, we evaluate the ICTR against these criteria and highlight areas of its presumed success as well as highlight some of its core limitations. We do the same in Part V with respect to the SCSL and the Sierra Leone situation. Part VI examines the unique situation of Liberia. Here, the assessment was necessarily brief, partly because that country opted to have a truth commission process as a deliberate policy choice of the parties to the conflict who wished to avoid any criminal prosecutions. This might have been the cost-benefit calculus that made the cessation of hostilities possible. Yet, the truth commission that was later established in Liberia strongly recommended criminal prosecutions on the basis that that it is only after such accountability that the prospects for long-term peace and stability will be strengthened.

2 Preliminary Issues and Methodology

As a preliminary matter, it is imperative to define the parameters of this assessment. The ICTR and SCSL differed dramatically in their scope, breadth, budget, funding mechanisms, location, international involvement and novelty. The task at hand is not to assess which flavor of international justice is preferable. Instead, the goal is to assess the strengths and weaknesses of each mechanism so that an informed decision can be made wherever an ad hoc tribunal becomes necessary in the future. Such a mechanism may become necessary for many reasons, including a failure to act on the part of an unwilling or unable national jurisdiction or, if the concerned state is a party to the Rome Statute, the ICC has not shown a preliminary interest in investigating or prosecuting.

That said, in international criminal law, before the simultaneous establishment of the two for the first time ever in Sierra Leone, ad hoc international criminal tribunals and truth commissions were traditionally considered as alternatives to each other. The former is generally focused on retribution or deterrence while the latter aims at discerning the truth and creating an accurate historical record with the view to fostering reconciliation. Going beyond this conventional understanding of the general relationship of criminal tribunals to truth commissions, we argue that even amongst temporary international criminal courts which share many goals and similarity in features, it is plausible to conceive of each separate mechanism as a different tool. For one thing, the institutional design of each can vary considerably depending on the specific role envisaged for it and the mandate created by its founding instruments. For another, the given court's contribution to the wider post conflict dispensation would depend on the presence of other transitional mechanisms and the extent to which those are anticipated to relate or complement its mandate.

It would seem that although as the Africa-based tribunal the ICTR generally served as the basic blueprint for the SCSL,[2] it can probably be analogized to a hammer, which was intended to be used in the fight against impunity in post-genocide Rwanda. This claim derives from the statement of the United Nations Security Council (UNSC) that part of the role of the tribunal was to give retributive justice for the genocide. The SCSL, which had a more limited jurisdictional mandate compared to the ICTR, could be conceptualized as a chisel that was intended to scrape away some of the impunity in the notoriously brutal Sierra Leonean conflict. This claim too can be supported by the resolutions of the Security Council in the lead up to the establishment of the SCSL in collaboration with the government of Sierra Leone. With these analogies in place, one would not ask "which is a better tool: the hammer or the chisel?" for the simple reason that each tool has a special purpose for which it is suited and any number of other purposes for which it is wholly inappropriate. What's more, the utility and morality of the tasks for which a given tool are suited are independent of a tool's ability to accomplish those tasks. A hammer is equally well-suited to the tasks of building a school for orphans as it is for bludgeoning an innocent victim. The manner in which the tool is wielded, as well as its purpose, greatly changes the equation. The tasks for which a particular tool is well-suited are necessarily limited. Thus, just as one would not ask whether a hammer is a better tool than a chisel, one would also not ask whether a hammer or a chisel is better at solving complex mathematical equations. The answer is obvious: neither is suited to the task nor are they meant to be used as such. Such grandiose outcomes as restoring peace and security in a post-conflict state are frequently cited as goals for these criminal courts. True, these are important predicates for the criminal justice process to take place. But this paper will only briefly touch on the presumed impact of international criminal justice on peace and security in those countries under consideration since, to our minds, these are arenas that essentially fall outside of their core mandates

---

2 See, *Letter Dated Mar. 6, 2002 from the Secretary-General addressed to the President of the Security Council*, UN Doc. S/2002/246, Annex I, *Report of the Planning Mission on the Establishment of the Special Court for Sierra Leone*.

to prosecute particular crimes in fair trials comporting with the high standards contained in their statutes and customary international human rights law.

That said, whether particular courts can reasonably impact peace and security assumes that it is, firstly, possible for courts to do so. Secondly, it assumes that these are within the capability of these particular courts. These and other related assumptions seem problematic. After all, would we expect even the most mature and effective national criminal justice mechanism to decrease youth unemployment, increase agricultural yields or encourage sustainable economic development? While these ends may ultimately be beneficial to a post-conflict state, and can be both a symbol of and a byproduct of peace, stability and security, they are not within the idyllic ambit of even a perfect national criminal justice system. Further, it seems necessary to view our "tools" in a realistic social, political and economic context. It is simply not worth asking what an international tribunal could do with US$10 trillion, as that is an unrealistic funding target. Similarly, it is almost guaranteed that *some* constituency, local or international, victim or perpetrator, government or military or civilian, will be displeased with the brand of justice achieved. There is no criminal justice system in the world that has 100% buy-in from its people. An international mechanism is no exception. As international justice mechanisms operate between and among states, with national and international staff, and contemporaneously with other political, economic, and cultural activity and often in complex circumstances after or even during conflict, it appears likewise guaranteed that there will be *some* conflict between competing areas of forward progress. Stability is not peace. Peace is not justice. Justice is not prosperity. Prosperity is not stability. However, each can reasonably be said to be bolstered by the presence of the others.

Worse, even in the best of scenarios where we have defined limited expectations, there is some internal tension among the ambitions our "tools" are intended to achieve.[3] As some scholars have noted with regard to the International Criminal Tribunal for the former Yugoslavia (ICTY), "depending on their interests, the [court] may be expected to speak to the desire for victim's justice or guard against the perception of victor's justice. Similarly, the [court] must also prosecute alleged war criminals while simultaneously protecting the accused defendants in the process."[4] This tension exists not only

---

3 Mirjan R. Damaska, *What is the Point of International Criminal Justice?*, 83 Chi.-Kent L. Rev. 329 (2008).

4 Kimi L. King and James D. Meernik, *Assessing the Impact of the ICTY: Balancing International and Local Interests While Doing Justice*, in The Legacy of the International Criminal Tribunal for the Former Yugoslavia, 7, 12 (Bert Swart, et al, eds.) (hereinafter "the Legacy of the ICTY").

between local and international stakeholders, but also between the desire for efficient trials and the requirement for fair trials, and between the reasonable impulse to keep costs in control and the necessities of pursuing justice in a post-conflict society.

Lastly, the goal of assessing the efficacy of the tribunals as legal institutions is distinct from the task of assessing the impact they have had on the peace, reconciliation, and security in a given country. As Janine Clark has persuasively argued, an accurate assessment of whether an international justice mechanism has contributed to the restoration and maintenance of peace in a post-conflict society requires a thorough empirical study of on-the-ground conditions and the attitudes of the mechanisms' various constituencies.[5] This is not such a study, and we do not purport to evaluate the experiences of those affected by the conflicts in Rwanda, Sierra Leone, or Liberia, nor their individual or overarching perception of the justice delivered by these mechanisms. Justice "is a matter of both actions and the perceptions that they create."[6] A failing beyond the scope of a tribunal's mandate may greatly undermine even the best of criminal processes.[7] Moreover, delivering on some of a tribunal's goals (such as due process rights and humane sentencing) may run counter to other goals (such as reconciliation and local buy-in). Thus a thorough understanding of the justice achieved by the mechanisms would require an empirical study of those affected by the processes and a study of the actions undertaken by and in service to those processes. The latter category is where we focus our efforts.

3 Factors Used in Assessing Impact

As discussed above, the methodology of this paper will be to normatively assess the ICTR and the SCSL on eight different criteria relevant to their creation, their work, and their effect on the local community. These are initial criteria aimed at identifying the legal impact of the tribunals, and in that sense, we do

---

[5] Janine Natalya Clark, *The Impact Question: the ICTY and the Restoration and Maintenance of Peace*, in the Legacy of the ICTY, *supra* note 3, at 55–81.
[6] Erin Staub, *Reconciliation after Genocide, Mass Killing or Intractable Conflict: Understanding the Roots of Violence, Psychological Recovery and Steps toward a General Theory*, 27 Political Psychology 867, 884 (2006).
[7] For instance, Professor Clark interviewed subjects in Bosnia-Herzegovina who felt that proper justice would require "economic opportunities and creation of jobs." Clark, *supra* note 4 at 70. Nothing in the mandate of either the ICTR or SCSL would allow them to undertake large-scale employment or economic development initiatives, and thus would never be capable of delivering "justice" within the above meaning by themselves.

not aim to provide a comprehensive view of all frames or lens through which to view the courts, their legacies, and their impact. There is certainly great room for other scholars to consider the psychological, openly political, sociological or economic and other impacts of these mechanisms.

A Local Involvement in International Instrument

A primary factor to consider in assessing the international mechanisms is the degree of local involvement in the formation, organization, conduct, and decisions of the tribunal in question. This factor has both principled and practical implications.

The principle that war crimes and crimes against humanity should not go unpunished seems to be, at this point in history, widely accepted by all nations. In this sense, the desire to try perpetrators should be shared by both the putative international community and the state in question. The two are not in opposition, and often, the wishes of both the local and the international actors coincide with and complement each other. This helps to create a sense of a common goal to work towards. The desire and necessity of punishing perpetrators is just as much a local concern as it is an imposition of international high-mindedness from abroad.

From a practical standpoint, the evidence, witnesses, and often the accused, will be in the *locus commisi delicti* – the place where the crime was committed. A court, whether local, wholly international or internationalized, relies on the local community and its government to collect information and capture perpetrators. Thus, the degree to which the court is successful depends considerably on the cooperation of the local institutions. It is obvious that a court that attempts to function without witnesses, physical evidence, or a defendant will have a rough go of it. As such, local involvement, both at the level of the formal institutions of the state and outside of them in civil society and amongst individuals, has a very important practical impact on the conduct of the work of the penal tribunal.

Further, inasmuch it can be argued that one goal of international criminal justice is to bolster the reconstruction of post-conflict states and regions, it is necessary to assess the degree to which the affected population endorses the work of the court. However, local *involvement* in the tribunal and local *approval* of the court's work are separate and distinct things.[8] The former can be assessed using benchmarks such as participation in terms of numbers of local prosecutors, judges, defense counsel and other staff. The latter can be affected

---

8 See, Clark, *supra* note 4 (arguing that only empirical studies can validate the high-minded claims of ICJ proponents).

by both the perceptions of the tribunal's work and the extent of local involvement and local input, but it is ultimately a separate issue altogether. For instance, an authoritative study of the ICTY found that members of the affected populations (including Serbs, Bosnians, and Croats) in Bosnia held a wide variety of views about the Tribunal.[9] This, in one way, may not be that surprising. Many locals interviewed for the study took issue with the length of specific sentences,[10] the pace of the trials,[11] and the use of plea bargains in lieu of trials.[12] Although the respondents may not have approved of all of the actions of the court, the local populace was certainly involved – at least sufficiently to form opinions – about the work of the ICTY.

B *Competing National Proceedings*

It has been a given, going back to the first such prosecutions after World War II, that it is not possible for international justice to act as a replacement for national justice. For this reason, all international and internationalized courts have had a limited mandate to prosecute a certain class of crimes or actors. A system for selecting individuals that will be brought to account in the international forum is therefore inevitable. However, depending on the scale of the conflict, the commission of atrocities will involve dozens, if not hundreds or thousands and sometimes tens of thousands of actual perpetrators. Crimes associated with those within the ambit of the international court's personal jurisdiction, as well as others not within it, must be dealt with by local authorities in one way or another. As such, the degree to which the local authorities seek other avenues of redress, and the character of those efforts, inform the perceptions that will be generated about the efficacy of the international court. In other words, the inevitable division of labor between the national jurisdiction and the international(ized) jurisdiction has an impact on the perception of either and often both of the entities in question.

C *Competing International Proceedings*

Similarly, the efforts of other international organizations or third-party states to bring perpetrators to justice implicate the actual and presumed efficacy of an international criminal justice mechanism. For example, some countries might invoke universal jurisdiction, passive personality, or other permissible grounds of jurisdiction to prosecute offenders who have fled to their territories,

---

9 Diane F. Orenlichter, That Someone Guilty be Punished (Open Society, 2010).
10 Id., at 51–57.
11 Id., at 72–79.
12 Id., at 57–65.

as a number of countries such as Belgium, Canada and France have done with respect to alleged *genocidaires* from Rwanda.[13] On the one hand, such national level efforts that complement the court's work will allow the tribunal to focus on fulfilling its mandate. On the other, efforts that overlap with the tribunal's work may raise questions of jurisdictional conflict and primacy or even be a reflection of a lack of broader support for the court.

D   Impunity and "Victor's Justice"

A common concern since the establishment of the International Military Tribunals (IMTS) after World War II has been that the victor in a conflict will subject the vanquished to the victor's preferred justice. The choice to forgo outright execution of the enemy leaders and instead subject them to criminal trials in a court of law was a step forward in 1945, even if the practical consequence were the same for the convicted. Pragmatically, it is unlikely in the context of a widespread violent conflict that atrocities and violations of international law are limited to one side. Yet, in 1946, this meant that the Allies could choose to conveniently ignore the crimes that their own forces committed in favor of prosecuting 22 Nazi leaders and their associates. So, in this wider morally fraught context in which no victorious power will set up a court to prosecute itself instead of only its enemies, the firebombing of civilians in Dresden or the use of atomic weapons against the Japanese in Nagasaki and Hiroshima could be recast as unfortunate consequences of Axis aggression, but not prosecutable war crimes or crimes against humanity. The hypocrisy that results is self-evident and deeply problematic.

In the modern context, the reality of the victor's power to decide what will happen to the loser remains. Much as in the past, the parties that ultimately come to control the government of a post-conflict nation are likely to have had *some* hand in the conflict. Yet, as Victor Peskin has argued, "[a] corollary to [the principle of the universality of human rights] is that all victims of human rights abuses deserve justice regardless of which side they belong to.... There is no moral basis for immunizing victorious nations from scrutiny."[14] In this vein, in modern African conflicts and other transitions, the concern will arise whether the international criminal justice mechanism created to prosecute atrocities will privilege and effectively insulate the victors from criminal pro-

---

13   Charles Jalloh, *Universal Jurisdiction, Universal Prescription? A Preliminary Assessment of the African Union Perspective on Universal Jurisdiction*, 21 Crim L.F. 1 (2010).

14   Victor Peskin, *Beyond Victor's Justice? The Challenge of Prosecuting the Winners at the International Criminal Tribunals for the Former Yugoslavia and Rwanda*, 4 J. Hum. Rts. 213, 214 (2005).

cess, much like the Allies ensured at Nuremberg. On the other hand, and we pursue this admittedly controversial line of thought further below, it maybe – even if this at first blush seems counter-intuitive – that victor's justice is not only practically inevitable, but may also be practically desirable.

E   Breadth of Proceedings

If we mean to assess a court's success, we must necessarily examine what the court set out to accomplish. Of course, in the international criminal law area, there is no shortage of ambitions for these courts. Some of these ambitions are more consistent with the central mission of the tribunal as a criminal court while others are a bit more distant from it. We might, to have a useful conversation, seek to separate out the primary from the secondary goals and justifiably limit our assessment to those that are primary responsibilities of a criminal court: to render fair trials in accordance with the law.[15] For instance, it would be no failure of justice if a Nigerian court fails to prosecute a common criminal in Lesotho; that is not the Nigerian court's role. Similarly, we should consider the success of an ad hoc court within the context of its core mission and core purpose.[16]

The most fundamental statement of a court's intended purpose is its mandate. In the international context, some specific statute or instrument, or a set of instruments, must describe the jurisdiction. This sets out the framework for how the court is to be run, what rules will apply, and most importantly, what kinds of crimes, committed where, when, and by whom, the court is empowered to adjudicate. The ICTR and SCSL differ dramatically in this regard, as discussed below, as do those two Chapter VII courts from the permanent ICC.

A corollary to the court's explicit mandate is the number of trials the tribunal actually carries out. This has a nexus to the mandate in the sense that the manner in which jurisdiction is framed can narrow or widen the field of prosecutorial charging decisions. The terms "greatest responsibility"[17] and "most responsible"[18] are now becoming terms of art, suggesting a move away from a

---

15   Damaska, *supra* note 2.
16   This is not to say, however, that we have to accept the wisdom of the decision that set the court's goals. Rather, it is to say that a court explicitly established to try 30 particular defendants cannot be held accountable for failing to prosecute 100 more.
17   SCSL Statute, art. 1–1.
18   See e.g., Xabier Agirre Aranburu, *Prosecuting the Most Responsible for International Crimes: Dilemmas of Definition and Prosecutorial Discretion* in Protección Internacional de Derechos Humanos y Estado de Derecho, 381–404 (Bogotá: Grupo Editorial Ibanez, 2009).

"persons responsible" standard that appeared to apply in the heyday of international criminal courts.[19] Not only does the form of personal jurisdiction relate directly to the expected throughput of the court, they serve to either cabin or widen the prosecutorial mandate and ultimately influence the exercise of discretion in a given direction. These, in turn, affect the breadth or quantity of justice that is served. Those in turn impact on the perception of the justice that was rendered.

F   Quality of Proceedings

It should go without saying that a properly constituted justice mechanism seeks to ensure the highest quality legal proceedings. This is especially so with international criminal justice mechanisms, where a supplemental legal entity is created often out of concern for the poor condition of the default national mechanism. The so-called "international standards" that come into play in international criminal tribunals are therefore not necessarily always compatible with the standards in every local jurisdiction. They are not simply the subset of rules to which all international parties agree. Rather, they often are aspirational rules that aim to ensure a fair trial for the accused, just punishment, and a sufficient quantum of evidence to encourage faith in the process.

Given that international courts are set up with a goal of meeting international standards, they should be judged against that metric and not necessarily the standards of the local jurisdiction. Again, disagreement on these norms is not limited to the African context. Most American states, for instance, continue to provide for different rules on provision of grand juries or capital punishment, even though most other countries or international criminal justice does not. It would be patently unfair to criticize an international court for failing to apply American standards of punishment over the objections of American legislators.

A high-quality proceeding is not simply one that delivers the desired outcome (and, indeed, an impartial court should not prefer a specific outcome). It is equally true that an undesirable outcome is not the indicia of a low-quality proceeding. In both cases, the degree to which the proceedings complied with international standards for fair trial are wholly independent of the outcome in an individual case for the simple reason that the parties, constituencies, and observers often have differing views of which outcome is most desirable. Again, an empirical study of the perceptions of quality in the affected populations would yield valuable insight for future tribunals, but would not necessarily

---

19   Charles Jalloh, *Prosecuting Those Bearing 'Greatest Responsibility': The Lessons of the Special Court of Sierra Leone*, 96 Marq. L. Rev. 863 (2013).

speak to the question of whether the proceedings did, in fact, comport with international fair trial norms.

G Cost of Administration

There is, literally, a cost to international justice. It therefore seems fair to assess the cost of a particular implementation thereof. Again, the SCSL and the ICTR differed dramatically in this respect. A few different ways can be used to consider the cost of an international court. First, and most obvious, is the total amount of money spent by all parties (the total cost of the tribunal). Second is the cost per trial, per defendant, per situation, or otherwise reduced by a normalizing factor to facilitate comparison with other institutions. Third, we can consider the funding mechanism that provides money for the court's operation as it may greatly affect the way the tribunal does its work. Lastly, and least importantly perhaps, is the relative cost of courts vis-à-vis other national priorities. The latter issue may seem distant, but in many post conflict contexts, the very existence of the criminal tribunals and international involvement appears to have invited parallel comparison – a cost benefit analysis of whether the funds provided could have been better spent elsewhere. This is to be expected, considering that in many of those societies, international involvement comes about because of the failure of the national system in provisioning the relevant sectors of society adequately. Poverty and lack of resources may, in a world of finite resources, give rise to legitimate questions about what area must be given priority.

It is often said that the ICTR and ICTY were "expensive,"[20] and that the SCSL was set up as a cheaper alternative in the wake of "tribunal fatigue"[21] within the international community. True as that may be, neither the ICTY and ICTR spent what could be deemed an internationally significant amount of money when compared to the amounts that nations spend on warplanes, or what some developed countries spend on snack food, elective surgery, or movie tickets. On the other hand, one may rightly ask if the money spent on international criminal justice mechanisms would not have been better spent on food aid, capacity building, economic development or other beneficial endeavors. This seems like a fair question, but one that confused the hammer for the supercomputer. We submit that there is more than enough money to fund *both* international criminal justice and development efforts without seriously affecting the international community's bottom line. That being said, the

---

20   David Wippman, *The Costs of International Justice*, 100 Am. J. Int'l L. 861 (2006).
21   David Scheffer, *Challenges Confronting International Justice Issues*, 4 New Eng. Int'l & Comp. L. Ann. 1 (1998).

existence of that money, the question of political will, and the ability to convince states of the importance of these expenditures are separate questions beyond the scope of this paper. Ultimately, it maybe that in more ways than one, the work of international tribunals appear to follow the adage of project management "fast, cheap, and good: pick two."

H Jurisprudential Impact

One of the benefits of the push in the late 20th and early 21st centuries to establish norms of international criminal law is that newly constituted tribunals will not need to reinvent the wheel. With that in mind, the degree to which a court contributed to the goal of establishing this groundwork is often seen as relevant to assessing its legacy and efficacy as a legal institution. It is acknowledged that not all parties will agree on the accuracy or utility of any tribunal's contribution to the state of international criminal law.

Having identified the above factors, in what follows below, we will apply each of the above criteria to the situations in Rwanda, Sierra Leone, and Liberia.

4 Rwanda

A Background to the Genocide

Rwanda was colonized by both Germany and Belgium, the latter of which introduced a formal system of racial classification by separating the Rwandese population into three groups: the Hutu (roughly 84% of the population), the Tutsi (about 15%) and the Twa (the remaining 1%).[22] Broadly speaking, at the risk of oversimplification, the minority Tutsi population was favored by the colonial authorities over the majority Hutu. The Tutsi remained in positions of leadership until the UN Trusteeship-mandated universal elections in 1956, at which time the Hutus ushered in a Hutu-majority government and an era of civil unrest between ethnic groups.[23] Violence occasionally followed, with several targeted attacks against the minority Tutsis. After each attack, some Tutsis would flee the country. Some would end up in neighboring states as refugees. Rwandan Tutsi exiles in Uganda formed the Alliance Rwandaise pour l'Unite Nationale (ARUN) in 1979, and later renamed themselves the Rwandan Patriotic Front (RPF).[24]

---

22 Prosecutor v. Jean-Paul Akayesu, Case no. ICTR-96-4-T, Judgment, ¶83 (2 October 1998).
23 Id., at ¶¶ 86–89.
24 Id., at ¶ 93.

An attack from Uganda by the RPF into Rwanda on 1 October 1990 began a three-year conflict between the RPF and the Rwandese Armed Forces led by then-President Juvenal Habyarimana. The war was nominally ended by the Arusha Accords, a 1993 power-sharing agreement between the RPF and the Rwandese Government which provided for, *inter alia*, a transitional government that included the rebels, demobilization and integration of the armies, and deployment of a UN peace-keeping force in Rwanda (what later came to be known as the United Nations Assistance Mission for Rwanda – UNAMIR).[25]

Efforts to establish the transitional government led to a meeting in Dar-es-Salaam, Tanzania, on 6 April 1994 that included President Habyarimana, President Ntaryamirai of Burundi, and other regional heads of state. The plane carrying Habyarimana and Ntaryamirai crashed outside of the Kigali airport as it returned from the meeting around 8:30 p.m. on the night of 6 April 1994.[26] The government forces quickly blocked off entire areas of Kigali, and members of the Rwandan Army and the Presidential Guard began systematically killing moderates and other known prominent supporters of the Arusha Accords. Among these initial targets of the violence were Prime Minister Agathe Uwilingiyimana (MDR), a Hutu moderate politician, the president of the Supreme Court, and virtually the entire leadership of the *parti social democratie* (PSD).[27] This resulted in a constitutional power vacuum that was quickly filled by an avowedly pro-Hutu interim government made of extremists and led by Jean Kambanda.

Using the army and special battalions, as well as militia groups called *Interahamwe* and *Impuzamugambi*, a cadre of dedicated Hutu Power proponents led a series of genocidal attacks on Tutsi and moderate Hutu civilians throughout the country. Although UNAMIR forces were present in the country, their mandate was not extended to protection of civilians, despite repeated calls for such by the UN Force Commander General Rome Dallaire.[28] Instead, following the killing of 10 Belgian paratroopers, the UN peacekeeping mission was downgraded.[29] No other countries intervened, from Africa or elsewhere, giving sufficient space for the genocidal bloodbath to occur.[30] Over a period of 100 days,

---

25 Id.; Text of Accord *avilable at* https://peaceaccords.nd.edu/site_media/media/accords/Rwanda_Peace_Accord.pdf (last accessed 27 July 2014).
26 Id., at ¶ 106.
27 Id., at ¶ 107.
28 Romeo Dallaire, Shake Hands with the Devil: The Failure of Humanity in Rwanda, (Da Capo Press 2004).
29 Prosecutor v. Theoneste Bagosora, Case No. ICTR-96-4-A, Judgment (14 December 2011).
30 *Report of the Independent Inquiry into the actions of the United Nations during the 1994 genocide in Rwanda*, UN Doc S/1999/1257 (15 Dec. 1999); Organization of African Unity,

between 7 April 1994 and 18 July 1994, between 500,000 and 1 million Tutsis and moderate Hutus were killed in Rwanda.[31] The killings continued until the RPF, led by General Paul Kagame, captured the capital, Kigali, on 18 July 1994. Kagame was to later become Rwanda's president.

B   *Local Involvement*

Rwanda moved for UN support to create a tribunal to prosecute those who perpetrated the genocide. Yet, due to its dissatisfaction with a number of issues as discussed further below, it was the only government that ultimately voted against it. The ICTR was established by a resolution of the United Nations Security Council, and thus did not rely on formal consent from Rwanda.[32] In the simplest sense, though this was not inevitable, the creation of the Tribunal did not have the same level of local involvement as did the SCSL. Relying on the Security Council's broad powers to ensure the "maintain or restore international peace and security"[33] under Chapter VII of the UN Charter, the Tribunal, its mandate, and its governing statute were creations of the broader international community as represented by the United Nations.

Having voted against it in the Security Council, Rwanda's relationship with the Tribunal was predictably troubled from the start. Within a week of the beginning of the mass killings, the Representative of the RPF informed the President of the Security Council that genocide was being committed in Rwanda and requested Security Council action.[34] A few months later, on 8 June 1994, the Security Council adopted Resolution 925, which noted "with gravest concern the reports indicating that acts of genocide have occurred in Rwanda and recalling in this context that genocide constitutes a crime punishable under international law."[35] A panel of experts convened by the Secretary-General at the behest of the Security Council recommended, *inter alia*, that the Security Council "take all necessary and effective action to ensure that the individuals responsible for the serious violations of human rights in Rwanda ... are brought

---

International Panel of Eminent Personalities to Investigate the 1994 Genocide in Rwanda and the Surrounding Events, *Rwanda: The Preventable Genocide* (IPEP 2000).

31 Id., at ¶ 111.
32 S.C. Res. 955, UN Doc. S/RES/955 (8 November 1994).
33 UN Charter, art. 39.
34 *Letter Dated 15 December 199 from Members of the Independent Inquiry into the Actions of the United Nations during the 1994 Genocide in Rwanda Addressed to the Secretary-General*, UN Doc. S/1999/1257, Annex I at 68 (16 December 1999).
35 S.C. Res. 925, UN Doc. S/RES/925 (8 June 1994).

to justice before an independent and impartial international criminal tribunal."[36]

However, Rwanda's enthusiasm for the idea of an international tribunal faltered on the shoals of implementation. The Rwandese Government, as a rotating member of the Security Council at the time, was an active participant in the negotiation of the Statute of the Tribunal. Throughout the negotiations, Rwanda indicated serious misgivings about the form the Tribunal was taking. Evidently, its concerns were not addressed, an ominous sign of what was to come later. Ultimately, Resolution 955 passed over the objections of the Rwandese Government.[37]

Rwanda expressed seven primary points of concern over the form and substance of the Tribunal.[38] First, Rwanda objected to the limited temporal jurisdiction of the Tribunal because, in its view, the genocide that erupted in April 1994 was the result of a long period of planning and "pilot projects" that long predated the ICTR's limits.[39] Second, the Rwandese Government believed that the Tribunal as initially constituted lacked sufficient trial judges to fulfill its mandate. Rwanda's delegate suggested that "the establishment of so ineffective an international tribunal would only appease the conscience of the international community rather than respond to the expectations of the Rwandese people and the victims of the genocide[.]"[40] Third, the government was concerned that the Tribunal would expend its resources prosecuting crimes that were within the jurisdiction of national courts to the exclusion of the international crimes within its own jurisdiction.[41] Fourth, the government rejected some proposed judicial candidates who they believed had taken "a very active part in the civil war in Rwanda."[42] Fifth, the Rwandese Government felt that it was inappropriate that those convicted by the Tribunal should be imprisoned outside of Rwanda in accordance with the host country's laws.[43] Rwandan au-

---

36 *Preliminary Report of the Independent Commission of Experts Established in Accordance with Security Council Resolution 935 (1994)*, ¶ 150, UN Doc. S/1994/1125 (4 October 1994).

37 UN Doc. S/PV.3453 (8 November 1994). The Chinese Government abstained from the vote, noting that it may be "an incautious act" to proceed without the assent of Rwanda.

38 For more detailed analysis, see Payam Akhavan, *The International Criminal Tribunal for Rwanda: the Politics and Pragmatics of Punishment*, 90 Am. J. Int'l. L. 501, 505–08 (1996).

39 UN Doc. S/PV.3453, at 14.

40 Id., at 15.

41 Id.

42 Id.

43 This concern may have been borne out by the experience with Georges Ruggiu, the only non-Rwandan convicted by the ICTR. Ruggiu, an Italian-Belgian journalist for Radio Television Libre des Milles Collines, received a 12-year sentence in June 2000 after pleading

thorities argued that this would encourage countries inclined to free any convicted *genocidaires* to vie for the imprisonment assignments.[44] Sixth, the Rwandese delegation opposed the abolition of capital punishment in the Statute because of the possibility that those most responsible for the genocide would receive lighter treatment than those tried in Rwandan courts where capital punishment was legal.[45] Finally, the Rwandese Government disagreed with the decision to locate the Tribunal outside the country rather than in Rwanda itself. The government rightly argued that locating the court in Rwanda would serve to "fight against the impunity to which [the Rwandese people] have become accustomed ... and to promote the harmonization of international and national jurisprudence."[46] In many ways, some of these initial objections reflect typical concerns about sovereignty and a desire to influence, if not assert, a measure of control over the eventual mechanism that was being considered in the name of the people of Rwanda. With the benefit of hindsight, it seems that some of those concerns lacked merit while others proved to have some merit.

Though there were periods of smooth cooperation, especially with specific organs such as with the ICTR Office of the Prosecutor and the Registry, the overall on-off relationship between the ICTR and the Rwandese Government continued to be a challenge throughout the life of the Tribunal. This culminated in several high-profile conflicts, including standoffs over the ICTR's primacy in the extradition of Theoneste Bagosora and Foduald Karamira. Perhaps the most significant conflict, however, came in the case of Jean-Bosco Barayagwiza, who was accused of fomenting anti-Tutsi violence through his role in the Ministry of Foreign Affairs.[47] Finding that Barayagwiza's case had been marred by serious due process concerns, the Appeals Chamber dismissed the indictment with prejudice against the prosecution and ordered his uncondi-

---

guilty to direct and public incitement to genocide and persecution. In February 2008, Ruggiu was transferred to Italy to serve the remainder of his sentence. On 21 April 2009, he was released early by the Italian authorities despite the mandate in Article 27 of the ICTR statute giving the President sole authority to grant early release. See, The Hague Justice Portal, Convicted journalist released early in violation of ICTR Statute, available at http://www.haguejusticeportal.net/index.php?id=10688 (last accessed 27 July 2014).

44   Id.
45   Id., at 16.
46   Id.
47   Jean-Bosco Barayagwiza v. Prosecutor, Case No. ICTR-97–19-T, Amended Indictment (14 April 2000).

tional release in November of 1999.[48] The Rwandese Government responded by publicly declaring its intention to withhold cooperation with the Tribunal until the Appeals Chamber decision had been reversed. Eventually, the decision was reversed by the Appeals Chamber (citing "new facts"), and the cooperation between Rwanda and the Tribunal resumed.[49] Through this refusal to cooperate, and the subsequent Appeals Chamber decision that aligned with the Rwandese government's position, "[t]he government showed that it could effectively hold witnesses hostage and virtually bring the wheels of justice to a halt."[50] This tactic raises legitimate questions about the efficacy of the international regime especially given the state-centric nature of that system under which little if any action is possible without the support of the concerned state.[51] For this reason, without state cooperation, international criminal tribunals are unable to do any concrete work to achieve their mandates.[52]

After the active trials at the ICTR concluded, the Rwandese Minister of Justice confirmed that the national feelings of disassociation had continued through the end of the Tribunal's work. Minister Tharcisse Karugarama told the UN General Assembly that "international justice is in a crisis of credibility with regard to fostering national reconciliation in post-conflict situations," that international courts are "viewed as foreign, detached and contribute very little

---

[48] Jean-Bosco Barayagwiza v. Prosecutor, Decision (3 November 1999), *avilable at* http://unictr.org/Portals/0/Case/English/Barayagwiza/decisions/dcs991103.pdf (last visited 27 July 2014).

[49] Jean-Bosco Barayagwiza v. Prosecutor, Case No. ICTR-97-19-AR72, Decision (Prosecutor's Request for Review or Reconsideration) (31 March 2000), *avilable at* http://www.unictr.org/Portals/0/Case%5CEnglish%5CBarayagwiza%5Cdecisions%5Cdcs20000331.pdf (last visited 27 July 2014).

[50] Peskin, *supra* note 13 at 225.

[51] Prosecutor Carla Del Ponte told the Appeals Chamber that "her ability to continue with prosecutions and investigations depends on the government of Rwanda and that, unless the Appellant is tried, the Rwandan government will no longer be 'involved in any manner.'" Decision, *supra* note 48 at ¶ 24; See also, Transcript of the hearing on 22 February 2000, pp. 26–28; Decision, *supra* note 48, Declaration by Judge Rafael Nieto-Navia at ¶¶ 11, 16 (rejecting Del Ponte's accusations of political bias as well as what he perceived as the Rwandan desire to see every indictee convicted).

[52] The first president of the ICTY, Antonio Cassesse, famously described that court as "a giant without arms and legs." Cassesse declared that the ICTY needed "artificial limbs to walk and work. And these artificial limbs are state authorities. If the cooperation of states is not forthcoming, the ICTY cannot fulfill its functions. It has no means at its disposal to force states to cooperate with it." Antonio Cassese, *On Current Trends Towards Criminal Prosecution and Punishment of Breaches of International Humanitarian Law*, 9 Eur. J of Int'l L. 1 (1998).

to National reconciliation process," and that the objective of fostering national reconciliation and restoring peace in Rwanda had not been achieved.[53]

With that history in mind, it seems clear that the ICTR did not excel in the area of local involvement. There was no formal role for the government in the work of the ICTR such as appointing key staff, as there was at the SCSL.[54] Another problem is that the Tribunal missed opportunities to connect with Rwandans, with limited outreach to the country especially in the early years. The political and logistical conflicts between the Tribunal and Rwandese national institutions caused considerable difficulty during the court's tenure, and undermined each party's confidence in the other as a partner in achieving justice. As Minister Karugarama's statements at the UN indicate, the feeling that the Tribunal was not sufficiently focused on local needs, expressed by the Rwandese delegation during the negotiation of Resolution 955, continues to hold sway in official Rwandese circles. If this is the official position, it would seem unlikely that the ICTR would fare any better in assessments among the local population in the country.

On a related note, it is difficult to secure a statistical breakdown of the Tribunal's staff composition. But, the apparent absence of meaningful participation by Rwandans in the court's processes did not help bridge the physical and emotional gaps between the Tribunal and the national authorities. Based on one of the author's experience working in the judicial chambers of the tribunal as a legal officer, it was rather noticeable that there were hardly any Rwandese prosecutors in the ICTR, let alone judges or attorneys serving in other capacities. True, a handful of them were recruited at various stages of the process, but the numbers were so negligible that it smacked of tokenism. The reality is that the bulk of the prosecutors were from elsewhere, reflecting the UN-origins of the Tribunal. Of those there, few were senior trial attorneys leading teams or holding other senior positions. This implied that, whether deliberately or inadvertently, there was very little space created for or left in the Tribunal for nationals of the country most affected by the genocide. This was unfortunate for many reasons, not least that there was a failure to take advantage of their expertise and experiences with genocide to leave a legacy that could be useful to the national justice system (assuming those individuals returned home to

---

53 Statement by Hon. Tharcisse Karugarama, at the United Nations General Assembly, Thematic Debate on the Role of International Criminal Justice in Reconciliation (9 April 2013) *avilable at* http://rwandaun.org/site/2013/04/10/statement-by-honourable-tharcisse-karugarama-minister-of-justice-and-attorney-general-of-rwanda/ (last accessed 27 July 2014).

54 See, Part V.B. *supra*.

serve after the work of the ICTR concluded). The involvement of professionals with connections to the country might have served to increase local buy-in by carving out a role as informal ambassadors to disseminate information about the trials back in their home country. It seemed, in any event, that the bulk of those from Rwanda walking the hallways in Arusha were attorneys or investigators on the defense side, interpreters, or witness management officers. Those were important roles, but in some respects, they were hardly enough.

C   *Competing National Proceedings*

While the ICTR was tasked with trying those most responsible for the 1994 genocide, the Rwandese national authorities were responsible for prosecuting the vast majority of perpetrators in the national courts. This informal division of labor, between the tribunal and the domestic justice system, is a common and indeed inevitable feature of international criminal law. Some of the suspects and accused would of course have fallen within the jurisdiction of the ICTR. The remaining suspects would likely not have risen to the level of international humanitarian law violations, and where they did, they might not have been sufficiently high level to attract the ICTR's interest. This scenario is of course not unique to Rwanda; rather, all post-conflict societies can expect that the overwhelming majority of individual perpetrators would not be part of any international or internationalized prosecutions. The scope of such tribunals has, from Nuremberg to Arusha to Freetown to The Hague, been limited to higher ranking offenders.[55]

Thus, at the end of the day, the national institutions are given the more difficult task of ensuring justice is meted out to the bulk of the perpetrators. In Rwanda, after some experimentation, two principal methods were used to prosecute the alleged suspects. First, the national judiciary established specialized tribunals of first instance to deal with accused *genocidaires*. The national legal framework has been substantially modified since such trials started in 1996, including substantial moves toward an Anglo-American system of precedential decisions[56] and abolition of the death penalty in 2007. The national judiciary has handled roughly 15,000 cases over 17 years at a cost of US$ 17M.[57] Second, and more significantly, was the establishment of *gacaca* courts that acted at the local level independent of the formal courts. These community courts were created with the express purpose of incorporating local, tradition-

---

[55]   Jalloh, *Prosecuting Those Bearing 'Greatest Responsibility'*, supra note 18.

[56]   Nicholas A. Jones, The Courts of Genocide: Politics and the Rule of Law in Rwanda and Arusha, 91–93 (Routledge 2010).

[57]   Karugarama, *supra* note 52.

al understandings of justice into a modern justice framework. In this sense, the *gacaca* courts were an alternative both to formal criminal justice proceedings and non-retributive reconciliation methods such as truth and reconciliation commissions.[58]

Gacaca courts met weekly in each of the roughly 9,000 cellules and 1,500 sectors within Rwanda.[59] First, people in the community were encouraged to describe their experiences during the genocide as a way of collecting evidence against possible accused persons. Then, a trial phase has the accused questioned by judges and community members about their actions in 1994. Judgments were then rendered by a panel of judges drawn from the same broader community as the accused. Through this process, Rwanda has been able to handle nearly 2 million cases in 10 years at a cost of roughly US$ 52M.[60]

We hesitate to judge community trials like *gacaca*, which were effectively conceived of as a way to address the unprecedented crisis situation that Rwanda faced at the time, against formal justice processes with all their due process guarantees under the Rwandan constitution and international human rights law. Part of the reason is that regular criminal trials, let alone genocide trials, are hardly comparable to informal local community gatherings on the grass to talk about who did what to whom during a traumatic event – it is an apples-to-seahorses comparison. Second, that system by its very nature operates outside of the formal court system. It consequently would not likely comply nor purport to comply with the stringent demands we might expect of a formal criminal justice system. Yet, precisely because the choice to pursue *gacaca* effectively circumvents the government's obligations to comport itself with its constitutional, African and international human rights guarantees to its citizens, several observations are inevitable. All the more so given that the traditional *gacaca* approach has – as might be expected – both positive and negative elements that are worthy of consideration in future post-conflict scenarios.

On the one hand, the visibility, local sensitivity, and efficiency of these proceedings can be framed as effective counterweights to the perceived isolation, slow pace, and expense of the ICTR. On the other hand, this efficiency, and to some degree the emphasis on local community concerns, seem to apparently

---

[58] The modern incarnation of "gacaca" differs significantly from the pre-colonial form from which it takes its name. Notably, the prior incarnation dealt mainly with minor civil disputes and did not impose sentences of imprisonment. The modern analogue deals with "the crime of crimes" and routinely gives out prison sentences. Amaka Megwalu & Neophytos Loizides, *Dilemmas of Justice and Reconciliation: Rwandans and Gacaca Courts*, 18 Afr. J. of Int'l. & Comp. L. 1, 4–5 (2010).

[59] Id. at 3.

[60] Karugarama, *supra* note 52.

come at the expense of fair trial standards for individuals alleged to have been involved with the genocide. *Gacaca* courts are not courts of law *per se*, and their status as community courts creates the possibility of undue influence, double jeopardy, and even reversal of the burden of proof.[61] Further, decisions of the *gacaca* courts could only be appealed to the sector's appellate *gacaca* court, and thus decisions rendered in local communities were not reviewable by the national judiciary.[62]

D   *Competing International Proceedings*

As a creation of the UN Security Council, the ICTR relied mainly on the strength of the international community to support its core mission. Although that mission included the trial of those most responsible for the 1994 genocide, several domestic judiciaries conducted trials of Rwandan suspects that were likely within the ambit of the Tribunal. These domestic proceedings came about and garnered more political support as more countries internalized the anti-genocide norm at the national level. It could not have been timelier given David Scheffers's "tribunal fatigue"[63] in the Security Council following years of expensive trials at the ICTR and the ICTY. Inasmuch as the work of the ICTR relied on the support of domestic authorities to dispose of cases involving middle to high ranking offenders, the decision to try these perpetrators outside of the Tribunal system, and the ICTR's acquiescence to such arrangements, indicates that "tribunal fatigue" was an operative concern.[64]

Several countries tried suspected Rwandan *genocidaires* in their national systems during the operation of the ICTR. These cases mainly proceeded under the theory of universal jurisdiction, whereby states that do not have a nexus to the conflict, the victim or the accused could nonetheless try grave violations of international law.[65] National courts that tried suspects whose

---

61   Anne N. Kubai, *Between Justice and Reconciliation: The Survivors of Rwanda*, Afr. Sec. Rev. 16(1), 60 (2007).
62   Jones, *supra* note 55 at 94.
63   Scheffer, *supra* note 20.
64   See, e.g., *Report on the completion strategy of the International Criminal Tribunal for Rwanda*, UN Doc S/2008/322 (12 May 2008) (describing efforts to move cases to competent national jurisdictions); Erik Mose, *The ICTR's Completion Strategy – Challenges and Possible Solutions*, 6(4) J. In'tl. Crim. Just. 667(2008) (contemporaneous discussion of challenges of closing the ICTR).
65   Note that, many other countries, including the US and Canada also sought removal of those individual allegedly involved in genocide from their jurisdictions pursuant to the exclusion clauses of the Refugee Convention. See, e.g., Joseph Rikhof, *Complicity in International Criminal Law and Canadian Refugee Law*, 4 J. of Int'l Crim. Just. 702 (2006).

crimes were directly within the jurisdictional ambit of the ICTR have included Canada,[66] Germany,[67] Great Britain,[68] Belgium,[69] Norway,[70] and France.[71] It is notable here that, despite allegations of harboring several high level Rwandese fugitives from justice by countries such as Zaire, DRC, and Zambia, no African States have ever asserted universal jurisdiction to pursue prosecutions of the alleged *genocidaires* within their midst.[72] Save for a few instances, it is not entirely clear that these same individuals tried in foreign national courts would have been tried by the ICTR, especially in the latter stages of the court's life when the Completion Strategy appeared to have taken hold. Still, it can be concluded that the prosecutions by the mostly European countries mentioned may have played a useful role in the operation of the ICTR. The difficulty is that, where there were high level perpetrators involved, a separate question arises as to the motivations for the prosecutions. They were not always benign. For example, in some of the cases involving France, the Kagame regime has

---

66 R. v. Munyaneza [2009] QCCS 2201; Fannie LaFontaine, *Canada's Crimes against Humanity and War Crimes Act on Trial*, 8 J. of Int'l Crim. Just. 269 (2010).

67 Onesphore Rwabukombe, Oberlandesgericht Frankfurt am Main – Judgment of February 18, 2014 – reference number 5–3 StU 4/10–4–3/10..

68 Vincent Bajinya, Charles Munyaneza, Emmanuel Nteziryayo & Celestin Ugirashebuja. See, Brown v. Government of Rwanda [2009] EWHC 770 (Admin).

69 Vincent Ntezimana, Alphonse Higaniro, Consolata Mukangango and Julienne Mukabutera : see (Unreported, Cour d'Assises de l'Arrondissement Administratif de Bruxelles-Capital, President Maes, Judges Louveaux and Massart, 8 June 2001) available at http://www.asf.be/AssisesRwanda2/fr/ (last visited 27 July 2014); see also, Mathias Bushishi, http://www.trial-ch.org/en/resources/trial-watch/trial-watch/profiles/profile/1073/action/show/controller/Profile.html (last visited 27 July 2014); Etienne Nzabonimana, http://www.trial-ch.org/en/resources/trial-watch/trial-watch/profiles/profile/327/action/show/controller/Profile.html (last visited 27 July 2014); Samuel Ndashyikirwa, http://www.trial-ch.org/en/resources/trial-watch/trial-watch/profiles/profile/328/action/show/controller/Profile.html (last visited 27 July 2014).

70 Prosecutor v. Sadi Bugingo, TOSLO-2012–106377, Oslo District Court (15 February 2013) available at http://www.asser.nl/upload/documents/20130226T095633-Oslo%20District%20Court%20judgment%2014–02–2013%20Norwegian.pdf (last visited 27 July 2014).

71 Wenceslas Munyeshyaka, Rectification, Cass. Crim., No. 96-82491, (10 fevrier 1998) available at http://www.asser.nl/upload/documents/20120612T111630-Cour_de_Cassation_Chambre_criminelle_du_10_f%C3%A9vrier_1998.pdf.

72 Fatou Bensouda, *International Criminal Justice in Africa – The State of Play* in International Criminal Justice and Africa 24, 26 (Southern African Litigation Centre 2013) ("Save for the hybrid SCSL and Rwanda, African states have not for the most part been active in prosecuting international crimes domestically – despite ample opportunities to do so.").

argued more sinister motives might have being behind the push for domestic trials instead of voluntary transfer of all their accused to the Tribunal.[73]

E Impunity and "Victor's Justice"

Like the Nuremberg and Tokyo Tribunals, the ICTR has had a mixed record with regard to both impunity and victor's justice. Focusing on positive contributions, the list of accused before the Tribunal shows that a wide variety of actions were considered by the Prosecutor to have contributed to the genocide. Thus, the Tribunal has investigated and punished senior military officials, cabinet members of the civilian government, politicians, religious leaders. and media figures on genocide and genocide-related charges.[74] This view of the Tribunal's mandate to try those most responsible shows an acute understanding that organized violence on this scale does not arise solely through physical force.[75] Accordingly, the Tribunal removed the cloak of impunity, exposing most of the ring leaders in the public and the private spheres to some measure of accountability. On the other hand, as always, there is another side to the story. Much of the subsequent violence in the Great Lakes Region, including in the DRC and the CAR, have some nexus to the Rwandan conflict. It can be argued that, to the degree that the ICTR was unable to prevent participation in these neighboring conflicts by those who came within its jurisdiction is a strike against its war on impunity.[76] Yet, such an argument would need more to avoid being simplistic. For one thing, even though there seems to be a broad connection, it is not entirely clear based on publicly available evidence that the same leaders from Rwanda are the ones heading the activities of the militia and oth-

---

73 See, Karugarama, *supra* note 52; H.E. President Paul Kagame, *Statement to UN General Assembly 68th Session* (25 September 2013), *avilable at* http://gadebate.un.org/68/rwanda.

74 See, e.g., Trial Materials, Theoneste Bagosora v. Prosecutor, ICTR-96-7 (http://unictr.org/tabid/128/Default.aspx?id=10&mnid=4); Trial Materials, Jean Kambanda v. Prosecutor, ICTR-97-23 (http://unictr.org/tabid/128/Default.aspx?id=24&mnid=4); Trial Materials, Jean-Bosco Uwinkindi v. Prosecutor, ICTR-01-75 (http://unictr.org/tabid/128/Default.aspx?id=75&mnid=7); Trial Materials, Ferdinand Nahimana v. Prosecutor, ICTR-99-52 (http://unictr.org/tabid/128/Default.aspx?id=29&mnid=4).

75 Hassan B. Jallow, *Prosecutorial Discretion and International Criminal Justice*, 3 J. Int'l Crim. Just. 145 (2005) (arguing that "The primary targets for prosecution inevitably are therefore the political, administrative and military leadership at the time, which planned and oversaw the execution of the genocide. Any level of participation by any such persons is thus sufficient to bring them within the category of those to be prosecuted.").

76 At present, the ICTR has 9 accused for which indictments have been issued who remain at large. See, Accused at Large, http://unictr.org/Cases/tabid/77/Default.aspx?id=12&mnid=12 (last accessed 27 July 2014).

er fighters in those neighboring states. In this vein, and in any event, there is of course ICC involvement in prosecuting crimes from that region.[77]

But perhaps the biggest critique of the ICTR seems to be the claims by some human rights groups and academics that it has only dispensed "victor's justice."[78] This argument, made most forcefully by Human Rights Watch, echoes the experience of Nuremberg and apparently attempts to over correct for it. It is predicated on the simplest and perhaps noblest of ideas that justice has to be dispensed equally and to all sides involved in a given conflict. Notably, none of those tried at the ICTR came from the Rwandan Patriotic Front (RPF) camp.[79] Of course, the leader of the RPF, Paul Kagame, became the head of the post-genocide government of Rwanda, and remains in that post today. Allegedly, the attempts by then-Prosecutor Carla Del Ponte to bring charges against RPF leaders and commanders in 2002 preceded a political standoff that ended in the bifurcation of the Office of the Prosecutor at the ICTR and the ICTY.[80] Although then-Secretary-General Kofi Annan stated that the creation of separate prosecutor's offices was intended to increase efficiency and mitigate administrative concerns, "[t]he timing of the plan, in the face of intense Rwandan pressure, leaves the Security Council open to the charge that it sacrificed Del Ponte to appease Rwanda's anger and, perhaps, to stop the tribunal from issuing RPF indictments."[81]

With due respect, this appears to be a rather tenuous argument. For one thing, it buys into Del Ponte's broader claim that she was removed from her

---

[77] The Prosecutor of the ICC has brought cases against Thomas Lubanga Dyilo, Germain Katanga, Bosco Ntaganda, Callixte Mbarushimana, Sylvestre Mudacumura, and Mathieu Ngudjolo Chui for crimes committed or allegedly committed in the Democratic Republic of Congo, for instance. See, http://www.icc-cpi.int/en_menus/icc/situations%20and%20 cases/situations/situation%20icc%200104/Pages/situation%20index.aspx (last visited 27 July 2014).

[78] See, e.g., *Letter to the Prosecutor of the International Criminal Tribunal for Rwanda Regarding the Prosecution of RPF Crimes*, Human Rights Watch (26 May 2009), http://www.hrw.org/node/83536 (last visited 27 July 2014); Lars Waldorf, *'A Mere Pretense of Justice': Complementarity, Sham Trials, and Victor's Justice at the Rwanda Tribunal*, 33(4) Fordham Int'l L. J. 1221–77 (2010).

[79] UN Commission of Experts, *Final Report*, UN Doc. S/1994/1405 (Dec. 9, 1994); Peskin, *supra* note 13 at 216.

[80] See, in this regard, Carla Del Ponte, Madame Prosecutor: Confrontations with Humanity's Worst Criminals and the Culture of Impunity. A Memoir, 231–239 (2009).

[81] Peskin, *supra* note 13 at 226. For further criticisms by academics, see Filip Reyntjens, Political Governance in Post-Genocide Rwanda, 244 (Cambridge University Press, 2013); Luc Cote, *The Exercise of Prosecutorial Discretion in International Criminal Law*, 3 J. of Int'l Crim. Just. 162, 176–77 (2005).

post because she crossed the red line that the Kagame Government had drawn for her. Yet, it should be apparent that Madam Del Ponte was aggrieved, and having lost her job, may have been seeking an explanation to make sense of her situation. She is not exactly the most neutral person to make this claim. Furthermore, since Peskin's article was written, more information has emerged in the public domain suggesting that the non-renewal of Del Ponte's contract may have been, at least in part, for less sinister reasons.[82] This undermines the former prosecutor's arguments, and has led William Schabas, a leading scholar, to clarify that the decision may have had to do more with other factors than her desire to seek indictments against the RPF leadership for alleged crimes committed in 1994.[83]

In fact, going even further, there may well be explanations for a decision to not indict the RPF personnel that are less dramatic and perhaps even benign. According to the first Prosecutor of the ICTY and the ICTR, Richard Goldstone, the decision not to indict RPF crimes can be rationalized as a matter of prosecutorial policy.[84] This position was based on his professional assessment as an independent prosecutor. Thus, in Goldstone's view, the "Hutu crimes" ranked as a 9 or 10 while the "Tutsi crimes" ranked much lower. He, like many other national and international prosecutors, was faced with a difficult choice on which of many incidents to focus on in light of pragmatic constraints. "We didn't have enough resources to investigate all the nines and tens [a]nd the RPF, who acted in revenge, were at ones and twos and maybe even fours and fives."[85] Looked at in this way, the fact that the indictments did not include any RPF members could reasonably be construed as a function of the relative gravity of the crimes at issue, not a political or retributive decision, as Del Ponte and her supporters are inclined to suggest.[86] Ultimately, for whatever reason, whether political, security, or simply practical, the ICTR never filed any formal charges against alleged perpetrators of crimes committed by the RPF.

The ICTR Prosecutor has identified at least one incident in which several Hutu clergymen were killed under circumstances suggesting the perpetration

---

[82] United States Department of State, Diplomatic Cable, ICTY: President Meron urges USG to oppose Del Ponte renewal, 17 July 2003, 03THEHAGUE1827_A.

[83] William A. Schabas, *Selecting Cases at the ICTR* in Promoting Accountability for Gross Human Rights Violations Under International Law in Africa Essays in Honour of Prosecutor Hassan B. Jallow (Charles Jalloh and Alhagi Marong, eds., Brill Publishing, forthcoming 2015).

[84] Id., at 222.

[85] Id.

[86] Goldstone also stated, in the context of the ICTY, that he would issue indictments against Bosniak Muslims "for the sake of saying … what an even-handed chap I am." Id.

of war crimes, but Rwanda moved to prosecute those individuals in its domestic justice system. The Prosecutor of the ICTR, in light of that decision, stepped back and let the natural forum pursue the few perpetrators involved. As he reported to the Security Council, in June 2008, he was clear to the Prosecutor General of Rwanda that "any such prosecutions in and by Rwanda should be effective, expeditious, fair and open to the public." Furthermore, his office undertook to "monitor those proceedings", and if they were not satisfactory, he would invoke the primacy of the ICTR over those crimes.[87]

Between June and October 2008, Rwanda carried out the trial of four senior military officers and, as the ICTR did not have issues with the trial, the Prosecutor declared the matter closed from his perspective.[88] That trial has predictably been subject to criticism from both NGOs and scholars.[89] All to say, even though there was seemingly credible evidence supporting investigation of those crimes,[90] the ICTR's decision not to pursue them will continue to be a contentious point. The goal here is not to resolve that debate. Rather, it is sufficient for our purposes to note that Kagame's 20 year reign as president has also given some credence to the charge that the ICTR did not dispense blind justice during its tenure.

In the end, despite its alleged merits given the principle of equality of all persons (including victims) before the law, it seems rather simplistic to reduce a years-long, socio-economic-military conflict to "sides", and worse, to equate the criminal responsibility of the victims of the genocide to those who tried to wipe them out. At least, at a moral level, the argument comes off as deeply problematic if not downright offensive. From a legal point of view, the argument masks the fact that advocates are, by insisting on prosecuting those on the other side, effectively proposing to substitute their own views as to who should be prosecuted for those of the ICTR Prosecutor who is statutorily charged with that immense responsibility. Yet, even worse, as Goldstone's statements suggest, some of them have failed to account for the fact that charging decisions are made to reflect a number of different assessments including the likelihood of success in securing a conviction. That different prosecutors holding the same office might have taken a different approach, and exercised

---

87 UN Doc. S/PV.5904 (4 June 2008).
88 See, UN SCOR, 64th Sess., 6134th mtg. at 33, UN Doc. S/PV.6134 (4 June 2009).
89 See Human Rights Watch, *Rwanda: Tribunal Risks Supporting "Victor's Justice": Tribunal Should Vigorously Pursue Crimes of Rwandan Patriotic Front* (1 June 2009), http://www.hrw.org/news/2009/06/01/rwanda-tribunal-risks-supporting-victor-s-justice (last visited 27 July 2014).
90 See, e.g., UN Commission of Experts, *Final Report*, UN Doc. S/1994/1405 (9 Dec. 1994).

discretion differently, is beside the point. It is whether the decision taken can be justified as based on proper rather than improper criteria. Furthermore, supporters of the selectivity argument must bear the burden to satisfactorily answer an important practical question. That is, whether they would have been willing to forgo the prosecutions of the worst of the architects and planners of the genocide hauled before the ICTR just for the sake of securing the presumed benefits of equality of prosecutions of both sides to the Rwandan tragedy. Here, we assume for the sake of argument, that any attempt to prosecute in the ICTR a top RPF leader might practically have made it difficult if not impossible for the Tribunal to secure Rwanda's cooperation.

Finally, we note that some leniency for the sitting power in a post-conflict society may be justified as a boon to stability and security. In a country recovering from a debilitating conflict, the prior political and social infrastructure is no longer in place. The social order is stressed and often under some tension. In such a context, while there may be legal merit in doling out punishment without regard to post-conflict standing, *realpolitik* may argue for preserving what power structures remain as the basis for establishing long-term social peace and stability.

F Breadth of Proceedings

The UNSC's stated goal in establishing the ICTR was to prosecute "persons responsible for genocide and other serious violations of international humanitarian law committed in the territory of Rwanda and Rwandan citizens responsible for genocide and other such violations committed in the territory of neighboring States, between 1 January 1994 and 31 December 1994."[91] Accordingly, the ICTR's jurisdiction is limited temporally, geographically and substantively. The *ratione materiae* (subject-matter jurisdiction) of the Tribunal is limited to prosecuting the crimes of genocide,[92] crimes against humanity,[93] and violations of Common Article 3 and Additional Protocol II of the Geneva Conventions.[94] The *ratione temporis* (temporal jurisdiction) of the Tribunal is confined to crimes committed in the calendar year 1994. The Tribunal's *ratione personae* (personal jurisdiction) and *ratione loci* (territorial jurisdiction) are limited to 1) crimes committed by Rwandans in Rwanda and neighboring states, and 2) crimes committed by non-Rwandans in Rwanda.

---

91   ICTR Statute, art. 1.
92   ICTR Statute, art. 2.
93   ICTR Statute, art. 3.
94   ICTR Statute, art. 4.

These jurisdictional limitations created a highly focused mandate for the Tribunal. Notably, the mass killings broadly associated with the genocide in Rwanda did not begin until 6 April 1994, and were brought to an end in July 1994. As such, the court's temporal jurisdiction extends before and after the bulk of the overt criminal acts associated with the genocide, and is sufficient to capture *some* planning and preparation beforehand as well as some violence that accompanied the handover of power. The court's *ratione personae* allowed the Tribunal to bring charges against Rwandans who committed atrocities while fleeing Rwanda and the RPF takeover, limited to the aforementioned *ratione temporis*. In so structuring the Tribunal's mandate, the UNSC was able to avoid having the ICTR become responsible for litigating offenses that might have been precursors of the genocide.[95] Similarly, had the mandate been left open-ended, as was the case for the ICTY, it might have been possible to prosecute crimes that occurred subsequently in the neighboring states by individuals associated with either side of the Rwandan conflict.

In pursuit of its mandate, the ICTR indicted a total of 93 persons, of which 47 have been convicted or pleaded guilty, 16 are pending appeal, 12 were acquitted, 10 were transferred to national jurisdictions, and 9 remain at large.[96] By way of comparison, the ICTY (which has much broader temporal jurisdiction) indicted a total of 161 persons, and the SCSL indicted just 22. All said, the Tribunal was broad in its assessment of who to hold accountable for the genocide, and conducted a fair amount of business for an international tribunal.

Seen from a domestic perspective, a criminal institution that managed to try less than 100 defendants in 15 years would not be considered a resounding success if numbers of those prosecuted are our only calculus. But the quality, not the quantity, of justice also matters.[97] In any case, as one of the first international courts since the end of World War II, the ICTR had to lay a substantial amount of groundwork. Although this was a time-consuming and often frustrating process, it was ultimately a necessary one.

---

95 At the same time, the limited mandate created the somewhat perverse situation where significant international attention was focused on acts committed in basically 100 days in one small geographic area while, at the same time, serious violations of international law were on-going in neighboring countries. The Tribunal was simply not empowered to bring peace to the entire region; the Prosecutor was as unable to bring charges related to fresh atrocities in DRC as anyone else.

96 UN ICTR, *Status of Cases*, http://unictr.org/Cases/tabid/204/Default.aspx (last visited 27 July 2014).

97 Charles Jalloh, *Special Court for Sierra Leone: Achieving Justice?*, 32 Mich. J. Int'l. L. 395 (Spring 2011).

G   *Quality of Proceedings*

The ICTR expended great effort to ensure that its proceedings generally adhered to the highest international standards, and in that respect, is to be commended. The Statute of the Tribunal was revised several times to accommodate changes to court procedure. The Rules of Procedure and Evidence, which were amended every year of the Tribunal's operation,[98] would be recognizable to a lawyer in any national jurisdiction. The RPE and the Statute also incorporate elements of both civil and common law traditions, further harmonizing disparate notions of justice across the globe.

Further, the fact that 12 cases before the Tribunal resulted in acquittal shows that this adherence to international norms was not simply expensive and time-consuming window dressing. No system is perfect, and not every decision is justifiable in retrospect, but the ICTR deserves credit for pushing vigorously for fair trials that simultaneously respected the rights of the accused and international norms. That is not to say that there were not many, and in some cases, unacceptable delays between the indictment, arraignment, trial, issuance of judgment and finalization of some of its most important cases. Some of these undue delays led to serious and legitimate questions about whether justice had been served.[99]

This adherence to international norms is not, however, an unalloyed good. In terms of peace and security, there is understandably a sense that "those most responsible" were treated better than those not sufficiently responsible to merit international attention. For instance, the availability of capital punishment in Rwandan proceedings prior to 2007 ultimately means that some national defendants were treated "more harshly" than ICTR defendants, and thus the international community's insistence on fair trials ultimately benefited the most guilty. It is arguable that when the UN is involved, we cannot – or should not – have it any other way.

---

98   See Rules of Procedure and Evidence, http://unictr.org/Legal/RulesofProcedureandEvidence/tabid/95/Default.aspx (last visited 27 July 2014).

99   In a partially dissenting opinion in the Government II case, for instance, Judge Emile Short found that "the Accused have been incarcerated without judgement for more than 12 years" and concluded that "the right to trial without undue delay has been violated." Judge Short suggested a reduction in sentence for the convicted defendants would be appropriate as a result. Prosecutor v. Bizimungu et al., Case No. ICTR-99-50-T, Judgement and Sentence, p. 548 (30 September 2011). On appeal, Judge Patrick Robinson found that the nearly three years it took to prepare the trial judgment also breached the right to trial without undue delay. Mugenzi & Mugiraneza v. Prosecutor, Case No. ICTR-99-50-A, Judgement, p. 262 (4 February 2003).

H Cost of Administration

All of these international standards come, literally, at a cost. One frequent critique of the ICTR (and the ICTY) is that they were quite expensive.[100] All told, the Tribunal is expected to cost roughly US$1.75 billion over its lifetime, with a peak annual spending of US$150 million in 2008.[101] On an individualized basis, the ICTR spent approximately US$23.3 million per accused.[102]

Notably, the proceedings at the ICTR did not cost substantially more on a per-day basis than federal criminal trials in the United States.[103] However, the trials themselves lasted considerably longer than the average criminal trial, and thus the cost per *trial* is far greater than the average domestic proceeding (even in expensive jurisdictions).

Some of this expense is surely a product of the need to establish international precedent following the 45 year hibernation of international criminal law, the complexity of the subject matter, the need to translate witness testimony from Kinyarwanda to the working languages of the Tribunal, and to elicit testimony from witnesses about events that may have taken place 10 years in the past. It is equally true that some expense could have been avoided through better pre-trial management, limitations on witnesses, more frequent use of judicial notice, and more thorough sharing of evidence across cases. Furthermore, the decision to locate the Tribunal in Arusha created geographic distance between the *locus commisi delicti* and the seat of the court. It is clear that this ultimately made the process of gathering evidence and securing witness testimony much more expensive as it required arrangements, safe houses, and dedicated aircraft for witness travel.

Of course, the ICTR, the ICTY, and the Residual Mechanisms for those two courts are funded by the UN directly. The organization that created the court and gave it a mandate was also responsible for providing the resources necessary to accomplish those goals. This is not to say that the Tribunal did not experience budgetary pressures from New York, but only to say that the Tribunal had a substantially more stable funding base compared to others that came after it, such as the SCSL.[104]

---

100 As noted in the introduction, "expensive" is a relative term.
101 S. Ford, *How Leadership in International Criminal Law is Shifting from the United States to Europe and Asia: An Analysis of Spending On and Contributions to International Criminal Courts*, 55 St. Louis U. L. J. 953, 973 (2011).
102 The ICTR completed 47 cases, had 16 on appeal and 12 acquittals as of July 2014, for a total of 75. See, http://www.unictr.org/Cases/StatusofCases/tabid/204/Default.aspx.
103 Eric Posner, The Perils of Global Legalism (University of Chicago Press, 2009).
104 See, Part V.H. *supra*.

I   *Jurisprudential Impact*

The ICTR (and the ICTY), through individual proceedings and the appellate structure, did yeoman's legal work. Inasmuch as the only (and oft-cited) precedents were the Nuremberg and Tokyo Tribunals, the case law and normalization of fairly radical notions of international responsibility developed and normalized by the Tribunals is a real victory.

Several important contributions of the ICTR are worth noting, although a complete catalogue of its effects would be beyond the scope of this paper. First and foremost, the ICTR (and the ICTY) played an integral role in giving effect to the 1948 Convention on the Prevention and Punishment of the Crime of Genocide,[105] and in "confirming that genocide is an international crime, recognized as such in convention and custom, for which individual perpetrators may be held liable."[106] To that end, the ICTR delivered the first ever conviction for genocide before an international tribunal in the case of *Prosecutor v. Jean Paul Akayesu*.[107] The *Akayesu* case also created the important precedent that sexual violence and rape can be acts of genocide when committed with the requisite specialized intent.[108] This impact of the *Akayesu* case continues to reverberate today, including with the advancement of that crime as a supplemental element to close a normative gap in the genocide convention in Africa's proposed regional criminal court.

Second, the indictment and guilty plea of former Rwandese Prime Minister Jean Kambanda contributed to an emerging understanding that traditional notions of sovereign immunity were falling by the wayside in the modern era. Official capacity of an individual has no effect on his criminal responsibility, at least as it relates to core crimes such as genocide, war crimes, and crimes against humanity.[109]

Third, the ICTR contributed greatly to a working understanding of Common Article 3 and Additional Protocol II to the Geneva Conventions of 1949 as standards for armed conflict. Common Article 3 and Additional Protocol II both relate to *internal* armed conflict, and thus contain no implementation or enforcement provisions.[110] The explicit reference to these instruments in the ICTR Statute, and subsequent case law outlining the elements of each crime

---

105   78 UNTS 227 (9 December 1948).
106   M. Cherif Bassiouni, International Criminal Law 112 (3d Ed., Brill 2008).
107   Prosecutor v. Jean Paul Akayesu, Case No. ICTR-96-4-T, Judgment (2 September 1998).
108   Id., at para. 731–33.
109   See, ICTR Statute, Art. 6(2); Bassiouni, *supra* note 105 at 113. This is also a feature of the ICTY, ICC and SCSL statutes.
110   Bassiouni, *supra* note 105 at 114.

covered by the agreements, has helped to transform them into operating instruments of international criminal law.[111]

Lastly, the work of the both the Trial and Appeals Chambers has been cited on numerous occasions by other international criminal and national courts. In a certain respect, this is an accident of history; as one of the first tribunals, the ICTR had a better shot at laying the groundwork of modern genocide law. In the same way the ICTY had formed some kind of basis for the ICTR, so too did the ICTR affect the model of subsequent courts such as the SCSL.[112] However, that historical fact does not diminish the overall importance of the Tribunal to international justice.

5   Sierra Leone

A   *Brief History of the Conflict*

Sierra Leone was one of four British colonies in West Africa until it gained political independence in April 1961. After what seemed an auspicious start for democracy with the first transfer of power to an elected opposition party in an independent African State in 1967,[113] the country quickly degenerated into instability with a spate of military coups and counter-coups.[114] Ultimately, the civilian All People's Congress (APC) party formed a stable government around 1970. Unfortunately, the APC government stifled democracy by transforming itself into a despotic, one-party regime and sustaining its stranglehold on the country through massive corruption, nepotism, plunder of public assets, and

---

111   See, *Prosecutor v. Semanza*, Case No. ICTR-97-20-T, Judgment and Sentence (15 May 2003). Larissa van den Herik, Contribution of the Rwanda Tribunal to the Development of International Law (Brill, 15 May 2005); George Mugwanya, The Crime of Genocide in International Law: Appraising the Contribution of the UN Tribunal for Rwanda (Cameron May, 2007); Erik Mose, *Main Achievements of the ICTR*, 3 J. of Int'l Crim. Just. 920 (2005).

112   UN Security Council, *Report of the Secretary-General on the establishment of a Special Court for Sierra Leone*, S/2000/915 (4 October 2000) (addressing relationship between new SCSL and existing ad hoc tribunals); SCSL Statute, art. 14 (inheriting Rules of Procedure and Evidence from ICTR mutatis mutandi), art. 19 (looking to ICTR for guidance on sentencing), art. 20 (looking to ICTR and ICTY appellate decisions).

113   J.R. Cartwright, Politics in Sierra Leone: 1947–1967, 4 (University of Toronto Press 1970).

114   Sierra Leone Truth and Reconciliation Commission, *Report of the Commission Executive Summary*, Vol. 2, Chapter 1, *avilable at* http://www.sierraleonetrc.org/index.php/view-the-final-report/download-table-of-contents/volume-two/item/witness-to-the-truth-volume-two-chapter-1?category_id=12 (last visited 27 July 2014).

exacerbation of ethnic and regional cleavages.[115] By the 1990s, bad governance and economic decay, among other factors, had created sufficient malaise for the outbreak of conflict in the country.[116]

In March 1991, a mix of approximately 60 armed men attacked the village of Bomaru in eastern Sierra Leone.[117] The attack turned out to be the first salvo of the Revolutionary United Front (RUF) rebels apparently led by Foday Sankoh, a formerly low-ranking corporal in the Sierra Leone Army (SLA), whose ostensible goal was to overthrow the government of then-President Joseph Momoh. In a few weeks, the rebels quickly increased the intensity and frequency of their attacks, allegedly with logistical, financial, material, and even combat support from Liberian fighters donated by Charles Taylor of the National Patriotic Front of Liberia (NPFL).[118] The ill-equipped SLA, which had more experience putting down peaceful pro-democracy student demonstrations than fighting a war, proved unable to contain the unrelenting and devastating guerrilla attacks. In a few months, most of eastern Sierra Leone had fallen under rebel control. The war soon spread to other parts of the country.

President Momoh lacked a coherent strategy to deal with the war and was ousted from power in April 1992. Two successive military regimes failed to end the war. Under pressure from Sierra Leoneans clamoring to participate in their country's governance through the ballot box, democratic elections were finally held in 1996. Sierra Leone People's Party candidate Ahmad Tejan Kabbah, who had run on a platform of restoring peace, won the election. President Kabbah immediately entered into negotiations with the RUF and concluded a peace accord in Abidjan, Cote d'Ivoire. Despite this step toward the cessation of hostilities, the conflict resumed and yet another military coup took place. Kabbah fled to neighboring Guinea where he set up a government in exile in Conakry.

With strong international backing, especially from the regional Economic Community of West African States (ECOWAS), Kabbah was reinstated in 1998. Around mid-1999, his government negotiated the Lomé Peace Agreement with the RUF in another attempt to end the conflict. The Lomé Agreement included an amnesty provision, Article IX, granting Sankoh, and all other combatants and collaborators, "absolute and free pardon and reprieve" in respect of all

---

115 Id.
116 Id.
117 See, L. Gberie, A Dirty War in West Africa: The RUF and the Destruction of Sierra Leone (Indiana University Press 2006); D. Keen, Conflict and Collusion in Sierra Leone (Palgrave McMillan 2006).
118 Taylor started a guerrilla war in Liberia in 1989 similar to that led by Sankoh in Sierra Leone. He served as Liberia's President from 1997 to 2003.

their actions between the start of the war and the conclusion of the accords.[119] Despite this agreement, hostilities continued in the country until disarmament began in earnest in 2001. President Kabbah formally declared the war over in January 2002.

B   Local Involvement

Whereas the ICTR and the ICTY were established by the UN Security Council under its Chapter VII power, albeit with some limited input from the affected countries, the SCSL is a product of a bilateral treaty between Sierra Leone and the UN.[120] Thus, by its very nature as a consensual instrument, the SCSL incorporated more local concerns from its inception than the ICTR.

The Agreement establishing the Special Court was the culmination of a process that began with a letter from Sierra Leonean President Ahmad Kabbah to the UNSC via then-Secretary-General Kofi Annan requesting the international community's assistance in prosecuting those leaders who had planned and directed the brutal conflict in Sierra Leone.[121] President Kabbah maintained that international support was necessary to successfully prosecute those responsible for war-time atrocities due to the lack of legal, logistical and financial resources within the country.[122]

Through Resolution 1315, the UNSC formally endorsed President Kabbah's request to establish a "special court," although it did not take the same definitive action as in Rwanda or the former Yugoslavia. Rather than creating another fully international tribunal with a mandate to try "those persons responsible", the Security Council instead directed Secretary-General Kofi Annan to negotiate an agreement with the Sierra Leonean government to establish an *independent* tribunal to try those bearing "greatest responsibility."[123] The subsequent agreement between the UN and the government of Sierra Leone signaled that the Special Court would be a different animal than the

---

119   Peace Agreement between the Government of Sierra Leone and the Revolutionary Armed Front of Sierra Leone (May 18, 1999), *avilable at* http://www.sierraleonetrc.org/downloads/legalresources/lomepeaceaccord.pdf (hereinafter "Lome Accords") (last visited 27 July 2014).

120   *Agreement between the United Nations and the Government of Sierra Leone on the Establishment of a Special Court for Sierra Leone*, 2178 UNTS 127 (16 Jan. 2002) (hereinafter "SCSL Agreement").

121   President of the Republic of Sierra Leone, *Annex to the Letter dated Aug. 9, 2000 from the Permanent Representative of Sierra Leone to the United Nations addressed to the President of the Security Council*, UN Doc. S/2000/786 (10 Aug. 2000).

122   Id.

123   S.C. Res. 1315, UN Doc. S/RES/1315 (14 Aug. 2000).

previous ad hoc tribunals. Coming as it did after the international community had had experiences with the Chapter VII model, it also attempted to address some of the perceived deficiencies of the ICTY and ICTR.[124]

Perhaps the most important accession to local concerns was the decision to locate the Special Court in Freetown, the capital of Sierra Leone. Unlike the ICTR and ICTY before it, the Special Court did its work in the *locus commisi delicti*. While both of the International Tribunals have been criticized for delivering justice from afar,[125] the SCSL specifically undertook to be present in the affected communities.

In addition to its advantageous location, the SCSL also actively undertook to engage with the populace of Sierra Leone from the very beginning. As part of this effort, the Office of the Prosecutor and the Registry set up day-long "town hall" meetings in towns and cities around the country to discuss the work of the Special Court. In the first four months of the Special Court's existence, it is reported that the then-Prosecutor David Crane visited every district and every major town in Sierra Leone.[126] Calling himself "their prosecutor," Crane described the role of these meetings as one where he "would go out and listen to the people of Sierra Leone tell me what happened in their country."[127] One may rightly question whether the Outreach Office and the people "up country" took the same lessons away from their meetings.[128] However, the substantial efforts to reach out to the local population and to keep them abreast of the SCSL's work shows some concern for local engagement and perhaps even local acceptance and local endorsement of its work.

---

[124] Antonio Cassesse, *Independent Expert Report on the Special Court for Sierra Leone* (12 December 2006), *avilable at* http://www.rscsl.org/Documents/Cassese%20Report.pdf; Alison Smith, *The Expectations and Role of International and National Civil Society and the SCSL*, in The Sierra Leone Special Court and its Legacy 46 (Cambridge Univ. Press 2014, Charles Jalloh, Ed.) (hereinafter "Sierra Leone Special Court Legacy").

[125] See, e.g., Ralph Zacklin, *The Failings of Ad Hoc International Tribunals*, 2 J. Int'l. Crim. Just. 541, 544 (2004) (arguing that there was a perception among the victims that the ICTY was too remote and that there was little appreciation of its work at the grass roots level); Karugarama, *supra* note 52(arguing that the Tribunals were "viewed as foreign, detached and contribute very little to National reconciliation process").

[126] David M. Crane, *Dancing with the Devil: Prosecuting West Africa's Warlords: Building Initial Prosecutorial Strategy for an International Tribunal after Third World Armed Conflicts*, 37 Case W. Res. J. of Int'l Law 1 (2005).

[127] Id.

[128] See, e.g., Lydia A. Nkansah, *Justice within the Arrangement of the Special Court for Sierra Leone versus Local Perception of Justice: a Contradiction or Harmonious?*, 22 Afr. J. Int'l Comp. L. 103, 115 (2014) (reviewing a field study of attitudes amongst ordinary Sierra Leoneans about the Special Court).

The SCSL was also created with the participation of local jurists in mind. The Agreement establishing the tribunal provides that at least one-third of the Trial Chambers judges, two-fifths of the Appeals Chambers judges, and the Deputy Prosecutor would be from Sierra Leone, and that the Government of Sierra Leone would participate in the SCSL's Management Committee.[129] Additionally, the Secretary-General, who was responsible for appointing the key international staff, was to do so on the basis of recommendations of States, particularly member states of the Economic Community of West African States (ECOWAS).[130] The hope was that this would make the SCSL more relevant in the minds of Sierra Leoneans. But beyond the various positions reserved for Sierra Leone to appoint, there have been some questions about the extent of substantive local lawyer participation in the court's processes. The failure to meaningfully involve and/or to integrate them into the tribunal's processes is anecdotally reported to have created some friction between the tribunal and the local bar, when the national lawyers realized that there would be limited opportunities for them to serve in the tribunal.[131] Yet, international criminal law literature has been touting that one of the alleged benefits of the SCSL model was precisely that it enabled nationals and internationals to work side by side in service to a common cause.[132] It is unclear how much of this theory came out in the practice.

Nevertheless, the Special Court took at least four steps to involve the local community from its inception. First, the SCSL was located in Freetown. Second, it was given jurisdiction over some violations of Sierra Leonean law, thus bringing it home in a symbolic sense, even if in practice those offenses were never used to bring charges due to the prosecutorial decision not to so do.[133] Third, the SCSL undertook a serious outreach effort to inform the affected population about its mandate and work.[134] Here, in contrast to its predecessors, it

---

129 SCSL Agreement, *supra* note 119, art. 2,3,7.
130 Id.,, art. 2.
131 Smith, *supra* note 123.
132 Antonio Cassese, *The role of internationalized courts and tribunals in the fight against international criminality* in Internationalized Criminal Courts Sierra Leone, East Timor, Kosovo, And Cambodia (Oxford Univ. Press 2004) (Cesare P.R. Romano, Andre Nollkaemper, and Jann K. Kleffner eds); Laura A. Dickinson, *The Promise of Hybrid Courts*, 97 Am. J. Int' L. 295 (2003).
133 Jalloh, *supra* note 96.
134 Vincent Nmehielle and Charles Jalloh, *The Legacy of the Special Court for Sierra Leone*, 30 Fletcher Forum of World Aff. 107 (2006); Outreach and Public Affairs, http://www.rscsl.org/OPA.html; Stuart Ford, *How Special is the Special Court's Outreach Section?* in Sierra Leone Special Court Legacy, *supra* note 123 at 505.

benefited from its location in Freetown. This, however, is not to say that it did not face challenges in expanding its footprint in a country with limited road and other infrastructure.[135] Fourth, a certain number of places within the SCSL's hierarchy were reserved specifically for Sierra Leoneans by the Statute, thus ensuring a floor for the level of local involvement. This contrasts favorably with the ICTR model. Yet, due to the Kabbah Government choice not to use its appointments to put Sierra Leoneans in some of the key tribunal positions (especially that of Deputy Prosecutor), the extent of local involvement proved to be less than many would have predicted and gave rise to some disappointment in the local bar.

C *Competing National Proceedings*

As is evident by a review of the Special Court's mandate, the SCSL was not empowered to right all wrongs that may have been committed in the country during the decade-long conflict. Rather, the SCSL was limited to prosecuting serious violations of international law, war crimes, crimes against humanity, and a select set of national laws which occurred during the latter half of the conflict. The remainder of the work of helping to restore respect for the rule of law, healing open wounds, stabilizing the peace, and building the local legal capacity rested with the Sierra Leonean authorities. Of course, some of those goals were, presumably for political and optics reasons, mentioned in the Security Council Resolution preceding the creation of the Tribunal. They were frequently the result of discussions. This generated high expectations, in Sierra Leone and elsewhere, that could simply not be fulfilled. Espousing wider expectations for the SCSL was not unique, and in fact, is a common feature of UN involvement in the Yugoslavia and Rwanda contexts – a phenomenon that has led some scholars such as Marjan Damaska to call for a downgrading of expectations.[136] The argument is that such unrealistic expectations are not only unfair impositions on a criminal court, but that they also tend to inevitably lead to high disappointments.

The government of Sierra Leone took two important steps to address the conflict. First, Sierra Leone created a Truth and Reconciliation Commission (TRC) that operated in tandem with, and independent of, the SCSL. The TRC was established pursuant to Article VI of the Lomé Peace Accord[137] with the goals of creating "an impartial historical record of violations and abuses of human rights and international humanitarian law related to the armed conflict in

---

135   Nmehille and Jalloh, *supra* note 133.
136   Damaska, *supra* note 2.
137   Lome Accords, *supra* note 118, art. VI.

Sierra Leone [from 1991 to 1999], to respond to the needs of the victims, to promote healing and reconciliation and to prevent a repetition of the violations and abuses suffered."[138] Although the agreement included a blanket amnesty provision,[139] the TRC itself was not empowered to grant any pardons or extend amnesty to any combatants.[140]

While the Special Court and the TRC had complementary mandates, there were some operational conflicts. In particular, "some individuals were hesitant to testify before the TRC out of a fear, real or perceived, that they could be prosecuted" based on their testimony.[141] This problem was highlighted by the case of Samuel Hinga Norman, a former deputy minister in the custody of the SCSL who wished to testify publicly before the TRC. The Special Court ultimately found that Norman could testify, but that the proceedings must be closed in order to prevent diminution of the SCSL's process.[142] In its final report, the TRC issued several recommendations for future joint processes, including the establishment of "the basic rights of individuals in relation to each body in different circumstances. In particular, the right of detainees and prisoners, in the custody of a justice body, to participate in the truth and reconciliation process should be enshrined in law."[143]

In addition to the parallel reconciliation process, national courts also tried 31 members of an RUF splinter group, known as the West Side Boys, for conspiracy to commit murder. The prosecution initially filed 31 counts against a total of 27 accused. Charges against 16 of the accused were dismissed after the High Court found that there was no case for them to answer.[144] Of the remaining 11 defendants, 7 were convicted on six counts of conspiracy to commit

---

138   The Truth and Reconciliation Commission Act of 2000 (2000), *avilable at* http://www.sierraleonetrc.org/downloads/legalresources/trc_act_2000.pdf (last accessed 27 July2014) (hereinafter "TRC Act").

139   Lome Accords, art. IX.

140   William A. Schabas, *Truth Commissions and Courts Working in Parallel*, 93 Am. Soc'y Int'l L. Proc. 189, 191 (2004).

141   Linda E. Carter, *International Judicial Trials, Truth Commissions, And Gacaca: Developing a Framework for Transitional Justice from the Experiences in Sierra Leone and Rwanda*, in Sierra Leone Special Court Legacy, *supra* note 123 at 728.

142   Prosecutor v. Norman, Case No. SCSL-2003–08-PT-122, Decision on appeal by TRC and accused against the decision of His Lordship Justice Bankole Thompson to deny the TRC request to hold a public hearing with Chief Norman (28 November 2003), *avilable at* http://www.rscsl.org/Documents/Decisions/CDF/Appeal/122/SCSL-03–08-PT-122.pdf.

143   Sierra Leone Truth & Reconciliation Commission, 2 Witness to Truth: Report of the Sierra Leone Truth & Reconciliation Commission 1, 190 (2004).

144   S v. Kallay and Others [2006] SLHC 7 (5 April 2006).

murder and sentenced to 10 years imprisonment for each count, to run concurrently.[145]

Given the prosecution's inability to provide sufficient evidence against a majority of the accused, the West Side Boys case suggests that the national authorities were not up to the task of prosecuting crimes related to the conflict. The case can also be understood as a statement on the state of the judiciary. One of the principal justifications that the government used when it sought international support to establish the SCSL was that the local justice system lacked the capacity to prosecute.[146] But, it seemed that the members of the local bar who met with the UN felt that there was sufficient capacity to prosecute.[147] Thus, by holding the government to proof of the charges that it had brought, the local judiciary vindicated that view. Leaving practicalities aside, the question arises whether the government would have been able to prosecute more offenders, assuming it was willing to do so, in light of the amnesty clause contained in the Lomé Accord which granted amnesty to all combatants in the conflict.[148]

D Competing International Proceedings

There is anecdotal evidence suggesting that one or two jurisdictions carried out investigations of Sierra Leoneans who had arrived in their territories. They were alleged to have been involved in international crimes, although presumably because the evidence was weak, no trials ever materialized. In the end, in contrast to the Rwanda situation, there were no significant trials of combatants or leaders outside of the SCSL and the Sierra Leonean national judiciary. The only international action against a party connected loosely to that country's conflict was the trial of Chuckie Taylor, the son of former Liberian President Charles Taylor, on torture charges in the United States. The younger Taylor is a US citizen by dint of his being born in the US, and the criminal conduct with which he was charged was related to his actions as head of the Anti-Terrorism Unit in Liberia. Although his father was charged with crimes against humanity and war crimes by the SCSL, no explicit connection between Sierra Leone and Chuckie Taylor was made by the US Justice Department.[149] It is hard

---

145 Id.
146 See, Letter from President Alhaji Ahmad Tejan Kabbah to the United Nations Secretary-General dated 12 June 2000, *avilable at* http://www.rscsl.org/Documents/Establishment/S-2000–786.pdf (last visited 27 July 2014).
147 See, *Report of the Planning Mission on the Establishment of the Special Court for Sierra Leone*, *supra* note 1.
148 Charles Jalloh, *Conclusion* in Sierra Leone Special Court Legacy, *supra* note 123 at 770.
149 See, Superseding Indictment, United States v. Roy M. Belfast, Jr., Case No. 06–20758-

to establish why definitively, but part of the reason for this appears to be that the younger Taylor might not have been implicated in the violence in Sierra Leone. Another might be that there was already strong evidence of his involvement in crimes in Liberia.

E Impunity and "Victor's Justice"

The conflict which gave rise to the SCSL was a complex one which defies easy description for its motivations. Among other factors, it was tied to bad governance and the apparent desire by a few men to exploit the country's diamond wealth for personal gain.[150] The list of accused before the Special Court reflects this complexity to some degree. Of the 12 defendants tried by the Special Court for crimes related to the conflict, five were drawn from the Revolutionary United Front,[151] four were members of the Armed Forces Revolutionary Council,[152] and three were members of the Civil Defence Forces.[153] In a broad sense, the SCSL indicted combatants from "all sides" of the conflict, if we leave aside the alleged responsibility of West African peacekeepers who received an exemption from its jurisdiction.[154]

To mention this diversity is not to say that the number of prosecutions or the identity of the individual defendants is necessarily correct. Charles Jalloh, for instance, has argued that there was an over inclusiveness with respect to those that were actually prosecuted.[155] Yet, the argument can be made that the diversity in the list of defendants was a good step towards showing that no party to a conflict is above the law. In this sense, the practice at the Special Court arguably stands in contrast to that at the ICTR, where only one "side" of the underlying conflict was indicted, and where, consequently, allegations of "victor's justice" ran rampant throughout the Tribunal's tenure. Conversely, in Sierra Leone, the allegation has now surfaced in a new form about "White Mans" justice. On the other hand, as mentioned earlier in relation to the selectivity argument vis-à-vis non prosecution of any Tutsis before the ICTR, there

---

 CR-ALTONAGA(s), (S.D. Fl., 10 September 2007) *avilable at* http://www.justice.gov/criminal/hrsp/pr/2007/september/09-06-07ctaylor-indict.pdf (27 July 2014).

150 Lansana Gberie, A Dirty War in West Africa: The RUF and the Destruction of Sierra Leone (Indiana Univ. Press, December 1, 2005); Yusuf Bangura *Strategic Policy Failure and Governance in Sierra Leone*, 38(4) J. of Modern Afr. Stud. 551 (2001).

151 Foday Saybana Sankoh, Sam Bockarie, Issa Hassan Sesay and Morris Kallon.

152 Alex Tamba Brima, Ibrahim Bazzy Kamara, Santigie Borbor Kanu and Johnny Paul Koroma.

153 Sam Hinga Norma, Moinina Fofana and Allieu Kondewa.

154 SCSL Statute, art. 1.

155 Jalloh, *supra* note 96.

is perhaps a price to be paid for equality of prosecutions. That price suggests moral and legal equivalence to the individual criminal responsibility of those who fomented war (such as the RUF) for selfish reasons and those that tried to stop it in acts of patriotism for selfless reasons, but in the process, committed some crimes. It might have also undermined the long term peace in Sierra Leone given the controversy that since arose from the CDF Trial and the perception that it led to among many Sierra Leoneans.[156]

The Special Court's arguable achievements in breaking the trend of victor's justice after mass atrocity do not necessarily carry over into the realm of impunity. One of the consequences of the Tribunal's narrow mandate is that relatively few people were tried. This is the problem of under-inclusiveness.[157] The bulk of the combatants were left for the national judiciary to deal with, and assuming amnesty issues did not bar such prosecutions for international crimes before the domestic courts, these authorities simply lacked the resources to effectively try a significant portion of the country's population. As a result, people who were famous for their exploits during the conflict remain among the population. Some of them arguably fell within the "greatest responsibility" jurisdiction of the SCSL, but because the Special Court never prosecuted them and the neglect of the Sierra Leonean authorities, they are not within the reach of the national judiciary.[158]

F *Breadth of Proceedings*

Much like its predecessors, the *ratione materiae* (subject-matter jurisdiction) of the SCSL extended to crimes against humanity,[159] war crimes,[160] and other serious violations of international law.[161] However, the SCSL's jurisdiction was

---

156 Lansana Gberie, *The Civil Defense Forces Trial: Limit to International Justice?* in Sierra Leone Special Court Legacy, *supra* note 123 at 624; Charles Jalloh, *Prosecuting Those Bearing "Greatest Responsibility": The Contributions of the Special Court for Sierra Leone* in Sierra Leone Special Court Legacy, *supra* note 123 at 589; Jalloh, *supra* note 96.

157 Jalloh, *supra* note 96.

158 For instance, some international commentators have called for the arrest of Ibrahim Bah, an associate of Charles Taylor accused of, inter alia, supplying arms to the conflict. See, Centre for Accountability and Rule of Law, *CARL Calls for the Prosecution of former mercenary in the Sierra Leone Civil Conflict* (13 June 2013), *avilable at* http://www.carl-sl.org/home/press-releases/613-ibrahim-tommy-executive-director-carl (last visited 27 July 2014); Human Rights Watch, *Sierra Leone: Investigate Alleged Rebel Arms Supplier* (19 June 2013) *avilable at* http://www.hrw.org/news/2013/06/19/sierra-leone-investigate-alleged-rebel-arms-supplier (27 July 2014).

159 SCSL Statute, art. 2.

160 Id., at art. 3.

161 Id., at art. 4.

distinct from those of the International Tribunals in two important respects. First, the Special Court did not have jurisdiction over the crime of genocide. The international crimes are limited to those listed above. Second, as a hybrid tribunal, the SCSL was also granted jurisdiction over certain domestic, Sierra Leonean crimes, including the abuse of girls and wanton destruction of property.[162] Thus, the Special Court's role within the international and national judicial structure was markedly different than that of the ICTR and the ICTY. Of course, whereas the tribunal used the international crimes in its cases, no Sierra Leonean crimes were used. On the other side, we could not find evidence that the government used those same crimes from its national laws or international crimes to prosecute war related cases in its own courts.

Further, unlike the ICTR, the Special Court's *ratione temporis* (temporal jurisdiction) extended well before the end of hostilities. This was a function of the fact that the conflict was ongoing. Thus, the SCSL's jurisdiction includes all crimes committed after 30 November 1996, nearly four years before the signing of the Agreement and six years before the Statute entered into force. Although the Sierra Leonean government had wanted the jurisdiction to extend to the beginning of the war in March 1991, the UN disagreed largely for financial reasons.[163] Readers will recall that the ICTR's mandate was limited to crimes committed during the calendar year 1994, limiting the Tribunal's ability to address predicate crimes that culminated in the genocide. This innovation at the Special Court can be seen as either an attempt to address that deficiency, as a delegation of authority already held by the Sierra Leonean judiciary, or both.

Lastly, the SCSL's *ratione personae* (personal jurisdiction) and *ratione loci* (territorial jurisdiction) differ from those of the ICTR. While the ICTR had jurisdiction over both Rwandans and certain foreigners, the SCSL is empowered to try "persons who bear the greatest responsibility" without specific reference to nationality.[164] However, this broader personal jurisdiction is limited by a requirement that the crimes at issue must have taken place "in the territory of Sierra Leone."[165] This differs from the ICTR's mandate granting jurisdiction over crimes committed by Rwandans "in neighbouring States."[166] There was no provision for prosecution of crimes that might have been committed by the

---

162   Id., at art. 5.
163   Abdul Tejan Cole, *The Special Court for Sierra Leone: Conceptual concerns and alternatives*, 1(1) Afr. Hum. Rts. L. J. 107 (2001).
164   SCSL Statue, art. 1 (1). Those persons must also have been over the age of 15 at the time of the alleged crime. SCSL Statue, art 7.
165   Id.
166   ICTR Statute, art. 1.

same combatants involved in cross border attacks in Liberia and Guinea, a common occurrence during the war.

It may at first glance seem that the SCSL had a fairly broad mandate, at least over crimes that took place within Sierra Leone. However, the ultimate limiting factor was the term "greatest responsibility."[167] In normal parlance, this standard may be synonymous with the "most responsible" mandate of the ICTR. In practice, however, the term "greatest responsibility" operated as a limitation on the number and breadth of trials before the SCSL. A fair amount of energy at the court was devoted to discerning an operative meaning of "greatest responsibility."[168]

In the end, the Special Court tried only 12 defendants on charges related to the conflict.[169] One of those defendants, however, was the head of a neighboring state at the time he committed the charged crimes. This simple fact complicates the act of assessing the breadth of proceedings before the SCSL. On the one hand, relatively few trials were conducted. In this sense, the Special Court Prosecutor was either fulfilling his narrow mandate or using too restrictive an interpretation of "greatest responsibility" that unnecessarily limited the SCSL's reach. On the other hand, the indictment, trial, and ultimate conviction of Charles Taylor suggests that the SCSL attempted to move beyond national borders to bring one of the biggest of big-fish defendants to justice. In this sense, it can be argued perhaps, the limited number of prosecutions might not have undermined their *breadth*.

G   *Quality of Proceedings*

Like the ICTR and the ICTY before it, the SCSL took great pains to bring international standards of justice to bear. The Rules of Procedure and Evidence were amended fourteen times between 2003 and 2012 as court practice evolved.[170] This could be taken as an indication of adherence to that commitment. At the same time, there are legitimate questions that have been raised about the double role of judges as implementers and drafters of the rules that guide their processes in these tribunals. Nevertheless, besides the ICC, all other ad hoc tribunals going back to Nuremberg provided for judicial drafting of the rules of court. Arguably, this promotes efficiency in the process as the tribunals

---

167   SCSL Statute, art. 1(1).
168   For more detailed analysis and legal history, *see* Charles Jalloh, *Prosecuting Those Bearing "Greatest Responsibility": The Contributions of the Special Court for Sierra Leone*, in Sierra Leone Special Court Legacy, *supra* note 123 at 589.
169   The Special Court also heard several contempt cases related to the primary proceedings.
170   See, http://www.rscsl.org/Documents/RPE.pdf (showing amendment dates of all prior versions of the RPE).

learn by doing and improve their procedures over time in light of the practical challenges faced during the trials.

The structure and processes of the Special Court were apparently designed to incorporate local concerns from its inception, in contrast to the situation in the ICTR. In particular, the guarantee of a certain number of court appointments for Sierra Leoneans and for international lawyers[171] helped to ensure both that the court's proceedings adhered to international standards and took local viewpoints into account. Yet, as noted earlier, save for a small number of appointments to the judiciary the remainder of those positions were occupied by non-Sierra Leoneans. For example, the first two national appointments to the position of Deputy Prosecutor selected a Sri-Lankan (Desmond de Silva) and later on an Australian (Christopher Staker). It was only towards the end of the Tribunal's life, when for all intents and purposes the work was done, that the government proposed a Sierra Leonean (Joseph Kamara) for the position.

National law was also to be used in the Tribunal. The sources of law applicable to the Special Court includes "general principles of law derived from national laws of legal systems of the world including, as appropriate, the national laws of the Republic of Sierra Leone, provided that those principles are not inconsistent with the Statute, the Agreement, and with international customary law and internationally recognized norms and standards."[172] On one level, of course, this provision can be seen as a step towards making Sierra Leonean law relevant to the work of the SCSL – above and beyond the (unused) national crimes included in the subject matter jurisdiction. Another reading of this provision is that, even though it provided for the use of principles of law from all national legal systems, it mentioned Sierra Leone as a source with a qualifier (as appropriate), thereby limiting the potential use of such laws at the Special Court. The implication was that the use of such principles was to occur only if there was no clash between such laws and the applicable instruments (SCSL Statute and UN-Sierra Leone Agreement) and customary international law.

A similar rule provided for examination of Sierra Leonean practice in respect of determination of penalties before the Tribunal. But these too were subordinated to the international and appeared not to have been taken seriously in the Court's judgments. Ultimately, it seems cogent to argue that although lip service was paid towards Sierra Leonean laws, the practice differed dramatically. Nevertheless, as Charles Jalloh has argued more fully elsewhere, if the alternative to the creation of the SCSL was prosecution by the

---

171   SCSL Agreement, *supra* note 119, art. 2,3.
172   SCSL RPE, Rule 72(iii).

standards of the then-extant Sierra Leonean national justice system, the SCSL "would probably be deemed exemplary."[173]

Two main concerns undermine the generally positive assessment of the quality of the SCSL's work. First, the overly conservative interpretation of the Special Court's mandate by the Prosecutor, and eventually the Chambers, resulted in far fewer (and therefore more selective) prosecutions than many Sierra Leoneans would have hoped for. Second, the rights of the accused before the tribunal may have been negatively affected by the very limited funds available for their defense counsel, and the long period of pre-trial detention.

With respect to the Special Court's mandate, recall that the SCSL was tasked with prosecuting those who bore the "greatest responsibility" for the serious violations of international law and select provisions of national law, "including those leaders who, in committing such crimes, have threatened the establishment of and implementation of the peace process in Sierra Leone."[174] However, the term "greatest responsibility" was not explicitly defined by any of the court's constitutive documents, nor was there agreement among the contracting parties as to its precise definition.[175] Not even the various organs of the SCSL agreed on an operative definition. The Trial Chamber hearing the CDF case held that the phrase was both a jurisdictional limitation and a guidepost for prosecutorial discretion.[176] An accurate assessment of whether there are reasonable grounds to support a finding that a particular accused bore "greatest responsibility" should be, in the CDF Trial Chamber's view, conducted by the Confirming Judge at the pre-trial stage. "Whether or not *in actuality* the Accused could be said to bear the greatest responsibility can only be determined by the Chamber after considering all the evidence presented during trial."[177] The Armed Forces Revolutionary Council (AFRC) Trial Chamber, on the other hand, found that the phrase was meant solely to "streamline the focus of prosecutorial strategy."[178] The judges rejected the idea that the phrase created a limit on personal jurisdiction that would require them to dismiss a case if the threshold were not met.[179] Accordingly, the AFRC Chamber did not think itself competent to review the Prosecutor's decision to bring an indictment against a particular person because the Office of the Prosecutor is an in-

---

173   Jalloh, *supra* note 96 at 456.
174   SCSL Statute, art. 1.
175   Jalloh, *supra* note 173 at 413.
176   Prosecutor v. Fofana, Case No. SCSL-04–14-T, Judgment, ¶¶ 91–92 (2 August 2007).
177   Id. at ¶ 92.
178   Prosecutor v. Brima, Case no. SCSL-04–16-T Judgment, ¶ 653 (20 June 2007).
179   Id.

dependent organ charged with making such assessments.[180] Ultimately, the Appeals Chamber came down on the side of the AFRC Trial Chamber, finding that the phrase "greatest responsibility" was meant to guide the use of prosecutorial discretion, and not as a jurisdictional limitation. The Appeals Chamber concluded:

> It is evident that it is the Prosecutor who has the responsibility and competence to determine who are to be prosecuted as a result of investigation undertaken by him. It is the Chambers that have the competence to try such persons who the Prosecutor has consequently brought before it as persons who bear the greatest responsibility.[181]

As a result of this deference to prosecutorial discretion, the *raison d'etre* of the SCSL was essentially delegated to one of the Court's organs without judicial oversight.[182] Under serious political and fiscal constraints, the Prosecutor's interpretation of the mandate to try those bearing "greatest responsibility" limited the list of suspects from 30,000 to about twenty.[183] When combined with the Court's desire to avoid imposition of "victor's justice," this narrow interpretation of the mandate left "an unusually bottom-heavy" indictment list.[184] A number of combatants whose wartime conduct was especially brutal were not indicted,[185] nor were prominent international businessmen who benefited from the illicit diamond trade.[186]

The second significant issue for the Court's proceedings came as a result of funding constraints (discussed in more detail in Part VI.G. below). The SCSL Statute incorporates language from the International Covenant on Civil and Political Rights[187] guaranteeing certain rights to the accused, including the rights to be presumed innocent, to a fair and public hearing before an impar-

---

180 Id., at ¶ 654.
181 Prosecutor v. Brima, Case no. SCSL-04–16-A, Appeals Judgment, ¶ 281 (22 February 2008).
182 See, Jalloh *supra* note 173 at 415–430.
183 David M. Crane, *International Criminal Tribunals in the 21st Century: Terrorists, Warlords, and Thugs*, 21 Am. U. Int'l L. Rev. 505, 508–09, 511–12 (2006).
184 Phoebe Knowles, *The Power to Prosecute: The Special Court for Sierra Leone From a Defence Perspective*, 6 Int'l Crim. L. Rev. 387, 406–07 (2006);
185 Human Rights Watch, *Bringing Justice: the Special Court for Sierra Leone: Accomplishments, Shortcomings and Needed Support* (8 September 2004), *avilable at* http://www.hrw.org/reports/2004/09/07/bringing-justice-special-court-sierra-leone (last visited 27 July 2014).
186 Jalloh, *supra* note 173 at 424.
187 International Covenant on Civil and Political Rights, arts. 9(3), 14, 999 U.N. T.S 171 (23 March 1976).

tial tribunal, to counsel, to adequate time and facilities to prepare their defense, and to cross-examine witnesses.[188] In order to fulfill these guarantees, the SCSL undertook the innovative and unprecedented creation of a Defense Office.[189] As an organ of the Court, however, the Defense Office was under competing mandates to ensure the rights of the defendants and to keep costs down.[190] Ultimately, the "SCSL was, in practice, so constrained by the general lack of funding, that its treatment of the accused and defense rights gave the unfortunate impression of being setup with the sole purpose to convict."[191]

H   Cost of Administration

Unlike the ICTR and the ICTY before it, the SCSL relied on voluntary contributions of states to support its work. The prior, fully international tribunals received their funding from assessed UN dues.[192] All in, the SCSL was expected to spend US$257 million over its lifetime, with an annual peak of US$36 million in 2007.[193] On an individual basis, the SCSL will have spent roughly US$28.5 million per completed trial.[194] In absolute terms, then, the SCSL was markedly cheaper than the ICTR (which cost roughly US$1.75 billion). However, in relative terms, the SCSL's lower price tag was not a result of its efficiency; the per-defendant costs are substantially the same for either court.[195]

No doubt a function of what David Scheffer has called "tribunal fatigue" at the Security Council,[196] the SCSL was created with a voluntary funding mechanism whereby member states, IGOs, and NGOs would contribute funds,

---

188   SCSL Statute, art. 17.
189   SCSL RPE, art. 45.
190   Jalloh *supra* note 173 at 442.
191   Id., at 444 (*citing* Wayne Jordash & Scott Martin, *Due Process and Fair Trial Rights at the Special Court: How the Desire for Accountability Outweighed the Demands of Justice at the Special Court for Sierra Leone*, 23 Leiden J. Int'l L. 585, 587, 608 (2010)).
192   ICTR Statute, art. 30; ICTY Statute, art. 32.
193   S. Ford, *How Leadership in International Criminal Law is Shifting from the United States to Europe and Asia: An Analysis of Spending On and Contributions to International Criminal Courts*, 55 St. Louis U. L. J. 953, 975–6 (2011).
194   In practical terms, the SCSL has completed trials for only nine individuals. Prosecutor v. Brima, Kamara & Kanu, Case No. SCSL-04–16-T; Prosecutor v. Sesay, Kallon & Gbao, Case No. SCSL-04–15-T; Prosecutor v. Fofana & Kondewa, Case No. SCSL-04–14-T.
195   Would that $5 million could be called "trivial" in our everyday lives. However, the expenditure-per-defendant metric does not take into account many economic factors that may be important to an overall calculation. Thus, it is a rough measure of a rough estimate, and as such, the resultant numbers are not specific enough to warrant one-to-one scrutiny.
196   See, Helena Cobban, *International Courts*, Foreign Pol'y, Mar.–Apr. 2006, at 22–23 (noting that the ICTs had "ballooning" timelines and costs).

equipment, service, and expert personnel on their own accord.[197] In recognition of this unique funding structure, the "important contributors" to the SCSL would also be given a position on the Management Committee, which was charged with assisting "the Secretary-General in obtaining adequate funding, and provide advice and policy direction on all non-judicial aspects of the operation of the Special Court, including questions of efficiency, and to perform other functions as agreed by interested States."[198] In theory, then, the SCSL would be directly accountable to the states and groups who chose to support the Court's work, rather than the UN bureaucracy as a whole.[199] Former SCSL Prosecutor Stephen Rapp described this voluntary funding arrangement as a "compact model" wherein the "[t]hose involved with the court would essentially put together a plan and go to world capitals saying, 'This is what we want to do. If you think it is important, contribute your tax money to this cause. [...] If you provide us with contributions to meet [our] budget, you will see this quantity of justice.'"[200]

In practice, this voluntary funding mechanism meant that "the success of the Court depended upon the level of funding that it could generate from UN members."[201] The initial plan was that the SCSL would run for three years,[202] and thus the scope of the fund-raising task that the SCSL would undertake over the next decade was not well understood at the outset. The implication that the Special Court's work would only last three years "created high and unrealistic expectations as to what it could accomplish in the time it had."[203] Further, the reliance on third-party funding resulted in disconnection between the SCSL and its founding entities.[204]

The end result of implementing this voluntary funding mechanism was a general reduction in the efficacy and, to some extent, the perceived legitimacy

---

197 S.C. Res 1315 (2000) ¶ 8; SCSL Agreement, *supra* note 119, art. 6.

198 SCSL Agreement, *supra* note 119, art. 7.

199 Sara Kendall, *Marketing Accountability at the Special Court for Sierra Leone*, in Sierra Leone Special Court Legacy, *supra* note 123 at 389.

200 Stephen Rapp, *The Compact Model in International Criminal Justice: The Special Court for Sierra Leone*, 57 Drake L. Rev. 11–48, 21 (2008–09).

201 Jalloh *supra* note 173 at 430.

202 UN Secretary-General, *Letter dated Jan 12, 2001 from the Secretary-General to the President of the Security Council*, ¶ 12, UN Doc. S/2001/40 (12 Jan 2001).

203 Jalloh *supra* note 173 at 435.

204 Notably, the SCSL had to be rescued financially by the UN in 2004, after its voluntary funding mechanism failed to provide sufficient funding to support the Court's on-going work. Stuart Ford, *How Leadership in International Criminal Law is Shifting from the United States to Europe and Asia: An Analysis of Spending On and Contributions to International Criminal Courts*, 55 St. Louis U. L. J. 953, 993 (2011).

of the SCSL. The lack of funding, *inter alia*, affected the Prosecutor's interpretation of the mandate to try those bearing "greatest responsibility" as encompassing only 20 defendants;[205] the ability of the Outreach Office to bring the Court's message to the affected population;[206] the defense and fair trial rights of the accused;[207] and the ability of the Court's staff to devote their energies to the work of justice rather than fund-raising.[208]

The funding mechanism also adversely affected the perception of the Special Court, at least to some degree. In place of the charge of "victor's justice" leveled at previous tribunals, the SCSL was subject to charges of "donors' justice," wherein the concerns of the donors in securing a "return" on their "investment" and/or securing an efficient outcome were apparently considered paramount to the concerns of substantive justice.[209]

I   **Jurisprudential Impact**

The Special Court has made significant contributions to the state of international criminal law, despite having completed relatively few trials.

Perhaps the SCSL's most important contribution was its successful indictment, arrest, trial, and conviction of a head of state, Charles Taylor of Liberia.[210] Taylor was indicted by the Special Court on 11 counts of crimes against humanity, war crimes, and other serious violations of international law.[211] The Prosecutor alleged that Taylor planned, instigated, and/or ordered the com-

---

205   Human Rights Watch, *supra* note 185, at 4–6.
206   The Special Court for Sierra Leone, First Annual Report of the President of the Special Court for Sierra Leone for the Period December 2, 2002 – December 1, 2003, at 27.
207   Cesare P.R. Romano, *The Price of International Justice*, 4 L. & Prac. Int'l Cts & Tribunals 281, 304–05 (2005). See also, Jalloh *supra* note 173 at 437–444 (describing in detail various implications for the defendants and Defense Office as a result of "shoestring" funding).
208   The Special Court for Sierra Leone, Fifth Annual Report of the President of the Special Court for Sierra Leone for the Period June 2007 – May 2008, at 11. (documenting numerous fundraising trips to world capitals); The Special Court for Sierra Leone, Sixth Annual Report of the President of the Special Court for Sierra Leone for the Period June 2008 – May 2009 (noting that the global financial crisis had increased the difficulty of fundraising from voluntary donors).
209   Kendall, *supra* note 199 at 393–99.
210   See, Micaela Frulli, *Piercing the Veil of Head-of-State Immunity: The Taylor Trial and Beyond*, in Sierra Leone Special Court Legacy, *supra* note 123 at 325.
211   Prosecutor v. Charles Taylor, SCSL Case no. SCSL-03–01-PT, Second Amended Indictment (29 May 2007), *avilable at* http://www.sc-sl.org/LinkClick.aspx?fileticket=lrnobAAMVYM%3d&tabid=107 (last visited 27 July 2014).

mission of crimes within the SCSL's jurisdiction, invoking command responsibility and joint criminal enterprise bases. The Taylor defense team sought to quash the indictment based on Taylor's head of state immunity, traditionally recognized in international law.[212] The Trial Chamber, relying on Article 6(2) of the SCSL Statute, practice at the IMTs, ICTs, and ICC, and various *amici* briefs, found that Taylor was not immune from prosecution.[213] First, Taylor was no longer head of state at the time of his indictment, and hence personal immunity (*ratione personae*) was inapplicable.[214] Second, and more importantly, the functional immunities (*ratione materiae*) which protect activities of officials acting in their official capacity on behalf of their state, did not apply to cases before "certain international criminal courts."[215] The Appeals Chamber determined that the SCSL was, in fact, an international court because of its establishment by international treaty, the language of Security Council Resolution 1315, the similarity of its mandate to those of the ICTY, ICTR, and ICC.[216] After this important ruling, the SCSL proceeded with Taylor's prosecution largely as it would with any other defendant (location of the trial aside). The SCSL's decision helped "consolidate an emerging trend [...] that establishes an exception to personal immunities accruing to incumbent heads of state as far as the jurisdiction of an international criminal tribunal is concerned."[217]

Another important contribution is the SCSL's jurisprudence on child recruitment.[218] The use of underage soldiers has been a sadly consistent part of modern asymmetrical warfare. In the CDF Case, the SCSL held individual defendants liable for the recruitment and use of child soldiers as a crime under

---

[212] In particular, the Defense cited Case concerning Arrest Warrant of 11 April 2000 (Democratic Republic of Congo v. Belgium) 2002 ICJ 1 (14 February) (commonly, "*Yerodia*").

[213] Special Court for Sierra Leone, Prosecutor v. Charles Ghankay Taylor, Case No. SCSL-03-1-T, Appeals Chamber, Decision on Immunity from Jurisdiction (May 31, 2004); Sarah Nouwen, *The Special Court for Sierra Leone and the Immunity of Taylor: The Arrest Warrant Case Continued*, 18(2) Leiden J. Int. L. 645 (2005); Zsuzsanna Deen-Racsmany, *Prosecutor v. Taylor: The Status of the Special Court for Sierra Leone and Its Implications for Immunity*, 18(3) Leiden J. Int. L. 229 (2005); Charles Jalloh, *Immunity from Prosecution for International Crimes: The Case of Charles Taylor at the Special Court for Sierra Leone*, 8 ASIL Insights 21 (5 October 2004).

[214] Decision on Immunity from Jurisdiction, *supra* note 213 at ¶ 59.

[215] Id., at ¶ 50–53.

[216] Id., at ¶¶ 39–42.

[217] Frulli, *supra* note 210 at 328.

[218] Alison Smith, *Child Recruitment and the Special Court for Sierra Leone*, 2(4) J. Int'l Crim. Just. 1141 (2004); Cecil Aptel, *Unpunished Crimes: The Special Court for Sierra Leone and Children* in Sierra Leone Special Court Legacy, *supra* note 123 at 340.

international law. Among those indictees affiliated with the CDF was Samuel Hinga Norman, who had commanded the *Kamajors* (a militia of traditional hunters) in support of the Government's action against rebel factions. Part of the indictment against Norman alleged that he had systematically forced children under the age of 15 into combat. Norman argued that, even if proven, this did not amount to a recognized crime under customary international law during the relevant time frame, and if it had become a rule of international law, it did so only after the treaty establishing the ICC was signed in 1998.[219] As such, Norman contended that the indictment violated the principle of *nullum crimen sin lege* (no crime without law). The Appeals Chamber, in another important jurisdictional ruling, found that prior international agreements, including the Additional Protocols to the Geneva Convention of 1977, the Convention on the Rights of the Child of 1989, the Fourth Geneva Convention of 1949, and the African Charter on the Rights and Welfare of the Child, all contained sufficient indicia of state practice and *opinio juris* to support the assertion that child recruitment crystallized into a rule of customary international law prior to 1996.[220] This decision marks a first in international law.

The SCSL also made significant contributions to another disturbing facet of modern conflict, namely that of sexual violence targeting women. The species of this violence found in Sierra Leone was formulated as the crime against humanity of "forced marriage."[221] During the Sierra Leonean conflict (and others) women were forced to "marry" combatants and were "raped repeatedly; made to cook, clean, and care for their captor-husbands; beaten, branded, and cut; and many became pregnant and were forced to bear and then rear the children."[222] Defendants in both the RUF and AFRC cases were charged with independent counts of forced marriage. As with the interpretation of the Court's mandate (discussed at Part V.E. above), the Trial Chambers came to opposite conclusions in the face of challenges by the defendants. The RUF Trial

---

219 Noah Benjamin Novogrodsky, *After the Horror: Child Soldiers and the Special Court for Sierra Leone*, in Sierra Leone Special Court Legacy, *supra* note 123 at 361.

220 Prosecutor v. Norman, Case No. SCSL-2004–14-AR72(E), Appeals Chamber, Decision on Preliminary Motion Based on Lack of Jurisdiction (May 31, 2004).

221 This term has been highly contentious. It is used here not to endorse any particular interpretation, but as a restatement of the wording used by the Special Court.

222 Michael P. Scharf, *Forced Marriage as a Separate Crime Against Humanity*, in Sierra Leone Special Court Legacy, *supra* note 123 at 193; Valerie Oosterveld, *Forced Marriage and the Special Court for Sierra Leone: Legal Advances and Conceptual Difficulties* 2(1) J. of Int'l Humanitarian L. Stud. 127 (2011); Patricia Sellers, *Wartime Female Slavery: Enslavement?*, 44 Cornell Int'l. L. J. 115 (2011).

Chamber upheld the charge.[223] The AFRC Trial Chamber, on the other hand, found that the purported crime of "forced marriage" was subsumed by the other charges of "sexual slavery," and hence were redundant.[224]

It fell to the Appeals Chamber to resolve the deadlock. The judges of that chamber sided with the RUF Trial Chamber, holding that forced marriage is a separate crime against humanity:

> [B]ased on the evidence on record, the Appeals Chamber finds that no tribunal could reasonably have found that forced marriage was subsumed in the crime against humanity of sexual slavery. While forced marriage shares certain elements with sexual slavery such as non-consensual sex and deprivation of liberty, there are also distinguishable factors. First, forced marriage involves a perpetrator compelling a person by threat of force [...] into a conjugal association with another [.] Second, unlike sexual slavery, forced marriage implies a relationship of exclusivity between "husband" and "wife," which could lead to disciplinary consequences for breach of this exclusive relationship. These distinctions imply that forced marriage is not predominantly a sexual crime.[225]

Although not all commentators will accept the Appeals Chamber's reasoning regarding the existence of this crime at international law prior to the commission of the acts,[226] the Special Court's work in this area has nonetheless provided a bases for future prosecutions on these grounds.

Another significant contribution of the SCSL came in its treatment of the amnesty provisions of the treaty that signaled the cessation of hostilities in Sierra Leone.[227] That agreement, the Lomé Accord, granted blanket immunity to "absolute and free pardon and reprieve to all combatants and collaborators

---

223 Prosecutor v. Sesay, Kallon and Gbao, Case No. SCSL-04–15-T, Judgment, ¶. 168 (2 March 2009).

224 Prosecutor v. Brima, Kamara and Kanu, Case no. SCSL-03–06-T, Judgment, ¶ 174 (20 June 2007).

225 Prosecutor v. Brima, Kamara and Kanu, Case no. SCSL-03–06-A, Judgment, ¶ 195 (22 February 2008).

226 See, Nicholas A. Goodfellow, *The Miscategorization of 'Forced Marriage' as a Crime Against Humanity by the Special Court for Sierra Leone*, 11 Int'l Crim. L. Rev. 831, 848–53 (2011); Sidney Thompson, *Forced Marriage at the Special Court for Sierra Leone: Questions of Jurisdiction, Legality, Specificity, and Consistency*, in Sierra Leone Special Court Legacy, *supra* note 123 at 215.

227 Simon M. Meisenberg, *Legality of amnesties in international humanitarian law: the Lome Amnesty Decision of the Special Court for Sierra Leone*, 86 Int'l Rev. of Red Cross 856 (2004).

with respect to anything done by them in pursuit of their objectives, up to the time of the signing of the present Agreement."[228] This provision was quite understandably cited by defendants before the SCSL, who felt that the Special Court's personality as a creation of a treaty involving a signatory to the Lomé Accord prevented it from abrogating the amnesty granted by Sierra Leone. The Statue of the SCSL, for its part, specifically prohibits application amnesty to any of the international crimes within its jurisdiction.[229] The Appeals Chamber upheld application of this prohibition on amnesty, finding that:

> Where jurisdiction is universal [as with grave international crimes] a State [such as Sierra Leone] cannot deprive another State of its jurisdiction to prosecute the offender by the grant of amnesty. [...] A State cannot bring into oblivion and forgetfulness a crime, such as a crime against international law, which other States are entitled to keep alive and remember.[230]

This decision has made it "very clear that in international peace negotiations, amnesties are off the table for genocide, war crimes, and crimes against humanity."[231]

6 Liberia

A *A Brief History of the Conflict*

Liberia's history is to some extent unique. It was established in 1847 by freed American slaves who "returned" to Africa with the help of the US government and the assistance of the American Colonization Society.[232] These colonizers saw a future of self-determination in Africa that was denied to them in the land of their enslavement. Many in America, including those in favor of abolition,

---

228 Lome Accords at art. IX.
229 SCSL Statute, art. 10.
230 Prosecutor v. Kallon & Kamara, Case Nos. SCSL-2004–15-AR72(E), SCSL-2004–16-AR72(E), Decision on Challenged to Jurisdiction: Lome Accord Amnesty, ¶ 3 (Mar. 13, 2004).
231 Leila Nadya Sadat, *The Lome Amnesty Decision of the Special Court for Sierra Leone*, in Sierra Leone Special Court Legacy, *supra* note 123 at 311, 323; *But see*, William Schabas, *Amnesty, the Sierra Leone Truth and Reconciliation Commission and the Special Court for Sierra Leone*, 11 U.C. Davis J. Int'l L. & Pol'y 145 (2005) (criticizing the SCSL's decisions on the applicability of the amnesty provision because, inter alia, they were too absolute and went beyond existing law).
232 See, Truth and Reconciliation Commission of Liberia, *Final Report: Vol. One* at 49–50.

were troubled by what, exactly, was to be done with the freed slaves once the bonds of servitude were severed. Thus, "returning" to Africa became a perceived net positive for both the formerly enslaved and the race-sensitive American government.

Needless to say, the land that was chosen by the colonialists was not uninhabited. Rather, there were large and distinct native populations on the land at the time of the Americans' arrival. The freed American slaves unfortunately used their experience of the Western labor and economic structures which once used them as human grist against the native populations. The resultant history of the nation of Liberia is one in which these Americo-Liberians, which comprised less than 5% of the population, and their descendants controlled the nation's social, political and economic life to the exclusion of the indigenous populations.[233]

The last of these Americo-Liberian leaders, William Richard Tolbert, Jr., was deposed in a 1980 coup lead by a young Master Sergeant in the Liberian Army, Samuel Doe.[234] Doe ruled Liberia in a rather ruthless and corrupt fashion throughout the 1980s.[235] Several different factions sought to end Doe's rule through military means, and enlisted the assistance of Libya's Muamar Gaddaffi in training for a military confrontation with the entrenched regime. "The most prominent of these characters was Charles Taylor, leader of the National Patriotic Front of Liberia (NPFL)."[236] From December 1989 to July 1990, Taylor led rebel forces from Nimba County (near the border with Cote d'Ivoire) to the capital, Monrovia.[237] Signaling the ethnic character of the conflict, Taylor's march to Monrovia was characterized by "destruction, arson, burning, looting and the killing of members of ethnic groups associated with Doe, or opposed to his NPFL."[238]

The Economic Community of West African States (ECOWAS) organized a monitoring group (ECOMOG) to monitor the tentative peace secured by arms in Monrovia. The monitoring group was quickly drawn into conflict through attempts to enforce peace between the warring factions.[239] This international involvement led Taylor to form something of a partnership with Foday Sankoh,

---

[233] Ozonnia Ojielo, *Critical Lessons In Post-Conflict Security in Africa: the Case of Liberia's Truth and Reconciliation Commission*, Inst. for Just. & Reconciliation in Afr. Prog. Occassional Paper 1, 3 (2010).

[234] Truth and Reconciliation Commission of Liberia, *Final Report: Volume Two*, at 144.

[235] Id., at 144–49.

[236] Ojielo, *supra* note 233 at 3.

[237] TRC Final Report Vol. 2 at 152–53.

[238] Id.

[239] TRC Final Report Vol. 2 at 157–58.

the leader of the Revolutionary United Forces (RUF), then engaged in the conflict in neighboring Sierra Leone. The RUF and NPFL forces supported one another's actions in their respective theaters of conflict although there is compelling evidence that they had met and made common cause with each other during their days in Libya or not long afterwards.[240] In response to this cross-border partnership, the government of Sierra Leone created the United Liberation Movement for Democracy (ULIMO), composed of Liberian members of the Sierra Leonean armed forces, to fight against the RUF. These operations eventually drew ULIMO into the conflict in Liberia proper.[241]

In 1996, ECOWAS brokered a ceasefire between the parties, which preceded fresh presidential elections in 1997. Taylor won those elections by a large margin, although it was obvious that the elections took place in a context of fear in which it was clear to the population what failure to vote for the NPFL candidate would mean.[242] "Between 1997 and 2000, Taylor's regime continued the history of oppression, intimidation, torture, execution of political opponents, arbitrary detentions and extra-judicial killings characteristic of previous governments."[243] Two important factions were created to oppose Taylor's government in Monrovia. First, Liberians United for Reconciliation and Democracy (LURD), a predominantly Krahn group, formed in the Sierra Leonean capital Freetown in 2000. Second, an offshoot group of LURD associated with ULIMO-J from the First Civil War formed the Movement for Democracy in Liberia (MODEL) in 2003. LURD began to advance on Monrovia from bases in Guinea; MODEL operated out of bases in Cote d'Ivoire with the assistance of Ivorian President Laurent Gbagbo.[244]

In the summer of 2003, Taylor found himself in a precarious situation. LURD and MODEL had fought their way from their respective borders to the outskirts of Monrovia. Taylor had been indicted by the SCSL in March of that year. That indictment was unveiled as he attended ceasefire talks in Ghana. With pressure mounting, both militarily and politically, Taylor returned to Liberia and

---

240   2004 Witness to Truth: Report of the Truth and Reconciliation Commission of Sierra Leone, 3A.

241   Notably, ULIMO itself was fractionalized on ethnic grounds. ULIMO-J was composed primarily of ethnic Krahns loyal to General Roosevelt Johnson. ULIMO-K was composed mostly of ethnic Mandingos loyal to Alhaji Kromah. Id., at 3.

242   Taylor's the National Patriotic Party cleared more than 75% of the votes. See, International Foundation for Electoral Systems, Final Results of Liberia's 1997 Elections, *avilable at* http://www.ifes.org/~/media/Files/Publications/Election%20Results%20Evaluation%20of/1997/835/1997_Liberia_Election_Final_Results.pdf.

243   Ojielo, *supra* note 233 at 4–5.

244   Ojielo, *supra* note 233 at 5.

subsequently agreed to leave the capital in return for an offer of asylum in Nigeria.[245] The Comprehensive Peace Agreement (CPA) between the various combatants brought formal hostilities to a close in August 2003 and the creation of a transitional government.[246] Most notably for our purposes, the CPA provided for the creation of a Truth and Reconciliation Commission (TRC)[247] and did not provide any specific authority for either criminal prosecutions or international involvement.

B   No International or Internationalized Proceedings to Consider

The entirety of the proceedings related to the adjudication of the atrocities committed during the First and Second Civil Wars in Liberia (1989–1996 and 2000–2003, respectively) were conducted by the national Truth and Reconciliation Commission. For that simple reason, we are unable to consider in this paper several of the metrics we have previously applied to the ICTR and SCSL. In particular, local involvement, competing prosecutions, breadth of the proceedings, quality of the proceedings, cost of administration and jurisprudential impact are simply inapplicable to the situation in Liberia. Without diminishing the work of the Liberian TRC, formal criminal trials of either a national or international character were not part of the reconciliation process in that country. Yet, there have been and continues to be calls for prosecutions of war criminals responsible for atrocities in Liberia.[248]

C   Benefits of National Action

Acknowledging the inapplicability of criminal justice metrics is not to say that the TRC had no effect on the end goals of promoting peace and security. The Truth and Reconciliation process in Liberia yielded at least three significant benefits that were also served (or purportedly served) by the criminal justice processes discussed above.

First, the TRC's final report is a voluminous and authoritative account of the history, challenges, and internal tensions that led to the conflicts in 1990 and 2003. Among other things, the TRC report contains analysis of the historical antecedents to the conflict,[249] the effect of the conflict on women,[250] the role

---

245   TRC Final Report Vol. 2 at 168.
246   A copy of the agreement has been made available by the United States Institutes for Peace at http://www.usip.org/sites/default/files/file/resources/collections/peace_agreements/liberia_08182003.pdf.
247   Id., at Article XIII.
248   See, e.g., Jalloh & Marong, *supra* note 260.
249   TRC Final Report Vol. 1.
250   TRC Final Report Vol. 3 Appendices Title I.

of children in the wars,[251] and economic crimes, exploitation and abuse before during and after the conflict.[252] To the degree that the ICTR and SCSL were intended to act or de facto acted as the official historians of their respective conflicts, the TRC's final report shows that this function need not be inextricably linked to criminal prosecution.

Second, whatever its ultimate drawbacks, the TRC process was a domestic institution geared toward using local perceptions, context and sensitivities in assessing the brutal conflicts from which the country had recently emerged. To the degree that the ICTR, and (to a lesser degree) the SCSL were viewed as foreign institutions imposing inapplicable justice from afar, the Liberian effort to deal with the legacy of conflicts internally with only limited international assistance is laudable.

Third, the TRC explicitly recommended that its work be followed by criminal prosecutions of particular individuals in a newly-constituted Extraordinary Criminal Court for Liberia that would be empowered "to try all persons recommended by the TRC for the commission of gross human rights violations including violations of international humanitarian law, international human rights law, war crimes and economic crimes including but not limited to, killing, gang rape, multiple rape, forced recruitment, sexual slavery, forced labor, exposure to deprivation, missing, etc."[253] The Commission recommended that 116 individuals from the NPFL, ULIMO-J, ULIMO-K, MODEL, LURD and other groups be prosecuted in this mechanism,[254] and even provided a draft statute for such a court.[255] Drawing lessons from the SCSL, this draft statute provides for appointment of judges by the President of Liberia and the UN Secretary General, reserves a certain number of judicial appointments for women, and precluded appointment of those who participated in (or are perceived to have participated in) the conflicts.[256] This is to say that, despite the CPA's preference for resort to a TRC process rather than criminal trials, the Commission did not see its work as providing a full measure of justice to the victims of the conflict. Rather, it saw criminal prosecutions in cooperation with the international community as an advisable and necessary next step.

---

251   TRC Final Report Vol. 3 Appendices Title II.
252   TRC Final Report Vol. 3 Appendices Title III; TRC Final Report Vol. 2.
253   TRC Final Report Vol. 2 at 349. More broadly, see TRC Final Report Vol 2 at para. 12.0 (discussing "Recommendations on Accountability: Extraordinary Criminal Court").
254   TRC Final Report Vol. 2 at 349–52.
255   TRC Final Report, Annex 2, draft Statute Establishing The Extraordinary Criminal Court For Liberia.
256   Id., at article 3.

One may rightly ask what has become of this recommendation since the issuance of the final TRC Report in December 2009. Unfortunately, no such Extraordinary Court has been established to adjudicate the atrocities outlined in the TRC report. Ozonnia Ojielo, the former Chief of Operations and Officer in Charge of the Sierra Leone Truth and Reconciliation Commission, and a consultant to the Liberia TRC, has offered several reasons for the lack of criminal prosecutions.[257] In general, the country's dismal civil, judicial and economic capacities, in the wake of nearly 20 years of civil strife, conspire against widespread formal prosecutions. From a criminal justice standpoint, many of the nation's jurists fled and the actual physical infrastructure of the justice system was destroyed during the conflict. In essence, there are few courts in which to hold prosecutions and few judges or lawyers to staff them. From a civil standpoint, the lack of strong governmental control outside of the capital, the history of organized oppression and persistent ethnic tensions undermine the national government's ability to engage in potentially divisive criminal prosecutions. Lastly, in light of the country's tenuous economic situation, the government has declared criminal prosecutions to be of a lesser priority than simply reconstituting Liberia as a functional state.

This economic concern is essentially a recasting of the familiar criticism of the expense of administering the ICTR and SCSL (see above at Part H and Part G) from a prospective position. In the cases of the ICTR and SCSL, the decision to expend great sums of money prosecuting relatively few defendants was criticized afterward as being a misallocation of resources away from projects and programs that could provide more benefit to the post-conflict society. In the case of Liberia, the need to rebuild the country through exactly those types of projects and programs has been used as a reason for not undertaking the expenditure of resources on criminal prosecutions in the first place. In either event, the limited resources available to the national and international authorities has created the perception of an either/or competition between criminal proceedings and other laudable public projects.

D   *Impunity and Victor's Justice*

The Liberian situation differs from the situation in Rwanda, and to a much lesser degree that of Sierra Leone, inasmuch as there was no clear "victor" in the conflict. The CPA represents a political settlement between the warring factions that forestalled ultimate military conquest, and thus precluded the possibility that post-conflict mechanism would focus on the vanquished.

---

257   Ojielo, *supra* note 233 at 6–7.

In and of itself, this political compromise does not necessarily mean that some or "all sides" of the conflict could not be subjected to an equal measure of justice in proportion to their wartime atrocities. In practice, however, the post-conflict governments contained members of all of the warring factions, and thus as a pragmatic political matter no group was incentivized to seek prosecutions against another group (lest they themselves be subjected to similar calls).[258] Thus, despite the TRC's recommendation that criminal prosecutions to adjudicate conduct during the conflict, the political reality is such that these recommendations are unlikely to be seriously considered. None of those in power, including President Ellen Johnson Sirleaf, is keen to prosecute. This may not be surprising given that she and many other prominent individuals were named in the TRC Report for giving early support to those who fomented the war, such as Taylor.

This political impasse highlights a somewhat perverse aspect of the much-maligned notion of "victor's justice." From Nuremberg to Kigali, the charge that one side of a conflict enjoyed impunity for their conduct necessarily acknowledges that the other side did not enjoy such impunity. If a modicum of justice is better than no justice at all (which is not a given), the fact that there is a victorious side interested in pursuing its own interests, and capable of doing so, does mean that at least *some* justice will be meted out. Where no party enjoys such a position of authority, and no one has decisively won the war, it appears unreasonable to expect that leaders will fall on their swords out of a shared sense of legal rectitude.

E   *Lessons from Earlier Situations*

The situation in Liberia, which in many ways parallels that in Sierra Leone, differs from those discussed above inasmuch as no ad hoc, internationalized, hybrid or other international court has been created to deal with the reputable claims of mass atrocities in the country's fourteen years of civil war.[259] What lessons learned from the experience at the ICTR and the SCSL can be brought to bear in post-war Liberia?

First, the slow pace, high cost and exhausted political will at the ad hoc Tribunals, as well as the subsequent entry into force of the ICC's Rome Statute, make the establishment of a dedicated special ad hoc criminal tribunal for Li-

---

258   Ojielo, *supra* note 233 at 7.
259   See, e.g., Human Rights Watch, *Liberia: A Human Rights Disaster – Violations of the Laws of War by all Parties to the Conflict* (26 October 1990), *avilable at* http://www.hrw.org/sites/default/files/reports/liberia1990.pdf (last visited 27 July 2014).

beria a very unlikely possibility.²⁶⁰ In this regard, even if there was domestic political will in the Sirleaf government to call for criminal accountability supported by the international community, it is unclear whether it will obtain the support of the United Nations which for the most part is focused on advancing developmental and peacebuilding goals in Liberia. What might give better results is a bilateral approach, say with the support of the United States or the African Union, to create such a special court for Liberia. Such a position would accord with US interest in advancing ad hoc courts as alternatives to full-fledged international tribunals as it proposed with respect to Sudan and more recently the Democratic Republic of the Congo. In terms of the AU, the creation of a special chamber in the national courts of Senegal to prosecute former Chadian president Hissiene Habre might serve as a blue print for a similar effort in relation to Liberia. Yet, given the limitations of funding, such an undertaking would likely require the financial support of African states as well as other, more affluent ones further afield.

Second, it is true that the broader international community did, in fact, agree to establish a permanent International Criminal Court in the years after the creation of the ad hocs. The Rome Statute provides the ICC with jurisdiction over four crimes: genocide,²⁶¹ crimes against humanity,²⁶² war crimes,²⁶³ and aggression.²⁶⁴ "The crimes committed in Liberia include at least two (crimes against humanity and war crimes), and possibly a third (genocide), of the four within the ICC's jurisdiction."²⁶⁵ Further, Liberia is a party to the Rome Statute, signing in 1998 and ratifying in September 2004. However, the temporal jurisdiction of the ICC is limited to those crimes committed after the entry into force of the Rome Statute, namely 1 July 2002. Many, if not most, of the atrocities in Liberia were committed prior to the entry into force, and accordingly, the ICC Prosecutor would be limited to seeking justice for a fraction of those who were affected by the war.

Third, the experience with the SCSL could be duplicated in neighboring Liberia. This hybrid model that uses elements of both international and domestic justice systems was also employed in East Timor, Kosovo, and Cambodia following the establishment of the ICTs in the early 1990s. However, part of the

---

260 Charles Jalloh and Alhagi Marong, *Ending Impunity: The Case for War Crimes Trials in Liberia*, 1 Afr. J. Legal Stud. 2 (2005) 74.
261 Rome Statute, art. 6.
262 Rome Statute, art. 7.
263 Rome Statute, art. 8.
264 Rome Statute, arts 122, 123 (actual definition of "aggression" as a crime at international law is to be made by subsequent approval of the Assembly of States Party).
265 Jalloh & Marong, *supra* note 260 at 73.

theory of creating a hybrid tribunal is to allow the international system to piggyback to a certain degree on the national institutions. As such, creation of a hybrid court or a special chamber in the national courts of Liberia "would require that there be at least an effectively functional and adequately resourced judicial system" beyond what currently exists in the country.[266] As we have seen with the SCSL (above at Part V), the resources necessary to create such a hybrid tribunal, as well as to do some necessary capacity-building at the national level, do not come easily whether due to lack of political will or otherwise.

7 Conclusion

Throughout this paper, we have argued that the form and structure of a criminal justice mechanism must be assessed on its merits relative to a specific situation. Simply put, it should be self-evident there is no one-size-fits-all approach to post-conflict criminal justice. The nature of a mechanism necessarily depend on the nature of each situation, the scope of the conflict, the character of the crimes at issue, as well as the extent of political will amongst those in government. Add to this the existence of a robust civil society interest in seeing some justice done.

In the main, we have assessed two post-conflict criminal justice mechanisms, those of the International Criminal Tribunal for Rwanda and the Special Court for Sierra Leone, on eight metrics: local involvement, competing national proceedings, competing international proceedings, impunity and victor's justice, breadth of the proceedings, quality of the proceedings, the cost of administering the mechanism and their jurisprudential impact. Notably, these are factors geared toward assessing the impact of the tribunals as legal entities, and therefore do not address their impact on economic development, public perceptions of justice, or many other laudable and necessary goals in a post-conflict society. As conceded above, a thorough understanding of the impact of these criminal justice mechanisms on the maintenance of peace would require an on-the-ground empirical study. The ICTR had several commendable aspects and several where it fell short of its high aspirations. In a positive light, the ICTR was a transformational approach to addressing post-conflict justice. International criminal law, functionally dormant since the end of World War II, was given a renewed lease on life, focused on bringing international fair trial standards to bear on some of the worst atrocities of the 20th Century.

---

266   Jalloh & Marong, *supra* note 260 at 75.

Unlike the International Military Tribunals in Germany and Tokyo, the ICTR indicted a variety of players whose actions were essential to the conduct of the genocide, to include military leaders, civilian leaders, politicians, local officials, and media personalities. This broad view of the Tribunal's mandate serves as a beneficial guidepost for future efforts. The quality of the proceedings before the Tribunal was also largely consistent with international standards, arguably to the detriment of the court's pace and efficiency.

Several aspects of the ICTR, however, are perceived as less positive. First and foremost, the Tribunal had a strained relationship with the Rwandan government from its inception, and this had a discernibly negative impact on the Tribunal's work. The Rwandan government was never fully invested after it lost a chance to influence the form the Tribunal took, and perception of the court's work in Rwanda has generally been one of a foreign, remote, ponderously slow and expensive institution. To that end, Rwanda conducted many, many times more trials in their national courts and the specially-constituted *gacaca* courts than did the Tribunal. Perhaps the biggest strike against the ICTR is the charge of "victor's justice." The civil war that culminated in the 1994 genocide had been on-going since at least 1990, and there is some prima facie evidence that the RPF committed atrocities during the conduct of the war. However, no RPF officials or soldiers were indicted by the Tribunal. In the end, although this concern does not in our minds undermine its ultimate legacy, and for a variety of pragmatic and principled reasons, the victors in the conflict were not subjected to criminal proceedings. This is not unlike what was the case at Nuremberg and Tokyo.

Like the ICTR, the SCSL has a generally positive legacy. From a positive standpoint, the SCSL took the local challenges faced by the ICTR and ICTY seriously. As such, the Special Court took at least four significant steps toward involving the local community from its inception. First, the Court was located in Freetown, the *locus criminis*. Second, the Court was given jurisdiction over some violations of Sierra Leonean law, thus bringing it more in line with the local judiciary. Third, the Special Court undertook a serious outreach effort to inform the affected population. Fourth, a certain number of places within the Court's hierarchy were reserved specifically for Sierra Leoneans by the Statute, thus ensuring a floor for the level of local involvement. As a product of a treaty between the UN and the government of Sierra Leone, the hybrid international and national character of the Special Court addressed to an extent the sense of foreign justice common among the affected population in Rwanda (even if it did not eliminate such criticism entirely). The Special Court also took pains to indict parties from all sides of the conflict, and thus took a conscious step to avoid or diminish a charge of "victor's justice." The indictment, arrest and successful prosecution of the head of a neighboring state, Charles Taylor of Liberia, and the resultant diminution of immunities, is another feather in the SCSL's cap. Lastly, and despite some tense exchanges, the experience in Sierra Leone provided a working example of how a national truth and reconciliation commission could work in tandem with international (or internationalized) criminal proceedings. It also offered lessons on pitfalls to avoid wherever two such institutions are simultaneously used in the future, as they were in Sierra Leone.

From a more critical standpoint, the SCSL was created with a narrow (and apparently vague) mandate to try those "bearing greatest responsibility" for the crimes at issue. The effort to define and implement that restriction took up a considerable amount of the Court's energy and ultimately resulted in a scant few trials actually taking place at the SCSL. As such, the breadth of the proceedings suffered. The situation in Sierra Leone also demonstrated one of the problems in relying on local authorities to prosecute the bulk of the crimes committed during a conflict. This assumption, which undergirds the Rome Statute system, may be a false one premised on the affected state having the capacity and political will to prosecute. That, as we have seen, is not always the case. Despite the generally positive outcome of the Sierra Leone TRC findings, and unlike the experience in Rwanda, there remain many perpetrators of atrocities who have seen neither the inside of the SCSL or a national court.

In closing, we highlight that neither court has received positive reviews for their cost efficiency. One may rightly question, as we do, whether the measure of justice should be done in dollars and cents. Nonetheless, the ICTR's expenditure of US$1.75 billion and the SCSL's expected cost of US$257 million (with roughly equivalent per-defendant expenses) will likely be considered a chilling example in future negotiations over international justice.

PART 5

Africa and International Law

∴

CHAPTER 23

The Public Law of Africa and International Law: Broadening the Scope of Application of International Rules and Enriching Them for Intra-Africa Purposes

Abdulqawi A. Yusuf

I   Introduction

Following their accession to independence in the 1950s and 1960s, African States resolved to coordinate their efforts in international fora, particularly in the United Nations (UN) and its specialized agencies, in order to bring the ideals and aspirations of the Pan-African movement to bear on international relations and on the evolution of international law. Thus, the First Conference of Independent African States, held in Accra, Ghana in April 1958, decided that the representatives of the eight independent African Member States of the UN should act as a group to ensure that "a distinctive 'African personality' would exert influence on international relations".[1] With the creation of the OAU in 1963, the African group at the UN and in other international forums was formalized as a regional group and played a very important role in the process of decolonization and elimination of apartheid from the continent.

It was in this context that the African States made their first efforts, as subjects of international law, to influence the codification and development of international law as well as to bring about its reform. In addition to their cooperation with other formerly dependent States in Asia and Latin America in pursuance of those objectives, the newly independent African States formed their own Pan-African intergovernmental organizations – particularly the Organization of African Unity (OAU) and the African Union (AU) – and began to develop a public law of Africa consisting of rules, principles and practices applicable to intra-African relations. This public law of Africa provides a normative framework for the realization of the political, social and economic objectives of Pan-Africanism. It also tries to address the aspirations of the peoples

---

[1]   For the text of the resolutions adopted by the conference, see C. Legum, *Pan-Africanism: A Short Political Guide*, 1962, Appendix 4, pp. 139–140.

of the continent in terms of human rights protection, peace and security and political and economic integration. Some aspects of this public law possess, however, a universal vocation, in the sense that they may eventually influence the adoption of similar international legal rules outside the continent.

Two categories of norms may be distinguished in this respect. First, there is a category of norms that are quite innovative and original as compared to universal international law in that they only exist within the public law of Africa as binding rules or principles. A second category consists of norms that supplement existing international legal rules and principles and enrich them by broadening their scope of application with regard to African issues or by adding, through specific African conventions, rules and principles applicable only in the context of intra-African relations.

The first category includes certain principles of the Constitutive Act of the AU, such as the right of the Union to intervene in Member States in respect of grave circumstances, including war crimes, genocide and crimes against humanity; the prohibition of unconstitutional changes of government in the continent; and the promotion of democratic practices and good governance. It also includes conventions concluded among African States on subjects that have not been codified into binding law on the global level, such as the issue of internally displaced persons addressed in the 2009 Kampala Convention on the Protection of Internally Displaced Persons (IDPs), as well as norms that introduce into positive law, in the context of intra-African relations, certain rights and obligations that have not yet been recognized in international law.

The second category, which will be addressed in this paper, either broadens the scope of application of certain international conventions, or further elaborates certain rights and obligations recognized at the global level, through conventions specifically adopted for that purpose by the Pan-African organizations. Examples of these conventions are the African Charter on Human and Peoples' Rights, with its elaborate provisions on people's rights; the Convention Governing Specific Aspects of Refugee Problems in Africa, the African Charter on the Rights and Welfare of the Child, and the Protocol on the Rights of Women in Africa.

Judge Abdul Koroma has made a significant contribution to the efforts of African States, following their independence, to influence the reform and further development of international law both in his capacity as the Permanent Representative of his country to the United Nations and to the Organization of African Unity (OAU), and as a scholar and member of the UN International Law Commission. He has also actively participated in the elaboration of various intra-African Conventions through which the categories of norms described above were established. It is therefore a great pleasure for me to be able to contribute this paper to a collection of essays in his honour.

II   The Banjul Charter and Peoples' Rights

The struggle for the independence of African States started as a fight for the emancipation of the peoples of the African continent from colonial domination. The concept of peoples' rights was at the heart of the Pan-African movement, which repeatedly emphasized in its resolutions the right of African peoples to self-determination and the need to liberate the peoples of the continent from alien occupation and oppression. Following the independence of most African States in the early 1960's, the OAU also proclaimed in the preamble of its Charter that "it is the inalienable right of all people to control their own destiny", underlining the centrality of peoples' rights to the liberation struggle in the African continent. Thus, when in the late 1970's, the Member States of the OAU decided to elaborate an African Charter on Human rights, they immediately decided that it should also encompass peoples' rights.

It was widely felt among the African States that Western approaches to human rights, centred as they are on the individual, did not adequately address certain human rights considerations deemed important in African societies, such as collective rights. As a result, the Banjul Charter shifts the traditional paradigm of human rights theory through an extensive coverage of peoples' rights, placing these collective rights on an equal footing with the rights of the individual. In the words of Fatsah Ouguergouz, "through its emphatic enshrinement of the rights of peoples, the African Charter can be seen as a revolutionary legal instrument".[2]

The provisions of the Banjul Charter relating to peoples' rights are established in Articles 19–24. Article 19 deals with the equal rights of peoples. Besides its enunciation in the UN Charter, as part of the principle of "equal rights and self-determination of peoples", the concept of equal rights of peoples finds its most explicit articulation in the African Charter, which provides that "[a]ll peoples shall be equal; they shall enjoy the same respect and shall have the same rights. Nothing shall justify the domination of a people by another".[3] In a similar fashion, Article 20 codifies the right to self-determination, but it distinguishes between the right of colonized peoples to self-determination and the right of "[a]ll peoples to existence" encompassing "the unquestionable and inalienable right to self-determination" under which they "shall freely

---

[2] F. Ouguergouz, 'African Charter of Human and Peoples' Rights', *Max Planck Encyclopedia of Public International Law,* online edition www.mpepil.com, last updated in 2010, p. 372.

[3] Banjul Charter, Art. 19.

determine their political status and shall pursue their economic and social development according to the policy they have freely chosen".[4] According to the case law of the African Commission, the right to external self-determination under the Banjul Charter, though generally available to all peoples, cannot be claimed by peoples forming part of the population of a sovereign State, however ethnically or racially distinct they may be, so long as they are treated equally and in a non-discriminatory fashion as compared to other component peoples of the State, and are allowed to participate in the choice of a representative government.[5] The Commission has, however, emphasized on several occasions the right of peoples to internal self-determination within their own State.

Article 21 also addresses peoples' rights, but in the more specific context of the right of peoples to economic self-determination. It grants peoples sovereignty over natural resources, which, in the first instance, entails a fiduciary relationship between the State and its citizens in the management and utilization of natural resources. The fiduciary relationship implies that permanent sovereignty over natural resources and the right to dispose freely of such resources belongs to the people and not to the State, nor to its governmental authorities, and that it shall be exercised by such organs in the exclusive interest of the people. In addition, Article 21 provides that "[i]n case of spoliation, the dispossessed people shall have the right to the lawful recovery of the property as well as to an adequate compensation".[6]

Other articles of the Banjul Charter establish miscellaneous rights of peoples. Article 22 recognizes the right of peoples to their economic, social and cultural development, as well as the corresponding duty of States parties to the Charter, individually or collectively, to "ensure the exercise of the right to development",[7] which is articulated for the first time in a binding international instrument. Article 23 establishes the right of peoples to national and international peace and security, while Article 24 provides that "[a]ll peoples shall have the right to a general satisfactory environment favourable to their development".[8] As the African Commission on Human and Peoples' Rights observed in the *Endorois* case,[9] "the African Charter is an innovative and unique

---

4 Ibid., Art. 20.
5 Communication 266/03 *Kevin Mgwanga Gunme* et al, *Cameroon*, African Commission on Human and Peoples' Rights, 27 May 2009, available at http://caselaw.ihrda.org/doc/266.03/.
6 Banjul Charter, Art. 21.
7 Ibid., Art. 22.
8 Ibid., Arts. 23–24.
9 Communication 276/03 *Centre for Minority Rights Development (Kenya) and Minority Rights Group (on behalf of Endorois Welfare Council) v. Kenya*, 29 November 2009, African Commission on Human and Peoples' Rights.

human rights document compared to other regional human rights instruments, in placing special emphasis on the rights of peoples".[10] Indeed, no other international instrument provides for and protects peoples' rights as extensively as the African Charter, and thus the fundamental difference between the African Charter and other human rights instruments lies in its coverage of peoples' rights. Through this unique and extensive coverage, the Charter has undoubtedly contributed to the recognition and progressive development of peoples' rights at the international level.

It is understandable that a certain measure of doubt may have existed until recently as to the practical effect of the Charter's provisions on peoples' rights, because the Charter must be interpreted or applied in the domestic legal orders of African States, or in the case law of the judicial or quasi-judicial organs of the African Union. Moreover, as recognized by the African Commission itself, for more than two decades the Commission shied away from interpreting the notion of "people" in the Charter because it was not "at ease in developing rights where there was little concrete international jurisprudence".[11]

However, through its most recent case law, and in particular through the *Southern Cameroon*,[12] the *Darfur*[13] and the *Endorois*[14] cases, the Commission has overcome its initial reticence to define the attributes of a people and has provided a much needed clarification and interpretation not only of the notion of "people", but also of the normative content of peoples' rights in the Charter. One may not agree with the conclusions of the Commission in some of these cases with regard to the definition of "people", or the quality of "people" under the Charter of some of the groups characterized as such by the Commission. It cannot, however, be denied that the Commission, through its case law, has succeeded in applying the peoples' rights codified in the African Charter to concrete cases brought before it. As a result of the Commission's jurisprudence interpreting the rights of peoples, the recognition and protection of such rights may be accomplished with greater ease at the international level, thus contributing to the firm anchorage of peoples' rights in international law as well as in the public law of Africa.

---

10   Ibid., para. 149.
11   *Report of the African Commission's Working Group of Experts on Indigenous Populations/Communities*, Twenty-Eighth Session, 2003.
12   See above n. 5.
13   Communication 279/03–296/05 *Sudan Human Rights Organisation & Centre on Housing Rights and Evictions (COHRE) v. Sudan*, 27 May 2009, available at <http://caselaw.ihrda.org/ doc/279.03–296.05/>.
14   See above n. 9.

III   The Specificities of the African Convention on Refugees

The Convention Governing the Specific Aspects of Refugee Problems in Africa was adopted in 1969 and entered into force in 1974.[15] It was adopted, in part, to address comprehensively the unique aspects of the refugee situation on the African continent. It is not, however, the only instrument governing the protection of refugees on the continent. Most African States are parties to the 1951 UN Convention relating to the Status of Refugees (1951 Convention)[16] and to its 1967 Protocol.[17] The Banjul Charter also addresses the rights of refugees in Africa.

However, the African Refugee Convention, which states that the 1951 Convention is "the basic and universal instrument relating to the status of refugees", is the only legally binding regional refugee instrument. As its name suggests, it regulates specific aspects of refugee problems in Africa and supplements the regulatory framework of the 1951 Convention with regard to Africa. It is indeed the most significant regional supplement to the 1951 Convention in so far as it goes much further than the latter in advancing and protecting the rights of refugees, namely through the extension of the definition of "refugee", the recognition of the principle of "non-refoulement" in a very wide sense, and the emphasis on the voluntary character of any repatriation of refugees. The African Convention further strengthens the institution of asylum and broadens the scope of the 1951 Convention in this respect by providing for the "right to grant asylum".

One of the most recognized innovative features of the African Refugee Convention is the definition of refugee. The African Convention's definition is partly based on the definition codified in the 1951 Convention, which describes a "refugee" as a person who

> as a result of events occurring before 1 January 1951 and owing to well-founded fear of being persecuted for reasons of race, religion, nationality or political opinion is outside the country of his nationality and is unable or, owing to such fear, is unwilling to avail himself of the protection of that country, or who not having a nationality and being outside the

---

15   Convention Governing the Specific Aspects of Refugee Problems in Africa (hereinafter African Refugee Convention), 10 September 1969, 1001 UNTS 45.

16   Convention Relating to the Status of Refugees (hereinafter Refugee Convention), 28 July 1951, 189 UNTS 137. 145 States are parties to the Refugee Convention, and 45 of the States Parties are African States.

17   Protocol Relating to the Status of Refugees (hereinafter Refugee Convention Protocol), 4 October 1967, 606 UNTS 267. 146 States are parties to the Refugee Convention Protocol, and 46 of the States Parties are African States.

country of his former habitual residence as a result of such events is unwilling to return to it.[18]

However, the African Refugee Convention extends this definition of refugee by prescribing that:

> the term 'refugee' shall also apply to every person who, owing to external aggression, occupation, foreign domination or events seriously disturbing public order in either part or the whole of his country of origin or nationality, is compelled to leave his place of habitual residence in order to seek refuge in another place outside his country of origin or nationality.[19]

This comparatively liberal formulation of the term "refugee" is a direct response to the specific problems faced by African refugees, particularly at the time when the 1969 Convention was adopted. During that period, some African countries were still under colonial rule, while others, such as Zimbabwe and South Africa, were governed by minority racist regimes. The independent African States neighbouring these countries were occasionally subjected to aggression due to their support for liberation movements. Thus, the reference to "external aggression, occupation and foreign domination" was designed to extend protection to both freedom fighters and their supporters. Of course, this provision is also applicable to situations of external aggression among independent African States, but such conflicts have become rare, particularly since the advent of the AU and the establishment of various mechanisms for the peaceful settlement of disputes, including the Peace and Security Council.

A more topical situation, which distinguishes even today the African Refugee Convention from the 1951 UN Convention, is the reference to "events seriously disturbing public order in either part or the whole of [an individual's] country of origin or nationality".[20] This reference remains relevant for the internal conflicts that have plagued the African continent over the past two decades and that have motivated the AU to take measures to restore peace and security for African populations whose own governments have failed to protect them. According to Eze:

---

18   Refugee Convention, Art. 1(A)(2).
19   African Refugee Convention, Art. 1(2).
20   Ibid.

Whatever the problems of interpretation may be, it is submitted that Article I(2) of the African Convention must have been intended to cover all manner of refugees, whether they be those from independent or dependent African States, whether they are engaged in a liberation war or in a struggle for democracy.[21]

The expansive definition of a refugee in the African Convention extends protection to all those persons who are forced to leave their country of habitual residence, nationality or origin in order to escape violence, regardless of whether they are personally in danger due to political persecution. Unlike the Refugee Convention, which only provides legal protection to those who fear persecution for one of five stipulated reasons (race, religion, nationality, membership of a particular social group or political opinion), the African Convention protects persons fleeing from various kinds of conflicts who do not meet these requirements. The original character of the African Convention definition lies in its explicit introduction of objective criteria for determining refugee status that are based on the prevailing conditions in the country of origin. Because it requires an objective determination of the status of a refugee, the definition contained in the African Convention is better suited for mass movements of refugees than the 1951 Convention, which relies on a subjective test. While the African Refugee Convention permits refugee status to be accorded to groups of refugees without necessarily subjecting each person to individual screening, the 1951 Convention does not, in theory, establish such a process.

Moreover, the African Convention definition of refugee does not require a "well-founded" fear of persecution, which is one of the fundamental criteria established in the 1951 Convention for an individual to claim refugee status. Under the more expansive definition in the African Refugee Convention, the determination of refugee status depends on whether a specific situation falls within the prescribed reasons for flight, namely external aggression, occupation, foreign domination or events causing a serious disturbance to public order. Similarly, by prescribing that refugee status may be accorded for events or conflicts taking place "in either part or the whole of his country of origin or nationality", the African definition disposes of the requirement in the 1951 Convention that a person must first seek safety in another part of the country where possible and practical. In short, the deliberate decision on the part of the drafters of the African Convention to omit several elements of the

---

21   See O. Eze, "The Convention Governing the Specific Aspects of Refugee Problems in Africa", in Yusuf & Ouguergouz,(ed.), *The African Union: Legal And Institutional Framework*, 2012, p. 503.

definition of refugee in the 1951 Convention effectively broadens the class of persons who could qualify for refugee status under the African Refugee Convention.

The progressive character of the African Convention has influenced other regional bodies. In 1984, a colloquium of government representatives and distinguished Latin American jurists was convened in Cartagena, Colombia, to discuss the international protection of refugees in the region. This gathering adopted what became known as the Cartagena Declaration, which recommends that the definition of a refugee used throughout the Latin American region should include both the 1951 Refugee Convention definition and also persons who have fled their country "because their lives, safety or freedom have been threatened by generalized violence, foreign aggression, internal conflicts, massive violation of human rights or other circumstances which have seriously disturbed public order".[22]

Although the Cartagena Declaration is not legally binding on States, most Latin American States apply the definition as a matter of practice, and some have incorporated the definition into their own national legislation.[23] In light of the expansive definition of the Cartagena Declaration, it cannot be denied that the adoption of an objective standard for the determination of refugee status by the Latin American States was inspired by the African Convention of 1969.[24]

The African Convention also supplements the 1951 Convention with regard to asylum. The regime governing asylum consists of various elements, including (i) the admission of an individual to the territory of a State; (ii) the authorization for the individual to remain in that territory; (iii) the refusal to expel or extradite such an individual; and (iv) the avoidance of prosecution, punishment, or other restriction on the individual's liberty under Articles 31, 32 and 33 of the 1951 UN Convention, which together articulate the fundamental principle of "non-refoulement".[25]

Article 11 of the 1969 African Convention reads as follows:

---

[22] Cartagena Declaration on Refugees, Colloquium on the International Protection of Refugees in Central America, Mexico and Panama, 22 November 1984, OAS Doc. OEA/Ser.L/V/II.66/doc.10, Art. 3.

[23] L. Jubilut and F. Piovesan, "Regional Developments: Americas" in A. Zimmerman (ed.), *The 1951 Convention Relating to the Status of Refugees and Its 1967 Protocol: A Commentary*, 2011, pp. 219–220.

[24] Ibid., p. 219.

[25] Refugee Convention, Arts. 31–33.

1. Member States of the OAU shall use their best endeavours consistent with their respective legislations to receive refugees and to secure the settlement of those refugees who, for well-founded reasons, are unable or unwilling to return to their country of origin or nationality.

2. The grant of asylum to refugees is a peaceful and humanitarian act and shall not be regarded as an unfriendly act by any Member State.

3. No person shall be subjected by a Member State to measures such as rejection at the frontier, return or expulsion, which would compel him to return to or remain in a territory where his life, physical integrity or liberty would be threatened for the reasons set out in Article 1, paragraphs 1 and 2.

4. Where a Member State finds difficulty in continuing to grant asylum to refugees, such Member State may appeal directly to other Member States and through the OAU, and such other Member States shall in the spirit of African solidarity and international cooperation take appropriate measures to lighten the burden of the Member State granting asylum.

5. Where a refugee has not received the right to reside in any country of asylum, he may be granted temporary residence in any country of asylum in which he first presented himself as a refugee pending arrangement for his resettlement in accordance with the preceding paragraph.

6. For reasons of security, countries of asylum shall, as far as possible, settle refugees at a reasonable distance from the frontier of their country of origin.[26]

With respect to asylum practices, Article II of the African Convention contains a number of innovative provisions that provide a fuller and wider protection to refugees as compared to the corresponding provisions of the 1951 UN Convention. First, under paragraphs 1 and 2, the African Convention advances the right to asylum, although it does not go so far as to establish it as an individual right. However, it encourages States to grant asylum to refugees and it depoliticizes the asylum institution by characterizing it as a "peaceful and humanitarian act" that "shall not be regarded as an unfriendly act by any Member State".[27] Secondly, it recognizes, under paragraph 3, the principle of "non-refoulement" in a wider sense by excluding the national security exception found in the 1951 UN Convention and by extending the temporal scope of the "non-refoulement" principle so as to protect asylum seekers from the very moment that they present themselves for entry at the frontier.

---

26   African Refugee Convention, Art. 2.
27   Ibid., Art. 2(2).

Thirdly, it provides for burden sharing and for temporary protection of refugees. Thus, if an African State "finds difficulty in continuing to grant asylum to refugees", it may appeal to other African States either directly or through the AU, to take "appropriate measures" including regional resettlement, financial support, and political responsibility sharing.[28] This explicit call for cooperation in the resettlement of refugees is meant to strengthen the solidarity among African States in confronting massive influxes of refugees due to a conflict in a neighbouring State. The provision on temporary protection, which is another example of burden sharing among African States in the regional asylum regime, applies to persons who have been recognized as refugees but who have not been granted the right of residence for any duration.[29] In such cases, the Convention preserves their status as refugees until resettlement can be arranged or a voluntary repatriation is carried out.

The African Convention also distinguishes itself from the 1951 UN Convention through its insistence on the voluntary character of repatriation of refugees. Indeed, it is the first – and remains the only – international legal instrument to formally insist on the voluntariness of refugee repatriation. For example, Article 5(1) provides that: "The essentially voluntary character of repatriation shall be respected in all cases and no refugee shall be repatriated against his will".[30] This is an important corollary of the provisions in Article 2 on asylum, particularly the provision on "non-refoulement". In order to give effect to the principle of voluntary repatriation, the Convention requires countries of asylum, countries of origin, voluntary agencies, and international and intergovernmental organizations to assist refugees with the process of return and establishes modalities for voluntary repatriation.[31]

IV   The Added Value of the African Charter on the Rights and Welfare of the Child

The African Charter on the Rights and Welfare of the Child (Children's Charter) was adopted in 1990 and entered into force on 29 November 1999.[32] Although it was adopted less than a year after the adoption of the UN Convention on the Rights of the Child (CRC),[33] its process of elaboration was launched in

---

28   Ibid.
29   Ibid., Art. 2(5).
30   Ibid., Art. 5(1).
31   See generally, ibid., Art. 5.
32   African Charter on the Rights and Welfare of the Child, 11 July 1990, OAU Doc. CAB/LEG/24.9/49.
33   Convention on the Rights of the Child, 20 November 1989, UN Doc. A/44/49.

1979 during the 16th Ordinary Session of the Assembly of the Heads of State and Government of the Organization of African Unity (OAU) in Monrovia, Liberia.[34]

As stated by Peter & Mwalimu:

> the African Charter seeks to complement the UN Convention on the Rights of the Child, taking into account social and cultural values of Africa and offering protection against violations of children's rights. It combines African values with international norms by proclaiming collective rights and individual duties. These include the duty of individuals to their family, community and State. The uniqueness of the Charter is to be found in the originality of its normative content. It covers civil and political rights as well as economic, social and cultural rights and some protective rights that are specific to children. Furthermore, the African Charter covers third generation rights, and gives due importance to the assumption that a person has duties as well as rights in the community.[35]

It is the added value of the Children's Charter and the manner in which it supplements its universal counterpart, the UN Convention on the Rights of the Child, which is of particular interest to us in this Chapter. One significant contribution of the African instrument is the very definition of the "Child". While the Children's Charter applies to every person below the age of eighteen,[36] the CRC defines a child as "every human being below the age of eighteen years unless under the law applicable to the child, majority is attained earlier".[37] Unlike the CRC, the Children's Charter provides a clear-cut definition of a child that does not allow for any limitations on the concept of childhood by including phrases such as "unless majority is attained earlier".[38] Thus, every human being below the age of eighteen is regarded as a child under the Children's Charter.

As a consequence of this difference in definition, the African Charter sets a higher level of protection than its UN equivalent. The most notable examples are, first, in the area of participation of children in hostilities, where under the Children's Charter no person under the age of eighteen is allowed to take part

---

[34] Declaration on the Rights and Welfare of the African Child (hereinafter Children's Charter), 17–20 July 1979, OAU Doc. AHG/ST.4 Rev.I.

[35] C. Peter and U. Mwalimu, "The African Charter on the Rights and Welfare of the Child", in Yusuf & Ouguergouz, op. cit., p. 480.

[36] Children's Charter, Art. 2.

[37] CRC, Art. 1.

[38] Ibid.

in hostilities[39] while the CRC allows children between fifteen and eighteen to be used in direct hostilities.[40] An optional protocol on the rights of children in armed conflict, which prohibits persons under the age of eighteen from taking direct part in hostilities and from compulsory recruitment, has been adopted under the CRC. However, even the Protocol allows voluntary recruitment for persons under the age of eighteen.[41] In light of Africa's endemic problem with the use of child soldiers in armed conflict, the bright-line prohibition on the participation of persons under the age of eighteen in the Children's Charter was clearly warranted and should be interpreted as a response to the realities of armed conflict on the continent.

Secondly, child marriages are not allowed under the Children's Charter,[42] whereas the UN Convention may be interpreted as not prohibiting the practice in those situations where majority may be attained below the age of 18.[43] Thirdly, Article 11 of the Children's Charter provides that States parties are required to "take special measures in respect of female, gifted and disadvantaged children", and "to ensure that children who became pregnant before completing their education shall have an opportunity to continue on the basis of their individual ability".[44] On the other hand, the CRC makes no special provision for female children with respect to education.

Fourthly, pursuant to its consideration of the family as the natural unit and basis of society, the Children's Charter explicitly considers the penalization of expectant mothers and mothers of infants and young children, while the CRC is silent on this subject. To ensure that young children are not separated from their mothers, the Children's Charter provides that States parties ensure, *inter alia*, that non-custodial and alternative sentences are considered for offending mothers, that special alternative facilities are provided for them, and that no death sentence is pronounced on them.[45] In establishing this provision, the Charter considers and protects the child not as an individual entity, but within the context of the integrity of the family.

Moreover, the scope of protection of uprooted children appears to be broader under the Children's Charter, which allows for internally displaced children to qualify for protection since the prescribed causes of dislocation are not

---

39   Children's Charter, Art. 22(2).
40   CRC, Arts. 38(2)–(3).
41   Optional Protocol to the Convention on the Rights of the Child on the Involvement of Children in Armed Conflict, 25 May 2000, UN Doc. A/RES/54/263, Art. 3.
42   Children's Charter, Arts. 2, 21(2).
43   CRC, Art. 1.
44   Children's Charter, Art. 11(3).
45   Ibid., Art. 30.

restricted but may take any form, including civil strife, internal armed conflict or the breakdown of economic and social order.[46] In stark contrast, the CRC refers only to refugee children. This unqualified protection of the rights of the internally displaced responds to the plight of internally displaced children, which particularly affects African States, and cannot be addressed only by resort to refugee law, because the definition of refugee used in international law and mentioned in both instruments does not apply to internally displaced individuals.

The innovative character of the Children's Charter is further evidenced in its treatment of different categories of human rights. The Charter does not explicitly distinguish between civil and political rights and economic, social and cultural rights. For example, while it is stated in the UN Convention that socio-economic rights shall be given effect only to the maximum extent of the available resources,[47] the African Charter does not contain such a limitation. Nevertheless, as noted by Peter & Mwalimu:

> in the more specific provisions of the Charter dealing with socio-economic rights, limitations related to the availability of resources seem to be permissible. Article 11(3) on the right to education and Article 13(3) on the rights of handicapped children could illustrate this argument. These illustrative Articles contain rights that could be categorized as socio-economic and speak of progressive realization. It can be assumed, therefore, that even though the distinction between categories of rights is less obvious in the Charter, such a distinction can nonetheless be found underlying certain of the Charter's provisions.[48]

The Children's Charter does, however, stipulate that the rights enshrined therein shall be regarded as the minimum standard rights and shall not hinder the effectiveness of rights contained in other instruments which grant a higher level of protection than the Charter itself.[49] As a result, the levels of protection offered under the African Charter may be supplemented by other human rights instruments as well as national legislation likely to enhance the protection of the child with respect to socioeconomic rights.

On the subject of harmful cultural practices, the rule codified in the African Children's Charter is also broader than the rule in the CRC. Article 1(3) of the

---

46   Ibid., Art. 23(4).
47   CRC, Art. 4.
48   Peter and Mwalimu, op. cit., pp. 481–82.
49   Children's Charter, Art. 1(2).

Charter provides that: "Any custom, tradition, cultural or religious practice that is inconsistent with the rights, duties and obligations contained in the present Charter shall to the extent of such inconsistency be discouraged".[50] This is an important provision in the African context where certain practices detrimental to the rights of the child continue to be justified on the basis of custom or tradition or religious usage.

The Children's Charter is also unique in establishing responsibilities, as well as rights, of the child. Article 31 establishes that "every child shall have responsibilities towards his family and society, the State and other legally recognized communities and the international community".[51] These duties include, *inter alia*: to work for the cohesion of the family; to serve the national community; to preserve and strengthen social and national solidarity, to preserve and strengthen African values; and to contribute to the promotion and achievement of African Unity.[52] This set of obligations underscores the emphasis in the Charter on the broad cultural and developmental context of the child. The child is not just a holder of rights; he or she is a human resource, an actor who may have the capacity, like all African individuals, to implement and give effect to the Pan-African principles of unity, solidarity and community.

Finally, with regard to implementation, the Children's Charter establishes the African Committee on the Rights and Welfare of the Child (African Committee) as its implementing body with a mandate that is wider than the one conferred on the UN Committee on the Rights of the Child. While the latter has the authority to consider reports from State parties, the African Committee has, in addition to State reporting, an additional mechanism for protecting children which includes both an individual complaint review system and an investigative procedure.[53]

V   The Supplementary Character of the African Protocol on the Rights of Women

The African Charter on Human and Peoples' Rights (the Banjul Charter) contains only one sub-paragraph on women's rights, Article 18(3), which states that: "The State shall ensure the elimination of every discrimination against women and also ensure the protection of the rights of the woman and the child as stipulated in international declarations and conventions".[54] Although

---

50   Children's Charter, Art. 1(3).
51   Ibid., Art. 31.
52   Ibid., Arts. 31 (a)–(f).
53   See ibid., Arts. 42–45; CRC, Arts. 43–45.
54   Children's Charter, Art. 18(3).

Article 18(3) imposes clear obligations on States parties to end discrimination, the Banjul Charter has not been considered by women's groups in the continent as an adequate instrument for the promotion and protection of women's rights and freedoms. According to Mayanja, the scepticism of African women's groups towards the Banjul Charter derives from the broader context in which the Charter establishes women's rights.[55] Specifically, Article 18(3) is preceded by the following two paragraphs which emphasize the importance of the family as a microcosm of society:

> (1) The family shall be the natural unit and basis of society. It shall be protected by the State which shall take care of its physical and moral health.
> (2) The State shall have the duty to assist the family which is the custodian of morals and traditional values recognized by the community.

Mayanja further observes that:

> by placing the sole non-discrimination clause against women under the umbrella of the family, along with others considered vulnerable, such as the aged and disabled, Article 18 of the Banjul Charter signals the OAU's main concern over the vulnerability of the family and certain of its members in respect of which it imposes a duty on the State to assist and protect the family. This unfortunate placement undermined from the outset the importance and effectiveness of the clause purporting to establish a framework of human rights for African women.[56]

In view of these perceived shortcomings of the Banjul Charter with respect to women's rights, the Protocol on the Rights of Women in Africa was adopted in July 2003 and entered into force on 25 November 2005, one month after its fifteenth ratification. The adoption and subsequent entry into force of the Protocol constitute an important milestone in the recognition of the rights of women in Africa. However, as States parties attempt to implement and enforce these rights across the continent, questions remain as to whether the Protocol contributes to the creation of "rights specific to African women" or to an African approach dictated by the realities of the lives of African women and the particular challenges they face in enjoying their human rights and freedoms.

---

[55] R. Mayanja,"The Protocol on the Rights of Women in Africa", in Yusuf & Ouguergouz, op. cit., p. 457.

[56] Ibid., p. 458.

Does the Protocol innovate with respect to the UN Convention on the Elimination of All Forms of Discrimination against Women (CEDAW) or supplement it in some important respects, thus enhancing the protection of women's rights in the African context?

According to Viljoen:

> compared to CEDAW, the Protocol speaks in a clearer voice about issues of particular concern to African women, locates CEDAW in [an] African reality, and returns to its fold some casualties of quests for global consensus [which resulted] from the adoption of CEDAW. More specifically, the Protocol expands the scope of protected rights beyond those provided for under CEDAW and it deals with rights already covered in CEDAW with greater specificity.[57]

Indeed, the provisions of the African Protocol broaden and enrich the scope of corresponding provisions in CEDAW, beginning with the very definition of discrimination against women in the Protocol. The Protocol defines discrimination as:

> any distinction, exclusion or restriction or any differential treatment based on sex and whose objectives or effects compromise or destroy the recognition, enjoyment or the exercise by women, regardless of their marital status, of human rights and fundamental freedoms in all spheres of life.[58]

Although the Protocol's definition is consistent with Article 1, Part I, of CEDAW, two elements deserve particular attention. First, the Protocol's definition is much broader as it includes "differential treatment".[59] Secondly, as noted by Mayanja:

> the Protocol unlike CEDAW does not include the phrase 'on a basis of equality of men and women', suggesting a conscious and deliberate decision on the part of its drafters to recognize women's *rights* on their own

---

[57] F. Viljoen, "An Introduction to the Protocol to the African Charter on Human and Peoples' Rights on the Rights of Women in Africa", 16 *Wash. & Lee J. Civil Rts. Soc. Just.*, 2009, p. 21.

[58] African Union, Protocol to the African Charter on Human and Peoples' Rights on the Rights of Women in Africa (hereinafter African Women's Protocol), 11 July 2003, Art. 1(f).

[59] See Convention on the Elimination of All Forms of Discrimination against Women (hereinafter CEDAW), 18 December 1979, G.A. res. 34/180, UN Doc. A/34/46, Art. 1.

merits and distinctly from those of men. Thus, the central focus of the Protocol is to secure women's empowerment and their status as rights-holders and to ensure that those rights are central to the African human rights regime.[60]

With respect to the elimination of practices harmful to women, Article 2(f) of CEDAW requires States parties "to take all appropriate measures, including legislation, to modify or abolish existing laws, regulations, customs and practices".[61] This broad obligation is expanded in Article 5 of the African Women's Protocol, which calls for the prohibition of certain practices, "such as all forms of female genital mutilation, scarification, medicalization and para-medicalization of female genital mutilation", and the protection and rehabilitation of victims of these practices.[62] Thus, the African Women's Protocol broadens the scope of the CEDAW in identifying specific regional practices and establishing remedies for victims.

The two conventions also differ in their treatment of fundamental human rights as they apply to women. Under Article 3, the African Women's Protocol establishes that women have the right to dignity and the right to respect as a person.[63] Accordingly, it imposes obligations on the State to take measures prohibiting the degradation and exploitation of women, as well as measures protecting women from all forms of violence, particularly sexual violence. In addition, Article 4 of the Protocol requires States parties to adopt several measures to prevent violence against women including the promulgation and enforcement of "laws to prohibit all forms of violence against women including unwanted or forced sex whether the violence takes place in private or public".[64] This emphasis on violence as a form of discrimination is absent in CEDAW. While CEDAW focuses generally on discrimination faced by women in an institutional sense, the provisions of the African Women's Protocol on the "core rights" establish remedies for the problems African women face in the private sphere, particularly in the domestic sphere. Essentially, these rights address the silence on violence in international instruments as a form of discrimination to be resolved at the regional level.

With regard to marriage, both instruments contain similar provisions, but the African Women's Protocol is distinct in its prohibition of child marriage

---

60 Mayanja, op. cit., p. 461.
61 CEDAW, Art. 2(f).
62 African Women's Protocol, Art. 5(b).
63 Ibid., Art. 3.
64 Ibid., Art. 4.

(by prescribing that the minimum age of marriage is 18 years) and in its encouragement of monogamy while simultaneously protecting the marriage and family rights of women in polygamous relationships.[65] These distinctions are designed to establish protections for African women exposed to potentially discriminatory institutions of marriage, which are common in Africa, but are unrecognized in CEDAW. Thus, while CEDAW does not ban child marriage or consider which marriage rights should be accorded to women in polygamous relationships to prevent discrimination and abuse, the African Women's Protocol imposes an obligation on States parties to enact legislation for these purposes.

In its provisions establishing obligations on States to "accord to women equality with men before the law",[66] CEDAW focuses primarily on establishing and protecting the legal capacity of women. It does not consider the access of women to justice, which is the exclusive focus of the provisions of the African Women's Protocol on the status of women under the law. Article 8, *inter alia*, requires States parties to ensure "effective access by women to judicial and legal services, including legal aid"[67] and prescribes that "women are represented equally in the judiciary and law enforcement".[68] Similarly, whereas the CEDAW provision considers only the substantive capacity of women under the law, the African Protocol directs its attention at the multitudinous ways that women are discriminated against *vis-à-vis* unequal institutional and procedural factors such as: representation in the judiciary and law enforcement, the capacity of law enforcement organs to apply and interpret gender equality rights, and access to legal services – including legal aid.[69] Because these factors are particularly endemic in developing regions, the African Women's Protocol addresses many of the underlying reasons why women lack equal protection under the law.

Article 14 of the African Women's Protocol, which addresses health and reproductive rights, goes beyond other binding treaties, such as CEDAW, in outlining reproductive rights. If implemented by African States, it could constitute a tool for ensuring universal access to reproductive health for women in Africa. Three of the most important components of women's reproductive health rights under the Protocol are:

---

65   African Women's Protocol, Arts. 6(b)–(c).
66   CEDAW, Art. 15(1).
67   African Women's Protocol, Art. 8(a).
68   Ibid., Art. 8(e).
69   Ibid., Art. 8.

(a) Reproductive and sexual decision making, including the number and spacing of children, contraceptive choice, and the right to self-protection from HIV;
(b) Access to information about HIV/AIDS and reproductive health; and
(c) Access to reproductive health services, including antenatal services and abortion-related services.[70]

Article 14 also contains the first references to HIV/AIDS in an international treaty, and the first expression of a right to abortion, albeit limited to instances in which a pregnancy results from sexual assault, rape, or where a woman's mental or physical health is endangered.[71] Moreover, it specifically recognizes marital rape as a form of gender-based violence and "identifies protection from HIV and AIDS as a key component of women's sexual and reproductive rights".[72]

While CEDAW prescribes a limited set of economic and social rights exclusively available for rural women,[73] the African Protocol on Women establishes a number of economic and social welfare rights for all women, including vulnerable women. For all women, Articles 15 and 16 establish the right to food and water security and adequate housing.[74] With respect to vulnerable women, the African Women's Protocol provides for a social security system for women working in the informal sector, a minimum working age for children, particularly girl children, and the recognition of the economic value of the work of women in the home.[75] Thus, under the African Women's Protocol, the category of vulnerable women is broadened to reflect the particular forms of economic marginalization common in Africa, and to protect women that are so marginalized.

The Protocol also recognizes a category of women described as "women in distress" and provides that States parties undertake to ensure the protection of poor women and women heads of families including women from marginalized population groups, and provide them an environment suitable for their condition and for their special physical, economic and social needs.[76] It also requires States parties to ensure the rights of pregnant or nursing women and

---

70 Ibid., Art. 14.
71 Ibid., Arts 14(1)(d)–(e), Art. 14(2)(c).
72 Ibid.
73 CEDAW, Art. 14(1).
74 African Women's Protocol, Arts. 15–16.
75 Ibid., Art. 13.
76 Ibid., Art. 24.

women in detention by providing them with an environment which is suitable to their condition and their right to be treated with dignity.[77]

At the time of writing, 36 out of 54 Member States of the African Union (AU) have ratified the Protocol. Moreover, in many States, "legal and institutional measures, such as laws prosecuting perpetrators of sexual violence (Kenya, Liberia), criminalizing domestic violence (Ghana, Mozambique), prohibiting female genital mutilation (Uganda, Zimbabwe) and establishing mechanisms mandated to promote women's rights (Côte d'Ivoire, Senegal), have accompanied these ratifications".[78]

Despite the undeniable progress in many parts of the continent, several of the rights enshrined in the Protocol are yet to be fully implemented. Throughout the continent, thousands of women victims of sexual violence continue to demand justice and compensation, while others are still waiting for equality within the family to be recognized or their right to property to become a reality.[79] Unfortunately, several State parties do not respect their obligation, under Article 26 of the Protocol, to indicate, in their periodic reports submitted to the ACHPR, the measures undertaken for the full realization of women's rights as provided within the Maputo Protocol.[80]

Moreover, some of the States parties to the Protocol have placed reservations on certain articles deemed more controversial, such as those on early marriage, property rights, sexual and reproductive rights.[81] The decision of these States to ratify the African Women's Protocol with these reservations

---

77 Ibid.
78 Fédération internationale des ligues des droits de l'homme, "Women's Rights in Africa: 18 countries are yet to ratify the Maputo Protocol", 10 July 2013, *available at* http://www.fidh.org/en/africa/african-union/women-s-rights-in-africa-18-countries-are-yet-to-ratify-the-maputo-13644.
79 See A. Melo, 16–30 May 2007, Intersession Activity Report, Special Rapporteur on the Rights of Women in Africa, 41st Ordinary Session African Commission on Human and Peoples' Rights, *available at* http://www.achpr.org/sessions/41st/intersession-activity-reports/angela-melo/, para. 50.
80 B. Kombo, R. Sow, F. Mohamed (eds.), *Journey to Equality: 10 Years of the Protocol on the Rights of Women in Africa*, 2013, pp. 32–34.
81 See University of Pretoria Centre for Human Rights, "Instrument of Ratification – Gambia (2003)", *available at* http://www1.chr.up.ac.za/images/files/documents/ahrdd/theme40/women_instrument_ratification_gambia_2003.pdf; Ibid., "Instrument of Ratification – Namibia (2003)", *available at* http://www1.chr.up.ac.za/images/files/documents/ahrdd/theme40/women_instrument_ratification_namibia_2003.pdf; Ibid., "Instrument of Ratification – South Africa (2003)", *available at* http://www1.chr.up.ac.za/images/files/documents/ahrdd/theme40/women_instrument_ratification_southafrica_2003.pdf.

directly affects gender equality and erodes the normative force of the supplementary provisions of the Protocol with respect to CEDAW. Nevertheless, as observed by Mayanja:

> The message emanating from the adoption and speedy coming into force of the Protocol is clear. African women are no longer willing to accept the persisting discrimination and violation of their rights and freedoms. They are determined to hold States accountable for the promotion and protection of their human rights.[82]

It is perhaps as a result of such civil society mobilization and sensitization that the Gambia[83] withdrew its reservation to the Protocol and that three African States (Libya, Lesotho and Mauritania) that entered reservations to CEDAW did not make such reservations to the Protocol, although, as discussed above, the African instrument broadens the scope of the rights of women in many important respects as compared to CEDAW.

VI   Concluding Remarks

As shown in this paper, many of the African conventions concluded under the auspices of the Pan-African organizations – the now defunct OAU and the AU – either enrich corresponding universal instruments by widening the scope of their application or add to them through new rules and principles applicable among African States. In both cases, the rules enacted by the African States, which are part of a growing corpus of African public law, constitute considerable improvements in relation to the corresponding global international law instruments. Take, for example, the protection of peoples' rights in Africa. The African Charter of Human and Peoples' Rights not only expressly recognizes the rights of peoples within the Charter, it dedicates six articles to peoples' rights, including the right to self-determination, the right to natural resources, the right to economic, social and cultural development, the right to peace and security and the right to a safe and healthy environment. This recognition of peoples' rights is unprecedented and unmatched by any other multilateral human rights instrument. Moreover, the African Commission, a quasi-judicial body responsible for monitoring rights protection under the Charter, is the first

---

82   Mayanja, op. cit., p. 475.
83   See F. Viljoen, *International Human Rights Law in Africa*, 2012, p. 256.

such body to define the concept of "peoples" for the purposes of the African Charter, and to apply it to concrete cases brought before the Commission.

Other innovative norms produced under the auspices of the Pan-African organizations include the expanded conception of refugee status introduced by the 1969 OAU Convention on Refugees; the scope of application of the African Children's Charter and its clear-cut definition of a child; the Kampala Convention on the protection of displaced persons; and the supplementary provisions of the African protocol on women's rights which not only expand the scope of protected rights beyond those provided for under CEDAW, but also deal with rights already covered in CEDAW with greater specificity.

An important vector of diversity in the future of international law will be that of *regional diversity*. The application, interpretation and creation of international law by regional organizations and regional courts are likely to provide a key impetus in the development and evolution of international law. These regional forums can be likened to the "laboratories" of federal systems: experimentation and legal innovation often occurs at the decentralized level, where legislators (in this case, international yet regional legislators) are closer to their constituents. From there, effective legal principles and rules and best practices can be diffused to and copied by other systems and – eventually and progressively – seep into the fabric of universal international law. Therefore, regional diversity is likely to be an engine for the development of international law in the years to come.

Africa represents an excellent example of the potential contribution regional diversity can make to general international law. In recent years, the African Union assumed an important role in legal production and codification through the enactment of a growing corpus of African public law. There is reason to expect that some of the best practices and innovative norms developed through the public law of Africa may eventually find their way to the universal level, as they are taken up in new universal instruments or as international judicial bodies find inspiration in some of them to resolve international disputes. In any case, it cannot be excluded that these supplementary norms enacted in the context of the public law of Africa will have a positive influence in the future development and evolution of universal international law.

CHAPTER 24

The Development and Enforcement of Community Law in the African Regional Economic Communities: Conceptual Issues, Architecture and Institutions

Tiyanjana Maluwa

I am honoured to contribute to this *Festschrift* for Judge Abdul G. Koroma. Among the many admirable attributes that have characterized Judge Koroma's long career as a diplomat for his native country, Sierra Leone, and subsequently as a judge of the International Court of Justice (ICJ), two may be noted here. First, his commitment to the idea of African unity; and second, his abiding belief in the value of the contribution of African states to the development of international law and the relevance of African voices to international legal discourse.

Judge Koroma's commitment to African unity was not born out of starry-eyed, arm-chair Pan-Africanism – though his Pan-Africanist inclinations are not in question – but through his practical engagement with Africa's political liberation and the post-colonial project of African integration as Sierra Leone's ambassador, successively, to the United Nations (UN), the European Economic Community (EEC) and the Organization of African Unity (OAU), the predecessor to the African Union (AU), prior to his election to the ICJ in 1994. His tenure as his country's permanent representative to the OAU coincided with the period of negotiations leading to the adoption in 1991 of the Treaty establishing the African Economic Community (AEC Treaty), which provides the legal framework for Africa's continental economic integration. Earlier, as a foreign ministry officer in the Sierra Leone government, he had participated in UN meetings and other multilateral conferences on various aspects of international law. He also bore witness to some momentous regional political developments, such as the establishment of the Economic Community of West African States (ECOWAS) in 1975.

Judge Koroma's diplomatic career evolved alongside another professional trajectory: that of the international legal expert and jurist. Over the decades, starting in the late 1970s, as a member of Sierra Leone's delegations to the United Nations General Assembly's Sixth Committee and as a member of the

International Law Commission (ILC) from 1988 to 1994, and subsequently as a judge at the ICJ, he has contributed to the discourses on various aspects of international law and to shaping certain conceptual developments and practical positions in the process. His judicial opinions and contributions are the subject of other chapters in this volume.

My contribution, rather, seeks to explore an issue relevant to some aspects of Judge Koroma's work, though not directly connected to his judicial career: the project of African integration and the development of community law by African states. The definition of community law adopted in this discussion is the law of the various African regional economic communities (RECs) and the AEC as enshrined in their respective treaties and decisions of the courts established under these treaties. This discussion does not aim to suggest a conflation of community law with international law – Judge Koroma's life-long pre-occupation – as traditionally defined and understood. While I acknowledge the autonomous character of community law and its ontological relationship with international law, I do not examine here the various competing arguments and questions that arise in the debates on this issue. Among these are the following: that community law has morphed into a form of municipal law of the regional economic communities in question; or that it is a type of transnational legal order that stands completely aside from international law; or that it represents a supranational legal system whose boundaries with international law have become increasingly blurred. These debates are both important and interesting.[1] However, suffice it to say here that an inquiry into the development of African community law in the RECs is consistent with Judge Koroma's general position on the subject of Africa's contribution to the development of international law in general.

---

1 See, for example, T. Schilling, "The Autonomy of the Community Legal Order: An Analysis of Possible Foundations", 37 *Harv. Int'l. L.J.* 389 (1996); J. Boulouis, "Le droit des Communautés européenes dans ses rapports avec le droit international général", 235 (IV) *Hague Recueil* 9 (1992). See also, generally, B. Simma and D. Pulkowski, "Of Planets and the Universe: Self-contained Regimes in International Law", 17 *EJIL* 483 (2006); and J. Weiler and U. Haltern, "The Autonomy of the Community Legal Order – Through the Looking Glass", 37 *Harv. Int'l. L.J.* 411 (1996). See also A. Sari, "The Relationship between Community Law and International Law after *Kadi*: Did the ECJ Slam the Door on Effective Multilateralism?" in Matthew Happold (ed.), *International Law in a Multipolar World*, (2011), available at SSRN: http://ssrn.com/abstract=1635759.

1 **African Regional Economic Communities: The Challenge of Proliferation**

Africa has a proliferation of regional economic communities or organizations, with one estimate putting their number at fourteen.[2] Recognizing this multiplicity of institutions, in 2006 the AU Assembly decided to suspend the recognition of new RECs beyond the already recognized eight: Arab Maghreb Union (AMU), Common Market for Eastern and Southern Africa (COMESA), Community of Sahel-Saharan States (CEN-SAD), East African Community (EAC), Economic Community of Central African States (ECCAS), Economic Community of West African States (ECOWAS), Inter-Governmental Authority on Development (IGAD) and Southern African Development Community (SADC).[3]

Two preliminary observations about this proliferation of RECs may be noted from the outset. First, the membership of these RECs does not necessarily and completely coincide with the membership of the five geographical regions into which the AU is divided: Central Africa, East Africa, North Africa, Southern Africa and West Africa. Furthermore, there is a considerable degree of overlapping REC membership between the different geographical regions, with some countries belonging to as many as three or four different RECs, and some RECs drawing their membership from at least three different AU geographical regions.[4] Among the better known sub-regional groupings that have not yet acquired the status of AU-recognized RECs are: Economic and Monetary Community of Central Africa (CEMAC), Economic and Monetary Union of West Africa (UEMAO), Southern African Customs Union (SACU) and Economic Community of Great Lakes Countries (ECGLC). Secondly, while these RECs are intended to be the basis on which the linear progression of African integration envisaged under Article 6 of the AEC Treaty would proceed – from free trade areas to a continent-wide common market – the trajectory of African integration has not followed this logic faithfully. The RECs are neither progressing towards the goal of creating the AEC at the same pace nor with the same procedures, processes or determination. Progress towards the dual-vision of

---

[2] See United Nations Economic Commission for Africa (UNECA), *Assessing Regional Integration in Africa II: Rationalizing Regional Economic Communities*, (Addis Ababa: UNECA, 2006), p. x.

[3] See Decision on the Moratorium on the Recognition of Regional Economic Communities (RECs) Assembly/AU/Dec.112 (VII), adopted by the seventh ordinary session of the AU Assembly held in Banjul, Gambia, on 1–2 July, 2006.

[4] For membership of the RECs see *infra* Table 24.1. Although the choice of membership may at first sight appear arbitrary in some respects, for the most part shared history and colonial legacies have been significant factors.

achieving economic development and promoting intra-African trade through various stages of economic integration has been painfully slow. Many factors lie behind this slow progress, including the variable sizes of the RECs, multiple (and sometimes irreconcilable) legal commitments and occasional political conflicts among member states. Thus, for example, it has been noted that COMESA's creation of a customs union in 2009 had been delayed because some members were also members of the EAC and SADC customs unions.[5] The observation made by the AEC some eighteen years ago remains valid today:[6]

> [There] is no clear evidence that they have long-term continental integration in view, [although] trade liberalization is in the forefront and there seems to be an acceptance of the need for rationalization and programme harmonization [in most places].

That said, it is also important to note that, despite the slow progress and weak structures, the RECs remain the predominant mode for organizing international trade, although they vary in their ultimate goals. Moreover, the United Nations Economic Commission for Africa (UNECA) recently noted that, unlike previous efforts at economic integration, the current efforts are making significant, if slow, progress including in the area of intra-African trade liberalization.[7]

TABLE 24.1 *Membership of the African Economic Community (AU) and AU-recognized Regional Economic Communities (as at 30 June, 2014)*

Country	Regional Economic Community								
	ECOWAS	EAC	COMESA	SADC	IGAD	AMU	ECCAS	CENSAD	AEC
Algeria						x			x
Angola			x				x		x
Benin	x							x	x
Botswana				x					x

---

5 See, Richard F. Oppong, *The Law of Regional Integration in Africa*, (CUP, 2011), p. 27.
6 AEC Economic and Social Commission, First Session, 11–12 June, 1996: *Strategy and Approach to the Implementation of the Treaty establishing the African Economic Community*, OAU Doc. AEC/ECOSOC 3(I)Rev.1.
7 See United Nations Economic Commission for Africa (UNECA), *Assessing Regional Integration in Africa IV: Enhancing Intra-African Trade* (Addis Ababa: UNECA, 2010), pp. 7–35.

TABLE 24.1. *Membership of the African Economic Community* (cont.)

Country	Regional Economic Community								
	ECOWAS	EAC	COMESA	SADC	IGAD	AMU	ECCAS	CENSAD	AEC
Burkina Faso	x							x	x
Burundi		x	x				x		x
Cameroon							x		x
Cape Verde	x								x
CAR[1]							x	x	x
Chad							x	x	x
Comoros			x					x	x
Congo							x		x
Côte d'Ivoire	x							x	x
DRC[2]			x	x			x		x
Djibouti			x		x			x	x
Egypt			x					x	x
Equ. Guinea[3]							x		x
Eritrea			x		x			x	x
Ethiopia			x		x				x
Gabon							x		x
Gambia	x							x	x
Ghana	x							x	x
Guinea	x							x	x
Guinea-Bissau	x							x	x
Kenya		x	x		x			x	x
Lesotho				x					x
Liberia	x							x	x
Libya			x			x		x	x
Madagascar			x	x					x
Malawi			x	x					x
Mali	x							x	x
Mauritania						x		x	x
Mauritius			x	x					x
Mozambique				x					x
Namibia				x					x
Niger	x							x	x
Nigeria	x							x	x
Rwanda		x	x						x

Country	Regional Economic Community								
	ECOWAS	EAC	COMESA	SADC	IGAD	AMU	ECCAS	CENSAD	AEC
S.A.D.R.[4]									x
S. Tome & P.[5]							x	x	x
Senegal	x							x	x
Seychelles			x	x					x
Sierra Leone	x							x	x
Somalia					x			x	x
South Africa				x					x
South Sudan			x		x				x
Sudan			x		x			x	x
Swaziland			x	x					x
Tanzania		x		x					x
Togo	x							x	x
Tunisia						x		x	x
Uganda		x	x		x				x
Zambia			x	x					x
Zimbabwe			x	x					x
Total membership[6]	15	5	20	15	8	4	10	27	54

Notes:

[1] Central African Republic; [2] Democratic Republic of Congo; [3] Equatorial Guinea; [4] Sahrawi Arab Democratic Republic; [5] Sao Tome and Principe; [6] Morocco, currently not a member of the AU, is a member of AMU and CEN-SAD.

Table 24.1 above lists the AU-recognized RECs only and does not include the complex array of regional integration arrangements in Africa. The fuller continental integration map reveals that each geographical region of Africa contains an average of three to four organizations, each with its own mandate. As noted earlier, in a 2006 survey, the UNECA put the total number of these organizations at fourteen, and noted that out of the fifty-three (as they then were) AU member states twenty simultaneously belonged to three of them, and one country belonged to four.[8] It will also be noted from Table 24.1 that although membership of the RECs is, in original conception if not in principle, supposed to be based on geographical contiguity, this logic has not been followed with respect to one organization, namely CEN-SAD. Not only is CEN-SAD member-

---

8 See *supra*, note 2.

ship the biggest among all the RECs, it also includes, for example, states that are as geographically far flung as Morocco (which is not even an AU member), Libya and Tunisia in north Africa, Ghana and Sierra Leone in west Africa, Chad and Central African Republic in central Africa, as well as Kenya and Comoros in east Africa. Only the southern African region does not have a member in CEN-SAD. It seems clear from this that the original conception of this REC as a grouping of countries in the Sahel-Saharan belt has since been superseded. It has been anecdotally suggested that the singularly relentless advocacy for the organization by its founder and main driving force, the late Libyan leader Muammar Gaddafi, and the apparent largesse that accompanied his efforts may have succeeded in attracting to it members from other geographical regions. In the process it appears that CEN-SAD has re-invented itself as a REC defined not so much by the regional economic integration project but by its self-image as an organization for states with significant or majority Muslim populations in Africa.[9]

The proliferation of RECs and their overlapping membership have not always had a positive impact on the regional integration process and the development of community law in Africa. Regional integration results in a juxtaposition of states, legal systems, and institutions for the purpose of achieving a common economic vision, underpinned by community law. Not surprisingly, the more numerous the regional economic institutions, the more challenging the task of identifying the corpus of legal rules and norms constituting a common community law. Most of the literature on this subject reveals that the majority of scholars and commentators have tended to focus on studying the law of integration in Africa from the perspective of each individual REC. The focus has been more on studying the separate law of integration in or for each of these regional groupings – with particular attention being devoted to the two best developed, ECOWAS and SADC – rather than exploring commonalities among them that allow us to identify an integrated and interconnected body of African regional economic community law or the law of regional integration in Africa as a whole.[10] In this essay, I discuss the development of community law

---

9   CEN-SAD appears to have been set adrift by the Arab Spring uprisings which resulted in the killing of Muammar Gaddafi on 20 October, 2011. Gaddafi's demise seems to have changed the dynamic in CEN-SAD, with Morocco reportedly pushing to assume a more visible and influential role in the grouping.

10   A welcome development was the Second Annual Forum of the AU Commission on International Law held in Addis Ababa, Ethiopia, on 11–12 November, 2013 on the theme "The Law of Regional Integration in Africa". It drew presentations on current developments in the law of integration of all the individual AU-recognized RECs with the exception of COMESA.

in the African RECs in the context of international trade in the broad sense and explore, in particular, the requirements for its architecture and institutions.[11]

The argument that international trade is the central goal of regional integration invites many questions, one of which is whether regional integration arrangements in Africa should be based on enforceable legal arrangements. Erasmus has addressed this question. He has highlighted some of the challenges that have been encountered or may be anticipated, not least the vexing issue of perceived loss of sovereignty by states that are members of these regional communities, the obstacles faced by individuals or private sector entities to pursue the enforcement of their legal rights through their national or regional community courts or tribunals, and the very role of these courts in the project of regional integration.[12] To the question posed above, the answer must of course be an unequivocal yes. Not only should African regional integration be based on legally enforceable rules, as Erasmus has concluded, but regional tribunals must develop a coherent jurisprudence anchoring rule-based regimes and rule-based regional governance, forming the basis of African regional integration law or community law.

This paper focuses on two central and inter-related questions that arise from all this: first, how do we define or identify this community law? And, second, what are the foundational conceptual issues and requirements for its architecture and institutions? I shall first address some conceptual issues relating to the definition and development of community law in the African regional economic communities. Following this, I shall discuss the constitutional architecture and relational instruments for regional economic integration. Finally, I shall turn to the institutions for the enforcement of community law both through the RECs and the AEC.

At the root of these questions lies the challenge of what one African legal commentator on this subject has recently called the "relational issues of law in economic integration."[13] These are regarded as the common relational legal

---

[11] This essay is a slightly revised version of a paper delivered at the Workshop on Dispute Settlement in SADC organized by the Trade Law Centre, Cape Town, South Africa, on 26 May, 2014.

[12] See G. Erasmus, "Should African Regional Integration be Based on Enforceable Legal Arrangements?". Paper presented at the Second Annual Forum of the AU Commission on International Law; see *supra* note 10.

[13] See *supra* note 5, *passim*. Oppong's study offers a novel and insightful discussion of African regional integration law broadly speaking. For this discussion, I have drawn upon some of his insights and approach and his conceptualization of a relational theory of regional integration, and my own forthcoming extended review essay of the book and other studies on African regional integration and trade by other authors.

issues and principles that any regional integration scheme – and African regional economic communities in particular – must contend with in order to succeed. It is argued that these relational issues and principles form the basis of the general framework of the law of regional economic integration in Africa and are applicable across the various aspects of regional integration, and not just in the pursuance of the specific goals of international trade and dispute settlement.

II   Understanding African Regional Integration/Community Law

In essence, Oppong argues that the key to defining, identifying and understanding the law of regional integration or community law in Africa law lies in decoding the "relational issues of law". This claim is based on a three-fold proposition.

The first part of this proposition has three aspects. First, it is argued that regional integration "is the product of structuring and managing vertical-horizontal, horizontal-horizontal and vertical-vertical relations among states, laws, institutions and [legal systems];[14] secondly, that earlier African economic integration arrangements had neglected relational instruments, although the more recent ones have paid some, but not always full, attention to these issues; and, thirdly, that ultimately the success or failure of the economic integration initiatives in Africa will depend, in part, on how relational issues are approached and resolved, because they have a direct relationship with the stage of integration reached or envisioned – whether free trade areas, customs unions, common markets, or economic unions. As Oppong has put it in his admirable study on the subject, this proposition suggests that an economic community must have well-structured and well-managed relations between itself and other legal systems as a necessary condition for its effectiveness.[15] Oppong has generally argued that Africa's economic integration processes have not paid systematic or rigorous attention to relational issues:[16]

> The interactions between community and member states' legal systems, among the various communities, as well as among member states' legal systems, have neither been carefully thought through nor placed on a solid legal framework. Where attempts have been made to provide a solid

---

14   Ibid., p. 310.
15   Ibid.
16   Ibid.

legal framework, they have been incomplete, unsatisfactory and, sometimes, grounded on questionable assumptions.

He concludes with the observation that "[even] if all the socio-economic and political challenges that bedevil Africa's integration were to disappear, there remains much in the realm of law which, if unaddressed, will hinder its success and effectiveness."[17] So, in essence, the first problem that we confront here is the very absence of a fully developed body of African regional economic community law, without which the economic integration project remains a great challenge. This aspect has been noted by the UNECA which, a decade ago, identified "the absence of a supranational authority to enforce the commonly agreed policies of the [regional economic] communities as a principal weakness of African economic communities."[18] It is thus imperative to define or understand what the notion of African community law entails. This essay discusses only the proposed architecture of REC (or community) law and legal systems rather than their substantive content. It focuses on the *lex ferenda* and not the *lex lata*.

The second aspect of the proposition is that for international (or intra-African) trade dispute settlement, it is equally important to understand the architecture of the community law of the RECs. Sometimes RECs treaties provide for a preliminary reference procedure.[19] In other instances, they envisage a role for national courts in the implementation and enforcement of community laws and judgments;[20] or, better still, allow individuals (including private sector entities) to access their community courts.[21] These features are evident in the better developed, and more recent, RECs, but not across the board. Could there be room for harmonization here?

The third issue for consideration concerns the institutional requirements. There is a view that one major handicap with the African regional economic integration project is the fact that national institutions that are thought critical to the success of community law are sometimes either lacking or, if they exist, somewhat ineffective. Particularly relevant here are the national courts. It is

---

17 Ibid.
18 See United Nations Economic Commission for Africa (UNECA), *Assessing Regional Integration in Africa*, (Addis Ababa: UNECA, 2004), p. 7.
19 Article 30, COMESA Treaty; article 10(f), Protocol on ECOWAS Court of Justice; and article 34, EAC Treaty.
20 Article 44, EAC Treaty; article 40, COMESA Treaty; and article 24, Protocol on ECOWAS Court of Justice.
21 Article 26, COMESA Treaty; article 30, EAC Treaty; and article 10, Protocol on ECOWAS Court of Justice.

fair to say that, by and large, most national courts are unaware of their role in the integration processes and the nature of their relationships with the communities' legal systems. Conversely, some community institutions have not shown a proper understanding of the relational principles tying them to national institutions either. Ignorance straddles both sides.

In the work cited earlier, Oppong[22] offers a scheme and conceptualization of relational legal issues, some of which I reconceptualize and summarize in this paper. These include: relations between the laws and institutions of the REC (*community law*) and those of member states (*national law*); mechanisms for normative exchange or communication between the REC and the member states and member states *inter se*; potential jurisdictional conflicts between the REC and member states; ascription of competences between the REC and the member states; access of individuals and interest groups to the organization's institutions; recognition and enforcement of inter-state and community normative acts; and relations between the legal system of the REC (*community legal system*) and the legal systems of the member states (*national legal systems*), as well as between the legal systems of the member states.

The principal actors in these relations are the regional or community legal systems, national legal systems and the international legal system. It is argued that if there is no proper understanding or management of these relations, there is a risk that ambiguities in the relations between the community legal system and the international legal system may lead to disputes about the international legality of the community, its acts, or acts of member states founded on community law. Similarly, neglect of the relations between the community legal system and national legal systems may lead to fissures and a disjuncture between both systems, and hamper the effective implementation of community law and its other normative acts.

A proper understanding of the overarching law of regional integration in Africa thus needs to do at least three things: first, consider the proper nature and design of the constitutional architecture of economic integration arrangements: what are their constituent elements? Secondly, identify the necessary legal instruments that should determine the design of this architecture. Thirdly, articulate the various ways in which these instruments influence the relational issues referred to earlier, and thereby determine the effectiveness of regional integration. This approach is akin to what has been termed the concept of "normative supranationalism", which relates to the relationships and hierarchies that exist between community policies and legal acts, on the one hand, and competing policies and legal acts of the member states, on the other.

---

22   For an extensive discussion, see *supra* note 5, *passim*.

The key elements of supranationalism in the context of regional integration have been described as "direct effect", "supremacy", and "pre-emption".[23]

III Architecture and Relational Instruments of Regional Integration/Community Law

From the perspective of international trade dispute settlement, regional integration demands a rethink in three interrelated areas: the traditional approaches to the reception of international law into national legal systems; the characterization of individuals as non-actors on the international plane; and the rules for resolving conflicts between international and national laws. Designing the architecture of regional integration law requires a reconceptualization of all these areas.

A number of relational instruments have been suggested in the legal literature as prerequisites for the constitutional architecture of regional integration law or community law.[24] In the next section, partially following Oppong's schema, I discuss briefly what I consider to be the most critical of these proposed instruments. These are not treated in any hierarchical order.

1 *Respect for the Autonomy of the REC (Community) Legal System*

The first argument is that relations between the REC or community, national and international legal systems should be founded on the autonomy of the community legal system and its distinctiveness from other legal systems. Autonomy is a key aspect of the supranational character of the REC which determines the effectiveness of community laws in their relations with the laws of other legal systems, and should be respected as such. It also guarantees the autonomous personality of the REC (i.e. *existential personality*). As with other types of international organizations, the REC's personality may be expressly provided for in its constitutive instrument or deduced from the community's law-making powers, among other factors. A REC's autonomy from other legal systems may also be evidenced by conferring exclusive jurisdiction to its judicial bodies to interpret matters or laws in which the community's interests are engaged (i.e. *interpretive autonomy*).

---

23 J. Weiler, "The Community System: The Dual Character of Supranationalism", 1 *Yrbk Eur. L.* 267 (1981), at 276.

24 See, especially, Oppong, "A Relational Theory of Regional Economic Integration – Implications for Africa", Working Paper No. 50/08, *available at* http://www.ssrn.com/link/SIEL-Inaugural-Conference.html.

2 Recognition of the Principles of Direct Applicability and Direct Effect of Community Law

Secondly, it is argued that a REC's legal system should ideally be underpinned by the principle of direct applicability of community law. This allows for the integration of all or some community laws into national legal systems without the need for the intervening transformative measures usually employed for the reception of international law into national law (for example through the application of the doctrines of transformation or incorporation). If enshrined in the REC's constitutive treaty, this principle would provide a uniform procedure for the reception of community law into the national legal systems of all the REC member states. In this context, the European Court of Justice has ruled that direct applicability means that the entry into force of community law is "independent of any measure of reception into national law."[25] Acceptance of the principle arguably maintains the specificity of community law within national legal systems.

The next principle, on the direct effect of community law, is somewhat related to that of direct applicability, although quite different in operation and effect. It enables individuals to invoke provisions of community law before national courts and allows national courts to use community law as a direct and autonomous basis for judicial decisions. The principle thus provides a means for integrating community laws into national legal systems by turning national courts and individuals into "private enforcers" of community laws, and thereby enables individuals to become direct beneficiaries of the rights conferred by community laws. Conceivably, direct effect may be expressly denied by the REC's constitutive treaty or it could be either permitted within limits or denied completely by national law or jurisprudence.

3 Application of the Principle of the Supremacy of Community Law

The next issue relates to the supremacy of community law. It may be expected that relations between community law and national law will on some occasions necessarily entail instances of friction and conflict of laws. In such cases, it is argued that the principle of supremacy of community law is needed to provide a means for resolving conflicts. Ideally, supremacy of community law should be enshrined in the REC's constitutive instrument,[26] but it may also be inferred from its constitutional architecture and goals. The principle essential-

---

25   *Amsterdam Bulb v. Produktschap voor Siergewassen* [1976] E.C.R. 137 at 146.

26   See, e.g. article 8(4), EAC Treaty, and article 39(2) of the Protocol on the Establishment of the East African Customs Union.

ly mandates a choice of community law as the applicable law.[27] It is argued that this principle achieves three things: first, vis-à-vis national legal systems, it affirms the autonomy of the community legal system; second, it ensures that the legitimate interests of the community are not overridden by national laws; thirdly, it fosters a coherent and common community legal system. Consequently, the operational effect of the principle is merely to set aside the application of national law to the particular matter at hand without abrogating the law as such.

4 Recognition of the Rule of Exhaustion of Local Remedies

In its classical formulation, the well-known rule of exhaustion of local remedies provides that a state should be given the opportunity to redress an alleged wrong within the framework of its own domestic legal system before its international responsibility can be called into question at the international level by an international or regional court. Arguably, from a relational perspective, in regional integration the rule is a means of regulating the jurisdictional interaction between national and community courts. The exhaustion of local remedies rule is often expressly provided for in the constitutive treaties of RECs, as in Article 26 of the COMESA Treaty.[28]

5 Procedures for Preliminary Reference and/or Requests for Advisory Opinions

Some national legal systems provide for a procedure under which a lower court may seek guidance from a superior court on a point of law arising from a case before it prior to making a final determination, usually consistent with the ruling of the superior court. In the context of regional integration, such a procedure enables a national court to seek guidance from a community court and thus arguably facilitates the integration of legal systems. The European Court of Justice has significantly influenced the economic integration process in the EU largely through the use of this procedure, which is regarded by some commentators as the keystone of the EU's legal structure. Article 234 of the EC Treaty has inspired similar provisions in other economic integration instruments (e.g. article 30 of the COMESA Treaty; article 10(f) of the Protocol on the ECOWAS Court of Justice; and article 16 of the Protocol on the SADC Tribunal, now defunct). Yet, a related procedure for institutionalizing relations between

---

[27] In this sense, it operates like a private international law choice of law rule. See Oppong, *supra* note 5, p. 47.

[28] By contrast, the exhaustion of local remedies is not a precondition for petitions in the ECOWAS Court of Justice.

community and national legal systems, missing under all the African REC treaties, would be to allow national institutions to seek advisory opinions from community courts on issues of community law.

6 *Jurisprudential Communication between Legal Systems and Mutual Recognition and Enforcement of Normative Acts between RECs and Member States*

The principle of jurisprudential communication between legal systems allows for community law to borrow from the national legal systems of its member states as well as from regional and international legal systems. This may include reliance on national law in the resolution of disputes before community institutions. In addition, the principle also enjoins national legal systems to communicate with each other and thereby promote the harmonization of laws across the community, a necessary process for building the AEC. A related aspect to this is the recognition and enforcement of foreign or community "normative acts" – judicial decisions, legislation, laws and administrative acts which produce legal consequences. Jurisprudential communication and mutual recognition and enforcement of foreign normative acts provide a means through which legal systems relate to each other. In regional integration, this facilitates the effective implementation of judicial decisions in the community, and ensures that cross-border commercial activities are not frustrated. This is the essence of international trade which, in fact, lies at the core of economic integration projects. But, as noted earlier, Africa has no general convention for the mutual recognition and enforcement of foreign judgments.

7 *Principle of Access by Individuals to Community Institutions*

The last and final relational instrument for consideration here concerns access by individuals to community institutions. To enjoy legitimacy, legal systems must ensure that the content of their laws meets the needs and aspirations of their subjects and also that the subjects "participate" in the law-making and adjudication processes. In regional integration, participation entails granting natural and legal persons access to community institutions, especially the judicial bodies, for the enforcement of rights conferred by the community's laws. RECs vary in the extent to which they allow individuals to access their institutions and, in terms of litigation, over what matters are justiciable.[29] This prin-

---

29 Article 26, COMESA Treaty; article 30, EAC Treaty; and article 10, Protocol on ECOWAS Court of Justice. See also article 15(2), Protocol on SADC Tribunal (now suspended indefinitely, but referred to here for illustrative purposes only).

ciple is of critical importance for the settlement of trade disputes as these normally involve individual persons and private sector or business entities.

Three general observations on these relational issues would be in order here. To begin with, in terms of their architectural design some RECs have been more attentive than others to relational issues and have utilized some of the relational instruments discussed above. The EAC, ECOWAS, COMESA and SADC treaties, for example, variously provide for a preliminary reference procedure, envisage a role for national courts in the implementation and enforcement of community laws and judgments,[30] and allow individuals to access community institutions, including their judicial branches.[31] In particular, the EAC Treaty makes provision for the supremacy of community law; the other REC treaties envisage that the implementation of community law will be effected through national legislation.[32] In the latter case, the risk is that states may not prioritize implementation of community laws at all, which could lead to significant problems for the implementation of REC decisions at the national level, especially for individuals who seek to benefit from community laws.[33]

The second observation relates to the ambiguity surrounding the principles of direct applicability and direct effect in the AEC Treaty for which the RECs are building blocks. The AEC Treaty provides for the automatic enforceability of decisions and regulations of the Assembly and the Council of Ministers respectively.[34] Yet, as some commentators have rightly noted, the treaty is silent on where the enforceability is envisaged: at the community or national levels? And who is to enforce the decisions or regulations? Further, there is no stipulation of an explicit role for national courts in the integration process under the AEC Treaty.

Thirdly, within the various RECs some national courts have relied on interpretative relational principles and techniques to find a place for community law in their decisions. Thus, in *R v. Chikane*[35] the Swaziland High Court invoked the SADC position on serious cross-border crime. In *Jumbe v. Chimpando*[36] the

---

30 See article 44, EAC Treaty; article 40, COMESA Treaty; article 24, Protocol on ECOWAS Court of Justice (as amended); article 32, Protocol on SADC Tribunal.

31 Article 30, EAC Treaty; article 26 of the COMESA Treaty; article 18, Protocol on ECOWAS Court of Justice (as amended); article 32, Protocol on SADC Tribunal.

32 See, for example, article 5(2), AEC Treaty; article 5(2), COMESA Treaty; article 5(2), ECOWAS Treaty; and article 8(2) of EAC Treaty.

33 This in fact happened with the so-called implementation by Kenya, Tanzania and Uganda under article 8(2) of the EAC Treaty.

34 Articles 10 and 13, AEC Treaty. See also discussion *infra* in Part IV(ii)(A).

35 Crim. Case No. 41/2000 (Swaziland High Court, 2003, unreported).

36 [2005] High Court, Malawi, Constitutional Cases Nos. 1 and 2, unreported.

High Court of Malawi relied on the SADC Protocol against Corruption for guidance on principles relating to corruption. In a civil case, *Chloride Batteries Limited v. Viscocity*[37] the same court took judicial notice of Article 55 of the COMESA Treaty dealing with the competition policy of member states in granting an injunction restraining the defendant from marketing in Malawi alleged counterfeit batteries imported from Kenya. Similarly, in *Hoffman v. SAA*[38] the South African Constitutional Court referred to the SADC Code of Conduct on HIV/AIDS and Employment for guidance. In addition, it should be noted that while not expressly invoking the principles of direct effect and direct applicability, individuals have relied upon community law before national courts: in Kenya and Uganda (the EAC Treaty); and in Zimbabwe (SADC Principles and Guidelines on Elections).

Two conclusions, essentially drawn from the observations made earlier, can be made. First, some of the REC treaties, but not all, have paid attention to the relationships between the RECs and national legal systems. Secondly, although the RECs are said to be the building blocks of the AEC, there are no instruments setting out the structure of the legal relations between and among them. The Protocol on Relations between the AU and the RECs (Protocol on Relations), adopted in July 2007, is meant to provide the legal framework for coordinating and harmonizing the relations between them but there are no definitive provisions on the relations between the respective legal systems. This leads to a number of questions, some of which have been extensively addressed in Oppong's work on the subject:[39] Does AEC law enjoy supremacy over a conflicting law of a REC? Are RECs enjoined to observe the legal system of the AEC as are states under Article 3(e) of the AEC Treaty? Are there any subjects on which only the AEC can legislate? How are breaches of the decisions and directives of the AEC to the RECs (adopted under Article 21 of the Protocol) to be enforced? What is the competence of RECs before the African Court of Justice? Can the AEC intervene in an action before a community court in cases in which its interests are at stake? Fuller treatment of these issues merits a separate discussion.

The lack of attention in the Protocol on Relations to these complex relational issues is remarkable, given that Article 28 explicitly recognizes that external and internal policies of the RECs may conflict with the objectives of the

---

37   [2006] High Court, Malawi, Civil Cause No. 1896, unreported.
38   [2001] (1) S.A. 1.
39   See Oppong, "Observing the Legal System of the Community: The Relationship between Community and National Legal Systems under the African Economic Community Treaty", 15 *Tul. J. Int'l & Comp. L.* 41 (2006).

AEC Treaty. The oft repeated mantra that the RECs are the building blocks of the AEC has not led to the adoption of instruments specifically articulating the these relational issues and the framework for coordinating the legal relations among the RECs themselves, and between the RECs and the AEC. As has been observed:[40]

> The Protocol on Relations sheds dim light on some of these issues. [It] explicitly recognizes that external and internal policies of the RECs may conflict with the objectives of the AEC Treaty. [The] possibility of conflict of jurisdictions and laws is acknowledged, but concrete steps have not been taken to address them.

I couldn't agree more. The Protocol on Relations missed an opportunity to clarify this fundamental relational issue. Similarly, as already noted above, no attention has been paid to one of the most important inter-state relational issues which affect the effectiveness of the integration process: the recognition and enforcement of judgments. Apart from isolated bilateral treaties, there is no general African convention on this subject. This is critical in an era of increasing international trade, with the real likelihood of a rise in transnational commercial litigation.

As noted earlier, relational issues of law are a prominent feature of regional economic integration organizations. These issues focus on the relations between the legal system of the regional economic communities and the national, regional and international legal systems. The extent to which relational issues manifest themselves and the degree of attention devoted to them in the constitutive instruments and the legislative and administrative acts of the member states often vary with the level or stage of integration reached. In turn, they determine the constitutional architecture of the RECs or communities and the nature and breadth of the law of regional integration – or community law – that emerges from the integration process.

IV   Institutions for Enforcement of Community Law in Africa

The development of African regional integration or community law has at least three different aspects to it: the constitutional architecture, relational instruments of law, and institutions for enforcing the law. In this part of the discussion, I turn to the third aspect. Enforcement of laws is organically related to

---

40   See *supra* note 5, p. 77.

the issue of dispute settlement. In the context of economic integration in Africa the manner and methods of settling trade disputes are key to the success and efficacy of this project and the fundamental goal of trade liberalization.

1   Institutions for enforcing Regional Economic Community Laws

A   Primary Institutions: Regional Economic Community Courts

Dispute settlement in African regional integration and trade both implies and requires the existence of courts. These are provided for under the REC treaties. Shany has observed that:[41]

> [Economic] integration/trade liberalization courts have been created primarily in order to help sustain a very delicate equilibrium between the states and other stakeholders participating in a special legal regime, and between the states and other stakeholders and the regime's institutions.

Most of the AU-recognized RECs have established courts of justice as one of their principal organs, among these: EAC,[42] ECOWAS,[43] COMESA,[44] and SADC.[45] In addition to the obvious primary function of settling disputes, REC courts, as with almost all courts, also perform at least two other, less obvious, functions: norm-creation and regime maintenance and sustainability. This is not the place to describe in great detail the respective organizational structures and jurisdictions of these courts, save to make the following observations.

First, it has been noted that in complex regimes, such as those engendered by economic integration, there is an essential need for robust courts to moni-

---

[41] Y. Shany, "No Longer a Weak Department of Power? Reflections on the Emergence of a New International Judiciary", 20 *EJIL* 73 (2009), p. 82.

[42] Article 9, EAC Treaty.

[43] Article 6(e), Revised Treaty of Economic Community of West African States of 1993 (replacing the ECOWAS Treaty of 1975); see also Supplementary Protocol A/SP.1/01/05 granting the Court power to hear, *inter alia*, cases relating to violations of human rights.

[44] Article 7(c), COMESA Treaty.

[45] Article 9, SADC Treaty. The tribunal, which operated under the Protocol on Tribunal and the Rules of Procedure, was suspended in August 2010 by the SADC summit held in Windhoek, Namibia, following representations by Zimbabwe that the tribunal was not properly established and, as such, could not be legally recognised as an institution of SADC. The representations came after the tribunal had made decisions regarding the Zimbabwe Fast-Track Land Reform Programme, which the Zimbabwean government did not agree with. The suspension was extended indefinitely by the thirty-second SADC summit in Maputo, Mozambique, on 17 August, 2012.

tor aspects of the integration project through dispute settlement.[46] The presence of such courts is said to improve the chances of state compliance with their treaty obligations and inspires business confidence.[47]

Second, a number of commentators have categorized dispute settlement regimes used by international trade organizations into distinct groups. For example, Schneider[48] has identified four categories of regimes along the following lines: (i) direct effect; (ii) supremacy of the institution's law over the state's domestic law; (iii) *locus standi*; and (iv) transparency and enforcement. Schneider goes on to posit that the choice of regime in any given organization is influenced by a number of socio-economic, political and legal considerations – which might include the level of integration desired, the nature of the political system in a given member state, its legal culture, and the degree of control that member states wish to exercise over the dispute settlement process.[49] Other writers have categorized dispute settlement institutions along a spectrum that runs from diplomatic (or political) to purely legal (or legalistic) mechanisms.[50] In this respect it has been suggested that the more ambitious the level of the integration project, the more willing states (or their political leaders) should be to endorse legalistic dispute settlement.

The foregoing observation leads to the third one: the characterization of African regional economic community courts as supranational and legalistic, with treaty provisions that, on paper at least, to use Helfer's and Slaughter's terminology, "allow tribunals to interact directly with the principal players in national legal systems".[51] This has been described as "remarkable for a continent that is traditionally perceived as having no litigation culture and with a fetishist attachment to state sovereignty".[52] Yet, the claim that Africa has no

---

46 A. Keck and S. Schropp, "Indisputably Essential: The Economics of Dispute Settlement Institutions in Trade Agreements", 42 *Journal of World Trade* 785 (2008).

47 K. Nyman-Metcalf and I. Papageorgiou, *Regional Integration and Courts of Justice*, (2005), *passim*.

48 See A.K. Schneider, "Getting Along: The Evolution of Dispute Settlement Regimes in International Trade Organizations", 20 *Michigan Journal of Int'l Law* 679 (1998–9).

49 Ibid., pp. 727–52.

50 J. Smith, "Politics of Dispute Settlement Design: Explaining Legalism in Regional Trade Pacts', 54 *International Organization* 137 (2000), pp. 139–143.

51 L. Helfer and Annie-Marie Slaughter, "Towards a Theory of Effective Supranational Adjudication", 107 *Yale Law Journal* 273 (1997), p. 277.

52 Oppong, *supra* note 5, p. 119. While the REC courts may be characterized as "supranational and legalistic", it has also been noted that the lack of a "supranational authority" to enforce the commonly agreed policies of these RECs is their principal weakness. See *supra* note 18.

litigation culture is not altogether justified, even in the context of economic integration and international trade issues. For the jurisprudence that is emerging from these courts does point to a changing litigation landscape. While it is true that most of the cases that have been decided by the community courts, especially in ECOWAS and COMESA, have either involved internal staff matters or human rights violations, a number of cases have arisen around issues directly concerned with economic integration or have an indirect bearing on it. The EAC, COMESA and SADC tribunals have dealt with cases of this nature.[53] Although this jurisprudence is admittedly limited and in its nascent stages, it does signal that the community courts have a role to play in African economic integration and are an essential part of the institutional architecture of African community law.

B   Secondary Institutions: National Courts

The role of national courts in economic integration in Europe and other regions – but not so much in Africa – has been the focus of much discussion and study, as evidenced in the copious literature on the subject.[54] That domestic courts are an integral part of the institutional architecture of economic integration is a fact that has to date been honoured more in the treaties than in the practice of African RECs. Thus, while the treaties establishing the EAC, ECOWAS, COMESA, and SADC all envisage a role for national courts by providing that the latter can seek preliminary rulings from the community courts on questions of interpretation and application of the treaties, or the validity of community regulations, directives or decisions, to date no national courts have

---

53   For example, *Mwatela v. East African Community* [2007] 1 East Afr. LR 237; *Anyang' Nyong'o v. A-G of the Republic of Kenya (I and II)* [2008] 3 KLR 397; *Eastern and Southern African Trade and Development Bank v. Ogang* [2001] East Afr. LR 46; *Mike Campbell v. Republic of Zimbabwe* [2008] SADC (T) Case No. 2/2007. For a more detailed discussion of some of this emerging jurisprudence and its role in regional integration, see Oppong, ibid., pp. 134–142; O.C. Ruppel and F.-X. Bangamwabo, "The SADC Tribunal: A Legal Analysis of its Mandate and Role in Regional Integration", 8 Monitoring Regional Integration in Southern Africa Yearbook 179 (2008); and A.P. van der Mei, "The East African Community: The Bumpy Road to Supranationalism – Some Reflections on the Judgments of the Court of Justice of the East African Community in *Anyang' Nyong'o and others* and *East African Law Society and others*", Maastricht University Faculty of Law Working Paper No. 2009-7, available at http://ssrn.com/abstract=1392709. E. Tino, "The Role of Regional Judiciaries in Eastern and Southern Africa", in A. du Pisani, G. Erasmus and T. Hartzenberg, (eds.), *Monitoring Regional Integration*, (2013), pp. 140–174.

54   For a general overview of the subject, see M. Hilf, "The Role of National Courts in International Trade Relations", in E.-U. Petersmann, (ed.), *International Trade Law and GATT/WTO Dispute Settlement System*, (1997).

actually made use of this preliminary reference procedure. So there is an apparent paradox here. On the one hand, there is wide recognition that national courts provide a platform or medium through which community norms can be translated into domestic norms for the benefit of individuals and business entities in the member states. Yet, on the other hand, uncertainty regarding the legal nature of the community courts and their hierarchy and relationship to national judicial institutions and constitutional structures generates an inherent reluctance on the part of national courts to use the preliminary reference procedure and seek preliminary rulings from the community courts.

Some of the same factors that seem to render African national courts reluctant interlocutors of community courts were earlier identified in the European context, when national courts were initially reluctant to engage with and seek preliminary rulings from the European Court of Justice.[55] Part of the problem here is that the power of a national court to refer a matter to another court, whether national or international, is a jurisdictional matter. It is trite law that a national court can only do so if expressly authorized by a national statute. Consequently, it is not enough that the treaty establishing the community court of a REC provides for such reference procedure; the domestic law must also empower the national courts to resort to that procedure. Members of the RECs have not paid attention to this.

Of course, the preliminary reference procedure is only one aspect of the jurisdictional relationship between national and community courts. Other aspects include the role of national courts as fora in which individuals can pursue claims for remedies based on community law. The extent to which individuals can rely on community law in their own national courts will in part depend on the level of awareness of the citizens of the existence of the community law in question, as well as the appreciation by national courts of that law. A number of national courts in various regions in Africa have already had occasion to address issues that engage community law in the context of litigation brought before them by individuals or business entities. These case sinclude: *Movement for Democratic Change v. President of Zimbabwe*[56] (Zimbabwe), *Republic v. Kenya Revenue Authority, ex parte Aberdale Freight Services Ltd*[57] (Kenya), *Shah v. Manumara Ltd*[58] (Uganda), and *Muleya v. Common Market for Eastern and*

---

55 G. Bebr, "Article 177 of the EEC Treaty in the Practice of National Courts", 26 *ICLQ* 241 (1977).
56 HC 1291/05 (Zimbabwe, High Court, 2007).
57 [2004] 2KLR 530.
58 [2003] 1 East Afr. LR 294.

Southern Africa[59] (Uganda), *Friday Anderson Jumbe v. Humphrey Chimpango*[60] (Malawi), *Chloride Batteries Ltd v. Viscocity*[61] (Malawi), *Molifi v. Independent Electoral Commission*[62] (Lesotho) and *Hoffman v. South African Airways*[63] (South Africa).

2   Institutions for enforcing African Economic Community Law

As indicated earlier, the concept of African community law encompasses both the law of the individual RECs and the law of integration of the AEC. A discussion of the architecture of African community law must, therefore, pay some attention to the institutions for the enforcement of AEC law as well. The starting point is the AEC Treaty itself. But, first, some observations on the dual-role of AU institutions as AEC institutions.

In Africa the projects of economic integration and political integration have been treated as part of an integrated agenda. This conflation goes back to the adoption of the AEC Treaty. Article 98(1) provides that "the Community shall form an integral part of the [Organization of African Unity]". Article 99 goes further to provide that the AEC Treaty and any protocols adopted under it shall form an "integral part of the OAU Charter". The legal consequence of these provisions is that the AEC was not accorded a separate legal personality from that of the OAU, and the institutions of the latter were co-opted to perform the corresponding functions of the institutions of the former. Thus, the Assembly of the OAU would also operate as the Assembly of the AEC; so, too, the Council of Ministers of the OAU, the OAU General Secretariat, and so on. Heads of state and government summits and ministerial meetings of the OAU seamlessly went through the ritual of formally declaring that the sessions would be turned into summits and meetings of the AEC when the deliberations turned from the political to the economic integration agenda. The Constitutive Act of the AU did not change this situation when it superseded the OAU Charter on its entry into force and the AU replaced the OAU.[64] It simply provides in Article 33(2): "[the] Act shall take precedence over and supersede any inconsistent or contrary provisions of the Treaty establishing the African Economic Community".

---

59   [2003] 1 East Afr. LR 173.
60   [2005] High Court, Malawi, Constitutional Cases Nos. 1 and 2, unreported.
61   [2006] High Court, Malawi, Civil Cause No. 1896, unreported.
62   [2005] Lesotho, High Court, Civil No. 11/05, CC: 135/05 (Court of Appeal).
63   [2001] (1) SA 1.
64   Adopted on 11 July, 2000, in Lomé, Togo, the Constitutive Act entered into force on 26 May, 2001. However, the AU was only formally launched on 9 July, 2002 at its first summit in Durban, South Africa.

Today AU institutions, therefore, continue to double as AEC institutions. More significantly, in practice, *all* AU member states are automatically considered to be members of the AEC, even if such states may not have taken the formal steps of ratifying or acceding to the AEC Treaty. Djibouti, Eritrea, Madagascar, Somalia and South Sudan, all states that have not ratified or acceded to the treaty, participate in the activities of the AEC and enjoy the privileges, and are subject to the obligations, of membership along with all other states without any objection. The AU Commission, like the OAU General Secretariat previously, acknowledges this position and treats them as AEC member states (see Table 24.1).

Three institutions established pursuant to the provisions of the AEC Treaty are relevant for the development and enforcement of AEC law. First, the Assembly of Heads of State and Government ("Assembly"), established under Article 8(1) as the supreme organ of the Community. Second, the Pan-African Parliament whose creation was first provided for under Article 14 of the AEC Treaty and, subsequently, under Article 17 of the Constitutive Act of the AU. Its actual establishment was effected by the Protocol to the Treaty establishing the African Economic Community Relating to the Pan-African Parliament, which, *inter alia*, details its powers and functions.[65] The third institution is the African Court of Justice, envisioned under Article 18(2) of the AEC Treaty, and established subsequently by the Protocol of the Court of Justice of the African Union, adopted in Maputo, Mozambique, on 11 July, 2003. Since then a further protocol[66] has been adopted by the AU Assembly with the objective of merging this court and the African Court on Human and Peoples' Rights, which was established by an earlier protocol adopted on 10 June, 1998: the Protocol to the African Charter on Human and Peoples' Rights on the Estab-

---

[65] Adopted on 2 March, 2001 in Sirte, Libya; entered into force on 14 December, 2003.

[66] See Decision on the Seats of the African Union, Assembly/AU/Dec 45 (III) Rev. 1, 3rd sess (6–8 July, 2004, Addis Ababa, Ethiopia) and Decision on the Merger of the African Court on Human and Peoples' Rights and the Court of Justice of the African Union, Assembly/AU/Dec 45 (III) (4–5 July, 2005, Sirte, Libya). The move was widely viewed by most human rights advocates and observes in Africa as an attempt to dilute the impact of a judicial organ established solely for the purpose of dealing with human rights issues. The instrument on the merged court, the Protocol on the Statute of the African Court of Justice and Human Rights, was adopted by the AU Assembly at its 11th ordinary session held in Sharm El-Sheik, Egypt, on 1 July, 2008. See Decision on the Single Legal Instrument on the Merger of the African Court on Human and Peoples' Rights and the African Court of Justice, Assembly/AU/Dec.196(XI), 11th sess., AU Doc. Assembly/AU (XI) (30 June – 1 July, 2008).

lishment of an African Court on Human and Peoples' Rights.[67] I do not propose to discuss the functions, powers and procedures of all these institutions in detail here. Only a few pertinent points will be noted.

A   Primary Institutions: AEC Assembly and Council of Ministers

The Assembly is, among other things, responsible for implementing the Community's objectives. This entails determining the general policy and major guidelines of the Community; giving directives; coordinating and harmonizing the economic, scientific, technical, cultural and social policies of member states; and taking any action to attain the objectives of the Community. In discharging its functions, the Assembly is guided by recommendations of the Council of Ministers of the AEC. Article 10 the AEC Treaty provides that decisions of the Assembly are "automatically enforceable" thirty days after they are signed by the Chairman of the Assembly. Similarly, Article 13 provides that regulations of the Council of Ministers must be approved by the Assembly and once approved are "enforceable automatically" thirty days after they are signed by the Chairman of the Council.

The concept of "automatic enforceability" seems unique to the AEC Treaty and has not been replicated in the treaties establishing the various RECs. And even under the AEC Treaty itself, there is no clarity on what this means: are the decisions and regulations automatically enforceable at the community level of the AEC itself or at the national level within member states? Who is responsible for their implementation and enforcement? Another question not addressed in the AEC Treaty is whether the concept of "automatic enforceability" means the *direct applicability* of the decisions and regulations, in which case there is no need for enactment of national legislation for their implementation, or *direct effectiveness*, which would suggest that the decisions or regulations create rights that individuals can invoke directly in national courts. I share the view that the concept of "automatic enforceability" was used by the drafters with the aim of achieving the two ends of direct effect and direct applicability as discussed above.[68]

All this must be understood against the broader context of the Rules of Procedure of the Assembly regarding the methods of adopting its decisions and their nature. Rule 33 of the Rules of Procedure provides that decisions can be in the form of Regulations, Directives, Recommendations, Declarations, Resolutions and Opinions. Rule 33 (1)(a) provides that Regulations are applicable in

---

67   Adopted in Ouagadougou, Burkina Faso, on 9 June, 1998; entered into force on 25 January, 2004.
68   See also Oppong, *supra* note 5, p. 198.

"all member states that take the necessary measures to implement them". According to Rule 33(1)(b), Directives are addressed to any or all member states, undertakings or individuals; they bind member states to the objectives to be achieved, but give national authorities the power to determine the form and means to be used for their implementation. Rule 34(1)(a) reinforces the notion of automatic enforceability: Regulations and Directives are "automatically enforceable" thirty days after the date of publication in the *Official Journal* of the African Union or as specified in the particular decision. Finally, Rule 34(1)(b) states that Regulations and Directives are automatically binding on "member states, RECs and organs of the AU". The normative character and, arguably, supremacy of the Assembly decisions, at least those characterized as Regulations or Directives, as sources of or instruments for the implementation of community law cannot be doubted.[69] All this is well and impressive, at least on paper. The reality is that since 2002, when the AU superseded the OAU and the AEC became an integral part of the AU – as it had been of the OAU – the AEC Assembly has not consciously paid attention to the various categories of decisions provided for in its Rules of Procedure. While the Assembly has over the past decade or so adopted decisions termed Resolutions or Declarations, it has not adopted any Directives or Regulations nor has the envisaged *Official Journal* ever been published. The practical role of the Assembly as a principal institution in the architecture of AEC law thus remains to be practically realized.

B   Secondary Institutions: Pan-African Parliament and African Court of Justice

One singular feature of African RECs is their use of community parliamentary institutions. All the eight AU-recognized RECs with the exception of AMU have either a full-fledged parliament or parliamentary networks or fora. These institutions perform two functions, both of which advance the implementation of community law: they offer an avenue for citizens to participate in the legislative processes of the RECs, and they provide a bridge for engagement with national parliaments or other legislative bodies on matters of concern both to member states and the RECs in question. The Pan-African Parliament occupies a similar place and plays the same role for the AEC. In fact, because the Pan-African Parliament currently draws its members from national parliaments,

---

69   By contrast, in terms of Rule 33(1)(c) Recommendations, Declarations, Resolutions and Opinions are not binding and are intended to guide and harmonize the viewpoints of member states. It is also noteworthy that the Rules of Procedure of the Council of Ministers provide that the Regulations of the Council are "binding and applicable in all member states" [and] that "national law shall, where appropriate, be aligned accordingly".

nominated by the latter, it has an organic connection to the domestic constituencies represented by these national parliaments. It is thus well placed to advance the project of regional integration and the development of community law by familiarizing the continent's citizens with the objectives and policies of the AEC. The most significant shortcoming is that, as with the parliaments of the RECs, it currently only has consultative and advisory powers, in terms of Article 3(1) of the Protocol, and lacks actual legislative authority.[70]

The African Court of Justice of the AEC is the most important institution for the enforcement of AEC law. According to Article 18(2) of the AEC Treaty, the mandate of the Court is "to ensure the adherence to law in the interpretation and application of [the AEC Treaty] and [decide] on disputes submitted thereto pursuant to the [AEC Treaty]." Article 20 of the AEC Treaty envisaged the adoption of a protocol to establish the Court and, as mentioned above, this protocol was duly adopted by the AU Assembly in Maputo on 11 July, 2003: Protocol of the Court of Justice of the African Union. Although the court was formally established in terms of Article 5 of the Constitutive Act of the AU, it was in fact created as the court provided for under the AEC Treaty. Barely a year after the adoption of the protocol, the AU Assembly decided to merge this court with the African Court on Human and People's Rights, which is already operational, ostensibly in the interest of rationalizing the proliferation of institutions of the AU and in consideration of budgetary prudence. As noted earlier, the result was the adoption of a new protocol creating the African Court of Justice and Human Rights. This protocol has not yet entered into force. The operationalization of potentially the single most important institution in the implementation of AEC law lies in an uncertain abeyance.

As an institution for enforcing community law, in its role as the judicial organ of the AEC, the African Court of Justice (or the merged court when it is eventually established) shall stand in a unique position: it will be the only court established with a mandate to enforce an economic integration treaty, not endowed with compulsory jurisdiction. A party to the AEC Treaty cannot be subjected to the compulsory jurisdiction of the court if it has not also ratified the protocol establishing the African Court. Its role in enforcing community law will, therefore, be necessarily circumscribed. Will this court be well

---

70   A proposal for a limited amendment of the parliament's legislative authority was recently endorsed by the AU Assembly when it adopted a new Protocol to the Constitutive Act of the African Union relating to the Pan-African Parliament at its twenty-third ordinary session held in Malabo, Equatorial Guinea, on 24–27 June, 2014. Article 8(1) provides that "the Assembly shall determine the subjects/areas on which the Pan-African Parliament may legislate of propose draft model laws." See Assembly/AU/Dec. 529(XXIII).

placed to settle disputes related to economic integration issues? Will it complement or hinder the respective jurisdictions and roles of the REC courts? The jury is still out on these questions.

V A Concluding Observation

The development of community law in the African regional economic communities, or African community law broadly speaking, remains a journey yet to be completed. The current "spaghetti bowl arrangements"[71] of RECs, with competing and sometimes contradictory agendas and rules, do not augur well for this ultimate goal. African integration is characterized by fragmentation and, as shown at the outset of the discussion, attended by a certain arbitrariness of affiliation to various schemes. This fragmentation has been compounded by a lack of consistency on the part of member states in their commitment to the project of African integration. A more critical concern, which I share with other commentators, is the fact that the constitutive instruments of the RECs designated as the building blocks of the AEC have paid little, if any, attention to the relational issues and suggested relational instruments. The 2007 Protocol on Relations fails to address this gap in the architecture of African community law, which needs to be remedied. Equally significantly, while the mechanisms and institutions for the implementation of African regional integration law – courts and tribunals – have been put in place and are operating relatively effectively to varying degrees in the different RECs, those established under the AEC Treaty and relevant protocols are yet to perform their respective functions in this respect in any appreciable manner. As discussed in the preceding section, the most important of these institutions, the African Court of Justice, is yet to be established in its reconfigured form.

African regional economic integration has many goals. While economic development and trade liberalization are given the most prominence, states may be driven by other objectives, including protection of the "national interest",

---

71 I borrow this colourful descriptive term from Thandika Mkandawire. See his Keynote Address, "The Political Economy of Regional Integration in Africa", delivered at the Annual Conference of the Trade Law Centre (TRALAC) on 15 May, 2014, Cape Town, South Africa. Copy of PowerPoint presentation on file with the author. This is, of course, an adaptation of the well-known term, "spaghetti bowl effect", first used by the leading economist Jagdish Bhagwati in the mid-1990s to describe the proliferation of free trade agreements. See his "U.S. Trade Policy: The Infatuation with Free Trade Agreements", in Jagdish Bhagwati and Anne O. Krueger, The Dangerous Drift to Preferential Trade Agreements, (AEI Press, 1995), pp. 1-18.

sovereignty and collective self-reliance, as well as the interests of peace and conflict management, and the diplomacy of good neighbourliness.[72] The context of this discussion has been the specific objective of trade liberalization (and the related issue of dispute settlement), which both requires and presupposes the existence of a well-developed rule-based regime. Some African RECs have made progress and are well ahead of others in establishing rule-based regimes for regional integration and international trade. The EAC, ECOWAS, COMESA and SADC come to mind. However, the development of a continent-wide community law under the aegis of the AEC remains a bigger challenge that will remain largely unfulfilled until the project of continental integration fully comes to fruition. In the meantime, the RECs provide the *loci* for the development of African regional integration law and community law and sites of struggle for the litigation and settlement of disputes arising under these legal regimes, most prominently in the areas of international trade and human rights. The ultimate completion of the African economic integration project and the full development of regional integration or community law would represent the realization of some of the causes to which Judge Koroma has devoted his attention for most of his professional life: strengthening African unity and cooperation, building effective regional and sub-regional institutions, and deepening the role of African states and voices in the ever expanding evolution of international law. His commitment to these causes has remained as strong in retirement as it was during the long years of his admirable national and international public service.

---

72   See Mkandawire, ibid.

CHAPTER 25

Africa's Contribution to the Advancement of the Right to Development in International Law

Olajumoke O. Oduwole

1 Introduction

The Right to Development appears to mean many things to many people. Judge Keba M'Baye, the distinguished Senegalese jurist, is credited with initiating the discourse on the concept of 'development' as a human right in a 1972 lecture held at the International Institute of Human Rights in Strasbourg, where he asserted that 'every man has a right to live and a right to live better.'[1] The developing countries that promoted a right to development at the time referred primarily to economic development and sovereignty over natural resources, in essence seeking to re-attempt the push for a New International Economic Order (NIEO) movement.[2]

However, the conceptualization and application of the RTD experienced a metamorphosis within the global human rights agenda in the 1990s, when the idea of development shifted from economic growth to human development.[3] While it is important to consider the development of the human being as a

---

* This paper is based in part on the author's inaugural lecture to the Prince Clause Chair in Development and Equity delivered on May 20, 2014 at the International Institute of Social Studies, The Hague, The Netherlands.
1 Judge Kéba M'Baye, 'Le Droit au Développement Comme un Droit de L'Homme [The Right to Development as a Human Right]', *Leçon inaugurale de la Troisième Session d'enseignement de l'Institut International des Droits de L'Homme* [Inaugural Address of the Third Teaching Session of the International Institute of Human Rights] (July 3, 1972), in (1972) 5 *Revue des Droits de L'Homme* [Human Rights Journal] 503 cited in Stephen Marks, 'The Human Right to Development: Between Rhetoric and Reality' (2004) 17 Harvard Human Rights Journal 138; see also Isabella Bunn, 'The Right to Development: Implications for International Economic Law' (2000) 15 No. 6 American University International Law Review 1426.
2 Asbjorn Eide, 'Human Rights-Based Development in the Age of Economic Globalization: Background and Prospects in Bard Andreassen and Stephen Marks (eds.) *Development As a Human Right: Legal, Political and Economic Dimensions* (Nobel Symposium, Harvard School of Public Health 2006) 220, 228.
3 Report of the Secretary-General, 'The emergence of the Right to Development' in Office of the High Commissioner for Human Rights, *Realizing the Right to Development: Essays in*

whole as a priority, conceptual inflation and the need to balance North and South interests have resulted in less clarity. The RTD remains controversial to the present day, with debates continuing to rage in academia and policy circles, generating copious academic commentary on the nature and extent of the right,[4] but limited practical efficacy. The latter is due, among other things, to international political posturing in spite of sustained commitment from stakeholders to promote this right under the existing UN international law and sustainable development framework. As a result, legal analysis of the RTD remains critical because the persisting ambivalence about the nature of the right as well as the duties that it confers on individuals, peoples and governments impedes its realization.[5]

Remarkably, an element that is scarcely examined in the literature on the RTD is that, prior to the UNDRTD, Article 22 of the African Charter on Human and Peoples Rights (African Charter or Banjul Charter) of 1981 conferred a legally binding right to development on African peoples.[6] This Peoples' Right to Development (PRTD) is currently the only explicit hard law dedicated solely to the right to development.[7] The relevance of this regional right to the analysis of the universal RTD lies in its contextual guidance regarding the original intent of the African developing country players who initiated this right at the

---

Commemoration of 25 Years of the United Nations Declaration on the Right to Development (HR/PUB/12/4, United Nations, 2013) 7.

4 Isabella Bunn, 'The Right to Development: Implications for International Economic Law' (2000) 15 No. 6 American University International Law Review 1426; Stephen Marks, 'The Human Right to Development: Between Rhetoric and Reality' (2004) 17 Harvard Human Rights Journal 137. According to Marks, the RTD has been part of international law terminology for three decades, with limited practical output in terms of planning and implementation as 'states express rhetoric support but neglect basic precepts in development practice.' 137.

5 Isabella Bunn, 'The Right to Development: Implications for International Economic Law' (2000) 15 No. 6 American University International Law Review 1426, 1434. Judge Koroma has commented that "in the international law related to development and globalization, even if the law itself does not directly favour developed countries, the application of this law in the current geo-political realities disparately impacts developing countries in a negative way"; see also Abdul G. Koroma, "International Law and Multiculturalsm", in S. Yee and J.-Y. Morin (eds.), *International Law and Multiculturalism: Essays in Honour of Edward J. McWhinney* (2009), p. 79, Section IV.

6 Organization of African Unity (OAU), *African Charter on Human and Peoples' Rights*, 27 June 1981, CAB/LEG/67/3 rev. 5, 21 I.L.M. 58 (1982), Article 22 www.achpr.org/instruments/achpr/ accessed 14 April 2014.

7 Nienke van der Have, 'The right to development: Can states be held responsible?' in Dick Foeken et al. (eds.) *Development and Equity: An Interdisciplinary Exploration by Ten Scholars from Africa, Asia and Latin America* (Brill 2014) 157, 159.

regional level, as well as the continent's contribution in the area of jurisprudence on the PRTD so far. This paper explores how African jurisprudence can influence international human rights law in this area through a pragmatic application of the PRTD in contemporary African.

The paper focuses on the future of the RTD as a legally enforceable right, and Africa's contribution to this process. It is recognized that, as currently formulated, the RTD has failed to attain universal consensus on its nature and scope. After a comprehensive analysis of the emergence of the RTD, and how the conceptualization of the right has undergone a metamorphosis within the international law and development arena, I turn to the historical context of the continent as a backdrop to the right to development in its current state in Africa. Then I examine what development as a 'right' has meant within the African regional human rights system. Finally, I will introduce ideas as to the future direction of RTD jurisprudence in Africa, and the impact that these pronouncements could have on the implementation of the RTD within the global human rights system.

2   The Universal Right to Development

The milestones in the evolution of the universal Right to Development, and later rights-based development, are well demarcated in the literature.[8] Generally, the International Bill of Rights comprising the 1948 Universal Declaration of Human Rights (UDHR),[9] the International Covenant on Civil and Political Rights (ICCPR)[10] and the International Covenant on Economic, Social and Cultural Rights (ICESCR),[11] both from 1967, are presented as the precursors to

---

8   Arjun Sengupta, 'Conceptualizing the Right to Development for the Twenty-first Century' in Office of the High Commissioner for Human Rights, *Realizing the Right to Development: Essays in Commemoration of 25 Years of the United Nations Declaration on the Right to Development* (HR/PUB/12/4, United Nations, 2013) 67.

9   The Universal Declaration of Human Rights. The Declaration was proclaimed by the United Nations General Assembly in Paris on 10 December 1948 by General Assembly Resolution 217 A (III). See www.ohchr.org/en/udhr/pages/introduction.aspx accessed 14 April, 2014.

10   International Covenant on Civil and Political Rights, G.A. Res. 2200A, UN GAOR 3d Comm., 21st Sess., 1496th plen. mtg., Annex, Agenda Item 62, at 16 UN Doc. A/RES/2200 (XXI) (1967). http://treaties.un.org/

11   International Covenant on Economic, Social and Cultural Rights, G.A. Res. 2200A, UN GAOR 3d Comm., 21st Sess., 1496th plen. mtg., Annex, Agenda Item 62, at 3, UN Doc. A/RES/2200 (XXI) (1967). http://www.un-documents.net/icescr.htm accessed 14 April, 2014.

the RTD.¹² Although none of these international instruments expressly mentions the RTD, Article 22 of the UDHR states as follows:

> Everyone, as a member of society, has the right to social security and is entitled to realization, through national effort and international cooperation and in accordance with the organization and resources of each State, of the economic, social and cultural rights indispensable for his dignity and the free development of his personality.¹³

Furthermore, Article 28 of the UDHR states that: 'Everyone is entitled to a social and international order in which the rights and freedoms set forth in this Declaration can be fully realized.'¹⁴ Margot Salomon has noted that the RTD derives its 'intellectual origins and legal claims'¹⁵ jointly from Article 28 and Articles 55 and 56 of the United Nations Charter.¹⁶ It is upon this foundation that the building blocks of the United Nations Declaration on the Right to Development, and the RTD that it proclaims, are laid down under international law.

Originally perceived as a 'third generation' or 'solidarity' right,¹⁷ the RTD was explicitly established by Article 1(1) of the UNDRTD, which states as follows: 'The Right to Development is an inalienable human right by virtue of which every human person and all peoples are entitled to participate in, contribute

---

12 See Matthew Craven, *The International Covenant on Economic, Social, And Cultural Rights: A Perspective On Its Development* (Clarendon Press 1998).

13 See Article 22, UDHR www.ohchr.org/EN/UDHR/Documents/UDHR_Translations/eng.pdf accessed 14 April, 2014.

14 *Supra* UDHR.

15 Margot Salomon, Global Responsibility for Human Rights (Oxford University Press 2007) 4; Margot Salomon, 'Legal Cosmopolitanism and the Normative Contribution of the Right to Development' in Stephen Marks (ed), *Implementing The Right To Development: The Role of International Law* (The Friedrich-Ebert-Stiftung/Harvard School of Public Health 2008) 17.

16 United Nations, Charter of the United Nations, 24 October 1945, 1 UNTS XVI www.un.org/en/documents/charter/ accessed 14 April, 2014.

17 Stephen Marks, 'The Human Right to Development: Between Rhetoric and Reality' (2004) 17 Harvard Human Rights Journal 137. In the 1970s and 1980s the RTD was introduced as one of several rights belonging to a third 'generation' of human rights. The first generation consisted of civil and political rights conceived as freedom from state abuse. The second generation consisted of economic, social and cultural rights, claims made against exploiters and oppressors. The third generation consisted of solidarity rights belonging to peoples and covering global concerns such as development, environment, humanitarian assistance, peace, communication and common heritage.

to, and enjoy economic, social, cultural and political development, in which all human rights and fundamental freedoms can be fully realized.'[18] Furthermore, Articles 2(3) and 3(3) declare a duty on states to formulate appropriate national development policies, and to cooperate with each other in ensuring development and eliminating obstacles to development respectively.[19]

It is now generally accepted that these provisions allude to both an individual and a collective right, and that the actual holders of this collective right are 'the people', with obligations resting on national governments as well as a duty of international cooperation amongst governments.[20] From the outset, this issue caused tension between developing and developed countries over the RTD when the former argued that a collective right to development existed, as opposed to the traditional model of human rights, which confers rights on individuals, typically against abuses from their own governments.[21] Furthermore, the developing countries argued that they (the states) were the right-holders (presumably on behalf of their citizens) while developed countries were the duty-bearers under the Declaration.[22] These underlying tensions, inherited from deep-seated North-South disagreements over the years, have continued to simmer, and long-standing political posturing has infused both the rhetoric and the practical application of the RTD.[23] Within the UN

---

18 www.un.org/documents/ga/res/41/a41r128.htm Resolution 41/128.
19 Ibid.
20 Sakiko Fukuda-Parr, 'The Right to Development: Reframing a New Discourse for the Twenty-First Century' (2012) 79 No. 4 Social Research 839. RTD commitments have implications for numerous questions of public expenditure priorities, incentive policies, and regulation. They extend to both national and international domains, and apply to cooperative action with other states in areas of trade, migration, finance, technology transfer, environmental commons, peace and security.
21 Ibid. As the developing countries advocated for the creation of a treaty that would codify the RTD as a new legal right with additional obligations, the developed countries maintained the position that RTD is an amalgam of other rights and does not incur new legally-binding obligations.
22 Salma Yusuf and Jennifer Woodham, 'A Human Right to Development – Moving Beyond the Rhetoric' (2012) Institute of Human Rights Sri Lanka 1.
23 Stephen Marks, 'The Human Right to Development: Between Rhetoric and Reality' (2004) 17 Harvard Human Rights Journal 137, 141–42; The political positions in the UN RTD Working Group can be categorized roughly into four camps: The first camp comprises the most active members of the non-aligned group (NAM), a developing country relic of the Cold War era, sometimes called the 'Like-Minded Group' (LMG) namely Algeria, Bangladesh, Bhutan, China, Cuba, Egypt, India, Indonesia, Iran, Malaysia, Myanmar, Nepal, Pakistan, the Philippines, Sri Lanka, Sudan, and Vietnam. The LMG seeks to utilize the RTD to reduce inequities of international trade, the negative impacts of globalization, differential

system, progress in application of the RTD has been hindered by these political considerations, as developed countries have largely continued to refuse interpretations of the UNDRTD that legally require them to give aid to particular developing countries, while developing countries continue to clamour for more aid and concessions, a fairer international trade climate, access to technology and debt relief from developed counties, contending that they face serious developmental challenges as well as a real threat of marginalization in the globalization era.

Significantly, in the midst of (or perhaps because of) the political jostling, the conceptualization of 'development' as a universal, inalienable, justiciable right as well as the express definition, scope and delimitation of the RTD have both continued to be the subject of much discourse over the years.[24] As a result, since its formal initiation in the mid-1980s, the RTD has yet to live up to its full potential as a legal tool in the hands of lawyers, human rights activists, governments and others. A main reason for this is that the specificity of the right remains unclear, particularly in relation to the duty-bearers and their obligations. Furthermore, lawyers of the positivist school of thought believe that if a right is not legally enforceable, it cannot be regarded as a human right, and should only be accorded the status of a social aspiration.[25]

Although the UNDRTD is a declaratory statement of the UN General Assembly, elements of the RTD have subsequently been echoed in various treaties,[26]

---

access to technology, the crushing debt burden, and similar factors they see as detrimental to the enjoyment of human rights and development. They also strongly support the idea that the RTD creates obligations on the international community to create better conditions for development. The second camp consists of more moderate developing countries that seek to implement human rights policies at a national level and cooperate with the donor community, international development agencies, and financial institutions. The third camp is made up of countries in transition and developed nations, such as the European Union, which typically support the RTD as a vehicle for constructive engagement between developed and developing countries, and seek to implement the RTD. Members of this group will support conservative resolutions or abstain. The fourth camp, led by the United States, consistently votes against RTD resolutions. Other members of this camp have included Japan, Denmark, and Australia, and smaller countries under the influence of the United States.

24 Arjun Sengupta, 'Conceptualizing the Right to Development for the Twenty-first Century' in United Nations Human Rights Office of the High Commissioner (ed) *Realizing the Right to Development* (United Nations Publication HR/PUB/12/4, United Nations 2013) 67.

25 Ibid. 74.

26 Tamara Kunanayakam, 'The Declaration on the Right to Development in the context of United Nations standard-setting' in Office of the High Commissioner for Human Rights, *Realizing the Right to Development: Essays in Commemoration of 25 Years of the United*

THE RIGHT TO DEVELOPMENT IN INTERNATIONAL LAW   571

and arguments have been made that the UNDRTD has now attained the status of customary international law.²⁷ However, the RTD's direct justiciability has hardly been tested.²⁸

Leading commentators have viewed the RTD as a composite right of all universal human rights.²⁹ In fact, Judge Bedjaoui famously valorized the right as 'the alpha and omega of human rights.'³⁰ However, some critics of the RTD have not embraced it as a full legal right in itself, claiming it is more of an 'umbrella' right covering human rights that already exist in legally binding treaties.³¹ According to Peter Uvin, from its inception, the RTD has fundamentally lacked legitimacy.³² He wrote the following about the UNDRTD and the RTD it confers:

> This was the kind of rhetorical victory that diplomats cherish: the Third World got its right to development, while the First World ensured that the right ... was totally non-binding, and that it carried no resource transfer obligations ... even in its watered down form, the right to development

---

     Nations Declaration on the Right to Development (HR/PUB/12/4, United Nations, 2013) 17–48.

27   Nienke van der Have, 'The right to development: Can states be held responsible?' in Dick Foeken et al. (eds.) *Development and Equity: An Interdisciplinary Exploration by Ten Scholars from Africa, Asia and Latin America* (Brill 2014) 157.

28   Brigitte Hamm, 'A Human Rights Approach to Development' (2001) 23 No. 4 Human Rights Quarterly1005; Arjun Sengupta, 'Conceptualizing the Right to Development for the Twenty-first Century' in Office of the High Commissioner for Human Rights, *Realizing the Right to Development: Essays in Commemoration of 25 Years of the United Nations Declaration on the Right to Development* (HR/PUB/12/4, United Nations, 2013) 67, 74.

29   Fifth Report of the Independent Expert on the Right to Development, Prof Arjun Sengupta, Submitted in Accordance with Commission Resolution 2002/69, at 5, 6, UN Doc. E/CN.4/2002/WG.18/6 (2002); Forward by Ms Navi Pillay, UNHCHR in United Nations Human Rights Office of the High Commissioner (ed.) *Realizing the Right to Development* (United Nations Publication HR/PUB/12/4, United Nations 2013).

30   Mohammed Bedjaoui, 'The Right to Development' in Mohammed Bedjaoui (ed.), *International Law: Achievements and Prospects* (Dordrecht: Martinus Nijhoff and UNESCO 1991) 1177, 1182.

31   Pillay, Ibid. xxv; See Peter Uvin, Human Rights and Development (Kumarian Press 2004) 41; See also Arne Vandenbogaerde, 'The Right to Development in International Human Rights Law: A Call for its Dissolution' (2013) 31/2 NQHR 187; Yash Ghai, Whose Human Right to Development?, Occasional Paper, Commonwealth Human Rights Unit, 1989.

32   Peter Uvin, Human Rights and Development (Kumarian Press 2004) 41; See also Arne Vandenbogaerde, 'The Right to Development in International Human Rights Law: A Call for its Dissolution' (2013) 31/2 NQHR 187.

amounted to a rich country vs. poor country debate, as it had been from the beginning ... the DRD was politically engineered to be bad law – vague, internally contradictory, duplicative of other already codified rights, and devoid of identifiable parties bearing clear obligations. ... Affirming that all people have the right to development, and that such development consists of and is realized through the realization of every existing category of human rights, adds nothing to our knowledge. It adds only verbiage.[33]

Despite Uvin's extremely cynical viewpoint regarding its origins, the RTD has continued to evolve. When the concept was first expressed by developing countries in the early 1970s, 'development as a right' emerged in relation to economic development and sovereignty over natural resources on the heels of the New International Economic Order movement.[34] Since then the RTD has broadened far beyond the notion of economic growth to encompass human development in its totality and human development practitioners and international human rights advocates, which once co-existed in parallel, have begun to intermingle considerably.[35] The concept of human development was institutionalized by the United Nations Development Programme (UNDP) in 1990, with the launch of its Human Development Reports. These reports focus on human well-being, and not economic growth, as the purpose and end of development.[36] Today, human rights and human development both share a common goal of 'human freedom' based on the well-being and dignity of human beings everywhere.[37] This convergence has been termed a 'rights-based approach to development' and covers all human rights.[38] For instance, according to the UN Office of the High Commissioner for Human Rights: 'a rights-based approach to trade is a conceptual framework for the processes of trade reform that is normatively based on international human rights standards and opera-

---

33   Uvin, Ibid. 42–3.
34   See Declaration on the Establishment of a New International Economic Order (NIEO), G.A. Res. 3201 (S-VI), UN Doc. (May 1, 1974).
35   United Nations Development Programme (UNDP), *Applying A Human Rights-Based Approach to Development Cooperation and Programming* (Capacity Development Group Bureau for Development Policy UNDP 2006).
36   Kate Manzo, 'Africa in the Rise of Rights-Based Development', (2003) 34 Geoforum 34 (2003) 437.
37   UNDP Report 2001, Partnerships to Fight Poverty. www.undp.org/content/dam/undp/library/corporate/UNDP-in-action/2001/English/complete.pdf accessed 14 April, 2014.
38   Ibid.

tionally directed to promoting and protecting human rights.'[39] Nevertheless, the unresolved issues around the conceptualization, legality and justiciability of the RTD still persist.

In 1993, at the Vienna World Conference on Human Rights, the RTD was reaffirmed unanimously.[40] The conference also resolved some of the main controversies relating to the RTD at the time, and the right was main-streamed within the UN human rights system, enjoying a place of prominence on the agenda. Brigitte Hamm has noted that after the Vienna World Conference the RTD became part of the mandate of the UN High Commissioner for Human Rights (UNHCHR), and has since been a major topic of discussion within the Commission on Human Rights and other UN human rights organs.[41]

The renewed focus on the RTD then took the form of instituting a follow-up mechanism by the appointment of an Independent Expert in 1998 (and later a High Level Task Force) as well as the establishment of an Open-Ended Working Group on the RTD (WG) by the UN Economic and Social Council on the recommendation of the Commission on Human Rights.[42] The High Level Task Force (HLTF) supporting the WG also articulated the 'core norms' of the RTD as 'the right of peoples and individuals to the constant improvement of their well-being and to a national and global environment conducive to just, equitable, participatory and human-centred development respectful of all human

---

[39] United Nations Human Rights, Office of the High Commissioner for Human Rights www.ohchr.org/EN/Issues/Globalization/Pages/GlobalizationIndex.aspx accessed 14 April, 2014; Henry Steiner and Philip Alston, *International Human Rights In Context: Law, Politics, Morals* (2nd ed, Oxford University Press 2000) 1311. In 1999, Mrs Mary Robinson, the then UN High Commissioner for Human Rights (UNHCHR) outlined the human rights dimension of an international financial, trade and development architecture with the aim of giving life to the copious statements in support of the right to development already available by this time.

[40] Vienna Declaration and Programme of Action, UN General Assembly, *Vienna Declaration and Programme of Action*, 12 July 1993, A/CONF.157/23 endorsed by General Assembly Resolution 48/121, 20 December 1993.

[41] Brigitte Hamm, 'A Human Rights Approach to Development' (2001) 23 No. 4 Human Rights Quarterly 1005.

[42] Stephen Marks, 'The Human Right to Development: Between Rhetoric and Reality' (2004) 17 Harvard Human Rights Journal 137. The Independent Expert was to present a study on the current state of progress in the implementation of the right to development to the working group at each of its sessions as a basis for a focused discussion, taking into account the deliberations and suggestions of the working group. The purpose of the working group was to monitor and review the progress of the Independent Expert and report back to the Commission. 139.

rights.'[43] Prior to this, the Independent Expert on the RTD at the time, prominent Indian economist Arjun Sengupta, further articulated the RTD in his reports.[44] He stipulated four key components of the RTD, stating 'The human right to development is a right to a particular process of development in which all human rights and fundamental freedoms can be fully realized.'[45] He noted as follows:

> The process is not the same thing as the outcome of the process, although in the right to development both the process and the outcome of the process are human rights. It is possible for individuals to realize several rights separately, such as the right to food, the right to education or the right to housing. It is also possible that these rights are realized separately in full accordance with human rights standards, with transparency and accountability, in a participatory and non-discriminatory manner, and even with equity and justice. But even then, the right to development may not be realized as a process of development if the interrelationships between the different rights are not fully taken into account.[46]

Sengupta expounded on the wording of the UNDRTD,[47] and built on the seminal work of Amartya Sen theorizing development as freedom.[48] Sen views the RTD less as a legal entitlement and sees it more in terms of social ethics and public reasoning. He asks why complete feasibility should be a condition of cogency of human rights when the main objective of human rights is our working towards expanding both their feasibility and their actual realization. In sharing his understanding that some human rights are not yet fully recognized, and may never be fully attainable under present global conditions and circumstances, Sen reminds us that this does not negate their being 'rights.' He described this as follows:

---

43 Report of the High Level Task force A/HRC/15/WG.2/TF/2/Add.2, 8 March 2010 8.
44 Arjun Sengupta, 'Conceptualizing the Right to Development for the Twenty-first Century' in Office of the High Commissioner for Human Rights, *Realizing the Right to Development: Essays in Commemoration of 25 Years of the United Nations Declaration on the Right to Development* (HR/PUB/12/4, United Nations, 2013) 67.
45 Ibid.
46 Ibid. 78.
47 UN General Assembly, *Declaration on the Right to Development : Resolution / adopted by the General Assembly*, 4 December 1986, A/RES/41/128.
48 Amartya Sen, *Development As Freedom* (Oxford University Press 1999) 35.

> The duty of any third person in support of human rights cannot but be somewhat inexactly perceived, since much will depend on what others are doing and what can be effective and how. ... Ambiguity of obligation, however, whether in law or in ethics, does not indicate that there are no obligations at all ... indeed, such loosely formulated obligations belong to the important category of duties that Immanuel Kant called "imperfect obligations," to which he attached great importance.[49]

While the above may give some comfort to proponents of the RTD, Stephen Marks and Bard Andreassen have commented on this notion, stating that a human right is still required to create rights and obligations with a sufficient degree of justiciability in order to be considered a right properly so called.[50] Likewise, Arjun Sengupta has said that, while obligations can be fulfilled on the basis of ethics, without legal enforcement, we still need to formulate binding legal obligations on the RTD, stating that 'however long and arduous it may be to reach consensus, it is worth the effort to reach such a consensus in order to make the right to development a proper human right, comparable to the other internationally accepted human rights.'[51] In my opinion, this line of reasoning supports the position that the RTD as it currently stands ought to be curtailed into a more practicable legal obligation, which can be effectively implemented.

Indeed, in recognition of this need for legal clarity for the RTD, at the direction of the Human Rights Council, the WG and the HLTF have undertaken significant work on the legal issues pertaining to an international treaty on the RTD in recent years.[52] The HLTF was mandated to craft possibly legally binding

---

49 Amartya Sen, 'Human Rights and Development' in Bard Andreassen and Stephen Marks (eds.) *Development As a Human Right: Legal, Political and Economic Dimensions* (Nobel Symposium, Harvard School of Public Health 2006) 6–7.

50 Stephen Marks and Bard Andreassen, 'Introduction' in Bard Andreassen and Stephen Marks (eds.) *Development As a Human Right: Legal, Political and Economic Dimensions* (Nobel Symposium, Harvard School of Public Health 2006) ix.

51 Arjun Sengupta, Preface in Stephen Marks (ed) *Implementing the Right to Development: The Role of International Law* 10; Salma Yusuf and Jennifer Woodham, 'A Human Right to Development – Moving Beyond the Rhetoric' (2012) Institute of Human Rights Sri Lanka 1, 5. Yusuf and Woodham note that Sengupta's definition places the duty to protect the RTD on all stakeholders, from individuals to the international community, which means that practically speaking, it is necessary to identify the obligations of each stakeholder and adopt legal mechanisms for the successful actualization of the RTD.

52 Implementing Resolution 4/4 of the Human Rights Council, adopted March 30, 2007, which requires the HLTF to execute a work plan, the final phase of which might include

guidelines which may eventually become a treaty on the RTD, paying special attention to criteria for evaluating global partnerships, as identified in MDG8, which deals with global partnerships for development.[53] Unsurprisingly, the highly political nature of the assignment led to a particularly divisive manifestation of the usual political posturing of states.[54] More recently, there has been a persuasive call for a comprehensive Framework Convention on the RTD as a way of creatively delivering on the promises of the RTD while avoiding a political stalemate, but this solution is still being debated in academic circles.[55] However, the other side of the coin is that the adoption of a legally binding treaty for the RTD carries the risk of perpetuating the political deadlock whereby states refuse to ratify or implement such a treaty. As a result, the underlying structural issues pertaining to the difficulties of implementing a legally binding obligation on the RTD are not resolved.

As currently defined the RTD implies both internal and external state obligations. However, more attention is given to the external obligations particularly on the part of developed countries, because the global rhetoric of development as a right has far outpaced the reality of currently accepted levels of state responsibility in international relations. As a result, particularly within the ambit of international economic law, states are unwilling to bear any legal obligations with positive financial obligations linked to the implementation of the RTD.

Commentators, such as David Beetham, have questioned the 'inflationary tendencies' of the RTD over time.[56] Beetham sees the dangers of conceptual inflation or 'terminology creep' to which the RTD seems to be intrinsically

---

'consideration of an international legal standard of a binding nature.' Stephen Marks, A legal perspective on the evolving criteria of the HLTF on the right to development' in Stephen Marks (ed), *Implementing The Right To Development: The Role of International Law* (The Friedrich-Ebert-Stiftung/Harvard School of Public Health 2008) 72.

53 Ibid. See also Fateh Azzam, 'The right to development and implementation of the Millennium Development Goals' in Office of the High Commissioner for Human Rights, *Realizing the Right to Development: Essays in Commemoration of 25 Years of the United Nations Declaration on the Right to Development* (HR/PUB/12/4, United Nations, 2013) 355.

54 For a comprehensive analysis of the issue considered by the HLTF, see Stephen Marks (ed), *Implementing The Right To Development: The Role of International Law* (The Friedrich-Ebert-Stiftung/Harvard School of Public Health 2008).

55 Koen De Feyter, 'Towards a Framework Convention on the Right to Development' (2013) The Friedrich-Ebert-Stiftung International Policy Analysis Dialogue on Globalization 17.

56 David Beetham, 'The Right to Development and Its Corresponding Obligations' in Bard Andreassen and Stephen Marks (eds.) *Development As a Human Right: Legal, Political and Economic Dimensions* (Nobel Symposium, Harvard School of Public Health 2006) 79.

prone, particularly under the pressure of attempting to achieve political consensus. In identifying the current over-emphasis on the non-economic dimensions of development, as seen in the definitions of thought leaders in this area,[57] Beetham has suggested that this over-emphasis hinders our ability to decipher when the RTD has been infringed upon by international economic agreements or domestic policies.[58] He supports the claim that the RTD has experienced a metamorphosis since the 1990s with the advent of human development, and prefers to narrow the definition of the RTD to a minimum core meaning, which is clearly distinct from other human rights. Finally, Beetham finds the idea of concentrating on the original RTD concept floated by developing countries in the 1970s, promoting individuals' and people's right to economic development, appealing.[59]

In sum, the RTD has certainly succeeded in deepening the conversation on development as a right. In spite of its shortcomings, the RTD has brought important innovations to the universal human rights framework. It underlined the idea of collective rights (rights of peoples) at a universal level, where that concept was previously relatively unknown and unaccepted and the dominant ideology of a right-holder was an individual. The RTD also echoes Article 28 of the UDHR in seeking international cooperation among states.[60] It recognizes 'the structure and operation of the international economic system as essential determinants of development.'[61]

It has been demonstrated above how the RTD underwent a transformation from an economic right to a comprehensive human-centred process in the 1990s with the advent of human development. Nevertheless, tensions between near parallel areas of international law are still very much in evidence. As Olivier De Schutter has observed: 'The current system of global governance is fragmented among different and sometimes conflicting regimes that result in

---

57 See Bard Andreassen and Stephen Marks (eds.) *Development As a Human Right: Legal, Political and Economic Dimensions* (Nobel Symposium, Harvard School of Public Health 2006); Stephen Marks (ed), *Implementing The Right To Development: The Role of International Law* (The Friedrich-Ebert-Stiftung/Harvard School of Public Health 2008).

58 Stephen Marks and Bard Andreassen, 'Introduction' in Bard Andreassen and Stephen Marks (eds.) *Development As a Human Right: Legal, Political and Economic Dimensions* (Nobel Symposium, Harvard School of Public Health 2006) viii.

59 David Beetham, 'The Right to Development and Its Corresponding Obligations' in Bard Andreassen and Stephen Marks (eds.) *Development As a Human Right: Legal, Political and Economic Dimensions* (Nobel Symposium, Harvard School of Public Health 2006) 79.

60 Sakiko Fukuda-Parr, 'The Right to Development: Reframing a New Discourse for the Twenty-First Century' (2012) 79 No. 4 Social Research 839.

61 Arts 3.1, 3.3 and 4.1 UNDRTD.

an imbalance between states' obligations under trade and investment agreements on the one hand, and human rights treaties on the other hand.'[62] Nevertheless, there has been some traction, as rights-based development continues to penetrate into more areas of international human rights law. However, the desirability or otherwise of the incursion of rights-based development into international law remains debatable. Therefore, international lawyers are correct to remain concerned about the legality, efficacy and justiciability of the RTD for its continued relevance and effectiveness in international law over time.

The right to development in Africa under the African Charter of Human and Peoples' Rights of 1981 is perhaps the only legally binding provision on the right to development, which has actually been tested by adjudication. Due to the continent's socio-economic history and development, Africa's position in the current international order lends a strong voice to the need for a legally binding RTD at a global level, with clearly defined and implementable rights and duties; along with the required justiciability to foster accountability.

3 The Peoples' Right to Development in Africa

> A man who does not know where the rain began to beat him cannot say where he dried his body.
> IGBO PROVERB

Chinua Achebe, one of Nigeria's most notable literary icons, spent much of his life advocating through his writings the need for us to look back in history in an attempt to identify where we went wrong as a nation, and in a wider sense as a continent. Metaphorically speaking, he repeatedly stated that: 'we must know where the rain started beating us.'[63] It is only through balanced knowledge and appreciation of Africa's past that we might know who we are, and only then might we fully understand where we ought to be going and how to get there.

Starting with Ghana in 1957, at independence, African developing countries assumed all pre-existing international obligations entered into on their behalf

---

62   Oliver Dr De Schutter, 'The Role of Human Rights in Shaping International Regulatory Regimes' (2012) 79 No. 4 Social Research 785.
63   Chinua Achebe, 'Nigeria's Promise, Africa's Hope' The New York Times, January 15, 2011 www.nytimes.com/2011/01/16/opinion/16achebe.html?pagewanted=all&_r=0 accessed 14 April, 2014.

before independence, thus perpetrating existing trade patterns.[64] Yet, from decolonialization to independence and its immediate aftermath, Africa's founding fathers appeared to have clear visions and ideology for their countries' development.[65] As more former African colonies gained their independence in the 1950s and 1960s, they joined the ranks of other developing countries at the UN clamouring for growth and change, and helped ensure that developing countries had a numerical majority at UN General Assembly meetings. In support of this development quest, the 1960s were designated as the first UN Decade for Development. In addition, in 1964 the United Nations Conference on Trade and Development (UNCTAD) was established to promote the integration of developing countries into the world economy in a 'development-friendly' manner and in1967 the International Covenant on Civil and Political Rights (ICCPR)[66] and the International Covenant on Economic, Social and Cultural Rights (ICESCR) both came into force.[67]

In the 1970s, these young developing countries collectively called for a New International Economic Order (NIEO)[68] in an attempt to realign the balance of world trade rules in their favour.[69] In Africa, critics argued that the NIEO was not fully representative of the interests of the continent's producers and exporters.[70] The 1970s and 1980s saw rapid changes in world geopolitics, with the Cold War at play before its eventual demise.[71] Later, the 1990s saw many African countries groan under the weight of Structural Adjustment Pro-

---

64   Obafemi Awolowo, *The Problems of Africa: The Need for Ideological Reappraisal* (1st Series, University of Cape Coast Kwameh Nkrumah Memorial Lectures Series Macmillan 1977).
65   Ibid.
66   International Covenant on Civil & Political Rights, G.A. Res. 2200A, UN GAOR 3d Comm., 21st Sess., 1496th plen. mtg., Annex, Agenda Item 62, at 16 UN Doc. A/RES/2200 (XXI) (1967). http://treaties.un.org/.
67   International Covenant on Economic, Social & Cultural Rights, G.A. Res. 2200A, UN GAOR 3d Comm., 21st Sess., 1496th plen. mtg., Annex, Agenda Item 62, at 3, UN Doc. A/RES/2200 (XXI) (1967). www.un-documents.net/icescr.htm See Matthew Craven, The International Covenant On Economic, Social and Cultural Rights: A Perspective On Its Development (Clarendon Press 1998) 6–29.
68   See Declaration on the Establishment of a New International Economic Order (NIEO), G.A. Res. 3201 (S-VI), UN Doc. (May 1, 1974).
69   Michael Trebilcock and Robert Howse, The Regulation of International Trade, (3rd edn. Routledge Publishers 2005) 471. See Declaration on the Establishment of a New International Economic Order (NIEO), G.A. Res. 3201 (S-VI), UN Doc. (May 1, 1974).
70   Nsongurua Udombana, 'The Summer has Ended and We are Not Saved! Towards a Transformative Agenda for Africa's Development' (2005) San Diego International Law Journal 5, 17.
71   Joseph Stiglitz, *Globalization and Its Discontents* (Penguin Publishers 2003) 244; Nsongu-

grammes (SAPs) propagated by the Washington Consensus and neo-liberalists.[72] Globalization became unpopular because it was blamed for the growing inequity between as well as within countries.[73] By now it was well-established that there is a clear link between the international trading system and the enjoyment of human rights of peoples, because economic growth through globalization and trade liberalization may increase the supply of resources required for the furtherance of all human rights, thus leading to development. However, as Africa has experienced first-hand, the positive dividends of globalization are far from automatic.[74]

At the turn of the century, across the continent, prominent African leaders called for an African Renaissance, which materialized as the New Partnership for Africa's Development (NEPAD), a vision and strategic framework for Africa's renewal, presented through the auspices of the OAU/AU, along with its peer review mechanism.[75] The Millennium Development Goals (MDGs) were another set of development commitments, which African countries adopted, along with the rest of the world, and the region saw some progress in crucial development areas such as poverty eradication and education, especially in Sub-Saharan Africa, the world's least-developed region.[76]

It was in this environment that the African Charter on Human and Peoples' Rights of 1981 (African Charter, also known as the Banjul Charter) was adopted by African states to promote and protect the human rights and basic freedoms of Africans across the continent.[77] The African Charter was drafted with the intention of reflecting African traditions and values, and a uniquely African conceptualization of human rights.[78] Based on the wordings of the African

---

rua Udombana, 'The Summer has Ended and We are Not Saved! Towards a Transformative Agenda for Africa's Development' (2005) San Diego International Law Journal 5, 43.

72   Joseph Stiglitz, *Globalization and Its Discontents* (Penguin Publishers 2003).
73   Ibid. 20.
74   United Nations, Office of the High Commissioner for Human Rights, www.ohchr.org/EN/Issues/Globalization/Pages/GlobalizationIndex.aspx accessed 14 April, 2014.
75   NEPAD www.nepad.org/about; See Bronwen Manby, 'Development, good governance and South-South cooperation: the African Peer Review Mechanism' in Office of the High Commissioner for Human Rights, *Realizing the Right to Development: Essays in Commemoration of 25 Years of the United Nations Declaration on the Right to Development* (HR/PUB/12/4, United Nations, 2013) 217.
76   African Development Bank Group, Achieving the Millennium Development Goals Report 2013 www.afdb.org/knowledge/publications/millennium-development-goals-mdgs-report/ accessed 14 April, 2014.
77   African Charter www.achpr.org/instruments/achpr/ accessed 14 April, 2014.
78   Oji Umozurike, *The African Charter on Human and Peoples' Rights* (Brill 1997).

Charter and the duties it imposed on states as well as individuals (at least on paper) the African system became an example of a human rights regime that is more duty-oriented, particularly on individuals, than the universal human rights system.[79] Significantly, the Charter went further than the universal human rights framework of the day, as well as beyond both the European and American regional human rights systems, by pioneering the introduction of the first legally binding article expressly conferring an individual and collective right to development.[80]

Article 22(1) of the African Charter provides that: 'All peoples shall have the right to their economic, social and cultural development with due regard to their freedom and identity and in the equal enjoyment of the common heritage of mankind.' Article 22(2) complements this position by presenting the duty of states, individually or collectively, to ensure the exercise of the right to development.[81] In Article 22, the drafters of the Charter appear to draw from both Article 22 of the Universal Declaration of Human Rights of 1948 (UDHR)[82] and Article 1(1) of the International Covenant on Economic, Social and Cultural Rights (ICESCR)[83] in an attempt to convey a comprehensive right, with an attendant duty.

However, although the 'Peoples' Right to Development' (PRTD) had been long anticipated by African human rights activists since the 1960 and 1970s, the

---

79 Ibid; Henry Steiner and Philip Alston, *International Human Rights in Context: Law, Politics and Morals* (2nd edn, Oxford University Press 2000) 920.

80 T.F. Yerima, 'The African Charter on Human and Peoples' Rights: A Critique, and in Comparison with Other Regional and International Human Rights Instruments' in Akin Ibidapo-Obe and T.F. Yerima (eds.), International Law, Human Rights and Development (Petoa Educational Publishers 2004) 63.

81 See http://www.achpr.org/instruments/achpr/ accessed 14 April 2014. Other treaties of the era with development components include: the International Convention on the Elimination of all Forms of Racial Discrimination; Declaration on Permanent Sovereignty over Natural Resources; Convention for the Prevention and Punishment of the Crime of Genocide; the International Convention on the Suppression and Punishment of the Crime of Apartheid; the Convention Against Torture and Other Cruel, Inhuman or Degrading Treatment or Punishment, among others.

82 Article 22 of UDHR states: 'Everyone, as a member of society, has the right to social security and is entitled to realization, through national effort and international cooperation and in accordance with the organization and resources of each State, of the economic, social and cultural rights indispensable for his dignity and the free development of his personality.'

83 Article 1(1) ICESCR states: 'All peoples have the right of self-determination. By virtue of that right they freely determine their political status and freely pursue their economic, social and cultural development.'

volume of advocacy on Article 22 of the African Charter has been far less than expected. Out of over 220 Communications submitted to the African Commission on Human and Peoples' Rights (the African Commission) since its inauguration in 1987,[84] only a total of seven have expressly relied on Article 22 in their claims. The first of these claims was submitted in 1994 against the government of Zimbabwe, but was later withdrawn.[85] Furthermore, of these seven Communications, only four were decided on the basis of the merits of the case.[86] As a result, the African Commission has had only a handful of opportunities to make pronouncements on the PRTD.

For example, the African Commission was deprived of an important opportunity to make an express pronouncement on Article 22 in its landmark decision involving the Nigerian government in 2001, *Social and Economic Rights Action Centre (SERAC) v. Nigeria (Ogoni case)*,[87] when it made a number of important development-related pronouncements on the African Charter. In that case, SERAC alleged that the (then) military government of Nigeria had been directly involved in oil production through the state oil company, the Nigerian National Petroleum Company (NNPC), the majority shareholder in a consortium with Shell Petroleum Development Corporation (SPDC), and that these

---

[84] The African Commission was established to provide oversight and interpretation of the African Charter and is a quasi-judicial body. Although it only gives recommendations that are not legally enforceable judgments, these judgments are persuasive and generally well respected.

[85] Commission on Human and Peoples' Rights, comm. No. 155/96, (2001), 1. Centre for Minority Rights Development (Kenya) and Minority Group (on behalf of Endorois Welfare Council) v. Kenya (2009) Commission on Human and People's Rights comm. No. 276/03 **(decided on merits)**; 2. Sudan Human Rights Organisation & Centre on Housing Rights and Evictions (COHRE) v. Sudan (2009) Commission on Human and People's Rights comm 279/03–296/05 **(decided on merits)**; 3. Socio Economic Rights and Accountability Project v. Nigeria (2008) Commission on Human and People's Rights, comm 300/05 **(ruled inadmissible)**; 4. Bakweri Land Claims Committee v. Cameroon (2004) Commission on Human and People's rights, comm. No 260/02 **(ruled inadmissible)**; 5. Democratic Republic of Congo v.Burundi, Rwanda, Uganda **(2003) Commission on Human and People's Rights, comm. No 227/99 (decided on merits)**; 6. Association pour la sauvegarde de la paix au Burundi v. Kenya, Uganda, Rwanda, Tanzania, Zaire (DRC), Zambia **(2003) Commission on Human and People's Rights, Comm. 157/96 (decided on merits)**; 7. William A. Courson v. Zimbabwe **(1995) Commission on Human and People's Rights comm 136/94 (withdrawn)**.

[86] Four cases were decided on merit, two ruled inadmissible, and one was withdrawn.

[87] Social and Economic Rights Action Centre (SERAC) and Another v. Nigeria (2001) AHRLR 60 (ACHPR 2001) Communication 155/96, Decided at the 30th ordinary session, Oct 2001, 15th Annual Activity Report.

operations caused environmental degradation and health problems resulting from the contamination of the environment among the Ogoni People of Southern Nigeria. In finding the Nigerian government to be in violation of, *inter alia*, Articles 21 and 24 of the African Charter, the African Commission stated that:

> 45. Firstly, the obligation to respect entails that the state should refrain from interfering in the enjoyment of all fundamental rights; it should respect right-holders, their freedoms, autonomy, resources, and liberty of their action. With respect to socio-economic rights, this means that the state is obliged to respect the free use of resources owned or at the disposal of the individual alone or in any form of association with others, including the household or the family, for the purpose of rights-related needs. And with regard to a collective group, the resources belonging to it should be respected, as it has to use the same resources to satisfy its needs.
>
> 46. At a secondary level, the State is obliged to protect right-holders against other subjects by legislation and provision of effective remedies. This obligation requires the State to take measures to protect beneficiaries of the protected rights against political, economic and social interferences. Protection generally entails the creation and maintenance of an atmosphere or framework by an effective interplay of laws and regulations so that individuals will be able to freely realize their rights and freedoms. This is very much intertwined with the tertiary obligation of the State to promote the enjoyment of all human rights. The State should make sure that individuals are able to exercise their rights and freedoms, for example, by promoting tolerance, raising awareness, and even building Infrastructures.

The Commission went on to state that the last layer of obligation requires the state to fulfil the rights and freedoms it freely undertook under the various human rights regimes by actively deploying the state machinery towards the practical realization of such rights.[88]

The first two Communications in which Article 22 was directly raised and recommendations were given, based on the merits of the case, were delivered by the African Commission in 2003. *Association pour la sauvegarde de la paix*

---

88   *SERAC v. Nigeria* (2001), para. 47.

au Burundi v. Kenya, Uganda, Rwanda, Tanzania, Zaire (DRC), Zambia[89] was initiated in 1996 by a non-profit organization based in Belgium. The case was brought against all of Burundi's neighbours, comprising the countries in the Great Lakes region of Africa (Tanzania, Kenya, Uganda, Rwanda, Zaire (now Democratic Republic of Congo), Ethiopia, and Zambia), challenging an embargo imposed by them on Burundi. The embargo was instituted by a resolution adopted in July 1996 at the Great Lakes Summit following the unconstitutional change of government in Burundi after the overthrow of the country's democratically elected government and the installation of a government led by a retired military ruler, with the support of the country's military. The resolution was later supported by the UN Security Council and by the Organization of African Unity (OAU). The claimant relied on, *inter alia*, Article 22 of the African Charter because the embargo prevented Burundians from having access to means of transportation by air and sea. Correctly, the African Commission found no violation on the part of the respondent states, who had a legitimate interest in peace and security in the region.

The second case was *Democratic Republic of the Congo v. Burundi, Rwanda and Uganda*,[90] again stemming from a regional conflict.[91] Here, the African Commission found that the respondents' barbaric acts committed in violation of Congolese peoples' rights to cultural development guaranteed by article 22 of the African Charter, were also 'an affront on the noble virtues of the African historical tradition and values enunciated in the Preamble to the African Charter.'[92] In addition, paragraph 95 stated that, '[t]he deprivation of the right of the people of the Democratic Republic of Congo, in this case, to freely dispose of their wealth and natural resources, has also occasioned another violation – their right to their economic, social and cultural development and of the

---

89 Association pour la sauvegarde de la paix au Burundi v. Kenya, Uganda, Rwanda, Tanzania, Zaire (DRC), Zambia (2003) Commission on Human and People's Rights, Comm. 157/96. Decided at the 33rd Ordinary Session held in Niamey, Niger from 15th to 29th May 2003. (*Burundi case*).

90 Democratic Republic of the Congo v. Burundi, Rwanda and Uganda (2004) AHRLR 19 (ACHPR 2003), Communication 227/99, *DR Congo v. Burundi, Rwanda and Uganda*, Decided at the 33rd ordinary session May 2003, 20th Activity Report.

91 DRC alleged grave and massive violations of human and peoples' rights committed by the armed forces of these three respondent countries in the Congolese provinces where there had been rebel activities since 2nd August 1998, and for which the Democratic Republic of Congo blames Burundi, Uganda and Rwanda.

92 Organization of African Unity (OAU), *African Charter on Human and Peoples' Rights*, 27 June 1981, CAB/LEG/67/3 rev. 5, 21 I.L.M. 58 (1982), www.achpr.org/instruments/achpr/ accessed 14 April 2014.

general duty of states to individually or collectively ensure the exercise of the right to development, guaranteed under article 22 of the African Charter.'[93]

In 2009, the African Commission seized the opportunity presented by *Sudan Human Rights Organisation & Centre on Housing Rights and Evictions (COHRE) v. Sudan*,[94] to expound on the concept of peoples' rights.[95] In finding Sudan in violation of, *inter alia*, Article 22, the African Commission interpreted the content of a 'peoples' right' under the African Charter by stating that an important aspect of defining 'a people' would be identifying the characteristics which a particular people may use to identify themselves, through the principle of self-identification, or which other people may use to identify them. The African Commission indicated that such characteristics may include the language, religion, culture, the territory they occupy in a state, common history, and ethno-anthropological factors.[96] The significance of this articulation by the African Commission on the composition of a people lies in the attempt to crystallize the conceptualization of who a people are in order to determine those who can legitimately benefit from the peoples' rights conferred by the African Charter. The African Commission noted that the complainants do not deserve to be dominated by a people of another race in the same state, and that their claim for equal treatment arose from alleged underdevelopment and marginalization, a form of collective punishment which is prohibited by Article 22.[97]

These three Communications on the PRTD were primarily submitted as a result of regional or national conflict situations. It is a step in the right direction that advocates saw it fit to raise and rely on Article 22 of the African Charter as part of their claims. However, unlike the *Ogoni case*, these Communications did not present a solid opportunity for the African Commission to elaborate fully on the nature, rights and obligations attributable to the PRTD.

---

93 Ibid. Article 22.
94 Sudan Human Rights Organisation & Centre on Housing Rights and Evictions (COHRE) v. Sudan (2009) Commission on Human and People's Rights comm 279/03–296/05 (*COHRE case*).
95 The complainants alleged gross, massive and systematic violations of human rights by the Republic of Sudan against the indigenous Black African tribes in the Darfur region (Western Sudan), claiming that the Darfur region has been under a state of emergency since the government of General Omar Al-Bashir seized power in 1989. They further allege that this situation has given security and paramilitary forces a free hand to arrest, detain torture and carry out extrajudicial executions of suspected insurgents.
96 *COHRE case*, para. 220.
97 Ibid.

The situation has since been partly remedied by the African Commission's landmark decision in *Centre for Minority Rights Development (Kenya) and Minority Rights Group International on behalf of Endorois Welfare Council v. Kenya* (*Endorois case*).[98] Here, the complainants allege violations of the PRTD resulting from the displacement of the Endorois Community, an indigenous community in Kenya, from their ancestral lands without adequate consultation or compensation for their loss of property, the disruption of the community's pastoral enterprise or the right to practice their religion and culture as the Endorois people.[99] According to the Endorois people, by creating a game reserve on their land over 30 years ago, the Kenyan government disregarded national law, Kenyan Constitutional provisions and, most importantly, numerous articles of the African Charter, including the right to development.[100] Citing the African Commission's reasoning in the *Ogoni case*, the Endorois Community noted the importance of choice to the rights holders' well-being and the 'liberty of their action,' which is tantamount to the choice embodied in the right to development and must, therefore, be respected by the Kenyan government. In pronouncing their findings of violation of the complainants' PRTD by the respondents, the African Commission stated as follows:

> 277. The African Commission is of the view that the right to development is a two-pronged test, that it is both constitutive and instrumental, or useful as both a means and an end. A violation of either the procedural or substantive element constitutes a violation of the right to development. Fulfilling only one of the two prongs will not satisfy the right to development. The African Commission notes the Complainants arguments that recognising the right to development requires fulfilling five main criteria: it must be equitable, non discriminatory, participatory, accountable, and transparent, with equity and choice as important, overarching themes in the right to development.

> 278. In that regard it takes note of the report of the UN Independent Expert who said that development is not simply the state providing, for

---

[98] Centre for Minority Rights Development (Kenya) and Minority Group (on behalf of Endorois Welfare Council) v. Kenya (2009) Commission on Human and People's Rights comm. No. 276/03(adopted May 2009, approved by the African Union January 2010) paras 22 and 297–8.

[99] Citing itself in the *Ogoni case*, the African Commission ruled that the Endorois are a 'people', a status that entitles them to benefit from the importance of community and collective identity in African culture which is recognised throughout the African Charter.

[100] Endorois case, para. 75.

example, housing for particular individuals or peoples; development is instead about providing people with the ability to choose where to live. He states "... the state or any other authority cannot decide arbitrarily where an individual should live just because the supplies of such housing are made available". Freedom of choice must be present as a part of the right to development.

On the issue of development as a choice, the African Commission went on to quote a Report produced for the UN Working Group on Indigenous Populations requiring that 'indigenous peoples are not coerced, pressured or intimidated in their choices of development.'[101] The African Commission was of the view that, if the government of Kenya had created conditions to facilitate the PRTD in this context, the game reserve would have aided the development of the Endorois as they would have made an informed decision and actively benefited from it. However, the forced evictions eliminated any choice as to where they would live.[102]

Finally, the African Commission enumerated the duties of the Kenyan government, stating that it 'bears the burden for creating conditions favourable to a people's development. The Respondent State, instead, is obligated to ensure that the Endorois are not left out of the development process or benefits. The African Commission agrees that the failure to provide adequate compensation and benefits, or provide suitable land for grazing indicates that the Respondent State did not adequately provide for the Endorois in the development process. It finds against the Respondent State that the Endorois community has suffered a violation of Article 22 of the Charter.'[103]

While the jurisprudence from the *Endorois case* is extremely helpful, the PRTD is still being considered from the position of the state's internal obligations to its own citizens.[104] What remains untested is the external duty of an African state to any group of African people. Furthermore, the African Commission, correctly, drew from the RTD and other regional instruments and jurisprudence in reaching its decision. However, care should be taken not to import concept inflation and, along with it, the unresolved debates about the

---

101   Ibid., para. 279.
102   Ibid., para. 283, 290.
103   Ibid., para. 290.
104   Margot Salomon, Global Responsibility for Human Rights (Oxford University Press 2007); Margot Salomon, 'Legal Cosmopolitanism and the Normative Contribution of the Right to Development' in Stephen Marks (ed), *Implementing The Right To Development: The Role of International Law* (The Friedrich-Ebert-Stiftung/Harvard School of Public Health 2008) 17.

nature and duties of the RTD into the realm of the PRTD, which may distort its justiciability.[105]

At present, jurisprudence on the PRTD within Africa may not have had much impact in the universal human rights arena. However, as African states continue engage in practices which could affect African peoples, whether individually or collectively, such as entering into economic partnership agreements with non-African states, it would be interesting to see how the universal system of human rights would react to the pronouncement of a violation of the PRTD arising from such agreements.

Apart from the difficulty in adjudicating socio-economic cases on the continent,[106] this presumed lukewarm attitude from advocates might be attributed to the fact that while Article 22(2) of the African Charter confers an obligation on paper on African states, individually and collectively, to 'ensure' that the PRTD is protected or attained, there is insufficient guidance as to what this duty entails in practice and how the duty could or should be achieved. Thus, a perceived vagueness about the level of legally enforceable implementation of a state's duty to ensure African peoples' development could be responsible for the minimal application of Article 22 by advocates across the continent.

Despite these limitations of this regional framework for the RTD in Africa, the Commission's pronouncements are nonetheless crucial in this debate at the international level.[107] In practice, while the scope of the PRTD is still evolving, in particular with respect to the external obligations of states, the PRTD is the first right to development that, at least in theory, is legally enforceable. Although the external obligations of African states have not been tested yet, I believe that the African Commission might be willing to make a pronouncement on the extent of these obligations of African states because it has ex-

---

105   David Beetham, 'The Right to Development and Its Corresponding Obligations' in Bard Andreassen and Stephen Marks (eds.) *Development As a Human Right: Legal, Political and Economic Dimensions* (Nobel Symposium, Harvard School of Public Health 2006) 79.

106   Takele Bulto, 'The Indirect Approach to Promote Justiciability of Socio-Economic Rights of the African Charter on Human and Peoples' Rights' in Rachael Murray (ed.), *Human Rights Litigation and the Domestication of International Human Rights Standards in Africa* (PULP 2010) 134–167.

107   Chidi Odinkalu, 'Analysis of Paralysis or Paralysis by Analysis? Implementing Economic, Social, and Cultural Rights under the African Charter on Human and Peoples' Rights' (2001) 23 Human Rights Quarterly 347.

pressly stated that the African Charter confers rights to all African peoples without regard to their geographic location.[108]

As we look to the future of the PRTD and its contribution to international human rights law, more Africans must deliberately and actively engage in Article 22 advocacy with a view to realizing the continent's development. The justiciability of the PRTD presents a germane opportunity to African peoples, which should be fully maximized. The precedents being set by African jurisprudence in this area could be fundamental to the universal debate on the legalisation and justiciability of the RTD, therefore, African advocates and activists have a responsibility to nurture its development by testing the limits of Article 22 and giving ample opportunity to African courts to extend the limits of the current jurisprudence.

4 Conclusion

The universal Right to Development has undergone fundamental change in its meaning and scope since its inception almost thirty years ago. When the RTD was first introduced in the 1970s, development was synonymous with economic growth and GDP. However, by the 1990s, the concept of development was expanded to encompass human development in its totality. While this expansion was a welcome progression, it came at a significant cost to the RTD as the broadened scope diluted the ability to use and legally apply the RTD beyond state borders. In addition, while the scope has been broadened, there is still a lack of clarity with respect to what obligations states have.

As the brief overview of the history of African development has demonstrated, international obligations to support the development aspirations of smaller African states have not yielded the desired results but rather contributed to the perpetuation of the cycle of underdevelopment, particularly in economic terms. Furthermore, since the extent to which these declaratory obligations can be legally enforced is unclear, it is questionable whether they are suitable to address the critical development challenges of today.

If the extent of states' obligations regarding the RTD is concretely defined, the question becomes how these obligations can and should be enforced. The PRTD, though a regional concept, can be used as a case study of how such enforcement could work on an international level. While the PRTD in Africa

---

108   Koen De Feyter, 'Indigenous peoples' in United Nations Human Rights Office of the High Commissioner (eds.) *Realizing the Right to Development* (United Nations Publication HR/PUB/12/4, United Nations 2013) 159, 164.

shares some of the challenges of the universal RTD with respect to the definition of scope, it does take the concept of a right to development a step further by providing a stronger basis for legal enforcement of the right. Although the extent of existing jurisprudence is limited to internal obligations of states towards their own people and the extent of external obligations of states has not yet been tested, there are indications that the African Commission could adjudicate on external obligations in a similar vein in the future. The onus is now on the African people to leverage the existing framework to further refine the RTD on a regional level, which in turn can and should contribute to the strengthening of the global RTD.

CHAPTER 26

Aspects of Africa's Contribution to the Development of International Law

Adetola Onayemi and Olufemi Elias

1   Introduction

Following the expansion of the international community to include Latin American and African states in the nineteenth and twentieth centuries, international law has had to adapt to accommodate the divergent interests. Judge Abdul Koroma, a vocal advocate of the need for international law to reflect the full scope of these interests, noted that the growth of the United Nations and the globalization of the international community created a challenge for "multiculturalism"; for international law to be effective, "it should strive to accommodate potentially differing views of the international legal order in this new community of States and peoples".[1] He points out the several respects in which international does not adequately reflect the needs and interests of parts of the international community. The "new" members of the international community have participated actively in reshaping the international law system to reflect their interests and needs, even though that has not resulted in a complete overhaul of modern international law and its Western origins.[2] In addition to Judge Koroma's observation regarding their participation in the creation and development of rules of universal or general application, African states and other newly independent states have established legal frameworks and developed new principles and rules that are intended to operate on a regional level to address matters of particular concern or interest to their situation and

---

1   A.G. Koroma, "International Law and Multi-Culturalism", in S. Yee and J.-Y. Morin (eds.) *Multiculturalism and International Law: Essays in honour of Edward McWhinney* (2009), p. 79–84, at p. 79.
2   See, generally, S. Bhuiyan, P. Sands and N. Schrijver (eds.), *International Law and Developing Countries: Essays in Honour of Kamal Hossain* (2014). See also, e.g., C. Wilfred Jenks, *The Common Law of Mankind*, p. 74–77 (1958); M. Boisard, "On the Probable Influence of Islam on Western Public and International Law", 2 *Int'l J. Middle Eastern Studies*, p. 429 (1980); Ved P. Nanda, "International Law in Ancient Hindu India", in *Religion and International Law* 51 (M. Janis et. al., eds., 1999); UNESCO (ed.), *International Dimensions of Humanitarian Law* (1988).

reflect their interests. This paper will focus on the latter aspect of the contribution of African States. It will provide a brief overview of a number of significant areas in which the solutions adopted in Africa can be considered progressive and provide more robust methods of addressing the issues arising in those fields of law.[3]

2 International Protection of Refugee Rights and Internally Displaced People

2.1 Refugee Rights

The protection of refugee rights is a proper starting point for an analysis of areas in which international law in Africa has developed to address pertinent existing problems. This is because the international law rules on the protection of refugees and internally displaced people in Africa, as will be subsequently considered, have been strategically formulated to both clarify and improve on the extant international law rules on refugees and internally displaced people.

2.1.1 Expanding the Legal Definition

The United Nations Convention Relating to the Status of Refugees of 1951 ("1951 Convention") defines a refugee as a person who is outside the country of his or her nationality (or place of habitual residence, in the case of a stateless person) due to a well-founded fear of persecution on account of race, religion, nationality, membership of a particular social group or political opinion or owing to such fear is unwilling to avail himself or herself of the protection of that country.[4] There are two requirements for refugee status in the 1951 Convention:[5] the existence of a well-founded fear of personal persecution for

---

3   See also A. Yusuf, "The Public Law of Africa and International Law: Broadening the Scope of Application of International Rules and Enriching Them for Intra-African Purposes", *infra*, Chapter 23. This paper does not consider the historical contribution of pre-colonial African Kingdoms. See T.O Elias, "International Relations in Africa: A Historical Survey", in A.K. Mensah-Brown (ed.), *African International Legal History* (UNITAR, New York, 1975); M. Lachs, "A Reminder: Africa and Asia and the Development of International Law in the Past" in *Essays on International Law: 25th Anniversary Commemorative Volume of the Asian-African Legal Consultative Committee*, pp. 21–28; R. Numelin, *The Beginnings of Diplomacy* (Helsinki, 1951), pp. 141, 153; G.-C. Onyeledo, "International law among the Yoruba, Benin and the Hausa-Fulani", in *Survey in African International Legal History*, p. 153–160. Also see generally A. Abass and F. Ippolito (ed.), *Regional Approaches to the Protection of Asylum Seekers* (2014).
4   189 UNTS 150, Article 1(A)(2).
5   T. Maluwa, *International Law in Post-Colonial Africa* (1999) p. 178.

one or more of the enumerated reasons; and the movement of the person in question from his country or origin (or place of habitual residence, in the case of a stateless person) into another country. In the absence of the second requirement, the person is an "internally displaced person". The legal classification of a person determines the legal regime that applies. Impliedly, internally displaced people are not protected under the international refugee law regime. However, as Helton[6] and Maluwa[7] both note, the increasingly common practice has been for the UNHCR at the request of the UN Secretary General and the UN General Assembly to extend its mandate to internally displaced people.

The 1951 Convention definition has been criticized on several grounds. First, the definition of refugees based on the crossing of borders excludes internally displaced people from the protection offered.[8] Second, the requirement of "well-founded fear" of personal persecution is vague and ill-defined for application by states when attempting to determine who qualifies as a refugee for the purpose of asylum.[9] Third, some scholars argue that the 1951 Convention definition is limited in that it distinguishes between political refugees suffering political persecution, which is contemplated under this Convention, and persons fleeing economic and other life-threatening conditions such as drought and famine ("economic refugees").[10]

One of the major contributions to refugee protection in Africa is the elucidation of a definition that takes greater account of the reality of refugee situations. The Organisation of African Unity (OAU) adopted on 10 September 1969 the Convention governing the Specific Aspects of Refugee Problems in Africa ("1969 Convention").[11] Article 1(1) of the 1969 Convention restates the 1951 Convention definition, but unlike the 1951 Convention, does not exclude events occurring before 1951..[12] Article 1(2) of the 1969 Convention then states:

---

6 A.C. Helton, "What is Refugee Protection?", *International Journal of Refugee Law* (Special Issue, 1990) p. 119.

7 Maluwa, *supra* n. 5.

8 A. Shacknove, "Who is a Refugee?", 95 *Ethics* (1985), p. 274; Maluwa, *supra* n. 5.

9 L. Gordenker, *Refugees in International Politics* (Columbia University Press, 1987, New York); Maluwa, *supra* n. 5.

10 A. Dowty, *Closed Borders: The Contemporary Assault on Freedom of Movement* (1987); E. Ferris, "Overview: Refugees and World Politics", in E. Ferris (ed.), *Refugees and World Politics*, (1985); Maluwa, *supra* n. 5.

11 1001 UNTS 45; adopted 10 September 1969, entered into force 20 June 1974 (1969 Convention).

12 Article 1(A) (2) of the 1951 Convention includes a limiting time clause of "events occurring before 1 January 1951".

> The term 'refugee' shall also apply to every person who, owing to external aggression, occupation, foreign domination or events seriously disturbing public order in either part or the whole of his country of origin or nationality, is compelled to leave his place of habitual residence in order to seek refuge in another place outside his country of origin or nationality.[13]

Maluwa notes that need to respond to the reality of the African Continent at the time – armed conflict arising from anti-colonial struggles, internal civil wars and the resulting exoduses – were overriding considerations for the 1969 Convention definition.[14] The expansion of the legal connotation of "refugee" improves upon the 1951 Convention definition in that it explicitly introduces objective criteria which are dependent on prevailing situations in the country of origin for determining who can enjoy refugee status.[15] It has been said that the 1969 Convention "requires neither the elements of deliberateness nor discrimination inherent in the 1951 Convention".[16]

The new terminology in the 1969 Convention provides a pragmatic solution to the problem of determining refugee status during times of massive migrations when individual determinations are impractical and adequate decision-making infrastructure is absent.[17] Regarding the requirement of personal "well-founded" fear of persecution, Maluwa states that the definition contained in Article 1 of the OAU Convention "broke new ground in international law by recasting the traditional definition of a refugee in embracing, as it does, an additional category of persons as refugees, i.e. all those who are compelled to leave their country of origin in order to escape violence, regardless of whether they are in fact personally in danger of political persecution".[18]

One criticism of the definition offered in the 1969 Convention is the use of terms – such as "external aggression", "occupation", and "foreign domination" – that had not acquired "widely agreed or settled meanings in international law at the time".[19] It has been argued that the "drafters of the new definition

---

13 Article 1(2) of the 1969 Convention.
14 Maluwa, *supra* n. 5, p. 180.
15 M. Sharpe, "Analytical Overview of the 1969 (OAU) Convention for the Southern Refugee Legal Aid Network", (Available online at <http://www.refugeelegalaidinformation.org/african-union-refugee-definition#sthash.vVieaCaP.dpuf> accessed 22 October 2014).
16 Ruma Mandal, 'Protection Mechanisms Outside the 1951 Convention ("Complementary Protection")' 13 UNHCR *Legal and Protection Policy Research Series* (2005).
17 E. Arboleda, "Refugee Definition in Africa and Latin America: The Lessons of Pragmatism", 3 *International Journal of Refugee Law* (1991), pp. 185–207 at p. 195.
18 Maluwa, *supra* n. 5, p. 180.
19 Ibid.

gave secondary consideration to the strict legal meaning of its terminology and case law"[20] and rather aimed at providing a pragmatic solution to the refugee problem. This should not be taken to mean that the 1969 establishes a lax regime. The 1969 Convention, in Article 1, includes paragraphs on cessation and exclusion where it adds to the scope of the 1951 Convention. For instance, amongst others, the 1969 Convention shall cease to apply to any refugee who has "committed a serious non-political crime outside his country of refuge"[21] after his admission to that country as a refugee or has "seriously infringed"[22] the purposes and objectives of the Convention. It is important to note that in its African operations, the UNHCR applies both the definition in the 1951 Convention as well as the 1969 Convention.[23]

2.1.2   Asylum

The 1951 Convention does not establish a right of asylum; it has indeed been pointed out that the right to asylum has not been expressly recognized in any international human rights instrument of universal scope.[24] While a state may not return refugees who have been admitted to places where their lives or freedom may be endangered (non-refoulement), the state does not have an obligation to admit refugees.[25] It has been argued that Articles 1 and 33 of the 1951 Convention, read jointly, go only as far as placing an implied duty[26] on States parties to grant access to asylum procedures.[27] While not derogating from the international consensus that the grant of asylum is within the exclusive jurisdiction of each state, the 1969 Convention provides that "Member states ... shall use their best endeavours consistent with their respective legislations to receive refugees and to secure the settlement of those refugees who, for well-founded reasons, are unable or unwilling to return to their country of origin or

---

20   Arboleda, *supra* n. 17.
21   1969 Convention Article 1(4)(f).
22   1969 Convention Article 1(4)(g).
23   UNHCR, "Note on International Protection", UN. Doc. A/AC96/830 (7 September 1994) [32].
24   M.-T. Gil-Bazo, "Refugee Status, Subsidiary Protection, and the Right to Be Granted Asylum Under EC Law", UNHCR, New Issues in Refugee Research, Research Paper No. 136; Oxford Legal Studies Research Paper No. 54/2006, available at SSRN: http://ssrn.com/abstract=951097; G. Goodwin-Gill and J. McAdam, *The Refugee in International Law* (3rd edn. OUP 2007), concludes on the basis of state practice that there is no right of asylum.
25   Ibid., at p. 132.
26   A. Edwards, "Tampering with Refugee Protection: The Case of Australia", 15 *Int'l Journal of Refugee Law* ((2003), p. 198.
27   Ibid., at p. 302.

nationality".[28] It has been stated that this "strengthens the institution of asylum"[29] and serves as "a further inroad into the traditional international law perspective which has tended to regard asylum as an exclusive right of the sovereign state, and certainly not as a right to be enforced by an individual against a state".[30] While a clear right to asylum may not have been established by the 1969 Convention, it can be favourably argued that there are prospects under Article 2(1) for the right to asylum to be enforced by an individual against a state in which the 1969 Convention has been transformed into, or is otherwise applicable as, domestic law.

2.1.3 Strengthening Non-refoulement

Non-refoulement,[31] under refugee law, prohibits states from returning refugees to territories where there is risk that the life or freedom of the refugee may be threatened on account of race, religion, nationality, or membership of a particular social group or political opinion. It has been argued that the 1969 Convention expands non-refoulement in four main respects.[32]

First, there is an exception under the 1951 Convention according to which that Convention does not apply in respect of a person with no nationality if the circumstances that made him a refugee have ceased to exist and he is able to return to the country of his former habitual residence.[33] The 1969 Convention does not contain this exception. Second, while Article 33 of the 1951 Convention provides that "[n]o Contracting State shall expel or return ("refouler") a refugee in any manner whatsoever to the frontiers of territories where his life or freedom would be threatened", it does not provide that a state has a responsibility not to reject any refugee who presents himself or herself at its frontier. Instead, it limits the scope of non-refoulement to any refugee who is already

---

28 1969 Convention Article 2(1).
29 R. Hofmann, "Refugee Law in the African Context" 52 *Heidelberg Journal of International Law* (1992), p. 318, 324.
30 M. Rwelamira, "Some Reflections on the OAU Convention on Refugees: Some Pending Issues", 16 *Comparative and International Law Journal of Southern Africa*, (1983), p. 155, p. 170.
31 The principle of non-refoulement, provided for in Article 33(1) of the 1951 Convention, provides that "No Contracting State shall expel or return ("refouler") a refugee in any manner whatsoever to the frontiers of territories where his life or freedom would be threatened on account of his race, religion, nationality, membership or a particular social group or political opinion". Some have argued that non-refoulement is now a *jus jogens* norm under International law. See Goodwin-Gill and McAdam, *supra* n. 24, pp. 167–168.
32 M. Sharpe, *supra* n. 15.
33 1951 Convention Article 1(C) (6).

within the state's borders. Article 2(3) of the 1969 Convention, in contrast, expressly provides that non-refoulement applies at frontiers of the state's territory ("No person shall be subjected by a Member State to measures such as rejection at the frontier ... "). Based on the foregoing, some commentators have contended that the scope of non-refoulement under the 1969 Convention is textually broader than the 1951 Convention.[34] In practice,[35] however, states recognise that non-refoulement applies when the asylum seeker presents himself or herself at their borders, so that the difference between the 1951 and 1969 Conventions in this regard is not great.[36] Third, some commentators have noted that in identifying the party to which non-refoulement applies, the 1969 Convention uses the term "persons" while the 1951 Convention uses the term "refugee".[37] It has been argued that this means that the 1969 Convention may protect a broader class of persons from refoulement.[38] Fourth, the 1969 Convention, more than the 1951 Convention, appears to offer protection from a wider range of harm.[39] While non-refoulement under the 1951 Convention prohibits return to territories where life or freedom would be threatened, the 1969 Convention prohibits return to territories where life, *physical integrity* and liberty would be threatened.[40]

2.1.4 Temporary Protection

Article 2(5) of the 1969 Convention states that "where a refugee has not received the right to reside in any country of asylum, he may be granted temporary residence in any country of asylum in which he first presented himself as a refugee pending arrangement for his resettlement."[41] It has been contended that the foregoing provision implies only protection of a limited duration.[42]

---

34 G. Abi-Saab, "The Admission and Expulsion of Refugees with Special Reference to Africa", 8 *African Yearbook of International Law* (2000), p. 71, at p. 89; N. Okogbule, "The Legal Dimensions of the Refugee Problem in Africa", 10 *East African Journal of Peace and Human Rights* (2004), p. 176, at p. 184; UNHCR, *The State of the World's Refugees 2000: Fifty Years of Humanitarian* Action (OUP 2000) 57.

35 Goodwin-Gill and McAdam, *supra* n. 24, p. 208.

36 M. Sharpe, *supra* n. 15, para. 13.

37 W. van Hovell tot Westerflier, "Africa and the Refugees: the OAU Refugee Convention in Theory and Practice", 7 *Netherlands Quarterly of Human Rights* (1989), p. 172, at p. 176.

38 Ibid; see also M. Sharpe, *supra* n. 15, para. 14.

39 Ibid.

40 1969 Convention Article 2(3).

41 1969 Convention Article 2(5).

42 B. Rutinwa, "Prima Facie Status and Refugee Protection", New Issues in Refugee Research Working Paper No 69 (2002) (UNHCR). <http://www.unhcr.org/3db9636c4.html> ac-

However, it has rightly been pointed out that Article 2(5) "applies to persons who have been recognised as refugees but for one reason or another have not been granted the right of residence for any duration at all. It is not intended to determine the duration of residence for all refugees who have been recognised and granted asylum".[43] It follows that when a refugee is resettled in another African country from another, the resettlement simply continues his refugee status in a new country. It is submitted that the concept of temporary protection under the 1969 Convention does not operate to limit state obligations towards refugees but is rather a form of responsibility sharing.[44] Hence, the residence in the first country of asylum is all that is "temporary" in the protection afforded under Article 2(5) of the 1969 Convention.

2.1.5 Enshrining Voluntary Repatriation

Though the notion of voluntary repatriation appears in the Statute of the Office of the United Nations High Commissioner for Refugees,[45] it does not establish voluntary repatriation as a principle. Article 5(1) of the 1969 Convention, in contrast, provides that "the essentially voluntary character of repatriation shall be respected in all cases and no refugee shall be repatriated against his will".[46] This is an important corollary to non-refoulement.[47]

2.2 *Protection of Internally Displaced Persons*

When it adopted the African Union Convention for the Protection and Assistance of Internally Displaced Persons in Africa[48] ("Kampala Convention") in October 2009, the African Union became the first regional organisation to adopt a treaty that addresses internal displacement caused by armed conflicts, natural disasters and large scale development projects and which governs all

---

cessed 22 October 2014; The Refugee Research Unit, Centre for Refugee Studies, York University, 'The Temporary Protection of Refugees: A Solution-Oriented and Rights Regarding Approach', Discussion Paper prepared under the auspices of the research project Toward the Reformulation of International Refugee Law, July 17 1996, Section IV.A., at p. 22.

43 Ibid. p. 16.
44 Ibid. p. 16.
45 UNGA Resolution 428 (V), 14 December 1950 [Chapter 1, article 1].
46 1969 Convention Article 5(1).
47 Article 5(1) of the 1969 Convention has been praised as a "power statement of principle": see J.-F. Durieux and A. Hurwitz, "How Many is Too Many? African and European Legal Responses to Mass Influx of Refugees", 47 *German Yearbook of International Law* (2004), p. 105, at p. 130.
48 52 I.L.M. (2013), p. 397.

phases of internal displacement.[49] It has been written that "it positions Africa at the forefront of international norm-setting and legal development in one of the most controversial areas in international law, the governance of internal displacement".[50] The Kampala Convention is the first regional instrument to impose legal obligations on states to: a) protect people from arbitrary displacement; b) provide protection and assistance to internally displaced persons (IDPs) during displacement; c) seek durable solutions for them; d) grant access to IDPs in need of protection and assistance; and e) prohibit non-state armed groups from obstructing such access or violating their rights. The Convention also provides IDPs with a wide range of claimable rights while imposing obligations on both national and regional international actors.[51]

Furthermore, while refugee law attempts to provide protection by all other states in the event that a state fails to protect its citizens from persecution within its territory, the Kampala Convention goes further by placing an international obligation on other African states when the state hosting the IDPs – not just the state of nationality of the IDPs – fails in its responsibility to protect them.[52] Within Africa, the Convention complements and offers solutions for the practical interpretation of the 1998 United Nations Guiding Principles on Internally Displaced Persons (GPIDP). For example, the Convention includes all causes of displacement such as armed conflict, unrest, human rights violations, natural and man-made disasters and situations where the displaced were forced from their homes due to infrastructural development. In Maru's words, "the Kampala Convention further perfects the GPID not only by converting the guiding principles into binding provisions, but by eliminating its ["most"] critical shortcomings. By consolidating the applicable, but insufficient and scattered, provisions of IHL (International Humanitarian Law) and HRL (Human Rights Law), the Kampala Convention exhibits a legal regime

---

[49] F. Deng, "Africa's Internally Displaced and the Development of International Norms: Standards versus Implementation", in J. Levitt (ed.), *Africa: Mapping New Boundaries in International Law* (Oxford, Portland, Studies in International Law Series, 2008), pp. 80–82; M.T. Maru, *The Kampala Convention and its Contribution to International Law* (Eleven International Publishing, Netherlands, 2014), p. 13. According to C. Beyani, the UN Special Rapporteur on the Human Rights of Internally Displaced Persons, it represents "the will and determination of African States and peoples to address and resolve the problem of internal displacement in Africa"; Report of the Special Rapporteur on the Human Rights of Internally Displaced Persons at the Twenty-sixth session of the Human Rights Council, UN. Doc. A/HRC/26/33. 4 April 2014, para. 27.

[50] Maru, *supra* n. 49, p. 13.

[51] Ibid., p. 6.

[52] Ibid., p. 7. See, for instance, Articles 5 and 8 of the Kampala Convention, *supra* n. 48.

that governs all aspects and types of internal displacement".[53] States are also required to provide IDPs with information that will enable them to make free and informed choices on whether to return, integrate or relocate elsewhere in the country.

One of the many commendations of the Kampala Convention came from the President of the International Committee of the Red Cross (ICRC) who eulogised it for not only filling the protective gaps but also improving international law in many respects.[54] In his words, "the Convention goes further than international humanitarian law treaties in some aspects, for example in the rules it contains on safe and voluntary return and on access to compensation or other forms of reparation. This is of course very positive in terms of enhancing the protection of IDPs."[55]

3 The Rights of the Child

On the 20th November 1989, the United Nations adopted and open for signature the United Nations Convention on the Rights of the Child (UNCRC).[56] Two optional protocols were adopted on 25 May 2000 and a third in December 2011. Building on the UNCRC framework, in 1990, the Organisation for African Unity adopted the African Charter on the Rights and Welfare of the Child (the Children's Charter).[57] The Children's Charter was adopted to fill perceived gaps in the UNCRC.

First, the Children's Charter defines a child as any person below the age of eighteen,[58] while the UNCRC defines a child as "a human being below the age of 18 years unless under the law applicable to the child, majority is attained earlier".[59] The UNCRC does not address the age of majority under the laws of

---

53   Maru, *supra* n. 49, p. 7.
54   J. Kellenberger, "Root Causes and Prevention of Internal Displacement: The ICRC Perspective", Statement to the Special Summit on Refugees, Returnees and IDPs in Africa, 23 October 2009, Kampala, Uganda) available at <https://www.icrc.org/eng/resources/documents/statement/displacement-statement-231009.htm> [accessed 23 October, 2014].
55   Ibid.
56   28 I.L.M. (1989), p. 1448, 1456, with an addendum in 29 I.L.M. 1340 (entered into force September 2, 1990).
57   CAB/LEG/24.9/49 (1990), (available at <http://www.au.int/en/sites/default/files/Charter_En_African_Charter_on_the_Rights_and_Wlefare_of_the_Child_AddisAbaba_July1990.pdf> [accessed 23 October, 2014]).
58   Article 2, Children's Charter.
59   Article 1, UNCRC.

states; states whose laws set low ages of majority are therefore able to maintain such laws. In contrast, the Children's Charter internationalizes the age of majority within the African region, thereby preventing the any African state from reducing that age by domestic legislation. By deciding that a child under the African Charter is any person less than 18 years of age, African States parties to the Charter are under an obligation to change those laws to reflect the Charter requirement.

Secondly, the Children's Charter sets a higher standard than the UNCRC in respect of the age at which children can participate in armed conflicts. By defining a child as anyone under the age of 18, and clearly providing in Article 22(2) that "States Parties to the present Charter shall take any necessary measures to ensure that no child shall take a direct part in hostilities, and refrain in particular, from recruiting any child",[60] the participation of children in armed conflict is prohibited entirely. In contrast, Article 38(3) of the UNCRC provides that "States Parties shall refrain from recruiting any person who has not attained the age of 15 years into their armed forces. In recruiting among those persons who have attained the age of 15 years but who have not attained the age of eighteen years, State Parties shall *endeavour* to give priority to those who are oldest".[61] The age at which an individual can participate in armed conflicts was one of the points of contention during the drafting of the UNCRC, with divergent opinions expressed on a number of issues including the minimum age for recruitment into military service.[62] The United States, for example, argued that the Working Group [which Working Group] was not the proper forum at which to modify international human rights law. Consensus was not achieved on the matter.[63]

In addition to reflecting the African experience on such matters, the provisions of the Children's Charter transcend cultural boundaries and operate over and above custom, tradition or religious practices that are inconsistent with

---

60 Article 22(2), Children's Charter.
61 Article 38(3), UNCRC (our emphasis).
62 K. McSweeney, "The Potential for Enforcement of the United Nations Convention on the Rights of the Child: The Need to Improve the Information Base", 16 *Boston College International and Comparative Law Review* (1993), p. 467, at pp. 472–474.
63 Ibid., page 474, para. 1; see also T. Hammarberg, "The UN Convention on the Rights of the Child – and How to Make it Work", 12 *Human Rights Quarterly* (1990), p. 97, at p. 101. Argentina's ratification of the UNCRC was accompanied by a statement that its preference was for the UNCRC to prohibit completely the use of children in combat. Hence, under the Article 41 of the UNCRC, Argentina will continue to apply its domestic law, while other countries like Columbia, Spain and Uruguay among others have also shown their preference for age 18 instead of 15.

the obligations enumerated therein, as well and take pre-eminence in its application.[64] Going beyond the UNCRC, the Children's Charter covers issues such as trade in children, kidnapping or trafficking of children, and the protection of internally-displaced children.[65] Hence, while the UNCRC simply states that "States Parties shall take measures to combat the illicit transfer and non-return of children abroad",[66] the Children's Charter provides explicitly that "States Parties to the present Charter shall take appropriate measures to prevent (a) the abduction, the sale of, or traffick of children for any purpose or in any form, by any person including parents or legal guardians of the children; (b) the use of children in all forms of begging".[67] In sum, the Children's Charter sets up a progressive and advanced framework for the protection of the rights of the child when compared to the existing rules in other instruments.

4   The Right to Development

Nearly thirty years after the adoption of the United Nations Declaration on the Right to Development,[68] scepticism persists regarding the legal status and the practical implications of the right to development (RTD). Human rights activists have rarely resorted to RTD as an effective tool for enforcing or driving policy.[69] While some commentators view RTD as a "composite right of all uni-

---

64   Article 1(3), Children's Charter.
65   Articles 23 and 29 of the Children's Charter.
66   Article 11, UNCRC.
67   Article 29, Children's Charter.
68   Declaration on the Right to Development, U.N, GAOR, 41st Session, Annex, Agenda Item 101, 97th Plenary meeting at 1, UN Doc. A/RES/41/128 (1987), para. 2. For in-depth analysis of the right to development, see *Infra*, O. Oduwole, Chapter 25. See also I. Bunn, "The Right to Development: Implications for International Economic Law", 15 *American University International Law Review* (2000), p. 1427.
69   See T. Kunanayakam, "The Declaration on the Right to Development in the context of United Nations Standard-setting", in United Nations Human Rights Office of the High Commissioner (ed) *Realizing the Right to Development* (United Nations Publication) HR/PUB/12/4, United Nations 2013) 17–48; A. Vandenbogarde, "The Right to Development in International Human Rights: A Call for its Dissolution", 31 *Netherlands Quarterly of Human Rights*, p. 187.

versal human rights",[70] "the alpha and omega of human rights",[71] and an "umbrella right covering human rights that already exist in legally binding treaties",[72] the direct justiciability of RTD remains a challenge.[73] The Universal Declaration of Human Rights (UDHR),[74] the International Covenant on Civil and Political Rights (ICCPR)[75] and the International Covenant on Economic, Social and Cultural Rights (ICESCR)[76] do not ascribe clear legal status to RTD. While "development" is mentioned in the ICESCR, is not framed as a right with corresponding obligations on states; it is linked to the right to self-determination,[77] and at best can be described as a goal under the ICESCR.[78] Hence, while neither of the two 1966 UN covenants expressly contains a right to development as

---

[70] A. Sengupta "Fifth Report of the Independent Expert on the Right to Development", submitted in accordance with Commission Resolution 2002/69, at 5,6, UN Doc. E/CN.4/2002/WG.18/6; Foreword by N. Pillay, UNHCHR in United Nations Human Rights Office of the High Commissioner (ed.) *Realizing the Right to Development* (United Nations Publication) HR/PUB/12/4, United Nations 2013).

[71] M. Bedjaoui, "The Right to Development", in M. Bedjaoui (ed.), *International Law: Achievements and Prospects* (1991), p. 1177, at p. 1182.

[72] O. Oduwole, *supra* n. 68 *infra*; P. Uvin, *Human Rights and Development* (Kumarian Press 2004) 41; A. Vandenbogaerde, *supra* n. 69; Y. Ghai andY.R. Rao, "Whose Human Right to Development?", Occasional Paper, Commonwealth Human Rights Unit (1989). Indeed other elements of RTD can be found in various other treaties. T. Kunanayakam, "The Declaration on the Right to Development in the context of United Nations Standard-setting", in United Nations Human Rights Office of the High Commissioner (ed.), *Realizing the Right to Development* (United Nations Publication) HR/PUB/12/4, United Nations 2013), p. 17.

[73] B. Hamm, "A Human Rights Approach to Development", 23 *Human Rights Quarterly* (2001), p. 1005; A. Sengupta, "Conceptualizing the Right to Development for the Twenty-first Century", in United Nations Human Rights Office of the High Commissioner (ed), *Realizing the Right to Development* (United Nations Publication) HR/PUB/12/4, United Nations 2013), p. 67, at p. 74.

[74] UNGA Resolution 217 A (III) (10 December 1948).

[75] 999 UNTS, p. 171.

[76] 993 UNTS, p. 3.

[77] Article 1(1) of the ICESCR provides that "All peoples have the right of self-determination. By virtue of that right they freely determine their political status and freely pursue their economic, social and cultural development".

[78] The status of development as a goal under the ICESCR is best demonstrated by Article 6(2) which in reference to the right to work states that "The steps to be taken by a state party to the present covenant to achieve the full realization of this right shall include technical and vocational guidance and training programmes, policies and techniques to steady economic, social and cultural development and full and productive employment under conditions safeguarding fundamental political and economic freedoms to the indi-

such, many of the principles and rights enumerated in those treaties are crucial for a full appreciation of the RTD.[79] The European Convention on Human Rights[80] and the American Covenant on Human Rights[81] do not provide for RTD. RTD also exists in other soft law instruments such as the Declaration on the Right to Development (1986),[82] the Rio Declaration on Environment and Development (1992),[83] the Vienna Declaration and Programme of Action (1993),[84] and the Declaration on the Rights of Indigenous Peoples (2007).[85] In 2011, in its implementation plan presented to the UN Working Group on RTD at its twelfth session, the High-Level Task Force responsible for the implementation of the right to development reformulated[86] the right in context of the Millennium Development Goals, which does little to enhance the legal status of the right. The Non-Aligned Movement disagreed with this approach, stating that the task force had exceeded its mandate and had offered an "incomprehensible definition" of RTD, especially due to the non-recognition of collective

---

vidual". See Matthew Craven, The International Covenant On Economic, Social and Cultural Rights: A Perspective On Its Development (Clarendon Press 1998) 6–29.

79   I. Bunn, *supra* n. 68, p. 1430.

80   Council of Europe, *European Convention for the Protection of Human Rights and Fundamental Freedoms, as amended by Protocols Nos. 11 and 14*, 4 November 1950, ETS 5, available at <http://www.echr.coe.int/Documents/Convention_ENG.pdf> [accessed 21 October 2014] [another citation].

81   Organization of American States (OAS), *American Convention on Human Rights, "Pact of San Jose", Costa Rica*, 22 November 1969, available at <http://www.oas.org/dil/treaties_B-32_American_Convention_on_Human_Rights.htm> [accessed 21 October 2014].

82   UN General Assembly, Declaration on the Right to Development, 4 December 1986, UN. Doc. A/RES/41/128, available at <http://www.un.org/documents/ga/res/41/a41r128.htm> [accessed 26 October 2014]. Article 1 of the Declaration on the Right to Development states that "[T]he right to development is an inalienable human right by virtue of which every human person and all peoples are entitled to participate in, contribute to, and enjoy economic, social, cultural and political development, in which all human rights and fundamental freedoms can be fully realized".

83   UN Doc. A/CONF.151/26 (Vol. I). See, e.g., Principle 3: "[T]he right to development must be fulfilled so as to equitably meet developmental and environmental needs of present and future generations.

84   UN General Assembly, Vienna Declaration and Programme of Action, 12 July 1993, UN. Doc. A/CONF.157/23.

85   UN General Assembly, United Nations Declaration on the Rights of Indigenous Peoples: resolution / adopted by the General Assembly, 2 October 2007, UN. Doc. A/RES/61/295.

86   See UN General Assembly, Human Rights Council: Report of the high-level task force on the implementation of the right to development on its sixth session, 8 March 2010, UN. Doc. A/HRC/15/WG.2/TF/2/Add.2.

responsibility and the duty of states to cooperate in order to fulfil the necessary obligations.[87]

The African Charter on Human and Peoples' Rights, which was drafted to represent an African conceptualization of human rights,[88] stands in clear contrast to the instruments mentioned above in setting up a human rights framework with specific duties imposed on both states and individuals.[89] Article 22 of the 1981 African Charter provides:

> (1) All peoples shall have the right to their economic, social and cultural development with due regard to their freedom and identity and in the equal enjoyment of the common heritage.
>
> (2) States shall have the duty, individually or collectively, to ensure the exercise of the right to development.

Through this provision, African States committed themselves to a legal framework for the right to development, in clear contrast to the prevailing trend. Furthermore, Article 22(2) establishes a duty of states, individually and collectively, to ensure the exercise of the right to development.[90] It has been argued that by drawing from components of Article 22 of the 1948 UDHR and Article 1(1) of the ICESCR, the drafters of the African Charter achieved a more comprehensive obligation in Article 22 of the 1981 African Charter,[91] and that the African Charter more adequately caters for RTD than the global, European and American human rights systems.[92] Judge Koroma has suggested that it is safe to assume that, had more African states been involved and present at the drafting of the UDHR, they would have influenced the drafting to result similar to the African Charter.[93] The most significant African contribution to RTD, how-

---

[87] Submission by Egypt on behalf of the Non-Aligned Movement in follow-up to HRC resolution 15/25 "The Right to Development", <www.ohchr.org/Documents/Issues/Development/Session12/NAM.pdf> at P.2, Assessed 12 November, 2014.
[88] O. Umozurike, *The African Charter on Human and Peoples' Rights* (Brill 1997), pp. 63–66.
[89] Ibid.; H. Steiner and P. Alston, *International Human Rights in Context: Law, Politics and Morals* (2000), p. 920.
[90] O. Oduwole, *supra* n. 68, at p. 581.
[91] Ibid.
[92] T.F. Yerima, "The African Charter on Human and Peoples' Rights: A Critique, and in comparison with Other Regional and International Human Rights Instruments" in A. Ibidapo-Obe and T.F Yerima (eds.), *International Law, Human Rights and Development* (2004), p. 63.
[93] A. Koroma, *supra* n. 1, at p. 80–81.

ever, lies in its distillation and interpretation by regional bodies and tribunals. Three examples will be considered here.

In *Democratic Republic of Congo v. Burundi, Rwanda and Uganda*,[94] the communication filed against Burundi, Rwanda and Uganda by the Democratic Republic of Congo (DRC) in March 1999) alleged that the armed forces of the respondent states had committed serious violations of human and peoples' rights in the Congolese provinces where rebel activities had taken place since 2 August 1998. The DRC alleged, inter alia, that Burundi, Uganda and Rwanda had violated Article 22 of the African Charter, and that the respondent states had unlawfully exploited and looted the natural resources of the DRC by various means, including confiscation, extraction, forced monopoly and price-fixing at proportions that made the war in the DRC a very lucrative business.[95] The African Commission on Human and Peoples' Rights found that depriving the people of the DRC of their right to freely dispose of their wealth was a violation of their right to their economic, social and cultural development as well as the general duty of states to individually or collectively ensure the exercise of the RTD as guaranteed under Article 22 of the African Charter.[96] The African Commission found that the indiscriminate dumping and mass burial of victims of the massacres and killings perpetrated against the peoples of the eastern province of the DRC during the occupation by the armed forces of the respondent were "barbaric and in reckless violation of Congolese peoples' cultural development guaranteed by Article 22 of the African Charter, and an affront on the noble virtues of the African historical traditions and values enunciated in the preamble of the African Charter".[97]

In *Sudan Human Rights Organization & Centre on Housing Rights and Evictions v. Sudan*,[98] the African Commission, noting that RTD under Article 22 is a collective right of "peoples", considered whether the victims constituted a "people" for this purpose. At the relevant time, the Sudan was the largest state in Africa, with a majority of its population being of Arab stock. In contrast, the population of Darfur, a province in the Sudan, is made up of three major tribes (the Zaghawa, the Fur and the Marsalit) who have been described as "people of black African origin". While noting the jurisprudence on "peoples'" rights is quite fluid, the Commission stated that an important aspect of the process of

---

94 African Commission on Human and People's Rights Communication, 227/99, *available at* <http://www.achpr.org/communications/decision/227.99/> [Accessed on 13 October 2014].
95 Ibid., paragraphs 92 and 93.
96 Ibid., paragraph 95.
97 Ibid., paragraph 87.
98 African Commission on Human and Peoples' Rights Communication, 279/03–296/05.

defining "a people" is their "characteristics, which a particular people may use to identify themselves, through the principle of self-determination, or be used by other people to identify them".[99] The Commission went on to list such characteristics, which include language, religion, culture, occupied territory, common history, and ethno-anthropological factors; and in states with a mixed racial composition, race and ethnic identity become important factors in determining groups of "peoples". The African Commission disagreed with the view that the peoples' rights could only be asserted against external aggression, oppression or colonization. The African Commission held that the people of Darfur are a "people" under the African Charter and do not deserve to be dominated by people of another race in the same state and that their claim for equal treatment arose from the alleged underdevelopment and marginalization. The Commission then said "the response by the respondent state, while fighting the armed conflict, targeted the civilian populations, instead of the combatants. This in a way was a form of collective punishment, which is prohibited by international law. It is in that respect that the Commission views the alleged violation of Article 22.[100] The Commission further stated:

> The attacks and forced displacement of Darfurian people denied them the opportunity to engage in economic, social and cultural activities. The displacement interfered with the right to education for their children and pursuit of other activities. Instead of deploying its resources to address the marginalisation in the Darfur, which was the main cause of the conflict, the Respondent State instead unleashed a punitive military campaign which constituted a massive violation of not only the economic social and cultural rights, but other individual rights of the Darfurian people. Based on the analysis hereinabove, concerning the nature and magnitude of the violations, the Commission finds that the Respondent State is in violation of [Article] 22 of the African Charter.[101]

In the *Centre for Minority Rights Development (Kenya) and Minority Rights Group International (MRG) on behalf of Endorois Welfare Council v. Republic of Kenya* case,[102] the complaint alleged displacement of the Endorois, an indigenous community, from their ancestral lands without prior consultation or compensation for loss of property; disruption of the community's pastoral enterprise; violation of their right to practise their religion and culture; and dis-

---

99 Ibid. para. 220.
100 Ibid. para. 223.
101 Ibid., paragraph 224.
102 African Commission on Human and Peoples' Rights Communication, No. 276/03.

ruption of "the overall process of development of the Endorois people". The complaint alleged that the Government of Kenya was responsible for all these actions, which violated the African Charter on Human and People's Rights, the Kenyan Constitution and international law. The complaint also alleged that the Kenyan Government had continued to deny the Endorois community effective participation in decisions affecting their own land and failed to ensure the continued improvement of the Endorois community's well-being, hence violating their right to development.[103] They argued that since their eviction from their ancestral lands, there had been a lack of access to the lake, the salt licks and their usual pasture leading to death of their cattle in large numbers. This affected their ability to pay taxes, which led to confiscation of more cattle by the Kenyan authorities, and resulted in the diminution of their choices, which they argued violated Article 22.

The African Commission stated that

> The right to development is a two-pronged test, that it is both constitutive and instrumental, or useful as both a means and an end. A violation of either the procedural or substantive element constitutes a violation of the right to development. Fulfilling only one of the two prongs will not satisfy the right to development. The African Commission notes the Complainants arguments that recognising the right to development requires fulfilling five main criteria: it must be equitable, non-discriminatory, participatory, accountable, and transparent, with equity and choice as important, over-arching themes in the right to development.[104]

The Commission relied on the report of the UN Independent Expert who had stated that "development is not simply the state providing, for example, housing for particular individuals or peoples; development is instead about providing people with the ability to choose where to live. He states "... the state or any other authority cannot decide arbitrarily where an individual should live just because the supplies of such housing are made available". Freedom of choice must be present as a part of the right to development".[105] The Commission further stated that its own standards require that a government consult with indigenous peoples especially when dealing with sensitive issues such as land.[106]

---

103   Ibid., para. 125.
104   Ibid., at para. 277. For a full discourse on the criteria and principles guiding the fulfillment of the responsibilities under RTD, see Bunn, *supra* n. 68, p. 1442–1451.
105   Ibid., para. 278.
106   Ibid., para. 281.

The Commission spent a considerable part of the communication elucidating the contents of the right to development, developing the commission's jurisprudence on RTD while finding the respondent state in violation of Article 22 of the African Charter. The Commission's jurisprudence (in which it refers to its decisions in other cases) on RTD is unparalleled in the extent to which it elucidates applicable principles and criteria to be fulfilled in the protection of RTD, even though it is quite clear that the contours of RTD are yet to be established.

5 The Norm of Regional Intervention

The change in the policy of African states regarding the principle of non-interference is well-known; while the principle of non-interference in the internal affairs of States is enshrined in Article 3, paragraph 2 of the Charter of the Organization of African Unity, Article 4 of the African Union's Constitutive Act creates a right to intervene in the event of grave situations such as war crimes, genocide and other crimes against humanity, in the territory of a Member State. The AU Constitutive Act is the only international treaty which currently makes provisions for a binding right of intervention in the cases of genocide, crimes against humanity and war crimes against inhabitants of a state within its boundaries and making same a common obligation.[107] For the purposes of restoring peace and security, Article 4 of the AU Charter also allows a Member State to request intervention in its territory.

It is however important to recall that prior to the enactment of the African Union Constitutive Charter, Article 58 of the 1993 Treaty of the Economic Community of West African States (ECOWAS) already provided for the obligation of Member States to "undertake to co-operate with the Community in establishing and strengthening appropriate mechanisms for the timely prevention and resolution of intra-State and inter-State conflicts."[108] This has also spread to other sub-regions; the Southern African Development Community (SADC) unanimously endorsed a Mutual Defence Pact,[109] in 2003, that gives each nation the right to intervene in armed attacks on other Member States.

---

107   See G. Aneme, "The Institutionalisation of Cosmopolitan Justice: The Case of the African Union's Right of Intervention", 22 *Minnesota Journal of International Law* (2013), p. 5.
108   35 I.L.M. (1996), p. 660.
109   South African Development Community (SADC), Mutual Defence Pact, 1 August 2011, available <http://www.sadc.int/files/2913/5333/8281/SADC_Mutual_Defence_Pact 2003.pdf> [accessed 27 October 2014].

Also in 2003, the African Union created the AU Peace and Security Architecture (APSA) which includes an early warning mechanism and a standby force.[110] The right to intervene is therefore enshrined at the regional as well as sub-regional levels.

These international instruments reflect the willingness of member states of these regional and sub-regional bodies to commit to a process of crisis control and resolution within Africa. by the application of the right of intervention. Seemingly, the African states have consented and delegated authority to the African Union to authorise and undertake these interventions.[111] This right of intervention has been demonstrated both by the use of military, economic and political means to resolve internal strife and conflict. Examples of such interventions include: ECOWAS's interventions in Liberia,[112] Sierra Leone,[113] Guinea-Bissau[114] and Guinea;[115] the AU peacekeeping missions in Darfur,[116] Sudan,[117]

---

110 Article 12, The Protocol relating to the establishment of the Peace and Security Council provides or early warning information provide to the Chairperson of the Commission through the Continental Early Warning System (CEWS). In event of grave magnitude, Article 13 of the Protocol provides that the African Standby Force (ASF) is established to deal with such eventualities.

111 J. Levitt, *The Law on Intervention: Africa's Pathbreaking Model*, Global Dialogue (2005), Volume 7, Number 1/2, available at <http://www.worlddialogue.org/content.php?id=330> [accessed on 27 October, 2014].

112 C. Ero, "ECOWAS and the Subregional Peacekeeping in Liberia", *The Journal of Humanitarian Assistance* (1995) available at <http://sites.tufts.edu/jha/archives/66> [accessed on 27 October, 2014]; P. Arthur, "ECOWAS and Regional Peacekeeping Integration in West Africa: Lessons for the Future", 57 *Africa Today* (2010), pp. 3; Levitt, *supra* n. 111.

113 K. Nowot & E. Schbacker, "The Use of Force to Restore Democracy: International Legal Implications of the ECOWAS Intervention in Sierra Leone", 14 *American University International Law Review* (1998) p. 312; Levitt, *supra* n. 111; Arthur, *supra* n. 112.

114 G. Yabi, *The Role of ECOWAS in Managing Political Crisis and Conflict: The cases of Guinea and Guinea-Bissau* (2010: Friedrich-Ebert-Stiftung, Nigeria); Levitt, *supra* n. 111.

115 Yabi, *supra* n. 114; Levitt, *supra* n. 111.

116 International Coalition for the Responsibility to Protect, The Crisis in Darfur, available at <http://www.responsibilitytoprotect.org/index.php/crises/crisis-in-darfur> [accessed on 27 October, 2014]; A. Keith, "The African Union in Darfur: An African Solution to a Global Problem?", 1 *Journal of Public and International Affairs* (2007) pp. 149.

117 T. Murithi, "The African Union's evolving role in peace operations: the African Union in Burundi, the African Union Mission in Sudan and the African Union Mission in Somalia", 17 *African Security Review* (Pretoria, South Africa: Institute for Security Studies, 2008) p. 70, (available at <http://www.issafrica.org/uploads/17NO1MURITHI.PDF> [accessed on 27 October, 2014]).

Burundi[118] and Somalia;[119] the SADC's intervention in the Democratic Republic of Congo[120] and Lesotho;[121] the AU's 2007 Electoral and Security Assistance Mission to the Comoros (MAES)[122] to facilitate a peaceful democratic transition of power as well as Operation Democracy to ensure democratic elections in the Comorian islands. While the challenges remain significant in view of the extent of conflict and internal displacement in Africa, it is most welcome that the problem does not lie in the absence of an established framework for dealing with the problem. While referring to what has been created in Africa as the "unambiguously ... the world's most legally coherent frameworks to combat conflict and regional security",[123] Levitt notes that "the willingness of African States to codify criteria for military intervention and openly to condemn in the continent's foremost political body undemocratic seizures of power is astounding"[124] and has "added significant weight to the development of the corpus of international law".[125]

---

118 A. Peen Rodt, "The African Mission in Burundi: The Successful Management of Violent Ethno-Political Conflict?", *Ethnopolitics Papers No. 10* (2011) available at <http://centres.exeter.ac.uk/exceps/downloads/Ethnopolitics%20papers_No10_peen%20rodt%20-%20> [accessed on 27 October, 2014]; B. Nowrojee, "Africa on its Own: Regional Intervention and Human Rights", in Human Rights Watch, *World Report 2004; Human Rights and Armed Conflict* (2004) pp. 37 ; Murithi, *supra* n. 117; Centre for Humanitarian Dialogue, *The AU and the search for Peace and Reconciliation in Burundi and Comoros* (2011) A joint report by the African Union and the HD Centre (available at <http://dspace.africaportal.org/jspui/bitstream/123456789/32201/1/The%20AU%20and%20the%20search%20for%20Peace%20and%20Reconciliation.pdf?1> [as of 27 October 2014]).

119 Murithi, *supra* n. 117.

120 Institute for Security Studies, "Hawks, Doves or Penguins: A critical review of the SADC military intervention in the DRC", *Institute for Security Studies Occasional Paper 88* (Pretoria, South Africa: Institute for Security Studies, 2004) p. 4; Nowrojee, *supra* n. 118.

121 Levitt, *supra* n. 111; compare F. Likoti, "The 1998 Military Intervention in Lesotho: SADC Peace Mission or Resource War?", 14 *International Peacekeeping* (2007), p. 251.

122 E. Svensson, "The African Union's Operations in the Comoros: MAES and Operation Democracy", FOI, Swedish Defence Research Agency Report Defence R-2659-SE (2008); Centre for Humanitarian Dialogue, *supra* n. 118, pp. 51–55.

123 Levitt, *supra* n. 111, para. 41; B. Kioko, "The right of intervention under the African Union's Constitutive Act: From non-interference to non-intervention", 85 IRRC December 2003. pp. 807–824.

124 Levitt, *supra* n. 111, para. 39.

125 Ibid., para. 41.

6 Conclusion

As shown in the previous sections, fields such as the rights of the child, the protection of refugee rights and internally displaced people, the right to development and regional intervention are illustrative of the willingness of the African continent not to confine itself to the existing international legal norms and to establish, instead, legal frameworks that take into account and address regional challenges and problems. Although the more progressive character of such legal frameworks may derive from regional needs and circumstances, it cannot be disputed that what African countries have achieved and the way in which they have addressed issues of interest to the whole international community is of relevance to the corpus of general international law and find applicability outside the African regional context.

Admittedly, the progressiveness, innovativeness and law-shaping potential of some of these initiatives are often overshadowed by challenges regarding the fulfilment of these commitments both and the national and regional levels. Such situation is a result of several factors, such as the problems of access to justice, a lack of political will and constitutional barriers to the implementation of international treaties and the limited access to justice. For example, the SADC Tribunal was suspended following its controversial decisions against Zimbabwe,[126] whereas the continent's commitment to intervention and the responsibility to protect was put into question in light of the responses by the African Union to the crisis in Libya.[127] There is no doubt that challenges and issues remain to be dealt with by African states. However, despite the existence of these challenges and problems, and regardless of the difficulties or non-implementation of these legal norms, the establishment of these legal framework for the protection of rights and for addressing issues in the fields discussed in this paper[128] is a crucial step in the providing holistic and effective regulation of the issues.

The adoption of progressive legal norms cannot have only regional impact. Such norms and rules, having been adopted and established by a great number of states of the international community, may be put forward by repre-

---

126 M. Hansungule, "The suspension of the SADC Tribunal", 35 *Strategic Review for Southern Africa* (2013), p. 135.

127 Alex Dewaal, "The African Union and the Libya Conflict of 2011" (online), 19 December 2012, available at http://sites.tufts.edu/reinventingpeace/2012/12/19/the-african-union-and-the-libya-conflict-of-2011/ (accessed on 10/12/2014). For further discussion, see V. Nmehielle, *infra* Ch. 27.

128 See also the other issues discussed by Judge Yusuf, *infra* Ch. 23.

sentatives of the African states or African non-state entities to international conferences, summits, international organisations and other relevant fora, in the same way as the right to development was brought forward by the Foreign Minister of Senegal at the United Nations General Assembly in the 1960s.[129] Africa's contribution to the evolution of international law – in the sense identified at the outset of this paper – is an undeniable reality.

---

[129] A. Sengupta, A. Negi, M. Basu (eds.), *Reflections on the Right To Development* (2006), p. 130.

CHAPTER 27

The African Union and Questions Arising from Efforts to Resolve the Ivorian and Libyan Conflicts

Vincent O. Nmehielle

1   Introduction

As eruditely observed by Judge Abdul G. Koroma of the International Court of Justice (ICJ) in his dissenting opinion on the question of the *Legality of the Threat or Use of Nuclear Weapons*[1] which the United Nations (UN) General Assembly asked the ICJ for an advisory opinion, "resort to peaceful means for the settlement of ... disputes" is a very important means of shielding humanity from the drastic consequences of war and violent conflicts. There is no part of the world today in more need of shielding humanity from violent conflicts and wars than in Africa. Post-colonial Africa has experienced series of conflicts that have resulted in untold suffering for innocent and poor African masses. Virtually every region of the continent has experienced some form of conflict – some more brutal and other less so since independence. In West Africa, Nigeria was involved in a brutal civil war just six years after independence.[2] In the early 1990s Liberia and Sierra Leone were each involved in decade-long deadly wars, the impact of which still makes them countries in post-conflict transi-

---

*   This chapter is based on earlier versions of a paper delivered at the Third Annual Lecture on Human Rights and Global Justice of the Center for International Law and Justice (CILJ), Florida A & M University College of Law, Orlando, Florida, USA on 10 November 2011, as the Inaugural Distinguished Scholar-in-Residence of the CILJ and a public lecture at St. Augustine's College, Victory Park, Johannesburg on 13 July 2011. The views expressed in this chapter are entirely those of the author and do not in any way represent the official or unofficial views or positions of the African Union or any of its organs.

1   *Legality of the Threat or Use of Nuclear Weapons*, Advisory Opinion of 8 July 1996. See ICJ Reports (1996), at p. 335.

2   The Nigerian civil war is commonly referred to as the Nigeria-Biafra war. Biafra represented the aspirations of the old Eastern Region of Nigeria to secede from Nigeria following the power struggle that ensued between the Hausa-Fulani of the then Northern Region and the predominantly Igbo Eastern Region after the toppling of the first civilian government in post-independent Nigeria.

tion.[3] Cote d'Ivoire's internal conflict began in 2002[4] and escalated at the close of 2010 following an electoral contest between former president Laurent Gbagbo and current president Alassane Quatara. The resolution of this particular conflict is an important aspect of this chapter in terms of the part played by the African Union and other entities. East Africa witnessed one of the most horrendous displays of humankind's inhumanity to humankind as exemplified by the Rwandan genocidal war of the early 1990s.[5] In the same vein, Burundi burned in conflict as well as Democratic Republic of Congo (DRC),[6] Central African Republic, Uganda and most recently, Kenya – another election-based conflict.[7] In the East Horn of Africa, the Ethiopian-Eritrean conflict has not fully abated. The complexity of Sudan's many conflicts remains a very serious burden for the continent.[8] Similarly, Somalia presented almost a hopeless situation that defies human logic and has resulted in the country being referred to either as a failed or a collapsed state.[9] While southern Africa has remained relatively stable, there are some concerns that what presently appears to be

---

3 For details on the Liberian war, see Levitt, Jeremy, The Evolution of Deadly Conflict in Liberia: From 'Parternaltarianism' to State Collapse (Carolina Academic Press, 2005); Jalloh, Charles & Marong Alhaji. J, Ending Impunity: The Case for War Crimes in Liberia 1 AJLS 53–78 (2005); Levitt, Jeremy, Humanitarian Intervention by Regional Actors in Internal Conflicts: The Case of ECOWAS in Liberia and Sierra Leone 12 Tem p. Int'l & Comp. L J. 333–375 (1998). On Sierra Leone's war, see Keen, David, Conflict and Collusion in Sierra Leone (Palgrave, New York 2005), Bartholomew, E.E, Constructing Durable Peace: Lessons from Sierra Leone 38 Cal. W. Int'l. L. J. 117–175 (2007), Levitt, Jeremy, Illegal Peace: An Inquiry into the Legality of Power-Sharing with Warlords and Rebels in Africa 27 Mich. J. Int'l L. 495–577 (2006).
4 See Lamin, A.R., The Conflict in Cote D'Ivoire: South Africa's Diplomacy and Prospects for Peace, Institute for Global Dialogue Occasional Paper No. 49, Johannesburg (2005).
5 It is now well known all over the world that Rwanda witnesses the worst genocide in recent history in a 100-day conflict between ethnic Hutus and Tutsis in 1994. Rwanda is still struggling to rebuild from the ravages of the conflict.
6 The Democratic Republic of Congo (DRC) has been engaged in conflict since the demise of President Mobutu Seseseko. The conflict has taken its toll on the ordinary people of the DRC.
7 The Kenya 2007/2008 post-election conflict is now a subject of the International Criminal Court's trial of the current president and deputy president of Kenya Uhuru Kenyatta and William Ruto as representative members of the feuding factions.
8 The long war between Northern and Southern Sudan that recently led to an independent South Sudan, the conflict within the larger Sudan as represented by the Darfur crisis; and most recently the conflict in an independent South Sudan (intra South Sudan conflict).
9 See Vincent O. Nmehielle and John-Mark Iyi, Nation Building, State Reconstruction, and Inclusiveness: Issues on South Sudan as a New State and Somalia as a Failed but Re-emerging State in Fostering Development through Opportunity, Inclusion and Equity: The World Bank Legal Review, Vol. 5 (2014), 483.

some mid-level crises may escalate to full conflicts in countries like Zimbabwe and Madagascar.

Until recently, North Africa (which most times is grouped with Middle Eastern states rather than with African states in global geopolitics) was tightly governed, giving less room to the kind of conflicts that engulfed the rest of Africa. However, the recent phenomenon in North Africa that has been described as the "Arab spring"[10] has shown that the region is not immune to violent conflicts. The "revolution" that started in Tunisia was successfully replicated in Egypt with relatively minor disturbances, but the same cannot be said of Libya. The uprising in Libya escalated to a civil war between the government of Muammar Gadaffi and then 'rebels' largely situated in Benghazi under the auspices of a National Transitional Council (TNC) but now the de jure government of Libya. This conflict was complicated by the quick involvement of the North Atlantic Treaty Organization (NATO) under the guise of United Nations Security Council's (UNSC) mandate.

It must be observed from the outset that African regional efforts have been largely instrumental in resolving or managing the resolution of a number of the African conflicts enumerated above, of course with assistance from a number of international actors and the United Nations (UN) – whether it is the Liberia, Sierra Leone, DRC, Burundi, or the Sudan conflicts. In this world of geopolitical interests, dealing with African conflicts has largely been left to Africa as exemplified by the regrettably slow response to the Rwandan genocidal war, the Sierra Leonean and Liberian wars, among others by the international community. What is, however, disturbing with regard to Libya is that the African Union was not allowed to play any significant or effective role in terms of concrete efforts at resolving the conflict. Also, the quick intervention of the NATO alliance in Africa is quite unusual and leaves one to wonder. It is either a sign of good things to come in terms of renewed concern for Africa's wellbeing by the international community, or it is a dangerous omen designed to undermine Africa's sovereign integrity from the point of view of individual countries, or the umbrella body of the continent – the African Union.

We must recall that one of the major reasons for the formation of the African Union was to deal with "the scourge of conflicts in Africa" which "constitutes a major impediment to the socio-economic development of the continent

---

10   A term that the media invented to characterize the wave of civil protests and demonstrations in North Africa and the Middle East that began in Tunisia when protesters forced the fall of the president Ben Ali's regime in late 2010. The protests later spilled into Egypt forcing the demise of the Mubarak regime and then to Libya and other Arab Countries.

and of the need to promote peace, security and stability as a prerequisite for the implementation of our development and integration agenda"[11] Furthermore, the founders of the African Union were driven by a determination "to promote and protect human and peoples' rights, consolidate democratic institutions and culture, and to ensure good governance and the rule of law."[12] In more concrete terms, a cardinal principle of the African Union that is enshrined in the Constitutive Act of the Union is "the right of the Union to intervene in a Member State pursuant to a decision of the Assembly in respect of grave circumstances, namely: war crimes, genocide and crimes against humanity."[13] Similarly, a Member State of the African Union has a right under Article 4 (j) to 'request intervention from the Union to restore peace and security." In the same vein, the African Union condemns and rejects "unconstitutional changes of government."[14] These principles would be elaborated on later.

This chapter therefore, examines the complex issues of resolving conflicts in Africa with particular focus on the Ivorian and Libyan conflicts in their recent ramifications. It is quite clear that the African Union played different roles in the two conflicts – one of which is relatively old – Ivory Coast and the other quite recent – Libya. Granted that the two conflicts present different sets of circumstances and challenges, it is, however, also true that they have serious impact on and ramifications for the peace, security and stability of the continent as well as adverse effect on the human rights of the peoples of the two countries because of how the resolution of these conflicts unfolded. This chapter, therefore, has more questions than answers regarding the various efforts at resolving the Ivorian and Libyan conflicts. Why did it appear as though the African Union spoke with one voice in condemning Laurent Gabagbo's continued hold on power after the run-off Presidential elections of 28 November 2010? Why did France participate with such zeal in the Ivorian crisis? Did the United Nations compromise its neutrality in an internal conflict? With regard to Libya, further questions also arise: what made the Libyan situation different from the Tunisian and the Egyptian 'revolutions"? Why did NATO feel obliged to act in Libya as fast as it did? Did the United Nations, and NATO, as the instrumentality of the UNSC ignore the African Union? Why did it appear as though the African Union was a late comer to the party in resolving the Libyan conflict?

---

11 Constitutive Act of the African Union, Preamble 8.
12 Ibid., Preamble 9.
13 Ibid., Article 4(h).
14 Ibid., Article 4(p).

The answers to these questions are not easy and I cannot pretend to exhaustively answer them in this chapter. Rather, I will only offer my individual opinion from the perspective of how, as an international law expert, I read global events relative to Africa and how I read the African Union as a continental body that is yet to fully deal with the challenges inherent in its reformation from a liberation-minded Organization of African Unity (OAU)[15] to the African Union, which among other things, resolved "to take up the multifaceted challenges that confront our continent and peoples in the light of the social, economic and political changes taking place in the world."[16]

II   Contextual Background to Africa's Organizational Resolution of Conflicts

In line with the United Nation's Charter,[17] which prescribes peaceful means in the settlement of disputes, African umbrella organizations tend to believe more in political solutions such as negotiation, mediation, arbitration and other less controversial means of resolving conflicts. Article 2(4) of the United Nations Charter provides that "All Members shall settle their international disputes by peaceful means in such a manner that international peace and security, and justice are not endangered." In the same vein, Article 2(4) of the Charter admonishes all its members to "refrain in their international relations from the threat or use of force against the territorial or political independence of any state, or in any other manner inconsistent with the Purposes of the United Nations." The OAU as the first post-colonial African inter-governmental entity espoused this admonition of the constitutive instrument of the UN and made it one of its cardinal principles as enshrined in its Charter.[18] In this regard, Article III (4) of the Charter of the OAU represents the affirmation of its members to pursue "Peaceful settlement of disputes by negotiation, mediation, conciliation, or arbitration." The product of the acceptance of this principle was the creation of a Commission of Mediation, Conciliation and

---

15   It is true that the OAU was more concerned with the struggle for self-determination of African states against colonial rule. The effort of the regional body was therefore focused on ensuring the liberation of all counties from colonial rule and any other form of racial oppression. The culmination of this was the end of the apartheid regime in South Africa when Nelson Mandela was elected as the first democratic president of South Africa in 1994.
16   Constitutive Act of the African Union, Preamble 5.
17   Charter of the United Nations, Art. 33.
18   See Maluwa, Tiyanjana, International Law in Post-Colonial Africa 233–257, at 233 (1999).

Arbitration in 1964, which was greeted with great optimism by African leaders of that era.[19] Unfortunately, the Commission failed to deliver on its mandate. In fact, it fizzled out of existence due to inactivity and lack of interest by those elected to the Commission and the states they represented.[20] With the death of the Commission peaceful settlement of disputes and conflicts under the OAU mechanism assumed the dimension of *ad hoc* arrangements, good offices and Heads of States diplomacy.[21] It was through these means that a number of the conflicts mentioned in the introduction above were either dealt with or their resolution was attempted.

In the early 1990s, the OAU came to a realization of its inability to adequately guarantee peace and security and to effectively resolve conflicts as a continental organ.[22] This led to the establishment in 1993 of a Mechanism for Conflict Prevention, Management and Resolution (MCPMR).[23] This was within the period the Rwandan war was raging, which ultimately led to the genocidal massacre of 1994 under the watch of a reluctant international community. Some commentators have observed that the weakness of the MCPMR was in its preoccupation with conflict prevention rather than resolution of already-occurred conflicts through some form of intervention, and their management.[24] As Levitt argues, the OAU's emphasis on conflict prevention under the mechanism could have been "because averting conflict is far less expensive than attempting to forestall it."[25] Ultimately, due to lack of resources, the MCPMR was not very successful in preventing and managing conflicts as opposed to attempts to preventing them. The result of this was that sub-regional entities

---

19 Ibid., at 238.
20 Ibid., 239.
21 Ibid., 239–240.
22 See Bakwesegha, Chris J, Conflict Situations in Africa in the Context of the OAU Mechanism for Conflict Prevention, Management and Resolution 3, a paper delivered at the Africa Center, London, United Kingdom on 22 November 1994 (on file with this Author).
23 The MCPMR was established pursuant to the Declaration on the establishment, within the Organization of African Unity (OAU), adopted by the 29th Ordinary Session of the Assembly of Heads of State and Government of the OAU, held in Cairo, Egypt, from 28 to 30 June 1993. See Preamble 2 to Protocol Relating to the Establishment of the Peace and Security Council of the African Union, adopted by the 1st Ordinary Session of the Assembly of the African Union in Durban on 9 July 2002.
24 Omorogbe, Eki Yemisi, Can the African Union Deliver Peace and Security? Journal of Conflict & Security Law (2011) 1–28, at 3. See also Levitt, Jeremy, Conflict Prevention, Management and Resolution: Africa – Regional Strategies for the Prevention of Displacement and Protection of Displaced Persons: The Cases of the OAU, ECOWAS, SADC and IGAD 11 Duke Journal of Comparative & International Law 39, at 55 (2001).
25 Ibid.

such as the Economic Community of West African States (ECOWAS) and the Southern African Development Community (SADC) stepped up their conflict prevention roles as African regional blocks.[26] The ECOWAS played a pivotal role in resolving the conflicts in Sierra Leone, Liberia as well as in Guinea Bissau; just as the SADC undertook to see to the resolution of the conflict in the DRC.[27]

Despite laudable good sub-regional conflict resolution efforts, it was clear to the OAU that if Africa was to join the rest of the world in post-cold war changes, something needed to be seriously done about the prevalent conflicts in the African continent. The Rwanda massacre was indeed a gaping sore in the legacy of African conflicts and such atrocities must therefore, not be allowed to occur elsewhere in Africa. The dissolution of the OAU and the birth of the African Union on 9 July 2002 in Durban promised a new direction in this regard, at least in the exhortation of the Constitutive Act of the African Union. Three important principles of the AU already mentioned in the earlier part of this chapter need reiterating, namely, 1) the principle in Article 4(h) of the Constitutive Act of the AU that endows it with the right "to intervene in a Member State pursuant to a decision of the Assembly in respect of grave circumstances, namely: war crimes, genocide and crimes against humanity"; 2) a Member State's right under Article 4 (j) to "request intervention from the Union to restore peace and security"; and 3) the Union's "condemnation and rejection of unconstitutional changes of government" under Article 4(p).

The first principle above is a clear indication that the AU, having at the back of its mind what happened in Rwanda, would intervene in a manner that is more likely with force than not, in a member state where "war crimes, genocide and crimes against humanity occur" as long as the Assembly of the AU makes a decision in this regard. Getting the Assembly to make that decision in proper determination of the circumstances is the crux of the matter. I submit that a proper application of the second principle could only mean circumstances where the member state that is seeking the intervention of the Union to restore peace and security is itself functioning under the rule of law and good governance but is being overrun or threatened by a lawless and illegal rebellion. Finally, the third principle which is related to the second in my view, presupposes that the condemnation and rejection of an unconstitutional change of government are based on the premise that the changed or threatened government itself is either a constitutional democracy and/or one that is delivering "good governance" to its citizenry as reasonably understood. The

---

26 Omorogbe, Eki Yemisi, *supra,* note 24, at 3.
27 Ibid.

promise of these interpretations, while yet to be realized, in my view, is a new Africa that has resolved to get it right in the enthronement of good governance, home-grown democracy and the rule of law.

Another development that whetted our appetite in this new Africa was the adoption of the Protocol Relating to the Establishment of the Peace and Security Council of the African Union at the founding of the AU in Durban. This Protocol established the Peace and Security Council of the African Union (AUPSC).[28] It is, in addition to Constitutive Act of the African Union, the centrepiece of what is commonly referred to as the peace and security architecture of the African Union, which replaced the MCPMR. According to Article 2(1) of the Protocol the AUPSC is "a standing decision-making organ for the prevention, management and resolution of conflicts" and is in essence, "a collective security and early-warning arrangement to facilitate timely and efficient response to conflict and crisis situations in Africa." In other words, the AUPSC should do for Africa what the UNSC does to the entire world under the auspices of the United Nations. It is the pivotal organ of the AU that should ensure and enforce peace and security in the continent. The promise of an African Standby Force under Article 13 of the Protocol conveyed an indication of a new resolve by the African Union to deal with threats to African peace and security in a manner that was lacking in the 39 years of the OAU before it was replaced by the "new" AU in 2002.

With all the new regional international legal and political prescriptions as well as the peace and security structures in place, the expectation would be that the AU ought to have a clear direction on how to deal with conflicts in Africa. The Ivorian and Libyan conflicts, among others, have, however, tested the regional body in this regard. The question then is whether the theory of the new African resolve as exemplified in the AU matches the practical application to conflict situations as represented by the two conflicts.

III The Ivorian and Libyan Conflicts in Context

A discussion on questions that arise from the resolution or attempts at resolving the Ivorian and Libyan conflicts cannot be complete without an overview of the conflicts, albeit briefly, in context. This is important because each of the conflicts will need to be understood in their different contexts in order for us

---

28 See Protocol Relating to the Establishment of the Peace and Security Council of the African Union, Art. 2, Adopted at the 1st Ordinary Session of the Assembly of the African Union in Durban on 9 July 2002.

to be able to address the roles played by the African Union and other entities in attempting to resolve the conflicts. Since the Ivorian conflict is in a way older than the Libyan conflict, it is better to start with it.

A   Ivory Coast

The death in 1993 of the first president and father of Ivory Coast's independence, Felix Houphouet Boigny who had ruled Ivory Coast for thirty-three years since independence from France in 1960 exposed the fragility of the country which resulted in political instability.[29] The political battle to succeed President Houphouet Boigny was fierce among his top lieutenants like Henri Konan Bedie who was the President of the Ivorian National Assembly and Alassane Ouattara, whom the president had brought from the International Monetary Fund (IMF) to become Prime Minister in 1990 to the dislike of many political elites.[30] At the end of the struggle Ouattara lost out to Bedie as successor to Houphouet Boigny in circumstances that Ouattara and his supporters labelled fraudulent.[31] One of the alleged concerns of the political elites regarding Ouattara was his mixed parentage – he is "partly Burkinabe and partly Ivorian", which though was thought to be a concern, was not presented as the main reason for the objection of some to his being prime minister under Houphouet Biogny but rather his closeness to "the Bretton Woods institutions."[32] However, with the emergence of Bedie as the President after Houphouet Boigny began what Lamin calls the "politics of exclusion" through which Bedie hoped to consolidate political power.[33] This was via a controversial constitutional amendment that introduced a citizenship law known as *Ivorite*" that was "designed to exclude certain segments of the (Ivorian) population from full participation in the political process." As pointed out by Lamin:

> According to the now infamous article 35 of the national constitution, anyone seeking to run for the presidency must first show that they were born in Côte d'Ivoire to parents who were also born to Ivorian nationals. In other words, contrary to practice where citizenship was defined by birth within Ivorian territory, to at least one parent of Ivorian nationality,

---

29   Lamin, Adbul, The Conflict in Ivory Coast: South Africa's Diplomacy and Prospects for Peace, 9–10, Occasional Paper 49, Institute for Global Dialogue, Johannesburg South Africa (2005).
30   Ibid., at 11.
31   Ibid.
32   Ibid.
33   Ibid., at 13.

under the new law the conditions were more stringent, excluding a vital segment of the population.[34]

Indeed *Ivorite* effectively excluded Ouattara and many others like him and frustrated his supporters who were mainly from the northern part of the country, which was dominated by Moslems. This law laid the foundation for the political instability that engulfed Ivory Coast between 2002 to the present. Bedie was, however, toppled in a military *coup d'etat* in 1992 and the military invited a former military chief of staff, General Robert Guei, who himself, as Chief of Army Staff, was removed by Bedie when he became president.[35] The emergence of Guei as a military leader was criticised by the Assembly of Heads of State and Government of the OAU, which at that time had already endorsed the normative shift whereby unconstitutional changes of government in Africa was condemned and rejected. The OAU thus put pressure on Guei to return Ivory Coast to democratic rule, which pressure bore fruit when Guei announced the holding of multiparty elections in October 2000.[36] Guei, however, did not repeal those aspects of the constitution that were "prejudicial" to those who aspired to the highest political office like Ouattara despite such a recommendation by a national commission that he set up "to review the constitution and the electoral code."[37] In the ensuing election, a number of prominent aspirants were disqualified and the presidency became a race between Guei and Laurent Gbagbo who had founded a socialist-leaning party, the Ivorian Popular Front (FPI) Party in 1982. Guei's attempt to use the military to force himself on Ivorians as the winner of the election resulted in mayhem occasioned by protests led "by youth brigades and militias loyal to Gbagbo," which made Guei to flee into exile and Gbagbo emerged as president[38] for a five-year tenure that should have ended in 2005 for fresh elections to be conducted.

Gbagbo's emergence as president was an opportunity to unify Ivorians, but it was not to be. Despite initially opposing *Ivorite*, when he was a candidate for the presidency, as president he maintained the status quo,[39] thus perpetuating the political exclusion that characterized post-Houphouet Boigny Ivory Coast and the attendant political instability.[40] Gbagbo's hold on power was

---

34 Ibid.
35 Ibid., at 15.
36 Ibid.
37 Ibid.
38 Ibid.
39 Ibid.
40 Ibid., at 16.

threatened by a military coup in 2002, while he was on travel overseas, which was eventually foiled. That coup laid the foundation for the civil war that engulfed Ivory Coast in 2002 "with the emergence of a rebel group known as New Forces or *Force Nouvelle*" that showed loyalty to Ouattara in a struggle that tended to pit the predominantly Moslem North against the predominantly Christian South[41] as represented by the aspirations of Ouattara and Gbagbo, respectively.

That Ivory Coast was in a state of civil war since 2002 under the presidency of Laurent Gbagbo is no longer news. The war had serious implications for Africa. France, which had long influenced the politics and the economy of Ivory Coast since Houphouet Boigny, stepped in, sending troops to protect its interests in Ivory Coast as well as trying to broker peace in its former colony. The French-brokered peace resulted in the Linas-Marcousis Accord in 2003 that had the backing of the African Union and the UN.[42] The Accord was, however, criticised by Gbagbo's supporters as granting too many political concessions to the opposing side, an act they attributed to France.[43] The Accord also provided "for disarmament, demobilization, and reintegration of armed combatants"[44] into a single Ivorian military or force. To monitor the observance of the accord, the UN established a peacekeeping mission in Ivory Coast in 2004.[45] Unfortunately, the implementation of the Linas-Marcousis Accord failed; little or no disarmament of combatants was achieved and the integration of the forces into a single force was not realized. This led the ECOWAS to facilitate "Accra I and II", which were aimed at making the "parties to engage each other and recommit themselves to the Linas-Marcousis Accord."[46] The failure of Accra I and II led to a broader AU initiative whereby former President Thabo Mbeki was mandated to lead AU's effort to resolve the conflict in November 2004.[47] Mbeki's effort yielded fruit in "the Pretoria Agreement of April 2005, which reinforced the prior agreements, charging the parties to reunify the country and the rebel 'New Forces to rejoin the power-sharing government," among other aspects such as "the disarmament and demobilisation of all armed combatants, and their reintegration into a national force."[48] These commitments were not honoured, resulting in a second Pretoria talks aimed at committing the

---

41 Ibid.
42 Ibid., at 18.
43 Ibid., 18–19.
44 Ibid., at 20.
45 Ibid.
46 Ibid.
47 Ibid.
48 Ibid., at 24–25.

parties to commence the disarmament of their forces with the hope of reaching an agreement on 20 August 2005 to provide ample time for scheduled elections in October 2005.[49]

Again, the hope of Ivorians for peace and that of Africans in general were dashed, as the security situation in the country made it impossible for the planned elections in October 2005 to be conducted.[50] Effectively Gbagbo remained in power as President while processes for peace designed to end the conflict between the parties, which were endorsed by the ECOWAS, the Peace and Security Council of the African Union and the United Nations and to enable the conduct of elections, were explored. These efforts continued unabated until there was a firm agreement on 29 November 2009 as the date for the first round of the presidential election.[51] President Gbagbo was quite upbeat about prospects in this regard. During "his address on the eve of the Côte d'Ivoire independence celebrations on 7 August (2009) ... " he "reaffirmed that there would be no more political obstacles to holding the presidential election as scheduled."[52] Unfortunately, the election was postponed again by the Independent Electoral Commission due to "delays in preparing and publishing the provisional electoral list."[53] The Commission hoped to hold the election either at the end of February 2 or the beginning of March 2010.[54] This was, however, shifted to 31 October 2010,[55] when the first round of the presidential election finally held.[56] From the provisional result of the election Gbagbo scored 38.04 percent, Ouattara garnered 32.07 percent and Bedie 25.24 percent. This meant that no candidate obtained the majority constitutionally required for an outright win in the first round.[57] The Ivorian Constitutional Council certified and validated the provisional result as announced by the Electoral Commission and declared Gbagbo and Ouattara as candidates for a run-off presidential election in a second round, as the highest scoring candidates but with none of them obtaining outright majority as required by the constitution.[58] Thus, "in keeping with paragraph 6 of Security Council resolution 1765 (2007), the Special Representative of the Secretary-General ... certified the

---

49 Ibid., at 26.
50 UN SG Report on Ivory Coast.
51 21st Report of the UNSG 4 (2009).
52 22nd Report of the UNSG to the UNSC 4 (2009).
53 23rd Report of the UNSG to the UNSC 2 (2010).
54 Ibid., at 3.
55 Progress Report of the UNSG 3 (2010).
56 See 26th Rep of the UNSG 3–7 (2010).
57 Ibid., at 6.
58 Ibid.

results of the first round of the presidential elections."[59] The stage was therefore set for a second round run-off presidential election between Gbagbo and Ouattara.

The run-off election took place on 28 November 2010. Prior to the election, Bedie called on his supporters to support Ouattara for the run-off. At the conclusion of the election supporters of Gbagbo and Ouattara alleged electoral malpractices against each other, despite the general acceptance of various observers that the election was relatively free and fair, taking into account where Ivory Coast was coming from – years of conflict. However, because of electoral grievances, on 30 November, a supporter of Gbagbo was alleged to have prevented an official of the Electoral Commission from announcing partial results of the election.[60] The Commission then submitted the provisional results to the Constitutional Council on 1 December and announced the provisional results on 2 December declaring that Ouattara scored 54.10 percent as against Gbagbo's 45.90 percent and a total voter turnout of 81 percent.[61] The President of the Constitutional Council claimed that the Electoral Commission "had missed the deadline for announcing the provisional results" and as such the provisional result as announced, was "null and void".[62] According to the United Nations Secretary-General:

> On 3 December, the President of the Constitutional Council proclaimed the final results of the presidential elections, with Laurent Gbagbo having received 51.45 per cent of the vote and Alassane Ouattara 48.55 per cent, and with a voter turnout of 71.28 per cent. Invoking alleged irregularities, including the use of violence, which had prevented people from voting, and the absence of the signatures of LMP representatives on the tally sheets, the Constitutional Council cancelled the election results received from seven departments in the north of the country – Bouaké, Dabakala, Katiola, Boundiali, Ferkessédougou, Korhogo and Séguéla – all of which had voted overwhelmingly for Mr. Ouattara.[63]

The United Nations Secretary-General's Representative in Ivory Coast, on the other hand, certified the provisional result as announced by the Electoral Commission.[64] In this regard, the United Nations contended that: "the final

---

59   Ibid., at 7.
60   27 Report of the UNSG 3 (2011).
61   Ibid., at 4.
62   Ibid.
63   Ibid.
64   Ibid.

results announced by the President of the Constitutional Council, which had proclaimed Mr. Gbagbo the winner of the second round, had not been based on facts."[65] It maintained that "even if the complaints of Mr. Gbagbo had been found valid, candidate Alassane Ouattara would still be the winner of the polls."[66]

The result of the confused state of things regarding the final result of the run-off election was a situation in which Gbagbo "took an oath of office before the Constitutional Council in Abidjan" on 4 December 2010,[67] while "Ouattara, in a letter dated 3 December to the Constitutional Council, explained that, owing to the prevailing exceptional circumstances, he was unable to take the oath of office before the Council and therefore was taking his oath in writing." Thus, the die was cast for a renewed conflict in Ivory Coast based on an election that the ECOWAS, the AU and the United Nations had prepared for – for ten (10) years and hoped would set the stage for the final end to the conflict in Ivory Coast. Thus, began another series of frantic efforts by the guarantors of the peace process in Ivory Coast to resolve the new stalemate of 2011 following a brutal armed conflict between the Forces Nouvelle in support of Ouattara and the Ivory Coast Army in support of Gbagbo. Also engaged in the conflict in some sense were French forces as well as UN Peacekeeping forces that have had an operation in Ivory Coast from 2004 since the initial breakout of conflict in 2002. Attempts at resolving the most recent major conflict and how it was seemingly resolved would be dealt with later.

B Libya

The modern history of Libya begins with its independence on 24 December 1951 pursuant to a United Nations General Assembly Resolution of 21 November 1949 that had authorised the independence of the country from the domination of Italy before 1 January 1952.[68] Thus, in 1951, Libya became "the first country to achieve independence through the United Nations and one of the first former European possessions in Africa to gain independence."[69] On gaining independence, Libya became "a constitutional and a hereditary monarchy" as proclaimed by King Idris I, who was Libya's representative during the nego-

---

65   Ibid.
66   Ibid.
67   Ibid.
68   See US Department of State's Bureau of Near Eastern Affairs Background Note on Libya of 17 November 2010 on file with this Author. Also available at http://www.state.gov/r/pa/ei/bgn/5425.htm (accessed 10 July 2011 and o 10 October 2014) (Hereafter, Background Note on Libya).
69   Ibid.

tiations at the United Nations.[70] At the time of independence Libya was a very poor country until oil was discovered in 1959, which over the years changed the fortune of the country, making it "extremely wealthy, as measured by per capita GDP"[71] due its small population.

King Idris was overthrown on 1 September 1969 in a military coup led by a young Captain Muammar Gadaffi, who abolished the monarchy and established the Libyan Arab Republic, which would later be renamed "Great Socialist People's Libyan Arab Jamahiriya" in 1977 under the Revolutionary Command Council (RCC) with him as 'Leader'.[72] The new government had no formal structures of governance as understood in many other states. The regime espoused a mix of socialism, Arab nationalism and Islam as its political philosophy as elaborated in "The Green Book" – Gadaffi's "personal manifesto."[73] The country was governed by peoples' committees or bureaus.

Whatever the case, it is important to observe that the people of Libya saw steady growth and development based on their oil wealth that was tightly controlled by Gadaffi under his socialist and Arab-Islamic nationalist persuasions. As one commentator puts it:

> The arrogant and unorthodox Libyan leader, Colonel Qhadaffi has fairly done well for his Libyan people and did in fact use his country's oil wealth to advance and improve the material living condition of his people. Those who have visited Libya confirmed to this writer that despite his lunatic characteristics and pathological obsession with anti-imperialism and anti-America and his special predilection for fomenting conflicts in his sister African countries, Col Qhadaffi ... has done well for his Libyan people.[74]

Indeed the complexity and the enigmatic personality of Gadaffi did not win him many friends, particularly in the West. He was branded a supporter of terrorists, the result of which was the bombing of his residence by the Regan administration in 1986 as well as sanctions by that administration – sanctions

---

70 Ibid.
71 Ibid.
72 Ibid.
73 See History of Libya. *Available at*: http://www.historyworld.net/wrldhis/PlainTextHistories.asp?historyid=aa83 (accessed 10 July 2011 and on 10 October 2014). (Hereafter, History of Libya).
74 Clement Chigbo, commenting on the Libyan conflict. See http://saharareporters.com/article/libyan-conflict-perspective-clement-chigbo (Accessed 10 July 2011).

that remained throughout other successive American administrations.[75] Libya was accused of orchestrating and implicated in the Lockerbie bombing of Pan Am flight 103 in 1988, leading to UN sanctions in 1992 that politically and economically isolated Libya up to late 1990s. From 1999 Gadaffi began to turn a new leaf, from surrendering suspects in the Pan Am bombing, paying compensation for the victims of the bombing to riding Libya of weapons of mass destruction[76] and other such requirements. This brought Libya back into the good books of the West, resulting in the normalization of diplomatic and trade relations with the United States, the United Kingdom, France, etc, all of which had been dying to do business with the oil rich country – only hoping that Gaddafi would behave, which he finally did. From 2003, Libya was virtually a friendly country to the West even though he had been in power since 1969. There were hardly any noticeable political disturbances in Libya until the "Arab Spring" that began on 18 December 2010.

The "Arab Spring" that began in Tunisia, swept through Egypt and reverberated in Libya and other Arab lands brought new realities to Libya and Ghadaffi, the signs of which one can say Gadaffi clearly failed to read properly. On 15 February 2011, nationwide protests began in Libya and soon metamorphosed into an uprising and an armed rebellion under the auspices of the then NTC, which were met with violent response by Gadaffi and his government. The presumed NTC's main objective was to overthrow Gadaffi and his regime that had been in power for over 41 years and to lead Libya into a "democratic" dispensation. The brutal nature of the conflict in Libya attracted the attention of the United Nations, which pursuant to the UNSC Resolution 1970 of 26 February 2011 froze the assets of Gadaffi and a number of his lieutenants and imposed a number of sanctions, including arms embargo. The Resolution also referred the situation in Libya to the International Criminal Court for Investigation. Due to continued and unabated use of force, the UNSC adopted Resolution 1973 under its Chapter VII on 11 March 2011, which imposed a "no fly zone" over Libya with the aim of protecting civilians in the conflict. This Resolution became the basis for NATO allied countries to bomb and bombard Tripoli in apparent support of the NTC for a regime change (though explained away as humanitarian intervention to protect civilians) as a way of resolving the conflict. Finally, a pre-trial chamber of the ICC issued indictments against Gadaffi, his son and his brother-in-law for crimes against humanity.

---

75   See History of Libya, *supra*, note 73.
76   See Background Note on Libya.

IV   The African Union and Measures Taken to Resolve the Ivorian and Libyan Conflicts

The importance of this chapter is anchored on an evaluation of the measures that were taken or are being taken to resolve the Ivorian and Libyan conflicts relative to the role, perceived role or stance of the Africa Union. In this regard, it is necessary to answer the questions that we asked at the beginning of the chapter. With regard to the Ivory Coast, we asked the following questions – 1) why did the African Union speak with one voice in condemning Laurent Gbagbo's continued hold on power after the run-off Presidential elections of 28 November 2010. 2) Why did France participate with such zeal in the Ivorian crisis? 3) Did the United Nations compromise is neutrality in an internal conflict?

Regarding the AU's stance that Gbagbo had to go, some may argue that the AU did not initially speak with one voice in terms of what should be done until the ECOWAS, the 15-member sub-regional block in West Africa took a firm stand and called on Gbagbo to hand over power to Ouattara as the rightful winner of the election. The ECOWAS took a further step in suspending Ivory Coast from the body and threatened the use of military force against Gbagbo. This was against the background of the ECOWAS's principled and continued lack of tolerance for attempts to thwart democratic processes in the region given the regional body's experience in Sierra Leone and Liberia, among others. The African Union had to defer to the sub-regional bloc. It thus followed suit to suspend Ivory Coast from AU activities until the installation of the rightful winner of the election as president. In furtherance of the use of regional communities as the building blocks of AU's action, it was important for it to close ranks with the ECOWAS, which step served to reinforce and emphasize the AU's own ideals of respect for and endorsement of constitutional change of government as against an unconstitutional change of government under its constitutive Act. The practical realities of the Ivory Coast situation would also have worked on the minds of the AU Assembly due to the fact that under Gbagbo the presidential election had been continuously shifted during a process that lasted for five years after the expiration of his initial five year period in 2005. The situation warranted some kind of political "risk" on the part of the AU to dispense with Gbagbo who had rejected the counsel of emissaries from both the ECOWAS and the AU.

President Thabo Mbeki, a prominent player in the resolution of the Ivorian conflict, as an AU envoy was at odds with the way the Ivorian conflict was handled by the international community including the AU.[77] He opines that the

---

[77]   Thabo Mbeki, What the World got Wrong in Côte D'Ivoire, Foreign Policy 29 April

international community did not properly evaluate whether the 2010 elections "would create the conditions that would establish the basis for the best possible future for the Ivorian people."[78] He blamed the AU for failing "to assert itself to persuade everybody to work to achieve reconciliation among the Ivorians, and therefore durable peace."[79] He observes that "tragically, the outcome that has been achieved in Cote d'Ivoire further entrenches the conflict in this country".[80]

While I have no doubt that the former President Mbeki has a genuine concern for wellbeing of Ivory Coast, it is important to point out that the Ivorian people finally needed a definitive rallying point to start reconciliation talks that continuously failed under an atmosphere of a questionable government mandate and legitimacy. That point had to be in a definite outcome of the presidential election that is not based on the now-in – vogue power arrangement whereby a loser of an election continues to lay hold on power in the hope that he would at worst, share power. Of course, I accept as true, the fact that the position of the parties may remain entrenched, which is expected in a conflict that had lasted for almost 10 years without any meaningful resolution. One would expect that president Ouattara would exercise utmost wisdom in ensuring that nothing else matters than the unity of Ivory Coast and sincerely tackle the uphill task of effective and enduring national reconciliation. A one-sided referral of atrocities that were allegedly committed during the Ivorian conflict to the ICC as is currently the case, among other such decisions, has a bearing on any meaningful reconciliation. While the establishment of a Truth and Reconciliation Commission by the Ouattara government is one step toward dealing with the past and possibly achieving some reconciliation and redress, it is important for the process to be credible and that its recommendations should be implemented.

The second question on why France participated with such zeal in the Ivorian conflict must be answered within the context that president Mbeki properly articulates it – French economic interests in Ivory Coast – "its former colony".[81] It is an open secret that Gbagbo was a critic of undue French influence in Ivorian politics. I agree with Mbeki that France overplayed its hand in

---

2011. *Available at* http://www.foreignpolicy.com/articles/2011/04/29/what_the_world_got_wrong_in_cote_d_ivoire?wp_login_redirect=0 [Accessed 15 August 2011].
78   Ibid.
79   Ibid.
80   Ibid.
81   Ibid.

this conflict using "its privileged position in the (UN) Security Council".[82] The manner in which French soldiers participated in direct war in Ivory Coast and the disgraceful capture of Gbagbo with the assistance of its soldiers, smacks of colonial conquest. President Ouattara has a huge challenge in dispelling the perception that he is a stooge of France. There was no greater need for the African Union's Standby Force (ASF) than for the situation that Ivory Coast faced within that period. The AFS would have been a more appropriate force within AU mechanisms to handle the situation. One would expect that such a force would be made up of contingents from the ECOWAS, the affected regional bloc. This presupposes that important and much stronger countries such as Nigeria and Ghana, among others, would not be opposed to the deployment of their armies to restore civility in Ivory Coast. Any such opposition would only weaken the ECOWAS resolve to end the conflict and would convey a lack of unanimous and common position in Africa for dealing with conflicts of this nature.

Lastly on Ivory Coast, the question whether the UN had compromised its neutrality in an internal conflict as peacekeepers, President Mbeki believes so. According to him, the Special Representative of the United Nations Secretary-General exceeded his mandate when he certified the election result and declared the winner.[83] For the esteemed former President of South Africa, this "positioned the UN Mission in Cote d'Ivore (UNOCI) as a partisan in the Ivorian conflict, rather than a neutral peacemaker, equidistant from the belligerent parties."[84] Indeed, the United Nations Mission in Ivory Coast was required to be neutral in its handling of the process. If it did not, it compromised the neutrality of the UN as a peacemaker. However, a close examination of UNSC Resolution 1880 of 30 July 2009 clearly authorized the Representative of the Secretary-General to certify the electoral process. According to the resolution:

> The Security Council ... Acting under Chapter VII of the Charter of the United Nations ...
>
> 7. *Reiterates* that the Special Representative of the Secretary-General shall certify that all stages of the electoral process provide all the necessary guarantees for the holding of open, free, fair and transparent presidential and legislative elections in accordance with international standards and

---

82 Ibid.
83 Ibid.
84 Ibid.

reaffirms its full support to the Special Representative of the Secretary-General in his certification role;

8. *Stresses* that it will base its assessment of the electoral process on the certification that will be prepared by the Special Representative consistent with the five-criteria framework referred to in document S/2008/250 and after inclusive contacts with all stakeholders in Côte d'Ivoire, including the civil society;

There is no doubt that the UN is a political body and that often political considerations impact decisions that it makes. However, the case of the Ivorian elections should be put into the context of a ten-year old conflict that was principally based on what could be termed the manipulation of the constitution to exclude some sections of Ivorians on the basis of their birth. The continued lack of acceptance of the rightful birth of any Ivorian in his or her quest to aspire to the highest office in accordance with the constitution portended danger for the stability of the Ivory Coast as country and Africa in general, and must therefore not be allowed by the guarantors of the peace process. That the ECOWAS and the AU spoke out firmly in support of a democratic process in Ivory Coast cannot be oversimplified. There was a need to take a stand on the Ivorian crisis that accorded with the principles enshrined in the Constitutive Act of the AU that promotes constitutional changes of African governments rather than unconstitutional changes of such governments. That does not necessarily mean that the AU condones or accepts the excesses of France in its role in Ivorian conflict.

Resolving the Libyan conflict on the other hand, posed more challenges than many commentators were prepared to accept. I submit that attempts at resolving the Libyan conflict must be evaluated by sincerely answering the questions that we posed above relative to Libya, which I repeat here: 1) what makes the Libyan situation different from the Tunisian and the Egyptian 'revolutions"? 2) Why did NATO feel obliged to act in Libya as fast as it did? 3) Did the United Nations, and NATO, as the instrumentality of the UNSC ignore the African Union? 4) Why does it appear that the African Union was a late comer to the party in resolving the Libyan conflict? There is yet another question – why was Libya treated differently compared to Syria and Yemen by the UNSC at the time?

In terms of the similarities and differences between the Libyan uprising and the initial revolutions in Tunisia and Egypt, they are similar in one respect: they represented a quest and demand for political reforms from governments that may have been in power longer than necessary. The Libyan conflict in my view was, however poles apart from the former in terms of the violent responses from both sides. Gadaffi was unwise in violently responding to the protesters, having just watched the Tunisian and Egyptian situations unfold. In the same vein, the sudden arming of the then Libyan protesters in Benghazi and the transformation of the protests to an armed uprising appear to set it apart from the others. Could it be that the protest was an armed insurrection in disguise that may have been instigated by powers foreign to Libya from the outset? Given current realities, any observer and student of international law and international affairs can draw his or her own conclusions.

While the execution of NATO's military action under UNSC Res 1973 that imposed a no-fly zone over Libya could be an adherence to the new principle of the responsibility of the international community to protect civilians when a state cannot or fails to protect its own citizens, the UN and NATO failed to seek peaceful means of resolving the conflict as they did in Egypt. In assuming the responsibility to protect, the United Nations and its NATO allies should have used military force only as a last resort when all other means had failed. The enforcement of a no-fly zone should not have amounted to a bombardment of the house of the head of state. That was more like an orchestrated plan to get rid of an individual for whatever reason. Similarly, the enforcement of a no-fly zone did not give NATO allies authority to flout UNSC Resolution 1970 that placed an arms embargo over Libya. There was evidence that France was arming the then NTC by dropping arms and ammunition from the air while the arms embargo was subsisting.

I also submit that the UN and NATO ignored the African Union as a regional body that remained central to resolving the conflict irrespective of the misgivings that the West may have about the African Union. The UN and NATO rather pitched their tent with the Arab League. Important member states of the AU such as Nigeria and South Africa, as non permanent members of the UN Security Council participated in the UNSC Resolutions 1970 and 1973 and thus could not be accused of not wanting to hold Gaddafi (one of their own) accountable. The very fact that they participated in that process was enough reason for NATO to seriously consult with the African Union on finding lasting solution to the conflict. In my view, the reason why Nigeria and South Africa as well Gabon voted in favour of the of Resolutions 1970 and 1973 was to create an atmosphere for meaningful engagement with the parties for a peaceful resolution of the Libyan conflict as mandated by the UN Charter and the Constitutive Act of the African Union. NATO had little regard for the African Union as a continental body that would eventually be saddled with the political aftermath of a destroyed Libya. The current realities of Libya give credence to this view on the importance of the African Union in the resolution of the Libyan conflict.

On the part of the African Union, I agree with President Mbeki that "the popular uprisings" in "Tunisia, Egypt and Libya took the whole of Africa by surprise"[85] just as it took the rest of the world. Yet, the African Union embarked on a series of initiatives to find a way forward to tackle the ensuing conflict in its region even before the UN and NATO. It therefore begs the question why the African Union is touted as a late comer to resolving the Libyan Conflict. We need to recall that protests began in Libya on 15 February 2001. Eight days later on 23 February 2011, the Peace and Security Council of the AU met on the situation in Libya and took a decision that condemned "the indiscriminate and excessive use of force and lethal weapons against peaceful protestors, in violation of human rights and International Humanitarian Law, which continues to contribute to the loss of human life and the destruction of property."[86] The decision further called for the protection of civilians and emphasized "that the aspirations of the people of Libya for democracy, political reform, justice and socio-economic development are legitimate' and that they should be respected by the government.[87] The AUPSC at that meeting resolved to send a mission to Libya "to assess the situation on the ground."[88] The above decision of the AU did not receive any publicity, or as Mbeki puts it

> in reality the international media virtually ignored the AU PSC decisions. Rather the world was exposed to the dramatic television images of what was happening in Libya and the public communications of the actors in this drama, including those of Colonel Muammar Gaddafi and his son, Saif al-Islam. In other words, the AU and therefore African message withered on the vine, making no impact whatsoever on African and world opinion of what might be done to resolve the conflict in Libya."[89]

The UNSC Resolution 1970 that referred the situation in Libya to the ICC and placed arms embargo on Libya was passed on 26 February 2011 on the heels of the earlier AUPSC decision.

---

85   Thabo Mbeki's Letter on Libya (Libya and African Self-Determination, available at https://lakkal.wordpress.com/2011/04/29/thabo-mbekis-letter-on-libya/ (Last Accessed 10 October 2014) (hereinafter, Mbeki on Libya).
86   AU Peace and Security Council 261st Meeting Communiqué of 23 February 2011, Addis Ababa, Ethiopia, PSC/PR/COMM (CCLXI), para. 2.
87   Ibid., para. 5.
88   Ibid., para.6.
89   Mbeki on Libya.

In further engagement to find a way to resolve the Libyan crises, the AUPSC on 10 March 2011 reaffirmed its earlier decision and condemned "the indiscriminate use of force" and proposed a roadmap based on a

> conviction that the current situation in Libya calls for an urgent African action for: (i) the immediate cessation of all hostilities, (ii) the cooperation of the competent Libyan authorities to facilitate the timely delivery of humanitarian assistance to the needy populations, (iii) the protection of foreign nationals, including the African migrants living in Libya, and (iv) the adoption and implementation of the political reforms necessary for the elimination of the causes of the current crisis;[90]

As part of the roadmap, the AU PSC decided to constitute a five-nation 'AU Ad Hoc High Level Committee on Libya' at Heads of State level with a mandate to ensure an inclusive dialogue among the warring parties in Libya on the reforms necessary that could lead to peacefully resolving the conflict.[91] It was clear in its decision that the AU PSC rejected "any foreign military intervention, whatever its form."[92]

As the world watched, on 17 March 2011, which was exactly a week after, the UN Security Council passed its Resolution 1973, prescribing the "foreign military intervention" that Africa, speaking through the AUPSC, earlier rejected.[93] As underscored by Mbeki,

> the historical fact is that as should have been the case, the African Union moved ahead of the United Nations in terms of prescribing what should be done to address the Libyan, and therefore African, crisis. The reality, however, was that the UN Security Council made absolutely certain that it ignored the views of the African Continent about what needed to be done to resolve a crisis in a member state of the AU. This was later emphasised by the refusal of the UN to allow the AU Ad Hoc Committee to visit Tripoli and Benghazi on March 18 and 19 respectively, to promote a peaceful resolution of the Libyan crisis, precisely to reduce the loss of human lives while promoting democratic rule in Libya. This meant that had the

---

90   AU Peace and Security Council 265th Meeting Communiqué of 10 March 2011, Addis Ababa, Ethiopia, PSC/PR/COMM (CCLXV), para. 5; 7.
91   Mbeki on Libya, *supra*, note 85.
92   Ibid.
93   Ibid.

African peacemakers flown to Libya to carry out their mission, they stood the danger of their planes being shot down![94]

It cannot therefore, be said that the AU in actuality was a late comer to resolving the Libyan conflict. The AU was rather ignored from the beginning. This is quite worrying given Africa's colonial past.

I posit that the disdain for Gadaffi as an individual based on years of accumulated hatred for him coupled with oil-based economic interest fuelled the alliance between the US, Britain and France to see the end of Gadaffi more than the enthronement of democratic governance in Libya. Few months prior to the Arab Spring many of these leaders from were dancing around Gadaffi for trade deals. The current realities in Libya where state failure appears imminent are a clear testimony to what went wrong in the NATO intervention in Libya. That Gadaffi, a prisoner of war, could be executed and his body displayed in mockery for days with the blessing of leaders of the United States, France and the United Kingdom is international humanitarian law turned on its head. Some of us cannot wait to see the Prosecutor of the ICC lunch investigations on how Gadaffi was killed and bring to book those who may have violated international humanitarian law.

There is then the question why Libya was treated differently from how the Syrian conflict is currently being treated and how the Yemeni situation was treated. In the case of Syria, there is hardly any agreement on how the UN should proceed; not even an agreement on the wording of a UNSC resolution. On Yemen, the UNSC Resolution 2014 made mockery of what the UN and NATO did in Libya. This shows nothing but the hypocrisy and double standards of the international community in the practice of international law relative to Africa or other supposedly weak parts of the world. The often neglected issue in these kinds of exercise of big power is that the innocent ordinary people are left to bear the brunt rather than being shielded from catastrophe brought about by wars and conflicted in the spirit of Judge Koroma's dissenting opinion.

V   Conclusion

From the reality on the ground, resolving African conflicts will continue to be a challenge. The Ivorian and Libyan conflicts are recent manifestations of this challenge. It is indeed challenging for the African Union to live its new ideals as enshrined in the Constitutive Act of the Union if leaders hold tight to office

---

94   Ibid.

even when their ideologies and philosophies have clearly lost meaning. It will only serve to dampen the credibility of the AU's new ideals of an African renaissance. The yearning of all Africans is that the African Union should collectively speak with one voice in furtherance of democratic governance that caters to the collective wishes of the people. In its resolve to finding lasting solutions to the various conflicts on the continent, the early warning systems must be sensitive to triggers of conflict as in the sudden Arab Spring.

On the other hand, the international community must accept that Africa has the greatest stake in resolving conflicts on the continent irrespective of the resource challenges that it faces. There must be a partnership that does not undermine the sovereignty of the individual states in the continent or the sovereignty of the African Union as representative body of those states as a collective. Any insensitive action or policy in that regard would only lead to governance tensions in the continent, as those leaders would see themselves as standing against colonial tendencies. NATO and its allies should have come to the table with the AU on its roadmap for effectively resolving the Libyan conflict. It should not have been about Gadaffi, but the Libyan people. Destroying Libya because of Gadaffi made absolutely no sense. More importantly, as eruditely reasoned by our esteemed Judge Abdul Koroma, humanity must be shielded from the destruction that flows from violent conflicts and wars through the exercise of the option of peaceful settlement of disputes and conflicts.

CHAPTER 28

Democratic Succession in Africa: Enhancing Orderly Transition through the African Charter on Democracy, Elections and Governance

Lydia A. Nkansah

1   Introduction

Mankind's quest for good governance has yielded all forms of political organisations in different epochs in the political history of the world. This ranges from different shades of authoritarianism to democracy and socialism. In modern times, democracy is seen as being effective in safeguarding the fundamental human rights of citizens,[1] although the evidence for this assertion is mixed.[2] With the collapse of communism in Eastern Europe, democracy is considered unparalleled to any form of government and is believed to have brought an end to the history of the world as far as political organisations are concerned. Thus, democracy as a political value permeates through major international and regional instruments.[3] Africa's first democratic wave started at the inception of independence of several African countries from colonial domination. However, columns 2–5 on the attached Table 28.1 shows that there

---

1   For example, Article 36(2) (e) of the Constitution of Ghana states "The State shall, in particular, take all necessary steps to establish a sound and healthy economy whose underlying principles shall include – the recognition that the most secure democracy is the one that assures the basic necessities of life for its people as a fundamental duty". Articles 2(1) & 3(1) of the African Charter on Democracy, Elections and Governance, 2007 links democracy with human rights, likewise Article 7 of the Inter-American Democratic Charter.

2   Bohman, J. (2010) Introducing Democracy across Borders: From Demos to Demoi, *Ethics and Global Politics*, 3 (1), pp. 1–11; Gilbert, A. (2010). Equal rights as centre of democratization, *Ethics and Global Politics,* 3(1), 55–70; Ojakorotu, V. (2009). From "Authoritarian Rule" to "Democracy" in Nigeria: Citizens' Welfare a Myth or Reality. *Journal of Alternative Perspective in the Social Sciences, 1*(2), 152–192.

3   See Article 4 of the UN Charter, 1945; Article 21 of the International Covenant on Civil and Political Rights (ICCPR). Article 8 of the International Covenant on Economic, Social and Cultural Rights; the preamble to the African Charter on Human and People's Rights, 1981/1986; The Protocol to the African Charter on Human and People's Rights on the Rights of Women in Africa, 2003/2005; The African Union Constitutive Act 2000/2001.

was a reverse wave on the continent and several states drifted into autocracy shortly after becoming independent by becoming a one party state, or suffered a coup d'état or a combination of both.[4] For example, within the West African sub-region, Senegal is the only country which has not experienced a coup d'état. Similarly all the countries in East Africa at independence introduced multi-party systems, but all in no time became one party/authoritarian states.[5] Others produced dominant leaders who used their huge majority in parliament to make constitutional amendments to retain them in power by increasing or removing term limits.

Africa's second democratisation wave started at the end of 1989. Since the 1990s, African states have committed themselves to the institutionalization of democratic governance individually and collectively through regional and continental inter-governmental bodies.[6] At the continental level, the African Union (AU) has been in the driving seat for the democratisation of the continent since its inception in 2000. In Article 4 of its Constitutive Act, the AU has committed its Member States to democratic principles. Since the inception of the AU in 2000, the momentum of democratisation throughout the continent has been accelerated. The past two decades have witnessed several countries on the continent embarking on democratisation processes,[7] as Column 6 on Table 28.1 depicts. The process from autocracy to the path of democratization differed from country to country. In countries like Ghana, Burkina Faso and Togo, the military juntas metamorphosed into political parties to contest elections to form government.[8] In Liberia, Sierra Leone and others the aftermath of civil unrest and/or civil war saw the institutionalisation of democracy as part of the post-conflict reconstruction projects, whereas civil demonstrations and/

---

[4] Keller, E.J. (2007). Africa in Transition: Facing the Challenges of Globalization. *Harvard International Review: Social Science Module,* 29(2). 46–51.

[5] Wariobo, J.S. (2006). Political Succession in East Africa. In Peter, C.M. and Kopsieker, F. (Ed.), *Political Succession in East Africa: In Search for a Limited Leadership* (pp. 1–11) Friedrich Ebert Stiftung: Kenya, pp. 2–3.

[6] See, Article Art 4(m-p) of the Constitutive Act of the African Union (2000/2001). The Declaration on the Principles Governing Democratic Elections in Africa, 2002), The African Charter on Democracy, Elections and Governance, 2007.

[7] Moise, A. Adjangba (1999). Democratic Transition and African Renaissance in sub-Saharan Africa. *International Journal on World Peace,* 16(3), pp. 45–58, p. 47.

[8] See Banjor, A. (2008), Constitutional and Succession Crisis in West Africa: The Togo case. *The Journal of Legal Studies,* pp. 147–161. p. 149; Nkansah, L.A. Transfer of Power to a New Administration in Ghana's Democratic System: The Way Forward, Paper presented at the Fourth European Conference on African Studies, under the theme 'Africa's Engagement: On Whose Terms', organized by The Nordic Africa Institute from June 14–18, 2011 in Uppsala, Sweden.

or civil wars brought down long standing dictators in the Middle East. The underlying triggers for this transformation have been identified as globalisation and the end of the cold war, which relaxed the Western World and shifted their attention to the Third World Countries. The upsurge of information technology which opened the Third World to the liberties of the Western political societies/cultures inspired those oppressed by dictators to 'fight' to free themselves.[9] These triggers may also be linked to the historical struggles in the past which culminated in the adoption of the Magna Carter of 1215 in England which spurred revolutions in other parts of the World in their quest for freedom and protection of rights.[10]

The core element in democracy is the requirement of periodic elections. This happens when a change of the principal leader with personnel decision making power of hiring and firing as well as that of policy making occurs within the contemplation of the law. Succession involves a change in administration namely (a) the taking over by a new leader of the machinery of government, (b) the taking over of the administration of the country and (c) acquiring the status of the maximum leader. The outgoing leader relinquishes all of these. In its ramification, it involves transfer of power and administrative functions and responsibilities and national assets at the national, regional and district levels as the case may be.[11]

Succession is thus inevitable in the ongoing democratisation process in Africa. It covers policies, structures, processes, and procedures for electing the leader, for the outgoing to hand over the machinery of government to the incoming, and the incoming to take over power to form a government and the legal, political and socio-economic consequence of the appearance of a new president. The dynamics occasioned in each of these phases of succession may resonate positively or negatively to enhance or threaten democracy.

The experience of democratic succession in Africa is akin to a military takeover. In Ivory Coast, Uganda, Kenya, Zimbabwe, Sudan, Togo and others the process of determining the next leader has resulted in political upheavals and civil wars in some cases. The Council for Development and Social Research in Africa (CODESRIA) and Open Society Initiative for West Africa (OSIWA) in a study identified the politics of succession as a source of discontent in the West Africa sub-region.[12]

---

[9] See Moise, A. Adjangba (1999). Democratic Transition and African Renaissance in sub-Saharan Africa. *International Journal on World Peace*, 16(3), pp. 45–58, p. 47.

[10] Ibid.

[11] Ahwoi, K. (2009a). Towards a Peaceful Political and Administrative Transitions in Ghana. The Institute of Economic Affairs Policy Brief Number 2.p. 4).

[12] Cited in Banjor, A. (2008). Constitutional and succession crisis in West Africa: The Togo case. *The Journal of Legal Studies*, pp. 147–161. p. 149.

The difficulties with democratic successions in Africa notwithstanding, some writers to dismiss it as not worthy of study because there is "no ideological component to African government and succession" due to "personalism in African politics". They argued that government in Africa is "conducted for the leaders themselves". Therefore leadership change is nothing more than "a continuing parade of self-serving politicos".[13] Govea and Holm[14] took a contrary view and advocated for the study of leadership change even if it involves personalism, because it provides a yardstick by which democracy may be measured in terms of progress. It is probably the only time debates on ideological pursuits become possible in the African contexts. Again, personified leaders' approaches to linkage building for support from civil society may yield or depict an ideology which could be picked up by other or subsequent political systems. Segal sums up the importance of studying succession in Africa when he observed "Succession events in Africa are billiard balls bouncing on and off neighbouring and even distant states … Treating Africa as a network of political impacts and influences often centred on succession makes sense".[15] The position of this paper is that succession is a significant component of the ongoing democratisation processes in Africa and has been a major factor impeding democratisation and is therefore worth studying.

The paper examines democratic successions in Africa from 1989–2013. It seeks to identify succession challenges, the sources of the challenges and their implications for Africa's democracy and the way forward, in particular how international instruments on democracy can be adapted to strengthen national institutions for smooth democratic successions on the African continent. This paper is significant in that it will inform governments, political parties, and civil society organizations, as well as the general African populace as to the way forward in addressing the problem of political upheavals and civil unrest associated with democratic transitions in Africa.

II Democratic Succession and the African Union's Framework

Democracy has been defined by different people at different times within different political epochs with varied forms of democratic institutional designs

---

13   Jackson and Rosberg as cited in Govea, R.M. & Holm, J.D.(1998). Crisis, Violence and Political Succession in Africa. *Third World Quarterly; International Module*, 19(1), 129–148, p. 131; Zolberg as cited in Ibid. p. 131.
14   Ibid.
15   Segal, A. (1996). Can Democratic Transitions Tame Political Successions? *Africa Today*, 43(4), 369–384. p.371.

i.e. presidential, parliamentary, or a fusion of both.[16] The current theories of democracy recognise that the utopian view of democracy as self-legislation or self-rule is no longer tenable in view of the complexity of modernity and political realities on the ground.[17] Concepts of democracy have evolved. The new world view of democracy emphasises self-determination and reflective institutions which allow for revision of decisions and procedures by a "deliberative generation". Within the context of this paper, Bohman's definition of democracy is being adopted as a "set of institutions by which individuals are empowered as free and equal citizens to form and change the terms of the common life together, including democracy itself. In this sense, democracy is self reflexive and consists of procedures by which its rules and practices are made subject to the deliberation of citizens themselves."[18] By the African Charter on Democracy, Elections and Governance, 2007 (the Charter on Democracy), which may be classified as the AU Bill on democracy, the AU committed itself to promote the universal principles of democracy among others. The African Charter is the culmination of AU/OAU's attempt to frame and ground democracy as a way of positioning Africa in response to the end of the cold war.[19] Per Article 2(1), each State Party undertakes to promote adherence to the universal principle of democracy and respect for human rights. Article 2(6) enjoins State Parties to nurture, support and consolidate good governance by promoting democratic culture and practice, building and strengthening governance institutions and inculcating political pluralism and tolerance.

---

16   Huntington, S.P. (2009). How Countries Democratize. *Political Science Quarterly*, Spring, 124(1), 31–69.
17   Bohman, J. (2010). Introducing Democracy Across Borders: from Demos to Demoi, *Ethics and Global Politics*, 23 (1), pp. 1–11.
18   Ibid. p. 2.
19   Earlier on the OAU had in 1990 issued the Declaration on the Political and Socio-Economic Situation in Africa and the Fundamental Changes Taking Place in the World. OAU Doc. AHG/Decl. 1 (XXVI) (1990); See also the *Relaunching Africa's Economic and Social Development: The Cairo Agenda for Action*, OAU Doc. AHG/Res. 236 (XXXI) (1995); Algiers Declaration, OAU Doc. AHG/Decl. 1 (XXXV) (1999); the Declaration on the Framework for an OAU Response to Unconstitutional Changes in Government at the 2000 meeting of the OAU in Lomé, Togo/OAU Doc. AHG/Decl. 5 (XXXVI) (2000); Constitutive Act of the African Union, July 11, 2000, *available at* http://www.africa-union.org/root/au/AboutAu/Constitutive_Act_en.htm; the AU Declaration on the Principles Governing Democratic Elections in Africa/AU Doc. AHG/Decl. 1 at 1 (XXXVIII) (2002); New Partnership for Africa's Development, Declaration on Democracy, Political, Economic and Corporate Governance, NEPAD Doc. AHG/235 (XXXVIII), Annex 1 (2002); *Protocol Relating to the Establishment of the Peace and Security Council of the African Union*, July 10, 2002, available online at http://www.africa-union.org/root/au/Documents/Treaties/Text/Protocol_peace_and_security.pdf;

The structural frame for democracy is constitutionalism, a government whose powers are limited by law through constitutional supremacy, the rule of law and separation of powers. In this way the state is separated from its officers in order to avoid the incidence of the state officials becoming the state[20] in order to avoid arbitrariness and secure the protection of the human rights of the citizens – the very essence of democratic government. By Article 2(2), of the African Charter on Democracy each State Party pledges to uphold the principle of the rule of law, premised upon the respect for, and the supremacy of, the constitutional order in the political arrangements of the State Parties.

The ideological differences in the conceptualisation of democracy notwithstanding, one of the core features of democracy which is generally accepted as basic to all forms of democracy is periodic elections regulated by law.[21] Elections are the badge of democracy.[22] Thus, the executive and legislative arms of the political apparatus are subjected to periodic change and reconstitution. The term of office of the principal members is fixed and a process is put in place to determine the next leader, individual and/or collective. This allows for predetermined and orderly change of government. Article 2(3) of the Charter on Democracy promotes the holding of regular free and fair elections to institutionalise legitimate authority of representative government as well as democratic change of governments. The Declaration on the Principles Governing Democratic Elections in Africa (2002), another key instrument, gives the bench mark for democratic elections.[23] It insists that; 1) democratic elections are the basis of authority of any representative government; 2) regular elections constitute a key element in the democratisation process and therefore are essential ingredients for good governance, the rule of law, the maintenance and

---

20 Moise, A. Adjangba (1999). Democratic Transition and African Renaissance in sub-Saharan Africa. *International Journal on World Peace*, 16(3), pp. 45–58, p. 47.
21 Nkansah, L.A. (2011), op. cit.
22 Cited in Teshome, W. (2008). Democracy and elections in Africa: Critical analysis. *International Journal of Human Sciences* [Online]. 5:2 Retrieved June 21, 2010 from http://www.insanbilimleri.com atp. 3.
23 The Preamble requires that democratic elections should be free and fair, under democratic constitutions and in compliance with supportive legal instruments, under a system of separation of powers that ensures in particular, the independence of the judiciary, at regular intervals in accordance with national constitutions, by impartial, all inclusive competent accountable electoral institutions staffed by well trained, personnel and equipped with adequate logistics.

promotion of peace, security, stability and development; 3) that democratic elections are important in conflict prevention, management and resolution. In consequence each state party undertakes to take necessary measures to ensure the conscientious implementation of the above principles, in accordance with the constitutional processes of their respective countries. Citizens on the other hand have the right to participate freely in the government of their countries, either directly or through freely elected representatives in accordance with the provisions of the law.

Implicit in democracy therefore is the element of succession. The trigger for succession in democracy is elections or succession without elections. This occurs when the position of the maximum leader becomes vacant as a result of death, resignation or removal from office by impeachment based on misconduct or ill health and a designated officer assumes control over a country without elections and "accidental president" emerges.[24] The demise of Yar'Adua, a democratically elected president of Nigeria witnessed Goodluck Jonathan becoming the president without elections. Likewise, the death of John Evans Atta-Mills, the democratically elected President of Ghana witnessed the swearing in of John Dramani Mahama as president of Ghana. This should be distinguished from a situation where the leader could be replaced by other means not within the contemplation of the law i.e. coups d'état. Articles 2(4) and 3(10) of the Charter on Democracy prohibit, reject and condemn unconstitutional change of government in any member state as a serious threat to stability, peace, security and development. The Protocol on Democracy and Good Governance adopted by the Economic Community of West African States in 2002 provides among other things that one of the principles to be declared as constitutional principles shared by all Member States is that "[e]very accession to power must be made through free, fair and transparent elections".[25]

Govea and Holm distinguished between two types of leadership succession as regulated and unregulated succession. Regulated succession is achieved by

---

[24] Abbot, P. (2005). Accidental Presidents: Death, Assasination, Resignation, and Democratic Succession. *Presidential Studies Quarterly*, 34(4), 627–645. p. 627. In the United States there have been such presidents who assumed office either because their predecessors had been assassinated, died or removed from office Abbot (2005) identified nine such US accidental presidents; Fillmore, Andrew Johnson, Arthur, Theodore Roosevelt, Coolidge, Truman, Lyndon, Johnson and Ford.

[25] Article 1(b).

a selection process laid down by "rules understood at least by the major political players in the system"[26] and with a peaceful and orderly transition. Unregulated succession on the other hand is "driven by the use of force or threat of force or is otherwise bereft of identifiable rule-governed behaviour".[27] In this study, democratic succession refers to electoral succession; a regulated succession which envisages the appearance of a leader within the contemplation of the law.

Succession involves "a transition from one leader to another."[28] It does not involve only structures, processes and procedures for handing over. It also involves "dialoguing and confidence-building among the political elites and with the bureaucrats in order to improve the political conditions for post-election governance and restoration of national cohesion in the country".[29] Abbot et al[30] maintained that the processes leading to the installation of a new leader legitimises the succession. The institutionalisation of succession as shown by the nature of transition is a pointer to the prevailing condition of democratisation in a given context; it indicates whether the system is progressing towards liberalism or the reverse.[31] The institutionalisation should be anchored in a clear and unambiguous policy, laid down processes and procedures, and guided by a culture of tolerance, accommodation, and respect for fundamental human rights. These should be reflected in the applicable laws and policies, structures and processes, ideological goals, attitudes, behaviours and practices as discernible during the transitions. It should also be noted that the fact that an established process is used to select a leader does not make the process a pointer to institutionalisation. The process should be devoid of threats, use of force and or violence. Electoral violence here connotes "all forms of organized acts or threats – physical, psychological, structural – aimed at intimidating, harming, blackmailing a political stakeholder before, during, and after an election with a view to determining, delaying, or otherwise influencing an electoral process".[32] However, it should be noted that the absence of violence may

---

26 Govea, R.M. & Holm, J.D.(1998), op. cit. p. 135.
27 Ibid.
28 Ibid., p. 132.
29 Ahwoi, K. (2009a). Towards a Peaceful Political and Administrative Transitions in Ghana. The Institute of Economic Affairs Policy Brief Number 2. p. 4.
30 Abbot, P., Thompson, L., Sarbaugh-Thompson, M.(2002). The Social Construction of a Legitimate President. *Studies in American Political Development.* 208–230.
31 Govea, R.M. & Holm, J.D.(1998), op. cit.
32 Albert, I.O., Quoted in Omotola, S., Explaining Electoral Violence in Africa's Democracies, *African Journal on Conflict Resolution*, 10(3), 51–73, p. 55.

also mean the absence of an organised opposition or that the opposition may have been crushed into silence as opposed to constituting prima facie evidence of peaceful orderly transition.[33] Thus Article 2(13) of the Charter on Democracy promotes best practices in the management of elections for purposes of political stability and good governance. Critical to electoral success is the settlement of electoral disputes. In this respect Article 17 requires State Parties to establish "independent and impartial" national electoral management institutions, institutions that provide expeditious settlement of "election-related disputes".

When all is said and done there should be transfer of power. Accordingly Article 5 of the Charter on Democracy provides that "State Parties shall take all the necessary appropriate measures to ensure ... constitutional transfer of power".

Pursuant to Article 3, State parties are to implement the Charter on Democracy in accordance with the principles of respect for human rights and democratic principles, representative government, access to and exercise of state power in accordance with the constitution of the State Party and the principle of the rule of law among others. Article 14 charges State Parties to strengthen and institutionalise constitutional civilian control over armed and security forces to ensure the consolidation of democracy and constitutional order. Also, State parties are to take legislative and regulatory measures to ensure that those who attempt to remove an elected government or maintain power through unconstitutional means are dealt with in accordance with law. Again, per Article 15 State parties shall establish public institutions that promote and support democracy and constitutional order. Article 17 requires State Parties to establish "independent and impartial" national electoral management institutions, institutions that provide expeditious settlement of "election-related disputes". There should be equitable access by "contesting parties and candidates" to state-owned media and adopt a legally binding code of conduct on stakeholders during and after the election process.

Sanctions are to be invoked in situations of coup d'états,[34] replacement of democratically elected government by mercenaries or armed dissidents,[35] refusal of incumbent government to relinquish power to "the winning party or candidate after free and fair elections"[36] and "any amendment or revision of the constitution or legal instrument" contrary to "the principles of democratic

---

33   Govea, R.M. & Holm, J.D. op. cit.
34   Article 23(1) of the Charter on democracy.
35   Ibid. Article 23(2) &(3).
36   Ibid. Article 23(4).

change of government".[37] The enforcement mechanisms are provided for by Articles 24 and 25 by which the powers of the AU Peace and Security Council may be invoked to intervene in situations where for example democratic governance is interrupted. Diplomatic initiatives could be employed to restore democratic governance, failing which the State concerned may be suspended from AU's activities. Article 18 enjoins Members States to request for assistance or advisory service from the Commission of the African Union (The Commission) to strengthen their "electoral institutions and processes" through the Democracy and Election Assistance Unit Election Assistance Fund. Member States are required to furnish the Commission with the scheduled dates of their elections with request for the Commission to send an electoral observer mission.

III   A Sketch of Democratic Succession in Africa

A   *Constitutionalisation of Succession*

African Countries have sought to constitutionalise succession in their democratisation process. Consequently, the constitutions of several African countries provide for a multi-party democracy as a form of government with Swaziland being a non-partisan State and Eritrea being the only single party state in Africa since its independence. The constitutions provide for how a government should be formed and the process for the emergence of the maximum leader (s) as well as those who qualify to assume such position(s). The constitutions mandate periodic elections to choose the leader, the term of the leader and outline the succession plan of the presidency or the political leadership.[38]

In terms of how this has played out, first, thirty-one out of the forty one countries which had hitherto not held elections did so between 1990 and 1994.[39] As at 2007, there had been multiparty elections in 45 out of the 48 countries in the sub-Saharan Africa.[40] More countries have since embraced multiparty po-

---

37   Ibid. Article 23(5).
38   For example, see the Constitution of the Republic of Ghana, 1992; Constitution of Federal Republic of Nigeria.
39   Ibrahim, J. Transforming Elections in West Africa into Opportunities for Political Choice. Keynote Address, Nordic Africa Institute conference on "Post-Conflict Elections in West Africa: Challenges for Democracy and Reconstruction", Held in Accra, Ghana, 15to 17 May, 2006.
40   Brown, S & Kaiser, P. (2007). Democratisations in Africa: Attempts, Hindrances and Prospects. *Third World Quaterly,* 28(6), pp. 1131–1149, at 1131 and 1133.

litical systems. Increasingly, mono-party and military regimes which plagued the continent are becoming obsolete.[41] Second, succession politics has provided an avenue for the alternation of power within and between political parties and also for coalition parties.[42] Thus interparty or intraparty succession has occurred through the ballot box in places like Ghana, Benin, Malawi and others as column 7 on Table 28.1 depicts. The political landscape on the continent whereby political succession would have occurred through the force of arms (i.e. coup d'états or palace coups or even civil wars) is changing and citizens are also participating in choosing their leaders.

Third, the second wave of democratisation in Africa (third wave in Huntington's count) has witnessed a sign of democratic consolidation in consonance with Huntington widely accepted *two-turnover test* in some parts of the continent. Huntington maintained that democracy is consolidated when the government which wins power in the initial election loses power to another party in the second election and the winner of the second election also loses power in subsequent elections. This has been achieved in some countries as column 7 on the Table shows.[43]

Fourth, succession governing rules have not in all cases resulted in transitions from authoritarian rule to civilian rule in some countries.[44] There are situations where there is no term limit on the tenure of the presidency. In Cameroon, Togo, Burkina Faso, Chad, Uganda, Zimbabwe, Gabon, Lesotho, Algeria, Sudan, Comoros, Cote d'Ivoire, Guinea, Swaziland, Tunisia and Guinea-Bissau there are no term limits on their political leadership.[45] This leads to the dominance of one political party or leader for several years such as Cameroon (Paul Biya in power for about 30 years) and Zimbabwe (Robert Mugabe has also been in power for over 30 years). This prospect adds to instability and leads to authoritarian rule. Opposition parties are mostly not allowed fair competition (restricted democratic practice) leading to free but unfair elections as observed in the recent 2013 elections in Zimbabwe.

Some countries that did not have term limits for the office of the presidents have adopted such limits. Yet this has not resulted in democratic succession in those countries. For example, Zimbabwe and Burkina Faso have provided for a presidential term limit through constitutional amendments but this did not

---

41   Segal, A.(1996). op. cit.
42   CODESRIA and OSIWA as cited in Banjo, A. (2008). Constitutional and Succession Crisis in West Africa: The Case of Togo, *African Journal of Legal Studies*, 2, 147–161.
43   Huntington, S. (1993). Political Development in Ethiopia: A Peasant-Based Dominant-Party Democracy? Report to USAID/Ethiopia.
44   CODESRIA-OSIWA as cited in Banjo, *op. cit.*
45   Mostly have in place the number of years the president should serve but no limit to the number of times one can become president.

translate into alteration of power from dominant leaders ie Robert Mugabe and Blaise Campaore. In both cases there were agitations that these two leaders should not contest because they had already served the number of years the constitution permitted. These two leaders succeeded to contest for elections on the basis that they had not exhausted their term limits as introduced because they did not have retroactive effect. An attempt by Blaise Campore to secure constitutional amendment in 2014 to enable him contest election for a third term sparked off civil resistance that led to his removal as president.[46]

At the same time the constitutional limit on succession plans has been thwarted by some governments who had changed the rules to extend their stay in power or to designate their sons as successors.[47] Yoweri Museveni, the Ugandan president was elected for a third time after a constitutional amendment had been effected to remove a presidential term limit. In Cameroon a presidential two-term limit was removed to allow for the re-election of Paul Biya. Also Idriss Deby was allowed to run for a third term following a referendum to remove a presidential term limit.[48] In Namibia President Sam Nujoma personally effected an amendment to have a third term. Malawi did the same. According to Wariobo, "There ... were murmurs in Kenya before the ... 2000 general elections [about extending the term of the President] and there was a spirited attempt by President Frederick Chiluba to change the Zambia constitution".[49] Obasanjo of Nigeria failed in his attempt to secure additional term of office through a constitutional amendment. There have been agitations in Togo by the opposition party for a term limit of the presidency.

Even where leaders had wanted to take their exit as a result of constitutional term limits, the leadership of their parties had urged for constitutional amendment to extend their tenure in office. When the term of Mwinyi of Tanzania ended in 1995 political leaders agitated for the lengthening of his term likewise Zanzibar in 2000, but the attempts failed in both cases.[50] The above scenarios on succession challenges persist and attempts to extend the term of presidents have created tensions and discontent in the countries involved. There is the need to consolidate limitations on the term of political

---

46 Nkansah. L.A., *Protection for Citizens of Ghana who Resist Usurpers in Defence of Ghana's Fourth Republican Constitution*, accepted for presentation at the forthcoming Southern African Law Teachers conference which will be held from July 6-8, 2015, in Durban, South Africa.

47 Wariobo, J.S.(2006). Political Succession in East Africa. In Peter, C.M. and Kopsieker, F. (ed.), *Political Succession in East Africa: In Search for a Limited Leadership* (pp. 1–11) Friedrich Ebert Stiftung: Kenya, p. 6.

48 Elvy Stacy-Ann (2013). Towards a New Democratic Africa: The African Charter on Democracy, Election and Governance, *Emory International Law Review*, 27, 41–115.

49 Wariobo, J.S. *op. cit.*, pp. 5–6.

50 Ibid.

leaders. But as Elvy has observed, there is no consensus on what is an acceptable term limit for heads of states.[51] This should be done based on the basic democratic tenets taking into consideration the historical, political, and socio-economic conditions of a given country. The AU may provide guidelines to guide its Member States on presidential term limits. Fifth, succession has generated a call for a replacement of the older generation for a younger generation and a discourse that the old should give place to the young.

B   *The Elections: Churning out Political Leaders*
A typical electoral mechanism includes the demarcation of electoral boundaries and constituencies, voter registration processes, the voter register, filing of nomination by candidates, voting, and the declaration of the election results. There are laws in respective countries regulating these electoral activities. However, it emerged that the transitional processes including the election apparatus even in places where the constitutional order of succession were complied with have been characterised by anomalies and violence before, during and after elections. Election rules have been breached with impunity. There have been reports of irregularities in the voters register, over-voting, rigging of elections results and manipulation of the electoral apparatus by the government in power. For example, Omotola reported that elections in Kenya, Nigeria and Zimbabwe were characterised by "political assassinations, riots, assaults, arson, looting, bombing and hijacking of electoral materials at gun point".[52] In Nigeria in particular, the assassination and bombing of political aspirants have become rampant since 1999.[53] The conduct of elections also witnessed "open display and use of dangerous weapons such as guns, axes and cutlass to commit electoral frauds"[54] as a result of which many innocent people died.[55] In Senegal, the Deputy Chair of the Constitutional Council was assassinated on the eve of the declaration of the legislation result in 1993.[56] Other forms of violence reported in Kenya and Zimbabwe were battering, destruction of properties, torture, rape, unlawful arrest and "detention and destruction of public meetings and campaign rallies".[57] The incidence of psychological violence occurred in the form of intimidation which created fear in the electorates and

---

51   Elvy Stacy-Ann (2013). op. cit.
52   Omotola, p. 61.
53   Ibid.
54   Ibid.
55   Ibid.
56   See Fall, I.M., Hounkpe, M., Jinadu., A.L. & Kambale, P. (2011). Election Management Bodies in West Africa: A Comparative Study of the Contribution of Electoral Commissions to the Strengthening of Democracy. Open Society Foundations, Dakar, Senegal.
57   Ibid., p. 62.

aspirants alike. Electoral integrity is compromised. This encourages widespread disturbances and unrest with most cases leading to political upheavals, civil strife, and wars as observed in the case of Kenya, Cote d'Ivoire, Togo, Uganda and Zimbabwe, Guinea or Guinea Bissau, Angola, Burundi, Republic of Congo, and Sierra Leone. Electoral violence has included mass killing, rape and torture of women and children, economic instability leading to extreme poverty and hunger (Somalia), and citizenry of such countries fleeing to other states as refugees. A country like Somalia has not had an effective central government for the past two decades due to political instability. In other instances too the military intervened by declaring a coup. In short, in Africa "the ballot has turned to the equivalent of the barrel of the gun – the previously illegitimate instrument of ascending to power."[58]

c   *Weak Electoral Management Bodies*

Critical to the succession process is the conduct of the elections as shown. There are established election management bodies to conduct elections. The credibility of Electoral Management Bodies (EMBs) has been identified as critical to the succession process.[59] In the past two decades which marked the second wave of democratisation, African countries have established bodies to conduct and manage elections. The Open Society Initiative in West Africa (OSIWA) in a study on EMBs in West Africa identified three types of electoral management bodies. One is the hybrid/governmental model where an independent body supervises the conduct of the elections by civil servants. There is also the political model which is composed of political party representatives. The other model is the expert model whose members are chosen on the basis of experience, personal qualities etc.[60]

The mode of appointment of membership of EMB also differs. Some are appointed by the president in consultation with another constitutional advisory body (Ghana). Others are elected by national parliaments such (Cape Verde) while others are nominated by the political parties (Benin Republic). The effectiveness of any EMB by and large depends on the independence of the body, irrespective of the composition and mode of appointment. The factors that go to make them independent were identified by OSIWA as "strength of character of members, ... security of tenure, ... the stability of administrative person-

---

58   Gbesan, G. (ed.) (2010). Democratic Recession in West Africa: Challenges to Revivalism, Proceedings of the Open Society Initiative for West Africa, p. 10.
59   Ibid.
60   Kambale, P. Overview: The Contribution of Electoral Management Bodies to Credible Elections in West Africa, In Ismaila, M. F., Mathias, H. Adele, L., Pascale, K. (eds) *Election Man- agement Bodies in Africa; A comparative Study of the contribution of electoral commissions to the strengthening of democracy*. Open Society Foundations (2011) 1–11, pp. 5–8.

nel, ... The security of funding, ... " as well as "the degree to which the EMB has effective control over all the task that must be completed in the electoral process".[61] In addition the mandate of the EMB to relate with the political parties and the quality of collaboration between EMB and other institutions and stakeholders in the electoral process is critical. OSIWA established in their study that the common challenges of the EMBs in West Africa are "the creation and maintenance of a credible electoral roll, the high cost of elections, the lack of powers to sanction misconduct, and the low level of involvement of EMBs in the management of electoral dispute".

In several African countries if not all, the EMBs are not independent or may be independent on paper but are in fact compromised politically and are in some cases biased in favour of the government in power in the conduct of elections. They are also plagued with human resource challenges and other logistical shortcomings and are not able to carry out the task of conducting and supervising elections effectively. Their work has come under fierce criticisms often leading to tensions and political upheavals.

D *Electoral Disputes and Adjudication*

Disputes arise at any stage in the electoral process. The laws on the elections make room for dispute resolution of issues that emanate from the process.[62] This includes issues relating to the demarcation of constituencies, challenging the registration processes as well as challenging the election results. There are cases where losers and their affiliates reject the election outcome at any stage in the voting process or at the declaration of the results. Non-acceptance is registered in several ways such as demonstrations, outrages, and perpetration of violence which sometimes leads to civil conflicts. Others resort to judicial or quasi judicial remedies. The effective resolution of disputes emanating from the electoral process is critical to electoral integrity. The import of electoral adjudication is captured in the observation by the Chief Justice of Ghana when she said "I appreciate the sobering fact that an important safeguard of election integrity lies in an effective resolution of complaints and appeals with minimum delay".[63]

---

61 Kambale, P. Overview: The Contribution of Electoral Management Bodies to Credible Elections in West Africa, in Ismaila, M. F., Mathias, H. Adele, L., Pascale, K. (eds) *Election Management Bodies in Africa; A comparative Study of the contribution of electoral commissions to the strengthening of democracy.* Open Society Foundations (2011) 1–11, pp. 5–8.

62 See for instance Articles 106 and 117 of the Constitution of Benin; Article 219 of the 1999 constitution of Cape Verde; Section 285 (1) of 1999 Constitution of Nigeria and the Electoral Act of Nigeria, 2006; Articles L43, L44, R28 and R35 of the Electoral Code of Senegal.; sections 45(2)(a-b) and section 78 Constitution of Sierra Leone 1991 and Electoral Laws Act, 2002 of Sierra Leone (as amended); Article 21(1) of the Constitution of Tanzania

63 Quoted in Judicial Service of Ghana (2012). *Manual on Election Adjudication in Ghana.* Ghana: DPI Print Ltd. p. 2.

In Ghana, Kenya, Ivory Coast and Nigeria disputes of presidential elections were handled by their constitutional courts.

In Ghana the result of the 2012 presidential election was challenged. The Electoral Commission declared John Dramani Mahama, the then flagbearer of the National Democratic Congress, as a winner with 50.70 % of the votes casts with Nana Addo Dankwa-Akuffo Addo the flag bearer of the New National Patriotic Party (NPP), obtaining 47.74%. In *Nana Addo Dankwa Akuffo Addo & 2 Others v. John Dramani and Others*.[64] Akuffo-Addo, his running mate Mahamudu Buhamia and Jake Obetsebi-Lamptey, the National Chairman of the NPP, instituted an action against John Dramani Mahama, the Electoral Commission, and the National Democratic Congress to challenge the legitimacy of Mahama who was sworn into office on January 7, 2013 as president of Ghana. Akuffo-Addo and the others claimed that the said election was marred with irregularities and the results as declared by the Electoral Commission should be set aside. The particulars or irregularities complained of were:

I. Over-voting
II. Voting without biometric verification
III. Absence of the signature of a presiding officer
IV. Duplicate serial numbers i.e. occurrence of the same serial number on pink sheets for two different polling stations
V. Duplicate polling station codes i.e. occurrence of different results/pink sheets for polling stations with the same polling station codes;
VI. Unknown polling stations i.e. results recorded for polling stations which are not part of the list of 26,002 polling stations provided by 2nd respondent [Electoral Commission]

On the above issues the Supreme Court of Ghana unanimously dismissed the claims relating to IV, V, and VI. On the other issues the Supreme Court in a majority dismissed the claims in I, II, III and ruled that "In the circumstances the overall effect is that the 1st respondent was validly elected and the petition is therefore dismissed".[65] Akuffo Addo accepted the verdict of the court and congratulated Mahama as the winner of the elections.

The Kenyan 2013 presidential election resulted in a dispute before the Kenyan Supreme Court. In *Raila Odinga v. The Independent Electoral and Bound-*

---

64   *Nana Addo Dankwa Akuffo Addo & 2 Others v.John Dramani and Others*. Writ No. J/16/2013 retrieved on September 26, 2013 from www.judicial.gov.gh.
65   The abridged judgment of the Supreme Court of Ghana delivered on 29th August, 2013 in respect of *Nana Addo Dankwa Akuffo Addo& 2 Others v. John Dramani and Others*.

aries Commission and others.[66] Raila Odinga, who had contested and lost the 2013 presidential elections in Kenya, instituted an action against the Independent Electoral and Boundaries Commission (IEBC), Ahmed Issack Hassan as a returning Officer of presidential election, Uhuru Kenyatta as the beneficiary of flawed presidential election as president elect, and William Samoei Ruto as the beneficiary of the allegedly flawed presidential election as deputy president elect. This case was consolidated with 3 other cases on the same matter.[67] The issues for determination by the Court were;

1. Whether the 3rd Respondent [Uhuru Kenyatta] and 4th Respondent [William Samoei Ruto] were validly elected and declared as President-elect and Deputy President-elect respectively, in the Presidential elections held on the 4th March 2013.
2. Whether the Presidential election held on March 4th, 2013 was conducted in a free, fair, transparent and credible manner in compliance with the provisions of the Constitution and all relevant provisions of the law.[68]

In a unanimous decision by the judges, the Court held among other things that the conduct of the election was in accordance with the Constitution and the law, and that Uhuru Kenyatta and William Ruto were validly elected.

The presidential election in Cote d'Ivoire resulted in a dispute before the Constitutional Council. Gbagbo, whose mandate had expired in 2005, had delayed the election several times. On 28 November 2010, the second round of the presidential elections was held. Four days later the Ivorian Election Commission (CEI) declared Alassane Ouattara the winner with 54.1% of the vote. Gbagbo's party complained of fraud and ordered that votes from nine regions be annulled, but the claims were disputed by the Ivorian Electoral Commission and international election observers. The Constitutional Council, in accordance with its legal powers in article 94 of the Ivorian Constitution, nullified the CEI's declaration based on alleged voting fraud, and excluded votes from nine northern areas. The Constitutional Council concluded that without these votes Gbagbo won with 51% of the remaining vote. The constitutional restriction on Presidents serving more than ten years was not addressed. A significant portion of the country's vote was nullified, especially in areas where Ouattara polled well. In 2011, the Constitutional Council President Paul Yao N'Dre said

---

[66] (2013)e KLR National Council for Law Reporting – Kenya Law Reports retrieved on September 26, 2013 from www.kenyalaw.org.

[67] *Moses Kiarie Kuria& 2 Others v. Ahmed Issack Hassan & Another* (Petition No. 3 of 2013); Gladwell *Wathoni Otieno & Anor v. Ahmed Issack Hassan &3 Others* (Petition No. 4 of 2013).

[68] *Raila Odinga v. The Independent Electoral and Boundaries Commission Others* p. 7.

the top legal body now accepted that Ouattara won the election and proclaimed Alassane Ouattara President. The Constitutional Council nullified its earlier decision and invited Alassane Ouattara to take an oath in front of an official audience as soon as possible. The court had cancelled more than half a million votes in Ouattara strongholds to declare Gbagbo winner in December, prompting almost universal condemnation from world powers, African leaders and the United Nations. The resulting bloody power struggle between them was only resolved when Ouattara's forces captured Gbagbo.

This paper does not intend to offer a review of the decisions of the courts under consideration which is reserved for another paper but to make some observations about the implications of the emerging phenomenon of electoral adjudication in the succession process. The idea of instituting an election petition in court as opposed to the aggrieved persons resorting to mayhem is a positive sign in the democratisation process. The aggrieved choose the law as their arbiter and put their hope in the law. This practice will facilitate the institutionalisation of succession and entrench the rule of law and constitutionalism. The effective resolution would also mean a review of the work of the electoral management body by making them accountable. Thus, an EMB whose work has come under the scrutiny of the court is likely to improve upon its performance in the future. Such a review is likely to highlight the lapses in the system for possible reform.

Electoral adjudication therefore places a sacred responsibility on the judiciary to be candid, fair, and impartial in the resolution of such disputes expeditiously. Judicial independence is critical to the process. It should be observed that judicial independence is enshrined in the constitutions of African countries.[69] Article 128 of the Constitution of Uganda states;

1. In the exercise of judicial power, the courts shall be independent and shall not be subject to the direction of any person or authority.
2. No person or authority shall interfere with the courts or judicial officers in the exercise of their judicial functions.

Yet, the judiciary in some African countries are plagued by corruption, unfair trials, political influence, resource and capacity problems to handle such disputes effectively. As a result they do not have the confidence and trust of the people.[70] The handling of the petition of the presidential election by the

---

69 See Article 125 of the Constitution of Ghana, Article 78 of the Constitution of Namibia, and Article 79 B of the Constitution of Zimbabwe with similar provision on judicial independence.

70 Abuya, E. O., 'The Role of the Judiciary in Promotion of Free and Fair Elections', Unpublished Manuscript. Retrieved July 20, 2014 from http://www.juridicas.unam.mx/wccl/

Constitutional Council of Cote d'Ivoire attracted worldwide criticism and condemnation. The Supreme Court of Ghana's decision had been received with mixed sentiments and the idea persists that the decision was against the weight of evidence. It should be pointed out that electoral politics have polarised African countries so that decisions on electoral disputes are likely to receive mixed responses. But the judiciary should rise above partisan sentiments. Justice must not only be done but should be manifestly and undoubtedly be seen to be done, and this is more relevant in Africa now than ever before. Apart from civil actions being instituted by aggrieved persons, the electoral laws created several offences, but these are rarely enforced. There have not been enough prosecutions to warrant deterrence. Election related offences in Kenyan and Cote d'Ivoire are currently being handled by the International Criminal Court. The question is whether the international platform is effective in dealing with such situations.

E   *Transfer of Power from one Administration to the other*

When all is said and done transferring power from the outgoing governments to incoming government is the crux of succession. It means that the incumbent should hand over power to the winner as declared by the body in charge of conducting elections as determined by the court as the case may be.

Africa has witnessed inauguration ceremonies to usher in presidents/prime ministers. But there have been problems when the incumbent has to hand over power to the winner. There could be several scenarios involved, such as where. Where the incumbent participates and does not win the election, or where the incumbent does not participate and its party wins or loses the election. In any case, factors which influenced transfer of power from one administration to the other are the election results, power sharing, negotiations, completion of constitutional term limits by the incumbent, use of force, the influence of the international community, absence of fear of reprisals against the incumbent after taking their exit.

Transfer of power means that the one who emerges out of the competition should be accepted by the different groupings in the hope that they "will be able to get enough of what they want out of the process".[71] This is the *demo-*

---

ponencias/1/1.pdf > accessed 20 July2014; Aguda T. Akinola (1985) The Judiciary in Africa. *The Fletcher Forum*, 13–35; European Union Observation Mission in Nigeria, Final Report on General Elections, April 2011. Retrieved June 20, 2014 from http://eeas.europa.eu/eueom/pdf/missions/final-report-nigeria2011_en.pdf; Commonwealth Human Rights Initiative [NiobeThompson: Author] (2002). In pursuit of justice, A report on the judiciary in Sierra Leone, 2002; Karen A. Saharan Africa: An Analysis of Neglect *African Studies Review* 31 (1) 135–147.

71   Shively, W.P. (1997). Power of Choice: An introduction of political Science. United States of America: McGraw-Hill, p. 129

cratic bargain and agreement. In consequence therefore the democratic fibre of any society according to Shively is fragile. This is because "all that is needed to make a democracy collapse is for one or more important groups to reject the result of the democratic bargain and to have access to enough power to overthrow the system".[72] Hence, the government of the day is or should be the government of all the people to the extent that the respective groupings will realise their reasonable expectations of the bargain. This includes those who voted for the government, those who did not vote for the government, and those who did not vote at all. But they fail to transform into government but continue to behave as a party in power. There is lack of respect for democratic bargaining, which is why incumbents and their supporters are reluctant to leave the scene.

The management of the transitional processes is very important. According to Ahwoi it does not involve only structures, processes and procedures for handing over but "dialoguing and confidence-building among the political elites and with the bureaucrats in order to improve the political conditions for post-election governance and restoration of national cohesion in the country".[73] The management of transitions has been clumsy and in some cases violent. There has been arbitrary sacking of public servants from office and the handing and taking over of national assets has posed problems. In Ghana, for example, some of the outgoing officials during transitions attempted or took away national assets with them. The incoming governments and their supporters seized public assets in the possession of the outgoing officials. In the process property of some outgoing officials was mistakenly taken for public properties and seized and in some the police had in some cases been involved in this.[74] The end result has been tensions and upsurge of violence and a general state of insecurity on the continent. Ghana's approach to addressing this problem by the adoption of Presidential Succession Act of 2012 should be considered by other countries.[75]

IV   Sources of the Challenges

The problems of democratic succession identified first may be due to the absence of democratic norms, values and culture to anchor the change.[76] The laws are in place but they are breached with impunity. This can be traced to the

---

72   Ibid.
73   Nkansah, L.A. op. cit.
74   Ibid.
75   Presidential (Transition) Act of Ghana, 2012 (Act 845).
76   Gbesan, G. *op. cit.*, p. 63.

legacy of colonialism and the struggle for independence. The introduction of formal governance by the colonial masters was authoritarian, and they operated the state as an instrument of 'oppression'.[77] As this is what had been known to the political elites and freedom fighters, they seek to perpetuate it in democratic dispensation.

The incessant coups d'état which followed after independence did not allow any democratic government to serve their full term. Therefore many African countries had not changed government through the ballot box for the most part since independence. The known culture was to overthrow government. Therefore the attitudes and behaviours of the actors in the transitions were akin to that of an overthrow of government as opposed to changing government, hence the intolerance and violence.

The political structure in place may also breed a form of intolerance. For example, countries like Ghana, Nigeria and Burkina Faso which transitioned from military regimes did so with constitutions which reproduced the concentration of power and the command structure of military regimes, thereby creating executive dominance.[78] The political culture which is evolving around the system of political dominance is undemocratic. Thus, winners were not prepared to accommodate the losers in any way for they had no incentives to do so. In Ghana for example the two transitions "produced rancour bitterness and acrimony, rather than understanding, brotherliness, accommodation and cooperation".[79]

There is also a deficit of credible leaders committed to the advancement of democracy and the welfare of citizens. They are dominated by their self interest and often fail to distinguish between the self and the state. The effect had been the "second colonialism, an inherent slavery of the people by ... elected leaders".[80]

The people of Africa are transitioning from cultures that are undemocratic. African traditional leadership models of kingship and chiefdoms are dominant in nature. Political actors who are the product of their societies have just translated traditional leadership ethos into democracy. This has resulted in restricted democratic practice and regimes in which a dominant ruling party controls the levers of power, including access to the media, and the electoral process in ways that inhibits significant challenge or opposition to its political hegemony.

Second, there is also the socio-economic dimension. A change in government dislodges the sources of wealth in society; people lose sources of wealth and

---

77 Ibid.
78 Ake, C. (2000). The Feasibility of Democracy in Africa.
79 See Memorandum to the Presidential Transition Bill of Ghana, 2009, pp. 12 and 14.
80 Gbesan, *op. cit.*, p. 10.

social status and others acquire new sources of wealth. The winner takes all politics cuts a segment off from their sources of income. This is a threat to succession in Africa where political economy prevails and the government is the major employer. This creates animosity by the losing party and their sympathisers. The situation is compounded in Africa where efforts are made by the winning party to cripple the opposition and their affiliates financially.

Third, the absence of or at least an inadequate legal framework to guide the complex process of the transitions may also be a factor. Constitutions laid down succession plans for the presidency without regulating or being specific on how it should be carried out in most cases. Several countries as yet do not have laws specifically to guide transfer of power from one leader to the other. The area is therefore grey without any definite law to regulate it. In consequence the realm was governed by discretion hence, the arbitrariness and irregularities.[81] The idea of Woodrow Wilson, the former American president, of restraining discretion with definite law is instructive in this regard.[82]

v Enhancing Orderly Succession through the AU Charter on Democracy

The AU's framework could serve as a guide to enhance the institutionalisation of succession. As an a regional international framework, the African Charter on Democracy has the potential of inducing States Parties to conduct their affairs in line with its tenets and thereby build a democratic culture that will be reflected in political transitions. But the challenge international law faces as far as AU's framework on democracy and succession is concerned is lack of enforcement. It is one of the key instruments that would have facilitated the building of a democratic culture in Africa, but it has not been signed, ratified or acceded to by some States. The African Union has not been able to persuade every government to ratify its Charter on Democracy, Elections and Governance. As at February 2012, 39 countries had signed on, with 15 ratifications, bringing the Charter into force.[83] A major reason advanced for this failure to ratify is the lack of political will on the part of the leaders; many of the leaders do not possess democratic credentials, and they sign international instruments and continental ones for the wrong reasons – often donor-driven. There

---

[81] Ahwoi, K. (2009a). Towards a Peaceful Political and Administrative Transitions in Ghana. The Institute of Economic Affairs Policy Brief Number 2.
[82] As cited in Cook, 2002.
[83] Electoral Institute for Sustainable Democracy in Africa, (2012) "A U: Ratification status of the African Charter on Democracy, Elections and Governance". *Available at*: http://www.eisa.org.za/EISA/aucharter.htm, retrieved on September 19, 2012.

are also no strong sanctions for non-compliance. That is why they can sign up and delay ratification. As long as they do not ratify, they have no obligation to comply with the tenets of the instrument. This raises the issue of moral or political credibility and a clear evidence of the lack of political will to institutionalise democratic governance for smooth political successions. This is so notwithstanding the existence of a framework in place which serves as an anchor to democracy; there is the need for political will on the part of Member States to make it a reality. The Charter needs some tightening up through amendments of the African Charter on Democracy. There is the need to frame democracy as a right and for that matter an entitlement for the peoples of Africa and an obligation for their governments to "promote and defend as provided for by the Inter-American Democratic Charter for the Americas".[84]

Democratic rights should be made enforceable and individuals and groups should be able to seek redress for the breaches of their democratic rights. There is the need to create specific offences resulting from the breaches of the Charter and hold identifiable legal personalities/groups responsible for them. The enforcement mechanisms should be widened to include the platform of the juridical bodies of the AU. There is the need for specific guidelines on constitutional term limits for heads of states and also on transfer of power from one administration to the other.

VI Conclusion and the Way Forward

From the foregoing, it is clear that Africa has made some progress in its democratisation process with some countries changing government through the ballot box. This notwithstanding, the continent underwent upheaval during periods of political successions, because there is the lack of commitment to democracy as the AU's relevant instruments have not been complied with due to the failure of the Member States to ratify the instruments. There is the issue of weak national institutions and their inability to anchor the transitional process on the tenets of fair play. Other factors are the absence or inadequate frameworks to anchor transitions, the prevailing undemocratic cultures discernible in ideological goals, policies, structures, processes, attitudes, behaviours and practices during transitions. It should be pointed out that generally there are laws in place both at the national and continental level on democratic succession. But these are breached with impunity. Merely legislating

---

[84] Article 1 of the Inter-American Democratic Charter for the Americas, available at http://www.oas.org/charter/docs/resolution1_en_p4.htm).

would not bring about orderly political succession. They should be anchored in constitutionalism, the rule of law and fundamental human rights.

In terms of the way forward there is the need to sensitize aspiring and sitting presidents and their supporters on the terminal nature of a democratic government and prepare them for such an eventuality, and to also measures should be put in place to help outgoing heads of state to transform into statesmen after presidency.

There is the need for constitutional review in terms of the structure of power between the executive and legislature for balance structuring of power in order to address the issue of executive dominance as a way of facilitating the building of the culture of tolerance, accommodation and respect for human rights.

There is the need for definite, clear and simple law, which ensures individual responsibility for private and official accountability in political transitions. Those aggrieved should seek redress in the court and challenge impunity.

The security apparatus especially the police should be non-partisan and work for the security of all with regard to protecting life and property during transitions and curtail acts of hooliganism by bringing culprits to legal accountability.

The judiciary in Africa should rise above partisan politics and respect the requirements imposed on them by law and insulate itself from party sentiments. They should be sensitive to handling transitional issues in an expeditious manner. Special Courts should be designated for that purpose. This will bring about accountability.

"The winner takes all" politics should be abandoned. This can be achieved by the incoming governments allowing for continuity in office of public officers who are technically not part of the political class.

Incoming and outgoing regimes should respect the existing governance framework and structures. This has implications for political parties and the political elites, including incumbent governments and the opposition, as well as the populace.

Above all, the AU members should commit themselves to the tenets of democratic practice for the development of the continent to ensure that political succession is firmly institutionalised for an orderly transfer of power.

DEMOCRATIC SUCCESSION IN AFRICA 663

TABLE 28.1 *On Democratisation and Succession in Africa*

Name of country	1st wave of democratisation/ Independence	Democratic succession in the 1st wave of democratisation	One party status/one dominant political party	Military rule during the 1st wave of democratisation	2nd wave of democratisation / multiparty system from 1990	Democratic succession through the ballot box in the 2nd wave of democratisation	Military rule in the second wave of democratisation	Term limits of presidents	Political upheavals / tension in succession in the 2nd wave
Algeria	1962–1965			1965–1978 1978–1990	1990 (multiparty transition)	1995, 1999 (intra-party succession with same leader) 2004 (interparty succession) and re-election of same leader in 2009		5yr term with no limit	
Angola	1975		1975–1991 (one party state)		1991–1992 (multiparty transition)	1992, 2008 and 2012 (intraparty successions with same leader)		Two 5yr terms	Civil war from 1992 to 2002
Benin	1960–1961		1961–1963 (de facto one party state) 1964–1965 (de facto one party state)	1963–1964 1965–1968 1969–1970 1972–1975	1990–1991 (multiparty transition)	1996 and 2001 (interparty successions) 2006 (interparty succession) and re-election of same person in 2011		Two 5yr terms	Tension

TABLE 28.1 cont.

Name of country	1st wave of democratisation/ Independence	Democratic succession in the 1st wave of democratisation	One party status/one dominant political party	Military rule during the 1st wave of democratisation	2nd wave of democratisation / multiparty system from 1990	Democratic succession through the ballot box in the 2nd wave of democratisation	Military rule in the second wave of democratisation	Term limits of presidents	Political upheavals/tension in succession in the 2nd wave
Botswana	1966	One party dominant with elections in 1969, 1974, 1979, 1984, 1989, 1994, 1999, 2004, 2009	1968–1969; 1970–72 (restricted democratic practice) 1975–1990 (one party rule)					Two 5yr terms	
Burkina Faso	1960	1977–1978 (multiparty transition) 1978–1980 Democracy	1960–1966 (one party rule) 1970–1974 (restricted democratic practice)	1966–1970 1974–1977 1980–1991	1991 (multiparty transition) 1991–2002 (restricted democratic practice)	1998, 2005, 2010 (intraparty successions with same leader)		Two 5yr terms since 2000	Tension
Burundi	1962–1966		1974–1976 (one party rule) 1979–1987	1966–1974 1976–1979 1987–1992	1992–1993 (multiparty transition)	2001–2005 (transitional government)	1996	Two 5yr terms	Civil war from 1993–2005

DEMOCRATIC SUCCESSION IN AFRICA

Cameroon	1960–1966	1966–1990 (one party rule) 1992-date (dominant leader)	1990–1992 (multiparty transition) 1992 to date (restricted democratic practice)	successions with same leader 1997, 2004, 2011 (intraparty successions with same leader)	7yr term with no limit	Tension
Cape Verde	1975	1975–1990 (one party rule)	1990–1991 (multiparty transition)	1995, 2001 (intraparty succession with different leader) 2006 (interparty succession) 2011 (interparty succession)	Two 5yr terms	
Central African Republic	1960–1962	1962–1966 (one party) 1966–1976 1976–1979 (one party) 1979–1981 1980–1981 (one party) 1981–1987 1987–1991 (one party)	1992–1993 (multiparty transition)	1999 (intraparty success with same leader) 2005 (interparty succession), and re-election of the same person in 2011	Two 5yr terms 2003–2005, 2013	Tension
Chad	1960	1960–1962, (de facto one party rule) 1979–1982 (transitional government)	1975–1979 1982–1984 1993–1996	2001, 2006, 2011 (intraparty	5yr term with no limit	Tension

TABLE 28.1 cont.

Name of country	1st wave of democratisation / Independence	Democratic succession in the 1st wave of democratisation	One party status/one dominant political party	Military rule during the 1st wave of democratisation	2nd wave of democratisation / multiparty system from 1990	Democratic succession through the ballot box in the 2nd wave of democratisation	Military rule in the second wave of democratisation	Term limits of presidents	Political upheavals/tension in succession in the 2nd wave
			1962–1975 (one party) 1989–1990 (one party) 1996–2011 (dominant leader)	1984–1989 1990–1993		successions with same leader			
Comoros	1975		1975–1982 (restricted democratic practice) 1982–1990 (one party)		1990–1995 (emerging democracy) 1995–1996 (transitional government) 1996–1999 (emerging democracy)	2002 (interparty succession) 2006 (interparty succession) and 2010 (interparty succession)	1999–2002	5yr term with no limit	Tension
Congo-Brazzaville/	1960–1963		1963–1964 (de-facto	1968–1969 1977–1979	1990–1992 (multiparty	2002 and 2009 (intraparty		Two 7yr terms	Civil war 1997–

Congo-Kinshasa/ Democratic Republic of Congo	1960–1965	1965–1967 1997–2003	1967–1990 (one party rule) 1964–1968 (one party) 1969–1977 (one party) 1979–1990 (one party)	1990–1997 (multiparty transition) 1992–1997 (democracy)	2003–2006 (transitional government) 2006 (interparty succession) and re-election of the same person in 2011	Two 5yr terms	Civil War, National Fragmentation (1997–2003)
Côte d'Ivoire	1960		1960–1990 (one party rule)	1990 (multiparty transition) 1990–1999 (restricted democratic practice)	1995 (intraparty succession) and the re-election of same person in 1999 2000 (interparty succession) 2010 (interparty succession)	5yr term with no term limits	1999–2000 Civil war
Djibouti	1977		1977–1981 (de facto one party rule)	1992–1999 (restricted democratic practice)	2005 and 2011 (intraparty successions with same leader)	Two 5yr terms	Tension

TABLE 28.1 cont.

Name of country	1st wave of democratisation / Independence	Democratic succession in the 1st wave of democratisation	One party status/one dominant political party	Military rule during the 1st wave of democratisation	2nd wave of democratisation / multiparty system from 1990	Democratic succession through the ballot box in the 2nd wave of democratisation	Military rule in the second wave of democratisation	Term limits of presidents	Political upheavals/tension in succession in the 2nd wave
Egypt	1922–1952	Single candidate elections in 1987, 1993 and 1999	1981–1992 (one party rule) 1981–2011 (dominant leader)	1952–1953 1954–1956 1956–1970 1970–1981	2005 (multiparty transition)	2012	2013	Two 4yr terms starting from 2012 presidential election	Tension
Equatorial Guinea	1968–1969		1970–1979 (one party) 1987–1991 (one party) 1996–2009 (dominant leader)	1979–1982 (Military rule) 1982–1987 (non party state)	1991–1993 (multiparty transition)	1996, 2002 and 2009 (intraparty successions with same leader)		7yr term with no term limit	
Eritrea				-	1993 independence	1993- date one party state; (dominant leader)		-	

Traditional Monarchy		(one party state) 1995–2007 (one party dominant state)	1984–1987	government/ multiparty transition)	successions with same leader)
Gabon	1960–1968	1968–1990 (one party rule)	–	1991–1993 (multiparty transition)	1998, 2005, and 2009 (intraparty successions with different leader) and re-election of same person in 2011	7yr term with no limit
The Gambia	1965–1994			1994–1996	1996	2001, 2006, 2011 (intraparty successions with same leader)	5yr term with no limit
Ghana	1957–1958	1958–1964 (restricted democratic practice) 1969–1972; 1979–1981 (democracy)	1964–1966 (one party rule)	1966–1969 1972–1979 1981–1992	1992 (multiparty transition)	1996 (re-election of same person) 2000 (interparty succession and re-election of same person in 2004) 2008 (interparty succession) 2012 (intraparty succession with same leader)	Two 4yr terms

TABLE 28.1 cont.

Name of country	1st wave of democratisation / Independence	Democratic succession in the 1st wave of democratisation	One party status/one dominant political party	Military rule during the 1st wave of democratisation	2nd wave of democratisation / multiparty system from 1990	Democratic succession through the ballot box in the 2nd wave of democratisation	Military rule in the second wave of democratisation	Term limits of presidents	Political upheavals / tension in succession in the 2nd wave
Guinea	1958		1958–1984 (one party rule)	1984–1990 2008–2010	1990–1993 (multiparty transition) 1993–2008 (restricted democratic practice)	1999 and 2003 (intraparty successions with same leader) 2010 (interparty succession)		5yr terms with no limit	
Guinea-Bissau	1974		1974–1980 (one party) 1984–1991 (one party)	1980–1984	1991–1994 (multiparty transition) 2003–2005 (transitional government) 2012 (transitional government)	1999 and 2005 (interparty successions) 2009, 2012 (intraparty successions with different leaders)	2012	5yr term with no limit	
Kenya	1963–1966	1966–1969 (restricted	1969–1982 (de-facto		1991–1992 (multiparty	1997 (intraparty succession with		Two 5yr terms	Civil war

Lesotho	1966–1970		1986–1993	1993	2013 (interparty succession)
		1970–1986 (dominant leader) (restricted democratic practice)		1998 (interparty succession) and re-election of same leader in 2002 and 2007	5yr term with no limit	Tension
				2012 (interparty succession)		
Liberia	1847–1878	1984–1990 (restricted democratic practice)	1980–1984	1990–1997 (transitional government) 2003–2006 (transitional government)	2005 (interparty succession) and re-election of same leader in 2011	Two 6yr terms
Libya	1951	1951–1969 (constitutional monarchy)	1969–1972		2012 (transitional government)		Civil war (2011)
		1972–2011 (one party rule)					
Madagascar	1960–1972	1976–1989 (one party rule)	1972–1976	1989–1992 (multiparty transition)	1996 (interparty succession)	2009	Two 5yr terms	Tension
					2001 (interparty succession)		

TABLE 28.1 cont.

Name of country	1st wave of democratisation/ Independence	Democratic succession in the 1st wave of democratisation	One party status/one dominant political party	Military rule during the 1st wave of democratisation	2nd wave of democratisation / multiparty system from 1990	Democratic succession through the ballot box in the 2nd wave of democratisation	Military rule in the second wave of democratisation	Term limits of presidents	Political upheavals/tension in succession in the 2nd wave
Malawi	1964		1964–1966 (de facto one party rule) 1966–1993 (one party)		1993–1994 (multiparty transition)	re-election of same person in 2006 2009-date (transitional government) 1999 (intraparty succession with different leader) 2004 (intraparty succession with different leader) 2009 (interparty succession)		Two 5yr terms	Tension, civil strife
Mali	1960		1960–1968, (one party) 1979–1991 (one party)	1968–1976, 1976–1979	1991–1992 (transitional government and	1997 (intraparty succession with same leader) 2002 (interparty	2012 (interim government)	Two 5yr terms	Tension

DEMOCRATIC SUCCESSION IN AFRICA

Mauritania	1960–1961	1961–1978 (one party rule)	1978–1991	1991–1992 (multiparty transition)	1997,2003 (intraparty succession with same leader)	2005–2007 2008–2009	Two 5yr terms Tension
					2007 (interparty succession)		
					2009 (interparty succession)		
Mauritius	1968	Legislative elections which formed electoral college to choose the president took place in 1976,1982, 1983,1987, 1991,1995, 2000 and 2005			1992, 1997 (same party with same leader)		Two 5yr terms
					2002 (interparty succession)		
					2003 (intraparty succession with different leader) and re-election in 2008;		
					2012 (interparty succession)		
Morocco	1956 Parliamentary constitutional monarchy	Legislative elections which formed the electoral college to choose president were conducted in				–	

TABLE 28.1 cont.

Name of country	1st wave of democratisation / Independence	Democratic succession in the 1st wave of democratisation	One party status/one dominant political party	Military rule during the 1st wave of democratisation	2nd wave of democratisation / multiparty system from 1990	Democratic succession through the ballot box in the 2nd wave of democratisation	Military rule in the second wave of democratisation	Term limits of presidents	Political upheavals / tension in succession in the 2nd wave
		1963, 1970, 1977, 1984, 1993, 1997, 2002, with interparty successions in 2007 and 2011							
Mozambique	1975		1975–1990 (one party rule)		1990–1994 (multiparty transition)	1999, 2004 and 2009 (intraparty successions with different leaders)		Two 5yr terms	Tension
Namibia	1990				1990	1994,1999 and 2004 (intraparty successions with different leaders) and re-election of the same leader in 2009		Two 5yr terms	Tension

Nigeria	1960–1966	1979–1983 (democracy) 1989–1993 (restricted democratic practice)	1966–1979 1983–1989 1993–1998	1989–1991 (one party) transition) 2009–2010 (restricted democratic practice)	1999 and 2004 (intraparty successions with same leader) 2011 (interparty succession)	Two 4yr terms	Tension
Rwanda	1962–1965 (restricted democratic practice)		1965–1973 (one party) 1975–1978 (de facto one party) 1978–1991 (one party)	1973–1975 1991–1994 (multiparty transition) 1994–2003 (transitional government)	1998–1999 (transitional government) 1999, 2003, 2007, 2011 (intraparty successions with different leaders) 2003 (interparty succession) and re-election of same leader in 2010	Two 7yr terms	Civil war
São Tomé and Príncipe	1975		1975–1990 (one party rule)	1990–1991 (multiparty transition)	1996 (interparty succession) 2001 (interparty succession) and re-election of same person in 2006 2011 (interparty succession)	Two 5yr terms	

TABLE 28.1 cont.

Name of country	1st wave of democratisation / Independence	Democratic succession in the 1st wave of democratisation	One party status/one dominant political party	Military rule during the 1st wave of democratisation	2nd wave of democratisation / multiparty system from 1990	Democratic succession through the ballot box in the 2nd wave of democratisation	Military rule in the second wave of democratisation	Term limits of presidents	Political upheavals / tension in succession in the 2nd wave
Senegal	1960–1963	Presidential elections since 1963,1978,1983 1988,1993,2000 2007,2012 1963–1966; 1974–1978 (restricted democratic practice)	1966–1974 (one party rule)		1978–2000 (emerging democracy)	1993 (interparty succession) 2000,2007,2012 (intraparty successions with same leader)		Two 7yr terms	Tension
Seychelles	1976–1977		1977–1979 (de facto one party rule) 1979–1991 (one party rule)		1991–1993 (multiparty transition)	1998 and 2001 (intraparty successions with different leaders) 2006, 2011 (intraparty successions with same leader)		Three 5yr terms	
Sierra Leone	1961–1967	1968–1971 (emerging	1978–1991 (one party	1967–1968	1991–1992 (multiparty	1996, 2002 (intraparty	1992–1996, 1997–1998	Two 5y-r terms	Civil war from 1991

DEMOCRATIC SUCCESSION IN AFRICA

Somalia	1960–1969 (democratic practice)	1976–1991 (one party rule)	1969–1976 1976–1991	1991–2000 (no central government) 2000-date (transitional government)	(intraparty succession with different leader) - National Fragmentation (1991-date)
Somaliland				1991–2003 (transitional government)	2003, 2010 (interparty successions) 5yr term with no limit
South Africa	1934 (independence) 1994 (end of apartheid)	1948–1990 (apartheid whites and restricted democratic practice)		1990–1994 (transition to multiracial rule)	1999, 2004, 2009 (intraparty successions with different leaders) Two 5yr terms Tension
South Sudan				2010 referendum; 2011 (restricted democratic practice)	-
Sudan	1956–1958	1964–1965 (transitional government)	1971–1985 (one party) 1993–1999	1958–1964 1969–1971	2000 (multiparty elections) 2010 (intraparty succession with same leaders) 5yr term with no limit Civil war (1983–2005)

TABLE 28.1 cont.

Name of country	1st wave of democratisation / Independence	Democratic succession in the 1st wave of democratisation	One party status/one dominant political party	Military rule during the 1st wave of democratisation	2nd wave of democratisation / multiparty system from 1990	Democratic succession through the ballot box in the 2nd wave of democratisation	Military rule in the second wave of democratisation	Term limits of presidents	Political upheavals / tension in succession in the 2nd wave
		1965–1969 1986–1989 (democracy)	(de facto one party rule)	1985–1986 1989–1993	with (restricted democratic practice)				
Swaziland	1968–1973 Constitutional monarchy		1973–1993 Traditional monarchy from		Non-partisan elections 1993	Elections in 1998, 2003, and 2008		–	
Tanzania	1964		1964–1965 (de facto one party rule) 1965–1992 (one party)		1992–1995 (multiparty transition)	2000, 2005, 2010 (intraparty succession with different leaders)		Two 5yr terms	Tension
Togo	1960–1961	1963–1967 (emerging democracy)	1962–1963 (de facto one party rule) 1979–1991 (one party)	1967–1969 1969–1979	1991–1993 (multiparty transition)	1998, 2003, 2005 (intraparty successions with same leader); 2010 (intraparty succession with		5yr term with no term limit	

Uganda	1962–1966	1966–1969 1980–1985 (restricted democratic practice)	1969–1971 (one party rule)	1971–1979 1985–1989	1989–1996 (transitional period)	2006 and 2011 (intraparty successions with same leader)	-	Tension
Zambia	1964–1972		1972–1990 (one party rule)		1990–1991 (multiparty transition)	1996, 2001, 2006 (intraparty successions with different leaders) 2008 (intra party succession with same leader) 2011 (interparty succession)	1997	Two 5yr terms	Tension
Zimbabwe	1980–1987	1987–date (restricted democratic practice)			1990	1996, 2002, 2013 (intraparty successions with same leader)	before the 2011 revolution	6yr term with no limit	Tension

Compiled from Author's Research from 2010–2013 based on available data

CHAPTER 29

Secession: The African Experience

Gino J. Naldi

Secession is arguably one of the most controversial areas of international law. The possible dismemberment of a State is a subject that is not always amenable to rational discourse but it is a fact of life and hence can not easily be ignored. There are many examples in the post-war era of successful and unsuccessful attempts at secession, some unilateral, or contested, that is, without prior principled negotiation among all stakeholders, others consensual, that is, with the consent or approval of the parent State.[1] In the latter instance international recognition of the new State is largely a formality. Africa has not been immune from secessionist tendencies; Katanga and Biafra are well-known instances. This has been one of the unfortunate legacies of the, oft arbitrary, partition of Africa, a consequence of the colonial experience.[2] This essay will not revisit these two cases which have been studied in some depth;[3] neither will it debate secession in the context of colonial peoples asserting their independence since the law relating to decolonization is a distinct issue. Rather it examines more recent events, including Eritrea, Somaliland and South Sudan, concerned with secession from independent States. However, before focusing on Africa it is necessary to consider briefly the various dimensions of international law relating to secession.

---

1   J. Crawford, *The Creation of States in International Law* (2nd ed., Oxford University Press, Oxford, 2006) pp. 391–418. A recent example is that of Scotland; in 2012 the British and Scottish Governments reached agreement on a referendum on the independence of Scotland, Agreement between the United Kingdom Government and the British and the Scottish Government on a referendum on independence for Scotland (15 October 2012) <http://www.number10.gov.uk/wp-content/uploads/2012/10/ Agreement-final-for-signing.pdf> visited on 14 December 2012. The vote held in 2014 rejected independence by a reasonable majority, BBC News, 'Scottish referendum: Scotland votes "No" to independence' (19 September 2014) <http://www.bbc.co.uk/news/uk-Scotland-29270441) (accessed 4 March 2015)
2   I.Ll. Griffiths, *The African Inheritance* (Routledge, London, 1995) pp. 123–135.
3   See Crawford, *supra* note 1, pp. 56–58, 404–406; Griffiths, *supra* note 2, pp. 124–128, 128–131 respectively; V. Berny, 'La sécession du Katanga', 19 *Revue juridique et politique independence et cooperation* (1965) 563; D.A. Ijalaye, 'Was "Biafra" at Any Time a State in International Law?', 65 *American Journal of International Law* (1971) 551; T.D. Musgrave, *Self-Determination and National Minorities* (Oxford University Press, Oxford, 2000) pp. 195–199; F. Wodié, 'La sécession du Biafra et le droit international public', 73 *Revue Générale de Droit International Public* (1969) 1018.

1   The Status of Unilateral Secession – An Overview

An overwhelming body of academic opinion is of the view that international law does not prohibit or provide for a right to unilateral secession, it neither condemns nor condones it; secession *per se* is not contrary to international law.[4] Thus Franck writes that 'the law will neither prohibit nor authorize secession'.[5] According to Cassese 'the international community does not recognize the right of secession'.[6] But differing positions should also be acknowledged and the view has been expressed that there is a limited 'acceptance of the legitimacy of secession within international law norms.'[7] Nevertheless, the better view seems to be that not only is it the case that a general right of secession does not exist under international law but neither does it seem possible 'to agree on definite criteria under which secession may be justified in given circumstances.'[8] It has been asserted to the contrary that secession may be legitimate if four conditions exist: (a) a people distinct from the rest of the population by reason of ethnic, religious or national origin; (b) discrimination against those people amounting to a denial of internal self-determination; (c) the people must inhabit a readily severable part of the State; (d) the people

---

4   Crawford, *supra* note 1, pp. 388–390; Musgrave, *supra* note 3, pp. 209–210; A. Aust, *Handbook of International Law* (Cambridge University Press, Cambridge, 2005) p. 23; P. Malanczuk, *Akehurst's Modern Introduction to International Law* (7th rev. ed., Routledge, London, 1997) pp. 78, 339; 'Expert opinion prepared in 1992 by T.M. Franck, R. Higgins, A. Pellet, M.N. Shaw and C. Tomuschat, "The Territorial Integrity of Québec in the Event of the Attainment of Sovereignty"', in A.E. Bayefsky (ed.), *Self-Determination in International Law: Quebec and Lessons Learned* (Kluwer Law International, The Hague, 2000) pp. 241, 284; G. Abi-Saab, 'The Effectivity Required of an Entity that Declares its Independence in Order for it to be Considered a State in International Law', ibid., p. 69, p. 72; T.M. Franck, 'Opinion Directed at Question 2 of the Reference', ibid., p. 75, pp. 77–78, 83; M.N. Shaw, 'Re: Order in Council P.C. 1996–1497 of 30 September 1996', ibid., p. 125, p. 136; H. Hannum, 'The right of self-determination in the twenty-first century', 55 *Washington and Lee Law Review* (1998) 773, p. 776.
5   T.M. Franck, 'Postmodern Tribalism and the Right to Secession', in C. Brölmann, R. Lefeber, M. Zieck (eds.), *Peoples and Minorities in International Law* (Kluwer, The Hague, 1993) pp. 3, 14.
6   A. Cassese, *International Law* (2nd ed., Oxford University Press, Oxford, 2005) p. 68.
7   V.P. Nanda, 'Self-Determination under International Law: Validity of Claims to Secede', 13 *Case Western Reserve Journal of International Law* (1981) 257, p. 271. Franck observes that secession constitutes a 'lawful option', T.M. Franck, 'Opinion Directed at Response of Professor Crawford and Wildhaber', *supra* note 4, p. 179, p. 183.
8   L. Henkin, R.C. Pugh, O. Schacter, H. Smit, *International Law: Cases and Materials* (2nd ed., West Publishing Co., St. Paul, 1987), p. 282.

must have historic ties with the territory they inhabit.[9] Be that as it may, the critical element appears to be that of effectiveness. If the seceding entity can successfully defend its independent existence, and assuming it fulfils the criteria of statehood, it is likely that the international community will ultimately accept that reality.[10] Another consideration, which is more of a political or moral imperative, is that peace and security may be better served by accepting secession.[11]

State practice can be drawn upon in support of the initial premise. In the advisory proceedings before the International Court of Justice (ICJ) relating to Kosovo's unilateral declaration of independence France submitted that it 'is entirely clear that there is no right to secession in international law, it is equally apparent that international law does not prohibit secession'.[12] The United Kingdom's stated position was the same, that 'international law contains neither a right of unilateral secession nor the denial *per se* of such a right.'[13] This

---

[9] R.C.A. White, 'Self-Determination: Time for a Re-Assessment?' 28 *Netherlands International Law Review* (1981) 147, p. 161. For other critera see, Nanda, *supra* note 7, p. 275; L.-C. Chen, *An Introduction to Contemporary International Law* (2nd ed., Yale University Press, New Haven, 2000) pp. 35–36.

[10] Abi-Saab, *supra* note 4, pp. 73–74; Aust, *supra* note 4, p. 24; Franck, Higgins, Pellet, Shaw and Tomuschat, *supra* note 4, ibid.; A. Pellet, 'Legal Opinion on Certain Questions of International Law Raised by the Reference', in *Self-Determination in International Law*, *supra* note 4, p. 185, pp. 206–208; H. Lauterpacht, *Oppenheim's International Law*, vol. 1, (8th ed., Longmans, London, 1955) pp. 128–129; *Reference re Secession of Quebec* 37 ILM (1998) 1342, paras 140–143. Consequently, the nature of recognition, constitutive or declaratory, assumes an added significance which has led one writer to query whether secession can be described as a neutral act in international law, Musgrave, *supra* note 3, pp. 193–194.

[11] D. Murswiek, 'The Issue of a Right of Secession – Reconsidered', in C. Tomuschat (ed.), *Modern Law of Self-Determination* (Martinus Nijhoff, The Hague, 1993) p. 21, p. 36; Henkin et al., *supra* note 8, ibid. In *Accordance with International Law of the Unilateral Declaration of Independence in Respect of Kosovo*, 22 July 2010, International Court of Justice, Advisory Opinion, *ICJ Reports 2010*, p. 403, p. 618, para. 6, Judge Yusuf expressed the view that claims to secession can pose a threat to regional stability and international peace and security (Separate Opinion of Judge Yusuf).

[12] Written Statement by France to the ICJ *Accordance with International Law of the Unilateral Declaration of Independence by the Provisional Institutions of Self-Government of Kosovo*, para. 2.8 <http://www.icj.cij.org/docket/files/141/15607.pdf> visited 11 October 2013. See also Written Statement by Germany, Section VI <http://www.icj.cij.org/docket/files/141/15624.pdf> visited 11 October 2013.

[13] Written Statement by the United Kingdom, para. 1.14 <http://www.icj.cij.org/docket/files/141/15638.pdf> visited 11 October 2013.

stance was shared by the United States.[14] And Ireland expressed the view that 'international law is generally silent or neutral on the legality of secession.'[15] But Cassese writes that 'it cannot be denied that State practice and the overwhelming view of States remain opposed to secession.'[16]

Judicial opinion is of a similar view. In a landmark decision in 1998 concerning the future of the Canadian federation the Supreme Court of Canada addressed the issue of whether the province of Quebec would be able to secede from Canada.[17] Regarding the question whether international law conferred upon Quebec the right to effect its secession from Canada unilaterally, the Supreme Court observed that 'international law does not specifically grant component parts of sovereign states the legal right to secede unilaterally from their "parent" state'.[18] Judge Koroma expressed the view in the *Kosovo Case* that this statement was an accurate reflection of the present state of international law.[19] Nevertheless, the Supreme Court of Canada went on to observe that in the absence of a specific prohibition '[I]nternational law contains neither a right nor the explicit denial of such a right' but that secession could be validated only in exceptional circumstances.[20]

While the Advisory Opinion of the ICJ in the *Kosovo Case*[21] may well be considered as a missed opportunity to expound on this subject[22] the ICJ nevertheless did proceed to state that no prohibition of unilateral declarations of independence existed in general international law.[23] Additionally, state prac-

---

14 Written Statement by the United States, pp. 50–52 <http://www.icj.cij.org/docket/files/141/15640.pdf> visited 11 October 2013.
15 Written Statement by Ireland, para. 19 <http://www.icj.cij.org/docket/files/141/15662.pdf> visited 16 October 2013.
16 A. Cassese, *Self-Determination of Peoples: A Legal Reappraisal* (Cambridge University Press, Cambridge, 1995) p. 123. See also, Crawford, *supra* note 1, p. 390.
17 *Reference re Secession of Quebec, supra* note 10, para. 111.
18 Ibid. para. 111.
19 *Kosovo Case, supra* note 11, p. 467, para. 23 (Dissenting Opinion of Judge Koroma). See similarly the case decided by the Spanish Constitutional Court on the attempt by the Catalonian regional government to set in motion a process that could lead to the establishment of a sovereign Catalan state, Judgment No. 01389-2013, Tribunal Constitucional, 25 March 2014.
20 Ibid. para. 112.
21 *Kosovo Case, supra* note 11.
22 See, e.g., *Kosovo Case, supra* note 11, p. 491 (Separate Opinion of Judge Sepúlveda-Amor).
23 *Kosovo Case, supra* note 11, paras 79, 81. For comment see, R. Wilde, 'Case Report: Accordance with International Law of the Unilateral Declaration of Independence by the Provisional Institutions of Self-Government of Kosovo', 105 *American Journal of International Law* (2011) 301. According to a distinguished commentator, this did not mean that the ICJ

tice did not indicate the emergence of a new rule of international law prohibiting unilateral declarations of independence outside the contexts of colonialism or alien domination.[24] These pronouncements of the ICJ must be treated with due caution because it is unclear whether the ICJ equated secession with unilateral declarations of independence, something the United States had done in its Written Statements.[25] Indeed, as France and Switzerland observed, the two are not synonymous.[26] Certainly, Judge Koroma also drew a distinction.[27]

A further important point needs to be made. A secession that comes about in contravention of fundamental principles of international law, for example, through foreign armed subversion violating the territorial integrity of the State, or in breach of the right of self-determination, will be deemed unlawful and any de facto state, or quasi-state,[28] that emerges thereby will not attract recognition from the international community as a whole.[29] Into this category fall the quasi-states of Abkhazia, South Ossetia[30] and the Turkish Republic of

---

found the declaration acceptable under international law, R. Falk, 'The *Kosovo* Advisory Opinion: Conflict Resolution and Precedent', 105 *American Journal of International Law* (2011) 50, p. 50.

24   *Kosovo Case, supra* note 11, para. 79.
25   Written Statement by the United States, *supra* note 14, ibid.
26   Written Statement by France, *supra* note 12, para. 2.8; Written Statement by Switzerland, para. 27 <http://www.icj.cij.org/docket/files/141/15614.pdf > visited 11 October 2013. See also, Crawford, *supra* note 1, p. 35.
27   Describing the unilateral declaration of independence as 'tantamount' to an attempt at secession, Dissenting Opinion of Judge Koroma, *supra* note 19, para. 23.
28   Quasi-states are defined as 'regions that secede from another state, gain de facto control over the territory they lay claim to, but fail to achieve international recognition', P. Kolstø, 'The Sustainability and Future of Unrecognized States', 43 *Journal of Peace Research* (2006) 723, p. 723.
29   *Kosovo Case, supra* note 11, para. 81; Written Statement by France, *supra* note 12, para. 2.13; Written Statement by the United States, *supra* note 14, p. 56; Written Statement by Ireland, *supra* note 15, para. 22; Cassese, *supra* note 16, p. 158; Crawford, *supra* note 1, pp. 148, 388; Shaw, *supra* note 4, p. 136. See also, *EC Arbitration Commission on Yugoslavia (Opinion No. 10)* 31 ILM (1992) 1525, para. 4. And see UN General Assembly Resolution 68/262 (2014) on the Territorial integrity of Ukraine calling on States not to recognize changes in the status of the Crimea.
30   M. Shaw, *International Law* (6th ed. Cambridge University Press, Cambridge, 2008) p. 238; A. Tancredi, 'Neither Authorized nor Prohibited? Secession and International Law after Kosovo, South Ossetia and Abkhazia', 18 *Italian Yearbook of International Law* (2008) 37, pp. 59–62. See also, *Ilascu v. Moldova and Russia* (2004) 40 EHRR 1030, para. 392, with regard to the unrecognized Transnistrian Moldovan Republic.

Northern Cyprus.[31] Significant external destabilization was one of the reasons why Katanga's claim to statehood was rejected.[32]

2 The Impact of Self-Determination

The next question that must be addressed is concerned with the possible effect of self-determination on sovereign States beyond the colonial context, that is, whether unilateral secession is legitimized in international law by invoking the right to self-determination. Since the late 1960s, following the adoption of the International Covenant on Civil and Political Rights (ICCPR)[33] and the UN Declaration on Friendly Relations and Co-operation Among States 1970,[34] there has been a growing acceptance that the right to self-determination has become established as a universal human right which is no longer confined to the arena of decolonization.[35] But does such a right give rise to an entitlement

---

31 Crawford, *supra* note 1, pp. 143–147; Nanda, *supra* note 8, pp. 273–274; Shaw, *supra* note 30, pp. 235–236. The UN Security Council has declared Northern Cyprus to be 'legally invalid', Security Council Resolution 541 (1983). See further, Case C – 432/92, *R.* v. *Minister of Agriculture, Fisheries & Food, ex parte Anastasiou (Pissouri) Ltd.* [1994] ECR I – 3087; *Loizidou* v. *Turkey*, European Court of Human Rights, Merits, (1996) 23 EHRR 513, paras 42–43; *Cyprus* v. *Turkey*, European Court of Human Rights, Merits, (2001) 35 EHRR 731, para. 61.

32 Written Statement by the United Kingdom, *supra* note 13, para. 5.36.

33 1966 International Covenant on Civil and Political Rights 999 UNTS 171 (ICCPR).

34 UN General Assembly Resolution 2625 (XXV) 1970 Declaration on Friendly Relations and Co-operation Among States in Accordance with the Charter of the United Nations, 9 ILM (1970) 1292.

35 This is implicit in General Comment No. 12, Compilation of General Comments and General Recommendations Adopted by Human Rights Treaty Bodies, General Comments Adopted by the Human Rights Committee, HRI/GEN/1/Rev.9 (Vol. I). See further, Cassese, *supra* note 16, p. 109; Musgrave, *supra* note 3, pp. 98–100; A. Conte and R. Burchill *Defining Civil and Political Rights: The Jurisprudence of the United Nations Human Rights Committee* (2nd ed., Ashgate, Farnham, 2009) pp. 248–249; D. McGoldrick, *The Human Rights Committee: Its Role in the Development of the International Covenant on Civil and Political Rights* (Clarendon Press, Oxford, 1991) p. 15; H. Hannum, 'Rethinking Self-Determination', 34 *Virginia Journal of International Law* (1993) 1, pp. 19, 33; P. Thornberry, 'Self-Determination, Minorities, Human Rights: A Review of International Instruments', 38 *International & Comparative Law Quarterly* (1989) 867, p. 878. Self-determination has the status of an 'essential principle' of international law, *East Timor (Portugal* v. *Australia)*, 30 June 1995, International Court of Justice, ICJ Reports 1995, p. 90, p. 102; *Legal Consequences of the Construction of a Wall in the Occupied Palestinian Territory*, 9 July 2004, International Court of Justice, Advisory Opinion, ICJ Reports 2004, p. 136, pp. 171–172. See also, *Reference re Secession of Quebec*, *supra* note 10, para. 114.

to secede? It seems that international law may still not be able to provide a definitive answer to this crucial question.[36] The weight of scholarly opinion is that self-determination cannot sanction secession.[37] Thus Franck expresses the view that self-determination 'has not been endowed by states in texts or practice with anything remotely like an internationally-validated *right*, accruing to every secession-minded anywhere, to secede territorially, at will'.[38] According to Hannum, 'self-determination has never been considered an absolute right to be exercised irrespective of competing claims or rights'.[39] Shaw writes that self-determination 'cannot be utilised as a legal tool for the dismantling of sovereign states.'[40] As another writer puts it, 'A State-based international legal order cannot contain a rule that leads to the destruction of most of the States. That is why States would never have accepted self-determination as a legal principle that validates an unlimited right to secession.'[41]

Judicial and quasi-judicial authorities have reached the same conclusion. In the *Aaland Islands Case* the International Commission of Jurists reported that, 'Positive International Law does not recognize the right of national groups, as such, to separate themselves from the State of which they form part by the simple expression of a wish ... Generally speaking, the grant or the refusal of such a right to a portion of its population determining its own political fate by plebiscite or by some other method, is, exclusively, an attribute of the sovereignty of every State'.[42] In the *Kosovo Case* Judge Koroma drew attention to the

---

36 EC *Arbitration Commission on Yugoslavia (Opinion No. 2)* 31 ILM (1992) 1497, para. 1. According to Shaw, *supra* note 30, p. 257, the principle of seld-determination could evolve to encompass a right to secession but has not yet 'convincingly happened.'

37 Cassese, *supra* note 16, pp. 102–108, 122–124, 335; Franck, Higgins, Pellet, Shaw and Tomuschat, *supra* note 4, para. 3.15; Hannum, *supra* note 4, p. 776; Malanczuk, *supra* note 4, pp. 335–336, 339–340; Shaw, *supra* note 4, pp. 137–138; L.C. Buchheit, *Secession: The Legitimacy of Self-Determination* (Yale University Press, New Haven, 1978) pp. 86–87; D.J. Harris, *Cases and Materials on International Law* (7th ed., Sweet & Maxwell, London, 2010) p. 104; R. Higgins, *Problems and Process: International Law and How We Use It* (Oxford University Press, Oxford, 1994) pp. 117, 122; P. Hilpold, 'Self-Determination in the 21st Century – Modern Perspectives for an Old Concept', 36 *Israel Yearbook on Human Rights* (2006) 247. Cf. contra, Chen, *supra* note 9, pp. 32–38.

38 Franck, *supra* note 5, p. 16.

39 Hannum, *supra* note 35, p. 32.

40 Shaw, *supra* note 30, p. 291.

41 Murswiek, *supra* note 11, p. 36.

42 *Report of the International Commission of Jurists on the Legal Aspects of the Aaland Islands Question*, in M.W. Janis & J.E. Noyes, *Cases and Commentary on International Law* (West Publishing Co., St. Paul, 1997) p. 395, para. 2. See Cassese, *supra* note 16, pp. 27–31.

threat to international stability if the position were otherwise.[43] Echoing the words of the International Commission of Jurists Judge Koroma stated flatly that, 'International Law does not confer a right on ethnic, linguistic or religious groups to break away from the territory of a State of which they form part, without that State's consent, merely by expressing their wish to do so. To accept otherwise, to allow any ethnic, linguistic or religious group to declare independence and break away from the territory of the State of which it forms part, outside the context of decolonization, creates a very dangerous precedent.'[44] Judge Yusuf shared this standpoint. He stated, 'Surely, there is no general positive right under international law which entitles all ethnically or racially distinct groups within existing States to claim separate statehood ... Thus, a racially or ethnically distinct group within a State ... does not have the right to unilateral secession simply because it wishes to create its own separate State'.[45] In a similar vein the UN Committee on the Elimination of Racial Discrimination has stated that, 'international law has not recognized a general right of peoples unilaterally to declare secession from a State'.[46]

Numerous significant international instruments make it clear that no action that would dismember or impair the territorial integrity or political unity of a State can be justified on the basis of self-determination.[47] The right of exter-

---

43 Dissenting Opinion of Judge Koroma, *supra* note 19, para. 4. See also, Separate Opinion of Judge Yusuf, *supra* note 11, para. 10.

44 Dissenting Opinion of Judge Koroma, *supra* note 19, para. 4. See Franck, *supra* note 5, p. 11; Higgins, *supra* note 37, p. 124; Musgrave, *supra* note 3, p. 210. According to one commentator, the ICJ's perception of the *Kosovo Case* as exceptional that did not constitute a precedent was an attempt to meet Judge Koroma's criticisms that the Opinion would hearten separatists, Falk, *supra* note 23, p. 51. Judge Koroma's warnings seem prescient in light of Crimea's breakaway from Ukraine in 2014.

45 Separate Opinion of Judge Yusuf, *supra* note 11, para. 10.

46 Compilation of General Comments and General Recommendations Adopted by Human Rights Treaty Bodies, General Recommendations Adopted by the Committee on the Elimination of Racial Discrimination, General Recommendation XXI, para. 11 HRI/GEN/1/Rev.9 (Vol. II).

47 UN General Assembly Resolution 2625 (XXV) 1970 Declaration on Friendly Relations and Co-operation Among States in Accordance with the Charter of the United Nations, para. 7; 1975 Helsinki Final Act, 14 ILM (1975) 1292, Principle VIII (reaffirmed by the 1990 Charter of Paris for a New Europe, 30 ILM (1991) 190); 1993 Vienna Declaration and Programme of Action, Part I, para. 2, 32 ILM (1993) 1661. See J.P. Grant and J.C. Barker, *Parry & Grant Encyclopaedic Dictionary of International Law* (3rd ed., Oxford University Press, New York, 2009) p. 545. In Resolution 68/262 (2014) the UN General Assembly declared invalid the referendum held in the Crimea in March 2014 which resulted in an overwhelming vote to break away from Ukraine.

nal self-determination must be consistent with that of territorial integrity. This was a point made by Judge Koroma in the *Kosovo Case*. The fundamental importance of the principles of sovereignty and territorial integrity led to the conclusion that they prevailed over that of self-determination.[48] This was reiterated by Judge Yusuf who stated that the territorial integrity of States could otherwise be reduced to irrelevance.[49] The Supreme Court of Canada has reaffirmed this view, stating that 'international law expects that the right to self-determination will be exercised by peoples within the framework of existing sovereign states and consistently with the maintenance of the territorial integrity of those states.'[50] The UN Human Rights Committee has commented that the rights of minorities under Article 27 ICCPR do not prejudice the sovereignty and territorial integrity of State parties.[51] According to Franck this provision gives rise only to a limited right, 'Evidently, they are not given the right to secede.'[52] The African Commission on Human and Peoples' Rights (African Commission) has held that the exercise of self-determination under Article 20 of the African Charter on Human and Peoples' Rights (African Charter)[53] must be compatible with the sovereignty and territorial integrity of States and that it does not authorize secession.[54] According to the African Commission 'secession is not recognised as a variant of the right of self-determination within the con-

---

48 Dissenting Opinion of Judge Koroma, *supra* note 19, paras 21–22. The hierarchical relationship between these two principle continues to defy categorical classification but appears to be dependent on the circumstances of each particular case. Dicta in the *Western Sahara*, 16 October 1975, International Court of Justice, Advisory Opinion, *ICJ Reports 1975*, p. 12, p. 68, is open to the interpretation that territorial integrity takes precedence, M.N. Shaw, 'The Western Sahara Case', 49 *British Yearbook of International Law* (1978) 119, p. 148. The conventional view was that the principle of territorial integrity 'precluded internal attempts at secession', M. Weller, 'The International Response to the Dissolution of the Socialist Federal Republic of Yugoslavia', 86 *American Journal of International Law* (1992) 569, p. 572.

49 Separate Opinion of Judge Yusuf, *supra* note 11, para. 10.

50 *Reference re Secession of Quebec*, *supra* note 10, para. 122. See further, ibid., para. 127.

51 Compilation of General Comments and General Recommendations Adopted by Human Rights Treaty Bodies, General Comments Adopted by the Human Rights Committee, General Comment No. 23, para. 3.2 HRI/GEN/1/Rev.9 (Vol. I). See further, Malanczuk, *supra* note 4, pp. 338–339.

52 Franck, *supra* note 5, p. 11.

53 1981 African Charter on Human and Peoples' Rights 1520 UNTS 217.

54 *Katangese Peoples' Congress v. Zaire*, Communication No. 75/92, 8th Activity Report 1994–1995, para. 4; *Gunme* et al. v. *Cameroon*, Communication No. 266/2003, 26th Activity Report 2008–2009, paras 190, 200. During the break-up of Yugoslavia in the 1990s the EC Commission impliedly rejected the contention that the Serb populations of Croatia and

text of the African Charter.'[55] It has therefore stated that it 'cannot envisage, condone or encourage secession, as a form of self-determination'.[56] Reliance may also be placed on State practice.[57] However, the situation may well be different when a State is in the process of dissolution; in such a situation the right of self-determination may play a crucial role.[58]

However, in the *Kosovo Case* the ICJ chose to interpret the relationship between the principles of territorial integrity and self-determination in a different, and potentially destabilizing, way. It took the view that the principle of territorial integrity governs inter-State relations, an aspect of the duty of non-intervention, but is not opposable to affairs between States and national groups, a variant on the 'internal theory'.[59] In this particular subject area the unfortunate consequence is that non-state actors are conferred power without responsibility. This stance had been advanced by France which argued that the principle of territorial integrity does not 'stand in the way of the accession to independence of non-colonial peoples.'[60] The United Kingdom adopted a

---

Bosnia-Herzegovina could secede, EC *Arbitration Commission on Yugoslavia* (*Opinion No. 2*), *supra* note 36.

55 *Gunme et al. v. Cameroon, supra* note 54, para. 200.

56 Ibid. The African Commission has also rejected a secessionist claim to independence from Senegal by Casamance separatists, *Report on the Mission of Good Offices to Senegal of the African Commission on Human and Peoples' Rights* (1–7 June 1996), Tenth Annual Activity Report, 1996–1997, in R. Murray and M. Evans (eds.), *Documents of the African Commission on Human and Peoples' Rights* (Hart Publishing, Oxford, 2001) 530.

57 Written Statement by Ireland, *supra* note 15, para. 28; Written Statement by Switzerland, *supra* note 26, para. 62; Written Statement by China Parts II-III, <http://www.icj.cij.org/docket/files/141/15611.pdf> visited 16 October 2013; Written Statement by Egypt Parts III-IV, <http://www.icj.cij.org/docket/files/141/15622.pdf> visited 16 October 2013; Written Statement by The Netherlands para. 3.6 <http://www.icj.cij.org/docket/files/141/15652.pdf> visited 11 October 2013; Written Statement by the Russian Federation paras 76–88 <http://www.icj.cij.org/docket/files/141/15628.pdf> visited 11 October 2013; Written Statement by Spain pp. 19–24 <http://www.icj.cij.org/docket/files/141/15644.pdf> visited 11 October 2013. See also, OAU AHG/Res. 51(IV) (1967). See further, Musgrave, *supra* note 3, pp. 104–105.

58 *Aaland Islands Case, supra* note 42, para. 3; *Wildermann v. Stinnes* 2 ILR 224; *EC Arbitration Commission on Yugoslavia* (*Opinion No. 1*) 31 ILM (1992) 1494.

59 *Kosovo Case, supra* note 11, para. 80. Wilde, *supra* note 23, p. 304, who proceeds to opine that as a consequence whether or not non-state actors have a right of self-determination is irrelevant.

60 Written Statement by France, *supra* note 12, paras 2.6–2.7. See also, Franck, Higgins, Pellet, Shaw and Tomuschat, *supra* note 4, paras 3.14(iii), 3.15; A. Pellet, 'Legal Opinion on Certain Questions of International Law Raised by the Reference', in *Self-Determination in International Law, supra* note 4, p. 85, pp. 98–99; Musgrave, *supra* note 3, p. 182.

similar position. It stated that 'although a State's territorial integrity is protected under international law, as a general matter this protection has been extended only insofar as the use of force and intervention by third States is concerned. It has not been extended to the point of providing a guarantee of the integrity of a State's territory against internal developments which may lead over time to the dissolution or reconfiguration of the State.'[61] Poland has expressed a more nuanced view, stating that 'the subordination of the principle of self-determination to the principle of territorial integrity is by no means of absolute character. The latter does not always have priority irrespective of the particular conditions of a given situation.'[62] But while it is a truism that the law does not provide absolute guarantees, against murder, speeding, discrimination, theft, etc., it is quite another matter to adopt a permissive attitude, the Ukraine Crisis highlights that danger; a presumption must exist in favour of preserving the territorial integrity of States. As Judge Koroma observed, a State exercises sovereignty *within* its territory which involves an obligation on others to respect its territorial integrity.[63] But if, as the ICJ pointed out, States must refrain from violating the territorial integrity of other States it follows that their recognition of quasi-states must be compatible with this obligation.[64]

The 'remedial' or 'oppression' theory may constitute another exception. The right of self-determination has evolved to a principle guiding the external and internal dimensions of a people's right to determine their political status and to pursue their economic, social and cultural development. The internal facet of self-determination entails the fundamental human right of the people of the State to good and representative governance on the basis of full equality, including protecting the rights of national minorities.[65] This being so the territorial integrity of States must be upheld.[66] The generally accepted view is that there is no right to unilateral secession from a democratic State. However, secession may be justified *in extremis* in instances of egregious human rights abuses, crimes against humanity, persecution of minorities, discriminatory

---

61 Written Statement by the United Kingdom, *supra* note 13, para. 5.10.
62 Written Statement by Poland, para. 6.9 <http://www.icj.cij.org/docket/files/141/15632.pdf> visited 16 October 2013.
63 Dissenting Opinion of Judge Koroma, *supra* note 19, para. 21.
64 Wilde, *supra* note 23, p. 306. Of course, premature recognition constitutes a delict in international law, or at least unlawful intervention, J. Brierly, *The Law of Nations*, (5th ed., Clarendon Press, Oxford, 1955) p. 130; Cassese, *supra* note 6, pp. 74–75; Lauterpacht, *supra* note 10, p. 128; Grant and Barker, *supra* note 47, p. 509.
65 Charter of Paris, *supra* note 47; EC *Arbitration Commission on Yugoslavia (Opinion No. 2)*, *supra* note 36, para. 2; Separate Opinion of Judge Yusuf, *supra* note 11, paras 8–9.
66 Vienna Declaration and Programme of Action, *supra* note 47, Part I, para. 2(3).

and exclusive policies and practices. Or as Cassese puts it, 'extreme and unremitting persecution and the lack of any reasonable prospect for peaceful challenge'.[67] Consequently, a 'right to secession proper may only arise when a *racial group* is *forcibly* refused equal access to government.'[68] It is additionally argued that international law's condemnation of 'alien domination' in post-colonial times extends to *any* subjugated peoples, and is not limited to neo-colonial or racist regimes.[69] Considerable scholarly support exists for the remedial theory.[70] Judicial pronouncements go the same way.[71] It was endorsed by Judge Wildhaber in *Loizidou* v. *Turkey*[72] and in the *Kosovo Case* by Judge Yusuf[73] and fervently so by Judge Cançado-Trindade.[74] The remedial theory has also been accepted in principle by the African Commission.[75] It has stated that the African Charter prohibits the domination of one people over another in the same State.[76] But massive violations of human rights, caused by oppression and domination, under the African Charter must be established.[77] The capacity of the people to democratic participation in government is an important consider-

---

[67] Cassese, *supra* note 16, p. 120.

[68] Cassese, *supra* note 6, p. 68.

[69] Franck, *supra* note 5, p. 14. However, according to Cassese, *supra* note 16, pp. 90–99, 'alien domination' or 'subjugation' applies to control over foreign or occupied territory.

[70] Buchheit, *supra* note 37, pp. 18, 222; Cassese, *supra* note 16, pp. 108–125; Chen, *supra* note 9, p. 38; Franck, *supra* note 5, p. 14; Hannum, *supra* note 4, pp. 776–777; Hannum, *supra* note 35, p. 32; Murswiek, *supra* note 11, p. 27; Musgrave, *supra* note 3, p. 209; Nanda, *supra* note 8, p. 278; Shaw, *supra* note 4, p. 138; J. Klabbers and R. Lefeber, 'Lost Between Self-Determination and *Uti Possidetis*', in Brölmann, Lefeber, Zieck, *supra* note 5, p. 48.

[71] In the *Aaland Islands Case, supra* note 42, para. 2, the International Commission of Jurists felt unable to give an opinion as to whether a 'manifest and continued abuse of sovereign power, to the detriment of a section of the population of a State' gave rise to an international dispute.

[72] *Loizidou* v. *Turkey, supra* note 31, (Concurring Opinion of Judge Wildhaber, joined by Judge Ryssdal).

[73] Separate Opinion of Judge Yusuf, *supra* note 11, paras 11–12.

[74] *Kosovo Case, supra* note 11, p. 523, paras 173–176 (Separate Opinion of Judge Cançado-Trindade).

[75] D. Shelton, 'Self-Determination in Regional Human Rights Law: From Kosovo to Cameroon', 105 *American Journal of International Law* (2011) 60, p. 81.

[76] *Malawi African Association* et al. v. *Mauritania*, Communication Nos. 54/91, 61/91, 98/93, 164/97–196/97, 210/98, 13th Activity Report 1999–2000, para. 142, where discriminatory practices against the Black population of Mauritania was condemned. See also, *Sudan Human Rights Organization and Sudan Centre for Housing Rights and Evictions* v. *Sudan*, Communication Nos. 279/03, 296/05, 49 ILM (2010) 1573, para. 223.

[77] *Gunme* et al. v. *Cameroon, supra* note 54, paras 197, 199. See also, *Katangese Peoples' Congress* v. *Zaire, supra* note 54, para. 6.

ation in this regard.[78] The Supreme Court of Canada did not rule out the validity of the remedial theory in appropriate circumstances, expressing the view that it was unclear whether was it an established principle of international law, but it held that Canada in any case complied with the internal dimension of self-determination, it being demonstrably the case that Quebecers participated fully in Canadian public affairs, so that no recourse to a right to secession arose.[79] State practice can also be invoked in its support.[80] However, one eminent jurist cautions against too ready a recourse to secession, warning that 'secession can be only a step of last resort and should not be granted lightly as a remedy.'[81] This was a view shared by Judge Yusuf in the *Kosovo Case* who, while approving of the oppression theory in principle, did not believe that it could automatically lead to separate statehood without prior exhaustion of all possible remedies for the realization of internal self-determination.[82] Russia would admit of remedial secession only in 'truly extreme circumstances'.[83] Notwithstanding these authorities it cannot be said with conviction that this proposition actually reflects established international law or even *de lege ferenda*.[84] Nevertheless, ultimately the ICJ's Opinion in the *Kosovo Case* constitutes a hostage to fortune in that it is capable of being construed as authority for a postcolonial interpretation of self-determination that 'any "people" living in a geographically distinct area, if suffering from gross abuse of human rights, could claim sovereign independence and statehood.'[85]

3 Secessionism in Africa

Many African States have experienced instability, and the threat of secession, as they have wrestled with centrifugal forces caused by a variety of factors,

---

[78] *Katangese Peoples' Congress v. Zaire*, supra note 54, ibid.; *Gunme et al. v. Cameroon*, supra note 54, paras 194–195.

[79] *Reference re Secession of Quebec*, supra note 10, paras 135–136, 138.

[80] Written Statement by Ireland, *supra* note 15, paras 29–32; Written Statement by Switzerland, *supra* note 26, paras 63–67; Written Statement by Poland, *supra* note 62, paras 6.3–6.8; Written Statement by The Netherlands, *supra* note 57, paras 3.6–3.7, 3.9–3.11, describing it as 'an *ultimum remedium*.'

[81] C. Tomuschat, 'Self-Determination in a Post-Colonial World', in Tomuschat, *supra* note 11, p. 1, pp. 9–10. See also, Buchheit, *supra* note 37, pp. 93–94, 221–222.

[82] Separate Opinion of Judge Yusuf, *supra* note 11, paras 11–16. See also, Written Statement by The Netherlands, *supra* note 57, para. 3.11.

[83] Written Statement by the Russian Federation, *supra* note 57, para. 89.

[84] Tancredi, *supra* note 30, p. 62. See also, Malanczuk, *supra* note 4, p. 340, who suggests that these proposals are unlikely to succeed in practice.

[85] Falk, *supra* note 23, p. 58.

including misrule, undemocratic politics, unaccountable administrations, human rights abuses, ethnic and religious differences, inequitably distributed resources, corruption and mismanagement and underdevelopment.[86] Unsurprisingly therefore, that the preservation of stability and the avoidance of ethnic conflicts while at the same time discouraging separatism have been basic aims of the Organization of African Unity (OAU) and the African Union (AU). One of the abiding foundational principles of the AU, as of the OAU before it, has been that of the territorial integrity of States. Hence one of the essential objectives of the AU is to defend the sovereignty and territorial integrity of its Member States.[87] This has also found expression in the adoption of the principle of *uti possidetis*.[88] One commentator has therefore explained the stance of the OAU/AU, 'Because of the extreme ethnic heterogeneity of most African States and the resulting difficulties in developing a sense of statehood in the post-independence period, the principles of territorial integrity and national unity have been widely felt to be more fundamental than that of self-determination.'[89] But significant differences exist between the AU and the OAU, one important one being the right of the AU to intervene in a Member State's internal affairs given certain state of affairs. Thus the AU is authorised to intervene in a Member State in 'grave circumstances', albeit limited to war crimes, genocide and crimes against humanity.[90] If such crimes were committed in a war of secession the AU could take action.[91] But of greater practical sig-

---

86 Griffiths, *supra* note 2, p. 135.
87 Article 3(b) 2000 Constitutive Act of the African Union 2158 UNTS 3. See also, Art. 4(e) 2002 Protocol relating to the Establishment of the Peace and Security Council of the African Union <http://au.org> (PSC). In relation to the OAU see Arts. 2(1)(c), 3(3) 1963 Charter of the Organization of African Unity 479 UNTS 39. See further, AHG/Res. 51(IV) (1967) whereby the OAU condemned secession in Member States, reaffirmed its support for the principle of territorial integrity and declared that the right of self-determination did not apply to cases of secession.
88 See Art. 4(b) Constitutive Act; Art. 4(i) PSC Protocol. See also, G.J. Naldi, *The Organization of African Unity: An Analysis of its Role* (2nd ed., Mansell, London, 1999) pp. 12–13.
89 Hannum, *supra* note 35, p. 32.
90 Art. 4(h) Constitutive Act. See also, Art. 4(j) PSC Protocol.
91 In 2009 an AU High-Level Panel on Darfur acknowledged that atrocities had been committed in the Darfur conflict in Sudan, 'Report of the High Level Panel on Darfur', AU Doc. PSC/AHG/2(CCVII). Secessionist sentiment appears to have played a factor. In 2005 the *Report of the International Commission of Inquiry on violations of international humanitarian law and human rights law in Darfur* had concluded that violations of international human rights and humanitarian law had occurred but not acts of genocide, UN Doc. S/2005/60. Pursuant to UN Security Council Resolution 1593 (2005), 44 ILM (2005) 1008, 'the situation in Darfur' was referred to the Prosecutor of the International Criminal Court. The President of Sudan, Omar Al-Bashir, was indicted for crimes against humanity

nificance perhaps is the right of Member States to request intervention from the AU in order to restore peace and security.[92] Central governments are therefore in a lawful position to seek external assistance to combat attempted secessions. As will be seen below, this occurred in the case of the Comoros.

3.1 Azawad[93]

In April 2012 a Tuareg rebel group, the National Movement for the Liberation of Azawad (MNLA), taking advantage of the toppling of Mali's democratic government in a coup, declared the independence of Azawad, a region of north-west Mali, from Mali.[94] The Tuareg, a largely nomadic people who inhabit the Sahara Desert, have had troubled relations with the Malian authorities over the years, often spilling over into violence. Having a distinct ethnic, cultural and linguistic identity from its southern compatriots, the Tuareg have long complained about marginalization and discrimination. In fact, calls for an independent Tuareg state in North Africa were made during the French colonial era. The declaration of independence was condemned by the AU, the European Union and the Economic Community for West African States (ECOWAS).[95] The UN Security Council also condemned the purported independence of Azawad, categorizing it as 'null and void',[96] and expressed its commitment to Mali's unity and territorial integrity.[97] In June 2013 a peace agreement known as the Ouagadougou Preliminary Agreement between the government and the MNLA

---

and war crimes in March 2009, *Decision on the Prosecution's Application for a Warrant of Arrest against Omar Hassan Ahmad Al Bashir* ICC-02/05–01/09-3 P-T Ch I, 48 ILM (2009) 463. In 2011 the Prosecutor of the International Criminal Court advised the UN Security Council that President Al-Bashir had continued to commit crimes against humanity in Darfur, Office of the Prosecutor, UN Security Council, 'Statement to the United Nations Security Council on the situation in Darfur, the Sudan, pursuant to UNSCR 1593 (2005)', UN Doc. S/PV 6688. In *Sudan Human Rights Organization and Sudan Centre for Housing Rights and Evictions v. Sudan*, supra note 76, the African Commission found that massive violations of human rights had taken place in Darfur.

92   Art. 4(j) Constitutive Act. See also, Art. 4(k) PSC Protocol.
93   D.H. Flood, 'Between Islamization and Secession: The Contest for Northern Mali', 5 *CTC Sentinel* (2012) 1.
94   BBC News, 'Mali Tuareg rebels declare independence in the north' (6 April 2012) <http://www.bbc.co.uk/news/world/africa-17635437> (accessed 1 November 2013).
95   Ibid.
96   UN Security Council Resolution 2056 (2012).
97   See UN Security Council Resolution 2085 (2012).

was reached.[98] And in February 2015 a further ceasefire agreement was accepted between the parties.[99]

3.2 Casamance[100]

There has been a low-level conflict in the Casamance region of Senegal, the southernmost part of the country, since 1982. The Movement of Democratic Forces of Casamance (MFDC) has sought the independence of Casamance, whose population is religiously and ethnically distinct from the rest of Senegal, aggrieved about land seizures and economic neglect.[101] The MFDC additionally argues that Casamance was an autonomous region under French colonization and should have been granted independence by France.[102] The election of a new president, Macky Sall, in 2012, and it is important to note that Senegal is a functioning democracy, has brought fresh hope of a resolution of the conflict as he announced a decentralization policy for Casamance.

The African Commission played a mediating role in the Casamance conflict. In its *Report on the Mission of Good Offices to Senegal* of 1996, it rejected separatist claims of discriminatory economic policies, cultural subjugation or forcible land seizures.[103] At the same time, it found that the State's interpretation of 'national unity' was too rigid and urged it to ensure equality of participation in

---

[98] BBC News, 'Mali and Tuareg rebels sign peace deal' (18 June 2013) <http://www.bbc.co.uk/news/world/africa-22961519> (accessed 2 November 2013). The Ouagadougou Preliminary Agreement reaffirms Mali's sovereignty and territorial integrity and provides for a process of autonomy known as 'cantonment'. In September 2013 the MNLA suspended the agreement, accusing the government of failing to abide by its terms, BBC News, 'Mali Tuareg rebels pull out of peace deal' (26 September 2013) <http://www.bbc.co.uk/ news/world/africa-242961987> (accessed 2 November 2013). However, the Ouagadougou Preliminary Agreement continues to receive the support of the UN Security Council, see Resolution 2164 (2014).

[99] BBC News, 'Mali signs UN ceasefire to end conflict with northern rebels' (20 February 2015) <http://www.bbc.co.uk/news/world/africa-31544438> (accessed 18 March 2015).

[100] Griffiths, *supra* note 2, pp. 134–135; J. Grace and J. Laffin, *Fontana Dictionary of Africa Since 1960* (Fontana Press, London, 1991) pp. 298–299; L.S. Woocher, 'The "Casamance Question": An Examination of the Legitimacy of Self-Determination in Southern Senegal', 7 *International Journal of Minority and Group Rights* (2000) 341.

[101] *Report on the Mission of Good Offices to Senegal of the African Commission on Human and Peoples' Rights*, *supra* note 56, pp. 534–535.

[102] This argument does not appear convincing, Woocher, *supra* note 100, pp. 355–358.

[103] *Report on the Mission of Good Offices to Senegal of the African Commission on Human and Peoples' Rights*, *supra* note 56, pp. 535–536. Woocher, *supra* note 100, pp. 358–367, is also not persuaded by these arguments.

public affairs.[104] Implicit in the African Commission's conclusions is that a form of autonomy could provide an acceptable solution. This appears to be the policy being pursued by the current president.

3.3 Comoros[105]

In 1997 the islands of Anjouan (since renamed Nzwani) and Mohéli (now Mwali)[106] purported to break away from the then Federal Islamic Republic of the Comoros (now Union of the Comoros) amidst demands for a return to rule by France, the former colonial power. This event appears to have been prompted in particular by severe economic neglect and political instability. Geographically, the Comoro Islands form an archipelago in the Indian Ocean and consist of four main islands, Grand Comore (now Njazidja), Anjouan, Mohéli and Mayotte.[107] However, these islands do not form part of the same State. In 1912 France had proclaimed the colony of *Les Comores*. In 1974 a referendum declared overwhelming support for independence, except for Mayotte which voted against. On 6 July 1975 the Comoros unilaterally declared independence and was admitted both to the OAU and UN later in the year. France, however, did not relinquish control over Mayotte which it declared a French Overseas Territory.[108] In 2011, following a referendum in Mayotte in favour of integration, Mayotte became a *départment d'outre-mer*.[109]

Chronic crises seemed a permanent feature of life in the Comoros since independence.[110] In August 1997 Anjouan and Mohéli sought to secede. Resort to force in an attempt to bring this existential challenge to an end failed; the fol-

---

104 Ibid., p. 536.
105 See C. Ayangafac, 'Situation Critical: The Anjouan Political Crisis' (Situation Report, Institute for Security Studies, Pretoria, 2008); S. Massey and B. Baker, 'Comoros: External Involvement in a Small Island State', Chatham House Programme Paper AFP 2009/1 (Chatham House, London, 2009); G.J. Naldi, 'Separatism in the Comoros: Some Legal Aspects', 11 *Leiden Journal of International Law* (1998) 247, E. Svensson, 'The African Union's Operations in the Comoros: MAES and Operation Democracy', (Swedish Defence Research Agency, Stockholm, 2008).
106 However, to avoid confusion the original names will be used in this essay.
107 Grace and Laffin, *supra* note 100, pp. 81–84.
108 Musgrave, *supra* note 3, pp. 184–186.
109 This step was condemned by the AU which reaffirmed that Mayotte belongs to the Comoros, 'Decision on the Report of the Peace and Security Council on its Activities and the State of Peace and Security in Africa' (30 June-1 July 2011) Seventeenth Ordinary Session, Assembly/AU/Dec. 369(XVII) para. 6. The UN General Assembly had previously reaffirmed the sovereignty of Comoros over Mayotte, UN General Assembly Resolution 49/18 (1994). See Crawford, *supra* note 1, p. 645.
110 Grace and Laffin, *supra* note 100, pp. 83–84.

lowing month a seaborne invasion by government forces was repulsed. On 26 October 1997 Anjouan and Mohéli voted enthusiastically for independence and the following year a new constitution, endorsed by the people in a referendum, was adopted and a government formed. Notwithstanding the freely expressed wishes of the people the new State went unrecognized. OAU mediation resulted in the Antananarivo Agreement and in 2001 a new constitution was adopted, providing for partial autonomy for the three islands and a rotating presidency. However, discord persisted, in particular relating to the redistribution of resources. A serious crisis was precipitated in 2007 when the President of Anjouan, Mohammed Bacar, refused to leave office upon completion of his term of office. In May 2007 the PSC deployed the AU Electoral and Security Assistance Mission (MAES) to the Comoros; its mandate included assisting and facilitating the reinstatement of central government authority on Anjouan.[111] Bacar nevertheless proceeded with an election in Anjouan which confirmed him in office. However, the election was declared null and void not only by the Union government but significantly by the AU which, committed to the unity and territorial integrity of the Comoros, imposed targeted sanctions.[112] The AU described the Bacar regime in Anjouan as 'illegal' and called for the restoration of the Union government's authority.[113] Military intervention was pursued as the solution to this latest crisis. On 25 March 2008 a joint Comorian-AU led invasion of Anjouan, 'Operation Democracy in Comoros', to overthrow Bacar and restore governmental authority was launched successfully,[114] a development welcomed by the AU.[115] MAES's mandate was extended to assist the government in post-conflict reconstruction.[116] On 17 May 2009 a contested referendum approved amendments to the Constitution, *inter alia*, limiting the powers of the islands' presidents.[117] In 2010 presidential elections were held but tensions remain however.[118]

---

[111] PSC Communiqué PSC/MIN/COMM.1(LXXVIII) (9 May 2007). See also, PSC Communiqué PSC/PR/COMM(XCV) (10 October 2007). See Svensson, *supra* note 105, pp. 19–20.

[112] PSC Communiqué PSC/PR/COMM(XCV); Svensson, *supra* note 105, p. 14.

[113] 'Decision on the Situation in the Comoros' (31 January-2 February 2008) Tenth Ordinary Session Assembly/AU/Dec. 186(X).

[114] Massey and Baker, *supra* note 105, pp. 15–16; Svensson, *supra* note 105, pp. 20–21.

[115] 'Decision on the Report of the Peace and Security Council on its Activities and the State of Peace and Security in Africa' (30 June-1 July 2008) Eleventh Ordinary Session, Assembly/AU/Dec. 193(XI) para. 4.

[116] PSC Communiqué PSC/PR/COMM(CXXIV) (30 April 2008).

[117] Massey and Baker, *supra* note 105, pp. 5, 12.

[118] 'Country Analysis: Comoros', *Peace and Security Council Report* No. 8, March 2010 <http://www.issafrica.org> visited on 9 August 2013.

The root cause of secessionist sentiment in the Comoros appears to have been prolonged misrule which led to political alienation. A case can therefore be constructed for the argument that the purported secession in 1997 was an instance of remedial secession in that a section of the population, concentrated in the defined areas of Anjouan and Mohéli, rebelled against unrepresentative and arbitrary government. Whether that denial of internal self-determination met the threshold of a serious breach is open to question, however. Moreover, the fact that a negotiated political settlement was reached in 2001 providing for a measure of self-government satisfies the condition precedent that all effective remedies must be exhausted. The fact that the proposed secession of Anjouan and Mohéli attracted no international support is explicable against this background.

3.4 Eritrea[119]

Portrayed as an example of 'African imperialism',[120] Eritrea waged a long war to win its independence from Ethiopia. Eritrea had become an Italian colony in 1890. During the Second World War it was captured by British forces. Failing agreement after the Second World War Eritrea's future was put in the hands of the UN which established the UN Commission for Eritrea.[121] In accordance with UN guidelines a federation between Eritrea and Ethiopia was established in 1952 but this arrangement was terminated unilaterally in 1962 when Ethiopia effectively annexed Eritrea, giving rise to a guerrilla war of independence. In 1974 a doctrinaire neo-Marxist military clique, led by Colonel Mengistu, took power in a coup. Mengistu assumed dictatorial powers and instituted a period of misrule and systematic human rights abuses. In 1978 he intensified the military campaign against the separatists, and the fortunes of war see-sawed back and forth until the late 1980s when the Eritrean People's Liberation Front (EPLF) scored a number of spectacular successes. The EPLF gained the upper hand and in 1991 the Mengistu regime fell when the EPLF entered Addis Ababa. The new Transitional Government of Ethiopia accepted the Eritrean claims to self-determination.[122] Although independence had been effectively achieved

---

119 Cassese, *supra* note 16, pp. 218–222; Griffiths, *supra* note 2, pp. 148–153; E. Gayim, *The Eritrean Question: The Conflict Between the Right of Self-Determination and the Interests of States* (Iustus Forlag, Uppsala, 1993); M. Haile, 'Legality of Secessions: The Case of Eritrea', 8 *Emory International Law Review* (1994) 479.

120 Griffiths, *supra* note 2, pp. 148–151.

121 UN General Assembly Resolution 289 (IV) (1949).

122 Crawford, *supra* note 1, pp. 402; Haile, *supra* note 119, p. 531. It is argued that the Transitional Government of Ethiopia had no democratic mandate to allow Eritrea's secession, Haile, *supra* note 119, pp. 531–533.

by a thirty-year armed struggle the new State of Eritrea was legitimised by a referendum held under UN auspices in April 1993 which voted strongly in favour of Eritrea's independence,[123] which came into being on 24 May 1993. On 28 May 1993 Eritrea was admitted to the UN.[124]

The Eritrean claim to independence was based principally on self-determination.[125] It was argued that the UN Commission for Eritrea failed to ascertain properly the wishes of the people of Eritrea through a referendum and that the federation did not meet their aspirations;[126] and that in 1962 Ethiopia forcibly annexed Eritrea, thereby reviving the right to self-determination. These Eritrean claims have been challenged.[127] Whilst it is certainly unlikely that the way in which the federation came into being would be acceptable today in light of subsequent developments in law and practice[128] it must be borne in mind that these sorts of arrangements were not altogether unusual at the time.[129] It has additionally been argued that the Eritreans were neither a 'people' under 'alien subjugation' nor were they specifically singled out for human rights violations.[130] Regardless of the validity of these arguments the fact remains that at the end of the day Eritrea emerged as an independent State.

Eritrea was the first successful example in Africa of a seceding entity achieving statehood. But despite the lengthy war Eritrea is considered an example of consensual, rather than contested, secession, based on the peace agreement between the EPLF and Ethiopia and the latter's acceptance of the applicability of self-determination to Eritrea.

3.5 Somaliland[131]

The Republic of Somaliland, corresponding to the territory of the former British Protectorate of Somaliland, declared its independence in May 1991. On 1

---

123   Crawford, *supra* note 1, pp. 402.
124   See UN General Assembly Resolution 47/230 (1992).
125   Cassese, *supra* note 16, pp. 221–222; Gayim, *supra* note 107, Part III.
126   This failure on the part of the UN has been considered a mistake, Cassese, *supra* note 16, p. 222.
127   Haile, *supra* note 119, pp. 484–487.
128   In line with the ICJ's emphasis in the *Western Sahara Case, supra* note 48, p. 68, that the law of decolonization requires a free and genuine expression of the will of the people, optimally through a plebiscite, an internationally approved referendum would appear to be a necessity.
129   Crawford, *supra* note 1, pp. 336–337, 646.
130   Ibid., pp. 511–514, 516–517, 517–523.
131   Crawford, *supra* note 1, pp. 412–415; A.K. Eggers, 'When is a State a State? The Case for Recognition of Somaliland', 30 *Boston College International & Comparative Law Review*

July 1960 the newly independent British Somaliland had joined the Italian Somaliland in forming the Republic of Somalia. Aside from nationalist fervour, one of the principal reasons behind this move appears to have been ethnic and religious homogeneity.[132] Since the late 1970s Somalia was wracked by both internal and external conflict and in 1991 the central government collapsed.[133] As Somalia began its descent into anarchy, and in the view of many became the archetypal example of a failed state,[134] Somaliland broke away; in 2001 a referendum overwhelmingly supported the country's new constitution and, by extension, its independence.[135] To this day the quasi-state of Somaliland, despite its viability, remains unrecognized.

A variety of factors appear to have prompted Somaliland's secession, including tribal differences, economic disparity and different traditions inherited from colonial times.[136] Somalia's disintegration is an additional potent consideration. For some two decades there was no effective governmental authority in Somalia;[137] despite efforts by the international community,[138] the country continues to be racked by instability, rival militias vie for control of various parts of the country and engage in violence, banditry and terrorism, posing a threat to neighbouring States and international shipping. What little control the Somali Government exercises would not seem to be possible without external support, especially that provided by the AU's stabilization force, African Union Mission in Somalia (AMISOM).[139] Peace and national reconciliation still seem a distant prospect. By way of contrast, Somaliland appears to have developed a form of representative democracy.[140] The country has a stable political organization and an effective working civil administration;[141] it has a

---

(2007) 21; B.R. Farley, 'Calling a State a State: Somaliland and International Recognition', 24 *Emory International Law Review* (2010) 777; A. Kreuter, 'Self-determination, Sovereignty, and the Failure of States: Somaliland and the Case for Justified Secession', 19 *Minnesota Journal of International Law* (2010) p. 363; D. Lalos, 'Between Statehood and Somalia: Reflections of Somaliland Statehood', 10 *Washington University Global Studies Law Review* (2011) 789.

132   Griffiths, *supra* note 2, p. 165.
133   Ibid., pp. 141–142.
134   See Harris, *supra* note 37, p. 35.
135   Crawford, *supra* note 1, pp. 413–414; Lalos, *supra* note 131, p. 795.
136   Crawford, *supra* note 1, p. 413.
137   Farley, *supra* note 131, pp. 784–786; Harris, *supra* note 37, pp. 93–94; Kreuter, *supra* note 131, p. 377.
138   See Naldi, *supra* note 87, p. 8.
139   UN Security Council Resolution 1744 (2007). See C. Gray, *International Law and the Use of Force* (3rd ed., Oxford University Press, Oxford, 2008) pp. 379–380.
140   Farley, *supra* note 131, p. 787; Kreuter, *supra* note 131, p. 378.
141   Farley, *supra* note 131, p. 788.

functioning legal system based on the Somali Penal Code of 1962, with a Supreme Court.[142] It appears that the judiciary in Germany and the United States have acknowledged the effectiveness of the Somaliland polity.[143] It has been observed that Somaliland does in fact satisfy the factual criteria of statehood and in view of its prolonged survival therefore deserves to be recognized as a state.[144] Additionally, it complies with the principle of *uti possidetis*.[145] It has also been suggested that Somaliland's secession is justified in accordance with the remedial theory, that Somaliland was denied its internal right to self-determination and that the failed nature of the Somalian State left it with no means of pursuing its grievances.[146] These arguments have not proven sufficiently convincing for another writer[147] who suggests that Somaliland's secession is permissible only on the basis that Somalia is a failed state incapable of providing even the most basic state functions.[148] Perhaps the doctrine of reversion may be applicable. Notwithstanding the fact that Somaliland had been an independent State only for the briefest time before its merger it could be argued that, in compelling circumstances, Somaliland's leaders simply reversed the decision of thirty years previously and resumed its separate existence in 1991. However, the better view is that in such instances of voluntary merger the original States become extinct.[149]

3.6 South Sudan[150]

Sudan achieved independence in 1956. The largest country in Africa, it was ethnically and religiously diverse, the north largely Arab and Muslim, the population of the south mainly African and Christian or adherents of traditional beliefs.[151] Tensions between the two regions increased as independence

---

142 Naldi, *supra* note 87, p. 45.
143 Crawford, *supra* note 1, p. 414.
144 Eggers, *supra* note 131, pp. 219–222. See also, Farley, *supra* note 131, pp. 806–809.
145 Farley, *supra* note 131, pp. 802–805.
146 Lalos, *supra* note 131, pp. 809–810.
147 Kreuter, *supra* note 131, pp. 385–392.
148 Ibid., pp. 392–397.
149 Lauterpacht, *supra* note 10, pp. 155–156. Another example of voluntary merger was that of Tanganyika and Zanzibar in 1964 to form the United Republic of Tanzania. Secessionist sentiment exists in Zanzibar, see M.J. Maalim, 'The right of secession under international law and national laws: a case study of Zanzibar in United Republic of Tanzania', 1 *Journal of African and International Law* (2008) 107.
150 Griffiths, *supra* note 2, pp. 131–133; J. Vidmar, 'South Sudan and the International Legal Framework Governing the Emergence and Delimitation of New States', 47 *Texas International Law Journal* (2011–2012) 541.
151 Grace and Laffin, *supra* note 100, pp. 326–327.

loomed, as the south was apprehensive of its identity being subjugated by the stronger and more populous north. A state of civil war existed from the outset but the most significant rebel player that emerged was the Sudan People's Liberation Army/Movement (SPLA/M) in 1983, in response to the loss of autonomy and the imposition of *Shari'a* law.[152] In 1993 the regional African organization, the Inter-Governmental Authority for Development (IGAD), assumed the role of mediator in an attempt to resolve the enduring civil war and in April 1997 the Sudanese government concluded peace agreements, *inter alia*, granting self-determination to the people of the south.[153] In July 2002 a peace agreement between the Sudanese government and the SPLA/M, known as the Machakos Protocol, was signed.[154] Under its terms it was accepted that the people of South Sudan had a right to self-determination through a referendum to determine their future status.[155] Notwithstanding a difficult process a comprehensive peace agreement between the Sudanese government and the SPLA/M was eventually signed in 2005, under which the south was granted regional autonomy along with guaranteed representation in a national power-sharing government.[156] Significantly, the Machakos Protocol was reaffirmed. In January 2011 a referendum overwhelmingly supported the independence of South Sudan and formal independence followed on 9 July 2011,[157] although certain territorial disputes still remain.[158] South Sudan was admitted to both the AU and the UN.[159]

As has been mentioned, the population of Sudan was of a heterogeneous composition. There can be little doubt that the Sudanese government was unwise to pursue its illiberal policies to try to impose homogeneity on a distinct population.[160] The causes that motivated South Sudan's struggle for indepen-

---

[152] Ibid., p. 328.
[153] UN Doc. E/CN.4/1998/SR.48, paras 21, 64.
[154] Reprinted in 10 *Yearbook of Islamic & Middle Eastern Law* (2003–2004) 303.
[155] Ibid., para. 2.3.
[156] The Comprehensive Peace Agreement Between the Government of the Republic of Sudan and the Sudan People's Liberation Movement/Sudan People's Liberation Army <http://unmis.unmissions.org/Portals/UNMIS/Documents/General/cpa-en.pdf> visited on 18 October 2013. See Vidmar, *supra* note 150, pp. 551–552.
[157] Vidmar, *supra* note 150, pp. 552–553.
[158] Ibid., pp. 554–556. In October 2013 an unofficial referendum was held in the disputed territory of Abyei which voted overwhelmingly to be part of South Sudan, BBC News, 'Abyei opts to join South Sudan in unofficial referendum' (31 October 2013) <http://www.bbc.co.uk/ news/world/africa-24761524> (accessed 2 November 2013).
[159] UN General Assembly Resolution 65/308 (2010).
[160] Griffiths, *supra* note 2, p. 132.

dence therefore included self-determination and the role of religion in the State. It could thus be argued that this was an example of remedial secession. As with Eritrea, despite the protracted civil war South Sudan is classified as an example of consensual, rather than contested, secession, based on the negotiated peace agreements and Sudan's acceptance of the result of the independence referendum.[161] However, it seems unlikely that South Sudan's independence would have been achieved without resort to arms.

4   Conclusion

In view of the existential threat posed to States by secession it is little surprise that States cannot support a '*general* right of secession by territorial communities within their borders or to agree on definite criteria under which secession may be justified in given circumstances.'[162] Cases of consensual secession pose relatively few problems but contested secessions are another matter. The position on secession has been summed up by one writer thus, that secession 'is *per se* neither prohibited nor authorized by international law. What matters is that the new government possesses the requisites of effectiveness and independence that are normally required for the creation of States as international legal subjects.'[163]

Africa has not been spared from secessionist pressures. The African case studies that have been considered in this essay share factors in common, usually focused on economic grievances and misrule against the central government. If these grievances can be addressed the secessionist demands tend to lessen. The AU's commitment to good governance should help meet some of the concerns about misrule.[164] But the AU is not committed to an inflexible and static concept of government. It accepts that internal self-determination may be exercised in diverse, but equally acceptable, forms. The African Commission has taken the sensible position that some form of autonomy or devolution may in fact help bolster state sovereignty.[165] The AU has accepted the cases of consensual secession, Eritrea, South Sudan, even if they may amount to unhelpful precedents. But the AU remains staunchly opposed to cases of

---

161   Vidmar, *supra* note 150, p. 553.
162   Henkin et al., *supra* note 8, ibid.
163   Tancredi, *supra* note 30, p. 55.
164   Art. 3(g) Constitutive Act.
165   *Katangese Peoples' Congress v. Zaire*, *supra* note 54, para. 4; *Gunme* et al. v. *Cameroon*, *supra* note 54, paras 194–195.

contested secession. Somaliland makes a compelling case for international recognition but it seems that Western States would prefer to act in concert with the AU.[166] The AU's stance is explicable in light of Africa's historical legacy but the encouragement of enlightened politics encompassing self-government seems the way forward.

---

166   Farley, *supra* note 131, pp. 812–813.

CHAPTER 30

Can Regional and Sub-Regional African Courts Strengthen the Rule of Law in Africa? Questions of Impact and Enforcement

Mia Swart

1 Introduction

The question of whether international criminal justice can have an impact on domestic jurisdictions in Africa is closely related to the extent to which the rule of law gains respect on the African continent. The purpose of this Chapter is to ask whether the creation of African regional courts have set standards for the rule of law in Africa. What standards would be standards that strengthen the rule of law? The promotion of human rights would be one such standard. The following issues are particularly relevant in setting standards for the rule of law: (1) enforcement of judicial decisions, (2) judicial independence and co-ordination, (3) and coherence between the various regional and sub-regional African Courts.

This Chapter will further focus on the impact of the decisions of African regional and sub-regional institutions on individual African jurisdictions and will examine whether the judgments of African regional and sub-regional courts have had a positive trickle-down effect on domestic systems. Additionally, this chapter will consider the extent to which domestic courts have taken note of the regional and sub-regional jurisprudence. One way of measuring the impact of the regional and sub-regional courts is to explore the extent that domestic jurisdictions in Africa have cited the jurisprudence of these regional courts. However, in light of the relative newness of the sub-regional and regional courts it is not surprising that there have not been ample instances of such citation.

This chapter will also focus on the question of the enforcement of the judgments of the regional courts. The question of whether the monist/dualist debate remains relevant in this regard will be discussed. It will be argued that the monist/dualist debate is no longer the determining factor when it comes to the

---

* This paper was first presented at a workshop of the Bingham Centre for the Rule of Law, London in 2012.

extent of enforcement. The emphasis will be on the African Court of Human and People's Rights, the African Commission, and on the most prominent African sub-regional courts: the ECOWAS Court of Justice, the East African Court of Justice, and the Tribunal of the Southern African Development Community (SADC Tribunal).

Assessing whether the regional and sub-regional courts have set standards for the rule of law is partly a question of the *impact* of these courts. Whereas there can be no clear definition of 'impact', impact in the context of this chapter can be understood as the *influence* exerted by the existence, work and jurisprudence of the regional and sub-regional African courts. One reason the impact of the jurisprudence of regional African courts has been limited is because of the low enforcement rate of judgments. The extent to which impact can be equated with compliance or enforcement of judgments will be discussed. The meaning and relevance of the term 'rule of law' will be discussed first.

2 Relevance of the Rule of Law

International judicial institutions share a commitment to the rule of law. It is the view of Anne Marie Slaughter that the meshing of that commitment 'through increasingly direct interaction' is more likely to establish an international rule of law than a single international court.[1] As she eloquently puts it: 'transjudicial communication ... presupposes that the courts involved ... speak a sufficient common language to interact in terms of persuasion rather than compulsion.'[2]

Regional African Courts have the potential to play a significant role in promoting the international rule of law in Africa.[3] By cooperating with the regional African human rights system and by implementing the decisions of the regional African courts, African states will provide individuals with supranational fora for human rights protections when national fora fail. In so doing they will strengthen the rule of law.[4] Tom Bingham wrote that the international pro-

---

[1] Slaughter 'Transjudicial Communication' 137.
[2] Ibid. 136.
[3] Chesterman has described the international rule of law as the application of rule of law principles to relations between States and other subjects of international law. S Chesterman 'An International Rule of Law?' (2008) 56 *American Journal of Comparative Law* 2, 355.
[4] Tom Bingham emphasized the necessity of states to comply with international law. Tom Bingham 'The Rule of Law and the International Legal Order' in R McCorquodale (ed.) *The Rule of Law in International and Comparative Context* (2010) 4.

tection of human rights is important to the rule of law because human rights are founded on values that command widespread acceptance throughout most of the world.[5] In turn, the international protection of the rule of law is important because of the extent to which national courts are drawn into the process of determining questions of international law.[6] Bingham pointed out that this is a field in which individual claimants feature very prominently.[7] The existence of an individual complaints procedure at most of the regional African Courts makes it possible for African citizens to directly access the courts. African citizens can access the courts in their individual capacities to assert their rights as individuals. This is one of the most important and salient features of the African sub-regional courts.

3 Impact of Jurisprudence of Regional African Courts on Domestic Courts in Africa

Until international tribunals command a wider constituency, the courts of the various countries afford the best means for the development of a respected body of international law.[8]

What has been the impact of the regional African courts on domestic systems in Africa? There are different ways of measuring the impact of the regional African courts. One important measure of impact is to consider the extent to which domestic courts on the African continent have cited the decisions of the regional African courts.

Slaughter writes of an increasing cross-fertilization of ideas and precedent among constitutional judges around the world.[9] In Africa such cross-fertilization may not take the form of express judicial cooperation but of a more slow and subtle penetration of international human rights principles into the work of domestic courts. This same cross-fertilization can potentially occur between regional courts and domestic courts. Slaughter distinguishes between

---

5 In describing the closeness of the relationship between international protection of human rights and the rule of law Bingham wrote that 'no other field of law rests so directly on a moral foundation'. Tom Bingham *The Rule of Law* (2012) 117. The Security Council has frequently made reference to the rule of law in resolutions.
6 Ibid.
7 Ibid.
8 Judge Powell *First National City Bank v. Banco National de Cuba* 406 US 759, 775 (1971) per Powell J.
9 Anne Marie Slaughter 'A Global Community of Courts' *Harvard International Law Journal* 44 (2003) 202.

horizontal communication between courts and vertical communication. Horizontal communication takes place between courts of the same status (whether national or supranational).[10] There might be no formal relationship between such courts and courts may not even formally acknowledge the fruits of the communication by actual citation.[11] Supranational courts may also engage in this kind of horizontal communication. The citation of the European human rights jurisprudence by the Inter-American Court of Human Rights is the best example.[12] The communication between national and supranational courts is called vertical communication. Slaughter writes that the most developed form of such communication takes place within the framework of a treaty establishing a supranational tribunal with a specialized jurisdiction that overlaps with national jurisdiction. She regards the Rome Treaty as the prime example of a treaty that establishes such a framework. Although the decisions of the regional and sub-regional courts do not bind domestic courts, these courts create a framework for vertical communication. In Slaughter's view the citation of supranational courts by domestic courts that have no formal allegiance to the 'supranational authority' is a form of vertical communication that resembles horizontal communication.

As will be seen in the discussion of the case law below, courts occasionally refer to the case law of the regional courts or to the African Charter merely for cosmetic purposes. This means that judges in domestic jurisdictions would refer to these cases to create the impression that foreign jurisprudence has been considered but the cases would not necessarily be analysed in any depth or have a substantial impact on the ultimate decision.

This occurs for example when a court cites the African Charter as part of a list of international human rights instruments without the African Charter contributing to a human rights friendly outcome. If formal ratification or adherence to international instruments such as the African Charter ensured human rights compliance, one would not have seen the extent of human rights violations that have plagued the African continent over the last decades.

It is often difficult to determine the direct influence or effect of the citation of case law on domestic systems. Partly because of the dearth of case law emanating from the regional courts, there are but very few examples of cases of the regional courts having a direct and concrete impact on domestic jurisdictions. A trend towards democratization has been observed in many of the member

---

10   Anne Marie Slaughter 'A Typology of Transjudicial Communication' *University of Richmond Law Review* (1994) 103.
11   Ibid.
12   Ibid. 106.

states of the African sub-regional organisations and in Africa generally.[13] This leads to the question: Is there a link between the extent to which domestic states in Africa have explicitly incorporated the case law of regional and sub-regional African courts and democratization?

While I will not attempt to find every instance of citation of a regional court's *oeuvre* of cases, I will provide an overview of the extent to which the decisions of the regional African courts have been cited and incorporated in domestic judgments.

I African Charter

The African Court is not compelled to refer to the jurisprudence of the African Commission. However Viljoen is of the view that the Court would be wise to take note of and be persuaded by the Commission's progressive interpretation of the African Charter.[14]

Although, the African Court has hardly been cited by national courts in Africa reference has often been made to the African Charter. In most of the cases where domestic courts have cited the African Charter, the domestic courts did not rely solely on the African Charter in determining the outcome of a case but merely considered the African Charter alongside other international instruments.

Instances of African courts citing the African Charter are too many to mention. A prominent example is the reference by the High Court of Botswana to the African Charter in the well-known case of *Attorney General v. Unity Dow*.[15] This landmark case confirmed the guarantee of equality under the constitution in the context of citizenship rights. On appeal, the court used international human rights instruments to aid constitutional interpretation. The

---

[13] Whereas before 1990 there were only a few democracies in Africa (such as the Gambia, Mauritius and Botswana) by 2007, Freedom House classified half of the 48 African states as democracies. Democracy to Freedom House means regimes where citizens can choose their leaders and replace their leaders in reasonably free and fair elections, which in turn require some significant degree of personal and political freedom. 'Democratization in Africa, What Progress Towards Institutionalisation?' Conference Report, National Intelligence Council, February 2008.

[14] Frans Viljoen *International Human Rights Law in Africa* 425. Viljoen suggests that such reliance will be particularly fruitful in the areas of socio-economic and fair trial rights and with regard to 'exhaustion of local remedies rule' and with regard to its approach to 'limitations'.

[15] [1992] LRC (Const.) 623.

South African Constitutional Court has also referred to the African Charter in a considerable amount of cases.[16]

II African Commission

Of the regional institutions discussed in this paper, the African Commission has been the most active. Despite this fact, domestic African courts have not frequently cited the African Commission. One reason for this is the fact that the Commission does not have the status of a court and its decisions, therefore, have low precedential value. Decisions of the African Commission have however been cited by courts in jurisdictions such as Zambia and Gambia.

In *Attorney-General v. Clarke*[17] the Zambian Supreme Court referred to the African Commission regarding illegal deportation (and the right to criticize government).

In *Sabally v. Inspector General of Police and Others*,[18] a case on press freedom, the judges of the Supreme Court of Ghana, referred to an African Commission decision on media rights: *Constitutional Rights Project, the Civil Liberties Organization and Media Rights Agenda against Nigeria.*[19]

III ECOWAS

According to Nwauche, there is little doubt that national judicial institutions in West Africa are subordinate to community legal institutions (such as the ECOWAS Court). Despite this fact there are not many instances of domestic courts citing ECOWAS cases. The Sierra Leone Special Court, a court that is partly domestic and partly international in nature, has referred to ECOWAS on a few occasions, but mostly as an *institution* and not to case law emanating from the ECOWAS Court. In the Charles Taylor case, for example *Prosecutor v. Taylor* (SCSL 2007), the court referred to the ECOWAS cease-fire. In *Prosecutor*

---

16 See *S v. Makwanyane and Another* 1995 (3) SA 391 (CC); *Bhe v. Magistrate of Khayelitsha and Others* CCT 49/03 (2004) ZACC 17. For more on the topic of the impact of the African Charter on African domestic systems see http://www.pulp.up.ac.za/pdf/2012_07/2012_07.pdf.

17 (2008) AHRLR 259 (ZaSC 2008).

18 (2002) AHRLR 87 (GaSC 2001) In this 2005 case the Supreme Court of The Gambia nullified several provisions of the Indemnity (Amendment) Act 2001 for contravening the human rights provisions of the 1997 Constitution of the Republic of The Gambia and article 7 of the African Charter on Human and Peoples' Rights which guarantees the fundamental right of the individual to access the courts of the land.

19 The court had occasion to address the issue of legislative nullification of pending judicial proceedings. (assault and injury during public emergency).

v. Kallon (SCSL 2004), reference was made to ECOWAS's role in the implementation of the Lomé Agreement.

IV   EAC

Since the East African Court of Justice is still in its infancy it has not had a significant impact on domestic jurisdictions in East Africa yet. Two factors that seem to hamper the progress of the East African Court are the *ad hoc* nature of the Court (the fact that the court sits only during certain periods of the year and the judges are not permanently based in Arusha)[20] and the slowness of the adoption of the Protocol extending the Court's jurisdiction to human rights matters.[21] I could not find any instances of domestic courts citing the East African Court.

V   *SADC Tribunal*

The SADC Tribunal cases have not been cited by other African courts or by African domestic courts. Except for the *Gramara* case[22] the only references to SADC Tribunal in domestic African case law (on a number of databases)[23] are instances of SADC Tribunal cases citing other SADC Tribunal cases. The SADC Tribunal cases, which have been cited by SADC, are: *Tembani v. Republic of Zimbabwe*[24] and *Fick and Another v. Republic of Zimbabwe*.[25]

It was decided in the *Gramara* case that the Zimbabwean courts do not have to implement the decisions of the SADC Tribunal. The Court decided that the Zimbabwean government will not be constrained in its land redistribution program by a judgment of the SADC Tribunal and since *Gramara* was the only instance of a domestic African judgment taking note of a SADC case, it seems as if the political impact of the SADC Tribunal has been more significant than its legal impact.

African regional courts also cite *each other*. The *Campbell* judgment of the SADC Tribunal has cited two judgments of the African Commission.[26]

---

20   Ruhangisa writes that none of the judges of the Court reside in Arusha which causes delays. John Ruhangisa, John Eudes 'The East Africa Court of Justice: Ten Years of Operation' (2011) 24.

21   Ibid. 26.

22   *Gramara and another v. Government of Republic of Zimbabwe & Others* [2010] (ZHO).

23   Including SAFLII

24   [2010] SADCT (Namibia).

25   [2010] SADCT

26   In paragraph 42 of the *Campbell* judgment (SADC 2008) the Commission refers to *Constitutional Rights Project and Others v. Nigeria*, communications 140/94, 141/94 145/95 [(2000) AHRLR 227 (ACHPR 1999)] Paragraph 43 refers to *Zimbabwe Human Rights NGO Forum v.*

This phenomenon, however, does not extend to SADC judgments generally – there have not been other instances of the SADC Tribunal citing cases of the African Court or African Commission.

4 The Monist/Dualist Debate: The Impact of Legal Tradition and Diversity on Enforcement

Enforcement of the regional African courts' decisions in Africa is complicated by the variety of legal systems present in Africa. The enforcement of decisions often depends on whether a country adheres to a monist or dualist system of law. The monist school maintains that 'international law and municipal law, far from being essentially different, must be regarded as manifestations of a single conception of law.'[27] In monist systems there is no need for domestic implementing legislation. International law is immediately applicable within national law. In dualist systems international law and national law are viewed as distinct legal orders.[28] For international law to be applicable in dualist systems, it must be received through domestic legislative measures. The monist/dualist divide has been criticized on many different grounds,[29] but it has important implications for the way that international law is treated in domestic systems. Malcolm Shaw has noted '… it is precisely because of the inadequate

---

Zimbabwe, communication 245/2002 [(2006) AHRLR 128 (ACHPR 2006)], In paragraph 47 the Tribunal refers to *Attorney-General of the Commonwealth of the Bahamas v. Ryan* (1980) AC 718. In paragraph 49 the Tribunal refers to *Jackson v. Attorney-General* UKHL 56 (2006) 1 AC 262. Interestingly the Campbell judgment also referred to the Constitutional Court of South Africa in *Zondi v. MEC for Traditional and Local Government Affairs and Others* 2005 (3) SA 589 (CC).

27 'International Law and Municipal Law', E Lauterpacht (ed) *International Law: Being the Collected Papers of Hersch Lauterpacht* vol. 1 *The General Works* (1970) 216 at 217.

28 See also Richard Frimpong Oppong 'Re-Imagining International Law: An Examination of Recent Trends in the Reception of International law into National Legal Systems in Africa' http://eprints.lancs.ac.uk/21002/1/R-F-OPPONG-_RE-IMAGINING-INT_LAW-FORDHAM_INT_L_J.doc 3.

29 Hans Kelsen *The Pure Theory of Law* 328–347 (Max Knight trans., 1967). Paulus comments 'The vision of a hierarchical unity of international and domestic laws is more threatening than reassuring, in particular at a juncture where the temptations of superpower hegemony appear stronger than ever.' See Andreas Paulus, 'Beyond the Monism –Dualism Debate' (2003). He argues that the pluralism of the contemporary legal world requires a profound change of methodology. In an age of globalization a dualist insistence on separateness and closedness of legal orders is doomed to fail just as much as monist attempts at harmonization and hierarchisation.

enforcement facilities that lie at the disposal of international law that one must consider the relationship with municipal law as more than of marginal importance.'[30] The extent to which international law can compel or induce reform in national law has been said to hinge on the monist/dualist dichotomy.[31]

Too much should, however, not be made of the monist/dualist distinction. The Kenyan Court of Appeal stated in 2005 that the rigid distinction between monist and dualist jurisdictions is no longer tenable.[32] The Court stated that the 'current thinking on the common law theory is that both international customary law and treaty law can be applied by state courts where there is no conflict with existing state law, even in the absence of implementing legislation.'[33]

The question of whether a country is monist or dualist will often depend on whether a country has a common law tradition, Roman-Dutch heritage, or whether a particular jurisdiction is French- or Portuguese-oriented. ECOWAS provides a good illustration. French speaking ECOWAS countries such as Senegal and Benin are monist in orientation. Lusophone countries (including Cape Verde and Guinea Bissau) also generally follow the monist tradition.

An interesting shared feature of the fourteen SADC countries is that they all inherited their legal systems from their former colonial masters. In countries that inherited the common law tradition, the relevant common law principles and statutory provisions apply.[34] In civil law SADC countries (such as Angola, the DRC and Mozambique) the matter of enforcement is governed by the relevant provisions in the respective civil law and civil procedure codes.

In spite of the general position adopted by common law countries that a treaty will not have the force of law unless implemented by domestic legislation, some African national courts in common law jurisdictions have displayed a willingness to rely on international human rights conventions even if they have not been incorporated into the national legal systems. One such case is *Unity Dow v. Attorney General*,[35] a well-known case in which the applicant chal-

---

30   Malcolm Shaw *International Law* (2008) 161.
31   Richard Frimpong Oppong (note 27) 3.
32   *Mary Rono v. Jane Rono and Another,* Civil Appeal 66 of 2002, Court of Appeal at Eldoret, judgment of 26 April 2005; (2005) AHRLR 107 (KeCa 2005).
33   Ibid.para. 21.
34   Andre Thomashausen 'The enforcement and recognition of judgments and other forms of legal cooperation in the SADC' *CILSA* 2002 30.
35   (191) 13 (High Court of Botswana, Misca. 124/90) The Court also cited the UN General Assembly Declaration on the Elimination of Discrimination against Women (1967). Although the Attorney General specifically ok issue with the court's reliance on these

lenged the constitutionality of provisions of the Citizenship Act of 1984 as being discriminatory because it denied citizenship to children born to female citizens of Botswana who were married to foreign men. The High Court's interpretation of the relevant statutory provisions regarding citizenship was strengthened by the fact that Botswana was a signatory to the OAU's Convention on non-discrimination, even though Botswana had not ratified it. The court noted that Botswana, as one of the few liberal democracies in Africa, should not insulate itself from progressive movements in other states.[36]

And in the Ghanaian case of *New Patriotic Party v. Inspector General of Police*,[37] Chief Justice Archer held that the fact that Ghana had not passed specific legislation to give effect to the African Charter on Human and People's Rights did not mean that the Charter could not be relied upon.[38]

It is, however, a fallacy that monist countries in Africa directly and immediately incorporate international law into their domestic legal systems. Formal adherence to monism does not guarantee 'direct enforcement'.[39] The case of Senegal's efforts to prosecute Hisséne Habré provides a vivid illustration. As a state party to the UN Convention Against Torture (CAT), Senegal is (according to article 5 of CAT) under an obligation 'to take such measures as may be necessary to establish its jurisdiction' over offences of torture 'where the alleged offender is present in any territory under its jurisdiction and it does not extradite him.' However, the Senegalese *Cour de Cassation* held that 'enforcement of the Convention makes it necessary for Senegal to take prior legislative measures.'[40] Regardless of the fact that Senegal formally adhered to monism, legislative enactment was required for provisions that domestic courts do not automatically regard as municipal law. Interestingly, a Military Tribunal in Ituri directly applied international law in the context of the conflict in Congo.[41]

---

international instruments, the Court of Appeal affirmed the High Court's reliance of these instruments. See also *State v. Makwanyane* 1995 (6) BCLR 665 (CC) 72–73 and *Government of the Republic of South Africa v. Grootboom* 2000 (11) BCLR 116 (CC) on using international law as a guide to constitutional interpretation.

36   *Unity Dow v. Attorney General* [1992] L.R.C (Const). at 623.
37   [1993–94] 2 G.L.R 459, 466.
38   See also Neville Botha & Michelle Olivier *Ten Years of International Law in South African Courts, Reviewing the Past and Assessing the Future* 29 South African Yearbook of International Law 42 (2004).
39   See the discussion by Frans Viljoen (note 13) 520.
40   See Obligation to Prosecute and Extradite (See Belg v. Sen) Judgment 2012 ICJ 44, 117, July 20.
41   In a criminal matter the Tribunal placed reliance on the ICC Statute to fill in what is considered to be a gap in the domestic legislation (the Military Penal Code).

Benin forms an interesting exception to 'meaningless monism' (monism that exists more in theory than practice). The Constitution of Benin explicitly recognises the African Charter as an 'integral part' of the Constitution and of 'Beninese law' and it attaches the Charter as an annex to the Constitution.[42] The Charter's status as 'superior authority' to national legislation is thus assured.

Viljoen concludes that almost without fail monist African states have not adopted the required enactments.[43] Most monist African states require that states adopt procedures to domesticate international instruments. He writes that the tendency of African legislatures in "dualist" states not to domesticate international treaties and of judges in monist states not to enforce them, necessitates a new approach.[44] He suggests that the monist/dualist distinction be discarded in favour of an approach that identifies whether particular treaty provisions are self-executing. This would allow the provisions to serve as the basis for independent legal action in the absence of domestic enactment.[45] Self-execution means that judicial reliance is placed on an international treaty as the basis of a remedy, allowing the international agreement to be 'treated as part of domestic law for purposes of adjudication' in a domestic court.[46]

Viljoen draws an important distinction between the use of the word 'apply' in the sense of 'direct enforcement' and the use of 'apply' in the sense of providing 'interpretative guidance.'[47] Viljoen writes that focusing on these two manifestations of 'judicial application' may lead to a more nuanced discussion, than a mere focus on "monism" and "dualism". The well-known case of *Attorney General of Botswana v. Unity Dow*, is one of the few examples of a domestic case in which 'legislative effect' was given to the African Charter. This case involved the constitutionality of sex-based discrimination in the context of citizenship in Botswana. The judges referred to article 2 of the African Charter and a majority in the Botswana Court of Appeal found the law (Citizenship Act), which stated that children had to adopt the nationality of their fathers unconstitutional. As a result of the decision the Parliament of Botswana amended the Citizenship Act. This is a powerful example of a domestic court using international law as an interpretative source with the result of changing the domestic law.

---

42   Ibid.
43   521.
44   Viljoen (note 13) 524.
45   Ibid.
46   *Gwebu v. Rex* (2002) AHRLR 229 (SwCA 2002) para. 17.
47   Viljoen (note 13) 527.

The 1996 Constitution of South Africa affirms the dualist approach in that it requires treaty provisions to be enacted into national law before it becomes law.[48] If the treaty is self-executing and not inconsistent with the Constitution it becomes part of national law upon Parliament's mere approval, even in the absence of a domesticating enactment. But in practice lawyers are often not aware of the notion of the self-executing treaty. South Africa currently does not adhere to a strictly dualist approach.[49] The dualist approach has of course not always served South Africa well.[50] The neglect of international law during the Apartheid era has been attributed to the dualist approach.

5   Direct Effect

It has been suggested that the decisions of regional courts or 'community law' should have direct effect in member states. Nwauche proposes that a citizen in an ECOWAS state should be able to invoke ECOWAS law in a matter before the national courts. Nwauche calls this the 'direct effect' of community law – similar to the 'direct effect' acknowledged by the European Court of Justice.[51] At present, it seems as if national legislation may at times clash with the objectives of the Revised ECOWAS Treaty of 2003.

The Organisation for the Harmonisation of Business Law in Africa (OHADA)[52] provides a good example of successful enforcement in member states in West Africa as a result of its direct effect. The objective of the treaty establishing OHADA is to harmonize the business laws in the contracting states. Under the treaty member states relinquish some degree of national sovereignty in order

---

48   Section 231 (4) of the Constitution of South Africa, Act 108 of 1996.

49   Dikgand Moseneke writes that the 1996 Constitution has adopted a mixed approach to the incorporation of international law into our domestic law which assumes a dualist approach in relation to treaties and a monist stance in respect of customary international law. See Moseneke 'The role of comparative and public international law in domestic legal systems: a South African perspective', Middle Temple Conference *Advocate* (December 2010).

50   John Dugard, "International Law and the South African Constitution", *European Journal of International Law* 8 (1997) 78.

51   ES Nwauche, 'Enforcing ECOWAS Law in West African National Courts', *Journal of African Law*, Vol. 55 2.

52   Organisation pour l'Harmonisation en Afrique du Droit des Affaires. OHADA is a West and Central African initiative to harmonize business laws and implementing institutions. OHADA aims to alternative solutions to the lack of economic growth in sub-Saharan Africa.

to establish a single cross-border regime of uniform business laws called Uniform Acts.[53] The Uniform Acts of OHADA are directly applicable and overriding in the Contracting States. This is the case notwithstanding any conflict that may arise as a result of the subsequent enactment of municipal laws.[54] This means that these laws are automatically and immediately applicable within the national legal systems of each country and no national implementing legislate is necessary. Furthermore, the Common Court of Justice and Arbitration established under the treaty, states that the Uniform Acts abrogate national laws that are contrary to the OHADA laws.[55] The Common Court may also hear appeals from national courts or appeals directly from aggrieved individuals.[56] The decisions of the court are final and override the decisions of all national courts, including national Supreme Courts. Most OHADA countries are French-speaking[57] and their monist orientation might have played a role in the OHADA Treaty and Court. It has been speculated that the 'direct application' clause is a reason why common law countries have not become members of OHADA. The direct effect of the Uniform Acts has played a crucial role in promoting uniformity of application of the Uniform Acts and in the success of OHADA. It must, however, be kept in mind that OHADA deals exclusively with trade-related matters and not with human rights. It is unlikely that states will be prepared to sacrifice their sovereignty with regard to human rights questions to the same extent as they are prepared to do with regard to business and trade.

6 (ii) Enforcement and the Extent to which judgments of Regional Courts are Binding

Von Bogdandy and Venzke write that international courts are frequently embedded in contexts that may lever considerable enforcement mechanisms in support of their decisions, even if not to the same degree as many domestic

---

53   Oppong (note 27) 8. See Xavier Forneris *Harmonising Commercial Law in Africa*: the OHADA, *Juris Periodique* (July – September 2001) 6, commenting 'no one can deny that transfer of sovereignty occurs under OHADA.'

54   Treat for the Organisation for the Harmonisation of Business laws in Africa (OHADA Treaty), Article 10.

55   See Mamdou Kone, *Le Nouveau droit Commercial des Pays de la Zone OHADA: comparisons avec le droit francais* 5 (2003).

56   Oppong (note 27) 9.

57   The member states are Benin, Burkina Faso, Cameroon, the Central African Republic, the Comoros, Congo-Brazzaville, Cote d'Ivoire, Gabon, Guinea, Guinea Bissau, Equatorial Guinea, Mali, Niger, Senegal, Chad and Togo.

law contexts.[58] The authors refer to the WTO as an example of a court that levers such enforcement mechanisms. In the African context most regional courts are not embedded in such contexts. According to Abass, Africa suffers from the devastating consequences of ineffective implementation of international obligations.[59] He emphasizes the sacred duty of the African Court to uphold human rights particularly important in the African context where domestic courts are often prevented from effective functioning by governments.

The ECOWAS court and OHADA form exceptions. In the context of West Africa there seems to be greater political will to cooperate on a regional basis than elsewhere in Africa. This explains the relative success of ECOWAS as an economic unit and the ECOWAS Court member states have shown a commitment to regional solidarity that has not been shown in the context of East Africa or Southern Africa. The suspension of the SADC Tribunal at the behest of the Zimbabwean government[60] is the best illustration of the lack of such commitment in the Southern African context.

The enforcement of the decisions of regional African courts is important in determining the extent to which states adhere to the rule of law. Non-enforcement of decisions shows disregard for the rule of law.

1   *African Court*

Although, the African Court has the competence to make final and binding decisions on human rights violations, the Court lacks independent enforcement power over its own orders and judgements. The African Union is ulti-

---

58   Examples of this are the Committee of Ministers of the Council of Europe which oversees the implementation decisions of the ECtof HR, the member states of the ICC cooperate with the court and the fact that in the framework of the WTO member states may resort to countermeasures if their claims have succeeded in adjudication. In Von Bogdandy & Venzke 'Beyond Dispute: International Judicial Institutions as Lawmakers' in Von Bogdandy & Venzke (eds.)*International Judicial Lawmaking: On Public Authority and Democratic Legitimation*.

59   These consequences are felt in the areas of food security, corruption etc. Ademola Abass *Protecting Human Security in Africa* 362.

60   Zimbabwe refused to comply with the interim order in the *Campbell* case which resulted in a referral from the SADC Tribunal to the SADC summit. In response to the referral the Zimbabwean government prepared a discussion paper in which it raised fundamental challenges to the existence and functioning of the SADC Tribunal. Zimbabwe called for a review of the founding instruments of the SADC Tribunal. On 17 August 2010 the SADC authorities issued a communiqué to announce that a review of the 'role, functions and terms of reference of the SADC Tribunal' would be undertaken and concluded within six months. See 'Tackling Threats to the Existence of the SADC Tribunal', Malawi Law Journal, Vol. 4 (2010) 201. 202.

mately responsible for the enforcement of the African Court's orders and judgments. Pursuant to Article 31 of the Protocol, the African Court reports annually to the African Union's Assembly of Heads of State and Government, specifying which States have failed to comply with its orders or judgments. Pursuant to Article 29 of the Protocol, it is the Executive Council of the African Union which is ultimately responsible for monitoring the enforcement of these orders or judgments on behalf of the Assembly. State parties to the Court's Protocol undertake to implement the findings of the Court.[61]

The African Court's decision on the situation in Libya provides a good illustration of the difficulties surrounding enforcement of the Court's judgments.[62] In an interesting discussion on the African Court's ruling that Libya 'immediately refrain from any action that would result in loss of life or violation of physical integrity of persons,' Mulugeta addresses the issue of enforcement. He suggests that although the Court's order is binding, it 'can only be implemented through diplomatic pressure.'[63]

Rather ingeniously, Mulugeta argues that there may be other 'enforcement avenues' open to the Court and states.[64] On a generous interpretation of the Court's Statute two avenues exist: First, article 29 of the Court's Protocol states that the AU's Executive Council 'shall monitor [the Court's judgments] execution on behalf of the Assembly' of the AU. Again, if one considers 'interim measures' to be as binding as judgments, then arguably the Executive Council's responsibility under article 29 would extend to such measures as well. The question then becomes how 'monitor' is constructed.

---

61 African Court Protocol, art. 30.
62 *African Commission of Human and People's Rights v. The Great Socialist Libyan People's Republic of Arab Jamahiriya* The case against Libya did not come to the court directly. Instead, on February 24 a group of NGOs – including Human Rights Watch, Interights, and the Egyptian Initiative for Personal Rights – lodged a complaint with the African Commission on Human and Peoples' Rights. This complaint alleged that Gaddafi's forces had killed civilians, indiscriminately attacked protesters, and illegally detained opposition members – which amounted to serious violations of the right to life, integrity of the person, assembly, freedom of expression, and other fundamental human rights guaranteed under the African Charter.
63 Abebe A. Mulugeta, 'A Landmark Provisional Ruling of the African Court on Human and People's Rights on Libya', International Law Observer (2011).
64 See *International Law Observer* and Christopher Gevers, *Enforcing the African Court's Order on Libya* http://warandlaw. his-interesting-discussion-of.html. High Court of Zimbabwe (PATEL J), *Gramara (PRIVATE) limited and Colin Bailie Cloete v. Government* blogspot.com/2011/04/in-his-interesting-discussion-of.html?z#!/2011/04/in-his-interesting-discussion-of.html.

Second, and perhaps more generously, article 30 could be interpreted as placing an obligation on States Parties to the Court to guarantee the enforcement of the Court's decisions.[65]

II African Commission

Being a quasi-judicial body, the African Commission has no binding powers. In particular, under the African Charter, the Commission's functions are limited to examining state reports, considering communications alleging violations, and interpreting the Charter at the request of a State party, the OAU, or any organization recognized by the OAU. The scantiness of the enforcement and compliance control mechanism contained in the African Charter, however, is hardly surprising. At the time the OAU adopted the African Charter, very few African States (i.e. Gambia, Senegal, and Botswana), could vaunt of a democratic regime respectful of at least fundamental human rights. Since, the African Commission does not have the status of a court and since its decisions are not binding, enforcement is problematic.[66] The 2010 Rules of Procedure and Evidence of the African Commission put in place a new system in terms of which the implementation of decisions can be monitored by the Commission.[67] A 'Rapporteur for Communication' shall present a report during a public session on the implementation of the Commission's recommendations.

Wachira and Ayinla write that in general the attitude of state parties over the last twenty years has been to ignore the Commission's recommendations with no attendant consequences.[68] With regard to implementation it can be said that the efforts of the Commission have been inconsistent and *ad hoc*.[69] To date the Commission has also not commissioned a follow up system aimed

---

65   This can be done by reading the provision disjunctively; thereby creating two obligations on States Parties: The first being a specific obligation to 'comply with the judgment in any case to which they are parties within the time stipulated by the Court,' the second being a general obligation on all States Parties to guarantee the execution of decisions of the Court. This is a tenuous reading of the text, but two aspects of article 30 make a plain reading of it difficult and suggest it is open to a more constructive, *nuanced* interpretation.

66   George Wachira & Abiola Ayinla, 'Twenty years of elusive enforcement of the recommendations of the African Commission of Human and People's Rights: A possible remedy' *African Human Rights Law Journal* (2006) 6.

67   http://caselaw.ihrda.org/instrument/2010_acmhpr_rop.112/.

68   Wachira & Ayinla (note 54) 466.

69   Viljoen (note 13) 415.

at gathering information about the steps states have taken to implement decisions.[70]

The Commission faces many obstacles in terms of enforcement of its decisions. The Commission's inability to deal effectively with the most egregious human rights violations is partly attributed to enforcement obstacles.[71]

III ECOWAS

Article 19 (2) of ECOWAS Court Protocol makes decisions immediately binding. Article 15 (4) of the Revised ECOWAS Treaty of 1993[72] states that judgments of the Court are binding on member states, the institutions of the community, and on individuals and corporate bodies. Article 22 (3) requires member states and ECOWAS institutions to take all measures to ensure execution of the court's judgments. Article 24 of the Protocol requires execution of ECOWAS judgments to be in the form of a writ of execution, which the chief registrar is required to submit to the relevant member state that is then required to execute the judgment according to the civil procedure of that state. The state then has to determine the competent national authority to execute the judgment. The civil procedure rules of ECOWAS states recognize the registration and enforcement of foreign judgements.

The ECOWAS Court is unique in that its judgments are not that of a foreign court but of a court whose judgment is immediately binding on member states. The execution of its judgment by the highest courts of member states reinforces the fact that the judgment automatically becomes part of the national law and will be of the highest precedential value.

According to Nwauche,[73] there is little doubt that national judicial institutions in West Africa are subordinate to community legal institutions (such as the ECOWAS Court). The deepening of the integration in the ECOWAS region depends partly on the principles of direct effect and direct applicability. A significant part of ECOWAS community law could be said to have direct effect. According to Nwauche, it is open to the ECOWAS Court to recognise direct effect. The mandate of the Revised Treaty allows for the court to assert that community law has authority, which can be invoked in national courts. A practical

---

70   Viljoen (note 13) 416.
71   A.A.R Mohamed, 'Article 58 of the African Charter on Human and People's Rights: A Legal Analysis and How it can be Put into More Practical Use' (1996) ASICL proceedings 304–305.
72   The revised treaty was accepted in July 1993 in Cotonou, Benin. The text is available at: http://www.comm.ecowas.int/sec/index.php?id+treaty&lang=en.
73   Nwauche (note 48) 55.

illustration of this question arises in the landmark case *SERAP v. Federal Republic of Nigeria* (2009) regarding the right to education. If *SERAP* is of direct effect it will amount to amendment to the 1999 Constitution overruling landmark decisions.[74] The central problem in the *SERAP* case is that the right to education is not contained in chapter IV of the 1999 Constitution, which sets out enforceable constitutional rights. Instead, the right to education is contained in chapter II, which contains directive principles of state policy.[75] The ECOWAS Court dismissed the Nigerian government's objection that the right to education is a mere directive principle of government and not a citizen's right. It based its decision on the African Charter which contains a justiciable right to education and which has been ratified and domesticated by Nigeria.

If a decision of ECOWAS has precedential value in Nigeria, a large section of Nigerian law may change as a result of *SERAP*. However, it must be kept in mind that it was stated in a previous decision of the African Commission that a number of socio-economic rights are enforceable by virtue of the African Charter[76] and this has not changed the enforcement of socioeconomic rights in Nigeria.[77]

Recognizing the principle of direct effect in the context of ECOWAS has the potential to influence the development of the principle of direct effect for other regional courts such as the African Court.

IV   EAC

The East African Court has concurrent jurisdiction with national courts on the interpretation of the Treaty but decisions of the Court take precedence over national courts.[78] The execution of judgments of the Court, which imposes a pecuniary obligation on a person, shall be governed by the rules of civil procedure in force in the Partner State in which execution is to take place. Where there is no pecuniary obligation involved, the Partner States and the Council are under an obligation to implement the judgment of the Court without delay.

---

74   Such as *Adesanya v. Presiet of the FederalR epublic of Nigeria* 1981 and *Okogie v. Attorney General of Lagos State* (1981) 2 NCLR 350.
75   In terms of section 6(6) (c) of the Constitution these principles are not enforceable.
76   *Social and Economic Rights Centre v. Nigeria* (2001) AHRLR 60.
77   Nwauche (note 71) 199.
78   See *East Africa Law Society and 4 Others and the Attorney General of Kenya and 3 Others* By the provisions under article 23, 33 (2) the Treaty established the principle of overall supremacy of the Court over the interpretation and application of the Treaty, to ensure harmony and certainty.

V   SADC *Tribunal*

The decisions of the SADC Tribunal are final and binding. The SADC Summit's inactivity regarding the enforcement of the decisions of the Tribunal has led to the suspension and review of the Tribunal.[79]

Domestic courts were unwilling to enforce the decision in the *Campbell* case. Specifically, courts in Zimbabwe rejected the request to enforce the decision in the *Campbell* case. In its decision of January 26th 2010 the High Court of Zimbabwe declined the application to register the SADC decision for purposes of enforcement.[80] In *Gramara*, Judge Patel of the High Court held that the decision could not be registered since it was contrary to public policy (*ordre public*).[81] The High Court held that the Supreme Court had confirmed the constitutionality of the land reform program; thus to register the SADC Tribunal's judgement in Zimbabwe would be to undermine the Supreme Court's authority. The High Court felt bound by the Supreme Court as the supreme law of the land.[82] Essentially, the *Campbell* decision seemed to clash with the political and policy objectives of the Zimbabwean government. In this case there was no appreciation for the fact that regional courts could take priority over those of national courts. The decision of the Supreme Court of Zimbabwe was considered to trump that of the SADC Tribunal.

7   Conclusion and Recommendations

It is clear from this study that domestic jurisdictions have referred to the jurisprudence of regional courts only infrequently. Viljoen writes that 'the ultimate test of international human rights law is the extent to which it takes root in national soil.'[83] If one applies this test to regional courts it is clear that the regional courts have not yet measured up to this standard. The crucial question

---

79   Andreas R Ziegler 'Regional Economic Integration Agreements and Investor Protection in Africa – The Case of SADC' 13.

80   High Court of Zimbabwe (PATEL J) *Gramara (PRIVATE) limited and Colin Bailie Cloete v. Government of the Republic of Zimbabwe and Attorney general of Zimbabwe and Norman Kapanga* (Intervener), Opposed Application, Harare, 24 November 2009 and 26 January 2010.

81   *Gramara (Pvt.) Ltd and Other vs Government of the Republic of Zimbabwean and Others* [2010] 16. See also Jeremy Gauntlett's, 'Why was Southern Africa's House of Justice Pulled Down?' (24 September 2012) politicsweb available at http://www.politicsweb.co.za/politicsweb/view/politicsweb/en/page71656/page71619?oid=328350&sn=Detail&pid=71619.

82   Ibid.

83   Viljoen (note 13) 518.

is, therefore, not just whether the case law of the regional courts have trickled down into the case law of domestic systems, but what has also been the effect of citation by domestic courts: for example, has the reference to regional case law led to a human rights friendly outcome? At this stage very few cases have had the dramatic human rights-promoting impact of cases such as the ECOWAS slavery decision, *Hadijatou Mani Koraou v. Niger*.[84] And it is acknowledged that the fact that a domestic court cites regional jurisprudence does not mean that the norms or standards set by a regional court have necessarily changed the behavior or rules in a domestic jurisdiction.

This study further illustrates that although it cannot yet be said that the creation and existence of Regional African courts introduces a new layer of supranational protection of human rights in Africa, the potential to fulfil such role certainly exists.[85] Regional and sub-regional courts are increasingly becoming more active. Although, the African Commission has been particularly active in issuing decisions, the ECOWAS Court has been the most active African sub-regional court.

The citation of court cases are of course not the only measure of impact. The harmonization of legislation in the member states and the inculcation of human rights law principles into domestic legal systems (without necessarily explicitly referring to the African Charter or regional courts) as well as deliberations emanating from regional courts are all essential in enriching human rights discourse in African sub-regions.[86] The impact of the regional courts can also be assessed by looking at whether the regional courts have generally contributed to the building of democratic capacity.

Suggestions have been made for the reconsideration of the traditional monist/dualist debate. It seems the framing of enforcement along these lines does not always reflect the practical realities of enforcement by member states of the African Union.

Ultimately the future of the African Court, African Commission, and sub-regional courts depends on political will. The success of the court will depend on the will of African states, the judges of the regional and sub-regional courts, as well as domestic judges, and NGO's to make active use of the regional and sub-regional bodies. Since most of the African regional courts are still relatively new this applies to all the courts. Institutions such as the regional courts

---

84 AHRLR 182 (ECOWAS 2008).
85 Lucyline Nkata Murugi, *Revisiting the Role of Sub-Regional Courts in the Protection of Human Rights in Africa*, LLM Dissertation, University of the Western Cape (2009) 23.
86 Ibid. at 27.

are of the very few institutions in Africa that create a window of opportunity for citizens of African states to be heard and for their rights to vindicated, especially in the absence of domestic human rights protection. If the rule of law protects the vulnerable rather than the powerful, the optimal functioning and development of these courts is of pressing concern for the rule of law in Africa.

CHAPTER 31

Rethinking Anti-Corruption Strategies in Africa: Constitutional Entrenchment as Basis for Credible and Effective Anti-Corruption Clean-Ups

Charles Manga Fombad and Madeleine Choe-Amusimo Fombad

1   Introduction

Corruption is probably one of the biggest threats to peace and stability in Africa today. Worse still, it casts an ominous dark shadow over the future political, economic, and social progress of the continent given the deleterious effects it is having on the faltering efforts to establish a culture of constitutionalism, democracy, respect for the rule of law and good governance. The debilitating effects of corruption are sparing no African country. For example, in a letter of 3 May 2012, President Salva Kiir of South Sudan, Africa's youngest state (which barely celebrated the first year of its hard-earned independence from the Republic of Sudan in July 2012), wrote to 75 former and current government officials to return an estimated US$ 4 billion which had been stolen from the country which was now almost bankrupt. In it, he said:

> We fought for freedom, justice and equality. Yet, once we got to power, we forgot what we fought for and began to enrich ourselves at the expense of our people.[1]

South Sudan in many respects epitomises the African paradox; how African leaders have fought hard to liberate their people from exploitative, alien, cruel, despotic and undemocratic foreign powers but within a few years of getting

---

[1]   See, "S. Sudan asks officials to return stolen funds," http://www.aljazeera.com/news/africa/2012/06/201265233043136384.html (accessed in March 2015). On 8 July 2013, a "letter of concern to President Salva Kiir," was written by "several long-term friends of South Sudan" in which they expressed their concern about the "increasingly perilous fate of South Sudan," which barely two years after independence, has "become synonymous with corruption." See, *Pambazuka News* Issue 638 of 10 July 2013, http://www.pambazuka.org/en/category/comment/88191/print (accessed in March 2015).

to power, they become worse than these foreign oppressors. The cancer of corruption appears to have eroded the sense of fairness, rationality, compassion, patriotism and humanity in the ruling class in Africa.[2] The gravity of the corruption problem in Africa was succinctly summarised by Moseneke DJP and Cameron J in the South African case of *Glenister v. The State President of South Africa and others*[3] thus:

> There can be no gainsaying that corruption threatens to fell at the knees virtually everything we hold dear and precious in our hard-won constitutional order. It blatantly undermines the democratic ethos, the institutions of democracy, the rule of law and the foundational values of our nascent constitutional project. It fuels maladministration and public fraudulence, imperils the capacity of the state to fulfil its obligations to respect, protect, promote and fulfil all the rights enshrined in the Bill of Rights. When corruption and organised crime flourish, sustainable development and economic growth are stunted. And in turn, the stability and security of society is put at risk.

Corruption is neither a new phenomenon nor is it unique to Africa. As Transparency International's (TI) annual Corruption Perception Index (CPI) shows,[4] it is a feature of all countries both developed and underdeveloped. It is, however, the scale of corruption in Africa and the debilitating effect it is having on the continent that makes it different.[5] Not only does it undermine economic

---

[2] For example, how else can one explain the fact that the first major decision taken by the South African government soon after defeating apartheid was to devote billions of Rand to buying warships and warplanes when there was no conceivable foreign military threat to the country and when the real threat to the consolidation of democracy is poverty. Instead of building houses, schools and hospitals or seriously tackling the issue of HIV and AIDS the government preferred to enter into a huge arms deal that has been described as a betrayal of the struggle against apartheid, because, as we shall see later, of the huge kickbacks that many of the politicians made from the deal. See further, Terry Crawford-Browne, "The Arms Deal Scandal," 31(100) *Review of African Political Economy* (2004), pp. 329–342.

[3] 2011 (3) SA 347 (CC) at para. 166.

[4] See, http://www.transparency.org/ (accessed in March 2015).

[5] According to Edeard Hoseah, Chairman of the AU Advisory Board on Anti-Corruption (AU-ABC), and citing a recent report from the African Development Bank, Africa losses about USD 148billion a year through corruption. It also says that over 50% of tax revenue and USD 30 billion of foreign aid is lost through corruption. See, "Hoseah: Foreign banks fuel graft" http://dailynews.co.tz/archive/index.php/local-news/6393-hoseah-foreign-banks-fuel-graft, http://sabahionline.com/en_GB/articles/hoa/articles/newsbriefs/2012/06/20/newsbrief-06 Also see,

development and growth, it discourages foreign investment, diverts resources from priority areas in the economy and inflicts needless poverty and suffering, especially on the most vulnerable.

Over the last two decades, the pressure on African governments to clean up corruption has been relentless and strident. This has come from donor governments,[6] the World Bank, the International Monetary Fund, the UN, the UN Economic Commission for Africa (ECA), specialist NGOs such as TI and the International Group for Anti-corruption. This has led many African countries to sign and ratify numerous international and regional anti-corruption treaties. Many of these governments have also at various stages, especially from 1995 when TI started naming and shaming countries based on their corruption perception level, enacted legislation and established bodies to fight against corruption. Most of these measures have been inadequate and ineffective and turned out to be mere palliatives and tokenistic gestures designed to give the impression that something was being done. The anti-corruption institutions that have, from time to time been created, spend more time talking about corruption than actually dealing with it; and more often bark but do not bite. The anti-corruption measures never really went to the root of the problem, nor were they sufficiently robust to render corruption a high risk activity in which the chances of being caught and severely punished acted as a strong deterrent. As the example of South Sudan shows, corruption in Africa is like a cancer that is steadily destroying the continent. It has become so endemic that it is considered as a way of life: the stigma usually attached to it is almost non-existent. In some countries, such as Nigeria and Cameroon, bribes are requested openly as if it were a right.[7] It is almost irrational to be honest and straight. The regular

---

"Corruption costing Africa billions," http://zambia.co.zm/local-news/2010/11/26/corruption-costing-africa-billions/ (accessed in March 2015).

6 See for example, "Netherlands to Stop Budget aid to Mozambique," at http://www.news24.com/Africa/News/Netherlands-to-stop-budget-aid-to-Mozambique-20120713 (accessed in March 2015) where it was reported in mid July 2012 that the Netherlands government had decided to stop funding Mozambique's general budget with effect from 2013 because of the country's questionable governance record and its anti-corruption drive. In March 2010, a group of 19 donors had suspended their budget support to the country following the 2009 elections and only agreed to resume this after the government made firms commitments on electoral reforms and the fight against corruption.

7 A story was circulating in the social network media about how a Nigerian policeman arrested a man urinating at a place clearly marked: "Do not Urinate Here, Fine N500." The offender gives the policeman a N1000 note. The policeman turned around and said "urinate again, I don't have change … "

corruption scandals that dominate the headlines on television and in newspapers no longer shock or embarrass anybody.

It had been assumed that the spread of democratisation, economic liberalisation and the constitutional reforms that saw concerted attempts to entrench an ethos of constitutionalism, respect for the rule of law, good governance and respect for human rights will bring about greater transparency and scrutiny that will limit corruption. Instead, the level of corruption has intensified as opportunistic politicians have misused national resources to entrench themselves or their parties in power. The best opportunity to institutionalise effective anti-corruption measures came with the fever of constitutional reforms of the post 1990 era. After more than two decades under these new or revised constitutions, it is now clear that most of them failed to properly address some of the critical problems of African constitutional development.[8] One of these is the issue of corruption, which today constitutes one of the root causes of political instability, poor governance, under-development and poverty. In fact, very few African constitutions directly address in any meaningful manner the issue of corruption. The main contention in this Chapter is that only constitutionally entrenched measures and institutions, protected by certain entrenched fundamental principles, can provide a solid bedrock on which to launch any effective anti-corruption strategy that could bring Africa's troubling endemic corruption under control.

The Chapter starts by briefly considering the meaning and nature of corruption and some of the consequences it has on Africa. It then reviews some of the anti-corruption strategies that have been attempted in the past. This is followed by a consideration of the rationale for constitutionalising the principles and institutions needed to combat corruption and the possible scope of these anti-corruption principles. The final part in conclusion, points out that the scale of corruption in most African countries has reached a point where the only chance to begin to solve the problem is by taking fairly drastic and harsh measures designed to ensure that only those prepared to live with the severe penalties dare to indulge in corrupt practices.

What this Chapter proposes is a radical but robust and effective novel constitutional approach to curbing corruption. The aim is to change the present situation where corruption is a highly lucrative low risk activity that does not only guarantee wealth but has enabled politicians and their cronies to capture

---

[8] These are discussed in Charles Manga Fombad, "Constitutional Reforms and Constitutionalism in Africa: Reflections on Some Current Challenges and Future Prospects," 59(4) *Buffalo Law Review* (2011), pp. 1007–1107.

power, keep others out whilst making a farce of democracy, rule of law, good governance and accountability. In doing so, the constitution and constitutionalism has been progressively undermined and subverted. This Chapter proposes a constitutionalist response that will render corruption a high risk activity to all, regardless of their status, and make the risk of being caught and severely punished a potent deterrent. The justification for such a radical approach lies in the fact that it is time to recognise and sanction corruption for what it is. It is an act of evil and wickedness[9] because of its potential not only to subject people to needless destitution but even death through starvation, lack of basic medical care[10] or accidents,[11] and must therefore be treated with the utmost

---

9   An incident reported in the, 2011 Country Reports on Human Rights Practices – Nigeria," http://www.refworld.org/cgi-bin/texis/vtx/rwmain?page=country&category=&publisher=&type=&coi=NGA&rid=&docid=4fc75a7546&skip=0 (accessed in March 2015) underscores the point being made whether some of the corrupt individuals in Africa still have any human feelings. In this report, an incident of 14 August 2010 is reported where police in Anambra state shot five persons at a roadblock after they refused to pay a bribe of 20 Naira (approximately, USD 0.13).

10 A recent study by Amnesty International on maternal death in Burkina Faso reported that corruption amongst medical personnel is one of the main causes of the deaths of thousands of women during pregnancy. Poor women who are unable to make the illegal payments demanded by hospital staff to administer care to them are turned away from hospitals and end of relying on quack traditional healers. Data for 64 countries suggest that an increase in the demand for bribes is associated with an increase in maternal mortality. See George Fominyen, "Corruption undermines Burkina Faso efforts on maternal mortality," http://www.trust.org/trustlaw/news/corruption-undermines-burkina-faso-efforts-on-maternal-mortality/ (accessed in March 2015) ; and TI, "The Anti-corruption Catalyst: Realising the MDGs by 2015," http://www.transparency-usa.org/documents/AntiCorruptionCatalystRealisingtheMDGby2015.pdf (accessed in March 2015).

11 In Cameroon, it is only recently after a former minister of Territorial Administration and Decentralisation, Marafa Hamidou Yaya, a one-time favourite to take over from President Paul Biya was arrested, allegedly, for corruption and embezzlement that in a series of open letters to Paul Biya, the former minister has been narrating gory tales of corruption and its effects on the ordinary citizen. According to one of his letters, the death of 71 people in a Boeing 737–200 operated by Camair on 3 December 1995 was a direct result of the failure to carry out normal routine maintenance of the aircraft. A multi-million dollars maintenance contract was alleged to have been signed with South African Airways (SAA) under which several Cameroonian politicians and top officials at Camair received huge bribes. Because no maintenance was ever carried out, it is alleged that SAA admitted liability and negotiated a deal in which Camair received USD 65million as compensation but until Marafa wrote his explosive letters in June 2012, none of the victims' families had received anything. Nor is there any indication of where the money paid as compensation went to, especially since Camair eventually went bankrupt.

2 Meaning, Nature and Consequences of Corruption in Africa

It is necessary here to examine, albeit briefly, what is meant by corruption, its nature and manifestations before we consider its possible consequences. Understanding what corruption is and its diverse forms and manifestations is crucial to designing any effective anti-corruption remedy.

2.1 *Meaning, Nature and Manifestations of Corruption*

Corruption is an exceedingly complex phenomenon in terms of its definition, form and manifestation.[12] The literature on the topic is replete with numerous complex definitions each looking at the concept from one perspective or another but there is none which is either comprehensive or generally accepted. It is not necessary for our purposes here, to go into a discussion of the merits or otherwise of the different definitions.[13] For our purposes here, it will suffice to note that, in a general sense, corruption arises where an individual or group of individuals abuse a position of trust in which they are placed or find themselves, subverting existing rules whether legal or extra-legal, and generate undeserved benefits for themselves.

Corruption has many features and forms and may manifest itself in diverse ways. There is no exhaustive list of all the activities that could constitute corruption because this depends on the laws of each country. Nevertheless some of the common activities that are considered to amount to acts of corruption

---

[12] See, R.D. Pathak and R.S. Prasad, "The Role of E-Governance in Tackling Corruption: The Indian Experience," in Raza Ahmad (ed.), *The Role of Public Administration in Building a Harmonious Society,* Kuala Lumpur, Asia Development Bank (2006), pp. 434–463.

[13] For an excellent discussion of this, see John Mukum Mbaku, *Bureaucratic and Political Corruption in Africa. The Public Choice Perspective,* Florida, Krieger Publishing Co (2000), pp. 9–16.

include bribery,[14] embezzlement,[15] patronage,[16] nepotism and cronyism,[17] conflict of interest,[18] influence peddling,[19] kickbacks,[20] electoral fraud[21] and unholy alliance.[22]

A number of classifications have been made over the years in the attempts to understand the different types of corruption and determine how best to tackle them. Two of these are worth noting.[23] The first of these categorisa-

---

[14] Bribery can be defined as offering, promising, giving, accepting or soliciting of an advantage as an inducement for an action which is illegal, unethical or a breach of trust. Inducements can take the form of gifts, loans, fees, rewards or other advantages. Sometimes, active bribery is distinguished from passive bribery. The former involves the promising, offering or giving by any person, directly or indirectly, any undue advantage to any public official in order to induce him to act or refrain from acting in the exercise of his functions. Passive bribery on the other hand is the request or receipt by any public official directly or indirectly of any undue advantage or the acceptance of an offer or promise of such an advantage in order to act or refrain from acting in the exercise of his functions. See generally, TI's site, "What is Public Sector Corruption," http://blog.transparency.org/2011/12/02/what-is-public-sector-corruption/ (accessed in March 2015) and Jens Chr. Andvig et al., "Research on Corruption. A Policy Oriented Survey," http://www.icgg.org/downloads/contribution07_andvig.pdf (accessed in March 2015).

[15] Embezzlement is where a person holding office in an institution, organisation or company dishonestly and illegally appropriates uses or traffics the funds and goods they have been entrusted with for personal enrichment or other activities.

[16] Patronage is a form of favouritism in which a person is selected, regardless qualifications or entitlement, for a job or government benefit because of political affiliations or connections.

[17] This is a form of favouritism based on acquaintances and friendship (in the case of cronyism) or familiar relationships (in the case of nepotism) whereby someone in an official position exploits his authority and power to provide a job or favour to a family member or friend, even though he may not be qualified or deserving.

[18] This is a situation where an individual or the entity where he works, whether this be a government, business or civil society organisation is confronted with choosing between the duties and demands of their position and their private interests.

[19] Influence peddling or trading in influence refers to a situation where a person is selling his influence over the decision process involving a third party (individual or institution).

[20] This is an official's share of misappropriated funds allocated from his organisation to an organisation involved in corrupt bidding.

[21] Also called voter fraud, this entails all forms of illegal interference with the electoral process and therefore preventing a free and fair outcome.

[22] This is a coalition between seemingly antagonistic groups for an *ad hoc* or hidden opportunistic gain.

[23] Another categorisation is the distinction made by some writers between corruption in developing countries, which they describe as growth-retarding or a threat to political stability and corruption in developed countries which they describe as more benign and

tions distinguishes between grand and petty corruption. Grand corruption, which is often regarded as political corruption, although the two are not necessarily the same, reflects not the amount of money involved but rather the high level of the corruption. It is often associated with political corruption because it refers to acts committed at the highest level of government where policies and rules are formulated. Political or grand corruption occurs when politicians and senior civil servants responsible for making important policy decisions that affect the welfare of the state misuse their position and abuse the enormous powers that are at their disposal to make decisions that benefit them personally rather than the state. Grand corruption arises from the fact that high level decision makers either side-step the laws which they make or tailor them to suit their selfish interest. It is the most deadly form of corruption because once the top leadership is also involved in it, corruption tends to spread rapidly downwards and often spirals out of control. By contrast, petty corruption or bureaucratic corruption as it is usually referred to, is small scale everyday corruption that takes place at the implementation end. Because it often involves small sums, it is also sometimes referred to as low level or street level corruption. People experience this daily when they encounter the public administration and services such as police at road blocks, licensing authorities, hospitals and schools.[24] Whether or not such petty corruption is anything but a "petty nuisance" depends very much on how extensive it is. This links up with the other category of classification. Where petty corruption is extensive, it gives rise to another form of corruption covered by the second classification.

This second classification distinguishes between three types of corruption: incidental (individual) or sporadic, institutional, and systemic (societal or endemic) corruption.[25] Incidental corruption, which is also known as individual or sporadic corruption, is where corruption occurs irregularly or is confined to a few instances of malfeasance on the part of individual politicians or public officials in a manner that does not threaten the functioning of the administration or the economy of the country. Incidences of corruption are episodic rather than systemic. On the other hand, institutional corruption is where cor-

---

does not undermine the economic or political viability of the country. See, M. Johnson, "The Search for Definitions: The Vitality of Politics and the Issue of Corruption," 149 *International Social Science Journal* (1996), pp. 321–235, and P.D. Hutchcroft, "The Politics of Privilege: Assessing the Impact of Rents, Corruption and Clientelism in Third World Development," 45(3) *Political Studies* (1997), pp. 639–658.

24   See, Elaine Byrne, "Definitions and Types of Corruption," http://elaine.ie/2009/07/31/definitions-and-types-of-corruption/ (accessed in March 2015).

25   See, Mark Robinson, "Corruption and Development: An Introduction," in Mark Robinson (ed.), *Corruption and Development*, London, Frank Cass (1998), pp. 3–8.

ruption pervades particular institutions or sectors of activity. There may be many reasons for this. For instance, it could be because it is easier for public officials in those institutions or sectors of activity to extract rents or because the controls and regulations are weak and allow these officials too much discretion. An example of this is the police service which is regarded as the most corrupt institution in Africa.[26] The third form of corruption here, endemic, societal, entrenched or systemic corruption, as the names suggest, is the worst type of corruption. It describes a situation where corruption is virtually an integral and essential part of national life because it is all-pervasive, routinised and accepted by all. Such corruption pervades all aspects of economic, social and political life. The World Bank has sometimes described this as "quiet corruption."[27]

Properly identifying the type of corruption that operates in a particular country is critical to designing appropriate measures to counter it. The strategy to be adopted will differ depending on the type of corruption. Based on the classifications examined above, it can be said generally that corruption is endemic or deeply entrenched in most African countries. Two factors have made is particularly virulent. First, is the fact that it is grand or political corruption, which in many respects, is the mother of all corruption because of its tendency to breed, spread and intensify corruption. Corruption at the top creates expectations amongst bureaucrats that they will also share in the booty and reduces any moral or psychological authority on the top officials to constrain the lower level officials. Generalised low level corruption can hardly be kept under control by a corrupt leadership. Such state of unrestrained political corruption, as operates in many African countries, is known as kleptocracy, literally meaning, "rule by thieves."[28] Second, it manifests elements of petty corruption because

---

[26] See, "You are rotten! Survey declares police as most corrupt institution in Ghana," http://www.africaundisguised.com/newsportal/story/you-are-rotten-survey-declares-police-most-corrupt-institution-ghana (accessed in March 2015); and "Police most corrupt public institution," https://www.newsday.co.zw/2011/11/28/2011-11-28-police-most-corrupt-public-institution/ (accessed in March 2015).

[27] This is the pervasive and widespread failure across Africa by public servants to deliver goods and services paid for by government. This species of corruption hardly makes headline news but is extremely corrosive of society. See, "'Quiet Corruption' Undermining Development in Africa," http://web.worldbank.org/wbsite/external/countries/africaext/0,,contentmdk:22501207~pagePK:146736~piPK:146830~theSitePK:258644,00.html (accessed in March 2015).

[28] The late Mobutu Sese Seko who ruled the DR Congo (which he renamed Zaire) from 1965 to 1997 has probably been one of the most notorious cases of a kleptomania. For other examples, see Stephen Riley, "The Political Economy of Anti-corruption Strategies in

it operates from the lowest street level. This has had severe consequences on African development which we shall now proceed to look at.

2.2 Consequences of corruption in Africa

Almost all the voluminous literature on corruption in Africa concludes that it poses the greatest challenge to development on the continent.[29] In TI's CPI for 2011, all but four Sub-Saharan countries fall in the lower half with a score below 5.[30] Four of the ten most corrupt countries in the world (Libya, Equatorial Guinea, Sudan and Somalia) are from Africa, with Somalia having had the dubious reputation of being the most corrupt country in the world for the last five years. This is a slight improvement on 2010, when six of the ten most corrupt countries in the world were from Africa. It is particularly problematic because Africa is the poorest and least developed continent in the world and generally has the lowest aggregate level of human development. The negative consequences of corruption on economic, political, social and cultural development on the continent add to the numerous other problems such as disease and drought that afflict the continent.[31] And, as Kofi Annan, the former Secretary General of the UN, in lamenting about the destructive effects of corruption in developing countries said:

> Corruption hurts the poor disproportionately by diverting funds intended for development, undermining a government's ability to provide basic services, feeding inequality and injustice, and discouraging foreign investment and aid. Corruption is a key factor in economic underperformance and a major obstacle to poverty alleviation and development.[32]

Africa," in Mark Robinson (ed.), *Corruption and Development*, London, Frank Cass (1998), pp. 140–142, and 156.

29 Besides annual survey reports of Transparency International, see John Mukum Mbaku, op. cit.; Paul Heywood, *Political Corruption*, Oxford, Blackwell Press (1997).; UNDP, *Corruption and Good Governance. Discussion Paper 3*, New York, UNDP (1997); and Mark Robinson op. cit.; Donatella Porta and Alberto Vannucci, "The 'Perverse Effects' of Political Corruption, in *Paul Heywood*, op. cit. pp. 100–122; *UNDP, Corruption and Good Governance. Discussion Paper 3, New York, UNDP (1997); and Mark Robinson* op. cit.

30 Only Botswana, Cape Verde, Mauritius and Rwanda score above 5 in the index. See, http://www.transparency.org/cpi2011/results (accessed in March 2015).

31 See generally, John Mukum Mbaku, op. cit.;

32 In "foreword," "United Nations Convention Against Corruption," http://www.unodc.org/documents/treaties/UNCAC/Publications/Convention/08-50026_E.pdf (accessed in March 2015).

One of the main victims of corruption today in Africa has been democracy, good governance and constitutionalism. The great optimism that followed the wave of democratisation and the political and constitutional reforms that went with it in the early 1990s with the apparent opening up of political space for competitive elections has now been neutralised by the corruption of the electoral process by African leaders.[33] Through well organised and sophisticated processes of vote rigging, electoral fraud and other electoral malpractices, the pre-1990 one party systems have merely transformed themselves into multiparty dominant party dictatorships that have done little to replace the repressive, exploitative, corrupt and inefficient structures that provided a breeding ground for the rise of military dictatorships and political instability in the past. To maintain the façade of democracy and multipartyism, African leaders have squandered state resources to bribe voters through staging regular ritualistic elections with predictable outcomes. Ill-gotten state resources have also been used to co-opt and neutralise the opposition parties into sharing the spoils of power. However, the biggest threat posed by the regular electoral fraud and other malpractices that have marred recent elections in countries such as Cameroon, Côte d'Ivoire, DR. Congo, Ethiopia, Gabon, Kenya and Zimbabwe, is that it destroys faith in the ballot box and in democracy. The recent post-election violence in DR. Congo, Kenya and Zimbabwe are a timely reminder of the veracity of the late President John F. Kennedy's oft-quoted prediction that "those who make peaceful revolution impossible, will make violent revolution inevitable."[34] In other words, corruption of the electoral processes in Africa by the ruling elites is not only progressively undermining all the efforts towards establishing and entrenching an ethos of democracy, good governance and constitutionalism on the continent but threatening peace and stability as well.

Corruption is also a major obstacle to the efforts, since the 1990s, to establish credible, independent and effective judiciaries. Judges all over the con-

---

33 See, James D. Long, "Electoral Fraud and the Erosion of Democratic Gains in Kenya," http://www.sscnet.ucla.edu/polisci/wgape/papers/18_Long.pdf (accessed in March 2015); Rafael Lopez-Pintor, "Assessing Electoral Fraud in New Democracies: A Basic Conceptual Framework," http://www.ifes.org/~/media/Files/Publications/White%20Paper-Report/2010/RLP_Assessing_Electoral_Fraud_White_Paper_Dec2010.pdf (accessed in March 2015); and U.B. Ikpe, "The Impact of Manipulated Re-elections on Accountability and Legitimacy of Democratic Regimes in Africa: Observations from Nigeria, Zambia and Kenya," 3(7) *African Journal of Political Science and International Relations* (2009), pp. 300–310.

34 In a speech at the White House in 1962, http://www.quotationspage.com/quote/24966.html (accessed in March 2015).

tinent are reasonably well paid and receive salaries and pensions well above that of the average civil servants. Yet, after the police, the judiciary is generally considered to be the most corrupt institution in Africa. The case of Kenya is well documented. In 2003, the Kenyan judiciary was described as "pathologically sycophantic," "grossly incompetent" and "shamelessly corrupt."[35] A Ringera Committee Report of 2003 that investigated issues of integrity and corruption in the Kenyan judiciary contained a "price list" showing the cost of bribing a judge. According to this list, and depending on the seniority and nature of the case, the amounts were as follows:

- Appeals Court .... US$ 190,800
- High Court .... US$ 636 to US$ 20,356
- Magistrates' Court .... US$ 50 to US$ 1,908
- Murder/armed robbery ..... US$ 509 to US$ 17,723
- Manslaughter/rape/drugs ... US$ 255 to US$ 6,360

The report also indicated that corrupt magistrates expected 10 to 30% of any civil awards that they make.[36] Many Africans now openly wonder why they should bother to hire a lawyer when they can buy the judges. Some lawyers now openly make it clear that their fee includes the judge's bribe. Corruption, especially on the scale reported in Kenya destroys confidence in the judicial system and distracts judges from their sacred responsibility to do justice and see that justice is done. In spite of considerable steps taken during the constitutional revisions in the 1990s and thereafter to promote a culture of judicial independence and respect for the rule of law for the first time in African countries, this is largely being compromised in many countries such as Nigeria, Cameroon, DR Congo and Kenya by the inability of the judiciary in these countries to resist the lure of bribes. Justice in most African countries today no longer depends on the merits of the case but rather on who is able to pay the judge more.

It is perhaps the economic consequences of corruption in Africa that are particularly debilitating on the continent. The destructive consequences of corruption not only reinforce but daily increases the number and the plight of the millions of poor and marginalised people struggling to eke a living at a time of severe economic crisis on the continent. Generally, corruption hurts the poor and marginalised more than any other groups in society because it

---

[35] See, Linda Van De Vijver (ed.), *The Judicial Institution in Southern Africa. A Comparative Study of Common Law Jurisdictions*, Cape Town, Siber Ink (2006), at p. 50.
[36] Ibid. at p. 51.

restricts their access to basic services such as water, education, health care and many other crucial services necessary for survival. It is the poor who are vulnerable to extortion of bribes by public officials, especially the police. Generalised petty corruption hurts the poor most because they are forced to pay bribes for most of the essential services which are designed to lift them out of poverty. Payment of little bribes here and there eats into their meagre earnings and often makes apparently free social services more expensive. For example, the amounts needed to bribe head teachers and principals and their colleagues, in order to gain admission into the so-called free public schools in many African countries effectively makes nonsense of the much vaunted policy of free education.[37] In South Africa, an estimated 10% of the social security budget is lost due to fraud, theft and inefficiencies in the system. This compromises the goals of poverty alleviation because it has been estimated that one pension drawer supports 7 to 11 people with the meagre pension.[38] In many African countries, essential medicines, such as anti-retroviral drugs, which are supposed to be distributed free of charge at hospitals, are openly sold to patients. Corruption thus becomes a sort of regressive tax which hits the poor and needy hardest.

Corruption also causes enormous damage by distorting national priorities and diverting public expenditures away from less lucrative sectors such as health, education and other labour-intensive activities which traditionally employ the poor into capital-intensive projects which generate larger kickbacks. On 27 May 2012, a popular South African Sunday newspaper on its front page, under the title, "Suffer the children. Here is an image that should outrage the nation," carried photographs of primary school classes from grades R to 7 being conducted under trees in a hamlet in Limpopo since January 2012.[39] Meanwhile, President Jacob Zuma, in response to the criticism that the African National Congress (ANC) government is too busy enjoying the spoils of power to care about the people it was supposed to have fought against apartheid for,

---

[37] For example, TI in a seven-country study of African countries (Ghana, Madagascar, Morocco, Niger, Senegal, Sierra Leone and Uganda) where schools are supposed to be free and open to all students, found out that 44% of the parents surveyed had had to pay illegal fees as bribes to enable their children to be admitted in these schools. See, TI, "Africa Education Watch: Good Governance Lessons for Primary Education, February 2010," http://www.polity.org.za/article/africa-education-watch-good-governance-lessons-for-primary-education-february-2010-2010-02-23 (accessed in March 2015).

[38] See, "Corruption and Poverty" http://billyaportadera.com/?page=articles&action=read&id=5 (accessed in March 2015).

[39] See, *Sunday Times*, 27 May 2012.

promised in his state of the nation address of 9 February 2012, a "huge campaign of building the infrastructure nationwide," that will "boost the level of the economy and create job opportunities."[40] His Finance Minister, Pravin Gordhan duly obliged a few weeks later in the 2012 budget. If the evidence of the last few years is anything to go by, it is likely that this whole "huge campaign of building the infrastructure nationwide," will do nothing more than fuel the flames of corruption by "tenderpreneurs."[41] For example, the newspapers have reported how a company that was paid R 16 million to build more than 700 Reconstruction and Development Programme (RDP) houses for the homeless and poor ended up building only one house.[42] The Public Protector was asked in 2011 to investigate a transaction in which the government spent millions of Rands to buy land in a questionable deal that resulted in a businessman pocketing R24.5 million in a record two minutes.[43] One analyst has estimated that the amount of money lost in South Africa through corruption in 2011 was about a staggering R675 billion.[44] There have been similar accounts of

---

[40] See, "State of the Nation Address by His Excellency Jacob G Zuma, President of the Republic of South Africa on the occasion of the Joint Sitting of Parliament," http://www.thepresidency.gov.za/pebble.asp?relid=6381 (accessed in March 2015).

[41] Terry Mackenzie-hoy, "Tenderpreneurs frustrating legitimate contractors," http://www.engineeringnews.co.za/article/tenderpreneurs-frustrating-legitimate-contractors-2010-03-05 (accessed in March 2015), describes the South African word as referring to a person who has made an extraordinary sums of money from a contract (usually a national government, provincial government or municipal tender) that has been awarded for some sort of service. He explains that the reason why there is a lot of cash flows from these contracts is that the award value significantly exceeds the cost of the services, and the surplus goes into the pockets of the contractor and the officials who award the contract. Also see "Tenderpreneurs Cripple the Provinces," *Sowetan Live* 24 January 2012, http://www.sowetanlive.co.za/news/business/2012/01/24/tenderpreneurs-cripple-provinces (accessed in March 2015); and Stephan de la Harpe, "Combating Corruption in Public Procurement," (2011), http://suno25.sun.ac.za/portal/page/portal/law/index.english/public_proc/images/De%20la%20Harpe.pdf (accessed in March 2015) points out that tenders worth R 207 billion were awarded by local government to government employees, local government council members and mayors.

[42] See, "R 16m for One RDP house," *Sowetan Live*, 18 January 2012, http://www.sowetanlive.co.za/news/2012/01/18/r16m-for-one-rdp-house (accessed in March 2015).

[43] See, "How to make a cool R24.5m in a few minutes," *Sowetan Live* 29 September 2011, http://www.sowetanlive.co.za/news/2011/09/29/how-to-make-a-cool-r24.5m-in-a-few-minutes (accessed in March 2015).

[44] See Paul Hoffman, "Hawks or Eagles: What does South Africa deserve?" http://accountabilitynow.org.za/hawks-eagles-south-africa-deserve/ (accessed in March 2015).

massive amounts of money being lost in other African countries.[45] For example, it has been estimated that Nigeria lost about US $ 400 billion between 1960 and 1999 through corruption.[46]

Corruption usually distorts the public tendering system and as a result, the companies who win public contracts hardly ever have the requisite experience, equipment or expertise to deliver the quality of services for which they are often paid inflated amounts. It is therefore no surprise, as the examples from South Africa show, that these contracts are hardly ever completed. The capital and major cities in many African are littered with abandoned and partly completed schools, hospitals, public offices and other government infrastructure standing derelict for years, although the contractors would have been fully paid.[47] Even where the projects are completed, the quality of the work is usually substandard. It is thus ironic that although government budgets today are larger and many economies are reported to be growing (although in most cases these are jobless growths), the standard of healthcare, the infrastructure and quality of education is much lower than it was twenty years ago. The steady deterioration in the quality of government services and infrastructure is no surprise because corruption often compromises compliance with government regulations on matters such as buildings, road constructions and environmental standards.

The inefficiency and high cost of doing business combined with the unpredictability of legal outcomes that have been provoked by corruption has made investment in Africa a very risky undertaking. Corruption has also considerably increased the cost of government borrowing money. Besides this, foreign aid donors and international financial institutions are generally unwilling to lend money especially for projects in areas where corruption is rife. As a result, most African governments have over the years adopted diverse strategies to bring corruption under control. It is now necessary to see what these strategies have been and why they have not succeeded. This will provide the context to the radical proposals that are made about a constitutionally entrenched framework which combines incentives for good conduct and severe sanctions for

---

45   See, Mujwahuzi Njunwa, "Governance Initiatives to Fight Corruption. Combating Corruption in Tanzania's Public Service: Successes and Challenges," http://www.napsipag.org/PDF/MUJWAHUZI_NJUNWA.pdf (accessed in March 2015) where the author points out that in Tanzania, 90% of the contractors pay 10 to 15% of the contract value in bribes.

46   See, "Nigeria's Corruption Busters," http://www.unodc.org/unodc/en/frontpage/nigerias-corruption-busters.html (accessed in March 2015).

47   Government officials cannot complain because they would already have received their kickbacks. The main losers are usually the poor people whom these buildings are primarily supposed to serve.

those who abuse their positions by exploiting them to enrich themselves at the expense of the poor.

3 Brief Overview of Past Anti-corruption Strategies in Africa

Although the problem of corruption goes back to the pre – and post-independence period, it is only after the lifting of restrictions on the media in the 1990s that the details of the various corruption scandals were now being freely and regularly reported in the media. Regular media exposure of the scale of the problem and public pressure for action, especially from foreign donors and international financial institutions forced African governments for the first time, to take serious steps to curb corruption. Several African countries have also signed and ratified a number of international and regional anti-corruption treaties.[48] The fact that there has been no real improvement suggests that these measures have not been effective. Before considering what measures and strategies are likely going to be more effective, it is necessary here to briefly examine what strategies have been tried in the past and why they have not been effective. These have taken a wide variety of forms which are individually too numerous to catalogue. Nevertheless, one could conveniently summarise these diverse approaches under four main broad headings *viz,* the establishment of appropriate legal framework to combat corruption, the use of specialised anti-corruption agencies, the use of purges or crack-downs and other possibilities centred around the economic liberalisation and democratisation processes.

3.1 *The Establishment of an Appropriate Legal Framework*

Most African countries recognise the fact that a relatively comprehensive legal framework which identifies and sanctions the different forms of corrupt

---

48 At the global level, there is the UN Convention against Corruption (UNCAC), which entered into force on 14 December 2004 and has been ratified by 42 of the 54 African countries; the UN Convention against transnational organised crime which entered into force on 29 September 2003 and has been ratified by 42 of the 54 African countries. At the regional level, there is the African Union Convention on Preventing and Combating Corruption which entered into force on 5 August 2006 and has been ratified by only 33 of the 54 African countries. At the sub-regional level, there is the Southern African Development Community (SADC) Protocol against Corruption in force since 2005 which has been ratified by 8 countries and the Economic Community of West African States (ECOWAS) Protocol for the Fight against Corruption which was adopted since 21 December 2001 and has not yet come into force.

activities that take place in the country is crucial to any credible attempts to reduce corruption. As noted above, many of these countries are parties to international and regional instruments designed to combat corruption and therefore know exactly what needs to be done. In many of these countries, there is a wide range of legislation that not only criminalises corruption but also protects whistleblowers and witnesses, provide a access to information to ordinary citizens, provides for the establishment of independent institutions such as ombudsman, auditor-general, and public service commission, permits the proceeds of crimes including corruption to be seized and allows for international cooperation in criminal matters. Some of these matters are either regulated or reinforced by codes of conduct. Most countries have, in many instances, under pressure from aid donors and the international financial institutions developed management, accountability and internal control arrangements, including performance, employment and procurement policies designed to limit avenues for corruption.

A few examples are worth noting. South Africa probably has one of the most comprehensive anti-corruption legal framework on the continent. The foundation for this is laid down in the1996 constitution which *inter alia*, provides in chapter 9 for six specially protected "state institutions supporting constitutional democracy," which include the Public Protector, the South African Human Rights Commission, the Auditor-General and the Electoral Commission.[49] In addition to this, there are also other pieces of legislation which criminalise corruption, protect whistleblowers and witnesses, provide access to information, provide for the recovery of proceeds of crime including corruption and also provide for international co-operation in criminal matters. There are also codes of conduct for public officials.[50] In Nigeria[51] and Ghana,[52] multiple progressive anti-corruption laws have been enacted. In some countries, the law

---

49 They are specially protected against political interference by the safeguards provided in section 181(2)–(5) of the constitution.

50 See generally, Themba Godi, "Fighting Corruption: National Integrity Systems, Good Practice Examples," http://www.nacf.org.za/global_forum5/CVS/055.4%20e%20Godi.pdf (accessed in March 2015).

51 For example, the Money Laundering Prohibition Act, 2004; Public Procurement Act, 2007;Fiscal Responsibility Act, 2007; Code of Conduct Act, 1989; Independent Corrupt Practices Commission Act, 2000; and the Economic and Financial Commission Act,2004. The latter two laws establish and empower the two major anti-corruption institutions in the country.

52 Ghana enacted the Financial Administration Act, 2003; the Public Procurement Act, 2003; Audit Service Act, 2000; Internal Audit Agency Act, 2003; and the Money Laundering Act, 2007.

requires public officials to declare their income, assets and liabilities before assuming office and again when they leave office or even in some cases, on an annual basis.[53]

Although anti-corruption legislation and measures have become common practice in Africa today, these do not seem to be having any serious impact on the relentless spread of corruption on the continent. Three important recent high profile examples of corruption in high places will suffice to illustrate the challenges of controlling corruption in Africa. The first, is the case of a former Nigerian governor of one of its oil rich states, James Ibori, who was sentenced to 13 years in prison on 17 April 2012 by a London court for embezzling the staggering amount of 50 million pounds (US$ 79 million), which the Judge admitted was a "ludicrously low" fraction of his total booty.[54] It is speculated that confiscation proceedings may reveal that the real amount is in excess of 200 million pounds. There are two aspects of this case which make it a landmark decision, besides the incredible amount of money embezzled. First, he had used his powerful political connections to thwart the attempts of the Economic and Financial Crimes Commission (EFCC), Nigeria's anti-corruption agency, to prosecute him. Using his powerful position as a founding member and power-broker in the ruling People's Democratic Party, Ibori obtained the transfer of his court case from the northern Nigerian city of Kaduna to the Delta state capital Asaba, where a judge, who was also his cousin, dismissed all 170 charges against him. He also obtained court orders that prevented officers from the London Metropolitan Police from visiting the Delta state to collect evidence of money laundering against him. In 2007, he went to the office of Ribadu, the head of the EFCC's office and offered him US$15 million cash bribe in order for the investigations to be dropped. Ribadu refused the bribe and later went into exile because of threats to his life. Ibori was eventually arrested in Dubai where he had fled and was extradited to Britain. The second significance of this case is the fact that his wife, sister, mistress, lawyer, bankers and accountants were all tried and sentenced for their part in helping Ibori launder the money. Thus, the relevant British law made it possible not just for the embezzler but also all

---

53   This is the case in Ghana, under the Public Office Holders (Declaration of Assets and Disqualification) Act, 1998; in Tanzania under the Leadership Code of Conduct; in Uganda under the Leadership Code of Ethics Act (No. 13), and in Nigeria under the Code of Conduct Bureau and Tribunal Act.

54   See, Estelle Shirbon, "Corrupt Nigerian Governor gets 13 years UK Jail Term," http://www.reuters.com/article/2012/04/17/britain-nigeria-ibori-idUSL6E8FH3J820120417 (accessed in March 2015).

those who conspired or assisted him as well as benefited from his activities to be also punished.

The second example concerns the South African President, Jacob Zuma who became embroiled in the corruption scandal involving the now notorious South African arms deal. In 2004 Shabir Shaik, a Durban businessman and financial advisor to Zuma was tried for bribery in the course of the purchase of Valour class frigates as part of the arms deal. He was found guilty and sentenced to 15 years in prison.[55] During the trial, it was alleged that he had paid Zuma R 1.2 million to further their relationship and had also solicited a bribe of R500,000 per annum for Zuma in return for the latter's support for the defence contractor Thomson CSF. As a result some of the findings made by the judge in the course of his judgment in the Shabir Shaik case, Zuma who was then Deputy President, was relieved of his duties. He was later formally charged with corruption but the case was struck from the roll of the Pietermaritzburg High Court after the prosecution's application for a postponement to enable it to secure evidence was rejected.

In December 2007, the independent crime fighting unit, popularly known as the Scorpions, decided to indict Zuma on various counts of racketeering, money laundering, corruption and fraud. A conviction would have rendered him ineligible to stand for election to the South African parliament and thus not eligible to serve as president of the country. In September 2008, Judge Chris Nicholson of the Pietermaritzburg court dismissed the charges as unlawful on procedural grounds in that the National Directorate of Public Prosecutions (NDPP) had not given Zuma a chance to make representations as required by section 179(5)(d) of the constitution before the indictment and he added that he believed political interference had played a part in Zuma being recharged.[56]

---

55 See, *State v. Schabir Shaik & 11 Others,* http://blogs.timeslive.co.za/hartley/2008/03/23/judge-hillary-squires-judgment-on-schabir-shaik-full-text/ (accessed in March 2015) Just to support the point made earlier that powerfully connected perpetrators of corruption easily get away with it, Schabir Shaik was released in 2009 on medical parole designed to ensure that terminally ill offenders can be allowed to die in a dignified and consolatory manner in the presence of their family and friends. Not only have hundreds of terminally ill South African prisoners died in prison but Schabir Shaik, shortly after his release, was seen playing golf and since then has been enjoying surprisingly good health for a person who was supposed to be months away from death. See, "Opposition Slams Release of Schabir Shaik," http://mg.co.za/article/2009-03-03-opposition-slams-release-of-shaik (accessed in March 2015).

56 This was because Zuma was recharged shortly after he had defeated his main political rival, the then president, Thabo Mbeki to become leader of the ANC at a Polokwane conference.

In an appeal against this judgment by the NDPP in January 2009, the Supreme Court of Appeal reversed the High Court judgment and also declared that Judge Nicholson had "overstepped the limits of his authority," in making inferences of political meddling.

After reviewing tapes of intercepted telephone conversations between the former head of the Scorpions and the former Director of the NDPP suggesting that the charges against Zuma had been timed in order to assist his political rival, Thabo Mbeki, the National Prosecuting Authority (NPA), in April 2009, decided to drop the corruption charges. The acting head of the NPA stressed that the withdrawal was due to the legal process being "tainted" and did not amount to an acquittal. Since then, there have been questions about the justification for the charges being dropped. Nevertheless, the corruption charges have hung over Zuma's head like a sword of Damocles.

The main opposition party, the Democratic Alliance (DA) has, since 2009, been arguing that the decision to drop the charges against Zuma, was unconstitutional and invalid and wants the charges to be reinstated. In March 2012, the Supreme Court of Appeal in an action brought by the DA held that the decision to drop the corruption charges can be reviewed.[57] It also ordered the NPA to release the transcripts of the spy tapes that it got from the National Intelligence Agency which it claimed had informed the decision to drop the more than 700 charges of corruption that had been made against Zuma. The NPA ignored this decision. On 16 August 2013, the DA obtained another order from the High Court which gave the NPA five days within which to hand over the transcripts of the spy tapes to the DA.[58] If there is no rational justification for withdrawing the charges based on the documents that will handed over to the DA, there is a likelihood that it will apply for the decision to drop the charges to be invalidated and for the charges to be reinstated. However, the matter is still pending.

Perhaps the most dramatic and telling case of the callous extremes of corruption in Africa is that of Teodorin Obiang Mbasago, the son and heir apparent of President Teodoro Nguema Obiang Mbasogo of Equatorial Guinea, Africa's oldest dictator.[59] Teodorin Mbasago who, since May 2012, is Vice President for National Defence and State Security but as Minister of Agriculture on

---

57   See, "South African Jacob Zuma Corruption Case to be Reviewed," http://www.bbc.co.uk/news/world-africa-17442486 (accessed March 2015).
58   See, Ernest Mabuza, "Court Orders Prosecuting Authority to give 'Spy Tapes' to DA", http://www.bdlive.co.za/national/2013/08/16/court-orders-prosecuting-authority-to-give-spy-tapes-to-da (accessed in March 2015).
59   He has been in power for 34 years.

about USD 100,000 amassed so much wealth through money laundering that both the US and France issued international warrants for his arrest.[60] After the French Government ordered the seizure of some of his property based in France, his father decided to protect him by appointing him a delegate of UNESCO which gave him diplomatic immunity and restricted the scope of the investigations. However, his extensive wealth only contrasts with the extreme poverty of the country where 70% of the population of 680,000 live in extreme poverty without access to clean water, basic health facilities and education. Between 2000 and 2011, he spent over USD 300,000 million and later that year ordered a super yacht for £236 million.[61] It is the international life of opulence and wasteful extravagance of his life style[62] which makes it difficult to believe whether African countries are seriously committed to stamping out corruption, and this is just the tip of the iceberg because his father's own wealth is conservatively estimated at USD 600 million.[63] As the family fall over each other in this scramble to swindle the country's oil wealth which is predicted to start dropping dramatically after 2017, the future looks bleak.[64] It makes it very difficult to accept theories of African humanity captured in notions of *ubuntu* and *batho pele*[65] especially when these are sometimes propagated by the very

---

[60] See, "Judge Issue Warrant for Teodoro Nguema Obiang Mangue, son of Equatorial Guinea's President," http://oleafrica.com/corruption-2/judge-issue-warrant-of-arrest-for-teodoro-nguema-obiang-mangue-son-of-equatorial-guineas-president/4235 (accessed in March 2015); and See, "Teodorin Obiang: The Dictator's Son with a Malibu Mansion and a Warrant for his arrest," http://world.time.com/2012/07/16/teodorin-obiang-the-dictators-son-with-a-malibu-mansion-and-a-warrant-for-his-arrest/ (accessed in March 2015).

[61] See, "African Dictator's Son Orders £236 million Luxury Super Yacht," http://www.telegraph.co.uk/news/worldnews/africaandindianocean/equatorialguinea/8351343/African-dictators-son-orders-236-million-luxury-super-yacht.html (accessed in March 2015).

[62] His wealth includes the following: luxury cars valued at about USD 10, Michael Jackson items worth USD 3.2, furniture worth USD 52 million, wine worth USD 2.7million, art work worth USD 24 million, a mansion in Malibu worth USD 25 million, and a 101 room five-story private mansion on Avenue Foch in Paris' expensive 16th arrondissement. See further, "International Arrest Warrant Sought for Playboy son of Equatorial Guinea President," http://www.telegraph.co.uk/news/worldnews/africaandindianocean/equatorialguinea/9169755/International-arrest-warrant-sought-for-playboy-son-of-Equatorial-Guinea-president.html (accessed in March 2015); and the other sources referred in the preceding footnotes.

[63] See, "Jonathan is 6th Richest African Presidents" http://www.elombah.com/index.php/reports/26315-jonathan-is-6th-richest-african-presidents-richestlifestyle-com (accessed in March 2015).

[64] See, "Equatorial Guinea: L'etat, c'est nous." 54(14), *Africa Confidential* 5 July 2013.

[65] How can one reconcile this inhumanity with Archbishop Desmond Tutu's suggestion that *Ubuntu* is "the essence of being human, and that it is part of the gift that Africa will give

leaders who needlessly inflict extensive poverty and suffering on their people by looting the national wealth, hiding it in foreign accounts and in many cases hanging onto and dying in power without ever using this money.[66]

From the three examples given above, it is clear that in spite of the impressive array of legislation to combat corruption, there is still corruption at the highest level. The first and main problem that arises from these three cases is that if there is such high level corruption, then this makes it extremely difficult for any anti-corruption strategy to work. If there is one thing that the abundant literature on corruption is unequivocally agreed upon, it is the fact that the success of any anti-corruption strategy depends to a very large extent on a political leadership that is honest and perceived by the public as being of the highest integrity and committed to curbing corruption. Once the leadership itself is tainted with corruption, they will lack the will, moral authority and credibility to lead any effective fight to control corruption. For example, two former African leaders feature amongst the ten most corrupt leaders of all time. Mobutu Sese Seko who is third on the list having embezzled about US$ 5 billion and Sani Abacha (president of Nigeria from 1993–1998) who is fourth and alleged to have embezzled from US$ 2–5 billion.[67] Most other African leaders, both past and present ruthlessly exploit their positions to fraudulently amass wealth for themselves and therefore pay nothing more than lip service to anti-corruption campaigns.[68] In Malawi and Zambia, former presi-

---

the world."? Cited by John Hailey in, "Ubuntu: A Literature Review," http://www.tutufoundationuk.org/documents/UbuntuLiteratureReview_JH_Dec08.pdf (accessed in March 2015); and for the *batho pele* principles which are supposed to "put people first", see http://localgovernmentaction.org.dedi6.cpt3.host-h.net/content/batho-pele-principles (accessed in March 2015).

66   The most recent cases are those of Mobutu of DR. Congo, Omar Bongo of Gabon, Gaddafi of Libya and Eyadema of Togo.

67   See, "World's Ten Most Corrupt Leaders," http://www.infoplease.com/ipa/A0921295.html (accessed in March 2015). In fact, it has been estimated that Mobutu placed about a third of the state budget under his control and siphoned off a quarter of gross receipts from copper exports. See, Susan Rose-Ackerman, *Corruption and Government: Causes, Consequences and Reform,* Cambridge, Cambridge University Press (1999), at p. 116.

68   See for example, Lonce Ndikumana, "Rich Presidents of Poor Nations: An African Story of Oil and Capital Flight," http://truth-out.org/index.php?option=com_k2&view=item&id=6937:rich-presidents-of-poor-nations-an-african-story-of-oil-and-capital-flight (accessed in March 2015) who discusses the wealth of the presidents of Equatorial Guinea, Gabon and Republic of Congo. The case of Theodoro Obiang Nguema, the son of the President of Equatorial Guinea, whose family has accumulated massive wealth by mortgaging the country's oil. He has commissioned a personal super-yacht for US$ 380, an amount that is said to be three times the country's combined budget for health and education.

dents Bakili Muluzi and Frederick Chiluba have been tried for corruption.[69] As was pointed out earlier, in many countries, the law requires the president, ministers and other public officials to declare their income, assets and liabilities before assuming office or annually when in office and after the leave office. In most cases, these declarations are never made or done in secret so that the public have no opportunity to access the information and check its accuracy. For example, in Nigeria, President Goodluck Jonathan and several of his ministers have refused to declare their assets. On the other hand, some officials have devised sophisticated ways to circumvent this legislation by operating proxy accounts in the name of family members, friends and business allies.[70]

Besides the non-implementation of anti-corruption legislation, another problem is that the legislation adopted doesn't often go far enough to address the problem at its source. For example, although it has been noted that many African countries have ratified UN and AU anti-corruption conventions, the commitment in many instances has remained formal and symbolic rather than substantive because few of these countries have actually domesticated the conventions. Nor do they make any efforts to update and harmonise domestic laws to take account of these international conventions. There are particular problems with the specialised anti-corruption agencies that many African governments have established to display their commitment to fighting against corruption.

3.2 Use of Anti-corruption Agencies

Anti-corruption agencies (ACAs), have been established in many countries. Examples of these institutions are the Ombudsman (or Public Protector), Auditor-General, Public Service Commission, Audit Courts,[71] Parliamentary Accounts Committee and Judicial Service Commission (or Supreme Council of the Magistracy as it is often referred to in Francophone Africa). There have also been specialised stand-alone ACAs established in some countries to deal specifically with issues of corruption. A 2007 study has suggested that there are

---

69   Chiluba was found guilty of stealing and embezzlement in May 2007 by Judge Peter Smith in a London Court and the judge accused Chiluba of shamelessly defrauding his people. See, *Attorney-General v. Meer Care & Desai & others* http://www.bailii.org/ew/cases/EWCA/Civ/2008/1007.html (accessed in March 2015); and "Frederick Chiluba," http://www.assetrecovery.org/kc/node/4ec2e572-cd77-11dc-b471-db7db47931e5.0;jsessionid=B8A22224CC49CB3A09484DC6B8FCCFB9 (accessed in March 2015).

70   See, Fredrik Galtung, "Criteria for Sustainable Corruption Control," in Mark Robinson, op. cit., pp. 116–117.

71   Common under the constitutions of Francophone African states. See for example, article 141 of the Niger constitution of 2010 and article 41 of the Cameroon constitution of 1996.

about 18 stand-alone and six integrated ACAs operating in Africa.[72] Some well-known examples of stand-alone agencies are Botswana's Directorate on Corruption and Economic Crimes (DCEC), Nigeria's Independent Corrupt Practices and Other Related Offences Commission and the EFCC, and Kenya's Anti-Corruption Commission.[73]

The tremendous success of ACAs in pulling some countries such as Hong Kong and Singapore in South East Asia, and Argentina and a few countries in South America, which were previously subject to endemic corruption to relatively low levels of corruption, has encouraged many African countries to adopt this approach to curbing corruption.[74] A number of studies of some of the African ACAs show that they have had rather limited success.[75] From these studies, four main problems appear to have plagued African ACAs.

First, they have suffered from serious design faults that have limited their independence and therefore exposed them to manipulation by politicians. The main form of this interference has usually come through the politicisation of the appointment of the head and other senior officials of the ACAs. For example, Mwai Kibaki was elected president of Kenya in 2002 on an anti-corruption platform and named John Githongo a well-known anti-corruption campaigner to head the Kenyan Anti-corruption Commission. In 2005, he re-

---

[72] The Pan African Lawyers Union Pan African Yearbook of Law vol 1 (2012) file:///E:/Editing/Pan-African-Yearbook-of-Law-PAYL-Vol-1-of-2012.pdf p37. However this also cites the De Maria article (accessed in March 2015). Stand-alone or free standing ACAs refers to those agencies that have distinct organisational identities separate from the normal state bureaucracy as opposed to the integrated ACAs which are part of departmental structures within the normal bureaucracy.

[73] Besides those mentioned above, stand-alone ACAs are found in Angola, Benin, DR Congo, Ghana, Guinea, Lesotho, Malawi, Namibia, Sierra Leone, Sudan, Tanzania, Uganda, Zambia and Zimbabwe. Integrated ACAs are found in Burkina Faso, Cameroon, Egypt, Mozambique, Senegal, and South Africa.

[74] See for example, Susan Rose-Ackerman, *Corruption and Government. Causes, Consequences and Reform*, Cambridge, Cambridge University Press (1999), at pp. 158–162 and Andre Thomashausen, *Anti-corruption Measures: A Comparative Survey of Selected National and International Programmes*, Occasional Paper Series, Konrad-Adenauer-Stiftung, Johannesburg (2000), at p. 9.

[75] See for example, Charles Manga Fombad, "Curbing Corruption in Africa: Some Lessons from Botswana's experience," 51 *International Social Science Journal* (1999), pp. 241–254; Charles Manga Fombad and David Sebududubu, "The Framework for Curbing Corruption, Enhancing Accountability and Promoting Good Governance in Botswana," in Charles Manga Fombad (ed.), *Essays on the Law of Botswana*, Cape Town, Juta & Co (2007), pp. 82–126; "A Review of South Africa's National Anti-Corruption Agencies," http://www.psc.gov.za/documents/reports/corruption/01.pdf (accessed in March 2015) and Bill De Maria, op. cit.

signed and went into exile citing lack of government commitment to the fight against corruption. In response to this, the US, Germany and other donors immediately suspended their funding for the programme. There has been continuous political interference with other ACAs such as those of Malawi and Zimbabwe.[76] But even where the government does not interfere, they usually starve the agency of the funds that it needs to carry out its tasks. In many countries, these ACAs are only accountable to the politicians who appointed them and not to the people through parliament. This provides further avenues for political interference.

Second, the record of these ACAs in bringing those responsible for corruption has been less than impressive. Inevitably, because of the overbearing control exercised by the politicians, many of whom owe their positions to various forms of corrupt practices, the ACAs turn to avoid confrontation with their political masters by investigating only "safe" cases. Even in Botswana, which for over a decade has consistently appeared in TI's CPI as Africa's least corrupt country, its ACA, the Directorate of Corruption and Economic Crime is well noted for leaving the corrupt elites to swim undisturbed whilst it catches only the tiddlers.[77] Many ACAs have thus operated more like toothless bulldogs that protect the rich, powerful and well-connected wrongdoers but raise a storm about petty offenders who should ordinarily and routinely be dealt with by the police.[78]

Third, some of the heads and senior staff of the ACAs use their positions to also extort money from people that they are investigating. For example, in Nigeria, Farida Waziri, the head of the EFCC which has become largely ineffectual was dismissed by President Goodluck Jonathan after credible allegations showing that she had been involved in several corrupt practices.[79]

Finally, many of the ACAs do not have sufficient powers to target corrupt activities or even to instigate "own motion" investigations. The scope of their powers is often narrowly defined and they can only investigate matters reported to them and can do no more than recommend that a particular person be prosecuted.

---

76 See, The Pan African Lawyers Union Pan African Yearbook of Law vol 1 (2012) file:///E:/Editing/Pan-African-Yearbook-of-Law-PAYL-Vol-1-of-2012.pdf p37. However this also cites the De Maria article, op. cit. at pp. 14–15.

77 This is discussed in Charles Manga Fombad, "Curbing Corruption in Africa: Some Lessons from Botswana's experience," 51 *International Social Science Journal* (1999), pp. 241–254.

78 See, Mary Revesai, "Zimbabwe has leeches not scorpions," http://www.newzimbabwe.com/pages/mary.15044.html (accessed in March 2015).

79 See, "US Government Dismisses Nigeria's War Against Corruption as Hot Air," http://saharareporters.com/2012/06/07/us-government-dismisses-nigeria%E2%80%99s-war-against-corruption-hot-air (accessed in March 2015).

Bill de Maria uses the post-colonial theory to argue that the failure of the ACAs in Africa is a result of a "misapplication of western anti-corruption technologies to Africa," and therefore proposes a new corruption investigation model consistent with evolving pan-Africanism, administered by the" the AU. The irony however is that this author wants this new AU approach to be based on another western design, "the Anti-Fraud Office of the European Union."[80] As will shortly be seen, it is submitted that the ACAs in Africa could work as well as they have done in countries such as Hong Kong and Singapore if their design flaws are corrected. Replacing them with an office within the AU will not help. The AU, for all its good intentions and well drafted Constitutive Act which lays down a solid agenda to promote good governance, transparency and accountability, has had a dismal implementation record. At this stage, placing blind faith in an AU body might just create another opening for African politicians to reduce the fight against corruption into political gimmicks as they have done using purges and crack-downs.

3.3 Purges and Crack-downs

In many African countries, attempts to fight corruption have often taken the form of periodic populist measures such as purges or crack-downs. Since the 1970s, Nigeria has seen many purges as part of anti-corruption campaigns under various slogans such as "War Against indiscipline," "War Against Corruption," and "Operation Purge the Nation." During the course of these purges, thousands of civil servants, including police and military officers were either dismissed or retired.[81] In Ghana, during one of Jerry Rawlings sojourns as a military leader, he ordered the execution of three former military leaders (General Ignatius Acheampong, General Afrifa and General Akuffo) and five other senior military officers in June 1979 as part of a campaign to root out corruption. In Cameroon, *L' Opération Epervier* (Operation Sparrowhawk) has been in place since 2004 and has led to the arrest, trial and imprisonment of several prominent politicians including a former Prime Minister and a number of politicians who at one stage or another were seen as potential heirs of the 79 year old Cameroonian president, Paul Biya. Nevertheless, in spite of the purges and crack downs, the looting of public property in most African countries has

---

80   See, op. cit. at p. 2.
81   See generally, Stephen Riley, "The Political Economy of Anti-Corruption Strategies in Africa," op. cit. and R.A. Doig and S. Riley, "Corruption and Anti-Corruption Strategies: Issues and Case Studies from Developing Countries," in G.S. Cheema and J. Bonvin (eds.), *Corruption and Integrity Improvement Initiatives in Developing Countries*, Paris, OECD (1998).

continued unabated. This strategy has proven as ineffectual as a long term and credible anti – corruption strategy as the others. There are many reasons for this.[82]

First, purges and crack-downs have often been used by military leaders as a public relations exercise designed to assuage public or international revulsion at the overthrow of a democratically elected government. Such campaigns hardly ever last long, especially since there is usually no serious legal framework within which they are carried out.

Second, most of these campaigns are simply a reaction either to a scandal or series of scandals or to strong external pressure from donors. This is often the case where the government itself is deeply involved in the corruption. Through purges and crack-downs, it can go through the motions and ensure that it never really puts the right persons to do the job or commit the necessary resources required. In this way, the government can carefully select "safe" targets to go against without threatening its constituency. It is not surprise that one cynic has compared corruption purges to an unusual fishing net which only catches small fish whilst the big fish swim free.[83]

Third, in many countries, anti-corruption crusades of this nature have been used by governments to carry out a witch hunt of their opponents or to divert attention from more pressing problems. An excellent example of the former is Cameroon's *L'Opération Epervier*. Unlike most anti-corruption operations, it has netted lots of big fish but there is a growing perception by analyst that it has only been successful in neutralising any apposition to Biya by those who have benefited from his largesse over the last 30 years and yet had the imprudence to nurse ambitions to replace him. Thus, a number of former senior regime favourites who became too confident to manifest presidential ambitions are languishing in jail or detention, sometimes without charges for several years.[84] As a result, the exercise has hardly diminished the level of all-pervasive

---

82   Some of these are discussed in, "Why Anti-Corruption Crusades Often Fail to Win Lasting Victories," http://unpan1.un.org/intradoc/groups/public/documents/un/unpan010748.pdf (accessed March 2015).

83   See the novelist, A.K. Armah, quoted in Stephen Riley, "The Political Economy of Anti-Corruption Strategies in Africa," in Mark Robinson(ed.), op. cit. at p. 151.

84   See the analysis by Larry Luxner, "Former Ambassador Fights to Prove Innocence Behind Bars in Cameroon," 17(7) *The Washington Diplomat*, July 2010. Those in jail or detention include, Titus Edjoa who was formerly President Biya's physician, then Secretary General at the Presidency and Minister of Health. He has been serving a 15 year imprisonment term and was expected to be released in October but fresh, fresh charges have now been brought against him which is likely going to result in another long prison term. Two other former Secretary Generals in the Presidency, Jean-Marie Atangana Mebara and Marafa

endemic corruption in Cameroon. Besides this, many of these types of campaigns remain at the level of rhetoric and achieve no significant results because they are usually poorly planned, unconvincing, over-ambitious and set unrealistic goals.

Finally, purges and crack-downs do not often succeed in providing a sustainable solution, especially where corruption is deeply embedded in the fabric of society because there is the perception of it as something imposed from the top. Where no time or effort is taken to consult and get the buy-in of the different stakeholders, such as businesses and civil society, the anti-corruption strategy will be misconstrued and not be supported by the rest of the society. The non-involvement of the community, especially opposition parties is one of the reasons why most initiatives have underperformed. It is also the reason why the democratisation and economic liberalisation moves that started in the 1990s were thought by many as a possible way to tame the unruly corruption beast.

3.4 Possible Role of Democratisation and Economic Liberalisation

The wave of democratisation and economic liberalisation that swept through the African continent from the 1990s was considered by some analysts to contain the elements necessary for bringing corruption on the continent under control. However, this is a debatable matter because although to some, these processes have helped to curb corruption, there are others who feel that they have instead fuelled it.

Some political scientists argue that corruption is a function of the lack of durable political institutions and political competition and a weak and underdeveloped civil society.[85] They posit that political liberalisation has the potential to create an open, transparent and accountable system which will discourage corruption because of the potential for closer scrutiny of actions of politicians and government officials by citizens, the media and NGOs. However, the emerging evidence after more than two decades of democratisation

---

Hamidou Yaya, all of whom have manifestly expressed their presidential ambitions at one stage or another are also incarcerated. Recently, a former prime minister, Ephraim Inoni, who is the one who is launched the *L'Opération Epervier* has been caught in his own net. The long list of mainly former ministers include Polycarpe Abah Abah, Urbain Olanguena Awono, Edouard Etonde Ekotto, Alfonse Siyam Sewe, Seydou Mounchipou, Jean Baptiste Nguini Effa, Jerome Mendouga, Giles Roger Belinga, Abessolo, Catherine Abena, Haman Adama, Iya Mohamed and other prominent personalities such as Zachaeus Fornjidam, Yves Michael Fotso and Thierry Michel Atangana. This has given rise to what cynics term, "le gouvernement de Kondengui" (the Kondengui prison cabinet).

85   The different arguments are discussed in Mark Robinson, op. cit. at p. 4.

in Africa is that corruption does not only co-exist with the so-called democratic or quasi-democratic regimes on the continent but actually fuels them.[86] Political corruption of the electoral processes has now regularly been used to transform elections into a ritual with predictable results.[87] As a result, the democratic structures that could in theory have provided for greater transparency and accountability have increasingly proven ineffective to curb the misuse of state resources by politicians and their cronies.

Similarly, economists and public choice theorists have argued that economic liberalisation and downsizing the size of the state will reduce the avenues for corruption.[88] This view was strongly supported by the World Bank which in promoting deregulation and the expansion of markets, argue that markets generally discipline participants more effectively than the public sector can. The World Bank's view is that any effective anti-corruption strategy must aim to enlarge the scope and improve the functioning of markets, strengthen competitive forces in the economy and curtail rents and in this way eliminate the bribes public officials may be offered or may extort.[89] Since the late 1980s and 1990s, privatisation of state enterprises in order to downsize and increase efficiency and productivity was the buzzword. Public private partnerships are now the new strategy. However, privatisation led to massive corruption as politicians sold many state enterprises such as water and electricity bodies to their associates at far below market values and made hefty profits. In Tanzania, the Warioba Presidential Commission set up after a series of corruption scandals in the country in the mid-1990s concluded *inter alia*, that economic liberalisation had significantly contributed to the increase of corruption in the country.[90] Once again, a potentially useful anti-corruption strategy has in many African countries become a source of corruption instead.

---

86   Ibid. at pp. 146–149.
87   See generally, See for example, the analysis by Michael Bratton and Nicholas Van De Walle, *Democratic Experiments in Africa: Regime Transitions in Comparative Perspectives*, Cambridge, Cambridge University Press (1997); and U.B. Ikpe, "The Impact of Manipulated Re-elections on Accountability and Legitimacy of Democratic Regimes in Africa: Observations from Nigeria, Zambia and Kenya," 3(7) *African Journal of Political Science and International Relations* (2009), pp. 300–310.
88   Ibid. p. 5, 8, 142, 144–148,150; John Mukum Mbaku, op. cit.; and Robin Theobald, *Corruption and Underdevelopment*, Durham, Duke University Press (1990), pp. 156–158.
89   See, "Helping Countries Combat Corruption. The Role of the World Bank," http://www1.worldbank.org/publicsector/anticorrupt/corruptn/corrptn.pdf (accessed in March 2015).
90   See, Stephen Riley, op. cit. at p. 144.

In spite of the apparent failure of the democratisation and economic liberalisation processes to assist in dealing with the corruption cancer in most African countries, this does not necessarily mean that these processes are inherently incapable of checking the spread of corruption. What is clear is that both democratisation and economic liberalisation are necessary but not on their own, sufficient means for tackling corruption. The main contention of this Chapter is that it is the weak constitutional framework within which all the above measures have been tried in the past that has been problematic and necessitates a radically new approach. We will now see what this new approach.

4 The Rationale and Scope for Constitutionally Entrenched Anti-corruption Framework

There is no standard, ready-made solution to dealing with the problem of corruption. As noted above, and the point bears repeating, the success of anti-corruption measures in some countries, such as Hong Kong and Singapore testifies to the fact that the deeply entrenched corruption in African countries can be brought under control provided serious and credible strategies are adopted. Nevertheless, it is contended that the most credible and potentially successful strategies are those that are based on a constitutionally entrenched framework.

This section will consider two main issues, first, the rationale for constitutionally entrenched anti-corruption framework, and second, the possible scope of the relevant constitutional principles and the institutions needed to operationalize this.

4.1 *The Rationale for a Constitutionally Entrenched Anti-corruption Framework*

Generally, only principles and institutions which are entrenched in a constitution can provide the basis for an operational framework from which to gain a firm foothold to begin serious anti-corruption work, build capacity behind an anti-corruption strategy and enhance the sustainability of such a strategy over time. The concept of constitutional "entrenchment" in this context needs to be explained. There are at least three main senses in which the concept is used in constitutional law.

In one sense, it could be used to make the distinction between an entrenched constitution and a non-entrenched constitution. In this sense, an entrenched constitution refers to a constitution that is legally protected against arbitrary amendment unless a special procedure is followed. A non-entrenched constitution, on the other hand, refers to a constitution, such as the British constitution, which does not need any special procedure for its amendment and in fact is often amended as any ordinary piece of legislation. In a second sense, entrenchment may also refer to certain provisions in a constitution whose amendment have been made particularly difficult by requiring that such amendments will only be valid where they obtain the consent of a special supermajority in parliament and in some cases also need the approval of the people in a referendum.[91] A third meaning, and that in which the concept is used in this Chapter, refers to any constitutional provisions which contains legally enforceable obligations. This therefore excludes provisions which are essentially declaratory and hortatory in nature and which are explicitly or implicitly stated to contain principles which are non-justiciable.[92] There are a number of reasons for advocating for the constitutional entrenchment of the principles and institutions needed to effectively curb and bring the corruption that has eaten so deep and become part of life in almost all African countries, under control.

The first reason flows from the very nature and status of constitutions or more specifically written constitutions. Unlike any other law, the constitution is the supreme law of the land and is based on, as well as reflects, the sovereign will of the people. As the supreme law of the land, all other laws derive their validity from it and will be declared invalid to the extent to which they are inconsistent with the constitution. Also, because of its special status, constitutions are meant to endure and are often protected from careless, casual or arbitrary amendments by transient majorities or opportunistic leaders trying to promote a selfish political agenda.[93] From this perspective, the advantage of constitutional entrenchment is that it provides a greater a sense of durability, certainty and predictability than is the case with ordinary legislation.

---

91   See generally, Charles Manga Fombad, "Some Perspectives on Durability and Change Under Modern African Constitutions," 11(2) *International Journal of Constitutional Law* (2013), pp. 382–413.

92   For example, some constitutions put socio-economic rights under sections with labels such as "fundamental objectives and directive principles of state policy," or "principles of state policy," which are expressly stated not to be enforceable by the courts. See for example, section 25 of the constitution Lesotho of 1993, sections 6(6)(c) and (9)(3) of the constitution of Nigeria of 1999, section 14 of the constitution of Sierra Leone of 1991, and section 7(2) of the constitution of Tanzania of 1977.

93   See further, Charles Manga Fombad, "Some Perspectives on Durability and Change Under Modern African Constitutions," op. cit.

Second, to the extent to which robust anti-corruption principles and institutions are given a constitutional status, they impose obligations on both the legislature and executive in a manner that will limit their scope of action or inaction. If this is reinforced by a positive obligation to act,[94] rather than a mere discretion to act when possible, it opens the way for an action for violation of the constitution where the alleged "violation" consists of a failure to fulfil a constitutional obligation. This may therefore result in a declaration of unconstitutionality for the omission to carry out a constitutional obligation.[95] In this way, pressure can be brought to bear on both the legislature and executive, to take effective anti-corruption measures. It will no longer lie within the exclusive and absolute discretion of these two branches of government to decide either when to act or how to act. The courts will have the power to invalidate any legislation which fails to comply with the obligations imposed by the constitution. Although some scholars have argued that what is needed most are not new constitutions, laws or treaties but the political will and strong, independent institutions to implement them,[96] the reality is that once there is a legally enforceable constitutional obligation on the government to take effective measures to combat corruption, the political will must necessarily follow.

A third advantage of constitutional entrenchment of anti-corruption measures is that the nature of the action to be taken will no longer depend on the whims and caprices of opportunistic majorities who may want to arbitrarily change the law at any stage to suit their political agenda. The courts have the power to invalidate any legislation that goes against the constitution. Besides this, most constitutions usually provide a special procedure for amending their provisions to ensure that any amendments are sufficiently difficult and require

---

94 See an example of such an obligation in section 2 of the South African constitution of 1996 which states in section 2 that, "this constitution is the supreme law of the Republic; law or conduct inconsistent with it is invalid, *and the obligations imposed by it must be fulfilled.*" (emphasis added).

95 For a discussion of this interesting issue, see, Mendes, "Constitutional jurisdiction in Brazil: The problem of unconstitutional legislative omission," http://www.stf.jus.br/repositorio/cms/portalStfInternacional/portalStfDiscurso_en_US/anexo/Omisao_Legislativa_v__Ing.pdf (accessed in March 2015); and also, Paczolay, "Experience of the execution of Constitutional Court's decisions declaring legislative omission in Hungary," http://www.venice.coe.int/webforms/documents/default.aspx?pdffile=CDL-JU%282008%29029-e (accessed in March 2015).

96 See, Themba Godi, "Fighting Corruption: National Integrity Systems, Good Practice Examples," http://www.nacf.org.za/global_forum5/cvs/055.4%20e%20Godi.pdf (accessed in March 2015).

special majorities and sometimes, confirmation through a referendum.[97] In this way, self-serving legislation by dominant parties or transient majorities can be avoided.

The fourth advantage of constitutional entrenchment is that it may in some respects provide individuals or a group of individuals with an opportunity to take a direct action against those who are needlessly inflicting hardship and suffering on them through the looting of state resources. *Locus standi* rules could be expanded, as has happened under some constitutions, to make this possible.[98] The prosecution of those responsible for embezzlement and other corrupt activities would no longer depend exclusively on the discretion of the state prosecuting authorities but is open to the public. This is an aspect of what has been referred to by some writers as the privatisation of the public good although it is admittedly, "a more radical step than that involved in the sale of public assets and the commercialization of public services."[99]

Ultimately, the significance of constitutional entrenchment will depend on, amongst other factors, the exact nature and scope of the rights recognised and incorporated in the constitution. Where these are couched in clear language and in a manner that imposes a legal obligation covering both the scope of corrupt and potentially corrupt activities and the institutions that are required to enforce these anti-corruption measures, this is likely to be more effective than where the constitution merely empowers the legislature to take such measures without actually compelling it to do so. It is now necessary to consider what these possible measures are.

---

97 See generally, Charles Manga Fombad, "Some Perspectives on Durability and Change Under Modern African Constitutions," op. cit.

98 In this regard, article 22(2) of the Kenyan Constitution of 2010 states that proceedings could be instituted by: (a) a person acting on behalf of another person who cannot act in their own names; (b) a person acting as a member of, or in the interest of, a group or class of persons; (c) a person acting in the public interest; or (d) an association acting in the interest of one or more of its members. Article 22(2) even goes further to limit formalities relating to proceedings to a minimum and provide that the court shall, "if necessary, entertain proceedings on the basis of informal documentation," and that "no fee may be charged for commencing the proceedings." The Angolan constitution of 2010 in articles 73–75 also appears to broaden the rules of *locus standi* but the language in which this is couched and articles 228 and 230 which restricts access to certain specified personalities casts serious doubts about the effectiveness of this.

99 See, Timothy Macklem, "Entrenching Bills of Rights," 26(1) *Oxford Journal of Legal Studies* (2006), at p. 113.

4.2 The Nature and Possible Scope of Constitutionally Entrenched Anti-corruption Measures

The constitutional entrenchment of provisions designed to combat corruption is fairly new. The traditional view that has prevailed until recently is that trying to deal with corruption in a constitution might entail too many details for an issue that is at best an ordinary social misfeasance that can be dealt with through the normal legislative process.[100] But as we have seen, corruption can no longer be seen as an ordinary offence and the plethora of legislative enactments in different African countries have hardly scratched at the bottom of the problem. It is thus no surprise that although many modern African constitutions have no provisions dealing with the problem, there are many others that have recognised the importance of incorporating anti-corruption provisions in their constitutions. The best example of an African constitution with elaborate provisions designed to prevent, control and punish corruption and related activities, is the Kenyan Constitution of 2010.[101] Other constitutions which also contain a number of provisions dealing with corruption include the Constitution of Ghana of 1991,[102] the constitution of Uganda of 1995,[103] and the Nigerian Constitution of 1999.[104] In spite of this, both Nigeria and Uganda have, according to TI's CPI, consistently been ranked amongst the top corrupt countries in the world.[105] By contrast, a country like Botswana, which has no provision in the Constitution dealing with corruption, has, as noted above, recorded the lowest levels of corruption in Africa for more than a decade. Entrenching anti-corruption provisions in a constitution is therefore not a magic solution that will cause corruption to disappear overnight. The fact that both Nigeria

---

100   See, Andras Sajo, "Anti-Corruption Provisions in the Afghan Constitution?," http://www.constitutionnet.org/files/E19AMemoAntiCorruptionProvisionsSajo.pdf (accessed in March 2015).

101   See in particular chapter 6 on leadership and integrity and other provisions such as articles 228–259.

102   See for example articles 35, 69, 92, 94, 218, 284–286. Note in particular article 286 which is contains one of the most comprehensive provisions dealing with the declaration of property and assets.

103   See for example, articles 107, 128, 120, 165–176, 233–236. Worth noting under the Ugandan constitution is the provision providing an elaborate leadership code of conduct and a Leadership Code Tribunal.

104   See for example, sections 23, 66(10), 69, 107(1), 137(1), 143(2), 149, 152, 156(1)(b), 182(1), 188, 194, 196, 197 and 221–229.

105   For example, both countries were ranked 143rd out of the 182 surveyed in 2011, http://cpi.transparency.org/cpi2011/results/#CountryResults (accessed in March 2015), as compared to Nigeria's position of 134, and Uganda's 127 of the 178 countries surveyed the previous year. http://www.transparency.org/cpi2010/in_detail (accessed in March 2015).

and Uganda have fairly elaborate constitutional provisions trying to combat corruption and yet corruption remains as endemic in both countries as it is in most other African countries, is a clear indication that these provisions are inadequate and ineffective. It is suggested that three important issues must be covered by any constitutional provisions designed to prevent and control corruption for them to be effective. First, they must define the basic principles which provide a framework within which anti-corruption measures must be taken, second they must specify the nature of legislation that is necessary and finally they must spell out the institutions that are needed to fight against corruption. These will now be discussed separately but it must be noted that they are not necessarily distinct measures but are closely and intimately interrelated.

4.2.1 Fundamental Anti-corruption Principles

One of the major weaknesses of anti-corruption measures, even when these appear in the constitution, is that they fail to address the matter in a comprehensive manner or where they do, their enforcement depends, for the most part, on the very officials who are responsible for promoting the corruption. They thus have little incentive to take action against other corrupt officials because they themselves are corrupt. The purpose of constitutional provisions that spell out the general principles underlying the fight against corruption is to ensure that effective enforcement, whether in the form of enacting legislation or taking action against corrupt individuals will not depend on the good will of certain individuals or institutions. In this respect, the general constitutional principles that are absolutely necessary, can be succinctly summarised under a number of points which underscore the degree of revulsion against corruption and the need to severely punish those involved in it to discourage others from engaging in such activities.

First, is the need to criminalise corruption. All forms of corruption, such as bribery, embezzlement, fraud, extortion, abuse of power, misappropriation of public funds and all other forms of abuse of office and misuse of public property must be made to constitute offences punishable under the criminal law or any other special law. No person or his relatives, friends or other associates should be allowed to benefit whether directly or indirectly from the proceeds of corruption or any corrupt activities. All the proceeds and other assets resulting from or associated with corruption should be seized and confiscated by the state. Once there is an arguable case of corruption, the prosecuting authorities must be under an obligation to prosecute and should have no discretion or right to use technicalities, such as that used in the South African arms deal case discussed earlier, as an excuse for not prosecuting.

The second principle will require integrity and transparency from all public officers whether occupying an elective political office or an appointive position in the civil service. For both positions, those who have been found guilty of corruption should be barred from holding any public office for a period of 10–15 years depending on the gravity of the offence. All persons or businesses implicated in corruption or corrupt activities should also be barred for a period of 10–20 years from doing business with the state or any parastatal or organisation in which the government has a controlling interest. All public officials under investigation for, or charged with corruption, should automatically be suspended from office.[106]

Third, is the principle that recognises a right of individual and collective action for the removal from office, trial and prosecution of any public official alleged to be involved in corruption or corrupt activities. This should also extend to a right to take action requesting the blacklisting of any person or businesses that have been associated with corrupt activities. This needs to be reinforced by an obligation imposed on all individuals and institutions to promptly comply with court orders or directions.[107] The right of public interest action is a necessary response to the growing disenchantment with the ability and willingness of public institutions, such as the prosecuting authorities and other

---

[106] This is to ensure that the accused do not use their official positions to interfere with the evidence or the investigations taking place. The ruling ANC in South Africa, after its national policy conference of June 2012 resolved that any party leaders who are under investigations will have to "step aside" until the investigations are complete. See "Policy: Alleged Fraudsters will have to 'step aside' – ANC," in *Legalbrief Today*, Issue No. 3067 of Friday, 29 June 2012.

[107] The general record of African governments complying with court orders and decisions is quite poor. Even in South Africa, a recent report states that "although government generally shows a willingness to comply with court orders, there have been some instances of failures to comply with some court judgments, especially in relation to socio-economic rights ... " See, Lauren Paremoer, Cherrel Africa and Robert Mattes, *The Open Society Monitoring Index: Dimensions, Indicators and Available Evidence.* (January 2012), at p. 99. (Report made available to author by the Open Society Foundation for South Africa). It would therefore not help to make it easier for citizens to bring claims to compel governments to act unless there is a corresponding obligation on governments to comply with judicial orders or decisions. An excellent way of dealing with this is provided in the Ghanaian 1992 constitution, which in article 2(3)(3) imposes a duty on "any person or group of persons to whom an order or direction is addressed ... by the Supreme Court ... to obey and carry out the terms of the order or direction." Article 2(3)(4) provides that any "failure to obey or carry out the terms of the order or direction ... constitutes a crime under this Constitution ... in the case of the President or Vice President, constitute a ground for removal from office ... ".

anti-corruption agencies to secure and defend the public interest against the predatory activities of public officials.[108] This will strengthen the hands of those individuals, CBOs and NGOs that have been actively monitoring and exposing corruption. It is the activities of such individuals and organisations that have continuously put pressure on the South African government and its anti-corruption agencies to respond to the numerous incidences of corruption that regularly make news headlines in the country.[109] This move towards a self-enforcing constitution enhances each individual in the society's right for self-government and inevitably involves the transfer of some powers from the public into the private hands in a manner that is likely to promote greater efficiency and efficacy in dealing with corruption.[110] A cardinal principle of justice is that nobody, regardless of his status is above or beyond the reach of the law. Corruption, especially elite corruption, has flourished because most of the political leaders and their associates have been able to use their ill-gotten wealth to place themselves beyond the reach of the law. The state monopolisation of prosecutorial authority has meant that these people have been able to easily avoid accountability. Presidential immunities in many African countries are now qualified and allow for the impeachment of leaders who misuse their powers to embezzle government funds. However, operationalizing the impeachment processes remains complex and often impracticable.[111] One huge advantage of the right to individual and collective against corrupt individuals and institutions is that no one is now beyond the reach of the law. This is a powerful weapon in the hands of the main victims of corruption, namely, the poor and marginalised who can, with the assistance of NGOs and CBOs take action against their oppressors. There is no better way of reducing corruption

---

108 There should be no requirement of a personal interest for the action to be brought. See Bamford-Addo JSC in the Ghanaian case of *Sam (No. 2) v. Attorney-General* [2000] SCGLR 305 at p. 314.

109 See for example, Open Democracy Advice Centre (ODAC), the Right2Know Campaign, One Society Initiative, and the Institute for Accountability in Southern Africa.

110 It can be argued that this right of action is consistent with the right recognised in traditional African society for the people to rebel against an unjust and oppressive King who ignored his responsibilities. Even regicide was accepted and the people were free to kill such a ruler as a "mad dog". See, Funmilola Tolulope Abioye, "Rule Of Law In English Speaking African Countries: The Case Of Nigeria And South Africa: Chapter 2: History of Governance in Africa" http://repository.up.ac.za/bitstream/handle/2263/28459/Complete.pdf?sequence=9 (accessed in March 2015).

111 See further, Charles Manga Fombad and Enyinna Nwauche, "Africa's Imperial Presidents: Immunity, Impunity and Accountability," 5(2) *African Journal of Legal Studies* (2012), pp. 91–118.

than that of placing all politicians and government officials *in terrorem* for any acts of corruption at the instance of any citizen. In this way, individuals can have an opportunity to participate and contribute towards good governance.

Fourth, is the principle that excludes all persons convicted of corruption or corrupt activities from the benefit of any pardons or amnesties and the principle that statutes of limitations shall not apply to any person alleged to have been involved in corruption or corrupt activities.[112]

Fifth, is the principle of reward and punishment. This will seek to encourage and protect those who report corruption and punish not only those who are engaged in it but also those who negligently or deliberately refuse to report acts of corruption. All persons whose information led to the recovery of public funds that were illegally misappropriated through corrupt activities should be entitled to 3–10% of the monetary value of the assets forfeited. All such persons should be protected from persecution or any form of victimisation by law. On the other hand, all persons who knew or reasonably ought to know of the corrupt activities of another person and deliberately or negligently failed to report to the relevant authorities should be considered as accomplices to such corrupt activities. The extent of punishment should be determined by the level of culpability. A duty should also be imposed on all financial institutions to regularly review their transactions and report any suspicious activities to the police.

Sixth, there should be a duty to examine the assets of public officials who appear to be living beyond their means on grounds of suspicious wealth. Where the officials cannot satisfactorily explain such wealth, it should be confiscated by the state. The onus should be on the official to prove that the wealth was acquired in a legitimate manner.

Finally, members of the judiciary, the police service, the armed forces and custom services, from whom the highest standards of integrity is expected must be given a higher penalty than ordinary offenders, for any offence involving corruption and corrupt activities that they commit.

4.2.2 The Scope of Legislative Enactments

The transition towards a corruption-free society necessitates a series of legislative enactments based on the basic principles stated above. These should be drafted to deal in as comprehensive a manner as possible with the different forms and manifestations of corruption. As we have seen, the problem in Africa has not been the absence of anti-corruption legislation but rather their

---

[112] A proposed amendment to the 1991 Benin constitution will, *inter alia*, make economic crimes imprescriptible.

lack of effectiveness. The main advantage of constitutionalising the basic principles stated above is to ensure that all the pieces of legislation enacted conform to the basic principles, failing which, their constitutional validity can be impugned. Examples of important pieces of legislation needed to implement the basic principles and effectively deal with corruption are as follows:

i. Whistle blower protection law to encourage the reporting of cases.
ii. Conflict of interest laws.
iii. Freedom of information laws which gives citizens the right to demand the disclosure of information regarding government activities.
iv. Seizure and forfeiture of proceeds of crime and criminal activities legislation.
v. Declaration of assets by senior officials holding political office or civil service positions such as parliamentarians, ministers, the president and directors.
vi. Legislation providing for international co-operation in criminal matters.
vii. Legislation guaranteeing a system of fair and transparent appointment to positions in the public service.
viii. Party financing legislation.
ix. Procurement legislation.
x. Anti-laundering laws.
xi. Law to promote administrative justice, like South Africa's Promotion of Administrative Justice Act.[113]
xii. Enforceable code of conduct for public servants and politicians.[114]

This is not meant to be an exhaustive list of all legislation that can combat corruption. What is important is that the list of relevant legislation must be speci-

---

[113] Act No. 3 of 2000.
[114] Codes of conduct that serve to underline a new culture of non-tolerance of corruption in all its forms through a definition of the values and standards of behaviour expected of workers in their different professional settings is important. This should deal with unethical practices, such as misusing government resources (for example, photocopiers, computers and cars) which do not necessarily warrant sanctions entailing jail sentences and other forms of unethical conduct, such as drinking on duty, doing a private job during official hours and sexual harassment of a colleague, that may warrant more serious punishment, even including dismissal. The advantage of regulating some of these matters through codes of conduct drawn up by members of the profession themselves rather than legally enforceable rules is that these codes would set standards agreed upon by the professionals themselves and their enforcement would be easier to ensure and monitor than legal rules or even statutory codes imposed from outside the profession.

fied in the constitution to ensure that any legislative enactment conforms to the general principles discussed above. It is only within a fairly comprehensive anti-corruption legislative framework that independent institutions designed to fight corruption can effectively discharge their mandates. We now turn to these institutions.

4.2.3   Independent Anti-corruption Agencies

Two types of ACAs were noted earlier. The first is the free standing bodies that have separate and distinct operational identities and operate outside the normal state bureaucracy. They have the fight against corruption or crime in general, as their primary or exclusive responsibility.[115] The other type are those which are integrated into some departmental structures and usually complement the work of the free-standing institutions although their primary mandate may or may not be to combat corruption or crime. Both types of institutions will be more effective when they are specifically spelt out in the constitution and protected from being captured and manipulated by politicians.

The main ACAs, some of which feature in one form or another in some modern African constitutions are:

i.   Public Service Commission.
ii.   Auditor-General.[116]
iii. Public Accounts Committee of Parliament.
iv.   Special Parliamentary Committee on Governance and Accountability.[117]
v.   Public Procurement Commission[118]
vi.   Special Investigations Unit of the Police.
vii. Commissions of inquiry which may be established as and when the need arises.
viii. Independent electoral commission.
ix.   Electoral boundaries commission
x.   Human Rights commission.

---

115   See Bill De Maria, op. cit. at p. 31, explanatory notes to Appendix 1.
116   In Francophone Africa, some of the functions performed by the Auditor-General are performed by specialised courts called audit courts.
117   This is a novelty whose rationale is explained below.
118   A majority of corruption cases arise during the award of government contracts in disregard of public procurement regulations and procedures. A public procurement commission should be an independent body that will not only ensure that all public procurement regulations are followed but should deal expeditiously with all complaints of irregularities and recommend speedy action.

xi.   Judicial Service commission.
xii. Media and Access to information commission.
xiii. Minority rights commission.
xiv. National prosecuting authority or Public Prosecutor (whose functions are performed by the Attorney-General in some Anglophone countries).
xv.   Ombudsman (or the more descriptive word, Public Protector).
xvi. Specialised anti-corruption agency.

Two preliminary comments are in order here. The first is that one of the most important institutions – the judiciary – is not mentioned or discussed. Nevertheless, it must be made clear that no constitutional framework, however comprehensive or well-crafted it is, can function properly without an efficient and competent judiciary that is independent and has integrity. All what is said about the merits of constitutionally entrenched anti-corruption framework therefore depends on a fully functional and efficient judiciary that is ready to act as defender and enforcer of constitutional justice without fear or favour.[119] The second point to note is that the Special Parliamentary Committee on Governance and Accountability mentioned above does not appear in any modern African constitution. It is however considered as an important body to receive quarterly reports from all the constitutional ACAs, monitor their activities and ensure accountability. Institutions such as the specialised anti-corruption agency, the ombudsman, the national prosecuting authority and the judicial service commission should report to it rather than to the executive. The constitution should expressly determine how it is to be constituted. Ideally, it should have at least an equal number of representatives from the ruling party and from the opposition parties and be chaired by a member from the opposition parties. It should have the powers to subpoena anybody to appear before it and should be able to co-opt such experts as it might need to assist it discharge its functions.

Having said this, it is worthwhile pointing out that although many African constitutions provide for the establishment of some of the above-mentioned institutions, especially ombudsman, public service commissions and judicial

---

[119] We have pointed to the problem of judicial corruption in Africa. There have been significant attempts since the 1990s to enhance the prospects for judicial independence in Africa. Although there remain many problems, the radical changes introduced in the 2010 Kenyan constitution and the high reputation and prestige that judgments of South African courts, especially the Constitutional Court, have earned in the last decade has set a high standard which, in the globalised world of today, many other African judges cannot ignore. In the final analysis, if the constitutional framework is solid, African judges will be more inclined to allowing justice to prevail than give in to external pressure and corruption.

service commissions, they have hardly been able to operate effectively because of political interference in one form or another. The key to their success is therefore to insulate them against this. Five principles need to be constitutionally entrenched to protect these institutions from external interference and to ensure that they can function efficiently and effectively.

The best example of shielding ACAs from external interference appears in chapter 9 of the South African constitution dealing with a number of "state institutions supporting democracy." Although these institutions are expressly designed to strengthen the country's constitutional democracy, many of them, such as the Public Protector (ombudsman), the Auditor-General and the Electoral Commission also play a role in combatting corruption. What is unique about the South African approach is the four constitutionally entrenched legal principles that are spelt out to ensure that these institutions are an effective log to the constitutional wheel and not a political charade of symbolic value only. The four guiding principles provide that:

i. These institutions are independent and subject only to the constitution and the law, and they must be impartial and must exercise their powers and perform their functions without fear, favour or prejudice.
ii. Other organs of state, through legislative and other measures, must assist and protect these institutions, to ensure the independence, impartiality, dignity and effectiveness of these institutions.
iii. No person or organ of state may interfere with the functioning of these institutions.
iv. These institutions are accountable to the National Assembly, and must report on their activities and the performance of their functions to the Assembly at least once a year[120]

Something close to these principles are referred to in some constitutions as "directive principles of state policy,"[121] but these, unlike the principles in the South African constitution, are stated in purely hortatory terms. The fifth and critically important principle that needs to be entrenched should state that that any legislation, action, measures or mechanisms introduced to regulate any of these institutions, which undermines the essential purpose of combatting corruption and ensuring accountability and transparency shall be declared null and void by the courts. The fourth principle stated in the South African constitution is inevitably modified as discussed above to require that

---

120 See, Section 181(1), (2), (3) and (4) of the South African Constitution.
121 See for example, Articles 34–41 of the Constitution of Ghana; and Sections 13–24 of the Constitution of Nigeria.

quarterly reports should be submitted to the Special Parliamentary Committee on Governance and Accountability.

Creating so many institutions might lead to duplication, conflicts, unnecessary bureaucracy, and inefficiency due to cases falling between the cracks in turf identification wars.[122] There is certainly a risk of all this but careful draftsmanship could limit the potential for this. Arguably, the benefits of effectively controlling and limiting corruption will more than make up for all this. Besides this, there are several other advantages that cannot be lightly ignored.

First, each of these institutions will deal with different types (for example, bribery, gerrymandering of electoral constituencies, graft, and nepotism) and the diverse forms (for example, petty and grand corruption), and different avenues (for example, electoral corruption and corruption in the public service) through which corruption takes place. Their combined effect is to provide a comprehensive and holistic approach which will enable the institutions in their diverse ways not only to investigate and initiate the prosecution of corrupt persons but also to prevent corruption through education. This will also ensure that the institutions can be both proactive and reactive to issues of corruption and good governance.

Second, the variety of institutions will enable them to be accessible to all, especially the poor and marginalised in society. For instance, ombudsmen and specialised anti-corruption institutions are often decentralised and have offices in many parts of the country where they can be easily accessed by the poor. In this way, they can deal with the pervasive and perennial abuses of discretionary powers involving unjustified discrimination and extortion of money which a majority of Africans are subjected to on a daily basis, for example, the extraction of bribes by police officers at road blocks and the bribes extracted by civil servants in order to process official documents.

Third and perhaps most importantly, the five principles will provide a powerful bulwark against the persistent problem of political manipulation. Three South African cases will suffice to illustrate how the guiding principles spelt out in the constitution have protected the chapter 9 institutions from political interference. In *Independent Electoral Commission v. Langeberg Municipality*,[123] the Constitutional Court had no hesitation in pointing out that as a result of the constitutional guarantees of the independence and impartiality of the In-

---

122 See, Paul Hoffman, "Hawks or Eagles: What does South Africa deserve?" (Notes for an address to the Cape Town Press Club on 15 May 2012), http://accountabilitynow.org.za/hawks-eagles-south-africa-deserve/ (accessed in March 2015).

123 2001 (9) BCLR 883 (CC).

dependent Electoral Commission (IEC) Parliament had a duty in making the legislation regulating its activities to ensure its manifest independence and impartiality and that such legislation was justiciable for conformity to the constitution. In the absence of such guarantees, the courts will lack the power to review legislation on electoral commissions to ensure that it is not biased in favour of ruling parties. The importance of the independence of these institutions was again underscored in *New National Party of South Africa v. Government of the Republic of South Africa and Others.*[124] In this case, questions were raised about the independence of the IEC and the possibility of governmental interference with its proper functioning. The Constitutional Court, although concluding that the allegations had not been proven by the facts, nevertheless pointed out that the IEC was one of the institutions provided for under Chapter 9 of the South African constitution which are a product of a "new constitutionalism"[125] whose independence had to be jealously preserved by the courts. Two factors that were relevant to this independence were highlighted by the court. First, it pointed out that independence implied financial independence which required that the IEC should be given enough money to discharge its functions. This had to come, not from government but from parliament and the IEC had to be "afforded an adequate opportunity to defend its budgetary requirements before parliament and its relevant bodies."[126] Second, the IEC's status also implied administrative independence which meant that the IEC was subject only to the constitution and the law and answerable only to Parliament rather than the executive. The issue of adequate resources needs to be emphasised. An ACA that is understaffed and under-resourced may cause more harm than good because its over-stretched staff will be easy prey for those who want to bribe their way out of lengthy prison sentences. Hong Kong's success has not come cheap. In 1994, its ICAC had 1300 employees in a jurisdiction with just over five million people. In 2006, its budget was USD 86 million as compared to Botswana's DCEC budget of USD 2.8 million and Kenya's ACA with USD 14.7 million.[127]

Another decision of the South African Constitutional Court; *Glenister v. President of the Republic of South Africa,*[128] illustrates what is meant by these institutions being independent. The brief background to the case is that in December 2007, the ruling ANC in a historical conference swept aside the leader-

---

124 1999 (3) SA 191.
125 Per Langa DP at 224.
126 Ibid. at 231.
127 See, Bill de Maria, op. cit. pp. 15–16.
128 [2011] ZACC 6.

ship of then President, Thabo Mbeki. The Congress resolved that South Africa should have one single police force and a special corruption fighting unit, the Directorate of Special Operations, popularly known as the Scorpions, should be disbanded. There was widespread media speculation at the time of this resolution that the ANC had undertaken a vendetta against the Scorpions because they had investigated many senior officials in the party, including the then newly elected leader of the party, Jacob Zuma.[129] When the bill disbanding the Scorpions and establishing a new unit popularly known as the Hawks became law, Glenister, who had unsuccessfully challenged the cabinet decision to initiate the legislative process to disband the Scorpions, brought an action challenging the constitutionality of this new legislation. The Court by a majority of 5 to 4 declared that the amended Chapter 6A of the South African Police Service Act introducing the Scorpions was inconsistent with the constitution and invalid to the extent that it failed to provide for an adequate degree of independence for the corruption-fighting unit that it sought to establish. Although there was no specific provision in the constitution specifying that the unit must be independent, the majority held that the constitutional obligation to set up an independent unit could be inferred from the duty imposed by section 7(2) of the constitution to "respect, protect and fulfil" the rights in the bill of rights. It went further to point out that, based on section 39(1)(b) of the constitution which required the Court in interpreting the bill of rights to consider international law and section 231 which states that all international agreements approved by Parliament are binding, the establishment of a corruption-fighting unit ignoring binding international instruments which required such a unit to be independent was not a reasonable constitutional measure. In this indirect manner, the court declared legislation unconstitutional for violating international law which became relevant not only because it was based on instruments that are binding on the South African government but also because they reflect the ethos of constitutionalism. In other words, the constitutional duty to create a corruption fighting unit was not discharged by creating one which will be ineffective because it was placed under the control of politicians whom it is required to investigate. On the other hand, independence does not require complete insulation from political accountability. It rather requires insulation from a degree of management by political actors that would enable an ACA to operate without fear, favour or prejudice.

One other important point that emerges from the *Glenister* case is the importance that the courts ought to and should attach to the numerous inter-

---

[129] See, "Decision to Disband Scorpions made before National Conference," http://www.legalbrief.co.za/article.php?story=20080125083840869.

national treaties and conventions that African governments sign and ratify but hardly ever hurry to domesticate them. Corruption is now a global problem and international cooperation, especially through mutual legal assistance in criminal matters and extradition is crucial. The *Glenister* case and the famous Botswana case of *Attorney-General v. Dow*[130] suggest that whilst courts cannot compel governments to domesticate these international treaties and conventions, they can at least compel them not to act in breach of them. In dealing with the position where a treaty had been signed but had not been domesticated, Amissah JP in *Attorney-General v. Dow*, cited with approval the following passage from the judge *a quo* in the same case:

> I bear in mind that signing the Convention [the OAU Convention] does not give it the power of law in Botswana but the effect of the adherence by Botswana to the Convention must show that a construction of the section which does not do violence to the language but is consistent with and in harmony with the Convention must be preferable to a 'narrow construction' which results in a finding that section 15 of the Constitution permits discrimination on the basis of sex.[131]

In doing so, the Court basically followed the well-established presumption in statutory interpretation that courts will strive to interpret legislation in such manner that it will not conflict with international law. The judge went further to explain this thus:

> ... Botswana is a member of the community of civilised States which has undertaken to abide by certain standards of conduct, and, unless it is impossible to do otherwise, it would be wrong for its courts to interpret its legislation in a manner which conflicts with the international obligations Botswana has undertaken. This principle, used as an aid to construction as is quite permissible under section 24 of the Interpretation Act ... [132]

If courts are willing and able to rigorously enforce the five guiding principles, there is every likelihood that ACAs will be able to bring corruption under control.

---

130   [1992] BLR 119.
131   Ibid. at p. 154.
132   Ibid.

5 Conclusion

Attempts to control corruption are as old as corruption itself. No country has succeeded to eliminate it because its complex nature makes its total elimination impossible. Realistically, the goal of any effective anti-corruption strategy should at best aim not be to accomplish the impossible task of eliminating it but rather to control and limit its deleterious effects to as close to zero as possible.

In modern Africa, in spite of all the hype about fighting corruption and the regular noisy anti-corruption campaigns, it remains the single most serious obstacle to the eradication of poverty and inequality in African societies. It is not only discouraging foreign investment by creating an unstable and unpredictable legal and political environment but is also deepening poverty and impeding the attainment of the Millennium Development Goals.

This Chapter has reviewed the different types and forms of corruption in Africa and the diverse attempts to deal with this in the past. It was noted that the frequent and widely-publicised anti-corruption rhetoric and the campaigns and purges by African leaders was hardly matched by any concrete and effective action. Given the gravity of the corruption pandemic and the devastating effect it is having on the distressed and fragile economies already weakened by years of economic crisis and political instability, it has been argued in this Chapter that there is need for a radical, innovative and holistic anti-corruption strategy. It was shown that endemic corruption has declined in several countries in South East Asia and Latin America because of well-designed and well-targeted anti-corruption reforms sustained by committed political leaders and a vigilant civil society.

It has been the main contention of this Chapter that the key to unlocking the stranglehold of endemic corruption in Africa lies in reconfiguring the present constitutions to make corruption a high risk and unprofitable activity for everybody, whether rich or poor. The basic framework for a constitutionally entrenched anti-corruption strategy is built around three main pillars. First, a number of fundamental principles designed to criminalise corruption and ensure that everybody or institution, regardless of status who get involved in corrupt activities must be investigated, prosecuted and severely punished. Second, a comprehensive legislative agenda which imposes an obligation on the legislature, not merely to enact laws but ensure to that these laws sufficiently deal with the problem of corruption. And finally, a number of different anti-corruption agencies designed to ensure that they are able to deal with the different forms of corruption.

The massive amounts of money that are lost in Africa annually through corruption and the complacent attitude of many African leaders and their political cronies not only in countries adjudged to be relatively doing well from the perspective of corruption but also from those which appear to be terminally infected with the corruption virus is emblematic of the depth of the problem. Corruption is no longer just a simple crime or even just a crime against development,[133] as some have suggested, but justifies to be ranked amongst crimes against humanity. As we have seen, corruption inflicts needless and intolerable hardship on the voiceless poor and marginalised, some of whom are forced to live as destitutes or die from hunger and disease simply because the funds meant to remedy their situation and improve their lives have been siphoned off by powerful politicians and their associates. The suffering becomes wanton and inexplicable when the amounts embezzled and hidden in foreign banks are so massive that they could not possibly be exhausted in the perpetrator's lifetime. What is more, these leaders, such as Sani Abacha and Mobutu Sese Seko have died leaving most of this ill-gotten wealth in foreign bank account. It is therefore argued that people who loot government funds and in doing so deprive others of the basic necessities of life such as access to basic health facilities, drinking water, housing and food must now be ranked on the same par as murderers. However, short of treating them and punishing them as murderers, the argument of this paper is that all perpetrators of corruption must be severely punished; any assets and other benefits attributable to their corrupt activities should also be confiscated by the state. By constitutionalising the obligation to curb corruption, the duty to legislate as well as that to take action against corrupt individuals would no longer depend on the convenience of the legislature or executive but is spelt out in a legally enforceable manner in the constitution. Perhaps the main virtue of the new constitutional approach is that all persons involved in corrupt activities, regardless of their status in society are open to prosecution or legal action by the state as well as at the behest of individuals and CBOs. This will give the favourite slogan "zero tolerance of corruption" veritable teeth.

There is no better way for the constitution to protect the fundamental human rights of all citizens, address the problems of underdevelopment, backwardness, illiteracy, lack of basic necessities such as water, food and healthcare, than to lay in clear terms a strategy built around preventing, detecting, investigating and prosecuting those involved in corruption.

---

133   See, "Corruption is crime against development, says new UN campaign," http://www.unodc.org/unodc/en/frontpage/2009/November/corruption-is-a-crime-against-develop ment-says-new-un-campaign-.html (accessed March 2015).

Index

Aaland Islands Case 686, 689n58, 691n71
Abkhazia 56, 57, 684
Accordance with International Law of the Unilateral Declaration of Independence in Respect of Kosovo, 22 July 2010, International Court of Justice, Advisory Opinion, *I.C.J. Reports, 2010*, p. 403 36, 50, 52–60, 682, 683, 684n24, 684n29, 686, 687, 688, 689, 691, 692
Accountability
    For gender-based and sexual violence crimes, absence of 404, 406
    For Genocide 113, 381
    For Post-election violence 432, 617, 641
    In domestic courts or tribunals 427, 433, 434, 437, 438, 506
    In governance 711–54
    In ICTR 469
    In Right to Development 574, 578
    Of individuals for crimes at the International Criminal Court 430, 443
    Of States for *erga omnes* obligations 105
    Of the Seabed Disputes Chamber 204
    Of the Security Council 148
    Official accountability in political transitions 660, 661
    Truth Commission in lieu of criminal accountability 447–448
Actual and potential competition 249–52
Affirmative action 135, 137–139
African Charter on Human and Peoples' Rights, or Banjul Charter 255, 514, 515–18, 527–28, 529n57, 534–35, 559, 566, 578, 580–89, 605–09, 639n3, 688–89, 691, 708–10, 714–15, 719n62, 720, 721n71, 722, 724
African Commission on Human and Peoples' Rights, or ACHPR 253n26, 255, 516–17, 533n79, 534–35, 582–90, 606–09, 688, 689n56, 691, 694n91, 695–96, 703, 706, 709–12, 719n62, 720–24
    ACHPR-*Report on the Mission of Good Offices to Senegal* 688n56, 695n101, 695n103

African Court of Justice, or ACJ 406n2, 552, 559, 561–63, 709, 718-720
    Protocol of the Court of Justice of the African Union 559, 562
African Court of Justice and Human Rights, or ACJHR 406–25, 559n66, 562
    Protocol on the Statute of the African Court of Justice and Human Rights 406n2, 552, 559n66, 562
African Court on Human and Peoples' Rights, or ACHPR 254, 406n2, 559n66, 560, 562, 706
    Protocol to the African Charter on Human Rights and Peoples' Rights on the Establishment of an African Court on Human and Peoples' Rights 415n40, 559–60
African Economic Community, or AEC 536, 537–38, 539–40, 543, 550, 552–53, 558–59, 560–64
    Assembly of Heads of State and Government 551, 558–561
    Council of Ministers 551, 560–61
    Protocol on Relations between the African Economic Community and the Regional Economic Communities, or Protocol on Relations 552, 553, 563
    Protocol to the Treaty Establishing the African Economic Community Relating to the Pan-African Parliament 559
    Treaty Establishing the African Economic Community, or AEC Treaty 536–38, 551–53, 558–560, 562–63
African Economic Integration 538–39, 542–44, 547, 553–54, 556, 558, 562–64
African Union, or AU 34n47, 157–58, 247, 329, 333, 406, 414, 425, 427, 438, 439, 506, 513, 517, 519, 523, 533–35, 536, 538, 542, 554, 558–59, 561, 580, 598, 609–12, 614–38, 640, 642–43, 659–61, 693–95, 698, 703–04, 718–20, 724
    As a means for resolving disputes 34n47, 506, 614–38

776　　　　　　　　　　　　　　　　　　　　　　　　　　　　　　　　　INDEX

African Union, or AU (cont.)
   Assembly   406, 416n43, 444, 538, 559,
      561–62, 620, 630, 719
   AU Convention on Preventing and
      Combating Corruption   741n48
   AU Peace & Security Architecture, or APSA
      610, 621
   AU's Electoral and Security Assistance
      Mission to the Comoros, or MAES   611,
      696n105, 697
   AU's Mission in Somalia, or AMISOM   700
   AU's Standby Force, or ASF   610n110, 621,
      632
   Charter on Democracy, Elections and
      Governance   640n6, 643, 644–47, 659
   Commission   414, 559, 610n110, 647, 706
   Constitutive Act   333, 562 558, 559, 562,
      609, 617, 620–21, 630, 633, 634, 637, 639,
      640, 675n87, 675n88, 675n90, 676n92
   Legal Counsel and Director for Legal
      Affairs   414
   Official Journal of the African Union   561
   Peace and Security Council, or PSC, or
      AUPSC   519, 619n23, 621, 625, 635–36,
      647, 693n87, 696n109, 697n115 &n118
   Protocol relating to the Establishment of
      the Peace and Security Council of the
      African Union   621, 693n87 &n88
      &n90, 694n92
   Request for deferment of prosecution
      157
   Right of intervention   333, 514, 609–12,
      617, 647
   Specialized Technical Committee (STC) on
      Justice and Legal Affairs   418
   Tension with ICC   438–39, 444
African Union Commission on International
   Law   542n10, 543
American Convention on Human Rights
   604
Antarctic Mineral resources   7
Anti-corruption agencies   741–53, 765–72
Anti-corruption strategies   726, 729, 741–73
Apology   26
Arab Maghreb Union, or AMU   538–541, 561
Armed Conflict   7–11, 39, 43, 83, 242n1,
      254n40, 264n6, 265–67, 268–73, 277,
      281–82, 284, 339n234, 353, 365–66, 368,
      379, 385, 368, 390, 422n61, 477, 483,
      525–26, 594, 599, 615–17, 623–27, 629,
      631–32, 634–38
   Participation of Children   524–26, 601
Asylum
   Diplomatic Asylum   37–38, 502
   For Refugees   518, 521–23, 593, 595–98
Asymmetry (power relations of Global North
   and Global South)   150–162
Attack   29, 142, 340, 353–78, 385, 388, 391,
      458–59, 479–89, 607, 609, 719n62
   Widespread or systematic   353–72,
      372–77, 385
Avena case   40–43, 61–84, 130
Azawad   694–95
   National Movement for the Liberation of
      Azawad (MNLA)   694
   Ouagadougou Preliminary Agreement
      694
   Tuareg   694

Bakke case   138
Biafra   614n2, 680
Boundary disputes   42–46, 51, 174, 221

Cambodia   62, 68–71, 73, 286, 414, 506
Casamance   689n56, 695–96
   *Movement of Democratic Forces of
      Casamance* (MFDC)   695
Charter of Paris for a New Europe   687n47
Chechnya   57
Child and Child Welfare
   African Charter on the rights & welfare of
      the child   497, 514, 523–27, 535, 600–02
   African Committee on the Rights and
      Welfare of the Child   527
   Age of majority   524–25, 600–01
   Child marriages   525, 530–31
   Harmful cultural practice   526–27
   Internally Displaced Children, protection
      of   525–26
   Kidnapping   602
   Minimum working age for children   532
   Participation in armed conflicts   496–97,
      503, 524–25, 601
   Refugee children   526
   Responsibilities of the child   527
   Right of   523–27, 600–02, 612

Right to education   526, 574
Trafficking   602
UN Committee on the rights of the Child   527
UN Convention on the rights of the child   274, 523–26, 600–02
Civilians
  Attacks upon   279, 281, 400, 454, 459, 719n62
  Protection of   275, 281, 339n234, 400, 629, 634–35
Code of crimes   5, 359n28, 360, 363n41
Comity   231, 233, 241
Commission on the Limits of the Continental Shelf   182–85, 214, 216n122, 217, 218–19
Common Market for Eastern and Southern Africa, or COMESA   247, 538–541, 542n10, 551, 554, 556, 564
  Treaty Establishing the Common Market for Eastern and Southern Africa, or COMESA Treaty   545n19 &n20 &n21, 549, 550n29, 551n30 &n31 &n32, 552, 554n44
Community of Sahel-Saharan States, or CEN-SAD   538–42
Comoros   440, 540, 542, 611, 649, 694, 696–98, 717n57
  Anjouan and Mohéli   696–98
  AU Electoral and Security Assistance Mission, or MAES   611, 696n05, 697
  Bacar, Mohamed   697
  Mayotte   696
Compensation   25–26, 30, 39, 204, 222n43, 238–40, 254, 275, 338n31, 435, 516, 533, 586–87, 600, 607, 629, 730n1
Conduct of the belligerent powers   168, 264, 270, 272, 275, 277, 281–82, 287, 632, 634
Conflict Resolution   614–38, 629–38, 644
  Resolution of African Conflicts   615–38
Constitution
  Constitutional democracy   31, 138, 620, 623, 630, 633, 635, 645–47
  Constitutional term limits   640, 644, 648–50
Constitutional entrenchment   726, 729, 755–73
Constitutional law   230–41, 622, 755
Constitutionalism   643, 645–46

Convention on the Law of the Sea or UNCLOS   3, 7, 14, 23n8, 163–86, 187–229, 163, 256
Cornelius van Bynkershoek   165
Corruption   230, 415, 417n4, 420, 478, 552, 655, 693, 718n9, 744–73
  Consequences   729, 735–41
  Nature and types   729, 731–35
Crimes against humanity   290n4, 323, 329, 332–35, 340, 352–78, 382, 389, 391, 393, 410–11, 415, 420, 423n1, 427, 429, 452, 454, 473, 477, 483, 485, 487, 495, 499, 506, 514, 609, 617, 620, 629, 690, 693, 773
  Charters of the IMT, Nuremberg, Tokyo and Allied Control Council Law No. 10   354–57
  Definitional elements   369–77
  Evolution of   354-69
  International Law Commission, contributions to evolution   359–63
  Right to intervene   333, 514, 609, 617, 620, 629
  Rome Statute of the International Criminal Court, contribution of   367–69
  Statutes of UN ad hoc Tribunals, contribution to evolution of Crimes against Humanity   363–67
  United Nations War Crimes Commission, Works of   358–59
Cyprus v. Turkey, European Court of Human Rights, Merits, (2001) 35 EHRR   685n31, 731

Darfur case   517
Darfur   56, 158n76, 255, 336n222, 431–32, 438, 585n95, 606–07, 610, 615n8, 693n91
Decision on the Prosecution's Application for a Warrant of Arrest against Omar Hassan Ahmad Al Bashir ICC-02/05–01/09-3 P-T Ch I   48 ILM (2009) 463   693n91
Decolonization   54–55, 107–08, 118, 513, 680, 685–86, 699n128
Democracy
  Democratic consolidation   642, 648, 727
  Democratic elections   623, 630–32, 641, 643, 644–46, 660–61
  Democratic succession   639, 641–42, 644, 645, 647, 649

Democracy (cont.)
  Democratic transition 642, 646
  Democratization 636, 640, 642, 644–47, 729, 736
  Democratic governance 514, 621, 623, 629–30, 633, 635–38, 639–43, 645–47
Democratization of international law-making 142–162
Diallo Ahmadou Sadio case 118–24, 130
Diallo's case 139–40
Diplomatic and consular protection 29, 40, 104–130
Dispute Settlement Mechanism 105, 163–64, 170, 172–79, 183, 185–86, 187–229, 545, 550–51, 554–55, 618–19, 630–38
Dominant position 243–46, 254, 257–59

East African Community, or EAC 247, 538–541, 551, 554, 556, 564, 711, 722
  Treaty for the Establishment of the East African Community, or EAC Treaty 545n19 &n20 &n21, 548n26, 550n29, 551, 552, 554n42
East Timor 110, 482n132, 506
East Timor (Portugal v. Australia), 30 June 1995, International Court of Justice, I.C.J. Reports 1995 110, 111n15, 112, 221n138, 685n35
EC Arbitration Commission on Yugoslavia (*Opinion No. 1*) 31 ILM (1992) 1494 689n58
EC Arbitration Commission on Yugoslavia (*Opinion No. 10*) 31 ILM (1992) 1525 684n29
EC Arbitration Commission on Yugoslavia (*Opinion No. 2*) 31 ILM (1992) 1497 686n36, 689n54, 690n65
Economic and Monetary Community of Central Africa, or CEMAC 538
Economic and Monetary Community of West Africa, or UEMAO 538
Economic Community of Central African States, or ECCAS 538
Economic Community of Great Lakes Countries, or ECGLC 538
Economic Community of West African States, or ECOWAS 247, 248n14, 437, 479, 482, 501, 536, 538–542, 551, 554, 556, 564, 620, 624–25, 627, 630, 632–33, 710–11, 713, 716, 721–22
  ECOWAS Monitoring Group, or ECOMOG 500
  Protocol on Democracy and Good Governance 645
  Revised Treaty Establishing Economic Community of West African States (1993) 554n43, 721
  Treaty Establishing the Economic Community of West African States, or ECOWAS Treaty 551n32, 554n43, 609
Economic liberalization 539, 554, 563
ECOWAS Court of Justice 549n28, 706, 710, 718, 721–22, 724
  Protocol on ECOWAS Court of Justice 545n19 &n20 &n21, 549, 550n29, 551n30 &n31, 556, 721
Effectiveness principle 88–89, 96–100
Elections
  Democratic election 479, 611, 623, 630–32, 641, 643, 644–46, 648
  Election violence 624–26, 646, 650–51
  Electoral adjudication 652–55
  Electoral disputes 436, 615, 617, 626–27, 646–47, 652–55
  Electoral Management Bodies 646, 650–52
  Free and fair elections 417n44, 632, 641, 645, 649
  Presidential election 39, 437, 501, 617, 625–27, 630–32, 649
Empire 60, 88, 91, 100–01
Endorois case 516–17, 582n85, 586–87, 607–09
Enslavement 355–56, 358–59, 362n40, 363, 365–67, 371n79, 394, 396–98, 402, 499
Environment 6–9, 11–13, 47, 144, 172, 178, 180, 188, 196–98, 205, 228, 248, 516, 583, 740
Environmental Impact Assessment, or EIA 47
Eritrea 540, 559, 615, 647, 680, 698–99, 703
  Eritrean People's Liberation Front, or EPLF 698
  UN Commission for Eritrea 698–99
Ethiopia 540, 584, 615, 648n36, 698–99, 736
European Community, or EC 549
European Convention on Human Rights 30, 110, 282n82, 604

INDEX 779

European Court of Justice, or Court of Justice of the European Union, or ECJ or CJEU 66, 147, 232, 256n49, 318n166, 548–49, 557, 716
European Economic Community, or EEC 147, 174n20, 180, 245, 251, 536
European Union, or EU 25, 245–46, 248, 251, 253n35, 255, 277, 329, 549, 570n23, 694, 751
Exhaustion of local remedies 178, 549, 692, 709n14
Expropriation 235, 237n32, 238, 240n49
Extraordinary Chambers in the Courts of Cambodia, or ECCC 414

Fair and equitable treatment 230–38, 241
Fluvial navigational rights 47–48, 172
Forced Marriage 380, 390–95, 399, 400–05, 497–98
Foreign judgments
  mutual recognition and enforcement of 550
Forum shopping 144n2, 256–57
Fragmentation of International law 144, 146n11, 173n17, 189n10, 321n180

Gadaffi, Muammar 440, 616, 628–29, 634–35, 637–38
Gender 368, 382–83, 387, 391, 395, 405, 531, 534
Gender-based violence 379–405, 435, 530, 532–33
General Assembly, or United Nations General Assembly, or UNGA 3, 5, 7, 9, 12, 14, 21, 36, 51n1, 52, 55, 112, 149n23, 153n50, 154, 161, 169, 253n38, 267–68, 271–72, 276n57, 293, 306, 311–12, 332, 463, 536, 570, 579, 593, 613, 614, 627
Genocide
  Prevention of 105, 107, 112, 289–351, 352–53, 361, 415, 420, 427, 429, 447, 488, 499, 506, 514, 617
  Genocide Convention 112–13, 277, 279, 286n94, 289, 291, 292–93, 295, 297, 302–16, 318–19, 323, 330–37, 339–49
  Georgia 56–57, 250, 251n25, 255, 440–42
  Rwandan Genocide 113, 292, 324–30, 333, 348–49, 379–84, 387–88, 405, 458–78, 615–16, 620

State and Individual responsibility 26, 114–15, 422
Group of 77 246, 252, 257–59
Grutter case 137–39
Gunme et al. v. *Cameroon,* Communication No. 266/2003, 26th Activity Report 2008–2009 688n54, 689n55, 691n77, 692n78, 703n165

Hague Codification Conference 167–69
Helsinki Final Act 687n47
Host-State 231–33, 238–41
Hugo Grotius 10, 164–65, 318n168
Human rights
  Protection of 144, 514–35, 565–90, 592–609, 612, 617, 635, 639, 641, 646, 707n5, 724
Humanitarian intervention 150, 156n65, 289–351, 333, 620, 629, 636
Humanitarian law 10, 12, 263–288, 289–351, 352–378, 379–405, 406–425, 426–446, 447–512, 599–600, 635, 637

Ilascu v. *Moldova and Russia* (2004) 40 EHRR 1030 334n219, 684n30
Individual responsibility 25, 30, 334, 376n95, 386
Informal deference 231–38
Instrumental values 134–43
Inter-Governmental Authority on Development, or IGAD 247, 538–541, 619n24, 702
Internally Displaced People, or IDP
  AU Convention for the protection and assistance of IDP in Africa, or Kampala Convention 514, 535, 598–600
  Protection of 514, 592, 593, 598–600, 612
  UN Guiding Principles on IDPS or GPIDP 599
International Community 3–4, 12–13, 36, 46, 61, 84, 104–14, 155, 170, 172, 227–28, 259, 268, 318–21, 329n202, 332, 348, 352, 359, 363, 412, 414, 417, 428, 447, 452, 457, 460–61, 467, 475, 480–81, 503, 506, 527, 570, 575n51, 591, 612, 616, 619, 631, 634, 637–38, 656, 681–82, 684, 700

International Court of Justice, or ICJ   3, 7–12,
    14–17, 22, 28, 35–49, 51–60, 61–84,
    85–103, 104–126, 130, 151n44, 152, 153,
    172–73, 176–177, 178n21, 536–37, 182, 184,
    194–95, 205, 206n90, 208–15, 221,
    222n143, 224n146, 226, 228n160, 242,
    255, 256n50 &n51, 263–88, 289–90, 302,
    312n147, 332n210, 338n230 –n232, 339,
    344n248 &n249, 347, 348n267, 410, 412,
    424, 452n8, 536–37, 614, 682–83
  Statute of the International Court of
    Justice, or ICJ Statute   28, 78–80,
    256n51, 331
International Covenant on Civil and Political
    Rights, or ICCPR   136–37, 567, 579, 603,
    685, 688
International Covenant on Economic, Social
    and Cultural Rights, or ICESCR   135,
    567, 579, 581, 603, 605
International Criminal Court, or ICC   5,
    157–59, 179, 253, 350, 354, 401, 405, 410,
    414, 425, 426–46, 447, 496–97, 506, 629,
    631, 635, 637
  Office of the Prosecutor, or OTP   427–28,
    430–33, 439–44, 506
  Statute of International Criminal Court, or
    Rome Statute or ICC Statute   21, 352n1
    &n2, 367–69, 370n77, 411, 412, 426–30,
    439, 505–06
International Criminal Tribunal for Rwanda,
    or ICTR   354, 366–69, 379–88, 370–77,
    405, 410, 414, 447–49, 451n7, 455, 457,
    462–78, 480–81, 483, 486, 488–89, 493,
    496, 502–05, 507–9
  Statute of the International Criminal
    Tribunal for Rwanda, or ICTR Statute
    352n1 &n2, 366–69, 370–77, 411, 412, 473
International Criminal Tribunal for the
    former Yugoslavia, or ICTY   290, 381,
    385n21, 405, 410, 414, 450, 453, 457,
    463n51, 467, 470–71, 474, 476–78,
    480–81, 489, 493, 496
  Statute for the International Criminal
    Tribunal for the former Yugoslavia, or
    ICTY Statute   352n1 &n2, 368, 411, 412
International Law Commission or ILC   3,
    4n4, 5–7, 12–13, 14, 16, 32–33, 39, 117n33,
    120, 127n49, 129n55, 144n2, 146n11,
    147n14, 153, 169, 210, 286, 319n170, 321,
    333n215, 334n215, 342n238, 342n240,
    349n258, 351n261, 359–63, 409, 421, 514,
    537
International Law
  Development by Africa   513–35, 536,
    565–90, 591–613
  Development by the ICJ   21–34, 35–49,
    50–60, 104–132, 263–88, 513–14
  Media-made   151, 155, 161–62
  Participants   144–45, 155–62
  State-made   150–51, 154–55, 162
  Subjects   144n3, 145, 153, 155
International liability   6, 360n31
International Tribunal for the Law of the Sea,
    or ITLOS   73n24, 179–81, 187n3, 195–97,
    202, 204n86, 205–07, 221n137, 225, 228
International water-courses   6, 360n31
Intervention
  Democratic   142–43
Intra-African trade   539, 545
Intrinsic values   134–43
Investment arbitration   238, 240–41
Investor-State dispute   230–41
Israel   111, 255, 272–77, 287, 420n52, 428
Ivory Coast   436–37, 540, 617, 621–27, 630–33,
    637, 736
  Civil war   624–26

Joint criminal enterprise, or JCE   354, 371–72,
    375–76, 378, 387n26, 496
Judgment No. 01389–2013, Tribunal Constitu-
    cional 25 March 2014 (Spain)   683n19
Judicial settlement of international disputes
    21–34, 255, 646
Jurisdiction   5, 22–23, 36, 39, 42, 49, 61–84,
    110–14, 117–18, 126–27, 130, 158n76, 170,
    172, 174n20, 175–82, 189–228, 238,
    248n14, 256, 266, 277, 282–83, 286, 310,
    313–14, 330, 331n207, 332, 334, 338, 345,
    350n259, 355–57, 360, 365–68, 376, 383,
    406–19, 422n61, 424n64, 425, 426–32,
    435–38, 440–44, 446, 448–49, 453–56,
    461, 465, 467–69, 473–76, 482, 485–88,
    490–92, 496–99, 506, 508, 546–47, 549,
    553–54, 557, 562–63, 595, 705, 708,
    710–11, 713–14, 723–24, 741–43, 769
Jus cogens   12, 112–13, 149n23, 289–351

INDEX

Katanga 662, 685
  Katangese Peoples' Congress v. *Zaire*, Communication No. 75/92, 8th Activity Report 1994–1995 688n54, 691n77, 692n78, 703n165
Koroma, Abdul Gadire 1–13, 14–20, 35, 50–54, 59–60, 61, 83, 87n5, 92, 95, 98–99, 102n59, 106, 111n17, 112n19, 113n21, 115n28, 130, 133, 154n47, 189, 205n88, 206n90, 214n115, 228n160, 230, 242, 263, 267, 271, 276, 279–80, 288, 348n257, 360n32, 380n3, 486n152, 514, 536–37, 566n5 591, 605, 614, 637–38, 683–84, 686–88, 690
Kosovo 52–53, 56, 335n222, 482n132, 506, 684n30

Latin America 35–49, 108, 170, 513, 521, 591, 772
Law of Economic Integration 542, 545–46, 558
Legal Consequences of the Construction of a Wall in the Occupied Palestinian Territory 9 July 2004, International Court of Justice, Advisory Opinion, I.C.J. Reports 2004, 36, 58n34, 111, 272, 273–76, 284n89, 286n95, 287n98, 685n35
Legislative enactments 759
Legitimacy
  Of a government or State 88–89, 90–91, 93, 96–98, 631, 645, 653, 681
  Of the International Criminal Court, or ICC 426–446
Legitimate Statehood 85–103
Liberia 447, 499 – 509, 533, 540, 614, 616–17, 620, 630, 640
  Liberians United for Reconciliation and Democracy, or LURD 501, 503
  Movement for Democracy in Liberia, or MODEL 501, 503
  National Patriotic Front of Liberia, or NPFL 479, 500–01, 503
Libya 335n222, 430–32, 438–40, 444, 500, 540, 616–17, 621, 627–31, 633–38, 719, 735

Loizidou v. *Turkey*, European Court of Human Rights, Merits, (1996) 23 EHRR 513 685n31
Lunar Embassy 140–42

Malawi African Association et al. v. *Mauritania*, Communication Nos. 54/91, 61/91, 98/93, 164/97–196/97, 210/98, 13th Activity Report 1999–2000 691n76Mali 43, 432, 437–38, 444, 540, 694, 717n57
Mare clausum 164–65
Mare liberum 164–65
Marginality 156, 159, 162
Marginalization
  Of the Darfur 607
Maritime delimitation 44–46, 180, 189n10, 213–14
Maritime Disputes 22, 163–65, 170–71, 185, 218, 220
Market entry 257–59
Martens clause 269, 322
Mines 160, 264
Mining of ports 39, 182, 265–66
Multiculturalism 133n1, 230, 566n5, 591

National and International legal systems
  Nature of 88, 145, 147, 160, 232, 350, 403, 490, 546–47, 550, 553
National and International Peace and Security, right to 516
National unity 53, 55, 675, 677
North Atlantic Treaty Organization, or NATO 112, 249–51, 291n9, 440, 616–17, 629, 633–38
Nigeria 52, 85–86, 92, 97–99, 360n32, 432, 455, 502, 540, 578, 582–83, 614, 632, 634, 728, 737, 740, 742, 743, 747, 748, 749, 750–51, 756n92, 759
Non-Aligned Movement 246, 252, 257–58, 604
Non-intervention 39, 330, 441, 611n123, 636
Non-liquet 10
Non-State Actors 53, 55–59, 145, 160, 162, 547, 689
North American Free Trade Agreement, or NAFTA 231, 233, 234n18, 235–37

Nuclear Weapons
   Legal effects of the use   7–12, 36, 242, 267–71, 614
   Legality of the use   7–12, 36, 242, 267–71, 281–84, 614
   Opposition to development   30
Numerus clausus   135–36, 142

Organisation for the Harmonisation of Business Law in Africa, or OHADA   716–18
Organization of African Unity, or OAU   513–15, 522, 528, 534–36, 558, 561, 566n6, 580, 584, 593, 600, 618–21, 689n57, 693, 696–97, 714, 720–21
   Assembly   524, 558, 623
   Charter of the OAU   515, 558, 609, 618, 693n87
   Council of Ministers   558
   General Secretariat   558–59
   Convention on Non-Discrimination   714
Obligation to act   327, 330, 331n207, 335, 345, 757
Occupation   97, 251n25, 272–74, 276–78, 281, 283, 284–86, 314, 356n16, 515, 519–20, 594, 606

Palestine   272
Pan-African Parliament   559, 561, 562n70
Pan-Africanism   513–515, 527, 534–35, 536
Peace and security   5, 35–37, 39, 56, 81, 83–84, 147, 157, 188, 227–28, 247–48, 303, 310, 311n140, 359, 360–61, 363n41, 364, 412, 449–50, 460, 475, 502, 514, 516, 534, 615–21, 645
Peaceful Settlement of International Disputes   618, 638
   Context   21–34
   Dispute   21–34
   Parties   21–34
   Settlement   21–34, 255, 646
Peaceful Settlement of International Disputes, Method of
   Court or arbitration   21, 618
   Good offices   21, 619
   Mediation   21, 618
   National courts   23–24
   Negotiation   21, 618

Peaceful Settlement of International Disputes, Remedies
   Declaration of breach   25, 27, 29, 32
   Apology   26
   Compensation   25–26, 30, 39, 204, 222n143, 238–40, 254, 275, 338n231, 435, 516, 533, 586–87, 600, 607, 629, 730n11
Peer Review   88–89, 91, 95, 580
People's rights   514–17, 534, 585, 606–07
   Equal right and self-determination   515–16, 534, 606–07
Permanent Court of International Justice, or PCIJ   22, 23, 176, 221, 316n159
Pillage   279
Politics   13, 36, 188, 426–27, 445, 622, 624, 632, 641–42, 648, 656, 659, 660–61, 693, 704, 723
   Political transition, *see Transition*
Post-colonial   53, 59, 89, 97, 99, 101–03, 513–515, 536, 592n5, 614, 618, 632, 637–38, 639, 692n81, 751
Powell, Justice   138–39, 707n8
Power
   Transfer of   622–23, 641, 656–57
Preliminary reference procedure   545, 551, 557
Prisoners of War   265n6, 282, 339n234, 637
Public goods   248–49, 758
Public Law of Africa   513–35
Purges and crackdowns   741, 751–53, 772

R. v. *Minister of Agriculture, Fisheries & Food, ex parte Anastasiou (Pissouri) Ltd.* [1994] ECR I – 3087 685n31
Rape   356, 359, 362n40, 363, 365–66, 368, 376, 379–405, 477, 497, 503, 532, 650–51, 737
   Marital Rape   532
Regional Economic Communities, or RECs   536–39, 541–48, 550–52, 553, 554, 556–58, 560–64
   Proliferation of   538, 542
Reference re Secession of Quebec 37 ILM (1998) 1342   682n10, 683, 685n35, 688n50, 692
Refugees
   Asylum   518, 521–23, 593, 595–98
   Convention governing the specific aspects of refugee problems in Africa   514, 518–23, 593–98

INDEX

Diplomatic protection   125, 127
External aggression   519–21, 594
Foreign domination   519–20, 594
Non-refoulement   518, 521–23, 595–97
Responsibility sharing   522–23, 598
Rights of   108, 518–23, 592–98, 612
Statute of the Office of the UN High commissioner for refugees, or UNHCR   593, 595, 598
Temporary protection   521–23, 597–98
UN Convention relating to the Status of refugees   518–23, 592–97
Voluntary repatriation   518, 523, 598, 600
Regional Intervention
AU Peace & Security Architecture, or APSA   610, 621
AU's Electoral and Security Assistance Mission to the Comoros, or MAES   611, 696n105
Norm of   333, 514, 519, 609–12, 617, 620, 636, 647
SADC Mutual Defence Pact   609
Regionalism   35, 146n11, 147n18, 705–25
Rehnquist, Justice   138
Relational issues   543–44, 546, 551–53, 563
Relational instruments   543–44, 547, 550–51, 553, 563
Relevant geographic market   245–47, 251–52, 257–58
Relevant market   243–45, 247–49, 257–59
Relevant product market   245–46, 247–49, 251–55, 257
Remedial secession   53, 59, 60, 690–92, 698, 701, 703
Representativity   160
Responsibility to Protect, or RTP or R2P   12, 150, 290n4, 292, 332–33, 348, 349, 599, 610n116, 612, 634
Right to development, or RTD   516, 565–78, 581–82, 585–90, 602–09
Rio Declaration on Environment and Development   604
UN Declaration on the RTD, or UNDRTD   566, 568, 570–72, 574, 602, 604
UN working group on RTD   573, 575, 604
Rule of law   3, 5, 6, 13, 14–15, 21, 46, 49, 111, 114, 128–30, 234n17, 241, 389, 402–03, 483, 617, 620–21, 705–25, 727, 729

Rwanda   112–13, 158n75, 286, 322–30, 340, 351–52, 374, 378, 379–84, 458–78, 504, 508, 540, 619–20
Rwanda Patriotic Front, or RPF   458–59, 470, 473
Rwandan genocide   113, 292, 324–30, 333, 348–49, 379–84, 387–88, 405, 458–78, 615–16, 620
Rwandese Armed Forces   459

Satisfactory Environment, right to   516
Scotland   662n1
Special Court for Sierra Leone, or SCSL   379–82, 388–405, 412, 413, 447–49, 451n7, 455, 464, 480–91, 493–99, 501–09, 710
Statute for the Special Court for Sierra Leone, or SCSL Statute   352n1 &n2, 369n72 &n73, 370n78, 379n1, 392n41, 411, 412, 455n27, 483
Special Tribunal for Lebanon, or STL   414
Seabed Disputes Chamber   176–77, 179, 181–82
Secession   53–60, 680–704
Remedial theory   53, 59, 60, 690–92, 698, 701, 703
Self-determination   681, 684, 685–92, 692, 698–99, 701–03
Territorial integrity   50–60, 684, 687–90, 693–94, 697
Security Council, or United Nations Security Council, or UNSC   36, 38–39, 51n1, 55–57, 66–67, 73, 75–76, 81, 83, 147, 157, 174, 199, 221, 272, 301–06, 309–11, 315, 318n166, 326–28, 332–33, 340, 341n238, 349, 363–66, 403, 428, 431–32, 437, 445, 449, 460–61, 467, 470, 472–73, 480, 493, 584, 616–17, 621, 625, 629, 632–34, 636–37, 647, 685n31, 693n91, 694, 707n5
Self-defence
Individual's right of   139
State's right of   10, 11, 38, 242n1, 267, 271, 275, 283, 285
Self-determination   36, 51, 53–54, 58–60, 88, 101, 110–11, 136, 162, 275, 499, 515–16, 534, 581n83, 603, 607, 618n15, 643, 663, 681, 684, 685–92, 692, 698–99, 701–03

Senegal 102, 116, 180n22, 360n32, 432, 444, 506, 533, 541, 565, 613, 640, 650, 689n56, 695, 713–14, 717n57, 720, 738n37, 749n73
Serbia 26, 53, 114–15, 335n222
Sexual Slavery 368, 380, 389–404, 498, 503
Sexual Violence 368, 379–405, 477, 497, 530, 533
Sexual and Gender-Based Violence, or SGBV 368, 379–405, 477, 497, 530, 532–33
Shared natural resources
 Exploitation and use 42, 46–48
 Preservation of 46–48
Sierra Leone 3, 5, 13–14, 17, 51, 180n22, 286, 328, 352, 360n32, 381, 385, 388, 390–92, 394, 398–99, 402–05, 411–12, 445, 447–51, 458, 478–99, 501, 504–05, 507–09, 536, 614, 616, 620, 630, 640
 Armed Forces Revolutionary Council or AFRC 486, 491, 497–98
 Civil Defence Force 486
 Revolutionary United Front, or RUF 479, 486–87, 497, 501
 United Liberation Movement for Democracy, or ULIMO 501, 503
 Sierra Leone Army, or SLA 403, 479
Somalia 56, 541, 559, 610, 615, 652, 700–01, 735
 African Union Mission in Somalia, or AMISOM 610n117, 700
Somaliland 56, 680, 699–701, 704
South African Development Community, or SADC 247, 248n14, 538–542, 543, 551, 554, 554, 556, 556, 564, 620, 711–13, 723
 Code of Conduct on HIV/AIDS and Employment 552
 Principles and Guidelines on Elections 552
 Protocol against Corruption 552
 Protocol on the SADC Tribunal 549, 550n29, 551n30 &n31, 556n53
 SADC Mutual Defence Pact 609
 SADC Tribunal 549, 550n29, 551n30 &n31, 556n53, 706, 711–12, 718, 723
 Treaty of the Southern African Development Community, or SADC Treaty 554n45
South Ossetia 442, 684

South Sudan 34n47, 541, 559, 615n8, 680, 701–03, 726, 728
 Abyei 702n158
 Machakos Protocol 702
 Sudan People's Liberation Army/Movement (SPLA/M) 702
Southern African Customs Union, or SACU 538
Southern Cameroon case 517
Srebrenica 290, 323, 336
Standards of Civilization 161–62
State Responsibility 12, 25, 31–32, 39, 65, 104n2, 114, 279, 286–87, 308, 317, 321, 360n31, 421, 576
 Exclusion of wrongfulness 26, 32
 Relation to law of treaties 32
Succession 416, 639–61
 Electoral succession 644, 645
 Political succession 416
 Presidential succession 644–45, 648
 Regulated succession 416, 645
 Succession politics 648
 Unregulated succession 645
Sudan Human Rights Organization and Sudan Centre for Housing Rights and Evictions v. Sudan Communication Nos. 279/03, 296/05, 49 ILM (2010) 1573 585, 606, 691n76, 693n91
Sudan 34n47, 56, 158n76, 159n78, 255, 336n222, 411n25, 431, 438–39, 440, 506, 541, 569n23, 585, 606, 610, 615–16, 641, 649, 693n91, 702–03, 726, 735, 749n73
Tanzania 34n47, 156n66, 366n53, 432, 459, 541, 551n33, 582n85, 584, 649, 743n53, 749n73, 754, 756n92
 Secessionism in Zanzibar 701n149
Territorial Integrity 50–60, 161, 618, 681, 684, 687–90, 693–94, 697
Third World 3, 4, 13, 87, 88, 90, 96, 101–02, 108, 149, 156, 159, 160–62, 571, 641
Third World Approaches to International Law, or TWAIL 85–103, 156n66
Transition
 Orderly transition 645–46
 Political transition 614–15, 622, 645–46, 648, 650, 658

INDEX

Travaux préparatoires 169, 273, 292–93, 306n101, 312–16, 329n202
Turkish Republic of Northern Cyprus 684–85

Uganda 114, 277–79, 284n90, 285, 287, 432, 433–34, 445, 447, 458, 533, 541, 551n33, 552, 584, 606, 615, 641, 649–50, 656, 738n37, 743n53, 749n73, 759–60
   Lord's Resistance Army 433–34
   Uganda People's Defence Force, or UPDF, or Ugandan Army 433
Ukraine 60, 208, 213–14
Unilateral declaration of independence 36, 52–54, 682–85, 687, 690, 696
United Nations, or UN 3, 5, 12–13, 14, 16, 50n1, 51, 52n6, 55, 57–58, 67, 76, 83, 113, 166, 176, 195–96, 246, 252–54, 257–59, 294–98, 301, 303–32, 513, 536, 566, 573, 579, 586, 591, 600, 616–18, 621, 624–29, 632–35, 637, 728
   Charter 7, 10, 21, 30, 36, 39, 53–55, 57–58, 66–67, 110, 147, 150, 153, 157n70, 188n5, 191–93, 194–95, 199, 221, 229n162, 246n11, 265, 267, 269, 276, 277n61, 289, 291n9, 297, 302–04, 309, 311n143, 312–13, 332, 337–38, 340–45, 349, 364, 366n53, 412n31, 412n35, 429, 460, 568–69, 618, 632, 634, 639n3, 685n24, 687n47
   Committee on the Elimination of Racial Discrimination 687
   Convention Against Torture, or CAT 714
   Declaration on Right to Development 567, 602, 604
   Declaration on the rights of Indigenous people 604
   Economic Commission for Africa, or UNECA 538n2, 539, 541, 545, 728
   Human Rights Committee 685n35, 688
   Secretary-General 503, 593, 632–33, 656, 735
   Third Conference on the Law of the Sea 215
   UN Assistance Mission for Rwanda, or UNAMIR 459
   UN Conference on Trade and Development, UNCTAD 579
   UN Development Programme, or UNDP 572
   UN Mission in Cote d'Ivoire, or UNOCI 632
   UN Office of the High Commissioner for Human Rights, or UNHCHR 572–73
   Universal Declaration on Human Rights, or UDHR 567–68, 577, 581, 603, 605
   United Nations General Assembly Resolution, or UNGA Res
      289 (IV) (1949) 698n121
      2625 (XXV) 1970 Declaration on Friendly Relations and Co-operation among States 53, 685n24, 687n47
      47/230 (1992) 699n124
      49/18 (1994) 696n109
      65/308 (2010) 702n159
      68/262 (2014) 684n29, 687n47
   United Nations Security Council Resolution, or UNSC Res
      541 (1983) 685n31
      1744 (2007) 700n139
      1880 (2009) 632
      1970 (2011) 629, 634–35
      1973 (2011) 629, 634, 636
      2056 (2012) 694n96
      2085 (2012) 694n97
      2164 (2014) 695n98
Use of force 4n4, 10, 12, 36, 38, 53, 75–76, 81, 83, 150, 188, 205, 246, 267, 270, 277, 284–85, 291–92, 315, 328, 329n203, 332, 340, 340–51, 618, 620, 629, 634–36, 645–46, 656, 690
Uti possidetis 42, 43, 51, 60, 693, 701
Uti possidetis juris 42–43

Values 133–43
   Competition of 136–143;
Vienna Declaration and Programme of Action 58n35, 573n40, 604, 687n47, 690n66
Vox populi 156, 159, 162

Western Sahara 16 October 1975, International Court of Justice, Advisory Opinion, *I.C.J. Reports* 1975, p. 12 688n48, 699n128

Whistle-blowers
    Protection law for   732, 764
Wildermann v. *Stinnes*   2 ILR   224   689n58
Women's rights
    Criminal penalization of expectant (pregnant) mothers   525, 532–33
    Health and reproductive right   531–33
    Marriage of female child, prohibition of   530–31, 533
    Minimum working age for girl children   532
    Property rights   533
    Protection of   527–34
    Protocol on the rights of women in Africa   514, 528–35
    Sexual violence, prevention of   368, 379–405, 477, 497, 530, 533
    The education of pregnant Female children   525
    UN Convention on the Elimination of All Forms of Discrimination against Women, or CEDAW   529–32, 534–35
    Women in distress/Vulnerable Women   532
World Health Organization, or WHO   7–9, 271

Printed in the United States
By Bookmasters